The Norton Anthology
of World Literature

SECOND EDITION

VOLUME D

1650–1800

WITHDRAWN

American River College Library
4700 College Oak Drive
Sacramento, California 95841

WITHDRAWN

John Bierhorst

Jerome Wright Clinton
PROFESSOR OF NEAR EASTERN STUDIES, PRINCETON UNIVERSITY

Robert Lyons Danly
LATE OF THE UNIVERSITY OF MICHIGAN

Kenneth Douglas
LATE OF COLUMBIA UNIVERSITY

Howard E. Hugo
LATE OF THE UNIVERSITY OF CALIFORNIA, BERKELEY

F. Abiola Irele
PROFESSOR OF AFRICAN, FRENCH, AND COMPARATIVE LITERATURE,
THE OHIO STATE UNIVERSITY

Heather James
ASSOCIATE PROFESSOR OF ENGLISH, UNIVERSITY OF SOUTHERN CALIFORNIA

Bernard M. W. Knox
DIRECTOR EMERITUS, CENTER FOR HELLENIC STUDIES

John C. McGalliard
LATE OF THE UNIVERSITY OF IOWA

Stephen Owen
PROFESSOR OF CHINESE AND COMPARATIVE LITERATURE,
HARVARD UNIVERSITY

P. M. Pasinetti
PROFESSOR OF ITALIAN AND COMPARATIVE LITERATURE EMERITUS, UNIVERSITY OF CALIFORNIA,
LOS ANGELES

Lee Patterson
F. W. HILLES PROFESSOR OF ENGLISH, YALE UNIVERSITY

Indira Viswanathan Peterson
PROFESSOR OF ASIAN STUDIES, MOUNT HOLYOKE COLLEGE

Patricia Meyer Spacks
EDGAR F. SHANNON PROFESSOR OF ENGLISH, UNIVERSITY OF VIRGINIA

William G. Thalmann
PROFESSOR OF CLASSICS, UNIVERSITY OF SOUTHERN CALIFORNIA

René Wellek
LATE OF YALE UNIVERSITY

The Norton Anthology
of World Literature

SECOND EDITION

Sarah Lawall, *General Editor*

PROFESSOR OF COMPARATIVE LITERATURE AND ADJUNCT PROFESSOR OF
FRENCH, UNIVERSITY OF MASSACHUSETTS, AMHERST

Maynard Mack, *General Editor Emeritus*

LATE OF YALE UNIVERSITY

VOLUME D

1650–1800

W • W • NORTON & COMPANY • *New York* • *London*

Editor: Peter J. Simon
Developmental Editor: Carol Flechner
Associate Managing Editor: Marian Johnson
Production Manager: Diane O'Connor
Editorial Assistant: Isobel T. Evans
Project Editors: Candace Levy, Vivien Reinart, Carol Walker, Will Rigby
Permissions Manager: Nancy Rodwan
Assistant Permissions Manager: Sandra Chin
Text Design: Antonina Krass
Art Research: Neil Ryder Hoos
Maps: Jacques Chazaud

Copyright © 2002, 1999, 1997, 1995, 1992, 1985, 1979, 1973, 1965, 1956 by
W. W. Norton & Company, Inc. Copyright © 1984 by Maynard Mack.
Previous edition published as THE NORTON ANTHOLOGY OF WORLD
MASTERPIECES, Expanded Edition

All rights reserved.
Printed in the United States of America.

Since this page cannot legibly accommodate all the copyright notices,
the Permissions Acknowledgments constitute an extension of the copyright page.

The text of this book is composed in Fairfield Medium
with the display set in Bernhard Modern.
Composition by Binghamton Valley Composition.
Manufacturing by R. R. Donnelley & Sons.
Cover illustration: *Truth-Sincerity* by Suzuki Harunobu. 18th century. Burstein Collection/
Corbis.

Library of Congress Cataloging-in-Publication Data

The Norton anthology of world lliterature / Sarah Lawall, general editor; Maynard
Mack, general editor emeritus. — 2nd ed.
    p. cm.
    Rev. ed. of: The Norton anthology of world masterpieces.
    Includes bibliographical references and index.
    Contents: v. A. Beginnings to A.D. 100 — v. B. A.D. 100–1500 — v. C. 1500–1650 — v.
D. 1650–1800 — v. E. 1800–1900 — v. F. The twentieth century.
    ISBN 0-393-97764-1 (v. 1) — ISBN 0-393-97765-X (v. 2)
    1. Literature — Collections.   I. Lawall, Sarah N.   II. Mack, Maynard, 1909–   III. Norton
anthology of world masterpieces.

PN6014 .N66 2001
808.8 — dc21   2001030824

ISBN 0-393-97758-7 (pbk.)

W. W. Norton & Company, Inc., 500 Fifth Avenue, New York, NY 10110
www.wwnorton.com

W. W. Norton & Company Ltd., Castle House, 75/76 Wells Street, London W1T 3QT

2 3 4 5 6 7 8 9 0

Contents

The Rise of Popular Arts in Premodern Japan   583

Preface

The first edition of the *Norton Anthology of World Literature* to appear in the twenty-first century offers many new works from around the world and a fresh new format that responds to contemporary needs. The global reach of this anthology encompasses important works from Asia and Africa, central Asia and India, the Near East, Europe, and North and South America—all presented in the light of their own literary traditions, as a shared heritage of generations of readers in many countries, and as part of a network of cultural and literary relationships whose scope is still being discovered. With this edition, we institute a shift in title that reflects the way the anthology has grown. The initial *Norton Anthology of World Masterpieces* (1956) aimed to present a broader "Western tradition of world literature" in contrast to previous anthologies confined to English and American works; it focused on the richness and diversity of Western literary tradition, as does the Seventh Edition of 1999. The present volume, which derives from the "Expanded" edition of 1995, contains almost all the texts of the Seventh Edition and also thousands of pages from works around the globe; it now logically assumes the broader title of "World Literature." In altering the current title to *The Norton Anthology of World Literature,* we do not abandon the anthology's focus on major works of literature or a belief that these works especially repay close study. It is their consummate artistry, their ability to express complex signifying structures, that gives access to multiple dimensions of meaning, meanings that are always rooted in a specific setting and cultural tradition but that further constitute, upon comparison, a thought-provoking set of perspectives on the varieties of human experience. Readers familiar with the anthology's two volumes, whose size increased proportionally with the abundance of new material, will welcome the new boxed format, in which each of the earlier volumes is separated into three slim and easily portable smaller books. Whether maintaining the chronological structure of the original boxed set or selecting a different configuration, you will be able to consult a new Web site, developed by Norton specifically for the world-literature anthologies and containing contextual information, audiovisual resources, exploratory analyses, and related material to illustrate and illuminate these compelling texts.

The six volumes represent six consecutive chronological periods from approximately 2500 B.C. to the present. Subsequently, and for pedagogical reasons, our structure is guided by the broad continuities of different cultural traditions and the literary or artistic periods they recognize for themselves. This means that chronology advises but does not dictate the order in which works appear. If Western tradition names a certain time slot "the Renaissance" or "the Enlightenment" (each term implying a shared set of beliefs), that designation has little relevance in other parts of the globe; similarly, "vernacular literature" does not have the same literary-historical status in all traditions; and "classical" periods come at different times in India, China, and Western Europe. We find that it is more useful to start from a tradition's own sense of itself and the specific shape it gives to the community memory embodied as art. Occasionally there are displacements of absolute chronology: Petrarch, for example, belongs chronologically with Boccaccio and Chaucer, and Rousseau is a contemporary of Voltaire. Each can be read as a new and dissonant voice within his own century, a foil and balance for accepted ideas, or he can be considered as part of a powerful new consciousness, along with those indebted to his thought and example. In the first and last volumes of the anthology, for different pedagogical purposes, we have chosen to present diverse cultural traditions together. The first section of the first volume, "The Invention of Writing and the Earliest Literatures," introduces students to the study of world literature with works from three different cultural traditions—Babylonian, Egyptian, Judaic—each among the oldest works that have come down to us in written form, each in its origins reaching well back into a preliterate past, yet directly accessible as an image of human experience and still provocative at the beginning of the twenty-first century. The last volume, *The Twentieth Century*, reminds us that separation in the modern world is no longer a possibility. Works in the twentieth century are demonstrably part of a new global consciousness, itself fostered by advances in communications, that experiences reality in terms of interrelationships, of boundaries asserted or transgressed, and of the creation of personal and social identity from the interplay of sameness and difference. As teachers, we have tried to structure an anthology that is usable, accessible, and engaging in the classroom—that clarifies patterns and relationships for your students, while leaving you free to organize selections from this wealth of material into the themes, genres, topics, and special emphases that best fit your needs.

Changes in this edition have taken several forms. Most visibly, there are many new selections to spark further combinations with works you have already been teaching and to suggest ways of extending your favorite themes with additional geographic, gendered, chronological, or cultural perspectives. Thus the volume on the twentieth-century adds five important Latin American authors who are pivotal figures in their own time and with an established international stature that, in a few cases, is just beginning to be recognized in the United States. In fiction, there is Juan Rulfo, whose landmark novel *Pedro Páramo* is at once an allegory of political power in modern Mexico and a magical narrative that introduced modernist techniques to Latin American fiction, and Clarice Lispector, the innovative Brazilian novelist and short-story writer who writes primarily about women's experience and is internationally known for her descriptions of psychological states of mind. In poetry, the vehicle for political and cultural revolution in so many European and Latin American countries, we introduce the Nicaraguan Rubén Darío, a charismatic diplomat-poet at home in Europe and Latin America who created the image of a Spanish cultural identity that included his own Indian ancestry and counteracted prevailing images of North American dominance. After Darío there is Alfonsina Storni, the Argentinian poet who was as well known in the 1920s and 1930s for her independent journal articles and her feminism as for the intensely personal poetry that assures her reputation today. Finally, the Nobel Prize winner and Chilean activist Pablo Neruda, who reinvigorated the concept of public poet and became the best-known Latin American poet of the twentieth century, is represented by selections from various periods and styles of his work—in particular, the epic vision of human history taken by many to be his crowning achievement, *The Heights of Macchu Picchu*. Works by all five authors add to our representation of Spanish and Latin American literature, but their importance is not limited to regional or cultural representation. Each functions within a broader framework that may be artistic convention; national, ethnic, or class identity; feminist or postcolonial perspectives; or a particular vision of human experience. Each resonates with other works throughout the volume and is an opportunity to enrich your world-literature syllabus with new comparisons and contrasts.

Many of the new selections draw attention to historical circumstances and the texture of everyday life. Biographical tales from records of the ancient Chinese historian Ssu-ma Ch'ien give a glimpse of contemporary attitudes and ideals, as does the dedicated historian's poignant *Letter in Reply to Jen An*, written after his official punishment by castration. Entries in Dorothy Wordsworth's *Grasmere Journals* express the very personal world of the intimate journal, and Virginia Woolf's passionate analysis of the woman writer's position, in *A Room of One's Own*, combines autobiography with essay and fiction. Still other texts focus on specific historical events or issues but employ fictional techniques for greater immediacy. There is a thin line between fiction and autobiography in Tadeusz Borowski's terrifying Holocaust story *Ladies and Gentlemen, to the Gas Chamber*. Nawal El Saadawi's chilling courtroom tale *In Camera* uses the victim's shifting and fragmented perspectives to evoke the harsh realities of twentieth-century political torture and repression. Zhang Ailing's novella of a difficult love, *Love in a Fallen City*, depicts the decline of traditional Chinese society and concludes with the Japanese bombing of Hong Kong in World War II, while Anita Desai's *The Rooftop Dwellers* follows the struggles of a single woman in Delhi to make a career for herself in the face of social disapproval and family pressure. African American realist author Richard Wright, describes an adolescent crisis related to specific social images of manliness in *The Man Who Was Almost a Man*. Yet there are always different ways of presenting historical circumstances and dealing with the questions they raise. A play from Renaissance Spain, Lope de Vega's *Fuente Ovejuna*, is a light romantic comedy that draws heavily on dramatic conventions for its humor; yet it is also set during a famous peasant uprising whose bloodshed, political repercussions, and torture of the entire citizenry are represented in the course of the play. Readers who follow historical and cultural themes throughout the anthology will find much provocative material in these diverse new selections.

In renewing this edition, we have taken several routes: introducing new authors (many previously mentioned); choosing an alternate work by the same author when it resonates with material in other sections or speaks strongly to current concerns; adding small sections to existing larger pieces in order to fill out a theme or narrative line, or to suggest connections with other texts; and grouping several works to bring out new strengths. Three stories by the African writer Bernard Dadié appear here for the first time, as do the romantic adventures of Ludovico Ariosto's epic parody *Orlando Furi-*

oso, an African tale by Doris Lessing—*The Old Chief Mshlanga*—and Alice Munro's complex evocation of childhood memories *Walker Brothers Cowboy*. Among the alternate works by existing authors, we present Gustave Flaubert's great realist novel *Madame Bovary*, James Joyce's Dublin tale *The Dead*, and William Faulkner's *The Bear*, the latter printed in its entirety to convey its full scope as a chronicle of the legacy of slavery in the American South. New plays include Bertolt Brecht's drama *The Good Woman of Setzuan* and William Shakespeare's *Othello* as well as *Hamlet*; each has its own special resonance in world literature. Derek Walcott is represented by a selection of his poetry, including excerpts from the modern epic *Omeros*. Five more magical tales are added to the *Thousand and One Nights* and three new essays from Montaigne, including his memorable *To the Reader*. Six new tales from Ovid (in a new translation by Allen Mandelbaum) round out a set of myths exploring different images of love and gender, themes that reappear in two of the best-known lays of Marie de France, *Lanval* and *Laüstic*, as well as in Boccaccio's famous "Pot of Basil" and the influential tale of patient Griselda and her tyrannical husband, all presented here. From Chaucer, there is the bawdy, popular *Wife of Bath's Tale*, and from the *Heptameron* of Marguerite de Navarre fresh tales of love and intrigue that emphasize the stereotyping of gender roles. To *The Cherry Orchard* by Anton Chekhov, we add his famous tale of uncertain love *The Lady with the Dog*. New selections from Books 4 and 8 of John Milton's *Paradise Lost* depict the drama of Satan's malevolent entry into Paradise, Adam and Eve's innocent conversation, and the angel's warning to Adam. Finally, the poignant tales of Abraham and Isaac and of Jacob and Esau (Genesis 22, 25, 27) are added to the Old Testament selections, as well as the glorious love poetry of the Song of Songs; and Matthew 13 [Why Jesus Teaches in Parables] is included among the selections from the New Testament.

Two founding works of early India, the *Rāmāyaṇa* and the *Mahābhārata*, are offered in greatly increased selections and with new and exceptionally accessible translations. Readers can now follow (in a new translation by Swami Venkatesananda) the trajectory of Rāma's exile and life in the forest, the kidnapping of his wife Sītā, and ensuing magical adventures up to the final combat between Rāma and the demon king Rāvaṇa. A lively narrative of the *Mahābhārata*'s civil war (in a new translation by C. V. Narasimhan) unfolds in sequential excerpts that include two sections of special interest to modern students: the insulted Draupadī's formal accusation of the rulers in the Assembly Hall and the tragic story of the heroic but ill-fated warrior Karṇa.

To increase our understanding of individual authors' achievement, we join to the Indian Rabindranath Tagore's story *Punishment* a selection of the Bengali poems with which he revolutionized literary style in his homeland, and to the Chinese Lu Xun's two tales, examples of his poetry from *Wild Grass*. Rousseau's *Confessions* gain historical and psychological depth through new passages that shed light on his early years and on the development of his political sympathies.

The epic poetry that acts as the conscience of a community—*The Iliad*, *The Mahābhārata*, the *Son-Jara*, among others—has long been represented in the anthology. It has been our practice, however, to minimize the presence of lyric poetry in translation, recognizing—as is so cogently argued in the "Note on Translation," printed at the end of each volume—that the precise language and music of an original poem will never be identical with its translation and that short poems risk more of their substance in the transfer. Yet good translations often achieve a poetry of their own and occupy a pivotal position in a second literary history; thus the Egyptian love songs, the Chinese *Classic of Poetry* (*Book of Songs*), the biblical Song of Songs, and the lyrics of Sappho, Catullus, Petrarch, Rumi, and Baudelaire have all had influence far beyond the range of those who could read the original poems. Some poetry collections—like the Japanese *Man'yōshū* and *Kokinshū*—are recognized as an integral part of the society's cultural consciousness, and others—notably, the European Romantics—embody a sea change in artistic and cultural consciousness.

New to this edition is a series of poetry clusters that complement existing collections and represent a core of important and influential poetry in five different periods. You may decide to teach them as part of a spectrum of poetic expression or as reference points in a discussion of cultural consciousness. Thus a newly translated series of early hymns by the Tamil Śaiva saints exemplifies the early mystical poetry of India, while the multifarious vitality of medieval Europe is recaptured in poems by men and women from Arabic, Judaic, Welsh, Spanish, French, Provençal, Italian, English, and German traditions. Those who have taught English Romantic poetry will find both contrast and comparison in Continental poets from France, Italy, Germany, Spain, and Russia, many of whom possess lasting influence in nineteenth- and twentieth-century literature. Symbolism, whose insights into the relation of language and reality have permeated modern poetry and linguistic theory, is represented by the great nineteenth-century poets Charles Baudelaire, Stéphane Mallarmé, Paul Verlaine, and Arthur Rimbaud. Finally, a cluster of Dada-Surrealist poems that range from slashing, rebellious humor to ecstatic love introduces the free association and dreamlike structures of this visionary movement, whose influence extends around the world and has strong links to modern art and film.

How to choose, as you turn from the library before you to the inevitable constraint of available time? There is an embarrassment of riches, an inexhaustible series of options, to fit whatever course pattern you wish. Perhaps you have already decided to proceed by theme or genre, in chronological order or by a selected comparative principle; or you have favorite titles that work well in the classroom, and you seek to combine them with new pieces. Perhaps you want to create modules that compare ideas of national identity or of bicultural identity and shifting cultural paradigms, that survey images of gender in different times and places or that examine the place of memory in a range of texts. In each instance, you have only to pick and choose among a variety of works from different countries, languages, and cultural backgrounds. If you are teaching the course for the first time or wish to try something different, you may find what you are looking for in the sample syllabi of the *Instructor's Guide* or on the new Web site, which will also contain supporting material such as maps, time lines, and audio pronunciation glossaries, resource links, guides to section materials, various exercises and assignments, and a series of teaching modules related to specific works. Throughout, the editors (who are all practicing teachers) have selected and prepared texts that are significant in their own area of scholarly expertise, meaningful in the larger context of world literature, and, always, delightful, captivating and challenging to students.

Clearly one can parcel out the world in a variety of ways, most notably geopolitical, and there is no one map of world literature. In order to avoid parochialism, some scholars suggest that we should examine cultural activity in different countries at the same period of time. Others attempt to deconstruct prevailing literary assumptions (often selected from Western literary theory) by using history or cultural studies as a framework for examining texts as documents. "Global" literary studies project a different map that depends on one's geopolitical view of global interactions and of the energies involved in the creation and dissemination of literature. *The Norton Anthology of World Literature*, Second Edition, takes a different point of departure, focusing first of all on literary texts—artifacts, if you will, that have a special claim on our attention because they have been read over a great period of time and are cherished by a wide variety of readers. Once such texts have been proposed as objects of knowledge—and enjoyment, and illumination— they are available for any and all forms of analysis. Situating them inside larger forms of textuality—linguistic, historical, or cultural—is, after all, an inevitable part of the meaning-making process. It is the primary task of this anthology, however, to present them as multidimensional objects for discussion and then to let our readers choose when and where to extend the analysis.

From the beginning, the editors of *The Norton Anthology of World Literature* have always balanced the competing—and, we like to think, complementary—claims of teaching and scholarship, of the specialist's focused expertise and the generalist's broader perspectives. The founding editors set the example, which guides their successors. We welcome three new successor editors to this edition: William G. Thalmann, Professor of Classics at the University of Southern California; Lee Patterson, Professor of English at Yale University; and Heather James, Associate Professor of English at the University of Southern California. Two founding editors have assumed Emeritus status: Bernard M. W. Knox, eminent classical scholar and legendary teacher and lecturer; and P. M. Pasinetti, who combines the intellectual breadth of the Renaissance scholar with a novelist's creative intuition. We also pay tribute to the memory of Robert Lyons Danly, translator and astute scholar of Japanese literature, whose lively interventions have been missed since his untimely death in 1995. Finally, we salute the memory of Maynard Mack, General Editor and presiding genius from the first edition through the Expanded Edition of 1995. An Enlightenment scholar of much wisdom, humanity, and gracefully worn knowledge, and a firm believer in the role of great literature—world literature—in illuminating human nature, he was also unstintingly dedicated to this anthology as a teaching enterprise. To him, therefore, and on all counts, we dedicate the first millennial edition of the anthology.

Acknowledgments

Among our many critics, advisers, and friends, the following were of special help in providing suggestions and corrections: Joseph Barbarese (Rutgers University); Carol Clover (University of California, Berkeley); Patrick J. Cook (George Washington University); Janine Gerzanics (University of Southern California); Matthew Giancarlo (Yale University); Kevis Goodman (University of California at Berkeley); Roland Greene (University of Oregon); Dmitri Gutas (Yale University); John H. Hayes (Emory University); H. Mack Horton (University of California at Berkeley); Suzanne Keen (Washington and Lee University); Charles S. Kraszewski (King's College); Gregory F. Kuntz; Michelle Latiolais (University of California at Irvine); Sharon L. James (Bryn Mawr College); Ivan Marcus (Yale University); Timothy Martin (Rutgers University, Camden); William Naff (University of Massachusetts); Stanley Radosh (Our Lady of the Elms College); Fred C. Robinson (Yale University); John Rogers (Yale University); Robert Rothstein (University of Massachusetts); Lawrence Senelick (Boston University); Jack Shreve (Alleghany Community College); Frank Stringfellow (University of Miami); Nancy Vickers (Bryn Mawr College); and Jack Welch (Abilene Christian University).

We would also like to thank the following people who contributed to the planning of the Second Edition: Charles Adams, University of Arkansas; Dorothy S. Anderson, Salem State College; Roy Anker, Calvin College; John Apwah, County College of Morris; Doris Bargen, University of Massachusetts; Carol Barrett, Austin Community College, Northridge Campus; Michael Beard, University of North Dakota; Lysbeth Em Berkert, Northern State University; Marilyn Booth, University of Illinois; George Byers, Fairmont State College; Shirley Carnahan, University of Colorado; Ngwarsungu Chiwengo, Creighton University; Stephen Cooper, Troy State University; Bonita Cox, San Jose State University; Richard A. Cox, Abilene Christian University; Dorothy Deering, Purdue University; Donald Dickson, Texas A&M University; Alexander Dunlop, Auburn University; Janet Eber, County College of Morris; Angela Esterhammer, University of Western Ontario; Walter Evans, Augusta State University; Fidel Fajardo-Acosta, Creighton University; John C. Freeman, El Paso Community College, Valle Verde Campus; Barbara Gluck, Baruch College; Michael Grimwood, North Carolina State University; Rafey Habib, Rutgers University, Camden; John E. Hallwas, Western Illinois College; Jim Hauser, William Patterson College; Jack Hussey, Fairmont State College; Dane Johnson, San Francisco State University; Andrew Kelley, Jackson State Community College; Jane Kinney, Valdosta State University; Candace Knudson, Truman State University; Jameela Lares, University of Southern Mississippi; Thomas L. Long, Thomas Nelson Community College; Sara MacDonald, Sterling College; Linda Macri, University of Maryland; Rita Mayer, San Antonio College; Christopher Morris,

Norwich University; Deborah Nestor, Fairmont State College; John Netland, Calvin College; Kevin O'Brien, Chapman University; Mariannina Olcott, San Jose State University; Charles W. Pollard, Calvin College; Pilar Rotella, Chapman University; Rhonda Sandford, Fairmont State College; Daniel Schenker, University of Alabama at Huntsville; Robert Scotto, Baruch College; Carl Seiple, Kutztown University; Glenn Simshaw, Chemeketa Community College; Evan Lansing Smith, Midwestern State University; William H. Smith, Piedmont College; Floyd C. Stuart, Norwich University; Cathleen Tarp, Fairmont State College; Diane Thompson, Northern Virginia Community College; Sally Wheeler, Georgia Perimeter College; Jean Wilson, McMaster University; Susan Wood, University of Nevada, Las Vegas; Tom Wymer, Bowling Green State University.

Phonetic Equivalents

for use with the Pronouncing Glossaries preceding most
selections in this volume

a as in *cat*
ah as in *father*
ai as in *light*
ay as in *day*
aw as in *raw*
e as in *pet*
ee as in *street*
ehr as in *air*
er as in *bird*
eu as in *lurk*
g as in *good*
i as in *sit*
j as in *joke*
nh a nasal sound (as in French *vin, vẽ*)
o as in *pot*
oh as in *no*
oo as in *boot*
oy as in *toy*
or as in *bore*
ow as in *now*
s as in *mess*
ts as in *ants*
u as in *us*
zh as in *vision*

The Norton Anthology
of World Literature

SECOND EDITION

VOLUME D

1650–1800

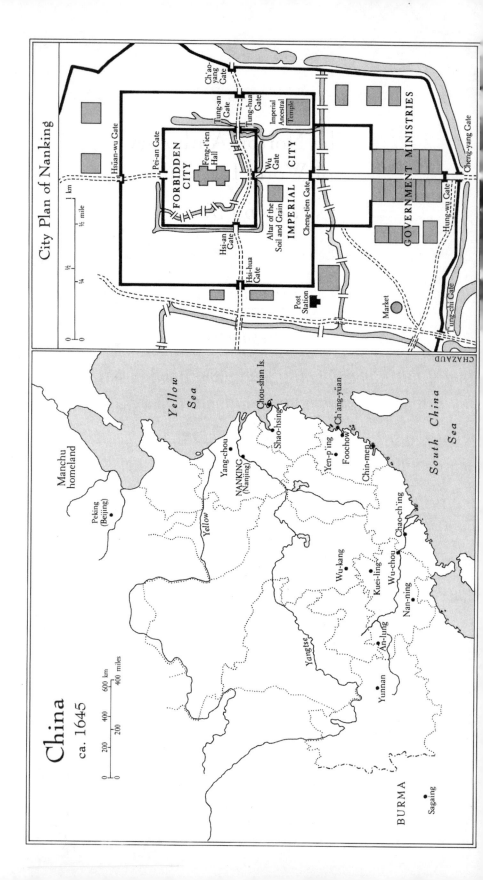

China
ca. 1645

City Plan of Nanking

Manchu homeland

Peking (Beijing)

Yellow Sea

Yellow

Chou-shan Is.

Shao-hsing

Yang-chou

NANKING (Nanjing)

Ch'ang-yüan

Yen-p'ing

Foochow

Chin-men

Yangtse

Wu-kang

Kuei-ling

Wu-chou

Chao-ch'ing

An-lung

Nan-ning

Yunnan

South China Sea

BURMA

Sagaing

0   200   400   600 km
0   200   400 miles

City Plan of Nanking

Ch'ao-yang Gate

Hsüan-wu Gate

Pei-an Gate

Tung-an Gate

Tung-hua Gate

Imperial Ancestral Temple

FORBIDDEN CITY

Feng-t'ien Hall

Wu Gate

IMPERIAL CITY

Cheng-yang Gate

Hsi-an Gate

Altar of the Soil and Grain

Hsi-hua Gate

Cheng-tien Gate

GOVERNMENT MINISTRIES

Hung-wu Gate

Post Station

Market

Tung-chi Gate

1 km
½ mile
½
¼
0

Vernacular Literature in China

Several decades after completing the conquest of north China, Mongol armies crossed the Yangtse River and conquered the Southern Sung Dynasty in 1279. At the time their empire stretched across all of Asia, but as a Chinese dynasty the Mongols were known as the Yüan. Although they assumed a Chinese dynastic title and some of the trappings of Chinese imperial government, the Mongols did not base their state on Confucian principles, for which they had the greatest contempt. To the everlasting shock of Chinese intellectuals, the Mongols suspended the examination system, by which members of the educated elite were recruited for government service. The long-established link between classical literature (poetry and nonfiction prose), an education in the Confucian classics, and service in the government was temporarily broken. Even after the civil service examinations were reestablished later in the dynasty, classical literature never regained its place as the core around which public, social, and private life was organized. Through the rest of the imperial period, classical literature remained an important part of the life of intellectuals, but its general role had been diminished to something like that of literature in Western civilization, an important adjunct of social life but not at its core.

As classical literature lost its importance, literature in vernacular Chinese (plays, verse romances, and prose fiction) began to be published. The steady rise of the bourgeoisie in the great cities and the spread of literacy in urban areas created a market for written versions of literary forms that already flourished in performance. In Europe and Great Britain the authority of classical drama could be used to defend the validity of Renaissance drama in the vernacular tongues. Greek and Latin prose romance, though with lesser prestige than drama, likewise informed the development of vernacular narrative prose. In China, by contrast, there was no ancient drama, and classical prose fiction was generally considered pure entertainment.

In the cities of China, however, rich traditions of theater, oral verse romance, and storytelling flourished. The thirteenth and fourteenth centuries produced the first published versions of these forms, with each written form carefully preserving the ambience of performance. Some intellectuals were fascinated by this urban popular literature, and what survives of it is the result of their efforts. Such literature grew steadily in volume and importance through the Ming Dynasty (1368–1644).

Although Yüan and Ming vernacular literature lacked the subtlety of classical literature, much that had been repressed in classical literature burst forth in the vernacular: sex, violence, satire, and humor. Plays, verse romances, and prose stories were often elaborations of some source in the classical language, spinning out a few pages into thirty or a thousand. This was a literature whose strength lay not in inventing plots but in filling in details and saying what had been omitted. In that strength, it became something different in kind from classical literature, with new virtues and new failings.

Chinese popular literature is largely a vast tissue of interrelated stories. The illiterate and semiliterate population had learned history from storytellers, who took a time period and elaborated it in the spoken tongue, including poems and songs. A dramatist might take one incident from a story cycle and develop it into a play. A fiction writer might cover an entire story cycle in a novel. A number of these historical romances survive, the most famous being *The Romance of the Three Kingdoms* (*San-kuo chih yen-yi*)—attributed to Lo Kuan-chung (earliest printed version 1522)—an elaboration of the official history of the period in which the Han Dynasty disintegrated, around the turn of the third century A.D. In *The Romance of the Three Kingdoms,* the somewhat dry historical account was transformed into a dazzling saga of battles and clever stratagems.

Popular literature worked with other materials as well. Murder mysteries, often based on recent cases, circulated, in which the wise magistrate, "Judge Pao," played a role equivalent to that of the modern detective. Stories of a famous group of twelfth-century bandits, like Robin Hood representing justice against corrupt authority, developed into the novel *Water Margin* (*Shui-hu chuan*) (early 1500s). One small incident in *Water Margin* was elaborated into the saga of a corrupt sensualist whose greed and sexual escapades give a vivid if skewed portrait of urban life in Ming China; this is *Golden Lotus* (*Chin P'ing Mei*) (1617). And the story of the Buddhist monk Hsuan Tsang who went west to India to get scriptures, guarded by a band of fantastic creatures headed by a wily monkey possessed of supernatural powers, became the novel *Monkey* (*Hsi-yu chi*) (1592).

As literature lost its role in public life, the vital link between literature and Confucian intellectual culture also gave way. High culture favored neo-Confucianism, at best prim and at worst dogmatic. Neo-Confucianism was an attempt to discover the philosophical grounds of the Confucian classics, and it developed into a system of private and social ethics that was to guide all aspects of life. Its rigid strictures on self-cultivation and ethical behavior failed in basic ways to address the complexities of human nature and the pressures of living in an increasingly complex world. Except among a very few committed thinkers, it was a philosophical position that invited gross hypocrisy. Vernacular literature, on the other hand, celebrated liberty, violent energy, and passion. Though such works often contained elements of neo-Confucian ethics and were later given pious neo-Confucian interpretations, by and large they either voiced qualities that neo-Confucianism sought to repress or savagely attacked society as a world of false appearances and secret evils.

In 1644 Manchu armies from the northeast descended into China and established a new dynasty, the Ch'ing, which would rule China until the revolution in 1911. Once again under non-Chinese rule and forced to wear the Manchu queue, a long ponytail, as a mark of submission, many Chinese harbored strong anti-Manchu sentiments. The Manchus, for their part, became very sensitive to native opposition. Censors set to survey current writings for hostility to the regime continually discovered slights, both real and imagined, against the dynasty. The late seventeenth and eighteenth centuries, known as the "literary inquisition," had a chilling effect on writing, especially in classical Chinese.

Such political realities may strongly affect, but do not entirely determine the intellectual and literary climate of an era. Ch'ing intellectual culture was a strong reaction against the radical individualism of the last part of the Ming, when personal freedom was celebrated at the expense of social responsibility. Early Ch'ing intellectuals held this late Ming ethos responsible for the decline of the Ming Dynasty. In the latter part of the seventeenth century and into the eighteenth century intellectuals turned away from Ming "subjectivism," the belief that each individual contained within himself or herself the grounds to make moral decisions and to interpret the authoritative texts of the tradition. The reaction saw not only a conservative public morality but also a new historical and philological rigor in the interpretation of early texts. This was closely analogous to the contemporary Western conflict in biblical studies between subjectivist "liberty of interpretation" and the development of historical philology—that is, the understanding of early texts by close study of how words were used at the time when the text was written. The new emphasis on historical scholarship had profound consequences for both China and the West, each of which had depended to some degree on the authority of received texts. This historical and philological approach to early texts was a form of empiricism, basing judgments on evidence and proof rather than tradition or private inclination. In China, as in the West at the same time, such empiricism in scholarship became linked to other forms of empiricism, such as interest in the natural sciences.

Ming subjectivist thought had found its strongest literary manifestation in a fascination with dreams, a world of illusion that was both a prominent theme in and a metaphor for the theater. And like Shakespeare, Chinese dramatists also observed that "all the world's a stage" and thus also a dream, as did the Spanish dramatist Calderón, author of *Life Is a Dream*. Drama, far more than prose fiction, dominated the literary world, both in the theater and in published texts. Social rituals and ceremonies had been one of the pillars of Confucian society, and these came increasingly to be represented in terms of theatrical performance. What had been norms of behavior became "roles," strongly suggesting awareness of their unreality and the presence of an individual who was only "playing" a role.

The eighteenth century was the last period of glory and self-confidence for traditional Chinese civilization. Although China had been in continuous contact with Europe since the sixteenth century, in the early nineteenth century European colonial powers began to make major inroads on Chinese autonomy. The opium trade, dominated by British merchants, drained away silver while producing a major social problem. In their campaign to stop the drug trade, the Chinese fired on a ship flying the British flag. From this followed the Opium War (1840–42), in which Great Britain inflicted a series of humiliating defeats on Chinese forces. In the treaty that followed, Hong Kong was ceded to Great Britain and five so-called treaty ports were established, subject to British law and control. Other European powers rushed to carve out their own enclaves. Christian missionaries, protected by treaty, spread throughout the country. One consequence was the T'ai-p'ing T'ien-kuo, the "Heavenly Kingdom of Great Peace," a political movement and religious sect that mingled Christianity and native Chinese beliefs. The T'ai-p'ing T'ien-kuo rose in rebellion against the Ch'ing government, and between 1850 and 1864 carried out a war that left central China in desolation.

Humiliated and exhausted, the Ch'ing government found itself unable to adapt, either culturally or technologically, to the world that had been thrust on it. Through the latter half of the nineteenth century and first decade of the twentieth, the Ch'ing Dynasty slowly disintegrated, until it was overthrown with remarkable ease in 1911, when the Republic of China was established.

FURTHER READING

A basic survey of the history of Chinese drama can be found in William Dolby, *A History of Chinese Drama* (1976). C. T. Hsia, *The Classic Chinese Novel: A Critical Introduction* (1968), remains one of the most readable introductions to the major novels. Patrick Hanan, *The Chinese Vernacular Story* (1981), provides an insightful study of the cultural background of vernacular fiction.

TIME LINE

TEXTS	CONTEXTS
1300–1350 Earliest printed versions of vernacular drama	
ca. 1350 Earliest publication of vernacular short stories	
	1368 Ming Dynasty is established with the capital at Nanking
	1405–1421 Ming admiral Cheng Ho explores southeast Asia, Sri Lanka, and the coast of Africa
	1421 The capital is moved to Peking
early 16th century Earliest edition of *Water Margin*, an episodic novel about a band of outlaws	
1522 Earliest edition of *Romance of the Three Kingdoms,* a long historical novel about the fall of the Han Dynasty	
1550–1617 T'ang Hsien-tsu, a major dramatist who developed the long *ch'uan-ch'i* play into a literary form	
1574–1646 Feng Meng-lung, collector and author of vernacular stories and popular songs, important in raising the status of vernacular literature	**1580–1644** Late Ming, a period of radical subjectivism and questioning of authority of tradition
	1583–1610 Matteo Ricci, Jesuit missionary, serves in China
1592 Earliest extant edition of **Monkey (*Journey to the West*)**	
1611–1680 Li Yü, comic dramatist, story writer, and champion of vernacular literature	
1617 Earliest edition of *Chin P'ing Mei* (Golden Lotus), a satirical novel of manners about a corrupt sensualist	
	1644–1645 Manchus conquer China • Ch'ing Dynasty is established • All Chinese males are forced to cut their hair and wear the queue

Boldface titles indicate works in the anthology.

TIME LINE

TEXTS	CONTEXTS
1648–1718 K'ung Shang-jen, author of *The Peach Blossom Fan* (1699)	
1715–1763 Cao Xueqin, author of *The Story of the Stone* (1740–50)	
	1736–1794 "Literary inquisition": earlier works are censored and many writers imprisoned for suspected critical references to the Ch'ing Dynasty
ca. 1750 *Ju-lin wai-shih* (The Scholars), a satirical novel; first extant edition 1803	
1788 The completion of the *Ssu-k'u ch'üan-shu,* a massive collection of all important earlier literature	

WU CH'ENG-EN
ca. 1506–1581

Like Malory's *Morte Darthur,* which combines Arthurian legends of the European Middle Ages, the novel or prose romance *Monkey* (properly, "Journey to the West," *Hsi-yu chi*) was not the work of a single person. First published in 1592, it represents a cumulative retelling and elaboration of materials that evolved over many centuries. Yet the final form of these stories in a vast, sprawling novel of one hundred chapters, often attributed to Wu Ch'eng-en, transformed the traditional material into a work of genius. The core of the story had a historical basis in the journey of the T'ang Buddhist monk Hsüan Tsang, or Tripitaka (596–664), from China to India in search of Buddhist scriptures. On his return, Hsüan Tsang left a short account of his experiences. The contents of this account had virtually nothing to do with the novel, but they may have served as the early basis from which the story began to be retold. Pilgrimages to India were by no means unique among Chinese monks of this era, but Tripitaka's journey somehow captured the popular imagination; it was retold in stories and plays, until it finally emerged as *Monkey.*

As Hsüan Tsang's journey was retold, the most important addition was his acquisition of a wondrous disciple Sun Wu-k'ung, Monkey Aware-of-Vacuity. Monkey had already made his appearance in a thirteenth-century version of the story and came to so dominate the full novel version that Arthur Waley named his condensation of the novel after this character.

It has long been debated whether *Monkey* is a work of exuberant play, celebrating Monkey's free spirit and turbulent ingenuity, or a serious allegory of Monkey and Tripitaka's journey toward Buddhist enlightenment. The novel is certainly something of both. An argument can be made, from a Buddhist point of view, that Tripitaka, however inept and timorous, is the novel's true hero. But for most readers, Chinese and Western, Monkey's splendid vitality and boundless humor remain the center of interest. Monkey's guardianship over Tripitaka is seconded by the ever-hungry and lustful Pigsy, who becomes increasingly unsympathetic as the journey progresses. Tripitaka's third disciple and protector is the gentle dragon Sandy, a former marshal of the hosts of Heaven who was sent to the bottom of a river to expiate the sin of having broken the Jade Emperor's (a Taoist divinity) crystal cup.

Above the four travelers is a divine machinery built of a synthesis of benign boddhisattvas (potential buddhas who linger in this world to help suffering humanity) and a Taoist pantheon of unruly and sometimes dangerous deities. On the earthly plane the pilgrims move through a landscape of strange kingdoms and monsters, stopping sometimes to help those in need or to protect themselves from harm. Some of the earthly monsters belong to the places where the pilgrims find them, but many of the demons and temptresses that the travelers encounter either are exiles and escapees from the heavenly realm or are sent on purpose to test the pilgrims.

Surrounded by three guardian disciples whose characters at the very least verge on the allegorical, Tripitaka is not only human but all too human. He is easily frightened, sometimes petulant, and never knows what to do. He is not so much driven on the pilgrimage by determined resolve as merely carried along by it. Yet he alone is the character destined for full buddhahood at the end, and his apparent lack of concern for the quest and for his disciples has been interpreted as the true manifestation of Buddhist detachment. Although Monkey grows increasingly devoted to his master through the course of the novel, Tripitaka never fully trusts him, however much he depends on him; and if there is a difficult Buddhist lesson in the novel, it is to grasp how Tripitaka, the ordinary man as saint, can be the novel's true hero. He is the empty center of the group, kept alive and carried forward by his more powerful and active disciples, both willing and unwilling. Yet he remains the master, and without him the pilgrimage would not exist.

Both Monkey and Pigsy are creatures of desire, though the nature of their desires differs greatly. Monkey, who had once lived an idyllic life with his monkey subjects in Water Curtain Cave, is, in the novel's early chapters, driven by a hunger for knowledge and immortality to search through the earth and the heavens. In the first stage of his existence, Monkey's hunger of the mind is never perfectly directed; it is a turbulence of spirit that always leads to mischief and an urge to create chaos. He acquires skills and magic tools that make him more powerful, but since he uses them unwisely, they only lead him to ever more outrageous escapades. After wreaking havoc in Heaven and being subdued by the god Erh-lang, he is imprisoned by the Buddha under a mountain for five hundred years; at last Monkey is given a chance to redeem himself by guarding Tripitaka on his pilgrimage to India.

During the course of the pilgrimage, Monkey becomes increasingly bound both to his master and to the quest itself, without ever losing his energy and humor. Despite occasional outbursts of his former mischief making, the quest becomes for Monkey a structured series of challenges by which he can focus and discipline his rambunctious intellect. The journey is driven forward by Monkey alone, with Tripitaka ever willing to give up in despair and Pigsy always ready to be seduced or return to his wife. Monkey understands the world with a comic detachment that is in some ways akin to Buddhist detachment, and this detachment makes him always more resourceful and often wiser than Tripitaka. Yet in his fierce energy and sheer joy in the use of his mind, Monkey falls short of the Buddhist ideal of true tranquility, while remaining the hero for unenlightened mortals.

Monkey is a complex character with many contradictions, as is perhaps fitting for a creature that may be seen in some sense as an allegory of the human mind. Pigsy, on the other hand, is a straightforward and predictable emblem of human sensual appetites. In his initial domestic setting, as the unwelcome son-in-law on Mr. Kao's farm, Pigsy was at least reliable and hardworking. But in the enforced celibacy of the pilgrimage, he grows increasingly slothful and undependable, always requiring Monkey's watchful prodding. Now and then on the journey he is permitted to gorge himself, but every time he finds a beautiful woman, something prevents him from satisfying his sexual appetite. Drafted into the quest, Pigsy did not freely choose it as expiation, as Monkey and Sandy did. And Pigsy wants to go home to his wife—or to take another along the way. Yet his Rabelaisian preoccupation with food and sex often makes him an endearing character.

The selections printed here treat Monkey's birth, his release by Tripitaka from imprisonment under the mountain, the gathering of the other disciples, and one of the early adventures in the kingdom of Cock-crow. Chapters II through XIII treat Monkey's acquisition of magical powers and his disruptions of Heaven and subsequent imprisonment as well as Tripitaka's commission from the T'ang emperor to go to India in search of scriptures. After leaving the kingdom of Cock-crow, the pilgrims continue on through numerous adventures, finally reaching India and acquiring the scriptures. In the last chapters all the pilgrims are whisked back to China by divine winds and are rewarded according to their merits (Pigsy, over his loud objections, is made janitor of the altars).

Like most Chinese novels, *Monkey* is very long. Arthur Waley's translation (1943) is an abridged version of thirty chapters out of the original one hundred, but Waley's gifts as a translator and the nature of his abridgement make this version a delight to read. In addition to Waley's abridgement, there is a complete and accurate four-volume translation of the novel by Anthony Yu, *Journey to the West* (1977–83), with a long introduction. There is also an excellent chapter on the novel in C. T. Hsia, *The Classic Chinese Novel: A Critical Introduction* (1968).

PRONOUNCING GLOSSARY

The following list uses common English syllables to provide rough equivalents of selected words whose pronunciation may be unfamiliar to the general reader.

Amitabha: *ah-mee-tahb-ha*

Ao-lai: *au–lai*

Chang Liang: *jahng lyahng*

Erh-lang: *ur–lahng*

Hsiao Ho: *shyau huh*

hsing: *shing*

Huang Shih Kung: *hwahng shir goong*

Hsüan Tsang: *shooahn dzahng*

Hui-yen: *hway–yen*

Jambudvīpa: *jahm-bood-vee-pah*

Kao Ts'ai: *gau tsai*

Kuan-yin: *gwahn–yin*

Lao Tzu: *lau dzuh*

Li Shih-min: *lee shir–min*

Lu Chia: *loo jyah*

Manjúsrī: *mahn-joosh-ree*

Sākyamuni: *shahk-yah-moo-nee*

śramana: *shrah-mah-nah*

Subodhi: *soo-bod-hee*

Sun Wu-k'ung: *swun woo-koong*

Trayaśimstra: *trah-ya-sheem-strah*

Wu Ch'eng-en: *woo chung-uhn*

Wu-ssu: *woo–suh*

Yü: *yoo*

Monkey[1]

CHAPTER I

There was a rock that since the creation of the world had been worked upon by the pure essences of Heaven and the fine savours of Earth, the vigour of sunshine and the grace of moonlight, till at last it became magically pregnant and one day split open, giving birth to a stone egg, about as big as a playing ball. Fructified by the wind it developed into a stone monkey, complete with every organ and limb. At once this monkey learned to climb and run; but its first act was to make a bow towards each of the four quarters. As it did so, a steely light darted from this monkey's eyes and flashed as far as the Palace of the Pole Star. This shaft of light astonished the Jade Emperor[2] as he sat in the Cloud Palace of the Golden Gates, in the Treasure Hall of the Holy Mists, surrounded by his fairy Ministers. Seeing this strange light flashing, he ordered Thousand-league Eye and Down-the-wind Ears[3] to open the gate of the Southern Heaven and look out. At his bidding these two captains went out to the gate and looked so sharply and listened so well that presently they were able to report, "This steely light comes from the borders of the small country of Ao-lai, that lies to the east of the Holy Continent, from the Mountain of Flowers and Fruit. On this mountain is a magic rock, which gave birth to an egg. This egg changed into a stone monkey, and when he made his bow to the four quarters a steely light flashed from his eyes with a beam that reached the Palace of the Pole Star. But now he is taking a drink, and the light is growing dim."

The Jade Emperor condescended to take an indulgent view. "These crea-

---

1. Translated by and with notes adapted from Arthur Waley.   2. The chief deity in the Taoist pantheon.
3. Here and throughout *Monkey* there are fantastic deities and places invented by the author.

tures in the world below," he said, "were compounded of the essence of heaven and earth, and nothing that goes on there should surprise us." That monkey walked, ran, leapt and bounded over the hills, feeding on grasses and shrubs, drinking from streams and springs, gathering the mountain flowers, looking for fruits. Wolf, panther and tiger were his companions, the deer and civet were his friends, gibbons and baboons his kindred. At night he lodged under cliffs of rock, by day he wandered among the peaks and caves. One very hot morning, after playing in the shade of some pine-trees, he and the other monkeys went to bathe in a mountain stream. See how those waters bounce and tumble like rolling melons!

There is an old saying, "Birds have their bird language, beasts have their beast talk." The monkeys said, "We none of us know where this stream comes from. As we have nothing to do this morning, wouldn't it be fun to follow it up to its source?" With a whoop of joy, dragging their sons and carrying their daughters, calling out to younger brother and to elder brother, the whole troupe rushed along the streamside and scrambled up the steep places, till they reached the source of the stream. They found themselves standing before the curtain of a great waterfall.

All the monkeys clapped their hands and cried aloud, "Lovely water, lovely water! To think that it starts far off in some cavern below the base of the mountain, and flows all the way to the Great Sea! If any of us were bold enough to pierce that curtain, get to where the water comes from and return unharmed, we would make him our king!" Three times the call went out, when suddenly one of them leapt from among the throng and answered the challenge in a loud voice. It was the Stone Monkey. "I will go," he cried, "I will go!" Look at him! He screws up his eyes and crouches; then at one bound he jumps straight through the waterfall. When he opened his eyes and looked about him, he found that where he had landed there was no water. A great bridge stretched in front of him, shining and glinting. When he looked closely at it, he saw that it was made all of burnished iron. The water under it flowed through a hole in the rock, filling in all the space under the arch. Monkey climbed up on to the bridge and, spying as he went, saw something that looked just like a house. There were stone seats and stone couches, and tables with stone bowls and cups. He skipped back to the hum of the bridge and saw that on the cliff there was an inscription in large square writing which said, "This cave of the Water Curtain in the blessed land of the Mountain of Flowers and Fruit leads to Heaven." Monkey was beside himself with delight. He rushed back and again crouched, shut his eyes and jumped through the curtain of water.

"A great stroke of luck," he cried, "A great stroke of luck." "What is it like on the other side?" asked the monkeys, crowding round him. "Is the water very deep?" "There is no water," said the Stone Monkey. "There is an iron bridge, and at the side of it a heaven-sent place to live in." "What made you think it would do to live in?" asked the monkeys. "The water," said the Stone Monkey, "flows out of a hole in the rock, filling in the space under the bridge. At the side of the bridge are flowers and trees, and there is a chamber of stone. Inside are stone tables, stone cups, stone dishes, stone couches, stone seats. We could really be very comfortable there. There is plenty of room for hundreds and thousands of us, young and old. Let us all go and live there; we shall be splendidly sheltered in every weather." "You go first and show us how!" cried the monkeys, in great delight. Once more he closed his eyes and was through at one bound. "Come along, all of you!" he cried. The bolder of them jumped at once; the more timid stretched out their heads and then drew them back, scratched their ears, rubbed their cheeks, and then with a great shout the whole mob leapt forward. Soon they were all seizing dishes and snatching cups, scrambling to the hearth or fighting for the beds, dragging things along or shifting them about, behaving indeed as monkeys with their mischievous nature might be expected to do, never quiet for an instant, till at last they were thoroughly worn out. The Stone Monkey took his seat at the head of them and said, "Gentlemen! 'With one whose word cannot be trusted there is nothing to be done!'[4] You promised that any of us who managed to get through the waterfall and back again, should be your king. I have not only come and gone and come again, but also found you a comfortable place to sleep, put you in the enviable position of being householders. Why do you not bow down to me as your king?"

Thus reminded, the monkeys all pressed together the palms of their hands and prostrated themselves, drawn up in a line according to age and standing, and bowing humbly they cried, "Great king, a thousand years!" After this the Stone Monkey discarded his old name and became king, with the title "Handsome Monkey King." He appointed various monkeys, gibbons and baboons to be his ministers and officers. By day they wandered about the Mountain of Flowers and Fruit; at night they slept in the Cave of the Water Curtain. They lived in perfect sympathy and accord, not mingling with bird or beast, in perfect independence and entire happiness.

The Monkey King had enjoyed this artless existence for several hundred years when one day, at a feast in which all the monkeys took part, the king suddenly felt very sad and burst into tears. His subjects at once ranged themselves in front of him and bowed down, saying, "Why is your Majesty so sad?" "At present," said the king, "I have no cause for unhappiness. But I have a misgiving about the future, which troubles me sorely." "Your Majesty is very hard to please," said the monkeys, laughing. "Every day we have happy meetings on fairy mountains, in blessed spots, in ancient caves, on holy islands. We are not subject to the Unicorn or Phoenix, nor to the restraints of any human king. Such freedom is an immeasurable blessing. What can it be that causes you this sad misgiving?" "It is true," said the Monkey King, "that today I am not answerable to the law of any human king, nor need I fear the menace of any beast or bird. But the time will come when I shall grow old and weak. Yama, King of Death, is secretly waiting to destroy me. Is there no way by which, instead of being born again on earth, I might live forever among the people of the sky?"

When the monkeys heard this they covered their faces with their hands and wept, each thinking of his own mortality. But look! From among the ranks there springs out one monkey commoner, who cries in a loud voice "If that is what troubles your Majesty, it shows that religion has taken hold upon your heart. There are indeed, among all creatures, three kinds that are not subject to Yama, King of Death." "And do you know which they are?" asked the Monkey King. "Buddhas, Immortals and Sages,"[5] he said. "These three

---

4. From Confucius's *Analects* II.22.   5. The highest stages of religious perfection in Buddhism, Taoism, and Confucianism, respectively.

are exempt from the Turning of the Wheel, from birth and destruction. They are eternal as Heaven and Earth, as the hills and streams." "Where are they to be found?" asked the Monkey King. "Here on the common earth," said the monkey, "in ancient caves among enchanted hills."

The king was delighted with this news. "To-morrow," he said, "I shall say good-bye to you, go down the mountain, wander like a cloud to the corners of the sea, far away to the end of the world, till I have found these three kinds of Immortal. From them I will learn how to be young forever and escape the doom of death." This determination it was that led him to leap clear of the toils of Re-incarnation and turned him at last into the Great Monkey Sage, equal of Heaven. The monkeys clapped their hands and cried aloud, "Splendid! Splendid! To-morrow we will scour the hills for fruits and berries and hold a great farewell banquet in honour of our king."

Next day they duly went to gather peaches and rare fruits, mountain herbs, yellow-sperm,[6] tubers, orchids, strange plants and flowers of every sort, and set out the stone tables and benches, laid out fairy meats and drinks. They put the Monkey King at the head of the table, and ranged themselves according to their age and rank. The pledge-cup[7] passed from hand to hand; they made their offerings to him of flowers and fruit. All day long they drank, and next day their king rose early and said, "Little ones, cut some pine-wood for me and make me a raft; then find a tall bamboo for pole, and put together a few fruits and such like. I am going to start." He got on to the raft all alone and pushed off with all his might, speeding away and away, straight out to sea, till favoured by a following wind he arrived at the borders of the Southern World. Fate indeed had favoured him; for days on end, ever since he set foot on the raft, a strong southeast wind blew and carried him at last to the north-western bank, which is indeed the frontier of the Southern World. He tested the water with his pole and found that it was shallow; so he left the raft and climbed ashore. On the beach were people fishing, shooting wild geese, scooping oysters, draining salt. He ran up to them and for fun began to perform queer antics which frightened them so much that they dropped their baskets and nets and ran for their lives. One of them, who stood his ground, Monkey caught hold of, and ripping off his clothes, found out how to wear them himself, and so dressed up went prancing through towns and cities, in market and bazaar, imitating the people's manners and talk. All the while his heart was set only on finding the Immortals and learning from them the secret of eternal youth. But he found the men of the world all engrossed in the quest of profit or fame; there was not one who had any care for the end that was in store for him. So Monkey went looking for the way of Immortality, but found no chance of meeting it. For eight or nine years he went from city to city and town to town till suddenly he came to the Western Ocean. He was sure that beyond this ocean there would certainly be Immortals, and he made for himself a raft like the one he had before. He floated on over the Western Ocean till he came to the Western Continent, where he went ashore, and when he had looked about for some time, he suddenly saw a very high and beautiful mountain, thickly wooded at the base. He had no fear of wolves, tigers or panthers, and made his way up to the very top. He was looking about him when he suddenly heard a man's voice coming from deep

6. Unidentified plant.   7. A cup used for offering toasts.

amid the woods. He hurried towards the spot and listened intently. It was some one singing, and these were the words that he caught:

> I hatch no plot, I scheme no scheme;
> Fame and shame are one to me,
> A simple life prolongs my days.
> Those I meet upon my way
> Are Immortals, one and all,
> Who from their quiet seats expound
> The Scriptures of the Yellow Court.[8]

When Monkey heard these words he was very pleased. "There must then be Immortals somewhere hereabouts," he said. He sprang deep into the forest and looking carefully saw that the singer was a woodman, who was cutting brushwood. "Reverend Immortal," said Monkey, coming forward, "your disciple raises his hands." The woodman was so astonished that he dropped his axe. "You have made a mistake," he said, turning and answering the salutation, "I am only a shabby, hungry woodcutter. What makes you address me as an 'Immortal'?" "If you are not an Immortal," said Monkey, "why did you talk of yourself as though you were one?" "What did I say," asked the woodcutter, "that sounded as though I were an Immortal?" "When I came to the edge of the wood," said Monkey, "I heard you singing 'Those I meet upon my way are Immortals, one and all, who from their quiet seats expound the Scriptures of the Yellow Court.' Those scriptures are secret, Taoist texts. What can you be but an Immortal?" "I won't deceive you," said the woodcutter. "That song was indeed taught to me by an Immortal, who lives not very far from my hut. He saw that I have to work hard for my living and have a lot of troubles; so he told me when I was worried by anything to say to myself the words of that song. This, he said, would comfort me and get me out of my difficulties. Just now I was upset about something and so I was singing that song. I had no idea that you were listening."

"If the Immortal lives close by," said Monkey, "how is it that you have not become his disciple? Wouldn't it have been as well to learn from him how never to grow old?" "I have a hard life of it," said the woodcutter. "When I was eight or nine I lost my father. I had no brothers and sisters, and it fell upon me alone to support my widowed mother. There was nothing for it but to work hard early and late. Now my mother is old and I dare not leave her. The garden is neglected, we have not enough either to eat or wear. The most I can do is to cut two bundles of firewood, carry them to market and with the penny or two that I get buy a few handfuls of rice which I cook myself and serve to my aged mother. I have no time to go and learn magic." "From what you tell me," said Monkey, "I can see that you are a good and devoted son, and your piety will certainly be rewarded. All I ask of you is that you will show me where the Immortal lives; for I should very much like to visit him."

"It is quite close," said the woodcutter. "This mountain is called the Holy Terrace Mountain, and on it is a cave called the Cave of the Slanting Moon and Three Stars. In that cave lives an Immortal called the Patriarch Subodhi. In his time he has had innumerable disciples, and at this moment there are

---

8. Texts of esoteric knowledge, containing secrets of immortality.

some thirty or forty of them studying with him. You have only to follow that small path southwards for eight or nine leagues,[9] and you will come to his home." "Honoured brother," said Monkey, drawing the woodcutter towards him, "come with me, and if I profit by the visit I will not forget that you guided me." "It takes a lot to make some people understand," said the woodcutter. "I've just been telling you why I can't go. If I went with you, what would become of my work? Who would give my old mother her food? I must go on cutting my wood, and you must find your way alone."

When Monkey heard this, he saw nothing for it but to say good-bye. He left the wood, found the path, went uphill for some seven or eight leagues and sure enough found a cave-dwelling. But the door was locked. All was quiet, and there was no sign of anyone being about. Suddenly he turned his head and saw on top of the cliff a stone slab about thirty feet high and eight feet wide. On it was an inscription in large letters saying, "Cave of the Slanting Moon and Three Stars on the Mountain of the Holy Terrace." "People here," said Monkey, "are certainly very truthful. There really is such a mountain, and such a cave!" He looked about for a while, but did not venture to knock at the door. Instead he jumped up into a pine-tree and began eating the pine-seed and playing among the branches. After a time he heard someone call; the door of the cave opened and a fairy boy of great beauty came out, in appearance utterly unlike the common lads that he had seen till now. The boy shouted, "Who is making a disturbance out there?" Monkey leapt down from his tree, and coming forward said with a bow, "Fairy boy, I am a pupil who has come to study Immortality. I should not dream of making a disturbance." "*You* a pupil!" said the boy laughing. "To be sure," said Monkey. "My master is lecturing," said the boy. "But before he gave out his theme he told me to go to the door and if anyone came asking for instruction, I was to look after him. I suppose he meant you." "Of course he meant me," said Monkey. "Follow me this way," said the boy. Monkey tidied himself and followed the boy into the cave. Huge chambers opened out before them, they went on from room to room, through lofty halls and innumerable cloisters and retreats, till they came to a platform of green jade, upon which was seated the Patriarch Subodhi, with thirty lesser Immortals assembled before him. Monkey at once prostrated himself and bumped his head three times upon the ground, murmuring, "Master, master! As pupil to teacher I pay you my humble respects." "Where do you come from?" asked the Patriarch. "First tell me your country and name, and then pay your respects again." "I am from the Water Curtain Cave," said Monkey, "on the Mountain of Fruit and Flowers in the country of Ao-lai." "Go away!" shouted the Patriarch. "I know the people there. They're a tricky, humbugging set. It's no good one of them supposing he's going to achieve Enlightenment." Monkey, kowtowing violently, hastened to say, "There's no trickery about this; it's just the plain truth I'm telling you." "If you claim that you're telling the truth," said the Patriarch, "how is it that you say you came from Ao-lai? Between there and here there are two oceans and the whole of the Southern Continent. How did you get here?" "I floated over the oceans and wandered over the lands for ten years and more," said Monkey, "till at last I reached here." "Oh well," said the Patriarch, "I suppose if you came by easy stages, it's not altogether impos-

9. One league was equal to 360 steps.

sible. But tell me, what is your *hsing?*"[1] "I never show *hsing*," said Monkey. "If I am abused, I am not at all annoyed. If I am hit, I am not angry; but on the contrary, twice more polite than before. All my life I have never shown *hsing*."

"I don't mean that kind of *hsing*," said the Patriarch. "I mean what was your family, what surname had they?" "I had no family," said Monkey, "neither father nor mother." "Oh indeed!" said the Patriarch. "Perhaps you grew on a tree!" "Not exactly," said Monkey. "I came out of a stone. There was a magic stone on the Mountain of Flowers and Fruit. When its time came, it burst open and I came out."

"We shall have to see about giving you a school-name,"[2] said the Patriarch. "We have twelve words that we use in these names, according to the grade of the pupil. You are in the tenth grade." "What are the twelve words?" asked Monkey. "They are Wide, Big, Wise, Clever, True, Conforming, Nature, Ocean, Lively, Aware, Perfect and Illumined. As you belong to the tenth grade, the word Aware must come in your name. How about Aware-of-Vacuity?" "Splendid!" said Monkey, laughing. "From now onwards let me be called Aware-of-Vacuity."

So that was his name in religion. And if you do not know whether in the end, equipped with this name, he managed to obtain enlightenment or not, listen while it is explained to you in the next chapter.

*　　*　　*

CHAPTER XIV

The hunter and Tripitaka were still wondering who had spoken, when again they heard the voice saying, "The Master has come." The hunter's servants said, "That is the voice of the old monkey who is shut up in the stone casket of the mountain side." "Why, to be sure it is!" said the hunter. "What old monkey is that?" asked Tripitaka. "This mountain," said the hunter, "was once called the Mountain of the Five Elements. But after our great T'ang Dynasty had carried out its campaigns to the West, its name was changed to Mountain of the Two Frontiers. Years ago a very old man told me that at the time when Wang Mang overthrew the First Han Dynasty, Heaven dropped this mountain in order to imprison a magic monkey under it. He has local spirits as his gaolers, who, when he is hungry give him iron pills to eat, and when he is thirsty give him copper-juice to drink, so that despite cold and short commons[3] he is still alive. That cry certainly comes from him. You need not be uneasy. We'll go down and have a look."

After going downhill for some way they came to the stone box, in which there was really a monkey. Only his head was visible, and one paw, which he waved violently through the opening, saying, "Welcome, Master! Welcome! Get me out of here, and I will protect you on your journey to the West." The hunter stepped boldly up, and removing the grasses from Monkey's hair and brushing away the grit from under his chin, "What have you got to say for yourself?" he asked. "To you, nothing," said Monkey. "But I have something to ask of that priest. Tell him to come here." "What do you want to ask me?" said Tripitaka. "Were you sent by the Emperor of T'ang to

---

1. This is a pun. *Hsing* can mean "surname" or "temper."　　2. A religious name assumed by a disciple.
3. Daily provisions.

look for Scriptures in India?" asked Monkey. "I was," said Tripitaka. "And what of that?" "I am the Great Sage Equal of Heaven," said Monkey. "Five hundred years ago I made trouble in the Halls of Heaven, and Buddha clamped me down in this place. Not long ago the Bodhisattva Kuan-yin,[4] whom Buddha had ordered to look around for someone to fetch Scriptures from India, came here and promised me that if I would amend my ways and faithfully protect the pilgrim on his way, I was to be released, and afterwards would find salvation. Ever since then I have been waiting impatiently night and day for you to come and let me out. I will protect you while you are going to get Scriptures and follow you as your disciple."

Tripitaka was delighted. "The only trouble is," he said, "that I have no axe or chisel, so how am I to get you out?" "There is no need for axe or chisel," said Monkey. "You have only to want me to be out, and I shall be out." "How can that be?" asked Tripitaka. "On the top of the mountain," said Monkey, "is a seal stamped with golden letters by Buddha himself. Take it away, and I shall be out." Tripitaka was for doing so at once, but the hunter took him aside and said there was no telling whether one could believe the monkey or not. "It's true, it's true!" screamed Monkey from inside the casket. At last the hunter was prevailed upon to come with him and, scrambling back again to the very top, they did indeed see innumerable beams of golden light streaming from a great square slab of rock, on which was imprinted in golden letters the inscription OM MANI PADME HUM.[5]

Tripitaka knelt down and did reverence to the inscription, saying, "If this monkey is indeed worthy to be a disciple, may this imprint be removed and may the monkey be released and accompany me to the seat of Buddha. But if he is not fit to be a disciple, but an unruly monster who would discredit my undertaking, may the imprint of this seal remain where it is." At once there came a gust of fragrant wind that carried the six letters[6] of the inscription up into the air, and a voice was heard saying, "I am the Great Sage's gaoler. To-day the time of his penance is ended and I am going to ask Buddha to let him loose." Having bowed reverently in the direction from which the voice came, Tripitaka and the hunter went back to the stone casket and said to Monkey, "The inscription is removed. You can come out." "You must go to a little distance," said Monkey. "I don't want to frighten you." They withdrew a little way, but heard Monkey calling to them "Further, further!" They did as they were bid, and presently heard a tremendous crushing and rending. They were all in great consternation, expecting the mountain to come hurtling on top of them, when suddenly the noise subsided, and Monkey appeared, kneeling in front of Tripitaka's horse, crying, "Master, I am out!" Then he sprang up and called to the hunter, "Brother, I'll trouble you to dust the grass-wisps from my cheek." Then he put together the packs and hoisted them on to the horse, which on seeing him became at once completely obedient. For Monkey had been a groom in Heaven, and it was natural that an ordinary horse should hold him in great awe.

Tripitaka, seeing that he knew how to make himself useful and looked as though he would make a pretty tolerable śramana,[7] said to him, "Disciple,

4. Associated with mercy and compassion. A *bodhisattva* is a potential buddha who remains in the world to help others achieve salvation.   5. A magic spell (in Sanskrit) that keeps Monkey imprisoned.   6. The inscription consists of six letters in devanagari, the script in which Sanskrit is written.   7. A Buddhist monk.

we must give you a name in religion." "No need for that," said Monkey, "I have one already. My name in religion is 'Aware-of-Vacuity.' " "Excellent!" said Tripitaka. "That fits in very well with the names of my other disciples. You shall be Monkey Aware-of-Vacuity."

The hunter, seeing that Monkey had got everything ready, said to Tripitaka, "I am very glad you have been fortunate enough to pick up this excellent disciple. As you are so well provided for, I will bid you good-bye and turn back." "I have brought you a long way from home," said Tripitaka, "and cannot thank you enough. Please also apologize to your mother and wife for all the trouble I gave, and tell them I will thank them in person on my return."

Tripitaka had not been long on the road with Monkey and had only just got clear of the Mountain of the Two Frontiers, when a tiger suddenly appeared, roaring savagely and lashing its tail. Tripitaka was terrified, but Monkey seemed delighted. "Don't be frightened, Master," he said. "He has only come to supply me with an apron."[8] So saying, he took a needle from behind his ear and, turning his face to the wind, made a few magic passes, and instantly it became a huge iron cudgel.[9] "It is five hundred years since I last used this precious thing," he said, "and to-day it is going to furnish me with a little much-needed clothing."

Look at him! He strides forward, crying, "Cursed creature, stand your ground!" The tiger crouched in the dust and dared not budge. Down came the cudgel on its head. The earth was spattered with its blood. Tripitaka rolled off his horse as best he could, crying with an awe-struck voice, "Heavens! When the hunter killed that stripy tiger yesterday, he struggled with it for hours on end. But this disciple of mine walked straight up to the tiger and struck it dead. True indeed is the saying 'Strong though he be, there is always a stronger.' " "Sit down a while," said Monkey, "and wait while I undress him; then when I am dressed, we'll go on." "How can you undress him?" said Tripitaka. "He hasn't got any clothes." "Don't worry about me," said Monkey. "I know what I am about." Dear Monkey! He took a hair from his tail, blew on it with magic breath, and it became a sharp little knife, with which he slit the tiger's skin straight down and ripped it off in one piece. Then he cut off the paws and head, and trimmed the skin into one big square. Holding it out, he measured it with his eye, and said, "A bit too wide. I must divide it in two." He cut it in half, put one half aside and the other round his waist, making it fast with some rattan that he pulled up from the roadside. "Now we can go," he said, "and when we get to the next house, I'll borrow a needle and thread and sew it up properly."

"What has become of your cudgel?" asked Tripitaka, when they were on their way again. "I must explain to you," said Monkey. "This cudgel is a piece of magic iron that I got in the Dragon King's palace, and it was with it that I made havoc in Heaven. I can make it as large or as small as I please. Just now I made it the size of an embroidery needle and put it away behind my ear, where it is always at hand in case I need it." "And why," asked Tripitaka, "did that tiger, as soon as it saw you, crouch down motionless and allow you to strike it just as you chose?" "The fact is," said Monkey, "that not only tigers but dragons too dare not do anything against me. But that is not all. I have such arts as can make rivers turn back in their course, and can raise

---

8. That is, Monkey will kill the tiger and take the tiger skin to wear around his waist.   9. A club.

tempests on the sea. Small wonder, then, that I can filch a tiger's skin. When we get into real difficulties you will see what I am really capable of."

"Master," said Monkey presently, "it is getting late. Over there is a clump of trees, and I think there must be a house. We had better see if we can spend the night there." Tripitaka whipped his horse, and soon they did indeed come to a farm, outside the gates of which he dismounted. Monkey cried "Open the door!" and presently there appeared a very old man, leaning on a staff. Muttering to himself, he began to push open the door, but when he saw Monkey, looking (with the tiger skin at his waist) for all the world like a thunder demon, he was terrified out of his wits and could only murmur "There's a devil at the door, sure enough there's a devil!" Tripitaka came up to him just in time to prevent him hobbling away. "Old patron," he said, "you need not be afraid. This is not a devil; it is my disciple." Seeing that Tripitaka at any rate was a clean-built, comely man, he took comfort a little and said, "I don't know what temple you come from, but you have no right to bring such an evil-looking fellow to my house." "I come from the Court of T'ang," said Tripitaka, "and I am going to India to get Scriptures. As my way brought me near your house, I have come here in the hope that you would consent to give me a night's lodging. I shall be starting off again tomorrow before daybreak." "You may be a man of T'ang," said the old man, "but I'll warrant that villainous fellow is no man of T'ang!" "Have you no eyes in your head," shouted Monkey. "The man of T'ang is my master. I am his disciple, and no man of T'ang or sugar-man[1] or honey-man either. I am the Great Sage Equal to Heaven. You people here know me well enough, and I have seen you before." "Where have you seen me?" he asked. "Didn't you when you were small cut the brushwood from in front of my face and gather the herbs that grew on my cheek?" "The stone monkey in the stone casket!" gasped the old man. "I see that you are a little like him. But how did you get out?" Monkey told the whole story, and the old man at once bowed before him, and asked them both to step inside. "Great Sage, how old are you?" the old man asked, when they were seated. "Let us first hear your age," said Monkey. "A hundred and thirty," said the old man. "Then you are young enough to be my great-great-grandson at least," said Monkey. "I have no idea when I was born. But I was under that mountain for five hundred years." "True enough," said the old man. "I remember my grandfather telling me that this mountain was dropped from Heaven in order to trap a monkey divinity, and you say that you have only just got out. When I used to see you in my childhood, there was grass growing out of your head and mud on your cheeks. I was not at all afraid of you then. Now there is no mud on your cheeks and no grass on your head. You look thinner, and with that tiger-skin at your waist, who would know that you weren't a devil?" "I don't want to give you all a lot of trouble," said Monkey presently, "but it is five hundred years since I last washed. Could you let us have a little hot water? I am sure my Master would be glad to wash too."

When they had both washed, they sat down in front of the lamp. "One more request," said Monkey. "Could you lend me a needle and thread?" "By all means, by all means," said the old man, and he told his old wife to bring them. Just then Monkey caught sight of a white shirt that Tripitaka had taken

1. *T'ang* can mean "sugar."

off when he washed and not put on again. He snatched it up and put it on. Then he wriggled out of the tiger-skin, sewed it up in one piece, made a "horse-face fold"[2] and put it round his waist again, fastening the rattan belt. Presenting himself to Tripitaka he said, "How do you like me in this garb? Is it an improvement?" "Splendid!" said Tripitaka. "Now you really do look like a pilgrim." "Disciple," added Tripitaka, "if you don't mind accepting an off-cast, you can have that shirt for your own."

They rose early next day, and the old man brought them washing-water and breakfast. Then they set out again on their way, lodging late and starting early for many days. One morning they suddenly heard a cry and six men rushed out at them from the roadside, all armed with pikes and swords. "Halt, priest!" they cried. "We want your horse and your packs, and quickly too, or you will not escape with your life."

Tripitaka, in great alarm, slid down from his horse and stood there speechless. "Don't worry," said Monkey. "This only means more clothes and travelling-money for us." "Monkey, are you deaf?" said Tripitaka. "They ordered us to surrender the horse and luggage, and you talk of getting clothes and money from them!" "You keep an eye on the packs and the horse," said Monkey, "while I settle matters with them! You'll soon see what I mean." "They are very strong men and there are six of them," said Tripitaka. "How can a little fellow like you hope to stand up against them single-handed?"

Monkey did not stop to argue, but strode forward and, folding his arms across his chest, bowed to the robbers and said, "Sirs, for what reason do you stop poor priests from going on their way?" "We are robber kings," they said, "mountain lords among the Benevolent.[3] Everyone knows us. How comes it that you are so ignorant? Hand over your things at once, and we will let you pass. But if half the word 'no' leaves your lips, we shall hack you to pieces and grind your bones to powder." "I, too," said Monkey, "am a great hereditary king, and lord of a mountain for hundreds of years; yet I have never heard your names." "In that case, let us tell you," they said. "The first of us is called Eye that Sees and Delights; the second, Ear that Hears and is Angry; the third, Nose that Smells and Covets; the fourth, Tongue that Tastes and Desires; the fifth, Mind that Conceives and Lusts; the sixth, Body that Supports and Suffers." "You're nothing but six hairy ruffians," said Monkey, laughing. "We priests, I would have you know, are your lords and masters, yet you dare block our path. Bring out all the stolen goods you have about you and divide them into seven parts. Then, if you leave me one part, I will spare your lives."

The robbers were so taken aback that they did not know whether to be angry or amused. "You must be mad," they said. "You've just lost all you possess, and you talk of sharing our booty with us!" Brandishing their spears and flourishing their swords they all rushed forward and began to rain blows upon Monkey's head. But he stood stock still and betrayed not the slightest concern. "Priest, your head must be very hard!" they cried. "That's all right," said Monkey, "I'm not in a hurry. But when your arms are tired, I'll take out my needle and do my turn." "What does he mean?" they said. "Perhaps he's a doctor turned priest. But we are none of us ill, so why should he talk about using the needle?"

2. Unclear; the modern edition reads "sewed it into a skirt." 3. The thieves' slang for "bandit."

Monkey took his needle from behind his ear, recited a spell which changed it into a huge cudgel, and cried, "Hold your ground and let old Monkey try his hand upon you!" The robbers fled in confusion, but in an instant he was among them and striking right and left he slew them all, stripped off their clothing and seized their baggage. Then he came back to Tripitaka and said laughing, "Master, we can start now; I have killed them all." "I am very sorry to hear it," said Tripitaka. "One has no right to kill robbers, however violent and wicked they may be. The most one may do is to bring them before a magistrate. It would have been quite enough in this case if you had driven them away. Why kill them? You have behaved with a cruelty that ill becomes one of your sacred calling." "If I had not killed them," said Monkey, "they would have killed you." "A priest," said Tripitaka, "should be ready to die rather than commit acts of violence." "I don't mind telling you," said Monkey, "that five hundred years ago, when I was a king, I killed a pretty fair number of people, and if I had held your view I should certainly never have become the Great Sage Equal of Heaven." "It was because of your unfortunate per-formances in Heaven," said Tripitaka, "that you had to do penance for five hundred years. If now that you have repented and become a priest you go on behaving as in old days, you can't come with me to India. You've made a very bad start." The one thing Monkey had never been able to bear was to be scolded, and when Tripitaka began to lecture him like this, he flared up at once and cried, "All right! I'll give up being a priest, and won't go with you to India. You needn't go on at me any more. I'm off!" Tripitaka did not answer. His silence enraged Monkey even further. He shook himself and with a last "I'm off!" he bounded away. When Tripitaka looked up, he had completely disappeared. "It's no use trying to teach people like that," said Tripitaka to himself gloomily. "I only said a word or two, and off he goes. Very well then. Evidently it is not my fate to have a disciple; so I must get on as best I can without one."

He collected the luggage, hoisted it on to the horse's back and set out on foot, leading the horse with one hand and carrying his priest's staff with the other, in very low spirits. He had not gone far, when he saw an old woman carrying a brocaded coat and embroidered cap. As she came near, Tripitaka drew his horse to the side of the road to let her pass. "Where are you off to all alone?" she asked. "The Emperor of China has sent me to India to fetch Scriptures," said Tripitaka. "The Temple of the Great Thunder Clap where Buddha lives," said she, "is a hundred and one thousand leagues away. You surely don't expect to get there with only one horse and no disciple to wait upon you?" "I picked up a disciple a few days ago," said Tripitaka, "but he behaved badly and I was obliged to speak rather severely to him; whereupon he went off in a huff, and I have not seen him since." "I've got a brocade coat and a cap with a metal band," said the old woman. "They belonged to my son. He entered a monastery, but when he had been a monk for three days, he died. I went and fetched them from the monastery to keep in mem-ory of him. If you had a disciple, I should be very glad to let you have them." "That is very kind of you," said Tripitaka, "but my disciple has run away, so I cannot accept them." "Which way did he go?" asked the old woman. "The last time I heard his voice, it came from the east," said Tripitaka. "That's the way that my house lies," said the old woman. "I expect he'll turn up there. I've got a spell here which I'll let you learn, if you promise not to teach it to anybody. I'll go and look for him and send him back to you. Make him wear this cap and coat. If he disobeys you, say the spell, and he'll give no more trouble and never dare to leave you." Suddenly the old woman changed into a shaft of golden light, which disappeared towards the east. Tripitaka at once guessed that she was the Bodhisattva Kuan-yin in disguise. He bowed and burned incense towards the east. Then having stored away the cap and coat he sat at the roadside, practising the spell.

After Monkey left the Master, he somersaulted through the clouds and landed right in the palace of the Dragon King of the Eastern Ocean. "I heard recently that your penance was over," said the dragon, "and made sure you would have gone back to be king in your fairy cave." "That's what I am doing," said Monkey. "But to start with I became a priest." "A priest?" said the dragon. "How did that happen?" "Kuan-yin persuaded me to accompany a priest of T'ang," said Monkey, "who is going to India to get Scriptures; so I was admitted to the Order." "That's certainly a step in the right direction," said the dragon. "I am sure I congratulate you. But in that case, what are you doing here in the east?" "It comes of my master being so unpractical," said Monkey. "We met some brigands, and naturally I killed them. Then he started scolding me. You may imagine I wasn't going to stand that. So I left him at once, and am going back to my kingdom. But I thought I would look you up on the way, and see if you could give me a cup of tea."

When he had been given his cup of tea, he looked round the room, and saw on the wall a picture of Chang Liang[4] offering the slipper. Monkey asked what it was about. "You were in Heaven at the time," said the dragon, "and naturally would not know about it. The immortal in the picture is Huang Shih Kung, and the other figure is Chang Liang. Once when Shih Kung was sitting on a bridge, his shoe came off and fell under the bridge. He called to Chang Liang to pick it up and bring it to him. Chang Liang did so, whereupon the Immortal at once let it fall again, and Chang Liang again fetched it. This happened three times, without Chang Liang showing the slightest sign of impatience. Huang Shih Kung then gave him a magic treatise, by means of which he defeated all the enemies of the House of Han, and became the greatest hero of the Han dynasty. In his old age he became a disciple of the Immortal Red Pine Seed and achieved Tao.[5] Great Sage, you must learn to have a little more patience, if you hope to accompany the pilgrim to India and gain the Fruits of Illumination." Monkey looked thoughtful. "Great Sage," said the dragon, "you must learn to control yourself and submit to the will of others, if you are not to spoil all your chances." "Not another word!" said Monkey, "I'll go back at once."

On the way he met the Bodhisattva Kuan-yin. "What are you doing here?" she asked. "The seal was removed and I got out," said Monkey, "and became Tripitaka's disciple. But he said I didn't know how to behave, and I gave him the slip. But now I am going back to look after him." "Go as fast as you can," said the Bodhisattva, "and try to do better this time." "Master," said Monkey, when he came back and found Tripitaka sitting dejectedly by the roadside, "what are you doing still sitting here?" "And where have you been?" asked Tripitaka. "I hadn't the heart to go on, and was just sitting here waiting for

4. A general who helped found the Han Dynasty; he was supposed to have had magical skills.   5. That is, immortality.

you." "I only went to the dragon of the eastern ocean," said Monkey, "to drink a cup of tea." "Now Monkey," said Tripitaka, "priests must always be careful to tell the truth. You know quite well that the dragon king lives far away in the east, and you have only been gone an hour." "That's easily explained," said Monkey. "I have the art of somersaulting through the clouds. One bound takes me a hundred and eight thousand leagues." "It seemed to me that you went off in a huff," said Tripitaka, "because I had to speak rather sharply to you. It's all very well for you to go off and get tea like that, if you are able to. But I think you might remember that I can't go with you. Doesn't it occur to you that I may be thirsty and hungry too?" "If you are," said Monkey, "I'll take a bowl and go and beg for you." "There isn't any need to do that," said Tripitaka. "There are some dried provisions in the pack." When Monkey opened the pack, his eye was caught by something bright. "Did you bring this coat and cap with you from the east?" he asked. "I used to wear them when I was young," replied Tripitaka, saying the first thing that came into his head. "Anyone who wears this cap can recite scriptures without having to learn them. Anyone who wears this coat can perform ceremonies without having practised them." "Dear Master," said Monkey, "let me put them on." "By all means," said Tripitaka. Monkey put on the coat and cap, and Tripitaka, pretending to be eating the dried provisions, silently mumbled the spell. "My head is hurting!" screamed Monkey. Tripitaka went on reciting, and Monkey rolled over on the ground, frantically trying to break the metal fillet of the cap. Fearing that he would succeed, Tripitaka stopped for a moment. Instantly the pain stopped. Monkey felt his head. The cap seemed to have taken root upon it. He took out his needle and tried to lever it up; but all in vain. Fearing once more that he would break the band, Tripitaka began to recite again. Monkey was soon writhing and turning somersaults. He grew purple in the face and his eyes bulged out of his head. Tripitaka, unable to bear the sight of such agony, stopped reciting, and at once Monkey's head stopped hurting.

"You've been putting a spell upon me," he said. "Nothing of the kind," said Tripitaka. "I've only been reciting the Scripture of the Tight Fillet."[6] "Start reciting again," said Monkey. When he did so, the pain began at once. "Stop, stop!" screamed Monkey. "Directly you begin, the pain starts; you can't pretend it's not you that are causing it." "In future, will you attend to what I say?" asked Tripitaka. "Indeed I will," said Monkey. "And never be troublesome again?" said Tripitaka. "I shouldn't dare," said Monkey. So he said, but in his heart there was still lurking a very evil intent. He took out his cudgel and rushed at Tripitaka, fully intending to strike. Much alarmed, the Master began to recite again, and Monkey fell writhing upon the ground; the cudgel dropped from his hand. "I give in, I give in!" he cried. "Is it possible," said Tripitaka, "that you were going to be so wicked as to strike me?" "I shouldn't dare, I shouldn't dare," groaned Monkey. "Master, how did you come by this spell?" "It was taught me by an old woman whom I met just now," said Tripitaka. "Not another word!" said Monkey. "I know well enough who she was. It was the Bodhisattva Kuan-yin. How dare she plot against me like that? Just wait a minute while I go to the Southern Ocean and give her a

---

6. A fillet is usually a strip of cloth—but here a band of metal—worn around the head. By reciting the scripture like a spell, Tripitaka can make the fillet tighten.

taste of my stick." "As it was she who taught me the spell," said Tripitaka, "she can presumably use it herself. What will become of you then?" Monkey saw the logic of this, and kneeling down he said contritely, "Master, this spell is too much for me. Let me go with you to India. You won't need to be always saying this spell. I will protect you faithfully to the end." "Very well then," said Tripitaka. "Help me on to my horse." Very crestfallen, Monkey put the luggage together, and they started off again towards the west.

If you do not know how the story goes on, you must listen to what is told in the next chapter.

CHAPTER XV

It was mid-winter, a fierce north wind was blowing and icicles hung everywhere. Their way took them up precipitous cliffs and across ridge after ridge of jagged mountain. Presently Tripitaka heard the roaring of a torrent and asked Monkey what this river might be. "I remember," said Monkey, "that there is a river near here called the Eagle Grief Stream." A moment later they came suddenly to the river side, and Tripitaka reined in his horse. They were looking down at the river, when suddenly there was a swirling sound and a dragon appeared in mid-stream. Churning the waters, it made straight for the shore, clambered up the bank and had almost reached them, when Monkey dragged Tripitaka down from the horse and turning his back to the river, hastily threw down the luggage and carried the Master up the bank. The dragon did not pursue them, but swallowed the horse, harness and all, and then plunged once more into the stream. Meanwhile Monkey had set down Tripitaka upon a high mound, and gone back to recover the horse and luggage. The luggage was there, but the horse had disappeared. He brought up the luggage to where Tripitaka was sitting. "The dragon has made off," he said. "The only trouble is that the horse has taken fright and bolted." "How are we to find it?" asked Tripitaka. "Just wait while I go and have a look," said Monkey. He sprang straight up into the sky, and shading his fiery eyes with his hand he peered down in every direction. But nowhere was the least sign of the horse. He lowered his cloud-trapeze. "I can't see it anywhere," he said. "There is only one thing that can have happened to it. It has been eaten by the dragon." "Now Monkey, what can you be thinking of?" said Tripitaka, "It would have to have a big mouth indeed to swallow a large horse, harness and all. It is much more likely that it bolted and is hidden by a fold of the hill. You had better have another look." "Master, you underrate my powers," said Monkey. "My sight is so good that in daylight I can see everything that happens a thousand leagues around. Within a thousand leagues a gnat cannot move its wings without my seeing it. How could I fail to see a horse?" "Well, suppose it has been eaten," said Tripitaka, "how am I to travel? It's a great deal too far to walk." And as he spoke his tears began to fall like rain. "Don't make such an object of yourself," shouted Monkey, infuriated by this exhibition of despair. "Just sit here, while I go and look for the wretch and make him give us back the horse." "You can't do anything unless he comes out of the water," said Tripitaka, "and if he does it will be me that he will eat this time." "You're impossible, impossible," thundered Monkey, angrier than ever. "You say you need the horse to ride, and yet you won't let me go and recover it. At this rate, you'll sit here staring at the luggage for ever."

He was still storming, when a voice spoke out of the sky, saying, "Monkey, do not be angry. Priest of T'ang, do not weep. We divinities have been sent by Kuan-yin to protect you in your quest." Tripitaka at once did obeisance.[7] "Which divinities are you?" cried Monkey. "Tell me your names, and I'll tick you off on the roll." "Here present are Lu Ting and Lu Chia," they said, "the Guardians of the Five Points, the Four Sentinels and the Eighteen Protectors of Monasteries. We attend upon you in rotation." "And which of you are on duty this morning?" asked Monkey. "Lu Chia, one Sentinel and the Protectors are on duty," they said, "and the Golden-headed Guardian is always somewhere about, night and day." "Those who aren't on duty can retire," said Monkey. "But Lu Ting, the Sentinel of the day, and all the Guardians had better stay and look after the Master, while I go to the river and look for that dragon, and see if I can get him to return the horse." Tripitaka, feeling somewhat reassured, sat down on the brink, begging Monkey to be careful. "Don't you worry about me!" said Monkey.

Dear Monkey! He tightened the belt of his brocade jacket, hitched up his tiger-skin, grasped his iron cudgel, and going straight down to the water's edge called in a loud voice, "Cursed fish, give me back my horse!" The dragon was lying quietly at the bottom of the river, digesting the white horse. But hearing some one cursing him and demanding his prey, he fell into a great rage, and leapt up through the waves crying, "Who is it that dares make such a hullabaloo outside my premises?" "Stand your ground," hissed Monkey, "and give me back my horse." He brandished his cudgel and struck at the dragon's head. The dragon advanced upon him with open jaws and threatening claws. It was a valiant fight that those two had on the banks of the river. To and fro they went, fighting for a long while, hither and thither, round and round. At last the dragon's strength began to fail, he could hold out no longer, and with a rapid twist of the tail he fled from the encounter and disappeared in the river. Monkey, standing on the bank, cursed and taunted him unceasingly, but he turned a deaf ear. Monkey saw nothing for it but to go back and report to Tripitaka. "Master," he said, "I taunted him till he came out and fought many bouts, and in the end he took fright and ran away. He is now at the bottom of the river and won't come out." "We are still not sure whether he did swallow the horse," said Tripitaka. "How can you say such a thing?" said Monkey. "If he hadn't eaten it, why should he have come out and answered my challenge?" "The other day when you dealt with that tiger," said Tripitaka, "you mentioned that you could also subdue dragons. I don't understand why you are having such difficulties with this dragon to-day." To such a taunt as this no one could be more sensitive than Monkey. "Not another word!" he cried, stung to the quick. "I'll soon show you which is master!"

He strode to the stream-side, and used a magic which stirred up the clear waters of the river till they became as turbulent as the waves of the Yellow River.[8] The dragon soon became very uncomfortable as he lay at the bottom of the stream. "Misfortunes never come singly," he thought to himself. "Hardly a year has passed since I barely escaped with my life from the Tribunal of Heaven and was condemned to this exile; and now I have fallen foul of this cursed monster, who seems determined to do me injury." The more he thought, the angrier he became. At last, determined not to give in,

7. Bowed.   8. The largest river in north China.

he leapt up through the waves and gnashing his teeth he snarled, "What monster are you, and where do you come from, that you dare affront me in this fashion?" "Never mind where I come from or don't come from," said Monkey. "Just give me back my horse, or you shall pay for it with your life." "Your horse," said the dragon, "is inside me. How am I to give it back to you? And anyhow, if I don't, what can you do to me?" "Have a look at this cudgel," said Monkey. "If you don't give me back the horse you shall pay for it with your life." Again they fought upon the bank, and after several rounds the dragon could hold out no longer, made one great wriggle and, changing itself into a water-snake, disappeared into the long grass. Beating the grass with his cudgel, Monkey pranced wildly about, trying to track it down, but all in vain. At last, fuming with impatience he uttered a loud OM, as a secret summons to the spirits of the locality. In a moment they were kneeling before him. "Hold out your shanks," said Monkey, "and I'll give you each five strokes with the cudgel just to relieve my feelings." "Great Sage," they besought him, "pray give us a chance to put our case to you. We had no idea that you had been released from your penance, or we should have come to meet you before. We humbly beg you to forgive us." "Very well then," said Monkey. "You shan't be beaten. But answer me this. Where does this dragon come from, who lives in the Eagle Grief River? Why did he swallow my Master's white horse?" "Great Sage," they said, "in old days you had no Master, and indeed refused obedience to any power in Heaven or Earth. What do you mean by your Master's horse?" "After I got into trouble about that affair in Heaven," said Monkey, "I had to do penance for five hundred years. But now I have been taken in hand by the Bodhisattva Kuan-yin and put in charge of a priest who is going to India to fetch Scriptures. I was travelling with him as his disciple, when we lost my Master's horse." "If you want to catch this dragon, surely your best plan would be to get the Bodhisattva to come and deal with it," they said. "There used not to be any dragon here, and it is she who sent it." They all went and told Tripitaka of this plan. "How long shall you be?" he asked. "Shan't I be dead of cold or starvation before you come back?" While he spoke, the voice of the Golden-headed Guardian was heard saying from the sky, "None of you need move a step. I will go and ask the Bodhisattva." "Much obliged," said Monkey. "Pray go at once." The Guardian soared up through the clouds and made straight for the Southern Ocean. Monkey told the local deities to look after the Master, and the Sentinels to supply food. Then he went back to the banks of the river. "What have you come for?" asked the Bodhisattva, when the Golden-headed Guardian was brought to her where she sat in her bamboo-grove. "The priest of T'ang," said he, "has lost his horse at the Eagle Grief River. It was swallowed by a dragon, and the Great Sage sent me for your help." "That dragon," said Kuan-yin, "is a son of the dragon-king of the Western Ocean. By his carelessness he set fire to the magic pearls in the palace and they were destroyed. His father accused him of subversive intents, and the Tribunal of Heaven condemned him to death. I saw the Jade Emperor about it, and asked that the sentence might be commuted if the dragon consented to carry the priest of T'ang on his journey to India. I cannot understand how he came to swallow the horse. I'll come and look into it." She got down from her lotus seat, left her fairy cave, and riding on a beam of magic light crossed the Southern Sea. When she came near the River of Eagle Grief, she looked down and saw

Monkey on the bank uttering ferocious curses. She sent the Guardian to announce her arrival. Monkey at once sprang into the air and shouted at her, "A fine 'Teacher of the Seven Buddhas,' a fine 'Founder of the Faith of Mercy' you are, to plot in this way against us!" "You impudent stableman, you half-witted red-bottom," said the Bodhisattva. "After all the trouble I have taken to find someone to fetch scriptures, and tell him to redeem you, instead of thanking me you make a scene like this!" "You've played a fine trick on me," said Monkey. "You might in decency, when you let me out, have allowed me to go round and amuse myself as I pleased. But you gave me a dressing down and told me I was to spend all my time and energy in looking after this T'ang priest. Very well! But why did you give him a cap that he coaxed me into putting on, and now I can't get it off, and whenever he says some spell or other I have frightful pains in the head?" "Oh Monkey," laughed Kuan-yin, "if you were not controlled in some such way as this, there would be no doing anything with you. Before long we should have you at all your old tricks again." "It's no good trying to put the blame on me," said Monkey. "How comes it that you put this dragon here, after he had been condemned by the Courts, and let him eat my Master's horse? It was you who put it in his way to continue his villainies here below. You ought to be ashamed of yourself!" "I specially asked the Jade Emperor," said Kuan-yin, "to let this dragon be stationed here, so that he might be used to carry the master on his way to India. No ordinary Chinese horse would be able to carry him all that way." "Well, now he is frightened of me and is hiding," said Monkey, "so what is to be done?" Kuan-yin called the Golden-haired Guardian and said to him, "Go to the edge of the river and cry 'Third son of the Dragon King, come out! The Bodhisattva is here.' He'll come out all right." The dragon leapt up through the waves and immediately assumed human form. "Don't you know that this is the Scripture-seeker's disciple?" Kuan-yin said, pointing at Monkey. "Bodhisattva," said the young dragon, "I've been having a fight with him. I was hungry yesterday and ate his horse. He never once mentioned anything about 'Scripture-seeking.' " "You never asked my name," said Monkey, "so why should I tell you?" "Didn't I ask you what monster you were and where you came from?" asked the dragon. "And didn't you shout at me 'Never mind where I came from or didn't come from, but just give me back my horse'? You never so much as mentioned the word T'ang." "Monkey is fonder of showing off his own powers than mentioning his connexion with other people," said Kuan-yin. "But in future if anyone questions him, he must be sure to say that he is seeking Scriptures. Then there will be no more trouble."

The Bodhisattva then went to the dragon and removed the jewel of wisdom from under his chin. Then she took her willow-spray[9] and sprinkled him all over with sweet dew, and blowing upon him with magic breath cried "Change!" Whereupon the dragon immediately changed into the exact image of the lost horse. She then solemnly called upon the once-dragon to turn from his evil ways, and promised that when his task was ended he should be given a golden body and gain illumination. The young dragon humbled himself and promised faithfully to do as he was bid. Then she turned to go, but Monkey grabbed at her, crying "This is not good enough! The way to the

9. A handful of willow twigs with the leaves still on them.

West is very bad going, and it would be difficult enough in any case to get an earthly priest over all those precipices and crags. But if we are going to have encounters like this all the time, I shall have hard work keeping alive at all, let alone any thought of achieving salvation. I'm not going on!" "That's odd," said the Bodhisattva, "because in the old days you used to be very keen on obtaining illumination. I am surprised that, having escaped from the punishment imposed upon you by Heaven, you should be so unwilling to take a little trouble. When you get into difficulties you have only to call upon Earth, and Earth will perform its miracles. If need be, I will come myself to succour you. And, by the way, come here! I am going to endow you with one more power." She took the willow leaves from her willow-spray, and dropping them down Monkey's back cried "Change." At once they changed into three magic hairs. "These," she said, "will get you out of any trouble, however menacing." Monkey thanked the Bodhisattva, who now set out for the Southern Heaven, and taking the horse by the forelock he led it to Tripitaka, saying, "Master, here's a horse any way!" "It's in much better condition than the old one," said Tripitaka. "However did you manage to find it?" "What have you been doing all the while? Dreaming?" said Monkey. "The Golden-haired Guardian sent for Kuan-yin, who changed the dragon into the exact image of our white horse. The only thing it lacks is harness." "Where is the Bodhisattva?" asked Tripitaka, very much surprised. "I should like to thank her." "You're too late," said Monkey. "By this time she is already crossing the Southern Ocean." However Tripitaka burned incense and bowed towards the south. Then he helped Monkey to put together the luggage, and they set out. "It's not going to be easy to ride a horse without saddle and reins," said Tripitaka. "I'd better find a boat to get across the river, and see if I can't get some harness on the other side." "That's not a very practical suggestion," said Monkey. "What chance is there of finding a boat in this wild, desolate place? The horse has lived here for some time and must know his way through the waters. Just sit tight on his back and let him carry you across." They had got to the river bank, Tripitaka astride the horse and Monkey carrying the luggage, when an old fisherman appeared upstream, punting a crazy old raft. Monkey waved to him, crying, "We have come from the east to fetch scriptures. My Master does not know how to get across, and would like you to ferry him." The old man punted rapidly towards them, and Monkey told Tripitaka to dismount. He then helped him on board, and embarked the horse and luggage. The old man punted them swiftly across to the far side, where Tripitaka told Monkey to look in the pack for some Chinese money to give to the old fisherman. But the old man pushed off again at once, saying he did not want money. Tripitaka felt very uncomfortable and could only press together his palms in token of gratitude. "Don't you worry about him," said Monkey. "Didn't you see who he really is? This is the river divinity who failed to come and meet us. I was on the point of giving him a good hiding, which he richly deserved. The fact that I let him off is payment enough. No wonder he hadn't the face to take your cash." Tripitaka was not at all sure whether to believe this story or not. He got astride the horse once more, and followed Monkey along the road to the west. And if you do not know where they got to, you must listen to what is told in the next chapter.

CHAPTER XVI

They had been travelling for several days through very wild country when at last, very late in the evening, they saw a group of houses in the far distance. "Monkey," said Tripitaka, "I think that is a farm over there. Wouldn't it be a good plan to see if we can't sleep there to-night?" "Let me go and have a look at it," said Monkey, "to see whether it looks lucky or unlucky, and we can then act accordingly." "You can proceed," Monkey reported presently. "I am certain that good people live there." Tripitaka urged on the white horse and soon came to a gate leading into a lane down which came a lad with a cotton wrap round his head, wearing a blue jacket, umbrella in hand and a bundle on his back. He was striding along, with a defiant air. "Where are you off to?" said Monkey stopping him. "There's something I want to ask you. What place is this?" The man tried to brush him aside, muttering, "Is there no one else on the farm, that you must needs pester me with questions?" "Now don't be cross," said Monkey laughing. "What harm can it do you to tell me the name of a place? If you're obliging to us, maybe we can do something to oblige you." Finding he could not get past, for Monkey was holding on to him tightly, he began to dance about in a great rage. "It's enough to put anyone out," he cried. "I've just been insulted by the master of the house, and then I run straight into this wretched bald-pate, and have to swallow his impudence!" "Unless you're clever enough to shake me off, which I very much doubt," said Monkey, "here you'll stay." The man wriggled this way and that, but all to no purpose. He was caught as though by iron pincers. In the struggle he dropped his bundle, dropped his umbrella, and began to rain blows on Monkey with both fists. Monkey kept one hand free to catch on to the luggage, and with the other held the lad fast. "Monkey," said Tripitaka, "I think there's someone coming over there. Wouldn't it do just as well if you asked him, and let this lad go?" "Master," said Monkey, "you don't know what you're talking about. There's no point in asking anyone else. This is the only fellow out of whom we can get what we want."

At last, seeing that he would never get free, the lad said, "This is called old Mr. Kao's farm. Most of the people that live and work here have the surname Kao, so the whole place is called Kao Farm. Now let me go!" "You look as if you were going on a journey," said Monkey. "Tell me where you are going, and on what business, and I will let you go."

"My name," he said, "is Kao Ts'ai. Old Mr. Kao has a daughter about twenty years old and unmarried. Three years ago she was carried off by a monster, who since has kept her as his wife, and lived with her here on the farm. Old Mr. Kao was not pleased. 'To have a monster as a son-in-law in the house,' he says, 'doesn't work very well. It's definitely discreditable to the house, and unpleasant not to be able to look forward to comings and goings between the two families.' He did everything in his power to drive away the monster, but it was no good; and in the end the creature took the girl and locked her away in that back building, where she has been for six months and no one in the family has seen her.

"Old Mr. Kao gave me two or three pieces of silver and told me to go and find an exorcist, and I spent a long time chasing round all over the country-side. I succeeded at last in getting the names of three or four practitioners, but they all turned out to be unfrocked priests or mouldy Taoists, quite incapable of dealing with such a monster. Mr. Kao only just now gave me a great scolding and accused me of bungling the business. Then he gave me five pieces of silver to pay for my travelling expenses and told me to go on looking till I found a really good exorcist, and I should be looking for one now if I hadn't run into this little scamp who won't let me pass. There! You have forced me to tell you how things are, and now you can let me go." "You've thrown a lucky number," said Monkey. "This is just my job. You needn't go a step further or spend an ounce of your silver. I'm no unfrocked priest or mouldy Taoist, I really do know how to catch monsters. You've 'got your stye cured on the way to the doctor's.' I'll trouble you to go to the master of the house, and tell him that a priest and his disciple have come, who are on their way to get scriptures in India, and that they can deal with any monster." "I hope you're telling me the truth," said the lad. "You'll get me into great trouble if you fail." "I'll positively guarantee," said Monkey, "that I'm not deceiving you. Make haste and lead us in."

The lad saw nothing for it but to pick up his bundle and go back to the house. "You half-wit," roared old Mr. Kao, "what have you come back for?" But as soon as he had heard the lad's story, he quickly changed into his best clothes and came out to greet the guests, smiling affably. Tripitaka returned his greeting, but Monkey did not bow or say a word. The old man looked him up and down, and not knowing quite what to make of him did not ask him how he did. "And how about me? Don't you want to know how I am?" said Monkey. "Isn't it enough to have a monster in the house as son-in-law," grumbled the old man, "without your bringing in this frightful creature to molest me?" "In all the years you've lived," said Monkey, "you've evidently learnt very little wisdom. If you judge people by their appearances, you'll always be going wrong. I'm not much to look at, I grant; but I have great powers, and if you are having any trouble with bogeys or monsters in the house, that's just where I come in. I'm going to get you back your daughter, so you had better stop grumbling about my appearance." Mr. Kao, trembling with fear, managed at last to pull himself together sufficiently to invite them both in. Monkey, without so much as by-your-leave, led the horse into the courtyard and tied it to a pillar. Then he drew up an old weather-beaten stool, asked Tripitaka to be seated, and taking another stool for himself calmly sat down at Tripitaka's side. "The little priest knows how to make himself at home," said Mr. Kao. "This is nothing," said Monkey. "Keep me here a few months and you'll see me really making myself at home!" "I don't quite understand," said the old man, "whether you've come for a night's lodging or to drive out the monster." "We've come for a night's lodging," said Monkey, "but if there are any monsters about I don't mind dealing with them, just to pass the time. But first, I should like to know how many of them there are?" "Heavens!" cried the old man, "isn't one monster enough to afflict the household, living here as my son-in-law?" "Just tell me about it from the beginning," said Monkey. "If I know what he's good for, I can deal with him." "We'd never had any trouble with ghosts or goblins or monsters on this farm before," said the old man. "Unfortunately I have no son, but only three daughters. The eldest is called Fragrant Orchid, the second Jade Orchid, and the third Blue Orchid. The first two were betrothed from childhood into neighbouring families. Our plan for the youngest was to marry her to some-one who would come and live with her here and help look after us in our old age. About three years ago a very nice-looking young fellow turned up, saying that he came from Fu-ling, and that his surname was Hog. He said he had no parents or brothers and sisters, and was looking for a family where he would be taken as son-in-law, in return for the work that he did about the place. He sounded just the sort we wanted, and I accepted him. I must say he worked very hard. He pushed the plough himself and never asked to use a bull; he managed to do all his reaping without knife or staff. For some time we were perfectly satisfied, except for one thing—his appearance began to change in a very odd way." "In what way?" asked Monkey. "When he first came," said the old man, "he was just a dark, stoutish fellow. But afterwards his nose began to turn into a regular snout, his ears became larger and larger, and great bristles began to grow at the back of his neck. In fact, he began to look more and more like a hog. His appetite is enormous. He eats four or five pounds of rice at each meal, and as a light collation in the morning I've known him get through over a hundred pasties.[1] He's not at all averse to fruit and vegetables either, and what with this and all the wine he drinks, in the course of the last six months he's pretty well eaten and drunk us out of house and home." "No doubt," said Tripitaka, "anyone who works so hard as he does needs a lot of nourishment." "If it were only this business of food," said the old man, "it wouldn't be so bad. But he frightens everybody round by raising magic winds, suddenly vanishing and appearing again, making stones fly through the air and suchlike tricks. Worst of all, he has locked up Blue Orchid in the back outhouse,[2] and it is six months since we set eyes on her. We don't even know if she is dead or alive. It is evident that he's an ogre of some kind, and that is why we were trying to get hold of an exorcist." "Don't you worry," said Monkey. "This very night I'll catch him and make him sign a Deed of Relinquishment[3] and give you back your daughter." "The main thing is to catch him," said Mr. Kao. "It doesn't so much matter about documents." "Perfectly easy," said Monkey. "To-night as soon as it is dark, you'll see the whole thing settled." "What weapons do you need, and how many men to help you?" asked Mr. Kao. "We must get on with the preparations." "I'm armed already," said Monkey. "So far as I can see, all you've got between you is a priest's staff," said the old man. "That wouldn't be much use against such a fiend as this." Monkey took his embroidery needle from behind his ear and once more changed it into a great iron cudgel. "Does this satisfy you?" he asked. "I doubt if your house could provide anything tougher." "How about followers?" said the old man. "I need no followers," said Monkey. "All I ask for is some decent elderly person to sit with my master and keep him company." Several respectable friends and relatives were fetched, and having looked them up and down Monkey said to Tripitaka, "Sit here quietly and don't worry. I'm off to do this job." "Take me to the back building," he said to Mr. Kao, grasping his cudgel. "I'd like to have a look at the monster's lodging-place." "Give me the key," he said, when they came to the door. "Think what you're saying," said the old man. "Do you suppose that if a key was all that was wanted, we should be troubling you?" "What's the use of living so long in the world if you haven't learnt even to recognize a joke when you hear one?" said Monkey laughing. Then he went up to the door and with a terrific blow of his cudgel smashed it down. Within, it was pitch dark. "Call

1. Meat pies. *Collation:* meal.   2. That is, outbuilding.   3. Divorce papers.

to your daughter and see if she is there," said Monkey. The old man summoned up his courage and cried, "Miss Three!" Recognizing her father's voice, she answered with a faint "Papa, I am here." Monkey peered into the darkness with his steely eyes, and it was a pitiable sight that he saw. Unwashed cheeks, matted hair, bloodless lips, weak and trembling. She tottered towards her father, flung her arms round him and burst into tears. "Don't make that noise," said Monkey, "but tell us where your monster is." "I don't know," she said. "Nowadays he goes out at dawn and comes back at dusk, I can't keep track of him at all. He knows that you're trying to find someone to exorcize him; that's why he keeps away all day." "Not a word more!" said Monkey. "Old man, take your darling back to the house and calm her down. I'll wait here for the monster. If he doesn't come, it is not my fault, and if he comes I'll pluck up your trouble by the roots."

Left alone, Monkey used his magic arts to change himself into the exact image of Blue Orchid, and sat waiting for the monster to return. Presently there was a great gust of wind; stones and gravel hurtled through the air. When the wind subsided there appeared a monster of truly terrible appearance. He had short bristles on his swarthy cheeks, a long snout and huge ears. He wore a cotton jacket that was green but not green, blue but not blue, and had a spotted handkerchief tied round his head. "That's the article," laughed Monkey to himself.

Dear Monkey! He did not go to meet the monster or ask him how he did, but lay on the bed groaning, as though he were ill. The monster, quite taken in, came up to the bed and grabbing at Monkey tried to kiss him. "None of your lewd tricks on old Monkey!" laughed Monkey to himself, and giving the monster a great clout on the nose sent him reeling. "Dear sister," said the monster, picking himself up, "why are you cross with me to-day? Is it because I am so late?" "I'm not cross," said Monkey. "If you're not cross," said the monster, "why do you push me away?" "You've got such a clumsy way of kissing," said Monkey. "You might have known that I'm not feeling well today, when you saw I did not come to the door to meet you. Take off your clothes and get into bed." Still suspecting nothing the monster began to undress. Monkey meanwhile jumped up and sat on the commode. When the monster got into bed he felt everywhere but could not find his bride. "Sister," he called, "what has become of you? Take off your clothes and get into bed." "You go to sleep first," said Monkey. "I'll follow when I've done my duties." Monkey suddenly began to sigh, murmuring "Was there ever such an unhappy girl as I?" "What are you grumbling about?" said the monster. "Since I came here, I've cost you something in food and drink, that I own. But I've more than earned what I have got. Haven't I cleaned the ground and drained ditches, carried bricks and tiles, built walls, ploughed fields, planted grain, and improved the farm out of all knowing? You've good clothes to wear and all the food you need. What's all this childish nonsense about being unhappy?" "That's not it at all," said Monkey. "To-day my parents came and made a fearful scene through the partition wall." "What did they make a scene about?" said the monster. "They don't like having you here as their son-in-law." said Monkey. "They say you've got an ugly face, and they don't know who your father is and haven't seen any of your relations. They say you come and go no one knows when or where, and it's bad for the credit of the house that we don't know your name or anything at all about you." That's what they said, and it has made me miserable." "What do looks matter?" said the monster. "It's a strong man they need about the place, and they can't say anything against me on that score. And if they think so ill of me, why did they accept me here at all? As for who I am, there's no mystery about it. I come from the Cloud-Ladder Cave at Fu-ling, and because I look a bit like a pig they call me Pigsy—Pigsy Bristles; next time they ask just tell them that." "Confiding monster!" thought Monkey. "It needs no tortures to get a confession from him. Now we know where he comes from and who he is. It only remains to catch him." "They are looking for an exorcist to drive you away," he said to the monster. "Go to sleep," said Pigsy, "and don't worry about them any more. Am not I strong enough, with my nine-pronged muck-rake, to frighten off any exorcist or priest or what-not? Even if your old man's prayers could bring down the master of all devils from the Ninth Heaven,[4] as a matter of fact he's an old friend of mine and wouldn't do anything against me." "He's done more than that," said Monkey. "He has called in the Great Sage, who five hundred years ago made turmoil in Heaven." "If that's so," said Pigsy, "I'm off! There'll be no more kissing to-night!" "Why are you going?" asked Monkey. "You don't know," said Pigsy. "That chap is terribly powerful, and I don't know that I could deal with him. I'm frightened of losing my reputation." He dressed hastily, opened the door and went out. But Monkey caught hold of him and making a magic pass changed himself back into his true form. "Monster, look round," he cried, "and you will see that I am he."

When Pigsy turned and saw Monkey with his sharp little teeth and grinning mouth, his fiery, steely eyes, his flat head and hairy cheeks, for all the world like a veritable thunder-demon, he was so startled that his hands fell limp beside him and his legs gave way. With a scream he tore himself free, leaving part of his coat in Monkey's hand, and was gone like a whirlwind. Monkey struck out with his cudgel; but Pigsy had already begun to make for the cave he came from. Soon Monkey was after him, crying, "Where are you off to? If you go up to Heaven I will follow you to the summit of the Pole Star, and if you go down into the earth I will follow you to the deepest pit of hell."

If you do not know how far he chased him or which of them won the fight, you must listen to what is told in the next chapter.

CHAPTER XVII

The monster fled with Monkey at his heels, till they came at last to a high mountain, and here the monster disappeared into a cave, and a moment later came back brandishing a nine-pronged muck-rake. They set to at once and battled all night long, from the second watch till dawn began to whiten in the sky. At last the monster could hold his ground no longer, and retreating into the cave bolted the door behind him. Standing outside the cave-door, Monkey saw that on a slab of rock was the inscription "Cloud-ladder Cave." As the monster showed no sign of coming out again and it was now broad daylight, Monkey thought to himself, "The Master will be wondering what has happened to me. I had better go and see him and then come back and

4. The highest level of Heaven.

catch the monster." So tripping from cloud to cloud he made his way back to the farm.

Tripitaka was still sitting with the old man, talking of this and that. He had not slept all night. He was just wondering why Monkey did not return when Monkey alighted in the courtyard, and suddenly stood before them. "Master, here I am," he said. The old men all bowed down before him, and supposing that he had accomplished his task thanked him for all his trouble. "You must have had a long way to go, to catch the creature," said Tripitaka. "Master," said Monkey, "the monster is not a common incubus[5] or elf. I have recognized him as a former inhabitant of Heaven, where he was in command of all the watery hosts. He was expelled to earth after an escapade with the daughter of the Moon Goddess, and though he was here re-incarnated with a pig-like form, he retains all his magic powers. I chased him to his mountain-cave, where he fetched out a nine-pronged muck-rake, and we fought together all night. Just at dawn he gave up the fight, and locked himself up in his cave. I would have beaten down the door and forced him to fight to a decision, but I was afraid the Master might be getting anxious, so I thought I had better come back first and report."

"Reverend Sir," said old Mr. Kao to Monkey, "I am afraid this hasn't helped matters much. True, you have driven him away; but after you have gone he's certain to come back again, and where shall we be then? We shall have to trouble you to catch him for us. That is the only way to pluck out our trouble by the root. I'll see to it that you have no cause to regret the trouble you take. You shall have half of all that is ours, both land and goods. If you like, my friends and relations shall sign a document to this effect. It will be well worth their while, if only we can remove this shame from our home."

"I think you make too much of the whole affair," said Monkey. "The monster himself admits that his appetite is large; but he has done quite a lot of useful work. All the recent improvements in the estate are his work. He claims to be well worth what he costs in keep, and does not see why you should be so anxious to get rid of him. He is a divinity from Heaven, although condemned to live on earth, he helps to keep things going, and so far as I can see he hasn't done any harm to your daughter." "It may be true," said old Mr. Kao, "that he's had no influence upon her. But I stick to it that it's very bad for our reputation. Wherever I go I hear people saying 'Mr. Kao has taken a monster as his son-in-law.' What is one to say to that?" "Now, Monkey," said Tripitaka, "don't you think you had better go and have one more fight with him and see if you can't settle the business once and for all?" "As a matter of fact," said Monkey, "I was only having a little game with him, to see how things would go. This time I shall certainly catch him and bring him back for you to see. Don't you worry!" "Look after my master," he cried to Mr. Kao, "I'm off!"

So saying, he disappeared into the clouds and soon arrived at the cave. With one blow of his cudgel he beat the doors to bits, and standing at the entrance he cried, "You noisome lout, come out and fight with Old Monkey." Pigsy lay fast asleep within, snoring heavily. But when he heard the door being beaten down and heard himself called a noisome lout, he was so much enraged that he snatched up his rake, pulled himself together and rushed

5. Demon.

out, crying, "You wretched stableman, if ever there was a rogue, you're he! What have I to do with you, that you should come and knock down my door? Go and look at the Statute Book.[6] You'll find that 'obtaining entry to premises by forcing a main door' is a Miscellaneous Capital Offence." "You fool," said Monkey. "Haven't I a perfectly good justification at law for forcing your door? Remember that you laid violent hands on a respectable girl, and lived with her without matchmaker or testimony, tea, scarlet,[7] wine or any other ceremony. Are you aware that heads are cut off for less than that?" "Stop that nonsense, and look at Old Pig's rake," cried Pigsy. He struck out, but Monkey warded off the blow, crying, "I suppose that's the rake you used when you worked on the farm. Why should you expect me to be frightened of it?" "You are very much mistaken," said Pigsy. "This rake was given to me by the Jade Emperor himself." "A lie!" cried Monkey. "Here's my head. Hit as hard as you please, and we'll see!" Pigsy raised the rake and brought it down with such force on Monkey's head that the sparks flew. But there was not a bruise or scratch. Pigsy was so much taken aback, that his hands fell limp at his side. "What a head!" he exclaimed. "You've still something to learn about me," said Monkey. "After I made havoc in Heaven and was caught by Erh-lang, all the deities of Heaven hacked me with their axes, hammered me with their mallets, slashed me with their swords, set fire to me, hurled thunderbolts at me, but not a hair of my body was hurt. Lao Tzu[8] put me in his alchemic stove and cooked me with holy fire. But all that happened was that my eyes became fiery, my head and shoulders hard as steel. If you don't believe it, try again, and see whether you can hurt me or not." "I remember," said Pigsy, "that before you made havoc in Heaven, you lived in the Cave of the Water-Curtain. Lately nothing has been heard of you. How did you get here? Perhaps my father-in-law asked you to come and deal with me." "Not at all," said Monkey, "I have been converted and am now a priest, and am going with a Chinese pilgrim called Tripitaka, who has been sent by the Emperor to fetch scriptures from India. On our way we happened to come past Mr. Kao's farm, and we asked for a night's lodging. In the course of conversation Mr. Kao asked for help about his daughter. That's why I'm after you, you noisome lout!"

No sooner did Pigsy hear these words than the rake fell from his hand. "Where is that pilgrim?" he gasped. "Take me to him." "What do you want to see him for?" asked Monkey. "I've been converted," said Pigsy. "Didn't you know? The Bodhisattva Kuan-yin converted me and put me here to prepare myself by fasting and abstention for going to India with a pilgrim to fetch scriptures; after which, I am to receive illumination. That all happened some years ago, and since then I have had no news of this pilgrim. If you are his disciple, what on earth possessed you not to mention this scripture-seeking business? Why did you prefer to pick a quarrel and knock me about in front of my own door?" "I suspect," said Monkey, "that you are just making all this up, in order to get away. If it's really true that you want to escort my Master to India, you must make a solemn vow to Heaven that you're telling the truth. Then I'll take you to him." Pigsy flung himself upon his knees and, kowtowing at the void,[9] up and down like a pestle in the mortar, he cried "I swear before

6. Law book.   7. Wedding gifts.   8. An ancient sage and one of the founders of Taoism. He was believed to have become immortal and occupied an important place in the Taoist pantheon.   9. Sky.

the Buddha Amitabha, praised be his name, that I am telling the truth; and if I am not, may I be condemned once more by the tribunals of Heaven and sliced into ten thousand pieces."

When Monkey heard him make this solemn vow, "Very well then," he said. "First take a torch and burn down your lair, and then I will take you with me." Pigsy took some reeds and brambles, lit a fire and soon reduced the cave to the state of a burnt-out kiln. "You've nothing against me now," he said. "Take me along with you." "You'd better give your rake to me," said Monkey. When Pigsy had handed over the rake, Monkey took a hair, blew on it with magic breath, and changed it into a three-ply hemp cord. Pigsy put his hands behind his back and let himself be bound. Then Monkey caught hold of his ear and dragged him along, crying, "Hurry up! Hurry up!" "Don't be so rough," begged Pigsy. "You're hurting my ear." "Rough indeed!" said Monkey. "I shouldn't get far by being gentle with you. The proverb says, 'The better the pig, the harder to hold.' Wait till you have seen the Master and shown that you are in earnest. Then we'll let you go."

When they reached the farm, Monkey twitched Pigsy's ear, saying, "You see that old fellow sitting so solemnly up there? That's my Master." Mr. Kao and the other old men, seeing Monkey leading the monster by the ear, were delighted beyond measure, and came out into the courtyard to meet him. "Reverend Sir," they cried, "that's the creature, sure enough, that married our master's daughter." Pigsy fell upon his knees and with his hands still tied behind his back, kowtowed to Tripitaka, crying, "Master, forgive me for failing to give you a proper reception. If I had known that it was you who were staying with my father-in-law I would have come to pay my respects, and all these unpleasantnesses would never have happened." "Monkey," said Tripitaka, "how did you manage to bring him to this state of mind?" Monkey let go his ear, and giving him a knock with the handle of the rake, shouted, "Speak, fool!" Pigsy then told how he had been commissioned by Kuan-yin. "Mr. Kao," said Tripitaka, when he heard the story, "this is the occasion for a little incense." Mr. Kao then brought out the incense tray, and Tripitaka washed his hands, and burning incense he turned towards the south and said, "I am much beholden, Bodhisattva!" Then he went up into the hall and resumed his seat, bidding Monkey to release Pigsy from his bonds. Monkey shook himself; the rope became a hair again and returned to his body. Pigsy was free. He again did obeisance, and vowed that he would follow Tripitaka to the west. Then he bowed to Monkey, whom as the senior disciple he addressed as "Elder Brother and Teacher."

"Where's my wife?" said Pigsy to Mr. Kao. "I should like her to pay her respects to my Father and Brother in the Law." "Wife indeed!" laughed Monkey. "You haven't got a wife now. There are some sorts of Taoists that are family men; but who ever heard of a Buddhist priest calmly talking about his 'wife'? Sit down and eat your supper, and early to-morrow we'll all start out for India." After supper Mr. Kao brought out a red lacquer bowl full of broken pieces of silver and gold, and offered the contents to the three priests, as a contribution towards their travelling expenses. He also offered them three pieces of fine silk to make clothes. Tripitaka said, "Travelling priests must beg their way as they go. We cannot accept money or silk." But Monkey came up and plunging his hand into the dish took out a handful of gold and silver, and called to the lad Kao Ts'ai, "You were kind enough yesterday to introduce my Master into the house and we owe it to you that we have found a new disciple. I have no other way of showing my thanks but giving you these broken pieces of gold and silver, which I hope you will use to buy yourself a pair of shoes. If you come across any more monsters, please bespeak them for me, and I shall be even further obliged to you." "Reverend Sirs," said Mr. Kao, "if I can't persuade you to accept silver or gold, I hope that you will at least let me show my gratitude by giving you these few pieces of coarse stuff, to make into cassocks." "A priest who accepts so much as a thread of silk," said Tripitaka, "must do penance for a thousand aeons to expiate his crime. All I ask is a few scraps left over from the household meal, to take with us as dry provisions." "Wait a minute," cried Pigsy. "If I get my due for all I've done on this estate since I married into the family, I should carry away several tons of provisions. That's by the way. But I think my father-in-law might in decency give me a new jacket. My old one was torn by Brother Monkey in the fight last night. And my shoes are all in pieces; I should be glad of a new pair."

Mr. Kao acceded to his request, and Pigsy, delighted by his new finery, strutted up and down in front of the company, calling to Mr. Kao, "Be so kind as to inform my mother-in-law, my sisters-in-law and all my kinsmen by marriage that I have become a priest and must ask their pardon for going off without saying good-bye to them in person. And father-in-law, I'll trouble you to take good care of my bride. For if we don't bring off this scripture business, I shall turn layman again and live with you as your son-in-law." "Lout!" cried Monkey. "Don't talk rubbish." "It's not rubbish," said Pigsy. "Things may go wrong, and then I shall be in a pretty pass! No salvation, and no wife either." "Kindly stop this silly argument," said Tripitaka. "It is high time we started." So they put together the luggage, which Pigsy was told to carry, and when the white horse was saddled Tripitaka was set astride. Monkey, with his cudgel over his shoulder, led the way. And so, parting from Mr. Kao and all his relations, the three of them set out for the West. And if you do not know what befell them, you must listen to what is told in the next chapter.

CHAPTER XVIII

So the three of them travelled on towards the West, and came at last to a great plain. Summer had passed and autumn come. They heard "the cicada singing in the rotten willow," saw "the Fire-Star rolling to the west." At last they came to a huge and turbulent river, racing along with gigantic waves. "That's a very broad river," cried Tripitaka from on horseback. "There does not seem to be a ferry anywhere about. How are we to get across?" "A boat wouldn't be much use in waters as rough as that," said Pigsy. Monkey leapt up into the air, and shading his eyes with his hand gazed at the waters. "Master," he cried, "this is going to be no easy matter. For me, yes. I should only have to shake my hips, and I should be across at one bound. But for you it's not going to be such easy work." "I can't even see the other side," said Tripitaka. "How far is it, do you suppose?" "About eight hundred leagues," said Monkey. "How do you come to that reckoning?" asked Pigsy. "I'll tell you frankly," said Monkey. "My sight is so good that I can see everything, lucky or unlucky, a thousand leagues away, and when I looked down on this river from above I could see well enough that it must be a good eight hundred leagues across." Tripitaka was very much depressed, and was just turning his horse when he saw a slab of stone on which was the inscription "River of Flowing Sands." Underneath in small letters was the verse:

> In the Floating Sands, eight hundred wide,
> In the Dead Waters, three thousand deep,
> A goose-feather will not keep afloat,
> A rush-flower sinks straight to the bottom.

They were looking at this inscription when suddenly a monster of horrifying aspect came surging through the mountainous waves. His hair was flaming red, his eyes were like two lanterns; at his neck were strung nine skulls, and he carried a huge priest's-staff. Like a whirlwind he rushed straight at the pilgrims. Monkey seized Tripitaka and hurried him up the bank to a safe distance. Pigsy dropped his load and rushed at the monster with his rake. The monster fended off the blow with his priest's-staff. The fight that followed was a good one, each displaying his powers on the shores of the River of Flowing Sands. They fought twenty bouts without reaching a decision. Monkey, seeing the grand fight that was in progress, itched to go and join in it. At last he said to Tripitaka, "You sit here and don't worry. I am going off to have a bit of fun with the creature." Tripitaka did his best to dissuade him. But Monkey with a wild whoop leapt into the fray. At this moment the two of them were locked in combat, and it was hard to get between them. But Monkey managed to put in a tremendous blow of the cudgel right on the monster's head. At once the monster broke away, and rushing madly back to the water's edge leapt in and disappeared. Pigsy was furious. "Heigh, brother," he cried. "Who asked you to interfere? The monster was just beginning to tire. After another three or four rounds he would not have been able to fend off my rake, and I should have had him at my mercy. But as soon as he saw your ugly face he took to his heels. You've spoilt everything!" "I'll just tell you how it happened," said Monkey. "It's months since I had a chance to use my cudgel, and when I saw you having such a rare time with him my feet itched with longing not to miss the fun, and I couldn't hold myself back. How was I to know that the monster wouldn't play?" So hand in hand, laughing and talking, the two of them went back to Tripitaka. "Have you caught the monster?" he asked. "He gave up the fight," said Monkey, "and went back again into the water." "It wouldn't be a bad thing," said Tripitaka, "if we could persuade him to show us how to get across. He's lived here a long time, and must know this river inside out. Otherwise I don't see how we are to get across an enormous river like this without a boat." "There is something in that," said Monkey. "Does not the proverb say 'You cannot live near cinnabar[1] without becoming red, or near ink without becoming black.' If we succeed in catching him we certainly ought not to kill him, but make him take the Master across this river and then dispose of him." "You shall have your chance this time," said Pigsy to Monkey. "I'll stay here and look after the Master."

"That's all very well," said Monkey, "but this job is not at all in my line. I'm not at my best in the water. To get along here, I have to change myself

---

1. A red ore of mercury.

into some water creature, such as a fish or crab. If it were a matter of going up into the clouds, I have tricks enough to deal with the ugliest situation. But in the water I confess I am at a disadvantage." "I used, of course," said Pigsy, "to be Marshal of the River of Heaven, and had the command of eighty thousand watery fellows, so that I certainly ought to know something about that element. My only fear is that if whole broods of water-creatures were to come to the monster's help, I might get myself into a bit of a fix." "What you must do," said Monkey, "is to lure the monster out, and not get yourself involved in more of a scrap than you can help. Once he is out, I'll come to your assistance." "That's the best plan," said Pigsy, "I'll go at once." So saying, he stripped off his blue embroidered jacket and shoes, and brandishing his rake plunged into the river. He found that he had forgotten none of his old water-magic, and lashing through the waves soon reached the bed of the stream and made his way straight ahead. After retiring from the fight, the monster lay down and had a nap. Soon however he was woken by the sound of someone coming through the water, and starting up he saw Pigsy pushing through the waves, rake in hand. Seizing his staff, he came towards him shouting, "Now then, shaven pate, just look where you're going or you'll get a nasty knock with this staff!" Pigsy struck the staff aside with his rake, crying, "What monster are you, that you dare to bar my path?" "I'm surprised that you don't recognize me," said the monster. "I am not an ordinary spook, but a divinity with name and surname." "If that is so," said Pigsy, "what are you doing here, taking human lives? Tell me who you are, and I'll spare you!"

"So great was my skill in alchemic arts," said the monster, "that I was summoned to Heaven by the Jade Emperor and became a Marshal of the Hosts of Heaven. One day, at a celestial banquet, my hand slipped and I broke a crystal cup. The Jade Emperor was furious, and I was hurried away to the execution ground. Fortunately for me the Red-legged Immortal begged for my release, and my sentence was changed to one of banishment to the River of Flowing Sands. When I am hungry I go ashore and eat whatever living thing comes my way. Many are the woodmen and fishermen who have fallen to me as my prey, and I don't mind telling you I am very hungry at this moment. Don't imagine that your flesh would be too coarse for me to eat. Chopped up fine and well sauced, you'll suit me nicely!" "Coarse indeed!" said Pigsy. "I'm a dainty enough morsel to make any mouth water. Mind your manners, and swallow your grandfather's rake!" The monster ducked and avoided the blow. Then both of them came up to the surface of the water, and treading the waves fought stubbornly for two hours without reaching a decision. It was a case of "the copper bowl meeting the iron broom, the jade gong confronted by the metal bell."[2]

After some thirty rounds Pigsy pretended to give in, and dragging his rake after him made for the shore, with the monster hard on his heels. "Come on!" cried Pigsy. "With firm ground under our feet we'll have a better fight than before." "I know what you're up to," cried the monster. "You've lured me up here, so that your partner may come and help you. We'll go back into the water and finish the fight there." The monster was too wily to come any further up the bank and they soon were fighting again, this time at the very edge of the water. This was too much for Monkey, who was watching them

2. A proverb for things different but equally matched.

from a distance. "Wait here," he said to Tripitaka, "while I try the trick called 'The ravening eagle pouncing on its prey.' " So saying, he catapulted into the air and swooped down on the monster, who swiftly turning his head and seeing Monkey pouncing down upon him from the clouds, leapt straight into the water and was seen no more. "He's given us the slip," said Monkey. "He's not likely to come out on the bank again. What are we going to do?" "It's a tough job," said Pigsy, "I doubt if I can beat him. Even if I sweat till I burst I can't get beyond quits." "Let's go and see the Master," said Monkey.

They climbed the bank, and finding Tripitaka they told him of their predicament. Tripitaka burst into tears. "We shall never get across," he sobbed. "Don't you worry," said Monkey. "It is true that with that creature lying in wait for us, we can't get across. But Pigsy, you stay here by the Master and don't attempt to do any more fighting. I am going off to the Southern Ocean." "And what are you going to do there?" asked Pigsy. "This scripture-seeking business," said Monkey, "is an invention of the Bodhisattva, and it was she who converted us. It is surely for her to find some way of getting us over this river. I'll go and ask her. It's a better idea than fighting with the monster." "Brother," said Pigsy, "when you're there you might say a word to her for me; tell her I'm very much obliged indeed for having been put on the right way." "If you are going," said Tripitaka, "you had better start at once and get back as soon as you can."

Monkey somersaulted into the clouds, and in less than half an hour he had reached the Southern Ocean and saw Mount Potalaka[3] rise before him. After landing, he went straight to the Purple Bamboo Grove, where he was met by the Spirits of the Twenty-Four Ways. "Great Sage, what brings you here?" they said. "My Master is in difficulties," said Monkey, "and I wish to have an interview with the Bodhisattva." "Sit down," they said, "and we will announce you." The Bodhisattva was leaning against the parapet of the Lotus Pool, looking at the flowers, with the Dragon King's daughter, bearer of the Magic Pearl, at her side. "Why aren't you looking after your Master?" she said to Monkey, when he was brought in. "When we came to the River of Flowing Sands," said Monkey, "we found it guarded by a monster formidable in the arts of war. My fellow-disciple Pigsy, whom we picked up on the way, did his best to subdue the creature, but was not successful. That is why I have ventured to come and ask you to take pity on us, and rescue my Master from this predicament." "You obstinate ape," said the Bodhisattva, "this is the same thing all over again. Why didn't you say that you were in charge of the priest of T'ang?" "We were both far too busy trying to catch him and make him take the Master across," said Monkey. "I put him there on purpose to help scripture-seekers," said Kuan-yin. "If only you had mentioned the fact that you had come from China to look for scriptures, you would have found him very helpful."

"At present," said Monkey, "he is skulking at the bottom of the river. How are we to get him to come out and make himself useful? And how is Tripitaka going to get across the river?" The Bodhisattva summoned her disciple Hui-yen, and taking a red gourd from her sleeve she said to him, "Take this gourd, go with Monkey to the river and shout "Sandy!" He will come out at once, and you must then bring him to the Master to make his submission. Next

---

3. Sacred mountain where the bodhisattva Kuan-yin lives.

string together the nine skulls that he wears at his neck according to the disposition of the Magic Square, with the gourd in the middle, and you will find you have a holy ship that will carry Tripitaka across the River of Flowing Sands."

Soon Hui-yen and Monkey alighted on the river-bank. Seeing who Monkey had brought with him, Pigsy led forward the Master to meet them. After salutations had been exchanged, Hui-yen went to the edge of the water and called, "Sandy, Sandy! The scripture-seekers have been here a long time. Why do you not come out and pay your respects to them?"

The monster Sandy, knowing that this must be a messenger from Kuan-yin, hastened to the surface, and as soon as his head was above water he saw Hui-yen and Monkey. He put on a polite smile and came towards them bowing and saying to Hui-yen, "Forgive me for not coming to meet you. Where is the Bodhisattva?" "She has not come," said Hui-yen. "She sent me to tell you to put yourself at Tripitaka's disposal and become his disciple. She also told me to take the skulls that you wear at your neck and this gourd that I have brought, and make a holy ship to carry the Master across."

"Where are the pilgrims?" asked Sandy. "Sitting there on the eastern bank," said Hui-yen. "Well," said Sandy, looking at Pigsy, "that filthy creature never said a word about scriptures, though I fought with him for two days." Then seeing Monkey, "What, is that fellow there too?" he cried. "He's the other's partner. I'm not going near them." "The first is Pigsy," said Hui-yen, "and the second is Monkey. They are both Tripitaka's disciples and both were converted by the Bodhisattva. You have nothing to fear from them. I myself will introduce you to the Master." Sandy put away his staff, tidied himself and scrambled up the bank. When they reached Tripitaka, Sandy knelt before him, exclaiming, "How can I have been so blind as not to rec-ognize you? Forgive me for all my rudeness!" "You brazen creature," said Pigsy, "why did you insist on having a row with us, instead of joining our party from the start?" "Brother," laughed Monkey, "don't scold him. It is we who are to blame, for never having told him that we were going to get scrip-tures." "Is it indeed your earnest desire to dedicate yourself to our religion?" asked Tripitaka. Sandy bowed his assent, and Tripitaka told Monkey to take a knife and shave his head.[4] He then once more did homage to Tripitaka, and in a less degree to Monkey and Pigsy. Tripitaka thought that Sandy shaped very well as a priest, and was thoroughly satisfied with him.

"You had better be quick and get on with your boat-building," said Hui-yen.

Sandy obediently took the skulls from his neck, and tying them in the pattern of the Magic Square he put the Bodhisattva's gourd in the middle, and called to Tripitaka to come down to the water. Tripitaka then ascended the holy ship, which he found as secure as any light craft. Pigsy supported him on the left, Sandy on the right, while Monkey in the stern held the halter of the white horse, which followed as best it could. Hui-yen floated just above them. They soon arrived in perfect safety at the other side.

And if you do not know how long it was before they got Illumination you must listen to what is told in the next chapter.

---

4. A sign of leaving the secular world and taking a Buddhist vow of monkhood.

CHAPTER XIX

Tripitaka sat in the Zen Hall[5] of the Treasure Wood Temple, under the lamp; he recited the Water Litany of the Liang Emperor and read through the True Scripture of the Peacock. It was now the third watch (12 p.m.), and he put his books back into their bag, and was just going to get up and go to bed when he heard a great banging outside the gate and felt a dank blast of ghostly wind. Fearing the lamp would be blown out, he hastened to screen it with his sleeve. But the lamp continued to flicker in the strangest way, and Tripitaka began to tremble. He was, however, very tired, and presently he lay down across the reading-desk and dozed. Although his eyes were closed, he still knew what was going on about him, and in his ears still sounded the dark wind that moaned outside the window. And when the wind had passed by, he heard a voice outside the Zen Hall whispering: "Master!"

Tripitaka raised his head, and in his dream he saw a man standing there, dripping from head to foot, with tears in his eyes, and continually murmuring, "Master, Master." Tripitaka sat up and said, "What can you be but a hobgoblin, evil spirit, monster or foul bogey, that you should come to this place and molest me in the middle of the night? But I must tell you that I am no common scrambler in the greedy world of man. I am a great and illustrious priest who at the bidding of the Emperor of T'ang am going to the West to worship the Buddha and seek scriptures. And I have three disciples, each of whom is adept in quelling dragons and subduing tigers, removing monsters and making away with bogeys. If these disciples were to see you, they would grind you to powder. I tell you this for your own good, in kindness and compassion. You had best hide at once, and not set foot in this place of Meditation." But the man drew nearer to the room and said, "Master, I am no hobgoblin, evil spirit, monster, nor foul bogey either." "If you are none of these things," said Tripitaka, "what are you doing here at depth of night?" "Master," said the man, "rest your eyes upon me and look at me well." Then Tripitaka looked at him with a fixed gaze and saw that there was a crown upon his head and a sceptre at his waist, and that he was dressed and shod as only a king can be.

When Tripitaka saw this he was much startled and amazed. At once he bowed down and cried out with a loud voice: "Of what court is your majesty the king? I beg of you, be seated." But the hand he stretched to help the king to his seat plunged through empty space. Yet when he was back in his seat and looked up, the man was still there. "Tell me, your majesty," he cried, "of what are you emperor, of where are you king? Doubtless there were troubles in your land, wicked ministers rebelled against you and at midnight you fled for your life. What is your tale? Tell it for me to hear." "Master," he said, "my home is due west of here, only forty leagues away. At that place, there is a city moated and walled, and this city is where my kingdom was founded." "And what is its name?" asked Tripitaka. "I will not deceive you," he said. "When my dynasty was set up there, a new name was given to it, and it was called Crow-cock." "But tell me," said Tripitaka, "what brings you here in such consternation?" "Master," he said, "five years ago there was a great drought. The grass did not grow and my people were all dying of hunger. It

5. Meditation room.

was pitiful indeed!" Tripitaka nodded. "Your majesty," he said, "there is an ancient saying, 'Heaven favours, where virtue rules.' I fear you have no compassion for your people; for now that they are in trouble, you leave your city. Go back and open your storehouses, sustain your people, repent your misdeeds, and do present good twofold to make recompense. Release from captivity any whom you have unjustly condemned, and Heaven will see to it that rain comes and the winds are tempered." "All the granaries in my kingdom were empty," he said, "I had neither cash nor grain. My officers civil and military were unpaid, and even at my own board no relish could be served. I have shared sweet and bitter with my people no less than Yü the Great[6] when he quelled the floods; I have bathed and done penance; morning and night I have burnt incense and prayed. For three years it was like this, till the rivers were all empty, the wells dry.

"Suddenly, when things were at their worst, there came a magician from the Chung-nan mountains[7] who could call the winds and summon the rain, and make stones into gold. First he obtained audience with my many officers, civil and military, and then with me. At once I begged him to mount the altar and pray for rain. He did so, and was answered; no sooner did his magic tablet resound than floods of rain fell. I told him three feet would be ample. But he said after so long a drought, it took a lot to soak the ground, and he brought down another two inches. And I, seeing him to be of such great powers, prostrated myself before him and treated him henceforth as my elder brother." "This was a great piece of luck," said Tripitaka. "Whence should my luck come?" asked he. "Why," said Tripitaka, "if your magician could make rain when you wanted it, and gold whenever you needed it, what did you lack that you must needs leave your kingdom and come to me here?"

"For two years," he said, "he was my fellow at board and bed. Then at spring time when all the fruit trees were in blossom and young men and girls from every house, gallants from every quarter, went out to enjoy the sights of spring, there came a time when my officers had all returned to their desks and the ladies of the court to their bowers. I with that magician went slowly stepping hand in hand, till we came to the flower-garden and to the eight-cornered crystal well. Here he threw down something, I do not know what, and at once there was a great golden light. He led me to the well-side, wondering what treasure was in the well. Then he conceived an evil intent, and with a great shove pushed me into the well; then took a paving-stone and covered the well-top and sealed it with clay, and planted a banana-plant on top of it. . . . Pity me! I have been dead three years; I am the phantom unavenged of one that perished at the bottom of a well."

When the man said that he was a ghost, Tripitaka was terrified; his legs grew flabby beneath him, and his hair stood on end. Controlling himself at last, he asked him saying, "Your Majesty's story is hard to reconcile with reason. You say you have been dead for three years. How is it that in all this time none of your officers civil and military, nor of your queens and concubines and chamberlains ever came to look for you?" "I have told you already," the man said, "of the magician's powers. There can be few others like him in all the world. He had but to give himself a shake, and there and

---

6. Mythical Chinese emperor of antiquity who carved the rivers of China to drain off floods.   7. A range south of the capital Ch'ang-an.

then, in the flower-garden, he changed himself into the exact image of me. And now he holds my rivers and hills, and has stolen away my kingdom. All my officers, the four hundred gentlemen of my court, my queens and concubines—all, all are his."

"Your Majesty is easily daunted," said Tripitaka. "Easily daunted?" he asked. "Yes," said Tripitaka, "that magician may have strange powers, turn himself into your image, steal your lands, your officers knowing nothing, and your ladies unaware. But you that were dead at least knew that you were dead. Why did you not go to Yama, King of Death, and put in a complaint?"

"The magician's power," he said, "is very great, and he is on close terms with the clerks and officers of Death. The Spirit of Wall and Moat is forever drinking with him; all the Dragon-kings of the Sea are his kinsmen. The God of the Eastern Peak is his good friend; the ten kings of Judgment are his cousins. I should be barred in every effort to lay my plaint before the King of Death."

"If your Majesty," said Tripitaka, "is unable to lay your case before the Courts of the Dead, what makes you come to the world of the living with any hope of redress?" "Master," he said, "how should a wronged ghost dare approach your door? The Spirit that Wanders at Night caught me in a gust of magic wind and blew me along. He said my three years' water-misery was ended and that I was to present myself before you; for at your service, he said, there was a great disciple, the Monkey Sage, most able to conquer demons and subdue impostors. I beg of you to come to my kingdom, lay hands on the magician and make clear the false from the true. Then, Master, I would repay you with all that will be mine to give."

"So then," said Tripitaka, "you have come to ask that my disciple should drive out the false magician?" "Indeed, indeed," he said. "My disciple," said Tripitaka, "in other ways is not all that he should be. But subduing monsters and evil spirits just suits his powers. I fear however that the circumstances make it hard for him to deal with this evil power." "Why so?" asked the king. "Because," said Tripitaka, "the magician has used his magic powers to change himself into the image of you. All the officers of your court have gone over to him, and all your ladies have accepted him. My disciple could no doubt deal with them; but he would hesitate to do violence to them. For should he do so, would not he and I be held guilty of conspiring to destroy your kingdom? And what would this be but to paint the tiger and carve the swan?"[8]

"There is still someone of mine at Court," he said. "Excellent, excellent," said Tripitaka. "No doubt it is some personal attendant, who is guarding some fastness[9] for you." "Not at all," he said. "It is my own heir apparent." "But surely," said Tripitaka, "the false magician has driven him away." "Not at all," he said. "He is in the Palace of Golden Bells, in the Tower of the Five Phoenixes, studying with his tutor, or on the steps of the magician's throne. But all these three years he has forbidden the prince to go into the inner chambers of the Palace, and he can never see his mother." "Why is that?" asked Tripitaka. "It is the magician's scheme," he said. "He fears that if they were to meet, the queen might in the course of conversation let drop some word that would arouse the prince's suspicions. So these two never meet, and he all this long time has lived secure."

8. The full proverb is: "A poorly drawn tiger looks like a dog; an ill-carved swan looks like a duck." That is, an ambitious undertaking, if not successful, may be worse than inaction.   9. That is, guarding some secure place.

"The disaster that has befallen you, no doubt at Heaven's behest, is much like my own misfortune. My own father was killed by brigands, who seized my mother, and after three months she gave birth to me. I at length escaped from their hands and by good chance met with kindness from a priest of the Golden Mountain Temple, who brought me up. Remembering my own unhappy state, without father or mother, I can sympathize with your prince, who has lost both his parents. But tell me, granted that this prince is still at Court, how can I manage to see him?" "What difficulty in that?" he said. "Because he is kept under strict control," said Tripitaka, "and is not even allowed to see the mother who bore him. How will a stray monk get to him?" "To-morrow," the king said, "he leaves the Court at daybreak." "For what purpose?" "To-morrow, early in the morning, with three thousand followers and falcons and dogs, he will go hunting outside the city, and it will certainly be easy for you to see him. You must then tell him what I have told you, and he cannot fail to believe you." "He is only a common mortal," said Tripitaka, "utterly deceived by the false magician in the palace, and at every turn calling him father and king. Why should he believe what I tell him?" "If that is what worries you," the king said, "I will give you a token to show to him." "And what can you give me?"

In his hand the king carried a tablet of white jade, bordered with gold. This he laid before Tripitaka saying, "Here is my token." "What thing is this?" asked Tripitaka. "When the magician disguised himself as me," said the king, "this treasure was the one thing he forgot about. When the queen asked what had become of it, he said that the wonder-worker who came to make rain took it away with him. If my prince sees it, his heart will be stirred towards me and he will avenge me." "That will do," said Tripitaka. "Wait for me a little, while I tell my disciple to arrange this matter for you. Where shall I find you?" "I dare not wait," he said. "I must ask the Spirit that wanders at Night to blow me to the inner chambers of the palace, where I will appear to the queen in a dream and tell her how to work with her son, and to conspire with you and your disciple." Tripitaka nodded and agreed, saying, "Go, if you will." Then the wronged ghost beat its head on the floor and turned as though to depart. Somehow it stumbled, and went sprawling with a loud noise that woke Tripitaka up. He knew that it had all been a dream, and finding himself sitting with the dying lamp in front of him, he hurriedly cried: "Disciple, disciple!" "Hey, what's that?" cried Pigsy, waking up and coming across to him. "In the old days when I was a decent chap and had my whack of human flesh whenever I wanted, and all the stinking victuals I needed, that was a happy life indeed. A very different matter from coddling an old cleric on his journey! I thought I was to be an acolyte, but this is more like being a slave. By day I hoist the luggage and lead the horse; by night I run my legs off bringing you your pot. No sleep early or late! What's the matter this time?" "Disciple," said Tripitaka, "I was dozing just now at my desk, and had a strange dream."

At this point Monkey sat up, and coming across to Tripitaka said, "Master, dreams come from waking thoughts. Each time we come to a hill before we have even begun to climb it, you are in a panic about ogres and demons. And you are always brooding about what a long way it is to India, and wondering if we shall ever get there; and thinking about Ch'ang-an,[1] and won-

1. The capital of T'ang China, from which Tripitaka had come.

dering if you will ever see it again. All this brooding makes dreams. You should be like me. I think only about seeing Buddha in the West, and not a dream comes near me." "Disciple," said Tripitaka, "this was not a dream of home-sickness. No sooner had I closed my eyes than there came a wild gust of wind, and there at the door stood an Emperor, who said he was the King of Crow-cock. He was dripping from head to foot, and his eyes were full of tears." Then he told Monkey the whole story. "You need say no more," said Monkey. "It is clear enough that this dream came to you in order to bring a little business my way. No doubt at all that this magician is an ogre who has usurped the throne. Just let me put him to the test. I don't doubt my stick will make short work of him." "Disciple," said Tripitaka, "he said the magician was terribly powerful." "What do I care how powerful he is?" said Monkey. "If he had any inkling that Monkey might arrive on the scene, he would have cleared out long ago." "Now I come to think of it," said Tripitaka, "he left a token." Pigsy laughed. "Now, Master," he said, "you must pull yourself together. A dream's a dream. Now it is time to talk sense again." But Sandy broke in, " 'He who does not believe that straight is straight must guard against the wickedness of good.' Let us light torches, open the gate, and see for ourselves whether the token has been left or not."

Monkey did indeed open the gate, and there, in the light of the stars and moon, with no need for torches, they saw lying on the ramp of the steps a tablet of white jade with gold edges. Pigsy stepped forward and picked it up, saying, "Brother, what's this thing?" "This," said Monkey, "is the treasure that the king carried in his hand. It is called a jade tablet. Master, now that we have found this thing, there is no more doubt about the matter. To-morrow it will be my job to catch this fiend."

Dear Monkey! He plucked a hair from his tail, blew on it with magic breath, cried out "Change!" and it became a casket lacquered in red and gold; he laid the tablet in it, and said, "Master, take this in your hand, and when day comes put on your embroidered cassock, and sit reading the scrip-tures in the great hall. Meanwhile I will inspect that walled city. If I find that an ogre is indeed ruling there, I will slay him, and do a deed by which I shall be remembered here. But if it is not an ogre, we must beware of meddling in the business at all." "You are right," said Tripitaka. "If," said Monkey, "the prince does not go out hunting, then there is nothing to be done. But if the dream comes true, I will bring him here to see you." "And if he comes here, how am I to receive him?" "When I let you know that he is coming, open the casket and wait while I change myself into a little priest two inches long, and put me in the casket. When the prince comes here, he will go and bow to the Buddha. Don't you take any notice of the prince or kneel down before him. When he sees that you, a commoner, do not bow down to him, he will order his followers to seize you. You will, of course, let yourself be seized, and beaten too, if they choose to beat you, and bound if they choose to bind you. Let them kill you, indeed, if they want to." "They will be well armed," said Tripitaka. "They might very well kill me. That is not a good idea at all." "It would not matter," said Monkey. "I could deal with that. I will see to it that nothing really serious happens. If he questions you, say that you were sent by the Emperor of China to worship Buddha and get scriptures, and that you have brought treasures with you. When he asks what treasures, show him your cassock and say it is the least of the three treasures, and that there are two others. Then show him the casket and tell him that there is a treasure within that knows what happened five hundred years ago, and what will happen in five hundred years long hence, and five hundred years between. One thousand five hundred years in all, of things past and present. Then let me out of the casket and I will tell the prince what was revealed in the dream. If he believes, I will go and seize the magician and the prince will be avenged upon his father's murderer and we shall win renown. But if he does not believe, I will show him the jade tablet. Only I fear he is too young, and will not recognize it." Tripitaka was delighted. "An excellent plan," he said. "But what shall we call the third treasure? The first is the embroidered cassock, the second the white jade tablet. What is your transformation[2] to be called?" "Call it," said Monkey, "the Baggage that makes Kings." Tripitaka agreed, and committed the name to memory.

Neither disciple nor teacher could sleep. How gladly would they have been able, by a nod, to call up the sun from the Mulberry Tree where it rests,[3] and by a puff of breath blow away the stars that filled the sky!

However, at last it began to grow white in the East, and Monkey got up and gave his orders to Pigsy and Sandy. "Do not," he said, "upset the other priests in the temple by coming out of your cell and rollicking about. Wait till I have done my work, and then we will go on again together."

As soon as he had left them he turned a somersault and leapt into the air. Looking due west with his fiery eyes he soon saw a walled and moated city. You may ask how it was that he could see it. Well, it was only forty leagues away from the temple, and being so high in the air he could see as far as that.

Going on a little way and looking closely, he saw that baleful clouds hung round the city and fumes of discontent surrounded it, and suspended in mid-air Monkey recited:

> Were he a true king seated on the throne,
> Then there would be a lucky gleam and fire-coloured clouds.
> But as it is, a false friend has seized the Dragon Seat,
> And coiling wreaths of black fume tarnish the Golden Gate.[4]

While he was gazing at this sad sight, Monkey suddenly heard a great clanging, and looking down he saw the eastern gate of the city open, and from it a great throng of men and horses come out; truly a host of huntsmen. Indeed, a brave show; look at them:

> At dawn they left the east of the Forbidden City;[5]
> They parted and rounded up in the fields of low grass,
> Their bright banners opened and caught the sun,
> Their white palfreys charged abreast the wind.
> Their skin drums clatter with a loud roll;
> The hurled spears fly each to its mark.

The hunters left the city and proceeded eastwards for twenty leagues towards a high plain. Now Monkey could see that in the midst of them was a little, little general in helmet and breast-plate, in his hand a jewelled sword, riding

2. Magic trick.   3. The Fu-sang Tree, where the sun rests before it rises.   4. The gate to the palace. *Dragon Seat*: the throne.   5. The palace compound.

a bay charger, his bow at his waist. "Don't tell me!" said Monkey in the air, "that is the prince. Let me go and play a trick on him."

Dear Monkey! He lowered himself on his cloud, made his way through the ranks of the huntsmen and, when he came to the prince, changed himself into a white hare and ran in front of the prince's horse. The prince was delighted, took an arrow from his quiver, strung it and shot at the hare, which he hit. But Monkey had willed the arrow to find its aim, and with a swift grab, just as it was about to touch him, he caught hold of it and ran on.

The prince, seeing that he had hit his mark, broke away from his companions and set out in pursuit. When the horse galloped fast, Monkey ran like the wind; when it slowed down, Monkey slowed down. The distance between them remained always the same, and so bit by bit he enticed the prince to the gates of the Treasure Wood Temple. The hare had vanished, for Monkey went back to his own form. But in the door-post an arrow was stuck.

"Here we are, Master," said Monkey, and at once changed again into a two-inch priest and hid in the casket.

Now when the prince came to the temple-gate and found no hare, but only his own arrow sticking in the gate-post, "Very strange!" said the prince, "I am certain I hit the hare. How is it that the hare has disappeared, but the arrow is here? I think it was not a common hare, but one that had lived too long and changed at last into a sprite."

He pulled out the arrow, and looking up saw that above the gate of the temple was an inscription which said "Treasure Wood Temple, erected by Royal Command." "Why, of course!" said the prince. "I remember years ago my father the king ordered an officer to take gold and precious stuffs to the priests of this temple, so that they might repair the chapel and images. I little thought that I would come here one day like this! A couplet says:

> Chance brought me to a priest's cell
> and I listened to his holy talk;
> From the life of the troubled world I got
> Half a day's rest.

I will go in."

The prince leapt from his horse's back and was just going in when three thousand officers who were in attendance upon him came galloping up in a great throng, and were soon pouring into the courtyard. The priests of the temple, much astonished, came out to do homage to the prince, and escort him into the Buddha Hall, to worship the Buddha. The prince was admiring the cloisters, when suddenly he came upon a priest who sat there and did not budge when he came past. "Has this priest no manners?" the prince cried in a rage. "As no warning was given that I was visiting this place, I could not expect to be met at a distance. But so soon as you saw men-at-arms approaching the gate, you ought to have stood up. How comes it that you are still sitting here without budging? Seize him!"

No sooner had he uttered the command than soldiers rushed from the sides, dragged Tripitaka off with them and made ready to bind him hand and foot. But Monkey in the casket soundlessly invoked the guardian spirits, Devas that protect the Law,[6] and Lu Ting and Lu Chia: "I am now on an

---

6. *Dharma*, the Buddhist "law." *Devas*: deities.

errand to subdue an evil spirit. But this prince, in his ignorance, has bade his servants bind my master, and you must come at once to his aid. If he is indeed bound, you will be held responsible!"

Thus secretly addressed by Monkey, how could they venture to disobey? They set a magic ring about Tripitaka, so that each time any one tried to lay hands on him, he could not be reached, any more than if he had been hedged in with a stout wall. "Where do you come from," the prince asked at last, "that you can cheat us like this, making yourself unapproachable?" Tripitaka now came forward and bowed. "I have no such art," he said. "I am only a priest from China, going to the West to worship Buddha and get scriptures."

"China?" said the prince. "Although it is called The Middle Land,[7] it is a most destitute place. Tell me, for example, if you have anything of value upon you." "There is the cassock on my back," said Tripitaka. "It is only a third-class treasure. But I have treasures of the first and second class, which are far superior."

"A coat like yours," said the prince, "that leaves half the body bare! It seems a queer thing to call that a treasure." "This cassock," said Tripitaka, "although it covers only half my body, is described in a poem:

Buddha's coat left one side bare,
But it hid the Absolute from the world's dust.
Its ten thousand threads and thousand stitches fulfilled the fruits of
    Meditation.
Is it a wonder that when I saw you come
              I did not rise to greet you?
You who call yourself a man, yet have failed to avenge a father's
    death!"

"What wild nonsense this priest is talking!" said the prince in a great rage. "That half-coat, if it has done nothing else for you, has given you the courage to babble ridiculous fustian.[8] How can my father's death be unavenged, since he is not dead? Just tell me that!"

Tripitaka came one step forward, pressed the palms of his hands together and said: "Your Majesty, to how many things does man, born into the world, owe gratitude?" "To four things," said the prince. "To what four things?" "He is grateful," said the prince, "to Heaven and Earth for covering and supporting him, to the sun and moon for shining upon him, to the king for lending him water and earth, and to his father and mother for rearing him."

Tripitaka laughed. "To the other three he owes gratitude indeed," he said. "But what need has he of a father and mother to rear him?" "That's all very well for you," said the prince, "who are a shaven-headed, disloyal, food-cadging wanderer. But if a man had no father or mother, how could he come into the world?" "Your Majesty," said Tripitaka, "I do not know. But in this casket there is a treasure called 'The baggage that makes kings.' It knows everything that happened during the five hundred years long ago, the five hundred years between, and the five hundred years to come, one thousand five hundred years in all. If he can quote a case where there was no gratitude to father and mother, then let me be detained captive here."

"Show him to me," said the prince. Tripitaka took off the cover and out

---

7. So-called because it was supposed to be the middle of the world.　8. Pompous, extravagant language.

jumped monkey, and began to skip about this way and that. "A little fellow like that can't know much," said the prince. Hearing himself described as too small, Monkey used his magic power and stretched himself till he was three feet four inches high. The huntsmen were astonished, and said, "If he goes on growing like this, in a few days he will be bumping his head against the sky." But when he reached his usual height, Monkey stopped growing. At this point the prince said to him, "Baggage who Makes Kings, the old priest says you know all things good and ill, in past and present. Do you divine by the tortoise or by the milfoil?[9] Or do you decide men's fates by sentences from books?" "Not a bit of it," said Monkey; "all I rely on is my three inches of tongue, that tells about everything."

"This fellow talks great nonsense," said the prince. "It has always been by the *Book of Changes*[1] that mysteries have been elucidated and the prospects of the world decided, so that people might know what to pursue and what to avoid. Is it not said: 'The tortoise for divination, the milfoil for prognostication?'[2] But so far as I can make out you go on no principle at all. You talk at random about fate and the future, exciting and misleading people to no purpose." "Now don't be in a hurry, Your Highness," said Monkey, "but listen to me. You are the Crown Prince of Crow-cock. Five years ago there was a famine in your land. The king and his ministers prayed and fasted, but they could not get a speck of rain. Then there came a wizard from the Chung-nan mountains who could call the winds, fetch rain, and turn stone into gold. The king was deceived by his wiles and hailed him as elder brother. Is this true?"

"Yes, yes, yes," said the prince. "Go on!" "For the last three years the magician has not been seen," said Monkey. "Who is it that has been on the throne?" "It is true about the wizard," said the prince. "My father did make this wizard his brother, and ate with him and slept with him. But three years ago, when they were walking in the flower garden and admiring the view, a gust of magic wind that the magician sent blew the jade tablet that the king carried out of his hand, and the magician went off with it straight to the Chung-nan mountains. My father still misses him and has no heart to walk in the flower garden without him. Indeed, for three years it has been locked up and no one has set foot in it. If the king is not my father, who is he?"

At this Monkey began to laugh, and did not stop laughing when the prince asked him what was the matter, till the prince lost his temper. "Why don't you say something?" he said, "instead of standing there laughing?" "I have quite a lot to say," said Monkey, "but I cannot say it in front of all these people." The prince thought this reasonable, and motioned to the huntsmen to retire. The leader gave his orders, and soon the three thousand men and horses were all stationed outside the gates. None of the priests of the temple were about. Monkey stopped laughing and said, "Your Highness, he who vanished was the father that begot you; he who sits on the throne is the magician that brought rain."

"Nonsense," cried the prince. "Since the magician left us, the winds have been favouring, the people have been at peace. But according to you it is not

<hr>

9. Yarrow. In ancient China prophecies were made from the cracks that formed in tortoiseshells when put in a fire. Divination was also done by casting stalks of milfoil.   1. One of the Confucian classics, also known as the *I Ching*; a book of prophecy and wisdom.   2. Actually, prognostication and divination are basically the same thing.

my father who is on the throne. It is all very well to say such things to me who am young and let it pass; but if my father were to hear you uttering this subversive talk, he would have you seized and torn into ten thousand pieces." He began railing at Monkey, who turned to Tripitaka and said, "What is to be done? I have told him and he does not believe me. Let's get to work. Show him your treasure, and then get your papers seen to, and go off to India." Tripitaka handed the lacquer-box to Monkey, and Monkey taking it gave himself a shake, and the box became invisible. For it was in reality one of Monkey's hairs, which he had changed into a box, but now put back again as a hair on his body. But the white jade tablet he presented to the prince.

"A fine sort of priest," the prince exclaimed. "You it was who came five years ago disguised as a magician, and stole the family treasure, and now, disguised as a priest, are offering it back again! Seize him!" This command startled Tripitaka out of his wits and pointing at Monkey, "It's you," he cried, "you wretched horse-groom, who have brought this trouble on us for no reason at all." Monkey rushed forward and checked him. "Hold your tongue," he said, "and don't let out my secrets. I am not called 'the Baggage that Makes Kings.' My real name is quite different." "I shall be glad to know your real name," said the prince, "that I may send you to the magistrate to be dealt with as you deserve."

"My name then," said Monkey, "is the Great Monkey Sage, and I am this old man's chief disciple. I was going with my Master to India to get scriptures, and last night we came to this temple and asked for shelter. My Master was reading scriptures by night, and at the third watch he had a dream. He dreamt that your father came to him and said he had been attacked by that magician, who in the flower garden pushed him into the eight-cornered crystal well. Then the wizard changed himself into your father's likeness. The court and all the officers were completely deceived; you yourself were too young to know. You were forbidden to enter the inner apartments of the Palace and the flower garden was shut up, lest the secret should get out. Tonight your father came and asked me to subdue the false magician. I was not sure that he was an evil spirit, but when I looked down from the sky I was quite certain of it. I was just going to seize him, when I met you and your huntsmen. The white hare you shot was me. It was I who led you here and brought you to my Master. This is the truth, every word of it. You have recognized the white tablet, and all that remains is for you to repay your father's care and revenge yourself on his enemy."

This upset the prince very much. "If I do not believe this story," he said to himself, "it must in any case have an unpleasant amount of truth in it. But if I believe it, how can I any longer look upon the present king as my father?" He was in great perplexity. "If you are in doubt," said Monkey, "ride home and ask your mother a question that will decide it. Ask whether she and the king, as man and wife, are on changed terms, these last three years."

"That is a good idea," said the prince. "Just wait while I go and ask my mother." He snatched up the jade tablet and was about to make off, when Monkey stopped him, saying, "If all your gentlemen follow you back to the palace, suspicions will be aroused, and how can I succeed in my task? You must go back all alone and attract no attention. Do not go in at the main gate but by the back gate. And when you get to the inner apartments and see your mother, do not speak loudly or clearly, but in a low whisper; for if the magician should hear you, so great is his power that your life and your mother's would be in danger."

The prince did as he was told, and as he left the temple he told his followers to remain there on guard and not to move. "I have some business," he said. "Wait till I have got to the city and then come on yourselves!" Look at him!

> He gives his orders to the men-at-arms,
> Flies on horseback home to the citadel.

If you do not know whether on this occasion he succeeded in seeing his mother, and if so what passed between them, you must listen to the next chapter.

CHAPTER XX

The prince was soon back at the city of Crow-cock, and as instructed he made no attempt to go in by the main gate, but without announcing himself went to the back gate, where several eunuchs were on guard. They did not dare to stop him, and (dear prince!) he rode in all alone, and soon reached the Arbour of Brocade Perfume, where he found his mother surrounded by her women, who were fanning her, while she leant weeping over a carven balustrade. Why, you will ask, was she weeping? At the fourth watch she had had a dream, half of which she could remember and half of which had faded; and she was thinking hard. Leaping from his horse, the prince knelt down before her and cried "Mother!" She forced herself to put on a happier countenance, and exclaimed, "Child, this is a joy indeed! For years past you have been so busy in the men's quarters at the Palace, studying with your father, that I have never seen you, which has been a great sorrow to me. How have you managed to find time to-day? It is an unspeakable pleasure! My child, why is your voice so mournful? Your father is growing old. Soon the time will come when the 'dragon returns to the pearl-gray sea, the phoenix to the pink mists'; you will then become king. Why should you be dispirited?"

The prince struck the floor with his forehead. "Mother, I ask you," he said, "who is it that sits upon the throne?" "He has gone mad," said the queen. "The ruler is your father and the king. Why should you ask?" "Mother," the prince said, "if you will promise me forgiveness I will speak. But if not, I dare not speak." "How can there be questions of guilt and pardon between mother and son? Of course, you are free to speak. Be quick and begin." "Mother," said the prince, "if you compare your life with my father these last three years with your life with him before, should you say that his affection was as great?" Hearing this question the queen altogether lost her presence of mind, and leaping to her feet ran down from the arbour and flung herself into his arms, saying, "Child, why, when I have not seen you for so long, should you suddenly come and ask me such a question?" "Mother," said the prince hotly, "do not evade this question. For much hangs upon the answer to it."

Then the queen sent away all the Court ladies, and with tears in her eyes said in a low voice, "Had you not asked me, I would have gone down to the Nine Springs[3] of Death without ever breathing a word about this matter. But since you have asked, hear what I have to say:

---

3. The underworld.

What three years ago was warm and bland,[4]
These last three years has been cold as ice.
When at the pillow's side I questioned him,
He told me age had impaired his strength
and that things did not work."

When he heard this, the prince shook himself free, gripped the saddle and mounted his horse. His mother tried to hold him back, saying, "Child, what is it that makes you rush off before our talk is done?" The prince returned and knelt in front of her. "Mother," he said, "I dare not speak. To-day at dawn I received a command to go hunting outside the city with falcon and dog. By chance I met a priest sent by the Emperor of China to fetch scriptures. He has a chief disciple named Monkey, who is very good at subduing evil spirits. According to him my father the king was drowned in the crystal well in the flower garden, and a wizard impersonated him and seized his throne. Last night at the third watch my father appeared in a dream to this priest and asked him to come to the city and seize the impostor. I did not believe all this, and so came to question you. But what you have just told me makes me certain that it is an evil spirit."

"My child," said the queen, "why should you believe strangers, of whom you have no knowledge?" "I should not," said the prince, "have dared to accept the story as true, had not the king my father left behind a token in the hands of these people." The queen asked what it was, and the prince took out from his sleeve the white jade tablet bordered with gold, and handed it to his mother. When she saw that it was indeed a treasure that had been the king's in old days, she could not stop her tears gushing out like a waterspring. "My lord and master," she cried, "why have you been dead three years and never come to me, but went first to a priest and afterwards to the prince?" "Mother," said the prince, "what do these words mean?" "My child," she said, "at the fourth watch I too had a dream. I dreamt I saw your father stand in front of me, all dripping wet, saying that he was dead, and that his soul had visited a priest of T'ang and asked him to defeat the false king and rescue his own body from where it had been thrown. That is all I can remember, and it is only half. The other half I cannot get clear, and I was puzzling about it when you came. It is strange that you should just at this moment come with this tale, and bring this tablet with you. I will put it away, and you must go and ask that priest to come at once and do what he promises. If he can drive away the impostor and distinguish the false from the true, you will have repaid the king your father for the pains he bestowed upon your upbringing."

The prince was soon back at the gates of the Treasure Wood Temple, where he was joined by his followers. The sun's red disc was now falling. He told his followers to stay quietly where they were, went into the temple alone, arranged his hat and clothes, and paid his respects to Monkey, who came hopping and skipping from the main hall. The prince knelt down, saying, "Here I am again, Father." Monkey raised him from his knees. "Did you ask anyone anything when you were in the city?" he said. "I questioned my mother," said the prince; and he told the whole story. Monkey smiled. "If it is as cold as that," he said, "he is probably a transformation of some chilly creature. No matter! Just wait while I mop him up for you. But to-day it is

4. Gentle.

growing late, and I cannot very well start doing anything. You go back now, and I will come early to-morrow."

"Master," said the prince, kneeling before him, "let me wait here till the morning, and then go along with you." "That will not do," said Monkey. "If I were to come into the city at the same time as you, the suspicions of the impostor would be aroused. He would not believe that I forced myself upon you, but would be sure you had invited me. And in this way the blame would fall on you."

"I shall get into trouble anyhow," said the prince, "if I go into the city now." "What about?" asked Monkey. "I was sent out hunting," said the prince, "and I have not got a single piece of game. How dare I face the king? If he accuses me of incompetence and casts me into prison, who will you have to look after you when you arrive to-morrow? There is not one of the officers who knows you." "What matter?" said Monkey. "You have only to mention that you need some game, and I will procure it for you." Dear Monkey! Watch him while he displays his arts before the prince. He gives himself a shake, jumps up on to the fringe of a cloud, performs a magic pass and murmurs a spell which compels the spirits of the mountain and the local deities to come before him and do obeisance. "Great Sage," they said, "what orders have you for us little divinities?" "I guarded a priest of T'ang on his way here," said Monkey. "I want to seize an evil spirit, but this prince here has nothing to show for his hunting, and does not dare return to Court. I have sent for you divinities to ask you to do me a favour. Find some musk deer, wild boar, hares and so on—any wild beasts or birds you can discover, and bring them here." The divinities dared not disobey. "How many do you require of each?" they asked. "It does not matter exactly how many," said Monkey. "Just bring some along; that is all."

Then these divinities, using the secret instruments that appertained to them, made a magic wind that drew together wild beasts. Soon there were hundreds and thousands of wild fowl, deer, foxes, hares, tigers, panthers and wolves collected in front of Monkey. "It is not I who want them!" he cried. "You must get them on the move again, and string them out on each side of the road for forty leagues. The hunters will be able to take them home without use of falcon or dog. That is all that is required of you."

The divinities obeyed, and spread out the game on each side of the road. Monkey then lowered his cloud and said to the prince, "Your Highness may now go back. There is game all along the road; you have only to collect it."

When the prince saw him floating about in the air and exercising magic powers, he was deeply impressed, and bent his head on the ground in prostration before Monkey, from whom he humbly took his leave. He then went out in front of the temple and gave orders to the huntsmen to return to Court. They were astonished to find endless wild game on each side of the road, which they took without use of falcon or dog, merely by laying hands upon it. They all believed that this blessing had been vouchsafed to the prince, and had no idea that it was Monkey's doing. Listen to the songs of triumph that they sing as they throng back to the city!

When the priests of the temple saw on what terms Tripitaka and the rest were with the prince, they began to treat them with a new deference. They invited them to refreshments, and again put the Zen Hall at Tripitaka's disposal. It was near the first watch; but Monkey had something on his mind and could not get to sleep at once. Presently he crept across to Tripitaka's bed and called, "Master!" Tripitaka was not asleep either; but knowing that Monkey liked giving people a start, he pretended to be asleep. Monkey rubbed his tonsure and shaking him violently, he said, "Master, why are you sleeping?" "The rogue!" cried Tripitaka crossly. "Why can't you go to sleep, instead of pestering me like this?" "Master," said Monkey, "there is something you must give me your advice about." "What is that?" said Tripitaka. "I talked very big to the prince," said Monkey, "giving him to understand that my powers were high as the hills and deep as the sea, and that I could catch the false wizard as easily as one takes things out of a bag—I had only to stretch out my hand and carry him off. But I cannot get to sleep, for it has occurred to me that it may not be so easy." "If you think it's too difficult, why do it?" said Tripitaka. "It's not that there's any difficulty about catching him," said Monkey. "The only question is whether it is legal." "What nonsense this monkey talks," said Tripitaka. "How can it be illegal to arrest a monster that has seized a monarch's throne?" "You only know how to read scriptures, worship Buddha and practise Zen, and have never studied the Code of Hsiao Ho.[5] But you must at least know the proverb 'Take robber, take loot.' The magician has been king for three years and not the slightest suspicion has been felt by anyone. All the late king's ladies sleep with him, and the ministers civil and military disport themselves with him. Even if I succeed in catching him, how am I to convince anyone of his guilt?" "What is the difficulty?" asked Tripitaka. "Even if he were as dumb as a calabash,[6] he would be able to talk one down. He would say boldly, 'I am the king of Crow-cock. What crime have I committed against Heaven that you should arrest me?' How would one argue with him then?" "And you," said Tripitaka, "what plan have you got?" "My plan is already made," said Monkey smiling. "The only obstacle is that you have a partiality." "A partiality for whom?" said Tripitaka. "Pigsy," said Monkey; "you have a preference for him because he is so strong." "What makes you think that?" asked Tripitaka. "If it were not so," said Monkey, "you would pull yourself together and have the courage to stay here with Sandy to look after you, while I and Pigsy go off to the city of Crow-cock, find the flower garden, uncover the well, and bring up the Emperor's body, which we will wrap in our wrapper, and next day bring to Court. There we will get our papers put in order, confront the Magician, and I will fell him with my cudgel. If he tries to exonerate himself, I will show him the body and say, 'Here is the man you drowned.' And I will make the prince come forward and wail over his father, the queen come out and recognize her husband, the officers civil and military look upon their lord, and then I and my brother will get to work. In this way the whole thing will be on a proper footing."

Tripitaka thought this was a splendid plan, but he was not sure that Pigsy would consent. "Why not?" said Monkey. "Didn't I say you were partial to him and did not want him to go? You think he would refuse to go because you know that when I call you it is often half an hour before you take any notice. You'll see when I start, that I shall only need a turn or two of my three-inch tongue, and no matter if he is Pigsy or Wigsy I am quite capable of making him follow me." "Very well," said Tripitaka, "call him when you go."

"Pigsy, Pigsy," cried Monkey at Pigsy's bedside. That fool did most of the

5. A minister of the Han Dynasty who established laws.   6. A type of gourd.

hard work when they were on the road, and no sooner did his head touch the pillow than he was snoring, and it took a great deal more than a shout to wake him.

Monkey pulled his ears, tweaked his bristles and dragged him from the pillow, shouting "Pigsy!" That fool pushed him away. Monkey shouted again. "Go to sleep and don't be so stupid," Pigsy said. "To-morrow we have got to be on the road again." "I am not being stupid," said Monkey, "there is a bit of business I want your help in." "What business?" asked Pigsy. "You heard what the prince said?" said Monkey. "No," said Pigsy, "I did not set eyes on him, or hear anything he said." "He told me," said Monkey, "that the magician has a treasure worth more than an army of ten thousand men. When we go to the city to-morrow, we are sure to fall foul of him, he will use it to overthrow us. Wouldn't it be much better if we got in first and stole the treasure?"

"Brother," said Pigsy, "are you asking me to commit robbery? If so, that's a business I have experience of and can really be of some help. But there is one thing we must get clear. If I steal a treasure or subdue a magician I expect more than a petty, skunking share. The treasure must be mine." "What do you want it for?" asked Monkey. "I am not so clever as you are at talking people into giving me alms. I am strong, but I have a very common way of talking, and I don't know how to recite the scriptures. When we get into a tight place, wouldn't this treasure be good to exchange for something to eat and drink?" "I only care for fame," said Monkey. "I don't want any treasures. You may have it all to yourself."

That fool, when he heard that it was all to be his, was in high glee. He rolled out of bed, hustled into his clothes and set out with Monkey.

> Clear wine brings a blush to the cheeks;
> Yellow gold moves even a philosophic heart.

The two of them opened the temple gate very quietly and, leaving Tripitaka, mounted a wreath of cloud and soon reached the city, where they lowered their cloud, just as the second watch was being sounded on the tower. "Brother! it's the second watch," said Monkey. "Couldn't be better," said Pigsy. "Everyone will just be deep in their first sleep."

They did not go to the main gate, but to the back gate, where they heard the sound of the watchman's clappers and bells. "Brother," said Monkey, "they are on the alert at all the gates. How shall we get in?" "When did thieves ever go in by a gate?" said Pigsy. "We must scramble over the wall." Monkey did so, and at a bound was over the rampart and wall. Pigsy followed, and the two stealthily made their way in, soon rejoining the road from the gate. They followed this till they came to the flower garden.

In front of them was a gate-tower with three thatched white gables, and high up was an inscription in shining letters, catching the light of the moon and stars. It said "Imperial Flower Garden." When Monkey came close, he saw that the locks were sealed up several layers deep, and he told Pigsy to get to work. That fool wielded his iron rake, which he brought crashing down upon the gate and smashed it to bits. Monkey stepped over the fragments, and once inside could not stop himself jumping and shouting for joy. "Brother," said Pigsy, "you'll be the ruin of us. Who ever heard of a thief making all that noise? You'll wake everyone up, we shall be arrested and taken before the judge, and if we are not condemned to death we shall certainly be sent back to where we came from and drafted into the army." "Why try to make me nervous?" said Monkey. "Look!

> The painted and carven balustrades are scattered and strewn;
> The jewel-studded arbours and trees are toppling down.
> The sedgy islands and knot-weed banks are buried in dust;
> The white peonies and yellow glove-flowers, all dust-destroyed.
> Jasmine and rose perfume the night;
> The red peony and tiger-lily bloom in vain,
> The hibiscus and Syrian mallow are choked with weeds;
> Strange plant and rare flower are crushed and die."

"And what does it matter if they do." said Pigsy. "Let's get on with our business." Monkey, although deeply affected by the scene, called to mind Tripitaka's dream, in which he was told that the well was underneath a banana-plant, and when they had gone a little further they did indeed discover a most singular banana-plant, which grew very thick and high.

"Now Pigsy," said Monkey. "Are you ready? The treasure is buried under this tree." That fool lifted his rake in both hands, beat down the banana-tree and began to nuzzle with his snout till he had made a hole three or four feet deep. At last he came to a slab of stone. "Brother," he cried, "here's luck. We've found the treasure. It's bound to be under this slab. If it's not in a coffer it will be in a jar." "Hoist it up and see," said Monkey. Pigsy went to work again with his snout and raised the slab till they could see underneath. Something sparkled and flashed. "Didn't I say we were in luck," said Pigsy. "That is the treasure glittering." But when they looked closer, it was the light of the stars and moon reflected in a well. "Brother," said Pigsy, "you should not think so much of the trunk that you forget the root." "Now, what does that mean?" asked Monkey. "This is a well," said Pigsy. "If you had told me before we started that the treasure was in a well, I should have brought with me the two ropes we tie up our bundles with, and you could have contrived to let me down. As it is, how are we to get at anything down there and bring it up again?" "You intend to go down?" said Monkey. "That's what I should do," said Pigsy, "if I had any rope." "Take off your clothes," said Monkey, "and I'll manage it for you." "I don't go in for much in the way of clothes," said Pigsy. "But I'll take off my jerkin, if that's any good."

Dear Monkey! He took out his metal-clasped cudgel, called to it "Stretch!" and when it was some thirty feet long he said to Pigsy, "You catch hold of one end, and I'll let you down." "Brother," said Pigsy, "let me down as far as you like, so long as you stop when I come to the water." "Just so," said Monkey. Pigsy caught hold of one end of the staff, and was very gently raised and let down into the well by Monkey. He soon reached the water. "I'm at the water," he called up. Monkey, hearing this, let him down just a little further. That fool Pigsy, when he felt the water touch him, began to beat out with his trotters, let go of the staff and flopped right into the water. "The rascal!" he cried, spluttering and blowing. "I told him to stop when I came to the water, and instead he let me down further."

Monkey only laughed, and withdrew the staff. "Brother," he said, "have you found the treasure?" "Treasure indeed!" said Pigsy. "There's nothing but well-water." "The treasure is under the water," said Monkey. "Just have a look."

Pigsy, it so happened, was thoroughly at home in the water. He took a great plunge straight down into the well. But, oh what a long way it was to the bottom! He dived again with all his might, and suddenly opening his eyes saw in front of him an entrance, above which was written "The Crystal Palace." This astonished him very much. "That finishes it," he cried. "I've come the wrong way and got into the sea! There is a Crystal Palace in the sea; but I never heard of one down a well." For he did not know that the Dragon King of the Well also has a Crystal Palace.

Pigsy was thus debating with himself when a yaksha,[7] on patrol-duty in the waters, opened the door, saw the intruder, and immediately withdrew to the interior, announcing: "Great King, a calamity! A long-snouted, long-eared priest has dropped down into our well, all naked and dripping. He is still alive, and speaks to himself rationally."

The Dragon King of the Well was, however, not at all surprised. "If I am not mistaken," he said, "this is General Pigsy. Last night the Spirit that Wanders by Night received orders to come here and fetch the soul of the king of Crow-cock and bring it to the priest of T'ang to ask the Monkey Sage to subdue the wicked magician. I imagine that Monkey has come, as well as General Pigsy. They must be treated with great consideration. Go at once and ask the General to come in." The Dragon King then tidied his clothes, adjusted his hat, and bringing with him all his watery kinsmen he came to the gate and cried in a loud voice: "General Pigsy, pray come inside and be seated!" Pigsy was delighted. "Fancy meeting with an old friend!" he said. And without thinking what he was in for, that fool went into the Crystal Palace. Caring nothing for good manners, all dripping as he was, he sat down in the seat of honour. "General," said the Dragon King, "I heard lately that your life was spared to you on condition you should embrace the faith of Sākyamuni[8] and protect Tripitaka on his journey to India. What then are you doing down here?" "It's just in that connection that I come," said Pigsy. "My brother Monkey presents his best compliments and sends me to fetch some treasure or other." "I am sorry," said the Dragon King, "but what should I be doing with any treasure? You're mixing me up with the dragons of the Yang-tze, the Yellow River, the Huai and the Chi, who soar about the sky and assume many shapes. They no doubt have treasures. But I stay down here all the time in this wretched hole never catching a glimpse of the sky above. Where should I get a treasure from?" "Don't make excuses," said Pigsy. "I know you have got it; so bring it out at once." "The one treasure I have," said the Dragon King, "can't be brought out. I suggest you should go and look at it for yourself." "Excellent," said Pigsy. "I'll come and have a look." The Dragon King led him through the Crystal Palace till they came to a cloister in which lay a body six feet long. Pointing at it the Dragon King said, "General, there is your treasure." Pigsy went up to it, and oh! what did he see before him? It was a dead Emperor, on his head a tall crown, dressed in a red gown, on his feet upturned shoes, girded with a belt of jades, who lay stretched full length upon the floor. Pigsy laughed. "You won't kid me like that," he said. "Since when did this count as a treasure? Why, when I was an ogre in the mountains I made my supper on them every day. When one

7. An Indian demigod, imported into China along with Buddhism.   8. The original name of the present buddha. Buddhas appear at intervals in the history of the universe; thus there are past, present, and future buddhas.

has not only seen a thing time after time, but also eaten it again and again, can one be expected to regard it as a treasure?"

"General," said the Dragon King, "you do not understand. This is the body of the King of Crow-cock. When he fell into the well I preserved him with a magic pearl, and he suffered no decay. If you care to take him up with you, show him to Monkey and succeed in bringing him back to his senses, you need worry no more about 'treasures,' you'll be able to get anything out of him that you choose to ask for." "Very well then," said Pigsy, "I'll remove him for you, if you'll let me know how much I shall get as my undertaker's fee." "I haven't got any money," said the Dragon King. "So you expect to get jobs done for nothing?" said Pigsy. "If you haven't got any money I won't remove him." "If you won't," said the Dragon King, "I must ask you to go away." Pigsy at once retired. The Dragon King ordered two powerful yakshas to carry the body to the gate of the Crystal Palace and leave it just outside. They removed from the gate its water-fending pearls, and at once there was a sound of rushing waters! Pigsy looked round. The gate had vanished, and while he was poking about for it, his hand touched the dead king's body, which gave him such a start that his legs gave way under him. He scrambled to the surface of the water, and squeezing against the well-wall, he cried, "Brother, let down your staff and get me out of this." "Did you find the treasure?" asked Monkey. "How should I?" said Pigsy. "All I found was a Dragon King at the bottom of the water, who wanted me to remove a corpse. I refused, and he had me put out at the door. Then his palace vanished, and I found myself touching the corpse. It gave me such a turn that I feel quite weak. Brother, you must get me out of this." "That was your treasure," said Monkey. "Why didn't you bring it up with you?" "I knew he had been dead a long time," said Pigsy. "What was the sense of bringing him?" "You'd better," said Monkey, "or I shall go away." "Go?" said Pigsy. "Where to?" "I shall go back to the temple," said Monkey, "and go to sleep like Tripitaka." "And I shall be left down here?" said Pigsy. "If you can climb out," said Monkey, "there is no reason why you should stay here; but if you can't there's an end of it." Pigsy was thoroughly frightened; he knew he could not possibly climb out. "Just think," he said, "even a city wall is difficult to get up. But this well-shaft has a big belly and a small mouth. Its walls slope in, and as no water has been drawn from it for several years they have become all covered with slime. It's far too slippery to climb. Brother, just to keep up a nice spirit between friends, I'll carry it up."

"That's right," said Monkey. "And be quick about it, so that we can both of us go home to bed."

That fool Pigsy dived down again, found the corpse, hoisted it on to his back, clambered up to the surface of the water, and propped himself and the body against the wall. "Brother," he called. "I've brought it." Monkey peered down, and seeing that Pigsy had indeed a burden on his back, he lowered his staff into the well.

That fool was a creature of much determination. He opened his mouth wide, bit hard on the staff, and Monkey pulled him gently up. Putting down the corpse, Pigsy pulled himself into his clothes. The Emperor, Monkey found on examining him, was indeed in the most perfect preservation. "Brother," he asked, "how comes it that a man who has been dead for three years can look so fresh?" "According to the Dragon King of the Well," said

Pigsy, "he used a magic pearl which prevented the body from decaying."
"That was a bit of luck," said Monkey. "But it still remains to take vengeance
upon his enemy and win glory for ourselves. Make haste and carry him off."
"Where to?" asked Pigsy. "To the temple," said Monkey, "to show him to
Tripitaka." "What an idea!" grumbled Pigsy to himself. "A fellow was having
a nice, sound sleep, and along comes this baboon with a wonderful yarn
about a job that must be done, and in the end it turns out to be nothing but
this silly game of carting about a corpse. Carry that stinking thing! It will
dribble filthy water all over me and dirty my clothes; there's no one to wash
them for me. There are patches in several places, and if the water gets
through I have nothing to change into." "Don't worry about your clothes,"
said Monkey. "Get the body to the temple, and I will give you a change of
clothes." "Impudence!" cried Pigsy. "You've none of your own. How can you
give me any to change into?" "Does that twaddle mean that you won't carry
it?" asked Monkey. "I'm not going to carry it," said Pigsy. "Then hold out
your paw and take twenty," said Monkey. "Brother," said Pigsy, much
alarmed, "that cudgel is very heavy; after twenty strokes of it there would not
be much to choose between me and this Emperor." "If you don't want to be
beaten," said Monkey, "make haste and carry it off."

Pigsy did indeed fear the cudgel, and sorely against his will he hoisted the
corpse on to his back and began to drag himself along towards the garden
gate. Dear Monkey! He performed a magic pass, recited a spell, traced a
magic square on the ground, and going to it blew a breath that turned into
a great gust of wind which blew Pigsy clean out of the palace grounds and
clear of the city moat. The wind stopped, and alighting they set out slowly
on their way. Pigsy was feeling very ill-used and thought of a plan to revenge
himself. "This monkey," he said to himself, "has played a dirty trick on me,
but I'll get even with him all right when we get back to the temple, I will tell
Tripitaka that Monkey can bring the dead to life. If he says he can't, I shall
persuade Tripitaka to recite the spell that makes this monkey's head ache,
and I shan't be satisfied till his brains are bursting out of his head." But
thinking about it as he went along, he said to himself, "That's no good! If he
is asked to bring the king to life, he won't have any difficulty; he will go
straight to Yama, King of Death, ask for the soul, and so bring the king to
life. I must make it clear that he is not to go to the Dark Realm, but must
do his cure here in the World of Light. That's the thing to do."

They were now at the temple gate, went straight in, and put down the
corpse at the door of the Zen Hall, saying, "Master, get up and look!" Tripitaka was not asleep, but was discussing with Sandy why the others were
away so long. Suddenly he heard them calling, and jumping up he said,
"Disciples, what is this I see?" "Monkey's father-in-law," said Pigsy; "he made
me carry him." "You rotten fool," said Monkey, "where have I any father-in-
law?" "Brother, if he isn't your father-in-law," said Pigsy, "why did you make
me carry him? It has been tiring work for me, I can tell you that!"

When Tripitaka and Sandy examined the body, and saw that the Emperor
looked just like a live man, Tripitaka suddenly burst into lamentation. "Alas,
poor Emperor," he cried, "in some forgotten existence you doubtless did great
wrong to one that in this incarnation has now confounded you, and brought
you to destruction. You were torn from wife and child; none of your generals
or counsellors knew, none of your officers were aware. Alas, for the blindness

of your queen and prince that offered no incense, no tea to your soul!" Here he broke down, and his tears fell like rain. "Master," said Pigsy, "what does it matter to you that he is dead? He is not your father or grandfather, why should you wail over him?" "Disciple," said Tripitaka, "for us who are followers of Buddha compassion is the root, indulgence the gate. Why is your heart so hard?" "It isn't that my heart is hard," said Pigsy. "But Brother Monkey tells me he can bring him to life. If he fails I am certainly not going to cart him about any more."

Now Tripitaka, being by nature pliable as water, was easily moved by that fool's story. "Monkey," he said, "if you can indeed bring this Emperor back to life, you will be doing what matters more than that we should reach the Holy Mountain and worship the Buddha. They say 'To save one life is better than to build a seven-storeyed pagoda.'" "Master," said Monkey, "do you really believe this fool's wild talk? When a man is dead, in three times seven, five times seven, or at the end of seven hundred days, when he has done penance for his sins in the World of Light, his turn comes to be born again. This king has been dead for three years. How can he possibly be saved?" "I expect we had better give up the idea," said Tripitaka, when he heard this. But Pigsy was not to be cheated of his revenge. "Don't let him put you off," he said to Tripitaka. "Remember, his head is very susceptible. You have only to recite that stuff of yours, and I guarantee that he'll turn the king into a live man."

Tripitaka accordingly did recite the headache spell, and it gripped so tight that Monkey's eyes started out of his head, and he suffered frightful pain.

If you do not know whether in the end this king was brought to life, you must listen to what is unfolded in the next chapter.

CHAPTER XXI

The pain in that great Monkey Sage's head was so great that at last he could bear it no longer and cried piteously, "Master, stop praying, stop praying! I'll doctor him." "How will you do it?" asked Tripitaka. "The only way is to visit Yama, King of Death, in the Land of Darkness, and get him to let me have the king's soul," said Monkey. "Don't believe him, Master," said Pigsy. "He told me there was no need to go to the Land of Darkness. He said he knew how to cure him here and now, in the World of Light." Tripitaka believed this wicked lie, and began praying again; and Monkey was so harassed that he soon gave in. "All right, all right," he cried. "I'll cure him in the World of Light." "Don't stop," said Pigsy. "Go on praying as hard as you can." "You ill-begotten idiot," cursed Monkey, "I'll pay you out for making the Master put a spell upon me." Pigsy laughed till he fell over. "Ho, ho, brother," he cried, "you thought it was only on me that tricks could be played. You didn't think that I could play a trick on you." "Master, stop praying," said Monkey, "and let me cure him in the World of Light." "How can that be done?" asked Tripitaka. "I will rise on my cloud-trapeze," said Monkey, "and force my way into the southern gate of Heaven. I shall not go to the Palace of the Pole and Ox, nor to the Hall of Holy Mists, but go straight up to the thirty-third heaven, and in the Trayaśimstra Courtyard of the heavenly palace of Quit Grief I shall visit Lao Tzu[9] and ask for a grain of his Nine

9. See n. 8, p. 35.

Times Sublimated Life Restoring Elixir, and with it I shall bring the king back to life."

This suggestion pleased Tripitaka very much. "Lose no time about it," he said. "It is only the third watch," said Monkey. "I shall be back before it is light. But it would look all wrong if the rest of you went quietly to sleep. It is only decent that someone should watch by the corpse and mourn." "You need say no more," said Pigsy. "I can see that you expect me to act as mourner." "I should like to see you refuse!" said Monkey. "If you don't act as mourner, I certainly shan't bring him to life." "Be off, Brother," said Pigsy, "and I'll do the mourning." "There are more ways than one of mourning," said Monkey. "Mere bellowing with dry eyes is no good. Nor is it any better just to squeeze out a few tears. What counts is a good hearty howling, with tears as well. That's what is wanted for a real, miserable mourning." "I'll give you a specimen," said Pigsy. He then from somewhere or other produced a piece of paper which he twisted into a paper-spill and thrust up his nostrils. This soon set him snivelling and his eyes running, and when he began to howl he kept up such a din that anyone would have thought he had indeed lost his dearest relative. The effect was so mournful that Tripitaka too soon began to weep bitterly. "That's what you've got to keep up the whole time I'm away," said Monkey laughing. "What I am frightened of is that this fool, the moment my back is turned, will stop wailing. I shall creep back and listen, and if he shows any sign of leaving off he will get twenty on the paw." "Be off with you," laughed Pigsy. "I could easily keep this up for two days on end."

Sandy, seeing that Pigsy had settled down to his job, went off to look for some sticks of incense to burn as an offering. "Excellent!" laughed Monkey. "The whole family is engaged in works of piety! Now's the time for Old Monkey to get to work."

Dear Monkey! Just at midnight he left his teacher and fellow-disciples, mounted his cloud-trapeze and flew in at the southern gate of Heaven. He did not indeed call at the Precious Hall of Holy Mists or go on to the Palace of the Pole and Ox, but only along a path of cloudy light went straight to the thirty-third heaven, to the Trayaśimstra Courtyard of the heavenly palace of Quit Grief. Just inside the gate he saw Lao Tzu in his alchemical studio, with a number of fairy boys holding banana-leaf fans, and fanning the fire in which the cinnabar was sublimating.[1]

As soon as Lao Tzu saw him coming, he called to the boys, "Be careful, all of you. Here's the thief who stole the elixir come back again." Monkey bowed, and said laughing, "Reverend Sir, there is no need to be in such a fret. You need take no precautions against me. I have come on quite different business." "Monkey," said Lao Tzu, "five hundred years ago you made great trouble in the Palace of Heaven, and stole a great quantity of my holy elixir; for which crime you were arrested and placed in my crucible, where you were smelted for forty-nine days, at the cost of I know not how much charcoal. Now you have been lucky enough to obtain forgiveness, enter the service of Buddha, and go with Tripitaka, the priest of T'ang, to get scriptures in India. Some while ago you quelled a demon in the Flat Topped Mountain and tricked disaster, but did not give me my share in the treasure. What

---

1. The boys were extracting mercury from cinnabar. Mercury was used in elixirs of immortality.

brings you here to-day?" "In those old days," said Monkey, "I lost no time in returning to you those five treasures of yours. You have no reason to be suspicious of me." "But what are you doing here?" asked Lao Tzu, "creeping into my palace instead of getting on with your journey?" "On our way to the West," said Monkey, "we came to a country called Crow-cock. The king of the country employed a wizard, who had disguised himself as a Taoist, to bring rain. This wizard secretly did away with the king, whose form he assumed, and now he is ensconced in the Hall of Golden Bells. My Master was reading the scriptures in the Treasure Wood Temple, when the soul of the king came to him and earnestly requested that I might be sent to subdue the wizard, and expose his imposture. I felt that I had no proof of the crime, and went with my fellow-disciple Pigsy. We broke into the flower garden by night, and looked for the crystal well into which the king had been thrown. We fished him up, and found him still sound and fresh. When we got back to the temple and saw Tripitaka, his compassion was aroused and he ordered me to bring the king to life. But I was not to go to the World of Darkness to recover his soul; I must cure him here in the World of Light. I could think of no way but to ask for your help. Would you be so kind as to lend me a thousand of your nine times sublimated life-restoring pills? Then I shall be able to set him right." "A thousand pills indeed!" exclaimed Lao Tzu. "Why not two thousand? Is he to have them at every meal instead of rice? Do you think one has only to stoop and pick them up like dirt from the ground? Shoo! Be off with you! I've nothing for you." "I'd take a hundred," said Monkey laughing. "I dare say," said Lao Tzu. "But I haven't any." "I'd take ten," said Monkey. "A curse on this Monkey!" said Lao Tzu, very angry. "Will he never stop haggling? Be off with you immediately." "If you really haven't got any," said Monkey, "I shall have to find some other way of bringing him to life." "Go, go, go!" screamed Lao Tzu. Very reluctantly Monkey turned away. But suddenly Lao Tzu thought to himself: "This monkey is very crafty. If he really went away and stayed away, it would be all right. But I am afraid he will slip back again and steal some." So he sent a fairy boy to bring Monkey back, and said to him, "If you are really so anxious to have some, I'll spare you just one pill." "Sir," said Monkey, "if you had an inkling of what I can do if I choose, you would think yourself lucky to go shares in it with me. If you hadn't given in, I should have come with my dredge and fished up the whole lot." Lao Tzu took a gourd-shaped pot and, tilting it up, emptied one grain of elixir and passed it across to Monkey, saying, "That's all you'll get, so be off with it. And if with this one grain you can bring the king back to life, you are welcome to the credit of it." "Not so fast," said Monkey. "I must taste it first. I don't want to be put off with a sham." So saying, he tossed it into his mouth. Lao Tzu rushed forward to stop him, and pressing his fists against his skull-cap he cried in despair, "If you swallow it, I shall kill you on the spot!" "Revolting meanness," said Monkey. "Keep calm; no one is eating anything of yours. And how much is it worth, anyhow? It's pretty wretched stuff, and come to that, I haven't swallowed it; it's here."

For the fact is that monkeys have a pouch under the gullet, and Monkey had stored the grain of elixir in his pouch. Lao Tzu pinched him and said, "Be off with you, be off with you, and don't let me find you hanging round here any more." So Monkey took leave of him, and quitted the Trayaśimstra Heaven. In a moment he had left by the Southern Gate, and turning eastward he saw the great globe of the sun just mounting. Lowering his cloud-seat, he soon reached the Treasure Wood Temple, where even before he entered the gate he could hear Pigsy still howling. He stepped briskly forward and cried "Master." "Is that Monkey?" said Tripitaka delightedly. "Have you got your elixir?" "Certainly," said Monkey. "What's the use of asking?" said Pigsy. "You can count on a sneak like that to bring back some trifle that doesn't belong to him." "Brother," laughed Monkey, "you can retire. We don't need you any more. Wipe your eyes, and if you want to do more howling do it elsewhere. And you, Sandy, bring me a little water." Sandy hurried out to the well behind the temple, where there was a bucket of water ready drawn. He dipped his bowl into it and brought half a bowlful of water. Monkey filled his mouth with water, and then spat out the elixir into the Emperor's lips. Next he forced open his jaws, and pouring in some clean water, he floated the elixir down into his belly. In a few moments there was a gurgling sound inside; but the body still did not move. "Master," said Monkey, "what will become of me if my elixir fails? Shall I be beaten to death?" "I don't see how it can fail," said Tripitaka. "It's already a miracle that a corpse that has been dead so long can swallow water. After the elixir entered his belly, we heard the guts ring. When the guts ring, the veins move in harmony. It only remains to get the breath into circulation. But even a piece of iron gets a bit rusty when it has been under water for three years; it is only natural that something of the same kind should happen to a man. All that's wrong with him is that he needs a supply of breath. If someone puts a mouthful of good breath into him, he would be quite himself again."

Pigsy at once offered himself for this service, but Tripitaka held him back. "You're no use for that," he cried. "Let Monkey do it." Tripitaka knew what he was talking about. For Pigsy had in his early days eaten living things, and even monstrously devoured human flesh, so that all his stock of breath was defiled. Whereas Monkey had always lived on pine-seeds, cypress cones, peaches and the like, and his breath was pure.

So Monkey stepped forward, and putting his wide mouth against the Emperor's lips he blew hard into his throat. The breath went down to the Two-Storeyed Tower, round the Hall of Light, on to the Cinnabar Field, and from the Jetting Spring went back again into the Mud Wall Palace.[2] Whereupon there was a deep panting sound. The king's humours concentrated, his spirits returned. He rolled over, brandished his fist, and bent his legs. Then with a cry "Master!" he knelt down in the dust and said, "Little did I think, when my soul visited you last night, that to-day at dawn I should again belong to the World of Light!" Tripitaka quickly raised him from his knees and said, "Your Majesty, this is no doing of mine. You must thank my disciple." "What talk is that?" said Monkey laughing. "The proverb says 'A household cannot have two masters.' There is no harm in letting him pay his respects to you."

Tripitaka, still feeling somewhat embarrassed, raised the Emperor to his feet and brought him to the Hall of Meditation, where he and his disciples again prostrated themselves, and set him on a seat. The priests of the temple had got ready their breakfast, and invited Tripitaka and his party to join them. Imagine their astonishment when they saw an Emperor, his clothes still drip-

---

2. All elegant terms for the internal organs.

ping. "Don't be surprised," said Monkey, coming forward. "This is the King of Crow-cock, your rightful lord. Three years ago he was robbed of his life by a fiend, and to-night I brought him back to life. Now we must take him to the city and surprise the impostor. If you have anything for us to eat, serve it now, and we will start as soon as we have breakfasted."

The priests brought the Emperor hot water to wash in, and helped him out of his clothes. The almoner[3] brought him a cloth jacket, and instead of his jade belt tied a silk sash round his waist; took off his upturned shoes, and gave him a pair of old priest's sandals. Then they all had breakfast, and saddled the horse. "Pigsy, is your luggage very heavy?" asked Monkey. "Brother, I've carried it so many days on end that I don't know whether it's heavy or not." "Divide the pack into two," said Monkey, "take one half yourself, and give the other to this Emperor to carry. In that way we shall get quicker to the city and dispose of our business." "That's a bit of luck," said Pigsy. "It was a nuisance getting him here. But now that he's been made alive, he is coming in useful as a partner."

Pigsy then divided the luggage after his own methods. Borrowing a hod[4] from the priests of the temple he put everything light into his own load, and everything heavy into the king's. "I hope your Majesty has no objection," said Monkey laughing, "to being dressed up like this, and carrying the luggage, and following us on foot." "Master," said the Emperor, instantly flinging himself upon his knees, "I can only regard you as my second progenitor, and let alone carrying luggage for you, my heartfelt desire is to go with you all the way to India, even if I were only to serve you as the lowest menial, running beside you whip in hand as you ride."

"There's no need for you to go to India," said Monkey. "That's our special concern. All you have to do is to carry the luggage forty leagues to the city and then let us seize the fiend. After which you can go on being Emperor again, and we can go on looking for scriptures."

"That's all very well," said Pigsy. "But in that case he gets off with forty leagues, while I shall be on the job all the time. "Brother," said Monkey, "don't talk nonsense, but be quick and lead the way out." Pigsy and the Emperor accordingly led the way, while Sandy supported Tripitaka on his horse and Monkey followed behind. They were accompanied to the gates by five hundred priests in gorgeous procession, blowing conches as they walked. "Don't come with us any further," said Monkey. "If some official were to notice, our plans might get out, and everything would go wrong. Go back at once, and have the Emperor's clothes well cleaned, and send them to the city to-night or early tomorrow. I will see to it that you are well paid for your pains."

They had not travelled for half a day when the walls and moat of the city of Crow-cock came into view. "Monkey," said Tripitaka, "I think this place in front of us must be the city of Crow-cock." "It certainly is," said Monkey. "Let us hurry on and do our business."

When they reached the city they found the streets and markets thronging with people, and everywhere a great stir and bustle. Soon they saw rising before them towers and gables of great magnificence. "Disciples," said Tripitaka, "let us go at once to Court and get our papers put in order. Then we

---

3. A court officer who dispenses alms.   4. A device for carrying heavy things on one's back.

shall have no more trouble hanging about in government offices." "That is a good idea," said Monkey. "We will all come with you; the more the tellers, the better the story." "Well, if you all come," said Tripitaka, "you must behave nicely, and not say anything till you have done homage as humble subjects of the throne." "But that means bowing down," said Monkey. "To be sure," said Tripitaka. "You have to bow down five times and strike your forehead on the ground three times." "Master," said Monkey, "that's not a good idea. To pay homage to a thing like that is really too silly. Let me go in first, and I will decide what we are to do. If he addresses us, let me answer him. If you see me bow, then you must bow too; if I squat, then you must squat."

Look at him, that Monkey King, maker of many troubles, how he goes straight up to the door and says to the high officer in charge: "We were sent by the Emperor of China to worship Buddha in India, and fetch scriptures. We want to have our papers put in order here, and would trouble you to announce our arrival. By doing so, you will not fail to gain religious merit." The eunuch went in and knelt on the steps of the throne, announcing the visitors and their request. "I did not think it right to let them straight in," he said. "They await your orders outside the door." The false king then summoned them in. Tripitaka entered, accompanied by the true king, who as he went could not stop the tears that coursed down his cheeks. "Alas," he sighed to himself, "for my dragon-guarded rivers and hills, my iron-girt shrines! Who would have guessed that a creature of darkness would possess you all?" "Emperor," said Monkey, "you must control your emotion, or we shall be discovered. I can feel the truncheon behind my ear twitching, and I am certain that I shall be successful. Leave it to me to slay the monster and when things are cleaned up, those rivers and hills will soon be yours again."

The true king dared not demur. He wiped away his tears, and followed as best he could. At last they reached the Hall of Golden Bells, where they saw the two rows of officials civil and military, and the four hundred Court officers, all of imposing stature and magnificently apparelled. Monkey led forward Tripitaka to the white jade steps, where they both stood motionless and erect. The officials were in consternation. "Are these priests so utterly bereft of decency and reason?" they exclaimed. "How comes it that, seeing our king, they do not bow down or greet him with any word of blessing? Not even a cry of salutation escaped their lips. Never have we seen such impudent lack of manners!" "Where do they come from?" interrupted the false king. "We were sent from the eastern land of T'ang in Southern Jambudvīpa," said Monkey haughtily, "by royal command, to go to India that is in the Western Region, and there to worship the Living Buddha in the Temple of the Great Thunder Clap, and obtain true scriptures. Having arrived here we dare not proceed without coming first to you to have our passports put in order." The false king was very angry. "What is this eastern land of yours?" he said. "Do I pay tribute to it, that you should appear before me in this rude fashion, without bowing down? I have never had any dealings with your country." "Our eastern land," said Monkey, "long ago set up a Heavenly Court and became a Great Power. Whereas yours is a Minor Power, a mere frontier land. There is an old saying, 'The king of a Great Country is father and lord; the king of a lesser country is vassal and son.' You admit that you have had no dealings with our country. How dare you contend that we ought to bow down?" "Remove that uncivil priest," the king called to his officers of war.

At this all the officers sprang forward. But Monkey made a magic pass and cried "Halt!" The magic of the pass was such that these officers all suddenly remained rooted to the spot and could not stir. Well might it be said:

> The captains standing round the steps became like figures of wood,
> The generals on the Royal Dais were like figures of clay.

Seeing that Monkey had brought his officers civil and military to a standstill, the false king leapt from his Dragon Couch and made as though to seize him. "Good," said Monkey to himself. "That is just what I wanted. Even if his hand is made of iron, this cudgel of mine will make some pretty dents in it!"

But just at this moment a star of rescue arrived. "Who can this have been?" you ask. It was no other than the prince of Crow-cock, who hastened forward and clutched at the false king's sleeve, and kneeling before him cried, "Father and king, stay your anger." "Little son," asked the king, "why should you say this?" "I must inform my father and king," said the prince. "Three years ago I heard someone say that a priest had been sent from T'ang to get scriptures in India, and it is he who has now unexpectedly arrived in our country. If my father and king, yielding to the ferocity of his noble nature, now arrests and beheads this priest, I fear that the news will one day reach the Emperor of T'ang, who will be furiously angry. You must know that after Li Shih-min had established this great dynasty of T'ang and united the whole land, his heart was still not content, and he has now begun to conquer far-away lands. If he hears that you have done harm to his favourite priest, he will raise his hosts and come to make war upon you. Our troops are few and our generals feeble. You will, when it is too late, be sorry indeed that you provoked him. If you were to follow your small son's advice, you would question these four priests, and only punish such of them as are proved not to travel at the King of China's bidding."

This was a stratagem of the prince's. For he feared that harm might come to Tripitaka, and therefore tried to check the king, not knowing that Monkey was ready to strike.

The false king believed him, and standing in front of the Dragon Couch, he cried in a loud voice: "Priest, how long ago did you leave China, and why were you sent to get scriptures?"

"My Master," said Monkey haughtily, "is called Tripitaka, and is treated by the Emperor of China as his younger brother. The Emperor in a vision went to the Realms of Death, and on his return he ordered a great Mass for all souls in torment. On this occasion my Master recited so well and showed such compassionate piety that the Goddess Kuan-yin chose him to go on a mission to the West. My Master vowed that he would faithfully perform this task in return for his sovereign's bounties, and he was furnished by the Emperor with credentials for the journey. He started in the thirteenth year of the Emperor's reign, in the ninth month, three days before the full moon. After leaving China, he came first to the Land of the Two Frontiers, where he picked up me, and made me his chief disciple. In the hamlet of the Kao family, on the borders of the country of Wu-ssu, he picked up a second disciple, called Pigsy; and at the river of Flowing Sands he picked up a third, whom we call Sandy. Finally a few days ago, at the Temple of the Treasure Wood, he found another recruit—the servant who is carrying the luggage."

The false king thought it unwise to ask any more questions about Tripitaka; but he turned savagely upon Monkey and addressed to him a crafty question. "I can accept," he said, "that one priest set out from China, and picked up three priests on the way. But your story about the fourth member of your party I altogether disbelieve. This servant is certainly someone whom you have kidnapped. What is his name? Has he a passport,[5] or has he none? Bring him before me to make his deposition!"

The true king shook with fright. "Master," he whispered, "what am I to depose?" "That's all right," said Monkey. "I'll make your deposition for you."

Dear Monkey! He stepped boldly forward and cried to the magician in a loud, clear voice: "Your Majesty, this old man is dumb and rather hard of hearing. But it so happens that when he was young, he travelled in India, and knows the way there. I know all about his career and origins and with your Majesty's permission I will make a deposition on his behalf." "Make haste," said the false king, "and furnish a true deposition or you will get into trouble."

Monkey then recited as follows:

> The subject of this deposition is far advanced in years; he is deaf and dumb, and has fallen upon evil days. His family for generations has lived in these parts; but five years ago disaster overtook his house. Heaven sent no rain; the people perished of drought, the lord king and all his subjects fasted and did penance. They burned incense, purified themselves and called upon the Lord of Heaven; but in all the sky not a wisp of cloud appeared. The hungry peasants dropped by the roadside, when suddenly there came a Taoist magician from the Chung-nan Mountains, a monster in human form. He called to the winds and summoned the rain, displaying godlike power; but soon after secretly destroyed this wretched man's life. In the flower-garden he pushed him down into the crystal well; then set himself on the Dragon Throne, none knowing it was he. Luckily I came and achieved a great success; I raised him from the dead and restored him to life without hurt or harm. He earnestly begged to be admitted to our faith, and act as carrier on the road, to join with us in our quest and journey to the Western Land. The false king who sits on the throne is that foul magician; he that now carries our load is Crow-cock's rightful king!

When the false king in the Palace of Golden Bells heard these words, he was so startled that his heart fluttered like the heart of a small deer. Then clouds of shame suffused his face, and leaping to his feet he was about to flee, when he remembered that he was unarmed. Looking round he saw a captain of the Guard with a dagger at his waist, standing there dumb and foolish as a result of Monkey's spell. The false king rushed at him and snatched the dagger; then leapt upon a cloud and disappeared into space.

Sandy burst into an exclamation of rage, and Pigsy loudly abused Monkey for his slowness. "It's a pity you didn't look sharp and stop him," he said. "Now he has sailed off on a cloud, and we shall never be able to find him." "Don't shout at me, brothers!" said Monkey laughing. "Let us call to the prince to come and do reverence to his true father, and the queen to her

---

5. Here, papers from the T'ang authorities, identifying the traveler and telling his or her mission.

husband." Then undoing by a magic pass the spell that he had put upon the officers, he told them to wake up and do homage to their lord, acknowledging him as their true king. "Give me a few facts to go upon," he said, "and as soon as I have got things clear, I will go and look for him."

Dear Monkey! He instructed Pigsy and Sandy to take good care of the prince, king, ministers, queen and Tripitaka; but while he was speaking he suddenly vanished from sight. He had already jumped up into the empyrean,[6] and was peering round on every side, looking for the wizard. Presently he saw that monster flying for his life towards the north-east. Monkey caught him up and shouted, "Monster, where are you off to? Monkey has come." The wizard turned swiftly, drew his dagger and cried, "Monkey, you scamp, what has it got to do with you whether I usurp someone else's throne? Why should you come calling me to account and letting out my secrets?" "Ho, ho," laughed Monkey. "You impudent rascal! Do you think I am going to allow you to play the emperor? Knowing who I am you would have done well to keep out of my way. Why did you bully my master, demanding depositions and what not? You must admit now that the deposition was not far from the truth. Stand your ground and take old Monkey's cudgel like a man!"

The wizard dodged and parried with a thrust of his dagger at Monkey's face. It was a fine fight! After several bouts the magician could no longer stand up against Monkey, and suddenly turning he fled back the way he had come, leapt into the city and slipped in among the officers who were assembled before the steps of the throne. Then giving himself a shake, he changed into an absolute counterpart of Tripitaka and stood beside him in front of the steps. Monkey rushed up and was about to strike what he supposed to be the wizard, when this Tripitaka said, "Disciple, do not strike! It is I!" It was impossible to distinguish between them. "If I kill Tripitaka, who is a transformation of the wizard, then I shall have achieved a glorious success; but supposing, on the other hand, it turns out that I have killed the real Tripitaka, that would not be so good. . . ." There was nothing for it but to stay his hand, and calling to Pigsy and Sandy he asked, "Which really is the wizard, and which is our master? Just point for me, and I will strike the one you point at." "We were watching you going for one another up in the air," said Pigsy, "when suddenly we looked round and saw that there were two Tripitakas. We have no idea which is the real one."

When Monkey heard this, he made a single pass and recited a spell to summon the *devas* that protect the Law, the local deities and the spirits of the neighbouring hills, and told them of his predicament. The wizard thought it time to mount the clouds again, and began to make towards the door. Thinking that Tripitaka was clearing the ground for him, Monkey raised his cudgel, and had it not been for the deities he had summoned he would have struck such a big blow at his master as would have made mince-meat of twenty Tripitakas. But in the nick of time the guardian deities stopped him, saying, "Great Sage, the wizard is just going to mount the clouds again." Monkey rushed after him, and was just about to cut off his retreat, when the wizard turned round, slipped back again into the crowd, and was once more indistinguishable from the real Tripitaka.

Much to Monkey's annoyance, Pigsy stood by, laughing at his discomfi-

6. The higher reaches of the sky.

ture. "You've nothing to laugh at, you hulking brute," he said. "This means you've got two masters to order you about. It's not going to do you much good." "Brother," said Pigsy, "you call me a fool, but you're a worse fool than I. You can't recognize your own Master, and it's a waste of effort to go on trying. But you would at least recognize your own headache, and if you ask our Master to recite his spell, Sandy and I will stand by and listen. The one who doesn't know the spell will certainly be the wizard. Then all will be easy." "Brother," said Monkey, "I am much obliged to you. There are only three people who know that spell. It sprouted from the heart of the Lord Buddha himself; it was handed down to the Bodhisattva Kuan-yin, and was then taught to our master by the Bodhisattva herself. No one else knows it. Good, then! Master, recite!"

The real Tripitaka at once began to recite the spell; while the wizard could do nothing but mumble senseless sounds. "That's the wizard," cried Pigsy. "He's only mumbling." And at the same time he raised his rake and was about to strike when the wizard sprang into the air and ran up along the clouds. Dear Pigsy! With a loud cry he set off in pursuit, and Sandy, leaving Tripitaka, hastened to the attack with his priest's staff. Tripitaka stopped reciting, and Monkey, released from his headache, seized his iron cudgel and sped through the air. Heigh, what a fight! Three wild priests beleaguered one foul fiend. With rake and staff Pigsy and Sandy assailed him from right and left. "If I join in," said Monkey, "and attack him in front, I fear he is so frightened of me that he will run away again. Let me get into position above him and give him a real garlic-pounding blow that will finish him off for good and all." He sprang up into the empyrean, and was about to deliver a tremendous blow when, from a many-coloured cloud in the north-east, there came a voice which said, "Monkey, stay your hand!" Monkey looked round and saw it was the Bodhisattva Manjuśrī. He withdrew his cudgel, and coming forward did obeisance, saying "Bodhisattva, where are you going to?" "I came to take this monster off your hands," said Manjuśrī. "I am sorry you should have the trouble," said Monkey. The Bodhisattva then drew from his sleeve a magic mirror that showed demons in their true form. Monkey called to the other two to come and look, and in the mirror they saw the wizard in his true shape. He was Manjuśrī's lion! "Bodhisattva," said Monkey, "this is the blue-maned lion that you sit upon. How comes it that it ran away and turned into an evil spirit? Can't you keep it under control?" "It did not run away," said Manjuśrī. "It acted under orders from Buddha himself." "You mean to tell me," said Monkey, "that it was Buddha who told this creature to turn into an evil spirit and seize the Emperor's throne? In that case all the troubles I meet with while escorting Tripitaka are very likely ordered by His Holiness. A nice thought!"

"Monkey," said Manjuśrī, "you don't understand. In the beginning this king of Crow-cock was devoted to good works and the entertaining of priests. Buddha was so pleased that he sent me to fetch him away to the Western Paradise, where he was to assume a golden body and become an Arhat.[7] As it was not proper for me to show myself in my true form I came disguised as a priest and begged for alms. Something I said gave him offence, and not knowing that I was anyone in particular he had me bound and cast into the

7. A Buddhist saint.

river, where I remained under water for three nights and three days, till at last a guardian spirit rescued me and brought me back to Paradise. I complained to Buddha, who sent this creature to throw the king into the well, and let him remain there three years as a retaliation for the three days that I was in the river. You know the saying: 'Not a sip, not a sup[8] . . .' But now you have arrived on the scene, the episode is successfully closed." "That is all very well," said Monkey. "All these 'sips and sups' may have enabled you to get even with your enemy. But what about all the unfortunate people whom this fiend has ruined?" "He hasn't ruined any one," said Manjuśrī. "During the three years that he was on the throne, rain has fallen, the crops have been good, and the people at perfect peace. How can you speak of his ruining people?" "That may be," said Monkey. "But how about all the ladies of the Court who have been sleeping with him and unwittingly been led into a heinous and unnatural offence? They would hardly subscribe to the view that he had done no harm." "He isn't in a position to defile anyone," said Manjuśrī. "He's a gelded lion!" At this Pigsy came up to the wizard and felt him. "Quite true," he announced, laughing. "This is a 'blotchy nose that never sniffed wine'; 'a bad name and nothing to show for it.' "

"Very well then," said Monkey. "Take him away. If you had not come just in time, he'd have been dead by now." Manjuśrī then recited a spell and said, "Creature, back to your true shape and look sharp about it!" The wizard at once changed into his real lion form, and Manjuśrī, putting down the lotus that he carried in his hand, harnessed the lion, mounted him and rode away over the clouds.

If you do not know how Tripitaka and his disciples left the city you must listen while it is explained to you in the next chapter.

*　　　*　　　*

8. That is, everything that happens depends on *karma. Karma* is the burden of deeds, both good and bad, that the soul carries from lifetime to lifetime.

K'UNG SHANG-JEN
1648–1718

Although there are indications of quasi-dramatic performances in China at an early period, drama grew in sophistication during the Sung Dynasty (960–1279). The earliest extant Chinese plays date from the thirteenth century.

Chinese theater has certain distinctive traits that contrast sharply with Western drama. Foremost among these is the alternation between prose dialogue and arias, which were sung in performance. Originally an act of a play was organized around a suite of arias, all in the same musical mode. In early northern plays only one character was allowed to sing in each act. The dialogue around the arias, often very lively, was given considerably less attention in early works, though when drama matured, the interplay between aria and fully developed dialogue was central to the artistic success of the play.

K'ung Shang-jen's *The Peach Blossom Fan* (1699) is a late work in a tradition of southern drama known as *ch'uan-ch'i* (the same term used for T'ang tales in the classical language). *Ch'uan-ch'i* are very long plays, most between thirty and fifty acts, and were performed either in single acts or in their entirety, spread out over a number of days. Drama also developed as a literary form with printed editions designed for reading. *The Peach Blossom Fan* is just such a play, circulating in manuscript long before it was performed. *Ch'uan-ch'i* plots are intricate and sprawling affairs, often weaving together numerous characters and multiple story lines. Although the plots have a degree of linear unity, it is clear that the primary sense of artistic coherence comes from parallel scenes and situations, in which each moment gains significance by echoes of corresponding moments in the play (and often echoes of earlier dramatic works). Drama was immensely popular in late imperial China, and audiences developed a high degree of connoisseurship and close knowledge of a wide range of plays.

K'ung Shang-jen was from the great K'ung family of Shan-tung, which claimed descent from Confucius (K'ung Ch'iu). He found favor with the K'ang-hsi emperor while visiting the great complex of Confucian temples at Ch'ü-fu, his home, and after a moderately successful official career turned to playwriting relatively late in his life.

Unlike most Chinese plays, which are set in a safely removed past, *The Peach Blossom Fan* treats one of the most politically sensitive events of recent history: the fall of the Ming and of its afterecho, the brief southern regime of the Ming prince Fu (1644–45) in Nanking. K'ung drew on a wide variety of historical sources to create a play that would function as a kind of history. It was an appropriate medium since Prince Fu's short-lived regime was itself a species of play-acting that begged comparison to the theater—though it is hard to say whether Prince Fu's inept government should be considered a tragedy or a farce. As K'ung has the master of ceremonies observe in the prologue to the second part:

> In bygone years, reality was the play;
> The play becomes reality today.
> Twice I have watched its progress: Heaven preserves
> This passive gazer with his cold clear eyes.

Versions of theatricality and performance occur throughout the play, for K'ung was much interested in the degree to which human acts and relationships involve playing roles. When we first meet the heroine, Fragrant Princess, she is a young courtesan being taught by her singing master to perform the arias sung by the heroine in another famous play, *Peony Pavilion*. At the same time she is given her adult name, Fragrant Princess, by the painter Yang Wen-ts'ung. Through the course of *The Peach Blossom Fan*, Fragrant Princess does indeed become the conventional heroine of romantic drama and goes beyond it. This act is framed by the first scene, in which the hero witnesses a performance by a storyteller, and the third scene, in which a ceremony in honor of Confucius, yet another performance, is disrupted by the appearance of the villain, Juan Ta-ch'eng. Juan himself is a playwright, producing immensely popular but vapid romantic comedies in the midst of national disaster. Prince Fu is an ardent admirer of Juan's plays and joins in the performance. Everywhere true identity is shaped by or revealed in performance.

The course of the play turns on the relation between art and a historical reality in which people bleed and suffer. Emblematic of this relation is the object from which the play takes its title: the peach blossom fan. The fan, bearing a love poem by the hero, Hou Fang-yü, is his wedding gift to Fragrant Princess. Since the other, more expensive wedding gifts must finally be rejected because they come from Juan Ta-ch'eng, the fan becomes the only external thing that symbolizes their union. Later, after Hou Fang-yü has been forced to flee Nanking, the fan is spattered with Fragrant Princess's blood when she is injured as she resists being carried away and forcibly married to another. Still later, as Fragrant Princess lies asleep, the painter Yang Wen-ts'ung comes in and sees the fan. Though knowing the source of the bloodstain, the true artist cannot help admiring its shade of red, and he paints green leaves and twigs around the splotches of blood to form peach blossoms: pain is transformed into art.

After this scene Fragrant Princess sends the fan off to her beloved, Hou Fang-yü, as a token of her faith. But at this point she is forced to enter the palace to serve in the emperor's acting troop, where the emperor (Prince Fu), admiring her beauty, gives her another fan painted with peach blossoms. Later, when Hou Fang-yü finally manages to get back to Nanking, he goes to Fragrant Princess's house, which in her absence has been taken over by the painter Lan Yin, who is painting a picture of peach blossoms. This painting comes into the hands of one Chang Wei, the commander of the Imperial Guard, and proves instrumental in saving Hou Fang-yü's life. The peach blossoms themselves have a double significance: as an image of a woman's beauty and young love and also as the symbol of Peach Blossom Spring, a mountain haven from the world's violence, discovered, as T'ao Ch'ien (fourth century) wrote, by a fisherman following a trail of peach blossoms in the water. And the play does indeed conclude in just such a location.

The character of the painter Yang Wen-ts'ung is central to the action. Yang moves easily between the villains and the virtuous, friends with both. The plot belongs to Yang: he is responsible both for the lovers coming together and for their being torn apart. He brings troubles on them and saves them from those same troubles.

Like Shakespeare, K'ung Shang-jen makes use of different classes and levels of language to give perspective and sometimes to call into question the values of the main characters. In the third scene, for example, the politically upright young scholars hold a solemn ceremony in honor of Confucius. This is interrupted by the intrusion of the villain Juan Ta-ch'eng, whose very presence is seen to corrupt the solemn purity of the occasion. The scene has begun, however, with a comic exchange between the servants taking inventory of the stocks of ritual goods, as if to remind the reader of the pragmatic details beneath the sacred rite. Again in the seventh scene, Fragrant Princess, playing the romantic heroine, grandly refuses the wedding gifts because they come from Juan Ta-ch'eng (arranged, of course, by Yang Wen-ts'ung). Her mother, Li Chen-li, observes:

> All the same, it was a pity to lose those valuable gifts. [Sings.]
>> When gold and pearls are in your hand,
>> Heedless you let them slip away
>> Daughter, you fail to understand
>> All that your mother had to pay.

If Li Chen-li were simply a greedy, unsympathetic character, these lines would not have the ring of truth, the reminder that someone has to pay for grand romantic gestures. In fact, she has great love for Fragrant Princess and ultimately sacrifices herself to protect her daughter from forced marriage.

The story of the lovers unfolds against the backdrop of major historical events: the suicide of the last Ming emperor after the rebel Li Tzu-ch'eng took Peking, the establishment of the corrupt and inept government of Prince Fu in Nanking, the Manchu conquest of north China and the crumbling of the Ming armies, Shih K'o-fa's desperate attempt to defend Yang-chou, and finally the fall of Nanking.

The play closes with the flight of all protagonists from Nanking to live as Taoist hermits in the mountains. Much like Elizabethan romantic comedy, Chinese romantic comedy always ends with the reunion of the separated hero and heroine. There among the Taoist nuns and acolytes, Hou Fang-yü and Fragrant Princess discover one another again. There the two lovers begin to play the reunion scene:

> HOU: [Speaking of those who had helped them to escape.] When we are home once more as man and wife, we shall endeavor to repay their kindness.

Chang Wei, now the abbot of the Taoist temple, interrupts to remind them that there is no home any more.

> CHANG: What is all this meaningless chatter? How laughable to cling to your amorous desires when the whole world has been turned upside down.

Or as he later sings:

> Are you not ashamed to hear
> The laughter your performance brings?

In this moment the lovers are enlightened to love's illusion, and they separate.

A biography of K'ung Shang-jen may be found in Richard E. Strassberg's *The World of K'ung Shang-jen: A Man of Letters in Early Ch'ing China* (1985).

PRONOUNCING GLOSSARY

The following list uses common English syllables to provide rough equivalents of selected words whose pronunciation may be unfamiliar to the general reader.

Chang Wei: *jahng way*

Chin: *jin*

Ch'in Shih-huang-ti: *chin shir–hwahng–dee*

Ch'ü-fu: *choo–foo*

Juan Ta-ch'eng: *rwahn dah–chuhng*

K'ang-hsi: *kahng–shee*

Kuei-te: *gway–duh*

K'ung Ch'iu: *koong chyoh*

K'ung Tzu: *koong dzuh*

Li Chen-li: *lee juhn–lee*

Li Tzu-ch'eng: *lee dzuh–chuhng*

Liu Ching-t'ing: *lyoh jing–ting*

Ma Shih-ying: *mah shir–ying*

Nanking: *nahn-jing*

Shan-tung: *shahn–doong*

Shih K'o-fa: *shir kuh–fah*

Sung: *soong*

T'ao Ch'ien: *tao chyen*

Tso Liang-yü: *dzwoh lyahng–yoo*

Yang-chou: *yahng–joh*

Yang Wen-ts'ung: *yahng wuhn–tsoong*

From The Peach Blossom Fan[1]

Prologue

1684

[*Enter an old man with a long white beard. He is the former* MASTER OF CEREMONIES[2] *of the Imperial Temple. He now wears a felt cap and a broad-sleeved Taoist robe.*[3]]

MASTER OF CEREMONIES: [*Sings.*]

> Where in the world is a quainter curio
> In jade or bronze than I, my face patined with age?
> Though superannuated, lone and lost,
> Why should I shrink when striplings mock at me?
> I extirpate old sorrows from my breast,　　　　　　5
> And where there's wine and song I'm apt to linger.
> When filial duty and loyalty reign, the universe will thrive
> And the fruit of longevity grow superfluous.

[*Speaks.*] The sun beams brightly on a world well governed. The flowers bloom in the first year of the cycle; the mountains are free　　10

---

1. Translated by and with notes adapted from Chen Shih-hsiang and Harold Acton, with the collaboration of Cyril Birch.　　2. An officer of the state who calls out the prescribed actions in a Confucian ritual.　　3. His clothes signify that he has retired from public office.

from bandits; the whole earth belongs to the blessed. Formerly an official of the Board of Rites,[4] I used to announce the ceremonies in the Imperial Temple of Nanking. Since my post was humble, I need not reveal my name. Happily I have been spared most calamities. During ninety-seven years of life I have seen the rise and fall of many generations. Now another cycle has dawned. Our ruler is supremely wise and virtuous, and his ministers are loyal and efficient. The people are quiet and contented after an uninterrupted succession of good harvests. During this twenty-third year of K'ang-hsi's[5] reign, twelve kinds of auspicious omens have appeared.

VOICE FROM BACKSTAGE: What were the omens?

MASTER OF CEREMONIES: [*Counting on his fingers.*] The Chart of Revelation emerged from the Yellow River, and the Holy Scripture from the River Lo.[6] We have seen both the Fortunate Star and the Felicitous Cloud; the sweet dew and the fruitful rain have fallen; the phoenix pair have returned and the unicorn roams at large. The bean-pods burst and the orchid flourishes; the sea is calm and the Yellow River clear. All the omens are complete. Is this not a matter for congratulation? My old body is glad to survive in so wondrous a world, and I have been enjoying innumerable excursions. Last night, in the Garden of Great Serenity, I saw a new play entitled *The Peach Blossom Fan*. The events it portrays took place in Nanking not long ago, during the last years of the Ming dynasty. The rise and fall of an empire are evoked in a story of meeting and separation. Both plot and protagonists were drawn from life. Not only did I hear tell of the originals; I saw them with my own eyes. How amusing it was to recognise my decrepit self in a minor role! I was stirred so deeply that I laughed and wept, raged and cursed by turns. Needless to say, the audience had no idea that I was included in the drama.

VOICE FROM BACKSTAGE: Who was the author of this remarkable play?

MASTER OF CEREMONIES: Perhaps you gentlemen do not realize that famous playwrights never divulge their names. Suffice it that in distributing praise and blame he follows the tradition of his ancestor, the author of the *Spring and Autumn Annals;* by melodic means he revives the lofty style of the classic Odes, and demonstrates the quality of his upbringing.[7]

VOICE FROM BACKSTAGE: It must be the Mountain Hermit of the Cloud Pavilion.[8]

MASTER OF CEREMONIES: You are not mistaken.

VOICE FROM BACKSTAGE: The play will be performed at today's assembly. Since you are one of the characters and a veteran familiar with the latest tunes, please favour us with a synopsis. We shall listen with rapt attention.

---

4. The government bureau in charge of conducting state rituals.   5. The reign title of Emperor Sheng-tsu; he ruled from 1662 to 1723—thus it is 1684.   6. These magical events were actually legendary happenings of high antiquity.   7. K'ung Shang-jen counted himself a descendant of Confucius in the sixty-fourth generation. Confucius (K'ung Tzu) wrote the *Spring and Autumn Annals* and compiled the *Classic Odes* (or *Book of Songs*).   8. One of K'ung Shang-jen's sobriquets.

MASTER OF CEREMONIES: It is summarized in a song by the Taoist   55
  priest Chang Wei. [*Sings.*]

> The young scholar Hou, residing in Mo-ling,[9]
> Lost his heart to a southern beauty there.
> But love was wounded; evil slandering
> Soon forced asunder this too happy pair.   60
> Chaos was loosened; warriors ran wild;
> A worthless debauchee the Throne defiled;
> Murderous traitors sprang from civil strife.
> Forever ended was the blissful life
> Of our fond lovers; he in fetters lay,   65
> While she true heroism did display.
> Aided by Su and Liu,[1] with all their might,
> The Emperor and his Premier fled by night.
> Over the misty waves I gaze and falter:
> Who is to chant the patriot's lament?   70
> The painted fan of peach blossoms was rent,
> And true love's token shattered at an altar.
> How matters went astray, we shall disclose.

VOICE FROM BACKSTAGE: Bravo, bravo! But your masterly trills sometimes made it difficult for us to follow the meaning. Please oblige   75
  us with a short outline of the plot.
MASTER OF CEREMONIES: [*Sings.*]

> Within and without the court, traitors Ma and Juan hide their blades;
> Liu and Su astutely plot to foil their machinations;
> Master Hou's life of rapture falls into ruin;
> Chang the Taoist tells the fates of dynasties in a song.   80

[*Speaks.*] Before I have finished speaking, Master Hou steps onto
the stage. Your attention please!

From *Part I*

SCENE 1

The Storyteller

1643, second month

[*Enter* HOU FANG-YÜ *in the robes of a scholar.*]
HOU: [*Sings.*]

> On Grieve-Not Lake beside the Poet's Tower,[2]
> The weeping willows burgeon once again.
> The sun is setting: hill and river blend
> In perfect beauty, and the traveller is tempted
> To drink, recalling beauties long ago,   5

---

9. Nanking.   1. Su K'un-sheng and Liu Ching-t'ing, respectively.   2. Built for the 4th-century poet
Sun Ch'u, located just to west of the city wall of Nanking.

Painted and powdered in the southern courts.
Sad thoughts come with twilight, while the swallows
Frolic regardless of the fall of kings.

[*Recites.*]

Hushed is the courtyard, cold the kitchen stove;
And I have risen late from heavy slumber.   10
Though flowers bloom, fatigue invades the limbs,
And while it rains at every dawn of day,
And trees around the royal tombs decay,
The river swollen with the melted snows
Washes away the palace's foundations.   15
I write new poems grieving for the past;
An exile's sorrow, dreaming dreams of home.
Where will the swallows choose to nest this year,
In my village home far west of the misty waters?

[*Speaks.*] My name is Hou Fang-yü, and I am a native of Kuei-te   20
in the heart of the empire. I am descended from a long line of scholars and officials; my father and grandfather were Ministers of State,
and both set up their standards in the Eastern Forest. Trained in
poetry and the classics, I have won distinction in the world of letters
and allied myself with the Revival Society.³ My early writings   25
were influenced by those master-spirits Pan Ku and Sung Yü; in
maturity I am drawing nearer to Han Yü and Su Tung-p'o.⁴ I have
written in praise of wine in the Yueh-hua Palace, despite my reluctance to plant more flowers in the garden at Loyang.⁵ Since finishing
my examinations last year, I have been staying on the shore of   30
Grieve-Not Lake. But the clouds of war continue to cover us, and
news from home is scarce. It is mid-spring and the green grass
stretches to the dim horizon, but where shall I find a companion for
my homeward journey? The yellow dust rises from the earth, but
here I sit in solitary exile. Oh! Grieve Not, Grieve Not! How   35
can I fail to grieve? Fortunately, my literary friends Ch'en Chen-hui
and Wu Ying-chi are staying over Ts'ai Yi-so's bookshop. We often
meet and cheer each other's solitude. Today we shall gather at
the Fair City Monastery and enjoy the splendour of the plum blossoms. I must start immediately or I shall be late. [*He proceeds*   40
to sing.]

New warmth invades the breeze,
Mist 'whelms the river glade.

---

3. The Tung-lin, or Eastern Forest Party, was a school of intellectuals who organized opposition to the corrupt dictatorship of the eunuch Wei Chung-hsien and his secret police. The Fu-she (*Revival*) Society for the revival of ancient learning was an offshoot of the Eastern Forest Party, whose aim was to "make friends by means of literature" and help its members prepare for the civil service examination. Wu Ying-chi, who appears in this play, in historical fact recorded more than two thousand members of this influential society.   **4.** Or Su Shih (1036–1101), leading poet and essayist of the Sung Dynasty. Pan Ku (died A.D. 92), eminent historian. Sung Yü (3rd century B.C.), statesman and poet whose works form part of the *Elegies of Ch'u.* Han Yü (768–824), poet and essayist, leader of the influential plain style movement of the T'ang Dynasty. The plain style movement advocated a more direct prose style that was conducive to serious argument.   **5.** Hou Fang-yü uses these allusions to compare himself with the poet Tsou Yang (ca. 206–129 B.C.), guest in the Yueh-hua Palace built by Prince Hsiao of Liang, and with the poet Shih Ch'ung (died A.D. 300), owner of a famous garden outside Loyang.

We stroll through flowery leas
With wine in jars of jade.
Thrilled by a sudden flute   45
The pilgrim's heart is mute.
Don't pass by Swallow Lane:
New owners are repainting
The lintels of your friends
Who will not come again. [*Exit.*]   50

[*Enter* CH'EN CHEN-HUI *and* WU YING-CHI.]
CH'EN: [*Sings.*]

The royal power is fading from Nanking.
The war-flags wave, the drums of battle beat.
One dreads to cross the river, though it flows
So placidly through willow groves and orchards.

[*Each announces his name.*]
CH'EN: What is the latest news of the roving bandits?   55
WU: Yesterday I saw an official report. After defeating the national
armies, the bandits are drawing near the capital. Tso Liang-yü, the
Earl of Ning-nan, has retreated to Hsiang-yang, and central China
is totally unprotected. The fate of the dynasty is sealed. We might
as well enjoy the spring while it lasts.   60
CH'EN *and* WU *together:* [*Singing.*]

Spring floods the air, but wind and rain
Have scattered petals of the pear,
And so dawn seems dishevelled and in pain.

HOU: [*Reentering.*] Greetings! So the two of you came betimes.
WU: Of course. We could not bear to keep you waiting.   65
CH'EN: I sent my servant ahead to sweep the monastery courtyard and
serve refreshments.
SERVANT: [*Entering in haste.*] When it is cold, the wine's not warm
enough; when flowers bloom, the trippers[6] are too many. . . .We
arrived too late, Your Honour. Let us all go home.   70
CH'EN: What do you mean, too late?
SERVANT: Master Hsu from the Wei Palace is giving a party in honour
of the blossoms. The whole monastery is crammed with his guests.
HOU: Let us go up the river then, and visit the beauties of the Water
Pavilion.   75
WU: Why trouble to go so far? Do you know that brilliant minstrel Liu
Ching-t'ing of T'ai-chou? He is highly esteemed by such connois-
seurs as the Ministers Fan Ching-wen and Ho Ju-ch'ung, and I hear
that he lives nearby. On this languid spring day, would it not be
pleasant to listen to him?   80
CH'EN: That is also a good suggestion.
HOU: [*Angrily.*] Pock-marked Liu was a toady of Juan Ta-ch'eng,
Bearded Juan, the eunuch's adopted son. I would rather avoid such
a creature.

6. Visitors.

WU: Apparently you do not know the facts. Since the despicable Juan 85
persisted in patronising singers and dancers and flattering the powerful at court instead of resigning, I wrote an impeachment exposing
his crimes and demanding his punishment. When at last his troupe
of artists discovered that he was a member of the treacherous Ts'ui
and Wei cliques, they all walked out on him in the middle 90
of a performance, and pock-marked Liu was among them. In my
opinion Liu deserves our respect.

HOU: I should never have expected to find such high principles in a
man of that sort. Let us pay him a visit. [*They proceed together.*]

HOU, WU, *and* CHEN *together:* [*Singing.*]

> Random pipe-notes in the Courts of the Transcendents 95
> Where the secluded Alchemist
> Watches "the vast sea turn into mulberry groves."[7]

SERVANT: Here we are. I'll knock at the door. [*Shouts.*] Is pock-marked
Liu at home?

CH'EN: Fie, fie! He is a celebrity: you should address him as *Master* 100
Liu.

SERVANT: Master Liu, open the door!

> [*Enters* LIU—*a "ch'ou" or comedian type with a white beard, a skull
> cap, and a blue gown.*]

LIU: [*Sings.*]

> Green moss and weeds grow rank and high
> Beside my long-locked door.
> Woodsmen and fishingfolk amble nigh 105
> To praise the times of yore.

[*Seeing the visitors, he exclaims.*] Oh, Masters Ch'en and Wu! Forgive
my ignorance of your arrival. Who is the gentleman you have brought
along with you?

CH'EN: This is our friend Hou Fang-yü of Honan, whose fame is in 110
the ascendant. He has long admired your art and hopes to hear you.

LIU: I am overwhelmed. Pray be seated and drink some tea. [*They sit,
and* LIU *continues.*] You gentlemen are such fine scholars, so familiar
with the *Records of the Historian*, the *Comprehensive Mirror*,[8] or
whatever; what pleasure or instruction could you hope to gain from 115
my vulgar discourse? [*He points at his courtyard and sings.*]

> In the forsaken garden, a withered pine leans over a broken wall;
> On the fragrant grass of the palace ruins, the silky showers fall.
> The Six Great Dynasties'[9] decay brings thoughts too sad to render;
> In telling tales I often weep, because my heart's too tender. 120

HOU: You are excessively modest. Please favour us with a sample of
your skill.

LIU: Since you honour me with your company, I dare not disappoint

---

7. A common Taoist (or alchemist) metaphor for the mutability of all phenomena. 8. The history of
China by Ssu-ma Kuang (1019–1086). The *Records of the Historian* (or *Historical Records*) is by Ssu-ma
Ch'ien (145–ca. 85 B.C.), who after his reformation of the calendar took up and completed the monumental
work begun by his father, the history of China from the earliest ages to his own time. 9. Those that
from the 3rd through the 6th centuries maintained their capital at Nanking.

you. But I fear that my crude versions of history and blind man's
tales are unworthy of your ears, so I shall comment on a chapter of   125
Confucius's *Analects* instead.

HOU: How strange! One would hardly expect you to choose such a
theme.

LIU: [*Laughing.*] You scholars discuss the *Analects*, why shouldn't I?
Today you will judge my slender claim to learning. [*Recites.*]   130

> "I dwell among green hills: you ask me why.
> My soul at ease, I smile without reply.
> The peach petals are swept along the stream
> To other lands outside this mortal dream."[1]

[*He claps his "wakener-board"*[2] *and continues, speaking.*] I shall tell   135
how the crime of three powerful clans who conspired against their
ruler was exposed. I shall also tell how wonderously Confucius succeeded in the reform of music. The great doctrine of the Way was
on the wane. Avarice and covetousness were deeply embedded in the
heart of man. On returning to Lu from the state of Wei, our   140
great Sage began to restore the true principles of music. So profoundly were performers affected by the result that they were
ashamed to realize they had been serving the wrong masters, and
abandoned those tribes of malefactors. The theatres of the mighty,
which had been full of glowing colour and vibrant melody, were   145
deserted in a twinkling. Truly fearsome, truly marvelous was the
influence of the Sage! [*He sings to drum or ta-ku*[3] *accompaniment,
keeping rhythmic time.*]

> The great Sage of antiquity was most versatile in magic;
> He could sway the wind and rain,
> And turn handfuls of peas into armies of warriors.   150
> When he saw that the turbulent nobles
> Had lost all sense of propriety in their dancing and music,
> He played a subtle trick on them.
> Hence the lowest of slaves
> Began to behave like the highest of heroes.   155

[LIU *claps his board and continues speaking.*] The first player to leave
for the state of Ch'i was good Master Chih. And why did he leave
for Ch'i? I'll tell you. [*He drums and sings.*]

> Alas, he exclaimed,
> Why should I ring the bell for these three clans?   160
> I must have been blind to wallow in such mire.
> I shall leave at once,
> Setting forth with long swift strides towards the northeast;
> There I shall join my old comrades and win fresh laurels.
> I shall play for the delight of Master K'ung himself,   165
> Who forgot the flavour of meat
> For three months after hearing my performance.
> And the virtuous Duke Ching

---

1. A poem by the great T'ang master Li Po (699–762).   2. A wooden clapper, used to punctuate story
telling.   3. A large drum.

Will also be moved to tears by my art.
Even if the usurpers have swallowed   170
The heart of a leopard and the gall of a bear,
I doubt if they would pursue me to Ch'i,
The land of Chiang T'ai-kung's[4] descendants!

[LIU *claps his board and continues speaking.*] The second master's
name was Kan. He left for the state of Ch'u. The third master, Liao,   175
retired to the state of Ts'ai. The fourth one was Ch'üeh, who went
to the state of Ch'in. Why did these three leave? I'll tell you. [*He
drums and sings.*]

All these musicians, who played at every banquet,
Had lost their leader now;
One by one they embarked on a new career.   180
The second master said: "See the usurper
Grasp his rice-bowl in the hall!
Why should we blow trumpets
And beat drums for his entertainment?
Our leader has left for the state of Ch'i;   185
Nobody can make him return.
As for me, I propose to play for Hsiung Yi, the King of Ch'u,
Committing myself to his powerful protection."
The third master said: "Though the state of Ts'ai,
South of the river, is not extensive,   190
It is near the capital
And in the heart of the central plain."
The fourth master gazed towards the south and said:
"I can see a new imperial spirit
Rising from the state of Ch'in,   195
Which has strong armies and fortifications;
Thither I shall take my lute."
All three of them pointed at the usurpers and said:
"We have endured your tyranny too long;
Henceforth we shall make you wince at the sound of our names."   200

[LIU *claps his board and continues speaking.*] One drummer named
Fang Shu went to the Yellow River region, and another named Wu
to the Han River region. The junior leader's name was Yang and the
gong-beater's name was Hsiang, and these repaired to the seacoast.
The manner of their leaving was different. I'll tell you. [*He*   205
drums and sings.]

Altogether there were four drummers and gong-beaters.
"Our theatre remains in confusion," said they,
"And we have no desire to stay.
Disgusted with our fiendish patrons,
We shall seek employment elsewhere,   210
Even though it is unlikely that we shall fare better.

---

4. Legendary octogenarian (12th century B.C.), who consolidated the Chou Dynasty. He was said to exercise authority over the spirits of the unseen universe and hence was often depicted over doors to frighten away evil spirits.

> Let us sail a light boat to the Peach Blossom Spring;[5]
> At least we may win renown
> As fishermen of the lakes and rivers."

[LIU *claps his board and continues speaking.*] These four made the 215
wisest decision. Hearken to their speech! [*He drums and sings.*]

> "The trees of coral soar a hundred feet, vermilion in the sunlight;
> The crystal palace of the sea-god is built on a terrace of pearls.
> The Dragon King will invite us to a banquet
> Where golden boys and jade girls excel earthly mortals. 220
> Phoenix flutes and ivory pipes
> Will be tuned to the dragon's most exquisite melodies;
> For this time, *others* will play while *we* shall listen.
> Though the usurpers may try to pursue us down the rivers,
> There will be thousands of leagues[6] between us 225
> In which they will lose their way.
> We need not fear to be friendless
> Among the mountains and distant waters,
> For all men within the four seas
> And beyond the horizon are our comrades. 230
> We should tear the paper windowpane
> And look at the real world.
> We have saved ourselves from the abyss by divine inspiration.
> Even if sea becomes land, and land sea,
> The vision of our Sage endures in the Six Canons.[7] 235

[*Standing up,* LIU *speaks.*] Thank you for listening! I have shown what
trifling talents I possess.

CH'EN: Superb! None of our modern pundits could express himself so
well. You are indeed a consummate artist.

WU: Since leaving Juan, Liu has not cared to seek another patron. This 240
last recital was autobiographical.

HOU: I perceive he has a noble character, untainted by worldliness.
He is truly one of us. Story-telling is merely one of his minor
accomplishments.

CH'EN, WU, *and* HOU *together:* [*Singing.*]

> The deep red dust is suddenly clear, 245
> And all shines bright as snow.
> The warm spring light is suddenly chill;
> The Sage solves all below.

---

5. During the Tsin Dynasty (265–420) the poet T'ao Ch'ien wrote of a fisherman of Wu-ling who, following
a stream without noticing its length, suddenly came to a grove of flowering peach trees. Fascinated by the
beauty of the trees and the abundance of scented plants, he wandered on until he reached a country of
well-tilled fields, clear water, and pleasant cottages. The inhabitants were highly civilized and law abiding.
He asked where they had come from and was told that their ancestors had fled from the tyranny of the
Ch'in Dynasty in the 3rd century B.C. and had found refuge in this country cut off from the rest of the
world. After leaving them, the fisherman reported his adventure. Men went out to investigate this unknown
region, but they lost their way. Hence the expression *Peach Blossom Spring* became a metaphor for a place
of retirement, far from the noise and turmoil of the world. The allusion is anachronistic here, coming from
the lips of a contemporary of Confucius (6th century B.C.).   6. Unit of distance, roughly equal to one-
third of a mile.   7. The oldest enumeration of Chinese classics gave only five canons: the *Book of
Changes,* the *Book of Documents,* the *Book of Songs,* the *Record of Rites,* and the *Spring and Autumn
Annals.* The *Record of Music* was later added as the sixth canon, but it is usually classed as one of the books
of the *Record of Rites.*

[*They laugh, and continue.*]

> Your mocking satire, our delight,
> Each phrase at once caress and bite,   250
> The triple beat of Yü-yang drum[8]
> To judgment come!

LIU: [*Sings.*]

> Please come another day;
> And if to Peach Blossom source
> You fail to find the way,   255
> To this old fisherman have recourse.

WU: Which of your other colleagues left the house of Juan?
LIU: We are all dispersed. Only the master-singer Su K'un-sheng
remains in this neighborhood.
HOU: I should like to meet him too, and hope you will both pay me a   260
visit.
LIU: Of course we should be most honoured.
    [*Each sings a line of the following quatrain.*]
LIU: After my song is sung, the sun is setting.
CH'EN: The fragrance of fallen petals fills the courtyard.
WU: Terraces and towers seem myriad blades of grass.   265
HOU: Spiritual discourse and imperial strategy melt into the void.

SCENE 2

The Singing-Master

1643, second month

[LI CHEN-LI, *the heroine's foster mother, enters. She is the hostess of
an elegant house of pleasure.*]
LI: [*Sings.*]

> With delicate firm strokes I paint my eyebrows.
> The doors of these red chambers are seldom closed;
> The drooping willows by the wooden bridge
> Cause riders to dismount.
> I shall embroider the bag of my reed-organ and
>   tighten the strings of my lute.   5

[*Recites a quatrain.*]

> The pear blossoms are like snow, the grass like mist;
> Spring settles on the banks of the Ch'in-huai River.
> A row of pleasure-chambers fronts on the water,
> Reflecting from each window a lovely face.

[*Speaks.*] My name is Li Chen-li. I have won fame in the world of   10
"mists and flowers," and high rank in the circles of "wind and
moon."[9] I was educated in the old tradition of my calling. Though I

---

8. Alludes to the drumming that accompanied Mi Heng when he cursed the tyrant Ts'ao Ts'ao in the time
of the Three Kingdoms (3rd century A.D.).   9. Metaphors for romantic love.

have escorted countless guests along the bridge to the pleasure-
quarters, the rose of my complexion has not faded and my charms
are as fresh as ever. I have adopted a daughter of exquisite grace, 15
who has recently begun to appear at social functions. She is very shy
and utterly enchanting; so far she has had no experience behind the
hibiscus-embroidered bed-curtains. I happen to know a former magistrate named Yang Wen-ts'ung who is the brother-in-law of Ma
Shih-ying, Governor of Feng-yang, and a sworn brother of Juan Ta- 20
ch'eng. Whenever he visits us, he lavishes praise on my adopted
daughter and promises to introduce an influential patron to "comb
her hair."[1] On such a fine spring day, I expect he will pay me a visit.
[Calls.] Draw the curtains, maid, and sweep the floor. See that everything is ready for our guests. 25

VOICE FROM BACKSTAGE: Aye, aye, ma'am.

    [YANG WEN-TS'UNG enters.]

YANG: This magnificent view of the three mounts is like a masterpiece
of painting. The romance of the Six Dynasties is a perennial theme
of poetry. I am Yang Wen-ts'ung, a retired magistrate. Since I am on
the best of terms with Mistress Li, the famous hostess of the 30
Ch'in-huai River, I'll take advantage of the fine weather to call on
her. Here is her house. [He enters it.] Where is Mistress Li? [On
seeing her.] The plum petals have fallen and the willow floss turned
yellow. The courtyard is filled with soft harmonies of spring. How
can we extract the utmost enjoyment from it? 35

LI: Let us climb to the upper chamber. Up there we can burn sweet
incense, sip tea, and enjoy some poetry.

YANG: That sounds delightful. [Both climb the stairs. He recites.]

> The bamboo screen suggests bars of a cage
> For the bird on his perch; 40
>
> Flower shadows seem like a cover
> For the fish in the bowl.

[Looking round, he says.] This must be the sitting-room of your
charming daughter. Where is she now?

LI: She has not finished dressing. 45

YANG: Please ask her to join us.

LI: [Calls.] Come out, my dear. His Honour Yang has arrived.

YANG: [Examining the poems hanging on the walls.] These are all gifts
from famous masters of calligraphy. What a choice collection! [He
reads them out loud to himself.]

    [The heroine, a GIRL of about sixteen, enters in an exquisite dress.]

GIRL: [Sings.]

1. That is, to deflower her. In the case of a young courtesan-to-be of exceptional beauty and talent—like
Fragrant Princess—this was an honor for which young men would eagerly vie. If the process led to a more
enduring attachment, there was the possibility that the young man might purchase the girl's freedom from
her adoptive mother (the madam of the house) and install her as his wife or secondary wife. This is what
indeed happens to Hou Fang-yü and Fragrant Princess. The vows of fidelity and plans to marry are to be
taken as serious intentions. Their union, however, was not regarded by others as totally binding.

Returning from the scented land of dreams,   50
I leave the red quilt embroidered with mandarin ducks,[2]
To redden my lips and dress my hair.
I shall con some recent poems
To dispel the languor of spring.

[*Says to* YANG.] Your Honour, a thousand blessings!   55
YANG: I have not seen you for several days, and you have grown much
  lovelier in the meantime. What profound truth the poems on this
  wall express! I see that some were written by my dearest friends.
  Since they have paid you such a compliment, I must join them.
    [MISTRESS LI *promptly brings him a brush and ink-slab.* YANG
    holds the brush in silence before saying.]
I doubt if I could ever compete with these masters. To conceal my   60
failings, I shall contribute a sketch of orchids.
LI: I can assure you it will be appreciated.
YANG: Here is a fist-shaped rock by Lan T'ien-shu.[3] I'll paint some
  orchids beside it. [*Sings.*]

The white wall gleams like silk for me to paint on: 65
Fresh leaves, sweet buds, an aura of mist and rain.
Here a fist-rock bursts with ink-splashed energy,
There specks of moss are elegantly scattered.

[*Standing back to survey his finished painting, he says.*] I believe it
will do. [*Sings.*]   70

No match for the splendid vigor of the Yuan masters,
But at least our ladies will have orchids to set them off.

LI: This is a genuine work of art. It vastly improves the room.
YANG: Don't mock me! [*To the* GIRL.] Please tell me your name so that
  I can inscribe it here.   75
GIRL: I am too young to have a name.[4]
LI: We should be obliged if Your Honour would choose one for her.
YANG: According to the *Tso chuan*,[5] "the fragrance of the orchid per-
  vades a whole nation, it captivates all mankind." Why not call her
  Fragrant Princess?   80
LI: That is perfect. Fragrant Princess, come and thank His Honour.
FRAGRANT PRINCESS: [*Curtseying.*] I thank Your Honour kindly.
YANG: [*Laughing.*] It provides us with a name for the house also. [*As
  he writes the inscription, he reads it aloud.*] In the springtime of the
  Year of the Horse during the reign of Ch'ung-chen,[6] I painted   85

---

2. Emblems of conjugal fidelity.   3. Or Lan Ying (1578–1660), one of the most accomplished painters
of his time, a last representative of the Che school; he appears later in the play.   4. The Chinese had a
number of personal names. At birth a male received a "milk name," which was used by relatives and
neighbors. On entering school, he was given a "book name" to be used by school masters, school fellows,
officials, and in literary connections. At marriage he was given a "great name" for use by acquaintances.
Every writer or scholar took one or more "studio names." If he won a literary degree, entered official life,
or had official rank, he took an "official name." After death he might be given a posthumous name. Names
usually had some appropriate significance. A female received a milk name, a marriage name, and perhaps
a nickname. "Fragrant Princess" corresponds to the last.   5. An important commentary on the *Spring
and Autumn Annals*, written in the 1st century A.D.   6. The last full reign of the Ming, from 1628 to
1644. *Year of the Horse*: 1643.

these orchids in the Abode of Entrancing Perfumes, in order to win a smile from Fragrant Princess. Signed, Yang Wen-ts'ung of Kweiyang.

LI: Both the calligraphy and brushwork are supreme. I can never thank you enough. [*All sit down.*]   90

YANG: Surely Fragrant Princess is the greatest beauty in the land. What training in the arts has she received?

LI: I brought her up so tenderly that she has only just begun to study in earnest. The day before yesterday I found a teacher to instruct her in the art of lyric.   95

YANG: Who is he?

LI: A certain Su K'un-sheng.

YANG: I know him well. He used to go by the name of Chou Ju-sung, and lived in Wusi. He deserves the highest praise. What tunes has he taught her so far?   100

LI: "The Four Dreams of the Jade Tea-House."[7]

YANG: How much has she learned?

LI: Only half "The Peony Pavilion." Dear daughter, as His Honour Yang is an old friend of ours, do bring your music book and sing a few tunes for him.   105

FRAGRANT PRINCESS: I dare not.

LI: Don't be silly. In our profession, sleeves and skirts are in constant motion. Why not sing when you have the chance? [*Sings.*]

> Born amid powdered faces and painted eyebrows,
> Nurtured as one of the orioles and flowers,   110
> A tuneful voice is your only source of wealth.
> Be not too prodigal with your emotions, but learn to sing
> Songs of the morning breeze and broken moon.
> Beat gentle time with your ivory castanets,
> Bear off the singer's prize,   115
> And princes will tether horses at your gate.

[SU K'UN-SHENG *enters, in everyday garb.*]

SU: On my way to the songbird in the emerald chamber, I stop to gaze at the peonies by the porch. Since leaving the house of Juan, I have been teaching music to the loveliest courtesans. Isn't this better than waiting on the whims of an eunuch's foster son? [*He steps in.*]   120 Ah! Your Honour Yang, it is an age since we have met!

YANG: I congratulate you on your entrancing pupil.

LI: Master Su has arrived. Run and welcome him, dear daughter.

[FRAGRANT PRINCESS *curtseys.*]

SU: Let us avoid formalities. Have you memorized the song we practised yesterday?   125

FRAGRANT PRINCESS: I have, sir.

SU: Since His Honour Yang is present, let us hear it. We should take advantage of his criticism.

YANG: I shall be content merely to listen.

SU *and* FRAGRANT PRINCESS: [*Sitting opposite each other, sing.*]

---

7. The studio name of T'ang Hsien-tsu (1550–1617), outstanding dramatist of the Ming period. *Four Dreams:* his plays.

Clusters of purple, witching hues of red,   130
Now blossom from below and overhead,
Even from dried-up wells and broken walls.
How shall we spend so glorious a day?

SU: [*Stopping.*] Your rhythm is weak. The accent should fall on "spend"
and "glorious"; don't run them together. Again! [*The last line is*   135
repeated. Then they continue.]
SU *and* FRAGRANT PRINCESS: [*Singing.*]

Where at this hour can perfect bliss be found?
Now twilight gathers, and the day has fled.
The many-coloured clouds are drifting round
The green-tiled roofs, and gusty showers fall. . . .

SU: [*Interrupting.*] The word "showers" should be stressed, and sung   140
from deep in the throat. [*The last line is repeated. Then they*
continue.]
SU *and* FRAGRANT PRINCESS: [*Singing.*]

Over the misty waves doth float
A fragile painted boat.
Yet by the cloistered maid these things are seen
Only as visions on a painted screen.   145

SU: Well done, well done! You have sung it without a mistake. Let us
continue.
SU *and* FRAGRANT PRINCESS: [*Singing.*]

The cuckoo's tears have stained the verdant hills,
The willow branches droop as drunk with wine;
New peonies reign; but when the spring is gone,   150
What will survive of their bright sovereignty?

SU: [*Interrupting.*] This line is new to you, try it again. [*They repeat the*
last line and then continue.]
SU *and* FRAGRANT PRINCESS: [*Singing.*]

Now feast your gaze in sheer serenity:
Behold the twittering swallows, how they fare,
Flashing their tails like scissors through the air,   155
While orioles drop their notes like rounded pearls.

SU: Better and better! Now we have mastered another melody.
YANG: [*To* LI.] I'm delighted to discover that your daughter has such
talent. She is certain to reach the peak of her profession. [*To* SU.]
Yesterday I met Hou Fang-yü, the son of Minister Hou. He has   160
brilliant prospects as well as literary genius, and he is looking for a
beautiful mate. Have you heard of him, old friend?
SU: He is a fellow countryman of mine, a youth of exceptional promise.
YANG: A match between such a couple should be very successful.
[*Sings.*]

The sixteen-year-old maid, as fair as emerald jade,   165
Is ripe for nuptial bliss—how ravishing her song!

Her suitor rides with silken gifts and trinkets for
   her hair.
Hand in hand they will drain the cups of wine,
While friends chant verses in congratulation;
The halls are freshly garnished for the wedding.   170
A couple perfectly matched,
Year after year they will abide together,
In a peace tree grove beside the sweet spring waters.

LI: I hope you will persuade this young gentleman to pay us a visit. It
   would be wonderful if such a match could be arranged.   175
YANG: I promise to keep it in mind.
LI: [*Sings.*]

My daughter is more precious to me than rarest pearls,
Her voice is purer than the new-born oriole's;
But her virgin youth is barred by many doors,
Unnoticed by the passing wanderer.   180

[*Speaks to all.*] This day should be celebrated. Let us drink some
wine below.
YANG: With the greatest pleasure.
    [*Exeunt, each one singing.*]
YANG: Outside the curtain, flowers fill the courtyard.
LI: The oriole feels drunk, the swallow drowsy.   185
FRAGRANT PRINCESS: My crimson kerchief holds a heap of cherries.
SU: Waiting to fling them at P'an's[8] chariot!

SCENE 3

The Disrupted Ceremonies

1643, third month

[*Enter two* TEMPLE SERVANTS, *both clowns.*]
FIRST SERVANT: For generations, the sacrificial peas have been symbols
   of this rite.[9]
SECOND SERVANT: Ever since the days of my old grandad's might.
FIRST SERVANT: The sacrificial vessels at each altar are catalogued in
   the books.   5
SECOND SERVANT: Count them like stooks.
FIRST SERVANT: In the beginning and middle of each month, we light
   the candles and open the door.
SECOND SERVANT: Sweep the floor.
FIRST SERVANT: Kneel down and greet the Master of Ceremonies as   10
   soon as he is sighted.
SECOND SERVANT: Make sure that everything is righted. But you have
   bungled all the words.
FIRST SERVANT: If you can do better, go ahead.

8. Poet (3rd century) renowned for his exceptional handsomeness; women would pelt his carriage with
flowers and fruits when he rode in the capital.   9. In early youth, Confucius was reputed to have used
peas to imitate the arrangement of a ritual altar, thereby indicating his precocious interest in the rites.

SECOND SERVANT: Grain tribute is brought to the treasury all the year   15
round.

FIRST SERVANT: Bragging of wealth by the pound.

SECOND SERVANT: The whole family lives under a green-tiled roof with
scarlet walls.

FIRST SERVANT: Leading a wife to the stalls.   20

SECOND SERVANT: Dry timber is felled as soon as an axe you seize.

FIRST SERVANT: Plundering neighbours' trees.

SECOND SERVANT: Year in, year out, no vegetable need you eat.

FIRST SERVANT: Nothing but salted meat.

SECOND SERVANT: Shame on you, you have made a hash of it with   25
your cheap rhymes. [Both laugh.]

FIRST and SECOND SERVANT together: We prepare the rites of the
Imperial Academy in Nanking. After six months of idleness, we are
back in the middle of spring, the season for sacrifice. All the ritual
vessels and provisions have arrived from the Minister's office. Let   30
us set them in proper order.

[They set out the altar.]

FIRST SERVANT: Chestnuts, dates, fresh water-roots.

SECOND SERVANT: Ox, sheep, pig, rabbit, and deer.

FIRST SERVANT: Fish, spinach, celery, bamboo shoots, and garlic.

SECOND SERVANT: Salt, wine, incense, silk, and candles.   35

FIRST SERVANT: The list is complete. Keep an eye on everything, for we
shall be blamed if the stewards pilfer.

MASTER OF CEREMONIES: [Entering.] Fie on you! If you don't pilfer,
well and good. Why cast aspersions on others?

FIRST SERVANT: [Bows with folded hands.] I beg your pardon. I was   40
referring to those who shall be nameless since they are shameless.
Of course a respectable person like you would be blameless.

MASTER OF CEREMONIES: Let us not waste words. It is already daybreak.
You should light the candles and incense.

SECOND SERVANT: Aye, aye, sir. [Exeunt.]   45

[LIBATIONER[1] appears in his official robes.]

LIBATIONER: [Sings.]

> The smoke of incense clouds the pillared hall
> Where scarlet candles flame beside the altar.
> And now the orchestra strikes up a prelude;
> The vessels, food and wine are all prepared.

[His ASSISTANT appears in his official robes.]

ASSISTANT: [Sings.]

> The ranks are drawn up   50
> For the observance of ceremonies in the Southern Academy.

LIBATIONER: I am the Libationer in the Imperial Academy of Nanking.

ASSISTANT: I am the Assistant Libationer. Today is the day of sacrifice
at the Temple of Confucius, and we are about to begin the cere-   55
mony.

---

1. The official who pours out ritual offerings.

[*They stand on either side of the stage.* WU YING-CHI *enters.*]
WU: [*Sings.*]

> The drum is booming; soon it will be dawn.
> The scholars file before the Almond Altar.

[*Enter* FOUR SCHOLARS *of the Imperial Academy.*]
FOUR SCHOLARS, *together:* [*Singing.*]

Of yore this music and these rites inspired three thousand disciples.
Today we shall again behold our Sage.   60

[JUAN TA-CH'ENG *enters in formal attire, his face covered with a heavy beard.*]
JUAN: [*Sings.*] I have brazened myself to join this solemn gathering.
WU: I, Wu Ying-chi, together with my comrades Yang Wei-tou, Liu Po-tsung, Shen K'un-t'ung, and Shen Mei-sheng, am ready to attend the sacrifice.
FOUR SCHOLARS: Let us take our appointed places.   65
JUAN: [*Hiding his face behind his sleeve.*] Having nothing else to do in Nanking, I came to see the ceremony. [*He takes up a position in the front rank.*]
MASTER OF CEREMONIES: [*Enters and calls.*] Go to your places. Stand in even ranks. Bow; kneel; prostrate yourselves; arise! [*Thrice repeated.*]
ALL *together:* [*Singing.*]

> A hundred feet above the clouds, the golden tablet gleams;   70
> Behold our Sage enthroned in majesty,
> His four supreme disciples sit beside him,
> While strains of music bid his spirit welcome.
> Let us prostrate ourselves below the steps,
> We who have studied poetry and the classics   75
> That we may come into his heritage.
> Now tremble in his presence, struck with awe.

[*After burning paper offerings, all salute each other.*]
LIBATIONER *and* ASSISTANT: [*Singing.*]

> Facing the north, we celebrate together
> Our Sage's glory with the spring's return;
> Observing all the hallowed regulations,   80
> The time and order of each sacrifice.

WU: [*Leading the* SCHOLARS' *chorus.*]

> Let us unite in worship of the Sage,
> Like his disciples in a nobler age.

JUAN: [*Sings.*]

> What joy to stroll the capital,
> A man of pleasure,   85
> Without official duties
> To rob me of my leisure.

[*Exeunt* LIBATIONER *and* ASSISTANT. JUAN *bows to all.*]

WU: [*Startled.*] Are you not whiskered Juan? What are you doing at the sacrifice? This is an insult to the Sage. You are a disgrace to the world of letters. [*Shouting.*] Away with you! 90

JUAN: [*Angrily.*] I am a distinguished Doctor of Literature, descended from a famous family. Why should I not be allowed to attend the sacrifice? What sin have I committed?

WU: At court and outside it, your guilt is notorious. You have covered your face with a mask and lost your conscience. How dare you set 95 foot in this temple? Did not my public impeachment say enough about your crimes?

JUAN: That was precisely why I attended these ceremonies, to confess what is in my heart.

WU: Let me tell you plainly who and what you are. [*Sings.*] 100

> Godson of Wei, godson of K'o,[2]
> To any family you will go.
> With Ts'ui Ch'eng-hsiu, and T'ien Erh-ching,[3]
> Consorting in stealth,
> You guzzle iniquities and gobble filth. 105
> Shooting secret arrows into the Eastern Forest,[4]
> Weaving your plots in the Western Shed,[5]
> Beware, beware—men will not be misled.

SCHOLARS: [*Singing in unison.*]

> Ha! behold the melting glacier,
> The baseless, toppling iron pillar! 110

JUAN: Brothers, you revile me without trying to understand my motives. You do not realize that I am a disciple of the great Chao Chung-i. When the Grand Eunuch Wei rose to power, I had retired to the country to mourn the death of my parents. How could I have harmed anyone? On what grounds do you accuse me? 115 [*Sings.*]

> To such injustice Heaven once responded
> By sending frost in midsummer.
> Hide me under no black bowl[6]
> To suffer slander
> No more substantial than a shadow. 120
> Why did I cultivate Wei Chung-hsien?
> To try to save the upright censors,
> Wei Ta-chung, Chou Ch'ao-jui!
> For their sake, my good name
> Gladly I sacrificed. 125

2. K'o-shih, Emperor Hsi-tsung's wet nurse. Wei Chung-hsien (1568–1637), one of the most powerful eunuchs in Chinese history, whose persecution of able generals and ministers weakened the Chinese defenses against the threatening Manchus. On the emperor's death, Wei hanged himself to escape trial and K'o-shih was executed. **3.** Leading associates of Wei's clique. **4.** See n. 3, p. 77. **5.** The notorious torture chamber of the court secret police. **6.** An image for an impenetrable cloud of unwarranted suspicion. *Frost in midsummer:* sent down by Heaven, in an ancient legend, to convince the emperor of the loyalty of an unjustly slandered minister.

[*Speaks.*] Have you forgotten Master K'ang Hai of yore, who curried favour with the eunuch Liu Chin[7] in order to save the life of an upright man? If I associated with Wei Chung-hsien, it was to protect my noble friends of the Eastern Forest Party. How can I be blamed for this? [*Sings.*]

130

> Every problem demands a fair solution,
> But I have been ten times wronged,
> Yet no one rises to defend me;
> I am vilified by all.
> These giddy striplings break wind in my face. . . .

135

WU: How dare you use such language here!

ALL: It is insufferable that a traitor like you should speak so foully in the temple of Confucius.

MASTER OF CEREMONIES: It is absolutely monstrous. Old as I am, I long to thrash the traitor! [*Beats* JUAN.]

140

WU: Pummel his face and pull out all his hair!

> [*Everybody attacks* JUAN.]

ALL: [*Singing.*]

> Damned spawn of a eunuch!
> You should not even be allowed
> To worship the Sage;
> A disgrace to the world of letters!
> We shall wage war against you and your like
> And drive you to the farthest wilderness,
> To feed wolves and tigers with your swinish carcass.

145

JUAN: Have you done with assaulting me? [*To* MASTER OF CEREMONIES.] Even an old gaffer like you has the nerve to strike me!

150

MASTER OF CEREMONIES: I can thrash you as vigorously as any man.

JUAN: [*Gazing ruefully at his beard.*] I have lost half my beard. How shall I ever appear in public again? [*He runs off the stage, singing.*]

> This volley of fists has laid me low,
> I am in agony;
> My arms feel broken, my back as well.
> I flee from this place of torment.

155

WU *and* ALL: [*Singing.*]

> Between the virtuous and the vile
> There is always a clear distinction,
> And this man's crimes are heavy and solid as lead.
> Not long ago his power could reach to Heaven—
> Today how ignominious was his flight!
> His scholar's hat was beaten flat;
> It is time for him to burn his ink and brushes.

160

WU: This incident has avenged the Eastern Forest Party and brought honour to the Academy of Nanking. We should persevere in this

165

---

7. A eunuch who became virtual head of the government under the Ming emperor Wu-tsung. A cabal formed against him, and he was executed in 1510.

resolute course, and prevent all such villains from showing themselves again in public.

CHORUS: Hear, Hear! We have done a righteous deed before the Sage's
 gate.   170

WU: Between light and darkness we should champion light.

CHORUS:

> Alas, 'tis never easy to decide
> Which be the winning, which the losing side.

WU:

> Heaven may loosen Chaos; 'tis for Man
> To conjure Order wheresoe'er he can. 175

SCENE 4

The Play Observed

1643, third month

[JUAN TA-CH'ENG *enters, in obvious distress.*]

JUAN: [*Sings.*]

> The old game is played out,
> My former colleagues scattered.
> The hair grows white upon my temples,
> No spirit is left in my song.
> Insulted by these upstarts without cease, 5
> How shall I ever sleep and eat in peace?

[*Speaks.*] Until recently I enjoyed a triumphant career. Power, fame,
and rank were within my grasp. Unfortunately, I was tempted by
vanity and greed to join the eunuch Wei's party. For a time I became
one of his foster sons. While his influence was spreading 10
like fire, I was like a wolf within sight of its prey. Now that it has
dwindled to cold ashes, I am more like a wretched owl in a withered
forest. Everybody curses me and spits in my face; I am assaulted
from every side. Alas, I am a scholar who has absorbed a whole
library of books. Why did I attach myself to that evil eunuch? 15
I was neither demented nor delirious, yet how could I have made
such a blunder as to become his henchman? [*Stamps his foot.*] When
I think of the past, I am filled with mortification. Luckily, this huge
city affords a shelter for all sorts. I have a spacious mansion in
Breeches' Bottom, which I have embellished with gardens 20
and pavilions, and here I have trained a private troupe of singers and
dancers. Should any high official deign to associate with me, I would
go to any expense to gratify him. Perhaps I may still win some good
man's sympathy, and the chance to amend past errors. . . . [*Whispers.*] But if Heaven allowed dead ashes to flare up again, 25
I would waste no further thought on my reputation. I would commit
every crime again to my heart's content! Yesterday I was grossly
insulted by the young urchins of the Revival Club in the temple
of Confucius. Though they were to blame, I was rash to expose

myself. But I am anxious to find a way to propitiate them. [*He*   30
scratches his head in thought and sings.]

> Coxcombs combined, a feather-pated crew,
> To cheat and slander my distinguished name.
> Like whirling winds they tore away the beard
> About my lips—these very lips, the same
> That uttered purest poetry; broke this wrist   35
> Whose calligraphic skill once brought me fame.
> Nor can I find revenge, but only hide
> Indoors in all my shame.

FIRST SERVANT: [*Entering with a letter.*] Few notabilities come this way;
all the fine birds are flown, alackaday! [*To* JUAN.] Your Hon-   40
our, here is a note requesting the loan of your troupe of players.
JUAN: [*Reading it aloud.*] "Your friend Ch'en Chen-hui salutes you."
Aha, this comes from a great celebrity. Why would such a great man
as this stoop to borrowing my troupe of players? What did his messenger have to say?   45
SERVANT: He says there are two other gentlemen named Fang Mi-chih
and Mao P'i-chiang who are drinking with him at the Crowing Cock
Inn. They are all agog to enjoy your new play, *The Swallow Letter.*
JUAN: Run upstairs, choose the best costumes, and summon the lead-
ing players. See that they brush themselves up and hasten to oblige   50
the scholars. You go with them, take my greetings, and keep a careful
eye on everything.
> [*Exit* FIRST SERVANT. *Several players cross the stage, followed by
> another* SERVANT *carrying costumes.* JUAN *beckons to him.*]
JUAN: [*Whispers.*] When you get there, listen carefully to their remarks
while they watch the play.
SERVANT: As you command, sir. [*Exit.*]   55
JUAN: [*Chuckling to himself.*] Ha-ha, I never expected them to apply to
me. This is an encouraging sign. I'll sit in my study and wait for the
servant's report. [*Exit.*]
> [YANG WEN-TS'UNG *enters.*]
YANG: In the hope of hearing the latest tunes, I have come to call on
my old crony. He excels in composing lyrics and plays as I do in   60
painting and calligraphy. Today I have a chance of hearing his latest
song for *The Swallow Letter.* Here is the Stone Nest Garden. How
exquisitely all the rocks and flowers are arranged. It must have been
designed by the famous Chang Nan-yüan.[8] [*Pointing at the rocks and
flowers, he sings.*]

> Flowering groves carefully spaced,   65
> Rocks mantled with moss,
> Create the effect of a landscape
> By Ni Tsan or Huang Kung-wang.[9]

---

8. Or Chang Lien, a landscape architect of the late Ming and early Ch'ing periods who designed many
famous gardens in Chekiang and Kiangsu.   9. Ni Tsan (1301–1374) and Huang Kung-wang (1269–
1354), two of the most celebrated artists of the Yuan Dynasty, which was a golden age of Chinese painting.

[*Looking up, he reads from a tablet.*] "The Hall of Lyrics. Calligraphy by Wang To."[1] What vigorous characters! Red carpets strew the 70 ground; this is where he rehearses his plays. [*Sings.*]

> A thatched pavilion completes the picture.
> There in his high black cap he directs the players
> With silver lute and crimson clappers.

[*Speaks.*] Maybe I shall find him in the flower garden. [*Sings.*] 75

> But why closed gates, a scene forlorn?
> Is he writing new poems or revising old ones?

[*Standing still, he listens and says.*] Somebody seems to be chanting; it must be old Juan reading aloud. Brother Juan, come and relax awhile. Don't give up all your time to literature! 80
JUAN: [*Enters, laughing.*] I was wondering who had come to see me. So it is you! Sit down, sit down.
YANG: Why shut yourself indoors on a fine spring day?
JUAN: My four plays are being printed, so I have to scrutinize the proofs for mistakes. 85
YANG: So that explains it. I heard you had finished rehearsing *The Swallow Letter*, and I long to see it.
JUAN: Unfortunately my actors are away.
YANG: Where have they gone?
JUAN: They have gone to entertain some friends of mine. 90
YANG: Would you let me see a copy of the script? I should enjoy nothing better than to read it with some wine beside me.
JUAN: [*To* SERVANTS.] Bring the wine. His Honour Yang and I will quench our thirst.
VOICES FROM BACKSTAGE: Aye, aye, sir. 95
[*Wine and refreshments are brought in.* YANG *and* JUAN *drink while reading the play.*]
YANG: [*Sings.*]

> Column by column, new poems flow onto paper,
> Each line as gold freshly sifted from sand.
> A beautiful woman speaks her reverie,
> As mist drifts over the sea and far clouds form.

[*Speaks.*] While reading this passage, I feel I have fallen in love! 100
[*Sings.*]

> Though willow buds whiten, and hair be sprinkled with snow,
> The swallow retains a fragment of spring in its beak.

JUAN: My doggerel and commonplace tunes must strike you as absurd. Pray drink some more wine.
FIRST SERVANT: [*Entering hastily.*] I bring my random words to allay my 105 master's concern. Your Honour, I have been watching the performance at the Crowing Cock Inn. They have finished three scenes, so I hurried back to report.

---

1. An eminent poet, painter, and calligrapher (1592–1652), who attained the exalted post of president of the Board of Rites, first under the Ming and then again under the Manchus.

JUAN: What were the comments of the audience?
SERVANT: All expressed the highest admiration. [*Sings.*] 110

> They nodded their heads and beat time in approval.
> They forgot their wine cups to lap every line of the play.

JUAN: Their approbation seems to have been genuine. What else did they say?
SERVANT: [*Sings.*]

> They exclaimed: 115
> "A true genius with a remarkable pen!"

JUAN: Oho! I am surprised that they were so complimentary. What else?
SERVANT: [*Sings.*]

> They said: "His style is that of an immortal,
> Expressing himself in human speech.
> In modern letters his art stands supreme." 120

JUAN: [*Feigning embarrassment.*] This is too much; they are exaggerating. But I shall look forward to hearing their comments when they have seen more of it. Be quick and find out, then run back and tell me. [SERVANT *obeys.* JUAN *laughs aloud.*] I never guessed those young men were so discerning! [*To* YANG.] No heel-taps! 125 [*Sings.*]

> Ah, I have seen
> All the landscapes of the southern school,
> Read all the old romances.
> I have toiled till dusk in my tower or rain pavilion,
> Toiled on from nightfall under a lamp; 130
> I have drained my heart's blood in solitary composing.
> At last I have found discriminating hearers!

YANG: Who are these gentlemen?
JUAN: Ch'en Ting-sheng, Fang Mi-chih, and Mao P'i-chiang—all men of the deepest culture. They have proved their esteem for me. 135
YANG: These persons are seldom addicted to praise, but your *Swallow Letter* is so fine in versification and melody that their admiration is natural.
FIRST SERVANT: [*Returning.*] I ran out like a rabbit; I fly back like a raven. Your Honour, now that they have seen half the play, I have 140 returned with another report.
JUAN: How did the audience respond?
SERVANT: [*Sings.*]

> They called Your Honour "Pride of the south,
> Chief ornament of the Eastern Forest,
> Worthy of the Han-lin Academy itself." 145

JUAN: Every sentence is so laudatory that I feel embarrassed. What else?
SERVANT: [*Sings.*]

They added: "But why did you join the traitors Ts'ui and Wei,
And turn against your old friends?"

JUAN: [*Frowning angrily.*] That was only a passing misjudgment; there   150
was no need to bring it up again. What else?
SERVANT: They said more in the same strain, but being your humble
servant I dare not repeat it.
JUAN: Never mind, proceed.
SERVANT: [*Sings.*]

> They said: "Your Honour called a stranger his father,   155
> And became his foster son;
> Utterly shameless and heartless,
> Fawning on your protector like a cur."

JUAN: [*Furiously.*] So they started reviling me again! I cannot endure
it. [*Sings.*]   160

> What have politics to do with art?
> I lent them my latest music and poetry
> To increase their enjoyment of wine and flowers.
> Alas, it was in vain.
> They never tried to fathom my motives,   165
> But only heaped on me the vilest abuse.
> I am overwhelmed by so many insults.

YANG: Why did they attack you?
JUAN: I cannot imagine. Recently I went to worship at the temple of
Confucius, where I was set upon and beaten by five young graduates.   170
Now I have lent them my play and private actors to propitiate them,
only to reap further calumnies. I must find a remedy, or I shall never
dare step out-of-doors.
YANG: Don't worry, elder brother, I have been pondering a solution.
JUAN: You give me a ray of hope. I shall be grateful for your advice.   175
YANG: The leaders of the graduates is Wu Tzu-wei, and the leader of
the nobles is Ch'en Ting-sheng. If these stop attacking you, your
peace will be restored.
JUAN: Of course; but who would venture to defend me?
YANG: I think Hou Fang-yü might be approached. He is their boon   180
companion in the literary club as well as at the wine table. Both are
influenced by his opinions. Only yesterday I heard that he was feeling
lonely for lack of employment. He longs for a girl companion, and I have found him one ideal in every respect. Her name is
Fragrant Princess. She excels in beauty as in the gentle arts; I am   185
sure he will be captivated by her. Now if you provide a dowry, he
would be obliged to show some gratitude. I could then ask him to
speak in your favour, which would lead to a general appeasement.
JUAN: [*Clapping his hands and laughing.*] Excellent! What a splendid
idea. Hou's father was my classmate, so he is almost a nephew to   190
me. I feel I should do whatever I can for him. But what will it cost
me?

YANG: About two hundred silver *taels*[2] should suffice for the wardrobe and banquet.

JUAN: I can easily afford it. I'll send three hundred over to your house. 195
Spend the money as you think fit.

YANG: That is too large a sum. [*Sings.*]

> A young willow leans over the gate
> For the lover to climb in late.

JUAN: [*Sings.*]

> My poems and music proved inadequate; 200
> Only this beauteous girl may serve as bait.

YANG: [*Sings.*]

> Upon your bounty will depend their fate.

SCENE 5

A Visit to the Beauty

1643, third month

[HOU FANG-YÜ, *elegantly gowned, enters singing.*]

HOU: [*Sings.*]

> The golden glory has not quite departed,
> The fragrance of the southern courts still lingers;
> These misty meadows melt into my soul,
> While breezes coax the budding flowers to open,
> But wind and rain will pass, and likewise spring. 5

[*Speaks.*] Too long I have been roving with only my books and sword for company, and no prospect of seeing my home. During this third month I have been steeped in nostalgia for the bygone Six Dynasties. As a wanderer I suffer from homesickness, nor can I help being stirred by the spring scenery. Yesterday I met Yang Wen- 10
ts'ung, who sang the praises of Fragrant Princess Li, of her youthful grace and exceptional beauty. He also told me that Su K'un-sheng was giving her singing lessons, and proposed that I should buy her trousseau. Alas, my purse is almost empty; I cannot afford what I ardently desire. Today is the Festival of Pure Brightness.[3] I feel so 15
lonely that I shall take a stroll through the meadows. Perhaps I may have a chance to visit the beauty's house.

[*Sings.*]

> I gaze towards the Forbidden City, where all the beauties dwell,
> Their gates concealed behind the drooping willows.
> Young cavaliers are riding down the highway, 20
> Flourishing elegant reins of purple silk,
> But where are the tender couples of young swallows?

---

2. The *tael* was the former monetary unit; it was worth approximately one ounce of silver. 3. The Ch'ing-ming Festival, corresponding to the Christian Easter, was usually in early April. On this day offerings were made to the dead, while their graves were put in good order; it was also a time for picnics and excursions into the country.

LIU CHING-T'ING: [*Entering.*]

> An oriole awoke me from my dreams;
> My white hair kindles memory's fading gleams.

[*To* HOU.] Where are you going, Master Hou? 25
HOU: Oh, it is Ching-t'ing! What a pleasant surprise! I set out for a
walk hoping to meet a companion like yourself.
LIU: I shall be glad to keep you company. [*As they stroll,* LIU *points and
says.*] There is the Water Pavilion, beyond the Ch'in Huai River.
HOU: [*Sings.*]

> Over the waves a green mist creeps, 30
> Brushing the windows; against the sky,
> Bright blossom of the almond peeps
> Above the house-wall high.

LIU: [*Pointing.*] Here is Long Bridge. Let us loiter on the way.
HOU: [*Sings.*]

> Passing the wine and tea shops 35
> And the noisy vendors of flowers . . .

LIU: Ha! This is the old quarter now.
HOU: [*Sings.*]

> We saunter across the wooden bridge
> To reach a labyrinth of lanes.

LIU: In yonder lane the most famous beauties dwell. 40
HOU: It has an air of voluptuous refinement. [*Sings.*]

> Over these twin black lacquered gates,
> A tender willow droops as if with dew.

LIU: That is the house of Mistress Li Chen-li.
HOU: And where does Fragrant Princess live? 45
LIU: She is Mistress Li's daughter.
HOU: How lucky! I have been longing to meet her, and here we are!
LIU: I'll knock at her door. [*Knocks.*]
VOICE FROM BACKSTAGE: Who's there?
LIU: It is old Liu, a regular visitor. I have brought a distinguished guest. 50
VOICE FROM BACKSTAGE: Mistress Li and Fragrant Princess are not at
home.
LIU: Where are they?
VOICE: They went to a hamper party at Mistress Pien's.
LIU: Oh, of course! I had quite forgotten about it. 55
HOU: Why did they have to go out today of all days?
LIU: My legs are tired. Let's sit on these stone steps and rest while I
explain. [*Both sit down.*] Just as men become sworn brothers by burn-
ing incense together, courtesans become sworn sisters by exchanging
kerchiefs. In due course, they hold parties in celebration 60
at times of festival. [*Sings.*]

> These beauties become sisters
> By knotting silken kerchiefs together.

> On days of festival,
> They meet in friendly rivalry. 65

HOU: I see; but why do they call it a hamper party?
LIU: Each must bring a hamper filled with delicacies. [*Sings.*]

> Dainty dishes from the sea,
> Succulent rarities from the rivers,
> And the choicest of wines. 70

HOU: What do they do on these occasions?
LIU: Usually they hold musical contests. [*Sings.*]

> They play the lute, The reed-organ, and
> the bamboo flute.

HOU: How fascinating! Are men allowed to join them? 75
LIU: No, at such times they shun male society. They bolt their doors and climb to an upper storey. Men are only allowed to admire them from below.
HOU: Supposing one glimpsed his heart's desire, how could a meeting be arranged? 80
LIU: In that case, a personal trinket might be thrown up into the tower, and the recipient might throw down fruit. [*Sings.*]

> If the girl is gratified,
> She will descend to offer wine
> And make an assignation. 85

HOU: I am tempted to go and see for myself.
LIU: There's no harm in trying.
HOU: But I don't know where Mistress Pien lives.
LIU: Her place is called the Halcyon Lodge; it isn't far from here. I'll show the way. [*As they proceed, each recites one line of a quatrain.*] 90
HOU: Before the worship at the tombs, each family hangs out a willow branch.
LIU: Everywhere the bamboo flute celebrates this festival.
HOU: Three miles of streets are adorned with birds and flowers.
LIU: We cross two bridges over the misty river. 95
    [*Points.*] Here is the house. Let's go in.
        [YANG WEN-TS'UNG *and* SU K'UN-SHENG *enter and meet* HOU *and* LIU.]
YANG: In my leisure I search for orioles and flowers.
SU: We have come to see powdered faces and painted eyebrows. [*They greet each other.*]
YANG: How astonishing to find you in such a resort!
HOU: All the more so since I heard you had gone to visit bearded Juan. 100
SU: We happened to come here expressly on your account.
LIU: Let us all sit down.
HOU: [*Looking up.*] What a charming lodge! [*Sings.*]

> The windows glowing on the spacious courtyard
> Transport one to a gentle land of dreams. 105

[*Speaks.*] But where is Fragrant Princess?
YANG: She is upstairs.

SU: Can you hear the music? [*A flute and a reed-organ are played offstage.*]

HOU: [*Listens and sings.*]

> The fairy organs and phoenix pipes echo among the clouds.

[*Lute and zither play.*]

> What subtle rhythm!   110
> What a harmony of strings!

[*A yün-lo or small gong is heard.*]

> What jade-like tinkling!
> Each note plucks at my heart.

[*Pan-pipes play.*]

> The phoenix pair soar fluttering through the air . . .

[*Speaks.*] These pipes have seized my soul and borne it away. I can   115 restrain myself no longer. I shall throw my pledge aloft. [*He removes the pendant from his fan and throws it into the upper room, singing.*]

> This treasure from the southern seas
> Is wafted high upon the breeze
> Into the lodge, my beauty's heart to tease.

[*A kerchief full of cherries is thrown down to him.*]

LIU: How curious! A shower of fruit.   120

SU: [*Opening the kerchief.*] Strange that there should be cherries at this season!

HOU: I wonder who threw them. If it was Fragrant Princess, I shall be overjoyed.

YANG: This kerchief is woven of the finest silk. I'll wager nine to one   125 that it is hers.

> [*Enter* LI CHEN-LI *with a teapot in her hand, followed by* FRAGRANT PRINCESS *with a vase of flowers.*]

LIU: The light grass trembles under the butterfly's wings, the beauty now descends the Phoenix Terrace.

SU: Look! They advance like goddesses.

LIU: [*With palms together as in prayer.*] Amida Buddha![4]   130

YANG: [*Whispering to* HOU.] Observe them carefully. [ALL *rise.*] That is Mistress Li, and that is Fragrant Princess.

HOU: [*Greeting* MISTRESS LI.] I am Hou Fang-yü of Honan. After hearing so much about you I am delighted to have this opportunity. [*To* FRAGRANT PRINCESS.] You are indeed a perfect beauty in the flush   135 of youth. My friend Yang's keen eyes have proved him a connoisseur.

LI: May I offer you gentlemen some fresh tea from Tiger Hill? [*She pours tea.*]

FRAGRANT PRINCESS: [*Showing her vase.*] These green willows and pink almond blossoms enhance the season's beauty.

ALL: [*In chorus of admiration.*] Delicious, to sip the rarest tea and gaze   140 upon such flowers!

---

4. An oath.

AMERICAN RIVER COLLEGE

YANG: On this occasion we should be drinking wine.

LI: I have already ordered it. Aunt Pien is occupied with guests in the lodge, so I shall act as hostess in her stead. [*Wine is brought by a* MAID.] Would it not be amusing to play some drinking games?   145

LIU: We await your orders.

MISTRESS LI: It is not for me to give orders.

SU: However, it is customary.

[MISTRESS LI *produces dice and a jar to throw them in.*]

LI: Fragrant Princess, you pour the wine when I ask you to, depending on the dice. The rule of the game is that each must give a sample of 150 his talent after every cup of wine. Number one stands for cherry, two for tea, three for willow, four for almond blossom, five for the pendant, and six for the silk handkerchief. Your Honour Hou comes first. [FRAGRANT PRINCESS *pours* HOU *a cup;* MISTRESS LI *throws the dice and says.*] It's the pendant. Drain your cup, Master Hou, and let 155 us hear your contribution.

HOU: [*Drinks and says.*] I'll improvise a verse. [*Chants.*]

> This came from the south for my beauty to wear;
> It should hang from her fan like a moon in midair,
> To sway and swing at her every turn,   160
> Catching the breeze from her fragrant hair.

YANG: How clever!

LIU: The pendant is a fine one, I'm only afraid it would sway once too often and get broken!

LI: Now it is His Honour Yang's turn to drink. [FRAGRANT PRINCESS 165 *pours and* YANG *drinks.* MISTRESS LI *throws the dice and says.*] It's the silk handkerchief.

YANG: I'll compose a verse about the handkerchief.

LI: Please change the metre for variety.

YANG: Then I'll make it an examination essay: "The silk that dabs off 170 perspiration evokes the lustrous skin of its possessor. The sweat that moistens the kerchief is spring's hot breath on a lovely face. And whose face is worthy of so fine a fabric? The rosy cheek and white silk blend, enhancing each other's perfection."

HOU: That's excellent.   175

LIU: What subtle talent! For this you should pass both provincial and metropolitan examinations at once!

FRAGRANT PRINCESS: [*Serving wine to* LIU.] Your turn, please, Master Liu.

LI: [*Throwing dice.*] Number two; that stands for tea.   180

LIU: [*Drinks, but jokes.*] You mean I only get tea to drink, while you drink wine?

LI: No, your *forfeit*[5] must be about tea.

LIU: Shall I tell the tale of Chang San-lang, drinking tea with his paramour Yen P'o-hsi in *The Men of the Marshes*?   185

---

5. Drinking games like those described were common at parties. The loser had to drink a *forfeit*, usually wine.

LI: That's too long-winded. Just tell us a joke.

LIU: All right. Su Tung-p'o and Huang T'ing-chien went to visit the Buddhist monk Fo Yin.[6] Su brought a pot of fine Ting-yao porcelain, and Huang a pound of excellent Yang-hsien tea. All three sat under a spreading pine to savour the brew. The monk said: "Master Huang has a notorious passion for tea, but I don't know about bearded Su's tea-drinking capacities. Why not have a competition now?" Su asked: "How shall we arrange it?" The monk replied, "You ask him a riddle. If he cannot answer at once, I'll put it on record that the Beard[7] has beaten the Graduate. He will then ask you a riddle, and if you fail to give a prompt reply, I'll put down that the Graduate has beaten the Beard. In the end we shall make a count. Each must drink a cup of tea on being defeated." "Very well," said Su, and asked: "How can you run a thread through a pin without a hole?" "Scratch away the pinpoint," Huang replied.[8] "Well answered," said Fo Yin. Huang asked: "How can you hold a gourd without a handle?" "By throwing it into the water," said Su. "Another good answer," said Fo Yin. Su asked: "If there is a louse in your breeches, will you see it or won't you?" Before Huang could reply, Su seized a stick to beat him. At that moment Huang was holding the teapot, and it slipped and was shattered on the ground. Su shouted: "Remember this, you monk, the Beard has beaten the Graduate." Fo Yin laughed and said: "But I only heard a crash. The Graduate broke the pot; the Beard[9] did not break the Graduate." [*General laughter.*] This is no laughing matter. Graduates can be dangerous fellows. [*Fingering the teapot.*] They can break a hardware pot, not to mention a soft one![1]

HOU: He deserves another drink for his rollicking wit and humour.

LI: Fragrant Princess, pour your teacher some wine.

> [LIU *drinks.* MISTRESS LI *throws dice and gets number four, almond blossom.*]

SU: [*Sings.*]

> The almond blossoms droop within the tower,
> And clothes grow thin at this cool evening hour.

FRAGRANT PRINCESS: [*Pouring wine for* MISTRESS LI.] It is your turn now, Mama.

> [MISTRESS LI *drinks and throws dice, getting number one, the cherry.*]

SU: Let me sing for you.

> "Those cherry lips the pearly teeth betray,
> Before a single syllable they say."

LIU: Master Su should be fined. The cherries he sings of are not the edible kind.

---

6. A rollicking Buddhist monk and convivial associate. For Su Tung-p'o, see n. 4, p. 77. Huang T'ing-chien (1045–1105), a poet and disciple of Su. 7. That is, Su. 8. There are many anecdotes about Su Tung-p'o and Fo Yin. These riddles are intended to be pointless, deliberate non sequiturs to confound the logical processes and thereby liberate true understanding, in approved Zen fashion. 9. A pun; the Chinese word *hu-tzu* means both "pot" and "beard." 1. Another pun: in Chinese, *juan hu-tzu*, which plays on "Bearded Juan."

SU: I accept the fine. [*He pours and drinks.*]

LI: Fragrant Princess, you will have to pour your own wine.   225

HOU: No, allow me. [*He pours and she drinks.*]

LI: [*Throwing dice.*] Number three. Fragrant Princess must sing about the willow. [*But* FRAGRANT PRINCESS *coyly declines.*] My daughter is too shy. Would somebody else perform in her stead? Perhaps Master Liu would oblige us?   230

SU: We are really making him work today!

LIU: My name means willow, and I have been afraid of that word all my life. On this Festival of Pure Brightness, there are willow garlands everywhere. Might as well put one on me as a "dog-collar."[2] [ALL *roar with laughter.*]

SU: Oh, that's enough of your jokes!   235

HOU: Having finished the wine, we ought to be taking our leave.

LIU: It is seldom that a handsome young genius is brought together with such a radiant girl. [*He pulls* HOU *and* FRAGRANT PRINCESS *together.*] Why don't you exchange vows over a cup of wine?

> [FRAGRANT PRINCESS *hides her face behind her sleeve and runs out covered with confusion.*]

SU: The girl is sensitive. You shouldn't have talked like that in front of her. What is to be done about her trousseau? Has His Excellency Hou any suggestions to offer?   240

HOU: [*Laughing.*] Would a Graduate object to becoming a Prize Candidate? My case is similar.

LI: Since you are so favourably disposed, let us choose an auspicious day.   245

YANG: The fifteenth of the third month is the best time for flowers and the full moon; it is also the best time for mating.

HOU: The only drawback is that, being a traveller, I'm short of ready cash. I'm afraid I couldn't make a suitable offer.   250

YANG: Never mind, you can leave that to me.

HOU: How could I put you to so much trouble?

YANG: I shall be only too pleased to assist you.

HOU: I am overwhelmed. [*Sings.*]

> Now fate has led me towards the magic peak.   255
> My passions rise like clouds, and in their tumult
> My eyes cannot discern the radiant goddess.
> This night of spring, these flowers, and the moon
> Lighting the silent land, are they illusions?
> Nay, for the joyful moment hurries near;   260
> Now for this blessed union I'll prepare.

> [HOU *bows farewell.*]

LI: I dare not detain you. Let us decide on the fifteenth provisionally. I shall send out the invitations and ask several fair sisters to join us. The finest music should be played for this occasion. [*Exit.*]

LIU: Alas, I had forgotten a previous engagement.   265

YANG: Couldn't you postpone it?

---

2. It was a local custom on this festival for children to wear willow garlands, which they called dog collars.

SU: Admiral Huang's warship is anchored west of the city, and on the fifteenth he is holding a flag ceremony. We shall have to attend it.

HOU: What a pity! We shall miss you.

YANG: There are plenty of others to make up a merry party. I suggest   270
Ting Chi-chih, Shen Kung-hsien, and Chang Yen-chu.
[*Exeunt, singing.*]

SU: Powdered cheeks are fragrant before the boudoir bright,

YANG: The grace of bygone ages returns to our delight,

LIU: Our outing of today found only hints of spring;

HOU: We think of the fair blossom tomorrow's warmth will bring.   275

SCENE 6

The Fragrant Couch

1643, third month

[*Enter* MISTRESS LI *in gorgeous attire.*]

LI: [*Sings.*]

> In short spring jacket, sleeves folded back,
> She tunes the zither in the fairy park.
> Today in expectation her curtains are raised;
> Let not the willow fronds
> Hide from view the groom's magnolia-wood boat.   5

[*Speaks.*] Since Fragrant Princess turned sixteen, I have been worrying night and day about her future. Luckily, Master Yang introduced us to Master Hou, who came to drink wine with us the other day—a distinguished young man of good family. Today is the auspicious day of their union banquet. Soon the guests will arrive, and I   10
am expecting all our fair sisters. To entertain so large a party is quite a responsibility. Where is the maid?

MAID: [*A clown, enters waving a fan.*] How I love cracking jokes at a banquet, and eavesdropping under a blanket! But mum, the mistress is calling me! [*To* MISTRESS LI.] What are your orders now,   15
ma'am? More pillows and quilts to be brought for some itching couple?

LI: Fie! The guests are due to arrive, and there you dawdle in a stupid daze. Make haste and draw the curtains, sweep the floor and arrange the chairs.   20

MAID: Always at your service, ma'am. [MISTRESS LI *directs her.*]

YANG WEN-TS'UNG: [*Entering in festive garb, singing.*]

> Like red embroidery, the peach blossoms
> Make patterns on the lady's banquet board;
> The screens are spread like golden peacocks' tails;
> Scent floats from the heraldic incense-burner.   25
> The crimson lady seated by the stove[3]
> Is the ideal mate for him to cherish.

---

3. An allusion to Ssu-ma Hsiáng-ju (died 117 B.C.), a Han Dynasty poet whose singing so captivated the young widow Cho Wen-chün that she eloped with him. They set up a small wine shop, where she served the customers and he washed the cups. Shamed by such bohemian conduct, her wealthy father took them back into his favor. Ssu-ma's fame as a poet reached Emperor Wu-ti, who appointed him to high office.

[*Speaks.*] I have come on behalf of Juan Ta-ch'eng to deliver the wedding gifts. Where is Mistress Li?

LI: [*Coming to greet him.*] A thousand thanks for helping to arrange this match. The feast is ready, but where is His Honour Hou? 30

YANG: I imagine he will soon be with us. I have brought a selection of dresses for Fragrant Princess's wardrobe. [*To* MAID, *who brings in chests containing hair ornaments and gowns.*] Take them into the bridal chamber and set them out neatly. [MAID *exits.*] 35

LI: Such an expense—how kind of you!

YANG: [*Drawing silver bars from his sleeve.*] Here are thirty *taels* of silver, to provide the best wines and dishes for the banquet.

LI: You are far too generous! [*She calls* FRAGRANT PRINCESS, *who enters magnificently dressed.*] His Honour Yang has showered so many 40 presents on you that you ought to thank him. [FRAGRANT PRINCESS *curtseys.*]

YANG: These are mere trifles, no need for such ceremony. Please retire to your boudoir. [*Exit* FRAGRANT PRINCESS.]

MAID: [*Entering breathlessly.*] The bridegroom has arrived.

HOU: [*Entering in his best clothes, followed by several* SERVANTS.] Though I did not win the highest degree in the examinations, I 45 now belong to the realm of the Moon Goddess.[4]

YANG: Congratulations, brother! You have won the paragon of feminine beauty. In token of my regard for you, I could only bring these paltry offerings as a contribution to your household expenses. I only hope they will add to the evening's enjoyment. 50

HOU: I am struck speechless by your munificence.

LI: Pray sit down and have some tea. [ALL *sit down. The* MAID *waits on them.*]

YANG: Is everything ready for the feast?

LI: Thanks to Your Honour, the arrangements are complete.

YANG: [*To* HOU.] I won't intrude on your private rejoicings. Tomorrow 55 I shall return to congratulate you again.

HOU: Why don't you join the party?

YANG: In my position that would not be proper.[5] [*He takes his leave.*]

MAID: May I remind the bridegroom that it is time for him to change? [HOU, *onstage, is assisted in removing his gown and donning a new one.*]

LI: I must go and help the bride to dress for the banquet. [*Exit.*] 60 [*Three male guests appear:* TING CHI-CHIH, SHEN KUNG-HSIEN, *and* CHANG YEN-CHU.]

THREE GUESTS: [*Recite.*]

> Poet-singers are we
> Like Chang Hsien and Li Erh[6] of old.

[*Each announces his name. Then, together, they say*]:
We have come to attend the auspicious banquet for His Honour Hou, and we are punctual to the minute.

CHANG: I wonder which of the girls I shall sit next to? 65

---

4. Successful examination candidates were eulogized as having plucked the blossoms of the mythical cassia tree tended by the goddess in the moon.   5. Yang had been the principal matchmaker.   6. A dramatist (14th century). Chang Hsien (11th century), a song lyricist.

SHEN: I hear that there will be several queens of their profession.

CHANG: Then we should have no difficulty in winning their favours.

TING: But are you rich enough to afford such luxuries?

CHANG: Everybody can get some outside help. Look at His Honour Hou. Has he had to spend a penny of his own on this? 70

SHEN: Stop gossiping. He is changing his clothes upstairs. Let us go and greet him. [*Together bowing to* HOU, *who is still on stage.*]

THREE GUESTS: Congratulations!

HOU: I thank you all for coming.

[*Enter three singing-girls:* PIEN YÜ-CHING, K'OU PAI-MEN, *and* CHENG T'O-NIANG.]

THREE GIRLS: Our passions run riot like grass, ever in a pleasant state 75 of titillation. And though we are as delicate as willow catkins, we are kept busy night and day. [*They greet the guests.*]

CHANG: From which pavilion of delight have you ladies sprung? Please announce your names.

FIRST GIRL: Are you the director of the conservatoire[7] to ask us such a 80 question?

HOU: [*Laughing, to* FIRST GIRL.] I should be happy to learn your honourable name.

FIRST GIRL: Your humble servant's name is Pien Yü-ching, "Jade Capital." 85

HOU: "Fairy from the Jade Capital" would be more suitable.

SECOND GIRL: And my name is K'ou Pai-men, "White Gate."

HOU: You truly deserve it.

THIRD GIRL: [*A clown.*] And I'm Cheng T'o-niang, "Lady Safety."

HOU: You certainly look quite safe. 90

CHANG: I'm afraid I don't agree.

SHEN: Why not?

CHANG: She would never be safe, from her husband's point of view.

CHENG: You should be ashamed of yourself. If I had not stuck to my job, you would never have grown so fat on overfeeding! [*General* 95 *laughter.*]

PIEN: Since the bridegroom is ready, let us ask Fragrant Princess to join him. [MISTRESS LI *leads* FRAGRANT PRINCESS *in.*]

SHEN: We should welcome the bride with music.

[CHANG, TING, *and* SHEN *play music on the right side of the stage.* BRIDE *and* GROOM *greet each other.*]

CHENG: It isn't the custom in our houses to perform the ceremonies of worship, so we can go straight to the celebration wine.[8] 100

[BRIDE *and* GROOM *take their seats, center; the* THREE SINGING-GIRLS *sit near, at left. The* MAID *brings wine, which is served from the left.*]

HOU: [*Sings.*]

> In the company of famous flowers and willows,
> Daily I write of love in jewelled rhymes,

---

7. The state-sponsored orchestra.   8. Since Hou and Fragrant Princess have not performed the ceremonies of obeisance to Heaven and earth and the ancestors, their "marriage" is more an expression of intention than a strict legal contract. This is why Fragrant Princess can later be urged to "marry again"— without need of divorce from Hou.

Like Tu Mu[9] of Yangchow, clad in silken robes,
Entirely given to painting my beauty's eyebrows
And teaching her perfection on the flute.   105
This very moment spring begins anew;
My fevered thirst will soon be quenched.
But oh, how slowly sinks the setting sun!
Meantime I'll drink another cup of wine.

FRAGRANT PRINCESS: [*Sings.*]

Flowers tremble on the terrace, curtains flutter.   110
My lord, so handsome and so elegant,
Withholds no mark of favour;
I shall be wife, not slave-girl, in his eyes,
And worthy must I prove;
A random flower still lovely,   115
A wild herb no less fragrant.
Under the glow of many scarlet lanterns,
Tonight I am to be the chosen bride.
Even adepts in the art of love would quail—
How fearful then a virgin's trepidation!   120

TING: Now that the red sun is swallowing the mountains and the crows are choosing their roosts, we should escort the young couple to their chamber.

SHEN: Why such haste? His Honour Hou is a distinguished man of letters who has won the heart of an exceptional beauty. He has   125
celebrated his happy union with wine, but poetry should not be neglected.

CHANG: You are right. I'll fetch ink and paper to wait upon his inspiration.

HOU: I need no paper, since I have a fan. I shall write a poem on it   130
for Fragrant Princess to keep as a lifelong token of my love.

CHENG: Marvelous! Let me hold the ink-slab for you.

LI: Such a freak is only fit to remove His Honour's shoes.

PIEN: Fragrant Princess should hold the ink-slab.

ALL: That is correct.   135

[FRAGRANT PRINCESS *does accordingly, while* HOU *writes on the fan.*
ALL *chant the words of his poem.*]

ALL: [*Chanting.*]

On a path between two rows of crimson towers,
The lucky Prince advances in his chariot.
From the magnolias he turns aside
To gaze in rapture at the breeze-blown peach blossoms.

ALL: What an exquisite poem! Fragrant Princess, mind you keep it   140
carefully. [FRAGRANT PRINCESS *puts the fan in her sleeve.*]

CHENG: Though we may not be as pretty as peach blossoms, why should he call us magnolias?

CHANG: Don't worry; the magnolia withers, but returns to life in the spring.   145

9. T'ang poet (803–852), famous for the number and beauty of his concubines and singing girls.

CHENG: That's as may be, but who will water my blossom?
MAID: [*Entering with a scroll.*] His Honour Yang has sent you these verses.
HOU: [*Takes it and reads aloud.*]

> Lady Fragrance was born with a beauty to overwhelm cities,
> Yet how demurely she yields to her lord's embrace! 150
> In his arms she is like the goddess of the twelve Magic Mountains,
> Appearing in a dream to the King of Ch'u.

HOU: That old gentleman shows a profound understanding of love. His verse is admirable.
CHANG: It is a fine evocation of Fragrant Princess's slender grace. She 155
reminds me of the jade pendant of a scented fan.
CHENG: Well, what's a jade pendant worth, anyway? At least I'm an amber one! [ALL *laugh.*]
TING: Let us have more music to inspire the young couple to drink.
CHENG: And excite them all the more to enter the love nest. 160
[*Wine and music follow.*]
HOU *and* FRAGRANT PRINCESS: [*Singing a duet.*]

> These golden cups create a thirst for wine,
> And friendly voices urge us on to drink.
> The hour is late; we droop with drowsiness,
> Furtively clasping hands, our eager eyes
> Look forward to a night of endless bliss, 165
> Longing to loosen our hibiscus clothes.
> Burn out, oh candles! Let the feast be done
> Ere the palace water-clock[1] its course has run!

TING: The second watch is announced; it is growing late. Let the banquet be cleared away. 170
CHANG: But we have not finished all the dishes. It would be a pity to remove them.
CHENG: I haven't eaten enough, either. Please wait awhile.
PIEN: Stop fussing. Let us escort the young couple with music to their chamber. 175
ALL: [*Singing.*]

> To the strains of pipes and flutes we descend the stair,
> Swaying to the lilt of songs under glowing lamplight.
> On yonder heavenly terrace the comely pair
> Will enter the 'broidered haven of scented curtains
> While others knit their brows with envy. Lo, 180
> How beautiful their wine-flushed self-abandon!
> Such love as this was certainly predestined.

[*Exeunt* HOU *and* FRAGRANT PRINCESS *hand in hand.*]
CHANG: Let us divide into couples and all go to bed together.
CHENG: Old Chang, you'd better not delude yourself. I'll take nothing

---

1. Used before mechanical clocks became widespread, it marked time by the slow draining of a fixed amount of water. Here the reference is to the passing of the night.

less than hard cash for favours. [CHANG *hands her ten coppers*[2] *and*   185
she counts them.]
ALL: [*Singing in chorus.*]

> The misty moon above the Ch'in-huai River
> Abides forever,
> Yet how much powder and rouge are washed away
> Day after day!
> Irrevocably love's supreme delight   190
> Is lost each night.

TING: South of the river grow the flowers, the current flows fast away.
K'OU: All who live on the river's banks are debonair and gay.
SHEN: Though your home be distant many a league, through clouds of
dust and spray,   195
PIEN: Here ballads of love are sung till break of day.

SCENE 7

The Rejected Trousseau

1643, third month

MAID: [*A clown, entering with a chamberpot, sings.*]

> Turtle-piss, turtle-piss,
> Little turtles come of this;
> Tortoise-blood, tortoise-blood,
> Turning into tortoise brood.
> Mixing, mating, copulating,   5
> Wholly undiscriminating,
> Never know who fathered who;
> Wouldn't matter if they knew.

[*Speaks.*] Ha, ha, hee hee! Yesterday Fragrant Princess lost her maid-
enhead and I lost half a night's sleep. Today I must rise early   10
to empty the chamberpot, but who knows how late the lucky lovebirds will slumber on? [*She scrubs out the pot.*]
YANG: [*Enters and sings.*]

> They sleep serene behind the willow screen.
> Flower-vendors cry outside the door, "Come buy!"
> Yet they dream on; the curtains never open.   15
> At last you hear the tinkling of jade hooks;[3]
> All spring is wrapped within those folds of silk.

[*Speaks.*] I have returned to congratulate His Honour Hou, but the
doors are closed and nobody seems to be stirring. They must be fast
asleep. [*Calls.*] Maid, please run to the young couple's window and   20
tell them that I have come to congratulate them.
MAID: They retired very late; I doubt if they have risen. Would you
mind returning tomorrow?
YANG: [*Laughing.*] Nonsense, you do as you're bid.

---

2. Coins.   3. Used to hold up the curtains when they were raised.

LI: [*From inside.*] Maid, who is there?   25
MAID: It's His Honour Yang come to offer congratulations.
LI: [*Still inside.*] Once heads touch pillow, how short the spring night
   seems! Then comes a knock at the door, always someone to inter-
   rupt! [*Greeting* YANG.] I must thank Your Honour for arranging this
   match.   30
YANG: Don't mention it. Where are the young couple?
LI: Please sit down while I call them. They have not risen yet.
YANG: Pray don't disturb them. [*Exit* MISTRESS LI. YANG *sings.*]

> Young love's like liquid honey fresh from flowers,
> So beautiful, so innocent and pure,   35
> Gently distilled in a dark world of dreams.

[*Says.*] Thanks to myself. [*Again singing.*]

> Pearls and emeralds glow
> And silken dresses flow,
> And every precious toy   40
> Is here for lover's joy.

LI: It was as pretty as a picture. The two of them were buttoning each
   other's clothes and gazing at each other's reflection in a mirror. They
   have just finished dressing. Will Your Honour step through to call
   them out for a cup of wine?   45
YANG: I am sorry to have interrupted their sweet dreams. [*Exeunt.*]
   [HOU *and* FRAGRANT PRINCESS *enter, dressed in their finest and singing together.*]
HOU *and* FRAGRANT PRINCESS: [*Singing.*]

> Cloud after cloud and shower after shower—
> Desire fulfilled without satiety!
> Who comes to rouse the lovebirds at this hour?
> The scarlet quilt is rolled into a billow;[4]   50
> Scent lingers on the coverlet and pillow;
> Throbbing with joy we rise as from a trance.

[*Enter* YANG *and* MISTRESS LI.]
YANG: So at last your have succeeded in rising! Congratulations! [*Sit-
   ting down.*] How did you like the poem I sent last night?
HOU: [*Bowing.*] It was a splendid composition. My only criticism is that   55
   Fragrant Princess, slender as she is, deserves to be kept in a house
   of pure gold.[5] How could I keep her under these sleeves of mine?

YANG: I expect you were also inspired to write poetry last night.
HOU: I merely improvised a little stanza.   60
YANG: Where is it?
FRAGRANT PRINCESS: On this fan. [*Drawing the fan from her sleeve.*]
YANG: [*Examining it.*] White silk, and what a graceful shape, what a
   subtle aroma! [*He chants the poem inscribed on it, and then recites.*]

---

4. Wave; here a metaphor for the bedcovers.   5. A reference to the Han emperor Wu-ti (140–87 B.C.),
a great patron of literature and student of Taoism. When he fell in love with his future consort, he remarked,
"If I could only win A-chiao, I would build a house of gold to keep her in."

> Like Tso Szu, your verse   65
> Sends up the price of paper in Loyang;
> Like P'an Yueh,[6]
> Your carriage draws all eyes.
> Beauteous and fragrant are the peach and apricot blossoms;
> Their very souls are captured on this fan.   70
> But of outer storms and treacherous winds beware!
> Preserve it under your sleeve with tender care!

[*Looking at* FRAGRANT PRINCESS, *he says.*] You are even lovelier since your nuptials. [*To* HOU.] How fortunate you are to have won such a prize.   75

HOU: Fragrant Princess was destined to be the beauty of her age, but today the pearls and emeralds in her hair and apparel display her charms to perfection.

FRAGRANT PRINCESS: [*To* YANG.] Thanks entirely to your munificence! [*Sings.*]

> You gave me the fillets to weave in my hair,   80
> And a casket of a hundred precious stones,
> Jewelled tassels for my curtain, and silver candlesticks,
> Lanterns of silk to shine all through the night,
> And golden cups for the wine that flows with song.

[*Speaks.*] And then, coming so soon to greet us like this! [*Sings.*]   85

> You have treated me as a daughter of your own,
> Having filled my wardrobe, you come to bless my union.

[*Speaks.*] Though related to General Ma, you are a stranger in this region. Why should you have incurred such expense for people like us? I feel deeply embarrassed, since you have been so extravagant   90 without any apparent motive. Please explain, so that I may make amends in future.

HOU: Fragrant Princess's question is opportune. Brother Yang and I chanced to meet like duckweed floating on water. These lavish gifts have made me quite uneasy.   95

YANG: Since you ask, I'll be candid. The dresses and banquet cost over two hundred *taels* of silver, all of which came from Huai-ning.

HOU: How do you mean, "from Huai-ning"?

YANG: From the former Minister Juan Ta-ch'eng, who is from Huai-ning.   100

HOU: Why should he have done this for me?

YANG: He is anxious to gain your friendship. [*Sings.*]

> He admires your talent and reputation,
> The fame of which is spreading far and wide.
> Since you sought a fair companion on the banks of the Ch'in-huai   105
>   River,
> Hibiscus wardrobe and mandarin duck quilts were indispensable.

---

6. P'an Yueh (see n. 8, p. 88) and Tso Szu won renown for their elegant rhapsodies in the last decades of the 3rd century. So many people wanted copies of Tso Szu's *Rhapsody on the Three Capitals* that, according to legend, the price of paper soared.

These were presented by Master Juan,
Your good neighbour from the south.

HOU: Old Juan was a classmate of my father's, but I have always   110
despised and avoided him. I am puzzled why he should show me
such kindness now.

YANG: He has various private troubles, and thinks you may be able to
help him.

HOU: What is the matter?   115

YANG: Juan was originally associated with our comrades. He only joined
the eunuch Wei Chung-hsien's faction to protect his friends of the
Eastern Forest Party, never dreaming that these would treat him so
shockingly since Wei's downfall. The Revival Club launched a campaign against him, and he was attacked and reviled by all its   120
members. It is just like a family feud. Juan's old cronies are so suspicious that none will step forward in his defence. In his utter
dejection, he keeps on saying: "That old friends should fall out like
this is deplorable. Only Master Hou can save me." Hence his anxiety
to gain your goodwill.   125

HOU: Now I understand. If he is in such distress as to need my help, I
pity him. Although he belonged to Wei's faction, he has repented of
it since. I disapprove of such violent extremes. Wu and Ch'en are
both close friends of mine. If I see them tomorrow, I shall try and
explain the situation to them.   130

YANG: That would be doing him a great kindness, and it would benefit
all concerned.

FRAGRANT PRINCESS: [*Indignantly to* HOU.] How can you say such
things, my honoured lord? Juan Ta-ch'eng shamelessly supported the
traitors; even women and children would gladly spit in his face. Yet   135
when others justly attack him, you propose to defend him. Consider
how this will affect your own position. [*Sings.*]

> How can you make such promises
> So thoughtlessly?
> Though you wish to save that creature from ruin,   140
> You must also bear in mind
> How others will judge yourself!

[*Speaks.*] Merely because he has done you a personal favour, you
forget the commonweal. Can't you see that I am indifferent to all
this finery? [*She removes her headdress and outer gown, singing.*]   145

> I care not whether I seem poor,
> Of lowly birth and station;
> In humble homespun I may win a virtuous reputation.

YANG: Dear me, what a fiery temper!

LI: The pity of it, the pity of it! Fancy throwing such precious things   150
all over the floor! [*She picks them up.*]

HOU: No! No! This is well done! Fragrant Princess has shown such
excellent judgment that I feel she is my superior in this. She is a
friend to be looked up to with respect and trembling! [*To* YANG.]
Please do not blame me, elder brother. Much as I should like to   155

oblige you, I am afraid I would be scorned by a woman if I did so. [*Sings.*]

> Though frivolous her profession,
> How keen her sense of justice and propriety.
> Shame on those
> Who belong to the Academy and the Emperor's Court,   160
> Yet cannot distinguish between blue and yellow!

[*Speaks.*] In the past I have won the respect of my colleagues on account of my firm convictions. If I compromised with a traitor, I would become a target myself. Why should I defend such a villain? [*Sings.*]

> One should never risk losing   165
> One's character and reputation.
> The serious and the trivial
> Must be clearly distinguished.

YANG: But old Juan has taken such pains to please you. I beg you not to send him a flat refusal.   170
HOU: I may be foolish, but I won't throw myself into a well on his behalf.
YANG: Then I had better say goodbye.
HOU: All those things in the wardrobe belong to old Juan. Since Fragrant Princess will not use them, please take them away.   175
YANG: This is a bitter disappointment. [*Exit, while* FRAGRANT PRINCESS *stares angrily after him.*]
HOU: My Fragrant Princess was born a great beauty without jewelled ornaments, and she is even lovelier without her satin gown.
LI: All the same, it was a pity to lose those valuable gifts. [*Sings.*]

> When gold and pearls are in your hand,   180
> Heedless you let them slip away
> Daughter, you fail to understand
> All that your mother had to pay.

HOU: Those trifles are not worth worrying about. I shall find others for her.   185
LI: That will be ample compensation. [*Sings.*]

> For the cost of powder and rouge do have a care.

FRAGRANT PRINCESS: I do not mind what simple clothes I wear.
HOU: Only such beauty could have such wisdom rare.
FRAGRANT PRINCESS: Distinction's free from fashion's passing flare.   190

*   *   *

Scenes 8 to 22 Summary   The plot becomes complicated, as Hou Fang-yü is drawn into political intrigues and the ever-worsening military crisis that besets the empire. The scene shifts to the camp of one of the Ming armies stationed near Nanking. General Tso Liang-yü, who had once been a protégé of Hou Fang-yü's father, is faced with the threat of mutiny because of lack of provisions. To placate his troops Tso Liang-yü is forced to violate his orders and move the army to the east. This move suggests rebellion and greatly worries the commandant of Nanking. Yang Wen-ts'ung reports this news to Hou Fang-yü and asks him, as the son of Tso Liang-yü's former commanding officer, to write a letter to Tso asking him to halt his advance. A story-teller, Liu Ching-t'ing, offers to carry the letter and persuade the general.

The civil and military officials of Nanking, including Juan Ta-ch'eng and Yang Wen-ts'ung, meet to decide what action to take in face of the situation. Because of his grudge against Hou, Juan denounces Hou Fang-yü as plotting rebellion with Tso, but Yang protests, and General Shih K'o-fa does not believe the charge. Nevertheless the military governor, Ma Shih-ying (eventually revealed as a major villain together with Juan Ta-ch'eng), is persuaded and orders Hou Fang-yü's arrest. Yang Wen-ts'ung hurries off to warn Hou, who is forced to part from Fragrant Princess and to flee to Shih K'o-fa for protection.

Eventually grain arrives for Tso's army, but news also comes that rebels have taken Peking, the Ming emperor has hanged himself, and the crown prince has disappeared. When one clique in Nanking wishes to put Prince Fu on the throne, Hou Fang-yü presents a strong case against it to General Shih K'o-fa. Nevertheless, Ma Shih-ying, working with Juan Ta-ch'eng, succeeds in enthroning Prince Fu; for he knows Prince Fu's weaknesses and believes he can manipulate the new emperor. Among the many appointments made by the new government is a kinsman of Yang Wen-ts'ung, and Yang suggests that he purchase Fragrant Princess as his concubine. Fragrant Princess absolutely refuses, determined to keep faith with Hou Fang-yü. Meanwhile to the north, the Manchus have moved into China and ousted the Chinese rebels from Peking; the Ming armies under the command of Shih K'o-fa are torn apart by internal rivalries and will prove ineffective in blocking the Manchus' southward advance. With this ends the first part of the play.

An interlude follows, beginning with a discussion at an inn between three travelers making their way south to Nanking on the Night of All Souls Festival, when the dead walk the earth. The three will play important roles in the second half of the play. The first is Lan Ying, a painter; the second is Ts'ai Yi-so, a bookseller; and the third is Chang Wei, an officer in the Imperial Guard, who has personally buried the last Ming emperor. After they fall asleep, a storm blows up, bringing with it the ghosts of the Ming emperor and empress, along with all who died in the wars in the north. Chang Wei, who rises and sees the procession of souls, vows to carry out a proper memorial service for the dead Ming emperor in Nanking on the same day in the following year.

As the second half of the play begins, the villain Ma Shih-ying, now prime minister, and Juan Ta-ch'eng hear from Yang Wen-ts'ung of Fragrant Princess's refusal to accept the proposal. Juan Ta-ch'eng is enraged and orders that she be forced to marry Yang's kinsman. When Yang Wen-ts'ung and Li Chen-li try to drag her downstairs, Fragrant Princess bangs her head on the floor until she knocks herself out, spattering her fan with blood. Horrified, Li Chen-li offers to take Fragrant Princess's place.

From *Part II*

SCENE 23

The Message on the Fan

1644, eleventh month

[FRAGRANT PRINCESS *enters, looking pale and wan.*]
FRAGRANT PRINCESS: [*Sings.*]

> The cold wind pierces my thin gown,
> I am too weary to burn incense.

A streak of bright blood still glistens on my eyebrow.
My languid soul floats over my lone shadow;
My life is spring gossamer in this frosty moonlit tower.   5
The night seems endless:
When dawn appears, the same grief lingers on.

[*Speaks.*] In a moment of despair, I tore my flesh to defend my virtue.
Alone, I peek and pine in my empty room. I have lost my sole companion. [*Sings.*]   10

> Long Bridge is wrapped in cloud and frozen snow,
> My tower is closed and visitors are few.
> Beyond the balustrade, a line of wild geese;
> Outside the curtain, icicles are dripping.
> The brazier is burnt out, all perfume faded—   15
> I shrink and shiver in the biting wind.

[*Speaks.*] Though I live in a pleasure resort, the flowers and moon
have ceased to bring me joy. I have done with worldly vanities.
[*Sings.*]

> My 'broidered window curtain is forlorn,
> Though the parrot's foolish voice cries "Serving tea,"   20
> And the white cat sleeps serenely on its cushion.
> So loose my skirt, it flaps about my waist;
> So tired my feet, their phoenix-patterned shoes
> Feel tossed upon the crests of boisterous waves.
> Excess of grief breeds sickness. Love and joy   25
> Have fled this chamber never to return.

[*Speaks.*] I never cease thinking of my beloved lord. Since his flight
I have had no news of him, but I shall preserve my chastity for his
sake. [*Sings.*]

> In a twinkling, our song of rapture was interrupted;   30
> At midnight the passionate lovers had to part.
> Neither at Swallow Cliff nor Peach-leaf Wharf⁷
> Shall my true love be seen.
> Over the mazy clouds and windy mountains
> The solitary swan has taken flight.   35
> Each year the blossoms of the plum return,
> Each year my love is ever more remote.
> From my balcony, I gaze into the distance,
> My falling tears like pools of autumn rain
> Which only the harsh wind will ever dry.   40

[*Speaks.*] The Prime Minister's sycophants would have forced me to
marry, but how could I betray my lord? [*Sings.*]

> They persecute me, feeble blossom afloat on the mist,
> Helpless before the arrogance of these ministers.
> But to preserve my purity, jade without flaw,   45
> Gladly I wound the flower-like bloom of my cheeks.

---

7. Famous beautiful spots where lovers used to meet.

[*Speaks.*] My poor mother is most to be pitied! Suddenly she left without a word, to take my place on that disastrous night. Her bed remains, but when will she return? [*Sings.*]

> Like a peach petal adrift in a snowstorm, 50
> Like a willow catkin wafted by the wind,
> Hiding her face behind her sleeve, she left at dead of night.
> Now I am left alone,
> No one to brush the dust from my coverlet,
> Desolate, 55
> A flower that opens for none to view.

[*Speaks.*] When I think of all this, I am heartbroken. [*She weeps and sings.*]

> A broken heart,
> How many tears that fall!
> And never a companion's cheery call, 60
> Only the knocking of the curtain-hooks.

[*Speaks.*] I shall take out my precious fan again and read my beloved's poem. Ah me, it is stained with blood. What shall I do? [*Sings.*]

> The bloodstains spread in bright confusion,
> Some thick, some thin, some heavy and some light; 65
> Not the cuckoo's tears of blood,
> But raindrops reddened by the peachbloom of my cheeks
> Spattering this silken fan.

[*Speaks.*] My lord, my lord! All this was for your sake! [*Sings.*]

> I tore my cloudy hair and bruised my limbs 70
> Until I swooned into a world of darkness,
> Like a long-buried queen beneath a hill-slope.
> Dripping with blood, my body seemed to fall
> As from the summit of the highest tower,
> Unconscious of the voices calling me; 75
> My melting soul past human invocation.
> The red clouds darken in the setting sun:
> I wake to find my pillow drenched with tears.
> Sorrow is graven on my heart and brow,
> Washing the rouge from my face, 80
> Staining the silk of my robe.

[*Speaks.*] I'm so overwhelmed with weariness that I shall fall asleep at this table. [*She dozes off, clutching her fan.*]

YANG WEN-TS'UNG: [*Enters and recites.*]

> The tower a slanting shadow throws
> Over the stream, and nesting crows 85
> Caw in the withered willow boughs.

SU K'UN-SHENG: [*Entering.*]

> This chamber where sweet music used to flow,
> Is now a hermit's cell where wild winds blow.

YANG: Oh Master Su, I'm so glad to see you again.

SU: Since Mistress Li's departure, Fragrant Princess has been living 90
here alone. I felt anxious about her, so I came to pay her a visit.

YANG: The night of Mistress Li's departure, I kept vigil with Fragrant
Princess till dawn. Since then I have been so occupied with official
business that I have not been able to see her. [*They enter the house
together.*]

SU: Fragrant Princess will never come downstairs. Let us go up and 95
see her. [*Both walk upstairs to find* FRAGRANT PRINCESS *asleep.*]

YANG: How ill and woebegone she looks in her sleep. We ought not to
wake her.

SU: The fan lies open before her. But why is it splashed with red?

YANG: This was Brother Hou's gift of betrothal. She treasured it above 100
everything in the world and was always reluctant to show it. Finding
it stained with her blood, she must have intended to dry it. [*Examining it.*] The stains are still very bright. I'll paint a few leaves and
twigs around them, so that it will resemble a picture of peach blossoms. Unfortunately, I lack green paint. 105

SU: If I squeeze some sap from the plant in yonder vase, perhaps you
may use it instead.

YANG: What a clever idea. [SU *procures him some, and* YANG *proceeds
to paint, reciting.*]

> The leaves are green with the sap of a fragrant plant
> To protect the blossoms dyed in a beauty's blood. 110

SU: This is the finest picture of peach blossoms I have seen.

YANG: It is a genuine peach blossom fan.

FRAGRANT PRINCESS: [*Waking up.*] O gentlemen, forgive my lack of
courtesy! Pray sit down.

YANG: The wound on your forehead looks almost healed. [*Laughing.*] 115
I have brought you a little gift—on which I have painted some peach
blossoms. [*Hands it to her.*]

FRAGRANT PRINCESS: But this is my old fan. As it is covered with bloodstains, I would rather not look at it. [*Puts it in her sleeve.*]

SU: But there is an exquisite picture which you really ought to see. 120

FRAGRANT PRINCESS: When was it painted?

YANG: Forgive me for not asking permission. I fear I might have spoiled
it.

FRAGRANT PRINCESS: [*Opening and examining it.*] Alas, peach blossom
is the most ill-fated of flowers, condemned to float forever on 125
this fan. I thank Your Honour. You have almost painted a portrait of
myself. [*Sings.*]

> Each branch a swaying sorrow in the wind,
> Each petal a lost soul swept by the rising tide.
> Only a master's hand could render thus 130
> A vivid line so natural, evoking
> The lips of beauty and the lotus cheek.
> A few bold strokes, and the tree springs to life,
> Red petals and green leaves; but evil fate
> Awaits the pictured flower and its possessor. 135

YANG: Now that you have this peach blossom fan, you need a partner
to appreciate it with you. Why turn yourself into a widow? Do you
want to be like the Moon Goddess who flew from the world?[8]

FRAGRANT PRINCESS: What is the use of discussing it? The famous
Kuan P'an-p'an[9] was also a professional singing-girl, but she lived   140
alone in her Swallow Tower until extreme old age.

SU: Supposing Master Hou returned tomorrow, would you promptly
recover your spirits and come downstairs?

FRAGRANT PRINCESS: Ah, then the whole world would be different. I
should feel as if my future were spread out like a beautiful tapestry.   145
Not only would I leave this tower, I would travel anywhere.

YANG: Such steadfast resolve is most unusual. Master Su, to prove your
devoted relationship as teacher to pupil, would you try to find
Brother Hou and bring them together again? I am sure it would be
a blessing for all concerned.   150

SU: After repeated inquiries, I finally discovered that he spent half a
year in Huai-an-fu with Minister Shih, whence he proceeded to
Yang-chou by way of Nanking. He is at present with General Kao's
army defending the Yellow River. I had intended to return to my
home, so I may search for him on the journey. But I should have a   155
letter from Fragrant Princess to take with me.

FRAGRANT PRINCESS: [To YANG.] Though my thoughts and emotions
are boundless, I have never been trained to express them in writing.
Would Your Honour be so kind as to write the letter for me?

YANG: How could I express what lies in the depths of your heart?   160

FRAGRANT PRINCESS: [Pensively.] All my fears and sorrows are associated with this fan. Perhaps it will suffice if you merely take it to him.

SU: What an original notion, to use a fan as a letter!

FRAGRANT PRINCESS: I'll seal it now. [She seals it, singing.]   165

> The poem he will recognize as the fruit of his flourishing brush,
> The red blossoms he will see as a new picture.
> So small a space holds the blood of a faithful heart,
> Ten thousand longings bound with silken strands—
> It is worth a volume of characters on paper.   170

SU: I promise to deliver it safely to his hands.

FRAGRANT PRINCESS: When will you start on the journey, Master?

SU: Within the next few days.

FRAGRANT PRINCESS: I hope you will set out as soon as possible.

YANG: It is time for our departure. Fragrant Princess, take care of your-   175
self! The hardship you have suffered for purity's sake deserves the
highest credit. When Brother Hou hears of it, he will certainly hasten
to see you.

SU: I may not have time to say goodbye before I leave. Truly, a new
message on the peach blossom fan.   180

YANG: An old constancy, locked in the Swallow Tower.

---

8. According to legend, Ch'ang O, the goddess of the moon, stole the elixir of immortality and flew away
to the moon, where she lives alone for all eternity.   9. Brilliant dancer and singer who became the favorite
of Chang Chien (died 651), a great-nephew of the founder of the T'ang Dynasty. When he died, P'an-p'an
refused to marry and lived alone in the Swallow Tower for ten years.

[*Exeunt* YANG *and* SU.]

FRAGRANT PRINCESS: [*Weeping.*] My mother has left me, and now my
dear teacher has gone. Alone in this room, my sorrows will seem
eternal. [*Sings.*]

I have ceased to sing the ballads of north and south,   185
My lute is silent, nor do I touch the flute:
I have thrust aside my instruments, and left them to rot away.
If only my fan could reach him soon, and my teacher were on his way!
When my lord returns, upon that joyful day,
Hand in hand we shall leave the tower together.   190
I hope my message reaches him before the snow has melted,
Though hills and vales seem endless on the voyage.

*   *   *

Scenes 24 to 27 Summary   At a party attended by Yang Wen-ts'ung, Juan Ta-
ch'eng and Ma Shih-ying, a group of singing girls—including Fragrant Princess—is
called to perform. Fragrant Princess denounces Juan and Ma, and they have her sent
to the palace, where she will be forced to play the role of clown in Juan Ta-ch'eng's
play *Swallow Letter*, for the newly enthroned Prince Fu, who is a devotee of the
theater. Prince Fu admires her and decides to keep her as an actress in the imperial
troupe.

Meanwhile in the north Hou Fang-yü has been sent by Shih K'o-fa to serve on the
staff of one of his subordinate generals. The general is killed in a private feud, and
Hou is forced to flee. On the river, Hou chances to meet Li Chen-li, who has been
sold again by the man who bought her as a concubine. At the same time, they encounter Su K'un-sheng, who is carrying the peach blossom fan as a token from Fragrant
Princess to show her love. Hou returns to Nanking and goes to Fragrant Princess's
lodgings only to discover that they are occupied by the painter Lan Ying.

SCENE 28

The Painting Inscribed

1645, third month

[*Enter* LAN YING *in the garb of a mountain hermit.*]

LAN: [*Recites.*]

Listless she sits, the incense cold, her embroidery neglected,
The peach-flowers open, but the garden gate is shut.
In the limitless mists and rain of the rising spring,
All that's left of the Southern courts are these painted hills.

[*Speaks.*] From early youth I have won fame as a painter. I heard   5
that my old friend Yang Wen-ts'ung has recently been appointed to
a post in the Ministry of War, and I bought a boat and came to visit
him. He has persuaded me to lodge in this Tower of Enchanted
Fragrance, which used to be the home of the celebrated singing-girl
Fragrant Princess. Since her departure the house has been   10
empty, but it is quiet enough to suit me. I shall now return to my
painting. [*He washes his ink-stone and painting-brush, and mixes the
pigment.*] But where can I find pure water? Ah, I had almost for-

gotten that the morning dew on leaves and flowers is the purest
for mixing colours. I'll gather some in the garden. [*Exits with a*   15
cup.]

HOU: [*Enters and sings.*]

> I have roamed between earth below and Heaven above,
> My heart ever bound by a thread of perfect love.
> Now the lanes are full of willow catkins; lo,
> They float while swallows flutter to and fro.
> Seeing the familiar house, the crimson tower,   20
> My tenderest feelings like green meadows flower,
> Fresh longings rise and fall in a misty shower.

[*Speaks.*] After meeting Su K'un-sheng on the Yellow River, I curbed
my excitement and travelled with him to Nanking. This morning I
left him at an inn, and came alone to look for Fragrant Princess.   25
How wonderful to see the Old House again! [*Sings.*]

> So little trace of human habitation,
> The birds are twittering in consternation.
> The walls are crumbling among weeds in piles,
> And green moss gathers on the lustrous tiles   30
> Beside the blossoms which should harmonize
> With her fair features. Now my spirit flies
> To meet my love and gaze into her eyes.

[*Pushing the door, he says.*] Oh, the doors are not locked! I'll walk in
and see who is there. [*Sings.*]   35

> My footsteps startle the birds and raise a squall,
> While mud from nests drops down into the hall;
> It seems this empty hall, where no man follows,
> Provides the perfect mating-place for swallows.
> I'll steal on tiptoe till I reach her room . . .   40

[*Speaks.*] Here is the Tower of Enchanted Fragrance—but oh, how
desolate! Though it is daytime, the curtains are drawn. Perhaps she
is still asleep. Instead of rousing her, I shall creep up the Tower and
stand beside her bed. When she wakes up and recognizes me, what
rapture we shall share! [*Sings.*]   45

> Clutching my gown, I part the drooping branches,
> And climb the crumbling staircase step by step,
> Among the dust and cobwebs. Out-of-doors
> The spring is all-pervading.
> Why does my love retire behind her curtains?   50

[*Seeing the bare table, he sings.*]

> Since when has she banished her lute?
> And all these pigments in boxes and jars:
> Has she become a recluse who paints for a living?

[*Speaks.*] The tower of song and dance has been turned into a studio.
How strange! I wonder why. . . . Perhaps to protect her virtue,   55
she wished to forget the arts of her vocation. Perhaps she hoped to

express her lonely thoughts with her brush. Here is her bedroom. I'll open the door gently. Why is it barred? It seems to have been so for ages. This is very strange. Is there no caretaker in the house? [*Sings.*]

> The room is forlorn; my beauty's far away, 60
> Where has she fled beyond the myriad hills,
> Locking her door? Maybe the birds can tell.
> Light-heartedly they frolic in the air,
> Heedless of my fond question. In despair
> I turn; by yonder hedge the twigs are stirring, 65
> A curtain rustles: do I hear her breathe?

[LAN *enters with a jar. Seeing* HOU, *he starts with surprise.*]

LAN: Who are you, sir? And why do you come to my tower?

HOU: It belongs to my beloved Fragrant Princess. I was about to ask you the same question.

LAN: I am an artist, and my name is Lan Ying. My friend Yang Wen- 70
ts'ung invited me to stay here.

HOU: So you are the eminent painter! I have long been your distant admirer. [LAN *asks his name, and* HAN *answers.*] I am also acquainted with Master Yang, and my name is Hou Fang-yü.

LAN: Your literary fame has even reached my ears. What good fortune 75
has brought us together? Pray sit down.

HOU: First of all, please tell me where is my Fragrant Princess?

LAN: I have heard that she has been removed to the Inner Palace.

HOU: [*In amazement.*] But how and when did that happen?

LAN: I'm afraid I do not know. 80

HOU: [*Wiping away tears, sings.*]

> After searching everywhere,
> I stand alone in the east wind.
> It is clear noon,
> But she is not to be seen.

[*Looking round.*]

> The window-paper and the curtain-gauze are torn. 85
> No relic of her remains;
> Neither an old scarf or hairpin,
> Nor the familiar flute.
> Her mandarin-duck quilts are put away;
> The mirrors are turned face down. 90
> There is no beauty left for the flowers to compete with.

[*Speaks.*] The peach trees were in full blossom on our marriage day. This tower had been newly decorated; now, no sooner has she left than it looks desolate again. I return to find the peach trees again in flower. How can I check my tears at the sight of them? [*Sings.*] 95

> Their petals flutter in the light spring breeze.
> Gossamer fills the air like snowflakes,
> Petals fall and scatter.

[*Speaks.*] I'll look at the peach blossoms on my fan. [*Sings.*]

> Painted in blood, 100
> Brighter petals are here than on the trees.

[*Speaks.*] And I was responsible for them. [*Sings.*]

> Opening this fan,
> Here in the desolation of her boudoir,
> I realize it was this very peach bloom 105
> That joined her fate with mine, to live or die.

LAN: Who painted this fan of yours?
HOU: Your distinguished patron, Master Yang.
LAN: But why does it make you weep?
HOU: This fan is the tangible token of our vow. [*Sings.*] 110

> Full of tenderness she held the ink-stone;
> In the candlelight she asked me for a poem.
> Thus line by line, I wrote a vow of love.

[*Speaks.*] But within less than a month, I had to escape my foes. Fragrant Princess segregated herself for my sake, and by doing so 115 she offended the ruling powers. They sent bloodhounds after her and drove her from her tower, so that in despair she tried to destroy her beauty. Still clutching this fan, she stained it with her blood.
LAN: Your story has moved me deeply.
HOU: Our friend Yang painted in a few leaves and converted it into a 120 peach blossom fan. It is my only keepsake of my beloved.
LAN: The brushwork is so skillful that one cannot detect the blood-stains. How did you recover it?
HOU: Fragrant Princess sent her teacher to search for me, taking it instead of a letter. Immediately upon receiving it, I made this jour- 125 ney, never dreaming that she would have been removed to the Imperial Palace. [*Weeps.*]

[*Enter* YANG WEN-TS'UNG, *with attendants to clear the way for him.*]
YANG: The Beauty is long gone from her tower, but in her place is installed a famous painter.
SERVANT: [*Comes in and announces.*] His Honour Yang has come to 130 visit Master Lan.

[YANG *steps out of his sedan-chair.* LAN *advances to meet him and escorts him upstairs.*]
YANG: [*Seeing* HOU.] When did you arrive, Brother Hou?
HOU: This very day, so I have not yet had time to visit you.
YANG: I heard that you were on the staff of His Excellency Shih, and also that you accompanied Kao Chieh to the Yellow River. This 135 morning I read an official report that Kao was murdered last month by Hsu Ting-kuo. Where were you in the meantime?
HOU: At home in my native village. On hearing of that disaster, I had to escape with my father into the hills, and there we stayed a month. Then I was warned that Hsu might send soldiers in pursuit 140 of me, so I hired a boat and came south. On the way I chanced to

meet Su K'un-sheng, who was searching for me. So I hurried to Nanking to find Fragrant Princess, or rather to find her gone. Where is she now?[1]

YANG: She was taken to the palace on the eighth of the first month.   145

HOU: When will she be able to leave it?

YANG: I cannot tell.

HOU: Then I shall have to wait here until she is set free.

YANG: There is no sense in that. You should find some other beauty to replace her.   150

HOU: How could I break my vow? You do not understand. If I could only obtain a message from her I would have a grain of comfort. [*Sings.*]

> Her dwelling, close at hand,
> Seems as remote as the sky.
> How can I find a fairy maiden   155
> To smuggle a letter to her?
> She has left the blossom-shaded tower,
> The wine pavilions, shrouded in mist and rain,
> And languishes unwilling in the palace;
> While I, her husband, wait at the far horizon   160
> Where each day seems a year.

YANG: Don't distress yourself unduly, Brother Hou. Let us watch Brother Lan at his painting. [YANG *and* HOU *sit beside* LAN *as he paints.* YANG *asks.*] Is this a picture of the Peach Blossom Fountain?[2]

LAN: You are right.   165

YANG: For whom are you painting it?

LAN: For Chang Wei, the Commanding Officer of the Imperial Guard. The picture is to be mounted on a screen for the Pine Wind Pavilion he has recently finished building.

HOU: I congratulate you on its fine qualities. Both the color and the   170
composition are extremely original, quite different from the traditional school of Nanking.

LAN: Thank you for taking so much notice of it. Would you kindly grace it with an inscription? That would increase its value considerably.   175

HOU: If you are not afraid of my spoiling such a work of art, I shall practice my lame calligraphy upon it. [*He composes a quatrain for the inscription.*]

> "I dwelt in the hidden cave by Peach Blossom Fountain,
> But on my way back I could not find the road.
> For the fisherman had misled me over the mountain,   180
> To keep this sanctuary for his own abode."

[*He signs his name to it.*]

YANG: Three are several recondite[3] allusions in your poem. You appear to blame me somewhat.

HOU: No, there you are mistaken. [*Points to the painting and sings.*]

---

1. Though aware of the facts, he evidently requires verbal confirmation from Yang, whose conduct has been ambiguous.   2. See n. 5, p. 82.   3. Obscure.

> How lovely the rippling brook,   185
> Where thousands of crimson petals fall,
> And streaks of cloud drift over
> Dense woods and far blue hills!
> The place remains the same,
> But no love is there to welcome me.   190
> The cave at Peach Blossom Spring is desolate;
> I turn back my boat as the sun sets.

[HOU *rises*.]

YANG: It is useless to repine, brother. Now Ma and Juan are in power, and you know how vindictive they are. Though intimate with both of them, I dare not appeal on behalf of either of you, especially since   195
the New Year's banquet when Fragrant Princess was asked to sing. Instead of singing, she pointed at Ma and Juan and denounced them to their faces.

HOU: Alas! I fear she must have been tortured in consequence.

YANG: Luckily I was present. I tried my best to calm their indignation,   200
so she was only cast out into the snow. No doubt she was distressed, but as long as she is in the Inner Court her life will be protected. But your connection with her is too well known, and you had better not remain here.

HOU: Thank you for the warning. [*Sings.*]   205

> Though my enemies use all their power against me,
> I'll clasp the peach blossom fan to my heart.

[*He turns abruptly to leave.*]

YANG: Let us bid Brother Lan farewell and leave together.

HOU: Forgive me; I had forgotten to say goodbye.
[*Farewells are exchanged. Exit* LAN *first, closing the door.* HOU *and* YANG *walk off together, singing.*]

HOU: Bewildered by this return to the crimson tower,   210

YANG: Idly we watched the painter at his task.

HOU: The beauty and her lover are cast asunder,

YANG: But peach flowers are as fine this year as last.

SCENE 29

The Club Suppressed

1645, third month

[*Enter* TS'AI YI-SO, *the bookseller.*]

TS'AI: [*Sings.*]

> In my shop, like the famous caves of Yu-shan,
> A myriad precious volumes are assembled;
> My labours as a collector have won for me
> Both learned reputation and hard cash.
> A scholar-merchant, I, who only hope   5
> To avoid any book-burning First Emperor of Ch'in!

[*Speaks.*] Nanking ranks first among cities for the wealth of its books, and most of these are in Three Mountain Street, where I keep the

largest bookshop. [*Points.*] Here are the Thirteen Canons, the
twenty-one Dynastic Histories,[4] all the tomes of the nine schools   10
of philosophy, of the three religions and the hundred thinkers,
besides collections of eight-legged essays[5] and fashionable modern
novels. They cram the shelves and innumerable boxes and rooms. I
have travelled north and south to gather this collection, minutely
examining old editions to make fine reprints with scholarly anno-   15
tations. As well as earning a handsome profit by these transactions,
I have helped to preserve and circulate the noblest thoughts of mankind. Even the doctors and masters of literature greet me with deference. I have reason to be satisfied with my reputation. [*He laughs.*]
This year the general civil service examination will be held again,   20
and the finest literary talents will receive due honour. The government has endorsed a proposal by the Minister of Ceremonies, Ch'ien
Ch'ien-i, advocating a new style of writing to express the spirit of the
new reign. Consequently I have invited several leading critics to com-
pile anthologies as models for composition. They will start work   25
today. I'll hang up my latest advertisement. [*He hangs a couplet on
each side of the door, which he reads.*]

> "The style in vogue was created by men of renown,
> Imitation of these models will please the chief examiner."

[*Exit.*]

[*Enter* HOU FANG-YÜ *and* SU K'UN-SHENG, *with baggage.*]
HOU: [*Sings.*]

> The moonlit tower of those bygone years
> Is far off as a dream;   30
> And the sound of pipes is stilled,
> Remote from each other as the star-lovers
> Across the Milky Way,
> Will no one bear a message,
> No one aid us in our distress?   35

[*Speaks.*] Master Su, we have travelled hundreds of miles to answer
the summons of my Fragrant Princess, but we arrived too late. She
is now immured in the palace, and it is impossible even to reach her
with a message. Last night I was warned to leave my lodgings. I don't
know where we can stay in safety until we get news of her.   40
[*Sings.*]

> If needs be,
> I shall wait for her till my hair turns white.
> But perhaps that happy day
> Is reserved for another lifetime.

---

4. The dynastic histories have by now reached a total of twenty-four. See n. 7, p. 82, for the Six Canons;
later subdivisions and additions led to a corpus of thirteen works, which remain canonical to this day.
5. The examination essay of Ming and Ch'ing times was christened *eight-legged* because it developed a
prescribed form in eight sections.

SU: It is clear that the political situation is going from bad to worse. 45
Public opinion has also changed considerably. Those in authority
are launching an offensive against the virtuous to settle old scores.
It would be wiser to keep out of their way and practise patience.

HOU: You may be right; I have hardly any friends left in this neighbourhood. My old comrades Ch'en and Wu have retired to their 50
native provinces. Perhaps I should follow them. [Sings.]

> My friends are seagulls by the shore.
> Prouder than kings,
> They turn aside from the dusty world,
> And frown at the muddled chess-game in the capital. 55
> Why not sail to the south
> And seek them among the hills?

SU: We are near the book market in Three Mountain Street, where
there is always a large crowd. We had better avoid it. [He quickens
his pace, singing.]

> Keep away from the leopards and wolves, 60
> The apes who wear the robes of government.
> On Three Mountain Street the mob is like a torrent.

HOU: [Stopping.] Here is Ts'ai Yi-so's bookshop, where my old comrades used to stay. Let us inquire whether they are still here. [Look-
ing up.] I see two new advertisements posted on these pillars. 65
[Reads.] "The Revival Club reopened." And there's a small notice
beside it: "New selections of model examination essays by Messrs.
Ch'en Chen-hui and Wu Ying-chi. Do you think they are here
now?

SU: I'll ask. [Calls.] Is the worthy proprietor at home? 70

TS'AI: [Entering.] Welcome. Are you gentlemen looking for books?

HOU: No, sir. I come for some information. Have you seen Messrs.
Ch'en and Wu?

TS'AI: They are inside at the moment. I'll go and call them. [Exit.]

CH'EN and WU: [Entering.] Oh, it's Brother Hou and Master Su as well. 75
What a delightful surprise! [Mutual bows.]

CH'EN: Where have you come from?

HOU: I have been in my native village.

WU: When did you arrive in the capital?

HOU: Only yesterday. [Sings.] 80

> The smoke of war has covered half the land.
> I have been with the army north and south,
> One camp after another, three wasted years.
> Now I return; who pities this wasted body?
> I have lingered by the Ch'in-huai River, 85
> Among the peach blossoms of my former haunt,
> But the shore no longer extends its former welcome.

[Speaks.] So I see that you, brothers, are creating a new literary style.

CH'EN and WU: You mock us. [Sing.]

Here in Chin-ling,[6] seat of ancient learning,   90
We labour side by side on compilations
To hold up T'ang and Sung as worthy models
And discourage the decadent Six Dynasties styles.
Studying our selections from the Eastern Forest,
All will acknowledge our classic purity.   95

TS'AI: [*From backstage.*] Please join me for a cup of tea.
CH'EN *and* WU: Thank you, we are coming.

[*They accompany* HOU *and* SU *to a room at the back. A* SERVANT
of JUAN TA -CH'ENG *enters with a bundle of large visiting cards.*]
SERVANT: My master, His Excellency Juan, has just been promoted to
Vice-Minister of War, and has received a new python robe and jade
belt as tokens of Imperial favour. He will be sent to direct the   100
defence of the river, so he is paying a round of farewell visits to his
friends.

[JUAN *enters in python robe and jade belt, sitting proudly in his sedan
chair, followed by retainers with fans and official umbrellas.*]
JUAN: [*Sings.*]

See my attendants, rank on rank,
Fans waving, parasols held high.
And who is this, in lofty state?   105
The man you scorned in years gone by.

SERVANT: Let Your Excellency's chair be halted. We are near the residence of His Excellency Yueh. [*Leaves a card at the latter's gate.*]
JUAN: You need not clear the street. Allow the public to gather round
and admire me. [*Waving his fan, brags.*] Having received this high   110
appointment from His Majesty, I'm paying a series of ceremonious
visits. My foes of the Eastern Forest Party will be arrested by Imperial
decree. They seem to have fled, for I see no sign of them. [*Sings.*]

Now I'll show them power and glory!
At last the wrinkles on my brow will vanish.   115

[*Noting the sign on the bookshop.*] What's this advertisement? Revival
Club? Tear it down and show it to me. [SERVANT *does so.* JUAN *reads.*]
"Reopening of the Revival Club. Ch'en Chen-hui and Wu Ying-
chi are editing new selections." How now! That Club is an offshoot
of the Eastern Forest Party which has been in close collaboration   120
with the rebels Chou and Lei. Now that a warrant is out for their
arrest, who dares invite them to make anthologies? This book dealer
is a rash fellow. Stop my chair! [*Steps out of the sedan, sits before the
bookshop, and says.*] Summon the local official in charge of the book
trade. [*The* OFFICIAL *is summoned.*]   125
OFFICIAL: [*Kneeling before* JUAN.] What is Your Excellency's wish?
JUAN: [*Sings.*]

6. One of the ancient names of Nanking.

> This bookseller defies the law
> By conspiring with the Revival Club.
> My duty is to suppress these rebels,
> Yours, to expose them root and branch.   130

OFFICIAL: Don't worry, Your Excellency. I'm an expert at making arrests. [*Exits and re-enters with* TS'AI YI-SO.] The criminal Ts'ai Yi-so is here, Your Excellency.

TS'AI: [*Kneeling.*] As a loyal subject of His Majesty, I protest that I have not violated any law.   135

JUAN: You have commissioned members of the Revival Club to work for you.

TS'AI: New selections of model essays are made every year before the civil service examination.

JUAN: Fie! Are you ignorant of the Imperial decree, whereby all rebels   140 are to be arrested? The law knows no mercy. You have harboured these rebels in your shop, yet you refuse to admit your guilt. You had better plead guilty at once.

TS'AI: I did not give them shelter. The gentlemen came of their own accord, because they are interested in the new anthologies.   145

JUAN: So you admit that they are inside your shop. [*To his* ATTEN-DANTS.] Make sure that none of them slip out.
        [*Exeunt* ATTENDANTS.]

JUAN: [*Whispers to the* OFFICIAL.] Send an immediate message to the City Marshal, who has the exclusive duty to deal with rebels. He must send his guards to arrest them. [*Sings.*]   150

> The Scarlet Guard will see the prisons filled,
> As these new rebels are in turn suppressed.

OFFICIAL: Yes, Your Excellency. [*Exit hurriedly.* JUAN *re-enters his sedan.*]

HOU, CH'EN, *and* WU: [*Enter, shouting.*] What crime have we committed that we should be kept in custody? Whoever you are, you have no   155 regard for justice.

JUAN: [*Smiling.*] I have given you no offence. Why are you all so indignant? What are your names? [*They announce them.*] Aha, so it's you three gentlemen. Don't you recognize this humble official? [*Sings.*]

> How imposing now my dignity must appear,   160
> How overwhelming my majestic frame!

[*To* WU.] Do you remember how you prevented me from joining the sacrifice at the Temple of Confucius? [*To* CH'EN.] Do you remember borrowing my troupe of actors? Why did you call me ugly names while enjoying my "Swallow Letter"? [*To* HOU.] When I bought you   165 a valuable wardrobe, you threw it away.

HOU: So it is Bearded Juan gloating on his revenge!

CH'EN *and* WU: Indeed. Let us drag him to the palace and tell what sort of man he is.

JUAN: [*Laughing.*] No need to hurry: you will have ample opportunity   170 to tell. [*Pointing.*] See who is coming to fetch you! [*Exit in sedan.*]

FOUR GUARDS: [*Enter, shouting.*] Which is Ts'ai Yi-so?
TS'AI: I am. What is the matter?
GUARD: We have come from the Marshal's headquarters to make cer-
tain arrests.   175
TS'AI: Who are you arresting?
GUARD: The three graduates Ch'en, Wu, and Hou.
HOU: We are all present. On what grounds do you arrest us?
GUARD: Come at once to headquarters. There you will discover. [*He
leads them out in chains.*]
TS'AI: What is behind all this? [*Calls.*] Brother Su, come quickly.   180
SU: [*Entering.*] What has happened?
TS'AI: It is terrible, terrible! The two scholars who were making selec-
tions for me have been arrested, and Master Hou as well.
SU: So it has really come to this! [*Sings.*]

> Hawks swoop down on innocent citizens;   185
> The Revival Club is an unprotected babe.
> Ma and Juan are now omnipotent.
> Woe to the world
> When the savage Prime Minister of a foolish Emperor
> Gives public pretexts for private revenge!   190

[*Speaks.*] Let us find out what is happening. We may yet be able to
save them.
TS'AI: We must. I'll inquire where they are being kept, so that I can
take them some food. [*They sing.*]
TS'AI: Court officers are furthering private feuds.   195
SU: Like the man of Ch'i, we fear the sky will fall.
TS'AI: Who can prevent this new Burning of Books?[7]
SU: On the Commander-in-Chief, Earl Tso, we call.

SCENE 30

The Return to the Hills

1645, third month

[CHANG WEI *enters; he wears a long white beard.*]
CHANG: [*Sings.*]

> Aged retainer of the Imperial court,
> I look back in vain towards my northern home.
> Mist and rain shroud the city of Nanking.
> Alas, the hopeful notes of restoration
> Have changed into the wail of a new tyranny,   5
> And the old court robes cannot hide the new decline.

[*Speaks.*] Formerly a Commander of the Imperial Guard in Peking,
I came south after the downfall of the old capital. Here the new
Emperor rewarded me with the same rank I held before, but evil
counsels sway the government. The condition of the country   10

---

7. The most infamous burning of books in Chinese history was the work of the first emperor, Ch'in Shih-
huang-ti (259–209 B.C.), the unifier of the country whose name became a byword for ferocious despotism.

deteriorates. As for me, I have built myself a house in the southern suburbs, with a pavilion called Pine Wind Hall, where I hope to retire and enjoy a calm old age. Unfortunately I have charge of two state prisoners, the so-called rebels Chou and Lei. These are sworn adversaries of Ma and Juan, who are determined to have them convicted. I am aware that this is grossly unjust, but I have not been able to find a way to save them. This harasses me day and night, so that I cannot decide to retire. [*Sings.*]

> The court is all intrigue and party strife:
> All honest men retire from such a life.
> Wherefore should I uphold the butcher's knife
> For malefactors? Quickly would I flee
> To my thatched Pine Pavilion and be free,
> Singing aloud to every passing cloud.
> But a terrible injustice haunts my breast,
> Until I stave it off I cannot rest.

SERVANT: [*Entering.*] Your Excellency, the City Marshal has captured three rebels, who await your immediate judgment.

> [*Four* GUARDS *carrying instruments of torture enter and stand on either side of the stage.* CHANG *ascends the tribune of justice. A* GUARD *leads in* HOU, WU, *and* CH'EN, *and kneels before* CHANG *to hand him the written warrant.* CHANG *examines it.*]

CHANG: According to a report from the local official in charge of the book trade, you are accused of organizing a secret society and plotting to purchase the freedom of Chou and Lei with bribes. Therefore you have been arrested. What have you to say in self-defense?

CH'EN *and* WU: [*Sing.*]

> We plead not guilty.
> Scholars of the Revival Club,
> Our friends are none but literary men.
> Only the tyranny of Ch'in Shih-huang[8]
> Would convict such innocent people as ourselves.

HOU: [*Sings.*]

> Do not torture us.
> I came to Nanking to visit old friends,
> And have no part in any clandestine meeting.
> Why should we be destroyed
> Like fish in a pond or swallows on a beam?

CHANG: You allege that you have been arrested without cause. It is impossible that the City Marshal should have committed such a blunder. [*Pounding on the table with a wooden block.*] Bring out the whips. Make them confess the truth.

CH'EN: [*Kneeling.*] Please do not take umbrage, Your Honour. I am Ch'en Chen-hui from I-hsing. My only crime is to have selected literary models at Ts'ai Yi-so's bookshop. I can think of no other offence.

8. See n. 7, p. 130.

WU: [*Kneeling.*] I am Wu Ying-chi from Juei-ch'ih, and a colleague of Ch'en Chen-hui. I was engaged in the same work, apart from which I did nothing.

CHANG: [*To* GUARD.] If these men are accused of organizing a secret society and plotting at Ts'ai's bookshop, Ts'ai himself should know the truth. Why was he not arrested? [*Throwing a warrant to the* GUARD.] Make haste and fetch Ts'ai Yi-so. [*Exit* GUARD.] 55

HOU: [*Kneeling.*] I am Hou Fang-yü from Kuei-te in Honan, and I travelled to Nanking with the sole purpose of visiting friends. When I heard that these old schoolmates of mine were in the bookshop, I called to visit them and was promptly arrested. 60

CHANG: [*Pondering.*] Recently the artist Lan Ying brought me a picture of the Peach Blossom Fountain for my Pine Wind Pavilion. It contained an inscription signed Hou Fang-yü of Kuei-te. Are you the same individual? 65

HOU: It is I, the accused, Your Honour.

CHANG: [*With a faint bow.*] This is most regrettable. I was greatly impressed by your calligraphy, and your verse is full of subtle import. I am sure you had nothing to do with this business. Please stand by. 70

HOU: I thank Your Honour for your kind expression of sympathy. [*He is offered a chair and sits down.*]

GUARD: [*Re-entering with warrant.*] Your Honour, Ts'ai Yi-so has bolted his shop and fled.

CHANG: How can this case be judged without any proof of the organization or of the alleged bribery? 75

GUARD: [*Entering with a letter.*] Here is a letter from Their Excellencies Wang and Ch'ien for Your Honour's perusal.

CHANG: So it comes from two highly respected Ministers of State. [*After reading it.*] They are absolutely right. I did not realize that Ch'en and Wu were leaders of the Revival Club. [*Sings.*] 80

> One is an essayist of renown;
> The other has won fame as a poet.
> What harm have they done to deserve arrest,
> And why should I serve as the agent of vile intrigues?
> As a judge, I hold independent authority; 85
> I should bring the light of the sun to the darkest hell.
> Let not the righteous be persecuted,
> Or art and literature decay in consequence.

[*Politely, to* CH'EN *and* WU.] Gentlemen, excuse my lack of courtesy. Are Their Excellencies Wang Chueh-ssu and Ch'ien Mu-chai old friends of yours? 90

CH'EN *and* WU: We have never had the pleasure of knowing them personally.

CHANG: Even so, they have written to me about your lofty characters and literary attainments. 95

CH'EN *and* WU: Perhaps it was due to Their Excellencies' sense of justice.

CHANG: Precisely. Though a member of the military profession, I am also devoted to literature and learning. How can I sacrifice worthy

men just to please the powers that be? I understand how deeply 100
you have been wronged. Please stand by and wait until I pronounce
the verdict. You will then be released. [CH'EN *and* WU *are given seats
while he writes the verdict. A* GUARD *arrives with a court bulletin.*]

GUARD: [*To* CHANG.] Today's bulletin contains an important new
decree. Please read it, Your Honour.

CHANG: [*Reading it aloud.*] "In accordance with Prime Minister Ma's 105
memorial concerning the swift execution of rebels to pacify the
country, Chou Piao and Lei Yin-tso, who plotted with the Prince of
Lu and have been conclusively proved traitors, should promptly be
executed to vindicate justice. A decree is hereby issued to that effect.
Furthermore, a memorial has been presented by Vice-Minister 110
of War Juan which runs as follows: 'Concerning the extermina-
tion of secret societies and the pacification of the country: it has
been discovered that the former members of the Eastern Forest Party
are still as numerous as locusts darkening the sun, and the young
upstarts of the Revival Club are breeding like their larvae. 115
The locusts have already become a plague and must be wiped out.
Their larvae are the calamity of the future and should be exterminated as a precaution. I, Your Majesty's servant Juan Ta-ch'eng,
possess a blacklist of these locusts and larvae. Mass arrests will be
effected with the guidance of the aforesaid list.' The decree is 120
hereby issued that those enumerated on the list aforesaid are to be
searched for and arrested. The urgent attention of authorities concerned is called with regard to these matters." [CHANG, *deeply
shocked.*] Ma and Juan are growing more and more vindictive. I'm
afraid no good man will survive. [*Sings.*] 125

> While I try to serve justice and mitigate penalties,
> They impose iniquitous laws and persecutions.
> A foul torrent has invaded our clean rivers,
> Every action of theirs is a monument of infamy.
> Soon they will catch everyone of worth in their evil snare; 130
> Few dare resist their authority.
> The members of the Revival Club and Eastern Forest Party
> Will be hunted down as victims of the new tyranny.

[*To* HOU, CH'EN, *and* WU.] Sympathising with the wrongs you have
suffered, I was about to release you, but the latest decrees prevent 135
me. Not only are Masters Chou and Lei to be executed but all members of the Eastern Forest Party and Revival Club are proscribed.

HOU, CH'EN *and* WU: [*Kneeling.*] We implore your Honour to save us.

CHANG: If I released you, you might be caught by others. Then you
would certainly be doomed. I advise you to be patient. [*Reading aloud* 140
as he writes.] "After cross-examination, no evidence of secret organizations or bribery could be discovered. The accused should be kept
in temporary custody. When Ts'ai Yi-so becomes available as a witness, the verdict will be given." [*To* HOU, CH'EN, *and* WU.] Although he is mainly concerned with self-advancement, the City 145
Marshal is not devoid of conscience. I shall send him a personal
letter. [*Reading aloud as he writes.*] "Having served for many years

in the Imperial Guard, I have seen more than most people of victims sacrificed to intrigue. I have reached the conclusion that the good and the evil are in perpetual conflict: they rise and fall alter- 150 nately. Every situation changes after a crisis. We who are responsible for preserving justice and the law should beware of favouritism. It is not our business to wield the butcher's knife for those in temporary power. There is a heaven above, and public opinion never dies. Let us avoid mistakes we shall never cease to regret." [*He bows to* 155 HOU, CH'EN, *and* WU.] Please wait patiently in confinement for the day when these wrongs will be righted. [*The prisoners are led off, and* CHANG *continues.*] I served the late Emperor throughout his reign, but now that the country is ruined and my home destroyed, I have given up all hope of a future career. Why should I continue 160 in the service of tyrants? There is an old proverb, "When you make a decision, don't wait till the day is over." I can hesitate no longer. [*Calls.*] Groom, bring my horse. I shall ride to my Pine Wind Pavilion. [GROOM *leads in horse.* CHANG *mounts it, singing.*]

> In the Spring, evening petals fill the sky, 165
> Green undulating mountains soothe the eye.
> South of the city, I waken from a dream
> As a tired traveller finds a gushing stream.

[*Speaks.*] Here I am back in my Pine Wind Pavilion. It seems as far from the world as the Peach Blossom Spring. I'll go and enjoy 170 the view. [*Sings as he goes upstairs.*]

> Few people approach this stream among the rocks.
> The wind in the pines recalls the murmur of waves.

[*Calls.*] Tell the gardener to open the windows and sweep the porch. 175
GARDENER: [*Entering, sweeps and recites.*]

> Catkins have flown where the swallow settles,
> Cobwebs have caught the flying petals.

[*Speaks.*] The porch is swept clean, Your Honour. [*Exit.*]
CHANG: [*Gazing out from the porch.*] How the shadows of the pines caress the window. My heart feels calm and rested. This would be a 180 suitable place to put my couch. [*Wanders across to the balcony.*] Spring water fills the pond and casts a green reflection on my beard. Here I ought to set up a tea-stove. [*Laughing.*] What a hurry I was in! I am still wearing my official uniform, most unbecoming to this hermitage. I must look ridiculous. [*To* SERVANT.] Open my bamboo 185 chest. I shall change into my loose robe, straw sandals, and bamboo hat. [*Changes and sings.*]

> This is my compensation for old age.
> Once my three houses are roofed with plain bamboo
> I'll pack my uniform. 190

[*Enter* GUARD *with* TS'AI YI-SO.]

GUARD: Among pines he must still preside over the law, and among the bamboos over documents pore. I have just captured Ts'ai Yi-so. Though His Honour Chang has left his office, I must report that his order has been executed. [*Calls.*] Is anybody there?

SERVANT: What urgent business has brought you so far from the city? 195

GUARD: Please report that Ts'ai Yi-so is at His Honour's disposal.

SERVANT: [*Goes upstairs and announces.*] The guard has caught Ts'ai Yi-so, and he is waiting for Your Honour's instructions.

CHANG: Now that this has happened, what can I do about the others? Tell the guard to wait downstairs and listen to me. [*To* GUARD *from* 200 *the porch.*] This is a very serious case and it must be kept secret. Ts'ai Yi-so is one of the chief witnesses; he will have to remain here. I shall question him presently.

GUARD: Yes, Your Honour. [GUARD *fastens* TS'AI *to a tree, and is about to leave when he is recalled.*]

CHANG: Come back. You may take my horse to the city as well as my 205 official cap, belt, robe, and boots. I wish to meditate in peace. Remember not to disturb me here again. [*Exit* GUARD *with horse, etc.* CHANG *stamps his foot.*] What an outrage, that a guard should trespass in my private garden and tie a witness to my favourite pine-tree! What sort of a hermitage is this? I shall have to see the prisoner. 210 [*Seeing* TS'AI.] So it is you, Ts'ai Yi-so.

TS'AI: Perhaps Your Honour may remember meeting me before?

CHANG: Of course I do, but that has nothing to do with the case. You have been accused of violating the new decree by harbouring rebels of the Revival Club. 215

TS'AI: [*Trying to kowtow.*] Yes, Your Honour.

CHANG: The latest books in your shop have some connection with the members of that club. They will be held as evidence against you.

TS'AI: [*Again trying to kowtow.*] Please be merciful, Your Honour!

CHANG: Your life can only be saved if you are willing to sacrifice your 220 fortune.

TS'AI: I'm willing to give up everything.

CHANG: [*Delighted.*] Then everything will turn out well. [*To servant.*] Unbind him quickly. [TS'AI *is released.* CHANG *says to him.*] If you are willing to give up your property, why not follow me to the hills? 225

TS'AI: My life depends on Your Honour.

CHANG: [*Pointing.*] Look towards the northeast. How white the clouds are and how blue the hills. [*To* SERVANT.] Take good care of the house. Master Ts'ai and I are going to view the scenery. We shall soon return. 230

[*Exit* SERVANT. CHANG *and* TS'AI *walk along together.*]

CHANG: [*Points.*] We shall spend tonight in the green forest.

TS'AI: If Your Honour wants to enjoy mountain scenery, you should send a servant to prepare lodgings in advance. Otherwise where can you stay except in some secluded temple?

CHANG: You are still in the dark. Once I have surrendered my official 235 cap, I shall become a poor Taoist priest. Any mountain cave will serve me for a dwelling.

TS'AI: What does Your Honour mean?

CHANG: Come, hesitate no longer. Ask no questions. Follow me.
[Sings.]

> My eyes are fixed upon the floating clouds,   240
> Regardless of the rocky distances.
> Slowly the pine woods darken, peace descends.
> Deep in the forest men are very few;
> A lonely path will wind between the peaks.
> Over the hills I'll walk with open heart,   245
> Visiting all the temples and forgetting
> Whatever dynasty may rule the land.
> In the realm of Immortals, far from the world's dust,
> A few wild peaches will be my nourishment.
> Now I know how easy it is to escape the turmoil.   250
> At dawn we shall leave our hut among the clouds;
> When we reach the summit the sun will still be high.

*   *   *

Scenes 31 to 39 Summary Su K'un-sheng goes off to seek General Tso, the
protégé of Hou Fang-yü's father, to tell him of the unjust imprisonment of Hou Fang-
yü and the evils being worked by the Juan Ta-ch'eng faction. Tso, enraged, decides
to move his army against Nanking but is blocked by armies sent out of the city and
dies. Meanwhile Juan Ta-ch'eng and Ma Shih-ying hold a memorial service for the
former Ming emperor, and their theatrical hypocrisy is a mockery of the service that
Chang Wei had earlier vowed to hold.

With the Ming armies in total disarray, Shih-k'o Fa prepares for a desperate defense
of the great city of Yang-chou against the advancing Manchu armies. Yang-chou falls,
and the Manchu army moves down on the southern capital Nanking, from which
everyone is trying to flee. Ma Shih-ying and Juan Ta-ch'eng are attacked by rioters,
beaten, and stripped of their possessions. Fragrant Princess escapes from the inner
palace, and Hou Fang-yü and his friends in the Revival Club are released from jail.
The puppet emperor, Prince Fu, flees to one of his generals, but the general's sub-
ordinates kill the general and plan to offer the prince to the Manchus. By different
routes Hou Fang-yü, his friends, and Fragrant Princess all reach refuge in two Taoist
temples in the mountains.

SCENE 40

Entering the Way[9]

1645, seventh month

[*Enter* CHANG WEI. *He wears the broad-sleeved robe and gourd-
shaped hat of a Taoist priest, and carries a whisk.*[1]]

CHANG: [Sings.]

> The blush of youth had faded from my cheeks
> Ere half a life-span in the dusty world.
> Too long I watched the puppet-play,
> Wept tears, and then in turn laughed loud.

---

9. The life of a Taoist hermit.   1. Held as a religious sign.

> No more of folly. In these secluded haunts, 5
> Few men have ever cherished worldly sorrows.

[*Speaks.*] Ever since I retired from the official world, I have lived in seclusion in this White Cloud Temple under the name of Chang the Taoist. This is my lot, to cultivate the Way and have no more to do with the world's affairs. It was my good fortune to be 10 accompanied here by Ts'ai Yi-so, the bookseller, who brought five cartloads of classics and histories. Lan Ying the painter made the same resolution, and he has painted scrolls depicting our rustic retreat. So, since in these bare hills I can study and let my fancy roam to my heart's content, when the time comes for my Transfor- 15 mation[2] it will be no doltish ignoramus who ascends to the clouds. The one regret that persists from my former life is my failure to repay the gracious favour of His Majesty the Emperor Ch'ung-chen. Therefore today, the fifteenth day of the seventh month, I have invited many celebrants to a major memorial service for His 20 late Majesty. I have been fortunate enough also to secure the attendance of a former Master of Ceremonies from Nanking, who with some of the local elders will offer the prayers. Now let me call my disciple to make sure all is ready. Boy!

TS'AI *and* LAN: [*Entering in Taoist garb, recite.*]

> Farewell to dusty world; 25
> In the clouds we gather as followers of the Way.
> Greetings from Ts'ai Yi-so and Lan Ying.

CHANG: Do you both prepare the altars and lead our brethren in the ritual. I will purify myself and change my garments so that I may offer up prayer with the utmost devotion. Truly a pure repast before 30 the gods, an offering from the chaste hearts of men.

> [CHANG *exits.* TS'AI *and* LAN *set up a triple altar which they furnish with incense, flowers, fruits, and tea. They set up banners and tablets, and then sing.*]

TS'AI *and* LAN *together:* [*Singing.*]

> As the sun rises from the sea, we build our high altar.
> All spirits of the sky, appear!
> Lords of the stars and planets, come to audience!
> Your banners float on the breeze 35
> As prayers ascend for the seventh-month sacrifices.

TS'AI: The altar is raised and furnished. All is ready.

LAN: And lo, here comes a throng of village elders with gifts of wine and incense.

> [*Enter* MASTER OF CEREMONIES *at the head of a crowd of* VILLAGERS. *They bear wine, incense, paper money, and embroidered banners.*]

VILLAGERS: [*Sing.*]

> Home-brewed wines we bear, 40
> Incense purple and yellow

2. Becoming immortal.

We've wrapped in broidered kerchiefs.
Upward we gaze, to the royal Throne
In the Jade Palace of the Purest Void,
And ask: How came our Emperor   45
To leave us villagers fatherless? [*They weep.*]
Now in the seventh month, deep in the folded hills,
Offerings we burn to His late Majesty.

[*They greet* TS'AI *and* LAN, *and say.*] Reverend Sirs, we of the laity are
all present and prepared for the service. Please ask His Rever-   50
ence the Abbot to come forth and circumambulate the altar.

TS'AI *and* LAN: [*Calling offstage.*] All is in readiness for Your Reverence to circumambulate the altar and perform the rites of
purification.

> [*Three drumbeats. Four* TAOIST MUSICIANS *appear.* TS'AI *and* LAN
> *put on robes decorated with magic symbols, and follow behind bear-*
> *ing censers. Last comes* CHANG, *in similar robe and gold mitre. He*
> *walks around the altar, carrying a vial of water and a pine branch*
> *with which he conducts the rituals of purification.*]

ALL: [*Singing.*]

> Hands new purified   55
> Flourish branch of pine,
> Scatter healing dew
> In droplets superfine.
> Round the altar and around,
> Thrice threefold and nine: 60
> Banish dust, vanish lust,
> From this place divine.
> Incense smoke ascending,
> Cloud with cloud entwine,
> Airy palace towers   65
> For his royal line.

> [*Exit* CHANG.]

TS'AI *and* LAN: [*Calling to* CHANG, *offstage.*] The ritual of purification
is complete. Now let Your Reverence change your robe and offer the
memorial prayer at the altar.

> [TS'AI *and* LAN *proceed to set up the tablet of the Emperor Ch'ung-*
> *chen on the central altar. On the left are set the tablets of the civil*
> *martyrs of the year 1644, and on the right the tablets of the military*
> *martyrs of the same year. Soft music plays.* CHANG *enters wearing a*
> *nine-ridged hat (indicating highest rank in the bureaucracy) and a*
> *crane-embroidered robe of audience. His thick-soled boots also are*
> *such as are worn in Imperial audience. He wears a golden girdle and*
> *carries an ivory tablet.*]

CHANG: [*Kneeling.*] Let the stars of the heavens lend brightness to the   70
vision of the Land of the Immortals. Let the winds and the thunder
bear word that the gates of Heaven be opened. Here in all reverence
we implore the attendance of His Imperial Majesty Ch'ung-chen and
of all noble martyrs, both civil and military. Let the Imperial procession now appear in all its splendour, flanked by gleaming   75

banners and followed by the attendant throng. Ride the white clouds
to where we humbly await Your Imperial Presence with offerings of
sacred music and hallowed wine.

> [*Music sounds.* CHANG *makes a triple libation*[3] *and prostrates himself four times.* MASTER OF CEREMONIES *and* VILLAGERS *join in his prostrations.*]

CHANG: [*Sings.*]

> Adepts here assembled
> Implore Your Majesty to descend from the azure clouds.   80
> Leave Coal Hill,[4] the fatal tree,
> Untie the silken sash,
> Come relish pepper wine,
> Breathe incense of the pine,
> Lament no more the crimes of bandit rogues.   85
> No earthly pomp can last a thousand years,
> But in these hills your spirit lives forever.

> [CHANG *exits.* TS'AI *and* LAN *make libations at either side of the stage, then prostrate themselves.* MASTER OF CEREMONIES *and* VILLAGERS *join in the prostrations.*]

TS'AI *and* LAN *together*: [*Singing.*]

> For every martyr's soul we pray
> Who died on that ill-fated day.
> All who found death by slow starvation,   90
> Knife, or well, or strangulation,
> Let no more rage your bosoms fill,
> Join us here and feast at will.

[*They speak.*] Now pour libations and burn the spirit offerings, that
the spirits may be escorted to their heavenly home.   95

> [*All present burn paper offerings, make libations, and wail.*]

MASTER OF CEREMONIES: Now for the first time they have been fittingly
bewailed.

VILLAGERS: Having expressed our devotion, let us go to our own pure
repast. [*Exeunt.*]

TS'AI *and* LAN: [*Calling to* CHANG, *offstage.*] The ceremonies of invita-   100
tion are completed. Now is the time for Your Reverence to change
your robes and ascend to the altar to offer food to the wandering
souls.

> [TS'AI *and* LAN *set out the food offerings. To soft music,* CHANG *re-enters, now wearing a turban and a cloak trimmed with crane's down, and carrying his whisk. After prostrating himself, he ascends the steps of the altar. When* TS'AI *and* LAN *have assumed their positions behind him, he strikes the altar with his fist.*]

CHANG: Though endless spread the sandy battlefields, raising our eyes
we see the mansions of Heaven; lost as we are in the boundless   105
ocean of sorrows, turning our heads we see the Isles of Blessing. We
commemorate the host of those who gave their lives for their coun-

---

3. Pours out wine three times as an offering.   4. Where the Ming emperor Ch'ung-chen hanged himself.

try, whether they fought hard by the capital or in the central plains, south of the great lakes or far in the desert northwest; whether to them came death by water, death by fire, death by sword's edge, death by arrow, death beneath trampling feet, or death from sickness and starvation. Though your bones lie tangled in thorny thickets, though your spirits flicker as will-o'-the-wisps, come to our holy hill, our sacred altar. Come drink the cup that agelong will quench your thirst. Come taste the grain that for a thousand springs will be your nourishment. [*He scatters grains of rice, sprinkles water, and burns paper offerings. Then he sings.*]

> Out on the dusty battlefield
> With wild herbs overgrown,
> Crimson stains of blood must yield
> To slowly whitening bone.
> In howl of wind, rage of rain,
> Homeward gazing, they gaze in vain.
> Poor ghosts who linger drear and chill:
> Come eat this once, come eat your fill.

TS'AI *and* LAN: Now the gifts of food have been made, it is time for Your Reverence to send forth the rays of holy light which will illumine the Three Realms,[5] so that the wandering spirits may be guided each to his proper altar.

CHANG: They have been long in Heaven, the souls of the martyrs of last year's disaster.

TS'AI *and* LAN: But what of the victims of this year's struggle, Prince and ministers pitted against the north? We entreat you to seek a sign of what fates have befallen them.

CHANG: Then attend with steadfast hearts while I offer incense and enter meditation, closing my eyes to see the more intently. [TS'AI *and* LAN *stand with bowed heads, incense sticks held before them. A long pause ensues.*] No, I find no manifestation of the Emperor Hung-kuang, the two Generals Liu, T'ien Hsiung, and the rest. They must still be among the living.

TS'AI *and* LAN: What of Shih K'o-fa, Tso Liang-yü, and Huang Te-kung, who died in this year's fighting?

CHANG: Let me see.

> [*He closes his eyes, whereupon there enters, to soft music, a* WHITE-BEARDED FIGURE *wearing court headdress and crimson robe. His face is covered with a yellow silk cloth, and he has a retinue of* ATTENDANTS *carrying streamers of silk such as decorate shrines.*]

FIRST APPARITION: I, Shih K'o-fa, former Field Marshal and President of the Board of War, am newly appointed Original of the Purple Void, in the Palace of Great Purity. To this post I now ride.

> [*He mimes the act of riding, and exits. A* SECOND FIGURE, *in gold armour and with a red silk cloth over his face, enters to drums and pipes. His retinue carries banners.*]

SECOND APPARITION: I, Tso Liang-yü, former Earl of Southern Peace, am newly appointed Heaven-soaring Envoy. To this post I now ride.

---

5. From Buddhism, the realms of Desire, Form, and Formlessness.

[*He exits. A* THIRD FIGURE *enters with banners, drums, and pipes. His armour is silver, and the cloth over his face is black.*]

THIRD APPARITION: I, Huang Te-kung, former Earl of Southern Tranquillity, am newly appointed Heaven-roaming Envoy. To this post I now ride. [*Exit.*]

CHANG: [*Opens his eyes.*] Wonderful! I have just had visions of Their   150
Excellencies Shih K'o-fa, Tso Liang-yü, and Huang Te-kung, each riding to assume a glorious new appointment in Heaven. [*Sings.*]

> Celestial steeds astride the clouds,
> In heroes' pride they go.
> Heavenly music sounds on every side,   155
> Banners and parasols wave,
> Swords, robes, and insignia befit
> The majesty of other-worldly office.
> High Heaven recognized their worth,
> And now they ride in glory.   160

TS'AI *and* LAN: [*Bowing with folded hands.*] Homage to Heaven's Lord! Thus virtue reaps reward, and the justice of Heaven is displayed for all to see. [*Turning to* CHANG.] But what retribution has befallen the traitors Ma Shih-ying and Juan Ta-ch'eng?

CHANG: Let me see.   165
[*Enter, running, a* FOURTH FIGURE, *with dishevelled hair and clothes.*]

FOURTH APPARITION: After a lifetime of misdeeds, I, Ma Shih-ying, met my end in the T'aichou Mountains. [*Following him comes the* SPIRIT OF THE THUNDERCLAP, *who chases him around the stage. The* APPARITION *kneels, clutching his head.*] Have mercy! Have mercy!
[*The* SPIRIT *strikes him dead, strips his body, and departs. Enter a* FIFTH FIGURE *in court robes and girdle.*]

FIFTH APPARITION: Done it! A superb achievement for Juan Ta-ch'eng, to cross this Ridge of the Immortals!   170
[*He climbs a peak, whereupon the* MOUNTAIN SPIRIT *and* ATTENDANT YAKSHAS[6] *enter and push him off. He falls to his death.*]

CHANG: [*Opens his eyes.*] Horror, horror! A vision of Ma Shih-ying struck dead by a thunderbolt in the T'aichou Mountains, and Juan Ta-ch'eng fallen to his death from the Ridge of the Immortals. Each with his skull cracked open, terrible to behold. [*Sings.*]

> Bright is the image in the karmic mirror,[7]   175
> Close is the mesh of Heaven's all-compassing net.
> Flee where you may over a thousand hills,
> Thunder Spirit and Yakshas will hunt you down.
> Those who have scooped the brains from so many skulls,
> Will scarcely feed a dog with their remains.   180

TS'AI *and* LAN: [*Hands folded.*] Homage to Heaven's Lord! Thus evil meets retribution, and the justice of Heaven is displayed for all to see. [*Turning to* CHANG.] Your attendants still lack the fullest

---

6. Demon messengers from the underworld, in popular Buddhist belief.   7. A metaphor for seeing the fate suffered by those who committed misdeeds during their lifetimes.

understanding. We beseech Your Reverence to fill our ears with
truth.   185
  [*While* CHANG *raises his whisk and sings at the top of his voice,*
  MASTER OF CEREMONIES *and* VILLAGERS *re-enter to listen respect-*
  fully, incense sticks held before them.]
CHANG: [*Sings.*]

> Every mortal creature's
> Misdeeds, however small,
> However closely hidden,
> To his account must fall.
> And yet the karmic circle   190
> Each merit will recall,
> Reward and retribution
> Made visible to all.
> North succeeds to South,
> State gives way to state,   195
> Each dynastic cycle
> Predeterminate.
> Just men and the ungodly
> Meet their appointed fate,
> Sure of resolution,   200
> Whether soon or late.

  [MASTER OF CEREMONIES *and* VILLAGERS *kowtow and exit. Enter*
  FRAGRANT PRINCESS *with* PIEN YÜ-CHING.]
PIEN: Happiest in all this world are those who devote themselves to
  acts of piety. In the company of Taoist priestesses we have set up
  banners before the altar to the Empress Chou, and now we come to
  hear the Abbot in his sermon hall.   205
FRAGRANT PRINCESS: Am I permitted to accompany you?
PIEN: See, here is a throng of Taoist priests and laymen, there can be
  no harm in our presence as observers.
  [PIEN *prostrates herself before the altar, then takes up a position at*
  one side, with FRAGRANT PRINCESS. *Enter the minstrel* TING CHI-
  CHIH.]
TING: Hard to ensure return in mortal form; mysterious and secret is
  the Way. [*He prostrates himself before the altar, then rises and calls* 210
  offstage.] Master Hou, come see the sermon hall.
  [HOU FANG-YÜ *hastens onstage.*]
HOU: At last! Long have I suffered in the dusty world. Now to seek
  bliss beyond its narrow confines. [*He follows* TING *to a position at the*
  other side of the stage from FRAGRANT PRINCESS.]
CHANG: [*Pounds his lectern.*] You, my hearers, hearts turned to piety:
  know that only the total voidance of your dusty desires can free you   215
  to rise towards purity. One single speck of lingering mortal passion,
  and you are condemned to a thousand further revolutions of the
  wheel of karma.
  [*Concealing his face with his fan,* HOU *peers at* FRAGRANT PRINCESS,
  and starts in astonishment.]

HOU: That is my Fragrant Princess! How can it be that I find her standing here? [*He hurries over to* FRAGRANT PRINCESS *and tugs at her* 220
hand. She is equally startled to see him.]

FRAGRANT PRINCESS: It is Master Hou! Oh, the longing for you has
almost caused my death! [*Sings.*]

> Ah, when I recall
> The abruptness of our parting!
> No bridge was ours, to cross the Milky Way; 225
> Higher than Heaven seemed the walls between us.
> No letters could we exchange,
> Dreams were a vain recourse,
> Longing was endless;
> And when I left the palace, 230
> Ever more distant wanderings seemed to face me.

HOU: [*Points to the fan.*] Gazing on the peach blossoms of this fan, I
have asked myself how I could ever requite you. [*Sings.*]

> The blossoms on this fan:
> Were they really formed from bloodstains? 235
> Or are they the petals that rained down
> When the holy Abbot preached?[8]

[HOU *and* FRAGRANT PRINCESS *look at the fan together. Then they
are dragged apart by* TING *and* PIEN.]

TING: You should not discuss private matters while the Abbot is in the
middle of his sermon.

[HOU *and* FRAGRANT PRINCESS *take no notice, and* CHANG *pounds
his lectern again.*]

CHANG: Tchah! What kind of fractious children are these who babble 240
of love before this sacred altar? [*He hastens down, tears the fan from
the hands of* HOU *and* FRAGRANT PRINCESS, *and flings it to the
ground.*] This a place of sanctity, not to be defiled by wanton
youths.

TS'AI: Ai-ya! But Your Reverence knows this man. It is Hou Fang-yü of
Honan. 245

CHANG: And the girl?

LAN: I know her. She is Fragrant Princess, who became Master Hou's
bride.

CHANG: And what has brought them here?

TING: Master Hou is residing at my Gather Purity Temple. 250

PIEN: And Fragrant Princess at my Foster Purity Temple.

HOU: [*Bowing to* CHANG.] And you, sir, are Chang Wei, from whom in
former days I received much favour.

CHANG: Master Hou, I am delighted to see you released from prison.
Did you know it was because of you that I left the world to follow 255
the Way?

HOU: No, I had no means of knowing that.

---

8. According to Buddhist legend, when Abbot Kuang-ch'ang reached the climax of this exposition of the
sutras, a shower of flower petals fell from the sky.

TS'AI: I also left the world on your account. I shall tell you the story all in good time.

LAN: And I came here as escort to Fragrant Princess in her search for you. I little dreamed that we should find you at last. 260

HOU: How shall Fragrant Princess and I ever repay the debts we owe to you, Ting Chi-chih and Pien Yü-ching, who gave us refuge, or to you, Ts'ai Yi-so and Lan Ying, who aided our search for each other?

FRAGRANT PRINCESS: And Su K'un-sheng also accompanied me here. 265

HOU: And Liu Ching-t'ing came in my company.

FRAGRANT PRINCESS: We owe so much to Su and Liu, who stayed loyally beside us in defiance of all hardships.

HOU: When we are home once more as man and wife, we shall endeavour to repay their kindness. 270

CHANG: What is all this meaningless chatter? How laughable to cling to your amorous desires when the world has been turned upside down!

HOU: Sir, you are mistaken. The marriage of man with maid is the source of human relationship. Sorrows of separation, joys of reunion, 275 all these are the fruits of love. Why should you object to our discussion of them?

CHANG: [Angrily.] Pshaw! Two piteous passion-clinging bugs! Where now is the nation, where the home, where the prince, where the father? Can't you get rid of this miserable infatuation? [Sings.] 280

> Alas for silly youths,
> Ignorant of the changing of their world.
> A stream of lascivious chatter,
> Hand in hand they plan their marital bliss,
> Here, in the very presence of the spirits! 285
> Can't you divine love's final dissolution,
> Hear the flapping of wings
> As the mandarin ducks fly apart,
> See the shattered fragments
> Of the jewelled mirror of union? 290
> Are you not ashamed to hear
> The laughter your performance brings?
> Are you not ready to follow
> The broad highway of Escape?

HOU: [Bows.] I hear your words and wake from my dream, drenched 295 in a chilling sweat.

CHANG: Do you understand them?

HOU: I understand.

CHANG: Then if you do, salute Ting Chi-chih as your tutor. [HOU does so.]

FRAGRANT PRINCESS: I also understand. 300

CHANG: If you also understand, salute Pien Yü-ching as your tutor. [She does so.]

CHANG: [To TING and PIEN.] Help them change into Taoist robes. [They do so.]

TING and PIEN: Ascend to your seat, Your Reverence, so that we may present our disciples.

[CHANG *takes his seat, and* TING *and* PIEN *lead* HOU *and* FRAGRANT PRINCESS *to prostrate themselves before him.*]

TING *and* PIEN *together:* [*Singing.*]

> Crop the sprouts of love   305
> And see them wither, the sprigs of gold and jade.
> Root out passion
> From these descendants of the dragon and phoenix.
> Life is brief as bubble of foam,
> Short as spark, struck from stone.   310
> Let them spend their remnant years
> Following our doctrine.

CHANG: For the male, let the south be his direction. Let Hou Fang-yü depart for the southernmost hills, there to cultivate the Way.

HOU: I go. Understanding the Way, I perceive the depths of my folly.   315
   [TING *leads* HOU *offstage.*]

CHANG: For the female, let her direction be the north. Let Fragrant Princess depart for the northernmost hills, there to cultivate the Way.

FRAGRANT PRINCESS: I go. All is illusion; I know not that man before me.   320

> [PIEN *leads* FRAGRANT PRINCESS *offstage, the opposite side from* HOU'*s exit.* CHANG *descends from his seat and utters three great shouts of laughter.*]

CHANG: [*Sings.*]

> See them take their leave
> With never a backward glance.
> My task it was to shred the peach blossom fan,
> That never more the strands of folly
> Shall bind the heart of man and maid.   325
>
> White bones are laid in the dust,
> The southern realm concludes its span.
> Dreams of revival fall to earth
> In shreds with the peach blossom fan.

*   *   *

Summary   An epilogue follows (not printed here) in which Su K'un-sheng, Liu Ching-t'ing, and the Master of Ceremonies meet in the mountains three years later. Each recalls the events of the past, with Su K'un-sheng singing a long ballad about the ruins of Nanking, which he had recently visited. An emissary of the Ch'ing government makes an appearance and says that he is seeking virtuous men who are hiding in the mountains, so that he can bring them back to serve in the new government. When he tries to bring them in, they run off in different directions.

CAO XUEQIN (TS'AO HSÜEH-CH'IN)
1715–1763

Of all the world's novels perhaps only *Don Quixote* rivals *The Story of the Stone* as the embodiment of a nation's cultural identity in recent times, much as the epic once embodied cultural identity in the ancient world. For Chinese readers of the past two centuries *The Story of the Stone* (also known as the *Dream of the Red Chamber*) has come to represent the best and worst of traditional China in its final phase. It is the story of an extended family, centered around its women, and of the relationships within the family. Even after nearly a century of war, revolution, and social experiment, a century that has seen the dissolution of the traditional extended family, *The Story of the Stone* has retained its hold on the Chinese imagination.

As the title tells us, the novel is also, on a basic level, the story of a magical and conscious stone, the one block left over when the goddess Nü-wa repaired the damaged vault of the sky in the mythic past. Transported into the mortal world by a pair of priests, one Buddhist and one Taoist, Stone is destined to find enlightenment by suffering the pains of love, loss, and disillusion as a human being. In his incarnation, Stone is born as the sole legitimate male heir of a wealthy and powerful household, the Jias, which is about to pass from the height of prosperity into decline. Miraculously, the baby is born with an inscribed piece of jade in his mouth, from which he is given his name Bao-yu (Precious Jade) and which he wears always.

The novel itself has a peculiar genesis. The first eighty chapters are the work of Cao Xueqin, himself the scion of a once-wealthy family fallen on hard times. It is believed that he wrote the novel, in at least five drafts, between 1740 and 1750. There is another figure in the process of the novel's composition, someone who used the pseudonym "Red Inkstone" (or more properly "He of Red Inkstone Studio") and who added commentary and made corrections to the manuscript versions. He was obviously a close friend or relative of Cao Xueqin and acted the role of virtual collaborator. His comments suggest that the characters in the main portion of the novel are based on real people.

The novel was left unfinished and probably was never intended for publication, but it did circulate widely in Peking in manuscript copies, whose many variations show a complex process of revision. One version of the manuscript came into the hands of the writer Gao E (ca. 1740–ca. 1815), who completed the story by adding another 40 chapters, publishing the full 120-chapter version in 1791, about a half century after Cao Xueqin began to write. The transformations of the novel in its manuscript versions, the role of the mysterious Red Inkstone (and of another early commentator who calls himself "Odd Tablet"), and the relation of the characters to Cao's life are questions that continue to engage professional and amateur scholars.

Chinese novels are, as a rule, very long, and *The Story of the Stone* is longer than most, taking up five substantial volumes in its complete English translation. The narrative is impossible to summarize and difficult to excerpt. It has a huge cast of characters, both major and minor, who appear and disappear in intricately interwoven incidents. But, in part because of its very magnitude, the novel gradually draws its readers into the details of everyday life and the complexities of human relationships, occasionally punctuated by reminders that the intense emotions and the values given to things are all illusory. That sense of illusion is underscored by the family name Jia, a real Chinese surname that happens to be homophonous with another character meaning "false" or "feigned."

In addition to Bao-yu, the human metamorphosis of Stone, one other central character originates in the supernatural frame story and its fanciful landscape. This is Crimson Pearl Flower, a semidivine plant that grew near the Rock of Rebirth. In the opening chapter, while Stone is serving at the court of the goddess Disenchantment, he takes a fancy to this flower and waters it with sweet dew. This eventually brings the flower to life in the form of a fairy girl, who is obsessed with repaying the kindness of Stone, and for his gift of sweet dew she owes him the "debt of tears." This character is born as Bao-yu's cousin, the delicate and high-strung Lin Dai-yu (*Dai-yu* means "Black Jade").

The early chapters are devoted to the supernatural frame story and to bringing the characters together. In chapters seventeen and eighteen, Bao-yu's elder sister, an imperial concubine, has been permitted to pay a visit to her home. The women of the emperor's harem were usually confined to the palace; in permitting her to return, the emperor is displaying his favor to her and to her family. In her honor a huge garden (Prospect Garden) is constructed on the grounds of the family compound. After the imperial concubine's departure, the adolescent girls of the extended family are allowed to take up residence in the various buildings in the garden, and by special permission Bao-yu is also permitted to live there with his maids. The world of the garden is one of adolescent love in full flower, though we never forget the violent and ugly world outside, a world that often creeps into the garden world.

The adolescent love between Bao-yu and Dai-yu forms the core of the novel. Each is intensely sensitive to the other, and neither can express what he or she feels. Communication between them often depends on subtle gestures with implicit meanings, meanings that are inevitably misunderstood. Both, and particularly Dai-yu, believe in a perfect understanding of hearts; but even in the charmed world of the garden, closeness eludes them. The novel often juxtaposes brutish characters (usually male) with those possessed of a finer sensibility; but in the case of Dai-yu, sensibility is carried to the extreme. Dai-yu's relation to Bao-yu is balanced by that of another distant relation, Xue Bao-chai, whose plump good looks and gentle common sense are the very opposite of Dai-yu's frailty and histrionic morbidity. Bao-chai ("Precious Hairpin") has a golden locket with an inscription that matches Bao-yu's jade, and the marriage of "jade and gold" is a possibility seriously considered by older members of the family. Eventually, in Gao E's ending for the novel, as Dai-yu is dying of consumption, Bao-yu will be tricked into marrying Bao-chai. Bao-yu will finally carry out his obligation to continue the family line and at last renounce the world to become a Buddhist monk.

Although the triangle of Bao-yu, Dai-yu, and Bao-chai stands at the center of the novel, scores of subplots involve characters of all types. *The Story of the Stone* is, as noted, a novel about family, its internal relationships and its place in the larger social world. The reader easily becomes absorbed in the intensity of the family's internal relationships, always to be reminded how those relationships touch and are touched by the world outside. Because this family has social power, the actions taken by family members to serve its interests and loyalties can also be seen as corruption. In some cases the corruption is obvious, but in a far subtler way the reader comes to identify with the family and takes many acts of power and privilege for granted. At the same time, the outside world has the capacity to impinge on the protected space of the family, and the reader sees these forces from the point of view of the insider, as intrusions. It is a world of concentric circles of proximity, both of kinship and affinity. Petty details and private loves and hates grow larger and larger as they approach the center. And above this is the Buddhist and Taoist lesson about the illusion of care, of a world driven by blind but powerful emotions that at last cause only suffering, both to self and others.

The reader will find much unfamiliar about the Jia household, a vast establishment of close and distant family members, personal maids, and servants, each with his or her own level of status. Although the personal maids had some responsibilities, it will be obvious that the number of maids attached to each family member was primarily a mark of status. For a girl from a poor family, the position of personal maid was very desirable, providing room, board, and income to send to her own family. Bao-yu often flirts with his maids, but he has sexual relations only with his chief maid, Aroma.

The selection printed here includes part of the opening frame story and a series of chapters on Bao-yu and his female relations in Prospect Garden, with the blossoming of the love between him and Dai-yu.

Following these chapters the family declines, even as the young lovers grow more deeply bound to one another. The selection concludes with the end of Chapter 96 and Chapter 97, in which Dai-yu learns that Bao-yu is to be married to Bao-chai and sinks into her final illness. Bao-yu, meanwhile, is told that he is to marry Dai-yu; and, filled with hope, he revives from a fit of madness. The charade is carried through, with Bao-chai's face hidden behind a veil, even as Dai-yu is dying.

There is a complete translation of *The Story of the Stone* in five volumes (1973–82), the first three volumes by David Hawkes and the last two by John Minford. Andrew Plaks, *Archetype and Allegory in the Dream of the Red Chamber* (1976), is a useful study.

PRONOUNCING GLOSSARY

The following list uses common English syllables to provide rough equivalents of selected words whose pronunciation may be unfamiliar to the general reader.

Cao Xueqin: *tsao shueh-chin*

Feng-shi: *fuhng–shir*

Feng Zi-ying: *fuhng dzuh–ying*

Gao E: *gau uh*

Jia Yu-cun: *jyah yow–tswuhn*

Jia Zheng: *jyah juhng*

Kong Mei-xi: *koong may–shee*

qiang: *chyahng*

Shi Xiang-yun: *shir shyahng–yoon*

Wang Ji-ren: *wahng jee–ruhn*

Wu Yu-feng: *woo yow–fuhng*

Xi-feng: *shee–fuhng*

Xue Bao-chai: *shooeh bau–chai*

Ying-lian: *ying–lyen*

Zhao: *jau*

Zhen Shi-yin: *juhn shir–yin*

Zhi-xiao: *juhr–shyau*

From The Story of the Stone[1]

From *Volume 1*

FROM CHAPTER 1

*Zhen Shi-yin makes the Stone's acquaintance in a dream
And Jia Yu-cun finds that poverty is not incompatible with romantic
feelings*

Gentle Reader,

What, you may ask, was the origin of this book?

Though the answer to this question may at first seem to border on the absurd, reflection will show that there is a good deal more in it than meets the eye.

Long ago, when the goddess Nü-wa was repairing the sky, she melted down a great quantity of rock and, on the Incredible Crags of the Great Fable Mountains, moulded the amalgam into thirty-six thousand, five hundred and one large building blocks, each measuring seventy-two feet by a hundred and

---

1. Translated by David Hawkes. Note that Hawkes used the pinyin system of spelling (whereas this volume usually uses the Wade-Giles system).

forty-four feet square. She used thirty-six thousand five hundred of these blocks in the course of her building operations, leaving a single odd block unused, which lay, all on its own, at the foot of Greensickness Peak in the aforementioned mountains.

Now this block of stone, having undergone the melting and moulding of a goddess, possessed magic powers. It could move about at will and could grow or shrink to any size it wanted. Observing that all the other blocks had been used for celestial repairs and that it was the only one to have been rejected as unworthy, it became filled with shame and resentment and passed its days in sorrow and lamentation.

One day, in the midst of its lamentings, it saw a monk and a Taoist approaching from a great distance, each of them remarkable for certain eccentricities of manner and appearance. When they arrived at the foot of Greensickness Peak, they sat down on the ground and began to talk. The monk, catching sight of a lustrous, translucent stone—it was in fact the rejected building block which had now shrunk itself to the size of a fan-pendant[2] and looked very attractive in its new shape—took it up on the palm of his hand and addressed it with a smile:

"Ha, I see you have magical properties! But nothing to recommend you. I shall have to cut a few words on you so that anyone seeing you will know at once that you are something special. After that I shall take you to a certain

> brilliant
> successful
> poetical
> cultivated
> aristocratic
> elegant
> delectable
> luxurious
> opulent
> locality on a little trip."

The stone was delighted.

"What words will you cut? Where is this place you will take me to? I beg to be enlightened."

"Do not ask," replied the monk with a laugh. "You will know soon enough when the time comes."

And with that he slipped the stone into his sleeve and set off at a great pace with the Taoist. But where they both went to I have no idea.

Countless aeons went by and a certain Taoist called Vanitas in quest of the secret of immortality chanced to be passing below that same Greensickness Peak in the Incredible Crags of the Great Fable Mountains when he caught sight of a large stone standing there, on which the characters of a long inscription were clearly discernible.

Vanitas read the inscription through from beginning to end and learned that this was a once lifeless stone block which had been found unworthy to repair the sky, but which had magically transformed its shape and been taken

---

2. Jade decoration strung from the bottom of a fan.

down by the Buddhist mahāsattva[3] Impervioso and the Taoist illuminate Mysterioso into the world of mortals, where it had lived out the life of a man before finally attaining nirvana and returning to the other shore.[4] The inscription named the country where it had been born, and went into considerable detail about its domestic life, youthful amours, and even the verses, mottoes and riddles it had written. All it lacked was the authentication of a dynasty and date. On the back of the stone was inscribed the following quatrain:

> Found unfit to repair the azure sky
> Long years a foolish mortal man was I.
> My life in both worlds on this stone is writ:
> Pray who will copy out and publish it?

From his reading of the inscription Vanitas realized that this was a stone of some consequence. Accordingly he addressed himself to it in the following manner:

"Brother Stone, according to what you yourself seem to imply in these verses, this story of yours contains matter of sufficient interest to merit publication and has been carved here with that end in view. But as far as I can see (a) it has no discoverable dynastic period, and (b) it contains no examples of moral grandeur among its characters—no statesmanship, no social message of any kind. All I can find in it, in fact, are a number of females, conspicuous, if at all, only for their passion or folly or for some trifling talent or insignificant virtue. Even if I were to copy all this out, I cannot see that it would make a very remarkable book."

"Come, your reverence," said the stone (for Vanitas had been correct in assuming that it could speak), "must you be so obtuse? All the romances ever written have an artificial period setting—Han or Tang for the most part. In refusing to make use of that stale old convention and telling my *Story of the Stone* exactly as it occurred, it seems to me that, far from *depriving* it of anything, I have given it a freshness these other books do not have.

"Your so-called 'historical romances,' consisting, as they do, of scandalous anecdotes about statesmen and emperors of bygone days and scabrous attacks on the reputations of long-dead gentlewomen, contain more wickedness and immorality than I care to mention. Still worse is the 'erotic novel,' by whose filthy obscenities our young folk are all too easily corrupted. And the 'boudoir romances,' those dreary stereotypes with their volume after volume all pitched on the same note and their different characters undistinguishable except by name (all those ideally beautiful young ladies and ideally eligible young bachelors)—even they seem unable to avoid descending sooner or later into indecency.

"The trouble with this last kind of romance is that it only gets written in the first place because the author requires a framework in which to show off his love-poems. He goes about constructing this framework quite mechanically, beginning with the names of his pair of young lovers and invariably adding a third character, a servant or the like, to make mischief between them, like the *chou*[5] in a comedy.

"What makes these romances even more detestable is the stilted, bom-

---

3. Wise man.   4. That is, achieving enlightenment and passing beyond the cycles of rebirth.   5. The stock role of the clown in a play.

bastic language—inanities dressed in pompous rhetoric, remote alike from nature and common sense and teeming with the grossest absurdities.

"Surely my 'number of females,' whom I spent half a lifetime studying with my own eyes and ears, are preferable to this kind of stuff? I do not claim that they are better people than the ones who appear in books written before my time; I am only saying that the contemplation of their actions and motives may prove a more effective antidote to boredom and melancholy. And even the inelegant verses with which my story is interlarded could serve to entertain and amuse on those convivial occasions when rhymes and riddles are in demand.

"All that my story narrates, the meetings and partings, the joys and sorrows, the ups and downs of fortune, are recorded exactly as they happened. I have not dared to add the tiniest bit of touching-up, for fear of losing the true picture.

"My only wish is that men in the world below may sometimes pick up this tale when they are recovering from sleep or drunkenness, or when they wish to escape from business worries or a fit of the dumps, and in doing so find not only mental refreshment but even perhaps, if they will heed its lesson and abandon their vain and frivolous pursuits, some small arrest in the deterioration of their vital forces. What does your reverence say to that?"

For a long time Vanitas stood lost in thought, pondering this speech. He then subjected *The Story of the Stone* to a careful second reading. He could see that its main theme was love; that it consisted quite simply of a true record of real events; and that it was entirely free from any tendency to deprave and corrupt. He therefore copied it all out from beginning to end and took it back with him to look for a publisher.

As a consequence of all this, Vanitas, starting off in the Void (which is Truth) came to the contemplation of Form (which is Illusion); and from Form engendered Passion; and by communicating Passion, entered again into Form; and from Form awoke to the Void (which is Truth). He therefore changed his name from Vanitas to Brother Amor, or the Passionate Monk, (because he had approached Truth by way of Passion), and changed the title of the book from *The Story of the Stone* to *The Tale of Brother Amor*.

Old Kong Mei-xi from the homeland of Confucius called the book *A Mirror for the Romantic*. Wu Yu-feng called it *A Dream of Golden Days*. Cao Xueqin in his Nostalgia Studio worked on it for ten years, in the course of which he rewrote it no less than five times, dividing it into chapters, composing chapter headings, renaming it *The Twelve Beauties of Jinling,* and adding an introductory quatrain. Red Inkstone restored the original title when he recopied the book and added his second set of annotations to it.

This, then, is a true account of how *The Story of the Stone* came to be written.

> Pages full of idle words
> Penned with hot and bitter tears:
> All men call the author fool;
> None his secret message hears.

The origin of *The Story of the Stone* has now been made clear. The same cannot, however, be said of the characters and events which it recorded. Gentle reader, have patience! This is how the inscription began:

Long, long ago the world was tilted downwards towards the south-east;

and in that lower-lying south-easterly part of the earth there is a city called Soochow; and in Soochow the district around the Chang-men Gate is reckoned one of the two or three wealthiest and most fashionable quarters in the world of men. Outside the Chang-men Gate is a wide thoroughfare called Worldly Way; and somewhere off Worldly Way is an area called Carnal Lane. There is an old temple in the Carnal Lane area which, because of the way it is bottled up inside a narrow *cul-de-sac,* is referred to locally as Bottle-gourd Temple. Next door to Bottle-gourd Temple lived a gentleman of private means called Zhen Shi-yin and his wife Feng-shi, a kind, good woman with a profound sense of decency and decorum. The household was not a particularly wealthy one, but they were nevertheless looked up to by all and sundry as the leading family in the neighbourhood.

Zhen Shi-yin himself was by nature a quiet and totally unambitious person. He devoted his time to his garden and to the pleasures of wine and poetry. Except for a single flaw, his existence could, indeed, have been described as an idyllic one. The flaw was that, although already past fifty, he had no son, only a little girl, just two years old, whose name was Ying-lian.

Once, during the tedium of a burning summer's day, Shi-yin was sitting idly in his study. The book had slipped from his nerveless grasp and his head had nodded down onto the desk in a doze. While in this drowsy state he seemed to drift off to some place he could not identify, where he became aware of a monk and a Taoist walking along and talking as they went.

"Where do you intend to take that thing you are carrying?" the Taoist was asking.

"Don't you worry about him!" replied the monk with a laugh. "There is a batch of lovesick souls awaiting incarnation in the world below whose fate is due to be decided this very day. I intend to take advantage of this opportunity to slip our little friend in amongst them and let him have a taste of human life along with the rest."

"Well, well, so another lot of these amorous wretches is about to enter the vale of tears," said the Taoist. "How did all this begin? And where are the souls to be reborn?"

"You will laugh when I tell you," said the monk. "When this stone was left unused by the goddess, he found himself at a loose end and took to wandering about all over the place for want of better to do, until one day his wanderings took him to the place where the fairy Disenchantment lives.

"Now Disenchantment could tell that there was something unusual about this stone, so she kept him there in her Sunset Glow Palace and gave him the honorary title of Divine Luminescent Stone-in-Waiting in the Court of Sunset Glow.

"But most of his time he spent west of Sunset Glow exploring the banks of the Magic River. There, by the Rock of Rebirth, he found the beautiful Crimson Pearl Flower, for which he conceived such a fancy that he took to watering her every day with sweet dew, thereby conferring on her the gift of life.

"Crimson Pearl's substance was composed of the purest cosmic essences, so she was already half-divine; and now, thanks to the vitalizing effect of the sweet dew, she was able to shed her vegetable shape and assume the form of a girl.

"This fairy girl wandered about outside the Realm of Separation, eating the Secret Passion Fruit when she was hungry and drinking from the Pool of Sadness when she was thirsty. The consciousness that she owed the stone something for his kindness in watering her began to prey on her mind and ended by becoming an obsession.

" 'I have no sweet dew here that I can repay him with,' she would say to herself. 'The only way in which I could perhaps repay him would be with the tears shed during the whole of a mortal lifetime if he and I were ever to be reborn as humans in the world below.'

"Because of this strange affair, Disenchantment has got together a group of amorous young souls, of which Crimson Pearl is one, and intends to send them down into the world to take part in the great illusion of human life. And as today happens to be the day on which this stone is fated to go into the world too, I am taking him with me to Disenchantment's tribunal for the purpose of getting him registered and sent down to earth with the rest of these romantic creatures."

"How very amusing!" said the Taoist. "I have certainly never heard of a debt of tears before. Why shouldn't the two of us take advantage of this opportunity to go down into the world ourselves and save a few souls? It would be a work of merit."

"That is exactly what I was thinking," said the monk. "Come with me to Disenchantment's palace to get this absurd creature cleared. Then, when this last batch of romantic idiots goes down, you and I can go down with them. At present about half have already been born. They await this last batch to make up the number."

"Very good, I will go with you then," said the Taoist. Shi-yin heard all this conversation quite clearly, and curiosity impelled him to go forward and greet the two reverend gentlemen. They returned his greeting and asked him what he wanted.

"It is not often that one has the opportunity of listening to a discussion of the operations of *karma*[6] such as the one I have just been privileged to over-hear," said Shi-yin. "Unfortunately I am a man of very limited understanding and have not been able to derive the full benefit from your conversation. If you would have the very great kindness to enlighten my benighted under-standing with a somewhat fuller account of what you were discussing, I can promise you the most devout attention. I feel sure that your teaching would have a salutary effect on me and—who knows—might save me from the pains of hell."

The reverend gentlemen laughed. "These are heavenly mysteries and may not be divulged. But if you wish to escape from the fiery pit, you have only to remember us when the time comes, and all will be well."

Shi-yin saw that it would be useless to press them. "Heavenly mysteries must not, of course, be revealed. But might one perhaps inquire what the 'absurd creature' is that you were talking about? Is it possible that I might be allowed to see it?"

"Oh, as for that," said the monk: "I think it is on the cards for you to have a look at *him*," and he took the object from his sleeve and handed it to Shi-yin.

Shi-yin took the object from him and saw that it was a clear, beautiful jade

---

6. The accumulation of good and bad deeds that determines a soul's future lives.

on one side of which were carved the words "Magic Jade." There were several columns of smaller characters on the back, which Shi-yin was just going to examine more closely when the monk, with a cry of "Here we are, at the frontier of Illusion," snatched the stone from him and disappeared, with the Taoist, through a big stone archway above which

THE LAND OF ILLUSION

was written in large characters. A couplet in smaller characters was inscribed vertically on either side of the arch:

> Truth becomes fiction when the fiction's true;
> Real becomes not-real where the unreal's real.

Shi-yin was on the point of following them through the archway when suddenly a great clap of thunder seemed to shake the earth to its very foundations, making him cry out in alarm.

And there he was sitting in his study, the contents of his dream already half forgotten, with the sun still blazing on the ever-rustling plantains outside, and the wet-nurse at the door with his little daughter Ying-lian in her arms. Her delicate little pink-and-white face seemed dearer to him than ever at that moment, and he stretched out his arms to take her and hugged her to him.

*   *   *

Chapters 1 to 25 Summary   After waking from his dream in the middle of the first chapter, Zhen Shi-yin meets the monk and the Taoist in the flesh, and they seek to take his daughter Ying-lian from him, informing him that otherwise she will be involved in misfortune. Zhen Shi-yin refuses and subsequently, in a series of misadventures, the baby is stolen from her nurse and will reappear in Chapter 4 as "Caltrop," raised by kidnappers and eventually sold to be the concubine of Xue Pan in the Jia household.

In Chapter 3 the scene shifts to the Jia household, which has made a home for the young Lin Dai-yu after her mother's death and for the Xue family, including Xue Pan and his sister Xue Bao-chai. The Xues had been a powerful family in Nanjing; but in acquiring Caltrop as his concubine, Xue Pan had another suitor beaten to death, and after Xue Pan had bribed his way out of a murder charge, the family thought it prudent to move to the capital to stay with their powerful relatives, the Jias.

The Jia household is dominated by Grandmother Jia, whose favorite is the adolescent Bao-yu, the only surviving son of Jia Zheng and his wife Lady Wang. Bao-yu, born with a piece of jade in his mouth, is the metamorphosis of Stone. Jia Zheng has another son, Jia Huan, by his concubine, known as Aunt Zhao. Note that concubinage was commonly practiced in large households, though normally only the sons of the legitimate wife could inherit.

In Chapter 17 Prospect Garden is constructed to receive the visit of the imperial concubine, one of Lady Wang's daughters and Bao-yu's sister. After the visit, all the young girls of the household are given lodgings in the various buildings in the garden; Bao-yu, who is very close to his sisters and cousins and prefers the company of girls to boys, is also allowed to take up residence in the garden.

As we pick up the story in Chapter 26, Jia Huan has spilled hot wax on his half brother Bao-yu's face in a fit of jealousy. Lady Wang rebukes Aunt Zhao for the behavior of her son, and Aunt Zhao, in a rage, pays a sorceress to cast a spell on Bao-yu. Bao-yu is ill for a while, but recovers.

CHAPTER 26

*A conversation on Wasp Waist Bridge is a cover for
communication of a different kind
And a soliloquy overhead in the Naiad's House reveals
unsuspected depths of feeling.*

By the time the thirty-three days' convalescence had ended, not only were Bao-yu's health and strength completely restored, but even the burn-marks on his face had vanished, and he was allowed to move back into the Garden.

It may be recalled that when Bao-yu's sickness was at its height, it had been found necessary to call in Jia Yun[7] with a number of pages under his command to take turns in watching over him. Crimson[8] was there too at that time, having been brought in with the other maids from his apartment. During those few days she and Jia Yun therefore had ample opportunity of seeing each other, and a certain familiarity began to grow up between them.

Crimson noticed that Jia Yun was often to be seen sporting a handkerchief very much like the one she had lost. She nearly asked him about it, but in the end was too shy. Then, after the monk's visit, the presence of the menfolk was no longer required and Jia Yun went back to his tree-planting. Though Crimson could still not dismiss the matter entirely from her mind, she did not ask anyone about it for fear of arousing their suspicions.

A day or two after their return to Green Delights,[9] Crimson was sitting in her room, still brooding over this handkerchief business, when a voice outside the window inquired whether she was in. Peeping through an eyelet in the casement she recognized Melilot,[1] a little maid who belonged to the same apartment as herself.

"Yes, I'm in," she said. "Come inside!"

Little Melilot came bounding in and sat down on the bed with a giggle.

"I'm in luck!" she said. "I was washing some things in the yard when Bao-yu asked for some tea to be taken round to Miss Lin's for him and Miss Aroma[2] gave *me* the job of taking it. When I got there, Miss Lin had just been given some money by Her Old Ladyship[3] and was sharing it out among her maids; so when she saw me she just said 'Here you are!' and gave me two big handfuls of it. I've no idea how much it is. Will you look after it for me, please?"

She undid her handkerchief and poured out a shower of coins. Crimson carefully counted them for her and put them away in a safe place.

"What's been the matter with you lately?" said Melilot. "If you ask me, I think you ought to go home for a day or two and call in a doctor. I expect you need some medicine."

"Silly!" said Crimson. "I'm perfectly all right. What should I want to go home for?"

"I know what, then," said Melilot. "Miss Lin's very weakly. She's always taking medicine. Why don't you ask her to give you some of hers? It would probably do just as well."

"Oh, nonsense!" said Crimson. "You can't take other people's medicines just like that!"

---

7. A poor relation of the Jias employed in the household.   8. One of Bao-yu's maids.   9. Bao-yu's residence in the garden.   1. One of Bao-yu's maids.   2. Bao-yu's chief maid. Miss Lin is Lin Dai-yu.
3. Bao-yu's grandmother.

"Well, you can't go on in this way," said Melilot, "never eating or drinking properly. What will become of you?"

"Who *cares?*" said Crimson. "The sooner I'm dead the better!"

"You shouldn't say such things," said Melilot. "It isn't right."

"Why not?" said Crimson. "How do you know what is on my mind?"

Melilot shook her head sympathetically.

"I can't say I really blame you," she said. "Things *are* very difficult here at times. Take yesterday, for example. Her Old Ladyship said that as Bao-yu was better now and there was to be a thanksgiving for his recovery, all those who had the trouble of nursing him during his illness were to be rewarded according to their grades. Well now, I can understand the very young ones like me not being included, but why should they leave *you* out? I felt really sorry for you when I heard that they'd left you out. Aroma, of course, you'd expect to get more than anyone else. I don't blame *her* at all. In fact, I think it's owing to her. Let's be honest: none of us can compare with Aroma. I mean, even if she didn't always take so much trouble over everything, no one would want to quarrel about *her* having a bigger share. What makes me so angry is that people like Skybright and Mackerel should count as top grade when everyone knows they're only put there to curry favour with Bao-yu. Doesn't it make you angry?"

"I don't see much point in getting angry," said Crimson. "You know what they said about the mile-wide marquee: 'Even the longest party must have an end'? Well, none of us is here for ever, you know. Another four or five years from now when we've each gone our different ways it won't *matter* any longer what all the rest of us are doing."

Little Melilot found this talk of parting and impermanence vaguely affecting and a slight moisture was to be observed about her eyes. She thought shame to cry without good cause, however, and masked her emotion with a smile:

"That's perfectly true. Only yesterday Bao-yu was going on about all the things he's going to do to his rooms and the clothes he's going to have made and everything, just as if he had a hundred or two years ahead of him with nothing to do but kill time in."

Crimson laughed scornfully, though whether at Melilot's simplicity or at Bao-yu's improvidence is unclear, since just as she was about to comment, a little maid came running in, so young that her hair was still done up in two little girl's horns. She was carrying some patterns and sheets of paper.

"You're to copy out these two patterns."

She threw them in Crimson's direction and straightway darted out again. Crimson shouted after her:

"Who are they for, then? You might at least finish your message before rushing off. What are you in such a tearing hurry about? Is someone steaming wheatcakes for you and you're afraid they'll get cold?"

"They're for Mackerel." The little maid paused long enough to bawl an answer through the window, then picking up her heels, went pounding off, *plim-plam, plim-plam, plim-plam,* as fast as she had come.

Crimson threw the patterns crossly to one side and went to hunt in her drawer for a brush to trace them with. After rummaging for several minutes she had only succeeded in finding a few worn-out ones, too moulted for use.

"Funny!" she said. "I could have sworn I put a new one in there the other day . . ."

She thought a bit, then laughed at herself as she remembered:

"Of course. Oriole[4] took it, the evening before last." She turned to Melilot. "Would you go and get it for me, then?"

"I'm afraid I can't," said Melilot. "Miss Aroma's waiting for me to fetch some boxes for her. You'll have to get it yourself."

"If Aroma's waiting for you, why have you been sitting here gossiping all this time?" said Crimson. "If I hadn't asked you to go and get it, she wouldn't have been waiting, would she? Lazy little beast!"

She left the room and walked out of the gate of Green Delights and in the direction of Bao-chai's courtyard. She was just passing by Drenched Blossoms Pavilion when she caught sight of Bao-yu's old wet-nurse, Nannie Li, coming from the opposite direction and stood respectfully aside to wait for her.

"Where have you been, Mrs. Li?" she asked her. "I didn't expect to see you here."

Nannie Li made a flapping gesture with her hand:

"What do you think, my dear: His Nibs has taken a fancy to the young fellow who does the tree-planting—'Yin' or 'Yun' or whatever his name is—so Nannie has to go and ask him in. Let's hope Their Ladyships don't find out about it. There'll be trouble if they do."

"Are you really going to ask him in?"

"Yes. Why?"

Crimson laughed:

"If your Mr. Yun knows what's good for him, he won't agree to come."

"He's no fool," said Nannie Li. "Why shouldn't he?"

"Anyway, if he *does* come in," said Crimson, ignoring her question, "you can't just bring him in and then leave him, Mrs. Li. You'll have to take him back again yourself afterwards. You don't want him wandering off on his own. There's no knowing *who* he might bump into."

(Crimson herself, was the secret hope.)

"Gracious me! I haven't got *that* much spare time," said Nannie Li. "All I've done is just to tell him that he's got to come. I'll send someone else to fetch him in when I get back presently—one of the girls, or one of the older women, maybe."

She hobbled off on her stick, leaving Crimson standing there in a muse, her mission to fetch the tracing-brush momentarily forgotten. She was still standing there a minute or two later when a little maid came along, who, seeing that it was Crimson, asked her what she was doing there. Crimson looked up. It was Trinket, another of the maids from Green Delights.

"Where are you going?" Crimson asked her.

"I've been sent to fetch Mr. Yun," said Trinket. "I have to bring him inside to meet Master Bao."

She ran off on her way.

At the gate to Wasp Waist Bridge Crimson ran into Trinket again, this time with Jia Yun in tow. His eyes sought Crimson's; and hers, as she made

4. One of Bao-chai's maids.

pretence of conversing with Trinket, sought his. Their two pairs of eyes met and briefly skirmished; then Crimson felt herself blushing, and turning away abruptly, she made off for Allspice Court.

Our narrative now follows Jia Yun and Trinket along the winding pathway to the House of Green Delights. Soon they were at the courtyard gate and Jia Yun waited outside while she went in to announce his arrival. She returned presently to lead him inside.

There were a few scattered rocks in the courtyard and some clumps of jade-green plantain. Two storks stood in the shadow of a pine-tree, preening themselves with their long bills. The gallery surrounding the courtyard was hung with cages of unusual design in which perched or fluttered a wide variety of birds, some of them gay-plumaged exotic ones. Above the steps was a little five-frame[5] penthouse building with a glimpse of delicately-carved partitions visible through the open doorway, above which a horizontal board hung, inscribed with the words

CRIMSON JOYS AND GREEN DELIGHTS

"So that's why it's called 'The House of Green Delights,' " Jia Yun told himself. "The name is taken from the inscription."

A laughing voice addressed him from behind one of the silk gauze casements:

"Come on in! It must be two or three months since I first forgot our appointment!"

Jia Yun recognized the voice as Bao-yu's and hurried up the steps inside. He looked about him, dazzled by the brilliance of gold and semi-precious inlay-work and the richness of the ornaments and furnishings, but unable to see Bao-yu in the midst of it all. To the left of him was a full-length mirror from behind which two girls now emerged, both about fifteen or sixteen years old and of much the same build and height. They addressed him by name and asked him to come inside. Slightly overawed, he muttered something in reply and hurried after them, not daring to take more than a furtive glance at them from the corner of his eye. They ushered him into a tent-like summer "cabinet" of green net, whose principal furniture was a tiny lacquered bed with crimson hangings heavily patterned in gold. On this Bao-yu, wearing everyday clothes and a pair of bedroom slippers, was reclining, book in hand. He threw the book down as Jia Yun entered and rose to his feet with a welcoming smile. Jia Yun swiftly dropped knee and hand to floor in greeting. Bidden to sit, he modestly placed himself on a bedside chair.

"After I invited you round to my study that day," said Bao-yu, "a whole lot of things seemed to happen one after the other, and I'm afraid I quite forgot about your visit."[6]

Jia Yun returned his smile:

"Let's just say that it wasn't my luck to see you then. But you have been ill since then, Uncle Bao. Are you quite better now?"

"Quite better, thank you. I hear you've been very busy these last few days."

"That's as it should be,' said Jia Yun. "But I'm glad you are better, Uncle. That's a piece of good fortune for *all* of us."

---

5. A unit for measuring space in a building; a *five-frame* building is relatively small.   6. Earlier, Jia Yun had been invited to pay a visit on Bao-yu.

As they chatted, a maid came in with some tea. Jia Yun was talking to Bao-yu as she approached, but his eyes were on her. She was tall and rather thin with a long oval face, and she was wearing a rose-pink dress over a closely pleated white satin skirt and a black satin sleeveless jacket over the dress.

In the course of his brief sojourn among them in the early days of Bao-yu's illness, Jia Yun had got by heart the names of most of the principal females of Bao-yu's establishment. He knew at a glance that the maid now serving him tea was Aroma. He was also aware that she was in some way more important than the other maids and that to be waited on by her in the seated presence of her master was an honour. Jumping hastily to his feet he addressed her with a modest smile:

"You shouldn't pour tea for *me*, Miss! I'm not like a visitor here. You should let me pour for myself!"

"Oh *do* sit down!" said Bao-yu. "You don't have to be like that in front of the *maids!*"

"I know," said Jia Yun. "But a body-servant![7] I don't like to presume."

He sat down, nevertheless, and sipped his tea while Bao-yu made conversation on a number of unimportant topics. He told him which household kept the best troupe of players, which had the finest gardens, whose maids were the prettiest, who gave the best parties, and who had the best collection of curiosities or the strangest pets. Jia Yun did his best to keep up with him. After a while Bao-yu showed signs of flagging, and when Jia Yun, observing what appeared to be fatigue, rose to take his leave, he did not very strongly press him to stay.

"You must come again when you can spare the time," said Bao-yu, and ordered Trinket to see him out of the Garden.

Once outside the gateway of Green Delights, Jia Yun looked around him on all sides, and having ascertained that there was no one else about, slowed down to a more dawdling pace so that he could ask Trinket a few questions. Indeed, the little maid was subjected to quite a catechism: How old was she? What was her name? What did her father and mother do? How many years had she been working for his Uncle Bao? How much pay did she get a month? How many girls were there working for him altogether? Trinket seemed to have no objection, however, and answered each question as it came.

"That girl you were talking to on the way in," he said, "isn't her name 'Crimson'?"

Trinket laughed:

"Yes. Why do you ask?"

"I heard her asking you about a handkerchief. Only it just so happens that I picked one up."

Trinket showed interest.

"She's asked me about that handkerchief of hers a number of times. I told her, I've got better things to do with my time than go looking for people's handkerchiefs. But when she asked me about it again today, she said that if I could find it for her, she'd give me a reward. Come to think of it, you were there when she said that, weren't you? It was when we were outside the gate of Allspice Court. So you can bear me out. Oh Mr. Jia, please let me have it if you've picked it up and I'll be able to see what she will give me for it!"

---

7. A personal servant of higher status than maids.

Jia Yun had picked up a silk handkerchief a month previously at the time when his tree-planting activities had just started. He knew that it must have been dropped by one or another of the female inmates of the Garden, but not knowing which, had not so far ventured to do anything about his discovery. When earlier on he had heard Crimson question Trinket about her loss, he had realized, with a thrill of pleasure, that the handkerchief he had picked up must have been hers. Trinket's request now gave him just the opening he required. He drew a handkerchief of his own from inside his sleeve and held it up in front of her with a smile:

"I'll give it to you on one condition. If she lets you have this reward you were speaking of, you've *got* to let me know. No cheating, mind!"

Trinket received the handkerchief with eager assurances that he would be informed of the outcome, and having seen him out of the Garden, went back again to look for Crimson.

Our narrative returns now to Bao-yu.

After disposing of Jia Yun, Bao-yu continued to feel extremely lethargic and lay back on the bed with every appearance of being about to doze off to sleep. Aroma hurried over to him and, sitting on the edge of the bed, roused him with a shake:

"Come on! Surely you are not going to sleep *again*? You need some fresh air. Why don't you go outside and walk around for a bit?"

Bao-yu took her by the hand and smiled at her.

"I'd like to go," he said, "but I don't want to leave you."

"Silly!" said Aroma with a laugh. "Don't say what you don't mean!"

She hoicked[8] him to his feet.

"Well, where am I going to go then?" said Bao-yu. "I just feel so *bored*."

"Never mind where, just go out!" said Aroma. "If you stay moping indoors like this, you'll get even more bored."

Bao-yu followed her advice, albeit half-heartedly, and went out into the courtyard. After visiting the cages in the gallery and playing for a bit with the birds, he ambled out of the courtyard into the Garden and along the bank of Drenched Blossoms Stream, pausing for a while to look at the goldfish in the water. As he did so, a pair of fawns came running like the wind from the hillside opposite. Bao-yu was puzzled. There seemed to be no reason for their mysterious terror. But just then little Jia Lan came running down the same slope after them, a tiny bow clutched in his hand. Seeing his uncle ahead of him, he stood politely to attention and greeted him cheerfully:

"Hello, Uncle. I didn't know you were at home. I thought you'd gone out."

"Mischievous little blighter, aren't you?" said Bao-yu. "What do you want to go shooting them for, poor little things?"

"I've got no reading to do today," said Jia Lan, "and I don't like to hang about doing nothing, so I thought I'd practise my archery and equitation."[9]

"Goodness! You'd better not waste time jawing, then," said Bao-yu, and left the young toxophilite[1] to his pursuits.

Moving on, without much thinking where he was going, he came presently to the gate of a courtyard.

> Denser than feathers on the phoenix' tail
> The stirred leaves murmured with a pent dragon's moan.

8. Yanked.   9. Horseback riding.   1. Archer.

The multitudinous bamboos and the board above the gate confirmed that his feet had, without conscious direction, carried him to the Naiad's House. Of their own accord they now carried him through the gateway and into the courtyard.

The House seemed silent and deserted, its bamboo door-blind hanging unrolled to the ground; but as he approached the window, he detected a faint sweetness in the air, traceable to a thin curl of incense smoke which drifted out through the green gauze of the casement. He pressed his face to the gauze; but before his eyes could distinguish anything, his ear became aware of a long, languorous sigh and the sound of a voice speaking:

"Each day in a drowsy waking dream of love."

Bao-yu felt a sudden yearning for the speaker. He could see her now. It was Dai-yu, of course, lying on her bed, stretching herself and yawning luxuriously.

He laughed:

"Why 'each day in a drowsy waking dream of love'?" he asked through the window (the words were from his beloved *Western Chamber*²); then going to the doorway he lifted up the door-blind and walked into the room.

Dai-yu realized that she had been caught off her guard. She covered her burning face with her sleeve, and turning over towards the wall, pretended to be asleep. Bao-yu went over intending to turn her back again, but just at that moment Dai-yu's old wet-nurse came hurrying in with two other old women at her heels:

"Miss Lin's asleep, sir. Would you mind coming back again after she's woken up?"

Dai-yu at once turned over and sat up with a laugh:

"Who's asleep?"

The three old women laughed apologetically.

"Sorry, miss. We thought you were asleep. Nightingale! Come inside now! Your mistress is awake."

Having shouted for Nightingale, the three guardians of morality retired.

"What do you mean by coming into people's rooms when they're asleep?" said Dai-yu, smiling up at Bao-yu as she sat on the bed's edge patting her hair into shape.

At the sight of those soft cheeks so adorably flushed and the starry eyes a little misted with sleep a wave of emotion passed over him. He sank into a chair and smiled back at her:

"What was that you were saying just now before I came in?"

"I didn't say anything," said Dai-yu.

Bao-yu laughed and snapped his fingers at her:

"Put that on your tongue, girl! I heard you say it."

While they were talking to one another, Nightingale came in.

"Nightingale," said Bao-yu, "what about a cup of that excellent tea of yours?"

"Excellent tea?" said Nightingale. "There's nothing very special about the tea we drink here. If nothing but the best will do, you'd better wait for Aroma to come."

"Never mind about *him*!" said Dai-yu. "First go and get me some water!"

---

2. A 13th-century romantic play.

"He *is* our guest," said Nightingale. "I can't fetch you any water until I've given him his tea." And she went to pour him a cup.

"Good girl!" said Bao-yu.

> "If with your amorous mistress I should wed,
> 'Tis you, sweet maid, must make our bridal bed."

The words, like Dai-yu's languorous line, were from *Western Chamber*, but in somewhat dubious taste. Dai-yu was dreadfully offended by them. In an instant the smile had vanished from her face.

"*What* was that you said?"

He laughed:

"I didn't say anything."

Dai-yu began to cry.

"This is your latest amusement, I suppose. Every time you hear some coarse expression outside or read some crude, disgusting book, you have to come back here and give me the benefit of it. I am to become a source of entertainment for the *menfolk* now, it seems."

She rose, weeping, from the bed and went outside. Bao-yu followed her in alarm.

"Dearest coz, it was very wrong of me to say that, but it just slipped out without thinking. Please don't go and tell! I promise never to say anything like that again. May my mouth rot and my tongue decay if I do!"

Just at that moment Aroma came hurrying up:

"Quick!" she said. "You must come back and change. The Master[3] wants to see you."

The descent of this thunderbolt drove all else from his mind and he rushed off in a panic. As soon as he had changed, he hurried out of the Garden. Tealeaf[4] was waiting for him outside the inner gate.

"I suppose you don't know what he wants to see me about?" Bao-yu asked him.

"I should hurry up, if I were you," said Tealeaf. "All I know is that he wants to see you. You'll find out why soon enough when you get there."

He hustled him along as he spoke.

They had passed round the main hall, Bao-yu still in a state of fluttering apprehensiveness, when there was a loud guffaw from a corner of the wall. It was Xue Pan,[5] clapping his hands and stamping his feet in mirth.

"Ho! Ho! Ho! You'd never have come this quickly if you hadn't been told that Uncle wanted you!"

Tealeaf, also laughing, fell on his knees. Bao-yu stood there looking puzzled. It was some moments before it dawned on him that he had been hoaxed. Xue Pan was by this time being apologetic—bowing repeatedly and pumping his hands to show how sorry he was:

"Don't blame the lad!" he said. "It wasn't his fault. I talked him into it."

Bao-yu saw that he could do nothing, and might as well accept with a good grace.

"I don't mind being made a fool of," he said, "but I think it was going a bit far to bring my father into it. I think perhaps I'd better tell Aunt Xue and see what *she* thinks about it all."

---

3. Jia Sheng, Bao-yu's father.   4. One of Bao-yu's male pages.   5. A troublemaker, Xue Bao-chai's brother.

"Now look here, old chap," said Xue Pan, getting agitated, "it was only because I wanted to fetch you out a bit quicker. I admit it was very wrong of me to make free with your Parent, but after all, you've only got to mention *my* father next time you want to fool *me* and we'll be quits!"

"Aiyo!" said Bao-yu. "Worse and worse!" He turned to Tealeaf: "Treacherous little beast! What are you still kneeling for?"

Tealeaf kotowed and rose to his feet.

"Look," said Xue Pan. "I wouldn't have troubled you otherwise, only it's my birthday on the third of next month and old Hu and old Cheng and a couple of the others, I don't know where they got them from but they've given me:

> a piece of fresh lotus root, ever so crisp and crunchy, as thick as that, look, and as long as that;
> a huge great melon, look, as big as that;
> a freshly-caught sturgeon as big as that;
> and a cypress-smoked Siamese sucking-pig as big as that that came in the tribute from Siam.

Don't you think it was clever of them to get me those things? Maybe not so much the sturgeon and the sucking-pig. They're just expensive. But where would you go to get a piece of lotus root or a melon like that? However did they get them to *grow* so big? I've given some of the stuff to Mother, and while I was about it I sent some round to your grandmother and Auntie Wang, but I've still got a lot left over. I can't eat it all myself: it would be unlucky. But apart from me, the only person I can think of who is *worthy* to eat a present like this is you. That's why I came over specially to invite you. And we're lucky, because we've got a little chap who sings coming round as well. So you and I will be able to sit down and make a day of it, eh? Really enjoy ourselves."

Xue Pan, still talking, conducted Bao-yu to his "study," where Zhan Guang, Cheng Ri-xing, Hu Si-lai and Dan Ping-ren (the four donors of the feast) and the young singer he had mentioned were already waiting. They rose to welcome Bao-yu as he entered. When the bowings and courtesies were over and tea had been taken, Xue Pan called for his servants to lay.[6] A tremendous bustle ensued, which seemed to go on for quite a long time before everything was finally ready and the diners were able to take their places at the table.

Bao-yu noticed sliced melon and lotus root among the dishes, both of unusual quality and size.

"It seems wrong to be sharing your presents with you before I have given you anything myself," he said jokingly.

"Yes," said Xue Pan. "What are you planning to give me for my birthday next month? Something new and out of the ordinary, I hope."

"I haven't really *got* anything much to give you," said Bao-yu. "Things like money and food and clothing I don't want for, but they're not really mine to give. The only way I could give you something that would *really* be mine would be by doing some calligraphy or painting a picture for you."

"Talking of pictures," said Xue Pan genially, "that's reminded me. I saw a set of dirty pictures in someone's house the other day. They were real beauties. There was a lot of writing on top that I didn't pay much attention to,

6. That is, to set the table.

but I did notice the signature. I think it was 'Geng Huang,' the man who painted them. They were really good!"

Bao-yu was puzzled. His knowledge of the masters of painting and calligraphy both past and present was not inconsiderable, but he had never in all his experience come across a "Geng Huang." After racking his brains for some moments he suddenly began to chuckle and called for a writing-brush. A writing-brush having been produced by one of the servants, he wrote two characters with it in the palm of his hand.

"Are you quite *sure* the signature you saw was 'Geng Huang'?" he asked Xue Pan.

"What do you mean?" said Xue Pan. "Of course I'm sure."

Bao-yu opened his hand and held it up for Xue Pan to see:

"You sure it wasn't these two characters? They *are* quite similar."

The others crowded round to look. They all laughed when they saw what he had written:

"Yes, it must have been 'Tang Yin.'[7] Mr. Xue couldn't have been seeing straight that day. Ha! Ha! Ha!"

Xue Pan realized that he had made a fool of himself, but passed it off with an embarrassed laugh:

"Oh, Tankin' or wankin'," he said, "what difference does it make, anyway?"

Just then "Mr. Feng" was announced by one of the servants, which Bao-yu knew could only mean General Feng Tang's son, Feng Zi-ying. Xue Pan and the rest told the boy to bring him in immediately, but Feng Zi-ying was already striding in, talking and laughing as he went. The others hurriedly rose and invited him to take a seat.

"Ha!" said Feng Zi-ying. "No need to go out then. Enjoyin' yourselves at home, eh? Very nice too!"

"It's a long time since we've seen you around," said Bao-yu. "How's the General?"

"Fahver's in good health, thank you very much," said Feng Zi-ying, "but Muvver hasn't been too well lately. Caught a chill or somethin'."

Observing with glee that Feng Zi-ying was sporting a black eye, Xue Pan asked him how he had come by it:

"Been having a dust-up, then? Who was it this time? Looks as if he left his signature!"

Feng Zi-ying laughed:

"Don't use the mitts any more nowadays—not since that time I laid into Colonel Chou's son and did him an injury. That was a lesson to me. I've learned to keep my temper since then. No, this happened the other day durin' a huntin' expedition in the Iron Net Mountains. I got flicked by a goshawk's wing."

"When was this?" Bao-yu asked him.

"We left on the twenty-eighth of last month," said Feng Zi-ying. "Didn't get back till a few days ago."

"Ah, that explains why I didn't see you at Shen's party earlier this month," said Bao-yu. "I meant at the time to ask why you weren't there, but I forgot. Did you go alone on this expedition or was the General there with you?"

---

7. This joke shows Xue Pan's ignorance: he has misread the Chinese characters for one of the most famous of all Ming painters.

"Fahver most certainly *was* there," said Feng Zi-ying. "I was practically dragged along in tow. Do you think I'm mad enough to go rushin' off in pursuit of hideous hardships when I could be sittin' comfortably at home eatin' good food and drinkin' good wine and listenin' to the odd song or two? Still, some good came of it. It was a lucky accident."

As he had now finished his tea, Xue Pan urged him to join them at table and tell them his story at leisure, but Feng Zi-ying rose to his feet again and declined.

"I ought by rights to stay and drink a few cups with you," he said, "but there's somethin' very important I've got to see Fahver about now, so I'm afraid I really must refuse."

But Xue Pan, Bao-yu and the rest were by no means content to let him get away with this excuse and propelled him insistently towards the table.

"Now look here, this is too bad!" Feng Zi-ying good-humouredly protested. "All the years we've been knockin' around togevver we've never before insisted that a fellow should have to stay if he don't want to. The fact is, I really *can't*. Oh well, if I *must* have a drink, fetch some decent-sized cups and I'll just put down a couple of quick ones!"

This was clearly the most he would concede and the others perforce acquiesced. Two sconce-cups were brought and ceremoniously filled, Bao-yu holding the cups and Xue Pan pouring from the wine-kettle.[8] Feng Zi-ying drank them standing, one after the other, each in a single breath.

"Now come on," said Bao-yu, "let's hear about this 'lucky accident' before you go!"

Feng Zi-ying laughed:

"Couldn't tell it properly just now," he said. "It's somethin' that needs a special party all to itself. I'll invite you all round to my place another day and you shall have the details then. There's a favour I want to ask too, by the bye, so we'll be able to talk about that then as well."

He made a determined movement towards the door.

"Now you've got us all peeing ourselves with curiosity!" said Xue Pan. "You might at least tell us when this party is going to be, to put us out of our suspense."

"Not more than ten days' time and not less than eight," said Feng Zi-ying; and going out into the courtyard, he jumped on his horse and clattered away.

Having seen him off, the others went in again, reseated themselves at table, and resumed their potations. When the party finally broke up, Bao-yu returned to the Garden in a state of cheerful inebriation. Aroma, who had had no idea what the summons from Jia Zheng might portend and was still wondering anxiously what had become of him, at once demanded to know the cause of his condition. He gave her a full account of what had happened.

"Well really!" said Aroma. "Here were we practically beside ourselves with anxiety, and all the time you were there enjoying yourself! You might at least have sent word to let us know you were all right."

"I was going to send word," said Bao-yu. "Of course I was. But then old Feng arrived and it put it out of my mind."

At that moment Bao-chai walked in, all smiles.

"I hear you've made a start on the famous present," she said.

---

8. Chinese wine was heated before it was drunk. *Sconce-cups:* large wine cups.

"But surely you and your family must have had some already?" said Bao-yu.

Bao-chai shook her head:

"Pan was very pressing that I should have some, but I refused. I told him to save it for other people. I know I'm not really the right sort of person for such superior delicacies. If *I* were to eat any, I should be afraid of some frightful nemesis overtaking me."

A maid poured tea for her as she spoke, and conversation of a desultory kind proceeded between sips.

Our narrative returns now to Dai-yu.

Having been present when Bao-yu received his summons, Dai-yu, too, was greatly worried about him—the more so as the day advanced and he had still not returned. Then in the evening, some time after dinner, she heard that he had just got back and resolved to go over and ask him exactly what had happened. She was sauntering along on the way there when she caught sight of Bao-chai some distance ahead of her, just entering Bao-yu's courtyard. Continuing to amble on, she came presently to Drenched Blossoms Bridge, from which a large number of different kinds of fish were to be seen swimming about in the water below. Dai-yu did not know what kinds of fish they were, but they were so beautiful that she had to stop and admire them, and by the time she reached the House of Green Delights, the courtyard gate had been shut for the night and she was obliged to knock for admittance.

Now it so happened that Skybright had just been having a quarrel with Emerald, and being thoroughly out of temper, was venting some of her ill-humour on the lately arrived Bao-chai, complaining *sotto voce* behind her back about "people who were always inventing excuses to come dropping in and who kept other people staying up half the night when they would like to be in bed." A knock at the gate coming in the midst of these resentful mutterings was enough to make her really angry.

"They've all gone to bed," she shouted, not even bothering to inquire who the caller was. "Come again tomorrow!"

Dai-yu was aware that Bao-yu's maids often played tricks on one another, and it occurred to her that the girl in the courtyard, not recognizing her voice, might have mistaken her for another maid and be keeping her locked out for a joke. She therefore called out again, this time somewhat louder than before:

"Come on! Open up, please! It's me."

Unfortunately Skybright had still not recognized the voice.

"I don't care who you are," she replied bad-temperedly. "Master Bao's orders are that I'm not to let *anyone* in."

Dumbfounded by her insolence, Dai-yu stood outside the gate in silence. She could not, however much she felt like it, give vent to her anger in noisy expostulation. "Although they are always telling me to treat my Uncle's house as my own," she reflected, "I am still really an outsider. And now that Mother and Father are both dead and I am on my own, to make a fuss about a thing like this when I am living in someone else's house could only lead to further unpleasantness."

A big tear coursed, unregarded, down her cheek.

She was still standing there irresolute, unable to decide whether to go or stay, when a sudden volley of talk and laughter reached her from inside. It resolved itself, as she listened attentively, into the voices of Bao-yu and Bao-chai. An even bitterer sense of chagrin took possession of her. Suddenly, as she hunted in her mind for some possible reason for her exclusion, she remembered the events of the morning and concluded that Bao-yu must think she had told on him to his parents and was punishing her for her betrayal.

"But I would never betray you!" she expostulated with him in her mind. "Why couldn't you have asked first, before letting your resentment carry you to such lengths? If you won't see me today, does that mean that from now on we are going to stop seeing each other altogether?"

The more she thought about it the more distressed she became.

> Chill was the green moss pearled with dew
> And chill was the wind in the avenue;

but Dai-yu, all unmindful of the unwholesome damp, had withdrawn into the shadow of a flowering fruit-tree by the corner of the wall, and grieving now in real earnest, began to cry as though her heart would break. And as if Nature herself were affected by the grief of so beautiful a creature, the crows who had been roosting in the trees round about flew up with a great commotion and removed themselves to another part of the Garden, unable to endure the sorrow of her weeping.

> Tears filled each flower and grief their hearts perturbed,
> And silly birds were from their nests disturbed.

The author of the preceding couplet has given us a quatrain in much the same vein:

> Few in this world fair Frowner's looks surpassed,
> None matched her store of sweetness unexpressed.
> The first sob scarcely from her lips had passed
> When blossoms fell and birds flew off distressed.

As Dai-yu continued weeping there alone, the courtyard door suddenly opened with a loud creak and someone came out.

But in order to find out who it was, you will have to wait for the next chapter.

From *Volume 2*

CHAPTER 27

*Beauty Perspiring sports with butterflies
by the Raindrop Pavilion
And Beauty Suspiring weeps for fallen blossoms
by the Flowers' Grave*

As Dai-yu stood there weeping, there was a sudden creak of the courtyard gate and Bao-chai walked out, accompanied by Bao-yu with Aroma and a bevy of other maids who had come out to see her off. Dai-yu was on the point of stepping forward to question Bao-yu, but shrank from embarrassing him in front of so many people. Instead she slipped back into the shadows to let Bao-chai pass, emerging only when Bao-yu and the rest were back inside and the gate was once more barred. She stood for a while facing it, and shed a few silent tears; then, realizing that it was pointless to remain standing there, she turned and went back to her room and began, in a listless, mechanical manner, to take off her ornaments and prepare herself for the night.

Nightingale and Snowgoose had long since become habituated to Dai-yu's moody temperament; they were used to her unaccountable fits of depression, when she would sit, the picture of misery, in gloomy silence broken only by an occasional gusty sigh, and to her mysterious, perpetual weeping, that was occasioned by no observable cause. At first they had tried to reason with her, or, imagining that she must be grieving for her parents or that she was feeling homesick or had been upset by some unkindness, they would do their best to comfort her. But as the months lengthened into years and she still continued exactly the same as before, they gradually became accustomed and no longer sought reasons for her behaviour. That was why they ignored her on this occasion and left her alone to her misery, remaining where they were in the outer room and continuing to occupy themselves with their own affairs.

She sat, motionless as a statue, leaning against the back of the bed, her hands clasped about her knees, her eyes full of tears. It had already been dark for some hours when she finally lay down to sleep.

Our story passes over the rest of that night in silence.

Next day was the twenty-sixth of the fourth month, the day on which, this year, the festival of Grain in Ear was due to fall. To be precise, the festival's official commencement was on the twenty-sixth day of the fourth month at two o'clock in the afternoon. It has been the custom from time immemorial to make offerings to the flower fairies on this day. For Grain in Ear marks the beginning of summer; it is about this time that the blossom begins to fall; and tradition has it that the flowerspirits, their work now completed, go away on this day and do not return until the following year. The offerings are therefore thought of as a sort of farewell party for the flowers.

This charming custom of "speeding the fairies" is a special favourite with the fair sex, and in Prospect Garden all the girls were up betimes on this day making little coaches and palanquins[9] out of willow-twigs and flowers and little banners and pennants from scraps of brocade and any other pretty material they could find, which they fastened with threads of coloured silk to the tops of flowering trees and shrubs. Soon every plant and tree was decorated and the whole garden had become a shimmering sea of nodding blossoms and fluttering coloured streamers. Moving about in the midst of it all, the girls in their brilliant summer dresses, beside which the most vivid hues of plant and plumage became faint with envy, added the final touch of brightness to a scene of indescribable gaiety and colour.

All the young people—Bao-chai, Ying-chun, Tan-chun, Xi-chun, Li Wan,

9. Sedan chairs, carried on poles by bearers.

Xi-feng[1] and her little girl and Caltrop, and all the maids from all the different apartments—were outside in the Garden enjoying themselves—all, that is, except Dai-yu, whose absence, beginning to be noticed, was first commented on by Ying-chun:

"What's happened to Cousin Lin? Lazy girl! Surely she can't *still* be in bed at this hour?"

Bao-chai volunteered to go and fetch her:

"The rest of you wait here; I'll go and rout her out for you," she said; and breaking away from the others, she made off in the direction of the Naiad's House.

While she was on her way, she caught sight of Élégante and the eleven other little actresses, evidently on their way to join in the fun. They came up and greeted her, and for a while she stood and chatted with them. As she was leaving them, she turned back and pointed in the direction from which she had just come:

"You'll find the others somewhere over there," she said. "I'm on my way to get Miss Lin. I'll join the rest of you presently."

She continued, by the circuitous route that the garden's contours obliged her to take, on her way to the Naiad's House. Raising her eyes as she approached it, she suddenly became aware that the figure ahead of her just disappearing inside it was Bao-yu. She stopped and lowered her eyes pensively again to the ground.

"Bao-yu and Dai-yu have known each other since they were little," she reflected. "They are used to behaving uninhibitedly when they are alone together. They don't seem to care what they say to one another; and one is never quite sure what sort of mood one is going to find them in. And Dai-yu, at the best of times, is always so touchy and suspicious. If I go in now after him, *he* is sure to feel embarrassed and *she* is sure to start imagining things. It would be better to go back without seeing her."

Her mind made up, she turned round and began to retrace her steps, intending to go back to the other girls; but just at that moment she noticed two enormous turquoise-coloured butterflies a little way ahead of her, each as large as a child's fan, fluttering and dancing on the breeze. She watched them fascinated and thought she would like to play a game with them. Taking a fan from inside her sleeve and holding it outspread in front of her, she followed them off the path and into the grass.

To and fro fluttered the pair of butterflies, sometimes alighting for a moment, but always flying off again before she could reach them. Once they seemed on the point of flying across the little river that flowed through the midst of the garden and Bao-chai had to stalk them with bated breath for fear of startling them out on to the water. By the time she had reached the Raindrop Pavilion she was perspiring freely and her interest in the butterflies was beginning to evaporate. She was about to turn back when she became aware of a low murmur of voices coming from inside the pavilion.

Raindrop Pavilion was built in such a way that it projected into the middle of the pool into which the little watercourse widened out at this point, so that on three of its sides it looked out on to the water. It was surrounded by

1. The wife of Bao-yu's uncle; she manages the household.

a verandah, whose railing followed the many angles formed by the bays and projections of the base. In each of its wooden walls there was a large paper-covered casement of elegantly patterned latticework.

Hearing voices inside the pavilion, Bao-chai halted and inclined her ear to listen.

"Are you *sure* this is your handkerchief?" one of the voices was saying. "If it is, take it; but if it isn't, I must return it to Mr. Yun."

"Of course it's mine," said the second voice. "Come on, let me have it!"

"Are you going to give me a reward? I hope I haven't taken all this trouble for nothing."

"I promised you I would give you a reward, and so I shall. Surely you don't think I was deceiving you?"

"All right, I get a reward for bringing it to you. But what about the person who picked it up? Doesn't *he* get anything?"

"Don't talk nonsense," said the second voice. "He's one of the masters. A master picking up something belonging to one of us should give it back as a matter of course. How can there be any question of *rewarding* him?"

"If you don't intend to reward him, what am I supposed to tell him when I see him? He was most insistent that I wasn't to give you the handkerchief unless you gave him a reward."

There was a long pause, after which the second voice replied:

"Oh, all right. Let him have this other handkerchief of mine then. That will have to do as his reward—But you must swear a solemn oath not to tell anyone else about this."

"May my mouth rot and may I die a horrible death if I ever tell anyone else about this, amen!" said the first voice.

"Goodness!" said the second voice again. "Here we are talking away, and all the time someone could be creeping up outside and listening to every word we say. We had better open these casements;[2] then even if anyone outside sees us, they'll think we are having an ordinary conversation; and *we* shall be able to see *them* and know in time when to stop."

Bao-chai, listening outside, gave a start.

"No wonder they say 'venery and thievery sharpen the wits,' " she thought. "If they open those windows and see me here, they are going to feel terribly embarrassed. And one of those voices sounds like that proud, peculiar girl Crimson who works in Bao-yu's room. If a girl like that knows that I have overheard her doing something she shouldn't be doing, it will be a case of 'the desperate dog will jump a wall, the desperate man will hazard all': there'll be a great deal of trouble and I shall be involved in it. There isn't time to hide. I shall have to do as the cicada does when he jumps out of his skin: give them something to put them off the scent—"

There was a loud creak as the casement yielded. Bao-chai advanced with deliberately noisy tread.

"Frowner!" she called out gaily. "I know where you're hiding."

Inside the pavilion Crimson and Trinket, who heard her say this and saw her advancing towards them just as they were opening the casement, were speechless with amazement; but Bao-chai ignored their confusion and addressed them genially:

2. That is, casement windows.

"Have you two got Miss Lin hidden away in there?"

"I haven't *seen* Miss Lin," said Trinket.

"I saw her just now from the river-bank," said Bao-chai. "She was squatting down over here playing with something in the water. I was going to creep up and surprise her, but she spotted me before I could get up to her and disappeared round this corner. Are you *sure* she's not hiding in there?"

She made a point of going inside the pavilion and searching; then, coming out again, she said in a voice loud enough for them to hear:

"If she's not in the pavilion, she must have crept into that grotto. Oh well, if she's not afraid of being bitten by a snake—!"

As she walked away she laughed inwardly at the ease with which she had extricated herself from a difficult situation.

"I think I'm fairly safely out of *that* one," she thought. "I wonder what those two will make of it."

What indeed! Crimson believed every word that Bao-chai had said, and as soon as the latter was at a distance, she seized hold of Trinket in alarm:

"Oh, how terrible! If Miss Lin was squatting there, she must have heard what we said before she went away."

Her companion was silent.

"Oh dear! What do you think she'll *do?*" said Crimson.

"Well, suppose she *did* hear," said Trinket, "it's not *her* backache. If we mind our business and she minds hers, there's no reason why anything should come of it."

"If it were Miss Bao that had heard us, I don't suppose anything *would*," said Crimson; "but Miss Lin is so critical and so intolerant. If *she* heard it and it gets about—oh dear!"

But just at that moment Caltrop, Advent, Chess and Scribe were seen approaching the pavilion, and Crimson and Trinket had to drop the subject in a hurry and join in a general conversation. Crimson noticed Xi-feng standing half-way up the rockery above the little grotto, beckoning. Breaking away from the others, she bounded up to her with a smiling face:

"What can I do for you, madam?"

Xi-feng ran an appraising eye over her. A neat, pretty, pleasantly-spoken girl, she decided, and smiled at her graciously:

"I have come here without my maids and need someone to take a message back to my apartment. I wonder if you are clever enough to get it right."

"Tell me the message, madam. If I don't get it right and make a mess of it, it will be up to you to punish me."

"Which of the young ladies do you work for?" said Xi-feng. "I'd better know, so that I can explain to her if she asks for you while you are doing my errand."

"I work for Master Bao," said Crimson.

Xi-feng laughed.

"Ah ha! You work for Master Bao. No wonder. Very well, then, if he asks for you while you are away, I shall explain. I want you to go to my apartment and tell Patience that there is a roll of money under the stand of the Ru-ware dish on the table in the outside room. There are a hundred and twenty taels[3] of silver in it to pay the embroiderers with. Tell her that when Zhang Cai's wife comes for it, she is to weigh it out in front of her before handing

---

3. A unit of currency. *Ru-ware:* fine porcelain.

it over. And there's one other thing. There's a little purse at the head of the bed in my inside room. I want you to bring it to me."

"Yes madam," said Crimson, and hurried off.

Returning shortly afterwards, she found that Xi-feng was no longer on the rockery; but Chess had just emerged from the little grotto beneath it and was standing there doing up her sash. Crimson ran down to speak to her:

"Excuse me, did you see where Mrs. Lian went to?"

" 'Fraid I didn't notice," said Chess.

Crimson looked around her. Bao-chai and Tan-chun were standing at the edge of the pool looking at the fish. She went up to them:

"Excuse me, does either of you young ladies happen to know where Mrs. Lian went to just now, please?"

"Try Mrs. Zhu's place," said Tan-chun.

Crimson hurried off in the direction of Sweet-rice Village. On her way she ran head-on into a party of maids consisting of Skybright, Mackerel, Emerald, Ripple, Musk, Scribe, Picture and Oriole.

"Here, what are you gadding about like this for?" said Skybright as soon as she saw who it was. "The flowers want watering; the birds need feeding; the stove for the tea-water needs seeing to. You've no business to go wandering around outside!"

"Master Bao gave orders yesterday that the flowers were only to be watered every other day," said Crimson. "I fed the birds when you were still fast asleep in bed."

"What about the stove?" said Emerald.

"It isn't my day for the stove," said Crimson. "The tea-water today has nothing to do with me."

"Listen to Miss Pert!" said Mackerel. "I wouldn't bother about her, if I were you—just leave her to wander about as she pleases."

"I'm *not* 'wandering about,' if you really want to know," said Crimson. "If you really want to know, Mrs. Lian sent me outside to take a message and to fetch something for her."

She held up the purse for them to see; at which they were silent. But when they had passed each other, Skybright laughed sneeringly:

"You can see why she's so uppity. She's on the climb again. Look at her— all cock-a-hoop because someone's given her a little message to carry! And she probably doesn't even know who it's about. Well, one little message isn't going to get her very far. It's what happens in the long run that counts. Now if she were clever enough to climb her way right out of this Garden and stay there, that would be really something!"

These words were spoken for Crimson to hear, but in such a way that she was unable to answer them. She had to swallow her anger and hurry on to look for Xi-feng.

Xi-feng was in Li Wan's room, as Tan-chun had predicted, and Crimson found the two of them in conversation. She went up to Xi-feng and delivered her message:

"Patience says that she found the silver just after you had gone and took care of it; and she says that when Zhang Cai's wife came for it she did weigh it out in front of her before giving it to her to take away."

Crimson now produced the purse and handed it to Xi-feng.

Then she added:

"Patience told me to tell you that Brightie has just been in to inquire what your instructions were for his visit, and she said that she gave him a message to take based on the things she thought you would want him to say."

"Oh?" said Xi-feng, amused. "And what *was* this message 'based on the things she thought I would want him to say'?"

"She said he was to tell them: 'Our lady hopes your lady is well and she says that the Master is away at present and may not be back for another day or two, but your lady is not to worry; and when the lady from West Lane is better, our lady will come with their lady to see your lady. And our lady says that the lady from West Lane sent someone the other day with a message from the *elder* Lady Wang[4] saying that she hopes our lady is well and will she please see if *our* Lady Wang can let her have a few of her Golden Myriad Macrobiotic Pills; and if she can, will our lady please send someone with them to *her*, because someone will be going from there to the *elder* Lady Wang's in a few days' time and they will be able to take them for her—' "

Crimson was still in full spate when Li Wan interrupted her with a laugh:

"What an extraordinary number of 'ladies'! I hope you can understand what it's all about, Feng. I'm sure *I* can't!"

"I'm not surprised," said Xi-feng. "There are four or five different house-holds involved in that message." She smiled graciously at Crimson. "You're a clever girl, my dear, to have got it all right—not like the simpering little ninnies I usually have to put up with. You have no idea, cousin," she said, turning to Li Wan again. "Apart from the one or two girls and one or two older women that I always keep about me, I just dread talking to servants nowadays. They take such an *interminable* time to tell you anything—*so* long-winded! And the airs and graces they give themselves! and the simpering! and the um-ing and ah-ing! If they only knew how it makes me *fume!* Our Patience used to be like that when she first came to me. I used to say to her, 'Do you think it makes you seem glamorous, all that affected humming?—like a little gnat!' I had to talk to her several times about it before she would mend her ways."

Li Wan laughed.

"I suppose if they were all peppercorns like you, it would be all right."

"This girl's all right," said Xi-feng. "Those two messages she gave me just now may not have been very long ones, but you could see how clear-cut her delivery of them was."

She smiled at Crimson again.

"How would you like to come and work for me and be my god-daughter? With a little grooming from me you could go far."

Crimson suppressed a giggle.

"Why do you laugh?" said Xi-feng. "I suppose you think I'm too young to be your god-mother. You're very silly if you think that. You just ask around a bit: there are plenty much older than you who'd give their ears to be my god-daughter. What I'm offering you is a very special favour."

Crimson smiled.

"I wasn't laughing because of that, madam. I was laughing because you had got the generation wrong. My mother is your god-daughter already. If you made me your god-daughter too, I should be my own mother's sister!"

4. Lady Wang's mother and Bao-yu's grandmother.

"Who *is* your mother?" said Xi-feng.

"Do you mean to say that you don't know who this girl is that you've been talking to all this time?" said Li Wan. "This is Lin Zhi-xiao's daughter."

Xi-feng registered surprise:

"You mean to tell me that this is the *Lins'* daughter?" She laughed. "*That* couple of old sticks? I can never get a peep out of either of them. I've always maintained that Lin Zhi-xiao and his wife were the perfect match: one *hears* nothing and the other *says* nothing. Well! To think they should have produced a bright little thing like this between them!—How old are you?" she asked Crimson.

"Sixteen."

"And what's your name?"

" 'Crimson,' madam. I used to be called 'Jade,' but they made me change it on account of Master Bao."

Xi-feng looked away with a frown of displeasure.

"I should think so too," she muttered. "Odious people! One can hear them saying it: 'We've got a "Jade" in our family the same as you,' or some such impertinence."

She turned to Li Wan again:

"I don't think you know, Wan, but I told this girl's mother that as Lai Da's wife is so busy nowadays that she doesn't even know who half the girls in the household *are* any longer, I wanted *her* to pick out a couple of likely-looking girls to work under me. Now she promised that she would do this; but you see, not only has she not done so, but she's actually gone and sent her own daughter to work for someone else. Do you suppose she *really* thinks her girl would have had such a terrible time with me?"

"Don't be so touchy," said Li Wan. "Her mother is not to blame. The girl had already started service in the Garden before you ever spoke to her about it."

"Oh well, in that case," said Xi-feng, recovering her good humour, "I'll have a word with Bao-yu about it tomorrow. I'll tell him to find someone else and let me have this girl to work under *me*. Still—" she turned to Crimson, "perhaps we ought to ask the party most concerned if she is willing."

Crimson smiled.

"As to being willing or not, madam, I don't think it's my place to say. But I do know this: that if I was to work for you, I should get to know what's what and all the inside and outside of household management. I'm sure it would be wonderful experience."

Just then a maid arrived from Lady Wang's asking for Xi-feng, who promptly excused herself to Li Wan and left. Crimson returned to Green Delights—where our story now leaves her.

We now return to Dai-yu, who, having slept so little the night before, was very late getting up on the morning of the festival. Hearing that the other girls were all out in the garden "speeding the fairies" and fearing to be teased by them for her lazy habits, she hurried over her toilet and went out as soon as it was completed. A smiling Bao-yu appeared in the gateway as she was stepping down into the courtyard.

"Well, coz," he said, "I hope you *didn't* tell on me yesterday. You had me worrying about it all last night."

Dai-yu turned back, ignoring him, to address Nightingale inside:

"When you do the room, leave one of the casements open so that the parent swallows can get in. And put the lion doorstop on the bottom of the blind to stop it flapping. And don't forget to put the cover back on the burner after you've lighted the incense."

She made her way across the courtyard, still ignoring him.

Bao-yu, who knew nothing of the little drama that had taken place outside his gate the night before, assumed that she was still angry about his unfortunate lapse earlier on that same day, when he had offended her susceptibilities with a somewhat risqué quotation from *The Western Chamber*. He offered her now, with energetic bowing and hand-pumping, the apologies that the previous day's emergency had caused him to neglect. But Dai-yu walked straight past him and out of the gate, not deigning so much as a glance in his direction, and stalked off in search of the others.

Bao-yu was nonplussed. He began to suspect that something more than he had first imagined must be wrong.

"Surely it can't only be because of yesterday lunchtime that she's carrying on in this fashion? There must be something else. On the other hand, I didn't get back until late and I didn't see her again last night, so how *could* I have offended her?"

Preoccupied with these reflections, he followed her at some distance behind.

Not far ahead Bao-chai and Tan-chun were watching the ungainly courtship dance of some storks. When they saw Dai-yu coming, they invited her to join them, and the three girls stood together and chatted. Then Bao-yu arrived. Tan-chun greeted him with sisterly concern:

"How have you been keeping, Bao? It's three whole days since I saw you last."

Bao-yu smiled back at her.

"How have *you* been keeping, sis? I was asking Cousin Wan about you the day before yesterday."

"Come over here a minute," said Tan-chun. "I want to talk to you."

He followed her into the shade of a pomegranate tree a little way apart from the other two.

"Has Father asked to see you at all during this last day or two?" Tan-chun began.

"No."

"I thought I heard someone say yesterday that he had been asking for you."

"No," said Bao-yu, smiling at her concern. "Whoever it was was mistaken. He certainly hasn't asked for *me*."

Tan-chun smiled and changed the subject.

"During the past few months," she said, "I've managed to save up another ten strings or so of cash.[5] I'd like you to take it again like you did last time, and next time you go out, if you see a nice painting or calligraphic scroll or some amusing little thing that would do for my room, I'd like you to buy it for me."

"Well, I don't know," said Bao-yu. "In the trips I make to bazaars and temple fairs, whether it's inside the city or round about, I can't say that I

---

5. Chinese copper coins had holes in the center and thus could be strung together.

ever see anything *really* nice or out of the ordinary. It's all bronzes and jades and porcelain and that sort of stuff. Apart from that it's mostly dress-making materials and clothes and things to eat."

"Now what would I want things like that for?" said Tan-chun. "No, I mean something like that little wickerwork basket you bought me last time, or the little box carved out of bamboo root, or the little clay burner. I thought they were sweet. Unfortunately the others took such a fancy to them that they carried them off as loot and wouldn't give them back to me again."

"Oh, if *those* are the sort of things you want," said Bao-yu laughing, "it's very simple. Just give a few strings of cash to one of the boys and he'll bring you back a whole cartload of them."

"What do the boys know about it?" said Tan-chun. "I need someone who can pick out the interesting things and the ones that are in good taste. You get me lots of nice little things, and I'll embroider a pair of slippers for you like the ones I made for you last time—only this time I'll do them more carefully."

"Talking of those slippers reminds me," said Bao-yu. "I happened to run into Father once when I was wearing them. He was Most Displeased. When he asked me who made them, I naturally didn't dare to tell him that *you* had, so I said that Aunt Wang had given them to me as a birthday present a few days before. There wasn't much he could do about it when he heard that they came from Aunt Wang; so after a very long pause he just said, 'What a pointless waste of human effort and valuable material, to produce things like that!' I told this to Aroma when I got back, and she said, 'Oh, that's nothing! You should have heard your Aunt Zhao complaining about those slippers. She was *furious* when she heard about them: "Her own natural brother so down at heel he scarcely dares show his face to people, and she spends her time making things like that!" ' "

Tan-chun's smile had vanished:

"How *can* she talk such nonsense? Why should *I* be the one to make shoes for him? Huan[6] gets a clothing allowance, doesn't he? He gets his clothing and footwear provided for the same as all the rest of us. And fancy saying a thing like that in front of a roomful of servants! For whose benefit was this remark made, I wonder? I make an occasional pair of slippers just for something to do in my spare time; and if I give a pair to someone I particularly like, that's my own affair. Surely no one else has any business to start telling me who I should give them to? Oh, she's so *petty!*"

Bao-yu shook his head:

"Perhaps you're being a bit hard on her. She's probably got her reasons."

This made Tan-chun really angry. Her chin went up defiantly:

"Now you're being as stupid as her. Of *course* she's got her reasons; but they are ignorant, stupid reasons. But she can think what she likes: as far as *I* am concerned, Sir Jia is my father and Lady Wang is my mother, and who was born in whose room doesn't interest me—the way I choose my friends inside the family has nothing to do with that. Oh, I know I shouldn't talk about her like this; but she is *so* idiotic about these things. As a matter of fact I can give you an even better example than your story of the slippers. That last time I gave you my savings to get something for me, she saw me a

6. Jia Huan, Bao-yu's half-brother, born to his father and the concubine Aunt Zhao.

few days afterwards and started telling me how short of money she was and how difficult things were for her. I took no notice, of course. But later, when the maids were out of the room, she began attacking me for giving the money I'd saved to other people instead of giving it to Huan. Really! I didn't know whether to laugh or get angry with her. In the end I just walked out of the room and went round to see Mother."

There was an amused interruption at this point from Bao-chai, who was still standing where they had left her a few minutes before:

"Do finish your talking and come back soon! It's easy to see that you two are brother and sister. As soon as you see each other, you get into a huddle and start talking about family secrets. Would it *really* be such a disaster if anything you are saying were to be overheard?"

Tan-chun and Bao-yu rejoined her, laughing.

Not seeing Dai-yu, Bao-yu realized that she must have slipped off elsewhere while he was talking.

"Better leave it a day or two," he told himself on reflection. "Wait until her anger has calmed down a bit."

While he was looking downwards and meditating, he noticed that the ground where they were standing was carpeted with a bright profusion of wind-blown flowers—pomegranate and balsam for the most part.

"You can see she's upset," he thought ruefully. "She's neglecting her flowers. I'll bury this lot for her and remind her about it next time I see her."

He became aware that Bao-chai was arranging for him and Tan-chun to go with her outside.

"I'll join you two presently," he said, and waited until they were a little way off before stooping down to gather the fallen blossoms into the skirt of his gown. It was quite a way from where he was to the place where Dai-yu had buried the peach-blossom on that previous occasion,[7] but he made his way towards it, over rocks and bridges and through plantations of trees and flowers. When he had almost reached his destination and there was only the spur of a miniature "mountain" between him and the burial-place of the flowers, he heard the sound of a voice, coming from the other side of the rock, whose continuous, gentle chiding was occasionally broken by the most pitiable and heart-rending sobs.

"It must be a maid from one of the apartments," thought Bao-yu. "Someone has been ill-treating her, and she has run here to cry on her own."

He stood still and endeavoured to catch what the weeping girl was saying. She appeared to be reciting something:

> The blossoms fade and falling fill the air,
> Of fragrance and bright hues bereft and bare.
> Floss drifts and flutters round the Maiden's bower,
> Or softly strikes against her curtained door.
>
> The Maid, grieved by these signs of spring's decease,
> Seeking some means her sorrow to express,
> Has rake in hand into the garden gone,
> Before the fallen flowers are trampled on.

---

7. A reference to an incident in Chap. 23. Dai-yu explains that she is burying the blossoms to return them to the earth, rather than letting them be simply swept away. Because beautiful women were commonly compared to flowers, this foreshadows her own death.

Elm-pods and willow-floss are fragrant too;
Why care, Maid, where the fallen flowers blew?
Next year, when peach and plum-tree bloom again,
Which of your sweet companions will remain?

This spring the heartless swallow built his nest
Beneath the eaves of mud with flowers compressed.
Next year the flowers will blossom as before,
But swallow, nest, and Maid will be no more.

Three hundred and three-score the year's full tale:
From swords of frost and from the slaughtering gale
How can the lovely flowers long stay intact,
Or, once loosed, from their drifting fate draw back?

Blooming so steadfast, fallen so hard to find!
Beside the flowers' grave, with sorrowing mind,
The solitary Maid sheds many a tear,
Which on the boughs as bloody drops appear.

At twilight, when the cuckoo sings no more,
The Maiden with her rake goes in at door
And lays her down between the lamplit walls,
While a chill rain against the window falls.

I know not why my heart's so strangely sad,
Half grieving for the spring and yet half glad:
Glad that it came, grieved it so soon was spent.
So soft it came, so silently it went!

Last night, outside, a mournful sound was heard:
The spirits of the flowers and of the bird.
But neither bird nor flowers would long delay,
Bird lacking speech, and flowers too shy to stay.

And then I wished that I had wings to fly
After the drifting flowers across the sky:
Across the sky to the world's farthest end,
The flowers' last fragrant resting-place to find.

But better their remains in silk to lay
And bury underneath the wholesome clay,
Pure substances the pure earth to enrich,
Than leave to soak and stink in some foul ditch.

Can I, that these flowers' obsequies attend,
Divine how soon or late *my* life will end?
Let others laugh flower-burial to see:
Another year who will be burying me?

As petals drop and spring begins to fail,
The bloom of youth, too, sickens and turns pale.
One day, when spring has gone and youth has fled,
The Maiden and the flowers will both be dead.

All this was uttered in a voice half-choked with sobs; for the words recited
seemed only to inflame the grief of the reciter—indeed, Bao-yu, listening on

the other side of the rock, was so overcome by them that he had already flung himself weeping upon the ground.

But the sequel to this painful scene will be told in the following chapter.

CHAPTER 28

*A crimson cummerbund becomes a pledge of friendship
And a chaplet of medicine-beads becomes a source of
embarrassment*

On the night before the festival, it may be remembered, Lin Dai-yu had mistakenly supposed Bao-yu responsible for Skybright's refusal to open the gate for her. The ceremonial farewell to the flowers of the following morning had transformed her pent-up and still smouldering resentment into a more generalized and seasonable sorrow. This had finally found its expression in a violent outburst of grief as she was burying the latest collection of fallen blossoms in her flower-grave. Meditation on the fate of flowers had led her to a contemplation of her own sad and orphaned lot; she had burst into tears, and soon after had begun a recitation of the poem whose words we recorded in the preceding chapter.

Unknown to her, Bao-yu was listening to this recitation from the slope of the near-by rockery. At first he merely nodded and sighed sympathetically; but when he heard the words

> "Can I, that these flowers' obsequies attend,
> Divine how soon or late *my* life will end?"

and, a little later,

> "One day when spring has gone and youth has fled,
> The Maiden and the flowers will both be dead."

he flung himself on the ground in a fit of weeping, scattering the earth all about him with the flowers he had been carrying in the skirt of his gown.

Lin Dai-yu dead! A world from which that delicate, flower-like countenance had irrevocably departed! It was unutterable anguish to think of it. Yet his sensitized imagination *did* now consider it—went on, indeed, to consider a world from which the others, too—Bao-chai, Caltrop, Aroma and the rest—had also irrevocably departed. Where would *he* be then? What would have become of him? And what of the Garden, the rocks, the flowers, the trees? To whom would they belong when he and the girls were no longer there to enjoy them? Passing from loss to loss in his imagination, he plunged deeper and deeper into a grief that seemed inconsolable. As the poet says:

> Flowers in my eyes and bird-song in my ears
> Augment my loss and mock my bitter tears.

Dai-yu, then, as she stood plunged in her own private sorrowing, suddenly heard the sound of another person crying bitterly on the rocks above her.

"The others are always telling me I'm a 'case,'" she thought. "Surely there can't be another 'case' up there?"

But on looking up she saw that it was Bao-yu.

"Pshaw!" she said crossly to herself. "I thought it was another girl, but all the time it was that cruel, hate—"

"Hateful" she had been going to say, but clapped her mouth shut before uttering it. She sighed instead and began to walk away.

By the time Bao-yu's weeping was over, Dai-yu was no longer there. He realized that she must have seen him and have gone away in order to avoid him. Feeling suddenly rather foolish, he rose to his feet and brushed the earth from his clothes. Then he descended from the rockery and began to retrace his steps in the direction of Green Delights. Quite by coincidence Dai-yu was walking along the same path a little way ahead.

"Stop a minute!" he cried, hurrying forward to catch up with her. "I know you are not taking any notice of me, but I only want to ask you one simple question, and then you need never have anything more to do with me."

Dai-yu had turned back to see who it was. When she saw that it was Bao-yu still, she was going to ignore him again; but hearing him say that he only wanted to ask her one question, she told him that he might do so.

Bao-yu could not resist teasing her a little.

"How about *two* questions? Would you wait for two?"

Dai-yu set her face forwards and began walking on again.

Bao-yu sighed.

"If it has to be like this now," he said, as if to himself, "it's a pity it was ever like it was in the beginning."

Dai-yu's curiosity got the better of her. She stopped walking and turned once more towards him.

"Like *what* in the beginning?" she asked. "And like what now?"

"Oh, the *beginning*!" said Bao-yu. "In the *beginning*, when you first came here, I was your faithful companion in all your games. Anything I had, even the thing most dear to me, was yours for the asking. If there was something to eat that I specially liked, I had only to hear that you were fond of it too and I would religiously hoard it away to share with you when you got back, not daring even to touch it until you came. We ate at the same table. We slept in the same bed. I used to think that because we were so close then, there would be something special about our relationship when we grew up— that even if we weren't particularly affectionate, we should at least have more understanding and forbearance for each other than the rest. But how wrong I was! Now that you *have* grown up, you seem only to have grown more touchy. You don't seem to care about *me* any more at all. You spend all your time brooding about outsiders like Feng and Chai. I haven't got any *real* brothers and sisters left here now. There are Huan and Tan, of course; but as you know, they're only my half-brother and half-sister: they aren't my mother's children. I'm on my own, like you. I should have thought we had so much in common—But what's the use? I try and try, but it gets me nowhere; and nobody knows or cares."

At this point—in spite of himself—he burst into tears.

The palpable evidence of her own eyes and ears had by now wrought a considerable softening on Dai-yu's heart. A sympathetic tear stole down her own cheek, and she hung her head and said nothing. Bao-yu could see that he had moved her.

"I know I'm not much use nowadays," he continued, "but however bad you may think me, I would never wittingly do anything in your presence to offend you. If I *do* ever slip up in some way, you ought to tell me off about it and warn me not to do it again, or shout at me—hit me, even, if you feel like it; I shouldn't mind. But you don't do that. You just ignore me. You leave me utterly at a loss to know what I'm supposed to have done wrong, so that I'm driven half frantic wondering what I ought to do to make up for it. If I were to die now, I should die with a grievance, and all the masses and exorcisms in the world wouldn't lay my ghost. Only when you explained what your reason was for ignoring me should I cease from haunting you and be reborn into another life."

Dai-yu's resentment for the gate incident had by now completely evaporated. She merely said:

"Oh well, in that case why did you tell your maids not to let me in when I came to call on you?"

"I honestly don't know what you are referring to," said Bao-yu in surprise. "Strike me dead if I ever did any such thing!"

"Hush!" said Dai-yu. "Talking about death at this time of the morning! You should be more careful what you say. If you did, you did. If you didn't, you didn't. There's no need for these horrible oaths."

"I really and truly didn't know you had called," said Bao-yu. "Cousin Bao came and sat with me a few minutes last night and then went away again. That's the only call I know about."

Dai-yu reflected for a moment or two, then smiled.

"Yes, it must have been the maids being lazy. Certainly they can be very disagreeable at such times."

"Yes, I'm sure that's what it was," said Bao-yu. "When I get back, I'll find out who it was and give her a good talking-to."

"I think some of your young ladies could *do* with a good talking-to," said Dai-yu, "—though it's not really for me to say so. It's a good job it was only me they were rude to. If Miss Bao or Miss Cow were to call and they behaved like that to *her,* that would be really serious."

She giggled mischievously. Bao-yu didn't know whether to laugh with her or grind his teeth. But just at that moment a maid came up to ask them both to lunch and the two of them went together out of the Garden and through into the front part of the mansion, calling in at Lady Wang's[8] on the way.

"How did you get on with that medicine of Dr. Bao's," Lady Wang asked Dai-yu as soon as she saw her, "—the Court Physician? Do you think you are any better for it?"

"It didn't seem to make very much difference," said Dai-yu. "Grandmother has put me back on Dr. Wang's prescription."

"Cousin Lin has got a naturally weak constitution, Mother," said Bao-yu. "She takes cold very easily. These strong decoctions are all very well provided she only takes one or two to dispel the cold. For regular treatment it's probably best if she sticks to pills."

"The doctor was telling me about some pills for her the other day," said Lady Wang, "but I just can't remember the name."

"I know the names of most of those pills," said Bao-yu. "I expect he wanted her to take Ginseng Tonic Pills."[9]

"No, that wasn't it," said Lady Wang.

---

8. Bao-yu's mother.   9. This passage plays on the fantastic names of Chinese medicines.

"Eight Gem Motherwort Pills?" said Bao-yu. "Zhang's Dextrals? Zhang's Sinistrals? If it wasn't any of them, it was probably Dr. Cui's Adenophora Kidney Pills."

"No," said Lady Wang, "it was none of those. All I can remember is that there was a 'Vajra'[1] in it."

Bao-yu gave a hoot and clapped his hands:

"I've never heard of 'Vajra Pills.' If there are 'Vajra Pills,' I suppose there must be 'Buddha Boluses'!"[2]

The others all laughed. Bao-chai looked at him mockingly.

"I should think it was probably 'The Deva-king Cardiac Elixir Pills,' " she said.

"Yes, yes, that's it!" said Lady Wang."Of course! How stupid of me!"

"No, Mother, not stupid," said Bao-yu. "It's the strain. All those Vajra-kings and Bodhisattvas have been overworking you!"

"You're a naughty boy to make fun of your poor mother," said Lady Wang. "A good whipping from your Pa is what you need."

"Oh, Father doesn't whip me for that sort of thing nowadays," said Bao-yu.

"Now that we know the name of the pills, we must get them to buy some for your Cousin Lin," said Lady Wang.

"None of those things are any good," said Bao-yu. "You give me three hundred and sixty taels of silver and I'll make up some pills for Cousin Lin that I guarantee will have her completely cured before she has finished the first boxful."

"Stuff!" said Lady Wang. "Whoever heard of a medicine that cost so much?"

"No, honestly!" said Bao-yu. "This prescription is a very unusual one with very special ingredients. I can't remember all of them, but I know they include

the caul[3] of a first-born child;
a ginseng root shaped like a man, with the leaves still on it;
a turtle-sized polygonum[4] root;

and

lycoperdon from the stump of a thousand-year-old pine-tree.

—Actually, though, there's nothing so *very* special about those ingredients. They're all in the standard pharmacopoeia. For 'sovereign remedies' they use ingredients that would *really* make you jump. I once gave the prescription for one to Cousin Xue. He was more than a year begging me for it before I would give it to him, and it took him another two or three years and nearly a thousand taels of silver to get all the ingredients together. Ask Bao-chai if you don't believe me, Mother."

"I know nothing about it," said Bao-chai. "I've never heard it mentioned. It's no good telling Aunt to ask *me*."

"You see! Bao-chai is a *good* girl. *She* doesn't tell lies," said Lady Wang.

---

1. The thunderbolt of the Indian god Indra, a conventional image for something hard and powerful.
2. A large pill given to a horse. 3. The membrane around the newborn. 4. The translator is using the Latin names of the plants used in the prescription.

Bao-yu was standing in the middle of the floor below the kang. He clapped his hands at this and turned to the others appealingly.

"But it's the *truth* I'm telling you. This is no lie."

As he turned, he happened to catch sight of Dai-yu, who was sitting behind Bao-chai, smiling mockingly and stroking her cheek with her finger—which in sign-language means, "You are a great big liar and you ought to be ashamed of yourself."

But Xi-feng, who happened to be in the inner room supervising the laying of the table and had overheard the preceding remarks, now emerged into the outer room to corroborate:

"It's quite true, what Bao says. I don't think he *is* making it up," she said. "Not so long ago Cousin Xue came to me asking for some pearls, and when I asked him what he wanted them for, he said, 'To make medicine with.' Then he started grumbling about the trouble he was having in getting the right ingredients and how he had half a mind not to make this medicine up after all. I said, 'What medicine?' and he told me that it was a prescription that Cousin Bao had given him and reeled off a lot of ingredients—I can't remember them now. 'Of course,' he said, 'I could easily enough *buy* a few pearls; only these have to be ones that have been worn. That's why I'm asking *you* for them. If you haven't got any loose ones,' he said, 'a few pearls broken off a bit of jewellery would do. I'd get you something nice to replace it with.' He was so insistent that in the end I had to break up two of my ornaments for him. Then he wanted a yard of Imperial red gauze. That was to put over the mortar to pound the pearls through. He said they had to be ground until they were as fine as flour."

"You see!" "You see!" Bao-yu kept interjecting throughout this recital.

"Incidentally, Mother," he said, when it was ended, "even *that* was only a substitute. According to the prescription, the pearls ought really to have come from an ancient grave. They should really have been pearls taken from jewellery on the corpse of a long-buried noblewoman. But as one can't very well go digging up graves and rifling tombs every time one wants to make this medicine, the prescription allows pearls worn by the living as a second-best."

"Blessed name of the Lord!" said Lady Wang. "What a *dreadful* idea! Even if you *did* get them from a grave, I can't believe that a medicine made from pearls that had been come by so wickedly—desecrating people's bones that had been lying peacefully in the ground all those hundreds of years—could possibly do you any good."

Bao-yu turned to Dai-yu.

"Did you hear what Feng said?" he asked her. "I hope you're not going to say that *she* was lying."

Although the remark was addressed to Dai-yu, he winked at Bao-chai as he made it.

Dai-yu clung to Lady Wang.

"Listen to him, Aunt!" she wailed. "Bao-chai won't be a party to his lies, but he still expects *me* to be."

"Bao-yu, you are very unkind to your cousin," said Lady Wang.

Bao-yu only laughed.

"You don't know the reason, Mother. Bao-chai didn't know a half of what Cousin Xue got up to, even when she was living with her mother outside;

and now that she's moved into the Garden, she knows even less. When she said she didn't know, she *really* didn't know: she wasn't giving me the lie. What you don't realize is that Cousin Lin was all the time sitting behind her making signs to show that she didn't believe me."

Just then a maid came from Grandmother Jia's apartment to fetch Bao-yu and Dai-yu to lunch.

Without saying a word to Bao-yu, Dai-yu got up and, taking the maid's hand, began to go. But the maid was reluctant.

"Let's wait for Master Bao and we can go together."

"He's not eating lunch today," said Dai-yu. "Come on, let's go!"

"Whether he's eating lunch or not," said the maid, "he'd better come with us, so that he can explain to Her Old Ladyship about it when she asks."

"All right, you wait for him then," said Dai-yu. "I'm going on ahead." And off she went.

"I think I'd rather eat with *you* today, Mother," said Bao-yu.

"No, no, you can't," said Lady Wang. "Today is one of my fast-days:[5] I shall only be eating vegetables. You go and have a proper meal with your Grandma."

"I shall share your vegetables," said Bao-yu. "Go on, you can go," he said, dismissing the maid; and rushing up to the table, he sat himself down at it in readiness.

"You others had better get on with your own lunch," Lady Wang said to Bao-chai and the girls. "Let him do as he likes."

"You really ought to go," Bao-chai said to Bao-yu. "Whether you have lunch there or not, you ought to keep Cousin Lin company. She is very upset, you know. Why don't you?"

"Oh, leave her alone!" said Bao-yu. "She'll be all right presently."

Soon they had finished eating, and Bao-yu, afraid that Grandmother Jia might be worrying and at the same time anxious to rejoin Dai-yu, hurriedly demanded tea to rinse his mouth with. Tan-chun and Xi-chun were much amused.

"Why are you always in such a hurry, Bao?" they asked him. "Even your eating and drinking all seems to be done in a rush."

"You should let him finish quickly, so that he can get back to his Dai-yu," said Bao-chai blandly. "Don't make him waste time here with us."

Bao-yu left as soon as he had drunk his tea, and made straight for the west courtyard where his Grandmother Jia's apartment was. But as he was passing by the gateway of Xi-feng's courtyard, it happened that Xi-feng herself was standing in her doorway with one foot on the threshold, grooming her teeth with an ear-cleaner and keeping a watchful eye on nine or ten pages who were moving potted plants about under her direction.

"Ah, just the person I wanted to see!" she said, as soon as she caught sight of Bao-yu. "Come inside. I want you to write something down for me."

Bao-yu was obliged to follow her indoors. Xi-feng called for some paper, an inkstone and a brush, and at once began dictating:

"Crimson lining-damask forty lengths, dragonet figured satin forty lengths, miscellaneous Imperial gauze one hundred lengths, gold necklets four,—"

---

5. Days when no meat is eaten; a Buddhist practice.

"Here, what *is* this?" said Bao-yu. "It isn't an invoice and it isn't a presentation list. How am I supposed to write it?"

"Never you mind about that," said Xi-feng. "As long as *I* know what it is, that's all that matters. Just put it down anyhow."

Bao-yu wrote down the four items. As soon as he had done so, Xi-feng took up the paper and folded it away.

"Now," she said, smiling pleasantly, "there's something I want to talk to you about. I don't know whether you'll agree to this or not, but there's a girl in your room called 'Crimson' whom I'd like to work for me. If I find you someone to replace her with, will you let me have her?"

"There are so many girls in my room," said Bao-yu. "Please take any you have a fancy to. You really don't need to ask me about it."

"In that case," said Xi-feng, "I'll send for her straight away."

"Please do," said Bao-yu, and started to go.

"Hey, come back!" said Xi-feng. "I haven't finished with you yet."

"I've got to see Grandma now," said Bao-yu. "If you've got anything else to say, you can tell me on my way back."

When he got to Grandmother Jia's apartment, they had all just finished lunch. Grandmother Jia asked him if he had had anything nice to eat with his mother.

"There wasn't anything nice," he said. "But I had an extra bowl of rice."

Then, after the briefest pause:

"Where's Cousin Lin?"

"In the inner room," said Grandmother Jia.

In the inner room a maid stood below the kang[6] blowing on a flat-iron. Up on the kang two maids were marking some material with a chalked string, while Dai-yu, her head bent low over her work, was engaged in cutting something from it with her shears.

"What are you making?" he asked her. "You'll give yourself a headache, stooping down like that immediately after your lunch."

Dai-yu took no notice and went on cutting.

"That corner looks a bit creased still," said one of the maids. "It will have to be ironed again."

"*Leave it alone!*" said Dai-yu, laying down her shears. "*It will be all right presently.*"

Bao-yu found her reply puzzling.

Bao-chai, Tan-chun and the rest had now arrived in the outer room and were talking to Grandmother Jia. Presently Bao-chai drifted inside and asked Dai-yu what she was doing; then, when she saw that she was cutting material, she exclaimed admiringly.

"What a lot of things you can do, Dai! Fancy, even dress-making now!"

Dai-yu smiled malignantly.

"Oh, it's all lies, really. I just do it to fool people."

"I've got something to tell you that I think will amuse you, Dai," said Bao-chai pleasantly. "When our cousin was holding forth about that medicine just now and I said I didn't know about it, I believe actually he was rather wounded."

---

6. A brick platform, heated by a small fire underneath, that could be used for sitting on or as a bed.

"*Oh, leave him alone!*" said Dai-yu. "*He will be all right presently.*"

"Grandma wants someone to play dominoes with," said Bao-yu to Bao-chai. "Why don't you go and play dominoes?"

"Oh, is *that* what I came for?" said Bao-chai; but she went, notwithstanding.

"Why don't *you* go?" said Dai-yu. "There's a tiger in this room. You might get eaten."

She said this still bending over her cutting, which she continued to work away at without looking up at him.

Finding himself once more ignored, Bao-yu nevertheless attempted to remain jovial.

"Why don't you come out for a bit too? You can do this cutting later."

Dai-yu continued to take no notice.

Failing to get a response from her, he tried the maids:

"Who told her to do this dress-making?"

"Whoever told her to do it," said Dai-yu, "it has nothing whatever to do with Master Bao."

Bao-yu was about to retort, but just at that moment someone came in to say that he was wanted outside, and he was obliged to hurry off.

Dai-yu leaned forward and shouted after him:

"Holy name! By the time you get back, I shall be dead."

Outside the gateway to the inner quarters Bao-yu found Tealeaf waiting.

"Mr. Feng invites you round to his house," said Tealeaf.

Bao-yu realized that this must be in connection with the matter Feng Zi-ying had spoken of on the previous day. He told Tealeaf to send for his going-out clothes, and went into his outer study to wait for them.

Tealeaf went back to the west inner gate to wait for someone who would carry a message inside to the maids. Presently an old woman came out:

"Excuse me, missus," said Tealeaf. "Master Bao is waiting in the outer study for his going-out clothes. Could you take a message inside to say that he wants them?"

"—your mother's twat!"[7] said the old woman. "Master Bao lives in the Garden now. All his maids are in the Garden. What do you want to come running round here for?"

Tealeaf laughed at his own mistake.

"You're quite right. I'm going cuckoo."

He ran round to the gate of the Garden. As luck would have it, the boys on that gate were playing football[8] in the open space below the terraced walk, and when Tealeaf had explained his errand, one of them ran off inside for him. He returned after a very long wait, carrying a large bundle, which he handed to Tealeaf, and which Tealeaf carried back to the outer study.

While he was changing, Bao-yu asked for his horse to be saddled, and presently set off, taking only Tealeaf, Ploughboy, Two-times and Oldie as his attendants. When they reached Feng Zi-ying's gate, someone ran in to announce his arrival, and Feng Zi-ying came out in person to greet him and led him inside to meet the company.

This comprised Xue Pan, who had evidently been waiting there for some

---

7. The casual use of vulgarity marks the woman's low class and reminds the reader of an uglier world surrounding the garden.   8. Here, a game similar to soccer.

time, a number of boy singers, a female impersonator called Jiang Yu-han and a girl called Nuageuse from the Budding Grove, a high-class establishment specializing in female entertainers. When everyone had been introduced, tea was served.

"Now come on!" said Bao-yu, as he picked up the proffered cup of tea. "What about this 'lucky accident' you mentioned yesterday? I've been waiting anxiously to hear about it ever since I saw you. That's why I came so promptly when I got your invitation."

Feng Zi-ying laughed.

"You and your cousin are such simple souls—I find it rahver touchin'! Afraid it was pure invention, what I said yesterday. I said it to make you come, because I fought that if I asked you outright to come and drink wiv me, you'd make excuses. Anyway, it worked."

The company joined in his merriment.

Wine was now brought in and everyone sat down in the places assigned to them. Feng Zi-ying first got one of the singing-boys to pour for them; then he called on Nuageuse to drink with each of the guests in turn.

Xue Pan, by the time he had three little cupfuls of wine inside him, was already beginning to be obstreperous. He seized Nuageuse by the hand and drew her towards him:

"If you'd sing me a nice new song—one of your specials, I'd drink a whole jarful for you. How about it, eh?"

Nuageuse had to oblige him by taking up her lute and singing the following song for him to her own accompaniment:

> Two lovely boys
> Are both in love with me
> And I can't get either from my mind.
> Both are so beautiful
> So wonderful
> So marvellous
> To give up either one would be unkind.
> Last night I promised I would go
> To meet one of them in the garden where the roses grow;
> The other came to see what he could find.
> And now that we three are all
> Here in this tribunal,
> There are no words that come into my mind.

"There you are!" she said. "Now drink your jarful!"

"That one's not worth a jarful," said Xue Pan. "Sing us a better one."

"Now just a minute," said Bao-yu. "Just guzzling like this will make us drunk in no time without giving us any real enjoyment. I've got a good new drinking-game for you. Let me first drink the M.C.'s starting-cup,[9] and I'll tell you the rules. After that, anyone who doesn't toe the line will be made to drink ten sconce-cups straight off as a forfeit, give up his seat at the party, and spend the rest of the time pouring out drinks for the rest of us."

Feng Zi-ying and Jiang Yu-han agreed enthusiastically, and Bao-yu picked up one of the extra large cups that had now been provided and drained its contents at a single draught.

---

9. Bao-yu is going to set up the drinking games, so he drinks first.

"Now," he said. "We're going to take four words—let's say 'upset,' 'glum,' 'blest' and 'content.' You have to begin by saying 'The girl is—,' and then you say one of the four words. That's your first line. The next line has to rhyme with the first line and it has to give the reason why the girl is whatever it says—'upset' or 'glum' or 'blest' or 'content.' When you've done all four, you're entitled to drink the wine in front of you. Only, before drinking it, you've first got to sing some new popular song; and *after* you've drunk it, you've got to choose some animal or vegetable object from the things in front of us and recite a line from a well-known poem, or an old couplet, or a quotation from the classics—"

Before he could finish, Xue Pan was on his feet, protesting vigorously:

"You can count *me* out of this. *I'm* taking no part in this. This is just to make a fool of me, isn't it?"

Nuageuse, too, stood up and attempted to push him back into his seat:

"What are you so afraid of, a practised drinker like you? You can't be any worse at this sort of thing than I am, and *I'm* going to have a go when *my* turn comes. If you do it all right, you've got nothing to worry about, and even if you can't, you'll only be made to drink a few cups of wine; whereas if you refuse to follow the rules at the very outset, you'll have to drink ten sconces straight off in a row and then be thrown out of the party and made to pour drinks for the rest of us."

"Bravo!" cried the others, clapping; and Xue Pan, seeing them united against him, subsided.

Bao-yu now began his own turn:

> "The girl's upset:
>   The years pass by, but no one's claimed her yet.
> The girl looks glum:
>   Her true-love's gone to follow ambition's drum.
> The girl feels blest:
>   The mirror shows her looks are at their best.
> The girl's content:
>   Long summer days in pleasant pastimes spent."

The others all applauded, except Xue Pan, who shook his head disapprovingly:

"No good, no good!" he said. "Pay the forfeit."

"Why, what's wrong with it?" they asked him.

"I couldn't understand a word of it."

Nuageuse gave him a pinch:

"Keep quiet and try to think what *you're* going to say," she advised him; "otherwise you'll have nothing ready when your own turn comes and you'll have to pay the forfeit yourself."

Thereupon she picked up her lute and accompanied Bao-yu as he sang the following song:

> "Still weeping tears of blood about our separation:
> Little red love-beans of my desolation.
> Still blooming flowers I see outside my window growing.
> Still awake in the dark I hear the wind a-blowing.
> Still oh still I can't forget those old hopes and fears.
> Still can't swallow food and drink, 'cos I'm choked with tears.

Mirror, mirror on the wall, tell me it's not true:
Do I look so thin and pale, do I look so blue?
Mirror, mirror, this long night how shall I get through?
                    Oh—oh—oh!
Blue as the mist upon the distant mountains,
Blue as the water in the ever-flowing fountains."

General applause—except from Xue Pan, who objected that there was "no rhythm."

Bao-yu now drank his well-earned cup—the "pass cup" as they call it—and, picking up a slice of pear from the table, concluded his turn with the following quotation:

"Rain whips the pear-tree, shut fast the door."

Now it was Feng Zi-ying's turn:

"The girl's upset:
    Her husband's ill and she's in debt.
The girl looks glum:
    The gale has turned her room into a slum.
The girl feels blest:
    She's got twin babies at the breast.
The girl's content:
    Waiting a certain pleasurable event."

Next, holding up his cupful of wine in readiness to drink, he sang this song:

"You're so exciting,
    And so inviting;
You're my Mary Contrary;
You're a crazy, mad thing.
You're my goddess, but oh! you're deaf to my praying:
Why won't you listen to what I am saying?
If you don't believe me, make a small investigation:
You will soon find out the true depth of my admiration."

Then he drained his bumper and, picking up a piece of chicken from one of the dishes, ended the performance, prior to popping it into his mouth, with a line from Wen Ting-yun:[1]

"From moonlit cot the cry of chanticleer."

Next it was the turn of Nuageuse:

"The girl's upset:"

she began,

"Not knowing how the future's to be met—"

Xue Pan laughed noisily.

"That's all right, my darling, don't you worry! Your Uncle Xue will take care of you."

---

1. Poet (9th century).

"Shush!" said the others. "Don't confuse her."
She continued:

> "The girl looks glum:
>   Nothing but blows and hard words from her Mum—"

"I saw that Mum of yours the other day," said Xue Pan, "and I particularly told her that she wasn't to beat you."

"Another word from you," said the others, "and you'll be made to drink ten cups as a punishment."

Xue Pan gave his own face a slap.

"Sorry! I forgot. Won't do it again."

> "The girl feels blest:"

said Nuageuse,

> "Her young man's rich and beautifully dressed.
> The girl's content:
>   She's been performing in a big event."

Next Nuageuse sang her song:

> "A flower began to open in the month of May.
> Along came a honey-bee to sport and play.
> He pushed and he squeezed to get inside,
> But he couldn't get in however hard he tried.
> So on the flower's lip he just hung around,
>   A-playing the see-saw up and down.
>   Oh my honey-sweet,
>   Oh my sweets of sin,
>   If I don't open up,
>   How will you get in?"

After drinking her "pass cup," she picked up a peach:

> "So bonny blooms the peach-tree-o."[2]

It was now Xue Pan's turn.

"Ah yes, now, let's see! *I* have to say something now, don't I?"

> "The girl's upset—"

But nothing followed.

"All right, what's she upset about then?" said Feng Zi-ying with a laugh. "Buck up!"

Xue Pan appeared to be engaged in a species of mental effort so frightful that his eyes seemed about to pop out of his head. After glaring fixedly for an unconscionable time, he said:

> "The girl's upset—"

He coughed a couple of times. Then at last it came:

> "The girl's upset:
>   She's married to a marmoset."

---

2. From the *Book of Songs*.

The others greeted this with a roar of laughter.

"What are you laughing at?" said Xue Pan. "That's perfectly reasonable, isn't it? If a girl was expecting a proper husband and he turned out to be one of *them*, she'd have cause to be upset, wouldn't she?"

His audience were by now doubled up.

"That's perfectly true," they conceded. "Very good. Now what about the next bit?"

Xue Pan glared a while very concentratedly, then:

> "The girl looks glum—"

But after that was silence.

"Come on!" said the others. "Why was she glum?"

> "His dad's a baboon with a big red bum."

"Ho! Ho! Ho! Pay the forfeit," they cried. "The first one was bad enough. We really can't let this one go."

The more officious of them even began filling the sconce-cups for him. But Bao-yu allowed the line.

"As long as it rhymes," he said, "we'll let it pass."

"There you are!" said Xue Pan. "The M.C. says it's all right. What are the rest of you making such a fuss about?"

At this the others desisted.

"The next two are even harder," said Nuageuse. "Shall I do them for you, dear?"

"Piss off!" said Xue Pan. "D'you think I haven't got any good lines of my own? Listen to this:

> The girl feels blest:
> In bridal bower she takes her rest."

The others stared at him in amazement:

"I say, old chap, that's a bit poetical for you, isn't it?"

Xue Pan continued unconcernedly:

> "The girl's content:
> She's got a big prick up her vent."

The others looked away with expressions of disgust.

"Oh dear, oh dear! Hurry up and get on with the song, then."

> "One little gnat went hum hum hum,"

Xue Pan began tunelessly. The others looked at him open-mouthed:

"What sort of song is that?"

Xue Pan droned on, ignoring the question:

> "Two little flies went bum bum bum,
> Three little—"

"Stop!" shouted the others.

"Sod you lot!" said Xue Pan. "This is the very latest new hit. It's called the Hum-bum Song. If you can't be bothered to listen to it, you'll have to let me off the other thing. I'll agree not to sing the rest of the song on that condition."

"Yes, yes, we'll let you off," they said. "Just don't interfere with the rest of us, that's all we ask."

This meant that it was now Jiang Yu-han's turn to perform. This is what he said:

> "The girl's upset:
>   Her man's away, she fears he will forget.
> The girl looks glum:
>   So short of cash she can't afford a crumb.
> The girl feels blest:
>   Her lampwick's got a lucky crest.
> The girl's content:
>   She's married to a perfect gent."

Then he sang this song:

> "A mischievous bundle of charm and love,
> Or an angel come down from the skies above?
>   Sweet sixteen
>   And so very green,
> Yet eager to see all there is to be seen.
>   Aie aie aie
>   The galaxy's high
>   In the roof of the sky,
>   And the drum from the tower
>   Sounds the midnight hour.
> So trim the lamp, love, and come with me
> Inside the bed-curtains, and you shall see!"

He raised the pass cup to his lips, but before drinking it, smiled round at his auditors and made this little speech:

"I'm afraid my knowledge of poetry is strictly limited. However, I happened to see a couplet on someone's wall yesterday which has stuck in my mind; and as one line in it is about something I can see here, I shall use it to finish my turn with."

So saying, he drained the cup and then, picking up a spray of cassia, recited the following line:

> "The flowers' aroma breathes of hotter days."

The others all accepted this as a satisfactory conclusion of the performance. Not so Xue Pan, however, who leaped to his feet and began protesting noisily:

"Terrible! Pay the forfeit. Where's the little doll? I can't see any doll on the table."

"I didn't say anything about a doll," said Jiang Yu-han. "What are you talking about?"

"Come on, don't try to wriggle out of it!" said Xue Pan. "Say what you said just now again."

> "The flowers' aroma breathes of hotter days."

"There you are!" said Xue Pan. " 'Aroma.' That's the name of a little doll.[3] Ask *him* if you don't believe me."—He pointed to Bao-yu.

---

3. Aroma is also the name of Bao-yu's chief maid.

Bao-yu looked embarrassed.

"Cousin Xue, this time I think you *do* have to pay the forfeit."

"All right, all right!" said Xue Pan. "I'll drink."

And he picked up the wine in front of him and drained it at a gulp.

Feng Zi-ying and Jiang Yu-han were still puzzled and asked him what this was all about. But it was Nuageuse who explained. Immediately Jiang Yu-han was on his feet apologizing. The others reassured him.

"It's not your fault. 'Ignorance excuses all,' " they said.

Shortly after this Bao-yu had to take temporary leave of the company to ease his bladder and Jiang Yu-han followed him outside. As the two of them stood side by side under the eaves, Jiang Yu-han once more offered Bao-yu his apologies. Much taken with the actor's winsome looks and gentleness of manner, Bao-yu impulsively took his hand and gave it a squeeze.

"Do come round to our place some time when you are free," he said. "There's something I want to ask you about. You have an actor in your company called 'Bijou' whom everyone is talking about lately. I should so much like to meet him, but so far I haven't had an opportunity."

"That's me!" said Jiang Yu-han. " 'Bijou' is my stage-name."

Bao-yu stamped with delight.

"But this is wonderful! I must say, you fully deserve your reputation. Oh dear! What am I going to do about a First Meeting present?"[4]

He thought for a bit, then took a fan from his sleeve and broke off its jade pendant.

"Here you are," he said, handing it to Bijou. "It's not much of a present, I'm afraid, but it will do to remind you of our meeting."

Bijou smiled and accepted it ceremoniously:

"I have done nothing to deserve this favour. It is too great an honour. Well, thank you. There's rather an unusual thing I'm wearing—I put it on today for the first time, so it's still fairly new: I wonder if you will allow me to give it to you as a token of my warm feelings towards you?"

He opened up his gown, undid the crimson cummerbund with which his trousers were fastened, and handed it to Bao-yu.

"It comes from the tribute sent by the Queen of the Madder Islands. It's for wearing in summer. It makes you smell nice and it doesn't show perspiration stains. I was given it yesterday by the Prince of Bei-jing, and today is the first time it's ever been worn. I wouldn't give a thing like this to anyone else, but I'd like *you* to have it. Will you take your own sash off, please, so that I can put it on instead?"

Bao-yu received the crimson cummerbund with delight and quickly took off his own viridian-coloured sash to give to Bijou in exchange. They had just finished fastening the sashes on again when Xue Pan jumped out from behind and seized hold of them both.

"What are you two up to, leaving the party and sneaking off like this?" he said. "Come on, take 'em out again and let's have a look!"

It was useless for them to protest that the situation was not what he imagined. Xue Pan continued to force his unwelcome attentions upon them until Feng Zi-ying came out and rescued them. After that they returned to the party and continued drinking until the evening.

Back in his own apartment in the Garden, Bao-yu took off his outer

4. Exchanged when people become friends.

clothes[5] and relaxed with a cup of tea. While he did so, Aroma noticed that the pendant of his fan was missing and asked him what had become of it. Bao-yu told her that it had come off while he was riding, and she gave the matter no more thought. But later, when he was going to bed, she saw the magnificent blood-red sash round his waist and began to put two and two together.

"Since you've got a better sash now," she said, "do you think I could have mine back, please?"

Bao-yu remembered, too late, that the viridian sash had been Aroma's and that he ought never to have given it away. He now very much regretted having done so, but instead of apologizing, attempted to pass it off with a laugh.

"I'll get you another," he told her lightly.

Aroma shook her head and sighed.

"I knew you still got up to these tricks,"[6] she said, "but at least you might refrain from giving *my* things to those disgusting creatures. I'm surprised you haven't got more sense."

She was going to say more, but checked herself for fear of provoking an explosion while he was in his cups.[7] And since there was nothing else she could do, she went to bed.

She awoke at first daylight next morning to find Bao-yu smiling down at her:

"We might have been burgled last night for all you'd have known about it—Look at your trousers!"

Looking down, Aroma saw the sash that Bao-yu had been wearing yesterday tied round her own waist, and knew that he must have exchanged it for hers during the night. She tore it off impatiently.

"*I* don't want the horrible thing. The sooner you take it away the better."

Bao-yu was anxious that she should keep it, and after a great deal of coaxing she consented, very reluctantly, to tie it on again. But she took it off once and for all as soon as he was out of the room and threw it into an empty chest, having first found another one of her own to put on in its place.

Bao-yu made no comment on the change when they were together again. He merely inquired whether anything had happened the day before, while he was out.

"Mrs. Lian sent someone round to fetch Crimson," said Aroma. "She wanted to wait for you; but it seemed to me that it wasn't all that important, so I took it on myself to send her off straight away."

"Quite right," said Bao-yu. "I already knew about it. There was no need to wait till I got back."

Aroma continued:

"Her Grace[8] sent that Mr. Xia of the Imperial Bedchamber yesterday with a hundred and twenty taels of silver to pay for a three-day *Pro Viventibus* by the Taoists of the Lunar Queen temple starting on the first of next month. There are to be plays performed as part of the Offering, and Mr. Zhen and all the other gentlemen are to go there to burn incense. Oh, and Her Grace's presents for the Double Fifth[9] have arrived."

She ordered a little maid to get out Bao-yu's share of the things sent. There were two Palace fans of exquisite workmanship, two strings of red musk-

5. Clothes were worn in multiple layers.   6. This may suggest that Aroma suspects him of engaging in homosexual acts.   7. That is, he was drunk.   8. Bao-yu's elder sister, the imperial concubine.   9. A holiday that falls on the fifth day of the Fifth Month.

scented medicine-beads, two lengths of maidenhair chiffon and a grass-woven "lotus" mat to lie on in the hot weather.

"Did the others all get the same?" he asked.

"Her Old Ladyship's presents were the same as yours with the addition of a perfume-sceptre and an agate head-rest, and Sir Zheng's, Lady Wang's and Mrs. Xue's were the same as Her Old Ladyship's but without the head-rest; Miss Bao's were exactly the same as yours; Miss Lin, Miss Ying-chun, Miss Tan-chun and Miss Xi-chun got only the fans and the beads; and Mrs. Zhu and Mrs. Lian both got two lengths of gauze, two lengths of chiffon, two perfume sachets and two moulded medicine-cakes."

"Funny!" said Bao-yu. "I wonder why Miss Lin didn't get the same as me and why only Miss Bao's and mine were the same. There must have been some mistake, surely?"

"When they unpacked them yesterday, the separate lots were all labelled," said Aroma. "I don't see how there could have been any mistake. Your share was in Her Old Ladyship's room and I went round there to get it for you. Her Old Ladyship says she wants you to go to Court at four o'clock tomorrow morning to give thanks."

"Yes, of course," said Bao-yu inattentively, and gave Ripple instructions to take his presents round to Dai-yu:

"Tell Miss Lin that I got these things yesterday and that if there's anything there she fancies, I should like her to keep it."

Ripple went off with the presents. She was back in a very short time, however.

"Miss Lin says she got some yesterday too, and will you please keep these for yourself."

Bao-yu told her to put them away. As soon as he had washed, he left to pay his morning call on Grandmother Jia; but just as he was going out he saw Dai-yu coming towards him and hurried forward to meet her.

"Why didn't you choose anything from the things I sent you?"

Yesterday's resentments were now quite forgotten; today Dai-yu had fresh matter to occupy her mind.

"I'm not equal to the honour," she said. "You forget, I'm not in the gold and jade class like you and your Cousin Bao. I'm only a common little wall-flower!"

The reference to gold and jade immediately aroused Bao-yu's suspicions.

"I don't know what anyone else may have been saying on the subject," he said, "but if any such thought ever so much as crossed *my* mind, may Heaven strike me dead, and may I never be reborn as a human being!"

Seeing him genuinely bewildered, Dai-yu smiled in what was meant to be a reassuring manner.

"I wish you wouldn't make these horrible oaths. It's so disagreeable. Who *cares* about your silly old 'gold and jade,' anyway?"

"It's hard to make you *see* what is in my heart," said Bao-yu. "One day perhaps you will know. But I can tell you this. My heart has room for four people only. Grannie and my parents are three of them and Cousin Dai is the fourth. I swear to you there isn't a fifth."

"There's no need for you to swear," said Dai-yu. "I know very well that Cousin Dai has a place in your heart. The trouble is that as soon as Cousin Chai comes along, Cousin Dai gets forgotten."

"You imagine these things," said Bao-yu. "It really isn't as you say."

"Yesterday when Little Miss Bao wouldn't tell lies for you, why did you turn to *me* and expect *me* to? How would you like it if I did that sort of thing to you?"

Bao-chai happened to come along while they were still talking and the two of them moved aside to avoid her. Bao-chai saw this clearly, but pretended not to notice and hurried by with lowered eyes. She went and sat with Lady Wang for a while and from there went on to Grandmother Jia's. Bao-yu was already at his grandmother's when she got there.

Bao-chai had on more than one occasion heard her mother telling Lady Wang and other people that the golden locket she wore had been given her by a monk, who had insisted that when she grew up the person she married must be someone who had "a jade to match the gold." This was one of the reasons why she tended to keep aloof from Bao-yu. The slight embarrassment she always felt as a result of her mother's chatter had yesterday been greatly intensified when Yuan-chun singled her out as the only girl to receive the same selection of presents as Bao-yu. She was relieved to think that Bao-yu, so wrapped up in Dai-yu that his thoughts were only of her, was unaware of her embarrassment.

But now here was Bao-yu smiling at her with sudden interest.

"Cousin Bao, may I have a look at your medicine-beads?"

She happened to be wearing one of the little chaplets[1] on her left wrist and began to pull it off now in obedience to his request. But Bao-chai was inclined to plumpness and perspired easily, and for a moment or two it would not come off. While she was struggling with it, Bao-yu had ample opportunity to observe her snow-white arm, and a feeling rather warmer than admiration was kindled inside him.

"If that arm were growing on Cousin Lin's body," he speculated, "I might hope one day to touch it. What a pity it's hers! Now I shall never have that good fortune."

Suddenly he thought of the curious coincidence of the gold and jade talismans and their matching inscriptions, which Dai-yu's remark had reminded him of. He looked again at Bao-chai—

> that face like the full moon's argent bowl;
> those eyes like sloes;
> those lips whose carmine hue no Art contrived;
> and brows by none but Nature's pencil lined.

This was beauty of quite a different order from Dai-yu's. Fascinated by it, he continued to stare at her with a somewhat dazed expression, so that when she handed him the chaplet, which she had now succeeded in getting off her wrist, he failed to take it from her.

Seeing that he had gone off into one of his trances, Bao-chai threw down the chaplet in embarrassment and turned to go. But Dai-yu was standing on the threshold, biting a corner of her handkerchief, convulsed with silent laughter.

"I thought you were so delicate," said Bao-chai. "What are you standing there in the draught for?"

"I've been in the room all the time," said Dai-yu. "I just this moment went

---

1. Strings of beads.

to have a look outside because I heard the sound of something in the sky. It was a gawping goose."

"Where?" said Bao-chai. "Let *me* have a look."

"Oh," said Dai-yu, "as soon as I went outside he flew away with a *whir-r-r—*"

She flicked her long handkerchief as she said this in the direction of Bao-yu's face.

"Ow!" he exclaimed—She had flicked him in the eye.

The extent of the damage will be examined in the following chapter.

CHAPTER 29

In which the greatly blessed pray for yet greater blessings
And the highly strung rise to new heights of passion

We told in the last chapter how, as Bao-yu was standing lost in one of his trances, Dai-yu flicked her handkerchief at him and made him jump by inadvertently catching him in the eye with it.

"Who did that?" he asked.

Dai-yu laughingly shook her head.

"I'm sorry. I didn't mean to. Bao-chai wanted to look at a *gawping goose,* and I accidently flicked you while I was showing her how it went."

Bao-yu rubbed his eye. He appeared to be about to say something, but then thought better of it.

And so the matter passed.

Shortly after this incident Xi-feng arrived and began talking about the arrangements that had been made for the purification ceremonies, due to begin on the first of next month at the Taoist temple of the Lunar Goddess. She invited Bao-chai, Bao-yu and Dai-yu to go with her there to watch the plays.

"Oh *no!*" said Bao-chai. "It's too *hot.* Even if they were to do something we haven't seen before—which isn't likely—I think I should still not want to go."

"But it's *cool* there," said Xi-feng. "There are upstairs galleries on all three sides that you can watch from in the shade. And if we go, I shall send someone a day or two in advance to turn the Taoists out of that part of the temple and make it nice and clean for us and get them to put up blinds.[2] And I'll ask them not to let any other visitors in on that day. I've already told Lady Wang I'm going, so if you others won't come with me, I shall go by myself. I'm so bored lately. And it's such a business when we put on our own plays at home, that I can never enjoy them properly."

"All right then, *I'll* come," said Grandmother Jia, who had been listening.

"*You'll* come, Grannie? Well that's splendid, isn't it! That means it will be just as bad for me as it would be if I were watching here at home."

"Now look here," said Grandmother Jia, "I shan't want you to stand and wait on me. Let me take the gallery facing the stage and you can have one

2. Although Taoist religious observances were respected, Taoist priests themselves were rarely of high status. When an important family like the Jias visited the temple, it had to be specially cleaned and a large section was set off.

of the side galleries all to yourself; then you can sit down and enjoy yourself in comfort."

Xi-feng was touched.

"*Do* come!" Grandmother Jia said to Bao-chai. "I'll see that your mother comes too. The days are so long now, and there's nothing to do at home except go to sleep."

Bao-chai had to promise that she would go.

Grandmother Jia now sent someone to invite Aunt Xue. The messenger was to call in on the way at Lady Wang's and ask her if the girls might go as well.

Lady Wang had already made it clear that she would not be going herself, partly because she was not feeling very well, and partly because she wanted to be at home in case any further messages arrived from Yuan-chun; but when she learned of Grandmother Jia's enthusiasm, she had word carried into the Garden that not just the girls but anyone else who wanted to might go along with Grandmother Jia's party on the first.

When this exciting news had been transmitted throughout the Garden, the maids—some of whom hardly set foot outside their own courtyards from one year's end to the next—were all dying to go, and those whose mistresses showed a lethargic disinclination to accept employed a hundred different wiles to make sure that they did so. The result was that in the end *all* the Garden's inhabitants said that they would be going. Grandmother Jia was quite elated and at once issued orders for the cleaning and preparation of the temple theatre.

But these are details with which we need not concern ourselves.

On the morning of the first sedans,[3] carriages, horses and people filled all the roadway outside Rong-guo[4] House. The stewards in charge knew that the occasion of this outing was a *Pro Viventibus* ordered by Her Grace the Imperial Concubine and that Her Old Ladyship was going in person to burn incense—quite apart from the fact that this was the first day of the month and the first day of the Summer Festival; consequently the turnout was as splendid as they could make it and far exceeded anything that had been seen on previous occasions.

Presently Grandmother Jia appeared, seated, in solitary splendour, in a large palanquin carried by eight bearers. Li Wan, Xi-feng and Aunt Xue followed, each in a palanquin with four bearers. After them came Bao-chai and Dai-yu sharing a carriage with a splendid turquoise-coloured canopy trimmed with pearls. The carriage after them, in which Ying-chun, Tan-chun and Xi-chun sat, had vermilion-painted wheels and was shaded with a large embroidered umbrella. After them rode Grandmother Jia's maids, Faithful, Parrot, Amber and Pearl; after them Lin Dai-yu's maids, Nightingale, Snow-goose and Delicate; then Bao-chai's maids, Oriole and Apricot; then Ying-chun's maids, Chess and Tangerine; then Tan-chun's maids, Scribe and Ebony; then Xi-chun's maids, Picture and Landscape; then Aunt Xue's maids, Providence and Prosper, sharing a carriage with Caltrop and Caltrop's own maid, Advent; then Li Wan's maids, Candida and Casta; then Xi-feng's own maids, Patience, Felicity and Crimson, with two of Lady Wang's maids, Golden and Suncloud, whom Xi-feng had agreed to take with her, in the carriage behind. In the carriage after them sat another couple of maids and a nurse holding Xi-feng's little girl. Yet more carriages followed carrying the nannies and old women from the various apartments and the women whose duty it was to act as duennas when the ladies of the household went out of doors. The street was packed with carriages as far as the eye could see in either direction, and Grandmother Jia's palanquin was well on the way to the temple before the last passengers in the rear had finished taking their places. A confused hubbub of laughter and chatter rose from the line of carriages while they were doing so, punctuated by an occasional louder and more distinctly audible protest, such as:

"I'm not sitting next to *you!*"

or,

"You're squashing the Mistress's bundle!"

or,

"Look, you've trodden on my spray!"

or,

"You've ruined my fan, clumsy!"

Zhou Rui's wife walked up and down calling for some order:

"Girls! Girls! You're out in the street now, where people can see you. A little behaviour, *please!*"

She had to do this several times before the clamour subsided somewhat.

The footmen and insignia-bearers at the front of the procession had now reached the temple, and as the files of their column opened out to range themselves on either side of the gateway, the onlookers lining the sides of the street were able to see Bao-yu on a splendidly caparisoned white horse riding at the head of the procession immediately in front of his grandmother's great palanquin with its eight bearers. As Grandmother Jia and her party approached the temple, there was a crash of drums and cymbals from the roadside. It was the Taoists of the temple come out to welcome them, with old Abbot Zhang at their head, resplendent in cope and vestments and with a burning joss-stick[5] in his hand.

The palanquin passed through the gateway and into the first courtyard. From her seat inside it Grandmother Jia could see the terrifying painted images of the temple guardians, one on each side of the inner gate, flanked by that equally ferocious pair, Thousand League Eye with his blue face and Favourable Wind Ear with his green one, and farther on, the benigner forms of the City God and the little Local Gods. She ordered the bearers to halt, and Cousin Zhen[6] at the head of the younger male members of the clan came forward from the inner courtyard to meet her.

Xi-feng, whose palanquin was nearest to Grandmother Jia's, realized that Faithful and the other maids were too far back in the procession to be able to reach the old lady in time to help her out, and hurried forward to perform this service herself. Unfortunately a little eleven- or twelve-year-old acolyte, who had been going round with a pair of snuffers trimming the wicks of the numerous candles that were burning everywhere and whom the arrival of the procession had caught unawares, chose this very moment to attempt a getaway and ran head-on into her. Out flew Xi-feng's hand and dealt him a resounding smack on the face that sent him flying.

"Clumsy brat!" she shouted. "Look where you're going!"

---

5. A stick of incense.   6. Jia Zhen is the acting head of a branch of the Jia clan, one to which Bao-yu does not belong.

The little acolyte picked himself up and, leaving his snuffers where they had fallen, darted off in the direction of the gate. But by now Bao-chai and the other young ladies were getting down from their carriages and a phalanx of women-servants clustered all round them, making egress impossible. Seeing a little Taoist running towards them, the women began to scream and shout:

"Catch him! Catch him! Hit him! Hit him!"

"What is it?" asked Grandmother Jia in alarm, hearing this hubbub behind her, and Cousin Zhen went forward to investigate.

"It's one of the young acolytes," said Xi-feng as she helped the old lady from her conveyance. "He was snuffing the candles and didn't get away in time and now he's rushing around trying to find a way out."

"Bring him to me, poor little thing!" said Grandmother Jia. "And don't frighten him. These children from poorer families have generally been rather spoiled. You can't expect them to stand up to great occasions like this. It would be a shame to frighten the poor little thing out of his wits. Think how upset his mother and father would be. Go on!" she said to Cousin Zhen. "Go and fetch him yourself."

Cousin Zhen was obliged to retrieve the little Taoist in person and led him by the hand to Grandmother Jia. The boy knelt down in front of her, the snuffers—now restored to him—clutched in one hand, trembling like a leaf. Grandmother Jia asked Cousin Zhen to raise him to his feet.

"Don't be afraid," she told the boy. "How old are you?"

But the little boy's mouth was hurting him too badly to speak.

"*Poor* little thing!" said Grandmother Jia. "You'd better take him away, Zhen. Give him some money to buy sweeties with and tell the others that they are not to grumble at him."

Cousin Zhen had to promise, and led the boy away, while the old lady led *her* party inside to begin a systematic tour of the shrines.

The pages in the outer courtyard, who had a moment before witnessed Grandmother Jia and her train trooping through the gateway that led into the inner courtyard, were surprised to see Cousin Zhen now emerging from it again with a little Taoist in tow. They heard him say that the boy was to be taken out and given a few hundred cash and that he was to be treated kindly. A few of them came forward and led the child away in obedience to his instructions.

Still standing at the top of the steps to the inner gate, Cousin Zhen inquired what had become of the stewards.

"Steward! Steward!" shouted the pages in unison, and almost immediately Lin Zhi-xiao came running out from heaven knows where, adjusting his hat with one hand as he ran.

"This is a big place," said Cousin Zhen when Lin Zhi-xiao was standing in front of him, "and we weren't expecting so many here today. I want you to take all the people you need and stay here in this courtyard with them. Those you don't need here can wait in the second courtyard. And pick some reliable boys to go on this gate and the two posterns to pass word through to those outside if those inside need anything. Do you understand? All the ladies are here today and I don't want any outsiders to get in. Is that understood?"

"Yessir!" said Lin Zhi-xiao. "Sir!"

"Well get on with it!" said Cousin Zhen. "Where's Rong got to?"

The words were scarcely out of his mouth when Jia Rong came bounding out of the bell-tower, buttoning his jacket as he ran.

"Look at him!" said Cousin Zhen irately. "Enjoying himself in the cool while I am roasting down here! Spit at him, someone."

Long familiarity with Cousin Zhen's temper had taught the boys that he would brook no opposition when roused. One of them obediently stepped forward and spat in Jia Rong's face; then, as Cousin Zhen continued to glare at him, he rebuked Jia Rong for presuming to be cool while his father was still sweating outside in the sun. Jia Rong was obliged to stand with his arms hanging submissively at his sides throughout this public humiliation, not daring to utter a word.

The other members of Jia Rong's generation who were present—Jia Yun, Jia Ping, Jia Qin and the rest—were greatly alarmed by this outburst; indeed, even the clansmen of Cousin Zhen's own generation—the Jia Bins and Jia Huangs and Jia Qiongs—were to be seen putting their hats on and slinking out, one by one, from the shadow of the walls.

"What are you standing here for?" said Cousin Zhen to Jia Rong. "Why don't you get on your horse and go back home and tell your mother and that new wife of yours that Her Old Ladyship is here with all the Rong-guo girls. Tell them they must come here at once to wait on her."

Jia Rong ran outside and began bawling impatiently for his horse. "What on earth can have got into him that he should suddenly have picked on me like that?" he muttered to himself resentfully; then, as his horse had still not arrived, he shouted angrily at the grooms:

"Come on, bring that horse, damn you! Are your hands tied or something?"

He would have liked to send a boy in his place, but was afraid that if he did, his father would find out when he went back later to report; and so, when the horse arrived, he mounted and rode off home.

Cousin Zhen was about to turn and go in again when he discovered old Abbot Zhang at his elbow, smiling somewhat unnaturally.

"Perhaps I don't come in quite the same category as the others," said the old Taoist. "Perhaps I should be allowed inside to wait on Her Old Ladyship. However. In this inclement heat, and with so many young ladies about, I shouldn't like to presume. I will do whatever you say. I *did* just wonder whether Her Old Ladyship might ask for me, or whether she might require a guide to take her round the shrines . . . However. Perhaps it would be best if I waited here."

Cousin Zhen was aware that, though Abbot Zhang had started life a poor boy and entered the Taoist church as "proxy novice" of Grandmother Jia's late husband, a former Emperor had with his own Imperial lips conferred on him the title "Doctor Mysticus," and he now held the seals of the Board of Commissioners of the Taoist Church, had been awarded the title "Doctor Serenissimus"[7] by the reigning sovereign, and was addressed as "Holiness" by princes, dukes and governors of provinces. He was therefore not a man to be trifled with. Moreover he was constantly in and out of the two mansions and on familiar terms with most of the Jia ladies. Cousin Zhen at once became affable.

"Oh, *you're* one of the family, Papa Zhang, so let's have no more of that

---

7. The translator is imitating the pompous titles of the Taoist clergy.

kind of talk, or I'll take you by that old beard of yours and give it a good pull. Come on, follow me!"

Abbot Zhang followed him inside, laughing delightedly.

Having found Grandmother Jia, Cousin Zhen ducked and smiled deferentially.

"Papa Zhang has come to pay his respects, Grannie."

"Help him, then!" said Grandmother Jia; and Cousin Zhen hurried back to where Abbot Zhang was waiting a few yards behind him and supported him by an elbow into her presence. The abbot prefaced his greeting with a good deal of jovial laughter.

"Blessed Buddha of Boundless Life! And how has Your Old Ladyship been all this while? In rude good health, I trust? And Their Ladyships, and all the younger ladies?—also flourishing? It's quite a while since I was at the mansion to call on Your Old Ladyship, but I declare you look more blooming than ever!"

"And how are *you*, old Holy One?" Grandmother Jia asked him with a pleased smile.

"Thank Your Old Ladyship for asking. I still keep pretty fit. But never mind about that. What *I* want to know is, how's our young hero been keeping, eh? We were celebrating the blessed Nativity of the Veiled King[8] here on the twenty-sixth. Very select little gathering. Tasteful offerings. I thought our young friend might have enjoyed it; but when I sent round to invite him, they told me he was out."

"He really *was* out," said Grandmother Jia, and turned aside to summon the "young hero"; but Bao-yu had gone to the lavatory. He came hurrying forward presently.

"Hallo, Papa Zhang! How are you?"

The old Taoist embraced him affectionately and returned his greeting.

"He's beginning to fill out," he said, addressing Grandmother Jia.

"He looks well enough on the outside," said Grandmother Jia, "but underneath he's delicate. And his Pa doesn't improve matters by forcing him to study all the time. I'm afraid he'll end up by *making* the child ill."

"Lately I've been seeing calligraphy and poems of his in all kinds of places," said Abbot Zhang, "—all quite remarkably good. I really can't understand why Sir Zheng is concerned that the boy doesn't study enough. If you ask me, I think he's all right as he is." He sighed. "Of course, you know who this young man reminds me of, don't you? Whether it's his looks or the way he talks or the way he moves, to me he's the spit and image of Old Sir Jia."

The old man's eyes grew moist, and Grandmother Jia herself showed a disposition to be tearful.

"It's quite true," she said. "None of our children or our children's children turned out like him, except my Bao. Only my little Jade Boy is like his grandfather."

"Of course, your generation wouldn't remember Old Sir Jia," Abbot Zhang said, turning to Cousin Zhen. "It's before your time. In fact, I don't suppose even Sir She and Sir Zheng can have a very clear recollection of what their father was like in his prime."

He brightened as another topic occurred to him and once more quaked with laughter.

---

8. The Taoist pantheon was filled with literally thousands of deities with such grandiloquent names.

"I saw a most attractive young lady when I was out visiting the other day. Fourteen this year. Seeing her put me in mind of our young friend here. It must be about time we started thinking about a match for him, surely? In looks, intelligence, breeding, background this girl was ideally suited. What does Your Old Ladyship feel? I didn't want to rush matters. I thought I'd better first wait and see what Your Old Ladyship thought before saying anything to the family."

"A monk who once told the boy's fortune said that he was not to marry young," said Grandmother Jia; "so I think we had better wait until he is a little older before we arrange anything definite. But do by all means go on inquiring for us. It doesn't matter whether the family is wealthy or not; as long as the girl *looks* all right, you can let me know. Even if it's a poor family, we can always help out over the expenses. Money is no problem. It's looks and character that count."

"Now come on, Papa Zhang!" said Xi-feng when this exchange had ended. "Where's that new amulet for my little girl? You had the nerve to send someone round the other day for gosling satin, and of course, as we didn't want to embarrass the old man by refusing, we had to send you some. So now what about that amulet?"

Abbot Zhang once more quaked with laughter.

"Ho! ho! ho! You can tell how bad my eyes are getting; I didn't even see you there, dear lady, or I should have thanked you for the satin. Yes, the amulet has been ready for some time. I was going to send it to you two days ago, but then Her Grace unexpectedly asked us for this *Pro Viventibus* and I stupidly forgot all about it. It's still on the high altar being sanctified. I'll go and get it for you."

He went off, surprisingly nimbly, to the main hall of the temple and returned after a short while carrying the amulet on a little tea-tray, using a red satin book-wrap as a tray-cloth. Baby's nurse took the amulet from him, and he was just about to receive the little girl from her arms when he caught sight of Xi-feng laughing at him mockingly.

"Why didn't you bring it in your hand?" she asked him.

"The hands get so sweaty in this weather," he said. "I thought a tray would be more hygienic."

"You gave me quite a fright when I saw you coming in with that tray," said Xi-feng. "I thought for one moment you were going to take up a collection!"

There was a loud burst of laughter from the assembled company. Even Cousin Zhen was unable to restrain himself.

"Monkey! Monkey!" said Grandmother Jia. "Aren't you afraid of going to the Hell of Scoffers when you die and having your tongue cut out?"

"Oh, Papa and I say what we like to each other," said Xi-feng. *He's* always telling *me* I must 'acquire merit' and threatening me with a short life if I don't pay up quickly. That's right, isn't it Papa?"

"As a matter of fact I *did* have an ulterior motive in bringing this tray," said Abbot Zhang, laughing, "but it wasn't in order to make a collection, I assure you. I wanted to ask this young gentleman here if he would be so very kind as to lend me the famous jade for a few minutes. The tray is for carrying it outside on, so that my Taoist friends, some of whom have travelled long distances to be here, and my old students, and *their* students, all of whom are gathered here today, may have the privilege of examining it."

"My dear good man, in that case let the boy go with it round his neck and show it to them himself!" said Grandmother Jia. "No need for all this running to and fro with trays—at your age, too!"

"Most kind! Most considerate!—But Your Old Ladyship is deceived," said the abbot. "I may look my eighty years, but I'm still hale and hearty. No, the point is that with so many of them here today and the weather so hot, the smell is sure to be somewhat overpowering. Our young friend here is certainly not used to it. We shouldn't want him to be overcome by the—ah—effluvia, should we?"

Hearing this, Grandmother Jia told Bao-yu to take off the Magic Jade and put it on the tray. Abbot Zhang draped the crimson cloth over his hands, grasped the tray between satin-covered thumbs and fingers, and, holding it like a sacred relic at eye level in front of him, conveyed it reverently from the courtyard.

Grandmother Jia and the others now continued their sightseeing. They had finished with everything at ground level and were about to mount the stairs into the galleries when Cousin Zhen came up to report that Abbot Zhang had returned with the jade. He was followed by the smiling figure of the abbot, holding the tray in the same reverential manner as before.

"Well, they've all seen the jade now," he said, "—and very grateful they were. They agreed that it really is a most remarkable object, and they regretted that they had nothing of value to show their appreciation with. Here you are!—this is the best they could do. These are all little Taoist trinkets they happened to have about them. Nothing very special, I'm afraid; but they'd like our young friend to keep them, either to amuse himself with or to give away to his friends."

Grandmother Jia looked at the tray. It was covered with jewellery. There were golden crescents, jade thumb-rings and a lot of "motto" jewellery—a tiny sceptre and persimmons with the rebus-meaning "success in all things," a little quail and a vase with corn-stalks meaning "peace throughout the years,"[9] and many other designs—all in gold- or jade-work, and much of it inlaid with pearls and precious stones. Altogether there must have been about forty pieces.

"What have you been up to, you naughty old man?" she said. "Those men are all poor priests—they can't afford to give things like *this* away. You really shouldn't have done this. We can't possibly accept them."

"It was their own idea, I do assure you," said the abbot. "There was nothing I could do to stop them. If you refuse to take these things, I am afraid you will destroy my credit with these people. They will say that I cannot really have the connection with your honoured family that I have always claimed to have."

After this Grandmother Jia could no longer decline. She told one of the servants to receive the tray.

"We obviously can't refuse, Grannie, after what Papa Zhang has just said," said Bao-yu; "but I really have no use for this stuff. Why not let one of the boys carry it outside for me and I'll distribute it to the poor?"

"I think that's a very good idea," said Grandmother Jia.

But Abbot Zhang thought otherwise and hastily intervened:

9. The names or forms of the objects in the jewelry would take on different meanings through puns and other kinds of wordplay.

"I'm sure it does our young friend credit, this charitable impulse. However. Although these things are, as I said, of no especial value, they are—what shall I say—objects of *virtù*, and if you give them to the poor, in the first place the poor won't have much use for them, and in the second place the objects themselves will get spoiled. If you want to give something to the poor, a largesse of money would, I suggest, be far more appropriate."

"Very well, look after this stuff for me, then," said Bao-yu to the servant, "and this evening you will distribute a largesse."

This being now settled, Abbot Zhang withdrew, and Grandmother Jia and her party went up to the galleries. Grandmother Jia sat with Bao-yu and the girls in the gallery facing the stage and Xi-feng and Li Wan sat in the east gallery. The maids all sat in the west gallery and took it in turns to go off and wait on their mistresses.

Not long after they were all seated, Cousin Zhen came upstairs to say that the gods had now chosen which plays were to be performed—by which was meant, of course, that the names had been shaken from a pot in front of the altar, since this was the only way in which the will of the gods could be known. The first play selected was *The White Serpent*.

"What's the story?" said Grandmother Jia.

Cousin Zhen explained that it was about the emperor Gao-zu, founder of the Han dynasty, who began his rise to greatness by decapitating a monstrous white snake.

The second choice was *A Heap of Honours,* which shows the sixtieth birth-day party of the great Tang general Guo Zi-yi, attended by his seven sons and eight sons-in-law, all of whom held high office, the "heap of honours" of the title being a reference to the table in his reception-hall piled high with their insignia.

"It seems a bit conceited to have this second one played," said Grand-mother Jia. "Still, if that's what the gods chose, I suppose we'd better have it. What's the third one going to be?"

"*The South Branch*,"[1] said Cousin Zhen.

Grandmother Jia was silent. She knew that *The South Branch* likens the world to an ant-heap and tells a tale of power and glory which turns out in the end to have been a dream.

Hearing no reply, Cousin Zhen went off downstairs again to see about the Offertory Scroll, which had to be ceremonially burnt in front of the holy images along with paper money and paper ingots before the theatrical per-formance could begin.

Our record omits any description of that ceremony and moves back to Bao-yu, who was sitting in the central gallery beside his grandmother, and who now called for a maid to bring the tray up so that he could put on his Magic Jade again. When he had done so, he began to pick over the other trinkets with which the tray was covered and to hand them one by one to Grandmother Jia for her inspection. Her attention was taken by a little red-gold kylin[2] with kingfisher-feather inlay. She stretched out her hand to take it.

"Now where have I seen something like this before?" she said. "I feel certain I've seen some girl wearing an ornament like this."

1. A play by T'ang Hsien-tsu (1550–1617).　　2. A unicorn, considered good luck.

"Cousin Shi's got one," said Bao-chai. "It's the same as this one only a little smaller."

"Funny!" said Bao-yu. "All the times she's been to our house, I don't remember ever having seen it."

"Cousin Bao is observant," said Tan-chun. "No matter what it is, she remembers everything."

"Well, perhaps not quite *everything*," said Dai-yu wryly. "But she's certainly very observant where things like *this* are concerned."

Bao-chai turned her head away and pretended not to have heard.

Now that he knew the kylin on the tray was like one that Shi Xiang-yun[3] wore, Bao-yu hurriedly picked it up and thrust it inside his jacket. But no sooner had he done so than it occurred to him that his action might be misconstrued; so instead of dropping it into his inside pocket, he continued to hold it there, at the same time glancing about him furtively to see if he had been observed. None of the others seemed to have noticed except Dai-yu, who was staring at him fixedly and nodding her head in mock approval.

Bao-yu felt suddenly embarrassed. Drawing his hand out again with the ornament still in it, he returned her look and laughed sheepishly:

"It's rather nice, isn't it? I thought I'd keep it for you," he said. "When we get home we can thread it on a ribbon and you'll be able to wear it."

Dai-yu tossed her head.

"*I* don't want it!"

"If *you* don't want it, I'll keep it for myself, then," said Bao-yu, and popped it once more inside his jacket.

He was about to add something, but just at that moment Cousin Zhen's wife, You-shi, and his new daughter-in-law, Hu-shi, arrived and came upstairs to pay their respects to Grandmother Jia.

"Now why have *you* come here? You really shouldn't have bothered," said Grandmother Jia. "We only came to amuse ourselves. It isn't a formal visit."

No sooner had she said this than it was announced that representatives from General Feng's household had arrived. It appeared that Feng Zi-ying's mother, hearing that the Jia ladies were having a *Pro Viventibus* performed at the Taoist temple, had immediately prepared an offering of pork, mutton, incense, tea and cakes and sent it post-haste to the temple with her compliments. Xi-feng, hearing the announcement, came hurrying round to the central gallery. She clapped her hands and laughed.

"Dear oh dear! This is something I hadn't bargained for. My idea was a quiet little outing for us girls; but here is everyone sending offerings and behaving as if we'd come here for a high mass or something. It's all your fault, Grannie! And we haven't even got any vails[4] ready to give to the bearers."

Even as she said this, two stewardesses from the Feng household were already mounting the stairs. And before *they* had gone, other messengers arrived with offerings from Vice-president Zhao's lady. From then on it was a steady stream: friends, kinsmen, family connections, business associates—all who had heard that the Jia ladies were holding a *Pro Viventibus* sent their representatives along with offerings and complimentary messages. Grandmother Jia began to regret that she had ever come.

3. An orphaned great-niece of Grandmother Jia.   4. Tips.

"It isn't as if we'd come here for the ceremony," she grumbled. "We only wanted to enjoy ourselves. But all we seem to have done is to have stirred up a lot of fuss."

Consequently, although she stayed and watched the plays for that day, she returned home fairly early in the afternoon and next day professed herself too lacking in energy to go again. Xi-feng reacted differently. "In for a penny, in for a pound" was her motto. They had already had the fuss; and since the players were there anyway, they might as well go again today and enjoy themselves in peace.

For Bao-yu the whole of the previous day had been spoilt by Abbot Zhang's proposal to Grandmother Jia to arrange a match for him. He came home in a thoroughly bad temper and kept telling everyone that he would "never see Abbot Zhang again as long as he lived." Not associating his ill-humour with the abbot's proposal, the others were mystified.

Grandmother Jia's unwillingness was further reinforced by the fact that Dai-yu, since her return home yesterday, had been suffering from mild sunstroke. What with one thing and another, the old lady declined absolutely to go again, and Xi-feng had to make up her own party and go by herself.

But Xi-feng's play-going does not concern us.

Bao-yu, believing that Dai-yu's sunstroke was serious and that she might even be in danger of her life, was so worried that he could not eat, and rushed round in the middle of the lunch-hour to see how she was. He found her neither as ill as he had feared nor as responsive as he might have hoped.

"Why don't you go and watch your plays?" she asked him. "What are you mooning about at home for?"

Abbot Zhang's recent attempt at match-making had profoundly distressed Bao-yu and he was shocked by her seeming indifference.

"I can forgive the others for not understanding what has upset me," he thought; "but that *she* should want to trifle with me at a time like this . . . !"

The sense that she had failed him made the annoyance he now felt with her a hundred times greater than it had been on any previous occasion. Never could any other person have stirred him to such depths of atrabilious[5] rage. Coming from other lips, her words would scarcely have touched him. Coming from hers, they put him in a passion. His face darkened.

"It's all along been a mistake, then," he said. "You're not what I took you for."

Dai-yu gave an unnatural little laugh.

"Not what you took me for? That's hardly surprising, is it? I haven't got that *little something* which would have made me worthy of you."

Bao-yu came right up to her and held his face close to hers:

"You do realize, don't you, that you are deliberately willing my death?"

Dai-yu could not for the moment understand what he was talking about.

"I swore an oath to you yesterday," he went on. "I said that I hoped Heaven might strike me dead if this 'gold and jade' business meant anything to me. Since you have now brought it up again, it's clear to me that you *want* me to die. Though what you hope to gain by my death I find it hard to imagine."

Dai-yu now remembered what had passed between them on the previous

---

5. Literally "black bile"; here, dark mood.

day. She knew that she was wrong to have spoken as she did, and felt both ashamed and a little frightened. Her shoulders started shaking and she began to cry.

"May Heaven strike *me* dead if I ever willed your death!" she said. "But I don't see what you have to get so worked up about. It's only because of what Abbot Zhang said about arranging a match for you. You're afraid he might interfere with your precious 'gold and jade' plans; and because you're angry about that, you have to come along and take it out on me—That's all it is, isn't it?"

Bao-yu had from early childhood manifested a streak of morbid sensibility, which being brought up in close proximity with a nature so closely in harmony with his own had done little to improve. Now that he had reached an age when both his experience and the reading of forbidden books had taught him something about "worldly matters," he had begun to take a rather more grown-up interest in girls. But although there were plenty of young ladies of outstanding beauty and breeding among the Jia family's numerous acquaintance, none of them, in his view, could remotely compare with Dai-yu. For some time now his feeling for her had been a very special one; but precisely because of this same morbid sensibility, he had shrunk from telling her about it. Instead, whenever he was feeling particularly happy or particularly cross, he would invent all sorts of ways of probing her to find out if this feeling for her was reciprocated. It was unfortunate for him that Dai-yu herself possessed a similar streak of morbid sensibility and disguised her real feelings, as he did his, while attempting to discover what *he* felt about *her*.

Here was a situation, then, in which both parties concealed their real emotions and assumed counterfeit ones in an endeavour to find out what the real feelings of the other party were. And because

> When false meets false the truth will oft-times out,

there was the constant possibility that the innumerable little frustrations that were engendered by all this concealment would eventually erupt into a quarrel.

Take the present instance. What Bao-yu was actually thinking at this moment was something like this:

"In my eyes and in my thoughts there is no one else but you. I can forgive the others for not knowing this, but surely *you* ought to realize? If at a time like this you can't share my anxiety—if you can think of nothing better to do than provoke me with that sort of silly talk, it shows that the concern I feel for you every waking minute of the day is wasted: that you just don't care about me at all."

This was what he *thought*; but of course he didn't *say* it. On her side Dai-yu's thoughts were somewhat as follows:

"I know you must care for me a little bit, and I'm sure you don't take this ridiculous 'gold and jade' talk seriously. But if you cared *only* for me and had absolutely no inclination at all in another direction, then every time I mentioned 'gold and jade' you would behave quite naturally and let it pass almost as if you hadn't noticed. How is it, then, that when I do refer to it you get so excited? It shows that it must be on your mind. You *pretend* to be upset in order to allay my suspicions."

Meanwhile a quite different thought was running through Bao-yu's mind:

"I would do anything—absolutely *anything*," he was thinking, "if only you would be nice to me. If you would be nice to me, I would gladly die for you this moment. It doesn't really matter whether you know what I feel for you or not. Just be nice to me, then at least we shall be a little closer to each other, instead of so horribly far apart."

At the same time Dai-yu was thinking:

"Never mind me. Just be your own natural self. If *you* were all right, *I* should be all right too. All these manoeuvrings to try and anticipate my feelings don't bring us any closer together; they merely draw us farther apart."

The percipient reader will no doubt observe that these two young people were already of one mind, but that the complicated procedures by which they sought to draw together were in fact having precisely the opposite effect. Complacent reader! Permit us to remind you that your correct understanding of the situation is due solely to the fact that we have been revealing to you the secret, innermost thoughts of those two young persons, which neither of them had so far ever felt able to express.

Let us now return from the contemplation of inner thoughts to the recording of outward appearances.

When Dai-yu, far from saying something nice to him, once more made reference to the "gold and jade," Bao-yu became so choked with rage that for a moment he was quite literally bereft of speech. Frenziedly snatching the "Magic Jade" from his neck and holding it by the end of its silken cord he gritted his teeth and dashed it against the floor with all the strength in his body.

"*Beastly* thing!" he shouted. "I'll smash you to pieces and put an end to this once and for all."

But the jade, being exceptionally hard and resistant, was not the tiniest bit damaged. Seeing that he had not broken it, Bao-yu began to look around for something to smash it with. Dai-yu, still crying, saw what he was going to do.

"Why smash a dumb, lifeless object?" she said. "If you want to smash something, let it be me."

The sound of their quarrelling brought Nightingale and Snowgoose hurrying in to keep the peace. They found Bao-yu apparently bent on destroying his jade and tried to wrest it from him. Failing to do so, and sensing that the quarrel was of more than usual dimensions, they went off to fetch Aroma. Aroma came back with them as fast as she could run and eventually succeeded in prising the jade from his hand. He glared at her scornfully.

"It's my own thing I'm smashing," he said. "What business is it of yours to interfere?"

Aroma saw that his face was white with anger and his eyes wild and dangerous. Never had she seen him in so terrible a rage. She took him gently by the hand:

"You shouldn't smash the jade just because of a disagreement with your cousin," she said. "What do you think she would feel like and what sort of position would it put her in if you really *were* to break it?"

Dai-yu heard these words through her sobs. They struck a responsive chord in her breast, and she wept all the harder to think that even Aroma seemed to understand her better than Bao-yu did. So much emotion was too much for her weak stomach. Suddenly there was a horrible retching noise and up came the tisane of elsholtzia[6] leaves she had taken only a short while before. Nightingale quickly held out her handkerchief to receive it and, while Snow-goose rubbed and pounded her back, Dai-yu continued to retch up wave upon wave of watery vomit, until the whole handkerchief was soaked with it.

"However cross you may be, Miss, you ought to have more regard for your health," said Nightingale. "You'd only just taken that medicine and you were beginning to feel a little bit better for it, and now because of your argument with Master Bao you've gone and brought it all up again. Suppose you were to be *really* ill as a consequence. How do you think Master Bao would feel?"

When Bao-yu heard these words they struck a responsive chord in *his* breast, and he reflected bitterly that even Nightingale seemed to understand him better than Dai-yu. But then he looked again at Dai-yu, who was sobbing and panting by turns, and whose red and swollen face was wet with perspiration and tears, and seeing how pitiably frail and ill she looked, his heart misgave him.

"I shouldn't have taken her up on that 'gold and jade' business," he thought. "I've got her into this state and now there's no way in which I can relieve her by sharing what she suffers." As he thought this, he, too, began to cry.

Now that Bao-yu and Dai-yu were both crying, Aroma instinctively drew towards her master to comfort him. A pang of pity for him passed through her and she squeezed his hand sympathetically. It was as cold as ice. She would have liked to tell him not to cry but hesitated, partly from the consideration that he might be suffering from some deep-concealed hurt which crying would do something to relieve, and partly from the fear that to do so in Dai-yu's presence might seem presumptuous. Torn between a desire to speak and fear of the possible consequences of speaking, she did what girls of her type often do when faced with a difficult decision: she avoided the necessity of making one by bursting into tears.

As for Nightingale, who had disposed of the handkerchief of vomited tisane and was now gently fanning her mistress with her fan, seeing the other three all standing there as quiet as mice with the tears streaming down their faces, she was so affected by the sight that she too started crying and was obliged to have recourse to a second handkerchief.

There the four of them stood, then, facing each other; all of them crying; none of them saying a word. It was Aroma who broke the silence with a strained and nervous laugh.

"You ought not to quarrel with Miss Lin," she said to Bao-yu, "if only for the sake of this pretty cord she made you."

At these words Dai-yu, ill as she was, darted forward, grabbed the jade from Aroma's hand, and snatching up a pair of scissors that were lying nearby, began feverishly cutting at its silken cord with them. Before Aroma and Nightingale could stop her, she had already cut it into several pieces.

"It was a waste of time making it," she sobbed. "He doesn't really care for it. And there's someone else who'll no doubt make him a better one!"

"What a shame!" said Aroma, retrieving the jade. "It's all my silly fault. I should have kept my mouth shut."

6. Unidentified. *Tisane:* a tea or infusion.

"Go on! Cut away!" said Bao-yu. "I shan't be wearing the wretched thing again anyway, so it doesn't matter."

Preoccupied with the quarrel, the four of them had failed to notice several old women, who had been drawn by the sound of it to investigate. Apprehensive, when they saw Dai-yu hysterically weeping and vomiting and Bao-yu trying to smash his jade, of the dire consequences to be expected from a scene of such desperate passion, they had hurried off in a body to the front of the mansion to report the matter to Grandmother Jia and Lady Wang, hoping in this way to establish in advance that whatever the consequences might be, *they* were not responsible for them. From their precipitate entry and the grave tone of their announcement Grandmother Jia and Lady Wang assumed that some major catastrophe had befallen and hurried with them into the Garden to find out what it was.

Their arrival filled Aroma with alarm. "What did Nightingale want to go troubling Their Ladyships for?" she thought crossly, supposing that the talebearer had been sent to them by Nightingale; while Nightingale for her part was angry with Aroma, thinking that the talebearer must have been one of Aroma's minions.

Grandmother Jia and Lady Wang entered the room to find a silent Bao-yu and a silent Dai-yu, neither of whom, when questioned, would admit that anything at all was the matter. They therefore visited their wrath on the heads of the two unfortunate maids, insisting that it was entirely owing to their negligence that matters had got so much out of hand. Unable to defend themselves, the girls were obliged to endure a long and abusive dressing-down, after which Grandmother Jia concluded the affair by carrying Bao-yu off to her own apartment.

Next day, the third of the fifth month, was Xue Pan's birthday and there was a family party with plays, to which the Jias were all invited. Bao-yu, who had still not seen Dai-yu since his outburst—which he now deeply regretted—was feeling far too dispirited to care about seeing plays, and declined to go on the ground that he was feeling unwell.

Dai-yu, though somewhat overcome on the day previous to this by the sultry weather, had by no means been seriously ill. Arguing that if *she* was not ill, it was impossible that *he* should be, she felt sure, when she heard of Bao-yu's excuse that it must be a false one.

"He usually enjoys drinking and watching plays," she thought. "If he's not going, it must be because he is still angry about yesterday; or if it isn't that, it must be because he's heard that I'm not going and doesn't want to go without me. Oh! I should *never* have cut that cord! Now he won't ever wear his jade again—unless I make him another cord to wear it on."

So she, too, regretted the quarrel.

Grandmother Jia knew that Bao-yu and Dai-yu were angry with each other, but she had been assuming that they would see each other at the Xues' party and make it up there. When neither of them turned up at it, she became seriously upset.

"I'm a miserable old sinner," she grumbled. "It must be my punishment for something I did wrong in a past life to have to live with a pair of such obstinate, addle-headed little geese! I'm sure there isn't a day goes by without their giving me some fresh cause for anxiety. It must be fate. That's what it says in the proverb, after all:

'Tis Fate brings foes and lo'es[7] tegither.

I'll be glad when I've drawn my last breath and closed my old eyes for the last time; then the two of them can snap and snarl at each other to their hearts' content, for *I* shan't be there to see it, and 'what the eye doesn't see, the heart doesn't grieve.' The Lord knows, it's not *my* wish to drag on this wearisome life any longer!"

Amidst these muttered grumblings the old lady began to cry.

In due course her words were transmitted to Bao-yu and Dai-yu. It happened that neither of them had ever heard the saying

'Tis Fate brings foes and lo'es tegither,

and its impact on them, hearing it for the first time, was like that of a Zen "perception": something to be meditated on with bowed head and savoured with a gush of tears. Though they had still not made it up since their quarrel, the difference between them had now vanished completely:

In Naiad's House one to the wind made moan,
In Green Delights one to the moon complained,

to parody the well-known lines. Or, in homelier verses:

Though each was in a different place,
Their hearts in friendship beat as one.

On the second day after their quarrel Aroma deemed that the time was now ripe for urging a settlement.

"Whatever the rights and wrongs of all this may be," she said to Bao-yu, "*you* are certainly the one who is *most* to blame. Whenever in the past you've heard about a quarrel between one of the pages and one of the girls, you've always said that the boy was a brute for not understanding the girl's feelings better—yet here you are behaving in exactly the same way yourself! Tomorrow will be the Double Fifth. Her Old Ladyship will be really angry if the two of you are still at daggers drawn on the day of the festival, and that will make life difficult for *all* of us. Why not put your pride in your pocket and go and say you are sorry, so that we can all get back to normal again?"

But as to whether or not Bao-yu followed her advice, or, if he did so, what the effect of following it was—those questions will be dealt with in the following chapter.

CHAPTER 30

Bao-chai speaks of a fan and castigates her deriders
Charmante scratches a "qiang" and mystifies a beholder

Dai-yu, as we have shown, regretted her quarrel with Bao-yu almost as soon as it was over; but since there were no conceivable grounds on which she could run after him and tell him so, she continued, both day and night, in a state of unrelieved depression that made her feel almost as if a part of her was lost. Nightingale had a shrewd idea how it was with her and resolved at last to tackle her:

"I think the day before yesterday you were too hasty, Miss. *We* ought to

7. Loves.

know what things Master Bao is touchy about, if no one else does. Look at
all the quarrels we've had with him in the past on account of that jade!"

"Poh!" said Dai-yu scornfully. "You are trying to make out that it was my
fault because you have taken his side against me. Of course I wasn't too
hasty."

Nightingale gave her a quizzical smile.

"No? Then why did you cut that cord up? If three parts of the blame was
Bao-yu's, I'm sure at least seven parts of it was yours. From what I've seen
of it, he's all right with you when you allow him to be; it's because you're so
prickly with him and always trying to put him in the wrong that he gets
worked up."

Dai-yu was about to retort when they heard someone at the courtyard gate
calling to be let in. Nightingale turned to listen:

"That's Bao-yu's voice," she said. "I expect he has come to apologize."

"I forbid you to let him in," said Dai-yu.

"There you go again!" said Nightingale. "You're going to keep him standing
outside in the blazing sun on a day like this. Surely *that*'s wrong, if nothing
else is?"

She was moving outside, even as she said this, regardless of her mistress's
injunction. Sure enough, it *was* Bao-yu. She unfastened the gate and welcomed him in with a friendly smile.

"Master Bao! I was beginning to think you weren't coming to see us any
more. I certainly didn't expect to see you here again so soon."

"Oh, you've been making a mountain out of a molehill," said Bao-yu,
returning her smile. "Why ever shouldn't I come? Even if I died, my *ghost*
would be round here a hundred times a day. How is my cousin? Quite better
now?"

"Physically she's better," said Nightingale, "but she's still in very poor
spirits."

"Ah yes—I know she's upset."

This exchange took place as they were crossing the forecourt. He now
entered the room. Dai-yu was sitting on the bed crying. She had not been
crying to start with, but the bittersweet pang she experienced when she heard
his arrival had started the tears rolling. Bao-yu went up to the bed and smiled
down at her.

"How are you, coz? Quite better now?"

As Dai-yu seemed to be too busy wiping her eyes to make a reply, he sat
down close beside her on the edge of the bed:

"I know you're not *really* angry with me," he said. "It's just that if the others
noticed I wasn't coming here, they would think we had been quarrelling; and
if we waited for them to interfere, we should be allowing other people to
come between us. It would be better to hit me and shout at me now and get
it over with, if you still bear any hard feelings, than to go on ignoring me.
Coz dear! Coz dear!—"

He must have repeated those same two words in the same tone of passionate entreaty upwards of twenty times. Dai-yu had been meaning to ignore
him, but what he had just been saying about other people "coming between"
them seemed to prove that he must in *some* way feel closer to her than the
rest, and she was unable to maintain her silence.

"You don't have to treat me like a child," she blurted out tearfully. "From now on I shall make no further claims on you. You can behave exactly as if I had gone away."

"Gone away?" said Bao-yu laughingly. "Where would you go to?"

"Back home."

"I'd follow you."

"As if I were dead then."

"If you died," he said, "I should become a monk."

Dai-yu's face darkened immediately:

"What an utterly idiotic thing to say! Suppose your own sisters were to die? Just how many times can one person become a monk? I think I had better see what the others think about that remark."

Bao-yu had realized at once that she would be offended; but the words were already out of his mouth before he could stop them. He turned very red and hung his head in silence. It was a good thing that no one else was in the room at that moment to see him. Dai-yu glared at him for some seconds —evidently too enraged to speak, for she made a sound somewhere between a snort and a sigh, but said nothing—then, seeing him almost purple in the face with suppressed emotion, she clenched her teeth, pointed her finger at him, and, with an indignant "Hmn!", stabbed the air quite savagely a few inches away from his forehead:

"You—!"

But whatever it was she had been going to call him never got said. She merely gave a sigh and began wiping her eyes again with her handkerchief.

Bao-yu had been in a highly emotional state when he came to see Dai-yu and it had further upset him to have inadvertently offended her so soon after his arrival. This angry gesture and the unsuccessful struggle, ending in sighs and tears, to say what she wanted to say now affected him so deeply that he, too, began to weep. In need of a handkerchief but finding that he had come out without one, he wiped his eyes on his sleeve.

Although Dai-yu was crying, the spectacle of Bao-yu using the sleeve of his brand-new lilac-coloured summer gown as a handkerchief had not escaped her, and while continuing to wipe her own eyes with one hand, she leaned over and reached with the other for the square of silk that was draped over the head-rest at the end of the bed. She lifted it off and threw it at him—all without uttering a word—then, once more burying her face in her own handkerchief, resumed her weeping. Bao-yu picked up the handkerchief she had thrown him and hurriedly wiped his eyes with it. When he had dried them, he drew up close to her again and took one of her hands in his own, smiling at her gently.

"I don't know why you go on crying," he said. "I feel as if all my insides were shattered. Come! Let's go and see Grandmother together."

Dai-yu flung off his hand.

"Take your hands off me! We're not children any more. You really can't go on mauling me about like this all the time. Don't you understand any-thing—?"

"Bravo!"

The shouted interruption startled them both. They spun round to look just as Xi-feng, full of smiles, came bustling into the room.

"Grandmother has been grumbling away something *awful*," she said. "She insisted that I should come over and see if you were both all right. 'Oh,' I said, 'there's no need to go and look, Grannie; they'll have made it up by now without any interference from *us*.' So she told me I was lazy. Well, here I am—and of course it's *exactly* as I said it would be. *I* don't know. I don't understand you two. What is it you find to argue about? For every three days that you're friends you must spend at least two days quarrelling. You really are a couple of babies. And the older you get, the worse you get. Look at you *now*—holding hands crying! And a couple of days ago you were glaring at each other like fighting-cocks. Come on! Come with me to see Grandmother. Let's put the old lady's mind at rest."

As she said this, she seized Dai-yu's hand and began marching off with her. Dai-yu turned back and called for her maids, but there was no response.

"What do you want to call *them* for?" said Xi-feng. "You've got *me* to wait on you, haven't you?"

She continued to walk away, still holding Dai-yu by the hand. Bao-yu followed a little way behind. They went out of the Garden and through into Grandmother Jia's apartment.

"I *told* you they could be left to themselves to make it up and that there was no need for you to worry," said Xi-feng to Grandmother Jia when they were all in the old lady's presence; "but you wouldn't believe me, would you? You insisted on my going there to act the peacemaker. Well, I went there; and what did I find? I found the two of them together *apologizing* to each other. It was like the kite and the kestrel[8] holding hands: they were positively *locked in a clinch!* No need of a peacemaker that *I* could see."

There was a burst of laughter from all present. Bao-chai was among these, but Dai-yu slipped past her without speaking and took a seat next to Grandmother Jia. Bao-yu, rather at a loss for something to say, turned to Bao-chai.

"I'm afraid I wasn't very well on your brother's birthday; so apart from not giving him a present, I couldn't even make him a kotow this year. I'm afraid he may not have realized I was ill and thought that I was merely making excuses. If you can spare a moment next time you see him, I do hope you will explain to him for me."

Bao-chai looked amused.

"That seems a trifle excessive. I am sure he would have felt uncomfortable about your kotowing[9] to him, even if you had been able to come; so I'm quite sure he wouldn't have wanted you to come when you weren't feeling well. It would be rather unfriendly, surely, if cousins who see each other all the time were to start worrying about trifles like *that*?"

Bao-yu smiled.

"Well, as long as *you* understand, that's all right—But why aren't you watching the players?"

"I can't stand the heat," said Bao-chai. "I did watch a couple of acts of something, but it was so hot that I couldn't stay any longer. Unfortunately none of the guests showed any sign of going, so I had to pretend I was ill in order to get away."

"*Touché!*" thought Bao-yu; but he hid his embarrassment in a stupid laugh.

"No wonder they compare you to Yang Gui-fei,[1] cousin. You are well-covered like her, and they always say that plump people fear the heat."

---

8. Two types of hawks.   9. Bowing the head to the ground, here as congratulations.   1. The favorite consort of the Tang emperor Xuan-zong, known for her plump beauty.

The colour flew into Bao-chai's face. An angry retort was on her lips, but she could hardly make it in front of company. Yet reflection only made her angrier. Eventually, after a scornful sniff or two, she said:

"I may be like Yang Gui-fei in some respects, but I don't think there is much danger of my cousin becoming a Prime Minister."[2]

It happened that just at that moment a very young maid called "Prettikins" jokingly accused Bao-chai of having hidden a fan she was looking for.

"I *know* Miss Bao's hidden it," she said. "Come on, Miss! *Please* let me have it."

"You be careful," said Bao-chai, pointing at the girl angrily and speaking with unwonted stridency. "When did you last see *me* playing games of this sort with anyone? If there are other young ladies who are in the habit of *romping about* with you, you had better ask *them*."

Prettikins fled.

Bao-yu realized that he had once again given offence by speaking thoughtlessly; and as this time it was in front of a lot of people, his embarrassment was correspondingly greater. He turned aside in confusion and began talking nervously to someone else.

Bao-yu's rudeness to Bao-chai had given Dai-yu secret satisfaction. When Prettikins came in looking for her fan, she had been on the point of adding some facetiousness of her own at Bao-chai's expense; but Bao-chai's brief explosion caused her to drop the prepared witticism and ask instead what play the two acts were from that Bao-chai said she had just been watching.

Bao-chai had observed the smirk on Dai-yu's face and knew very well that Bao-yu's rudeness must have pleased her. The smiling answer she gave to Dai-yu's question was therefore not without a touch of malice.

"The play I saw was *Li Kui Abuses Song Jiang and Afterwards Has to Say He Is Sorry*."

Bao-yu laughed.

"What a mouthful! Surely, with all your learning, cousin, you must know the proper name of that play? It's called *The Abject Apology*."

"*The Abject Apology?*" said Bao-chai. "Well, no doubt you clever people know all there is to know about abject apology. I'm afraid it's something I wouldn't know about."

Her words touched Bao-yu and Dai-yu on a sensitive spot, and by the time she had finished, they were both blushing hotly with embarrassment.

Xi-feng was insufficiently educated to have understood all these nuances, but by studying the speakers' expressions she had formed a pretty good idea of what they were talking about.

"Rather hot weather to be eating raw ginger, isn't it?" she asked.

No one present could understand what she meant.

"No one's been eating raw ginger," they said.

Xi-feng affected great surprise and rubbed her cheek meaningfully with her hand:

"If no one's been eating raw ginger, then why are they looking so hot and bothered?"

At this Bao-yu and Dai-yu felt even more uncomfortable. Bao-chai was about to add something, but seeing the abject look on Bao-yu's face, she

---

2. Yang Gui-fei's cousin became a corrupt prime minister. The comparison is a pointed reference to Bao-yu's neglect of his studies.

laughed and held her tongue. None of the others present had understood what the four of them were talking about and treated these exchanges as a joke.

Shortly after this, when Bao-chai and Xi-feng had gone out of the room, Dai-yu said to Bao-yu.

"You see? There are people even more dangerous to trifle with than I. If I weren't such a tongue-tied, slow-witted creature, you wouldn't get away with it quite so often, my friend."

Bao-yu was still smarting from Bao-chai's testiness. To be set upon now by Dai-yu as well seemed positively the last straw. But though he wanted to reply, he knew how easily she would take offence and controlled himself with an effort. Feeling in very low spirits, he left the room himself now and went off on his own.

It was the hottest part of the day. Lunch had long been over, and in every apartment mistress and maids alike had succumbed to the lassitude of the hour. As he sauntered slowly by, hands clasped behind his back, everywhere he went was hushed in the breathless silence of noon. From the back of Grandmother Jia's quarters he passed eastwards through the gallery that ended near the wall of Xi-feng's courtyard. He went up to the gate, but it was closed, and remembering that it was her invariable custom when the weather was hot to take two whole hours off in the middle of the day for her siesta, he thought he had better not go in. He continued, instead, through the corner gate that led into his parents' courtyard.

On entering his mother's apartment, he found several maids dozing over their embroidery. Lady Wang herself was lying on a summer-bed[3] in the inner room, apparently fast asleep. Her maid Golden, who was sitting beside her gently pounding her legs, also seemed half asleep, for her head was nodding and her half-closed eyes were blinking drowsily. Bao-yu tiptoed up to her and tweaked an ear-ring. She opened her eyes wide and saw that it was Bao-yu.

He smiled at her and whispered.

"So sleepy?"

Golden pursed her lips up in a smile, motioned to him with her hand to go away, and then closed her eyes again. But Bao-yu lingered, fascinated. Silently craning forward to make sure that Lady Wang's eyes were closed, he took a Fragrant Snow "quencher"[4] from the embroidered pouch at his waist and popped it between Golden's lips. Golden nibbled it dreamily without opening her eyes.

"Shall I ask Her Ladyship to let me have you, so that we can be together?" he whispered jokingly.

Golden made no reply.

"When she wakes up, I'll talk to her about it," he said.

Golden opened her eyes wide and gave him a little push.

"What's the hurry?" she said playfully. " 'Yours is yours, wherever it be,' as they said to the lady when she dropped her gold comb in the well. Haven't you ever heard that saying?—I'll tell you something to do, if you want a bit of fun. Go into the little east courtyard and you'll be able to catch Sunset and Huan together."

"Who cares about *them*?" said Bao-yu. "Let's talk about *us*."

3. A couch set up to catch the breeze.   4. A type of candy.

At this point Lady Wang sat bolt upright and dealt Golden a slap in the face.

"Shameless little harlot!" she cried, pointing at her wrathfully. "It's you and your like who corrupt our innocent young boys."

Bao-yu had slipped silently away as soon as his mother sat up. Golden, one of whose cheeks was now burning a fiery red, was left without a word to say. The other maids, hearing that their mistress was awake, came hurrying into the room.

"Silver!" said Lady Wang. "Go and fetch your mother. I want her to take your sister Golden away."

Golden threw herself, weeping, upon her knees:

"No, Your Ladyship, please! Beat me and revile me as much as you like, but please, for pity's sake, don't send me away. I've been with Your Ladyship nigh on ten years now. How can I ever hold up my head again if you dismiss me?"

Lady Wang was not naturally unkind. On the contrary, she was an exceptionally lenient mistress. This was, in fact, the first time in her life that she had ever struck a maid. But the kind of "shamelessness" of which—in her view—Golden had just been guilty was the one thing she had always most abhorred. It was the uncontrollable anger of the morally outraged that had caused her to strike Golden and call her names; and though Golden now begged and pleaded, she refused to retract her dismissal. When Golden's mother, old Mrs. Bai, had eventually been fetched, the wretched girl, utterly crushed by her shame and humiliation, was led away.

But of her no more.

Embarrassed by his mother's awakening, Bao-yu had slipped hurriedly into the Garden.

The burning sun was now in the height of heaven, the contracted shadows were concentrated darkly beneath the trees, and the stillness of noon, filled with the harsh trilling of cicadas, was broken by no human voice; but as he approached the bamboo trellises of the rose-garden, a sound like a suppressed sob seemed to come from inside the pergola. Uncertain what it was that he had heard, he stopped to listen. Undoubtedly there was someone there.

This was the fifth month of the year, when the rambler roses are in fullest bloom. Peeping through the fragrant panicles[5] with which the pergola was smothered, he saw a girl crouching down on the other side of the trellis, scratching at the ground with one of those long, blunt pins that girls use for fastening their back hair with.

"Can this be some silly maid come here to bury flowers like Frowner?"[6] he wondered.

He was reminded of Zhuang-zi's story of the beautiful Xi-shi's ugly neighbour, whose endeavours to imitate the little frown that made Xi-shi captivating produced an aspect so hideous that people ran from her in terror. The recollection of it made him smile.

"This is 'imitating the Frowner' with a vengeance," he thought, "—if that is really what she is doing. Not merely unoriginal, but downright disgusting!"

---

5. Bunches of flowers.   6. That is, Dai-yu.

"Don't imitate Miss Lin," he was about to shout; but a glimpse of the girl's face revealed to him just in time that this was no maid, but one of the twelve little actresses from Peartree Court—though which of them, since he had seen them only in their make-up on the stage, he was unable to make out. He stuck out his tongue in a grimace and clapped a hand to his mouth.

"Good job I didn't speak too soon," he thought. "I've been in trouble twice already today for doing that, once with Frowner and once with Chai. It only needs me to go and upset these twelve actresses as well and I shall be well and truly in the cart!"[7]

His efforts to identify the girl made him study her more closely. It was curious that he should have thought her an imitator of Dai-yu, for she had much of Dai-yu's ethereal grace in her looks: the same delicate face and frail, slender body; the same

> . . . brows like hills in spring,
> And eyes like autumn's limpid pools;

—even the same little frown that had often made him compare Dai-yu with Xi-shi of the legend.

It was now quite impossible for him to tear himself away. He watched her fascinated. As he watched, he began to see that what she was doing with the pin was not scratching a hole to bury flowers in, but writing. He followed the movements of her hand, and each vertical and horizontal stroke, each dot and hook that she made he copied with a finger on the palm of his hand. Altogether there were eighteen strokes. He thought for a moment. The character he had just written in his hand was QIANG. The name of the roses which covered the pergola contained the same character: "Qiang-wei."

"The sight of the roses has inspired her to write a poem," he thought. "Probably she's just thought of a good couplet and wants to write it down before she forgets it; or perhaps she has already composed several lines and wants to work on them a bit. Let's see what she writes next."

The girl went on writing, and he followed the movements of her hand as before. It was another QIANG. Again she wrote, and again he followed, and again it was a QIANG. It was as though she were under some sort of spell. As soon as she had finished writing one QIANG she began writing another.

QIANG QIANG QIANG QIANG QIANG QIANG QIANG . . .

He must have watched her write several dozen QIANG's in succession. He seemed to be as much affected by the spell on his side of the pergola as the girl herself was on hers, for his eyeballs continued to follow her pin long after he had learned to anticipate its movements.

"This girl must have something on her mind that she cannot tell anyone about to make her behave in this way," he thought. "One can see from her outward behaviour how much she must be suffering inwardly. And she looks so frail. Too frail for suffering. I wish I could bear some of it for you, my dear!"

In the stifling dog-days of summer the transition from clear to overcast is often sudden, and a little cloudlet can sometimes be the harbinger of a heavy shower. As Bao-yu watched the girl, a sudden gust of cool wind blew by,

---

7. That is, in big trouble.

followed, within moments, by the hissing downpour of rain. He could see the water running off her head in streams and soaking into her clothes.

"Oh, it's raining! With her delicate constitution she ought not to be outside in a downpour like this."

In his anxiety he cried out to her involuntarily:

"Don't write any more. Look! You're getting soaked."

The girl looked up, startled, when she heard the voice. She could see someone amidst the roses saying "Don't write"; but partly because of Bao-yu's almost girlishly beautiful features, and partly because she could in any case only see about half of his face, everything above and below being hidden by flowers and foliage, she took him for a maid; so instead of rushing from his presence as she would have done if she had known that it was Bao-yu, she smiled up at him gratefully:

"Thank you for reminding me. But what about you? You must be getting wet too, surely?"

"Aiyo!"—her words made him suddenly aware that the whole of his body was icy cold, and when he looked down, he saw that he was soaked.

"Oh lord!"

He rushed off in the direction of Green Delights; but all the time he was worrying about the girl, who had nowhere where she could shelter from the rain.

As this was the day before the Double Fifth festival, Élégante and the other little actresses—including the one whom Bao-yu had just been watching— had already started their holiday and had gone into the Garden to amuse themselves. Two of them, Trésor—one of the two members of the company who played Principal Boy parts—and Topaze—one of the company's two soubrettes[8]—happened to be in the House of Green Delights playing with Aroma when the rain started and prevented their leaving. They and the maids amused themselves by blocking up the gutters and letting the water collect in the courtyard. When it was nicely flooded, they rounded up a number of mallards, sheldrakes, mandarin ducks and other waterfowl, tied their wings together, and having first closed the courtyard gate, set them down in the water to swim about. Aroma and the girls were all in the outside gallery enjoying this spectacle when Bao-yu arrived at the gate. Finding it shut, he knocked on it for someone to come and open up for him. But there was little chance of a knock being heard above the excited laughter of the maids. He had to shout for some minutes and pound the gate till it shook before anyone heard him inside.

Aroma was not expecting him back so soon.

"I wonder who it can be at this time," she said. "Won't someone go and answer it?"

"It's *me!*" shouted Bao-yu.

"That's Miss Bao's voice," said Musk.

"Nonsense!" said Skybright. "What would *she* be doing visiting us at this time of day?"

"Let me just take a peep through the crack," said Aroma. "If I think it's all right, I'll let them in. We don't want to turn anyone away in the pouring rain."

8. Young actresses, who are often cast as maids.

Keeping under cover of the gallery, she made her way round to the gate and peered through the chink between the double doors. The sight of Bao-yu standing there like a bedraggled hen with the water running off him in streamlets was both alarming and—she could not help but feel—very funny. She opened the gate as quickly as she could, then, when she saw him fully, clapped her hands and doubled up with laughter.

"Master Bao! I *never* thought it would be you. What did you want to come running back in the pouring rain for?"

Bao-yu was by now in a thoroughly evil temper and had fully resolved to give whoever opened the gate a few kicks. As soon as it was open, therefore, he lashed out with his foot, not bothering to see who it was—for he assumed that the person answering it would be one of the younger maids—and dealt Aroma a mighty kick in the ribs that caused her to cry out in pain.

"Worthless lot!" he shouted. "Because I always treat you decently, you think you can get away with *anything*. I'm just your laughing-stock."

It was not until he looked down and saw Aroma crying that he realized he had kicked the wrong person.

"Aiyo! It's you! Where did I kick you?"

Up to this moment Aroma had never had so much as a harsh word from Bao-yu, and the combination of shame, anger and pain she now felt on being kicked and shouted at by him in front of so many people was well-nigh insupportable. Nevertheless she forced herself to bear it, reflecting that to have made an outcry would be like admitting that it was *her* he had meant to kick, which she knew was almost certainly not the case.

"You didn't; you missed me," she said. "Come in and get changed."

When Bao-yu had gone indoors and was changing his clothes, he said to her jokingly:

"In all these years this is the first time I've ever struck anyone in anger. Too bad that *you* should have been the one to get in the way of the blow!"

In spite of the pain, which it cost her some effort to master, Aroma was helping him with his changing. She smiled when he said this.

"I'm the person you always begin things with," she said. "Whether it's big things or little things or pleasant ones or unpleasant ones, it's only natural that you should try them out first on me. Only in this instance I hope that now you've hit me you won't from now on go around hitting other people."

"I didn't mean to kick *you*, you know," said Bao-yu.

"Who said you did?" said Aroma. "It's the younger ones who normally see to the gate; and they've grown so insolent nowadays, it's enough to put *anyone* in a rage. If you'd given one of *them* a few kicks and put the fear of God into them, it would have been a very good thing. No, it was my own silly fault. I should have made *them* open the gate and not gone to open it myself."

While they were speaking, the rain had stopped and Trésor and Topaze had left. The pain in Aroma's side was such that it was giving her a feeling of nausea and she could eat no dinner. At bedtime, when she took off her clothes, she saw a great black bruise the size of a rice-bowl spreading over the side of her chest. The extent of it frightened her, but she forbore to cry out. Nevertheless even her dreams that night were full of pain and she several times uttered an "Aiyo" in the midst of her sleep.

Although it was understood that he had not kicked her deliberately, Bao-yu had felt a little uneasy when he saw how sluggish Aroma seemed in her movements; and when, during the night, he heard her groaning in her sleep, he knew that he must have kicked her really hard. Getting out of bed, he picked up a lamp and tiptoed over to have a look. Just as he reached the foot of her bed, he heard her cough a couple of times and spit out a mouthful of something.

"Aiyo!"

She opened her eyes wide and saw Bao-yu. Startled, she asked him what he was doing there.

"You've been groaning in your sleep," he said. "I must have hurt you badly. Let me have a look."

"My head feels giddy," said Aroma, "and I've got a sweet, sickly taste in my throat. Have a look on the floor."

Bao-yu shone his lamp on the floor. Beside the bed, where she had spat, there was a mouthful of bright red blood. He was horrified.

"Oh, help!"

Aroma looked too, and felt the grip of fear on her heart.

The outcome will be told in the following chapter.

CHAPTER 31

A torn fan is the price of silver laughter
And a lost kylin is the clue to a happy marriage

A cold fear came over Aroma when she saw the fresh blood on the floor. She had often heard people say that if you spat blood when you were young, you would die early, or at the very least be an invalid all your life; and remembering this now, she felt all her bright, ambitious hopes for the future turn into dust and ashes. Tears of misery ran down her cheeks. The sight of them made Bao-yu, too, distressed.

"What is it?" he asked her.

"It's nothing." She forced herself to smile. "I'm all right."

Bao-yu was all for calling one of the maids and getting her to heat some rice wine, so that Aroma could be given hot wine and Hainan kid's[9]-blood pills; but Aroma, smiling through her tears, caught at his hand to restrain him.

"It's all right for *you* to make a fuss," she said; "but if you go involving the others, they are sure to accuse me of putting on airs. And besides, it will do neither of us any good to draw attention to ourselves—especially when so far no one seems to have noticed anything. The sensible thing would be for you to send one of the boys round tomorrow to Dr. Wang's and get me some medicine to take. I shall probably be all right again after a few doses, without a single soul knowing anything about it. Surely that's best, isn't it?"

Bao-yu knew that she was right and abandoned his intention of rousing the others. Instead he poured her a cup of tea from a pot on the table and gave it to her to rinse her mouth with. Aroma was uneasy about being waited on by her master; but fearing that if she refused his services he would insist on disturbing everybody, she lay back and allowed him to fuss over her.

As soon as it was daylight, Bao-yu threw on his clothes and, without even waiting to wash or comb, went out of the Garden to his study in the front part of the mansion, whither he summoned the doctor Wang Ji-ren for

9. A kid is a young goat.

detailed questioning. When this worthy had elicited the information that the haemorrhage inquired about had been caused by a blow, he seemed less disposed to take a serious view of the case, merely naming some pills and giving perfunctory instructions for taking them internally and for applying them in solution as a poultice. Bao-yu made a note of these instructions and went back into the Garden to carry them out.

But that is no part of our story.

It was now the festival of the Double Fifth. Sprays of calamus and artemisia crowned the doorways and everyone wore tiger amulets fastened on their clothing at the back. At noon Lady Wang gave a little party at which Aunt Xue and Bao-chai were the guests.

Bao-yu, finding Bao-chai somewhat glacial in her manner and evidently unwilling to talk to him, knew that it must be because of his rudeness to her of the day before.

Lady Wang, observing Bao-yu's dejected appearance, attributed it to embarrassment about yesterday's episode with Golden and ignored him even more pointedly than Bao-chai.

Dai-yu, seeing how morose Bao-yu looked assumed that it was because Bao-chai was offended with him and, feeling resentful that he should care, at once became as morose as he was.

Xi-feng, having been told all about Bao-yu and Golden the night before by Lady Wang, could scarcely be her usual laughing and joking self when she knew of her aunt's displeasure and, taking her cue from the latter, was if anything even more glacial than the others.

And Ying-chun, Tan-chun and Xi-chun, seeing everyone else so uncomfortable, soon began to feel just as uncomfortable themselves.

The result was that after sitting for only a very short time, the party broke up.

Dai-yu had a natural aversion to gatherings, which she rationalized by saying that since the inevitable consequence of getting together was parting, and since parting made people feel lonely and feeling lonely made them unhappy, *ergo* it was better for them not to get together in the first place. In the same way she argued that since the flowers, which give us so much pleasure when they open, only cause us a lot of extra sadness when they die, it would be better if they didn't come out at all.

Bao-yu was just the opposite. He always wanted the party to go on for ever and flowers to be in perpetual bloom; and when at last the party did end and the flowers did wither—well, it was infinitely sad and distressing, but it couldn't be helped.

And so today, while everyone else left the party with feelings of gloom, Dai-yu alone was completely unaffected. Bao-yu, on the other hand, returned to his room in a mood of black despondency, sighing and muttering as he went.

Unfortunately it was the sharp-tongued Skybright who came forward to help him change his clothes. With provoking carelessness she dropped a fan while she was doing so and snapped the bone fan-sticks by accidentally treading on it.

"Clumsy!" said Bao-yu reproachfully. "You won't be so careless with things when you have a household of your own."

Skybright gave a sardonic sniff.

"You're getting quite a temper lately, Master Bao. Almost every time we move nowadays we get a nasty look from you. Yesterday even Aroma caught it. Today you're finding fault with me, so I suppose I can expect a few kicks too. Well, kick away. But I must say, I shouldn't have thought treading on a *fan* was such a very terrible thing to do. In the past any number of glass bowls and agate cups have got broken without your turning a hair. Why this fuss about a fan, then? If you're not satisfied with my service, you ought to dismiss me and get someone better. Easy come, easy go. No need for beating about the bush."

By the time she had finished, Bao-yu was so angry that he was shaking all over.

"You'll *go* soon enough, don't you worry!" he said.

Aroma had heard all this from the adjoining room and now came hurrying in.

"Now what's all this about?" she said, addressing herself to Bao-yu. "Didn't I tell you? As soon as I turn my back there's trouble."

"If you knew that already," said Skybright, "it's a pity you couldn't have come in a bit sooner and saved me from provoking him. Of course, we all know that you're the only one who knows how to serve him properly. None of the rest of us knows how it's done. I suppose it's because you serve him so well that he gave you a kick in the ribs yesterday. Heaven knows what he's got in store for *me* for having served him so badly!"

Angry, and at the same time ashamed, Aroma was about to retort; but the sight of Bao-yu's face, now white with anger, made her restrain herself.

"Be a good girl—just go away and play for a bit. It's *we* who are in the wrong."

Skybright naturally assumed that "we" meant Aroma and Bao-yu. Her jealousy was further inflamed.

"What do you mean, 'we'?" she said. "You two make me feel ashamed for you, you really do—because you needn't think you deceive *me*. *I* know what goes on between you when you think no one is looking. But when all's said and done, in actual fact, when you come down to it, you're not even a 'Miss' by *rights*. By *rights* you're no better than any of the rest of us. I don't know where you get this 'we' from."

Aroma blushed and blushed with shame, until her face had become a dusky red colour. Too late she realized her slip. By "we" she had meant no more than "you and I"; not "Bao-yu and I" as Skybright imagined. But the pronoun had invited misunderstanding.

It was Bao-yu who retorted, however.

"I'll make her a 'Miss' then; I'll make her my chamber-wife[1] tomorrow, if that's all that's worrying you. You can spare your jealousy on *that* account."

Aroma seized his hand impulsively.

"Don't argue with her, she's only a silly girl. In any case, you've put up with much worse than this in the past; why be so touchy today?"

Skybright gave a harsh little laugh.

"Oh, yes. *I'm* too stupid to talk to. *I'm* only a slave."

"Are you arguing with me, Miss, or with Master Bao?" said Aroma. "If it's

1. A concubine, which would raise her status.

me you've got it in for, you'd better address your remarks to me elsewhere. There's no cause to go quarrelling with me in front of Master Bao. But if it's Master Bao you want to quarrel with, then at least you might do it a bit more quietly and not let everyone else know about it. When I came in just now, it was for everyone's sake, so that we could have a bit of peace and quiet. I don't know why you had to turn on *me* and start picking on *my* shortcomings. It seems as if you can't make up your mind whether you're angry with me or with Master Bao. Slipping in a dig here and a dig there. I don't know what you think you're up to. Anyway, I shan't say any more; I'll just leave you here to get on with it."

She walked out.

"There's no need for you to be so angry," Bao-yu said to Skybright. "I can guess what it is that's bothering you. I shall go and tell Her Ladyship that you're old enough to leave us now and ask her to send you away. That's what you really want, isn't it?"

"I don't want to go away. Why should I want to go away?" said Skybright with tears in her eyes—now more upset than ever. "You're inventing this as a means of getting rid of me, aren't you, because I'm in your way? But you won't get away with it."

"Look, I've never had to put up with scenes like *this* before," said Bao-yu. "What other reason *can* there be but that you want to leave? I really think I *had* better go and see Her Ladyship about this."

He got up and began to go; but Aroma came in again and barred his way.

"Where are you off to?" she asked him smilingly.

"To see Her Ladyship."

"Oh, that's silly," said Aroma. "I wonder you're not ashamed to. Even if Skybright really does want to leave, there will be plenty of time to tell Her Ladyship about it when everyone has cooled down a bit and you are feeling calm and collected. If you go rushing off in your present state, Her Ladyship will suspect something."

"Her Ladyship won't suspect anything," said Bao-yu. "I shall tell her quite openly that Skybright has been agitating to leave."

"When have I ever agitated to leave?" said Skybright, weeping now in earnest. "Even if you're angry with me, you ought not to twist things round in order to get the better of me. But you go and tell her! I don't care if I have to beat my own brains out, I'm not going out of that door."

"Now that's really strange," said Bao-yu. "You don't want to go, yet at the same time you won't keep quiet. It's no good; I really can't stand this quarrelling. I shall really *have* to see Her Ladyship about this and get it over with."

This time he seemed quite determined to go.

Seeing that she was unable to hold him back, Aroma went down on her knees. Emerald, Ripple, Musk and the other maids, aware that a quarrel of more than usual magnitude was going on inside, were waiting together outside in breathless silence. When word reached them that Aroma was now on her knees interceding for Skybright, they came silently trooping in to kneel down behind her. Bao-yu raised Aroma to her feet, sighed, sat down on the edge of the bed, and told the other maids to get up.

"What do you want me to do?" he asked Aroma. "My heart is destroyed inside me, but none of you knows or cares."

Tears started from his eyes and rolled down his cheeks unheeded. Seeing his tears, Aroma too began to cry. Skybright, who stood crying beside them, was about to say something; but just at that moment Dai-yu walked in and she slipped outside.

Dai-yu beamed at the weeping pair:

"Crying on a holiday? What's all this about? Have you been quarrelling over the rice-cakes?"

Bao-yu and Aroma both burst out laughing.

"Well, if Cousin Bao won't tell me," she went on, "I'm sure that *you* will. Come!" she said, slapping Aroma familiarly on the shoulder. "Tell sis all about it. It's obvious that the two of you have been having an argument. Tell me what it's all about and I'll make it up between you."

"Oh, Miss!" Aroma gave her a push. "Don't carry on so! I'm only a maid; you shouldn't say such things to me."

"Only a maid?" said Dai-yu. "I always think of you as my sister-in-law."

"Don't you see that you're simply *encouraging* people to be nasty to her?" Bao-yu protested. "Even as it is, people already gossip about her. How can she stand up to them if *you* come along and lend your weight to what they are saying?"

"You don't know what I feel, Miss," said Aroma. "If I only knew how to stop breathing, I'd gladly die."

Dai-yu smiled.

"If you were to die, I don't know about anyone else, but I know that *I* should die of grief."

"*I* should become a monk," said Bao-yu.

"Try to be a bit more serious," said Aroma. "You and Miss Lin are both laughing at me."

Dai-yu held up two fingers and looked at Bao-yu with a quizzical expression.

"That's twice you're going to become a monk. From now on I'm keeping the score."

Bao-yu recognized the allusion to what he had said to her the day before. Fortunately he was able to pass it off with a laugh. Shortly after that, Dai-yu left them.

No sooner had Dai-yu gone than someone arrived with an invitation from Xue Pan. Bao-yu thought that this time he had better go. It turned out to be only a drinking-party, but Xue Pan refused to release him and kept him there until it was over. He returned home in the evening more than a little drunk.

As he came lurching into his courtyard, he saw that someone in quest of coolness had taken a bed outside and was lying down on it asleep. Assuming that it must be Aroma, he sat down on the edge of it and gave her a push.

"Is the pain any better?"

"Can't you leave me alone?" she said, rising up wrathfully.

He looked again and saw that it was not Aroma after all but Skybright. Taking her by the hand, he drew her down on the bed beside him.

"You're getting so self-willed," he said laughingly. "When you trod on that fan this morning, I only made a harmless little remark, but look how you flew up in the air about it! And then when Aroma, out of the kindness of her heart, tried to reason with you, look how you pitched into *her*! Seriously, now, don't you think it was all a bit uncalled-for?"

"I'm so *hot*," said Skybright. "Do you *have* to maul me about like this? Suppose someone were to see us? Anyway, it's not right for me to be sitting here."

"If you know it's not right to be sitting here," he said teasingly, "what were you doing lying down?"

"Che-e-e!" Unable at once to reply, she gave a little laugh. Then she said: "When you are not here it doesn't matter. It's *your* being here that makes it wrong. Anyway, let me get up now, because I want to have a bath. Aroma and Musk have had theirs already. I'll send *them* out to you."

"I've just had rather a lot to drink and I could do with a bath myself," said Bao-yu. "As you haven't had yours yet, bring the water out here and we'll have a bath together."

Skybright laughed and declined with a vigorous gesture of her hand.

"*Oh* no! I daren't start you off on that caper. I still remember that time you got Emerald to help you bath. You must have been two or three hours in there, so that we began to get quite worried. We didn't like to go in while you were there, but when we did go in to have a look afterwards, we found water all over the floor, pools of water round the legs of the bed, and even the mat on the bed had water splashed all over it. Heaven only knows what you'd been up to. We laughed about it for days afterwards. I haven't got time to fetch *that* amount of water. And in any case, you don't want to go taking baths with *me*. As a matter of fact it's cooler now, so I don't think I shall have a bath after all. Why don't you let me fetch you a bowl of water so that you can have a nice wash and comb your hair? Faithful just sent a lot of fruit round and we've got it soaking in iced water in the big glass bowl. I'll tell them to bring some out to you, shall I?"

"All right," said Bao-yu. "If you're not having a bath yourself, I'll just wash my hands; and you can get me some of that fruit to eat."

Skybright smiled.

"You've already told me once today how clumsy I am. I can't even drop a fan without treading on it. So I'm much too clumsy to get your fruit for you. Suppose I were to break a plate. That would be terrible!"

"If you *want* to break it, by all means break it," said Bao-yu. "These things are there for our use. What we use them *for* is a matter of individual taste. For example, fans are made for fanning with; but if you prefer to tear them up because it gives you pleasure, there's no reason why you shouldn't. What you *mustn't* do is to use them as objects to vent your anger on. It's the same with plates and cups. Plates and cups are made to put food and drink in. But if you want to smash them on purpose because you like the noise, it's perfectly all right to do so. As long as you don't get into a passion and start taking it out on *things*—that is the golden rule."

"All right then," said Skybright with a mischievous smile. "Give me your fan to tear. I love the sound of a fan being torn."

Bao-yu held it out to her. She took it eagerly and—*chah!*—promptly tore it in half. And again—*chah! chah! chah!*—she tore it several more times. Bao-yu, an appreciative onlooker, laughed and encouraged her.

"Well torn! Well torn! Now again—a really loud one!"

Just then Musk appeared. She stared at them indignantly.

"Don't do that!" she said. "It's *wicked* to waste things like that."

But Bao-yu leaped up to her, snatched the fan from her hand, and passed it to Skybright, who at once tore it into several pieces. The two of them, Bao-yu and Skybright, then burst into uproarious laughter.

"What do you think you're doing?" said Musk. "That's *my fan* you've just ruined."

"What's an old fan?" said Bao-yu. "Open up the fan box and get yourself another."

"If that's your attitude," said Musk, "we might as well carry out the whole boxful and let her tear away to her heart's content."

"All right. Go and get it," said Bao-yu.

"And be born a beggar in my next life?" said Musk. "No thank you! She hasn't broken her arm. Let her go and get it herself."

Skybright stretched back on the bed, smiling complacently.

"I'm rather tired just now. I think I shall tear some more tomorrow."

Bao-yu laughed.

"The ancients used to say that for one smile of a beautiful woman a thousand taels are well spent. For a few old fans it's cheap at the price!"

He called to Aroma, who had just finished changing into clean clothes, to come outside and join them. Little Melilot came and cleared away the broken bits of fan, and everyone sat for a while and enjoyed the cool.

But our narrative supplies no further details of that evening.

About noon next day, while Lady Wang, Bao-chai, Dai-yu and the girls were sitting in Grandmother Jia's room, someone came in to announce that "Miss Shi" had arrived. Shortly afterwards Shi Xiang-yun appeared in the courtyard, attended by a bevy of matrons and maids. Bao-chai, Dai-yu and the rest hurried out to the foot of the steps to welcome her.

For young girls like the cousins a reunion after a mere month's separation is an occasion for touching demonstrations of affection. After these initial transports, when they were all indoors and the greetings, introductions and salutations had been completed, Grandmother Jia suggested that, as the weather was so hot, Xiang-yun should remove her outer garments. Xiang-yun rose to her feet with alacrity and divested herself of one or two layers. Lady Wang was amused.

"Gracious, child! What a lot you have on! I don't think I've ever seen anyone wearing so much."

"It's my Aunt Shi who makes me wear it all," said Xiang-yun. "You wouldn't catch me wearing this stuff if I didn't have to."

"You don't know our Xiang-yun, Aunt," Bao-chai interposed. "She's really happiest in boy's clothes. That time she was here in the third or fourth month last year, I remember one day she dressed up in one of Bao-yu's gowns and put a pair of his boots on and one of his belts round her waist. At first glance she looked exactly like Cousin Bao. It was only the ear-rings that gave her away. When she stood behind that chair over there, Grandmother was completely taken in. She said, 'Bao-yu, come over here! You'll get the dust from that hanging lamp in your eyes if you're not careful.' But Xiang-yun just smiled and didn't move. It was only when everyone couldn't hold it in any longer and started laughing that Grandmother realized who it was and joined in the laugh. She told her that she made a very good-looking boy."

"That's nothing," said Dai-yu. "What about that time last year when she came to stay for a couple of days with us in the first month and it snowed? Grandma and Auntie Wang had just got back from somewhere—I think it was from visiting the ancestors' portraits[2]—and she saw Grandma's new scarlet felt rain-cape lying there and put it on when no one was looking. Of course, it was much too big and much too long for her, so she hitched it up and tied it round her waist with a sash and went out like that into the back courtyard to help the maids build a snowman. And then she slipped over in it and got covered all over with mud—"

The others all laughed at the recollection.

Bao-chai asked Xiang-yun's nurse, Mrs. Zhou, whether Xiang-yun was still as tomboyish as ever. Nurse Zhou laughed but said nothing.

"I don't mind her being tomboyish," said Ying-chun, "but I do wish she wasn't such a chatterbox. You wouldn't believe it—even when she's in bed at night it still goes on. Jabber-jabber, jabber-jabber. Then she laughs. Then she talks a bit more. Then she laughs again. And you never heard such a lot of rubbish in your life. I don't know where she gets it all from."

"Well, perhaps she'll have got over that by now," said Lady Wang. "I hear that someone was round the other day to talk about a betrothal. Now that there's a future mother-in-law to think about, she can't be *quite* as tomboyish as she used to be."

"Are you staying this time, or do you have to go back tonight?" asked Grandmother Jia.

"Your Old Ladyship hasn't seen all the clothes she's brought," said Nurse Zhou. "She'll be staying two days here at the very least."

"Isn't Bao at home?" said Xiang-yun.

"Listen to her!" said Bao-chai. "Cousin Bao is the only one she thinks about. He and she get on well together because they are both fond of mischief. You can see she hasn't really changed."

"Perhaps now that you're getting older you had better stop using baby-names," said Grandmother Jia, reminded by the talk of betrothal that her babies were rapidly turning into grown-ups.

Just then Bao-yu came in.

"Ah! Hallo, Yun! Why didn't you come when we sent for you the other day?"

"Grandmother has just this moment been saying that it is time you all stopped using baby-names," said Lady Wang. "I must say, this isn't a very good beginning."

"Our cousin has got something nice to give you," said Dai-yu to Xiang-yun.

"Oh? What is it?" said Xiang-yun.

"Don't believe her," said Bao-yu. "Goodness! It's no time since you were here last, but you seem to have grown taller already."

Xiang-yun laughed.

"How's Aroma?"

"She's fine. Thank you for asking."

"I've brought something for her," said Xiang-yun. She produced a knotted-up silk handkerchief.

"What treasure have you got wrapped up in there?" said Bao-yu. "The best present you could have brought Aroma would have been a couple of those cheap agate rings like the ones you sent us the other day."

"What are these, then?"

2. Kept in shrines and honored as part of Chinese ancestor worship.

With a triumphant smile she opened her little bundle and revealed four rings, each inset with the veined red agate they had so much admired on a previous occasion.

"What a girl!" said Dai-yu. "These are exactly the same as the ones you sent us the other day by messenger. Why didn't you get him to bring these too and save yourself some trouble? I thought you must have got some wonderful rarity tied up in that handkerchief, seeing that you'd gone to all the trouble of bringing it here yourself—and all the time it was only a few more of *those!* You really are rather a silly."

"Thilly yourthelf!" said Xiang-yun. "The others can decide which of us is the silly one when I have explained my reason. If I send things for you and the girls, it's assumed that they are for you without the messenger even needing to say anything; but if I send things for any of the maids, I have to explain very carefully to the messenger which ones I mean. Now if the messenger is someone intelligent, that's all right; but if it's someone not so bright who has difficulty in remembering names, they'll probably make such a mess of it that they'll get not only the maids' presents mixed up, but yours as well. Then again, if the messenger is a woman, it's not so bad; but the other day it was one of the boys—and you know how hopeless *they* are over girls' names. So you see, I thought it would be simpler if I delivered the maids' ones myself. There!"—she laid the rings down one after another on the table—"One for Aroma; one for Faithful; one for Golden; and one for Patience. Can you imagine one of the boys getting those four names right?"

The others laughed.

"Clever! Clever!" they said.

"You're always so eloquent," said Bao-yu. "No one else gets a chance."

"If she weren't so eloquent, she wouldn't be worthy of the gold kylin," said Dai-yu huffily, rising from her seat and walking off as she spoke.

Fortunately no one heard her but Bao-chai, who made a laughing grimace, and Bao-yu, who immediately regretted having once more spoken out of turn, but who, suddenly catching sight of Bao-chai's expression, could not help laughing himself. Seeing him laugh, Bao-chai at once rose from her seat and hurried off to joke with Dai-yu.

"When you've finished your tea and rested a bit," said Grandmother Jia to Xiang-yun, "you can go and see your married cousins. After that, you can amuse yourself in the Garden with the girls. It's nice and cool there."

Xiang-yun thanked her grandmother. She wrapped up three of the rings again, and after sitting a little longer, went off, attended by her nannies and maids, to call on Wang Xi-feng. After chatting a while with her, she went into the Garden and called on Li Wan. Then, after sitting a short while with Li Wan, she went off in the direction of Green Delights in quest of Aroma. Before doing so, however, she turned to dismiss her escort.

"You needn't stay with me any longer," she said. "You can go off now and visit your relations. I'll just keep Fishy to wait on me."

The others thanked her and went off to look for various kith and kin, leaving Xiang-yun alone with Kingfisher.

"Why aren't these water-lilies out yet?" said Kingfisher.

"It isn't time for them yet," said Xiang-yun.

"Look, they're going to be 'double-decker' ones, like the ones in our lily-pond at home," said Kingfisher.

"Our ones are better," said Xiang-yun.

"They've got a pomegranate-tree here which has four or five lots of flowers growing one above the other on each branch," said Kingfisher. "That's a double-double-double-decker. I wonder what makes them grow like that."

"Plants are the same as people," said Xiang-yun. "The healthier their constitution is, the better they grow."

"I don't believe that," said Kingfisher with a toss of her head. "If that were so, why don't we see people walking around with one head growing on top of the other?"

Xiang-yun was unable to avoid laughing at the girl's simplicity.

"I've told you before, you talk too much," she said. "Let's see: how can one answer a question like that? Everything in the world is moulded by the forces of Yin and Yang. That means that, besides the normal, the abnormal, the peculiar, the freakish—in fact all the thousands and thousands of different variations we find in things—are caused by different combinations of Yin and Yang. Even if something appears that is so rare that no one has ever seen it before, the principle is still the same."

"So according to what you say," said Kingfisher, "all the things that have ever existed, from the time the world began right up to the present moment, have just been a lot of Yins and Yangs."

"No, stupid!" said Xiang-yun. "The more you say, the sillier you get. 'Just a lot of Yins and Yangs' indeed! In any case, strictly speaking Yin and Yang are not two things but one and the same thing. By the time the Yang has become exhausted, it *is* Yin; and by the time the Yin has become exhausted, it *is* Yang. It isn't a case of one of them coming to an end and then the other one growing out of nothing."

"That's too deep for me," said Kingfisher. "What sort of thing is a Yin-yang, I'd like to know? No one's ever seen one. You just answer that, Miss. What does a Yin-yang look like?"

"Yin-yang is a sort of *force*," said Xiang-yun. "It's the force in things that gives them their distinctive forms. For example, the sky is Yang and the earth is Yin; water is Yin and fire is Yang; the sun is Yang and the moon is Yin."

"Ah yes! *Now* I understand," said Kingfisher happily. "That's why astrologers call the sun the 'Yang star' and the moon the 'Yin star.' "

"Holy name!" said Xiang-yun. "She understands."

"That's not so difficult," said Kingfisher. "But what about things like mosquitoes and fleas and midges and plants and flowers and bricks and tiles? Surely you are not going to say that they are all Yin-yang too?"

"Certainly they are!" said Xiang-yun. "Take the leaf of a tree, for example. That's divided into Yin and Yang. The side facing upwards towards the sky is Yang; the underside, facing towards the ground, is Yin."

Kingfisher nodded.

"I see. Yes. I can understand that. But take these fans we are holding. Surely *they* don't have Yin and Yang?"

"Yes they do. The front of the fan is Yang; the back of the fan is Yin."

Kingfisher nodded, satisfied. She tried to think of some other object to ask about, but being for the moment unable to, she began looking around her for inspiration. As she did so, her eye chanced to light on the gold kylin fastened in the intricate loopings of her mistress's girdle.

"Well, Miss," she said, pointing triumphantly to the kylin, "you're not going to say that *that's* got Yin and Yang?"

"Certainly. In the case of birds and beasts and males are Yang and the females are Yin."

"Is this a daddy one or a mummy one?" said Kingfisher.

" 'A daddy one or a mummy one'! Silly girl!"

"All right, then," said Kingfisher. "But why is it that everything else has Yin and Yang but we haven't?"

"Get along with you, naughty girl! What subject will you get on to next?"

"Why? Why can't you tell me?" said Kingfisher. "Anyway, I know; so there's no need for you to be so nasty to me."

Xiang-yun suppressed a giggle.

"You're Yang and I'm Yin," said Kingfisher.

Xiang-yun held her handkerchief to her mouth and laughed.

"Well, that's right, isn't it?" said Kingfisher. "What are you laughing at?"

"Yes, yes," said Xiang-yun. "That's quite right."

"That's what they always say," said Kingfisher: "the master is Yang and the servant is Yin. Even I can understand that principle."

"I'm sure you can," said Xiang-yun. "Very good."

While they were talking, a glittering golden object at the foot of the rose pergola caught Xiang-yun's eye. She pointed it out to Kingfisher.

"Go and see what it is."

Kingfisher bounded over and picked it up.

"Ah ha!" she said, examining the object in her hand. "Now we shall be able to see whether it's Yin or Yang."

She took hold of the kylin fastened to Xiang-yun's girdle and held it up to look at it more closely. Xiang-yun wanted to see what it was that she held in her hand, but Kingfisher wouldn't let her.

"It's *my* treasure," she said with a laugh. "I won't let you see it, Miss. Funny, though. I wonder where it came from. I've never seen anyone here wearing it."

"Come on! Let me look," said Xiang-yun.

"There you are, Miss!" Kingfisher opened her hand.

Xiang-yun looked. It was a beautiful, shining gold kylin, both larger and more ornate than the one she was wearing. Reaching out and taking it from Kingfisher, she held it on the palm of her hand and contemplated it for some moments in silence.

Whatever reverie the contemplation inspired was broken by the sudden arrival of Bao-yu.

"What are you doing, standing out here in the blazing sun?" he asked her. "Why don't you go and see Aroma?"

"We were on our way," said Xiang-yun, hurriedly concealing the gold kylin.

The three of them entered the courtyard of Green Delights together.

Aroma had gone outside to take the air and was leaning on the verandah railings at the foot of the front door steps. As soon as she caught sight of Xiang-yun, she hurried down into the courtyard to welcome her, and taking her by the hand, led her into the house, animatedly exchanging news with her as they went.

"You should have come sooner," said Bao-yu when they were indoors and Aroma had made Xiang-yun take a seat. "I've got something nice for you here and I've been waiting for you to come so that I could give it to you."

He had been hunting through his pockets as he said this. Not finding what he was searching for, he exclaimed in surprise.

"Aiyo!" He turned to Aroma. "Have you put it away somewhere?"

"Put what away?"

"That little kylin I got the other day."

"You've been carrying it around with you everywhere," said Aroma. "Why ask *me* about it?"

Bao-yu clapped his hands together in vexation.

"Oh, I've lost it! Wherever am I going to look for it?"

He got up to begin searching.

Xiang-yun now realized that it must have been Bao-yu who dropped the kylin she had only a few minutes earlier discovered outside.

"Since when have *you* had a kylin?" she asked him.

"Oh, several days now," said Bao-yu. "What a shame! I'll never get another one like that. And the trouble is, I don't know when I can have lost it. Oh dear! How stupid of me!"

"It's only an ornament you're getting so upset about," said Xiang-yun. "What a good job it wasn't something more serious!"

She opened her hand:

"Look! Is that it?"

Bao-yu looked and saw, with extravagant delight, that it was.

The remainder of this episode will be told in the following chapter.

CHAPTER 32

Bao-yu demonstrates confusion of mind by making
his declaration to the wrong person
And Golden shows an unconquerable spirit by ending
her humiliation in death

Our last chapter told of Bao-yu's delight at seeing the gold kylin again. He reached out eagerly and took it from Xiang-yun's hand.

"Fancy *your* finding it!" he said. "How did you come to pick it up?"

"It's a good job it was only this you lost," she said. "One of these days it will be your seal of office—and then it won't be quite so funny."[3]

"Oh, losing one's seal of office is nothing," said Bao-yu. "Losing a thing like this is much more serious."

Aroma meanwhile was pouring tea.

"I heard your good news the other day," she said, handing Xiang-yun a cup. "Congratulations!"

Xiang-yun bent low over the cup to hide her blushes and made no reply.

"Why so bashful, Miss?" said Aroma. "Have you forgotten the things you used to tell me at night all those years ago, when we used to sleep together in the little closet-bed[4] at Her Old Ladyship's? You weren't very bashful then. What makes you so bashful with me now, all of a sudden?"

Xiang-yun's face became even redder. She gave a forced little laugh.

"Who's talking? That was a time when you and I were very close to each other. Then I had to go back home when my uncle's first wife died and you

---

3. The assumption is that Bao-yu will someday become a government official. All officials had seals with which to stamp documents, and such stamps had authorizing power, like a signature. Hence the loss of a seal was a serious matter.   4. A small temporary bed, like a cot.

were given Cousin Bao to look after, and I don't know why, but whenever I came back here after that, you seemed somehow changed towards me."

It was now Aroma's turn to blush and protest.

"When you first came to live here it was 'Pearl dear this' and 'Pearl dear that' all the time. You were always coaxing me to do things for you—do your hair, wash your face, or I don't know what. But now that's all changed. Now you're the young lady, aren't you? You can't act the young lady with me and expect me to stay on the same familiar terms as before."

"Holy name!" said Xiang-yun, now genuinely indignant. "That's *tho* unfair. I wish I may die if I ever 'acted the young lady' with you, as you put it. I come here in this frightful heat, and the very first person I want to see when I get here is you. Ask Fishy if you don't believe me. *She* can tell you. At home I'm *always* going on about you."

Aroma and Bao-yu both laughed.

"Don't take it to heart so, it was only a joke. You shouldn't be so excitable."

"Don't, whatever you do, admit that what *you* said was wounding," said Xiang-yun. "Say I'm 'excitable' and put *me* in the wrong!"

While she said this, she was undoing the knotted silk handkerchief and extracting one of the three rings from it. She handed it to Aroma. Aroma was greatly touched.

"I've got one like this already," she said. "It was given to me when you sent those ones the other day to the young ladies. But fancy your bringing this one here specially! Now I *know* you haven't forgotten me. It's little things like this that show you what a person really is. The ring itself isn't worth much, I know. It's the thought behind it."

"Who gave you the one you've already got?" said Xiang-yun.

"Miss Bao," said Aroma.

"Ah," said Xiang-yun, "Miss Bao. And I was thinking it must have been Miss Lin. Often when I'm at home I think to myself that of all my cousins Bao-chai is the one I like best. It's a pity we couldn't have been born of the same mother. With her for an elder sister it wouldn't matter so much being an orphan."

Her eyelids reddened as she said this and she seemed to be on the verge of tears.

"Now, now, now!" said Bao-yu. "Don't say things like that."

"And why not?" said Xiang-yun. "Oh, I know your trouble. You're afraid that Cousin Lin might hear and get angry with me again for praising Cousin Bao. That's what's worrying you, isn't it?"

Aroma giggled.

"Oh Miss Yun! You're just as outspoken as you used to be."

"Well, I've said that you lot are difficult to talk to," said Bao-yu, "and I was certainly right!"

"Don't make me sick," said Xiang-yun. "You say what you like to us. It's with your Cousin Lin that you have to be so careful."

"Never mind about that," said Aroma. "Joking apart, now: I want to ask you a favour."

"What is it?" said Xiang-yun.

"I've got a pair of slipper-tops here that I've already cut the openwork pattern in, but as I haven't been very well this last day or two, I haven't been able to sew them on to the backing material. Do you think you'd have time to do them for me?"

"That's rather a strange request," said Xiang-yun. "Quite apart from all the clever maids this household employs you have your own full-time tailors and embroiderers. Why ask *me* to do your sewing? You could give it to anyone here you liked. They could hardly refuse you."

"You can't be serious," said Aroma. "None of the sewing in this room is allowed to go outside.[5] Surely you knew that?"

Xiang-yun inferred from this that the slippers in question were for Bao-yu.

"Oh well," she said, "in that case I suppose I'd better do them for you. On one condition, though: I'll do them if they are for *you* to wear, but if they are for anyone else, I'm afraid I can't."

"Get along with you!" said Aroma. "Ask you to make slippers for *me?* I wouldn't have the nerve. No, I'll be honest with you, they're not for me. Never mind who they're for. Just tell yourself that I'm the one you'll be doing the favour."

"It isn't *that*," said Xiang-yun. "In the past I've done lots of things for you. Surely you must *know* what makes me unwilling now?"

"I'm sorry, I don't," said Aroma.

"What about the person who got in a temper the other day when that fan-case I made for you was compared with hers and cut it up with a pair of scissors? *I* heard all about that, so don't start protesting. If you expect me to do sewing for you after *that*, you're just treating me as your drudge."

"I didn't know at the time it was you who made it," Bao-yu put in hurriedly.

"He really didn't," said Aroma. "I pretended there was someone outside we'd just discovered who could do very fine and original needlework. I told him I'd got them to do that fan-case for him as a sample. He believed what I said and went around showing it to everyone. Unfortunately while he was doing this he upset you know who and she took a pair of scissors and cut it in pieces. Afterwards he was very anxious to have some more work done by the same person, so I had to tell him who it really was. He was very upset when he heard that it was you."

"I still think this is a very strange request," said Xiang-yun. "If Miss Lin can cut things up, she can sew them for him, too. Why not ask *her* to do them for you?"

"Oh, *she* wouldn't want to do them," said Aroma. "And even if she did, Her Old Ladyship wouldn't let her, for fear of her tiring herself. The doctors say she needs rest and quiet. I wouldn't want to trouble *her* with them. Last year she took practically the whole year embroidering one little purse, and this last six months I don't think she's picked up a needle."

Their conversation was interrupted by a servant with a message:

"Mr. Jia of Rich Street is here. The Master says will Master Bao receive him, please?"

Recognizing the "Mr. Jia" of the message as Jia Yu-cun, Bao-yu was more than a little vexed. While Aroma hurried off for his going-out clothes, he sat pulling his boots on and grumbling.

---

5. Bao-yu wants all his sewing done by only those who are close to him.

"He's got Father to talk to, surely that's enough for him? Why does he always have to see me?"

Xiang-yun laughed at his disgruntlement:

"I'm sure you're very good at entertaining people," she said. "That's why Sir Zheng asks you to see him."

"That message didn't come from Father," said Bao-yu. "He'll have made it up himself."

" 'When the host is refined, the callers are frequent,' " said Xiang-yun. "There must be something about you that has impressed him, otherwise he wouldn't want to see you."

"I make no claim to being refined, thanks all the same," said Bao-yu. "I'm as common as dirt. And furthermore I have no wish to mix with people of his sort."

"You're incorrigible," said Xiang-yun. "Now that you're older, you ought to be mixing with these officials and administrators as much as you can. Even if you don't want to take the Civil Service examinations and become an administrator yourself, you can learn a lot from talking to these people about the way the Empire is governed and the people who govern it that will stand you in good stead later on, when you come to manage your own affairs and take your place in society. You might even pick up one or two decent, respectable friends that way. You'll certainly never get anywhere if you spend all your time with us girls."

Bao-yu found such talk highly displeasing.

"I think perhaps you'd better go and sit in someone else's room," he said. "I wouldn't want a *decent, respectable* young lady like you to get contaminated."

"Don't try reasoning with him, Miss," Aroma put in hurriedly. "Last time Miss Bao tried it, he was just as rude to her. No consideration for her feelings whatever. He just said 'Hai!', picked up his heels, and walked out of the room, leaving her still half-way through her sentence. Poor Miss Bao! She was so embarrassed she turned bright red. She didn't know *what* to say. A good job it was her, though, and not Miss Lin. If it had been Miss Lin, there'd have been weeping and carrying on and I don't know what. I really admire the way Miss Bao behaved on that occasion. She just stood there a while collecting herself and then walked quietly out of the room. Myself, I was quite upset, thinking she must be offended. But not a bit of it. Next time she came round, it was just as if nothing had happened. A real little lady, Miss Bao—and generous-hearted, too. And yet the funny thing is that his lordship seems to have fallen out with her, whereas Miss Lin, who is always getting on her high horse and ignoring him, has him running round and apologizing to her all the time."

"Have you ever heard Miss Lin talking that sort of stupid rubbish?" said Bao-yu. "I'd long since have fallen out with *her* if she did."

Aroma and Xiang-yun shook their heads pityingly.

"So that's 'stupid rubbish,' is it?" they said, laughing.

Dai-yu rightly surmised that now Xiang-yun had arrived, Bao-yu would lose no time in telling her about his newly-acquired kylin.

Now Dai-yu had observed that in the romances which Bao-yu smuggled in to her and of which she was nowadays an avid consumer, it was always some trinket or small object of clothing or jewellery—a pair of lovebirds, a male and female phoenix, a jade ring, a gold buckle, a silken handkerchief, an embroidered belt or what not—that brought the heroes and heroines together. And since the fate and future happiness of those fortunate beings seemed to depend wholly on the instrumentality of such trifling objects, it was natural for her to suppose that Bao-yu's acquisition of the gold kylin would become the occasion of a dramatic rupture with *her* and the beginning of an association with Xiang-yun in which he and Xiang-yun would do together all those delightful things that she had read about in the romances.

It was with such apprehensions that she made her way stealthily towards Green Delights, her intention being to observe how the two of them were behaving and shape her own actions accordingly. Imagine her surprise when, just as she was about to enter, she heard Xiang-yun lecturing Bao-yu on his social obligations and Bao-yu telling Xiang-yun that "Cousin Lin never talked that sort of rubbish" and that if she did he would have "fallen out with her long ago." Mingled emotions of happiness, alarm, sorrow and regret assailed her.

Happiness:

Because after all (she thought) I wasn't mistaken in my judgement of you. I always thought of you as a true friend, and I was right.

Alarm:

Because if you praise me so unreservedly in front of other people, your warmth and affection are sure, sooner or later, to excite suspicion and be misunderstood.

Regret:

Because if you are my true friend, then I am yours and the two of us are a perfect match. But in that case why did there have to be all this talk of "the gold and the jade"? Alternatively, if there had to be all this talk of gold and jade, why weren't we the two to have them? Why did there have to be a Bao-chai with her golden locket?

Sorrow:

Because though there are things of burning importance to be said, without a father or a mother I have no one to say them for me. And besides, I feel so muzzy lately and I know that my illness is gradually gaining a hold on me. (The doctors say that the weakness and anaemia I suffer from may be the beginnings of a consumption.) So even if I *am* your true-love, I fear I may not be able to wait for you. And even though you are mine, you can do nothing to alter my fate.

At that point in her reflections she began to weep; and feeling in no fit state to be seen, she turned away from the door and began to make her way back again.

Bao-yu had finished his hasty dressing and now came out of the house. He saw Dai-yu slowly walking on ahead of him and, judging by her appearance from behind, wiping her eyes. He hurried forward to catch up with her.

"Where are you off to, coz? Are you crying again? Who has upset you this time?"

Dai-yu turned and saw that it was Bao-yu.

"I'm perfectly all right," she said, forcing a smile. "What would I be crying for?"

"Look at you! The tears are still wet on your face. How can you tell such fibs?"

Impulsively he stretched out his hand to wipe them. Dai-yu recoiled several paces:

"You'll get your head chopped off!" she said. "You really *must* keep your hands to yourself."

"I'm sorry. My feelings got the better of me. I'm afraid I wasn't thinking about my head."

"No, I forgot," said Dai-yu. "Losing your head is nothing, is it? It's losing your kylin—the famous *gold* kylin—that is really serious!"

Her words immediately put Bao-yu in a passion. He came up to her and held his face close to hers.

"Do you say these things to put a curse on me? or is it merely to make me angry that you say them?"

Remembering their recent quarrel, Dai-yu regretted her careless reintroduction of its theme and hastened to make amends:

"Now don't get excited. I shouldn't have said that—oh come now, it really isn't *that* important! Look at you! The veins are standing out on your forehead and your face is all covered with sweat."

She moved forward and wiped the perspiration from his brow. For some moments he stood there motionless, staring at her. Then he said:

"Don't worry!"

Hearing this, Dai-yu herself was silent for some moments.

"Why *should* I worry?" she said eventually. "I don't understand you. Would you mind telling me what you are talking about?"

Bao-yu sighed.

"Do you really not understand? Can I really have been all this time mistaken in my feelings towards you? If you don't even know your *own* mind, it's small wonder that you're always getting angry on *my* account."

"I really don't understand what you mean about not worrying," said Dai-yu.

Bao-yu sighed again and shook his head.

"My dear coz, don't think you can fool me. If you don't understand what I've just said, then not only have *my* feelings towards *you* been all along mistaken, but all that *you* have ever felt for *me* has been wasted, too. It's because you worry so much that you've made yourself ill. If only you could take things a bit easier, your illness wouldn't go on getting more and more serious all the time."

Dai-yu was thunderstruck. He had read her mind—had seen inside her more clearly than if she had plucked out her entrails and held them out for his inspection. And now there were a thousand things that she wanted to tell him; yet though she was dying to speak, she was unable to utter a single syllable and stood there like a simpleton, gazing at him in silence.

Bao-yu, too, had a thousand things to say, but he, too, stood mutely gazing at her, not knowing where to begin.

After the two of them had stared at each other for some considerable time in silence, Dai-yu heaved a deep sigh. The tears gushed from her eyes and she turned and walked away. Bao-yu hurried after her and caught at her dress.

"Coz dear, stop a moment! Just let me say one word."

As she wiped her eyes with one hand, Dai-yu pushed him away from her with the other.

"There's nothing to say. I already know what you want to tell me."

She said this without turning back her head, and having said it, passed swiftly on her way. Bao-yu remained where he was standing, gazing after her in silent stupefaction.

Now Bao-yu had left the apartment in such haste that he had forgotten to take his fan with him. Fearing that he would be very hot without it, Aroma hurried outside to give it to him, but when she noticed him standing some way ahead of her talking to Dai-yu, she halted. After a little while she saw Dai-yu walk away and Bao-yu continue standing motionless where he was. She chose this moment to go up and speak to him.

"You've gone out without your fan," she said. "It's a good job I noticed. Here you are. I ran out to give it to you."

Bao-yu, still in a muse, saw Aroma there talking to him, yet without clearly perceiving who it was. With the same glazed look in his eyes, he began to speak.

"Dearest coz! I've never before dared to tell you what I felt for you. Now at last I'm going to pluck up courage and tell you, and after that I don't care what becomes of me. Because of you I, too, have made myself ill—only I haven't dared tell anyone about it and have had to bear it all in silence. And the day that your illness is cured, I do believe that mine, too, will get better. Night and day, coz, sleeping and dreaming, you are never out of my mind."

Aroma listened to this declaration aghast.

"Holy saints preserve us!" she exclaimed. "He'll be the death of me."

She gave him a shake.

"What are you talking about? Are you bewitched? You'd better hurry."

Bao-yu seemed suddenly to waken from his trance and recognized the person he had been speaking to as Aroma. His face turned a deep red with embarrassment and he snatched the fan from her and fled.

After he had gone, Aroma began thinking about the words he had just said and realized that they must have been intended for Dai-yu. She reflected with some alarm that if things between them were as his words seemed to indicate, there was every likelihood of an ugly scandal developing, and wondered how she could arrange matters to prevent it. Preoccupied with these reflections, she stood as motionless and unseeing as her master had done a few moments before. Bao-chai found her in this state on her way back from the house.

"What are you brooding on, out in the burning sun?" she asked her, laughing.

Aroma laughed back.

"There were two little sparrows here having a fight. They were so funny, I had to stand and watch them."

"Where was Cousin Bao rushing off to just now, all dressed up for going out?" said Bao-chai. "I was going to call out and ask him, but he is getting so crotchety lately that I thought I had better not."

"The Master sent for him," said Aroma.

"Oh dear!" said Bao-chai. "I wonder why he should send for him in heat like this? I hope he hasn't thought of something to be angry about and called him over to be punished."

"No, it isn't that," said Aroma. "I think it's to receive a visitor."

"It must be a very tiresome visitor," said Bao-chai, "to go around bothering people on a boiling day like this instead of staying at home and trying to keep cool."

"You can say that again!" said Aroma.

"What's young Xiang-yun been doing at your place?" said Bao-chai, changing the subject.

"We were having a chat," said Aroma, "and after that she had a look at some slipper-tops that I've got ready pasted and have asked her to sew for me."

"You're an intelligent young woman," said Bao-chai, having first looked to right and left of her to make sure that no one else was about, "I should have thought you'd have sense enough to leave her a few moments in peace. I've been watching our Yun lately, and from what I've observed of her and various stray remarks I've heard, I get the impression that back at home she can barely call her soul her own. I know for a fact that they are too mean to pay for professional seamstresses and that nearly all the sewing has to be done by the women of the household, and I'm pretty sure that's why, whenever she's found herself alone with me on these last few visits, she's told me how tired she gets at home. When I press her for details, her eyes fill with tears and she answers evasively, as though she'd like to tell me but daren't. It must be very hard for her, losing both her parents when she was so young. It quite wrings my heart to see her so exploited."

Aroma smote her hands together as understanding dawned.

"Yes, I *see*. I see now why she was so slow with those ten butterfly bows I asked her to sew for me last month. It was ages before she sent them, and even then there was a message to say that she'd only been able to do them roughly. She told me I'd better use them on something else. 'If you want nice, even ones,' she said, 'you'll have to wait until next time I come to stay with you.' Now I can see why. She didn't like to refuse when I asked her, but I suppose she had to sit up till midnight doing them, poor thing. Oh, how stupid of me! I'd never have asked her if I'd realized."

"Last time she was here, she told me that it's quite normal for her to sit up sewing until midnight," said Bao-chai; "and if her aunt or the other women catch her doing the slightest bit of work for anyone else, they are angry with her."

"It's all the fault of that pig-headed young master of mine," said Aroma. "He refuses to let any of his sewing be done by the seamstresses outside. Every bit of work, large or small, has to be done in his room—and I just can't manage it all on my own."

Bao-chai laughed.

"Why do you take any notice of him? Why not simply give it to the seamstresses without telling him?"

"He's not so easy to fool," said Aroma. "He can tell the difference. I'm afraid there's nothing for it. I shall just have to work through it all gradually on my own."

"Now just a minute!" said Bao-chai. "We'll think of a way round this. Suppose *I* were to do some of it for you?"

"Would you really?" said Aroma. "I'd be so grateful if you would. I'll come over with some this evening then."

She had barely finished saying this when an old woman came rushing up to them in a state of great agitation.

"Isn't it dreadful? Miss Golden has drowned herself in the well."

"Which Golden?" said Aroma, startled.

"Which Golden?" said the old woman. "There aren't two Goldens that I know of. Golden from Her Ladyship's room, of course, that was dismissed the day before yesterday. She'd been crying and carrying on at home ever since, but nobody paid much attention to her. Then suddenly, when they went to look for her, she wasn't there, and just now someone going to fetch water from the well by the south-east corner found a body in it and rushed inside for help, and when they fished it out, they found that it was Golden. They did all they could to revive her, but it was too late. She was dead."

"How strange!" said Bao-chai.

Aroma shook her head wonderingly and a tear or two stole down her cheek. She and Golden had been like sisters to each other.

Bao-chai hurried off to Lady Wang's to offer her sympathy. Aroma went back to Green Delights.

When Bao-chai arrived at Lady Wang's apartment she found the whole place hushed and still and Lady Wang sitting in the inner room on her own, crying. Deeming it an unsuitable moment to raise the subject of her visit, Bao-chai sat down beside her in silence.

"Where have you just come from?" Lady Wang asked her.

"The Garden."

"The Garden," Lady Wang echoed. "Did you by any chance see your cousin Bao-yu there?"

"I saw him going out just now wearing his outdoor clothes, but I don't know where he was going to."

Lady Wang nodded and gave a sigh.

"I don't know if you've heard. Something very strange has happened. Golden has drowned herself in a well."

"That *is* strange," said Bao-chai. "Why ever did she do that?"

"The day before yesterday she broke something of mine," said Lady Wang, "and in a moment of anger I struck her a couple of times and sent her back to her mother's. I had only been meaning to leave her there a day or two to punish her. After that I would have had her back again. I never dreamed that she would be so angry with me as to drown herself. Now that she has, I feel that it is all my fault."

"It's only natural that a kind person like you should see it in that way," said Bao-chai, "but in my opinion Golden would never have drowned herself in anger. It's much more likely that she was playing about beside the well and slipped in accidentally. While she was in service her movements were restricted and it would be natural for her to go running around everywhere during her first day or two outside. There's no earthly reason why she should have felt angry enough with you to drown herself. If she did, all I can say is that she was a stupid person and not worth feeling sorry for!"

Lady Wang sighed and shook her head doubtfully.

"Well, it may be as you say, but I still feel very uneasy in my mind."

"I'm sure you have no cause, Aunt," said Bao-chai, "but if you feel *very* much distressed, I suggest that you simply give her family a little extra for the funeral. In that way you will more than fulfil any moral obligation you may have towards her as a mistress."

"I have just given her mother fifty taels," said Lady Wang. "I wanted to give her two new outfits as well from one of the girls' wardrobes, but it just so happens that at the moment none of them apart from your Cousin Lin has got anything new that would do. Your Cousin Lin has got two sets that we had made for her next birthday, but she is such a sensitive child and has had so much sickness and misfortune in her life that I'm afraid she would almost certainly feel superstitious about the clothes made for her birthday being used for dressing a corpse with, so I've had to ask the tailors to make up a couple in a hurry. Of course, if it were any other maid, I should have given the mother a few taels and that would have been the end of the matter. But though Golden was only a servant, she had been with me so long that she had become almost like a daughter to me."

She began to cry again as she said this.

"There's no need to hurry the tailors about this," said Bao-chai. "I've got two new outfits that I recently finished making for myself. Why not let her mother have *them* and save them the trouble? Golden once or twice wore old dresses of mine in the past, so I know they will fit her."

"That's very kind of you, but aren't you superstitious?" said Lady Wang. Bao-chai laughed.

"Don't worry about *that*, Aunt. That sort of thing has never bothered me."

At that she rose and went off to fetch them. Lady Wang hurriedly ordered two of the servants to go after her.

When Bao-chai returned with the clothes, she found Bao-yu sitting beside his mother in tears. Lady Wang was evidently in the midst of rebuking him about something, but as soon as she caught sight of Bao-chai, she closed her mouth and fell silent. From the scene before her eyes and the word or two she had overheard, Bao-chai was able to form a pretty good idea of what had been happening. She handed the clothes over to Lady Wang and Lady Wang summoned Golden's mother to come and fetch them.

What happened after that will be told in the following chapter.

CHAPTER 33

An envious younger brother puts in a malicious word or two
And a scapegrace elder brother receives a terrible chastisement

Our story last told how Golden's mother was summoned to take away the clothing that Bao-chai had brought for Golden's laying-out. When she arrived, Lady Wang called her inside, and after making her an additional present of some jewellery, advised her to procure the services of some Buddhist monks to recite a *sūtra*[6] for the salvation of the dead girl's soul. Golden's mother kotowed her thanks and departed with the clothes and jewellery.

The news that Golden's disgrace had driven her to take her own life had reached Bao-yu as he was returning from his interview with Jia Yu-cun, and

6. A Buddhist scripture.

he was already in a state of shock when he went in to see his mother, only to be subjected by her to a string of accusations and reproaches, to which he was unable to reply. He availed himself of the opportunity presented by Bao-chai's arrival to slip quietly out again, and wandered along, scarcely knowing where he was going, still in a state of shock, hands clasped behind him, head down low, and sighing as he went.

Without realizing it he was drifting towards the main reception hall, and was in fact just emerging from behind the screen-wall that masked the gateway leading from the inner to the outer part of the mansion, when he walked head-on into someone coming from the opposite direction.

"Stand where you are!" said this person in a harsh voice.

Bao-yu looked up with a start and saw that it was his father. He gave an involuntary gasp of fear and, dropping his hands to his sides, hastily assumed a more deferential posture.

"Now," said Jia Zheng, "will you kindly explain the meaning of these sighs and of this moping, hang-dog appearance? You took your time coming when Yu-cun called for you just now, and I gather that when you did eventually vouchsafe your presence, he found you dull and listless and without a lively word to say for yourself. And look at you now—sullenness and secret depravity written all over your face! What are these sighings and groanings supposed to indicate? What have *you* got to be discontented or displeased about? Come, sir! What is the meaning of this?"

Bao-yu was normally ready enough with his tongue, but on this occasion grief for Golden so occupied his mind (at that moment he would very willingly have changed places with her) that though he heard the words addressed to him by his father, he failed to take in their meaning and merely stared back at him stupidly.

Seeing him too hypnotized by fear—or so it appeared—to answer with his usual promptness, Jia Zheng, who had not been angry to start with, was now well on the way to becoming so; but the irate comment he was about to make was checked when a servant from the outer gate announced that a representative of "His Highness the Prince of Zhong-shun" had arrived.

Jia Zheng was puzzled.

"The Prince of Zhong-shun?" he thought. "I have never had any dealings with the Prince of Zhong-shun. I wonder why *he* should suddenly send someone to see me . . . ?"

He told the man to invite the prince's messenger to sit in the hall, while he himself hurried inside and changed into court dress. On entering the hall to receive his visitor, he found that it was the Prince of Zhong-shun's chamberlain who had come to see him. After an exchange of bows and verbal salutations, the two men sat down and tea was served. The chamberlain cut short the customary civilities by coming straight to the point.

"It would have been temerity on my part to have intruded on the leisure of an illustrious scholar in the privacy of his home, but in fact it is not for the purpose of paying a social call that I am here, but on orders from His Highness. His Highness has a small request to make of you. If you will be so good as to oblige him, not only will His Highness be extremely grateful himself, but I and my colleagues will also be very much beholden to you."

Jia Zheng was totally at a loss to imagine what the purpose of the man's visit might be; nevertheless he rose to his feet out of respect for the prince and smiled politely.

"You have orders from His Highness for me? I shall be happy to perform them if you will have the goodness to instruct me."

"I don't think any *performing* will be necessary," said the chamberlain drily. "All we want from you is a few words. A young actor called Bijou—a female impersonator—has gone missing from the palace. He hasn't been back now for four or five days; and though we have looked everywhere we can think of, we can't make out where he can have got to. However, in the course of the very extensive inquiries we have made both inside and outside the city, eight out of ten of the people we have spoken to say that he has recently been very thick with the young gentleman who was born with the jade in his mouth. Well, obviously we couldn't come inside here and search as we would have done if this had been anyone else's house, so we had to go back and report the matter to His Highness; and His Highness says that though he could view the loss of a hundred ordinary actors with equanimity, this Bijou is so skilled in anticipating his wishes and so essential to his peace of mind that it would be utterly impossible for him to dispense with his services. I have therefore come here to request you to ask your son if he will be good enough to let Bijou come back again. By doing so he will not only earn the undying gratitude of the Prince, but will also save me and my colleagues a great deal of tiring and disagreeable searching."

The chamberlain concluded with a sweeping bow.

Surprised and angered by what he had heard, Jia Zheng immediately sent for Bao-yu, who presently came hurrying in, ignorant of what the reason for his summons might be.

"Miserable scum!" said Jia Zheng. "It is not enough, apparently, that you should neglect your studies when you are at home. It seems that you must needs go perpetrating enormities outside. This Bijou I have been hearing about is under the patronage of His Royal Highness the Prince of Zhong-shun. How could you have the unspeakable effrontery to commit an act of enticement on his person—involving *me,* incidentally, in the consequences of your wrong-doing?"

The question made Bao-yu start.

"I honestly know nothing about this," he said. "I don't even know who or what 'Bijou' is, let alone what you mean by 'enticement.' "

Jia Zheng was about to exclaim, but the chamberlain forestalled him.

"There is really no point in concealment, young gentleman," he said coldly. "Even if you are not hiding him here, we are sure that you know where he is. In either case you had much better say straight out and save us a lot of trouble. I'd be greatly obliged if you would."

"I really don't know," said Bao-yu. "You must have been misinformed."

The chamberlain gave a sardonic laugh.

"I have, of course, got evidence for what I am saying and I'm afraid you are doing yourself little good by forcing me to mention it in front of your father. You say you don't know who Bijou is. Very well. Then will you kindly explain how his red cummerbund came to find its way around your waist?"

Bao-yu stared at him open-mouthed, too stunned to reply.

"If he knows even a private thing like that," he thought, "there's little likelihood of my being able to hoodwink him about anything else. I'd better get rid of him as quickly as possible, before he can say any more."

"Since you have managed to find out so much about him," he said, finding his tongue at last, "I'm surprised that so important a thing as buying a house should have escaped you. From what I've heard, he recently acquired a little villa and an acre or so of land at Fort Redwood, seven miles east of the walls. I suppose he could be there."

The chamberlain smiled.

"If you say so, then no doubt that is where we shall find him. I shall go and look there immediately. If I do find him there, you will hear no more from me; if not, I shall be back again for further instructions."

So saying, he hurriedly took his leave.

Jia Zheng, his eyes glaring and his mouth contorted with rage, went after the chamberlain to see him out. He turned briefly towards Bao-yu as he was leaving the hall.

"You stay where you are. I shall deal with you when I get back."

As he was on his way in again after seeing the chamberlain off the premises, Jia Huan with two or three pages at his heels came stampeding across the courtyard.

"Hit that boy!" Jia Zheng shouted, outraged. But Jia Huan, reduced to a quivering jelly of fear by the sight of his father, had already jolted to a halt and was standing with bowed head in front of him.

"And what is the meaning of this?" said Jia Zheng. "What has become of the people who are supposed to look after you? Why do they allow you to gallop around in this extraordinary fashion?" His voice rose to a shout: "Where are the people responsible for taking this boy to school?"

Jia Huan saw in his father's anger an opportunity of exercising his malice.

"I didn't mean to run, Father, but just as I was going by the well back there I saw the body of a maid who had drowned herself—all swollen up with water, and her head all swollen. It was *horrible*. I just couldn't help myself."

Jia Zheng heard him with incredulous horror.

"*What* are you saying? *Who* has drowned herself? Such a thing has never before happened in our family. Our family has always been lenient and considerate in its treatment of inferiors. It is one of our traditions. I suppose it is because I have been too neglectful of household matters during these last few years. Those in charge have felt encouraged to abuse their authority, until finally an appalling thing like this can happen—an innocent young life cut off by violence. What a terrible disgrace to our ancestors if this should get about!" He turned and shouted a command.

"Fetch Jia Lian and Lai Da!"

"Sir!" chorused the pages, and were on the point of doing so when Jia Huan impulsively stepped forward, threw himself on his knees and clung to his father's skirts.

"Don't be angry with me, Father, but apart from the servants in Lady Wang's room, no one else knows anything about this. I heard my mother say—"

He broke off and glanced around behind him. Jia Zheng understood and signalled with his eyes to the pages, who obediently withdrew some distance back to either side of the courtyard. Jia Huan continued in a voice lowered almost to a whisper.

"My mother told me that the day before yesterday, in Lady Wang's room, my brother Bao-yu tried to rape one of Her Ladyship's maids called Golden, and when she wouldn't let him, he gave her a beating; and Golden was so upset that she threw herself in the well and was drowned—"

Jia Zheng, whose face had now turned to a ghastly gold-leaf colour, interrupted him with a dreadful cry.

"Fetch Bao-yu!"

He began to stride towards his study, shouting to all and sundry as he went.

"If anyone tries to stop me *this* time, I shall make over my house and property and my post at the Ministry and everything else I have to him and Bao-yu. I absolutely refuse to be responsible for the boy any longer. I shall cut off my few remaining hairs (those that worry and wretchedness have left me) and look for some clean and decent spot to end my days in. Perhaps in that way I shall escape the charge of having disgraced my ancestors by rearing this unnatural monster as my son."

When they saw the state he was in, the literary gentlemen and senior menservants who were waiting for him in the study, guessed that Bao-yu must be the cause of it and, looking at each other with various grimaces, biting their thumbs or sticking their tongues out, hastily retreated from the room. Jia Zheng entered it alone and sat down, stiffly upright, in a chair. He was breathing heavily and his face was bathed in tears. Presently, when he had regained his breath, he barked out a rapid series of commands:

"Bring Bao-yu here. Get a heavy bamboo. Get some rope to tie him with. Close the courtyard gates. If anyone tries to take word through inside, kill him!"

"Sir!—Sir!—Sir!" the terrified pages chorused in unison at each of his commands, and some of them went off to look for Bao-yu.

Jia Zheng's ominous "Stay where you are" as he went out with the chamberlain had warned Bao-yu that something dire was imminent—though just how much more dire as a result of Jia Huan's malicious intervention he could not have foreseen and as he stood where his father had left him, he twisted and turned himself about, anxiously looking for some passer-by who could take a message through to the womenfolk inside. But no one came. Even the omnipresent Tealeaf was on this occasion nowhere to be seen. Then suddenly, in answer to his prayers, an old woman appeared—a darling, precious treasure of an old woman (or so she seemed at that moment)—and he dashed forward and clung to her beseechingly.

"Quickly!" he said. "Go and tell them that Sir Zheng is going to beat me. Quickly! Quickly! Go and tell. GO AND TELL."

Partly because agitation had made him incoherent and partly because, as ill luck would have it, the old woman was deaf, almost everything he said had escaped her—except for the "Go and tell," which she misheard as "in the well." She smiled at him reassuringly.

"Let her jump in the well then, young master. Don't you worry your pretty head about it!"

Realizing that he had deafness, too, to contend with, he now became quite frantic.

"GO AND TELL MY PAGES."

"Her wages?" the old woman asked in some surprise. "Bless you, of course they paid her wages! Her Ladyship gave a whole lot of money towards the funeral as well. And clothes. Paid her wages, indeed!"

Bao-yu stamped his feet in a frenzy of impatience. He was still wondering despairingly how to make her understand when Jia Zheng's pages arrived and forced him to go with them to the study.

Jia Zheng turned a pair of wild and bloodshot eyes on him as he entered. Forgetting the "riotous and dissipated conduct abroad leading to the unseemly bestowal of impudicities on a theatrical performer" and the "neglect of proper pursuits and studies at home culminating in the attempted violation of a parent's maidservant" and all the other high-sounding charges he had been preparing to hurl against him, he shouted two brief orders to the pages.

"Gag his mouth. Beat him to death."

The pages were too frightened not to comply. Two held Bao-yu face downwards on a bench while a third lifted up the flattened bamboo sweep and began to strike him with it across the hams. After about a dozen blows Jia Zheng, not satisfied that his executioner was hitting hard enough, kicked him impatiently aside, wrested the bamboo from his grasp, and, gritting his teeth, brought it down with the utmost savagery on the places that had already been beaten.

At this point the literary gentlemen, sensing that Bao-yu was in serious danger of life and limb, came in again to remonstrate; but Jia Zheng refused to hear them.

"Ask him what he has done and then tell me if you think I should spare him," he said. "It is the encouragement of people like you that has corrupted him; and now, when things have come to this pass, you intercede for him. I suppose you would like me to wait until he commits parricide, or worse. Would you still intercede for him then?"

They could see from this reply that he was beside himself. Wasting no further time on words, they quickly withdrew and looked for someone to take a message through inside.

Lady Wang did not stop to tell Grandmother Jia when she received it. She snatched up an outer garment, pulled it about her, and, supported by a single maid, rushed off, not caring what menfolk might see her, to the outer study, bursting into it with such suddenness that the literary gentlemen and other males present were unable to avoid her.

Her entry provoked Jia Zheng to fresh transports of fury. Faster and harder fell the bamboo on the prostrate form of Bao-yu, which by now appeared to be unconscious, for when the boys holding it down relaxed their hold and fled from their Mistress's presence, it had long since ceased even to twitch. Even so Jia Zheng would have continued beating it had not Lady Wang clasped the bamboo to her bosom and prevented him.

"Enough!" said Jia Zheng. "Today you are determined, all of you, to drive me insane."

"No doubt Bao-yu deserved to be beaten," said Lady Wang tearfully, "but it is bad for you to get over-excited. Besides, you ought to have some consideration for Lady Jia. She is not at all well in this frightful heat. It may not seem to you of much consequence to kill Bao-yu, but think what the effect would be on *her.*"

"Don't try that sort of talk with me!" said Jia Zheng bitterly. "Merely by fathering a monster like this I have proved myself an unfilial son; yet whenever in the past I have tried to discipline him, the rest of you have all conspired against me to protect him. Now that I have the opportunity at last, I may as well finish off what I have begun and put him down, like the vermin he is, before he can do any more damage."

So saying, he took up a rope and would have put his threat into execution, had not Lady Wang held her arms around him to prevent it.

"Of course you should discipline your son," she said, weeping, "but you have a wife too, Sir Zheng, don't forget. I am nearly fifty now and this wretched boy is the only son I have. If you insist on making an example of him, I dare not do much to dissuade you. But to kill him outright—that is deliberately to make me childless. Better strangle me first, if you are going to strangle him. Let the two of us die together. At least I shall have some support then in the world to come, if all support in this world is to be denied me!"

With these words she threw herself upon Bao-yu's body and, lifting up her voice, began weeping with noisy abandon. Jia Zheng, who had heard her with a sigh, sank into a chair and himself broke down in a fit of weeping.

Presently Lady Wang began to examine the body she was clasping. Bao-yu's face was ashen, his breathing was scarcely perceptible, and the trousers of thin green silk which clothed the lower part of his body were so soaked with blood that their colour was no longer recognizable. Feverishly she unfastened his waistband and drew them back. Everywhere, from the upper part of his buttocks down to his calves, was either raw and bloody or purplish black with bruises. Not an inch of sound flesh was to be seen. The sight made her cry out involuntarily.

"Oh my son! My unfortunate son!"

Once more she broke down into uncontrollable weeping.

Her own words reminded her of the son she had already lost, and now, with added bitterness, she began to call out his name.

"Oh, Zhu! Zhu! If only you had lived, I shouldn't have minded losing a *hundred* other sons!"

By this time news of Lady Wang's *démarche*[7] had circulated to the other members of the inner mansion and Li Wan, Xi-feng, Ying-chun, Tan-chun and Xi-chun had come to join her. The invocation of her dead husband's name, painful to all of them, was altogether too much for Li Wan, who broke into loud sobs on hearing it. Jia Zheng himself was deeply affected, and tears as round as pumpkins rolled down both his cheeks. It was beginning to look as if they might all go on weeping there indefinitely, since no one would make a move; but just then there was a cry of "Her Old Ladyship—!" from one of the maids, interrupted by a quavering voice outside the window.

"Kill me first! You may as well kill both of us while you are about it!"

As much distressed by his mother's words as he was alarmed by her arrival, Jia Zheng hurried out to meet her. She was leaning on the shoulder of a little maid, her old head swaying from side to side with the effort of running, and panting as she ran.

Jia Zheng bowed down before her and his face assumed the semblance of a smile.

"Surely, Mother, in such hot weather as this there is no need for you to come here? If you have any instructions, you should call for me and let *me* come to *you*."

---

7. A strategically chosen course of action.

Grandmother Jia had stopped when she heard this voice and now stood panting for some moments while she regained her breath. When she spoke, her voice had an unnatural shrillness in it.

"Oh! Are you speaking to *me*?—Yes, as a matter of fact I *have* got 'instructions,' as you put it; but as unfortunately I've never had a good son who cares for me, there's no one I can give them to."

Wounded in his most sensitive spot, Jia Zheng fell on his knees before her. The voice in which he replied to her was broken with tears.

"How can I bear it, Mother, if you speak to me like that? What I did to the boy I did for the honour of the family."

Grandmother Jia spat contemptuously.

"A single harsh word from me and you start whining that you can't bear it. How do you think Bao-yu could bear your cruel rod? And you say you've been punishing him for the honour of the family, but you just tell me this: did your own father ever punish *you* in such a way?—I think not."

She was weeping now herself.

"Don't upset yourself, Mother," said Jia Zheng, with the same forced smile. "I acted too hastily. From now on I'll never beat him again, if that's what you wish."

"Hoity-toity, keep your temper!" said Grandmother Jia. "He's your son. If you want to beat him, that's up to you. If we women are in your way, we'll leave you alone to get on with it." She turned to her attendants. "Call my carriage. Your Mistress and I and Bao-yu are going back to Nanking. We shall be leaving immediately."

The servants made a show of compliance.

"No need for you to cry," she said, turning to Lady Wang. "You love Bao-yu now that he's young, but when he's grown up and become an important official, he'll like enough forget that you're his mother. Much better force yourself not to love him now and save yourself some anguish later on."

Jia Zheng threw himself forward on his face.

"Don't say that, Mother! Don't reject your own son!"

"On the contrary," said Grandmother Jia, "it is *you* who have rejected *me*. But don't worry. When I have gone back to Nanking, there will be no one here to stop you. You can beat away to your heart's content." She turned to the servants.

"Come on, hurry up with that packing! And get the carriage and horses ready so that we can be on our way."

Jia Zheng's kotows were by now describing the whole quarter-circle from perpendicular to ground. But the old lady walked on inside, ignoring him.

From the sight that met her eyes she could tell that this had been no ordinary beating. It filled her with anguish for the sufferer and fresh anger for the man who had inflicted it, and for a long time she clung to the inert form and wept, only gradually calming down under the combined coaxing of Lady Wang, Xi-feng and Li Wan.

At this point several of the maids and womenservants came forward and attempted to raise Bao-yu to his feet.

"Idiots!" said Xi-feng. "Haven't you got eyes in your heads? Can't you *see* that he's in no fit state to walk? Go and get that wicker summer-bed from inside and carry him in on that."

The servants rushed out and presently reappeared carrying a long, narrow couch of woven rattan between them, on to which they lifted Bao-yu. Then, with Grandmother Jia, Lady Wang and the rest of the womenfolk leading the way, they carried him to Grandmother Jia's apartment and set him down inside it.

Jia Zheng, conscious that his mother's wrath against him had not abated and unwilling to leave things where they stood, had followed the little procession inside. His eyes travelled from Bao-yu, who, he now saw, really *had* been beaten very badly, to Lady Wang. She was sobbing bitterly, interspersing her sobs with cries of "My child!" and "My son!" Presently she broke off and began railing at the object of her sorrow: "Why couldn't you have died instead of Zhu? Zhu wouldn't have made his father angry the way you do and I should have been spared this constant anxiety. What is to become of me if *you* go away and leave me, too?" Then, with a cry of "Poor, worthless boy!" she fell once more to weeping. When Jia Zheng heard this, his own heart was softened and he began to wish that he had not beaten the boy quite so savagely. He tried to find words of comfort for his old mother, but she answered him tearfully.

"A father *ought* to punish his son if he's done wrong, but not like *that!*— Why don't you go now? Won't you be content until you've seen the boy die under your own eyes?"

Jia Zheng, with flustered deference, withdrew.

By now Aunt Xue, Bao-chai, Caltrop, Aroma and Shi Xiang-yun were there too. Aroma was deeply distressed, but could not show the extent of her feelings in the presence of so many others. Indeed, Bao-yu was so ringed around with people fanning him or forcing water through his lips that there was nothing she could have done for him if she had tried. Feeling somewhat superfluous, she left the apartment and went out to the inner gate, where she asked the pages to look for Tealeaf, so that she could find out what had happened.

"Why did the Master suddenly beat him like that?" she asked Tealeaf when he arrived. "He hadn't been doing anything. And why couldn't you have warned us in time?"

Tealeaf was indignant.

"I couldn't help it, I wasn't *there*. He was half-way through beating him before I even got to hear about it. I did my best to find out the reason, though. It seems that there were two things the Master was upset about: one was to do with Bijou and the other was to do with Golden."

"How did the Master get to know about them?" said Aroma.

"Well, the Bijou business he probably knew about indirectly through Mr. Xue," said Tealeaf. "Mr. Xue had been feeling very jealous, and it looks as though he may have put someone else up to telling the Master about it out of spite. And Golden he probably heard about from Master Huan— leastways, that's what the Master's own people told me."

The two reasons Tealeaf had given corresponded well enough with Aroma's own observations, and she was more than half inclined to believe them. Fairly confident, therefore, that she now knew the cause of what had happened, she returned once more to the apartment. The ministrations of those surrounding Bao-yu had by now restored him to full consciousness, and Grandmother Jia was instructing the servants to carry him back to his own room. There was an answering cry and something of a scramble as many willing hands lifted up the cane bed. Then, preceded as before by Grandmother Jia,

Lady Wang and the rest, they carried him through into the Garden and back to Green Delights, where they finally got him on to his own bed. After a good deal more bustle they gradually all drifted away and Aroma at last had Bao-yu alone to herself.

But in order to know what happened then, you must refer to the following chapter.

CHAPTER 34

A wordless message meets with silent understanding
And a groundless imputation leads to undeserved rebukes

When she saw that Grandmother Jia, Lady Wang and the rest had all gone, Aroma went and sat down at Bao-yu's bedside and asked him, with tears in her eyes, the reason why he had been beaten so severely.

Bao-yu sighed.

"Oh, the usual things. Need you ask? I wish you'd take a look down below, though, and tell me if anything's broken. It's hurting so dreadfully down there."

Very gently Aroma inserted her fingers into the top of his trousers and began to draw them off. She had barely started when he gritted his teeth and let out a cry, and she had to stop immediately. This happened three or four times before she finally succeeded in getting them off. The sight revealed made her grit her own teeth.

"Mother of mine!" she gasped, "he must have hit you savagely. If only you'd listened to me a bit in the past, it would never have come to *this*. Why, you might have been crippled for life. It doesn't bear thinking of."

Just then Bao-chai's arrival was announced by one of the maids. Since putting his trousers on again was out of the question, Aroma snatched up a lightweight coverlet and hurriedly threw it over him. Bao-chai came in carrying a large tablet of some sort of solid medicine which she instructed Aroma to pound up in wine and apply to Bao-yu's injuries in the evening.

"This is a decongestant," she said, handing it to her. "It will take away the inflammation by dispersing the bad blood in his bruises. After that, he should heal quite quickly."

She turned to Bao-yu.

"Are you feeling any better now?"

Bao-yu thanked her. "Yes," he said, he was feeling a little better, and invited her to sit down beside him. Bao-chai was relieved to see him with his eyes open and talking again. She shook her head sadly.

"If you had listened to what one said, this would never have happened. Everyone is so upset now. It isn't only Grandmother and Lady Wang, you know. Even—"

She checked herself abruptly, regretting that she had allowed her feelings to run away with her, and lowered her head, blushing. Bao-yu had sensed hidden depths of feeling in the passionate earnestness of her tone, and when she suddenly faltered and turned red, there was something so touching about the pretty air of confusion with which she dropped her head and played with the ends of her girdle, that his spirits soared and his pain was momentarily forgotten.

"What have I undergone but a few whacks of the bamboo?" he thought,

"—yet already they are so sad and concerned about me! What dear, adorable, sweet, noble girls they are! Heaven knows how they would grieve for me if I were actually to die! It would be almost worth dying, just to find out. The loss of a life's ambitions would be a small price to pay, and I should be a peevish, ungrateful ghost if I did not feel proud and happy when such darling creatures were grieving for me."

He was roused from this reverie by the sound of Bao-chai's voice asking Aroma what it was that had moved his father to such violent anger against him. Aroma's low reply, in which she merely repeated what Tealeaf had told her, was his first inkling of the part that Jia Huan had played in his misfortune. Her mention of Xue Pan's involvement, however, made him apprehensive that Bao-chai might feel embarrassed, and he hastily interrupted Aroma to prevent her from saying more.

"Old Xue would never do a thing like that," he said. "It's silly to make these wild assertions."

Bao-chai knew that it was out of respect for her feelings that he was silencing Aroma, and she wondered at his considerateness.

"What delicacy of feeling!" she thought, "—after so terrible a beating and in spite of all the pain, to be still able to worry about the possibility of someone else's being offended! If only you could apply some of that thoughtfulness to the more important things of life, my friend, you would make my Uncle so happy; and then perhaps these awful things would never happen. And when all's said and done, this sensibility on my behalf is rather wasted. Do you *really* think I know my own brother so little that I am unaware of his unruly nature? Nothing has ever been allowed to stand in the way of Pan's desires. Look at the terrible trouble he made for you that time over Qin Zhong. That was a long time ago, and I am sure he has got much worse since then."

Those were her thoughts, but what she said was:

"There's really no need to look around for someone to blame. If you ask me, the mere fact that Cousin Bao has been willing to keep such company was in itself quite enough to make Uncle angry. And though my brother can be very tactless and may well have let something out about Cousin Bao in the course of conversation, I'm sure it wouldn't have been deliberate troublemaking on his part. In the first place, it is, after all, true, what he is supposed to have said: Cousin Bao *has* been going around with that actor. And in the second place, my brother simply hasn't got it in him to be discreet. You have lived all your life with sensitive, considerate people like Cousin Bao, my dear Aroma. You have never had to deal with a crude, forthright person like my brother—someone who says whatever comes into his head with complete disregard for the consequences."

When Bao-yu cut short her remarks about Xue Pan, Aroma had realized at once that she was being tactless and inwardly prayed that Bao-chai had not taken exception to them. To her, therefore, these words of Bao-chai's were a source of tongue-tied embarrassment. Bao-yu, on the other hand, could see in them only the refusal of a frank and generous nature to admit deviousness in others and a sensibility capable of matching and responding to his own. As a consequence his spirits soared yet higher. He was about to say something, but Bao-chai rose to her feet and anticipated him.

"I'll come and see you again tomorrow. You must rest now and give yourself a chance to get well. I've given Aroma something to make a lotion with. Get her to put it on for you in the evening. I can guarantee that it will hasten your recovery."

She was moving towards the door as she said this. When she was outside, Aroma hurried after her to see her off and to thank her for her trouble.

"As soon as he's better," she said, "Master Bao will come over and thank you himself, Miss."

"It's nothing at all," said Bao-chai, turning back to her with a smile. "Do tell him to rest properly, though, and not to brood. And if there's anything at all he wants, just quietly come round to my place for it. Don't go bothering Lady Jia or Lady Wang or any of the others, in case my uncle gets to hear of it. It probably wouldn't matter at the time, but it might do later on, next time there is any trouble."

With that she left, and Aroma turned back into the courtyard, her heart full of gratitude for Bao-chai's kindness. Re-entering Bao-yu's room, she found him lying back quietly, plunged in thought. From the look of it, he was already half asleep. Tiptoeing out again, she went off to wash her hair.

But it was difficult for Bao-yu to lie quietly for very long. The pain in his buttocks was like the stabbing and pricking of knives and needles and there was a burning sensation in them as if he were being grilled over a fire, so that the slightest movement made him cry out. Already it was growing late. Aroma appeared to have gone away, but two or three maids were still in attendance. As there was nothing that they could do for him, he told them that they might go off and prepare themselves for the night, provided that they remained within call. The maids accordingly withdrew, leaving him on his own.

He had dozed off. The shadowy form of Jiang Yu-han had come in to tell him of his capture by the Prince of Zhong-shun's men, followed, shortly after, by Golden, who gave him a tearful account of how she had drowned herself. In his half-dreaming, half-awake state he was having the greatest difficulty in attending to what they were saying, when suddenly he felt someone pushing him and became dimly aware of a sound of weeping in his ear. He gave a start. Fully awake now, he opened his eyes. It was Lin Dai-yu. Suspecting this, too, to be a dream, he raised his head to look. A pair of eyes swollen like peaches met his own, and a face that was glistening with tears. It was Dai-yu all right, no doubt about that. He would have looked longer, but the strain of raising himself was causing such excruciating pain in his nether parts, that he fell back again with a groan. The groan was followed by a sigh.

"Now what have *you* come for?" he said. "The sun's not long set and the ground must still be very hot underfoot. You could still get a heat-stroke at this time of day, and that would be a fine how-do-you-do. Actually, in spite of the beating, I don't feel very much pain. This fuss I make is put on to fool the others. I'm hoping they'll spread the word around outside how badly I've been hurt, so that Father gets to hear of it. It's all shamming, really. You mustn't be taken in by it."

Dai-yu's sobbing had by this time ceased to be audible; but somehow her strangled, silent weeping was infinitely more pathetic than the most clamorous grief. At that moment volumes would have been inadequate to contain the things she wanted to say to him; yet all she could get out, after struggling for some time with her choking sobs, was:

"I suppose you'll change now."

Bao-yu gave a long sigh.

"Don't worry, I shan't change. People like that are worth dying for. I wouldn't change if he killed me."

The words were scarcely out of his mouth when they heard someone outside in the courtyard saying:

"Mrs. Lian has come."

Dai-yu had no wish to see Xi-feng, and rose to her feet hurriedly.

Bao-yu seized hold of her hand.

"Now that's funny. Why should you start being afraid of *her* all of a sudden?"

She stamped with impatience.

"Look at the state my eyes are in!" she said. "I don't want them all making fun of me again."

At that Bao-yu released her hand and she bounded round to the back of the bed, slipping into the rear courtyard just as Xi-feng was entering the room from the front.

"A bit better now?" said Xi-feng. "Is there anything you feel like eating yet? If there is, tell them to come round to my place and get it."

As soon as Xi-feng had gone, Bao-yu was visited by Aunt Xue, and shortly after that by someone whom his grandmother had sent to see how he was getting on. At lighting-up time, after taking a few mouthfuls of soup, he settled down into a fitful sleep.

Just then a new group of visitors arrived, consisting of Zhou Rui's wife, Wu Xin-deng's wife, Zheng Hao-shi's wife, and those other members of the mansion's female staff who had had most to do with Bao-yu in the past and who, having heard of his beating, were anxious to see how he was. Aroma came out smiling on to the verandah to welcome them.

"You're just too late to see him, ladies," she told them in a low voice. "He's just this minute dropped off."

She ushered them into the outer room, invited them to be seated, and served them with tea. After sitting there very quietly for several minutes, they got up to take their leave, requesting Aroma as they did so that she would inform Bao-yu when he waked that they had been round to ask about him. Aroma promised to do so and showed them out. Just as she was about to go in again, an old woman arrived from Lady Wang's to say that "Her Ladyship would like to see one of Master Bao's people." After reflecting for a moment, Aroma turned to the house and called softly to Skybright, Musk and Ripple inside.

"Her Ladyship wants to see someone, so I'm going over. Stay indoors and keep an eye on things while I'm away. I shan't be long."

Then she followed the old woman out of the Garden and round to Lady Wang's apartment in the central courtyard. She found Lady Wang sitting on a cane summer-bed and fanning herself with a palm-leaf fan. She appeared not entirely pleased when she saw that it was Aroma.

"You could have sent one of the others," she said. "There was no need for *you* to come and leave him unattended."

Aroma smiled reassuringly.

"Master Bao has just settled down for the night, Madam. If he *should* want anything, the others are nowadays quite capable of looking after him on their own. Your Ladyship has no need to worry. I thought I had better come myself and not send one of the others, in case Your Ladyship had something important to tell us. I was afraid that if I sent one of the others, they might not understand what you wanted."

"I have nothing in particular to tell you," said Lady Wang. "I merely wanted to ask about my son. How is the pain now?"

"Much better since I put on some of the lotion that Miss Bao brought for him," said Aroma. "It was so bad before that he couldn't lie still, but now he's sleeping quite soundly, so you can tell it must be better than it was."

"Has he had anything to eat yet?" said Lady Wang.

"He had a few sips of some soup Her Old Ladyship sent," said Aroma, "but that's all he would take. He kept complaining that he felt dry. He wanted me to give him plum bitters to drink, but of course that's an astringent, and I thought to myself that as he'd just had a beating and not been allowed to cry out during it, a lot of hot blood and hot poison must have been driven inwards and still be collected round his heart, and if he were to drink some of that stuff, it might stir them up and bring on a serious illness, so I talked him out of it. After a lot of persuading, I got him to take some rose syrup instead, that I mixed up in water for him; but after only half a cup of it he said it tasted sickly and he couldn't get it down."

"Oh dear, I wish you'd told me sooner," said Lady Wang. "We were sent some bottles of flavouring the other day that I could have let you have. As a matter of fact I *was* going to send him some of them, but then I thought that if I did they would probably only get wasted, so I didn't. If he can't manage the rose syrup, I can easily give you a few of them to take back with you. You need only mix a teaspoonful of essence in a cupful of water. The flavours are quite delicious." She called Suncloud to her. "Fetch me a few of those bottles of flavouring essence that were sent us the other day."

"Two will be enough," said Aroma, "otherwise it will only get wasted. If we run out, I can always come back for more later."

Suncloud was gone for a considerable time. Eventually she returned with two little glass bottles, each about three inches high, which she handed to Aroma. They had screw-on silver tops and yellow labels. One of them was labelled "Essence of Cassia Flower" and the other one "Essence of Roses."

"What tiny little bottles!" said Aroma. "They can't hold very much. I suppose the stuff inside them must be very precious."

"It was made specially for the Emperor," said Lady Wang. "That's what the yellow labels mean. Haven't you seen labels like that before? Mind you look after them and don't let the stuff in them get wasted."

Aroma promised to be careful and began to go.

"Just a minute!" said Lady Wang. "I've thought of something else that I wanted to ask you."

Aroma returned. Lady Wang first glanced about her to make sure that no one else was in the room, then she said:

"I think I heard someone say that Bao-yu's beating today was because of something that Huan had said to Sir Zheng. I suppose *you* don't happen to have heard anything about that?"

"No. I haven't heard anything about *that*," said Aroma. "What *I* heard was that it was because Master Bao had been going around with one of Prince Somebody-or-other's players and the Master was told about it by someone who called."

Lady Wang nodded her head mysteriously.

"Yes, that was one of the reasons. But there was another reason as well."

"I really know nothing about any other reason, Your Ladyship," said Aroma. She dropped her head and hesitated a moment before going on. "I wonder if I might be rather bold and say something very outspoken to Your Ladyship? Really and truly—" She faltered.

"Please go on."

"I will if Your Ladyship will promise not to be angry with me."

"That's all right," said Lady Wang. "Just tell me what you have to say."

"Well, really and truly," said Aroma, "Master Bao *needed* punishing. If the Master didn't keep an eye on him, there's no knowing *what* he mightn't get up to."

"My child," said Lady Wang with a warmth rarely seen in her, "those are exactly my own sentiments. How clever of you to have understood! Of course, I know perfectly well that Bao-yu is in need of discipline; and anyone who saw how strict I used to be with Mr. Zhu would realize that I am capable of exercising it. But I have my reasons. A woman of fifty cannot expect to bear any more children and Bao-yu is now the only son I have. He is not a very strong boy; and his Grannie dotes on him. I daren't *risk* being strict. I daren't risk losing another son. I daren't risk angering Her Old Ladyship and upsetting the whole household. I do once in a while have it out with him: but though I have argued and pleaded and wept, it doesn't do any good. He *seems* all right at the time, but he'll be just the same again a short while afterwards and I always know that I have failed to reach him. I am afraid he *has* to suffer before he can learn—but suppose it's too much for him?—suppose he doesn't get over *this* beating? What will become of *me?*"

She began to cry.

Seeing her mistress so distressed, Aroma herself was affected and began to cry too.

"I can understand Your Ladyship being so upset," she said, "when he's your own son. Even we servants that have been with him for a few years get worried about him. The most that *we* can ever hope for is to do our duty and get by without too much trouble—but even *that* won't be possible if he goes on the way he has been doing. I'm always telling him to change his ways. Every day—every hour—I tell him. But it's no use; he won't listen. Of course, if these people *will* make so much fuss of him, you can hardly blame him for going round with them—though it does make our job more difficult. But now that Your Ladyship has spoken like this, it puts me in mind of something that's been worrying me which I should like to have asked Your Ladyship's advice about, only I was afraid you might take it amiss, and then not only should I have spoken to no purpose, but I should leave myself without even a grave to lie in . . ."

It was evident to Lady Wang that what she was struggling to get out was a matter of some consequence.

"What is it you want to tell me, my child?" she said kindly. "I've heard a lot of people praising you recently, and I confess that I assumed it must be because you took special pains in serving Bao-yu or in making yourself agreeable to other people—little things of that sort. But I see that I was wrong. These are not at all little things that you have been talking about. What you have said so far makes very good sense and entirely accords with my own opinion of the matter. So if you have anything to tell me, I should like to hear it. But I must ask you not to discuss it with anyone else."

"All I really wanted to ask," said Aroma, "was if Your Ladyship could advise me how later on we can somehow or other contrive to get Master Bao moved back outside the Garden."

Lady Wang looked startled and clutched Aroma's hand in some alarm.

"I hope Bao-yu hasn't been doing something dreadful with one of the girls?"

"Oh no, Your Ladyship, please don't suspect that!" said Aroma hurriedly. "That wasn't my meaning at all. It's just that—if you'll allow me to say so— Master Bao and the young ladies are beginning to grow up now, and though they are all cousins, there *is* the difference of sex between them, which makes it very awkward sometimes when they are all living together, especially in the case of Miss Lin and Miss Bao, who aren't even of the same clan. One can't help feeling uneasy. Even to outsiders it looks like a very strange sort of family. They say 'where nothing happens, imagination is busiest,' and I'm sure lots of unaccountable misfortunes begin when some innocent little thing we did unthinkingly gets misconstrued in someone else's imagination and reported as something terrible. We just have to be on our guard against that sort of thing happening—especially when Master Bao has such a peculiar character, as Your Ladyship knows, and spends all his time with girls. He only has to make the tiniest slip in an unguarded moment, and whether he really did anything or not, with so many people about—and some of them no better than they should be—there is sure to be scandal. For you know what some of these people are like, Your Ladyship. If they feel well-disposed towards you, they'll make you out to be a saint; but if they're not, then Heaven help you! If Master Bao lives to be spoken well of, we can count ourselves lucky; but the way things are, it only needs someone to breathe a word of scandal and—I say nothing of what will happen to us servants—it's of no consequence if *we*'re all chopped up for mincemeat—but what's more important, Master Bao's reputation will be destroyed for life and all the care and worry Your Ladyship and Sir Zheng have had on his account will have been wasted. I know Your Ladyship is very busy and can't be expected to think of everything, and I probably shouldn't have thought of this myself, but once I *had* thought of it, it seemed to me that it would be wrong of me not to tell Your Ladyship, and it's been preying on my mind ever since. The only reason I haven't mentioned it before is because I was afraid Your Ladyship might be angry with me."

What Aroma had just been saying about misconstructions and scandals so exactly fitted what had in fact happened in the case of Golden that for a moment Lady Wang was quite taken aback. But on reflection she felt nothing but love and gratitude for this humble servant-girl who had shown so much solicitude on her behalf.

"It is very perceptive of you, my dear, to have thought it all out so carefully," she said. "I have, of course, thought about this matter myself, but other things have put it from my mind, and what you have just said has reminded me. It is most thoughtful of you. You are a very, very good girl— Well, you may go now. I think I now know what to do. There is just one thing before you go, though. Now that you have spoken to me like this, I am going to place Bao-yu entirely in your hands. Be very careful with him, won't you?

Remember that anything you do for him you will be doing also for me. You will find that I am not ungrateful."

Aroma stood for a moment with bowed head, weighing the import of these words. Then she said:

"I will do what Your Ladyship has asked me to the utmost of my ability."

She left the apartment slowly and made her way back to Green Delights, pondering as she went. When she arrived, Bao-yu had just woken up, so she told him about the flavourings. He was pleased and made her mix some for him straight away. It was quite delicious. He kept thinking about Dai-yu and wanted to send someone over to see her, but he was afraid that Aroma would disapprove, so, as a means of getting her out of the way, he sent her over to Bao-chai's place to borrow a book. As soon as she had gone, he summoned Skybright.

"I want you to go to Miss Lin's for me," he said. "Just see what she's doing, and if she asks about me, tell her I'm all right."

"I can't go rushing in there bald-headed without a reason," said Skybright. "You'd better give me *some* kind of a message, just to give me an excuse for going there."

"I have none to give," said Bao-yu.

"Well, give me something to take, then," said Skybright, "or think of something I can ask her for. Otherwise it will look so silly."

Bao-yu thought for a bit and then, reaching out and picking up two of his old handkerchiefs, he tossed them towards her with a smile.

"All right. Tell her I said you were to give her these."

"That's an odd sort of present!" said Skybright. "What's she going to do with a pair of your old handkerchiefs? Most likely she'll think you're making fun of her and get upset again."

"No she won't," said Bao-yu. "She'll understand."

Skybright deemed it pointless to argue, so she picked up the handkerchiefs and went off to the Naiad's House. Little Delicate, who was hanging some towels out to dry on the verandah railings, saw her enter the courtyard and attempted to wave her away.

"She's gone to bed."

Skybright ignored her and went on inside. The lamps had not been lit and the room was in almost total darkness. The voice of Dai-yu, lying awake in bed, spoke to her out of the shadows.

"Who is it?"

"Skybright."

"What do you want?"

"Master Bao has sent me with some handkerchiefs, Miss."

Dai-yu seemed to hesitate. She found the gift puzzling and was wondering what it could mean.

"I suppose they must be very good ones," she said. "Probably someone gave them to him. Tell him to keep them and give them to somebody else. I have no use for them just now myself."

Skybright laughed.

"They're not new ones, Miss. They're two of his old, everyday ones."

This was even more puzzling. Dai-yu thought very hard for some moments. Then suddenly, in a flash, she understood.

"Put them down. You may go now."

Skybright did as she was bid and withdrew. All the way back to Green Delights she tried to make sense of what had happened, but it continued to mystify her.

Meanwhile the message that eluded Skybright had thrown Dai-yu into a turmoil of conflicting emotions.

"I feel so happy," she thought, "that in the midst of his own affliction he has been able to grasp the cause of all *my* trouble.

"And yet at the same time I am sad," she thought; "because how do I know that my trouble will end in the way I want it to?

"Actually, I feel rather amused," she thought. "Fancy his sending a pair of old handkerchiefs like that! Suppose I hadn't understood what he was getting at?

"But I feel alarmed that he should be sending presents to me in secret.

"Oh, and I feel so ashamed when I think how I am forever crying and quarrelling," she thought, "and all the time he has understood! . . . ."

And her thoughts carried her this way and that, until the ferment of excitement within her cried out to be expressed. Careless of what the maids might think, she called for a lamp, sat herself down at her desk, ground some ink, softened her brush, and proceeded to compose the following quatrains, using the handkerchiefs themselves to write on:

1

Seeing my idle tears, you ask me why
These foolish drops fall from my teeming eye:
Then know, your gift, being by the merfolk[8] made,
In merman's currency must be repaid.

2

Jewelled drops by day in secret sorrow shed
Or, in the night-time, in my wakeful bed,
Lest sleeve or pillow they should spot or stain,
Shall on these gifts shower down their salty rain.

3

Yet silk preserves but ill the Naiad's tears:
Each salty trace of them fast disappears.
Only the speckled bamboo[9] stems that grow
Outside the window still her tear-marks show.

She had only half-filled the second handkerchief and was preparing to write another quatrain, when she became aware that her whole body was burning hot all over and her cheeks were afire. Going over to the dressing-table, she removed the brocade cover from the mirror and peered into it.

"Hmn! 'Brighter than the peach-flower's hue,'" she murmured complacently to the flushed face that stared out at her from the glass, and, little

8. Mythical beings who live in the sea. They were famous for the fine fabric they wove, and when they wept, their tears formed pearls.   9. This bamboo was supposed to have gotten its spots by the tears once shed on it by the two goddesses of the Hsiang River, who were lamenting the death of their husband, the sage-king Shun.

imagining that what she had been witnessing was the first symptom of a serious illness, went back to bed, her mind full of handkerchiefs.

* * *

Chapters 35 to 96 Summary   The love between Bao-yu and Dai-yu continues to grow as the world outside Prospect Garden becomes ever more threateningly intrusive. Various machinations on the part of members of the Jia household, particularly Wang Xi-feng, are seen by the authorities as corruption and abuse of power, and the family's fortunes steadily decline. As Bao-yu's adolescence progresses, the older members of the household grow apprehensive about the possibility of scandal if he continues to share the garden with the young women of the household, and Bao-yu is moved out of the garden. There had long been talk of the "pairing of gold and jade," marrying Bao-chai with her golden locket to Bao-yu with his jade. The match with Xue Bao-chai is finally agreed upon, but the news is withheld from both Bao-yu and Dai-yu, who believes that she herself will marry Bao-yu. As we approach Chapter 96, Bao-yu has just lost his precious jade and has lapsed into a state of idiocy. To bring him to his senses, a deception is planned: Bao-yu is told that he will be marrying Dai-yu (Bao-chai will be hidden behind a veil in the wedding ceremony), and he revives somewhat. Dai-yu, however, accidentally learns of the impending wedding and lapses into her final illness.

FROM CHAPTER 96

Xi-feng conceives an ingenious plan of deception
And Frowner is deranged by an inadvertent disclosure

* * *

A day or two after these events, Dai-yu, having eaten her breakfast, decided to take Nightingale with her to visit Grandmother Jia. She wanted to pay her respects, and also thought the visit might provide some sort of distraction for herself. She had hardly left the Naiad's House, when she remembered that she had left her handkerchief at home, and sent Nightingale back to fetch it, saying that she would walk ahead slowly and wait for her to catch up. She had just reached the corner behind the rockery at Drenched Blossoms Bridge—the very spot where she had once buried the flowers with Bao-yu—when all of a sudden she heard the sound of sobbing. She stopped at once and listened. She could not tell whose voice it was, nor could she distinguish what it was that the voice was complaining of, so tearfully and at such length. It really was most puzzling. She moved forward again cautiously and as she turned the corner, saw before her the source of the sobbing, a maid with large eyes and thick-set eyebrows.

Before setting eyes on this girl, Dai-yu had guessed that one of the many maids in the Jia household must have had an unhappy love-affair, and had come here to cry her heart out in secret. But now she laughed at the very idea. "How could such an ungainly creature as this know the meaning of love?" she thought to herself. "This must be one of the odd-job girls, who has probably been scolded by one of the senior maids." She looked more closely, but still could not place the girl. Seeing Dai-yu, the maid ceased her weeping, wiped her cheeks, and rose to her feet.

"Come now, what are you so upset about?" inquired Dai-yu.

"Oh Miss Lin!" replied the maid, amid fresh tears. "Tell me if you think it fair. *They* were talking about it, and how was I to know better? Just because I say one thing wrong, is that a reason for sister to start hitting me?"

Dai-yu did not know what she was talking about. She smiled, and asked again:

"Who is your sister?"

"Pearl," answered the maid.

From this, Dai-yu concluded that she must work in Grandmother Jia's apartment.

"And what is your name?"

"Simple."

Dai-yu laughed. Then:

"Why did she hit you? What did you say that was so wrong?"

"That's what I'd like to know! It was only to do with Master Bao marrying Miss Chai!"

The words struck Dai-yu's ears like a clap of thunder. Her heart started thumping fiercely. She tried to calm herself for a moment, and told the maid to come with her. The maid followed her to the secluded corner of the garden, where the Flower Burial Mound was situated. Here Dai-yu asked her:

"Why should she hit you for mentioning Master Bao's marriage to Miss Chai?"

"Her Old Ladyship, Her Ladyship and Mrs. Lian," replied Simple, "have decided that as the Master is leaving soon, they are going to arrange with Mrs. Xue to marry Master Bao and Miss Chai as quickly as possible. They want the wedding to turn his luck, and then . . ."

Her voice tailed off. She stared at Dai-yu, laughed and continued:

"Then, as soon as those two are married, they are going to find a husband for you, Miss Lin."

Dai-yu was speechless with horror. The maid went on regardless:

"But how was I to know that they'd decided to keep it quiet, for fear of embarrassing Miss Chai? All I did was say to Aroma, that serves in Master Bao's room: 'Won't it be a fine to-do here soon, when Miss Chai comes over, or Mrs. Bao . . . what *will* we have to call her?' That's all I said. What was there in that to hurt sister Pearl? Can *you* see, Miss Lin? She came across and hit me straight in the face and said I was talking rubbish and disobeying orders, and would be dismissed from service! How was I to know their Ladyships didn't want us to mention it? Nobody told me, and she just hit me!"

She started sobbing again. Dai-yu's heart felt as though oil, soy-sauce, sugar and vinegar had all been poured into it at once. She could not tell which flavor predominated, the sweet, the sour, the bitter or the salty. After a few moments' silence, she said in a trembling voice:

"Don't talk such rubbish. Any more of that, and you'll be beaten again. Off you go!"

She herself turned back in the direction of the Naiad's House. Her body felt as though it weighed a hundred tons, her feet were as wobbly as if she were walking on cotton-floss.[1] She could only manage one step at a time. After an age, she still had not reached the bank by Drenched Blossoms Bridge. She was going so slowly, with her feet about to collapse beneath her, and in her giddiness and confusion had wandered off course and increased

---

1. That is, unsteady, as if she were walking on deep fluff.

the distance by about a hundred yards. She reached Drenched Blossoms Bridge only to start drifting back again along the bank in the direction she had just come from, quite unaware of what she was doing.

Nightingale had by now returned with the handkerchief, but could not find Dai-yu anywhere. She finally saw her, pale as snow, tottering along, her eyes staring straight in front of her, meandering in circles. Nightingale also caught sight of a maid disappearing in the distance beyond Dai-yu, but could not make out who it was. She was most bewildered, and quickened her step.

"Why are you turning back again, Miss?" she asked softly. "Where are you heading for?"

Dai-yu only heard the blurred outline of this question. She replied:

"I want to ask Bao-yu something."

Nightingale could not fathom what was going on, and could only try to guide her on her way to Grandmother Jia's apartment. When they came to the entrance, Dai-yu seemed to feel clearer in mind. She turned, saw Nightingale supporting her, stopped for a moment, and asked:

"What are you doing here?"

"I went to fetch your handkerchief," replied Nightingale, smiling anxiously. "I saw you over by the bridge and hurried across. I asked you where you were going, but you took no notice."

"Oh!" said Dai-yu with a smile. "I thought you had come to see Bao-yu. What else did we come here for?"

Nightingale could see that her mind was utterly confused. She guessed that it was something that the maid had said in the garden, and only nodded with a faint smile in reply to Dai-yu's question. But to herself she was trying to imagine what sort of an encounter this was going to be, between the young master who had already lost his wits, and her young mistress who was now herself a little touched. Despite her apprehensions, she dared not prevent the meeting, and helped Dai-yu into the room. The funny thing was that Dai-yu now seemed to have recovered her strength. She did not wait for Nightingale but raised the portière[2] herself, and walked into the room. It was very quiet inside. Grandmother Jia had retired for her afternoon nap. Some of the maids had sneaked off to play, some were having forty winks themselves and others had gone to wait on Grandmother Jia in her bedroom. It was Aroma who came out to see who was there, when she heard the swish of the portière. Seeing that it was Dai-yu, she greeted her politely:

"Please come in and sit down, Miss."

"Is Master Bao at home?" asked Dai-yu with a smile.

Aroma did not know that anything was amiss, and was about to answer, when she saw Nightingale make an urgent movement with her lips from behind Dai-yu's back, pointing to her mistress and making a warning gesture with her hand. Aroma had no idea what she meant and dared not ask. Undeterred, Dai-yu walked on into Bao-yu's room. He was sitting up in bed, and when she came in made no move to get up or welcome her, but remained where he was, staring at her and giving a series of silly laughs. Dai-yu sat down uninvited, and she too began to smile and stare back at Bao-yu. There were no greetings exchanged, no courtesies, in fact no words of any kind. They just sat there staring into each other's faces and smiling like a pair of half-wits. Aroma stood watching, completely at a loss.

2. A curtain covering a doorway.

Suddenly Dai-yu said:

"Bao-yu, why are you sick?"

Bao-yu laughed.

"I'm sick because of Miss Lin."

Aroma and Nightingale grew pale with fright. They tried to change the subject, but their efforts only met with silence and more senseless smiles. By now it was clear to Aroma that Dai-yu's mind was as disturbed as Bao-yu's.

"Miss Lin has only just recovered from her illness," she whispered to Nightingale. "I'll ask Ripple to help you take her back. She should go home and lie down." Turning to Ripple, she said: "Go with Nightingale and accompany Miss Lin home. And no stupid chattering on the way, mind."

Ripple smiled, and without a word came over to help Nightingale. The two of them began to help Dai-yu to her feet. Dai-yu stood up at once, unassisted, still staring fixedly at Bao-yu, smiling and nodding her head.

"Come on, Miss!" urged Nightingale. "It's time to go home and rest."

"Of course!" exclaimed Dai-yu. "It's time!"

She turned to go. Still smiling and refusing any assistance from the maids, she strode out at twice her normal speed. Ripple and Nightingale hurried after her. On leaving Grandmother Jia's apartment, Dai-yu kept on walking, in quite the wrong direction. Nightingale hurried up to her and took her by the hand.

"This is the way, Miss."

Still smiling, Dai-yu allowed herself to be led, and followed Nightingale towards the Naiad's House. When they were nearly there, Nightingale exclaimed:

"Lord Buddha be praised! Home at last!"

She had no sooner uttered these words when she saw Dai-yu stumble forwards onto the ground, and give a loud cry. A stream of blood came gushing from her mouth.

To learn if she survived this crisis, please read the next chapter.

CHAPTER 97

Lin Dai-yu burns her poems
to signal the end of her heart's folly
And Xue Boa-chai leaves home
to take part in a solemn rite

We have seen how Dai-yu, on reaching the entrance of the Naiad's House, and on hearing Nightingale's cry of relief, slumped forward, vomited blood and almost fainted. Luckily Nightingale and Ripple were both at hand to assist her into the house. When Ripple left, Nightingale and Snowgoose stood by Dai-yu's bedside and watched her gradually come round.

"Why are you two standing round me crying?" asked Dai-yu, and Nightingale, greatly reassured to hear her talking sense again, replied:

"On your way back from Her Old Ladyship's, Miss, you had quite a nasty turn. We were scared and did not know what to do. That's why we were crying."

"I am not going to die yet!" said Dai-yu, with a bitter smile. But before she could even finish this sentence, she was doubled up and gasping for breath once more.

When she had learned earlier that day that Bao-yu and Bao-chai were to be married, the shock of knowing that what she had feared for so long was now about to come true, had thrown her into such a turmoil that at first she had quite taken leave of her senses. Now that she had brought up the blood, her mind gradually became clearer. Though at first she could remember nothing, when she saw Nightingale crying, Simple's words slowly came back to her. This time she did not succumb to her emotions, but set her heart instead on a speedy death and final settlement of her debt with fate.

Nightingale and Snowgoose could only stand by helplessly. They would have gone to inform the ladies, but were afraid of a repetition of the last occasion, when Xi-feng had rebuked them for creating a false alarm. Ripple had already given all away, however, by the look of horror on her face when she returned to Grandmother Jia's apartment. The old lady, who had just risen from her midday nap, asked her what the matter was, and in her shocked state Ripple told her all that she had just witnessed.

"What a terrible thing!" exclaimed Grandmother Jia, aghast. She sent for Lady Wang and Xi-feng at once, and told them both the news.

"But I gave instructions to everyone to observe strict secrecy," said Xi-feng. "Who can have betrayed us? Now we have another problem on our hands."

"Never mind that for the moment," said Grandmother Jia. "We must first find out how she is."

She took Lady Wang and Xi-feng with her to visit Dai-yu, and they arrived to find her barely conscious, breathing in faint little gasps, her face bloodless and white as snow. After a while she coughed again. A maid brought the spittoon and they watched with horror as she spat out a mouthful of blood and phlegm. Dai-yu faintly opened her eyes, and seeing Grandmother Jia standing at her bedside, struggled to find breath to speak.

"Grandmother! Your love for me has been in vain."

Grandmother Jia was most distraught.

"There now, my dear, you must rest. There is nothing to fear."

Dai-yu smiled faintly and closed her eyes again. A maid came in to tell Xi-feng that the doctor had arrived. The ladies withdrew, and doctor Wang came in with Jia Lian. He took Dai-yu's pulses, and said:

"As yet, there is no cause for alarm. An obstruction of morbid humours has affected the liver,[3] which is unable to store the blood, and as a consequence her spirit has been disturbed. I shall prescribe a medicine to check the Yin, and to halt the flow of blood. I think all will be well."

Doctor Wang left the room, accompanied by Jia Lian, to write out his prescription.

Grandmother Jia could tell that this time Dai-yu was seriously ill, and as they left the room, she said to Lady Wang and Xi-feng:

"I do not wish to sound gloomy or bring her bad luck, but I fear she has small hope of recovery, poor child. You must make ready her grave-clothes and coffin. Who knows, such preparations may even turn her luck. She may recover, which will be a mercy for us all. But it would be sensible anyway to be prepared for the worst, and not be taken unawares. We shall be so busy over the next few days."

---

3. In Chinese medicine, a negative energy (qi, "morbid humours") has entered the liver and is preventing it from functioning.

Xi-feng said she would make the necessary arrangements. Grandmother Jia then questioned Nightingale, but she had no idea who it was that had upset Dai-yu. The more she thought about it, the more it puzzled Grandmother Jia, and she said to Xi-feng and Lady Wang:

"I can understand that the two of them should have grown rather fond of one another, after growing up together and playing together as children. But now that they are older and more mature, the time has come for them to observe a certain distance. She must behave properly, if she is to earn my love. It's quite wrong of her to think she can disregard such things. Then all my love *will* have been in vain! What you have told me troubles me."

She returned to her apartment and sent for Aroma again. Aroma repeated to her all that she had told Lady Wang on the previous occasion, and in addition described the scene earlier that day between Dai-yu and Bao-yu.

"And yet, when I saw her just now," said Grandmother Jia, "she still seemed able to talk sense. I simply cannot understand it. Ours is a decent family. We do not tolerate unseemly goings-on. And that applies to foolish romantic attachments. If her illness is of a respectable nature, I do not mind how much we have to spend to get her better. But if she is suffering from some form of lovesickness, no amount of medicine will cure it and she can expect no further sympathy from me either."

"You really shouldn't worry about Cousin Lin, Grandmother," said Xi-feng. "Lian will be visiting her regularly with the doctor. We must concentrate on the wedding arrangements. Early this morning I heard that the finishing touches were being put to the bridal courtyard. You and Aunt Wang and I should go over to Aunt Xue's for a final consultation. There is one thing that occurs to me, however: with Bao-chai there, it will be rather awkward for us to discuss the wedding. Maybe we should ask Aunt Xue to come over here tomorrow evening, and then we can settle everything at once."

Grandmother Jia and Lady Wang agreed that her proposal was a good one, and said:

"It is too late today. Tomorrow after lunch, let us all go over together."

Grandmother Jia's dinner was now served, and Xi-feng and Lady Wang returned to their apartments.

Next day, Xi-feng came over after breakfast. Wishing to sound out Bao-yu according to her plan, she advanced into his room and said:

"Congratulations, Cousin Bao! Uncle Zheng has already chosen a lucky day for your wedding! Isn't that good news?"

Bao-yu stared at her with a blank smile, and nodded his head faintly.

"He is marrying you," went on Xi-feng, with a studied smile, "to your cousin Lin. Are you happy?"

Bao-yu burst out laughing. Xi-feng watched him carefully, but could not make out whether he had understood her, or was simply raving. She went on:

"Uncle Zheng says, you are to marry Miss Lin, *if* you get better. But not if you carry on behaving like a half-wit."

Bao-yu's expression suddenly changed to one of utter seriousness, as he said:

"I'm not a half-wit. You're the half-wit."

He stood up.

"I am going to see Cousin Lin, to set her mind at rest."

Xi-feng quickly put out a hand to stop him.

"She knows already. And, as your bride-to-be, she would be much too embarrassed to receive you now."

"What about when we're married? Will she see me then?"

Xi-feng found this both comic and somewhat disturbing.

"Aroma was right," she thought to herself. "Mention Dai-yu, and while he still talks like an idiot, he at least seems to understand what's going on. I can see we shall be in real trouble, if he sees through our scheme and finds out that his bride is not to be Dai-yu after all."

In reply to his question, she said, suppressing a smile:

"If you behave, she will see you. But not if you continue to act like an imbecile."

To which Bao-yu replied:

"I have given my heart to Cousin Lin. If she marries me, she will bring it with her and put it back in its proper place."

Now this was madman's talk if ever, thought Xi-feng. She left him, and walked back into the outer room, glancing with a smile in Grandmother Jia's direction. The old lady too found Bao-yu's words both funny and distressing.

"I heard you both myself," she said to Xi-feng. "For the present, we must ignore it. Tell Aroma to do her best to calm him down. Come, let us go."

Lady Wang joined them, and the three ladies went across to Aunt Xue's. On arrival there, they pretended to be concerned about the course of Xue Pan's affair. Aunt Xue expressed her profound gratitude for this concern, and gave them the latest news. After they had all taken tea, Aunt Xue was about to send for Bao-chai, when Xi-feng stopped her, saying:

"There is no need to tell Cousin Chai that we are here, Auntie."

With a diplomatic smile, she continued:

"Grandmother's visit today is not purely a social one. She has something of importance to say, and would like you to come over later so that we can all discuss it together."

Aunt Xue nodded.

"Of course."

After a little more chat, the three ladies returned.

That evening Aunt Xue came over as arranged, and after paying her respects to Grandmother Jia, went to her sister's apartment. First there was the inevitable scene of sisterly commiseration over Wang Zi-teng's death. Then Aunt Xue said:

"Just now when I was at Lady Jia's, young Bao came out to greet me and seemed quite well. A little thin perhaps, but certainly not as ill as I had been led to expect from your description and Xi-feng's."

"No, it is really not that serious," said Xi-feng. "It's only Grandmother who will worry so. Her idea is that it would be reassuring for Sir Zheng to see Bao-yu married before he leaves, as who knows when he will be able to come home from his new posting. And then from Bao-yu's own point of view, it might be just the thing to turn his luck. With Cousin Chai's golden locket to counteract the evil influence, he should make a good recovery."

Aunt Xue was willing enough to go along with the idea, but was concerned that Bao-chai might feel rather hard done by.

"I see nothing against it," she said. "But I think we should all take time to think it over properly."

In accordance with Xi-feng's plan, Lady Wang went on:

"As you have no head of family present, we should like you to dispense with the usual trousseau. Tomorrow you should send Ke to let Pan know that while we proceed with the wedding, we shall continue to do our utmost to settle his court-case."

She made no mention of Bao-yu's feelings for Dai-yu, but continued:

"Since you have given your consent, the sooner they are married, the sooner things will look up for everyone."

At this point, Faithful came in to take back a report to Grandmother Jia. Though Aunt Xue was still concerned about Bao-chai's feelings, she saw that in the circumstances she had no choice, and agreed to everything they had suggested. Faithful reported this to Grandmother Jia, who was delighted and sent her back again to ask Mrs. Xue to explain to Bao-chai why it was that things were being done in this way, so that she would not feel unfairly treated. Aunt Xue agreed to do this, and it was settled that Xi-feng and Jia Lian would act as official go-betweens. Xi-feng retired to her apartment, while Aunt Xue and Lady Wang stayed up talking together well into the night.

Next day, Aunt Xue returned to her apartment and told Bao-chai the details of the proposal, adding:

"I have already given my consent."

At first Bao-chai hung her head in silence. Then she began to cry. Aunt Xue said all that she could to comfort her, and went to great lengths to explain the reasoning behind the decision. Bao-chai retired to her room, and Bao-qin went in to keep her company and cheer her up. Aunt Xue also spoke to Ke, instructing him as follows:

"You must leave tomorrow. Find out the latest news of Pan's judgement, and then convey this message to him. Return as soon as you possibly can."

Xue Ke was away for four days, at the end of which time he returned to report to Aunt Xue.

"The Circuit Judge has ratified the verdict of manslaughter, and after the next hearing his final memorial will be presented to the Provincial Supreme Court for confirmation. We should have the commutation money ready. As for Cousin Chai's affair, Cousin Pan approves entirely of your decision, Aunt. And he says that curtailing the formalities will save us a lot of money too. You are not to wait for him, but should do whatever you think best."

Aunt Xue's mind was greatly eased by the knowledge that Xue Pan would soon be free to come home, and that there were now no further obstacles to the marriage. She could see that Bao-chai was unwilling to be married in this way, but reasoned with herself: "Even if this is not what she ideally wants, she is my daughter and has always been obedient and well-bred. She knows I have agreed to it, and will not go against my wishes."

She instructed Xue Ke:

"We must prepare the betrothal-card. Take some fine gold-splash paper and write on it the Stems and Branches of Bao-chai's birth. Then take it to Cousin Lian. Find out which day has been fixed for the exchange of presents and make all the necessary preparations for sending ours.[4] We shall not be

---

4. One system for naming days and years was a sixty-unit sequence formed by combining two sequences, the "ten heavenly stems" and the "twelve earthly branches." This was particularly important in Chinese fortune-telling, permitting one to decide which days were lucky. By comparing the birthdays of Bao-yu and Bao-chai, given in terms of *Stems and Branches*, the proper day for the *exchange of presents* between families, an essential part of the wedding ceremony, could be determined. *Gold-splash paper:* a gilded notepaper, appropriate for formal cards.

inviting any friends or relatives to the wedding. Pan's friends are a worthless lot, as you yourself said, while our relations consist mainly of the Jias and the Wangs. The Jias are groom's family, and there are no Wangs in the capital at present. When Xiang-yun was engaged, the Shis did not invite us, so we need not get in touch with them. The only person I think we should invite is our business manager, Zhang De-hui. He is an older man and experienced in such things, and will be a help to us."

Xue Ke carried out these instructions, and sent a servant over with the betrothal-card. Next day, Jia Lian came to visit Aunt Xue. After paying his respects, he said:

"I have consulted the almanac, and tomorrow is a most propitious day. I have come here today to propose that our two families exchange presents tomorrow. And please, Aunt Xue, do not be too critical about the arrangements."

He presented the groom's notice, which bore the date of the wedding. Aunt Xue said a few polite words of acceptance and nodded her assent. Jia Lian returned at once and reported to Jia Zheng.

"Report to your Grandmother," said Jia Zheng, "and say that as we are not inviting anybody, the wedding should be kept very simple. She can exercise her discretion over the presents. There is no need to consult me any further."

Jia Lian bowed, and went in to convey this message to Grandmother Jia. Meanwhile Lady Wang had told Xi-feng to bring in the presents that were being given on Bao-yu's behalf, for Grandmother Jia's inspection. She also told Aroma to bring Bao-yu in to see them. He seemed highly amused by the whole business, and said:

"It seems such a waste of everyone's time, to send all these things from here to the Garden, and then have them brought all the way back, when it's all in the family anyway!"

This seemed to Lady Wang and Grandmother Jia sufficient proof that, whatever anyone might have said to the contrary, Bao-yu still had his wits about him, and they said as much to each other in tones of some satisfaction. Faithful and the other maids could not help but smile too. They brought the presents in and displayed them one by one, describing them as they went along:

"A gold necklace and other jewellery in gold and precious stones—altogether eighty pieces; forty bolts of dragon-brocade[5] for formal wear and one hundred and twenty bolts of silks and satins in various colors; one hundred and twenty costumes for the four seasons of the year. They have not had time in the kitchen to prepare the sheep and wine, so this is money in lieu."

Grandmother Jia expressed her approval, and said softly to Xi-feng:

"You must tell Mrs. Xue not to think of this as an empty formality. In due course, when Pan is back and she has that weight off her mind, she can have these made up into dresses for Chai. In the meantime, we shall take care of all the bedcovers for the wedding-day."

"Yes Grandmother," replied Xi-feng, and returned to her apartment. She sent Jia Lian over first to Aunt Xue's, then summoned Zhou Rui and Brightie to receive their instructions.

---

5. A brocade woven with figures of dragons, appropriate for formal gowns for men.

"When delivering the presents," she said, "you are not to use the main gate. Use the little side-gate in the garden, that used to be kept open. I shall be going over myself shortly. The side-gate has the advantage of being a long way from the Naiad's House. If anyone from any other apartment notices you, you are to tell them on no account to mention it at the Naiad's House."

"Yes ma'am."

The two men departed for Aunt Xue's apartment at the head of a contingent of servants bearing the presents.

Bao-yu was quite taken in by all this. His new feeling of happy anticipation had caused a general improvement in his health, though his manner of speech remained rather eccentric at times. When the present-bearers returned, the whole thing was accomplished without a single name being mentioned. The family and all the staff knew, but were under orders from Xi-feng to maintain absolute secrecy, and no one dared disobey.

Dai-yu meanwhile, for all the medicine she took, continued to grow iller with every day that passed. Nightingale did her utmost to raise her spirits. Our story finds her standing once more by Dai-yu's bedside, earnestly beseeching her:

"Miss, now that things have come to this pass, I simply must speak my mind. We know what it is that's eating your heart out. But can't you see that your fears are groundless? Why, look at the state Bao-yu is in! How can he possibly get married, when he's so ill? You must ignore these silly rumours, stop fretting and let yourself get better."

Dai-yu gave a wraithlike smile, but said nothing. She started coughing again and brought up a lot more blood. Nightingale and Snowgoose came closer and watched her feebly struggling for breath. They knew that any further attempt to rally her would be to no avail, and could do nothing but stand there watching and weeping. Each day Nightingale went over three or four times to tell Grandmother Jia, but Faithful, judging the old lady's attitude towards Dai-yu to have hardened of late, intercepted her reports and hardly mentioned Dai-yu to her mistress. Grandmother Jia was preoccupied with the wedding arrangements, and in the absence of any particular news of Dai-yu, did not show a great deal of interest in the girl's fate, considering it sufficient that she should be receiving medical attention.

Previously, when she had been ill, Dai-yu had always received frequent visits from everyone in the household, from Grandmother Jia down to the humblest maidservant. But now not a single person came to see her. The only face she saw looking down at her was that of Nightingale. She began to feel her end drawing near, and struggled to say a few words to her:

"Dear Nightingale! Dear sister! Closest friend! Though you were Grandmother's maid before you came to serve me, over the years you have become as a sister to me . . ."

She had to stop for breath. Nightingale felt a pang of pity, was reduced to tears and could say nothing. After a long silence, Dai-yu began to speak again, searching for breath between words:

"Dear sister! I am so uncomfortable lying down like this. Please help me up and sit next to me."

"I don't think you should sit up, Miss, in your condition. You might get cold in the draught."

Dai-yu closed her eyes in silence. A little later she asked to sit up again.

Nightingale and Snowgoose felt they could no longer deny her request. They propped her up on both sides with soft pillows, while Nightingale sat by her on the bed to give further support. Dai-yu was not equal to the effort. The bed where she sat on it seemed to dig into her, and she struggled with all her remaining strength to lift herself up and ease the pain. She told Snowgoose to come closer.

"My poems . . ."

Her voice failed, and she fought for breath again. Snowgoose guessed that she meant the manuscripts she had been revising a few days previously, went to fetch them and laid them on Dai-yu's lap. Dai-yu nodded, then raised her eyes and gazed in the direction of a chest that stood on a stand close by. Snowgoose did not know how to interpret this and stood there at a loss. Dai-yu stared at her now with feverish impatience. She began to cough again and brought up another mouthful of blood. Snowgoose went to fetch some water, and Dai-yu rinsed her mouth and spat into the spittoon. Nightingale wiped her lips with a handkerchief. Dai-yu took the handkerchief from her and pointed to the chest. She tried to speak, but was again seized with an attack of breathlessness and closed her eyes.

"Lie down, Miss," said Nightingale. Dai-yu shook her head. Nightingale thought she must want one of her handkerchiefs, and told Snowgoose to open the chest and bring her a plain white silk one. Dai-yu looked at it, and dropped it on the bed. Making a supreme effort, she gasped out:

"The ones with the writing on . . ."

Nightingale finally realized that she meant the handkerchiefs Bao-yu had sent her, the ones she had inscribed with her own poems. She told Snowgoose to fetch them, and herself handed them to Dai-yu, with these words of advice:

"You must lie down and rest, Miss. Don't start wearing yourself out. You can look at these another time, when you are feeling better."

Dai-yu took the handkerchiefs in one hand and without even looking at them, brought round her other hand (which cost her a great effort) and tried with all her might to tear them in two. But she was so weak that all she could achieve was a pathetic trembling motion. Nightingale knew that Bao-yu was the object of all this bitterness but dared not mention his name, saying instead:

"Miss, there is no sense in working yourself up again."

Dai-yu nodded faintly, and slipped the handkerchiefs into her sleeve.

"Light the lamp," she ordered.

Snowgoose promptly obeyed. Dai-yu looked into the lamp, then closed her eyes and sat in silence. Another fit of breathlessness. Then:

"Make up the fire in the brazier."

Thinking she wanted it for the extra warmth, Nightingale protested:

"You should lie down, Miss, and have another cover on. And the fumes from the brazier might be bad for you."

Dai-yu shook her head, and Snowgoose reluctantly made up the brazier, placing it on its stand on the floor. Dai-yu made a motion with her hand, indicating that she wanted it moved up onto the kang. Snowgoose lifted it and placed it there, temporarily using the floor-stand, while she went out to fetch the special stand they used on the kang. Dai-yu, far from resting back in the warmth, now inclined her body slightly forward—Nightingale had to support her with both hands as she did so. Dai-yu took the handkerchiefs in one hand. Staring into the flames and nodding thoughtfully to herself, she dropped them into the brazier. Nightingale was horrified, but much as she would have liked to snatch them from the flames, she did not dare move her hands and leave Dai-yu unsupported. Snowgoose was out of the room, fetching the brazier-stand, and by now the handkerchiefs were all ablaze.

"Miss!" cried Nightingale. "What are you doing?"

As if she had not heard, Dai-yu reached over for her manuscripts, glanced at them and let them fall again onto the kang. Nightingale, anxious lest she burn these too, leaned up against Dai-yu and freeing one hand, reached out with it to take hold of them. But before she could do so, Dai-yu had picked them up again and dropped them in the flames. The brazier was out of Nightingale's reach, and there was nothing she could do but look on helplessly.

Just at that moment Snowgoose came in with the stand. She saw Dai-yu drop something into the fire, and without knowing what it was, rushed forward to try and save it. The manuscripts had caught at once and were already ablaze. Heedless of the danger to her hands, Snowgoose reached into the flames and pulled out what she could, throwing the paper on the floor and stamping frantically on it. But the fire had done its work, and only a few charred fragments remained.

Dai-yu closed her eyes and slumped back, almost causing Nightingale to topple over with her. Nightingale, her heart thumping in great agitation, called Snowgoose over to help her settle Dai-yu down again. It was too late now to send for anyone. And yet, what if Dai-yu should die during the night, and the only people there were Snowgoose, herself and the one or two other junior maids in the Naiad's House? They passed a restless night. Morning came at last, and Dai-yu seemed a little more comfortable. But after breakfast she suddenly began coughing and vomiting, and became tense and feverish again. Nightingale could see that she had reached a crisis. She called Snowgoose and the other juniors in and told them to mount watch, while she went to report to Grandmother Jia. But when she reached Grandmother Jia's apartment, she found it almost deserted. Only a few old nannies and charladies were there, keeping an eye.

"Where is Her Old Ladyship?" asked Nightingale.

"We don't know," came the reply in chorus.

That was very odd, thought Nightingale. She went into Bao-yu's room and found that too quite empty, save for a single maid who answered with the same "Don't know." By now Nightingale had more or less guessed the truth. How could they be so heartless and so cruel? And to think that not a soul had come to visit Dai-yu during the past few days! As the bitterness of it struck her with full force, she felt a great wave of resentment break out within her, and turned abruptly to go.

"I shall go and find Bao-yu, and see how *he* is faring! I wonder how he will manage to brazen it out in front of me! I remember last year, when I made up that story about Miss Lin going back to the South, he fell sick with despair. To think that now he should be openly doing a thing like this! Men must have hearts as cold as ice or snow. What hateful creatures they are!"

She was already at Green Delights, and found the courtyard gate ajar. All was quiet within. Suddenly she realized:

"Of course! If he is getting married, he will have a new apartment. But where?"

She was looking around her in uncertainty, when she saw Bao-yu's page boy Inky rush past, and called to him to stop. He came over, and with a broad smile asked:

"What are you doing here, Miss Nightingale?"

"I heard that Master Bao was getting married," replied Nightingale, "and I wanted to watch some of the fun. But I can see I've come to the wrong place. And I don't know when the wedding is taking place, either."

"If I tell you," said Inky in a confidential tone, "you must promise not to tell Snowgoose. We've been given orders not to let any of you know. The wedding's to be tonight. Of course it's not being held here. The Master told Mr. Lian to set aside another apartment."

"What's the matter?" continued Inky, after a pause.

"Nothing," replied Nightingale. "You can go now."

Inky rushed off again. Nightingale stood there for a while, lost in thought. Suddenly she remembered Dai-yu. She might already be dead! Her eyes filled with tears, and clenching her teeth, she said fiercely:

"Bao-yu! If she dies, you may think you can wash your hands of her in this callous way: but when you are happily married, and have your heart's desire, you needn't think you can look *me* in the face again."

As she walked, she began to weep. She made her way, sobbing pitifully, across the Garden. She was not far from the Naiad's House, when she saw two junior maids standing at the gate, peeping out nervously. They saw her coming, and one of them cried out:

"There's Miss Nightingale! At last!"

Nightingale could see that all was not well. Gesturing to them anxiously to be silent, she hurried in, to find Dai-yu red in the face, the fire from her liver having risen upwards and inflamed her cheeks. This was a dangerous sign, and Nightingale called Dai-yu's old wet-nurse, Nannie Wang, to come and take a look. One glance was enough to reduce this old woman to tears. Nightingale had turned to Nannie Wang as an older person, who could be expected to lend them some courage in this extremity. But she turned out to be quite helpless, and only made Nightingale more distraught than before. Suddenly she thought of someone else she could turn to, and sent one of the younger maids to fetch her with all speed. Her choice might seem a strange one; but Nightingale reasoned that as a widow, Li Wan would certainly be excluded from Bao-yu's wedding festivities. Besides she was in general charge of affairs in the Garden, and it would be in order to ask her to come.

Li Wan was at home correcting some of Jia Lan's poems, when the maid came rushing frantically in and cried:

"Mrs. Zhu! Miss Lin's dying! Everyone over there is in tears!"

Li Wan rose startled to her feet and without a word set off at once for the Naiad's House, followed by her maids Candida and Casta. As she walked, she wept and lamented to herself:

"When I think of all the times we have spent together—oh my poor cousin! So lovely, so gifted! There is hardly another like her. Only Frost Maiden and the Goddess of the Moon could rival her. How can she be leaving us at such a tender age, for that distant land from whence no travelers return. . . . And to think that because of Xi-feng's deceitful scheme, I have not been able to show myself at the Naiad's House and have done nothing to show my sisterly affection! Oh the poor, dear girl!"

She was already at the gate of the Naiad's House. There was no sound from within. She began to fret.

"I must be too late! She must have died already and they are resting between their lamentations, I wonder if her grave-clothes and coverlet are ready?"

She quickened her step and hurried on into the room. A young maid standing at the inner doorway had already seen her, and called out:

"Mrs. Zhu is here!"

Nightingale hurried out to meet her.

"How is she?" asked Li Wan.

Nightingale tried to answer but all she could muster was a choked sob. Tears poured down her cheeks like pearls from a broken necklace, as she pointed silently to where Dai-yu lay. Realizing with a pang what Nightingale's pitiable condition must portend, Li Wan asked no more, but went over at once to see for herself. Dai-yu no longer had the strength to speak. When Li Wan said her name a few times, her eyes opened a slit as if in recognition of the voice. But her eyelids and lips could only make a trembling suggestion of a movement. Although she still breathed, it was now more than she could manage to utter a single word, or shed a single tear.

Li Wan turned around and saw that Nightingale was no longer in the room. She asked Snowgoose where she was, and Snowgoose replied:

"In the outer room."

Li Wan hurried out, to find Nightingale lying on the empty bed, her face a ghastly green, her eyes closed, tears streaming down her cheeks. Where her head lay on the embroidered pillow, with its border of fine brocade, was a patch the size of a small plate, wet with her tears and the copious effusions of her nose. When Li Wan called to her, she opened her eyes slowly, and raised herself slightly on the bed.

"Silly girl!" Li Wan upbraided her. "Is this a time for tears? Fetch Miss Lin's grave-clothes and dress her in them. Are you going to leave it till it is too late? Would you have her go naked from the world? Would you ruin her honor?"

This released a fresh flood of tears on Nightingale's part. Li Wan wept herself, fretfully wiping her eyes and patting Nightingale on the shoulder.

"Dear girl! Look how you are upsetting me now, and making me cry. Hurry and get her things ready. If we delay much longer, it will all be over."

They were in this state of trepidation, when they heard footsteps outside, and someone came running into the room in a great flurry, causing Li Wan to start back in alarm. It was Patience. When she saw their tear-stained faces, she stopped abruptly and stared at them aghast for a while.

"Why aren't you over there?" asked Li Wan. "What do you want here?"

As she spoke, Steward Lin's wife also came into the room. Patience answered:

"Mrs. Lian was worried, and sent me to see how things were. As you are here, Mrs. Zhu, I can tell her to set her mind at rest."

Li Wan nodded. Patience went on:

"I should like to see Miss Lin myself." So saying, she walked into Dai-yu's bed-chamber, with tears on her cheeks. Li Wan turned to Steward Lin's wife and said:

"You have come just in time. Go and find your husband, and tell him to prepare Miss Lin's coffin and whatever else is necessary. When everything has been satisfactorily arranged, he is to let me know. There is no need to go over to the house."

"Yes, ma'am," replied Lin's wife, but made no move to go.

"Well? Is there something else?" asked Li Wan.

"Mrs. Lian and Her Old Ladyship," replied the steward's wife, "have decided that they need Miss Nightingale in attendance over there."

Before Li Wan could say anything, Nightingale spoke up for herself:

"Mrs. Lin, will you be so kind as to leave now? Can't you even wait until she is dead? We will leave her then, you need not fear. How can you be so . . ."

She stopped short, thinking it inadvisable to be so rude, and changing her tone somewhat, said:

"Besides, after waiting on a sick person, I fear we would not be fit for such an occasion. And while Miss Lin is still alive, she may ask for me at any time."

Li Wan tried to make the peace between them.

"The truth is," she said, "that this maid and Miss Lin have an affinity from a past life. Snowgoose, I know, was Miss Lin's original maid from home, but even she is not so indispensable as Nightingale. We really cannot separate them just now."

Lin's wife, who had been considerably put out by Nightingale's outspoken response, was obliged to contain herself when Li Wan came to the maid's defence. Seeing Nightingale reduced to floods of tears, she eyed her with a hostile smile and said:

"I shall ignore Miss Nightingale's rudeness. But am I to report what you have just said to Her Old Ladyship? And am I to tell Mrs. Lian?"

As she was speaking, Patience came out of Dai-yu's bedchamber, wiping her eyes.

"Tell Mrs. Lian what?" she asked.

Lin's wife told her the substance of their conversation. Patience lowered her head in thought. After a moment, she said:

"Why can't you take Snowgoose?"

"Would she do?" asked Li Wan. Patience went up to her and whispered a few words in her ear. Li Wan nodded, and said:

"Well in that case, it will be just as good if we send Snowgoose."

"Will Miss Snowgoose do?" Lin's wife asked Patience.

"Yes," replied Patience. "She will do just as well."

"Then will you please tell her to come with me straight away," said Lin's wife. "I shall report to Her Old Ladyship and Mrs. Lian. I shall say that you are both responsible for the arrangement, mind. And later you can tell Mrs. Lian yourself, Miss Patience."

"Of course," replied Li Wan curtly. "Do you mean to say that someone as old and experienced as you cannot even take the responsibility for a small thing like this?"

Lin's wife smiled.

"It is not that I can't take the responsibility. It is just that Her Old Ladyship and Mrs. Lian have arranged everything and the likes of us don't really know what's going on. In the circumstances, it seems only right to mention you and Miss Patience."

Patience had already told Snowgoose to come out. Over the past few days Snowgoose had fallen rather into disfavor with Dai-yu, who had called her a "silly, ignorant child," and her feelings of loyalty towards her mistress had as a consequence been rather blunted. Besides there was no question of her disobeying an order from Her Old Ladyship and Mrs. Lian. She therefore tidied her hair quickly and made ready to go. Patience told her to change into her smartest clothes and to go with Mrs. Lin. Patience herself stayed on and spoke for a short while with Li Wan. Before she left, Li Wan instructed her to call in on Lin's wife on her way and tell her that her husband should make the necessary preparations for Dai-yu with all possible speed. This Patience agreed to do and went on her way. As she turned a corner in the Garden, she caught sight of Lin's wife walking ahead of her with Snowgoose and called to her to wait.

"I will take Snowgoose with me. You go and tell your husband to prepare Miss Lin's things. I will report to Mrs. Lian for you."

"Yes, Miss Patience," said Lin's wife, and went on her errand.

Patience then took Snowgoose to the bridal apartment, and reported there herself before going to see to her own affairs.

When Snowgoose saw the wedding preparations in full swing and thought of Dai-yu lying at death's door, she felt a pang of grief. But she dared not show her feelings in the presence of Grandmother Jia and Xi-feng. "What can they want me for?" she wondered. "I must see what is going on. I know Bao-yu used to be head over heels in love with Miss Lin. And yet now he seems to have deserted her. I begin to wonder if this illness of his is genuine or just a pretence. He may have made the whole thing up so as to avoid upsetting Miss Lin. By pretending to lose his jade and acting like an idiot, perhaps he thinks he can put her off, and marry Miss Chai with a clear conscience? I must watch him closely, and see if he acts the fool when he sees me. Surely he won't keep up the pretence on his wedding-day?" She slipped in and stood spying at the inner doorway.

Now, though Bao-yu's mind was still clouded from the loss of his jade, his sense of joy at the prospect of marrying Dai-yu—in his eyes the most blessed, the most wonderful thing that had happened in heaven or earth since time began—had caused a temporary resurgence of physical well-being, if not a full restoration of his mental faculties. Xi-feng's ingenious plan had had exactly the intended effect, and he was now counting the minutes till he should see Dai-yu. Today was the day when all his dreams were to come true, and he was filled with a feeling of ecstasy. He still occasionally let slip some tell-tale imbecile remark, but in other respects gave the appearance of having completely recovered. All this Snowgoose observed, and was filled with hatred for him and grief for her mistress. She knew nothing of the true cause of his joy.

While Snowgoose slipped away unobserved, Bao-yu told Aroma to hurry and dress him in his bridegroom's finery. He sat in Lady Wang's chamber, watching Xi-feng and You-shi bustling about their preparations, himself bursting with impatience for the great moment.

"If Cousin Lin is coming from the Garden," he asked Aroma, "why all this fuss? Why isn't she here yet?"

Suppressing a smile, Aroma replied:

"She has to wait for the propitious moment."

Xi-feng turned to Lady Wang and said:

"Because we are in mourning, we cannot have music in the street. But the traditional ceremony would seem so drab without any music at all, so I have told some of the women-servants with a bit of musical knowledge, the ones who used to look after the actresses, to come and play a little, to add a bit of festive touch."

Lady Wang nodded, and said she thought this a good idea. Presently the great bridal palanquin was born in through the main gate. The little ensemble of women-servants played, as it entered down an avenue of twelve pairs of palace-lanterns, creating a passably stylish impression. The Master of Ceremonies requested the bride to step out of her palanquin, and Bao-yu saw the Matron of Honour, all in red, lead out his bride, her face concealed by the bridal veil. There was a maid in attendance, and Bao-yu saw to his surprise that it was Snowgoose. This puzzled him for a moment.

"Why Snowgoose, and not Nightingale?" he asked himself. Then: "Of course. Snowgoose is Dai-yu's original maid from the South, whereas Nightingale was one of our maids, which would never do."

And so, when he saw Snowgoose, it was as if he had seen the face of Dai-yu herself beneath the veil.

The Master of Ceremonies chanted the liturgy, and the bride and groom knelt before Heaven and Earth. Grandmother Jia was called forth to receive their obeisances, as were Sir Zheng, Lady Wang and other elders of the family, after which they escorted the couple into the hall and thence to the bridal chamber. Here they were made to sit on the bridal bed, were showered with dried fruit and subjected to the various other practices customary in old Nanking families such as the Jias, which we need not describe in detail here.

Jia Zheng, it will be remembered, had gone along with the plan grudgingly, in deference to Grandmother Jia's wishes, retaining grave though unspoken doubts himself as to her theory of "turning Bao-yu's luck." But today, seeing Bao-yu bear himself with a semblance of dignity, he could not help but be pleased.

The bride was now sitting alone on the bridal bed, and the moment had come for the groom to remove her veil. Xi-feng had made her preparations for this event, and now asked Grandmother Jia, Lady Wang and others of the ladies present to step forward into the bridal chamber to assist her. The sense of climax seemed to cause Bao-yu to revert somewhat to his imbecile ways, for as he approached his bride he said:

"Are you better now, coz? It's such a long time since we last saw each other. What do you want to go wrapping yourself up in that silly thing for?"

He was about to raise the veil. Grandmother Jia broke into a cold sweat. But he hesitated, thinking to himself:

"I know how sensitive Cousin Lin is. I must be very careful not to offend her."

He waited a little longer. But soon the suspense became unbearable, and he walked up to her and lifted the veil. The Matron of Honour took it from him, while Snowgoose melted into the background and Oriole came forward to take her place. Bao-yu stared at his bride. Surely this was Bao-chai? Incredulous, with one hand holding the lantern, he rubbed his eyes with the other and looked again. It *was* Bao-chai. How pretty she looked, in her wedding-gown! He gazed at her soft skin, the full curve of her shoulders, and her hair done up in tresses that hung from her temples! Her eyes were moist, her lips quivered slightly. Her whole appearance had the simple elegance of a white lily, wet with pendant dew; the maidenly blush on her cheeks resembled apricot-blossom wreathed in mist. For a moment he stared at her in utter astonishment. Then he noticed that Oriole was standing at her side, while Snowgoose had quite vanished. A feeling of helpless bewilderment seized him, and thinking he must be dreaming, he stood there in a motionless daze. The maids took the lamp from him and helped him to a chair, where he sat with his eyes fixed in front of him, still without uttering a single word. Grandmother Jia was anxious lest this might signal the approach of another of his fits, and herself came over to rally him, while Xi-feng and You-shi escorted Bao-chai to a chair in the inner part of the room. Bao-chai held her head bowed and said nothing.

After a while, Bao-yu had composed himself sufficiently to think. He saw Grandmother Jia and Lady Wang sitting opposite him, and asked Aroma in a whisper:

"Where am I? This must all be a dream."

"A dream? Why, it's the happiest day of your life!" said Aroma. "How can you be so silly? Take care: Sir Zheng is outside."

Pointing now to where Bao-chai sat, and still whispering, Bao-yu asked again:

"Who is that beautiful lady sitting over there?"

Aroma found this so comical that for a while she could say nothing, but held her hand to her face to conceal her mirth. Finally she replied:

"That is your bride, the new Mrs. Bao-yu."

The other maids also turned away, unable to contain their laughter.

Bao-yu: "Don't be so silly! What do you mean, 'Mrs. Bao-yu?' Who *is* Mrs. Bao-yu?"

Aroma: "Miss Chai."

Bao-yu: "But what about Miss Lin?"

Aroma: "The Master decided you should marry Miss Chai. What's Miss Lin got to do with it?"

Bao-yu: "But I saw her just a moment ago, and Snowgoose too. They couldn't have just vanished! What sort of trick is this that you're all playing on me?"

Xi-feng came up and whispered in his ear:

"Miss Chai is sitting over there, so please stop talking like this. If you offend her, Grannie will be very cross with you."

Bao-yu was now more hopelessly confused than ever. The mysterious goings-on of that night, coming on top of his already precarious mental state, had wrought him up to such a pitch of despair that all he could do was cry—"I must find Cousin Lin!"—again and again. Grandmother Jia and the other ladies tried to comfort him but he was impervious to their efforts. Furthermore, with Bao-chai in the room, they had to be careful what they said. Bao-yu was clearly suffering from a severe relapse, and they now abandoned their attempts to rally him and instead helped him to bed, while ordering several sticks of gum benzoin incense to be lit, the heavy, sedative fumes of which soon filled the room. They all stood in awesome hush. After a short while, the incense began to take effect and Bao-yu sank into a heavy slumber, much to the relief of the ladies, who sat down again to await the dawn. Grandmother Jia told Xi-feng to ask Bao-chai to lie down and rest, which she did, fully dressed as she was, behaving as though she had heard nothing.

Jia Zheng had remained in an outer room during all of this, and so had seen nothing to disillusion him of the reassuring impression he had received earlier on. The following day, as it happened, was the day selected according to the almanac for his departure to his new post. After a short rest, he took formal leave of the festivities and returned to his apartment. Grandmother Jia, too, left Bao-yu sound asleep and returned to her apartment for a brief rest.

The next morning, Jia Zheng took leave of the ancestors in the family shrine and came to bid his mother farewell. He bowed before her and said:

"I, your unworthy son, am about to depart for afar. My only wish is that you should keep warm in the cold weather and take good care of yourself. As soon as I arrive at my post, I shall write to ask how you are. You are not to worry on my account. Bao-yu's marriage has now been celebrated in accordance with your wishes, and it only remains for me to beg you to instruct him, and impart to him the wisdom of your years."

Grandmother Jia, for fear that Jia Zheng would worry on his journey, made no mention of Bao-yu's relapse but merely said:

"There is one thing I should tell you. Although the rites were performed last night, Bao-yu's marriage was not properly consummated. His health would not allow it. Custom, I know, decrees that he should see you off today. But in view of all the circumstances, his earlier illness, the luck turning, his still fragile state of convalescence and yesterday's exertions, I am worried that by going out he might catch a chill. So I put it to you: if you wish him to fulfil his filial obligations by seeing you off, then send for him at once and instruct him accordingly; but if you love him, then spare him and let him say goodbye and make his kotow to you here."

"Why should I want him to see me off?" returned Jia Zheng. "All I want is that from now on he should study in earnest. That would bring me greater pleasure by far."

Grandmother Jia was most relieved to hear this. She told Jia Zheng to be seated and sent Faithful, after imparting to her various secret instructions, to fetch Bao-yu and to bring Aroma with him. Faithful had not been away many minutes, when Bao-yu came in and with the usual promptings, performed his duty to his father. Luckily the sight of his father brought him, for a few moments, sufficient clarity to get through the formalities without any gross lapses. Jia Zheng delivered himself of a few exhortatory words, to all of which his son gave the correct replies. Then Jia Zheng told Aroma to escort him back to his room, while he himself went to Lady Wang's apartment. There he earnestly enjoined Lady Wang to take charge of Bao-yu's moral welfare during his absence.

"There must be none of his previous unruliness," he added. "He must now prepare himself to enter for next year's provincial examination."

Lady Wang assured him that she would do her utmost, and without mentioning anything else, at once sent a maid to escort Bao-chai into the room. Bao-chai performed the rite proper to a newly-married bride seeing off her father-in-law, and then remained in the room when Jia Zheng left. The other women-folk accompanied him as far as the inner gate before turning back. Cousin Zhen and the other young male Jias received a few words of exhortation, drank a farewell toast, and, together with a crowd of other friends and relatives, accompanied him as far as the Hostelry of the Tearful Parting, some three or four miles beyond the city walls, where they bid their final farewell.

But of Jia Zheng's departure no more. Let us return to Bao-yu, who on leaving his father, had suffered an immediate relapse. His mind became more and more clouded, and he could swallow neither food nor drink. Whether or not he was to emerge from this crisis alive will be revealed in the next chapter.

Chapters 98 to 120 Summary   Many Chinese readers have profoundly disliked the last 40 chapters of the 120-chapter novel, written by a different hand. In the first 80 chapters, there are no solutions and no conclusions; the last 40 chapters try to resolve the various narrative lines set in motion, including the marriage of Bao-yu and Bao-chai. After his marriage, Bao-yu does his duty to the family by passing the examination, then renounces the world, following the Buddhist monk and the Taoist. In perhaps the best scene in the last chapters, Bao-yu appears one more time, dressed in red amid the snow, to take his final leave of his father, then vanishes forever. Stone has learned his lesson about the human world.

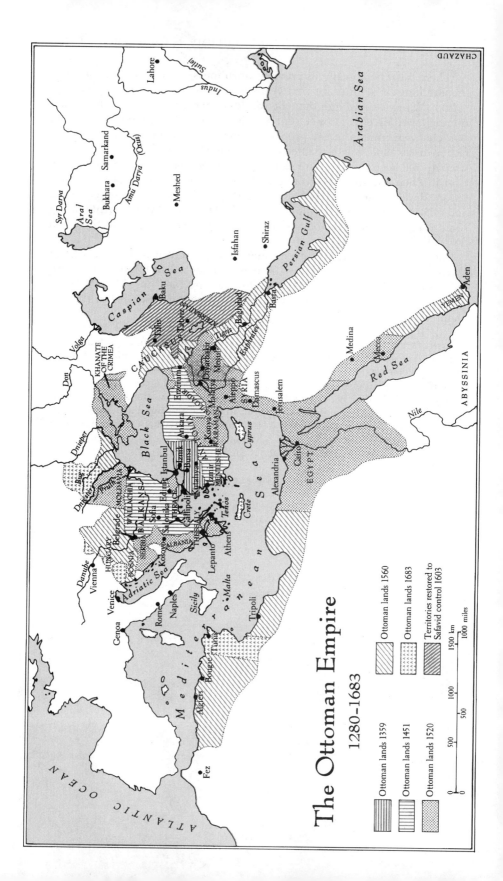

The Ottoman Empire
1280–1683

Ottoman lands 1359

Ottoman lands 1451

Ottoman lands 1520

Ottoman lands 1560

Ottoman lands 1683

Territories restored to
Safavid control 1603

0   500   1000   1500 km
0   500   1000 miles

The Ottoman Empire: Çelebi's *Book of Travels*

EVLIYA ÇELEBI
1611–1684

On the tenth night of the Muslim month of Muharram in the year 1040 of the Prophet's flight to Madina (August 19, 1630) and the twentieth year of his life, Evliya Çelebi had a dream in which the Prophet Muhammad appeared to him and encouraged him to pursue the life of a wanderer. The dream occurred at an opportune moment for the young Evliya. His family wished him to choose the settled life of an official in the imperial Ottoman administration at Istanbul, but his own inclination was to follow his wanderlust. The Prophet's encouragement both strengthened his resolve and silenced his family's objections, and for the next forty-odd years he journeyed throughout the Ottoman empire. Sometimes he traveled in the retinue of a high officer of the state (*pasha*), sometimes he went as an official himself, and sometimes he traveled as a private individual. But always he was an acute observer of the life around him, and he recorded what he saw in a vivid, anecdotal style. These observations, collected in ten volumes as the *Book of Travels* (*Seyâhatnâme*), provide us with a detailed, panoramic view of the Ottoman Empire in the mid-seventeenth century, when its geographic extent was greatest and its power had declined only a little from its apogee. There is no comparable record for any other Islamic state.

Evliya Çelebi, the son of Dervish Mehmet Zilli, was born in Istanbul on March 25, 1611, and died in the same city late in 1684. (*Mehmet* is Turkish for "Muhammad.") His father's family was originally from the city of Kutahya, in northwestern Anatolia, but had moved to Istanbul sometime after the Ottoman conquest of that city in 1453. Evliya's father was the chief jeweler of the court, a position of considerable distinction. He was a wealthy man as well, with houses and estates in several cities and four shops in Istanbul itself. These easy circumstances made it possible for his son to indulge his passion for travel. Evliya's mother was from the Caucasus and came to the royal household in the time of Sultan Ahmet I (1603–1617), where she married. She was related through her mother to the imperial son-in-law and high-ranking official of the court Melek Ahmet Pasha. This connection was a fortunate one for Evliya since it allowed him to join the retinue of the pasha during his embassies to Tabriz and his stints as governor of one or another of the Ottoman empire's far-flung provinces: Bosnia, Diyarbakir, Baghdad, and Damascus among them. Ahmet Pasha's assistance to his younger relative served his ends as well since Evliya wrote glowingly of his patron's character and abilities in his journals.

As a boy, Evliya attended an elementary school for seven years and then, for another eleven years, a school where he was trained in the art of reciting the Koran. His father also taught him the manual skills associated with jewelry making. When he was twenty-five he so distinguished himself by an especially beautiful recitation of the Koran that Ahmet Pasha presented him to Sultan Murat IV, and as a result, he was accepted into the palace school for extensive training in music, calligraphy, Arabic grammar, and advanced Koranic recitation.

Evliya began his travels at about this time, although initially his journeys did not take him far from home. The first volume of his *Book of Travels* is devoted to extensive descriptions of Istanbul and its environs. The plan of the remaining nine volumes is not systematic but dictated by the accidents of opportunity. A single volume may take him from Bosnia to Azerbaijan (Volume 2) or be devoted to travels in a single region. In Volume 8, from which the selection printed here is taken, Evliya travels exclusively in the Balkan peninsula, and Volume 10 is devoted to Cairo, upper Egypt, the Sudan, and Abyssinia. Inevitably, there are cities and regions he visited more than once. Egypt is the region he most enjoyed, or at least, it is the one where he lived longest, staying there for eight or nine years.

Although Evliya often traveled in an official capacity and was concerned about giving detailed and accurate descriptions of the places he visited, he was not a historian, and he had a penchant for the legendary and the miraculous. He exaggerates his adventures, sometimes to comic effect, and recounts journeys that he cannot possibly have taken. At times he seems to include anecdotes and stories merely to leaven the more pedestrian descriptions of forts and cities. His audience was the literate members of the Ottoman community, who wished to be amused as well as instructed. He suits his style to their taste in that he writes in a language that approximates the colloquial usage of the seventeenth century but also draws on the more formal style of the court and chancery. The hero of a travel journal is inevitably the author, and the man who emerges from the *Book of Travels* is one who must have made an appealing travel companion—lively, imaginative, inquisitive, and sensible.

THE OTTOMAN EMPIRE

The Ottoman state was the last of the great Muslim empires and the one whose effect on the history of both modern Europe and the modern Middle East has been the most consequential. The Ottomans were originally leaders of an Oghuz (Turkomen) tribal confederation that came to Anatolia (Turkey) from central Asia as part of the Saljuqid army sometime in the eleventh or twelfth century. After the destruction of the Saljuqid state in the thirteenth century, they established themselves as an independent dynasty in northwestern Anatolia. From there they expanded into Europe, crossing the strait to Gallipoli in 1354 and rapidly extending their rule into northern Greece, Macedonia, and Bulgaria. In 1389 they defeated the Serbs at Kosovo (in Serbia) and so gained mastery of the western Balkans as well. In their rapid conquest of the region the Ottomans were aided by their ready access to numbers of Turkomen warriors in Anatolia, by the deep dissension among the Balkan Slavs, and by the religious enmity between the Eastern Orthodox and Catholic Churches. From their secure base in the Balkans (which they called Rumelia), the Ottomans launched an aggressive campaign to extend their rule over their Turkomen neighbors to the east. Tamurlaine's invasion of Anatolia in 1402 checked their advance, but only briefly. They soon retook their former possessions. In 1453 Ottoman armies under Mehmed II the Conqueror (1444–1446, 1451–1481) vanquished Constantinople (which they pronounce *Istanbul*), the city that had defeated every Muslim army since the time of Muhammad.

Mehmed was the first of the Ottoman sultans to see himself as the successor to both the Muslim caliphs and the Byzantine emperors. His ambition was to found, like them, a universal empire. He adopted a style in architecture that symbolized that imperial ambition, constructing magnificent palaces and great congregational mosques that rivaled the finest monuments of Byzantine art. He also established a new legal code, and, most important, he initiated the policy of imperial expansion that ultimately gave the Ottoman state dominance over a region almost as vast as that of the Abbasid state, which ruled Islam in its golden age (eighth to thirteenth centuries). At its peak, the Ottoman empire extended from the Crimea in the north to

Aden on the Indian Ocean and from the borders of Iran to Morocco. Throughout the sixteenth and seventeenth centuries the Ottoman state waged war successfully against its European rivals to the west and north as well as against the Iranian Safavid state to the east. Ottoman ships controlled the eastern Mediterranean and provided the sole successful challenge to the Portuguese expansion into the Indian Ocean.

Although they were descended from the leaders of an Oghuz tribal confederation and spoke a Turkish language, the Ottomans saw themselves primarily not as Turkomans but as heirs to Abbasid imperial culture. They continued and enriched the Arabic and Persian tradition in literature, science, and the arts and established a rich and cosmopolitan court society in which learned and accomplished men of many origins were welcome. Ottoman literature was linguistically Turkish but drew heavily on both Arabic and Persian vocabulary, themes, and literary forms. Ottoman poets were often masters of all three languages. At its height, the poetry and prose of Ottoman Turkish achieved a richness and complexity that made it the third great literature of the Islamic tradition, after the Arabic and Persian.

The Ottoman empire reached its apogee in the mid-seventeenth century and then began a slow process of decline. By the eighteenth century Europe had developed the military and economic strength to check further Ottoman advances and, probably, to defeat the empire outright, but rivalries between the various European states helped to preserve the ailing Ottoman empire through its gradual dissolution over the next two centuries. Under the Albanian governor Muhammad Ali, Egypt became effectively autonomous in 1829. In the Balkans, powerful nationalist ambitions engendered by the French Revolution inspired the Balkan communities to rebel against Ottoman rule throughout the nineteenth century. Greece won its independence in 1829, and one by one the other states did as well until at the end of the Second Balkan War (1912–13) Turkey retained control of only one small province of Greece (eastern Thrace) from all its former vast empire in Europe. After World War I the victorious Allies stripped Turkey of its Arab provinces by reason of its support for the Central Powers. Within the remaining fragment of the Ottoman state itself, the nationalist leader Mustafa Kemal (later Atatürk) led a movement to establish a Turkish national state, repudiating the Ottoman heritage and distancing the Turkish people from the humiliations of the previous two centuries. In 1924 the caliphate was ended and the last Ottoman sultan, Abd al-Majid, was deposed.

THE CITY OF BOUDONÍTZA

The selection from the *Book of Travels* printed here displays, if not the full range, at least the polar extremes of Evliya's style. It begins with a factual account of the state of Boudonítza's fortifications, with the helpful suggestion that they could be repaired easily should the need or desire arise. Evliya then moves quickly to a vivid and detailed account of a pirate raid and to a somewhat despairing description of this remote and unpromising outpost of the empire where Muslims are outnumbered by Christians, the economy is depressed, and the community is at the mercy of the European pirates who ravage the coast. One can see the mind of the imperial official at work in his emphasizing that the raid originated as much in the cruelty and injustice of the chief judge as it did in the rapacity of the pirates. Following immediately on the heels of these shrewd and careful observations we have one of his most extraordinary flights of fantasy—the description of how Saint Veliüllah was miraculously saved from a horrible death and, as a result, converted an entire community to Islam.

Accounts of how a community was converted to Islam were of continuing interest to Muslims generally, and to the Ottomans in particular, since their proximity to the Christian world and the presence of large Christian communities within their borders gave them a sense of being in competition with Christians for the loyalties of their subjects and the control of their western provinces. Finally, this wonderful story is brought home by visiting God's curse on both the pirates and those greedy members of the community who wished either to despoil the saint's tomb or to carry away the property of the dervishes (pious mendicants). Although Evliya recounts this story as though he had viewed it with his own eyes, he frequently includes hearsay materials, and what we have here may simply be a wonderful anecdote he picked up in the local tea house. That is not to say that he is himself skeptical of the tale. Belief in the miraculous powers of saints was as widespread in Islam as it was in the Christian world to the west and not at all incongruous even in a man of Evliya's learning and sophistication. Saint Veliüllah was a Shi'ite who, like the Imams of Shi'ism, claimed descent from the Prophet Muhammad through his daughter Fatima and son-in-law Ali. By reciting the names of the saint's illustrious ancestors, Evliya invokes the divine authority of that lineage and lends a note of probability to this miraculous occurrence.

It is striking that he should celebrate this poor, small and depressed community with one of his richest imaginative flights. Although Evliya himself lived comfortably, he had a romantic and quite genuine admiration for the simple, hard-bitten residents of remote and impoverished outposts like Boudonítza. It would be completely in character for him to compose this heroic fantasy as a gesture of gratitude for the hospitality he received.

The Book of Travels circulated in manuscript during Evliya's lifetime; the first printed editions appeared in the nineteenth century. Though the bulk of the *Book of Travels* is still unavailable in English, Robert Dankoff has translated extensive selections from Volumes 1 to 8 in *The Intimate Life of an Ottoman Statesman* (1991). The focus of his selections is Evliya's relative and long-time patron Melek Ahmet Pasha. There is a sketch of Evliya's life, a listing of the contents of the *Book of Travels,* and a guide to translations of his work into English and other European languages in the *Encyclopedia of Islam* (1954–), where his name is transliterated as Ewliyā Čelebī. The selection printed here is excerpted from a fuller translation being prepared by Pierre A. MacKay.

PRONOUNCING GLOSSARY

The following list uses common English syllables and stress accents to provide rough equivalents of selected words whose pronunciation may be unfamiliar to the general reader.

Boudonítza: *boo'-doe-nitz'-uh*

Diyarbakir: *dee-ar'-buh-keer'*

Esed: *e-said'*

Evliya Çelebi: *ev-lee'-uh che'-luh-bee*

Fatiha: *fa'-ti-huh*

Haji: *haw'-jee*

Ibrahim: *eeb-ruh-heem'*

Kutahya: *koo-tah'-yuh*

Mehmed Bektash Veli: *me'-met bek'-tash ve'-lee*

Mehmet Zilli: *me'-met zil'-lee*

Melek Ahmet Pasha: *me'-lek ah'-met pa'-shuh*

Muharram: *mu-har-ram'*

Safavids: *sa'-fuh-vids*

Saljuqids: *sal-joo'-kids*

Seyâhatnâme: *say-ah-hat'-nah-may*

Sheyh: *shay*

Suleyman Dede: *sue-lay-mahn' de'-de*

Umayyad: *oo-my'-yad*

Veliüllah: *ve-lee'-uh-lah'*

Yezid: *ye-zeed'*

Zeyn al-Abidin: *zay'-n ol–ah'-bi-deen'*

Zitúni: *zee-too'-nee*

TIME LINE

TEXTS	CONTEXTS
16th century The leading poets of the time leave Iran for the more hospitable courts of India and central Asia	**1502** Shah Ismâ'il founds the Safavid Dynasty, which rules Iran until 1732. The Safavids make Shi'ism the official faith of Iran and defend Iran's borders against the Ottomans to the west and the Özbegs to the northeast
	1520–1566 During Sultan Suleymân's reign, the Ottomans add Hungary to their empire, besiege Vienna, and engage the Portuguese navy in the Indian Ocean
	1589–1629 Shah Abbâs creates the splendid architectural monuments that still survive in Isfahan and establishes diplomatic contacts with Europe
1611–1684 Evliya Çelebi, who decides at about age 25 to devote his life to travel and begins to work on **The Book of Travels**	
	1683 The second unsuccessful siege of Vienna marks the limits of Ottoman power and heralds its decline
1720–1730 The Ottomans make their first attempts at Westernization, importing a printing press	**1726** The Safavids are defeated by the Turkoman, Nader Shah, founder of the Afshar Dynasty, which rules Iran until 1795
	1729 Nader Shah sacks Delhi, further weakening the Mughals
	1750 Karim Khân Zand takes control of Iran from the last Afshar and establishes a dynasty that rules Iran until 1779
1757–1790 Sheyh Galip, the last great master of Ottoman court poetry	
	1779–1924 The Qajars under Agha Muhammad Khan gradually take control of Iran from the Zands; they will rule into the modern period
	1798 Napoleon invades Egypt, marking the beginning of the modern period in the Middle East

Boldface titles indicate works in the anthology.

From The Book of Travels[1]

The City of Boudonítza

DESCRIPTION OF THE POWERFUL TOWERS AND MIGHTY WALLS OF THE STRONG CASTLE OF BOUDONÍTZA[2]

The castle is less than two hours distance westward from the seashore. It is a strongly built circular castle, with four subdivisions, on a high place in the mountains, and it is altogether four thousand paces round in circumference. The two lower divisions of the castle, however, were destroyed after the conquest, and since that event the walls have stood in ruins in several places. But it would be an easy matter, if there were money and interest enough, to restore them. As for the third subdivision and the inner keep, they are very strong indeed.

By the will of the Lord, before arriving at this castle, your poor servant heard the noise of cannonfire and musketry on the road in front of us. Since we also heard the shouting of the Muhammadan war-cry,[3] however, we were not frightened off, but as we came up, slowly slowly, towards the city, we encountered several thousand of Muhammad's people, together with their entire households, who had fled from the place, with rags bound around their heads and feet. It appeared that the infidel[4] fleet had disembarked an army which came up from the sea-shore into the residential section of the castle. Together with a certain infidel named Captain Giorgio,[5] who had come from the landward side, they attacked the city; sacked and plundered it; and after throwing everything into confusion, set fire to it and departed with two hundred prisoners, thousands of groats[6] worth of commercial goods and supplies, and the chief judge himself, whom they had taken prisoner along with his entire household.

CAUSE OF THE ASSAULT ON THE CASTLE OF BOUDONÍTZA.

The judge is alleged to have been a tyrant so manifestly oppressive in his infringement of the rights of both the tributary and the exempt populace that the tributary subjects,[7] because of the judge's oppression, went off in boats to Captain Giorgio, whom they found cruising near the Venetian island of Tenos. When they got there, they complained of the judge, saying, "He has taken all our property from us so, in the name of our Lord Jesus, restore our rights to us." So saying, they gave this Captain Giorgio the pretext by which he came by land and sea, and for the sake of a single oppressive judge, the infidels destroyed and devastated this charming city, looted it, and took all those many prisoners.

We made so bold as to come into the city in the midst of this turmoil, and saw that the infidels were still busy binding and chaining their captives, poor creatures of the Lord, and sending them off. Those of Muhammad's people who were shut up in the castle opened the castle gate as soon as they saw us, and cried out to us, "Hey Heroes, what shall we do, when so many of our families, our wives and our children, are taken prisoner, and now, see, they are taking them away."

---

1. Translated by and with notes adapted from Pierre A. MacKay.   2. A small city on the coast of the island of Morea in southern Greece.   3. Probably the phrase *Allahu akbar!* (God is great!).   4. Christian.   5. A known pirate of the region.   6. An English silver coin widely used in commerce.   7. Christians. *Exempt populace:* Muslims.

Then, making up a party together with my servants and the men of the town, we extinguished such fires as we could in some of the neighborhoods, and while we were doing so, we saw the warlike hero warriors from Zitúni,[8] horse and foot, coming to help. Then all the people of the city gathered together and attacked the low-born infidels where they had assembled their forces near the sea-shore, and rescued much wealth and property and many prisoners, elderly men and women of Muhammad's people. There were also forty-five infidels whose strength was exhausted from running and from carrying their heavy load of loot. These remained behind, and thanks be to the Lord, we took them prisoner. But as we went further on and arrived close to the infidels' boats at the sea-shore, the accursed infidels let loose at us from their galleons and six gunnery barges, with their large cannon, and we were forced to take all our prisoners and retire once again. Having liberated so many of Muhammad's people, and repossessed so much material and heavy baggage, we made them very happy when we went back to the city with our infidel prisoners and in keeping with our exploits they gave your humble servant one of the infidel prisoners. Praise be to God, we found ourselves thus in a purely fortuitous battle, but what good was there in it, since all those people of Muhammad had been taken captive? There came news too that there were infidels lying in ambush in the mountains, so all the men from Boudonítza, from Zitúni and from Molo[9] came in, several thousands of them, and gathering together they patrolled through the hills and valleys around the city, and remained on watch there.

CONCLUDING DESCRIPTION OF THE CITY.

One ruinous old mosque in the lower residential quarter escaped the fire, and one inn. One dirty bath, ten shops, a hundred Muslim houses and a hundred and fifty infidel houses remained, all with tile roofs, and gardens and orchards. The rest were all set afire and burned.

Later on, the warriors from Boudonítza and Zitúni who had gone out into the mountains and valleys came back with the news that there was no trace or sign of infidels to be found, but we were still too fearful to sleep in the outer city, and so went into the middle redoubt,[1] where we were hospitably entertained. It is indeed a castle which rises level with the very sky, but the hills along the road that leads to Molo give artillery command over it. In the inner redoubt there are fifty dwellings for the poor wretches of garrison personnel, supplies of produce, and stores and depositories for weapons. But the arsenal is a small one, containing only five long brass falconets.[2] There is only the one small mosque, and no other public edifices. Here and there outside the castle there are gardens and orchards.

DESCRIPTION OF PLACES OF PILGRIMAGE TO THE GREAT SAINTS OF GOD IN THE CASTLE OF BOUDONÍTZA.

Outside the city, in the high lands to the east, there is an elevated parkland of cypresses and tall trees. Here, in a meadow from which the entire world may be observed, under a huge lead-roofed cupola, is buried that source of sacred knowledge, who is sprung from an illustrious stock, the seed of Musa

8. A town just to the north of Boudonítza.   9. A coastal village to the north of Boudonítza.   1. Fortification   2. Small cannons.

Reza, the venerated offspring of Kâzim, who is buried in the heavenly paradise of Baghdad, that recourse of the righteous, entranced by the uniqueness of God, and annihilated in his power, that guide through the stations of sanctity and mirror of illustrious generosity, that son of the noblest of princes, the chosen servant of God, the Sheyh[3] Sultan Veliüllah, son of the Imam Ali Musa Reza, son of the Imam Kâzim, son of the Imam Ja'fer Sadik, son of the Imam Bâkir, son of the Imam Zeyn al-Abidin, son of the Imam Hüseyin, son of the Imam Ali Murteza and his wife, the glorious Lady Fatima, daughter of the excellent Muḥammad, who is Ahmed, Mahmud, and Mustafa, may God exalt him, and be pleased with all of them.[4]

This excellent Sultan Veliüllah, being of such an illustrious line, found a final repose in this city of Boudonítza, and lies here in tranquillity, buried with all his dependents, children and friends in a brilliant shrine beneath a luminous dome.

THE EMINENT GLORIES OF THE SAINT, VELIÜLLAH.

Because of the abuse and persecution which the family of Yezid the Umayyad visited on the Imam Hüseyin after the disaster on the plains of Kerbela,[5] this Sultan Veliüllah departed from his homeland and, desiring to become a member of the spiritual brethren in Greece, he wandered and traveled over the earth. When he came to this city of Boudonítza, which was at that time in the hands of the great King of Spain,[6] he performed the Sultani celebration of God's unity for this perverted and evil-doing king. When they had all gathered together before him to the beat of the great kettledrums, the king asked about their condition and circumstances, their origins and their quality. Once made cognizant of their secrets, this cursed king was inflamed with poisonous rage and said, "What business have you in my country? For what reason have you set your foot in this land, making your call to prayer and performing the celebration of the unity of God? Is it not because of you that the Turkish race will march into this land after you, and that you have come to show them the way?" So saying, he thrust Sultan Veliüllah into a huge cannon, but just as he was on the point of firing it, the saint, in perfect conviction and belief, began the continuous recitation of the sacred verse from the Sura "The Prophets" of the Glorious Koran, "We said, Oh fire, be cold and harmless to Ibrahim."[7] While he was reciting this verse, at the very moment when the great crowd of followers at his side was totally absorbed in the celebration of the unity of God, the decision of the infidels who are consigned to Hell was no longer stayed, and the cannon was fired. By the will of God, the Imam Veliüllah blew higher and higher into the air, and as he appeared out of the sky, his voice could be heard crying, "O God, O my protector." And so, by the will of God, he floated down to land standing upright on the earth, having suffered not the slightest injury to his delicate

---

3. Or sheikh. **4.** This somewhat eccentric genealogy traces the descent of the Shi'ite Imam from Muhammad. *Ahmed* (most praiseworthy), *Mahmud* (praised), and *Mustafa* (chosen [by God]) are attributes of *Muhammad* (praised). **5.** A reference to the disastrous uprising of the Shi'a under the leadership of Hüseyin (Hussein), the grandson of the prophet Muhammad. Hüseyin was defeated and beheaded near Kerbela, southwest of Baghdad. The shrine built there in memory of his martyrdom is the most sacred of all the special Shi'a places of worship. Shi'as believed that the son-in-law of Muhammad should have been the first caliph and that the caliphate should have stayed in his family. **6.** The Spanish Catalans took over east-central Greece and ruled both Athens and Thebes during the first half of the 14th century. **7.** Sura 21.68. A sura is a section of the Koran, similar to a chapter.

body at impact. As soon as he had busied himself with an act of thanksgiving to All-glorious God, all the infidels ran to see the condition of the saint, and on that occasion seven thousand unbelieving infidels produced the words of witness and, having become believers and followers of the saint, stood to be led in worship. Even the king, on seeing this, produced the forefinger of attestation and on his recalling the verse that speaks the unity of God, he was honored with the welcome into Islam.[8] All his children and household too became faithful believers in God's unity, and so the first beginnings of Islam in Greece took place among those people of Boudonítza who were thus converted.

Afterwards they built a great shrine, which is still in use, on the place where the saint came down after being fired from the cannon, and gave the rations of food and drink which he established. Infidels from all the seven regions of the world used to come here and visit the saint but, for his own part, this same saint did not survive for long after he had made manifest his blessedness, but soon made the transition to the ultimate world. When he had gone to his pardon, his many thousands of followers buried him here at this palatial edifice, which is still a place of pilgrimage for men of all conditions, an immense hall full of ascetic followers and a cloister for the devotees of Haji Mehmed Bektash Veli.[9]

There are seventy Bektashis here. Wealthy in their want and poverty, rich in the skills of self-annihilation into God, brethren in the arts of self-abandonment and contemplative abstraction, they are all wonderfully kind, cultivated and wholesome spirits. Each of them is appointed to a specific task as they perform all services for the horses of every wayfarer. No matter how many horses a person may have, they do not leave it to him to deal with the blankets and nose-bags, but they bring the horses into the cloister stables and, after they have watered them, they hang a nosebag of feed on them. Then they make coffee for the traveler, and from their kitchens they offer the good things of their hospitable dining halls: soups, stewed meats, pilavs and saffron rice, to rich and poor, old and young, yea even to Jew and heathen, for theirs is an immense bequest, from which they distribute their goods to all wandering travelers in accordance with the holy Sura, "There is no creature on the earth, but God has given it sustenance."[1]

All the kings of infideldom, and other infidels as well, are believers in this important Sultan (Veliüllah), and every year old women come from infideldom, and traveling at the time of the new year, after the sounding of the festival kettledrum, under sacred Muhammadan sanctions, they make collections of money and provisions to provide for the sustenance of travelers.

This is a convent with a world-wide prospect which must be visited. All the buildings are roofed over with pure lead, which is one of the good works and benefactions of . . .[2] Pasha. On all sides of the sarcophagus of Saint Veliüllah, where he lies at rest under the luminous cupola, there are any number of glorious phrases written in a beautiful hand, and any number of precious incense burners, rosewater flasks, candle-holders and suspended

8. One of the ways a Muslim may express the unity of God is to raise the right-hand forefinger while saying "God is One." The gesture has particular resonance in Greek Orthodox lands, where it contrasts directly and intentionally with the ritual Christian attestation of the Trinity, which is to raise three fingers side by side in blessing.   9. Founder of a major and still-flourishing Sufi order. A sufi is a Muslim mystic.
1. Sura 11.6.   2. Evliya left lacunae in his writings to be filled in later. He died before completing the task.

lamps of every sort. There are rare and precious hangings too, and beautifully written inscriptions where each devout traveler by sea has left his mark. And there are articles from the apparatus of mendicant dervishes,[3] such as staffs, begging bowls, halters and gourd flasks. Besides these, there are all sorts of drums, pennants, iron clappers, banners, tambourines, kettledrums, trumpets, cymbals, . . . and whips. The Bektashis sprinkle rosewater over each pilgrim as he arrives. Beside Sultan Veliüllah is buried . . . sultan, one of his venerable sons, and beside him, . . . sultan, is buried. In the outer court also, there are great numbers of blessed saints buried. May God have mercy on them all.

AN ACCOUNT OF THE VERIFICATION OF THE SAINT'S
BLESSED EFFICACY

Your lowly servitor himself and with his own eyes witnessed it, and we have ventured to recount it here that during the previous day's raid and pillaging by the many thousands of despicable and accursed infidels, there was a dull-witted, obstinate and impious detachment of several hundred infidels which came up to the sacred tomb chapel, where they saw a detachment of dervishes standing with hands clasped before them. Since all infidels are believers in this saint, they did not take his followers captive, but many of them fell upon the raw foodstuffs and set their minds to looting various articles from the cellars of the kitchen building and the dervish quarters, and stuffing them in their sacks to carry them off as booty. Now the infidels imagined that mere looting posed no danger of harm to those who were carrying off goods and possessions, so a large number of them went in and seized the dishes, stew-pots, kettles and ladles from the kitchen, and some came out wearing the black stew-pots on their heads, on top of their black hats. On seeing this another lot of vicious infidels ventured to enter the blessed shrine itself, where they stole some items of dervish apparatus and some beautiful copies of sacred writ.[4] One infidel, however, made a particular show of defiance by laying his hands on the sacred headdress set up over the blessed head of the saint. At this moment, an aged follower named Suleyman Dede cried out distractedly, "O Saint, why do you lie there? If only you would see what is happening! Where now is the honor of Muhammad."

Glory be to God, as soon as he spoke, there came seven separate flashes and bright tongues of fire which struck each of the seven enemy infidels who were outside the luminous dome. All seven of those wretched unbelievers, condemned to eternal fire, were then destroyed within that brilliant shrine, set burning on the spot, like blackest coals. As for your humble servant, when I arrived to make my pilgrimage to the shrine, the seven human carcasses of those infidels who had been set afire, looking like skins full of black pitch, were lying like refuse under foot in the shade of the cypress trees. Your humble servant, together with my retinue and the dervishes themselves, got ropes around the feet of these stinking infidel carcasses and dragged them off away from the shrine into the open, where we left them, and when the

---

3. Muslim religious mendicants, usually sufis.   4. The Koran.

infidels from the city saw these burned infidel cadavers they acquired the most absolute and complete belief in the sultan Veliüllah.

Many of the other infidels, seeing that these were being burnt black as pitch, dropped the things they had just picked up and ran to tell the others, those who had earlier looted the kitchen of its dishes and pots, about these extremely depressing events. Some of the looters then dropped their booty but others dared to hold on to it and, while the latter were carrying it off, it happened by the will of God that the stew-pots on the heads of those infidels who were wearing them like black hats became suddenly hot. At once their black hair and their black heads began to ignite under their black hats from the red heat of the cooking pots. At this they dropped the pots and ran, but some remained stubbornly determined and carried their booty until their strength was at an end. They passed on their loads to other infidels, but these in turn as their bodies became powerless left the load to be taken up by others and, in the end, whatever they had taken from the shrine of Veliüllah they left strewn around the plain while they rushed onto the ships for dear life, crying out, "Let's be done with it!"

At the same time or just previously we had prevailed against the infidels . . . with what army we had and had made them drop much of their spoils, had freed many prisoners, and had captured forty-five infidel prisoners. And now, glory be to God, all the apparatus and paraphernalia came back to where it belonged. Not a single thing was lost and the worthy dervishes were recently still engaged in the task of putting all the various sorts of dervish apparatus back in their proper places. The significant inference to be drawn from all these noteworthy events is that all the blessed efficacy of the saint as written about in various books of belief is absolutely true. For the soul of the eminent Sheyh Veliüllah and for the souls of his family and his sons, that God may be pleased with them, a recitation of the Fatiha.[5]

Your humble servant spent an evening being entertained by these mendicants at the gates of God and engaging in uplifting conversation. Truly these are an orthodox people here, a community of the purest law and a congregation of poor followers of the truest belief. Their spiritual leader most particularly, that Hafiẓ Arslan Dede who is their leader in the true way of religious adoration, is the very essence of a dervish who keeps the fast assiduously, in David's manner,[6] and utters an invocation to God in his every breath. . . . He gave us a few dervishes to take along as companions and all of our party bade farewell, but just as we were leaving, there occurred a most extraordinary spectacle as several hundred people of Boudonítza arrived with the judge from Zitúni and began to lay claim to the wealth, the apparatus and the apparel of the dervishes from this chapel.

It would seem that this lot of people from Boudonítza were all of the Greek race, a company of stubborn recusant doubters, and it was alleged that since they did not believe in Sultan Veliüllah or in any other great saints they had appropriated for their own use and enjoyment any number of gardens, orchards and cultivable fields which they treated as their own property. These doubters stated in the judge's presence that the infidel raiders had come and

---

5. The first sura of the Koran, often recited independently as a prayer. 6. King David is exemplary for his piety in Muslim tradition.

had robbed them and made prisoners of their entire families and households at the same time as they, the infidels, were assaulting the dervishes. They alleged further that, "As the infidels were carrying off your property, they dropped it because it was too heavy a load, but they also dropped our property as well and you, on the pretext that it was all the saint's property, gathered up all our things from the fields and brought them all to this chapel." When they made this claim, the dervishes answered, "Misguided men, the infidels went off with our dervish apparel and the pots and dishes from our kitchen, except that the infidels who came into the shrine and were taking the lamps and candle-holders and the copies of holy writ—those infidels caught fire and are left behind here burned black as cinders."

Now just as they were saying this, one man announced that, "Those Korans are mine, and just such an amount of my belongings was taken," and with that he went straight into the sacred sepulchre and in the presence of the judge and of my humble self, he took three large copies of the Koran from off the reading stand saying, "These are mine."

But just as he was going out the door he was struck down into a neat little heap, and his soul was burned black as hell-fire. The dervishes picked up the holy writings from the spot and put them back where they belonged. Your humble servant was left in a state of rapturous ecstasy, unable to draw breath, but then, together with my servants, we got this doubter's corpse by head and feet, and dragged it out among the above-mentioned infidels' carcasses and left it there. All the people from Boudonítza, on seeing this occurrence, took to their heels.

The poor judge was very distressed to have come from Zitúni, and he too, saying, "Glory be to God," remounted his horse and traced his steps back to Zitúni. There are any number of trustworthy witnesses to the outcome of this matter.

We ourselves, at that very time, mounted our own horses and set out once again from Boudonítza in a southeasterly direction. Taking God as our refuge, we crossed through difficult rocky hills and gulleys and over mountains and valleys and came in 4 hours to Esed Abad.

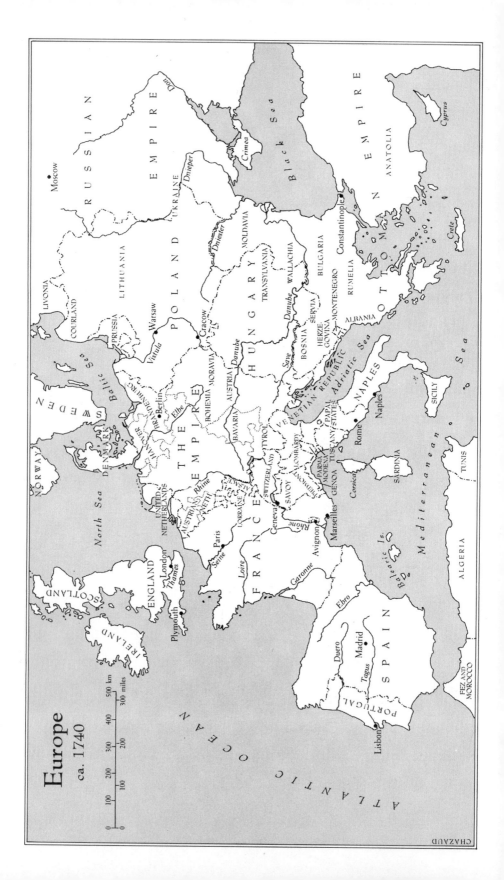

Europe
ca. 1740

CHAZAUD

The Enlightenment in
Europe

"I wonder if it is not better to try to correct and moderate men's passions than to try to suppress them altogether." The sentence, from Jean-Baptiste Molière's 1669 preface to his biting comedy about religious hypocrisy, *Tartuffe*, captures something of the anxiety and the optimism of a period for which subsequent generations have found no adequate single designation. "The Neo-Classic Period," "The Age of Reason," "The Enlightenment": such labels suggest, accurately enough, that thinkers between (roughly) 1660 and 1770 emphasized the powers of the mind and turned to the Roman past for models. But these terms do not convey the awareness of limitation expressed in Molière's sentence, an awareness as typical of the historical period to which the sentence belongs as is the expressed aspiration toward correctness and moderation. The effort to correct and moderate the passions might prove less foolhardy than the effort to suppress them, but both endeavors would involve human nature's struggle with itself, a struggle necessarily perpetual. "On life's vast ocean diversely we sail, / Reason the card, but Passion is the gale," Alexander Pope's *Essay on Man* (1733) pointed out. One could hope to steer with reason as guide only by remembering the omnipresence of passion as impetus. Eighteenth-century thinkers analyzed, and eighteenth-century imaginative writers dramatized, intricate interchanges and conflicts between these aspects of our selves.

The drama of reason and passion played itself out in society, the system of association human beings had devised partly to control passion and institutionalize reason. Structured on the basis of a rigid class system, the traditional social order began to face incipient challenges in the eighteenth century as new commerce generated new wealth, whose possessors felt entitled to claim their own share of social power. The threat to established hierarchies extended even to kings. Thomas Hobbes, in *Leviathan* (1651), had argued for the secular origins of the social contract. Kings arise, he said, not by divine ordinance but out of human need; they exist to prevent what would otherwise be a war of all on all. Monarchs still presided over European nations in the eighteenth century, but with less security than before. The English had executed their ruler in 1649; the French would perform another royal decapitation before the end of the eighteenth century. The mortality of kings had become a political fact, a fact implying the conceivable instability of the social order over which kings presided.

A sense of the contingencies of the human condition impinged on many minds in a world where men and women no longer automatically assumed God's benign supervision of human affairs or the primacy of their own Christian obligations. The fierce strife between Protestants and Catholics lapsed into relative quiescence by the end of the seventeenth century, but the Protestant English deposed their king in 1688 because of his marriage to a Catholic princess and their fear of a Catholic dynasty; and in France Louis XIV in 1685 revoked the Edict of Nantes, which had granted religious toleration to Protestants. The overt English struggle of Cavaliers and Puritans ended with the restoration of Charles II to the throne in 1660. Religious differences now became translated into divisions of social class and of political conviction—

divisions no less powerful for lacking the claim of supernatural authority. To England, the eighteenth century brought two unsuccessful but bitterly divisive rebellions on behalf of the deposed Stuart succession, as well as the cataclysmic American Revolution. In France, the century ended in revolution. Throughout the eighteenth century, wars erupted over succession to European thrones and over nationalistic claims, although no fighting took place on such a scale as that of the devastating Thirty Years' War (1618–48). On the whole, divisions *within* nations (in France and England) assumed greater importance than those between nations.

Philosophers now turned their attention to defining the possibilities and limitations of the human position in the material universe. "I think, therefore I am," René Descartes pronounced, declaring the mind the source of individual being. But this idea proved less reassuring than it initially seemed. Subsequent philosophers, exploring the concept's implications, realized the possibility of the mind's isolation in its own constructions. Perhaps, Wilhelm Leibniz suggested, no real communication can take place between one consciousness and another. Possibly, according to David Hume, the idea of individual identity itself derives from the mind's efforts to manufacture continuity out of discontinuous memories. Philosophers pointed out the impossibility of knowing for sure even the reality of the external world: the only certainty is that we think it exists. If contemplating the nature of human reason thus led philosophic skeptics to restrict severely the area of what we can know with certainty, other contemplations induced other thinkers to insist on the existence, beyond ourselves, of an entirely rational physical and moral universe. Isaac Newton's demonstrations of the order of natural law greatly encouraged this line of thought. The fullness and complexity of the perceived physical world testified, as many wrote, to the sublime rationality of a divine plan. The Planner, however, did not necessarily supervise the day-to-day operations of His arrangements; He might rather, as a popular analogy had it, resemble the watchmaker who winds the watch and leaves it running.

Deism, evoking a depersonalized deity, insisted on the logicality of the universe and encouraged the separation of ethics from religion. Ethics, too, could be understood as a matter of reason. "He that thinks reasonably must think morally," Samuel Johnson observed, echoing the noble horses Jonathan Swift had imagined in the fourth book of *Gulliver's Travels*. But such statements expressed wish more than perception. Awareness of the passions continued to haunt thinkers yearning for rationality. Swift's Houyhnhnms, creatures of his imagination, might achieve flawless rationality (with accompanying wisdom and benevolence) but actual human beings could only dream of such an ideal, while experiencing—as men and women have always experienced—the confusion of conflicting impulses often at war with the dictates of reason.

Although the social, economic, and political organizations in which the thinkers of this period participated hardly resemble our own, the questions they raised about the human condition have plagued the Western mind ever since. If we no longer locate the solution to all problems in an unattainable ideal of "reason," we too struggle to find the limits of certainty, experience problems of identity and isolation, and recognize the impossibility of altogether controlling internal forces now identified as "the unconscious" rather than "the passions." But we confront such issues largely from the position of isolated individuals. In the late seventeenth and early eighteenth centuries, in England and on the Continent, the sense of obligation to society had far more power than it possesses today. Society provided the standards and the instruments of control that might help to counter the tumult of individual impulse.

SOCIETY

Society, in this period, designates both a powerful idea and an omnipresent fact of experience. Prerevolutionary French society, like English society of the same period, depended on clear hierarchical structures. The literature of both countries issued from a small cultural elite, writing for others of their kind and assuming the rightness of their own knowledge of how people should feel and behave.

For the English and French upper classes, as for the ancient Romans they admired, public life mattered more than private. At one level, the "public" designated the realms of government and diplomacy: occupations allowing and encouraging oratory, frequent travel, negotiation, the exercise of political and economic power. In this sense, the public world belonged entirely to men, who determined the course of government, defined the limits of the important, enforced their sense of the fitness of things. By another definition, "public" might refer to the life of formal social intercourse. In France, such social life took place often in "salons," gatherings to engage in intellectual, as well as frivolous, conversation. Women typically presided over these salons, thus declaring both their intellectual authority and their capacity to combine high thought with high style. Until rather late in the eighteenth century, on the other hand, England allowed women no such commanding position; there, men controlled intellectual and political discourse. The male voice, accordingly, dominated English literature until the development of the novel provided new opportunities for women writers and for the articulation of domestic values.

Both the larger and the more limited public spheres depended on well-defined codes of behavior. The discrepancy between the forms of self-presentation dictated by these codes and the operations such forms might disguise—a specific form of the reason-versus–passion conflict—provides one of the insistent themes of French and English literature in the century beginning around 1660. Molière, examining religious sham; Swift, lashing the English for institutionalized hypocrisy; Pope, calling attention to ambiguities inherent in sexual mores; Voltaire, sending a naïve fictional protagonist to encounter the world's inconsistencies of profession and practice—such writers call attention to the deceptiveness and the possible misuses of social norms, as well as to their necessity. None suggests that the codes themselves are at fault. If people lived up to what they profess, the world would be a better place; ideally, they would modify not their standards of behavior but their tendency to hide behind them.

We in the twenty-first century have become accustomed to the notion of the sacredness of the individual, encouraged to believe in the high value of expressiveness, originality, specialness. Eighteenth-century writers, on the other hand, assumed the superior importance of the social group and of shared opinion. "Expressiveness," in their view, should provide an instrument for articulating the will of the community, not the eccentric desires of individuals. Society implies subordination: not only class hierarchy but individual submission to the good of the group.

French writers of imaginative literature often used domestic situations as ways to examine larger problems. Marriage, an institution at once social and personal, provides a useful image for human relationship as social and emotional fact. The developing eighteenth-century novel, in England and France alike, would assume marriage as the normal goal for men and women; Molière and Racine, writing before the turn of the century, examine economic, psychological, moral, and social implications of specific imagined marriages. The sexual alliances of rulers, Racine's subject in *Phaedra,* have literal consequences far beyond the individuals involved. Molière evokes a private family to suggest how professed sentiment can obscure the operations of ambition. Both understand marriage as social microcosm, a society in miniature, not merely as a structure for fulfillment of personal desire.

In England, writers in genres other than the novel typically focus their attention on a broader panorama. Pope and Swift, like Voltaire satirists of the human scene, consider varied operations of social law and pressure. In *The Rape of the Lock,* Pope uses a card party to epitomize social structures. Swift imagines idealized forms of social institutions ranging from marriage to Parliament, contrasting the ideals with evocations of their actual English counterparts; or he fantasizes the horrifying consequences of venture capitalism in the processing of infants for food. Voltaire's world tourists witness and participate in a vast range of sobering experience. In general, women fill subordinate roles in the harsh social environments evoked by these satiric works. As the evoked social scene widens, erotic love plays a less important part and the position of women becomes increasingly insignificant: women's sphere is the home, and home life matters less than does public life. It is perhaps not irrelevant to note that no work in this section (with the horrifying exception of *A Modest Proposal*) describes or evokes children. Only in adulthood do people assume social responsibility; only then do they provide interesting substance for social commentary.

NATURE

Society establishes one locus of reality for eighteenth-century thinkers, although they understand it as a human construct. Nature comprises another assumed measure of the real. The meanings of the word *nature* vary greatly in eighteenth-century usage, but two large senses are most relevant to the works here included: nature as the inherent order of things, including the physical universe, hence evidence of the deity's plan; and nature meaning specifically *human* nature.

Despite their pervasive awareness of natural contingency (vividly dramatized by Voltaire among others, in his account of the disastrous Lisbon earthquake), writers of this period locate their sense of permanence particularly in the idea of nature. Pope's *Essay on Man* comprises one of the most extensive—as well as intensive— examinations of the concept of natural order and its implications. Emphasizing the inadequacy of human reason, the poem insistently reminds the reader of limitation. We cannot hope to grasp the arrangement of the universe, Pope tells us: how can a part comprehend the whole? Human pride in reason only obscures from its possessors the great truths of a universal structure as flawlessly articulated in every detail as the stellar systems Newton and others had revealed. Contemplation of nature can both humble and exalt its practitioner, teaching the insufficiency of human powers in comparison with divine but also reminding human beings that they inhabit a wondrous universe in which all functions precisely as it should.

The notion of a permanent, divinely ordained natural order offers a good deal of comfort to those aware of flaws in actual social arrangements. It embodies an ideal of harmony, of order in variety, which, although it cannot be fully grasped by human intelligence, can yet provide a model for social complexities. It posits a *system,* a structure of relationships that at some theoretical level necessarily makes sense; thus it provides an assumed substructure of rationality for all experience of irrationality. It supplies a means of valuing all appearances of the natural world: every flower, every minnow, has meaning beyond itself, as part of the great pattern. The ardency with which the period's thinkers cling to belief in such a pattern suggests once more a pervasive anxiety about what human reason could not do. Human beings create a vision of something at once sublimely reasonable and beyond reason's grasp to reassure themselves that the limits of the rational need not coincide with the limits of the human.

The permanence of the conceptual natural order corresponds to that of human nature, as conceived in the eighteenth century. Human nature, it was generally believed, remains in all times and places the same. Thus Racine could re-present a fable from Greek tragedy, using classical setting and characters, with complete assurance that his imagining of Phaedra's conflict and suffering would speak to his contemporaries without falsifying the classical original. Despite social divergencies, fundamental aspects of personality do in fact remain constant: all people hope and fear, feel envy and lust, possess the capacity to reason. All suffer loss, all face death. Thinkers of the Enlightenment emphasized these common aspects of humanity far more than they considered cultural divergencies. Readers and writers alike could draw on this conviction about universality. It provided a test of excellence: if an author's imagining of character failed to conform to what eighteenth-century readers understood as human nature, a work might be securely judged inadequate. Conversely, the idea of a constant human nature held out the hope of longevity for writers who successfully evoked it. Moral philosophers could define human obligation and possibility in the conviction that they too wrote for all time; ethical standards would never change. Like the vision of order in the physical universe, the notion of constancy in human nature provided bedrock for an increasingly secularized society.

CONVENTION AND AUTHORITY

Eighteenth-century society, like all societies, operated, and its literary figures wrote, on the basis of established conventions. Manners are social conventions: agreed-on systems of behavior declared appropriate for specific situations. Guides to manners proliferated in the eighteenth century, expressing a widespread sense that commitment to decorum helped preserve society's important standards. Literary conventions—agreed-on systems of verbal behavior—served comparable purposes in another sphere. Like established codes of manners, such conventions declare continuity between present and past.

The literary conventions of the past, like outmoded manners or styles of dress, may strike the twenty-first-century reader as antiquated and artificial. A woman who curtseyed in a modern living room, a man who appeared in a wig, would seem to us ridiculous, even insane; but, of course, a young woman in jeans would strike our predecessors as equally perverse. The plaintive lyrics of current country music, like the extravagances of rap, operate within restrictive conventions that affect their hearers as "natural" only because they are familiar. Eighteenth-century writers had at their disposal an established set of conventions for every traditional literary genre. As the repetitive rhythms of the country ballad tell listeners what to expect, these literary conventions provided readers with clues about the kind of experience they could anticipate in a given poem or play.

Underlying all specific conventions was the classical assumption that literature existed to delight and to instruct its readers. The various genres represented in this period embody such belief in literature's dual function. Stage comedy and tragedy, the early novel, satire in prose and verse, didactic poetry, the philosophic tale: each form developed its own set of devices for involving audiences and readers in situations requiring moral choice, as well as for creating pleasure. The insistence in drama on unity of time and place (stage action occupying no more time than its representation, with no change of scene) exemplifies one such set, intended to facilitate in audiences the kind of belief encouraging maximum emotional and moral effect. The elevated diction of the *Essay on Man* ("Mark how it mounts, to Man's imperial race, / From the green myriads in the peopled grass"), like the mannered but less dignified language of *The Rape of the Lock* ("Here thou, great Anna! whom three realms obey, / Dost sometimes counsel take—and sometimes tea"), and the two-dimensional characters of Voltaire's tales: such (to us) unfamiliar aspects of these texts provide signals about authorial intention and about anticipated reader response.

One dominant convention of twenty-first-century poetry and prose is something we call "realism." In fiction, verse, and drama, writers often attempt to convey the literal feel of experience, the shape in which events actually occur in the world, the way people really talk. Racine, Pope, Voltaire pursued no such goal. Despite their concern with permanent patterns of thought and feeling, they employed deliberate and obvious forms of artifice as modes of emphasis and of indirection. The sonorous verse in which Racine's characters reflect on their passions ("I hate my life, abominate my lust; / Longing by death to rescue my good name / And hide my black love from the light of day") embodies a characteristic form of stylization. Artistic transformation of life, the period's writers believed, involves the imposition of formal order on the endless flux of event and feeling. The formalities of this literature constitute part of its meaning: its statement that what experience shows as unstable, art makes stable.

Reliance on convention as a mode of control expressed an aspect of the period's constant effort toward elusive stability. The classical past, for many, provided an emblem of that stability, a standard of permanence. But some felt a problem inherent in the high valuing of the past, a problem dramatized by the so-called quarrel of Ancients and Moderns in England and in France. At stake in this controversy was the value of permanence as against the value of change. Proponents of the Ancients believed that the giants of Greece and Rome had not only established standards applicable to all subsequent accomplishment but provided models of achievement never to be excelled. Homer wrote the first great epics; subsequent endeavors in the same genre could only imitate him. Innovation came when it came by making the old new, as Pope makes a woman's dressing for conquest new by comparing it to the arming of Achilles. Moderns who valued originality for its own sake, who multiplied worthless publications, who claimed significance for what time had not tested thereby testified to their own inadequacies and their foolish pride.

Those proud to be Moderns, on the other hand, held that men (possibly even women) standing on the shoulders of the Ancients could see farther than their predecessors. The new conceivably exceeded in value the old; one might discover flaws even in revered figures of the classic past. Not everything had yet been accomplished; fresh possibilities remained always possible. This view, of course, corresponds to one widely current since the eighteenth century, but it did not triumph easily: many powerful thinkers of the late seventeenth and early eighteenth century adhered to the more conservative position.

Also at issue in this debate was the question of authority. What position should one assume who hoped to write and be read? Did authority reside only in tradition? If so, one must write in classical forms, rely on classical allusions. Until late in the eighteenth century, virtually all important writers attempted to ally themselves with the authority of tradition, declaring themselves part of a community extending through time as well as space. The problems of authority became particularly important in connection with satire, a popular Enlightenment form. Satire involves criticism of vice and folly; Molière, Pope, Swift, and Voltaire, at least on occasion, wrote in the satiric mode. To establish the right to criticize fellow men and women, the satirist must establish a rhetorical ascendancy such as the pulpit gives the priest—an ascendancy most readily obtained by at least implicit alliance with literary and moral tradition. The satirist, like the moral philosopher, cannot afford to seem idiosyncratic when prescribing and condemning the behavior of others. The fact that satire flourished so richly in this period suggests another version of the central conflict between reason and passion, the forces of stability and of instability. In its heightened description of the world (people eating babies, young women initiating epic battles over the loss of a lock of hair), satire calls attention to the powerful presence of the irrational, opposing to that presence the clarity of the satirist's own claim to reason and tradition. As it chastises human beings for their eruptions of passion, urging resistance and control, satire reminds its readers of the universality of the irrational as well as of opposition to it. The effort "to correct and moderate men's [and women's] passions," that great theme of the Enlightenment, can equally generate hope or despair: opposed moods richly expressed throughout this period.

FURTHER READING

Useful books on the Enlightenment include, for English background, H. Nicolson, *The Age of Reason: The Eighteenth Century* (1960), and, for an opposed view, D. Greene, *The Age of Exuberance: Backgrounds to Eighteenth-Century English*

Literature (1970). Also useful is F. C. Beiser, *The Sovereignty of Reason: The Defense of Rationality in the Early English Enlightenment* (1996). For the intellectual and social situation in France, L. Crocker, *An Age of Crisis: Man and World in Eighteenth-Century French Thought* (1959); L. Gossman, *French Society and Culture: Background for Eighteenth-Century Literature* (1972); S. Gearhart, *The Open Boundary of History and Fiction: A Critical Approach to the French Enlightenment* (1984); and J. C. Hayes, *Reading the French Enlightenment: System and Subversion* (1999). An excellent treatment of the period's literature in England is M. Price, *To the Palace of Wisdom: Studies in Order and Energy from Dryden to Blake* (1964). M. Williamson, *Raising Their Voices, 1650–1750* (1990), discusses women's contributions to the English Enlightenment. A good introduction to the intellectual situation of eighteenth-century England is J. Sambrook, *The Eighteenth Century: The Intellectual and Cultural Context of English Literature, 1700–1789* (1986). For the artistic situation of France, see T. M. Kavanaugh, *Esthetics of the Moment: Literature and Art in the French Enlightenment* (1996).

TIME LINE

TEXTS	CONTEXTS
	1660 Civil War in England ends with Charles II's ascension to the throne (the "Restoration")
1664 Jean-Baptiste Poquelin Molière, *Tartuffe*	
1665 François de La Rochefoucauld, *Reflections*	**1666** Isaac Newton uncovers laws of gravitation • London, already stricken by plague, is destroyed in the Great Fire and subsequently rebuilt in more orderly fashion
1667 Publication of John Milton's ***Paradise Lost***	
	1670 The London-based Hudson's Bay Company is incorporated by royal charter to trade in North America
1677 Jean Racine, ***Phaedra***	
1678 Marie de la Vergne de La Fayette, *The Princess of Clèves*	
1690 John Locke, *Essay Concerning Human Understanding*	
1691 Sor Juana Inés de la Cruz, ***Reply to Sor Filotea de la Cruz***	**1694** Bank of England is chartered, forerunner of modern national banks and treasury systems; London stock exchange follows in 1698
	1697 Russian czar Peter the Great visits Western Europe and England, resolves to Westernize Russia
	1707 United Kingdom of Great Britain formed by union of England and Scotland
1710 First British copyright law, transferring rights of property in a published work from publisher to author	**1709** Up to 100,000 slaves a year cross the Atlantic, 20,000 to Britain's Caribbean colonies alone
1717 Alexander Pope, ***The Rape of the Lock***	
1719 Daniel Defoe publishes *Robinson Crusoe*, often called the first true novel in English	
1726 Jonathan Swift, ***Gulliver's Travels***	**1721** J. S. Bach, *The Brandenburg Concertos*

Boldface titles indicate works in the anthology.

TIME LINE

TEXTS	CONTEXTS
1729 Swift, *A Modest Proposal*	
1733–1734 Alexander Pope, *An Essay on Man*	
1751 First edition of French *Encyclopédie*, edited by Denis Diderot	
	1753 British Museum founded
1755 Samuel Johnson publishes the *Dictionary of the English Language,* the first comprehensive English dictionary on historical principles	1756–1763 Seven Years' War, involving nine European powers; Britain acquires Canada and Florida, Spain gets Cuba and the Philippines, France wins colonies in India and Africa as well as Guadeloupe and Martinique
1759 François-Marie Arouet de Voltaire, *Candide* • Samuel Johnson, *The History of Rasselas, Prince of Abissinia*	
	1765 James Watt, a Scott, invents the steam engine, first in a series of mechanical innovations ushering in the industrial revolution
1771 First publication of *Encyclopaedia Britannica* and complete French *Encyclopédie* testify to characteristic "Enlightenment" impulse to organize knowledge	1775–1783 American War of Independence; Declaration of Independence, 1776 • Constitution of the United States, 1787, the year of Mozart's opera *Don Giovanni*
1792 Mary Wollstonecraft, *Vindication of the Rights of Woman,* makes feminist case for female equality	1789 French Revolution begins; French National Assembly adopts the Declaration of the Rights of Man
	1799 After successful conquests throughout Europe, Napoleon Bonaparte becomes first consul—in effect, dictator—of France • Ludwig van Beethoven writes his first symphony (1799–1800)

JEAN-BAPTISTE POQUELIN MOLIÈRE
1622–1673

Son of a prosperous Paris merchant, Jean-Baptiste Molière (originally named Poquelin) devoted his entire adult life to the creation of stage illusion, as playwright and as actor. At about the age of twenty-five, he joined a company of traveling players established by the Béjart family; with them he toured the provinces for about twelve years. In 1658 the company was ordered to perform for Louis XIV in Paris; a year later, Molière's first great success, *The High-Brow Ladies (Les Précieuses ridicules)*, was produced. The theatrical company to which he belonged, patronized by the king, became increasingly successful, developing finally (1680) into the Comédie Française. In 1662, Molière married Armande Béjart. He died a few hours after performing in the lead role of his own play *The Imaginary Invalid*.

Molière wrote both broad farce and comedies of character, in which he caricatured some form of vice or folly by embodying it in a single figure. His targets included the miser, the aspiring but vulgar middle class, female would-be intellectuals, the hypochondriac, and in *Tartuffe,* the religious hypocrite.

In *Tartuffe* (1664), as in his other plays, Molière employs classic comic devices of plot and character—here, a foolish, stubborn father blocking the course of young love; an impudent servant commenting on her superiors' actions; a happy ending involving a marriage facilitated by implausible means. He often uses such devices, however, to comment on his own immediate social scene, imagining how universal patterns play themselves out in a specific historical context. *Tartuffe* had contemporary relevance so transparent that the Catholic Church forced the king to ban it, although Molière managed to have it published and produced once more by 1669.

The play's emotional energy derives not from the simple discrepancy of man and mask in Tartuffe ("Is not a face quite different from a mask?" inquires the normative character Cléante, who has no trouble making such distinctions) but from the struggle for erotic, psychic, and economic power in which people employ their masks. One can readily imagine modern equivalents for the stresses and strains within Orgon's family. Orgon, an aging man with grown children, seeks ways to preserve control. His mother, Madame Pernelle, encourages his efforts, thus fostering her illusion that *she* still runs things. Orgon identifies his own interests with those of the hypocritical Tartuffe, toward whom he plays a benevolent role. Because Tartuffe fulsomely hails him as benefactor, Orgon feels utterly powerful in relation to his fawning dependent. When he orders his passive daughter Mariane to marry Tartuffe, he reveals his vision of complete domestic autocracy. Tartuffe's lust, one of those passions forever eluding human mastery, disturbs Orgon's arrangements; in the end, the will of the offstage king orders everything, as though a benevolent god had intervened.

To make Tartuffe a specifically religious hypocrite is an act of inventive daring. Orgon, like his mother, conceals from himself his will to power by verbally subordinating himself to that divinity which Tartuffe too invokes. Although one may easily accept Molière's defense of his intentions (not to mock faith but to attack its misuse), it is not hard to see why the play might trouble religious authorities. Molière suggests how readily religious faith lends itself to misuse, how high-sounding pieties allow men and women to evade self-examination and immediate responsibilities. Tartuffe deceives others by his grandiosities of mortification ("Hang up my hair shirt") and charity; he encourages his victims in their own grandiosities. Orgon can indulge a fantasy of self-subordination (remarking of Tartuffe, "He guides our lives") at the same time that he furthers his more hidden desire for power. Religion offers ready justification for a course manifestly destructive as well as self-seeking.

Cléante, before he meets Tartuffe, claims (accurately) to understand him by his effects on others. Throughout the play, Cléante speaks in the voice of wisdom, counseling moderation, common sense, and self-control, calling attention to folly. More important, he emphasizes how the issues Molière examines in this comedy relate to dominant late seventeenth-century themes:

> Ah, Brother, man's a strangely fashioned creature
> Who seldom is content to follow Nature,
> But recklessly pursues his inclination
> Beyond the narrow bounds of moderation,
> And often, by transgressing Reason's laws,
> Perverts a lofty aim or noble cause.

To follow Nature means to act appropriately to the human situation in the created universe. Humankind occupies a middle position, between beasts and angels; such aspirations as Orgon's desire to control his daughter completely, or his apparent wish to submit himself absolutely to Tartuffe's claim of heavenly wisdom, imply a hope to surpass limitations inherent in the human condition. As Cléante's observations suggest, "to follow Nature," given the rationality of the universe, implies adherence to "Reason's laws." All transgression involves failure to submit to reason's dictates. Molière, with his stylized comic plot, makes that point as insistently as does Racine, who depicts grand passions and cataclysmic effects from them.

Although Cléante understands and can enunciate the principles of proper conduct, his wisdom has no direct effect on the play's action. Although the comedy suggests a social world in which women exist in utter subordination to fathers and husbands, in the plot, two women bring about the clarifications that unmask the villain. The virtuous wife, Elmire, object of Tartuffe's lust, and the articulate servant girl, Dorine, confront the immediate situation with pragmatic inventiveness. Dorine goads others to response; Elmire encourages Tartuffe to play out his sexual fantasies before a hidden audience. Both women have a clear sense of right and wrong, although they express it in less resounding terms than does Cléante. Their concrete insistence on facing what is really going on, cutting through all obfuscation, rescues the men from entanglement in their own abstract formulations.

The women's clarifications, however, do not resolve the comedy's dilemmas. Suddenly the context shifts: economic terms replace erotic ones. It is as though Tartuffe were only playing in his attempt to seduce Elmire; now we get to what really matters: money. For all his claims of disinterestedness, Tartuffe has managed to get control of his dupe's property. Control of property, the action gradually reveals, amounts to power over life itself: prison threatens Orgon, and the prospect of expulsion from their home menaces him and his family alike. Only the convenient and ostentatious artifice of royal intervention rescues the victims and punishes their betrayer.

Comedies conventionally end in the restoration of order, declaring that good inevitably triumphs; rationality renews itself despite the temporary deviations of the foolish and the vicious. At the end of *Tartuffe*, Orgon and his mother have been chastened by revelation of their favorite's depravity, Mariane has been allowed to marry her lover, Tartuffe has been judged, the king's power and justice have reasserted themselves and been acknowledged. In the organization of family and nation (metaphorically a larger family), order reassumes dominion. Yet the arbitrary intervention of the king leaves a disturbing emotional residue. The play has demonstrated that Tartuffe's corrupt will to power (as opposed to Orgon's merely foolish will) can ruthlessly aggrandize itself. Money speaks, in Orgon's society as in ours; possession of wealth implies total control over others. Only a kind of miracle can save Orgon. The miracle occurs, given the benign world of comedy, but the play reminds its readers of the extreme precariousness with which reason finally triumphs, even given the presence of such reasonable people as Cléante and Elmire. Tartuffe's monstrous lust, for women, money, power, genuinely endangers the social structure. *Tartuffe* enforces recognition of the constant threats to rationality, of how much we have at stake in trying to use reason as principle of action.

H. Walker, *Molière* (1990), provides a general biographical and critical introduction to the playwright. Useful critical studies include L. Gossman, *Men and Masks: A Study of Molière* (1963); Jacques Guicharnaud, ed., *Molière: A Collection of Critical Essays* (1964); N. Gross, *From Gesture to Idea: Esthetics and Ethics in Molière's Comedy* (1982); J. F. Gaines, *Social Structures in Molière's Theater* (1984); and L. F. Norman, *The Public Mirror: Molière and the Social Commerce of Depiction* (1999). An excellent treatment of Molière in his historical context is W. D. Howarth, *Molière: A Playwright and His Audience* (1984). Harold C. Knutson, *The Triumph of Wit* (1988), examines Molière in relation to Shakespeare and Ben Jonson. Martin Turnell, *The Classical Moment: Studies of Corneille, Molière, and Racine* (1975), offers useful insight into French dramatic tradition.

PRONOUNCING GLOSSARY

The following list uses common English syllables and stress accents to provide rough equivalents of selected words whose pronunciation may be unfamiliar to the general reader.

Cléante: *clay-ahnt'*

Damis: *dah-meece'*

Dorine: *do-reen'*

Elmire: *el-meer'*

Flipote: *flee-pot'*

Laurent: *lor-awnh'*

Loyal: *lwah-al'*

Molière: *moh-lyehr'*

Orante: *oh-rahnt'*

Orgon: *or-gohnh'*

Pernelle: *payr-nel'*

Tartuffe: *tahr-tewf'*

Valère: *vah-lehr'*

Vincennes: *vanh-sahnhz*

Tartuffe[1]

Preface

Here is a comedy that has excited a good deal of discussion and that has been under attack for a long time; and the persons who are mocked by it have made it plain that they are more powerful in France than all whom my plays have satirized up to this time. Noblemen, ladies of fashion, cuckolds, and doctors all kindly consented to their presentation, which they themselves seemed to enjoy along with everyone else; but hypocrites do not understand banter: they became angry at once, and found it strange that I was bold enough to represent their actions and to care to describe a profession shared by so many good men. This is a crime for which they cannot forgive me, and they have taken up arms against my comedy in a terrible rage. They were careful not to attack it at the point that had wounded them: they are too crafty for that and too clever to reveal their true character. In keeping with their lofty custom, they have used the cause of God to mask their private interests; and *Tartuffe*, they say, is a play that offends piety: it is filled with abominations from beginning to end, and nowhere is there a line that does not deserve to be burned. Every syllable is wicked, the very gestures are criminal, and the slightest glance, turn of the head, or step from right to left conceals mysteries that they are able to explain to my disadvantage. In vain

---

1. Translated by Richard Wilbur. The first version of *Tartuffe* was performed in 1664 and the second in 1667. When a second edition of the third version was printed in June 1669, Molière added his three petitions to Louis XIV; they follow the Preface.

did I submit the play to the criticism of my friends and the scrutiny of the public: all the corrections I could make, the judgment of the king and queen[2] who saw the play, the approval of great princes and ministers of state who honored it with their presence, the opinion of good men who found it worthwhile, all this did not help. They will not let go of their prey, and every day of the week they have pious zealots abusing me in public and damning me out of charity.

I would care very little about all they might say except that their devices make enemies of men whom I respect and gain the support of genuinely good men, whose faith they know and who, because of the warmth of their piety, readily accept the impressions that others present to them. And it is this which forces me to defend myself. Especially to the truly devout do I wish to vindicate my play, and I beg of them with all my heart not to condemn it before seeing it, to rid themselves of preconceptions, and not aid the cause of men dishonored by their actions.

If one takes the trouble to examine my comedy in good faith, he will surely see that my intentions are innocent throughout, and tend in no way to make fun of what men revere; that I have presented the subject with all the precautions that its delicacy imposes; and that I have used all the art and skill that I could to distinguish clearly the character of the hypocrite from that of the truly devout man. For that purpose I used two whole acts to prepare the appearance of my scoundrel. Never is there a moment's doubt about his character; he is known at once from the qualities I have given him; and from one end of the play to the other, he does not say a word, he does not perform an action which does not depict to the audience the character of a wicked man, and which does not bring out in sharp relief the character of the truly good man which I oppose to it.

I know full well that by way of reply, these gentlemen try to insinuate that it is not the role of the theater to speak of these matters; but with their permission, I ask them on what do they base this fine doctrine. It is a proposition they advance as no more than a supposition, for which they offer not a shred of proof; and surely it would not be difficult to show them that comedy, for the ancients, had its origin in religion and constituted a part of its ceremonies; that our neighbors, the Spaniards, have hardly a single holiday celebration in which a comedy is not a part; and that even here in France, it owes its birth to the efforts of a religious brotherhood who still own the Hôtel de Bourgogne, where the most important mystery plays of our faith were presented;[3] that you can still find comedies printed in gothic letters under the name of a learned doctor[4] of the Sorbonne; and without going so far, in our own day the religious dramas of Pierre Corneille[5] have been performed to the admiration of all France.

If the function of comedy is to correct men's vices, I do not see why any should be exempt. Such a condition in our society would be much more dangerous than the thing itself; and we have seen that the theater is admirably suited to provide correction. The most forceful lines of a serious moral

2. Louis XIV was married to Marie Thérèse of Austria.   3. A reference to the *Confrérie de la Passion et Résurrection de Notre-Seigneur* (Fraternity of the Passion and Resurrection of Our Savior), founded in 1402. The Hôtel de Bourgogne was a theater in rivalry with Molière's.   4. Probably Maître Jehân Michel, a medical doctor who wrote mystery plays.   5. Corneille (1606–1684) and Racine were France's two greatest writers of classic tragedy. The two dramas Molière doubtlessly had in mind were *Polyeucte* (1643) and *Théodore, vierge et martyre* (1645).

statement are usually less powerful than those of satire; and nothing will reform most men better than the depiction of their faults. It is a vigorous blow to vices to expose them to public laughter. Criticism is taken lightly, but men will not tolerate satire. They are quite willing to be mean, but they never like to be ridiculed.

I have been attacked for having placed words of piety in the mouth of my impostor. Could I avoid doing so in order to represent properly the character of a hypocrite? It seemed to me sufficient to reveal the criminal motives which make him speak as he does, and I have eliminated all ceremonial phrases, which nonetheless he would not have been found using incorrectly. Yet some say that in the fourth act he sets forth a vicious morality; but is not this a morality which everyone has heard again and again? Does my comedy say anything new here? And is there any fear that ideas so thoroughly detested by everyone can make an impression on men's minds; that I make them dangerous by presenting them in the theater; that they acquire authority from the lips of a scoundrel? There is not the slightest suggestion of any of this; and one must either approve the comedy of *Tartuffe* or condemn all comedies in general.

This has indeed been done in a furious way for some time now, and never was the theater so much abused.[6] I cannot deny that there were Church Fathers who condemned comedy; but neither will it be denied me that there were some who looked on it somewhat more favorably. Thus authority, on which censure is supposed to depend, is destroyed by this disagreement; and the only conclusion that can be drawn from this difference of opinion among men enlightened by the same wisdom is that they viewed comedy in different ways, and that some considered it in its purity, while others regarded it in its corruption and confused it with all those wretched performances which have been rightly called performances of filth.

And in fact, since we should talk about things rather than words, and since most misunderstanding comes from including contrary notions in the same word, we need only to remove the veil of ambiguity and look at comedy in itself to see if it warrants condemnation. It will surely be recognized that as it is nothing more than a clever poem which corrects men's faults by means of agreeable lessons, it cannot be condemned without injustice. And if we listened to the voice of ancient times on this matter, it would tell us that its most famous philosophers have praised comedy—they who professed so austere a wisdom and who ceaselessly denounced the vices of their times. It would tell us that Aristotle spent his evenings at the theater[7] and took the trouble to reduce the art of making comedies to rules. It would tell us that some of its greatest and most honored men took pride in writing comedies themselves;[8] and that others did not disdain to recite them in public; that Greece expressed its admiration for this art by means of handsome prizes and magnificent theaters to honor it; and finally, that in Rome this same art also received extraordinary honors; I do not speak of Rome run riot under the license of the emperors, but of disciplined Rome,

---

6. Molière had in mind Nicole's two attacks on the theater: *Visionnaires* (1666) and *Traité de la Comédie* (1667), as well as the prince de Conti's *Traité de la Comédie* (1666).   7. A reference to Aristotle's *Poetics* (composed between 335 and 322 B.C., the year of his death).   8. Scipio Africanus Minor (ca. 185–129 B.C.), the Roman consul and general responsible for the final destruction of Carthage in 146 B.C., collaborated with Terence (Publius Terentius Afer, ca. 195 or 185–ca. 159 B.C.), a writer of comedies.

governed by the wisdom of the consuls, and in the age of the full vigor of Roman dignity.

I admit that there have been times when comedy became corrupt. And what do men not corrupt every day? There is nothing so innocent that men cannot turn it to crime; nothing so beneficial that its values cannot be reversed; nothing so good in itself that it cannot be put to bad uses. Medical knowledge benefits mankind and is revered as one of our most wonderful possessions; and yet there was a time when it fell into discredit, and was often used to poison men. Philosophy is a gift of Heaven; it has been given to us to bring us to the knowledge of a God by contemplating the wonders of nature; and yet we know that often it has been turned away from its function and has been used openly in support of impiety. Even the holiest of things are not immune from human corruption, and every day we see scoundrels who use and abuse piety, and wickedly make it serve the greatest of crimes. But this does not prevent one from making the necessary distinctions. We do not confuse in the same false inference the goodness of things that are corrupted with the wickedness of the corrupt. The function of an art is always distinguished from its misuse; and as medicine is not forbidden because it was banned in Rome,[9] nor philosophy because it was publicly condemned in Athens,[1] we should not suppress comedy simply because it has been condemned at certain times. This censure was justified then for reasons which no longer apply today; it was limited to what was then seen; and we should not seize on these limits, apply them more rigidly than is necessary, and include in our condemnation the innocent along with the guilty. The comedy that this censure attacked is in no way the comedy that we want to defend. We must be careful not to confuse the one with the other. There may be two persons whose morals may be completely different. They may have no resemblance to one another except in their names, and it would be a terrible injustice to want to condemn Olympia, who is a good woman, because there is also an Olympia who is lewd. Such procedures would make for great confusion everywhere. Everything under the sun would be condemned; now since this rigor is not applied to the countless instances of abuse we see every day, the same should hold for comedy, and those plays should be approved in which instruction and virtue reign supreme.

I know there are some so delicate that they cannot tolerate a comedy, who say that the most decent are the most dangerous, that the passions they present are all the more moving because they are virtuous, and that men's feelings are stirred by these presentations. I do not see what great crime it is to be affected by the sight of a generous passion; and this utter insensitivity to which they would lead us is indeed a high degree of virtue! I wonder if so great a perfection resides within the strength of human nature, and I wonder if it is not better to try to correct and moderate men's passions than to try to suppress them altogether. I grant that there are places better to visit than the theater; and if we want to condemn every single thing that does not bear directly on God and our salvation, it is right that comedy be included, and I should willingly grant that it be condemned along with everything else. But if we admit, as is in fact true, that the exercise of piety will permit interrup-

---

9. Pliny the Elder says that the Romans expelled their doctors at the same time that the Greeks did theirs.
1. An allusion to Socrates' condemnation to death.

tions, and that men need amusement, I maintain that there is none more innocent than comedy. I have dwelled too long on this matter. Let me finish with the words of a great prince on the comedy, *Tartuffe*.[2]

Eight days after it had been banned, a play called *Scaramouche the Hermit*[3] was performed before the court; and the king, on his way out, said to this great prince: "I should really like to know why the persons who make so much noise about Molière's comedy do not say a word about *Scaramouche*." To which the prince replied, "It is because the comedy of *Scaramouche* makes fun of Heaven and religion, which these gentlemen do not care about at all, but that of Molière makes fun of *them*, and that is what they cannot bear."

THE AUTHOR

FIRST PETITION[4]

(*Presented to the King on the Comedy of Tartuffe*)

Sire,

As the duty of comedy is to correct men by amusing them, I believed that in my occupation I could do nothing better than attack the vices of my age by making them ridiculous; and as hypocrisy is undoubtedly one of the most common, most improper, and most dangerous, I thought, Sire, that I would perform a service for all good men of your kingdom if I wrote a comedy which denounced hypocrites and placed in proper view all of the contrived poses of these incredibly virtuous men, all of the concealed villainies of these counterfeit believers who would trap others with a fraudulent piety and a pretended virtue.

I have written this comedy, Sire, with all the care and caution that the delicacy of the subject demands; and so as to maintain all the more properly the admiration and respect due to truly devout men, I have delineated my character as sharply as I could; I have left no room for doubt; I have removed all that might confuse good with evil, and have used for this painting only the specific colors and essential lines that make one instantly recognize a true and brazen hypocrite.

Nevertheless, all my precautions have been to no avail. Others have taken advantage of the delicacy of your feelings on religious matters, and they have been able to deceive you on the only side of your character which lies open to deception: your respect for holy things. By underhanded means, the Tartuffes have skillfully gained Your Majesty's favor, and the models have succeeded in eliminating the copy, no matter how innocent it may have been and no matter what resemblance was found between them.

Although the suppression of this work was a serious blow for me, my misfortune was nonetheless softened by the way in which Your Majesty

---

2. One of Molière's benefactors who liked the play was the prince de Condé; de Condé had *Tartuffe* read to him and also privately performed for him.   3. A troupe of Italian comedians had just performed the licentious farce, in which a hermit dressed as a monk makes love to a married woman, announcing that *questo e per mortificar la carne* (this is to mortify the flesh).   4. The first of the three *petitions* or *placets* to Louis XIV concerning the play. On May 12, 1664, *Tartuffe*—or at least the first three acts roughly as they now stand—was performed at Versailles. A cabal unfavorable to Molière, including the archbishop of Paris, Hardouin de Péréfixe, Queen Mother Anne of Austria, certain influential courtiers, and the Brotherhood or Company of the Holy Sacrament (formed in 1627 to enforce morality), arranged that the play be banned and Molière censured.

explained his attitude on the matter; and I believed, Sire, that Your Majesty removed any cause I had for complaint, as you were kind enough to declare that you found nothing in this comedy that you would forbid me to present in public.

Yet, despite this glorious declaration of the greatest and most enlightened king in the world, despite the approval of the Papal Legate[5] and of most of our churchmen, all of whom, at private readings of my work, agreed with the views of Your Majesty, despite all this, a book has appeared by a certain priest[6] which boldly contradicts all of these noble judgments. Your Majesty expressed himself in vain, and the Papal Legate and churchmen gave their opinion to no avail: sight unseen, my comedy is diabolical, and so is my brain; I am a devil garbed in flesh and disguised as a man,[7] a libertine, a disbeliever who deserves a punishment that will set an example. It is not enough that fire expiate my crime in public, for that would be letting me off too easily: the generous piety of this good man will not stop there; he will not allow me to find any mercy in the sight of God; he demands that I be damned, and that will settle the matter.

This book, Sire, was presented to Your Majesty; and I am sure that you see for yourself how unpleasant it is for me to be exposed daily to the insults of these gentlemen, what harm these abuses will do my reputation if they must be tolerated, and finally, how important it is for me to clear myself of these false charges and let the public know that my comedy is nothing more than what they want it to be. I will not ask, Sire, for what I need for the sake of my reputation and the innocence of my work: enlightened kings such as you do not need to be told what is wished of them; like God, they see what we need and know better than we what they should give us. It is enough for me to place my interests in Your Majesty's hands, and I respectfully await whatever you may care to command.

(August, 1664)

SECOND PETITION[8]

(*Presented to the King in His Camp Before the City of Lille, in Flanders*)

Sire,

It is bold indeed for me to ask a favor of a great monarch in the midst of his glorious victories; but in my present situation, Sire, where will I find protection anywhere but where I seek it, and to whom can I appeal against the authority of the power[9] that crushes me, if not to the source of power and authority, the just dispenser of absolute law, the sovereign judge and master of all?

---

5. Cardinal Legate Chigi, nephew to Pope Alexander VII, heard a reading of *Tartuffe* at Fontainebleau on August 4, 1664.   6. Pierre Roullé, the curate of St. Barthélémy, who wrote a scathing attack on the play and sent his book to the king.   7. Molière took some of these phrases from Roullé.   8. On August 5, 1667, *Tartuffe* was performed at the Palais-Royal. The opposition—headed by the first president of parliament—brought in the police, and the play was stopped. Because Louis was campaigning in Flanders, friends of Molière brought the second *placet* to Lille. Louis had always been favorable toward the playwright; in August 1665 Molière's company, the *Troupe de Monsieur* (nominally sponsored by Louis's brother Philippe, duc d'Orléans), had become the *Troupe du Roi*.   9. President de Lanvignon, in charge of the Paris police.

My comedy, Sire, has not enjoyed the kindnesses of Your Majesty. All to no avail, I produced it under the title of *The Hypocrite* and disguised the principal character as a man of the world; in vain I gave him a little hat, long hair, a wide collar, a sword, and lace clothing,[1] softened the action and carefully eliminated all that I thought might provide even the shadow of grounds for discontent on the part of the famous models of the portrait I wished to present; nothing did any good. The conspiracy of opposition revived even at mere conjecture of what the play would be like. They found a way of persuading those who in all other matters plainly insist that they are not to be deceived. No sooner did my comedy appear than it was struck down by the very power which should impose respect; and all that I could do to save myself from the fury of this tempest was to say that Your Majesty had given me permission to present the play and I did not think it was necessary to ask this permission of others, since only Your Majesty could have refused it.

I have no doubt, Sire, that the men whom I depict in my comedy will employ every means possible to influence Your Majesty, and will use, as they have used already, those truly good men who are all the more easily deceived because they judge of others by themselves.[2] They know how to display all of their aims in the most favorable light; yet, no matter how pious they may seem, it is surely not the interests of God which stir them; they have proven this often enough in the comedies they have allowed to be performed hundreds of times without making the least objection. Those plays attacked only piety and religion, for which they care very little; but this play attacks and makes fun of them, and that is what they cannot bear. They will never forgive me for unmasking their hypocrisy in the eyes of everyone. And I am sure that they will not neglect to tell Your Majesty that people are shocked by my comedy. But the simple truth, Sire, is that all Paris is shocked only by its ban, that the most scrupulous persons have found its presentation worthwhile, and men are astounded that individuals of such known integrity should show so great a deference to people whom everyone should abominate and who are so clearly opposed to the true piety which they profess.

I respectfully await the judgment that Your Majesty will deign to pronounce: but it's certain, Sire, that I need not think of writing comedies if the Tartuffes are triumphant, if they thereby seize the right to persecute me more than ever, and find fault with even the most innocent lines that flow from my pen.

Let your goodness, Sire, give me protection against their envenomed rage, and allow me, at your return from so glorious a campaign, to relieve Your Majesty from the fatigue of his conquests, give him innocent pleasures after such noble accomplishments, and make the monarch laugh who makes all Europe tremble!

(*August, 1667*)

---

1. There is evidence that in 1664 Tartuffe played his role dressed in a cassock, thus allying him more directly to the clergy.   2. Molière apparently did not know that de Lanvignon had been affiliated with the Company of the Holy Sacrament for the previous ten years.

THIRD PETITION

(*Presented to the King*)

Sire,

A very honest doctor[3] whose patient I have the honor to be, promises and will legally contract to make me live another thirty years if I can obtain a favor for him from Your Majesty. I told him of his promise that I do not deserve so much, and that I should be glad to help him if he will merely agree not to kill me. This favor, Sire, is a post of canon at your royal chapel of Vincennes, made vacant by death.

May I dare to ask for this favor from Your Majesty on the very day of the glorious resurrection of *Tartuffe*, brought back to life by your goodness? By this first favor I have been reconciled with the devout, and the second will reconcile me with the doctors.[4] Undoubtedly this would be too much grace for me at one time, but perhaps it would not be too much for Your Majesty, and I await your answer to my petition with respectful hope.

(February, 1669)

CHARACTERS

MADAME PERNELLE, *Orgon's mother*
ORGON, *Elmire's husband*
ELMIRE, *Orgon's wife*
DAMIS, *Orgon's son, Elmire's stepson*
MARIANE, *Orgon's daughter, Elmire's stepdaughter, in love with Valère*

VALÈRE, *in love with Mariane*
CLÉANTE, *Orgon's brother-in-law*
TARTUFFE,[5] *a hypocrite*
DORINE, *Mariane's lady's-maid*
M. LOYAL, *a bailiff*
A POLICE OFFICER
FLIPOTE, *Mme Pernelle's maid*

The SCENE *throughout:* ORGON's *house in Paris*

Act I

SCENE 1[6]

MADAME PERNELLE *and* FLIPOTE, *her maid*, ELMIRE, MARIANE, DORINE, DAMIS, CLÉANTE

MADAME PERNELLE   Come, come, Flipote; it's time I left this place.
ELMIRE   I can't keep up, you walk at such a pace.
MADAME PERNELLE   Don't trouble, child; no need to show me out.
  It's not your manners I'm concerned about.
ELMIRE   We merely pay you the respect we owe.   5

3. A physician friend, M. de Mauvillain, who helped Molière with some of the medical details of *Le Malade imaginaire*.   4. Doctors are ridiculed to varying degrees in earlier plays of Molière: *Dom Juan, L'Amour médecin,* and *Le Médecin malgré lui*.   5. The name *Tartuffe* has been traced back to an older word associated with liar or charlatan: *truffer,* "to deceive" or "to cheat." Then there was also the Italian actor Tartufo, physically deformed and truffle shaped. Most of the other names are typical of this genre of court comedy and possess rather elegant connotations of pastoral and *bergerie. Dorine:* a *demoiselle de compagne* and not a mere maid, that is, a female companion to Mariane of roughly the same social status. This in part accounts for the liberties she takes in conversation with Orgon, Madame Pernelle, and others. Her name is short for Théodorine.   6. In French drama, the scene changes every time a character enters or exits.

But, Mother, why this hurry? Must you go?
MADAME PERNELLE   I must. This house appals me. No one in it
  Will pay attention for a single minute.
  I offer good advice, but you won't hear it.
  Children, I take my leave much vexed in spirit.   10
  You all break in and chatter on and on.
  It's like a madhouse with the keeper gone.
DORINE   If . . .
MADAME PERNELLE
               Girl, you talk too much, and I'm afraid
  You're far too saucy for a lady's-maid.
  You push in everywhere and have your say.   15
DAMIS   But . . .
MADAME PERNELLE
            You, boy, grow more foolish every day.
  To think my grandson should be such a dunce!
  I've said a hundred times, if I've said it once,
  That if you keep the course on which you've started,
  You'll leave your worthy father broken-hearted.   20
MARIANE   I think . . .
MADAME PERNELLE   And you, his sister, seem so pure,
  So shy, so innocent, and so demure.
  But you know what they say about still waters.
  I pity parents with secretive daughters.
ELMIRE   Now, Mother . . .
MADAME PERNELLE   And as for you, child, let me add   25
  That your behavior is extremely bad,
  And a poor example for these children, too.
  Their dear, dead mother did far better than you.
  You're much too free with money, and I'm distressed
  To see you so elaborately dressed.   30
  When it's one's husband that one aims to please,
  One has no need of costly fripperies.
CLÉANTE   Oh, Madam, really . . .
MADAME PERNELLE   You are her brother, Sir,
  And I respect and love you; yet if I were
  My son, this lady's good and pious spouse,   35
  I wouldn't make you welcome in my house.
  You're full of worldly counsels which, I fear,
  Aren't suitable for decent folk to hear.
  I've spoken bluntly, Sir; but it behooves us
  Not to mince words when righteous fervor moves us.   40
DAMIS   Your man Tartuffe is full of holy speeches . . .
MADAME PERNELLE   And practises precisely what he preaches.
  He's a fine man, and should be listened to.
  I will not hear him mocked by fools like you.
DAMIS   Good God! Do you expect me to submit   45
  To the tyranny of that carping hypocrite?
  Must we forgo all joys and satisfactions
  Because that bigot censures all our actions?

DORINE   To hear him talk—and he talks all the time—
  There's nothing one can do that's not a crime.   50
  He rails at everything, your dear Tartuffe.
MADAME PERNELLE   Whatever he reproves deserves reproof.
  He's out to save your souls, and all of you
  Must love him, as my son would have you do.
DAMIS   Ah no, Grandmother, I could never take   55
  To such a rascal, even for my father's sake.
  That's how I feel, and I shall not dissemble.
  His every action makes me seethe and tremble
  With helpless anger, and I have no doubt
  That he and I will shortly have it out.   60
DORINE   Surely it is a shame and a disgrace
  To see this man usurp the master's place—
  To see this beggar who, when first he came,
  Had not a shoe or shoestring to his name
  So far forget himself that he behaves   65
  As if the house were his, and we his slaves.
MADAME PERNELLE   Well, mark my words, your souls would fare far better
  If you obeyed his precepts to the letter.
DORINE   You see him as a saint. I'm far less awed;
  In fact, I see right through him. He's a fraud.   70
MADAME PERNELLE   Nonsense!
DORINE   His man Laurent's the same, or worse;
  I'd not trust either with a penny purse.
MADAME PERNELLE   I can't say what his servant's morals may be;
  His own great goodness I can guarantee.
  You all regard him with distaste and fear   75
  Because he tells you what you're loath to hear,
  Condemns your sins, points out your moral flaws,
  And humbly strives to further Heaven's cause.
DORINE   If sin is all that bothers him, why is it
  He's so upset when folk drop in to visit?   80
  Is Heaven so outraged by a social call
  That he must prophesy against us all?
  I'll tell you what I think: if you ask me,
  He's jealous of my mistress' company.
MADAME PERNELLE   Rubbish!
  [To ELMIRE.]
                    He's not alone, child, in complaining   85
  Of all of your promiscuous entertaining.
  Why, the whole neighborhood's upset, I know,
  By all these carriages that come and go,
  With crowds of guests parading in and out
  And noisy servants loitering about.   90
  In all of this, I'm sure there's nothing vicious;
  But why give people cause to be suspicious?
CLÉANTE   They need no cause; they'll talk in any case.
  Madam, this world would be a joyless place
  If, fearing what malicious tongues might say,   95

We locked our doors and turned our friends away.
And even if one did so dreary a thing,
D' you think those tongues would cease their chattering?
One can't fight slander; it's a losing battle;
Let us instead ignore their tittle-tattle.   100
Let's strive to live by conscience' clear decrees,
And let the gossips gossip as they please.
DORINE   If there is talk against us, I know the source:
It's Daphne and her little husband, of course.
Those who have greatest cause for guilt and shame   105
Are quickest to besmirch a neighbor's name.
When there's a chance for libel, they never miss it;
When something can be made to seem illicit
They're off at once to spread the joyous news,
Adding to fact what fantasies they choose.   110
By talking up their neighbor's indiscretions
They seek to camouflage their own transgressions,
Hoping that others' innocent affairs
Will lend a hue of innocence to theirs,
Or that their own black guilt will come to seem   115
Part of a general shady color-scheme.
MADAME PERNELLE   All this is quite irrelevant. I doubt
That anyone's more virtuous and devout
Than dear Orante; and I'm informed that she
Condemns your mode of life most vehemently.   120
DORINE   Oh, yes, she's strict, devout, and has no taint
Of worldliness; in short, she seems a saint.
But it was time which taught her that disguise;
She's thus because she can't be otherwise.
So long as her attractions could enthrall,   125
She flounced and flirted and enjoyed it all,
But now that they're no longer what they were
She quits a world which fast is quitting her,
And wears a veil of virtue to conceal
Her bankrupt beauty and her lost appeal.   130
That's what becomes of old coquettes today:
Distressed when all their lovers fall away,
They see no recourse but to play the prude,
And so confer a style on solitude.
Thereafter, they're severe with everyone,   135
Condemning all our actions, pardoning none,
And claiming to be pure, austere, and zealous
When, if the truth were known, they're merely jealous,
And cannot bear to see another know
The pleasures time has forced them to forgo.   140
MADAME PERNELLE [*Initially to* ELMIRE.]
That sort of talk[7] is what you like to hear;

---

7. In the original, a reference to a collection of novels about chivalry found in *La Bibliothèque bleue* (The Blue Library), written for children.

Therefore you'd have us all keep still, my dear,
While Madam rattles on the livelong day.
Nevertheless, I mean to have my say.
I tell you that you're blest to have Tartuffe   145
Dwelling, as my son's guest, beneath this roof;
That Heaven has sent him to forestall its wrath
By leading you, once more, to the true path;
That all he reprehends is reprehensible,
And that you'd better heed him, and be sensible.   150
These visits, balls, and parties in which you revel
Are nothing but inventions of the Devil.
One never hears a word that's edifying:
Nothing but chaff and foolishness and lying,
As well as vicious gossip in which one's neighbor   155
Is cut to bits with épée, foil, and saber.
People of sense are driven half-insane
At such affairs, where noise and folly reign
And reputations perish thick and fast.
As a wise preacher said on Sunday last,   160
Parties are Towers of Babylon,[8] because
The guests all babble on with never a pause;
And then he told a story which, I think . . .
[To CLÉANTE.] I heard that laugh, Sir, and I saw that wink!
Go find your silly friends and laugh some more!   165
Enough; I'm going; don't show me to the door.
I leave this household much dismayed and vexed;
I cannot say when I shall see you next.
         [Slapping FLIPOTE.]
Wake up, don't stand there gaping into space!
I'll slap some sense into that stupid face.   170
Move, move, you slut.

SCENE 2

CLÉANTE, DORINE

CLÉANTE   I think I'll stay behind;
    I want no further pieces of her mind.
    How that old lady . . .
DORINE   Oh, what wouldn't she say
    If she could hear you speak of her that way!
    She'd thank you for the *lady*, but I'm sure   5
    She'd find the *old* a little premature.
CLÉANTE   My, what a scene she made, and what a din!
    And how this man Tartuffe has taken her in!
DORINE   Yes, but her son is even worse deceived;
    His folly must be seen to be believed.   10

8. Tower of Babel. Madame Pernelle's malapropism is the cause of Cléante's laughter.

In the late troubles,[9] he played an able part
And served his king with wise and loyal heart,
But he's quite lost his senses since he fell
Beneath Tartuffe's infatuating spell.
He calls him brother, and loves him as his life,   15
Preferring him to mother, child, or wife.
In him and him alone will he confide;
He's made him his confessor and his guide;
He pets and pampers him with love more tender
Than any pretty maiden could engender,   20
Gives him the place of honor when they dine,
Delights to see him gorging like a swine,
Stuffs him with dainties till his guts distend,
And when he belches, cries "God bless you, friend!"
In short, he's mad; he worships him; he dotes;   25
His deeds he marvels at, his words, he quotes,
Thinking each act a miracle, each word
Oracular as those that Moses heard.
Tartuffe, much pleased to find so easy a victim,
Has in a hundred ways beguiled and tricked him,   30
Milked him of money, and with his permission
Established here a sort of Inquisition.
Even Laurent, his lackey, dares to give
Us arrogant advice on how to live;
He sermonizes us in thundering tones   35
And confiscates our ribbons and colognes.
Last week he tore a kerchief into pieces
Because he found it pressed in a *Life of Jesus*:
He said it was a sin to juxtapose
Unholy vanities and holy prose.   40

SCENE 3

ELMIRE, MARIANE, DAMIS, CLÉANTE, DORINE

ELMIRE [*To* CLÉANTE.]   You did well not to follow; she stood in the door
And said *verbatim* all she'd said before.
I saw my husband coming. I think I'd best
Go upstairs now, and take a little rest.
CLÉANTE   I'll wait and greet him here; then I must go.   5
I've really only time to say hello.
DAMIS   Sound him about my sister's wedding, please.
I think Tartuffe's against it, and that he's
Been urging Father to withdraw his blessing.
As you well know, I'd find that most distressing.   10
Unless my sister and Valère can marry,
My hopes to wed *his* sister will miscarry.

9. A series of political disturbances during the minority of Louis XIV. Specifically, these consisted of the *Fronde* ("opposition") of the Parlement (1648–49) and the *Fronde* of the Princes (1650–53). Orgon is depicted as supporting Louis XIV in these outbreaks and their resolution.

And I'm determined . . .

DORINE   He's coming.

SCENE 4

ORGON, CLÉANTE, DORINE

ORGON   Ah, Brother, good-day.

CLÉANTE   Well, welcome back, I'm sorry I can't stay.
How was the country? Blooming, I trust, and green?

ORGON   Excuse me, Brother; just one moment.
[*To* DORINE.]   Dorine . . .
[*To* CLÉANTE.] To put my mind at rest, I always learn   5
The household news the moment I return.
[*To* DORINE.] Has all been well, these two days I've been gone?
How are the family? What's been going on?

DORINE   Your wife, two days ago, had a bad fever,
And a fierce headache which refused to leave her.   10

ORGON   Ah. And Tartuffe?

DORINE   Tartuffe? Why, he's round and red.
Bursting with health, and excellently fed.

ORGON   Poor fellow!

DORINE   That night, the mistress was unable
To take a single bite at the dinner-table.
Her headache-pains, she said, were simply hellish.   15

ORGON   Ah. And Tartuffe?

DORINE   He ate his meal with relish,
And zealously devoured in her presence
A leg of mutton and a brace of pheasants.

ORGON   Poor fellow!

DORINE   Well, the pains continued strong,
And so she tossed and tossed the whole night long,   20
Now icy-cold, now burning like a flame.
We sat beside her bed till morning came.

ORGON   Ah. And Tartuffe?

DORINE   Why, having eaten, he rose
And sought his room, already in a doze,
Got into his warm bed, and snored away   25
In perfect peace until the break of day.

ORGON   Poor fellow!

DORINE   After much ado, we talked her
Into dispatching someone for the doctor.
He bled her, and the fever quickly fell.

ORGON   Ah. And Tartuffe?

DORINE   He bore it very well.   30
To keep his cheerfulness at any cost,
And make up for the blood Madame had lost,
He drank, at lunch, four beakers full of port.

ORGON   Poor fellow.

DORINE   Both are doing well, in short.

I'll go and tell Madame that you've expressed   35
Keen sympathy and anxious interest.

SCENE 5

ORGON, CLÉANTE

CLÉANTE   That girl was laughing in your face, and though
  I've no wish to offend you, even so
  I'm bound to say that she had some excuse.
  How can you possibly be such a goose?
  Are you so dazed by this man's hocus-pocus   5
  That all the world, save him, is out of focus?
  You've given him clothing, shelter, food, and care;
  Why must you also . . .
ORGON   Brother, stop right there.
  You do not know the man of whom you speak.
CLÉANTE   I grant you that. But my judgment's not so weak   10
  That I can't tell, by his effect on others . . .
ORGON   Ah, when you meet him, you two will be like brothers!
  There's been no loftier soul since time began.
  He is a man who . . . a man who . . . an excellent man.
  To keep his precepts is to be reborn,   15
  And view this dunghill of a world with scorn.
  Yes, thanks to him I'm a changed man indeed.
  Under his tutelage my soul's been freed
  From earthly loves, and every human tie:
  My mother, children, brother, and wife could die,   20
  And I'd not feel a single moment's pain.
CLÉANTE   That's a fine sentiment, Brother; most humane.
ORGON   Oh, had you seen Tartuffe as I first knew him,
  Your heart, like mine, would have surrendered to him.
  He used to come into our church each day   25
  And humbly kneel nearby, and start to pray.
  He'd draw the eyes of everybody there
  By the deep fervor of his heartfelt prayer;
  He'd sigh and weep, and sometimes with a sound
  Of rapture he would bend and kiss the ground;   30
  And when I rose to go, he'd run before
  To offer me holy-water at the door.
  His serving-man, no less devout than he,
  Informed me of his master's poverty;
  I gave him gifts, but in his humbleness   35
  He'd beg me every time to give him less.
  "Oh, that's too much," he'd cry, "too much by twice!
  I don't deserve it. The half, Sir, would suffice."
  And when I wouldn't take it back, he'd share
  Half of it with the poor, right then and there.   40
  At length, Heaven prompted me to take him in
  To dwell with us, and free our souls from sin.
  He guides our lives, and to protect my honor

Stays by my wife, and keeps an eye upon her;
He tells me whom she sees, and all she does,   45
And seems more jealous than I ever was!
And how austere he is! Why, he can detect
A moral sin where you would least suspect;
In smallest trifles, he's extremely strict.
Last week, his conscience was severely pricked   50
Because, while praying, he had caught a flea
And killed it, so he felt, too wrathfully.[1]
CLÉANTE   Good God, man! Have you lost your common sense—
Or is this all some joke at my expense?
How can you stand there and in all sobriety . . .   55
ORGON   Brother, your language savors of impiety.
Too much free-thinking's made your faith unsteady,
And as I've warned you many times already,
'Twill get you into trouble before you're through.
CLÉANTE   So I've been told before by dupes like you: 60
Being blind, you'd have all others blind as well;
The clear-eyed man you call an infidel,
And he who sees through humbug and pretense
Is charged, by you, with want of reverence.
Spare me your warnings, Brother; I have no fear   65
Of speaking out, for you and Heaven to hear,
Against affected zeal and pious knavery.
There's true and false in piety, as in bravery,
And just as those whose courage shines the most
In battle, are the least inclined to boast,   70
So those whose hearts are truly pure and lowly
Don't make a flashy show of being holy.
There's a vast difference, so it seems to me,
Between true piety and hypocrisy:
How do you fail to see it, may I ask?   75
Is not a face quite different from a mask?
Cannot sincerity and cunning art,
Reality and semblance, be told apart?
Are scarecrows just like men, and do you hold
That a false coin is just as good as gold?   80
Ah, Brother, man's a strangely fashioned creature
Who seldom is content to follow Nature,
But recklessly pursues his inclination
Beyond the narrow bounds of moderation,
And often, by transgressing Reason's laws,   85
Perverts a lofty aim or noble cause.
A passing observation, but it applies.
ORGON   I see, dear Brother, that you're profoundly wise;
You harbor all the insight of the age.
You are our one clear mind, our only sage,   90

1. In the *Golden Legend* (*Legenda sanctorum*), a popular collection of the lives of the saints written in the 13th century, it is said of St. Marcarius the Elder (d. 390) that he dwelt naked in the desert for six months, a penance he felt appropriate for having killed a flea.

The era's oracle, its Cato[2] too,
And all mankind are fools compared to you.
CLÉANTE   Brother, I don't pretend to be a sage,
Nor have I all the wisdom of the age.
There's just one insight I would dare to claim: 95
I know that true and false are not the same;
And just as there is nothing I more revere
Than a soul whose faith is steadfast and sincere,
Nothing that I more cherish and admire
Than honest zeal and true religious fire,   100
So there is nothing that I find more base
Than specious piety's dishonest face—
Than these bold mountebanks, these histrios
Whose impious mummeries and hollow shows
Exploit our love of Heaven, and make a jest   105
Of all that men think holiest and best;
These calculating souls who offer prayers
Not to their Maker, but as public wares,
And seek to buy respect and reputation
With lifted eyes and sighs of exaltation;   110
These charlatans, I say, whose pilgrim souls
Proceed, by way of Heaven, toward earthly goals,
Who weep and pray and swindle and extort,
Who preach the monkish life, but haunt the court,
Who make their zeal the partner of their vice—   115
Such men are vengeful, sly, and cold as ice,
And when there is an enemy to defame
They cloak their spite in fair religion's name,
Their private spleen and malice being made
To seem a high and virtuous crusade,   120
Until, to mankind's reverent applause,
They crucify their foe in Heaven's cause.
Such knaves are all too common; yet, for the wise,
True piety isn't hard to recognize,
And, happily, these present times provide us   125
With bright examples to instruct and guide us.
Consider Ariston and Périandre;
Look at Oronte, Alcidamas, Clitandre;[3]
Their virtue is acknowledged; who could doubt it?
But you won't hear them beat the drum about it.   130
They're never ostentatious, never vain,
And their religion's moderate and humane;
It's not their way to criticize and chide:
They think censoriousness a mark of pride,
And therefore, letting others preach and rave,   135
They show, by deeds, how Christians should behave.
They think no evil of their fellow man,

---

2. Roman statesman (95–46 B.C.) with an enduring reputation for honesty and incorruptibility.
3. Vaguely Greek and Roman names derived from the elegant literature of the day.

But judge of him as kindly as they can.
They don't intrigue and wangle and conspire;
To lead a good life is their one desire;   140
The sinner wakes no rancorous hate in them;
It is the sin alone which they condemn;
Nor do they try to show a fiercer zeal
For Heaven's cause than Heaven itself could feel.
These men I honor, these men I advocate   145
As models for us all to emulate.
Your man is not their sort at all, I fear:
And, while your praise of him is quite sincere,
I think that you've been dreadfully deluded.
ORGON   Now then, dear Brother, is your speech concluded?   150
CLÉANTE   Why, yes.
ORGON   Your servant, Sir.
      [*He turns to go.*]
CLÉANTE   No, Brother; wait.
   There's one more matter. You agreed of late
   That young Valère might have your daughter's hand.
ORGON   I did.
CLÉANTE   And set the date, I understand.
ORGON   Quite so.
CLÉANTE   You've now postponed it; is that true?   155
ORGON   No doubt.
CLÉANTE   The match no longer pleases you?
ORGON   Who knows?
CLÉANTE   D'you mean to go back on your word?
ORGON   I won't say that.
CLÉANTE   Has anything occurred
   Which might entitle you to break your pledge?
ORGON   Perhaps.
CLÉANTE   Why must you hem, and haw, and hedge?   160
   The boy asked me to sound you in this affair . . .
ORGON   It's been a pleasure.
CLÉANTE   But what shall I tell Valère?
ORGON   Whatever you like.
CLÉANTE   But what have you decided?
   What are your plans?
ORGON   I plan, Sir, to be guided
   By Heaven's will.
CLÉANTE   Come, Brother, don't talk rot.   165
   You've given Valère your word; will you keep it, or not?
ORGON   Good day.
CLÉANTE   This looks like poor Valère's undoing;
   I'll go and warn him that there's trouble brewing.

Act II

SCENE 1

ORGON, MARIANE

ORGON Mariane.

MARIANE Yes, Father?

ORGON A word with you; come here.

MARIANE What are you looking for?

ORGON [*Peering into a small closet.*] Eavesdroppers, dear.
  I'm making sure we shan't be overheard.
  Someone in there could catch our every word.
  Ah, good, we're safe. Now, Mariane, my child,   5
  You're a sweet girl who's tractable and mild,
  Whom I hold dear, and think most highly of.

MARIANE I'm deeply grateful, Father, for your love.

ORGON That's well said, Daughter; and you can repay me
  If, in all things, you'll cheerfully obey me.   10

MARIANE To please you, Sir, is what delights me best.

ORGON Good, good. Now, what d'you think of Tartuffe, our guest?

MARIANE I, Sir?

ORGON Yes. Weigh your answer; think it through.

MARIANE Oh, dear. I'll say whatever you wish me to.

ORGON That's wisely said, my Daughter. Say of him, then,   15
  That he's the very worthiest of men,
  And that you're fond of him, and would rejoice
  In being his wife, if that should be my choice.
  Well?

MARIANE What?

ORGON What's that?

MARIANE I . . .

ORGON Well?

MARIANE Forgive me, pray.

ORGON Did you not hear me?

MARIANE Of *whom*, Sir, must I say   20
  That I am fond of him, and would rejoice
  In being his wife, if that should be your choice?

ORGON Why, of Tartuffe.

MARIANE But, Father, that's false, you know.
  Why would you have me say what isn't so?

ORGON Because I am resolved it shall be true.   25
  That it's my wish should be enough for you.

MARIANE You can't mean, Father . . .

ORGON Yes, Tartuffe shall be
  Allied by marriage[4] to this family,

---

4. This assertion is important and more than a mere device in the plot of the day. The second *placet*, or petition, insists that Tartuffe be costumed as a layman, and Orgon's plan for him to marry again asserts Tartuffe's position in the laity. In the 1664 version of the play Tartuffe had been dressed in a cassock, suggesting the priesthood, and Molière was now anxious to avoid any suggestion of this kind.

And he's to be your husband, is that clear?
It's a father's privilege . . .   30

SCENE 2

DORINE, ORGON, MARIANE

ORGON [*To* DORINE.]   What are you doing in here?
Is curiosity so fierce a passion
With you, that you must eavesdrop in this fashion?
DORINE   There's lately been a rumor going about—
Based on some hunch or chance remark, no doubt—   5
That you mean Mariane to wed Tartuffe.
I've laughed it off, of course, as just a spoof.
ORGON   You find it so incredible?
DORINE   Yes, I do.
I won't accept that story, even from you.
ORGON   Well, you'll believe it when the thing is done.   10
DORINE   Yes, yes, of course. Go on and have your fun.
ORGON   I've never been more serious in my life.
DORINE   Ha!
ORGON   Daughter, I mean it; you're to be his wife.
DORINE   No, don't believe your father; it's all a hoax.
ORGON   See here, young woman . . .
DORINE   Come, Sir, no more jokes;   15
You can't fool us.
ORGON   How dare you talk that way?
DORINE   All right, then: we believe you, sad to say.
But how a man like you, who looks so wise
And wears a moustache of such splendid size,
Can be so foolish as to . . .
ORGON   Silence, please!   20
My girl, you take too many liberties.
I'm master here, as you must not forget.
DORINE   Do let's discuss this calmly; don't be upset.
You can't be serious, Sir, about this plan.
What should that bigot want with Mariane?   25
Praying and fasting ought to keep him busy.
And then, in terms of wealth and rank, what is he?
Why should a man of property like you
Pick out a beggar son-in-law?
ORGON   That will do.
Speak of his poverty with reverence.   30
His is a pure and saintly indigence
Which far transcends all worldly pride and pelf.
He lost his fortune, as he says himself,
Because he cared for Heaven alone, and so
Was careless of his interests here below.   35
I mean to get him out of his present straits
And help him to recover his estates—
Which, in his part of the world, have no small fame.

Poor though he is, he's a gentleman just the same.
DORINE   Yes, so he tells us; and, Sir, it seems to me   40
    Such pride goes very ill with piety.
    A man whose spirit spurns this dungy earth
    Ought not to brag of lands and noble birth;
    Such worldly arrogance will hardly square
    With meek devotion and the life of prayer.   45
    . . . But this approach, I see, has drawn a blank;
    Let's speak, then, of his person, not his rank.
    Doesn't it seem to you a trifle grim
    To give a girl like her to a man like him?
    When two are so ill-suited, can't you see   50
    What the sad consequence is bound to be?
    A young girl's virtue is imperilled, Sir,
    When such a marriage is imposed on her;
    For if one's bridegroom isn't to one's taste,
    It's hardly an inducement to be chaste,   55
    And many a man with horns upon his brow
    Has made his wife the thing that she is now.
    It's hard to be a faithful wife, in short,
    To certain husbands of a certain sort,
    And he who gives his daughter to a man she hates   60
    Must answer for her sins at Heaven's gates.
    Think, Sir, before you play so risky a role.
ORGON   This servant-girl presumes to save my soul!
DORINE   You would do well to ponder what I've said.
ORGON   Daughter, we'll disregard this dunderhead.   65
    Just trust your father's judgment. Oh, I'm aware
    That I once promised you to young Valère;
    But now I hear he gambles, which greatly shocks me;
    What's more, I've doubts about his orthodoxy.
    His visits to church, I note, are very few.   70
DORINE   Would you have him go at the same hours as you,
    And kneel nearby, to be sure of being seen?
ORGON   I can dispense with such remarks, Dorine.
    [To MARIANE.] Tartuffe, however, is sure of Heaven's blessing.
    And that's the only treasure worth possessing.   75
    This match will bring you joys beyond all measure;
    Your cup will overflow with every pleasure;
    You two will interchange your faithful loves
    Like two sweet cherubs, or two turtle-doves.
    No harsh word shall be heard, no frown be seen,   80
    And he shall make you happy as a queen.
DORINE   And she'll make him a cuckold, just wait and see.
ORGON   What language!
DORINE   Oh, he's a man of destiny;
    He's *made* for horns, and what the stars demand
    Your daughter's virtue surely can't withstand.   85
ORGON   Don't interrupt me further. Why can't you learn
    That certain things are none of your concern?

DORINE It's for your own sake that I interfere.

    [*She repeatedly interrupts* ORGON *just as he is turning to speak to
his daughter.*]

ORGON Most kind of you. Now, hold your tongue, d'you hear?

DORINE If I didn't love you . . .

ORGON   Spare me your affection.   90

DORINE I'll love you, Sir, in spite of your objection.

ORGON Blast!

DORINE   I can't bear, Sir, for your honor's sake,

    To let you make this ludicrous mistake.

ORGON You mean to go on talking?

DORINE   If I didn't protest

    This sinful marriage, my conscience couldn't rest.   95

ORGON If you don't hold your tongue, you little shrew . . .

DORINE What, lost your temper? A pious man like you?

ORGON Yes! Yes! You talk and talk. I'm maddened by it.

    Once and for all, I tell you to be quiet.

DORINE Well, I'll be quiet. But I'll be thinking hard.   100

ORGON Think all you like, but you had better guard

    That saucy tongue of yours, or I'll . . .

    [*Turning back to* MARIANE.]   Now, child,

    I've weighed this matter fully.

DORINE [*Aside.*]   It drives me wild

    That I can't speak.

    [ORGON *turns his head, and she is silent.*]

ORGON   Tartuffe is no young dandy,

    But, still, his person . . .

DORINE [*Aside.*]   Is as sweet as candy.   105

ORGON Is such that, even if you shouldn't care

    For his other merits . . .

    [*He turns and stands facing* DORINE, *arms crossed.*]

DORINE [*Aside.*]   They'll make a lovely pair.

    If I were she, no man would marry me

    Against my inclination, and go scot-free.

    He'd learn, before the wedding-day was over,   110

    How readily a wife can find a lover.

ORGON [*To* DORINE.] It seems you treat my orders as a joke.

DORINE Why, what's the matter? 'Twas not to you I spoke.

ORGON What *were* you doing?

DORINE   Talking to myself, that's all.

ORGON Ah! [*Aside.*] One more bit of impudence and gall,   115

    And I shall give her a good slap in the face.

    [*He puts himself in position to slap her;* DORINE, *whenever he
glances at her, stands immobile and silent.*]

    Daughter, you shall accept, and with good grace,

    The husband I've selected . . . Your wedding-day . . .

    [*To* DORINE.] Why don't you talk to yourself?

DORINE   I've nothing to say.

ORGON Come, just one word.

DORINE   No thank you, Sir. I pass.   120

ORGON   Come, speak; I'm waiting.
DORINE   I'd not be such an ass.
ORGON [*Turning to* MARIANE.]
  In short, dear Daughter, I mean to be obeyed,
  And you must bow to the sound choice I've made.
DORINE [*Moving away.*]   I'd not wed such a monster, even in jest.
        [ORGON *attempts to slap her, but misses.*]
ORGON   Daughter, that maid of yours is a thorough pest;   125
  She makes me sinfully annoyed and nettled.
  I can't speak further; my nerves are too unsettled.
  She's so upset me by her insolent talk,
  I'll calm myself by going for a walk.

SCENE 3

DORINE, MARIANE

DORINE [*Returning.*]   Well, have you lost your tongue, girl? Must I play
  Your part, and say the lines you ought to say?
  Faced with a fate so hideous and absurd,
  Can you not utter one dissenting word?
MARIANE   What good would it do? A father's power is great.   5
DORINE   Resist him now, or it will be too late.
MARIANE   But . . .
DORINE   Tell him one cannot love at a father's whim;
  That you shall marry for yourself, not him;
  That since it's you who are to be the bride,
  It's you, not he, who must be satisfied;   10
  And that if his Tartuffe is so sublime,
  He's free to marry him at any time.
MARIANE   I've bowed so long to Father's strict control,
  I couldn't oppose him now, to save my soul.
DORINE   Come, come, Mariane. Do listen to reason, won't you?   15
  Valère has asked your hand. Do you love him, or don't you?
MARIANE   Oh, how unjust of you! What can you mean
  By asking such a question, dear Dorine?
  You know the depth of my affection for him;
  I've told you a hundred times how I adore him.   20
DORINE   I don't believe in everything I hear;
  Who knows if your professions were sincere?
MARIANE   They were, Dorine, and you do me wrong to doubt it;
  Heaven knows that I've been all too frank about it.
DORINE   You love him, then?
MARIANE   Oh, more than I can express.   25
DORINE   And he, I take it, cares for you no less?
MARIANE   I think so.
DORINE   And you both, with equal fire,
  Burn to be married?
MARIANE   That is our one desire.
DORINE   What of Tartuffe, then? What of your father's plan?
MARIANE   I'll kill myself, if I'm forced to wed that man.   30

DORINE   I hadn't thought of that recourse. How splendid!
  Just die, and all your troubles will be ended!
  A fine solution. Oh, it maddens me
  To hear you talk in that self-pitying key.
MARIANE   Dorine, how harsh you are! It's most unfair.   35
  You have no sympathy for my despair.
DORINE   I've none at all for people who talk drivel
  And, faced with difficulties, whine and snivel.
MARIANE   No doubt I'm timid, but it would be wrong . . .
DORINE   True love requires a heart that's firm and strong.   40
MARIANE   I'm strong in my affection for Valère,
  But coping with my father is his affair.
DORINE   But if your father's brain has grown so cracked
  Over his dear Tartuffe that he can retract
  His blessing, though your wedding-day was named,   45
  It's surely not Valère who's to be blamed.
MARIANE   If I defied my father, as you suggest,
  Would it not seem unmaidenly, at best?
  Shall I defend my love at the expense
  Of brazenness and disobedience?   50
  Shall I parade my heart's desires, and flaunt . . .
DORINE   No, I ask nothing of you. Clearly you want
  To be Madame Tartuffe, and I feel bound
  Not to oppose a wish so very sound.
  What right have I to criticize the match?   55
  Indeed, my dear, the man's a brilliant catch.
  Monsieur Tartuffe! Now, there's a man of weight!
  Yes, yes, Monsieur Tartuffe, I'm bound to state,
  Is quite a person; that's not to be denied;
  'Twill be no little thing to be his bride.   60
  The world already rings with his renown;
  He's a great noble—in his native town;
  His ears are red, he has a pink complexion,
  And all in all, he'll suit you to perfection.
MARIANE   Dear God!
DORINE   Oh, how triumphant you will feel   65
  At having caught a husband so ideal!
MARIANE   Oh, do stop teasing, and use your cleverness
  To get me out of this appalling mess.
  Advise me, and I'll do whatever you say.
DORINE   Ah, no, a dutiful daughter must obey   70
  Her father, even if he weds her to an ape.
  You've a bright future; why struggle to escape?
  Tartuffe will take you back where his family lives,
  To a small town aswarm with relatives—
  Uncles and cousins whom you'll be charmed to meet.   75
  You'll be received at once by the elite,
  Calling upon the bailiff's⁵ wife, no less—

5.· A high-ranking official in the judiciary, not simply a sheriff's deputy as today.

Even, perhaps, upon the mayoress,[6]
Who'll sit you down in the *best* kitchen chair.[7]
Then, once a year, you'll dance at the village fair   80
To the drone of bagpipes—two of them, in fact—
And see a puppet-show, or an animal act.[8]
Your husband . . .
MARIANE   Oh, you turn my blood to ice!
Stop torturing me, and give me your advice.
DORINE [*Threatening to go.*]
Your servant, Madam.
MARIANE.   Dorine, I beg of you . . .   85
DORINE   No, you deserve it; this marriage must go through.
MARIANE   Dorine!
DORINE   No.
MARIANE   Not Tartuffe! You know I think him . . .
DORINE   Tartuffe's your cup of tea, and you shall drink him.
MARIANE   I've always told you everything, and relied . . .
DORINE   No. You deserve to be tartuffified.   90
MARIANE   Well, since you mock me and refuse to care,
I'll henceforth seek my solace in despair:
Despair shall be my counsellor and friend,
And help me bring my sorrows to an end. [*She starts to leave.*]
DORINE   There now, come back; my anger has subsided.   95
You do deserve some pity, I've decided.
MARIANE   Dorine, if Father makes me undergo
This dreadful martyrdom, I'll die, I know.
DORINE   Don't fret; it won't be difficult to discover
Some plan of action . . . But here's Valère, your lover.   100

SCENE 4

VALÈRE, MARIANE, DORINE

VALÈRE   Madam, I've just received some wondrous news
Regarding which I'd like to hear your views.
MARIANE   What news?
VALÈRE   You're marrying Tartuffe.
MARIANE   I find
That Father does have such a match in mind.
VALÈRE   Your father, Madam . . .
MARIANE   . . . has just this minute said   5
That it's Tartuffe he wishes me to wed.
VALÈRE   Can he be serious?
MARIANE   Oh, indeed he can;
He's clearly set his heart upon the plan.
VALÈRE   And what position do you propose to take,

---

6. The wife of a tax collector (*élue*), an important official controlling imports, elected by the Estates General.   7. In elegant society of Molière's day, there was a hierarchy of seats, and the use of each was determined by rank. The seats descended from *fauteuils* to *chaises, perroquets, tabourets,* and *pliants.* Thus Mariane would get the lowest seat in the room.   8. In the original, *fagotin,* literally "a monkey dressed up in a man's clothing."

Madam?
MARIANE Why—I don't know.
VALÈRE   For heaven's sake—   10
    You don't know?
MARIANE   No.
VALÈRE   Well, well!
MARIANE   Advise me, do.
VALÈRE Marry the man. That's my advice to you.
MARIANE That's your advice?
VALÈRE   Yes.
MARIANE   Truly?
VALÈRE   Oh, absolutely.
    You couldn't choose more wisely, more astutely.
MARIANE Thanks for this counsel; I'll follow it, of course.   15
VALÈRE Do, do; I'm sure 'twill cost you no remorse.
MARIANE To give it didn't cause your heart to break.
VALÈRE I gave it, Madam, only for your sake.
MARIANE And it's for your sake that I take it, Sir.
DORINE [*Withdrawing to the rear of the stage.*]
    Let's see which fool will prove the stubborner.   20
VALÈRE So! I am nothing to you, and it was flat
    Deception when you . . .
MARIANE   Please, enough of that.
    You've told me plainly that I should agree
    To wed the man my father's chosen for me,
    And since you've deigned to counsel me so wisely,   25
    I promise, Sir, to do as you advise me.
VALÈRE Ah, no, 'twas not by me that you were swayed.
    No, your decision was already made;
    Though now, to save appearances, you protest
    That you're betraying me at my behest.   30
MARIANE Just as you say.
VALÈRE   Quite so. And I now see
    That you were never truly in love with me.
MARIANE Alas, you're free to think so if you choose.
VALÈRE I choose to think so, and here's a bit of news:
    You've spurned my hand, but I know where to turn   35
    For kinder treatment, as you shall quickly learn.
MARIANE I'm sure you do. Your noble qualities
    Inspire affection . . .
VALÈRE   Forget my qualities, please.
    They don't inspire you overmuch, I find.
    But there's another lady I have in mind   40
    Whose sweet and generous nature will not scorn
    To compensate me for the loss I've borne.
MARIANE I'm no great loss, and I'm sure that you'll transfer
    Your heart quite painlessly from me to her.
VALÈRE I'll do my best to take it in my stride.   45
    The pain I feel at being cast aside
    Time and forgetfulness may put an end to.

Or if I can't forget, I shall pretend to.
No self-respecting person is expected
To go on loving once he's been rejected.   50
MARIANE   Now, that's a fine, high-minded sentiment.
VALÈRE   One to which any sane man would assent.
   Would you prefer it if I pined away
   In hopeless passion till my dying day?
   Am I to yield you to a rival's arms   55
   And not console myself with other charms?
MARIANE   Go then; console yourself; don't hesitate.
   I wish you to; indeed, I cannot wait.
VALÈRE   You wish me to?
MARIANE   Yes.
VALÈRE   That's the final straw.
   Madam, farewell. Your wish shall be my law.   60
         [*He starts to leave, and then returns: this repeatedly.*]
MARIANE   Splendid.
VALÈRE [*Coming back again.*]   This breach, remember, is of your making;
   It's you who've driven me to the step I'm taking.
MARIANE   Of course.
VALÈRE [*Coming back again.*]   Remember, too, that I am merely
   Following your example.
MARIANE   I see that clearly.
VALÈRE   Enough. I'll go and do your bidding, then.   65
MARIANE   Good.
VALÈRE [*Coming back again.*]   You shall never see my face again.
MARIANE   Excellent.
VALÈRE [*Walking to the door, then turning about.*]
                          Yes?
MARIANE   What?
VALÈRE   What's that? What did you say?
MARIANE   Nothing. You're dreaming.
VALÈRE   Ah. Well, I'm on my way.
   Farewell, Madame.
         [*He moves slowly away.*]
MARIANE   Farewell.
DORINE [*To* MARIANE.]   If you ask me,
   Both of you are as mad as mad can be.   70
   Do stop this nonsense, now. I've only let you
   Squabble so long to see where it would get you.
   Whoa there, Monsieur Valère!
         [*She goes and seizes* VALÈRE *by the arm; he makes a great show of
         resistance.*]
VALÈRE   What's this, Dorine?
DORINE   Come here.
VALÈRE   No, no, my heart's too full of spleen.
   Don't hold me back; her wish must be obeyed.   75
DORINE   Stop!
VALÈRE   It's too late now; my decision's made.
DORINE   Oh, pooh!

MARIANE [*Aside.*]   He hates the sight of me, that's plain.
   I'll go, and so deliver him from pain.
DORINE [*Leaving* VALÈRE, *running after* MARIANE.]
   And now *you* run away! Come back.
MARIANE   No, no
   Nothing you say will keep me here. Let go!   80
VALÈRE [*Aside.*]   She cannot bear my presence, I perceive.
   To spare her further torment, I shall leave.
DORINE [*Leaving* MARIANE, *running after* VALÈRE.]
   Again! You'll not escape, Sir; don't you try it.
   Come here, you two. Stop fussing and be quiet.
      [*She takes* VALÈRE *by the hand, then* MARIANE, *and draws them
      together.*]
VALÈRE [*To* DORINE.]   What do you want of me?   85
MARIANE [*To* DORINE.]   What is the point of this?
DORINE   We're going to have a little armistice.
   [*To* VALÈRE.] Now, weren't you silly to get so overheated?
VALÈRE   Didn't you see how badly I was treated?
DORINE [*To* MARIANE.]   Aren't you a simpleton, to have lost your
     head?   90
MARIANE   Didn't you hear the hateful things he said?
DORINE [*To* VALÈRE.]   You're both great fools. Her sole desire, Valère,
   Is to be yours in marriage. To that I'll swear.
   [*To* MARIANE.] He loves you only, and he wants no wife
   But you, Mariane. On that I'll stake my life.   95
MARIANE [*To* VALÈRE.]   Then why you advised me so, I cannot see.
VALÈRE [*To* MARIANE.]   On such a question, why ask advice of *me*?
DORINE   Oh, you're impossible. Give me your hands, you two.
   [*To* VALÈRE.] Yours first.
VALÈRE [*Giving* DORINE *his hand.*]   But why?
DORINE [*To* MARIANE.]   And now a hand from you.   100
MARIANE [*Also giving* DORINE *her hand.*]
   What are you doing?
DORINE   There: a perfect fit.
   You suit each other better than you'll admit.
     [VALÈRE *and* MARIANE *hold hands for some time without looking at
     each other.*]
VALÈRE [*Turning toward* MARIANE.]
   Ah, come, don't be so haughty. Give a man
   A look of kindness, won't you, Mariane?
     [MARIANE *turns toward* VALÈRE *and smiles.*]
DORINE   I tell you, lovers are completely mad!   105
VALÈRE [*To* MARIANE.]   Now come, confess that you were very bad
   To hurt my feelings as you did just now.
   I have a just complaint, you must allow.
MARIANE   *You* must allow that you were most unpleasant . . .
DORINE   Let's table that discussion for the present;   110
   Your father has a plan which must be stopped.
MARIANE   Advise us, then; what means must we adopt?
DORINE   We'll use all manner of means, and all at once.

[*To* MARIANE.] Your father's addled; he's acting like a dunce.
Therefore you'd better humor the old fossil.   115
Pretend to yield to him, be sweet and docile,
And then postpone, as often as necessary,
The day on which you have agreed to marry.
You'll thus gain time, and time will turn the trick.
Sometimes, for instance, you'll be taken sick,   120
And that will seem good reason for delay;
Or some bad omen will make you change the day—
You'll dream of muddy water, or you'll pass
A dead man's hearse, or break a looking-glass.
If all else fails, no man can marry you   125
Unless you take his ring and say "I do."
But now, let's separate. If they should find
Us talking here, our plot might be divined.
[*To* VALÈRE.] Go to your friends, and tell them what's occurred,
And have them urge her father to keep his word.   130
Meanwhile, we'll stir her brother into action,
And get Elmire,[9] as well, to join our faction.
Good-bye.
VALÈRE [*To* MARIANE.]   Though each of us will do his best,
   It's your true heart on which my hopes shall rest.   135
MARIANE [*To* VALÈRE.]   Regardless of what Father may decide,
   None but Valère shall claim me as his bride.
VALÈRE   Oh, how those words content me! Come what will . . .
DORINE   Oh, lovers, lovers! Their tongues are never still.
   Be off, now.
VALÈRE [*Turning to go, then turning back.*]
                  One last word . . .
DORINE   No time to chat: 140
   You leave by this door; and *you* leave by that.
         [DORINE *pushes them, by the shoulders, toward opposing doors.*]

Act III

SCENE 1

DAMIS, DORINE

DAMIS   May lightning strike me even as I speak,
   May all men call me cowardly and weak,
   If any fear or scruple holds me back
   From settling things, at once, with that great quack!
DORINE   Now, don't give way to violent emotion.   5
   Your father's merely talked about this notion,
   And words and deeds are far from being one.
   Much that is talked about is never done.

---

9. Orgon's second wife.

DAMIS   No, I must stop that scoundrel's machinations;
  I'll go and tell him off; I'm out of patience.   10
DORINE   Do calm down and be practical. I had rather
  My mistress dealt with him—and with your father.
  She has some influence with Tartuffe, I've noted.
  He hangs upon her words, seems most devoted,
  And may, indeed, be smitten by her charm.   15
  Pray Heaven it's true! 'Twould do our cause no harm.
  She sent for him, just now, to sound him out
  On this affair you're so incensed about;
  She'll find out where he stands, and tell him, too,
  What dreadful strife and trouble will ensue   20
  If he lends countenance to your father's plan.
  I couldn't get in to see him, but his man
  Says that he's almost finished with his prayers.
  Go, now. I'll catch him when he comes downstairs.
DAMIS   I want to hear this conference, and I will.   25
DORINE   No, they must be alone.
DAMIS   Oh, I'll keep still.
DORINE   Not you. I know your temper. You'd start a brawl,
  And shout and stamp your foot and spoil it all.
  Go on.
DAMIS   I won't; I have a perfect right . . .
DORINE   Lord, you're a nuisance! He's coming; get out of sight.   30
        [DAMIS *conceals himself in a closet at the rear of the stage.*]

SCENE 2

TARTUFFE, DORINE

TARTUFFE [*Observing* DORINE, *and calling to his manservant off-stage.*]
  Hang up my hair-shirt, put my scourge in place,
  And pray, Laurent, for Heaven's perpetual grace.
  I'm going to the prison now, to share
  My last few coins with the poor wretches there.
DORINE [*Aside.*]   Dear God, what affectation! What a fake!   5
TARTUFFE   You wished to see me?
DORINE   Yes . . .
TARTUFFE [*Taking a handkerchief from his pocket.*]
                                 For mercy's sake,
  Please take this handkerchief, before you speak.
DORINE   What?
TARTUFFE   Cover that bosom,[1] girl. The flesh is weak.
  And unclean thoughts are difficult to control.
  Such sights as that can undermine the soul.   10
DORINE   Your soul, it seems, has very poor defenses,
  And flesh makes quite an impact on your senses.

---

1. The Brotherhood of the Holy Sacrament practiced alms giving to prisoners and kept a careful, censorious check on women's clothing if they deemed it lascivious. Thus Molière's audience would have identified Tartuffe as sympathetic—hypocritically—to the aims of the organization.

It's strange that you're so easily excited;
My own desires are not so soon ignited,
And if I saw you naked as a beast,   15
Not all your hide would tempt me in the least.
TARTUFFE   Girl, speak more modestly; unless you do,
  I shall be forced to take my leave of you.
DORINE   Oh, no, it's I who must be on my way;
  I've just one little message to convey.   20
  Madame is coming down, and begs you, Sir,
  To wait and have a word or two with her.
TARTUFFE   Gladly.
DORINE [*Aside.*]   *That* had a softening effect!
  I think my guess about him was correct.
TARTUFFE   Will she be long?
DORINE   No: that's her step I hear.   25
  Ah, here she is, and I shall disappear.

SCENE 3

ELMIRE, TARTUFFE

TARTUFFE   May Heaven, whose infinite goodness we adore,
  Preserve your body and soul forevermore,
  And bless your days, and answer thus the plea
  Of one who is its humblest votary.
ELMIRE   I thank you for that pious wish. But please,   5
  Do take a chair and let's be more at ease.
      [*They sit down.*]
TARTUFFE   I trust that you are once more well and strong?
ELMIRE   Oh, yes: the fever didn't last for long.
TARTUFFE   My prayers are too unworthy, I am sure,
  To have gained from Heaven this most gracious cure;   10
  But lately, Madam, my every supplication
  Has had for object your recuperation.
ELMIRE   You shouldn't have troubled so. I don't deserve it.
TARTUFFE   Your health is priceless, Madam, and to preserve it
  I'd gladly give my own, in all sincerity.   15
ELMIRE   Sir, you outdo us all in Christian charity.
  You've been most kind. I count myself your debtor.
TARTUFFE   'Twas nothing, Madam. I long to serve you better.
ELMIRE   There's a private matter I'm anxious to discuss.
  I'm glad there's no one here to hinder us.   20
TARTUFFE   I too am glad; it floods my heart with bliss
  To find myself alone with you like this.
  For just this chance I've prayed with all my power—
  But prayed in vain, until this happy hour.
ELMIRE   This won't take long, Sir, and I hope you'll be   25
  Entirely frank and unconstrained with me.
TARTUFFE   Indeed, there's nothing I had rather do
  Than bare my inmost heart and soul to you.
  First, let me say that what remarks I've made

About the constant visits you are paid   30
Were prompted not by any mean emotion,
But rather by a pure and deep devotion,
A fervent zeal . . .

ELMIRE   No need for explanation.
Your sole concern, I'm sure, was my salvation.

TARTUFFE [*Taking* ELMIRE's *hand and pressing her fingertips.*]
Quite so; and such great fervor do I feel . . .   35

ELMIRE   Ooh! Please! You're pinching!

TARTUFFE   'Twas from excess of zeal.
I never meant to cause you pain, I swear.
I'd rather . . .
      [*He places his hand on* ELMIRE's *knee.*]

ELMIRE   What can your hand be doing there?

TARTUFFE   Feeling your gown: what soft, fine-woven stuff!

ELMIRE   Please, I'm extremely ticklish. That's enough.   40
    [*She draws her chair away;* TARTUFFE *pulls his after her.*]

TARTUFFE [*Fondling the lace collar of her gown.*]
My, my, what lovely lacework on your dress!
The workmanship's miraculous, no less.
I've not seen anything to equal it.

ELMIRE   Yes, quite. But let's talk business for a bit.
They say my husband means to break his word   45
And give his daughter to you, Sir. Had you heard?

TARTUFFE   He did once mention it. But I confess
I dream of quite a different happiness.
It's elsewhere, Madam, that my eyes discern
The promise of that bliss for which I yearn.   50

ELMIRE   I see: you care for nothing here below.

TARTUFFE   Ah, well—my heart's not made of stone, you know.

ELMIRE   All your desires mount heavenward, I'm sure,
In scorn of all that's earthly and impure.

TARTUFFE   A love of heavenly beauty does not preclude   55
A proper love for earthly pulchritude;
Our senses are quite rightly captivated
By perfect works our Maker has created.
Some glory clings to all that Heaven has made;
In you, all Heaven's marvels are displayed.   60
On that fair face, such beauties have been lavished,
The eyes are dazzled and the heart is ravished;
How could I look on you, O flawless creature,
And not adore the Author of all Nature,
Feeling a love both passionate and pure   65
For you, his triumph of self-portraiture?
At first, I trembled lest that love should be
A subtle snare that Hell had laid for me;
I vowed to flee the sight of you, eschewing
A rapture that might prove my soul's undoing;   70
But soon, fair being, I became aware
That my deep passion could be made to square

With rectitude, and with my bounden duty,
I thereupon surrendered to your beauty.
It is, I know, presumptuous on my part   75
To bring you this poor offering of my heart,
And it is not my merit, Heaven knows,
But your compassion on which my hopes repose.
You are my peace, my solace, my salvation;
On you depends my bliss—or desolation;   80
I bide your judgment and, as you think best,
I shall be either miserable or blest.
ELMIRE   Your declaration is most gallant, Sir,
    But don't you think it's out of character?
    You'd have done better to restrain your passion   85
    And think before you spoke in such a fashion.
    It ill becomes a pious man like you . . .
TARTUFFE   I may be pious, but I'm human too:
    With your celestial charms before his eyes,
    A man has not the power to be wise.   90
    I know such words sound strangely, coming from me,
    But I'm no angel, nor was meant to be,
    And if you blame my passion, you must needs
    Reproach as well the charms on which it feeds.
    Your loveliness I had no sooner seen   95
    Than you became my soul's unrivalled queen;
    Before your seraph glance, divinely sweet,
    My heart's defenses crumbled in defeat,
    And nothing fasting, prayer, or tears might do
    Could stay my spirit from adoring you.   100
    My eyes, my sighs have told you in the past
    What now my lips make bold to say at last,
    And if, in your great goodness, you will deign
    To look upon your slave, and ease his pain,—
    If, in compassion for my soul's distress,   105
    You'll stoop to comfort my unworthiness,
    I'll raise to you, in thanks for that sweet manna,
    An endless hymn, an infinite hosanna.
    With me, of course, there need be no anxiety,
    No fear of scandal or of notoriety.   110
    These young court gallants, whom all the ladies fancy,
    Are vain in speech, in action rash and chancy;
    When they succeed in love, the world soon knows it;
    No favor's granted them but they disclose it
    And by the looseness of their tongues profane   115
    The very altar where their hearts have lain.
    Men of my sort, however, love discreetly,
    And one may trust our reticence completely.
    My keen concern for my good name insures
    The absolute security of yours;   120
    In short, I offer you, my dear Elmire,
    Love without scandal, pleasure without fear.

ELMIRE   I've heard your well-turned speeches to the end,
  And what you urge I clearly apprehend.
  Aren't you afraid that I may take a notion   125
  To tell my husband of your warm devotion,
  And that, supposing he were duly told,
  His feelings toward you might grow rather cold?
TARTUFFE   I know, dear lady, that your exceeding charity
  Will lead your heart to pardon my temerity;   130
  That you'll excuse my violent affection
  As human weakness, human imperfection;
  And that—O fairest!—you will bear in mind
  That I'm but flesh and blood, and am not blind.
ELMIRE   Some women might do otherwise, perhaps,   135
  But I shall be discreet about your lapse;
  I'll tell my husband nothing of what's occurred
  If, in return, you'll give your solemn word
  To advocate as forcefully as you can
  The marriage of Valère and Mariane,   140
  Renouncing all desire to dispossess
  Another of his rightful happiness,
  And . . .

SCENE 4

DAMIS, ELMIRE, TARTUFFE

DAMIS [*Emerging from the closet where he has been hiding.*]
      No! We'll not hush up this vile affair;
  I heard it all inside that closet there,
  Where Heaven, in order to confound the pride
  Of this great rascal, prompted me to hide.
  Ah, now I have my long-awaited chance   5
  To punish his deceit and arrogance,
  And give my father clear and shocking proof
  Of the black character of his dear Tartuffe.
ELMIRE   Ah no, Damis; I'll be content if he
  Will study to deserve my leniency.   10
  I've promised silence—don't make me break my word;
  To make a scandal would be too absurd.
  Good wives laugh off such trifles, and forget them;
  Why should they tell their husbands, and upset them?
DAMIS   You have your reasons for taking such a course,   15
  And I have reasons, too, of equal force.
  To spare him now would be insanely wrong.
  I've swallowed my just wrath for far too long
  And watched this insolent bigot bringing strife
  And bitterness into our family life.   20
  Too long he's meddled in my father's affairs,
  Thwarting my marriage-hopes, and poor Valère's.
  It's high time that my father was undeceived,
  And now I've proof that can't be disbelieved—

Proof that was furnished me by Heaven above.   25
It's too good not to take advantage of.
This is my chance, and I deserve to lose it
If, for one moment, I hesitate to use it.
ELMIRE Damis . . .
DAMIS   No, I must do what I think right.
Madam, my heart is bursting with delight,   30
And, say whatever you will, I'll not consent
To lose the sweet revenge on which I'm bent.
I'll settle matters without more ado;
And here, most opportunely, is my cue.[2]

SCENE 5

ORGON, DAMIS, TARTUFFE, ELMIRE

DAMIS Father, I'm glad you've joined us. Let us advise you
Of some fresh news which doubtless will surprise you.
You've just now been repaid with interest
For all your loving-kindness to our guest.
He's proved his warm and grateful feelings toward you;   5
It's with a pair of horns he would reward you.
Yes, I surprised him with your wife, and heard
His whole adulterous offer, every word.
She, with her all too gentle disposition,
Would not have told you of his proposition;   10
But I shall not make terms with brazen lechery,
And feel that not to tell you would be treachery.
ELMIRE And I hold that one's husband's peace of mind
Should not be spoilt by tattle of this kind.
One's honor doesn't require it: to be proficient   15
In keeping men at bay is quite sufficient.
These are my sentiments, and I wish, Damis,
That you had heeded me and held your peace.

SCENE 6

ORGON, DAMIS, TARTUFFE

ORGON Can it be true, this dreadful thing I hear?
TARTUFFE Yes, Brother, I'm a wicked man, I fear:
A wretched sinner, all depraved and twisted,
The greatest villain that has ever existed.
My life's one heap of crimes, which grows each minute;   5
There's naught but foulness and corruption in it;
And I perceive that Heaven, outraged by me,
Has chosen this occasion to mortify me.
Charge me with any deed you wish to name;

---

2. In the original stage directions, Tartuffe now reads silently from his breviary—in the Roman Catholic Church, the book containing the Divine Office for each day, which those in holy orders are required to recite.

I'll not defend myself, but take the blame.   10
Believe what you are told, and drive Tartuffe
Like some base criminal from beneath your roof;
Yes, drive me hence, and with a parting curse:
I shan't protest, for I deserve far worse.

ORGON [*To* DAMIS.]   Ah, you deceitful boy, how dare you try   15
   To stain his purity with so foul a lie?

DAMIS   What! Are you taken in by such a fluff?
   Did you not hear . . . ?

ORGON   Enough, you rogue, enough!

TARTUFFE   Ah, Brother, let him speak: you're being unjust.
   Believe his story; the boy deserves your trust.   20
   Why, after all, should you have faith in me?
   How can you know what I might do, or be?
   Is it on my good actions that you base
   Your favor? Do you trust my pious face?
   Ah, no, don't be deceived by hollow shows;   25
   I'm far, alas, from being what men suppose;
   Though the world takes me for a man of worth,
   I'm truly the most worthless man on earth.
   [*To* DAMIS] Yes, my dear son, speak out now: call me the chief
   Of sinners, a wretch, a murderer, a thief;   ·   30
   Load me with all the names men most abhor;
   I'll not complain; I've earned them all, and more;
   I'll kneel here while you pour them on my head
   As a just punishment for the life I've led.

ORGON [*To* TARTUFFE]
   This is too much, dear Brother.
   [*To* DAMIS.]   Have you no heart?   35

DAMIS   Are you so hoodwinked by this rascal's art . . . ?

ORGON   Be still, you monster.
   [*To* TARTUFFE.]   Brother, I pray you, rise.
   [*To* DAMIS.] Villain!

DAMIS: But . . .

ORGON   Silence!

DAMIS   Can't you realize . . . ?

ORGON   Just one word more, and I'll tear you limb from limb.

TARTUFFE   In God's name, Brother, don't be harsh with him.   40
   I'd rather far be tortured at the stake
   Than see him bear one scratch for my poor sake.

ORGON [*To* DAMIS.]   Ingrate!

TARTUFFE   If I must beg you, on bended knee,
   To pardon him . . .

ORGON [*Falling to his knees, addressing* TARTUFFE
            Such goodness cannot be!
   [*To* DAMIS.] Now, *there's* true charity!

DAMIS   What, you . . . ?

ORGON   Villain, be still!   45
   I know your motives; I know you wish him ill:
   Yes, all of you—wife, children, servants, all—

Conspire against him and desire his fall,
Employing every shameful trick you can
To alienate me from this saintly man.   50
Ah, but the more you seek to drive him away,
The more I'll do to keep him. Without delay,
I'll spite this household and confound its pride
By giving him my daughter as his bride.

DAMIS   You're going to force her to accept his hand?   55
ORGON   Yes, and this very night, d'you understand?
  I shall defy you all, and make it clear
  That I'm the one who gives the orders here.
  Come, wretch, kneel down and clasp his blessed feet,
  And ask his pardon for your black deceit.   60
DAMIS   I ask that swindler's pardon? Why, I'd rather . . .
ORGON   So! You insult him, and defy your father!
  A stick! A stick! [*To* TARTUFFE.] No, no—release me, do.
  [*To* DAMIS.] Out of my house this minute! Be off with you,
  And never dare set foot in it again.   65
DAMIS   Well, I shall go, but . . .
ORGON   Well, go quickly, then.
  I disinherit you; an empty purse
  Is all you'll get from me—except my curse!

SCENE 7

ORGON, TARTUFFE

ORGON   How he blasphemed your goodness! What a son!
TARTUFFE   Forgive him, Lord, as I've already done.
  [*To* ORGON.] You can't know how it hurts when someone tries
  To blacken me in my dear brother's eyes.
ORGON   Ahh!
TARTUFFE   The mere thought of such ingratitude   5
  Plunges my soul into so dark a mood . . .
  Such horror grips my heart . . . I gasp for breath,
  And cannot speak, and feel myself near death.
ORGON [*He runs, in tears, to the door through which he has just driven
    his son.*]
  You blackguard! Why did I spare you? Why did I not
  Break you in little pieces on the spot?   10
  Compose yourself, and don't be hurt, dear friend.
TARTUFFE   These scenes, these dreadful quarrels, have got to end.
  I've much upset your household, and I perceive
  That the best thing will be for me to leave.
ORGON   What are you saying!
TARTUFFE   They're all against me here;   15
  They'd have you think me false and insincere.
ORGON   Ah, what of that? Have I ceased believing in you?
TARTUFFE   Their adverse talk will certainly continue,
  And charges which you now repudiate
  You may find credible at a later date.   20

ORGON No, Brother, never.
TARTUFFE   Brother, a wife can sway
  Her husband's mind in many a subtle way.
ORGON No, no.
TARTUFFE   To leave at once is the solution;
  Thus only can I end their persecution.
ORGON No, no, I'll not allow it; you shall remain.   25
TARTUFFE Ah, well; 'twill mean much martyrdom and pain,
  But if you wish it . . .
ORGON   Ah!
TARTUFFE   Enough; so be it.
  But one thing must be settled, as I see it.
  For your dear honor, and for our friendship's sake,
  There's one precaution I feel bound to take.   30
  I shall avoid your wife, and keep away . . .
ORGON No, you shall not, whatever they may say.
  It pleases me to vex them, and for spite
  I'd have them see you with her day and night.
  What's more, I'm going to drive them to despair   35
  By making you my only son and heir;
  This very day, I'll give to you alone
  Clear deed and title to everything I own.
  A dear, good friend and son-in-law-to-be
  Is more than wife, or child, or kin to me.   40
  Will you accept my offer, dearest son?
TARTUFFE In all things, let the will of Heaven be done.
ORGON Poor fellow! Come, we'll go draw up the deed.
  Then let them burst with disappointed greed!

Act IV

SCENE 1

CLÉANTE, TARTUFFE

CLÉANTE Yes, all the town's discussing it, and truly,
  Their comments do not flatter you unduly.
  I'm glad we've met, Sir, and I'll give my view
  Of this sad matter in a word or two.
  As for who's guilty, that I shan't discuss;   5
  Let's say it was Damis who caused the fuss;
  Assuming, then, that you have been ill-used
  By young Damis, and groundlessly accused,
  Ought not a Christian to forgive, and ought
  He not to stifle every vengeful thought?   10
  Should you stand by and watch a father make
  His only son an exile for your sake?
  Again I tell you frankly, be advised:
  The whole town, high and low, is scandalized;

This quarrel must be mended, and my advice is   15
Not to push matters to a further crisis.
No, sacrifice your wrath to God above,
And help Damis regain his father's love.
TARTUFFE   Alas, for my part I should take great joy
In doing so. I've nothing against the boy.   20
I pardon all, I harbor no resentment;
To serve him would afford me much contentment.
But Heaven's interest will not have it so:
If he comes back, then I shall have to go.
After his conduct—so extreme, so vicious—   25
Our further intercourse would look suspicious.
God knows what people would think! Why, they'd describe
My goodness to him as a sort of bribe;
They'd say that out of guilt I made pretense
Of loving-kindness and benevolence—   30
That, fearing my accuser's tongue, I strove
To buy his silence with a show of love.
CLÉANTE   Your reasoning is badly warped and stretched,
And these excuses, Sir, are most far-fetched.
Why put yourself in charge of Heaven's cause?   35
Does Heaven need our help to enforce its laws?
Leave vengeance to the Lord, Sir; while we live,
Our duty's not to punish, but forgive;
And what the Lord commands, we should obey
Without regard to what the world may say.   40
What! Shall the fear of being misunderstood
Prevent our doing what is right and good?
No, no: let's simply do what Heaven ordains,
And let no other thoughts perplex our brains.
TARTUFFE   Again, Sir, let me say that I've forgiven   45
Damis, and thus obeyed the laws of Heaven;
But I am not commanded by the Bible
To live with one who smears my name with libel.
CLÉANTE   Were you commanded, Sir, to indulge the whim
Of poor Orgon, and to encourage him   50
In suddenly transferring to your name
A large estate to which you have no claim?
TARTUFFE   'Twould never occur to those who know me best
To think I acted from self-interest.
The treasures of this world I quite despise;   55
Their specious glitter does not charm my eyes;
And if I have resigned myself to taking
The gift which my dear Brother insists on making,
I do so only, as he well understands,
Lest so much wealth fall into wicked hands,   60
Lest those to whom it might descend in time
Turn it to purposes of sin and crime,
And not, as I shall do, make use of it
For Heaven's glory and mankind's benefit.

CLÉANTE   Forget these trumped-up fears. Your argument   65
   Is one the rightful heir might well resent;
   It *is* a moral burden to inherit
   Such wealth, but give Damis a chance to bear it.
   And would it not be worse to be accused
   Of swindling, than to see that wealth misused?   70
   I'm shocked that you allowed Orgon to broach
   This matter, and that you feel no self-reproach;
   Does true religion teach that lawful heirs
   May freely be deprived of what is theirs?
   And if the Lord has told you in your heart   75
   That you and young Damis must dwell apart,
   Would it not be the decent thing to beat
   A generous and honorable retreat,
   Rather than let the son of the house be sent,
   For your convenience, into banishment?   80
   Sir, if you wish to prove the honesty
   Of your intentions . . .
TARTUFFE   Sir, it is a half past three.
   I've certain pious duties to attend to,
   And hope my prompt departure won't offend you.
CLÉANTE [*Alone.*]   Damn.

SCENE 2

ELMIRE, MARIANE, CLÉANTE, DORINE

DORINE   Stay, Sir, and help Mariane, for Heaven's sake!
   She's suffering so, I fear her heart will break.
   Her father's plan to marry her off tonight
   Has put the poor child in a desperate plight.
   I hear him coming. Let's stand together, now,   5
   And see if we can't change his mind, somehow,
   About this match we all deplore and fear.

SCENE 3

ORGON, ELMIRE, MARIANE, CLÉANTE, DORINE

ORGON   Hah! Glad to find you all assembled here.
   [*To* MARIANE.] This contract, child, contains your happiness,
   And what it says I think your heart can guess.
MARIANE [*Falling to her knees.*]
   Sir, by that Heaven which sees me here distressed,
   And by whatever else can move your breast,   5
   Do not employ a father's power, I pray you,
   To crush my heart and force it to obey you,
   Nor by your harsh commands oppress me so
   That I'll begrudge the duty which I owe—
   And do not so embitter and enslave me   10
   That I shall hate the very life you gave me.
   If my sweet hopes must perish, if you refuse

To give me to the one I've dared to choose,
Spare me at least—I beg you, I implore—
The pain of wedding one whom I abhor; 15
And do not, by a heartless use of force,
Drive me to contemplate some desperate course.
ORGON [*Feeling himself touched by her.*]
Be firm, my soul. No human weakness, now.
MARIANE   I don't resent your love for him. Allow
Your heart free rein, Sir; give him your property, 20
And if that's not enough, take mine from me;
He's welcome to my money; take it, do,
But don't, I pray, include my person too.
Spare me, I beg you; and let me end the tale
Of my sad days behind a convent veil. 25
ORGON   A convent! Hah! When crossed in their amours,
All lovesick girls have the same thought as yours.
Get up! The more you loathe the man, and dread him,
The more ennobling it will be to wed him.
Marry Tartuffe, and mortify your flesh! 30
Enough; don't start that whimpering afresh.
DORINE   But why . . . ?
ORGON   Be still, there. Speak when you're spoken to.
Not one more bit of impudence out of you.
CLÉANTE   If I may offer a word of counsel here . . .
ORGON   Brother, in counselling you have no peer; 35
All your advice is forceful, sound, and clever;
I don't propose to follow it, however.
ELMIRE [*To* ORGON.]   I am amazed, and don't know what to say;
Your blindness simply takes my breath away.
You are indeed bewitched, to take no warning 40
From our account of what occurred this morning.
ORGON   Madam, I know a few plain facts, and one
Is that you're partial to my rascal son;
Hence, when he sought to make Tartuffe the victim
Of a base lie, you dared not contradict him. 45
Ah, but you underplayed your part, my pet;
You should have looked more angry, more upset.
ELMIRE   When men make overtures, must we reply
With righteous anger and a battle-cry?
Must we turn back their amorous advances 50
With sharp reproaches and with fiery glances?
Myself, I find such offers merely amusing,
And make no scenes and fusses in refusing;
My taste is for good-natured rectitude,
And I dislike the savage sort of prude 55
Who guards her virtue with her teeth and claws,
And tears men's eyes out for the slightest cause:
The Lord preserve me from such honor as that,
Which bites and scratches like an alley-cat!
I've found that a polite and cool rebuff 60

Discourages a lover quite enough.

ORGON   I know the facts, and I shall not be shaken.

ELMIRE   I marvel at your power to be mistaken.
  Would it, I wonder, carry weight with you
  If I could *show* you that our tale was true?   65

ORGON   Show me?

ELMIRE   Yes.

ORGON   Rot.

ELMIRE   Come, what if I found a way
  To make you see the facts as plain as day?

ORGON   Nonsense.

ELMIRE   Do answer me; don't be absurd.
  I'm not now asking you to trust our word.
  Suppose that from some hiding-place in here   70
  You learned the whole sad truth by eye and ear—
  What would you say of your good friend, after that?

ORGON   Why, I'd say . . . nothing, by Jehoshaphat!
  It can't be true.

ELMIRE   You've been too long deceived,
  I'm quite tired of being disbelieved.   75
  Come now: let's put my statements to the test,
  And you shall see the truth made manifest.

ORGON   I'll take that challenge. Now do your uttermost.
  We'll see how you make good your empty boast.

ELMIRE [*To* DORINE.]   Send him to me.

DORINE   He's crafty; it may be hard   80
  To catch the cunning scoundrel off his guard.

ELMIRE   No, amorous men are gullible. Their conceit
  So blinds them that they're never hard to cheat.
  Have him come down.
  [*To* CLÉANTE *and* MARIANE.] Please leave us, for a bit.

SCENE 4

ELMIRE, ORGON

ELMIRE   Pull up this table, and get under it.

ORGON   What?

ELMIRE   It's essential that you be well-hidden.

ORGON   Why there?

ELMIRE   Oh, Heavens! Just do as you are bidden.
  I have my plans; we'll soon see how they fare.
  Under the table, now; and once you're there,   5
  Take care that you are neither seen nor heard.

ORGON   Well, I'll indulge you, since I gave my word
  To see you through this infantile charade.

ELMIRE   Once it is over, you'll be glad we played.
        [*To her husband, who is now under the table.*]
  I'm going to act quite strangely, now, and you   10
  Must not be shocked at anything I do.
  Whatever I may say, you must excuse

As part of that deceit I'm forced to use.
I shall employ sweet speeches in the task
Of making that impostor drop his mask;   15
I'll give encouragement to his bold desires,
And furnish fuel to his amorous fires.
Since it's for your sake, and for his destruction,
That I shall seem to yield to his seduction,
I'll gladly stop whenever you decide   20
That all your doubts are fully satisfied.
I'll count on you, as soon as you have seen
What sort of man he is, to intervene,
And not expose me to his odious lust
One moment longer than you feel you must.   25
Remember: you're to save me from my plight
Whenever . . . He's coming! Hush! Keep out of sight!

SCENE 5

TARTUFFE, ELMIRE, ORGON

TARTUFFE   You wish to have a word with me, I'm told.
ELMIRE   Yes, I've a little secret to unfold.
Before I speak, however, it would be wise
To close that door, and look about for spies.
           [TARTUFFE *goes to the door, closes it, and returns.*]
The very last thing that must happen now   5
Is a repetition of this morning's row.
I've never been so badly caught off guard.
Oh, how I feared for you! You saw how hard
I tried to make that troublesome Damis
Control his dreadful temper, and hold his peace.   10
In my confusion, I didn't have the sense
Simply to contradict his evidence;
But as it happened, that was for the best,
And all has worked out in our interest.
This storm has only bettered your position;   15
My husband doesn't have the least suspicion,
And now, in mockery of those who do,
He bids me be continually with you.
And that is why, quite fearless of reproof,
I now can be alone with my Tartuffe,   20
And why my heart—perhaps too quick to yield—
Feels free to let its passion be revealed.
TARTUFFE   Madam, your words confuse me. Not long ago,
You spoke in quite a different style, you know.
ELMIRE   Ah, Sir, if that refusal made you smart,   25
It's little that you know of woman's heart,
Or what that heart is trying to convey
When it resists in such a feeble way!
Always, at first, our modesty prevents
The frank avowal of tender sentiments: 30

However high the passion which inflames us,
Still, to confess its power somehow shames us.
Thus we reluct, at first, yet in a tone
Which tells you that our heart is overthrown,
That what our lips deny, our pulse confesses,   35
And that, in time, all noes will turn to yesses.
I fear my words are all too frank and free,
And a poor proof of woman's modesty;
But since I'm started, tell me, if you will—
Would I have tried to make Damis be still,   40
Would I have listened, calm and unoffended,
Until your lengthy offer of love was ended,
And been so very mild in my reaction,
Had your sweet words not given me satisfaction?
And when I tried to force you to undo   45
The marriage-plans my husband has in view,
What did my urgent pleading signify
If not that I admired you, and that I
Deplored the thought that someone else might own
Part of a heart I wished for mine alone?   50
TARTUFFE   Madam, no happiness is so complete
As when, from lips we love, come words so sweet;
Their nectar floods my every sense, and drains
In honeyed rivulets through all my veins.
To please you is my joy, my only goal;   55
Your love is the restorer of my soul;
And yet I must beg leave, now, to confess
Some lingering doubts as to my happiness.
Might this not be a trick? Might not the catch
Be that you wish me to break off the match   60
With Mariane, and so have feigned to love me?
I shan't quite trust your fond opinion of me
Until the feelings you've expressed so sweetly
Are demonstrated somewhat more concretely,
And you have shown, by certain kind concessions,   65
That I may put my faith in your professions
ELMIRE [*She coughs, to warn her husband.*]
Why be in such a hurry? Must my heart
Exhaust its bounty at the very start?
To make that sweet admission cost me dear,
But you'll not be content, it would appear,   70
Unless my store of favors is disbursed
To the last farthing, and at the very first.
TARTUFFE   The less we merit, the less we dare to hope,
And with our doubts, mere words can never cope.
We trust no promised bliss till we receive it;   75
Not till a joy is ours can we believe it.
I, who so little merit your esteem,
Can't credit this fulfillment of my dream,
And shan't believe it, Madam, until I savor

  Some palpable assurance of your favor.   80
ELMIRE My, how tyrannical your love can be,
  And how it flusters and perplexes me!
  How furiously you take one's heart in hand,
  And make your every wish a fierce command!
  Come, must you hound and harry me to death?   85
  Will you not give me time to catch my breath?
  Can it be right to press me with such force,
  Give me no quarter, show me no remorse,
  And take advantage, by your stern insistence,
  Of the fond feelings which weaken my resistance?   90
TARTUFFE Well, if you look with favor upon my love,
  Why, then, begrudge me some clear proof thereof?
ELMIRE But how can I consent without offense
  To Heaven, toward which you feel such reverence?
TARTUFFE If Heaven is all that holds you back, don't worry. 95
  I can remove that hindrance in a hurry.
  Nothing of that sort need obstruct our path.
ELMIRE Must one not be afraid of Heaven's wrath?
TARTUFFE Madam, forget such fears, and be my pupil,
  And I shall teach you how to conquer scruple.   100
  Some joys, it's true, are wrong in Heaven's eyes;
  Yet Heaven is not averse to compromise;
  There is a science, lately formulated,
  Whereby one's conscience may be liberated,[3]
  And any wrongful act you care to mention   105
  May be redeemed by purity of intention.
  I'll teach you, Madam, the secrets of that science;
  Meanwhile, just place on me your full reliance.
  Assuage my keen desires, and feel no dread:
  The sin, if any, shall be on my head.   110
    [ELMIRE *coughs, this time more loudly.*]
  You've a bad cough.
ELMIRE   Yes, yes, It's bad indeed.
TARTUFFE [*Producing a little paper bag.*]
  A bit of licorice may be what you need.
ELMIRE No, I've a stubborn cold, it seems. I'm sure it
  Will take much more than licorice to cure it.
TARTUFFE How aggravating.
ELMIRE   Oh, more than I can say.   115
TARTUFFE If you're still troubled, think of things this way:
  No one shall know our joys, save us alone,
  And there's no evil till the act is known;
  It's scandal, Madam, which makes it an offense,
  And it's no sin to sin in confidence.   120
ELMIRE [*Having coughed once more.*]
  Well, clearly I must do as you require,
  And yield to your importunate desire.

---

3. Molière created his own footnote to this line: "It is a scoundrel who speaks."

It is apparent, now, that nothing less
Will satisfy you, and so I acquiesce.
To go so far is much against my will;   125
I'm vexed that it should come to this; but still,
Since you are so determined on it, since you
Will not allow mere language to convince you,
And since you ask for concrete evidence, I
See nothing for it, now, but to comply.   130
If this is sinful, if I'm wrong to do it,
So much the worse for him who drove me to it.
The fault can surely not be charged to me.
TARTUFFE   Madam, the fault is mine, if fault there be,
And . . .
ELMIRE   Open the door a little, and peek out;   135
I wouldn't want my husband poking about.
TARTUFFE   Why worry about the man? Each day he grows
More gullible; one can lead him by the nose.
To find us here would fill him with delight,
And if he saw the worst, he'd doubt his sight.   140
ELMIRE   Nevertheless, do step out for a minute
Into the hall, and see that no one's in it.

SCENE 6

ORGON, ELMIRE

ORGON [*Coming out from under the table.*]
That man's a perfect monster, I must admit!
I'm simply stunned. I can't get over it.
ELMIRE   What, coming out so soon? How premature!
Get back in hiding, and wait until you're sure.
Stay till the end, and be convinced completely;   5
We mustn't stop till things are proved concretely.
ORGON   Hell never harbored anything so vicious!
ELMIRE   Tut, don't be hasty. Try to be judicious.
Wait, and be certain that there's no mistake.
No jumping to conclusions, for Heaven's sake!   10
[*She places* ORGON *behind her, as* TARTUFFE *re-enters.*]

SCENE 7

TARTUFFE, ELMIRE, ORGON

TARTUFFE [*Not seeing* ORGON.]
Madam, all things have worked out to perfection;
I've given the neighboring rooms a full inspection;
No one's about; and now I may at last . . .
ORGON [*Intercepting him.*]   Hold on, my passionate fellow, not so fast!
I should advise a little more restraint.   5
Well, so you thought you'd fool me, my dear saint!
How soon you wearied of the saintly life—
Wedding my daughter, and coveting my wife!

I've long suspected you, and had a feeling
That soon I'd catch you at your double-dealing.   10
Just now, you've given me evidence galore;
It's quite enough; I have no wish for more.
ELMIRE [*To* TARTUFFE.]   I'm sorry to have treated you so slyly,
  But circumstances forced me to be wily.
TARTUFFE   Brother, you can't think . . .
ORGON   No more talk from you;   15
  Just leave this household, without more ado.
TARTUFFE   What I intended . . .
ORGON   That seems fairly clear.
  Spare me your falsehoods and get out of here.
TARTUFFE   No, I'm the master, and you're the one to go!
  This house belongs to me, I'll have you know,
  And I shall show you that you can't hurt *me*   20
  By this contemptible conspiracy,
  That those who cross me know not what they do,
  And that I've means to expose and punish you,
  Avenge offended Heaven, and make you grieve   25
  That ever you dared order me to leave.

SCENE 8

ELMIRE, ORGON

ELMIRE   What was the point of all that angry chatter?
ORGON   Dear God, I'm worried. This is no laughing matter.
ELMIRE   How so?
ORGON   I fear I understood his drift.
  I'm much disturbed about that deed of gift.
ELMIRE   You gave him . . . ?
ORGON   Yes, it's all been drawn and signed.   5
  But one thing more is weighing on my mind.
ELMIRE   What's that?
ORGON   I'll tell you; but first let's see if there's
  A certain strong-box in his room upstairs.

Act V

SCENE 1

ORGON, CLÉANTE

CLÉANTE   Where are you going so fast?
ORGON   God knows!
CLÉANTE   Then wait;
  Let's have a conference, and deliberate
  On how this situation's to be met.
ORGON   That strong-box has me utterly upset;

This is the worst of many, many shocks.   5
CLÉANTE   Is there some fearful mystery in that box?
ORGON   My poor friend Argas brought that box to me
With his own hands, in utmost secrecy;
'Twas on the very morning of his flight.
It's full of papers which, if they came to light,   10
Would ruin him—or such is my impression.
CLÉANTE   Then why did you let it out of your possession?
ORGON   Those papers vexed my conscience, and it seemed best
To ask the counsel of my pious guest.
The cunning scoundrel got me to agree   15
To leave the strong-box in his custody,
So that, in case of an investigation,
I could employ a slight equivocation
And swear I didn't have it, and thereby,
At no expense to conscience, tell a lie.   20
CLÉANTE   It looks to me as if you're out on a limb.
Trusting him with that box, and offering him
That deed of gift, were actions of a kind
Which scarcely indicate a prudent mind.
With two such weapons, he has the upper hand,   25
And since you're vulnerable, as matters stand,
You erred once more in bringing him to bay.
You should have acted in some subtler way.
ORGON   Just think of it: behind that fervent face,
A heart so wicked, and a soul so base!   30
I took him in, a hungry beggar, and then . . .
Enough, by God! I'm through with pious men:
Henceforth I'll hate the whole false brotherhood,
And persecute them worse than Satan could.
CLÉANTE   Ah, there you go—extravagant as ever!   35
Why can you not be rational? You never
Manage to take the middle course, it seems,
But jump, instead, between absurd extremes.
You've recognized your recent grave mistake
In falling victim to a pious fake;   40
Now, to correct that error, must you embrace
An even greater error in its place,
And judge our worthy neighbors as a whole
By what you've learned of one corrupted soul?
Come, just because one rascal made you swallow   45
A show of zeal which turned out to be hollow,
Shall you conclude that all men are deceivers,
And that, today, there are no true believers?
Let atheists make that foolish inference;
Learn to distinguish virtue from pretense,   50
Be cautious in bestowing admiration,
And cultivate a sober moderation.
Don't humor fraud, but also don't asperse

True piety; the latter fault is worse,
And it is best to err, if err one must,   55
As you have done, upon the side of trust.

SCENE 2

DAMIS, ORGON, CLÉANTE

DAMIS   Father, I hear that scoundrel's uttered threats
Against you; that he pridefully forgets
How, in his need, he was befriended by you,
And means to use your gifts to crucify you.
ORGON   It's true, my boy. I'm too distressed for tears.   5
DAMIS   Leave it to me, Sir; let me trim his ears.
Faced with such insolence, we must not waver.
I shall rejoice in doing you the favor
Of cutting short his life, and your distress.
CLÉANTE   What a display of young hotheadedness!   10
Do learn to moderate your fits of rage.
In this just kingdom, this enlightened age,
One does not settle things by violence.

SCENE 3

MADAME PERNELLE, MARIANE, ELMIRE, DORINE, DAMIS,
ORGON, CLÉANTE

MADAME PERNELLE   I hear strange tales of very strange events.
ORGON   Yes, strange events which these two eyes beheld.
The man's ingratitude is unparalleled.
I save a wretched pauper from starvation,
House him, and treat him like a blood relation,   5
Shower him every day with my largesse,
Give him my daughter, and all that I possess;
And meanwhile the unconscionable knave
Tries to induce my wife to misbehave;
And not content with such extreme rascality,   10
Now threatens me with my own liberality,
And aims, by taking base advantage of
The gifts I gave him out of Christian love,
To drive me from my house, a ruined man,
And make me end a pauper, as he began.   15
DORINE   Poor fellow!
MADAME PERNELLE   No, my son, I'll never bring
Myself to think him guilty of such a thing.
ORGON   How's that?
MADAME PERNELLE   The righteous always were maligned.
ORGON   Speak clearly, Mother. Say what's on your mind.   20
MADAME PERNELLE   I mean that I can smell a rat, my dear.
You know how everybody hates him, here.
ORGON   That has no bearing on the case at all.
MADAME PERNELLE   I told you a hundred times, when you were small,

That virtue in this world is hated ever; 25
  Malicious men may die, but malice never.
ORGON   No doubt that's true, but how does it apply?
MADAME PERNELLE   They've turned you against him by a clever lie.
ORGON   I've told you, I was there and saw it done.
MADAME PERNELLE   Ah, slanderers will stop at nothing, Son. 30
ORGON   Mother, I'll lose my temper . . . For the last time,
  I tell you I was witness to the crime.
MADAME PERNELLE   The tongues of spite are busy night and noon,
  And to their venom no man is immune.
ORGON   You're talking nonsense. Can't you realize 35
  I saw it; saw it; saw it with my eyes?
  Saw, do you understand me? Must I shout it
  Into your ears before you'll cease to doubt it?
MADAME PERNELLE   Appearances can deceive, my son. Dear me,
  We cannot always judge by what we see. 40
ORGON   Drat! Drat!
MADAME PERNELLE   One often interprets things awry;
  Good can seem evil to a suspicious eye.
ORGON   Was I to see his pawing at Elmire
  As an act of charity?
MADAME PERNELLE   Till his guilt is clear, 45
  A man deserves the benefit of the doubt.
  You should have waited, to see how things turned out.
ORGON   Great God in Heaven, what more proof did I need?
  Was I to sit there, watching, until he'd . . .
  You drive me to the brink of impropriety. 50
MADAME PERNELLE   No, no, a man of such surpassing piety
  Could not do such a thing. You cannot shake me.
  I don't believe it, and you shall not make me.
ORGON   You vex me so that, if you weren't my mother,
  I'd say to you . . . some dreadful thing or other. 55
DORINE   It's your turn now, Sir, not to be listened to;
  You'd not trust us, and now she won't trust you.
CLÉANTE   My friends, we're wasting time which should be spent
  In facing up to our predicament.
  I fear that scoundrel's threats weren't made in sport. 60
DAMIS   Do you think he'd have the nerve to go to court?
ELMIRE   I'm sure he won't: they'd find it all too crude
  A case of swindling and ingratitude.
CLÉANTE   Don't be too sure. He won't be at a loss
  To give his claims a high and righteous gloss; 65
  And clever rogues with far less valid cause
  Have trapped their victims in a web of laws.
  I say again that to antagonize
  A man so strongly armed was most unwise.
ORGON   I know it; but the man's appalling cheek 70
  Outraged me so, I couldn't control my pique.
CLÉANTE   I wish to Heaven that we could devise
  Some truce between you, or some compromise.

ELMIRE   If I had known what cards he held, I'd not
　Have roused his anger by my little plot.   75
ORGON [*To* DORINE, *as* M. LOYAL *enters.*]
　What is that fellow looking for? Who is he?
　Go talk to him—and tell him that I'm busy.

SCENE 4

MONSIEUR LOYAL, MADAME PERNELLE, ORGON, DAMIS, MARIANE, DORINE,
ELMIRE, CLÉANTE

MONSIEUR LOYAL   Good day, dear sister. Kindly let me see
　Your master.
DORINE　　　　He's involved with company,
　And cannot be disturbed just now, I fear.
MONSIEUR LOYAL   I hate to intrude; but what has brought me here
　Will not disturb your master, in any event.   5
　Indeed, my news will make him most content.
DORINE   Your name?
MONSIEUR LOYAL　　Just say that I bring greetings from
　Monsieur Tartuffe, on whose behalf I've come.
DORINE [*To* ORGON.]   Sir, he's a very gracious man, and bears
　A message from Tartuffe, which, he declares,   10
　Will make you most content.
CLÉANTE　　　　　　　　　　Upon my word,
　I think this man had best be seen, and heard.
ORGON   Perhaps he has some settlement to suggest.
　How shall I treat him? What manner would be best?
CLÉANTE   Control your anger, and if he should mention   15
　Some fair adjustment, give him your full attention.
MONSIEUR LOYAL   Good health to you, good Sir. May Heaven confound
　Your enemies, and may your joys abound.
ORGON [*Aside, to* CLÉANTE.]   A gentle salutation: it confirms
　My guess that he is here to offer terms.   20
MONSIEUR LOYAL   I've always held your family most dear;
　I served your father, Sir, for many a year.
ORGON   Sir, I must ask your pardon; to my shame,
　I cannot now recall your face or name.
MONSIEUR LOYAL   Loyal's my name; I come from Normandy,   25
　And I'm a bailiff, in all modesty.
　For forty years, praise God, it's been my boast
　To serve with honor in that vital post,
　And I am here, Sir, if you will permit
　The liberty, to serve you with this writ . . .   30
ORGON   To—*what?*
MONSIEUR LOYAL　　Now, please, Sir, let us have no friction:
　It's nothing but an order of eviction.
　You are to move your goods and family out
　And make way for new occupants, without
　Deferment or delay, and give the keys . . .   35
ORGON   I? Leave this house?
MONSIEUR LOYAL　　　　　　Why yes, Sir, if you please.

This house, Sir, from the cellar to the roof,
Belongs now to the good Monsieur Tartuffe,
And he is lord and master of your estate
By virtue of a deed of present date,   40
Drawn in due form, with clearest legal phrasing . . .
DAMIS   Your insolence is utterly amazing!
MONSIEUR LOYAL   Young man, my business here is not with you
But with your wise and temperate father, who,
Like every worthy citizen, stands in awe   45
Of justice, and would never obstruct the law.
ORGON   But . . .
MONSIEUR LOYAL   Not for a million, Sir, would you rebel
Against authority; I know that well.
You'll not make trouble, Sir, or interfere
With the execution of my duties here.   50
DAMIS   Someone may execute a smart tattoo
On that black jacket[4] of yours, before you're through.
MONSIEUR LOYAL   Sir, bid your son be silent. I'd much regret
Having to mention such a nasty threat
Of violence, in writing my report.   55
DORINE [*Aside.*]   This man Loyal's a most disloyal sort!
MONSIEUR LOYAL   I love all men of upright character,
And when I agreed to serve these papers, Sir,
It was your feelings that I had in mind.
I couldn't bear to see the case assigned   60
To someone else, who might esteem you less
And so subject you to unpleasantness.
ORGON   What's more unpleasant than telling a man to leave
His house and home?
MONSIEUR LOYAL   You'd like a short reprieve?
If you desire it, Sir, I shall not press you,   65
But wait until tomorrow to dispossess you.
Splendid. I'll come and spend the night here, then,
Most quietly, with half a score of men.
For form's sake, you might bring me, just before
You go to bed, the keys to the front door.   70
My men, I promise, will be on their best
Behavior, and will not disturb your rest.
But bright and early, Sir, you must be quick
And move out all your furniture, every stick:
The men I've chosen are both young and strong,   75
And with their help it shouldn't take you long.
In short, I'll make things pleasant and convenient,
And since I'm being so extremely lenient,
Please show me, Sir, a like consideration,
And give me your entire cooperation.   80
ORGON [*Aside.*]   I may be all but bankrupt, but I vow
I'd give a hundred louis, here and now,

---

4. In the original, *justaucorps à longues basques,* a close-fitting, long black coat with skirts, the customary
dress of a bailiff.

Just for the pleasure of landing one good clout
Right on the end of that complacent snout.
CLÉANTE   Careful; don't make things worse.
DAMIS   My bootsole itches   85
To give that beggar a good kick in the breeches.
DORINE   Monsieur Loyal, I'd love to hear the whack
Of a stout stick across your fine broad back.
MONSIEUR LOYAL   Take care: a woman too may go to jail if
She uses threatening language to a bailiff.   90
CLÉANTE   Enough, enough, Sir. This must not go on.
Give me that paper, please, and then begone.
MONSIEUR LOYAL   Well, *au revoir.* God give you all good cheer!
ORGON   May God confound you, and him who sent you here!

SCENE 5

ORGON, CLÉANTE, MARIANE, ELMIRE, MADAME PERNELLE, DORINE, DAMIS

ORGON   Now, Mother, was I right or not? This writ
Should change your notion of Tartuffe a bit.
Do you perceive his villainy at last?
MADAME PERNELLE   I'm thunderstruck. I'm utterly aghast.
DORINE   Oh, come, be fair. You mustn't take offense   5
At this new proof of his benevolence.
He's acting out of selfless love, I know.
Material things enslave the soul, and so
He kindly has arranged your liberation
From all that might endanger your salvation.   10
ORGON   Will you not ever hold your tongue, you dunce?
CLÉANTE   Come, you must take some action, and at once.
ELMIRE   Go tell the world of the low trick he's tried.
The deed of gift is surely nullified
By such behavior, and public rage will not   15
Permit the wretch to carry out his plot.

SCENE 6

VALÈRE, ORGON, CLÉANTE, ELMIRE, MARIANE, MADAME PERNELLE,
DAMIS, DORINE

VALÈRE   Sir, though I hate to bring you more bad news,
Such is the danger that I cannot choose.
A friend who is extremely close to me
And knows my interest in your family
Has, for my sake, presumed to violate   5
The secrecy that's due to things of state,
And sends me word that you are in a plight
From which your one salvation lies in flight.
That scoundrel who's imposed upon you so
Denounced you to the King an hour ago   10
And, as supporting evidence, displayed
The strong-box of a certain renegade

Whose secret papers, so he testified,
You had disloyally agreed to hide.
I don't know just what charges may be pressed, 15
But there's a warrant out for your arrest;
Tartuffe has been instructed, furthermore,
To guide the arresting officer to your door.
CLÉANTE   He's clearly done this to facilitate
His seizure of your house and your estate. 20
ORGON   That man, I must say, is a vicious beast!
VALÈRE   You can't afford to delay, Sir, in the least.
My carriage is outside, to take you hence;
This thousand louis should cover all expense.
Let's lose no time, or you shall be undone; 25
The sole defense, in this case, is to run.
I shall go with you all the way, and place you
In a safe refuge to which they'll never trace you.
ORGON   Alas, dear boy, I wish that I could show you
My gratitude for everything I owe you. 30
But now is not the time; I pray the Lord
That I may live to give you your reward.
Farewell, my dears; be careful . . .
CLÉANTE   Brother, hurry.
We shall take care of things; you needn't worry.

SCENE 7

The OFFICER, TARTUFFE, VALÈRE, ORGON, ELMIRE, MARIANE,
MADAME PERNELLE, DORINE, CLÉANTE, DAMIS

TARTUFFE   Gently, Sir, gently; stay right where you are.
No need for haste; your lodging isn't far.
You're off to prison, by order of the Prince.
ORGON   This is the crowning blow, you wretch; and since
It means my total ruin and defeat, 5
Your villainy is now at last complete.
TARTUFFE   You needn't try to provoke me; it's no use.
Those who serve Heaven must expect abuse.
CLÉANTE   You are indeed most patient, sweet, and blameless.
DORINE   How he exploits the name of Heaven! It's shameless. 10
TARTUFFE   Your taunts and mockeries are all for naught;
To do my duty is my only thought.
MARIANE   Your love of duty is most meritorious,
And what you've done is little short of glorious.
TARTUFFE   All deeds are glorious, Madam, which obey 15
The sovereign prince who sent me here today.
ORGON   I rescued you when you were destitute;
Have you forgotten that, you thankless brute?
TARTUFFE   No, no, I well remember everything;
But my first duty is to serve my King. 20
That obligation is so paramount
That other claims, beside it, do not count;

And for it I would sacrifice my wife,
My family, my friend, or my own life.
ELMIRE   Hypocrite!
DORINE   All that we most revere, he uses   25
   To cloak his plots and camouflage his ruses.
CLÉANTE   If it is true that you are animated
   By pure and loyal zeal, as you have stated,
   Why was this zeal not roused until you'd sought
   To make Orgon a cuckold, and been caught?   30
   Why weren't you moved to give your evidence
   Until your outraged host had driven you hence?
   I shan't say that the gift of all his treasure
   Ought to have damped your zeal in any measure;
   But if he is a traitor, as you declare,   35
   How could you condescend to be his heir?
TARTUFFE [*To the* OFFICER.]
   Sir, spare me all this clamor; it's growing shrill.
   Please carry out your orders, if you will.
OFFICER[5]   Yes, I've delayed too long, Sir. Thank you kindly.
   You're just the proper person to remind me.   40
   Come, you are off to join the other boarders
   In the King's prison, according to his orders.
TARTUFFE   Who? I, Sir?
OFFICER   Yes.
TARTUFFE   To prison? This can't be true!
OFFICER   I owe an explanation, but not to you.
   [*To* ORGON.] Sir, all is well; rest easy, and be grateful.   45
   We serve a Prince to whom all sham is hateful,
   A Prince who sees into our inmost hearts,
   And can't be fooled by any trickster's arts.
   His royal soul, though generous and human,
   Views all things with discernment and acumen;   50
   His sovereign reason is not lightly swayed,
   And all his judgments are discreetly weighed.
   He honors righteous men of every kind,
   And yet his zeal for virtue is not blind,
   Nor does his love of piety numb his wits   55
   And make him tolerant of hypocrites.
   'Twas hardly likely that this man could cozen
   A King who's foiled such liars by the dozen.
   With one keen glance, the King perceived the whole
   Perverseness and corruption of his soul,   60
   And thus high Heaven's justice was displayed:
   Betraying you, the rogue stood self-betrayed.
   The King soon recognized Tartuffe as one
   Notorious by another name, who'd done
   So many vicious crimes that one could fill   65

---

5. In the original, *un exempt*. He would actually have been a gentleman from the king's personal bodyguard with the rank of lieutenant colonel or "master of the camp."

Ten volumes with them, and be writing still.
But to be brief: our sovereign was appalled
By this man's treachery toward you, which he called
The last, worst villainy of a vile career,
And bade me follow the impostor here   70
To see how gross his impudence could be,
And force him to restore your property.
Your private papers, by the King's command,
I hereby seize and give into your hand.
The King, by royal order, invalidates   75
The deed which gave this rascal your estates,
And pardons, furthermore, your grave offense
In harboring an exile's documents.
By these decrees, our Prince rewards you for
Your loyal deeds in the late civil war,[6]   80
And shows how heartfelt is his satisfaction
In recompensing any worthy action,
How much he prizes merit, and how he makes
More of men's virtues than of their mistakes.
DORINE   Heaven be praised!
MADAME PERNELLE.   I breathe again, at last.   85
ELMIRE   We're safe.
MARIANE   I can't believe the danger's past.
ORGON [*To* TARTUFFE.]   Well, traitor, now you see . . .
CLÉANTE   Ah, brother, please
Let's not descend to such indignities.
Leave the poor wretch to his unhappy fate,
And don't say anything to aggravate   90
His present woes; but rather hope that he
Will soon embrace an honest piety,
And mend his ways, and by a true repentance
Move our just King to moderate his sentence.
Meanwhile, go kneel before your sovereign's throne   95
And thank him for the mercies he has shown.
ORGON   Well said: let's go at once and, gladly kneeling,
Express the gratitude which all are feeling.
Then, when that first great duty has been done,
We'll turn with pleasure to a second one,   100
And give Valère, whose love has proven so true,
The wedded happiness which is his due.

6. A reference to Orgon's role in supporting the king during the *Frondes*.

JEAN RACINE
1639–1699

Jean Racine's capacity to communicate the full intensity of passion in tragedies marked by their formal decorum and their elevated tone gave him immediate and lasting fame among French dramatists. He brings to material adapted from classic texts an immediacy of psychological insight to which twenty-first-century audiences readily respond.

Born into the family of a government official in the Valois district, eighty miles from Paris, Racine attended the College de Beauvais. Later (1655–59) he studied in the Jansenist center of Port-Royal. (Jansenism, a strict Catholic movement emphasizing moral self-examination and severely controlled conduct, exercised a profound influence on Racine.) In 1660, encouraged by the poet Jean de la Fontaine, Racine came to Paris, where his early plays failed, driving him to a period of seclusion in Provence. When he returned to Paris in 1663, however, the Court and the nobility patronized him, and he rapidly developed a reputation as a major playwright. In 1677 he left Paris and returned to Port-Royal, an environment appropriate to his increasing interest in religious thought. He married Catherine de Romanet, with whom he had seven children, most of whom became nuns or priests. Remaining in the country, he wrote history, made short trips to Paris, and traveled as historiographer with Louis XIV's campaigns. Buried at Port-Royal, his body was exhumed in 1711 and reburied next to Pascal at the church of St. Étienne-du-Mont in Paris.

Only one of Racine's twelve plays, an early comedy, deviated from the tragic mode. His first tragedies imitated the work of his contemporary Pierre Corneille; later he chose biblical and classical models. *Phaedra* (1677) adapts, with new emphasis, the action of Euripides' *Hippolytus,* making the guilty woman rather than the relatively passive man the protagonist and using the highly charged sexual situation between the two to generate intense psychological drama. To twenty-first-century readers, the play's most immediately obvious aspect may be its conventional formalities: long declamatory speeches, stylized exchanges in compressed half lines, the artificiality of conveying such complicated relationships and histories through the action of a single day. Such devices, however—which would have seemed as artificial to seventeenth-century audiences as they do to us, although more familiar—intensify the impact of the central characters' anguish and their desperate attempts to deal with it. If the play's surface is formal, its depths seethe with passion.

Passion, of course, is the subject of *Phaedra.* The conflict between reason and passion that preoccupied many thinkers in the late seventeenth and early eighteenth centuries here plays itself out with stark urgency. Passion triumphs, in *Phaedra,* over all principles of control, bringing death to the two central characters and misery to their survivors. As in Greek tragedy, although by rather different means, the reader feels not only the self-destructiveness of the human psyche but the pathos and the heroism of the doomed effort to transcend the limits of the given.

The play opens not with Phaedra herself but with Hippolytus, meditating about his heroic father, Theseus. Like Molière, Racine uses the family as microcosm of larger social orders, but the intense conflicts that throb beneath the surface in many real-life families here undergo no comic transformation. Hippolytus has his own problems, quite apart from Phaedra. Blessed and burdened with a larger-than-life father, he must choose whether to try to imitate that father or to seek other ways of being a man. "I sucked that pride which seems so strange to you / From an Amazonian mother," he tells his friend Theramenes, alluding to the "austere and proud / Persuasions" that have prevented him from feeling interest in any woman. But matters cannot remain so simple. Theseus has distinguished himself in two ways: by heroic womanizing (he leaves a trail of women behind him wherever he goes) and by heroic action, the conquering and destruction of monsters human and inhuman. As the play opens, Hippolytus acknowledges in himself the first incursions of love. No longer can his adolescent defense, his refusal of any resemblance to his father, serve him. When Theseus returns, Hippolytus will beg permission to seek his own heroism:

> Before you'd lived as long as I have done,
> More than one tyrant, monsters more than one
> Had felt your strength of arm, your sword's keen blade . . .
> Let me at long last show my courage.

He wants, he says, even by death to "prove to all the world I was your son." By the time he makes this plea, however, his innocent desire to prove his manhood, to declare his separateness from and worthiness of his father, has been overwhelmed by darker forces.

Phaedra's impulses are less innocent—less "natural," she suggests. In a poignant passage, she imagines Hippolytus and his youthful beloved, Aricia, expressing their love in a natural setting, themselves a part of the natural world. She understands her own sin as an internal revolution of feeling against control; she speaks of desperately seeking her "lost reason" in the entrails of sacrifices she makes to Venus, trying to avert her fate. Never does she excuse herself, never does she believe herself justified in loving the son of the man who kidnapped her into marriage. When Theseus is thought dead, Phaedra declares herself unworthy to rule a nation because she cannot rule herself. Yet such moral awareness fails to help her: knowing her sin, she continues to enact it, at least in feeling. The play evokes the full torment of such experience.

As for powerful Theseus, conqueror of women, defier of the supernatural, ally of Neptune—this kingly figure returns to find himself powerless at home. The son and wife who by social convention exist in utter subordination to him turn into enemies he has no capacity to master. First his wife's nurse tells him that his son has attempted to seduce Phaedra. The rivalry of sons and fathers lies deep: if sons fear they can never equal their fathers, fathers fear that the young necessarily overcome the old. Theseus believes the nurse's bare assertion, unsupported by substantial evidence. He banishes his son and invokes Neptune's power to destroy him. Then Aricia's hints lead him to suspect his wife, who confesses her own emotional sin while already on the verge of self-inflicted death. Theseus remains alone, bereft, his tyrannical impulse now devoid of domestic object. His own passions, too quickly fired—jealous possessiveness of his wife, jealous rivalry with his son—have deprived him of two beings he loved.

The play provides no villains. Phaedra, in some versions of the story a monster of lust, here becomes a woman struggling against her nature, as profoundly committed to standards of control as to the violent feelings that overthrow them. Hippolytus, in the process of self-discovery, at a delicate balance point between youth and maturity, cannot protect himself against the alternations of closely linked love and hate in a woman whose passions, and whose self-awareness, far exceed his. Theseus, in the ignorance of success, fails in comprehension, not understanding himself, his wife, or his son. All three exemplify the pathos and the dignity of the human struggle to be human.

Phaedra dies with the word *purity* on her lips, seeking self-purification in death, the only course now possible to her. Hippolytus dies in the beauty of his youth, deprived of age's suffering and fulfillment. Theseus lives to try once more to rule adequately, perhaps chastened by suffering into greater awareness. The names of the Greek gods survive in this drama: Aphrodite torments Phaedra, Neptune serves Theseus's impetuous will. But the gods now function as projections of human passion: Phaedra's sexual lust, Theseus's lust for power. Phaedra's torment suggests a Christian effort at purification, a Christian ideal of self-denial. The drama, in Racine's handling of the ancient story, projects on a giant screen conflicts all men and women undergo, the surge of feeling warring with the ideal of self-restraint. By concentrating the play of passions within a small family group and a confined space of time, while recalling connections between the characters' feelings and historical events that lie behind them; by giving Theseus and Phaedra heroic dignity and stature; by linking this family with the fate of nations,

Racine forces his readers to feel the intensity and the large significance of feelings and happenings that might in other treatments seem merely sordid. He gives his characters timeless reality—speaking to his time, and to ours.

To translate Racine into English involves particularly difficult problems, since the French Alexandrine couplet, composed of twelve-syllable lines, does not adapt naturally to English verse. Richard Wilbur's version uses the common English pentameter, the ten-syllable line, to construct fluent, pointed, and dignified verse. His couplets by their formal elegance remind the reader steadily of the discipline that the play embodies and celebrates.

A useful biography of Racine is G. Brereton, *Jean Racine: A Critical Biography* (1951), which combines biography with literary criticism. Valuable critical insight is provided by O. de Mourgues, *Racine; or, The Triumph of Relevance* (1967); Richard Parish, *Racine: The Limits of Tragedy* (1993); H. Phillips, *Racine: Language and Theatre* (1994); and A. Wygant, *Towards a Cultural Philology: Phedre and the Construction of "Racine"* (1999). A treatment of French tragic drama that includes extensive and valuable material on Racine is Albert Cook, *French Tragedy: The Power of Enactment* (1981). For an interpretation that includes stage history of Racine's plays, see D. Maskell, *Racine: A Theatrical Reading* (1991). Intended especially for students is Philip Butler, *A Student's Guide to Racine* (1974).

PRONOUNCING GLOSSARY

The following list uses common English syllables and stress accents to provide rough equivalents of selected words whose pronunciation may be unfamiliar to the general reader.

Acheron: *ah-ker-awn'*

Ariadne: *ah-ree-ahd'-ne*

Aricia: *ah-ree'-sha*

Cocytus: *coh-sai'-tuhs*

Euripides: *yoo-rip'-uh-deez*

Hippolytus: *hip-pol'-i-tuhs*

Ismene: *is-mee'-ne*

Medea: *me-dee'-a*

Mycenae: *mai-see'-nee*

Oenone: *ee-noh'-ne*

Panope: *pah'-no-pe*

Pasiphaë: *pa-si'-fa-ee*

Peirithous: *pay-rith'-oo-uhs*

Peloponnesus: *pel-luh-puh-nee'-suhs*

Phaedra: *fee'-drah*

Scythia: *si'-thee-uh*

Taenarus: *ten'-a-ruhs*

Theramenes: *thee-ram'-uh-neez*

Theseus: *thee'-see-uhs*

Troezen: *troh'-zen*

Phaedra[1]

CHARACTERS

THESEUS, *son of Aegeus, King of Athens*

PHAEDRA, *wife of Theseus, daughter of Minos and Pasiphaë*

HIPPOLYTUS, *son of Theseus and Antiope, Queen of the Amazons*

ARICIA, *princess of the blood royal of Athens*

THERAMENES, *Hippolytus' tutor*

OENONE, *Phaedra's nurse and confidante*

ISMENE, *Aricia's confidante*

PANOPE, *lady-in-waiting to Phaedra*

GUARDS

---

1. Translated by Richard Wilbur.

The action takes place within and without a palace at Troezen, a town in the Peloponnesus.

Act I

SCENE 1

HIPPOLYTUS, THERAMENES

HIPPOLYTUS   No, dear Theramenes, I've too long delayed
　　In pleasant Troezen; my decision's made.
　　I'm off; in my anxiety, I commence
　　To tax myself with shameful indolence.
　　My father has been gone six months and more,　　　　　5
　　And yet I do not know what distant shore
　　Now hides him, or what trials he now may bear.
THERAMENES   You'll go in search of him, my lord? But where?
　　Already, to appease your fears, I've plied
　　The seas which lie on Corinth's either side;　　　　　10
　　I've asked for Theseus among tribes who dwell
　　Where Acheron[2] goes plunging into Hell;
　　Elis I've searched and, from Taenarus[3] bound,
　　Reached even that sea where Icarus[4] was drowned.
　　In what fresh hope, in what unthought-of places,　　　　15
　　Do you set out to find your father's traces?
　　Who knows, indeed, if he wants the truth about
　　His long, mysterious absence to come out,
　　And whether, while we tremble for him, he's
　　Not fondling some new conquest at his ease　　　　　20
　　And planning to deceive her like the rest? . . .
HIPPOLYTUS   Enough, Theramenes. In King Theseus' breast,
　　The foolish fires of youth have ceased to burn;
　　No tawdry dalliance hinders his return.
　　Phaedra need fear no rivals now; the King　　　　　25
　　Long since, for her sake, ceased philandering.
　　I go then, out of duty—and as a way
　　To flee a place in which I dare not stay.
THERAMENES   Since when, my lord, have you begun to fear
　　This peaceful place your childhood held so dear,　　　　30
　　And which I've often known you to prefer
　　To Athens' court, with all its pomp and stir?
　　What danger or affliction drives you hence?
HIPPOLYTUS   Those happy times are gone. All's altered since
　　The Gods dispatched to us across the sea　　　　　35
　　The child of Minos and Pasiphaë.[5]
THERAMENES   Ah. Then it's Phaedra's presence in this place

---

2. A river that flows into Hades.   3. A point of land in southern Greece, near Sparta. Elis is a district of Greece on the west coast of the Peloponnesus.   4. Son of Daedalus. Escaping from Crete by means of wings made by his father, Icarus flew so high that the sun melted the wax holding his wings together, and he fell to his death.   5. Phaedra was the daughter of King Minos of Crete and Pasiphaë, sister to Circe. Enamored of a white bull sent by Poseidon, Pasiphaë consequently gave birth to the Minotaur, the Cretan monster later killed by Theseus. Phaedra was thus half sister to the Minotaur.

That weighs on you. She'd hardly seen your face
When, as the King's new consort, she required
Your banishment, and got what she desired.   40
But now her hatred for you, once so great,
Has vanished, or has cooled, at any rate.
And why, my lord, should you feel threatened by
A dying woman who desires to die?
Sick unto death—with what, she will not say,   45
Weary of life and of the light of day,
Could Phaedra plot to do you any harm?
HIPPOLYTUS   Her vain hostility gives me no alarm.
It is, I own, another enemy.
The young Aricia, from whom I flee,   50
Last of a line which sought to overthrow
Our house.
THERAMENES   What! Will you also be her foe?
That gentle maiden, though of Pallas' line,
Had no part in her brothers' base design.[6]
If she is guiltless, why should you hate her, Sir?   55
HIPPOLYTUS   I would not flee her if I hated her.
THERAMENES   Dare I surmise, then, why you're leaving us?
Are you no longer that Hippolytus
Who spurned love's dictates and refused with scorn
The yoke which Theseus has so often borne?   60
Has Venus, long offended by your pride,
Contrived to see her Theseus justified
By making you confess her power divine
And bow, like other men, before her shrine?
Are you in love, Sir?
HIPPOLYTUS   What do you mean, dear man   65
You who have known me since my life began?
How can you wish that my austere and proud
Persuasions be so basely disvowed?
I sucked that pride which seems so strange to you
From an Amazonian mother,[7] and when I grew   70
To riper years, and knew myself, I thought
My given nature to be nobly wrought.
You then, devoted friend, instructed me
In all my father's brilliant history,
And you recall how glowingly I heard   75
His exploits, how I hung on every word
As you portrayed a sire whose deeds appease
Men's longing for another Hercules—
Those monsters slain, those brigands all undone,
Procrustes, Sciron, Sinis, Cercyon,—   80
The Epidaurian giant's scattered bones,
The Minotaur's foul blood on Cretan stones!

---

6. Theseus killed all fifty sons of Pallas because they threatened his kingdom of Athens. Aricia is Pallas's daughter.   7. Hippolytus's mother was Antiope, sister of Hippolyta, queen of the Amazons.

But when you told me of less glorious feats,
His far-flung chain of amorous deceits,
Helen of Sparta[8] kidnapped as a maid;   85
Sad Periboea[9] in Salamis betrayed;
Others, whose very names escape him now,
Too-trusting hearts, deceived by sigh and vow;
Wronged Ariadne,[1] telling the rocks her moan,
Phaedra abducted, though to grace a throne,—   90
You know how, loathing stories of that sort,
I begged you oftentimes to cut them short,
And wished posterity might never hear
The worser half of Theseus' great career.
Shall I, in my turn, be subjected so   95
To passion, by the Gods be brought so low—
The more disgraced because I cannot claim
Such honors as redeem King Theseus' name,
And have not, by the blood of monsters, won
The right to trespass as my sire has done?   100
And even if my pride laid down its arms,
Could I surrender to Aricia's charms?
Would not my wayward passions heed the ban
Forbidding her to me, or any man?
The King's no friend to her, and has decreed   105
That she not keep alive her brothers' seed;
Fearing some new shoot from their guilty stem,
He wants her death to be the end of them;
For her, the nuptial torch shall never blaze;
He's doomed her to be single all her days.   110
Shall I take up her cause then, brave his rage,
Set a rebellious pattern for the age,
Commit my youth to love's delirium . . . ?
THERAMENES   Ah, Sir, if love's appointed hour has come,
It's vain to reason; Heaven will not hear.   115
What Theseus bans, he makes you hold more dear.
His hate for her but stirs your flames the more,
And lends new grace to her whom you adore.
Why fear, my lord, a love that's true and chaste?
Of what's so sweet, will you not dare to taste?   120
Shall timid scruples make your blood congeal?
What Hercules once felt, may you not feel?
What hearts has Venus' power failed to sway?
Where would you be, who strive with her today,
If fierce Antiope had not grown tame[2]   125
And loved king Theseus with a virtuous flame?
But come, my lord, why posture and debate?

8. Daughter of Zeus and Leda, later the wife of Menelaus of Sparta (and the cause of the Trojan War). In her girlhood she was abducted by Theseus and Peirithoüs; her brothers rescued her and brought her back home.   9. The mother of Ajax, one of the women Theseus seduced and abandoned.   1. Phaedra's sister, who was abandoned by Theseus on the island of Naxos after she rescued him from the Minotaur. 2. As an Amazon, Antiope was committed to chastity.

Admit that you have changed, and that of late
You're seen less often, in your lonely pride,
Racing your chariot by the oceanside, 130
Or deftly using Neptune's[3] art to train
Some charger to obey the curb and rein.
The woods less often echo to our cries.
A secret fire burns in your heavy eyes.
No question of it: you're sick with love, you feel 135
A wasting passion which you would conceal.
Has fair Aricia wakened your desire?
HIPPOLYTUS   I'm off, Theramenes, to find my sire.
THERAMENES   Will you not see the Queen before you go,
  My lord?
HIPPOLYTUS
          I mean to. You may tell her so. 140
  Duty requires it of me. Ah, but here's
  Her dear Oenone; what new grief prompts her tears?

SCENE 2

HIPPOLYTUS, OENONE, THERAMENES

OENONE   Alas, my lord, what grief could equal mine?
  The Queen has gone into a swift decline.
  I nurse her, tend her day and night, but she
  Is dying of some nameless malady.
  Disorder rules within her heart and head. 5
  A restless pain has dragged her from her bed;
  She longs to see the light; but in her keen
  Distress she is unwilling to be seen. . . .
  She's coming.
HIPPOLYTUS   I understand, and I shall go.
  My hated face would but increase her woe. 10

SCENE 3

PHAEDRA, OENONE

PHAEDRA   Let's go no farther; stay, Oenone dear.
  I'm faint; my strength abandons me, I fear.
  My eyes are blinded by the glare of day,
  And now I feel my trembling knees give way.
  Alas!
       [She sits.]
OENONE   O Gods, abate our misery! 5
PHAEDRA   These veils, these baubles, how they burden me!
  What meddling hand has twined my hair, and made
  Upon my brow so intricate a braid?
  All things oppress me, vex me, do me ill.
OENONE   Her wishes war against each other still. 10
  'Twas you who, full of self-reproach, just now

---

3. Or Poseidon, god of the sea, who was also identified with Hippios, god of horses.

Insisted that our hands adorn your brow;
You who called back your strength so that you might
Come forth again and once more see the light.
Yet, seeing it, you all but turn and flee,   15
Hating the light which you came forth to see.

PHAEDRA   Founder of our sad race, bright god of fire,
You whom my mother dared to boast her sire,[4]
Who blush perhaps to see my wretched case,
For the last time, O Sun, I see your face.   20

OENONE   Can't you shake off that morbid wish? Must I
Forever hear you laying plans to die?
What is this pact with death which you have made?

PHAEDRA   Oh, to be sitting in the woods' deep shade!
When shall I witness, through a golden wrack   25
Of dust, a chariot flying down the track?

OENONE   What, Madam?

PHAEDRA   Where am I? Madness! What did I say?
Where have I let my hankering senses stray?
The Gods have robbed me of my wits. A rush
Of shame, Oenone, causes me to blush.   30
I make my guilty torments all too plain.
My eyes, despite me, fill with tears of pain.

OENONE   If you must blush, then blush for your perverse
Silence, which only makes your sickness worse.
Spurning our care, and deaf to all we say—   35
Is it your cruel design to die this way?
What madness dooms your life in middle course?
What spell, what poison has dried up its source?
Three times the night has overrun the skies
Since sleep last visited your hollow eyes,   40
And thrice the day has made dim night retreat
Since you, though starving, have refused to eat.
What frightful evil does your heart intend?
What right have you to plot your own life's end?
You thereby wrong the Gods who authored you;   45
Betray the spouse to whom your faith is due;
Betray your children by the selfsame stroke,
And thrust their necks beneath a heavy yoke.
Yes, on the day their mother's life is done,
Proud hopes will stir in someone else's son—   50
Your foe, the foe of all your lineage, whom
An Amazon once carried in her womb:
Hippolytus . . .

PHAEDRA   Gods!

OENONE   My words strike home at last.

PHAEDRA   Oh, wretched woman, what was that name which passed
Your lips?

OENONE   Ah, now you're roused to anger. Good.   55
That name has made you shudder, as it should.

---

4. Helios, the sun god, was the father of Phaedra's mother, Pasiphaë.

Live, then. Let love and duty fire your spirit.
Live, lest a Scythian's[5] son should disinherit
Your children, lest he crush the noblest fruit
Of Greece and of the Gods beneath his boot.   60
But lose no time; each moment now could cost
Your life; retrieve the strength that you have lost,
While still your feeble fires, which sink so low,
Smoulder and may be fanned into a glow.

PHAEDRA   Alas, my guilty flame has burnt too long.   65

OENONE   Come, what remorse can flay you so? What wrong
   Can you have done to be so crushed with guilt?
   There is no innocent blood your hands have spilt.

PHAEDRA   My hands, thank Heaven, are guiltless, as you say.
   Gods! That my heart were innocent as they!   70

OENONE   What fearful notion can your thoughts have bred
   So that your heart still shrinks from it in dread?

PHAEDRA   I've said enough, Oenone. Spare me the rest.
   I die, to keep that horror unconfessed.

OENONE   Then die, and keep your heartless silence, do;   75
   But someone else must close your eyes for you.
   Although your flickering life has all but fled,
   I shall go down before you to the dead.
   There are a thousand roads that travel there;
   I'll choose the shortest, in my just despair.   80
   O cruel mistress! When have I failed or grieved you?
   Remember: at your birth, these arms received you.
   For you I left my country, children, kin:
   Is this the prize my faithfulness should win?

PHAEDRA   What can you gain by this? Why rant and scold?   85
   You'd shake with terror if the truth were told.

OENONE   Great Gods! What words could match the terror I
   Must daily suffer as I watch you die?

PHAEDRA   When you have learnt my crime, my fate, my shame,
   I'll die no less, but with a guiltier name.   90

OENONE   My lady, by the tears which stain my face,
   And by your trembling knees which I embrace,
   Enlighten me; deliver me from doubt.

PHAEDRA   You've asked it. Rise.

OENONE   I'm listening. Come, speak out.

PHAEDRA   O Gods! What shall I say to her? Where shall I start?   95

OENONE   Speak, speak. Your hesitations wound my heart.

PHAEDRA   Alas, how Venus hates us! As Love's thrall,
   Into what vileness did my mother fall!

OENONE   Dear Queen, forget it; to the end of time
   Let silence shroud the memory of that crime.   100

PHAEDRA   O sister Ariadne! Through love, once more,
   You died abandoned on a barren shore![6]

---

5. Scythia, home of the Amazons, was for the Greeks associated with barbarians.   **6.** Ariadne died on Naxos after Theseus's desertion of her.

OENONE   Madame, what's this? What anguish makes you trace
  So bitterly the tale of all your race?
PHAEDRA   And now, since Venus wills it, I must pine   105
  And die, the last of our accursèd line.
OENONE   You are in love?
PHAEDRA   I feel love's raging thirst.
OENONE   For whom?
PHAEDRA   Of all dire things, now hear the worst.
  I love . . . From that dread name I shrink, undone;
  I love . . .
OENONE   Whom?
PHAEDRA   Think of a Scythian woman's son,   110
  A prince I long ill-used and heaped with blame.
OENONE   Hippolytus? Gods!
PHAEDRA   'Twas you who spoke his name.
OENONE   Just Heaven! All my blood begins to freeze.
  O crime, despair, most curst of families!
  Why did we voyage to this ill-starred land   115
  And set our feet upon its treacherous strand?
PHAEDRA   My ills began far earlier. Scarcely had I
  Pledged with Aegeus' son our marriage-tie,
  Secure in that sweet joy a bride should know,
  When I, in Athens, met my haughty foe.   120
  I stared, I blushed, I paled, beholding him;
  A sudden turmoil set my mind aswim;
  My eyes no longer saw, my lips were dumb;
  My body burned, and yet was cold and numb.
  I knew myself possessed by Venus, whose   125
  Fierce flames torment the quarry she pursues.
  I thought to appease her then by constant prayer,
  And built for her a temple, decked with care.
  I made continual sacrifice, and sought
  In entrails[7] for a spirit less distraught—   130
  But what could cure a lovesick soul like mine?
  In vain my hands burnt incense at her shrine:
  Though I invoked the Goddess' name, 'twas he
  I worshipped; I saw his image constantly,
  And even as I fed the altar's flame   135
  Made offering to a god I dared not name.
  I shunned him; but—O horror and disgrace!—
  My eyes beheld him in his father's face.
  At last I knew that I must act, must urge
  Myself, despite myself, to be his scourge.   140
  To rid me of the foe I loved, I feigned
  A harsh stepmother's malice, and obtained
  By ceaseless cries my wish that he be sent
  From home and father into banishment.
  I breathed once more, Oenone; once he was gone,   145

---

7. Examining the entrails of an animal sacrifice was a means of prophecy.

My blameless days could flow more smoothly on.
I hid my grief, was faithful to my spouse,
And reared the offspring of our luckless vows.
Ah, mocking Fate! What use was all my care?
Brought by my spouse himself to Troezen, there   150
I yet again beheld my exiled foe:
My unhealed wound began once more to flow.
Love hides no longer in these veins, at bay:
Great Venus fastens on her helpless prey.
I look with horror on my crime; I hate   155
My life; my passion I abominate.
I hoped by death to keep my honor bright,
And hide so dark a flame from day's pure light;
Yet, yielding to your tearful argument,
I've told you all; of that I'll not repent   160
Provided you do not, as death draws near,
Pour more unjust reproaches in my ear,
Or seek once more in vain to fan a fire
Which flickers and is ready to expire.

SCENE 4

PHAEDRA, OENONE, PANOPE

PANOPE   Madam, there's grievous news which I'd withhold
   If I were able; but it must be told.
   Death's claimed your lord, who feared no other foe—
   Of which great loss you are the last to know.
OENONE   You tell us, Panope . . . ?
PANOPE   That the Queen in vain   5
   Prays for her Theseus to return again;
   That mariners have come to port, from whom
   Hippolytus has learned his father's doom.
PHAEDRA   Gods!
PANOPE   Who'll succeed him, Athens can't agree.
   The Prince your son commands much loyalty,   10
   My lady; yet, despite their country's laws,[8]
   Some make the alien woman's son their cause;
   Some plot, they say, to put in Theseus' place
   Aricia, the last of Pallas' race.
   Of both these threats I thought that you should know. 15
   Hippolytus has rigged his ship to go,
   And if, in Athens' ferment, he appeared,
   The fickle mob might back him, it is feared.
OENONE   Enough. The Queen has heard you. She'll give thought
   To these momentous tidings you have brought.   20

8. Athenian law made the son of an Athenian and a non-Greek woman illegitimate. As noted, Hippolytus's mother was an Amazon. It is not clear why Phaedra's children are not similarly classified.

SCENE 5

PHAEDRA, OENONE

OENONE   Mistress, I'd ceased to urge you not to die;
  I thought to follow you to the grave, since my
  Dissuasions had no longer any force:
  But this dark news prescribes a change of course.
  Your destiny now wears a different face: 5
  The King is dead, and you must take his place.
  He leaves a son who needs your sheltering wing—
  A slave without you; if you live, a king.
  Who else will soothe his orphan sorrows, pray?
  If you are dead, who'll wipe his tears away?   10
  His innocent cries, borne up to Heaven, will make
  The Gods, his forebears, curse you for his sake.
  Live, then: there's nothing now you're guilty of.
  Your love's become like any other love.
  With Theseus' death, those bonds exist no more   15
  Which made your passion something to abhor.
  Hippolytus need no longer cause you fear;
  Seeing him now, your conscience can be clear.
  Perhaps, convinced that you're his bitter foe,
  He means to lead the rebels. Make him know   20
  His error; win him over; stay his hand.
  He's king, by right, of Troezen's pleasant land;
  But as for bright Minerva's⁹ citadel,
  It is your son's by law, as he knows well.
  You should, indeed, join forces, you and he: 25
  Aricia is your common enemy.
PHAEDRA   So be it. By your advice I shall be led;
  I'll live, if I can come back from the dead,
  And if my mother-love still has the power
  To rouse my weakened spirits in this hour.   30

Act II

SCENE 1

ARICIA, ISMENE

ARICIA   Hippolytus asks to see me? Can this be?
  He seeks me out to take his leave of me?
  There's no mistake, Ismene?
ISMENE   Indeed, there's not.
  This shows how Theseus' death has changed your lot.
  Expect now to receive from every side   5

9. The Greek goddess Athene, protector of Athens.

The homage which, through him, you've been denied.
At last, Aricia rules her destiny;
Soon, at her feet, all Greece shall bend the knee.
ARICIA This is no doubtful rumor, then? I've shed
The bonds of slavery? My oppressor's dead? 10
ISMENE The Gods relent, my lady. It is so.
Theseus has joined your brothers' shades below.
ARICIA And by what mishap did he come to grief?
ISMENE The tales are many, and they strain belief.
Some say that he, abducting from her home 15
A new beloved, was swallowed by the foam.
It's even thought, as many tongues now tell,
That, faring with Pirithoüs down to Hell,[1]
He walked alive amid the dusky ranks
Of souls, and saw Cocytus'[2] dismal banks, 20
But found himself a prisoner in that stern
Domain from which no mortal can return.
ARICIA Shall I believe that, while he still draws breath,
A man can penetrate the realms of death?
What spell could lure him to that fearsome tract? 25
ISMENE Theseus is dead. You, only, doubt the fact.
All Athens grieves; the news was scarcely known
When Troezen raised Hippolytus to its throne.
Here in this palace, trembling for her son,
Phaedra confers on what must now be done. 30
ARICIA You think Hippolytus will be more kind
Than Theseus was to me, that he'll unbind
My chains, and show me pity?
ISMENE   Madam, I do.
ARICIA Isn't the man's cold nature known to you?
What makes you think that, scorning women, he 35
Will yet show pity and respect to me?
He long has shunned us, and as you well know
Haunts just those places where we do not go.
ISMENE He's called, I know, the most austere of men,
But I have seen him in your presence, when, 40
Intrigued by his repute, I thought to observe
His celebrated pride and cold reserve.
His manner contradicted all I'd heard:
At your first glance, I saw him flushed and stirred.
His eyes, already full of languor, tried 45
To leave your face, but could not turn aside.
He has, though love's a thing he may despise,
If not a lover's tongue, a lover's eyes.
ARICIA Ismene, how your words delight my ear!
Even if baseless, they are sweet to hear. 50

1. Theseus went to Hades with Pentithoüs, king of the Lapiths—with whom he had earlier abducted Helen—to help his friend steal Persephone. Hercules freed Theseus, whom the god Hades had imprisoned, but could not free Pentithoüs, who was later killed. 2. River in Hades, tributary to Acheron.

O you who know me, can you believe of me,
Sad plaything of a ruthless destiny,
Forever fed on tears and bitterness,
That love could touch me, and its dear distress?
Last offspring of that king whom Earth once bore,[3]   55
I only have escaped the rage of war.
I lost six brothers, young and fresh as May,
In whom the hopes of our great lineage lay:
The sharp sword reaped them all; Earth, soaked and red,
Drank sadly what Erectheus' heirs had shed.   60
You know that, since their death, a harsh decree
Forbids all Greeks to pay their court to me,
Lest, through my progeny, I should revive
My brothers' ashes, and keep their cause alive.
But you know too with what disdain I bore   65
The ban of our suspicious conqueror.
You know how I, a lifelong enemy
Of love, gave thanks for Theseus' tyranny,
Since he forbade what I was glad to shun.
But then . . . but then I had not seen his son.   70
Not that my eyes alone, charmed by his grace,
Have made me love him for his form or face,
Mere natural gifts for which he seems to care
But little, or of which he's unaware.
I find in him far nobler gifts than these—   75
His father's strengths, without his frailties.
I love, I own, a heart that's never bowed
Beneath Love's yoke, but stayed aloof and proud.
Small glory Phaedra gained from Theseus' sighs!
More proud than she, I spurn the easy prize   80
Of love-words said a thousand times before,
And of a heart that's like an open door.
Ah, but to move a heart that's firm as stone,
To teach it pangs which it has never known,
To bind my baffled captive in a chain   85
Against whose sweet constraint he strives in vain:
There's what excites me in Hippolytus; he's
A harder conquest than was Hercules,
Whose heart, so often vanquished and inflamed,
Less honored those by whom he had been tamed.   90
But, dear Ismene, how rashly I have talked!
My hopes may all too easily be balked,
And I may humbly grieve in future days
Because of that same pride which now I praise.
Of fortune can it be . . . ?

ISMENE   You'll shortly learn;   95
    He's coming.

---

3. Erectheus, their ancestor, son of Earth and reared by Athene.

SCENE 2

HIPPOLYTUS, ARICIA, ISMENE

HIPPOLYTUS   Madam, I felt, ere leaving here,
That I should make your altered fortunes clear.
My sire is dead. My fears divined, alas,
By his long absence, what had come to pass.
Death only, ending all his feats and frays,   5
Could hide him from the world so many days.
The Gods have yielded to destroying Fate
Hercules' heir[4] and friend and battle-mate.
Although you hated him, I trust that you
Do not begrudge such praise as was his due.   10
One thought, however, soothes my mortal grief:
I now may offer you a just relief,
Revoking the most cruel of decrees.
Your heart, your hand, bestow them as you please;
For here in Troezen, where I now shall reign,   15
Which was my grandsire Pittheus' domain,
And which with one voice gives its throne to me,
I make you free as I; indeed, more free.
ARICIA   Your goodness stuns me, Sir. By this excess
Of noble sympathy for my distress,   20
You leave me, more than you could dream, still yoked
By those strict laws which you have just revoked.
HIPPOLYTUS   Athens, unsure of who should rule, divides
'Twixt you and me, and the Queen's son besides.
ARICIA   They speak of *me*?
HIPPOLYTUS   Their laws, I'm well aware,   25
Would seem to void my claim as Theseus' heir,
Because an alien bore me. But if my one
Opponent were my brother, Phaedra's son,
I would, my lady, have the better cause,
And would contest those smug and foolish laws.   30
What checks me is a truer claim, your own;
I yield, or, rather, give you back, a throne
And scepter which your sires inherited
From that great mortal whom the Earth once bred.
Aegeus,[5] though adopted, took their crown.   35
Theseus, his son, enlarged the state, cast down
Her foes, and was the choice of everyone,
Leaving your brothers in oblivion.
Now Athens calls you back within her walls.
Too long she's grieved for these dynastic brawls;   40
Too long your kinsmen's blood has drenched her earth,
Rising in steam from fields which gave it birth.
Troezen is mine, then. The domain of Crete

---

4. *Heir* in the sense of being, like Hercules, a destroyer of monsters.   5. Pandion's son by adoption, and Theseus's father.

Offers to Phaedra's son a rich retreat.
Athens is yours. I go now to combine   45
In your cause all your partisans and mine.
ARICIA   These words so daze me that I almost fear
Some dream, some fancy has deceived my ear.
Am I awake? This plan which you have wrought—
What god, what god inspired you with the thought?   50
How just that, everywhere, men praise your name!
And how the truth, my lord, exceeds your fame!
You'll press my claims, against your interest?
'Twas kind enough that you should not detest
My house and me, should not be governed by   55
Old hatreds. . . .
HIPPOLYTUS   Hate you, Princess? No, not I.
I'm counted rough and proud, but don't assume
That I'm the issue of some monster's womb.
What hate-filled heart, what brute however wild
Could look upon your face and not grow mild?   60
Could I withstand your sweet, beguiling spell?
ARICIA   What's this, my lord?
HIPPOLYTUS   I've said too much. Ah, well.
My reason can't rein in my heart, I see.
Since I have spoken thus impetuously,
I must go on, my lady, and make plain   65
A secret I no longer can contain.
You see before you a most sorry prince,
A signal case of blind conceit. I wince
To think how I, Love's enemy, long disdained
Its bonds, and all whom passion had enchained;   70
How, pitying poor storm-tossed fools, I swore
Ever to view such tempests from the shore;
And now, like common men, for all my pride,
Am lost to reason in a raging tide.
One moment saw my vain defenses fall: 75
My haughty spirit is at last in thrall.
For six months now, ashamed and in despair,
I've borne Love's piercing arrow everywhere;
I've striven with you, and with myself, and though
I shun you, you are everywhere I go;   80
In the deep woods, your image haunts my sight;
The light of day, the shadows of the night,
All things call up your charms before my eyes
And vie to make my rebel heart your prize.
What use to struggle? I am not as before: 85
I seek myself, and find myself no more.
My bow, my javelins and my chariot pall;
What Neptune taught me once, I can't recall;
My idle steeds forget the voice they've known,
And the woods echo to my plaints alone.   90
You blush, perhaps, for so uncouth a love

As you have caused, and which I tell you of.
What a rude offer of my heart I make!
How strange a captive does your beauty take!
Yet that should make my offering seem more rich.   95
Remember, it's an unknown tongue in which
I speak; don't scorn these words, so poorly turned,
Which, but for you, my lips had never learned.

SCENE 3

HIPPOLYTUS, ARICIA, THERAMENES, ISMENE

THERAMENES   My lord: the Queen, they tell me, comes this way.
  It's you she seeks.
HIPPOLYTUS   Me?
THERAMENES   Why, I cannot say.
  But Phaedra's sent ahead to let you know
  That she must speak with you before you go.
HIPPOLYTUS   I, talk with Phaedra? What should we talk about?   5
ARICIA   My lord, you can't refuse to hear her out.
  Malignant toward you as the Queen appears,
  You owe some pity to her widow's tears.
HIPPOLYTUS   But now you'll leave me! And I shall sail before
  I learn my fate from her whom I adore,   10
  And in whose hands I leave this heart of mine. . . .
ARICIA   Go, Prince; pursue your generous design.
  Make Athens subject to my royal sway.
  All of your gifts I gladly take this day.
  But that great empire, glorious though it be,   15
  Is not the offering most dear to me.

SCENE 4

HIPPOLYTUS, THERAMENES

HIPPOLYTUS   Are we ready, friend? But the Queen's coming: hark.
  Go, bid them trim our vessel; we soon embark.
  Quick, give the order and return, that you
  May free me from a vexing interview.

SCENE 5

PHAEDRA, HIPPOLYTUS, OENONE

PHAEDRA [To OENONE, at stage rear.]
  He's here. Blood rushes to my heart: I'm weak,
  And can't recall the words I meant to speak.
OENONE   Think of your son, whose one hope rests with you.
PHAEDRA   My lord, they say you leave us. Before you do,
  I've come to join your sorrows and my tears,   5
  And tell you also of a mother's fears.
  My son now lacks a father; and he will learn

Ere long that death has claimed me in my turn.
A thousand foes already seek to end
His hopes, which you, you only, can defend.   10
Yet I've a guilty fear that I have made
Your ears indifferent to his cries for aid.
I tremble lest you visit on my son
Your righteous wrath at what his mother's done.

HIPPOLYTUS   So base a thought I could not entertain.   15

PHAEDRA   Were you to hate me, I could not complain,
My lord. You've seen me bent on hurting you,
Though what was in my heart you never knew.
I sought your enmity. I would not stand
Your dwelling with me in the selfsame land.   20
I vilified you, and did not feel free
Till oceans separated you and me.
I went so far, indeed, as to proclaim
That none should, in my hearing, speak your name.
Yet if the crime prescribes the culprit's fate,   25
If I must hate you to have earned your hate,
Never did woman more deserve, my lord,
Your pity, or less deserve to be abhorred.

HIPPOLYTUS   It's common, Madam, that a mother spites
The stepson who might claim her children's rights.   30
I know that in a second marriage-bed
Anxiety and mistrust are often bred.
Another woman would have wished me ill
As you have, and perhaps been harsher still.

PHAEDRA   Ah, Prince! The Gods, by whom I swear it, saw   35
Fit to except me from that general law.
By what a different care am I beset!

HIPPOLYTUS   My lady, don't give way to anguish yet.
Your husband still may see the light of day;
Heaven may hear us, and guide his sail this way.   40
Neptune protects him, and that deity
Will never fail to heed my father's plea.

PHAEDRA   No one goes twice among the dead; and since
Theseus has seen those gloomy regions, Prince,
No god will bring him back, hope though you may,   45
Nor greedy Acheron yield up his prey.
But no! He is not dead; he breathes in you.
My husband still seems present to my view.
I see him, speak with him . . . Ah, my lord, I feel
Crazed with a passion which I can't conceal.   50

HIPPOLYTUS   In your strong love, what wondrous power lies!
Theseus, though dead, appears before your eyes.
For love of him your soul is still on fire.

PHAEDRA   Yes, Prince, I burn for him with starved desire,
Though not as he was seen among the shades,   55
The fickle worshiper of a thousand maids,
Intent on cuckolding the King of Hell;

But constant, proud, a little shy as well,
Young, charming, irresistible, much as we
Depict our Gods, or as you look to me.   60
He had your eyes, your voice, your virile grace,
It was your noble blush that tinged his face
When, crossing on the waves, he came to Crete
And made the hearts of Minos' daughters[6] beat.
Where were you then? Why no Hippolytus   65
Among the flower of Greece he chose for us?
Why were you yet too young to join that band
Of heroes whom he brought to Minos' land?
You would have slain the Cretan monster then,
Despite the endless windings of his den.[7]   70
My sister would have armed you with a skein
Of thread, to lead you from that dark domain.
But no: I'd first have thought of that design,
Inspired by love; the plan would have been mine.
It's I who would have helped you solve the maze,   75
My Prince, and taught you all its twisting ways.
What I'd have done to save that charming head!
My love would not have trusted to a thread.
No, Phaedra would have wished to share with you
Your perils, would have wished to lead you through   80
The Labyrinth, and thence have side by side
Returned with you; or else, with you, have died.
HIPPOLYTUS Gods! What are you saying, Madam? Is Theseus not
     Your husband, and my sire? Have you forgot?
PHAEDRA You think that I forget those things? For shame,   85
     My lord. Have I no care for my good name?
HIPPOLYTUS Forgive me, Madam. I blush to have misread
     The innocent intent of what you said.
     I'm too abashed to face you; I shall take
     My leave. . . .
PHAEDRA   Ah, cruel Prince, 'twas no mistake.   90
     You understood; my words were all too plain.
     Behold then Phaedra as she is, insane
     With love for you. Don't think that I'm content
     To be so, that I think it innocent,
     Or that by weak compliance I have fed   95
     The baneful love that clouds my heart and head.
     Poor victim that I am of Heaven's curse,[8]
     I loathe myself; you could not hate me worse.
     The Gods could tell how in this breast of mine
     They lit the flame that's tortured all my line,   100
     Those cruel Gods for whom it is but play
     To lead a feeble woman's heart astray.
     You too could bear me out; remember, do,
     How I not only shunned but banished you.

6. Phaedra and Ariadne. 7. The Minotaur inhabited the heart of a maze. Ariadne provided Theseus
with a ball of thread by which he left a trail behind him and could retrace his steps after killing the monster.
8. Phaedra feels herself a victim of Venus, the goddess of love; she loves Hippolytus against her will.

I wanted to be odious in your sight; 105
To balk my love, I sought to earn your spite.
But what was gained by all of that distress?
You hated me the more; I loved no less,
And what you suffered made you still more dear.
I pined, I withered, scorched by many a tear. 110
That what I say is true, your eyes could see
If for a moment they could look at me.
What have I said? Do you suppose I came
To tell, of my free will, this tale of shame?
No, anxious for a son I dared not fail, 115
I came to beg you not to hate him. Frail
Indeed the heart is that's consumed by love!
Alas, it's only you I've spoken of.
Avenge yourself, now; punish my foul desire.
Come, rid the world, like your heroic sire, 120
Of one more monster; do as he'd have done.
Shall Theseus' widow dare to love his son?
No, such a monster is too vile to spare.
Here is my heart. Your blade must pierce me there.
In haste to expiate its wicked lust, 125
My heart already leaps to meet your thrust.
Strike, then. Or if your hatred and disdain
Refuse me such a blow, so sweet a pain,
If you'll not stain your hand with my abhorred
And tainted blood, lend me at least your sword. 130
Give it to me!
OENONE   Just Gods! What's this, my Queen?
Someone is coming. You must not be seen.
Quick! Flee! You'll be disgraced if you delay.

SCENE 6

HIPPOLYTUS, THERAMENES

THERAMENES   Did I see Phaedra vanish, dragged away?
Why do I find you pale and overcome?
Where is your sword, Sir? Why are you stricken dumb?
HIPPOLYTUS   Theramenes, I'm staggered. Let's go in haste.
I view myself with horror and distaste. 5
Phaedra . . . but no, great Gods! This thing must not
Be told, but ever buried and forgot.
THERAMENES   Sir, if you wish to sail, our ship's prepared.
But Athens' choice already is declared.
Her clans have all conferred; their leaders name 10
Your brother; Phaedra has achieved her aim.
HIPPOLYTUS   Phaedra?
THERAMENES   A herald's come at their command
To give the reins of state into her hand.
Her son is king.
HIPPOLYTUS   Gods, what she is you know;
Is it her virtue you've rewarded so? 15

THERAMENES   Meanwhile, it's rumored that the King's not dead,
  That in Epirus he has shown his head.
  But I, who searched that land, know well, my lord . . .
HIPPOLYTUS   No, let all clues be weighed, and none ignored.
  We'll track this rumor down. Should it appear   20
  Too insubstantial to detain us here,
  We'll sail, and at whatever cost obtain
  Great Athens' crown for one who's fit to reign.

Act III

SCENE 1

PHAEDRA, OENONE

PHAEDRA   Ah, let their honors deck some other brow.
  Why urge me? How can I let them see me now?
  D'you think to soothe my anguished heart with such
  Vain solace? Hide me, rather. I've said too much.
  My frenzied love's burst forth in act and word.   5
  I've spoken what should never have been heard.
  And how he heard me! How, with many a shift,
  The brute pretended not to catch my drift!
  How ardently he longed to turn and go!
  And how his blushes caused my shame to grow!   10
  Why did you come between my death and me?
  Ah, when his sword-point neared my breast, did he
  Turn pale with horror, and snatch back the blade?
  No. I had touched it, and that touch had made
  Him see it as a thing defiled and stained,   15
  By which his pure hand must not be profaned.
OENONE   Dwelling like this on all you're grieved about,
  You feed a flame which best were beaten out.
  Would it not suit King Minos' child to find
  In loftier concerns her peace of mind,   20
  To flee an ingrate whom you love in vain,
  Assume the conduct of the State, and reign?
PHAEDRA   I, reign? You'd trust the State to my control,
  When reason rules no longer in my soul?
  When passion's overthrown me? When, from the weight   25
  Of shame I bear, I almost suffocate?
  When I am dying?
OENONE   Flee him.
PHAEDRA   How could I? How?
OENONE   You once could banish him; can't you shun him now?
PHAEDRA   Too late. He knows what frenzy burns in me.
  I've gone beyond the bounds of modesty.   30
  My conqueror has heard my shame confessed,
  And hope, despite me, has crept into my breast.

'Twas you who, when my life was near eclipse
And my last breath was fluttering on my lips,
Revived me with sweet lies that took me in.   35
You said that now my love was free of sin.

OENONE   Ah, whether or not your woes are on my head,
To save you, what would I not have done or said?
But if an insult ever roused your spleen,
How can you pardon his disdainful mien?   40
How stonily, and with what cold conceit
He saw you all but grovel at his feet!
Oh, but his arrogance was rude and raw!
Why did not Phaedra see the man I saw?

PHAEDRA   This arrogance which irks you may grow less.   45
Bred in the forests, he has their ruggedness,
And, trained in harsh pursuits since he was young,
Has never heard, till now, love's gentle tongue.
No doubt it was surprise which made him mute,
And we do wrong to take him for a brute.   50

OENONE   Remember that an Amazon gave him life.

PHAEDRA   True: yet she learned to love like any wife.

OENONE   He has a savage hate for womankind.

PHAEDRA   No fear of rivals, then, need plague my mind.
Enough. Your counsels now are out of season.   55
Oenone, serve my madness, not my reason.
His heart is armored against love; let's seek
Some point where his defenses may be weak.
Imperial rule was in his thoughts, I feel;
He wanted Athens; that he could not conceal;   60
His vessels' prows already pointed there,
With sails all set and flapping in the air.
Go in my name, then; find this ambitious boy;
Dangle the crown before him like a toy.
His be the sacred diadem; in its stead   65
I ask no honor but to crown his head,
And yield a power I cannot hold. He'll school
My son in princely arts, teach him to rule,
And play for him, perhaps, a father's role.
Both mother and son I yield to his control.   70
Sway him, Oenone, by every wile that's known:
Your words will please him better than my own.
Sigh, groan, harangue him; picture me as dying;
Make use of supplication and of crying;
I'll sanction all you say. Go. I shall find,   75
When you return, what fate I am assigned.

SCENE 2

PHAEDRA, *alone*

PHAEDRA   O you who see to what I have descended,
Implacable Venus, is your vengeance ended?

Your shafts have all struck home; your victory's
Complete; what need for further cruelties?
If you would prove your pitiless force anew, 5
Attack a foe who's more averse to you.
Hippolytus flouts you; braving your divine
Wrath, he has never knelt before your shrine.
His proud ears seem offended by your name.
Take vengeance, Goddess; our causes are the same. 10
Force him to love . . . Oenone! You've returned
So soon? He hates me, then; your words were spurned.

SCENE 3

PHAEDRA, OENONE

OENONE   Madam, your hopeless love must be suppressed.
Call back the virtue which you once possessed.
The King, whom all thought dead, will soon be here;
Theseus has landed; Theseus is drawing near.
His people rush to see him, rapturous. 5
I'd just gone out to seek Hippolytus
When a great cry went up on every hand. . . .
PHAEDRA   My husband lives, Oenone; I understand.
I have confessed a love he will abhor.
He lives, and I have wronged him. Say no more. 10
OENONE   What?
PHAEDRA   I foresaw this, but you changed my course.
Your tears won out over my just remorse.
I might have died this morning, mourned and chaste;
I took your counsels, and I die disgraced.
OENONE   You die?
PHAEDRA   Just Heaven! Think what I have done! 15
My husband's coming; with him will be his son.
I'll see the witness of my vile desire
Watch with what countenance I can greet his sire,
My heart still heavy with rejected sighs,
And tears which could not move him in my eyes. 20
Mindful of Theseus' honor, will he conceal
The scandal of my passion, do you feel,
Deceiving both his sire and king? Will he
Contain the horror that he feels for me?
His silence would be vain. What ill I've done 25
I know, Oenone, and I am not one
Of those bold women who, at ease in crime,
Are never seen to blush at any time.
I know my mad deeds, I recall them all.
I think that in this place each vault, each wall 30
Can speak, and that, impatient to accuse,
They wait to give my trusting spouse their news.
I'll die, then; from these horrors I'll be free.
It is so sad a thing to cease to be?

Death is not fearful to a suffering mind.   35
My only fear's the name I leave behind.
For my poor children, what a dire bequest!
Each has the blood of Jove within his breast,
But whatsoever pride of blood they share,
A mother's crime's a heavy thing to bear.   40
I tremble lest—alas, too truly!—they
Be chided for their mother's guilt some day.
I tremble lest, befouled by such a stain,
Neither should dare to lift his head again.
OENONE   I pity both of them; you could not be   45
    More justified in your anxiety.
    But why expose them to such insult? Why
    Witness against yourself? You've but to die,
    And folk will say that Phaedra, having strayed
    From virtue, flees the husband she betrayed.   50
    Hippolytus will rejoice that, cutting short
    Your days, you lend his charges your support.
    How shall I answer your accuser? He
    Will have no trouble in refuting me.
    I'll watch him gloating hatefully, and hear   55
    Him pour your shame in every listening ear.
    Let Heaven's fire consume me ere I do!
    But come, speak frankly; is he still dear to you?
    How do you see this prince so full of pride?
PHAEDRA   I see a monster, of whom I'm terrified.   60
OENONE   Then why should he triumph, when all can be reversed?
    You fear the man. Dare to accuse him first
    Of that which he might charge you with today.
    What could belie you? The facts all point his way:
    The sword which by good chance he left behind,   65
    Your past mistrust, your present anguished mind,
    His sire long cautioned by your warning voice,
    And he sent into exile by your choice.
PHAEDRA   I, charge an innocent man with doing ill?
OENONE   Trust to my zeal. You've only to be still.   70
    Like you I tremble, and feel a sharp regret.
    I'd sooner face a thousand deaths. And yet
    Since, lacking this sad remedy, you'll perish;
    Since, above all, it is your life I cherish,
    I'll speak to Theseus. He will do no more   75
    Than doom his son to exile, as before.
    A sire, when he must punish, is still a sire;
    A lenient sentence will appease his ire.
    But even if guiltless blood must flow, the cost
    Were less than if your honor should be lost.   80
    That honor is too dear to risk; its cause
    Is priceless, and its dictates are your laws.
    You must give up, since honor is at stake,
    Everything, even virtue, for its sake.

Ah! Here comes Theseus.
PHAEDRA   And Hippolytus, he   85
  In whose cold eyes I read the end of me.
  Do what you will; I yield myself to you.
  In my confusion, I know not what to do.

SCENE 4

THESEUS, HIPPOLYTUS, PHAEDRA, OENONE, THERAMENES

THESEUS Fortune has blessed me after long delay,
  And in your arms, my lady . . .
PHAEDRA   Theseus, stay,
  And don't profane the love those words express.
  I am not worthy of your tenderness.
  You have been wronged. Fortune or bitter fate   5
  Did not, while you were absent, spare your mate.
  Unfit to please you, or to be at your side,
  Henceforth my only thought must be to hide.

SCENE 5

THESEUS, HIPPOLYTUS, THERAMENES

THESEUS Why am I welcomed in this curious vein?
HIPPOLYTUS That, Father, only Phaedra can explain.
  But if my prayers can move you, grant me, Sir,
  Never again to set my eyes on her.
  Allow Hippolytus to say farewell   5
  To any region where your wife may dwell.
THESEUS Then you, my son, would leave me?
HIPPOLYTUS   I never sought her
  When to this land she came, 'twas you who brought her.
  Yes, you, my lord, when last you left us, bore
  Aricia and the Queen to Troezen's shore.   10
  You bade me be their guardian then; but how
  Should any duties here detain me now?
  Too long my youthful skill's been thrown away
  Amidst these woods, upon ignoble prey.
  May I not flee my idle pastimes here   15
  To stain with worthier blood my sword or spear?
  Before you'd lived as long as I have done,
  More than one tyrant, monsters more than one
  Had felt your strength of arm, your sword's keen blade;
  Already, scourging such as sack and raid,   20
  You had made safe the coasts of either sea.
  The traveler lost his fears of banditry,
  And Hercules, to whom your fame was known,
  Welcomed your toils, and rested from his own.
  But I, the unknown son of such a sire,   25
  Lack even the fame my mother's deeds inspire.[9]

---

9. Hippolytus's mother also performed brave deeds.

Let me at long last show my courage, and,
If any monster has escaped your hand,
Bring back its pelt and lay it at your feet,
Or let me by a glorious death complete   30
A life that will defy oblivion
And prove to all the world I was your son.
THESEUS   What have I found? What horror fills this place,
And makes my family flee before my face?
If my unwished return makes all grow pale,   35
Why, Heaven, did you free me from my jail?
I'd one dear friend. He had a hankering
To steal the consort of Epirus'[1] king.
I joined his amorous plot, though somewhat loath;
But outraged Fate brought blindness on us both.   40
The tyrant caught me, unarmed and by surprise.
I saw Pirithoüs with my weeping eyes
Flung by the barbarous king to monsters then,
Fierce beasts who drink the blood of luckless men.
Me he confined where never light invades,   45
In caverns near the empire of the shades.
After six months, Heaven pitied my mischance.
Escaping from my guardians' vigilance,
I cleansed the world of one more fiend, and threw
To his own beasts the bloody corpse to chew.   50
But now when, joyful, I return to see
The dearest whom the Gods have left to me;
Now, when my spirits, glad once more and light,
Would feast again upon that cherished sight,
I'm met with shudders and with frightened faces;   55
All flee me, all deny me their embraces.
Touched by the very terror I beget,
I wish I were Epirus' prisoner yet.
Speak! Phaedra says that I've been wronged. By whom?
Why has the culprit not yet met his doom?   60
Has Greece, so often sheltered by my arm,
Chosen to shield this criminal from harm?
You're silent. Is my own son, if you please,
In some alliance with my enemies?
I shall go in, and end this maddening doubt.   65
Both crime and culprit must be rooted out,
And Phaedra tell why she is so distraught.

SCENE 6

HIPPOLYTUS, THERAMENES

HIPPOLYTUS   How her words chilled me! What was in her thought?
Will Phaedra, who is still her frenzy's prey,
Accuse herself, and throw her life away?
What will the King say? Gods! What love has done

---

1. A district in western Greece, on the Ionian Sea.

To poison all this house while he was gone!   5
And I, who burn for one who bears his curse,
Am altered in his sight, and for the worse!
I've dark forebodings; something ill draws near.
Yet surely innocence need never fear.
Come, let's consider now how I may best   10
Revive the kindness in my father's breast,
And tell him of a love which he may take
Amiss, but all his power cannot shake.

Act IV

SCENE 1

THESEUS, OENONE

THESEUS What do I hear? How bold and treacherous
To plot against his father's honor thus!
How sternly you pursue me, Destiny!
Where shall I turn? I know not. Where can I be?
O love and kindness not repaid in kind!   5
Outrageous scheme of a degenerate mind!
To seek his lustful end he had recourse,
Like any blackguard, to the use of force.
I recognize the sword his passion drew—
My gift, bestowed with nobler deeds in view.   10
Why did our ties of blood prove no restraint?
Why too did Phaedra make no prompt complaint?
Was it to spare the culprit?
OENONE   It was rather
That she, in pity, wished to spare his father.
Ashamed because her beauty had begot   15
So foul a passion, and so fierce a plot,
By her own hand, my lord, she sought to die,
And darken thus the pure light of her eye.
I saw her raise her arm; to me you owe
Her life, because I ran and stayed the blow.   20
Now, pitying both her torment and your fears,
I have, against my will, spelled out her tears.
THESEUS The traitor! Ah, no wonder he turned pale.
When first he sighted me, I saw him quail.
'Twas strange to see no greeting in his face.   25
My heart was frozen by his cold embrace.
But did he, even in Athens, manifest
This guilty love by which he is possessed?
OENONE The Queen, remember, could not tolerate him.
It was his infamous love which made her hate him.   30
THESEUS That love, I take it, was rekindled here
In Troezen?
OENONE   I've told you all, my lord. I fear

I've left the Queen too long in mortal grief.
Let me now haste to bring her some relief.

SCENE 2

THESEUS, HIPPOLYTUS

THESEUS   Ah, here he comes. Gods! By that noble mien
What eye would not be duped, as mine has been!
Why must the brow of an adulterer
Be stamped with virtue's sacred character?
Should there not be clear signs by which one can   5
Divine the heart of a perfidious man?
HIPPOLYTUS   May I enquire what louring cloud obscures,
My lord, that royal countenance of yours?
Dare you entrust the secret to your son?
THESEUS   Dare you appear before me, treacherous one?   10
Monster, at whom Jove's thunder should be hurled!
Foul brigand, like those of whom I cleaned the world!
Now that your vile, unnatural love has led
You even to attempt your father's bed,
How dare you show your hated self to me   15
Here in the precincts of your infamy,
Rather than seek some unknown land where fame
Has never brought the tidings of my name?
Fly, wretch. Don't brave the hate which fills my soul,
Or tempt a wrath it pains me to control.   20
I've earned, forevermore, enough disgrace
By fathering one who'd do a deed so base,
Without your death upon my hands, to soil
A noble history of heroic toil.
Fly, and unless you wish to join the band   25
Of knaves who've met quick justice at my hand,
Take care lest by the sun's eye you be found
Setting an insolent foot upon this ground.
Now, never to return, be off; take flight;
Cleanse all my realms of your abhorrent sight.   30
And you, O Neptune, if by courage I
Once cleared your shores of murderers, hear my cry.
Recall that, as reward for that great task,
You swore to grant the first thing I should ask.
Pent in a cruel jail for endless hours,   35
I never called on your immortal powers.
I've hoarded up the aid you promised me
Till greater need should justify my plea.
I make it now. Avenge a father's wrong.
Seize on this traitor, and let your rage be strong.   40
Drown in his blood his brazen lust. I'll know
Your favor by the fury that you show.
HIPPOLYTUS   Phaedra accuses me of lust? I'm weak
With horror at the thought, and cannot speak;
By all these sudden blows I'm overcome;   45

They leave me stupefied, and stricken dumb.

THESEUS Scoundrel, you thought that Phaedra'd be afraid
To tell of the depraved assault you made.
You should have wrested from her hands the hilt
Of the sharp sword that points now to your guilt;   50
Or, better, crowned your outrage of my wife
By robbing her at once of speech and life.

HIPPOLYTUS In just resentment of so black a lie,
I might well let the truth be known, but I
Suppress what comes too near your heart. Approve,   55
My lord, a silence which bespeaks my love.
Restrain, as well, your mounting rage and woe:
Review my life; recall the son you know.
Great crimes grow out of small ones. If today
A man first oversteps the bounds, he may   60
Abuse in time all laws and sanctities;
For crime, like virtue, ripens by degrees;
But when has one seen innocence, in a trice,
So change as to embrace the ways of vice?
Not in a single day could time transmute   65
A virtuous man to an incestuous brute.
I had an Amazon mother, brave and chaste,
Whose noble blood my life has not debased.
And when I left her hands, 'twas Pitteus,² thought
Earth's wisest man, by whom my youth was taught.   70
I shall not vaunt such merits as I've got,
But if one virtue's fallen to my lot,
It is, my lord, a fierce antipathy
To just that vice imputed now to me.
It is for that Hippolytus is known   75
In Greece—for virtue cold and hard as stone.
By harsh austerity I am set apart.
The daylight is not purer than my heart.
Yet I, it's charged, consumed by lechery . . .

THESEUS This very boast betrays your guilt. I see   80
What all your vaunted coldness signifies:
Phaedra alone could please your lustful eyes;
No other woman moved you, or could inspire
Your scornful heart with innocent desire.

HIPPOLYTUS No, Father: hear what it's time I told you of;   85
I have not scorned to feel a blameless love.
I here confess my only true misdeed:
I am in love, despite what you decreed.
Aricia has enslaved me; my heart is won,
And Pallas' daughter has subdued your son.   90
I worship her against your orders, Sir,
Nor could I burn or sigh except for her.

THESEUS You love her? Gods! But no, I see your game.

---

2. The most learned man of his age, Theseus's guardian. After marrying Phaedra, Theseus sent Hippolytus to Pitteus (or Pitheus), who had adopted him as heir to the throne of Troezen.

You play the criminal to clear your name.
HIPPOLYTUS Six months I've shunned her whom my heart adored.   95
  I came in fear to tell you this, my lord.
  Why must you be so stubbornly mistaken?
  To win your trust, what great oath must be taken?
  By Earth, and Heaven, and all the things that be . . .
THESEUS A rascal never shrinks from perjury.   100
  Cease now to weary me with sly discourse,
  If your false virtue has but that resource.
HIPPOLYTUS My virtue may seem false and sly to you,
  But Phaedra has good cause to know it true.
THESEUS Ah, how your impudence makes my temper boil!   105
HIPPOLYTUS How long shall I be banished? On what soil?
THESEUS Were you beyond Alcides' pillars,[3] I
  Would think yet that a rogue was too nearby.
HIPPOLYTUS Who will befriend me now—a man suspected
  Of such a crime, by such a sire rejected?   110
THESEUS Go look for friends who think adultery cause
  For accolades, and incest for applause,
  Yes, ingrates, traitors, to law and honor blind,
  Fit to protect a blackguard of your kind.
HIPPOLYTUS Incest! Adultery! Are these still your themes?   115
  I'll say no more. Yet Phaedra's mother, it seems,
  And, as you know, Sir, all of Phaedra's line
  Knew more about such horrors than did mine.
THESEUS So! You dare storm and rage before my face?
  I tell you for the last time: leave this place.   120
  Be off, before I'm roused to violence
  And have you, in dishonor, driven hence.

SCENE 3

THESEUS, *alone*

THESEUS Poor wretch, the path you take will end in blood.
  What Neptune swore by Styx, that darkest flood
  Which frights the Gods themselves, he'll surely do.
  And none escapes when vengeful Gods' pursue.
  I loved you; and in spite of what you've done,   5
  I mourn your coming agonies, my son.
  But you have all too well deserved my curse.
  When was a father ever outraged worse?
  Just Gods, who see this grief which drives me wild,
  How could I father such a wicked child?   10

SCENE 4

PHAEDRA, THESEUS

PHAEDRA My lord, I hasten to you, full of dread.
  I heard your threatening voice, and what it said.

---

3. The Pillars of Hercules, the two points of land on either side of the Strait of Gibraltar, at the western end of the Mediterranean and thus representing one edge of the known world.

Pray Heaven no deed has followed on your threat.
I beg you, if there is time to save him yet,
To spare your son; spare me the dreadful sound   5
Of blood, your own blood, crying from the ground.
Do not impose on me the endless woe
Of having caused your hand to make it flow.

THESEUS   No, Madam, my blood's not on my hands. But he,
The thankless knave, has not escaped from me.   10
A God's great hand will be his nemesis
And your avenger. Neptune owes me this.

PHAEDRA   Neptune! And will your angry prayers be heard?

THESEUS   What! Are you fearful lest he keep his word?
No, rather join me in my righteous pleas.   15
Recount to me my son's black treacheries;
Stir up my sluggish wrath, that's still too cold.
He has done crimes of which you've not been told:
Enraged at you, he slanders your good name:
Your mouth is full of lies, he dares to claim;   20
He states that heart and soul, his love is pledged
To Aricia.

PHAEDRA   What, my lord!

THESEUS   So he alleged;
But I saw through so obvious a trick.
Let's hope that Neptune's justice will be quick.
I go now to his altars, to implore   25
A prompt fulfillment of the oath he swore.

SCENE 5

PHAEDRA, *alone*

PHAEDRA   He's gone. What news assails my ear? What ill-
Extinguished fire flares in my bosom still?
By what a thunderbolt I am undone!
I'd flown here with one thought, to save his son.
Escaping from Oenone's arms by force,   5
I'd yielded to my torturing remorse.
How far I might have gone, I cannot guess.
Guilt might perhaps have driven me to confess.
Perhaps, had shock not caused my voice to fail,
I might have blurted out my hideous tale.   10
Hippolytus can feel, but not for me!
Aricia has his love, his loyalty!
Gods! When he steeled himself against my sighs
With that forbidding brow, those scornful eyes,
I thought his heart, which love-darts could not strike,   15
Was armed against all womankind alike.
And yet another's made his pride surrender;
Another's made his cruel eyes grow tender.
Perhaps his heart is easy to ensnare.

It's me, alone of women, he cannot bear!   20
Shall I defend a man by whom I'm spurned?

SCENE 6

PHAEDRA, OENONE

PHAEDRA   Oenone dear, do you know what I have learned?
OENONE   No, but in truth I'm quaking still with fear
  Of the wild urge that sent you rushing here:
  I feared some blunder fatally adverse.
PHAEDRA   I had a rival. Who would have thought it, Nurse?   5
OENONE   What?
PHAEDRA   Yes, Hippolytus is in love; it's true.
  That savage creature no one could subdue,
  Who scorned regard, who heard no lovers' pleas,
  That tiger whom I viewed with trembling knees,
  Is tame now, broken by a woman's art: 10
  Aricia's found the way into his heart.
OENONE   Aricia?
PHAEDRA   O pain I never felt before!
  What new, sharp torments have I kept in store!
  All that I've suffered—frenzies, fears, the dire
  Oppression of remorse, my heart on fire,   15
  The merciless rebuff he gave to me—
  All were but foretastes of this agony.
  They love each other! By what magic, then,
  Did they beguile me? Where did they meet, and when?
  You knew. Why did you keep me unaware,   20
  Deceived as to their furtive love-affair?
  Were they much seen together? Were they known
  To haunt the deep woods, so as to be alone?
  Alas, they'd perfect liberty to meet.
  Heaven smiled on hearts so innocent and sweet;   25
  Without remorse, they savored love's delight;
  For them, each dawn arose serene and bright—
  While I, creation's outcast, hid away
  From the Sun's eye, and fled the light of day.
  Death was the only God I dared implore.   30
  I longed for him; I prayed to be no more.
  Quenching my thirst with tears, and fed on gall,
  Yet in my woe too closely watched by all,
  I dared not weep and grieve in fullest measure;
  I sipped in secret at that bitter pleasure;   35
  And often, wearing a serene disguise,
  I kept my pain from welling in my eyes.
OENONE   What will their love avail them? They will never
  Meet again.
PHAEDRA   But they will love forever.
  Even as I speak—ah, deadly thought!—they dare   40
  To mock my crazed desire and my despair.

Despite this exile which will make them part,
They swear forever to be joined in heart.
No, no, their bliss I cannot tolerate,
Oenone. Take pity on my jealous hate.   45
Aricia must die. Her odious house
Must once more feel the anger of my spouse.
Nor can the penalty be light, for her
Misdeeds are darker than her brothers' were.
In my wild jealousy I will plead with him.   50
I'll what? Has my poor reason grown so dim?
I, jealous! And it's with Theseus I would plead!
My husband lives, and still my passions feed
On whom? Toward whom do all my wishes tend?
At every word, my hair stands up on end.   55
The measure of my crimes is now replete.
I foul the air with incest and deceit.
My murderous hands are itching to be stained
With innocent blood, that vengeance be obtained.
Wretch that I am, how can I live, how face   60
That sacred Sun, great elder of my race?
My grandsire was, of all the Gods, most high;
My forebears fill the world, and all the sky.
Where can I hide? For Hades' night I yearn.
No, there my father holds the dreadful urn   65
Entrusted to his hands by Fate, it's said:
There Minos judges all the ashen dead.
Ah, how his shade will tremble with surprise
To see his daughter brought before his eyes—
Forced to confess a throng of sins, to tell   70
Of crimes perhaps unheard of yet in Hell!
What will you say then, Father? As in a dream,
I see you drop the fearful urn;[4] you seem
To ponder some new torment fit for her,
Yourself become your own child's torturer.   75
Forgive me. A cruel God destroys your line;
Behold her hand in these mad deeds of mine.
My heart, alas! not once enjoyed the fruit
Of its dark, shameful crime. In fierce pursuit,
Misfortune dogs me till, with my last breath,   80
My sad life shall, in torments, yield to death.
OENONE   My lady, don't give in to needless terror.
Look freshly at your pardonable error.
You love. But who can conquer Destiny?
Lured by a fatal spell, you were not free.   85
Is that a marvel hitherto unknown?
Has Love entrapped no heart but yours alone?
Weakness is natural to us, is it not?

---

4. After his death, Minos of Crete became, along with his brother Rhadamanthus, one of the judges of souls in the underworld. The urn held the lots determining to what abode in the underworld the souls of the dead were to be sent.

You are a mortal; accept your mortal lot.
To chafe against our frail estate is vain.   90
Even the Gods who on Olympus reign,
And with their thunders chasten men for crime,
Have felt illicit passions many a time.
PHAEDRA   Ah, what corrupting counsels do I hear?
Wretch! Will you pour such poison in my ear   95
Right to the end? Look how you've ruined me.
You dragged me back to all I sought to flee.
You blinded me to duty; called it no wrong
To see Hippolytus, whom I'd shunned so long.
Ah, meddling creature, why did your sinful tongue   100
Falsely accuse a soul so pure and young?
He'll die, it may be, if the Gods can bear
To grant his maddened father's impious prayer.
No, say no more. Go, monster whom I hate.
Go, let me face at last my own sad fate.   105
May Heaven reward you for your deeds! And may
Your punishment forever give dismay
To all who, like yourself, by servile arts
Nourish the weaknesses of princes' hearts,
Incline them to pursue the baser path,   110
And smooth for them the way to sin and wrath—
Accursèd flatterers, the worst of things
That Heaven's anger can bestow on kings!
OENONE   I've given my life to her. Ah, Gods! It hurts
To be thus thanked. Yet I have my just deserts.   115

Act V

SCENE 1

HIPPOLYTUS, ARICIA

ARICIA   Come, in this mortal danger, will you not make
Your loving sire aware of his mistake?
If, scorning all my tears, you can consent
To parting and an endless banishment,
Go, leave Aricia in her life alone.   5
But first assure the safety of your own.
Defend your honor against a foul attack,
And force your sire to call his prayers back.
There yet is time. What moves you, if you please,
Not to contest Queen Phaedra's calumnies?   10
Tell Theseus the truth.
HIPPOLYTUS   What more should I
Have told him? How she smirched their marriage-tie?
How could I, by disclosing everything,
Humiliate my father and my king?

It's you alone I've told these horrors to.   15
I've bared my heart but to the Gods and you.
Judge of my love, which forced me to confide
What even from myself I wished to hide.
But, mind you, keep this secret ever sealed.
Forget, if possible, all that I've revealed,   20
And never let those pure lips part to bear
Witness, my lady, to this vile affair.
Let us rely upon the Gods' high laws:
Their honor binds them to defend my cause;
And Phaedra, sooner or later brought to book,   25
Will blush for crimes their justice cannot brook.
To that restraint I ask you to agree.
In all things else, just anger makes me free.
Come, break away from this, your slavish plight;
Dare follow me, dare join me in my flight;   30
Be quit of an accursèd country where
Virtue must breathe a foul and poisoned air.
Under the cover of this turbulence
Which my disfavor brings, slip quickly hence.
I can assure a safe escape for you.   35
Your only guards are of my retinue.
Strong states will champion us; upon our side
Is Sparta; Argos' arms are open wide:
Let's plead then to these friends our righteous case,
Lest Phaedra, profiting by our disgrace,   40
Deny our lineal claims to either throne,
And pledge her son my birthright and your own.
Come, let us seize the moment; we mustn't wait.
What holds you back? You seem to hesitate.
It's zeal for you that moves me to be bold.   45
When I am all on fire, what makes you cold?
Are you afraid to join a banished man?
ARICIA   Alas, my lord, how sweet to share that ban!
What deep delight, as partner of your lot,
To live with you, by all the world forgot!   50
But since no blessèd tie unites us two,
Can I, in honor, flee this land with you?
The sternest code, I know, would not deny
My right to break your father's bonds and fly;
I'd grieve no loving parents thus; I'm free,   55
As all are, to escape from tyranny.
But, Sir, you love me, and my fear of shame . . .
HIPPOLYTUS   Ah, never doubt my care for your good name.
It is a nobler plan that I propose:
Flee with your husband from our common foes.   60
Freed my mischance, since Heaven so commands,
We need no man's consent to join our hands.
Not every nuptial needs the torch's light.
At Troezen's gate, amidst that burial site

Where stand our princes' ancient sepulchers,   65
There is a temple feared by perjurers.
No man there dares to break his faith, on pain
Of instant doom, or swear an oath in vain;
There all deceivers, lest they surely die,
Bridle their tongues and are afraid to lie.   70
There, if you trust me, we will go, and of
Our own accord shall pledge eternal love;
The temple's God will witness to our oath;
We'll pray that he be father to us both.
I shall invoke all deities pure and just.   75
The chaste Diana, Juno[5] the august,
And all the Gods who know my faithfulness
Will guarantee the vows I shall profess.
ARICIA   The king is coming. Go, Prince, make no delay.
To cloak my own departure, I'll briefly stay.   80
Go, go; but leave with me some faithful guide
Who'll lead my timid footsteps to your side.

SCENE 2

THESEUS, ARICIA, ISMENE

THESEUS   O Gods, bring light into my troubled mind;
  Show me the truth which I've come here to find.
ARICIA   Make ready for our flight, Ismene dear.

SCENE 3

THESEUS, ARICIA

THESEUS   Your color changes, Madame, and you appear
  Confused. Why was Hippolytus here with you?
ARICIA   He came, my lord, to say a last adieu.
THESEUS   Ah, yes. You've tamed his heart, which none could capture.
  And taught his stubborn lips to sigh with rapture.   5
ARICIA   I shan't deny the truth, my lord. No, he
  Did not inherit your malignity,
  Nor treat me as a criminal, in your fashion.
THESEUS   I see. He's sworn, no doubt, eternal passion.
  Put no reliance on the vows of such   10
  A fickle lover. He's promised others as much.
ARICIA   He, Sir?
THESEUS   You should have taught him not to stray.
  How could you share his love in that base way?
ARICIA   How could you let a shameful lie besmear
  The stainless honor of his young career?   15
  Have you so little knowledge of his heart?
  Can't you tell sin and innocence apart?
  Must some black cloud bedim your eyes alone

---

5. The wife of Jupiter and queen of the gods. Diana was goddess of the moon and of chastity.

To the bright virtue for which your son is known?
Shall slander ruin him? That were too much to bear. 20
Turn back: repent now of your murderous prayer.
Fear, my lord, fear lest the stern deities
So hate you as to grant your wrathful pleas.
Our sacrifices anger Heaven at times;
Its gifts are often sent to scourge our crimes. 25
THESEUS   Your words can't cover up that sin of his:
Love's blinded you to what the scoundrel is.
But I've sure proofs on which I may rely:
I have seen tears—yes, tears which could not lie.
ARICIA   Take care, my lord. You have, in many lands, 30
Slain countless monsters with your conquering hands;
But all are not destroyed; there still lives one
Who . . . No, I am sworn to silence by your son.
Knowing his wish to shield your honor, I'd
Afflict him if I further testified. 35
I'll imitate his reticence, and flee
Your presence, lest the truth should burst from me.

SCENE 4

THESEUS, *alone*

THESEUS   What does she mean? These speeches which begin
And then break off—what are they keeping in?
Is this some sham those two have figured out?
Have they conspired to torture me with doubt?
But I myself, despite my stern control— 5
What plaintive voice cries from my inmost soul?
I feel a secret pity, a surge of pain.
Oenone must be questioned once again.
I'll have more light on this. Not all is known.
Guards, go and bring Oenone here, alone. 10

SCENE 5

THESEUS, PANOPE

PANOPE   I don't know what the Queen may contemplate,
My lord, but she is in a frightening state.
Mortal despair is what her looks bespeak;
Death's pallor is already on her cheek.
Oenone, driven from her in disgrace, 5
Has thrown herself into the sea's embrace.
None knows what madness caused the thing she did;
Beneath the waves she lies forever hid.
THESEUS   What do you tell me?
PANOPE   This death has left the Queen
No calmer; her distraction grows more keen. 10
At moments, to allay her dark unrest,
She clasps her children, weeping, to her breast;

Then, with a sudden horror, she will shove
Them both away, and starve her mother-love.
She wanders aimlessly about the floor;   15
Her blank eye does not know us any more.
Thrice she has written; and thrice, before she'd done,
Torn up the letter which she had begun.
We cannot help her. I beg you, Sire, to try.
THESEUS   Oenone's dead? And Phaedra wants to die?   20
  O bring me back my son, and let him clear
  His name! If he'll but speak, I now will hear.
  O Neptune, let your gifts not be conferred
  Too swiftly; let my prayers go unheard.
  Too much I've trusted what may not be true,   25
  Too quickly raised my cruel hands to you.
  How I'd despair if what I asked were done!

SCENE 6

THESEUS, THERAMENES

THESEUS   Is it you, Theramenes? Where have you left my son?
  You've been his mentor since his tenderest years.
  But why do I behold you drenched in tears?
  Where's my dear son?
THERAMENES   Too late, Sire, you restore
  Your love to him. Hippolytus is no more.   5
THESEUS   Gods!
THERAMENES   I have seen the best of mortals slain,
  My lord, and the least guilty, I maintain.
THESEUS   My son is dead? What! Just when I extend
  My arms to him, Heaven's haste has caused his end?
  What thunderbolt bereaved me? What was his fate?   10
THERAMENES   Scarcely had we emerged from Troezen's gate:
  He drove his chariot, and his soldiery
  Were ranged about him, mute and grave as he.
  Brooding, he headed toward Mycenae. Lax
  In his hands, the reins lay on his horses' backs.   15
  His haughty chargers, quick once to obey
  His voice, and give their noble spirits play,
  Now, with hung head and mournful eye, seemed part
  Of the sad thoughts that filled their master's heart.
  Out of the sea-deeps then a frightful cry   20
  Arose, to tear the quiet of the sky,
  And a dread voice from far beneath the ground
  Replies in groans to that appalling sound.
  Our hearts congeal; blood freezes in our veins.
  The horses, hearing, bristle up their manes.   25
  And now there rises from the sea's calm breast
  A liquid mountain with a seething crest.
  The wave approaches, breaks, and spews before
  Our eyes a raging monster on the shore.

His huge brow's armed with horns; the spray unveils 30
A body covered all with yellow scales;
Half bull he is, half dragon; fiery, bold;
His thrashing tail contorts in fold on fold.
With echoing bellows now he shakes the strand.
The sky, aghast, beholds him; he makes the land 35
Shudder; his foul breath chokes the atmosphere;
The wave which brought him in recoils in fear.
All flee, and in a nearby temple save
Their lives, since it is hopeless to be brave.
Hippolytus alone dares make a stand. 40
He checks his chargers, javelins in hand,
Has at the monster and, with a sure-aimed throw,
Pierces his flank: a great wound starts to flow.
In rage and pain the beast makes one dread spring,
Falls near the horses' feet, still bellowing, 45
Rolls over toward them, with fiery throat takes aim
And covers them with smoke and blood and flame.
Sheer panic takes them; deaf now, they pay no heed
To voice or curb, but bolt in full stampede;
Their master strives to hold them back, in vain. 50
A bloody slaver drips from bit and rein.
It's said that, in that tumult, some caught sight
Of a God who spurred those dusty flanks to flight.
Fear drives them over rocks; the axletree
Screeches and breaks. The intrepid Prince must see 55
His chariot dashed to bits, for all his pains;
He falls at last, entangled in the reins.
Forgive my grief. That cruel sight will be
An everlasting source of tears for me.
I've seen, my lord, the heroic son you bred 60
Dragged by the horses which his hand had fed.
His shouts to them but make their fear more strong.
His body seems but one great wound, ere long.
The plain re-echoes to our cries of woe.
At last, their headlong fury starts to slow: 65
They stop, then, near that graveyard which contains,
In royal tombs, his forebears' cold remains.
I run to him in tears; his guards are led
By the bright trail of noble blood he shed;
The rocks are red with it; the briars bear 70
Their red and dripping trophies of his hair.
I reach him; speak his name; his hand seeks mine;
His eyelids lift a moment, then decline.
"Heaven takes," he says, "my innocent life away.
Protect my sad Aricia, I pray. 75
If ever, friend, my sire is disabused,
And mourns his son who falsely was accused,
Bid him appease my blood and plaintive shade
By dealing gently with that captive maid.

Let him restore . . ." His voice then died away,   80
And in my arms a mangled body lay
Which the God's wrath had claimed, a sorry prize
Which even his father would not recognize.
THESEUS   My son, dear hope whom folly made me kill!
O ruthless Gods, too well you did my will!   85
I'll henceforth be the brokenest of men.
THERAMENES   Upon this scene came shy Aricia then,
Fleeing your wrath, and ready to espouse
Your son before the Gods by holy vows.
She comes, and sees the red and steaming grass;   90
She sees—no sight for loving eyes, alas!—
Hippolytus sprawled there, lacking form or hue.
At first, she won't believe her loss is true.
Not recognizing her beloved, she
Both looks at him and asks where he may be.   95
At last she knows too well what's lying there;
She lifts to the Gods a sad, accusing stare;
Then, moaning, cold, and all but dead, the sweet
Maid drops unconscious at her lover's feet.
Ismene, weeping, kneels and seeks to bring   100
Her back to life—a life of suffering.
And I, my lord, have come, who now detest
This world, to bring a hero's last request,
And so perform the bitter embassy
Which, with his dying breath, he asked of me.   105
But look: his mortal enemy comes this way.

SCENE 7

THESEUS, PHAEDRA, THERAMENES, PANOPE, GUARDS

THESEUS   Well, Madam, my son's no more; you've won the day!
Ah, but what qualms I feel! What doubts torment
My heart, and plead that he was innocent!
But, madam, claim your victim. He is dead.
Enjoy his death, unjust or merited.   5
I'm willing to be evermore deceived.
You've called him guilty; let it be believed.
His death is grief enough for me to bear
Without my further probing this affair,
Which could not bring his dear life back again   10
And might perhaps but aggravate my pain.
No, far from you and Troezen, I shall flee
My dead son's torn and bloody memory.
It will pursue me ever, like a curse:
Would I were banished from the universe!   15
All seems to chide my wicked wrathfulness.
My very fame now adds to my distress.
How shall I hide, who have a name so great?
Even the Gods' high patronage I hate.

I go to mourn this murderous gift of theirs,   20
Nor trouble them again with useless prayers.
Do for me what they might, it could not pay
For what their deadly favor took away.

PHAEDRA   Theseus, my wrongful silence must be ended.
Your guiltless son must be at last defended.   25
He did no ill.

THESEUS   How curst a father am I!
I doomed him, trusting in your heartless lie!
Do you think to be excused for such a crime?

PHAEDRA   Hear me, my lord. I have but little time.
I was the lustful and incestuous one   30
Who dared desire your chaste and loyal son.
Heaven lit a fatal blaze within my breast.
Detestable Oenone did the rest.
She, fearing lest Hippolytus, who knew
Of my vile passion, might make it known to you,   35
Abused my weakness and, by a vicious ruse,
Made haste to be the first one to accuse.
For that she's paid; fleeing my wrath, she found
Too mild a death, and in the waves is drowned.
Much though I wished to die then by the sword,   40
Your son's pure name cried out to be restored.
That my remorse be told, I chose instead
A slower road that leads down to the dead.
I drank, to give my burning veins some peace,
A poison which Medea[6] brought to Greece.   45
Already, to my heart, the venom gives
An alien coldness, so that it scarcely lives;
Already, to my sight, all clouds and fades—
The sky, my spouse, the world my life degrades;
Death dims my eyes, which soiled what they could see,   50
Restoring to the light its purity.

PANOPE   She's dead, my lord!

THESEUS   Would that I could inter
The memory of her black misdeeds with her!
Let's go, since now my error's all too clear,
And mix my poor son's blood with many a tear,   55
Embrace his dear remains, and expiate
The fury of a prayer which now I hate.
To his great worth all honor shall be paid,
And, further to appease his angry shade,
Aricia, despite her brother's offense,   60
Shall be my daughter from this moment hence.

---

6. A sorceress who helped Jason get the Golden Fleece; later, deserted by him, she killed her rival and her own children and burned her palace before fleeing to Athens. According to one legend, she tried to poison Theseus.

SOR JUANA INÉS DE LA CRUZ
1648–1695

One hardly expects to find a spirited defense of women's intellectual rights issuing from the pen of a seventeenth-century Mexican nun, but *Reply to Sor Filotea de la Cruz,* by Sister Juana Inés de la Cruz, is exactly that. In the guise of declaring her humility and her religious subordination, this nun manages to advance claims for her sex more far-reaching and profound than any previously offered.

Born into an upper-class family, Sister Juana in her teens served as lady-in-waiting at the Viceregal court. She soon took the veil, however; her *Reply* suggests a reason in her desire for a safe environment in which to pursue her intellectual interests. Religious vocation did not prevent her from writing in secular forms: lyric poetry and drama. Indeed, she achieved an important literary reputation, later coming to be known throughout the Spanish-speaking world as the "Tenth Muse." Because her religious superiors intermittently rebuked her for her worldly interests, however, she appears to have developed a powerful sense of guilt. It is said that the natural disturbances and disasters—a solar eclipse, storms, and famine—plaguing Mexico City in the 1690s intensified her guilt; in 1694, she reaffirmed her faith, signing the statement in her own blood with the words, "I, Sister Juana Inés de la Cruz, the worst in the world." She died after nursing the sick in an epidemic.

The *Reply* stems directly from Sister Juana's venture into theological polemic. In 1690 she wrote a commentary on a sermon delivered forty years earlier by the Portuguese Jesuit Antonio de Vieira, a sermon in which he disputed with Saint Augustine and Saint Thomas about the nature of Christ's greatest expression of love at His life's end. Her commentary, in the form of a letter, was published, without her consent, by the bishop of Puebla. The bishop provided the title, *Athenagoric Letter,* or "letter worthy of the wisdom of Athena," but he also prefixed his own letter to Sister Juana, signed with the pseudonym "Filotea de la Cruz." Here he advised the nun to focus her attention and her talents more on religious matters. In her *Reply* (1691), she nominally accepted the bishop's rebuke; the smooth surface of her elegant prose, however, conceals both rage and determination to assert her right—and that of other women—to a fully realized life of the mind.

The artistry of this piece of self-defense demonstrates Sister Juana's powers and thus constitutes part of her justification. Systematically refusing to make any overt claims for herself, she declares her desire to do whatever her associates wish or demand of her. While asserting her own unimportance, she illustrates the range of her knowledge and of her rhetorical skill. The sheer abundance of her biblical allusions and of her quotations from theological texts, for instance, proves that she has mastered a large body of religious material and that she has not sacrificed religious to secular study. Her elaborate protestations of deference, her vocabulary of insignificance, her narrative of subservience: all show the verbal dexterity that enables her to achieve her own rhetorical ends even as she denies her commitment to purely personal goals.

If she acknowledges no self-seeking, she nevertheless declares and demonstrates her ungovernable passion for the life of the mind. She tells of how she joined the convent despite fears that the community "would intrude upon the peaceful silence of my books." "Certain learned persons," however, explained to her that her desire for solitary intellectual experience constituted "temptation." She therefore entered the religious life, believing, she says, "that I was fleeing from myself, but—wretch that I am!—I brought with me my worst enemy, my inclination, which I do not know whether to consider a gift or a punishment from Heaven; for once dimmed and encumbered by the many activities common to Religion, that inclination exploded in me like gunpowder." Although this sentence explicitly labels her intellectual inclinations her worst enemy and suggests that they might be considered divine punishment, the same sentence dramatizes the uncontrollable, explosive force of those inclinations and hints at the negative potential of religious experience, which dims and encumbers the mind. No matter how often Sister Juana admits that her longings amount to a form of "vice," she embodies in her prose the energy and the vividness they generate and makes her audience feel their positive weight.

The autobiographical aspects of Sister Juana's self-defense give it special imme-diacy for modern readers, who may recognize versions of their own dilemmas in her narrative of difficulties. Of course, girls no longer have to trick their way into learning or plead for permission to dress in boy's clothes to go to a university. But even twenty-first-century young women have been known to experience the kind of hostility Sister Juana reports as the response to her remarkable achievement. Yet more recognizable as a frequent form of female anxiety is the nun's concern to proclaim her responsiveness to others, her "tender and affable nature," which causes the other nuns, she says, to hold her "in great affection." She insists that she fills all the respon-sibilities of a woman as well as displays the kinds of capacity more generally associated with men, and she performs her womanly and her religious duties *first*, reserving her scholarly pursuits for leisure hours.

But, of course, her larger argument depends on her utter denial that intelligence or a thirst for knowledge should be considered a sex-limited characteristic. She draws on history for evidence of female intellectual power; one may feel the irony of the fact that her list of female worthies requires so much annotation today. The names of these notable women have hardly become household words. Still, these names, these histories, do exist, providing powerful support for Sister Juana's position. Even more forceful is the testimony of her own experience: her account of how, deprived of books, she finds matter for intellectual inquiry everywhere—in the yolk of an egg, the spinning of a top, the reading of the Bible. This is, the reader comes to believe, a woman born to think. If she arouses uneasiness when she implicitly equates herself, as object of persecution, with Christ, she also makes one feel directly the horror of women's official exclusion, in the past, from intellectual pursuits.

A volume in the Twayne series by Gerard Flynn, *Sor Juana Inés de la Cruz* (1971), provides a biographical, critical, and bibliographical introduction to Sister Juana. She is also treated in histories of Latin American literature: for example, J. Franco, *An Introduction to Spanish-American Literature* (1969). An important critical work, belatedly translated into English, is Octavio Paz, *Sor Juana; Or, The Traps of Faith* (1988). Other studies include F. Royer, *The Tenth Muse: Sor Juana Inés de la Cruz* (1952); S. Merrim, ed., *Feminist Perspectives on Sor Juana Inés de la Cruz* (1991), a collection of essays; P. Kirk, *Sor Juana Inés de la Cruz: Religion, Art, and Feminism* (1998); and S. Merrim, *Early Modern Women's Writing and Sor Juana Inés de la Cruz* (1999).

PRONOUNCING GLOSSARY

The following list uses common English syllables and stress accents to provide rough equiv-alents of selected words whose pronunciation may be unfamiliar to the general reader.

Albertus Magnus: *ahl-bayr'-tus mahg'-noos*

Arete: *ah-ray'-tee*

Atenagórica: *ah-tay-nah-goh'-ree-kah*

Duquesa of Abeyro: *doo-kay'-zah of ah-bay'-roh*

Machiavelli: *mah-kee-ah-vel'-ee*

señora: *sen-yoh'rah*

sueño: *swayn'-yoh*

Reply to Sor Filotea de la Cruz[1]

My most illustrious *señora*, dear lady. It has not been my will, my poor health, or my justifiable apprehension that for so many days delayed my response. How could I write, considering that at my very first step my clumsy pen encountered two obstructions in its path? The first (and, for me, the most uncompromising) is to know how to reply to your most learned, most prudent, most holy, and most loving letter. For I recall that when Saint Thomas, the Angelic Doctor of Scholasticism, was asked about his silence regarding his teacher Albertus Magnus,[2] he replied that he had not spoken because he knew no words worthy of Albertus. With so much greater reason, must not I too be silent? Not, like the Saint, out of humility, but because in reality I know nothing I can say that is worthy of you. The second obstruction is to know how to express my appreciation for a favor as unexpected as extreme, for having my scribblings printed, a gift so immeasurable as to surpass my most ambitious aspiration, my most fervent desire, which even as an entity of reason never entered my thoughts. Yours was a kindness, finally, of such magnitude that words cannot express my gratitude, a kindness exceeding the bounds of appreciation, as great as it was unexpected—which is as Quintilian[3] said: *aspirations engender minor glory; benefices,[4] major*. To such a degree as to impose silence on the receiver.

When the blessedly sterile—that she might miraculously become fecund—Mother of John the Baptist saw in her house such an extraordinary visitor as the Mother of the Word, her reason became clouded and her speech deserted her; and thus, in the place of thanks, she burst out with doubts and questions: *And whence is to me [that the mother of my Lord should come to me?]*[5] And whence cometh such a thing to *me*? And so also it fell to Saul when he found himself the chosen, the anointed, King of Israel: *Am I not a son of Jemini, of the least tribe of Israel, and my kindred the last among all the families of the tribe of Benjamin? Why then hast thou spoken this word to me?*[6] And thus say I, most honorable lady. Why do I receive such favor? By chance, am I other than an humble nun, the lowliest creature of the world, the most unworthy to occupy your attention? "Wherefore then speakest thou so to me?" "And whence is this to me?" Nor to the first obstruction do I have any response other than I am little worthy of your eyes; nor to the second, other than wonder, in the stead of thanks, saying that I am not capable of thanking you for the smallest part of that which I owe you. This is not pretended modesty, lady, but the simplest truth issuing from the depths of my heart, that when the letter which with propriety you called *Atenagórica*[7] reached

---

1. The Spanish text for this 17th-century declaration of women's intellectual freedom was discovered by Gabriel North Seymour during her Fulbright Scholarship in Mexico in 1980, following graduation from Princeton University. The English Language translation by Margaret Sayers Peden was commissioned by Lime Rock Press, Inc., a small independent press in Connecticut, and was originally published in 1982 in a limited edition that included Ms. Seymour's black-and-white photographs of Sor Juana sites, under the title "A Woman of Genius: The Intellectual Autobiography of Sor Juana Inés de la Cruz." The publication was honored at a special convocation of Mexican and American scholars at the Library of Congress. Copyright 1982 by Lime Rock Press, Inc. Reprinted by permission. 2. Saint Albert the Great (1193?–1280), scholastic philosopher, called the Universal Doctor; he exercised great influence on his student Thomas Aquinas. 3. Marcus Fabius Quintilianus (ca. A.D. 35–100), born in Spain, became a famous Roman orator and wrote on rhetoric. 4. I.e., good works. 5. Luke 1.43. 6. 1 Samuel 9.21. 7. Sister Juana's letter criticizing Father Vieira's sermon was retitled by the bishop *Carta Atenagórica* (Letter worthy of Athena). Athena was the Greek goddess of wisdom.

my hands, in print, I burst into tears of confusion (withal, that tears do not come easily to me) because it seemed to me that your favor was but a remonstrance God made against the wrong I have committed, and that in the same way He corrects others with punishment He wishes to subject me with benefices, with this special favor for which I know myself to be myself to be His debtor, as for an infinitude of others from His boundless kindness. I looked upon this favor as a particular way to shame and confound me, it being the most exquisite means of castigation, that of causing me, by my own intellect, to be the judge who pronounces sentence and who denounces my ingratitude. And thus, when here in my solitude I think on these things, I am wont to say: Blessed art Thou, oh Lord, for Thou hast not chosen to place in the hands of others my judgment, nor yet in mine, but hast reserved that to Thy own, and freed me from myself, and from the necessity to sit in judgment on myself, which judgment, forced from my own intellect, could be no less than condemnation, but Thou hast reserved me to Thy mercy, because Thou lovest me more than I can love myself.

I beg you, lady, to forgive this digression to which I was drawn by the power of truth, and, if I am to confess all the truth, I shall confess that I cast about for some manner by which I might flee the difficulty of a reply, and was sorely tempted to take refuge in silence. But as silence is a negative thing, though it explains a great deal through the very stress of not explaining, we must assign some meaning to it that we may understand what the silence is intended to say, for if not, silence will say nothing, as that is its very office: *to say nothing*. The holy Chosen Vessel, Saint Paul, having been caught up into paradise, and having heard the arcane secrets of God, *heard secret words, which it is not granted to man to utter*.[8] He does not say what he heard; he says that he cannot say it. So that of things one cannot say, it is needful to say at least that they cannot be said, so that it may be understood that not speaking is not the same as having nothing to say, but rather being unable to express the many things there are to say. Saint John says that if all the marvels our Redeemer wrought "were written every one, the world itself, I think, would not be able to contain the books that should be written."[9] And Vieyra[1] says on this point that in this single phrase the Evangelist said more than in all else he wrote; and this same Lusitanian[2] Phoenix speaks well (but when does he not speak well, even when he does not speak well of others?) because in those words Saint John said everything left unsaid and expressed all that was left to be expressed. And thus I, lady, shall respond only that I do not know how to respond; I shall thank you in saying only that I am incapable of thanking you; and I shall say, through the indication of what I leave to silence, that it is only with the confidence of one who is favored and with the protection of one who is honorable that I presume to address your magnificence, and if this be folly, be forgiving of it, for folly may be good fortune, and in this manner I shall provide further occasion for your benignity and you will better shape my intellect.

Because he was halting of speech, Moses thought himself unworthy to speak with Pharaoh, but after he found himself highly favored of God, and thus inspired, he not only spoke with God Almighty but dared ask the impossible: *shew me thy face*.[3] In this same manner, lady, and in view of how you

---

8. 2 Corinthians 12.4.   9. John 21.25.   1. Antonio Vieira (1608–1697), author of the sermon that Sister Juana had earlier criticized, was a Portuguese ecclesiastic whose most important work was converting the Indians of Brazil.   2. Roman name for Portugal.   3. Exodus 33.13.

favor me, I no longer see as impossible the obstructions I posed in the beginning: for who was it who had my letter printed unbeknownst to me? Who entitled it, who bore the cost, who honored it, it being so unworthy in itself, and in its author? What will such a person not do, not pardon? What would he fail to do, or fail to pardon? And thus, based on the supposition that I speak under the safe-conduct of your favor, and with the assurance of your benignity, and with the knowledge that like a second Ahasuerus[4] you have offered to me to kiss the top of the golden scepter of your affection as a sign of conceding to me your benevolent license to speak and offer judgments in your exalted presence, I say to you that I have taken to heart your most holy admonition that I apply myself to the study of the Sacred Books, which, though it comes in the guise of counsel, will have for me the authority of a precept, but with the not insignificant consolation that even before your counsel I was disposed to obey your pastoral suggestion as your direction, which may be inferred from the premise and argument of my Letter. For I know well that your most sensible warning is not directed against it, but rather against those worldly matters of which I have written.[5] And thus I had hoped with the Letter to make amends for any lack of application you may (with great reason) have inferred from others of my writings; and, speaking more particularly, I confess to you with all the candor of which you are deserving, and with the truth and clarity which are the natural custom in me, that my not having written often of sacred matters was not caused by disaffection or by want of application, but by the abundant fear and reverence due those Sacred Letters, knowing myself incapable of their comprehension and unworthy of their employment. Always resounding in my ears, with no little horror, I hear God's threat and prohibition to sinners like myself. *Why dost thou declare my justices, and take my covenant in thy mouth?*[6] This question, as well as the knowledge that even learned men are forbidden to read the Canticle of Canticles[7] until they have passed thirty years of age, or even Genesis—the latter for its obscurity; the former in order that the sweetness of those epithalamia not serve as occasion for imprudent youth to transmute their meaning into carnal emotion, as borne out by my exalted Father Saint Jerome,[8] who ordered that these be the last verses to be studied, and for the same reason: *And finally, one may read without peril the Song of Songs, for if it is read one may suffer harm through not understanding those Epithalamia of the spiritual wedding which is expressed in carnal terms.* And Seneca[9] says: *In the early years the faith is dim.* For how then would I have dared take in my unworthy hands these verses, defying gender, age, and, above all, custom? And thus I confess that many times this fear has plucked my pen from my hand and has turned my thoughts back toward the very same reason from which they had wished to be born: which obstacle did not impinge upon profane matters, for a heresy against art is not punished by the Holy Office but by the judicious with derision, and by critics with censure, and censure, *just or unjust, is not to be feared,* as it does not forbid the taking of communion or hearing of mass, and offers me little or

---

4. King of Persia, who stretched out his gold scepter to his queen, Esther, and said he would grant her whatever she wished (Esther 5.2–3).   5. Sister Juana had published secular poetry and drama. 6. Psalm 50.16.   7. The Song of Solomon (also called Song of Songs), which employs erotic imagery. 8. Eusebius Sophronius Hieronymus (ca. 342–420), ascetic and scholar, most learned of the Latin Church fathers, a prolific author of treatises and commentaries. Sister Juana belonged to a Jeronymite convent; Jerome had founded the order.   9. Lucius Annaeus Seneca (ca. 3 B.C.–A.D. 63), Roman philosopher and orator.

no cause for anxiety, because in the opinion of those who defame my art, I have neither the obligation to know nor the aptitude to triumph. If, then, I err, I suffer neither blame nor discredit: I suffer no blame, as I have no obligation; no discredit, as I have no possibility of triumphing—*and no one is obliged to do the impossible*. And, in truth, I have written nothing except when compelled and constrained, and then only to give pleasure to others; not alone without pleasure of my own, but with absolute repugnance, for I have never deemed myself one who has any worth in letters or the wit necessity demands of one who would write; and thus my customary response to those who press me, above all in sacred matters, is, what capacity of reason have I? what application? what resources? what rudimentary knowledge of such matters beyond that of the most superficial scholarly degrees? Leave these matters to those who understand them; I wish no quarrel with the Holy Office, for I am ignorant, and I tremble that I may express some proposition that will cause offense or twist the true meaning of some scripture. I do not study to write, even less to teach—which in one like myself were unseemly pride—but only to the end that if I study, I will be ignorant of less. This is my response, and these are my feelings.

I have never written of my own choice, but at the urging of others, to whom with reason I might say, *You have compelled me*.[1] But one truth I shall not deny (first, because it is well-known to all, and second, because although it has not worked in my favor, God has granted me the mercy of loving truth above all else), which is that from the moment I was first illuminated by the light of reason, my inclination toward letters has been so vehement, so overpowering, that not even the admonitions of others—and I have suffered many—nor my own meditations—and they have not been few—have been sufficient to cause me to forswear this natural impulse that God placed in me: the Lord God knows why, and for what purpose. And He knows that I have prayed that He dim the light of my reason, leaving only that which is needed to keep His Law, for there are those who would say that all else is unwanted in a woman, and there are even those who would hold that such knowledge does injury. And my Holy Father knows too that as I have been unable to achieve this (my prayer has not been answered), I have sought to veil the light of my reason—along with my name—and to offer it up only to Him who bestowed it upon me, and He knows that none other was the cause of my entering into Religion, notwithstanding that the spiritual exercises and company of a community were repugnant to the freedom and quiet I desired for my studious endeavors. And later, in that community, the Lord God knows—and, in the world, only the one who must know[2]—how diligently I sought to obscure my name, and how this was not permitted, saying it was temptation: and so it would have been. If it were in my power, lady, to repay you in some part what I owe you, it might be done by telling you this thing which has never before passed my lips, except to be spoken to the one who should hear it. It is my hope that by having opened wide to you the doors of my heart, by having made patent to you its most deeply-hidden secrets, you will deem my confidence not unworthy of the debt I owe to your most august person and to your most uncommon favors.

Continuing the narrations of my inclinations, of which I wish to give you a thorough account, I will tell you that I was not yet three years old when my mother determined to send one of my elder sisters to learn to read at a

---

1. 2 Corinthians 12.11.   2. Presumably her confessor, Father Antonio Núñez.

school for girls we call the *Amigas*. Affection, and mischief, caused me to follow her, and when I observed how she was being taught her lessons I was so inflamed with the desire to know how to read, that deceiving—for so I knew it to be—the mistress, I told her that my mother had meant for me to have lessons too. She did not believe it, as it was little to be believed, but, to humour me, she acceded. I continued to go there, and she continued to teach me, but now, as experience had disabused her, with all seriousness; and I learned so quickly that before my mother knew of it I could already read, for my teacher had kept it from her in order to reveal the surprise and reap the reward at one and the same time. And I, you may be sure, kept the secret, fearing that I would be whipped for having acted without permission. The woman who taught me, may God bless and keep her, is still alive and can bear witness to all I say. I also remember that in those days, my tastes being those common to that age, I abstained from eating cheese because I had heard that it made one slow of wits, for in me the desire for learning was stronger than the desire for eating—as powerful as that is in children. When later, being six or seven, and having learned how to read and write, along with all the other skills of needlework and household arts that girls learn, it came to my attention that in Mexico City there were Schools, and a University, in which one studied the sciences. The moment I heard this, I began to plague my mother with insistent and importunate pleas: she should dress me in boy's clothing and send me to Mexico City to live with relatives, to study and be tutored at the University. She would not permit it, and she was wise, but I assuaged my disappointment by reading the many and varied books belonging to my grandfather, and there were not enough punishments, nor reprimands, to prevent me from reading: so that when I came to the city many marveled, not so much at my natural wit, as at my memory, and at the amount of learning I had mastered at an age when many have scarcely learned to speak well.

I began to study Latin grammar—in all, I believe, I had no more than twenty lessons—and so intense was my concern that though among women (especially a woman in the flower of her youth) the natural adornment of one's hair is held in such high esteem, I cut off mine to the breadth of some four to six fingers, measuring the place it had reached, and imposing upon myself the condition that if by the time it had again grown to that length I had not learned such and such a thing I had set for myself to learn while my hair was growing, I would again cut it off as punishment for being so slow-witted. And it did happen that my hair grew out and still I had not learned what I had set for myself—because my hair grew quickly and I learned slowly—and in fact I did cut it in punishment for such stupidity: for there seemed to me no cause for a head to be adorned with hair and naked of learning—which was the more desired embellishment. And so I entered the religious order, knowing that life there entailed certain conditions (I refer to superficial, and not fundamental, regards) most repugnant to my nature; but given the total antipathy I felt for marriage, I deemed convent life the least unsuitable and the most honorable I could elect if I were to insure my salvation. Working against that end, first (as, finally, the most important) was the matter of all the trivial aspects of my nature which nourished my pride, such as wishing to live alone, and wishing to have no obligatory occupation that would inhibit the freedom of my studies, nor the sounds of a community that would intrude upon the peaceful silence of my books. These desires caused me to falter some while in my decision, until certain learned persons enlightened me, explaining that they were temptation, and, with divine favor, I overcame them, and took upon myself the state which now so unworthily I hold. I believed that I was fleeing from myself, but—wretch that I am!—I brought with me my worst enemy, my inclination, which I do not know whether to consider a gift or a punishment from Heaven, for once dimmed and encumbered by the many activities common to Religion, that inclination exploded in me like gunpowder, proving how *privation is the source of appetite.*

I turned again (which is badly put, for I never ceased), I continued, then, in my studious endeavour (which for me was respite during those moments not occupied by my duties) of reading and more reading, of study and more study, with no teachers but my books. Thus I learned how difficult it is to study those soulless letters, lacking a human voice or the explication of a teacher. But I suffered this labor happily for my love of learning. Oh, had it only been for love of God, which were proper, how worthwhile it would have been! I strove mightily to elevate these studies, to dedicate them to His service, as the goal to which I aspired was to study Theology—it seeming to me debilitating for a Catholic not to know everything in this life of the Divine Mysteries that can be learned through natural means—and, being a nun and not a layperson, it was seemly that I profess my vows to learning through ecclesiastical channels; and especially, being a daughter of a Saint Jerome and a Saint Paula,[3] it was essential that such erudite parents not be shamed by a witless daughter. This is the argument I proposed to myself, and it seemed to me well-reasoned. It was, however (and this cannot be denied) merely glorification and approbation of my inclination, and enjoyment of it offered as justification. And so I continued, as I have said, directing the course of my studies toward the peak of Sacred Theology, it seeming necessary to me, in order to scale those heights, to climb the steps of the human sciences and arts; for how could one undertake the study of the Queen of Sciences if first one had not come to know her servants?

How, without Logic, could I be apprised of the general and specific way in which the Holy Scripture is written? How, without Rhetoric, could I understand its figures, its tropes, its locutions? How, without Physics,[4] so many innate questions concerning the nature of animals, their sacrifices, wherein exist so many symbols, many already declared, many still to be discovered? How should I know whether Saul's being refreshed by the sound of David's harp was due to the virtue and natural power of Music, or to a transcendent power God wished to place in David? How, without Arithmetic, could one understand the computations of the years, days, months, hours, those mysterious weeks communicated by Gabriel to Daniel,[5] and others for whose understanding one must know the nature, concordance, and properties of numbers? How, without Geometry, could one measure the Holy Ark of the Covenant and the Holy City of Jerusalem, whose mysterious measures are foursquare in their dimensions, as well as the miraculous proportions of all their parts? How, without Architecture, could one know the great Temple

---

3. A Roman woman (d. 404), converted to Christianity after her daughter's death, who founded a nunnery next to Saint Jerome's monastery at Bethlehem and helped Jerome in his studies.   4. I.e., physic, or medicine.   5. While Daniel was praying, Gabriel came to him to interpret, in great chronological detail, a vision Daniel had previously had (Daniel 9.21–27).

of Solomon, of which God Himself was the Author who conceived the disposition and the design, and the Wise King but the overseer who executed it, of which temple there was no foundation without mystery, no column without symbolism, no cornice without allusion, no architrave without significance; and similarly others of its parts, of which the least fillet was never intended solely for the service and complement of Art, but as symbol of greater things? How, without great knowledge of the laws and parts of which History is comprised, could one understand historical Books? Or those recapitulations in which many times what happened first is seen in the narrated account to have happened later? How, without great learning in Canon and Civil Law, could one understand Legal Books? How, without great erudition, could one apprehend the secular histories of which the Holy Scripture makes mention, such as the many customs of the Gentiles, their many rites, their many ways of speaking? How without the abundant laws and lessons of the Holy Fathers could one understand the obscure lesson of the Prophets? And without being expert in Music, how could one understand the exquisite precision of the musical proportions that grace so many Scriptures, particularly those in which Abraham beseeches God in defense of the Cities,[6] asking whether He would spare the place were there but fifty just men therein; and then Abraham reduced that number to five less than fifty, forty-five, which is a ninth, and is as Mi to Re; then to forty, which is a tone, and is as Re to Mi; from forty to thirty, which is a diatessaron, the interval of the perfect fourth; from thirty to twenty, which is the perfect fifth; and from twenty to ten, which is the octave, the diapason; and as there are no further harmonic proportions, made no further reductions. How might one understand this without Music? And there in the Book of Job, God says to Job: *Shalt thou be able to join together the shining stars the Pleiades, or canst thou stop the turning about of Arcturus? Canst thou bring forth the day star in its time, and make the evening star to rise upon the children of the earth?*[7] Which message, without knowledge of Astrology, would be impossible to apprehend. And not only these noble sciences; there is no applied art that is not mentioned. And, finally, in consideration of the Book that comprises all books, and the Science in which all sciences are embraced, and for whose comprehension all sciences serve, and even after knowing them all (which we now see is not easy, nor even possible), there is one condition that takes precedence over all the rest, which is uninterrupted prayer and purity of life, that one may entreat of God that purgation of spirit and illumination of mind necessary for the understanding of such elevated matters: and if that be lacking, none of the aforesaid will have been of any purpose.

Of the Angelic Doctor Saint Thomas[8] the Church affirms: *When reading the most difficult passages of the Holy Scripture, he joined fast with prayer. And he was wont to say to his companion Brother Reginald that all he knew derived not so much from study or his own labor as from the grace of God.* How then should I—so lacking in virtue and so poorly read—find courage to write? But as I had acquired the rudiments of learning, I continued to study ceaselessly divers subjects, having for none any particular inclination, but for all in general; and having studied some more than others was not owing to

6. Abraham beseeches God to save Sodom for the sake of its just inhabitants (Genesis 18.23–33).   7. Job 38.31–32.   8. Thomas Aquinas (ca. 1225–1274), Dominican theologian, author of *Summa Theologica* (ca. 1266), and for centuries the most important authority on Church doctrine.

preference, but to the chance that more books on certain subjects had fallen into my hands, causing the election of them through no discretion of my own. And as I was not directed by preference, nor, forced by the need to fulfill certain scholarly requirements, constrained by time in the pursuit of any subject, I found myself free to study numerous topics at the same time, or to leave some for others; although in this scheme some order was observed, for some I deigned[9] study and others diversion, and in the latter I found respite from the former. From which it follows that though I have studied many things I know nothing, as some have inhibited the learning of others. I speak specifically of the practical aspect of those arts that allow practice, because it is clear that when the pen moves the compass must lie idle, and while the harp is played the organ is stilled, *et sic de caeteris.*[1] And because much practice is required of one who would acquire facility, none who divides his interest among various exercises may reach perfection. Whereas in the formal and theoretical arts the contrary is true, and I would hope to persuade all with my experience, which is that one need not inhibit the other, but, in fact, each may illuminate and open the way to others, by nature of their variations and their hidden links, which were placed in this universal chain by the wisdom of their Author in such a way that they conform and are joined together with admirable unity and harmony. This is the very chain the ancients believed did issue from the mouth of Jupiter, from which were suspended all things linked one with another, as is demonstrated by the Reverend Father Athanasius Kircher[2] in his curious book, *De Magnate.* All things issue from God, Who is at once the center and the circumference from which and in which all lines begin and end.

I myself can affirm that what I have not understood in an author in one branch of knowledge I may understand in a second in a branch that seems remote from the first. And authors, in their elucidation, may suggest metaphorical examples in other arts: as when logicians say that to prove whether parts are equal, the means is to the extremes as a determined measure to two equidistant bodies; or in stating how the argument of the logician moves, in the manner of a straight line, along the shortest route, while that of the rhetorician moves as a curve, by the longest, but that both finally arrive at the same point. And similarly, as it is when they say that the Exegetes are like an open hand, and the Scholastics like a closed fist.[3] And thus it is no apology, nor do I offer it as such, to say that I have studied many subjects, seeing that each augments the other; but that I have not profited is the fault of my own ineptitude and the inadequacy of my intelligence, not the fault of the variety. But what may be offered as exoneration is that I undertook this great task without benefit of teacher, or fellow students with whom to confer and discuss, having for a master no other than a mute book, and for a colleague, an insentient inkwell; and in the stead of explication and exercise, many obstructions, not merely those of my religious obligations (for it is already known how useful and advantageous is the time employed in them), rather, all the attendant details of living in a community: how I might be reading, and those in the adjoining cell would wish to play their instruments, and sing; how I might be studying, and two servants who had quar-

9. Deemed, considered.   1. And so for other things (Latin).   2. German Jesuit scientist (1601?–1680), author of *Magnes sive de arte magnetica* (The Magnet; or, Of the Magnetic Science).   3. The Exegetes emphasized interpretation; the Scholastics, logic.

reled would select me to judge their dispute; or how I might be writing, and a friend come to visit me, doing me no favor but with the best of will, at which time one must not only accept the inconvenience, but be grateful for the hurt. And such occurrences are the normal state of affairs, for as the times I set apart for study are those remaining after the ordinary duties of the community are fulfilled, they are the same moments available to my sisters, in which they may come to interrupt my labor; and only those who have experience of such a community will know how true this is, and how it is only the strength of my vocation that allows me happiness; that, and the great love existing between me and my beloved sisters, for as love is union, it knows no extremes of distance.

With this I confess how interminable has been my labor; and how I am unable to say what I have with envy heard others state—that they have not been plagued by the thirst for knowledge: blessed are they. For me, not the knowing (for still I do not know), merely the desiring to know, has been such torment that I can say, as has my Father Saint Jerome (although not with his accomplishment) . . . *my conscience is witness to what effort I have expended, what difficulties I have suffered, how many times I have despaired, how often I have ceased my labors and turned to them again, driven by the hunger for knowledge; my conscience is witness, and that of those who have lived beside me.* With the exception of the companions and witnesses (for I have been denied even this consolation), I can attest to the truth of these words. And to the fact that even so, my black inclination has been so great that it has conquered all else!

It has been my fortune that, among other benefices,[4] I owe to God a most tender and affable nature, and because of it my sisters (who being good women do not take note of my faults) hold me in great affection, and take pleasure in my company; and knowing this, and moved by the great love I hold for them—having greater reason than they—I enjoy even more *their* company. Thus I was wont in our rare idle moments to visit among them, offering them consolation and entertaining myself in their conversation. I could not help but note, however, that in these times I was neglecting my study, and I made a vow not to enter any cell unless obliged by obedience or charity; for without such a compelling constraint—the constraint of mere intention not being sufficient—my love would be more powerful than my will. I would (knowing well my frailty) make this vow for the period of a few weeks, or a month; and when that time had expired, I would allow myself a brief respite of a day or two before renewing it, using that time not so much for rest (for *not* studying has never been restful for me) as to assure that I not be deemed cold, remote, or ungrateful in the little-deserved affection of my dearest sisters.

In this practice one may recognize the strength of my inclination. I give thanks to God, Who willed that such an ungovernable force be turned toward letters and not to some other vice. From this it may also be inferred how obdurately against the current my poor studies have sailed (more accurately, have foundered). For still to be related is the most arduous of my difficulties—those mentioned until now, either compulsory or fortuitous, being merely tangential—and still unreported the more directly aimed slings and

4. Benefits or kindnesses.

arrows that have acted to impede and prevent the exercise of my study. Who would have doubted, having witnessed such general approbation, that I sailed before the wind across calm seas, amid the laurels of widespread acclaim. But our Lord God knows that it has not been so; He knows how from amongst the blossoms of this very acclaim emerged such a number of aroused vipers, hissing their emulation and their persecution, that one could not count them. But the most noxious, those who most deeply wounded me, have not been those who persecuted me with open loathing and malice, but rather those who in loving me and desiring my well-being (and who are deserving of God's blessing for their good intent) have mortified and tormented me more than those others with their abhorrence. "Such studies are not in conformity with sacred innocence; surely she will be lost; surely she will, by cause of her very perspicacity and acuity, grow heady at such exalted heights." How was I to endure? An uncommon sort of martyrdom in which I was both martyr and executioner. And for my (in me, twice hapless) facility in making verses, even though they be sacred verses, what sorrows have I not suffered? What sorrows not ceased to suffer? Be assured, lady, it is often that I have meditated on how one who distinguishes himself—or one on whom God chooses to confer distinction, for it is only He who may do so—is received as a common enemy, because it seems to some that he usurps the applause they deserve, or that he dams up the admiration to which they aspired, and so they persecute that person.

That politically barbaric law of Athens by which any person who excelled by cause of his natural gifts and virtues was exiled from his Republic in order that he not threaten the public freedom still endures, is still observed in our day, although not for the reasons held by the Athenians. Those reasons have been replaced by another, no less efficient though not as well founded, seeming, rather, a maxim more appropriate to that impious Machiavelli[5]—which is to abhor one who excels, because he deprives others of regard. And thus it happens, and thus it has always happened.

For if not, what was the cause of the rage and loathing the Pharisees[6] directed against Christ, there being so many reasons to love Him? If we behold His presence, what is more to be loved than that Divine beauty? What more powerful to stir one's heart? For if ordinary human beauty holds sway over strength of will, and is able to subdue it with tender and enticing vehemence, what power would Divine beauty exert, with all its prerogatives and sovereign endowments? What might move, what effect, what not move and not effect, such incomprehensible beauty, that beauteous face through which, as through a polished crystal, were diffused the rays of Divinity? What would not be moved by that semblance which beyond incomparable human perfections revealed Divine illuminations? If the visage of Moses, merely from conversation with God, caused men to fear to come near him,[7] how much finer must be the face of God-made-flesh? And among other virtues, what more to be loved than that celestial modesty? That sweetness and kindness disseminating mercy in every movement? That profound humility and gentleness? Those words of eternal life and eternal wisdom? How therefore

---

5. Niccolò Machiavelli (1469–1527), Italian statesman whose writings (notably *The Prince*) advocated political unscrupulousness.   6. Members of a strict Jewish sect that emphasized conformity to the law who were, according to the New Testament of the Bible, prominent in plotting the death of Jesus (Mark 3.6, John 11.47–57).   7. Exodus 34.30.

is it possible that such beauty did not stir their souls, that they did not follow after Him, enamored and enlightened?

The Holy Mother, my Mother Teresa,[8] says that when she beheld the beauty of Christ never again was she inclined toward any human creature, for she saw nothing that was not ugliness compared to such beauty. How was it then that in men it engendered such contrary reactions? For although they were uncouth and vile and had no knowledge or appreciation of His perfections, not even as they might profit from them, how was it they were not moved by the many advantages of such benefices as He performed for them, healing the sick, resurrecting the dead, restoring those possessed of the devil? How was it they did not love Him? But God is witness that it was for these very acts they did not love Him, that they despised Him. As they themselves testified.

They gather together in their council and say: *What do we? for this man doth many miracles.*[9] Can this be cause? If they had said: here is an evil-doer, a transgressor of the law, a rabble-rouser who with deceit stirs up the populace, they would have lied—as they did indeed lie when they spoke these things. But there were more apposite reasons for effecting what they desired, which was to take His life; and to give as reason that he had performed wondrous deeds seems not befitting learned men, for such were the Pharisees. Thus it is that in the heat of passion learned men erupt with such irrelevancies; for we know it as truth that only for this reason was it determined that Christ should die. Oh, men, if men you may be called, being so like to brutes, what is the cause of so cruel a determination? Their only response is that "this man doth many miracles." May God forgive them. Then is performing signal deeds cause enough that one should die? This "he doth many miracles" evokes *the root of Jesse, who standeth for an ensign of the people,*[1] and that *and for a sign which shall be contradicted.*[2] He is a sign? Then He shall die. He excels? Then He shall suffer, for that is the reward for one who excels.

Often on the crest of temples are placed as adornment figures of the winds and of fame, and to defend them from the birds, they are covered with iron barbs; this appears to be in defense, but is in truth obligatory propriety: the figure thus elevated cannot survive without the very barbs that prick it; there on high is found the animosity of the air, on high the ferocity of the elements, on high is unleashed the anger of the thunderbolt, on high stands the target for slings and arrows. Oh unhappy eminence, exposed to such uncounted perils. Oh sign, become the target of envy and the butt of contradiction. Whatever eminence, whether that of dignity, nobility, riches, beauty, or science, must suffer this burden; but the eminence that undergoes the most severe attack is that of reason. First, because it is the most defenseless, for riches and power strike out against those who dare attack them; but not so reason, for while it is the greater it is more modest and long-suffering, and defends itself less. Second, as Gracian[3] stated so eruditely, *favors in man's reason are favors in his nature.*

For no other cause except that the angel is superior in reason is the angel above man; for no other cause does man stand above the beast but by his

---

8. Saint Teresa de Ávila (1515–1582), a mystical writer, responsible for a great awakening of religious fervor.　9. John 11.47.　1. Isaiah 11.10.　2. Luke 2.34.　3. Baltasar Gracián (1601–1658), Spanish Jesuit philosopher.

reason; and thus, as no one wishes to be lower than another, neither does he confess that another is superior in reason, as reason is a consequence of being superior. One will abide, and will confess that another is nobler than he, that another is richer, more handsome, and even that he is more learned, but that another is richer in reason scarcely any will confess: *Rare is he who will concede genius.* That is why the assault against this virtue works to such profit.

When the soldiers mocked, made entertainment and diversion of our Lord Jesus Christ, they brought Him a worn purple garment and a hollow reed, and a crown of thorns to crown Him King of Fools.[4] But though the reed and the purple were an affront, they did not cause suffering. Why does only the crown give pain? Is it not enough that like the other emblems the crown was a symbol of ridicule and ignominy, as that was its intent? No. Because the sacred head of Christ and His divine intellect were the depository of wisdom, and the world is not satisfied for wisdom to be the object of mere ridicule, it must also be done injury and harm. A head that is a storehouse of wisdom can expect nothing but a crown of thorns. What garland may human wisdom expect when it is known what was bestowed on that divine wisdom? Roman pride crowned the many achievements of their Captains with many crowns: he who defended the city received the civic crown; he who fought his way into the hostile camp received the camp crown; he who scaled the wall, the mural;[5] he who liberated a beseiged city, or any army besieged either in the field or in the enemy camp, received the obsidional, the siege, crown; other feats were crowned with naval, ovation, or triumphal crowns, as described by Pliny and Aulus Gellius.[6] Observing so many and varied crowns, I debated as to which Christ's crown must have been, and determined that it was the siege crown, for (as well you know, lady) that was the most honored crown and was called obsidional after *obsidio,* which means siege; which crown was made not from gold, or silver, but from the leaves and grasses flourishing on the field where the feat was achieved. And as the heroic feat of Christ was to break the siege of the Prince of Darkness, who had laid siege to all the earth, as is told in the Book of Job, quoting Satan: *I have gone round about the earth, and walked through it,*[7] and as St. Peter says: *As a roaring lion, goeth about seeking whom he may devour.*[8] And our Master came and caused him to lift the siege: *Now shall the prince of this world be cast out.*[9] So the soldiers crowned Him not with gold or silver but with the natural fruit of the world, which was the field of battle—and which, after the curse *Thorns also and thistles shall it bring forth to thee,*[1] produced only thorns—and thus it was a most fitting crown for the courageous and wise Conqueror, with which His mother Synagogue crowned Him. And the daughters of Zion, weeping, came out to witness the sorrowful triumph,[2] as they had come rejoicing for the triumph of Solomon,[3] because the triumph of the wise is earned with sorrow and celebrated with weeping, which is the manner of the triumph of wisdom; and as Christ is the King of wisdom, He was the first to wear that crown; and as it was sanctified on His

---

4. Matthew 27.28–31.   5. Pertaining to walls; the word *crown* is understood.   6. Latin writer (2nd century A.D.), author of *Noctes Atticae,* valuable for its quotations from lost works. Pliny the Younger (62?– ca. 113) was a Roman orator and statesman and author of well-known letters about Roman life.   7. Job 1.7.   8. 1 Peter 5.8.   9. John 12.31.   1. The curse on Adam and Eve after the Fall (Genesis 3.18). 2. Luke 23.27–28.   3. Song of Solomon 3.11.

brow, it removed all fear and dread from those who are wise, for they know they need aspire to no other honor.

The Living Word, Life, wished to restore life to Lazarus, who was dead. His disciples did not know His purpose and they said to Him: *Rabbi, the Jews but now sought to stone thee; and goest thou thither again?* And the Redeemer calmed their fear: *Are there not twelve hours of the day?*[4] It seems they feared because there had been those who wished to stone Him when He rebuked them, calling them thieves and not shepherds of sheep.[5] And thus the disciples feared that if He returned to the same place—for even though rebukes be just, they are often badly received—He would be risking his life. But once having been disabused and having realized that He was setting forth to raise up Lazarus from the dead, what was it that caused Thomas, like Peter in the Garden, to say *Let us also go, that we may die with him?*[6] What say you, Sainted Apostle? The Lord does not go out to die; whence your misgiving? For Christ goes not to rebuke, but to work an act of mercy, and therefore they will do Him no harm. These same Jews could have assured you, for when He reproved those who wished to stone Him, *Many good works I have shewed you from my Father; for which of those works do you stone me?* they replied: *For a good work we stone thee not; but for blasphemy.*[7] And as they say they will not stone Him for doing good works, and now He goes to do a work so great as to raise up Lazarus from the dead, whence your misgiving? Why do you fear? Were it not better to say: let us go to gather the fruits of appreciation for the good work our Master is about to do; to see him lauded and applauded for His benefice; to see men marvel at His miracle. Why speak words seemingly so alien to the circumstance as *Let us also go?* Ah, woe, the Saint feared as a prudent man and spoke as an Apostle. Does Christ not go to work a miracle? Why, what *greater* peril? It is less to be suffered that pride endure rebukes than envy witness miracles. In all the above, most honored lady, I do not wish to say (nor is such folly to be found in me) that I have been persecuted for my wisdom, but merely for my love of wisdom and letters, having achieved neither one nor the other.

At one time even the Prince of the Apostles was very far from wisdom, as is emphasized in that *But Peter followed afar off.*[8] Very distant from the laurels of a learned man is one so little in his judgment that he was *Not knowing what he said.*[9] And being questioned on his mastery of wisdom, he himself was witness that he had not achieved the first measure: *But he denied him, saying: Woman, I know him not.*[1] And what becomes of him? We find that having this reputation of ignorance, he did not enjoy its good fortune, but, rather, the affliction of being taken for wise. And why? There was no other motive but: *This man also was with him*[2] He was fond of wisdom, it filled His heart, He followed after it, He prided himself as a pursuer and lover of wisdom; and although He followed from so *afar off* that He neither understood nor achieved it, His love for it was sufficient that He incur its torments. And there was present that soldier to cause Him distress, and a certain maidservant to cause Him grief. I confess that I find myself very distant from the goals of wisdom, for all that I have desired to follow it, even from *afar off.* But in this I have been brought closer to the fire of persecution, to the

4. John 11.8–9. 5. John 10.1–31. 6. John 11.16. 7. John 10.32–33. 8. Luke 22.54. 9. Refers to Peter (Luke 9.33). 1. Luke 22.57. 2. A serving maid says this of Peter, who thereupon denies knowing Jesus (Luke 22.56).

crucible of torment, and to such lengths that they have asked that study be forbidden to me.

At one time this was achieved through the offices of a very saintly and ingenuous Abbess who believed that study was a thing of the Inquisition, who commanded me not to study. I obeyed her (the three some[3] months her power to command endured) in that I did not take up a book; but that I study not at all is not within my power to achieve, and this I could not obey, for though I did not study in books, I studied all the things that God had wrought, reading in them, as in writing and in books, all the workings of the universe. I looked on nothing without reflection; I heard nothing without meditation, even in the most minute and imperfect things; because as there is no creature, however lowly, in which one cannot recognize that *God made me*, there is none that does not astound reason, if properly meditated on. Thus, I reiterate, I saw and admired all things; so that even the very persons with whom I spoke, and the things they said, were cause for a thousand meditations. Whence the variety of genius and wit, being all of a single species? Which the temperaments and hidden qualities that occasioned such variety? If I saw a figure, I was forever combining the proportion of its lines and measuring it with my reason and reducing it to new proportions. Occasionally as I walked along the far wall of one of our dormitories (which is a most capacious room) I observed that though the lines of the two sides were parallel and the ceiling perfectly level, in my sight they were distorted, the lines seeming to incline toward one another, the ceiling seeming lower in the distance than in proximity: from which I inferred that *visual* lines run straight but not parallel, forming a pyramidal figure. I pondered whether this might not be the reason that caused the ancients to question whether the world were spherical. Because, although it so seems, this could be a deception of vision, suggesting concavities where possibly none existed.

This manner of reflection has always been my habit, and is quite beyond my will to control; on the contrary, I am wont to become vexed that my intellect makes me weary; and I believed that it was so with everyone, as well as making verses, until experience taught me otherwise; and it is so strong in me this nature, or custom, that I look at nothing without giving it further examination. Once in my presence two young girls were spinning a top and scarcely had I seen the motion and the figure described, when I began, out of this madness of mine, to meditate on the effortless *motus*[4] of the spherical form, and how the impulse persisted even when free and independent of its cause—for the top continued to dance even at some distance from the child's hand, which was the causal force. And not content with this, I had flour brought and sprinkled about, so that as the top danced one might learn whether these were perfect circles it described with its movement; and I found that they were not, but, rather, spiral lines that lost their circularity as the impetus declined. Other girls sat playing at spillikins[5] (surely the most frivolous game that children play); I walked closer to observe the figures they formed, and seeing that by chance three lay in a triangle, I set to joining one with another, recalling that this was said to be the form of the mysterious ring of Solomon,[6] in which he was able to see the distant splendor and images

---

3. I.e., "the three or so."   4. Motion.   5. Jackstraws, or pickup sticks.   6. It may, like Solomon's seal, have contained the image of the Star of David, composed of triangles.

of the Holy Trinity, by virtue of which the ring worked such prodigies and marvels. And the same shape was said to form David's harp, and that is why Saul was refreshed at its sound; and harps today largely conserve that shape.

And what shall I tell you, lady, of the natural secrets I have discovered while cooking? I see that an egg holds together and fries in butter or in oil, but, on the contrary, in syrup shrivels into shreds; observe that to keep sugar in a liquid state one need only add a drop or two of water in which a quince or other bitter fruit has been soaked; observe that the yolk and the white of one egg are so dissimilar that each with sugar produces a result not obtainable with both together. I do not wish to weary you with such inconsequential matters, and make mention of them only to give you full notice of my nature, for I believe they will be occasion for laughter. But, lady, as women, what wisdom may be ours if not the philosophies of the kitchen? Lupercio Leonardo[7] spoke well when he said: how well one may philosophize when preparing dinner. And I often say, when observing these trivial details: had Aristotle prepared victuals, he would have written more. And pursuing the manner of my cogitations, I tell you that this process is so continuous in me that I have no need for books. And on one occasion, when because of a grave upset of the stomach the physicians forbade me to study, I passed thus some days, but then I proposed that it would be less harmful if they allowed me books, because so vigorous and vehement were my cogitations that my spirit was consumed more greatly in a quarter of an hour than in four days' studying books. And thus they were persuaded to allow me to read. And moreover, lady, not even have my dreams been excluded from this ceaseless agitation of my imagination; indeed, in dreams it is wont to work more freely and less encumbered, collating with greater clarity and calm the gleanings of the day, arguing and making verses, of which I could offer you an extended catalogue, as well as of some arguments and inventions that I have better achieved sleeping than awake. I relinquish this subject in order not to tire you, for the above is sufficient to allow your discretion and acuity to penetrate perfectly and perceive my nature, as well as the beginnings, the methods, and the present state of my studies.

Even, lady, were these merits (and I see them celebrated as such in men), they would not have been so in me, for I cannot but study. If they are faults, then, for the same reasons, I believe I have none. Nevertheless, I live always with so little confidence in myself that neither in my study, nor in any other thing, do I trust my judgment; and thus I remit the decision to your sovereign genius, submitting myself to whatever sentence you may bestow, without controversy, without reluctance, for I have wished here only to present you with a simple narration of my inclination toward letters.

I confess, too, that though it is true, as I have stated, that I had no need of books, it is nonetheless also true that they have been no little inspiration, in divine as in human letters. Because I find a Debbora[8] administering the law, both military and political, and governing a people among whom there were many learned men. I find a most wise Queen of Saba,[9] so learned that she dares to challenge with hard questions the wisdom of the greatest of all wise men, without being reprimanded for doing so, but, rather, as a conse-

---

7. Lupercio Leonardo de Argensola (1559–1639), poet, playwright, and historian.   8. Or Deborah, a prophetess who judged the Israelites (Judges 4.4–14).   9. Or Sheba, who tested King Solomon with questions (1 Kings 10.1–3).

quence, to judge unbelievers. I see many and illustrious women; some blessed with the gift of prophecy, like Abigail, others of persuasion, like Esther; others with pity, like Rehab; others with perseverance, like Anna,[1] the mother of Samuel; and an infinite number of others, with divers gifts and virtues.

If I again turn to the Gentiles, the first I encounter are the Sibyls,[2] those women chosen by God to prophesy the principal mysteries of our Faith, and with learned and elegant verses that surpass admiration. I see adored as a goddess of the sciences a woman like Minerva,[3] the daughter of the first Jupiter and mistress over all the wisdom of Athens. I see a Polla Argentaria, who helped Lucan, her husband, write his epic *Pharsalia*.[4] I see the daughter of the divine Tiresias, more learned than her father. I see a Zenobia, Queen of the Palmyrans, as wise as she was valiant. An Arete, most learned daughter of Aristippus.[5] A Nicostrate,[6] framer of Latin verses and most erudite in Greek. An Aspasia Milesia, who taught philosophy and rhetoric, and who was a teacher of the philosopher Pericles. An Hypatia, who taught astrology, and studied many years in Alexandria. A Leontium, a Greek woman, who questioned the philosopher Theophrastus, and convinced him. A Julia, a Corinna, a Cornelia;[7] and, finally, a great throng of women deserving to be named, some as Greeks, some as muses, some as seers; for all were nothing more than learned women, held, and celebrated—and venerated as well—as such by antiquity. Without mentioning an infinity of other women whose names fill books. For example, I find the Egyptian Catherine,[8] studying and influencing the wisdom of all the wise men of Egypt. I see a Gertrudis[9] studying, writing, and teaching. And not to overlook examples close to home, I see my most holy mother Paula, learned in Hebrew, Greek, and Latin, and most able in interpreting the Scriptures. And what greater praise than, having as her chronicler a Jeronimus Maximus,[1] that Saint scarcely found himself competent for his task, and says, with that weighty deliberation and energetic precision with which he so well expressed himself: "If all the members of my body were tongues, they still would not be sufficient to proclaim the wisdom and virtue of Paula." Similarly praiseworthy was the widow Blesilla; also, the illustrious virgin Eustochium,[2] both daughters of this same saint; especially the second, who, for her knowledge, was called the Prodigy of the World. The Roman Fabiola[3] was most well-versed in the Holy Scripture. Proba Fal-

---

1. Or Hannah, who after years of childlessness received the answer to her prayers in the birth of Samuel (1 Samuel 1.1–20). Abigail was the wife of a surly husband, Nabal. After Nabal insulted King David, she went to the king with presents and prophesied his future triumphs, thus saving her husband's life (1 Samuel 25.2–35). Esther persuaded her husband, King Ahasuerus, to protect the Jews (Esther 5–9). Rehab, or Rahab, was a harlot who protected two Israelites from the King of Jericho (Joshua 2.1–7).   2. Female prophets of the ancient world.   3. Or Athena, goddess of wisdom.   4. Epic poem on the civil war between Caesar and Pompey, properly called *Bellum Civile* (ca. A.D. 62–65).   5. Greek philosopher (ca. 435–ca. 360 B.C.). Tiresias was a legendary blind Theban seer. His daughter was Manto, known for her skill in divination by fire. Zenobia, the learned widow of Odenathus, declared her independence from Rome and expanded the Middle-Eastern territory under her rule, naming herself Augusta, empress of Rome. She was finally defeated and captured in 272.   6. Or Carmentis, legendary daughter of Pallas, king of Arcadia, and (in legend) inventor of the Roman alphabet.   7. Noted for her devotion to her children's education after her husband's death (2nd century B.C.); she was the second daughter of Scipio Africanus and wife of Tiberius Sempronius Gracchus. Julia Domna (2nd century A.D.), wife of the Roman emperor Septimius Severus, known for her learning as Julia the Philosopher. Corinna (ca. 500? B.C.), a lyric poet of Tanagra who wrote for a group of women.   8. Saint Catherine (4th century?), allegedly so wise she could refute fifty philosophers at once.   9. Saint Gertrude (d. 1302), Benedictine nun and visionary, an important mystic.   1. Saint Jerome.   2. Blesilla and Eustochium were daughters of Saint Paula and, like her, were taught by Saint Jerome.   3. One of Jerome's disciples.

conia, a Roman woman, wrote elegant centos,[4] containing verses from Virgil, about the mysteries of Our Holy Faith. It is well-known by all that Queen Isabel,[5] wife of the tenth Alfonso, wrote about astrology. Many others I do not list, out of the desire not merely to transcribe what others have said (a vice I have always abominated); and many are flourishing today, as witness Christina Alexandra, Queen of Sweden,[6] as learned as she is valiant and magnanimous, and the Most Honorable Ladies, the Duquesa of Abeyro and the Condesa of Villaumbrosa.

The venerable Doctor Arce[7] (by his virtue and learning a worthy teacher of the Scriptures) in his scholarly *Bibliorum* raises this question: *Is it permissible for women to dedicate themselves to the study of the Holy Scriptures, and to their interpretation?* and he offers as negative arguments the opinions of many saints, especially that of the Apostle: *Let women keep silence in the churches; for it is not permitted them to speak,* etc.[8] He later cites other opinions and, from the same Apostle, verses from his letter to Titus: *The aged women in like manner, in holy attire . . . teaching well,*[9] with interpretations by the Holy Fathers. Finally he resolves, with all prudence, that teaching publicly from a University chair, or preaching from the pulpit, is not permissible for women; but that to study, write, and teach privately not only is permissible, but most advantageous and useful. It is evident that this is not to be the case with all women, but with those to whom God may have granted special virtue and prudence, and who may be well advanced in learning, and having the essential talent and requisites for such a sacred calling. This view is indeed just, so much so that not only women, who are held to be so inept, but also men, who merely for being men believe they are wise, should be prohibited from interpreting the Sacred Word if they are not learned and virtuous and of gentle and well-inclined natures; that this is not so has been, I believe, at the root of so much sectarianism and so many heresies. For there are many who study but are ignorant, especially those who are in spirit arrogant, troubled, and proud, so eager for new interpretations of the Word (which itself rejects new interpretations) that merely for the sake of saying what no one else has said they speak a heresy, and even then are not content. Of these the Holy Spirit says: *For wisdom will not enter into a malicious soul.*[1] To such as these more harm results from knowing than from ignorance. A wise man has said: he who does not know Latin is not a complete fool; but he who knows it is well qualified to be.[2] And I would add that a fool may reach perfection (if ignorance may tolerate perfection) by having studied his tittle of philosophy and theology and by having some learning of tongues, by which he may be a fool in many sciences and languages: a great fool cannot be contained solely in his mother tongue.

For such as these, I reiterate, study is harmful, because it is as if to place a sword in the hands of a madman; which, though a most noble instrument for defense, is in his hands his own death and that of many others. So were

---

4. Compositions made up of verses from other authors.   5. Of Spain, wife of Alfonso X, Alfonso the Wise (1221–1284).   6. She attracted many scholars and artists to her court (1626–1689).   7. Juan Díaz de Arce (1594–1653), author of theological books.   8. 1 Corinthians 14.34.   9. Titus 2.3–5. 1. Book of Wisdom 1.4 (in the Apocrypha).   2. Alludes to the Spanish proverb "A fool, unless he knows Latin, is never a great fool."

the Divine Scriptures in the possession of the evil Pelagius and the intractable Arius, of the evil Luther, and the other heresiarchs like our own Doctor (who was neither ours nor a doctor) Cazalla.[3] To these men, wisdom was harmful, although it is the greatest nourishment and the life of the soul; in the same way that in a stomach of sickly constitution and adulterated complexion, the finer the nourishment it receives, the more arid, fermented, and perverse are the humors it produces; thus these evil men: the more they study, the worse opinions they engender, their reason being obstructed with the very substance meant to nourish it, and they study much and digest little, exceeding the limits of the vessel of their reason. Of which the Apostle says: *For I say, by the grace that is given me, to all that are among you, not to be more wise than it behoveth to be wise, but to be wise unto sobriety, and according as God hath divided to every one the measure of faith.*[4] And in truth, the Apostle did not direct these words to women, but to men; and that *keep silence* is intended not only for women, but for *all* incompetents. If I desire to know as much, or more, than Aristotle or Saint Augustine, and if I have not the aptitude of Saint Augustine or Aristotle, though I study more than either, not only will I not achieve learning, but I will weaken and dull the workings of my feeble reason with the disproportionateness of the goal.

Oh, that each of us—I, being ignorant, the first—should take the measure of our talents before we study, or, more importantly, write, with the covetous ambition to equal and even surpass others, how little spirit we should have for it, and how many errors we should avoid, and how many tortured intellects of which we have experience, we should have had no experience! And I place my own ignorance in the forefront of all these, for if I knew all I should, I would not write. And I protest that I do so only to obey you; and with such apprehension that you owe me more that I have taken up my pen in fear than you would have owed had I presented you more perfect works. But it is well that they go to your correction. Cross them out, tear them up, reprove me, and I shall appreciate that more than all the vain applause others may offer. *That just men shall correct me in mercy, and shall reprove me; but let not the oil of the sinner fatten my head.*[5] And returning again to our Arce, I say that in affirmation of his opinion he cites the words of my father, Saint Jerome: *To Leta, Upon the Education of Her Daughter.* Where he says: *Accustom her tongue, still young, to the sweetness of the Psalms. Even the names through which little by little she will become accustomed to form her phrases should not be chosen by chance, but selected and repeated with care; the prophets must be included, of course, and the apostles, as well, and all the Patriarchs beginning with Adam and down to Matthew and Luke, so that as she practices other things she will be readying her memory for the future. Let your daily task be taken from the flower of the Scriptures.* And if this Saint desired that a young girl scarcely beginning to talk be educated in this fashion, what would he desire for his nuns and his spiritual daughters? These beliefs are illustrated in the examples of the previously mentioned Eustochium and Fabiola, and Marcella, her sister, and Pacatula, and others whom the Saint honors

---

3. Augustino Cazallo (1510–1559), Spanish Protestant executed by the Inquisition for promulgating Lutheran doctrine. Pelagius was a heretical monk (ca. 355–ca. 425) who taught that people do not need divine grace because they have a natural tendency to seek the good. Arius was a Libyan theologian (ca. 256–336), founder of the Arian heresy that declared that Christ was neither eternal nor equal with God. Martin Luther (1483–1546), was the German leader of the Protestant Reformation and, from Sister Juana's point of view, another heretic. **4.** Romans 12.3. **5.** Psalm 141.5.

in his epistles, exhorting them to this sacred exercise, as they are recognized in the epistle I cited, *Let your daily task* . . . which is affirmation of and agreement with the *aged women . . . teaching well* of Saint Paul. My illustrious Father's *Let your daily task* . . . makes clear that the teacher of the child is to be Leta herself, the child's mother.

Oh, how much injury might have been avoided in our land if our aged women had been learned, as was Leta, and had they known how to instruct as directed by Saint Paul and by my Father, Saint Jerome. And failing this, and because of the considerable idleness to which our poor women have been relegated, if a father desires to provide his daughters with more than ordinary learning, he is forced by necessity, and by the absence of wise elder women, to bring men to teach the skills of reading, writing, counting, the playing of musical instruments, and other accomplishments, from which no little harm results, as is experienced every day in doleful examples of perilous association, because through the immediacy of contact and the intimacy born from the passage of time, what one may never have thought possible is easily accomplished. For which reason many prefer to leave their daughters unpolished and uncultured rather than to expose them to such notorious peril as that of familiarity with men, which quandary could be prevented if there were learned elder women, as Saint Paul wished to see, and if the teaching were handed down from one to another, as is the custom with domestic crafts and all other traditional skills.

For what objection can there be that an older woman, learned in letters and in sacred conversation and customs, have in her charge the education of young girls? This would prevent these girls being lost either for lack of instruction or for hesitating to offer instruction through such dangerous means as male teachers, for even when there is no greater risk of indecency than to seat beside a modest woman (who still may blush when her own father looks directly at her) a strange man who treats her as if he were a member of the household and with the authority of an intimate, the modesty demanded in interchange with men, and in conversation with them, is sufficient reason that such an arrangement not be permitted. For I do not find that the custom of men teaching women is without its peril, lest it be in the severe tribunal of the confessional, or from the remote decency of the pulpit, or in the distant learning of books—never in the personal contact of immediacy. And the world knows this is true; and, notwithstanding, it is permitted solely from the want of learned elder women. Then is it not detrimental, the lack of such women? This question should be addressed by those who, bound to that *Let women keep silence in the church,* say that it is blasphemy for women to learn and teach, as if it were not the Apostle himself who said: *The aged women . . . teaching well.* As well as the fact that this prohibition touches upon historical fact as reported by Eusebium:[6] which is that in the early Church, women were charged with teaching the doctrine to one another in the temples and the sound of this teaching caused confusion as the Apostles were preaching and this is the reason they were ordered to be silent; and even today, while the homilist is preaching, one does not pray aloud.

Who will argue that for the comprehension of many Scriptures one must

6. Probably Eusebius of Caesaria (ca. 263–339?), an early Church historian.

be familiar with the history, customs, ceremonies, proverbs, and even the manners of speaking of those times in which they were written, if one is to apprehend the references and allusions of more than a few passages of the Holy Word. *And rend your heart and not your garments.*[7] Is this not a reference to the ceremony in which Hebrews rent their garments as a sign of grief, as did the evil pontiff when he said that Christ had blasphemed? In many scriptures the Apostle writes of succour for widows; did they not refer to the customs of those times? Does not the example of the valiant woman, *Her husband is honourable in the gates,*[8] allude to the fact that the tribunals of the judges were at the gates of the cities? That *Dare terram Deo,* give of your land to God, did that not mean to make some votive offering? And did they not call the public sinners *hiemantes,* those who endure the winter, because they made their penance in the open air instead of at a town gate as others did? And Christ's plaint to that Pharisee who had neither kissed him nor given him water for his feet,[9] was that not because it was the Jews' usual custom to offer these acts of hospitality? And we find an infinite number of additional instances not only in the Divine Letters, but human, as well, such as *adorate purpuram,* venerate the purple, which meant obey the King; *manumittere eum,* manumit them, alluding to the custom and ceremony of striking the slave with one's hand to signify his freedom. That *intonuit coelum,* heaven thundered, in Virgil, which alludes to the augury of thunder from the west, which was held to be good.[1] Martial's *tu nunquam leporem edisti,*[2] you never ate hare, has not only the wit of ambiguity in its *leporem,*[3] but, as well, the allusion to the reputed propensity of hares [to bless with beauty those who dine on them]. That proverb, *maleam legens, que sunt domi obliviscere,* to sail along the shore of Malia is to forget what one has at home, alludes to the great peril of the promontory of Laconia.[4] That chaste matron's response to the unwanted suit of her pretender: "the hinge-pins shall not be oiled for my sake, nor shall the torches blaze," meaning that she did not want to marry, alluded to the ceremony of anointing the doorways with oils and lighting the nuptial torches in the wedding ceremony, as if now we would say, they shall not prepare the thirteen coins for my dowry, nor shall the priest invoke the blessing. And thus it is with many comments of Virgil and Homer and all the poets and orators. In addition, how many are the difficulties found even in the grammar of the Holy Scripture, such as writing a plural for a singular, or changing from the second to third persons, as in the Psalms, *Let him kiss me with the kiss of his mouth, for thy breasts are better than wine.*[5] Or placing adjectives in the genitive instead of the accusative, as in *Calicem salutaris accipiam,* I will take the chalice of salvation.[6] Or to replace the feminine with the masculine, and, in contrast, to call any sin adultery.

All this demands more investigation than some believe, who strictly as grammarians, or, at most, employing the four principles of applied logic, attempt to interpret the Scriptures while clinging to that *Let the women keep silence in the church,* not knowing how it is to be interpreted. As well as that

7. Joel 2.13. 8. Proverbs 31.23. 9. Luke 7.44–45. 1. Sister Juana possibly misremembers *Aeneid* 2.693: "thunder on the left." 2. Marcus Valerius Martialis (ca. 40–ca. 104), Roman epigrammatic poet; "Edisti numquam, Gellia, tu leporem" (*Epigrams* 5.29). 3. This word can also mean charm, grace, attractiveness. 4. The site of ancient Sparta, conquered by Macedonia in the 4th century B.C. 5. Song of Solomon 1.2. 6. Psalm 116.13.

other verse, *Let the women learn in silence*.[7] For this latter scripture works more to women's favor than their disfavor, as it commands them to learn; and it is only natural that they must maintain silence while they learn. And it is also written, *Hear, oh Israel, and be silent*.[8] Which addresses the entire congregation of men and women, commanding all to silence, because if one is to hear and learn, it is with good reason that he attend and be silent. And if it is not so, I would want these interpreters and expositors of Saint Paul to explain to me how they interpret that scripture, *Let the women keep silence in the church*. For either they must understand it to refer to the material church, that is the church of pulpits and cathedras,[9] or to the spiritual, the community of the faithful, which is the Church. If they understand it to be the former, which, in my opinion, is its true interpretation, then we see that if in fact it is not permitted of women to read publicly in church, nor preach, why do they censure those who study privately? And if they understand the latter, and wish that the prohibition of the Apostle be applied transcendentally—that not even in private are women to be permitted to write or study— how are we to view the fact that the Church permitted a Gertrudis, a Santa Teresa, a Saint Birgitta, the Nun of Agreda,[1] and so many others, to write? And if they say to me that these women were saints, they speak the truth; but this poses no obstacle to my argument. First, because Saint Paul's proposition is absolute, and encompasses all women not excepting saints, as Martha and Mary, Marcella, Mary, mother of Jacob, and Salome,[2] all were in their time, and many other zealous women of the early church. But we see, too, that the Church allows women who are not saints to write, for the Nun of Agreda and Sor María de la Antigua[3] are not canonized, yet their writings are circulated. And when Santa Teresa and the others were writing, they were not as yet canonized. In which case, Saint Paul's prohibition was directed solely to the public office of the pulpit, for if the Apostle had forbidden women to write, the Church would not have allowed it. Now I do not make so bold as to teach—which in me would be excessively presumptuous— and as for writing, that requires a greater talent than mine, and serious reflection. As Saint Cyprian[4] says: *The things we write require most conscientious consideration*. I have desired to study that I might be ignorant of less; for (according to Saint Augustine[5]) some things are learned to be enacted and others only to be known: *We learn some things to know them, others, to do them*. Then, where is the offense to be found if even what is licit to women—which is to teach by writing—I do not perform, as I know that I am lacking in means, following the counsel of Quintilian: *Let each person learn not only from the precepts of others, but also let him reap counsel from his own nature*.

If the offense is to be found in the *Atenagórica* letter, was that letter anything other than the simple expression of my feeling, written with the implicit

7. 1 Timothy 2.11.   8. Not a biblical quotation.   9. A cathedra is the throne of the bishop in his church.   1. Maria de Agreda (1602–1635), Spanish Franciscan nun, author of *The Mystic City of God* (1670), a work allegedly divinely inspired. Birgitta, or Bridget (1303–1373), of Sweden.   2. In the King James Bible, Mary, the mother of James (or Jacob), and Salome came to the empty sepulcher to anoint Jesus' body (Mark 16.1). Martha and Mary were sisters. Mary anointed Jesus' feet (John 12.3). Martha was preoccupied with household tasks (Luke 10.40–42). Marcella was one of the women taught by Jerome.   3. Spanish nun (1544–1617).   4. Thascius Caecilius Cyprianus (ca. 200–258), one of the Church fathers, known for his efforts to enforce Church discipline.   5. Aurelius Augustinus (354–430), baptized by Saint Ambrose in 387, author of *De Civitate Dei*, a vindication of the Church that long possessed great authority.

permission of our Holy Mother Church? For if the Church, in her most sacred authority, does not forbid it, why must others do so? That I proffered an opinion contrary to that of de Vieyra was audacious, but, as a Father, was it not audacious that he speak against the three Holy Fathers of the Church? My reason, such as it is, is it not as unfettered as his, as both issue from the same source? Is his opinion to be considered as a revelation, as a principle of the Holy Faith, that we must accept blindly? Furthermore, I maintained at all times the respect due such a virtuous man, a respect in which his defender was sadly wanting, ignoring the phrase of Titus Lucius:[6] *Respect is companion to the arts*. I did not touch a thread of the robes of the Society of Jesus; nor did I write for other than the consideration of the person who suggested that I write. And, according to Pliny, *how different the condition of one who writes from that of one who merely speaks*. Had I believed the letter was to be published I would not have been so inattentive. If, as the censor says, the letter is heretical, why does he not denounce it? And with that he would be avenged, and I content, for, which is only seemly, I esteem more highly my reputation as a Catholic and obedient daughter of the Holy Mother Church than all the approbation due a learned woman. If the letter is rash, and he does well to criticize it, then laugh, even if with the laugh of the rabbit, for I have not asked that he approve; as I was free to dissent from de Vieyra, so will anyone be free to oppose my opinion.

But how I have strayed, lady. None of this pertains here, nor is it intended for your ears, but as I was discussing my accusers I remembered the words of one that recently have appeared, and, though my intent was to speak in general, my pen, unbidden, slipped, and began to respond in particular. And so, returning to our Arce, he says that he knew in this city two nuns: one in the Convent of the Regina, who had so thoroughly committed the Breviary to memory that with the greatest promptitude and propriety she applied in her conversation its verses, psalms, and maxims of saintly homilies. The other, in the Convent of the Conception, was so accustomed to reading the Epistles of my Father Saint Jerome, and the Locutions of this Saint, that Arce says, *It seemed I was listening to Saint Jerome himself, speaking in Spanish*. And of this latter woman he says that after her death he learned that she had translated these Epistles into the Spanish language. What pity that such talents could not have been employed in major studies with scientific principles. He does not give the name of either, although he offers these women as confirmation of his opinion, which is that not only is it licit, but most useful and essential for women to study the Holy Word, and even more essential for nuns; and that study is the very thing to which your wisdom exhorts me, and in which so many arguments concur.

Then if I turn my eyes to the oft-chastized faculty of making verses—which is in me so natural that I must discipline myself that even this letter not be written in that form—I might cite those lines, *All I wished to express took the form of verse*.[7] And seeing that so many condemn and criticize this ability, I have conscientiously sought to find what harm may be in it, and I have not found it, but, rather, I see verse acclaimed in the mouths of the Sibyls; sanctified in the pens of the Prophets, especially King David, of whom the

6. Better known as Saturantius Apuleius (2nd century A.D.), greatly celebrated in his time for eloquence.
7. Ovid's *Tristia* 4.10.25ff.

exalted Expositor my beloved Father[8] says (explicating the measure of his meters): *in the manner of Horace and Pindar, now it hurries along in iambs, now it rings in alcaic, now swells in sapphic, then arrives in broken feet.* The greater part of the Holy Books are in meter, as is the Book of Moses; and those of Job (as Saint Isidore[9] states in his *Etymologiae*) are in heroic verse. Solomon wrote the Canticle of Canticles in verse; and Jeremias, his *Lamentations.* And so, says Cassiodorus:[1] *All poetic expression had as its source the Holy Scriptures.* For not only does our Catholic Church not disdain verse, it employs verse in its hymns, and recites the lines of Saint Ambrose,[2] Saint Thomas, Saint Isidore, and others. Saint Bonaventure[3] was so taken with verse that he writes scarcely a page where it does not appear. It is readily apparent that Saint Paul had studied verse, for he quotes and translates verses of Aratus: *For in him we live, and move, and are.*[4] And he quotes also that verse of Parmenides: *The Cretians are always liars, evil beasts, slothful bellies.*[5] Saint Gregory Nazianzen[6] argues in elegant verses the questions of matrimony and virginity. And, how should I tire? The Queen of Wisdom, Our Lady, with Her sacred lips, intoned the Canticle of the Magnificat;[7] and having brought forth this example, it would be offensive to add others that were profane, even those of the most serious and learned men, for this alone is more than sufficient confirmation; and even though Hebrew elegance could not be compressed into Latin measure, for which reason, although the sacred translator, more attentive to the importance of the meaning, omitted the verse, the Psalms retain the number and divisions of verses, and what harm is to be found in them? For misuse is not the blame of art, but rather of the evil teacher who perverts the arts, making of them the snare of the devil; and this occurs in all the arts and sciences.

And if the evil is attributed to the fact that a woman employs them, we have seen how many have done so in praiseworthy fashion; what then is the evil in my being a woman? I confess openly my own baseness and meanness; but I judge that no couplet of mine has been deemed indecent. Furthermore, I have never written of my own will, but under the pleas and injunctions of others; to such a degree that the only piece I remember having written for my own pleasure was a little trifle they called *El sueño.*[8] That letter, lady, which you so greatly honored, I wrote more with repugnance than any other emotion; both by reason of the fact that it treated sacred matters, for which (as I have stated) I hold such reverent awe, and because it seems to wish to impugn, a practice for which I have natural aversion; and I believe that had I foreseen the blessed destiny to which it was fated—for like a second Moses I had set it adrift, naked, on the waters of the Nile of silence, where you, a princess, found and cherished it[9]—I believe, I reiterate, that had I known, the very hands of which it was born would have drowned it, out of the fear that these clumsy scribblings from my ignorance appear before the light of

---

8. Jerome.   9. Spanish archbishop (ca. 560–636), who helped organize the Church in Spain. 1. Flavius Magnus Aurelius Cassiodorus (ca. 485–ca. 580), Roman monk and author of *Institutiones,* a course of studies for monks.   2. Bishop of Milan (339–397), who had an important share in the conversion of St. Augustine.   3. Franciscan bishop and cardinal (1221–1274), who preached the importance of study.   4. Acts 17.28.   5. Titus 1.12.   6. Gregorius Nazianzenus, bishop of Constantinople and associate of Jerome. The allusion is to the first of his forty moral poems, 732 lines eulogizing virginity. 7. Luke 1.46–55.   8. *The Dream,* one of Sister Juana's best-known poems, which tells of the flight of her soul toward learning.   9. Because Pharaoh had ordered all male Hebrew infants killed, Moses' mother placed him in a basket by the Nile, where he was found and rescued by Pharaoh's daughter (Exodus 2.1–10).

your great wisdom; by which one knows the munificence of your kindness, for your goodwill applauds precisely what your reason must wish to reject. For as fate cast it before your doors, so exposed, so orphaned, that it fell to you even to give it a name, I must lament that among other deformities it also bears the blemish of haste; both because of the unrelenting ill-health I suffer, and for the profusion of duties imposed on me by obedience, as well as the want of anyone to guide me in my writing and the need that it all come from my hand, and, finally, because the writing went against my nature and I wished only to keep my promise to one whom I could not disobey, I could not find the time to finish properly, and thus I failed to include whole treatises and many arguments that presented themselves to me, but which I omitted in order to put an end to the writing—many, that had I known the letter was to be printed, I would not have excluded, even if merely to satisfy some objections that have since arisen and which could have been refuted. But I shall not be so ill-mannered as to place such indecent objects before the purity of your eyes, for it is enough that my ignorance be an offense in your sight, without need of entrusting to it the effronteries of others. If they should wing your way (and they are of such little weight that this will happen), then you will command what I am to do; for, if it does not run contrary to your will, my defense shall be not to take up my pen, for I deem that one affront need not occasion another, if one recognizes the error in the very place it lies concealed. As my Father Saint Jerome says, *good discourse seeks not things,* and Saint Ambrose, *it is the nature of a guilty conscience to lie concealed.* Nor do I consider that I have been impugned, for one statute of the Law states: *An accusation will not endure unless nurtured by the person who brought it forth.* What *is* a matter to be weighed is the effort spent in copying the accusation. A strange madness, to expend more effort in denying acclaim than in earning it! I, lady, have chosen not to respond (although others did so without my knowledge); it suffices that I have seen certain treatises, among them one so learned I send it to you so that reading it will compensate in part for the time you squandered on my writing. If, lady, you wish that I act contrary to what I have proposed here for your judgment and opinion, the merest indication of your desire will, as is seemly, countermand my inclination, which, as I have told you, is to be silent, for although Saint John Chrysostom[1] says, *those who slander must be refuted, and those who question, taught,* I know also that Saint Gregory[2] says, *It is no less a victory to tolerate enemies than to overcome them.* And that patience conquers by tolerating and triumphs by suffering. And if among the Roman Gentiles it was the custom when their captains were at the highest peak of glory—when returning triumphant from other nations, robed in purple and wreathed with laurel, crowned-but-conquered kings pulling their carriages in the stead of beasts, accompanied by the spoils of the riches of all the world, the conquering troops adorned with the insignia of their heroic feats, hearing the plaudits of the people who showered them with titles of honor and renown such as Fathers of the Nation, Columns of the Empire, Walls of Rome, Shelter of the Republic, and other glorious names—a soldier went before these captains in this moment of the supreme apogee of glory and human

---

1. Syrian prelate (ca. 347–407), known as the greatest orator of the Church, author of many homilies and treatises.   2. Gregory the Great (ca. 540–604), pope from 590, deeply concerned with the reformation of the Church.

happiness crying out in a loud voice to the conqueror (by his consent and order of the Senate): Behold how you are mortal; behold how you have this or that defect, not excepting the most shameful, as happened in the triumph of Caesar, when the vilest soldiers clamored in his ear: *Beware, Romans, for we bring you the bald adulterer*. Which was done so that in the midst of such honor the conquerers not be swelled up with pride, and that the ballast of these insults act as counterweight to the bellying sails of such approbation, and that the ship of good judgment not founder amidst the winds of acclamation. If this, I say, was the practice among Gentiles, who knew only the light of Natural Law, how much might we Catholics, under the injunction to love our enemies, achieve by tolerating them? And in my own behalf I can attest that calumny has often mortified me, but never harmed me, being that I hold as a great fool one who having occasion to receive credit suffers the difficulty and loses the credit, as it is with those who do not resign themselves to death, but, in the end, die anyway, their resistance not having prevented death, but merely deprived them of the credit of resignation and caused them to die badly when they might have died well. And thus, lady, I believe these experiences do more good than harm, and I hold as greater the jeopardy of applause to human weakness, as we are wont to appropriate praise that is not our own, and must be ever watchful, and carry graven on our hearts those words of the Apostle: *Or what hast thou that thou hast not received? And if thou hast received, why doest thou glory as if thou hadst not received it?*[3] so that these words serve as a shield to fend off the sharp barbs of commendations, which are as spears which when not attributed to God (whose they are), claim our lives and cause us to be thieves of God's honor and usurpers of the talents He bestowed on us and the gifts that He lent to us, for which we must give the most strict accounting. And thus, lady, I fear applause more than calumny, because the latter, with but the simple act of patience becomes gain, while the former requires many acts of reflection and humility and proper recognition so that it not become harm. And I know and recognize that it is by special favor of God that I know this, as it enables me in either instance to act in accord with the words of Saint Augustine: *One must believe neither the friend who praises nor the enemy who detracts.* Although most often I squander God's favor, or vitiate with such defects and imperfections that I spoil what, being His, was good. And thus in what little of mine that has been printed, neither the use of my name, nor even consent for the printing, was given by my own counsel, but by the license of another who lies outside my domain, as was also true with the printing of the *Atenagórica* letter, and only a few *Exercises of the Incarnation* and *Offerings of the Sorrow* were printed for public devotions with my pleasure, but without my name; of which I am sending some few copies that (if you so desire) you may distribute them among our sisters, the nuns of that holy community, as well as in that city. I send but one copy of the *Sorrows* because the others have been exhausted and I could find no other copy. I wrote them long ago, solely for the devotions of my sisters, and later they were spread abroad; and their contents are disproportionate as regards my unworthiness and my ignorance, and they profited that they touched on matters of our exalted Queen; for I cannot explain what it is that inflames the coldest heart when one refers to

3. Corinthians 11.4.

the Most Holy Mary. It is my only desire, esteemed lady, to remit to you works worthy of your virtue and wisdom; as the poet said: *Though strength may falter, good will must be praised. In this, I believe, the gods will be content.*

If ever I write again, my scribbling will always find its way to the haven of your holy feet and the certainty of your correction, for I have no other jewel with which to pay you, and, in the lament of Seneca, he who has once bestowed benefices has committed himself to continue; and so you must be repaid out of your own munificence, for only in this way shall I with dignity be freed from debt and avoid that the words of that same Seneca come to pass: *It is contemptible to be surpassed in benefices.*[4] For in his gallantry the generous creditor gives to the poor debtor the means to satisfy his debt. So God gave his gift to a world unable to repay Him: He gave his son that He be offered a recompense worthy of Him.

If, most venerable lady, the tone of this letter may not have seemed right and proper, I ask forgiveness for its homely familiarity, and the less than seemly respect in which by treating you as a nun, one of my sisters, I have lost sight of the remoteness of your most illustrious person; which, had I seen you without your veil, would never have occurred; but you in all your prudence and mercy will supplement or amend the language, and if you find unsuitable the *Vos* of the address I have employed, believing that for the reverence I owe you, Your Reverence seemed little reverent, modify it in whatever manner seems appropriate to your due, for I have not dared exceed the limits of your custom, nor transgress the boundary of your modesty.

And hold me in your grace, and entreat for me divine grace, of which the Lord God grant you large measure, and keep you, as I pray Him, and am needful. From this convent of our Father Saint Jerome in Mexico City, the first day of the month of March of sixteen hundred and ninety-one. Allow me to kiss your hand, your most favored

JUANA INÉS DE LA CRUZ

4. *On Benefits* 5.2.1.

JONATHAN SWIFT
1667–1745

In virtually all his writing, Jonathan Swift displays his gift for making other people uncomfortable. He makes us uneasy by making us aware of our own moral inadequacies; and by his wit, energy, and inventiveness, he actually compels us to enjoy the process of being brought to such awareness.

Born in Dublin to English parents, Swift was educated at Trinity College, Dublin. In 1689, the young man went to England, where he served as secretary to the statesman Sir William Temple. During his residence at Moor Park, Sir William's estate, Swift became friendly with Esther Johnson, daughter of the steward there; he remained on close terms with her for the rest of his life. (His playful, intimate letters to her—he used the name "Stella"—were published in a collection called *Journal to Stella*.) In 1692, Swift received an M.A. from Oxford University; three years later, he took orders, becoming a clergyman in the Anglican Church but continuing in Sir

William's employ, although with intermittent stays in Ireland. Early in the eighteenth century, he began his career of political journalism; he also published brilliant satiric works, including *A Tale of a Tub* (1704), of which he is supposed to have said, late in his life, "What a genius I had when I composed that book!" Although he had hoped for church advancement in England, as a reward for his writings in the Tory cause, in 1713 he was instead named dean of St. Patrick's Cathedral, Dublin. He spent the rest of his life in Ireland (save for two brief visits to friends in England) writing passionately on behalf of the oppressed Irish people. In his final years, he was declared mentally incompetent, suffering, presumably, from senility. As he had prophesied in his verses *On the Death of Dr. Swift*, "He gave what little wealth he had / To build a house for fools and mad"; the mental hospital founded by his legacy still exists in Dublin.

For *Gulliver's Travels* (1726) Swift used the travel book, a form hovering between fact and fiction, as his model. Lemuel Gulliver, ship's surgeon, travels into four imagined nations. The first book takes him to Lilliput, where he duly observes the customs and traditions of a race of people six inches high. The narrative of their preoccupations and procedures mocks the pettiness of the English, although Gulliver, himself involved in the intrigues of his tiny hosts, fails to note the resemblance between Lilliput and his native land. His simple patriotism survives through the second book, where Gulliver encounters the giants of Brobdingnag, whose benevolent king, after hearing Gulliver's patriotic account of England, comments, "I cannot but conclude the bulk of your natives, to be the most pernicious race of little odious vermin that nature ever suffered to crawl upon the surface of the earth." The third book is more various, and Gulliver on the whole seems less gullible in his encounters with the ludicrous or dangerous results of abstract speculation divorced from practical concerns (philosophers, for instance, so deep in ratiocination that they have to be attended by "flappers," servants who "flap" them into awareness of immediate actuality), with the ghosts of great men from the past who stress the lies of historians and the moral and physical decline of their descendants, and with the terrifying Struldbrugs, who grow old but live forever in horrible senility.

Part IV, printed here, has always presented problems to critics. More directly than any other imaginative work of its period, it confronts problems inherent in the idealization of reason as sufficient guide to human conduct. It is easy enough to see that Swift has here imagined an absolute separation between the animal and the rational aspects of human nature. As Gulliver gradually and with horror realizes (the reader undergoing a comparable process), the disgusting Yahoos manifest degraded human form and embody characteristics of human beings deprived of all rational capacity. They act on the basis of pure—and ugly—passion: lust, envy, avarice, greed, rage. The Houyhnhnms, the governing class of horses, treat them as beasts, but consider them more ungovernable than other creatures; Gulliver, looking at them, sees a horrifying version of the human, become (by the absence of reason) subhuman.

As for the Houyhnhnms, those noble horses exemplify pure rationality. They lead monotonous, orderly lives, with no need for disagreement (the truth being self-evident to rational creatures) or excitement. Under their influence, Gulliver wants to stay forever in this land without literal or metaphorical salt. After the Houyhnhnms expel him, Gulliver can make no distinction among human beings: he condemns the benevolent Pedro Mendez as a Yahoo, resents his connection with his own wife and children, and spends as much time as possible in his stable. Life with the Houyhnhnms has driven him mad: he cannot adjust to English actuality.

The question is, Why? By one interpretation, Gulliver judges rightly in perceiving his fellow human beings as essentially Yahoos. His Houyhnhnm master concludes, Gulliver says, that humans are "a sort of animals to whose share . . . some small pittance of reason had fallen, whereof we made no other use than by its assistance to aggravate our natural corruptions, and to acquire new ones which nature had not given us." Perhaps he is right. The Houyhnhnms exemplify an ideal to which human beings should aspire, although they can never reach it; to call attention to the monotony of their lives or the failure of their curiosity only reveals the reader's participation in human depravity. Pedro Mendez is a good man, as men go, but the gulf between the best of humans and a Houyhnhnm gapes so hugely that Gulliver sees correctly in detesting all humans. If he implicitly excepts himself, he thus acknowledges the difference his education by Houyhnhnms has made: at least he knows the gulf's existence.

Another view has it that the Houyhnhnms exemplify a way of being utterly irrelevant to humankind, as well as deeply boring. To hate the animal and glorify the rational denies the inextricable mixture of our nature. Gulliver's pride leads him to aspire to an essentially inhuman state; he wishes, sinfully, to exceed ordained natural limits. Moreover, he ignores the Christian virtue of charity, the command to love one's neighbors. Captain Mendez demonstrates that virtue; Gulliver cannot perceive the moral distinction between the generous captain and the bloodthirsty natives who shoot the Englishman with an arrow shortly after he leaves the Houyhnhnms, producing a lasting scar. Gulliver's condemnation of pride in others emphasizes his blindness to his own flaws.

A compromise position might remind us that to declare the Houyhnhnms irrelevant perhaps leaves the reader in rather too comfortable a position, considering Swift's declared intention "to vex the world rather than divert it." Gulliver's Travels, this comment implies, involves serious attack. We can perhaps dismiss the Houyhnhnms as boring (they have virtually nothing to talk about) or heartless (they make no distinctions of parentage; they expel Gulliver despite his ardent desire to remain) because our natures include more than reason and we appropriately value principles of conduct beyond the rational. Gulliver becomes crazy when he returns to England, unable to accept his full human nature and to make necessary distinctions; given the limits of the human condition, men and women must find the way to operate within them. Gulliver fails and, failing, reminds us of necessities to which we must adapt. The Houyhnhnms provide no solution to human problems: their extirpation of passion, their narrow commitment to reason, prove "inhumane." (They are, after all, horses!) Humankind, as Swift suggested in a letter, is only capable of reason, not fully reasonable; perhaps the spontaneous generosity of the Portuguese captain exemplifies the greatest good to which human beings should aspire.

On the other hand, we claim to value reason; Gulliver has seen in pure form an ideal to which we pay lip service. His realization of the terrible discrepancy between ideal and actual has made it impossible for him to function in his own society. It has given him a harsh perspective by which he sees how morally intolerable social arrangements in fact are. The readiness of most people to compromise, given social necessity, shows how far they are from taking seriously the values they profess. Swift calls our attention to the divergences in our own lives between what we say we believe and how we actually behave. The reality of reason exceeds human capacities; Gulliver's Travels reminds us that we live by hypocrisies. The Houyhnhnms thus tell us something about ourselves despite their lack of humanity.

The problems in interpretation that Gulliver's Travels has always generated come partly from the fact that we receive all information about Gulliver's experience from the traveler himself, an untrustworthy source. In reading his narrative, we must assess his understanding—a slippery process, since we lack a point of reference. Gulliver's Travels abounds in allusions to such phenomena as corrupt lawyers and politicians, avaricious doctors, mass slaughter in wars over trivial pretexts—aspects of our experience and of Gulliver's and reminders that this narrative has something to do with us. The necessity of arriving at a coherent judgment of Gulliver and his experiences implicates the reader in the moral problem of how to judge—and perhaps how to change—society.

Such implication of the reader in often uncomfortable processes of judgment typifies an important aspect of satire. A Modest Proposal (1729), Swift's attack on the economic oppression of the Irish by the English, keeps the reader constantly off balance, trying to understand exactly who is being criticized and why. Swift is writing out of his firsthand awareness of the suffering caused by English policies in Ireland. Absentee landlords who never saw the actual situation of their tenants, British politicians who made policy at a distance, presumably did not know that Ireland had become a land of the starving. In Swift's view, however, the Irish people collaborated by their apathy with the oppressors. In *A Modest Proposal,* he attacks English and Irish alike.

Even more emphatically than Gulliver, the nameless speaker in *A Modest Proposal* proves an undependable guide, tempting us to identify with his tone of rationality and compassion, only to reveal that his plausible economic orientation leads to advocacy of cannibalism. He offers a series of morally sound and economically feasible suggestions for solutions to Ireland's problems, but draws back immediately, declaring them impossible, since no one will put them in practice. The satire indicts the English for inhumanity, the Irish for passivity, and the economically oriented proposer of remedies for moral blindness. But it also reaches out to criticize the reader as representative of all who endure calmly the intolerable actuality in the world (but not, perhaps, where we have to see it ourselves) of our own inhumanity to our fellow human beings. Swift's self-chosen epitaph, on his tomb, may be translated, "Where fierce indignation no longer tears the heart." *A Modest Proposal* exemplifies the lacerating power of that indignation.

A good introduction to Swift's life and character is I. Ehrenpreis, *The Personality of Jonathan Swift* (1958). For a more recent biography see J. McMinn, *Jonathan Swift: A Literary Life* (1991). An interpretation of the writer in his intellectual context is K. Williams, *Jonathan Swift and the Age of Compromise* (1959). E. Zimmerman, *Swift's Narrative Satires: Author and Authority* (1983), provides acute interpretation of the prose satires. Useful and varied collections of essays about Swift include C. Probyn, ed., *Jonathan Swift: The Contemporary Background* (1978); C. Rawson, ed., *The Art of Swift's Satire: A Revised Focus* (1983); C. Rawson, ed., *Swift: A Collection of Critical Essays* (1994); and Harold Bloom, ed., *Jonathan Swift's Gulliver's Travels* (1986). Specialized but illuminating analyses include J. McMinn and others, *Jonathan's Travels: Swift and Ireland* (1994), and C. Fabricant, *Swift's Landscape* (1995).

PRONOUNCING GLOSSARY

The following list uses common English syllables and stress accents to provide rough equivalents of selected words whose pronunciation may be unfamiliar to the general reader.

Brobdingnag: *brahb'-ding-nag*   Lilliput: *lil-ee-put*

Houyhnhnm: *whin'-im*   Psalmanazar: *sahl-mahn'-ah-zahr*

From Gulliver's Travels[1]

A Letter from Captain Gulliver to His Cousin Sympson[2]

I hope you will be ready to own publicly, whenever you shall be called to it, that by your great and frequent urgency you prevailed on me to publish a very loose and uncorrect account of my travels; with direction to hire some young gentlemen of either University to put them in order, and correct the

---

1. Swift's full title for this work was *Travels into Several Remote Nations of the World. In Four Parts. By Lemuel Gulliver, First a Surgeon, and then a Captain of several Ships.* The text is based on the Dublin edition of Swift's work (1735).   2. In this letter, first published in 1735, Swift complains, among other matters, of the alterations in his original text made by the publisher, Benjamin Motte, in the interest of what he considered political discretion.

style, as my Cousin Dampier[3] did by my advice, in his book called *A Voyage round the World*. But I do not remember I gave you power to consent that anything should be omitted, and much less that anything should be inserted: therefore, as to the latter, I do here renounce everything of that kind; particularly a paragraph about her Majesty the late Queen Anne, of most pious and glorious memory; although I did reverence and esteem her more than any of human species. But you, or your interpolator, ought to have considered that as it was not my inclination, so was it not decent to praise any animal of our composition before my master Houyhnhnm; and besides, the fact was altogether false; for to my knowledge, being in England during some part of her Majesty's reign, she did govern by a chief Minister; nay, even by two successively; the first whereof was the Lord of Godolphin, and the second the Lord of Oxford; so that you have made me *say the thing that was not.* Likewise, in the account of the Academy of Projectors, and several passages of my discourse to my master Houyhnhnm, you have either omitted some material circumstances, or minced or changed them in such a manner, that I do hardly know mine own work. When I formerly hinted to you something of this in a letter, you were pleased to answer that you were afraid of giving offense; that people in power were very watchful over the press; and apt not only to interpret, but to punish everything which looked like an *inuendo* (as I think you called it). But pray, how could that which I spoke so many years ago, and at above five thousand leagues distance, in another reign, be applied to any of the Yahoos, who now are said to govern the herd; especially, at a time when I little thought on or feared the unhappiness of living under them. Have not I the most reason to complain, when I see these very Yahoos carried by Houyhnhnms in a vehicle, as if these were brutes, and those the rational creatures? And, indeed, to avoid so monstrous and detestable a sight was one principal motive of my retirement hither.[4]

Thus much I thought proper to tell you in relation to yourself, and to the trust I reposed in you.

I do in the next place complain of my own great want of judgment, in being prevailed upon by the intreaties and false reasonings of you and some others, very much against mine own opinion, to suffer my travels to be published. Pray bring to your mind how often I desired you to consider, when you insisted on the motive of public good, that the Yahoos were a species of animals utterly incapable of amendment by precepts or examples; and so it hath proved; for instead of seeing a full stop put to all abuses and corruptions, at least in this little island, as I had reason to expect, behold, after above six months warning. I cannot learn that my book hath produced one single effect according to mine intentions; I desired you would let me know by a letter, when party and faction were extinguished; judges learned and upright; pleaders honest and modest, with some tincture of common sense; and Smithfield[5] blazing with pyramids of law books; the young nobility's education entirely changed; the physicians banished; the female Yahoos abounding in virtue, honor, truth, and good sense; courts and levees of great ministers thoroughly weeded and swept; wit, merit, and learning rewarded; all disgracers of the

---

3. William Dampier (1652–1715), the explorer, whose account of his circumnavigation of the globe Swift had read. 4. To Nottinghamshire in central England. 5. An area of London, used in the 16th century for burning heretics, that should now be used (Swift implies) to burn the incentives to litigation.

press in prose and verse, condemned to eat nothing but their own cotton,[6] and quench their thirst with their own ink. These, and a thousand other reformations, I firmly counted upon by your encouragement; as indeed they were plainly deducible from the precepts delivered in my book. And, it must be owned that seven months were a sufficient time to correct every vice and folly to which Yahoos are subject; if their natures had been capable of the least disposition to virtue or wisdom; yet so far have you been from answering mine expectation in any of your letters, that on the contrary, you are loading our carrier every week with libels, and keys, and reflections, and memoirs, and second parts; wherein I see myself accused of reflecting upon great statesfolk; of degrading human nature (for so they have still the confidence to style it) and of abusing the female sex. I find likewise, that the writers of those bundles are not agreed among themselves; for some of them will not allow me to be author of mine own travels; and others make me author of books to which I am wholly a stranger.

I find likewise that your printer hath been so careless as to confound the times, and mistake the dates of my several voyages and returns; neither assigning the true year, or the true month, or day of the month; and I hear the original manuscript is all destroyed, since the publication of my book. Neither have I any copy left; however, I have sent you some corrections, which you may insert, if ever there should be a second edition; and yet I cannot stand to them, but shall leave that matter to my judicious and candid readers, to adjust it as they please.

I hear some of our sea Yahoos find fault with my sea language, as not proper in many parts, nor now in use. I cannot help it. In my first voyages, while I was young, I was instructed by the oldest mariners, and learned to speak as they did. But I have since found that the sea Yahoos are apt, like the land ones, to become new fangled in their words; which the latter change every year; insomuch, as I remember upon each return to mine own country, their old dialect was so altered, that I could hardly understand the new. And I observe, when any Yahoo comes from London out of curiosity to visit me at mine own house, we neither of us are able to deliver our conceptions in a manner intelligible to the other.

If the censure of Yahoos could any way affect me, I should have great reason to complain that some of them are so bold as to think my book of travels a mere fiction out of mine own brain; and have gone so far as to drop hints that the Houyhnhnms and Yahoos have no more existence than the inhabitants of Utopia.

Indeed I must confess that as to the people of Lilliput, Brobdingrag (for so the word should have been spelled, and not erroneously Brobdingnag) and Laputa, I have never yet heard of any Yahoo so presumptuous as to dispute their being, or the facts I have related concerning them; because the truth immediately strikes every reader with conviction. And, is there less probability in my account of the Houyhnhnms or Yahoos, when it is manifest as to the latter, there are so many thousands even in this city, who only differ from their brother brutes in Houyhnhnmland, because they use a sort of a jabber, and do not go naked. I wrote for their amendment, and not their

6. The fiber favored for paper making.

approbation. The united praise of the whole race would be of less consequence to me, than the neighing of those two degenerate Houyhnhnms I keep in my stable; because, from these, degenerate as they are, I still improve in some virtues, without any mixture of vice.

Do these miserable animals presume to think that I am so far degenerated as to defend my veracity; Yahoo as I am, it is well known through all Houyhnhnmland, that by the instructions and example of my illustrious master, I was able in the compass of two years (although I confess with the utmost difficulty) to remove that infernal habit of lying, shuffling, deceiving, and equivocating, so deeply rooted in the very souls of all my species; especially the Europeans.

I have other complaints to make upon this vexatious occasion; but I forbear troubling myself or you any further. I must freely confess that since my last return, some corruptions of my Yahoo nature have revived in me by conversing with a few of your species, and particularly those of mine own family, by an unavoidable necessity; else I should never have attempted so absurd a project as that of reforming the Yahoo race in this kingdom; but I have now done with all such visionary schemes for ever.

The Publisher to the Reader

The author of these travels, Mr. Lemuel Gulliver, is my ancient and intimate friend; there is likewise some relation between us by the mother's side. About three years ago Mr. Gulliver, growing weary of the concourse of curious people coming to him at his house in Redriff,[7] made a small purchase of land, with a convenient house, near Newark, in Nottinghamshire, his native country; where he now lives retired, yet in good esteem among his neighbors.

Although Mr. Gulliver were born in Nottinghamshire, where his father dwelt, yet I have heard him say his family came from Oxfordshire; to confirm which, I have observed in the churchyard at Banbury, in that county, several tombs and monuments of the Gullivers.

Before he quitted Redriff, he left the custody of the following papers in my hands, with the liberty to dispose of them as I should think fit. I have carefully perused them three times; the style is very plain and simple; and the only fault I find is that the author, after the manner of travelers, is a little too circumstantial. There is an air of truth apparent through the whole; and indeed the author was so distinguished for his veracity, that it became a sort of proverb among his neighbors at Redriff, when anyone affirmed a thing, to say, it was as true as if Mr. Gulliver had spoke it.

By the advice of several worthy persons, to whom, with the author's permission, I communicated these papers, I now venture to send them into the world; hoping they may be, at least for some time, a better entertainment to our young noblemen, than the common scribbles of politics and party.

This volume would have been at least twice as large, if I had not made bold to strike out innumerable passages relating to the winds and tides, as well as to the variations and bearings in the several voyages; together with the minute descriptions of the management of the ship in storms, in the style

---

7. Rotherhithe, a district in south London then frequented by sailors.

of sailors; likewise the account of the longitudes and latitudes, wherein I have reason to apprehend that Mr. Gulliver may be a little dissatisfied; but I was resolved to fit the work as much as possible to the general capacity of readers. However, if my own ignorance in sea affairs shall have led me to commit some mistakes, I alone am answerable for them; and if any traveler hath a curiosity to see the whole work at large, as it came from the hand of the author, I will be ready to gratify him.

As for any further particulars relating to the author, the reader will receive satisfaction from the first pages of the book.

RICHARD SYMPSON

Part IV

A Voyage to the Country of the Houyhnhnms[8]

CHAPTER I

The Author sets out as Captain of a ship. His men conspire against him, confine him a long time to his cabin, set him on shore in an unknown land. He travels up into the country. The Yahoos, a strange sort of animal, described. The Author meets two Houyhnhnms.

I continued at home with my wife and children about five months in a very happy condition, if I could have learned the lesson of knowing when I was well. I left my poor wife big with child, and accepted an advantageous offer made me to be Captain of the *Adventure,* a stout merchantman of 350 tons; for I understood navigation well, and being grown weary of a surgeon's employment at sea, which however I could exercise upon occasion, I took a skillful young man of that calling, one Robert Purefoy, into my ship. We set sail from Portsmouth upon the 7th day of September, 1710; on the 14th we met with Captain Pocock of Bristol, at Tenariff, who was going to the Bay of Campeachy[9] to cut logwood. On the 16th he was parted from us by a storm; I heard since my return that his ship foundered and none escaped, but one cabin boy. He was an honest man and a good sailor, but a little too positive in his own opinions, which was the cause of his destruction, as it hath been of several others. For if he had followed my advice, he might at this time have been safe at home with his family as well as myself.

I had several men died in my ship of calentures,[1] so that I was forced to get recruits out of Barbadoes and the Leeward Islands,[2] where I touched by the direction of the merchants who employed me; which I had soon too much cause to repent, for I found afterwards that most of them had been buccaneers. I had fifty hands on board; and my orders were that I should trade with the Indians in the South Sea, and make what discoveries I could. These rogues whom I had picked up debauched my other men, and they all formed a conspiracy to seize the ship and secure me; which they did one morning,

8. The word suggests the sound of a horse neighing.   9. Probably Campeche, in southeast Mexico, on the western side of the Yucatán Peninsula. Tenariff (now Tenerife) is the largest of the Canary Islands, off northwest Africa in the Atlantic.   1. Tropical fever.   2. The northern group of the Lesser Antilles in the West Indies, extending southeast from Puerto Rico. Barbados is the easternmost of the West Indies.

rushing into my cabin, and binding me hand and foot, threatening to throw me overboard, if I offered to stir. I told them I was their prisoner, and would submit. This they made me swear to do, and then unbound me, only fastening one of my legs with a chair near my bed, and placed a sentry at my door with his piece charged, who was commanded to shoot me dead if I attempted my liberty. They sent me down victuals and drink, and took the government of the ship to themselves. Their design was to turn pirates and plunder the Spaniards, which they could not do, till they got more men. But first they resolved to sell the goods in the ship, and then go to Madagascar for recruits, several among them having died since my confinement. They sailed many weeks, and traded with the Indians; but I knew not what course they took, being kept close prisoner in my cabin, and expecting nothing less than to be murdered, as they often threatened me.

Upon the 9th day of May, 1711, one James Welch came down to my cabin; and said he had orders from the Captain to set me ashore. I expostulated with him, but in vain; neither would he so much as tell me who their new Captain was. They forced me into the longboat, letting me put on my best suit of clothes, which were as good as new, and a small bundle of linen, but no arms except my hanger;[3] and they were so civil as not to search my pockets, into which I conveyed what money I had, with some other little necessaries. They rowed about a league, and then set me down on a strand. I desired them to tell me what country it was; they all swore, they knew no more than myself, but said that the Captain (as they called him) was resolved, after they had sold the lading, to get rid of me in the first place where they discovered land. They pushed off immediately, advising me to make haste, for fear of being overtaken by the tide, and bade me farewell.

In this desolate condition I advanced forward, and soon got upon firm ground, where I sat down on a bank to rest myself, and consider what I had best to do. When I was a little refreshed, I went up into the country, resolving to deliver myself to the first savages I should meet, and purchase my life from them by some bracelets, glass rings, and other toys, which sailors usually provide themselves with in those voyages, and whereof I had some about me. The land was divided by long rows of trees, not regularly planted, but naturally growing; there was great plenty of grass, and several fields of oats. I walked very circumspectly for fear of being surprised, or suddenly shot with an arrow from behind, or on either side. I fell into a beaten road, where I saw many tracks of human feet, and some of cows, but most of horses. At last I beheld several animals in a field, and one or two of the same kind sitting in trees. Their shape was very singular, and deformed, which a little discomposed me, so that I lay down behind a thicket to observe them better. Some of them coming forward near the place where I lay, gave me an opportunity of distinctly marking their form. Their heads and breasts were covered with a thick hair, some frizzled and others lank; they had beards like goats, and a long ridge of hair down their backs, and the fore parts of their legs and feet; but the rest of their bodies were bare, so that I might see their skins, which were of a brown buff color. They had no tails, nor any hair at all on their buttocks, except about the anus; which, I presume Nature had placed there to defend them as they sat on the ground; for this posture they used,

3. A small sword.

as well as lying down, and often stood on their hind feet. They climbed high trees, as nimbly as a squirrel, for they had strong extended claws before and behind, terminating in sharp points, and hooded.[4] They would often spring, and bound, and leap with prodigious agility. The females were not so large as the males; they had long lank hair on their heads, and only a sort of down on the rest of their bodies, except about the anus, and pudenda. Their dugs hung between their forefeet, and often reached almost to the ground as they walked. The hair of both sexes was of several colors, brown, red, black, and yellow. Upon the whole, I never beheld in all my travels so disagreeable an animal, or one against which I naturally conceived so strong an antipathy. So that thinking I had seen enough, full of contempt and aversion, I got up and pursued the beaten road, hoping it might direct me to the cabin of some Indian: I had not gone far when I met one of these creatures full in my way, and coming up directly to me. The ugly monster, when he saw me, distorted several ways every feature of his visage, and stared as at an object he had never seen before; then approaching nearer, lifted up his forepaw, whether out of curiosity or mischief, I could not tell; but I drew my hanger, and gave him a good blow with the flat side of it; for I durst not strike him with the edge, fearing the inhabitants might be provoked against me, if they should come to know that I had killed or maimed any of their cattle. When the beast felt the smart, he drew back, and roared so loud, that a herd of at least forty came flocking about me from the next field, howling and making odious faces; but I ran to the body of a tree, and leaning my back against it, kept them off, by waving my hanger. Several of this cursed brood getting hold of the branches behind, leaped up into the tree, from whence they began to discharge their excrements on my head; however, I escaped pretty well, by sticking close to the stem of the tree, but was almost stifled with the filth, which fell about me on every side.

In the midst of this distress, I observed them all to run away on a sudden as fast as they could; at which I ventured to leave the tree, and pursue the road, wondering what it was that could put them into this fright. But looking on my left hand, I saw a horse walking softly in the field; which my persecutors having sooner discovered, was the cause of their flight. The horse started a little when he came near me, but soon recovering himself, looked full in my face with manifest tokens of wonder; he viewed my hands and feet, walking round me several times. I would have pursued my journey, but he placed himself directly in the way, yet looking with a very mild aspect, never offering the least violence. We stood gazing at each other for some time; at last I took the boldness, to reach my hand towards his neck, with a design to stroke it; using the common style and whistle of jockies when they are going to handle a strange horse. But, this animal seeming to receive my civilities with disdain, shook his head, and bent his brows, softly raising up his left forefoot to remove my hand. Then he neighed three or four times, but in so different a cadence, that I almost began to think he was speaking to himself in some language of his own.

While he and I were thus employed, another horse came up; who applying himself to the first in a very formal manner, they gently struck each other's right hoof before, neighing several times by turns, and varying the sound,

4. Concealed, or sheathed by flesh.

which seemed to be almost articulate. They went some paces off, as if it were to confer together, walking side by side, backward and forward, like persons deliberating upon some affair of weight; but often turning their eyes towards me, as it were to watch that I might not escape. I was amazed to see such actions and behavior in brute beasts; and concluded with myself that if the inhabitants of this country were endued with a proportionable degree of reason, they must needs be the wisest people upon earth. This thought gave me so much comfort, that I resolved to go forward until I could discover some house or village, or meet with any of the natives, leaving the two horses to discourse together as they pleased. But the first, who was a dapple grey, observing me to steal off, neighed after me in so expressive a tone that I fancied myself to understand what he meant; whereupon I turned back, and came near him, to expect his farther commands; but concealing my fear as much as I could; for I began to be in some pain, how this adventure might terminate; and the reader will easily believe I did not much like my present situation.

The two horses came up close to me, looking with great earnestness upon my face and hands. The grey steed rubbed my hat all round with his right fore hoof, and discomposed it so much that I was forced to adjust it better, by taking it off, and settling it again; whereat both he and his companion (who was a brown bay) appeared to be much surprised; the latter felt the lappet of my coat, and finding it to hang loose about me, they both looked with new signs of wonder. He stroked my right hand, seeming to admire the softness, and color; but he squeezed it so hard between his hoof and his pastern,[5] that I was forced to roar; after which they both touched me with all possible tenderness. They were under great perplexity about my shoes and stockings, which they felt very often, neighing to each other, and using various gestures, not unlike those of a philosopher, when he would attempt to solve some new and difficult phenomenon.

Upon the whole, the behavior of these animals was so orderly and rational, so acute and judicious, that I at last concluded, they must needs be magicians, who had thus metamorphosed themselves upon some design; and seeing a stranger in the way, were resolved to divert themselves with him; or perhaps were really amazed at the sight of a man so very different in habit, feature, and complexion from those who might probably live in so remote a climate. Upon the strength of this reasoning, I ventured to address them in the following manner: "Gentlemen, if you be conjurers, as I have good cause to believe, you can understand any language; therefore I make bold to let your worships know that I am a poor distressed Englishman, driven by his misfortunes upon your coast; and I entreat one of you, to let me ride upon his back, as if he were a real horse, to some house or village, where I can be relieved. In return of which favor, I will make you a present of this knife and bracelet" (taking them out of my pocket). The two creatures stood silent while I spoke, seeming to listen with great attention; and when I had ended, they neighed frequently towards each other, as if they were engaged in serious conversation. I plainly observed, that their language expressed the passions very well, and the words might with little pains be resolved into an alphabet more easily than the Chinese.

5. The part of a horse's foot between the joint at the rear and the hoof.

I could frequently distinguish the word *Yahoo,* which was repeated by each of them several times; and although it were impossible for me to conjecture what it meant, yet while the two horses were busy in conversation, I endeavored to practice this word upon my tongue; and as soon as they were silent, I boldly pronounced "Yahoo" in a loud voice, imitating, at the same time, as near as I could, the neighing of a horse; at which they were both visibly surprised, and the grey repeated the same word twice, as if he meant to teach me the right accent, wherein I spoke after him as well as I could, and found myself perceivably to improve every time, although very far from any degree of perfection. Then the bay tried me with a second word, much harder to be pronounced; but reducing it to the English orthography, may be spelt thus *Houyhnhnm.* I did not succeed in this so well as the former, but after two or three farther trials, I had better fortune; and they both appeared amazed at my capacity.

After some farther discourse, which I then conjectured might relate to me, the two friends took their leaves, with the same compliment of striking each other's hoof; and the grey made me signs that I should walk before him; wherein I thought it prudent to comply, till I could find a better director. When I offered to slacken my pace, he would cry, "Hhuun, Hhuun"; I guessed his meaning, and gave him to understand, as well as I could that I was weary, and not able to walk faster; upon which, he would stand a while to let me rest.

CHAPTER II

The Author conducted by a Houyhnhnm to his house. The house described. The Author's reception. The food of the Houyhnhnms. The Author in distress for want of meat is at last relieved. His manner of feeding in that country.

Having traveled about three miles, we came to a long kind of building, made of timber, stuck in the ground, and wattled across; the roof was low, and covered with straw. I now began to be a little comforted, and took out some toys, which travelers usually carry for presents to the savage Indians of America and other parts, in hopes the people of the house would be thereby encouraged to receive me kindly. The horse made me a sign to go in first; it was a large room with a smooth clay floor, and a rack and manger extending the whole length on one side. There were three nags, and two mares, not eating, but some of them sitting down upon their hams, which I very much wondered at; but wondered more to see the rest employed in domestic business; the last seemed but ordinary cattle; however this confirmed my first opinion, that a people who could so far civilize brute animals must needs excel in wisdom all the nations of the world. The grey came in just after, and thereby prevented any ill treatment, which the others might have given me. He neighed to them several times in a style of authority, and received answers.

Beyond this room there were three others, reaching the length of the house, to which you passed through three doors, opposite to each other, in the manner of a vista; we went through the second room towards the third; here the grey walked in first, beckoning me to attend; I waited in the second room, and got ready my presents, for the master and mistress of the house;

they were two knives, three bracelets of false pearl, a small looking glass and a bead necklace. The horse neighed three or four times, and I waited to hear some answers in a human voice, but I heard no other returns than in the same dialect, only one or two a little shriller than his. I began to think that this house must belong to some person of great note among them, because there appeared so much ceremony before I could gain admittance. But, that a man of quality should be served all by horses, was beyond my comprehension. I feared my brain was disturbed by my sufferings and misfortunes; I roused myself, and looked about me in the room where I was left alone; this was furnished as the first, only after a more elegant manner. I rubbed my eyes often, but the same objects still occurred. I pinched my arms and sides, to awake myself, hoping I might be in a dream. I then absolutely concluded that all these appearances could be nothing else but necromancy and magic. But I had no time to pursue these reflections; for the grey horse came to the door, and made me a sign to follow him into the third room; where I saw a very comely mare, together with a colt and foal, sitting on their haunches, upon mats of straw, not unartfully made, and perfectly neat and clean.

The mare soon after my entrance, rose from her mat, and coming up close, after having nicely observed my hands and face, gave me a most contemptuous look; then turning to the horse, I heard the word Yahoo often repeated betwixt them; the meaning of which word I could not then comprehend, although it were the first I had learned to pronounce; but I was soon better informed, to my everlasting mortification: for the horse beckoning to me with his head, and repeating the word, "Hhuun, Hhuun," as he did upon the road, which I understood was to attend him, led me out into a kind of court, where was another building at some distance from the house. Here we entered, and I saw three of those detestable creatures, which I first met after my landing, feeding upon roots, and the flesh of some animals, which I afterwards found to be that of asses and dogs, and now and then a cow dead by accident or disease. They were all tied by the neck with strong withes,[6] fastened to a beam; they held their food between the claws of their forefeet, and tore it with their teeth.

The master horse ordered a sorrel nag, one of his servants, to untie the largest of these animals, and take him into a yard. The beast and I were brought close together; and our countenances diligently compared, both by master and servant, who thereupon repeated several times the word "Yahoo." My horror and astonishment are not to be described, when I observed, in this abominable animal, a perfect human figure; the face of it indeed was flat and broad, the nose depressed, the lips large, and the mouth wide; but these differences are common to all savage nations, where the lineaments of the countenance are distorted by the natives suffering their infants to lie groveling on the earth, or by carrying them on their backs, nuzzling with their face against the mother's shoulders. The forefeet of the Yahoo differed from my hands in nothing else but the length of the nails, the coarseness and brownness of the palms, and the hairiness on the backs. There was the same resemblance between our feet, with the same differences, which I knew very well, although the horses did not, because of my shoes and stockings;

6. Fibers braided into rope.

the same in every part of our bodies, except as to hairiness and color, which I have already described.

The great difficulty that seemed to stick with the two horses was to see the rest of my body so very different from that of a Yahoo, for which I was obliged to my clothes, whereof they had no conception; the sorrel nag offered me a root, which he held (after their manner, as we shall describe in its proper place) between his hoof and pastern; I took it in my hand, and having smelled it, returned it to him again as civilly as I could. He brought out of the Yahoo's kennel a piece of ass's flesh, but it smelled so offensively that I turned from it with loathing; he then threw it to the Yahoo, by whom it was greedily devoured. He afterwards showed me a wisp of hay, and a fetlock[7] full of oats; but I shook my head, to signify that neither of these were food for me. And indeed, I now apprehended that I must absolutely starve, if I did not get to some of my own species; for as to those filthy Yahoos, although there were few greater lovers of mankind, at that time, than myself, yet I confess I never saw any sensitive being so detestable on all accounts; and the more I came near them, the more hateful they grew, while I stayed in that country. This the master horse observed by my behavior, and therefore sent the Yahoo back to his kennel. He then put his forehoof to his mouth, at which I was much surprised, although he did it with ease, and with a motion that appeared perfectly natural; and made other signs to know what I would eat; but I could not return him such an answer as he was able to apprehend; and if he had understood me, I did not see how it was possible to contrive any way for finding myself nourishment. While we were thus engaged, I observed a cow passing by; whereupon I pointed to her, and expressed a desire to let me go and milk her. This had its effect; for he led me back into the house, and ordered a mare-servant to open a room, where a good store of milk lay in earthen and wooden vessels, after a very orderly and cleanly manner. She gave me a large bowl full, of which I drank very heartily, and found myself well refreshed.

About noon I saw coming towards the house a kind of vehicle, drawn like a sledge by four Yahoos. There was in it an old steed, who seemed to be of quality; he alighted with his hind feet forward, having by accident got a hurt in his left forefoot. He came to dine with our horse, who received him with great civility. They dined in the best room, and had oats boiled in milk for the second course, which the old horse eat warm, but the rest cold. Their mangers were placed circular in the middle of the room, and divided into several partitions, round which they sat on their haunches upon bosses of straw. In the middle was a large rack with angles answering to every partition of the manger. So that each horse and mare eat their own hay, and their own mash of oats and milk, with much decency and regularity. The behavior of the young colt and foal appeared very modest; and that of the master and mistress extremely cheerful and complaisant to their guest. The grey ordered me to stand by him; and much discourse passed between him and his friend concerning me, as I found by the stranger's often looking on me, and the frequent repetition of the word Yahoo.

I happened to wear my gloves; which the master grey observing, seemed perplexed; discovering signs of wonder what I had done to my forefeet; he

---

7. The joint at the back of a horse's foot, just above the hoof, in which the Houyhnhnm holds the oats.

put his hoof three or four times to them, as if he would signify, that I should reduce them to their former shape, which I presently did, pulling off both my gloves, and putting them into my pocket. This occasioned farther talk, and I saw the company was pleased with my behavior, whereof I soon found the good effects. I was ordered to speak the few words I understood; and while they were at dinner, the master taught me the names for oats, milk, fire, water, and some others which I could readily pronounce after him, having from my youth a great facility in learning languages.

When dinner was done, the master horse took me aside, and by signs and words made me understand the concern he was in that I had nothing to eat. Oats in their tongue are called *hlunnh*. This word I pronounced two or three times; for although I had refused them at first, yet upon second thoughts, I considered that I could contrive to make a kind of bread, which might be sufficient with milk to keep me alive, till I could make my escape to some other country, and to creatures of my own species. The horse immediately ordered a white mare-servant of his family to bring me a good quantity of oats in a sort of wooden tray. These I heated before the fire as well as I could, and rubbed them till the husks came off, which I made a shift to winnow from the grain; I ground and beat them between two stones, then took water, and made them into a paste or cake, which I toasted at the fire, and eat warm with milk. It was at first a very insipid diet, although common enough in many parts of Europe, but grew tolerable by time; and having been often reduced to hard fare in my life, this was not the first experiment I had made how easily nature is satisfied. And I cannot but observe that I never had one hour's sickness, while I staid in this island. It is true, I sometimes made a shift to catch a rabbit, or bird, by springes made of Yahoos' hairs; and I often gathered wholesome herbs, which I boiled, or ate as salads with my bread; and now and then, for a rarity, I made a little butter, and drank the whey. I was at first at a great loss for salt; but custom soon reconciled the want of it; and I am confident that the frequent use of salt among us is an effect of luxury, and was first introduced only as a provocative to drink; except where it is necessary for preserving of flesh in long voyages, or in places remote from great markets. For we observe no animal to be fond of it but man;[8] and as to myself, when I left this country, it was a great while before I could endure the taste of it in anything that I eat.

This is enough to say upon the subject of my diet, wherewith other travelers fill their books, as if the readers were personally concerned whether we fare well or ill. However, it was necessary to mention this matter, lest the world should think it impossible that I could find sustenance for three years in such a country, and among such inhabitants.

When it grew towards evening, the master horse ordered a place for me to lodge in; it was but six yards from the house, and separated from the stable of the Yahoos. Here I got some straw, and covering myself with my own clothes, slept very sound. But I was in a short time better accommodated, as the reader shall know hereafter, when I come to treat more particularly about my way of living.

---

8. Gulliver's error; many animals are very fond of salt.

CHAPTER III

The Author studious to learn the language, the Houyhnhnm his master assists in teaching him. The language described. Several Houyhnhnms of quality come out of curiosity to see the Author. He gives his master a short account of his voyage.

My principal endeavor was to learn the language, which my master (for so I shall henceforth call him) and his children, and every servant of his house were desirous to teach me. For they looked upon it as a prodigy, that a brute animal should discover such marks of a rational creature. I pointed to everything, and enquired the name of it, which I wrote down in my journal book when I was alone, and corrected my bad accent, by desiring those of the family to pronounce it often. In this employment, a sorrel nag, one of the under servants, was very ready to assist me.

In speaking, they pronounce through the nose and throat, and their language approaches nearest to the High Dutch or German, of any I know in Europe; but is much more graceful and significant. The Emperor Charles V made almost the same observation, when he said, that if he were to speak to his horse, it should be in High Dutch.[9]

The curiosity and impatience of my master were so great, that he spent many hours of his leisure to instruct me. He was convinced (as he afterwards told me) that I must be a Yahoo, but my teachableness, civility, and cleanliness astonished him; which were qualities altogether so opposite to those animals. He was most perplexed about my clothes, reasoning sometimes with himself whether they were a part of my body; for I never pulled them off till the family were asleep, and got them on before they waked in the morning. My master was eager to learn from whence I came; how I acquired those appearances of reason, which I discovered in all my actions; and to know my story from my own mouth, which he hoped he should soon do by the great proficiency I made in learning and pronouncing their words and sentences. To help my memory, I formed all I learned into the English alphabet, and writ the words down with the translations. This last, after some time, I ventured to do in my master's presence. It cost me much trouble to explain to him what I was doing; for the inhabitants have not the least idea of books or literature.

In about ten weeks time I was able to understand most of his questions; and in three months could give him some tolerable answers. He was extremely curious to know from what part of the country I came, and how I was taught to imitate a rational creature; because the Yahoos (whom he saw I exactly resembled in my head, hands, and face, that were only visible) with some appearance of cunning, and the strongest disposition to mischief, were observed to be the most unteachable of all brutes. I answered that I came over the sea, from a far place, with many others of my own kind, in a great hollow vessel made of the bodies of trees; that my companions forced me to land on this coast, and then left me to shift for myself. It was with some difficulty, and by the help of many signs, that I brought him to understand me. He replied that I must needs be mistaken, or that I *said the thing which*

9. Charles was reputed to have said he would address God in Spanish, women in Italian, men in French, and his horse in German.

was not. (For they have no word in their language to express lying or falsehood.) He knew it was impossible that there could be a country beyond the sea, or that a parcel of brutes could move a wooden vessel whither they pleased upon water. He was sure no Houyhnhnm alive could make such a vessel, or would trust Yahoos to manage it.

The word Houyhnhnm, in their tongue, signifies a Horse; and in its etymology, the Perfection of Nature. I told my master that I was at a loss for expression, but would improve as fast as I could; and hoped in a short time I should be able to tell him wonders; he was pleased to direct his own mare, his colt, and foal, and the servants of the family to take all opportunities of instructing me; and every day for two or three hours, he was at the same pains himself; several horses and mares of quality in the neighborhood came often to our house, upon the report spread of a wonderful Yahoo, that could speak like a Houyhnhnm, and seemed in his words and actions to discover some glimmerings of reason. These delighted to converse with me; they put many questions, and received such answers as I was able to return. By all which advantages, I made so great a progress, that in five months from my arrival, I understood whatever was spoke, and could express myself tolerably well.

The Houyhnhnms who came to visit my master, out of a design of seeing and talking with me, could hardly believe me to be a right Yahoo, because my body had a different covering from others of my kind. They were astonished to observe me without the usual hair or skin, except on my head, face, and hands; but I discovered that secret to my master, upon an accident, which happened about a fortnight before.

I have already told the reader, that every night when the family were gone to bed, it was my custom to strip and cover myself with my clothes; it happened one morning early, that my master sent for me, by the sorrel nag, who was his valet; when he came, I was fast asleep, my clothes fallen off on one side, and my shirt above my waist. I awaked at the noise he made, and observed him to deliver his message in some disorder; after which he went to my master, and in a great fright gave him a very confused account of what he had seen; this I presently discovered; for going as soon as I was dressed, to pay my attendance upon his honor, he asked me the meaning of what his servant had reported; that I was not the same thing when I slept as I appeared to be at other times; that his valet assured him, some part of me was white, some yellow, at least not so white, and some brown.

I had hitherto concealed the secret of my dress, in order to distinguish myself as much as possible, from that cursed race of Yahoos; but now I found it in vain to do so any longer. Besides, I considered that my clothes and shoes would soon wear out, which already were in a declining condition, and must be supplied by some contrivance from the hides of Yahoos, or other brutes; whereby the whole secret would be known. I therefore told my master, that in the country from whence I came, those of my kind always covered their bodies with the hairs of certain animals prepared by art, as well for decency, as to avoid inclemencies of air both hot and cold; of which, as to my own person I would give him immediate conviction, if he pleased to command me; only desiring this excuse, if I did not expose those parts that nature taught us to conceal. He said, my discourse was all very strange, but especially the last part; for he could not understand why Nature should teach us to conceal what Nature had given. That neither himself nor family were ashamed of any parts of their bodies; but however I might do as I pleased. Whereupon, I first unbuttoned my coat, and pulled it off. I did the same with my waistcoat; I drew off my shoes, stockings, and breeches. I let my shirt down to my waist, and drew up the bottom, fastening it like a girdle about my middle to hide my nakedness.

My master observed the whole performance with great signs of curiosity and admiration. He took up all my clothes in his pastern, one piece after another, and examined them diligently; he then stroked my body very gently, and looked round me several times; after which he said, it was plain I must be a perfect Yahoo; but that I differed very much from the rest of my species, in the whiteness and smoothness of my skin, my want of hair in several parts of my body, the shape and shortness of my claws behind and before, and my affectation of walking continually on my two hinder feet. He desired to see no more; and gave me leave to put on my clothes again, for I was shuddering with cold.

I expressed my uneasiness at his giving me so often the appellation of Yahoo, an odious animal, for which I had so utter an hatred and contempt. I begged he would forbear applying that word to me, and take the same order in his family, and among his friends whom he suffered to see me. I requested likewise, that the secret of my having a false covering to my body might be known to none but himself, at least as long as my present clothing should last; for as to what the sorrel nag his valet had observed, his honor might command him to conceal it.

All this my master very graciously consented to; and thus the secret was kept till my clothes began to wear out, which I was forced to supply by several contrivances, that shall hereafter be mentioned. In the meantime, he desired I would go on with my utmost diligence to learn their language, because he was more astonished at my capacity for speech and reason, than at the figure of my body, whether it were covered or no; adding that he waited with some impatience to hear the wonders which I promised to tell him.

From thenceforward he doubled the pains he had been at to instruct me; he brought me into all company, and made them treat me with civility, because, as he told them privately, this would put me into good humor, and make me more diverting.

Every day when I waited on him, beside the trouble he was at in teaching, he would ask me several questions concerning myself, which I answered as well as I could; and by those means he had already received some general ideas, although very imperfect. It would be tedious to relate the several steps, by which I advanced to a more regular conversation, but the first account I gave of myself in any order and length was to this purpose:

That, I came from a very far country, as I already had attempted to tell him, with about fifty more of my own species; that we traveled upon the seas, in a great hollow vessel made of wood, and larger than his honor's house. I described the ship to him in the best terms I could; and explained by the help of my handkerchief displayed, how it was driven forward by the wind. That, upon a quarrel among us, I was set on shore on this coast, where I walked forward without knowing whither, till he delivered me from the persecution of those execrable Yahoos. He asked me who made the ship, and how it was possible that the Houyhnhnms of my country would leave it to the management of brutes? My answer was that I durst proceed no farther in my relation, unless he would give me his word and honor that he would not be offended; and then I would tell him the wonders I had so often promised. He agreed; and I went on by assuring him, that the ship was made by creatures like myself, who in all the countries I had traveled, as well as in my own, were the only governing, rational animals; and that upon my arrival hither, I was as much astonished to see the Houyhnhnms act like rational begins, as he or his friends could be in finding some marks of reason in a creature he was pleased to call a Yahoo; to which I owned my resemblance in every part, but could not account for their degenerate and brutal nature. I said farther, that if good fortune ever restored me to my native country, to relate my travels hither, as I resolved to do; everybody would believe that I *said the thing which was not*; that I invented the story out of my own head; and with all possible respect to himself, his family, and friends, and under his promise of not being offended, our countrymen would hardly think it probable, that a Houyhnhnm should be the presiding creature of a nation, and a Yahoo the brute.

CHAPTER IV

The Houyhnhnms' notion of truth and falsehood. The author's discourse disapproved by his master. The author gives a more particular account of himself, and the accidents of his voyages.

My master heard me with great appearances of uneasiness in his countenance; because *doubting* or *not believing* are so little known in this country, that the inhabitants cannot tell how to behave themselves under such circumstances. And I remember in frequent discourses with my master concerning the nature of manhood, in other parts of the world, having occasion to talk of *lying* and *false representation,* it was with much difficulty that he comprehended what I meant; although he had otherwise a most acute judgment. For he argued thus: that the use of speech was to make us understand one another, and to receive information of facts; now if anyone *said the thing which was not,* these ends were defeated; because I cannot properly be said to understand him; and I am so far from receiving information, that he leaves me worse than in ignorance; for I am led to believe a thing *black* when it is *white,* and *short* when it is *long.* And these were all the notions he had concerning that faculty of *lying,* so perfectly well understood, and so universally practiced among human creatures.

To return from this digression; when I asserted that the Yahoos were the only governing animals in my country, which my master said was altogether past his conception, he desired to know, whether we had Houyhnhnms among us, and what was their employment; I told him we had great numbers; that in summer they grazed in the fields, and in winter were kept in houses, with hay and oats, where Yahoo servants were employed to rub their skins smooth, comb their manes, pick their feet, serve them with food, and make their beds. "I understand you well," said my master; "it is now very plain from all you have spoken, that whatever share of reason the Yahoos pretend to, the Houyhnhnms are your masters; I heartily wish our Yahoos would be so tractable." I begged his honor would please to excuse me from proceeding any farther, because I was very certain that the account he expected from me would be highly displeasing. But he insisted in commanding me to let him know the best and the worst; I told him he should be obeyed. I owned that the Houyhnhnms among us, whom we called Horses, were the most generous[1] and comely animal we had; that they excelled in strength and swiftness; and when they belonged to persons of quality, employed in traveling, racing, and drawing chariots, they were treated with much kindness and care, till they fell into diseases, or became foundered in the feet; but then they were sold, and used to all kind of drudgery till they died; after which their skins were stripped and sold for what they were worth, and their bodies left to be devoured by dogs and birds of prey. But the common race of horses had not so good fortune, being kept by farmers and carriers, and other mean people, who put them to greater labor, and fed them worse. I described as well as I could, our way of riding; the shape and use of a bridle, a saddle, a spur, and a whip; of harness and wheels. I added, that we fastened plates of a certain hard substance called iron at the bottom of their feet, to preserve their hoofs from being broken by the stony ways on which we often traveled.

My master, after some expressions of great indignation, wondered how we dared to venture upon a Houyhnhnm's back; for he was sure, that the weakest servant in his house would be able to shake off the strongest Yahoo; or by lying down, and rolling upon his back, squeeze the brute to death. I answered that our horses were trained up from three or four years old to the several uses we intended them for; that if any of them proved intolerably vicious, they were employed for carriages; that they were severely beaten while they were young for any mischievous tricks; that the males, designed for the common use of riding or draught, were generally castrated about two years after their birth, to take down their spirits, and make them more tame and gentle; that they were indeed sensible of rewards and punishments; but his honor would please to consider that they had not the least tincture of reason any more than the Yahoos in this country.

It put me to the pains of many circumlocutions to give my master a right idea of what I spoke; for their language doth not abound in variety of words, because their wants and passions are fewer than among us. But it is impossible to express his noble resentment at our savage treatment of the Houyhnhnm race; particularly after I had explained the manner and use of castrating horses among us, to hinder them from propagating their kind, and to render them more servile. He said, if it were possible there could be any country where Yahoos alone were endued with reason, they certainly must be the governing animal, because reason will in time always prevail against brutal strength. But, considering the frame of our bodies, and especially of mine, he thought no creature of equal bulk was so ill-contrived for employing that reason in the common offices of life; whereupon he desired to know whether those among whom I lived resembled me or the Yahoos of his country. I assured him that I was as well shaped as most of my age; but the younger and the females were much more soft and tender, and the skins of the latter generally as white as milk. He said I differed indeed from other Yahoos, being much more cleanly, and not altogether so deformed; but in point of real advantage, he thought I differed for the worse. That my nails were of no use

1. Noble.

either to my fore or hinder feet; as to my forefeet, he could not properly call them by that name, for he never observed me to walk upon them; that they were too soft to bear the ground; that I generally went with them uncovered, neither was the covering I sometimes wore on them of the same shape, or so strong as that on my feet behind. That I could not walk with any security; for if either of my hinder feet slipped, I must inevitably fall. He then began to find fault with other parts of my body; the flatness of my face, the prominence of my nose, my eyes placed directly in front, so that I could not look on either side without turning my head; that I was not able to feed myself without lifting one of my forefeet to my mouth; and therefore nature had placed those joints to answer that necessity. He knew not what could be the use of those several clefts and divisions in my feet behind; that these were too soft to bear the hardness and sharpness of stones without a covering made from the skin of some other brute; that my whole body wanted a fence against heat and cold, which I was forced to put on and off every day with tediousness and trouble. And lastly, that he observed every animal in his country naturally to abhor the Yahoos, whom the weaker avoided, and the stronger drove from them. So that supposing us to have the gift of reason, he could not see how it were possible to cure that natural antipathy which every creature discovered against us; nor consequently, how we could tame and render them serviceable. However, he would (as he said) debate the matter no farther, because he was more desirous to know my own story, the country where I was born, and the several actions and events of my life before I came hither.

I assured him how extremely desirous I was that he should be satisfied in every point; but I doubted much whether it would be possible for me to explain myself on several subjects whereof his honor could have no conception, because I saw nothing in his country to which I could resemble them. That however, I would do my best, and strive to express myself by similitudes, humbly desiring his assistance when I wanted proper words; which he was pleased to promise me.

I said, my birth was of honest parents, in an island called England, which was remote from this country, as many days journey as the strongest of his honor's servants could travel in the annual course of the sun. That I was bred a surgeon, whose trade it is to cure wounds and hurts in the body, got by accident or violence. That my country was governed by a female man, whom we called a queen.[2] That I left it to get riches, whereby I might maintain myself and family when I should return. That in my last voyage, I was Commander of the ship and had about fifty Yahoos under me, many of which died at sea, and I was forced to supply them by others picked out from several nations. That our ship was twice in danger of being sunk; the first time by a great storm, and the second, by striking against a rock. Here my master interposed, by asking me, how I could persuade strangers out of different countries to venture with me, after the losses I had sustained, and the hazards I had run. I said, they were fellows of desperate fortunes, forced to fly from the places of their birth, on account of their poverty or their crimes. Some were undone by lawsuits; others spent all they had in drinking, whor-

2. Queen Anne (1665–1714), the last Stuart ruler.

ing, and gaming; others fled for treason; many for murder, theft, poisoning, robbery, perjury, forgery, coining false money; for committing rapes or sodomy; for flying from their colors, or deserting to the enemy; and most of them had broken prison. None of these durst return to their native countries for fear of being hanged, or of starving in a jail; and therefore were under a necessity of seeking livelihood in other places.

During this discourse, my master was pleased often to interrupt me. I had made use of many circumlocutions in describing to him the nature of the several crimes, for which most of our crew had been forced to fly their country. This labor took up several days conversation before he was able to comprehend me. He was wholly at a loss to know what could be the use or necessity of practicing those vices. To clear up which I endeavored to give him some ideas of the desire of power and riches; of the terrible effects of lust, intemperance, malice, and envy. All this I was forced to define and describe by putting of cases, and making suppositions. After which, like one whose imagination was struck with something never seen or heard of before, he would lift up his eyes with amazement and indignation. Power, government, war, law, punishment, and a thousand other things had no terms, wherein that language could express them; which made the difficulty almost insuperable to give my master any conception of what I meant; but being of an excellent understanding, much improved by contemplation and converse, he at last arrived at a competent knowledge of what human nature in our parts of the world is capable to perform; and desired I would give him some particular account of that land, which we call Europe, especially, of my own country.

CHAPTER V

The Author, at his master's commands, informs him of the state of England. The causes of war among the princes of Europe. The Author begins to explain the English Constitution.

The reader may please to observe that the following extract of many conversations I had with my master contains a summary of the most material points, which were discoursed at several times for above two years; his honor often desiring fuller satisfaction as I farther improved in the Houyhnhnm tongue. I laid before him, as well as I could, the whole state of Europe; I discoursed of trade and manufactures, of arts and sciences; and the answers I gave to all the questions he made, as they arose upon several subjects, were a fund of conversation not to be exhausted. But I shall here only set down the substance of what passed between us concerning my own country, reducing it into order as well as I can, without any regard to time or other circumstances, while I strictly adhere to truth. My only concern is that I shall hardly be able to do justice to my master's arguments and expressions; which must needs suffer by my want of capacity, as well as by a translation into our barbarous English.

In obedience therefore to his honor's commands, I related to him the Revolution under the Prince of Orange; the long war with France entered into by the said Prince, and renewed by his successor the present queen; wherein the greatest powers of Christendom were engaged, and which still continued. I computed at his request, that about a million of Yahoos might have been killed in the whole progress of it; and perhaps a hundred or more cities taken, and five times as many ships burned or sunk.[3]

He asked me what were the usual causes or motives that made one country to go to war with another. I answered, they were innumerable; but I should only mention a few of the chief. Sometimes the ambition of princes, who never think they have land or people enough to govern; sometimes the corruption of ministers, who engage their master in a war in order to stifle or divert the clamor of the subjects against their evil administration. Difference in opinions hath cost many millions of lives; for instance, whether flesh be bread, or bread be flesh; whether the juice of a certain berry be blood or wine; whether whistling be a vice or a virtue; whether it be better to kiss a post, or throw it into the fire; what is the best color for a coat, whether black, white, red, or grey; and whether it should be long or short, narrow or wide, dirty or clean;[4] with many more. Neither are any wars so furious and bloody, or of so long continuance, as those occasioned by difference in opinion, especially if it be in things indifferent.

Sometimes the quarrel between two princes is to decide which of them shall dispossess a third of his dominions, where neither of them pretend to any right. Sometimes one prince quarreleth with another, for fear the other should quarrel with him. Sometimes a war is entered upon, because the enemy is too strong, and sometimes because he is too weak. Sometimes our neighbors want the things which we have, or have the things which we want; and we both fight, till they take ours or give us theirs. It is a very justifiable cause of war to invade a country after the people have been wasted by famine, destroyed by pestilence, or embroiled by factions amongst themselves. It is justifiable to enter into a war against our nearest ally, when one of his towns lies convenient for us, or a territory of land, that would render our dominions round and compact. If a prince send forces into a nation, where the people are poor and ignorant, he may lawfully put half of them to death, and make slaves of the rest, in order to civilize and reduce them from their barbarous way of living. It is a very kingly, honorable, and frequent practice, when one prince desires the assistance of another to secure him against an invasion, that the assistant, when he hath driven out the invader, should seize on the dominions himself, and kill, imprison, or banish the prince he came to relieve. Alliance by blood or marriage is a sufficient cause of war between princes; and the nearer the kindred is, the greater is their disposition to quarrel; poor nations are hungry, and rich nations are proud; and pride and hunger will ever be at variance. For these reasons, the trade of a soldier is held the most honorable of all others: because a soldier is a Yahoo hired to kill in cold blood as many of his own species, who have never offended him, as possibly he can.

There is likewise a kind of beggarly princes in Europe, not able to make war by themselves, who hire out their troops to richer nations for so much a day to each man; of which they keep three fourths to themselves, and it is

---

3. Gulliver relates recent English history: the Glorious Revolution of 1688 and the War of the Spanish Succession (1703–13). He greatly exaggerates the casualties in the war.   4. Gulliver refers to the religious controversies of the Reformation and Counter-Reformation: the doctrine of transubstantiation, the use of music in church services, the veneration of the Crucifix, and the wearing of priestly vestments.

the best part of their maintenance; such are those in many northern parts of Europe.

"What you have told me," said my master, "upon the subject of war, doth indeed discover most admirably the effects of that reason you pretend to; however, it is happy that the shame is greater than the danger; and that Nature hath left you utterly uncapable of doing much mischief; for your mouths lying flat with your faces, you can hardly bite each other to any purpose, unless by consent. Then, as to the claws upon your feet before and behind, they are so short and tender, that one of our Yahoos would drive a dozen of yours before him. And therefore in recounting the numbers of those who have been killed in battle, I cannot but think that you have *said the thing which is not*."

I could not forebear shaking my head and smiling a little at his ignorance. And, being no stranger to the art of war, I gave him a description of cannons, culverins, muskets, carabines, pistols, bullets, powder, swords, bayonets, battles, sieges, retreats, attacks, undermines, countermines, bombardments, sea fights; ships sunk with a thousand men; twenty thousand killed on each side; dying groans, limbs flying in the air; smoke, noise, confusion, trampling to death under horses' feet; flight, pursuit, victory; fields strewed with carcasses left for food to dogs, and wolves, and birds of prey; plundering, stripping, ravishing, burning, and destroying. And, to set forth the valor of my own dear countrymen, I assured him that I had seen them blow up a hundred enemies at once in a siege, and as many in a ship; and beheld the dead bodies drop down in pieces from the clouds, to the great diversion of all the spectators.

I was going on to more particulars, when my master commanded me silence. He said, whoever understood the nature of Yahoos might easily believe it possible for so vile an animal, to be capable of every action I had named, if their strength and cunning equaled their malice. But, as my discourse had increased his abhorrence of the whole species, so he found it gave him a disturbance in his mind, to which he was wholly a stranger before. He thought his ears being used to such abominable words, might by degrees admit them with less detestation. That, although he hated the Yahoos of this country, yet he no more blamed them for their odious qualities, than he did a *gnnayh* (a bird of prey) for its cruelty, or a sharp stone for cutting his hoof. But, when a creature pretending to reason could be capable of such enormities, he dreaded lest the corruption of that faculty might be worse than brutality itself. He seemed therefore confident, that instead of reason, we were only possessed of some quality fitted to increase our natural vices; as the reflection from a troubled stream returns the image of an ill-shapen body, not only larger, but more distorted.

He added that he had heard too much upon the subject of war, both in this and some former discourses. There was another point which a little perplexed him at present. I had said that some of our crew left their country on account of being ruined by law: that I had already explained the meaning of the word; but he was at a loss how it should come to pass, that the law which was intended for every man's preservation, should be any man's ruin. Therefore he desired to be farther satisfied what I meant by law, and the dispensers thereof, according to the present practice in my own country; because he thought nature and reason were sufficient guides for a reasonable animal, as we pretended to be, in showing us what we ought to do, and what to avoid.

I assured his honor that law was a science wherein I had not much conversed, further than by employing advocates, in vain, upon some injustices that had been done me. However, I would give him all the satisfaction I was able.

I said there was a society of men among us, bred up from their youth in the art of proving by words multiplied for the purpose, that white is black, and black is white, according as they are paid. To this society all the rest of the people are slaves.

"For example. If my neighbor hath a mind to my cow, he hires a lawyer to prove that he ought to have my cow from me. I must then hire another to defend my right; it being against all rules of law that any man should be allowed to speak for himself. Now in this case, I who am the true owner lie under two great disadvantages. First, my lawyer being practiced almost from his cradle in defending falsehood is quite out of his element when he would be an advocate for justice, which as an office unnatural, he always attempts with great awkwardness, if not with ill-will. The second disadvantage is that my lawyer must proceed with great caution, or else he will be reprimanded by the judges, and abhorred by his breathren, as one who would lessen the practice of the law. And therefore I have but two methods to preserve my cow. The first is to gain over my adversary's lawyer with a double fee; who will then betray his client, by insinuating that he hath justice on his side. The second way is for my lawyer to make my cause appear as unjust as he can; by allowing the cow to belong to my adversary; and this if it be skillfully done, will certainly bespeak the favor of the bench.

"Now, your honor is to know that these judges are persons appointed to decide all controversies of property, as well as for the trial of criminals; and picked out from the most dextrous lawyers who are grown old or lazy; and having been biased all their lives against truth and equity, lie under such a fatal necessity of favoring fraud, perjury, and oppression, that I have known some of them to have refused a large bribe from the side where justice lay, rather than injure the faculty,[5] by doing anything unbecoming their nature or their office.

"It is a maxim among these lawyers, that whatever hath been done before may legally be done again; and therefore they take special care to record all the decisions formerly made against common justice and the general reason of mankind. These, under the name of *precedents*, they produce as authorities to justify the most iniquitous opinions; and the judges never fail of directing accordingly.

"In pleading, they studiously avoid entering into the merits of the cause; but are loud, violent, and tedious in dwelling upon all circumstances which are not to the purpose. For instance, in the case already mentioned, they never desire to know what claim or title my adversary hath to my cow; but whether the said cow were red or black; her horns long or short; whether the field I graze her in be round or square; whether she were milked at home or abroad; what diseases she is subject to, and the like. After which they

5. Profession.

consult precedents, adjourn the cause, from time to time, and in ten, twenty, or thirty years come to an issue.

"It is likewise to be observed, that this society hath a peculiar cant and jargon of their own, that no other mortal can understand, and wherein all their laws are written, which they take special care to multiply; whereby they have wholly confounded the very essence of truth and falsehood, of right and wrong; so that it will take thirty years to decide whether the field, left me by my ancestors for six generations, belong to me, or to a stranger three hundred miles off.

"In the trial of persons accused for crimes against the state, the method is much more short and commendable: the judge first sends to sound the disposition of those in power; after which he can easily hang or save the criminal, strictly preserving all the forms of law."

Here my master interposing said it was a pity that creatures endowed with such prodigious abilities of mind as these lawyers, by the description I gave of them must certainly be, were not rather encouraged to be instructors of others in wisdom and knowledge. In answer to which, I assured his honor that in all points out of their own trade, they were usually the most ignorant and stupid generation among us, the most despicable in common conversation, avowed enemies to all knowledge and learning; and equally disposed to pervert the general reason of mankind, in every other subject of discourse as in that of their own profession.

CHAPTER VI

A continuation of the state of England, under Queen Anne. The character of a first minister in the courts of Europe.

My master was yet wholly at a loss to understand what motives could incite this race of lawyers to perplex, disquiet, and weary themselves by engaging in a confederacy of injustice, merely for the sake of injuring their fellow animals; neither could he comprehend what I meant in saying they did it for hire. Whereupon I was at much pains to describe to him the use of money, the materials it was made of, and the value of the metals; that when a Yahoo had got a great store of this precious substance, he was able to purchase whatever he had a mind to; the finest clothing, the noblest houses, great tracts of land, the most costly meats and drinks; and have his choice of the most beautiful females. Therefore since money alone was able to perform all these feats, our Yahoos thought they could never have enough of it to spend or to save, as they found themselves inclined from their natural bent either to profusion or avarice. That the rich man enjoyed the fruit of the poor man's labor, and the latter were a thousand to one in proportion to the former. That the bulk of our people was forced to live miserably, by laboring every day for small wages to make a few live plentifully. I enlarged myself much on these and many other particulars to the same purpose, but his honor was still to seek, for he went upon a supposition that all animals had a title to their share in the productions of the earth; and especially those who presided over the rest. Therefore he desired I would let him know what these costly meats were, and how any of us happened to want[6] them. Whereupon I enu-

6. Lack.

merated as many sorts as came into my head, with the various methods of dressing them, which could not be done without sending vessels by sea to every part of the world, as well for liquors to drink, as for sauces, and innumerable other conveniencies. I assured him, that this whole globe of earth must be at least three times gone round, before one of our better female Yahoos could get her breakfast, or a cup to put it in. He said, "That must needs be a miserable country which cannot furnish food for its own inhabitants." But what he chiefly wondered at, was how such vast tracts of ground as I described, should be wholly without fresh water, and the people put to the necessity of sending over the sea for drink. I replied that England (the dear place of my nativity) was computed to produce three times the quantity of food, more than its inhabitants are able to consume, as well as liquors extracted from grain, or pressed out of the fruit of certain trees, which made excellent drink; and the same proportion in every other convenience of life. But, in order to feed the luxury and intemperance of the males, and the vanity of the females, we sent away the greatest part of our necessary things to other countries, from whence in return we brought the materials of diseases, folly, and vice, to spend among ourselves. Hence it follows of necessity, that vast numbers of our people are compelled to seek their livelihood by begging, robbing, stealing, cheating, pimping, foreswearing, flattering, suborning, forging, gaming, lying, fawning, hectoring, voting, scribbling, star gazing, poisoning, whoring, canting, libeling, freethinking, and the like occupations; every one of which terms, I was at much pains to make him understand.

That, wine was not imported among us from foreign countries, to supply the want of water or other drinks, but because it was a sort of liquid which made us merry, by putting us out of our senses; diverted all melancholy thoughts, begat wild extravagant imaginations in the brain, raised our hopes, and banished our fears; suspended every office of reason for a time, and deprived us of the use of our limbs, until we fell into a profound sleep; although it must be confessed, that we always awaked sick and dispirited; and that the use of this liquor filled us with diseases, which made our lives uncomfortable and short.

But beside all this, the bulk of our people supported themselves by furnishing the necessities or conveniencies of life to the rich, and to each other. For instance, when I am at home and dressed as I ought to be, I carry on my body the workmanship of an hundred tradesmen; the building and furniture of my house employ as many more; and five times the number to adorn my wife.

I was going on to tell him of another sort of people, who get their livelihood by attending the sick; having upon some occasions informed his honor that many of my crew had died of diseases. But here it was with the utmost difficulty that I brought him to apprehend what I meant. He could easily conceive that a Houyhnhnm grew weak and heavy a few days before his death; or by some accident might hurt a limb. But that nature, who worketh all things to perfection, should suffer any pains to breed in our bodies, he thought impossible; and desired to know the reason of so unaccountable an evil. I told him, we fed on a thousand things which operated contrary to each other; that we eat when we were not hungry, and drank without the provocation of thirst; that we sat whole nights drinking strong liquors without eating a bit, which disposed us to sloth, inflamed our bodies, and precipitated or prevented digestion. That, prostitute female Yahoos acquired a certain malady, which bred rottenness in the bones of those who fell into their embraces; that this and many other diseases were propagated from father to son; so that great numbers come into the world with complicated maladies upon them; that it would be endless to give him a catalogue of all diseases incident to human bodies; for they could not be fewer than five or six hundred, spread over every limb, and joint; in short, every part, external and intestine, having diseases appropriated to each. To remedy which, there was a sort of people bred up among us, in the profession or pretense of curing the sick. And because I had some skill in the faculty, I would in gratitude to his honor let him know the whole mystery and method by which they proceed.

Their fundamental is that all diseases arise from repletion; from whence they conclude, that a great evacuation of the body is necessary, either through the natural passage, or upwards at the mouth. Their next business is, from herbs, minerals, gums, oils, shells, salts, juices, seaweed, excrements, barks of trees, serpents, toads, frogs, spiders, dead men's flesh and bones, birds, beasts and fishes, to form a composition for smell and taste the most abominable, nauseous, and detestable, that they can possibly contrive, which the stomach immediately rejects with loathing, and this they call a vomit. Or else from the same storehouse, with some other poisonous additions, they command us to take in at the orifice above or below (just as the physician then happens to be disposed) a medicine equally annoying and disgustful to the bowels; which relaxing the belly, drives down all before it; and this they call a purge, or a clyster. For nature (as the physicians allege) having intended the superior anterior orifice only for the intromission of solids and liquids, and the inferior posterior for ejection, these artists ingeniously considering that in all diseases nature is forced out of her seat; therefore to replace her in it, the body must be treated in a manner directly contrary, but interchanging the use of each orifice; forcing solids and liquids in at the anus, and making evacuations at the mouth.

But, besides real diseases, we are subject to many that are only imaginary, for which the physicians have invented imaginary cures; these have their several names, and so have the drugs that are proper for them; and with these our female Yahoos are always infested.

One great excellency in this tribe is their skill at prognostics, wherein they seldom fail; their predictions in real diseases, when they rise to any degree of malignity, generally portending death, which is always in their power, when recovery is not, and therefore, upon any unexpected signs of amendment, after they have pronounced their sentence, rather than be accused as false prophets, they know how to approve[7] their sagacity to the world by a seasonable dose.

They are likewise of special use to husbands and wives, who are grown weary of their mates; to eldest sons, to great ministers of state, and often to princes.

I had formerly upon occasion discoursed with my master upon the nature of government in general, and particularly of our own excellent constitution,

7. Prove.

deservedly the wonder and envy of the whole world. But having here accidentally mentioned a minister of state, he commanded me some time after to inform him what species of Yahoo I particularly meant by that appellation.

I told him that a first or chief minister of state, whom I intended to describe, was a creature wholly exempt from joy and grief, love and hatred, pity and anger; at least makes use of no other passions but a violent desire of wealth, power, and titles; that he applies his words to all uses, except to the indication of his mind; that he never tells a truth, but with an intent that you should take it for a lie; nor a lie, but with a design that you should take it for a truth; that those he speaks worst of behind their backs are in the surest way to preferment; and whenever he begins to praise you to others or to yourself, you are from that day forlorn. The worst mark you can receive is a promise, especially when it is confirmed with an oath; after which every wise man retires, and gives over all hopes.

There are three methods by which a man may rise to be chief minister: the first is by knowing how with prudence to dispose of a wife, a daughter, or a sister; the second, by betraying or undermining his predecessor; and the third is by a furious zeal in public assemblies against the corruptions of the court. But a wise prince would rather choose to employ those who practice the last of these methods; because such zealots prove always the most obsequious and subservient to the will and passions of their master. That, these ministers having all employments at their disposal, preserve themselves in power by bribing the majority of a senate or great council; and at last by an expedient called an Act of Indemnity (whereof I described the nature to him) they secure themselves from after-reckonings, and retire from the public, laden with the spoils of the nation.

The palace of a chief minister is a seminary to breed up others in his own trade; the pages, lackies, and porter, by imitating their master, become ministers of state in their several districts, and learn to excel in the three principal ingredients, of insolence, lying, and bribery. Accordingly, they have a subaltern court paid to them by persons of the best rank; and sometimes by the force of dexterity and impudence, arrive through several gradations to be successors to their lord.

He is usually governed by a decayed wench, or favorite footman, who are the tunnels through which all graces are conveyed, and may properly be called, in the last resort, the governors of the kingdom.

One day, my master, having heard me mention the nobility of my country, was pleased to make me a compliment which I could not pretend to deserve: that, he was sure, I must have been born of some noble family, because I far exceeded in shape, color, and cleanliness, all the Yahoos of his nation, although I seemed to fail in strength, and agility, which must be imputed to my different way of living from those other brutes; and besides, I was not only endowed with the faculty of speech, but likewise with some rudiments of reason, to a degree, that with all his acquaintance I passed for a prodigy.

He made me observe, that among the Houyhnhnms, the white, the sorrel, and the iron grey were not so exactly shaped as the bay, the dapple grey, and the black; nor born with equal talents of mind, or a capacity to improve them; and therefore continued always in the condition of servants, without ever aspiring to match out of their own race, which in that country would be reckoned monstrous and unnatural.

I made his honor my most humble acknowledgements for the good opinion he was pleased to conceive of me; but assured him at the same time, that my birth was of the lower sort, having been born of plain, honest parents, who were just able to give me a tolerable education; that, nobility among us was altogether a different thing from the idea he had of it; that, our young noblemen are bred from their childhood in idleness and luxury; that, as soon as years will permit, they consume their vigor, and contract odious diseases among lewd females; and when their fortunes are almost ruined, they marry some woman of mean birth, disagreeable person, and unsound constitution, merely for the sake of money, whom they hate and despise. That, the productions of such marriages are generally scrofulous, rickety or deformed children; by which means the family seldom continues above three generations, unless the wife take care to provide a healthy father among her neighbors, or domestics, in order to improve and continue the breed. That a weak diseased body, a meager countenance, and sallow complexion are the true marks of noble blood; and a healthy robust appearance is so disgraceful in a man of quality, that the world concludes his real father to have been a groom or a coachman. The imperfections of his mind run parallel with those of his body; being a composition of spleen, dullness, ignorance, caprice, sensuality, and pride.

Without the consent of this illustrious body, no law can be enacted, repealed, or altered, and these nobles have likewise the decision of all our possessions without appeal.

CHAPTER VII

The Author's great love of his native country. His master's observations upon the constitution and administration of England, as described by the Author, with parallel cases and comparisons. His master's observations upon human nature.

The reader may be disposed to wonder how I could prevail on myself to give so free a representation of my own species, among a race of mortals who were already too apt to conceive the vilest opinion of humankind, from that entire congruity betwixt me and their Yahoos. But I must freely confess that the many virtues of those excellent quadrupeds placed in opposite view to human corruptions had so far opened my eyes, and enlarged my understanding, that I began to view the actions and passions of man in a very different light; and to think the honor of my own kind not worth managing; which, besides, it was impossible for me to do before a person of so acute a judgment as my master, who daily convinced me of a thousand faults in myself, whereof I had not the least perception before, and which with us would never be numbered even among human infirmities. I had likewise learned from his example an utter detestation of all falsehood or disguise; and truth appeared so amiable to me, that I determined upon sacrificing everything to it.

Let me deal so candidly with the reader as to confess that there was yet a much stronger motive for the freedom I took in my representation of things. I had not been a year in this country, before I contracted such a love and veneration for the inhabitants, that I entered on a firm resolution never to return to humankind, but to pass the rest of my life among these admirable Houyhnhnms in the contemplation and practice of every virtue; where I could have no example or incitement to vice. But it was decreed by fortune, my perpetual enemy, that so great a felicity should not fall to my share. However, it is now some comfort to reflect that in what I said of my countrymen, I extenuated their faults as much as I durst before so strict an examiner; and upon every article, gave as favorable a turn as the matter would bear. For, indeed, who is there alive that will not be swayed by his bias and partiality to the place of his birth?

I have related the substance of several conversations I had with my master, during the greatest part of the time I had the honor to be in his service; but have indeed for brevity sake omitted much more than is here set down.

When I had answered all his questions, and his curiosity seemed to be fully satisfied; he sent for me one morning early, and commanding me to sit down at some distance (an honor which he had never before conferred upon me), he said he had been very seriously considering my whole story, as far as it related both to myself and my country; that, he looked upon us as a sort of animal to whose share, by what accident he could not conjecture, some small pittance of reason had fallen, whereof we made no other use than by its assistance to aggravate our natural corruptions, and to acquire new ones which nature had not given us. That we disarmed ourselves of the few abilities she had bestowed; had been very successful in multiplying our original wants, and seemed to spend our whole lives in vain endeavors to supply them by our own inventions. That, as to myself, it was manifest I had neither the strength or agility of a common Yahoo; that I walked infirmly on my hinder feet; had found out a contrivance to make my claws of no use or defense, and to remove the hair from my chin, which was intended as a shelter from the sun and the weather. Lastly, that I could neither run with speed, nor climb trees like my brethren (as he called them) the Yahoos in this country.

That our institutions of government and law were plainly owing to our gross defects in reason, and by consequence, in virtue; because reason alone is sufficient to govern a rational creature; which was therefore a character we had no pretense to challenge, even from the account I had given of my own people; although he manifestly perceived, that in order to favor them, I had concealed many particulars, and often *said the thing which was not.*

He was the more confirmed in this opinion, because he observed that I agreed in every feature of my body with other Yahoos, except where it was to my real disadvantage in point of strength, speed, and activity, the shortness of my claws, and some other particulars where nature had no part; so, from the representation I had given him of our lives, our manners, and our actions, he found as near a resemblance in the disposition of our minds. He said the Yahoos were known to hate one another more than they did any different species of animals; and the reason usually assigned was the odiousness of their own shapes, which all could see in the rest, but not in themselves. He had therefore begun to think it not unwise in us to cover our bodies, and by that invention, conceal many of our deformities from each other, which would else be hardly supportable. But he now found he had been mistaken; and that the dissentions of those brutes in his country were owing to the same cause with ours, as I had described them. For, if (said he) you throw among five Yahoos as much food as would be sufficient for fifty, they will, instead of eating peaceably, fall together by the ears, each single one impatient to have all to itself; and therefore a servant was usually employed to stand by while they were feeding abroad, and those kept at home were tied at a distance from each other. That, if a cow died of age or accident, before a Houyhnhnm could secure it for his own Yahoos, those in the neighborhood would come in herds to seize it, and then would ensue such a battle as I had described, with terrible wounds made by their claws on both sides, although they seldom were able to kill one another, for want of such convenient instruments of death as we had invented. At other times the like battles have been fought between the Yahoos of several neighborhoods without any visible cause; those of one district watching all opportunities to surprise the next before they are prepared. But if they find their project hath miscarried, they return home, and for want of enemies, engage in what I call a civil war among themselves.

That, in some fields of his country, there are certain shining stones of several colors, whereof the Yahoos are violently fond; and when part of these stones are fixed in the earth, as it sometimes happeneth, they will dig with their claws for whole days to get them out, and carry them away, and hide them by heaps in their kennels; but still looking round with great caution, for fear their comrades should find out their treasure. My master said he could never discover the reason of this unnatural appetite, or how these stones could be of any use to a Yahoo; but now he believed it might proceed from the same principle of avarice, which I had ascribed to mankind. That he had once, by way of experiment, privately removed a heap of these stones from the place where one of his Yahoos had buried it, whereupon, the sordid animal missing his treasure, by his loud lamenting brought the whole herd to the place, there miserably howled, then fell to biting and tearing the rest; began to pine away, would neither eat nor sleep, nor work, till he ordered a servant privately to convey the stones into the same hole, and hide them as before; which when his Yahoo had found, he presently recovered his spirits and good humor; but took care to remove them to a better hiding place; and hath ever since been a very serviceable brute.

My master farther assured me, which I also observed myself; that in the fields where these shining stones abound, the fiercest and most frequent battles are fought, occasioned by perpetual inroads of the neighboring Yahoos.

He said it was common when two Yahoos discovered such a stone in a field, and were contending which of them should be the proprietor, a third would take the advantage, and carry it away from them both; which my master would needs contend to have some resemblance with our suits at law; wherein I thought it for our credit not to undeceive him; since the decision he mentioned was much more equitable than many decrees among us; because the plaintiff and defendant there lost nothing beside the stone they contended for; whereas our courts of equity would never have dismissed the cause while either of them had anything left.

My master continuing his discourse said there was nothing that rendered the Yahoos more odious, than their undistinguished appetite to devour everything that came in their way, whether herbs, roots, berries, corrupted flesh of animals, or all mingled together; and it was peculiar in their temper, that they were fonder of what they could get by rapine or stealth at a greater distance, than much better food provided for them at home. If their prey held out, they would eat till they were ready to burst, after which nature had pointed out to them a certain root that gave them a general evacuation.

There was also another kind of root very juicy, but something rare and difficult to be found, which the Yahoos fought for with much eagerness, and would suck it with great delight; it produced the same effects that wine hath upon us. It would make them sometimes hug, and sometimes tear one another; they would howl and grin, and chatter, and reel, and tumble, and then fall asleep in the mud.

I did indeed observe that the Yahoos were the only animals in this country subject to any diseases; which however, were much fewer than horses have among us, and contracted not by any ill treatment they meet with, but by the nastiness and greediness of that sordid brute. Neither has their language any more than a general appellation for those maladies; which is borrowed from the name of the beast, and called *Hnea Yahoo,* or the Yahoo's Evil; and the cure prescribed is a mixture of their own dung and urine, forcibly put down the Yahoo's throat. This I have since often known to have been taken with success, and do here freely recommend it to my countrymen, for the public good, as an admirable specific against all diseases produced by repletion.

As to learning, government, arts, manufactures, and the like, my master confessed he could find little or no resemblance between the Yahoos of that country and those in ours. For he only meant to observe what parity there was in our natures. He had heard indeed some curious Houyhnhnms observe that in most herds there was a sort of ruling Yahoo (as among us there is generally some leading or principal stag in a park) who was always more deformed in body, and mischievous in disposition, than any of the rest. That this leader had usually a favorite as like himself as he could get, whose employment was to lick his master's feet and posteriors, and drive the female Yahoos to his kennel; for which he was now and then rewarded with a piece of ass's flesh. This favorite is hated by the whole herd; and therefore to protect himself, keeps always near the person of his leader. He usually continues in office till a worse can be found; but the very moment he is discarded, his successor, at the head of all the Yahoos in that district, young and old, male and female, come in a body, and discharge their excrements upon him from head to foot. But how far this might be applicable to our courts and favorites, and ministers of state, my master said I could best determine.

I durst make no return to this malicious insinuation, which debased human understanding below the sagacity of a common hound, who hath judgment enough to distinguish and follow the cry of the ablest dog in the pack, without being ever mistaken.

My master told me there were some qualities remarkable in the Yahoos, which he had not observed me to mention, or at least very slightly, in the accounts I had given him of humankind. He said, those animals, like other brutes, had their females in common; but in this differed, that the she-Yahoo would admit the male while she was pregnant; and that the hes would quarrel and fight with the females as fiercely as with each other. Both which practices were such degrees of infamous brutality, that no other sensitive creature ever arrived at.

Another thing he wondered at in the Yahoos was their strange disposition to nastiness and dirt; whereas there appears to be a natural love of cleanliness in all other animals. As to the two former accusations, I was glad to let them pass without any reply, because I had not a word to offer upon them in defense of my species, which otherwise I certainly had done from my own inclinations. But I could have easily vindicated humankind from the imputation of singularity upon the last article, if there had been any swine in that country (as unluckily for me there were not) which although it may be a sweeter quadruped than a Yahoo, cannot I humbly conceive in justice pretend to more cleanliness; and so his honor himself must have owned, if he had seen their filthy way of feeding, and their custom of wallowing and sleeping in the mud.

My master likewise mentioned another quality, which his servants had discovered in several Yahoos, and to him was wholly unaccountable. He said, a fancy would sometimes take a Yahoo, to retire into a corner, to lie down and howl, and groan, and spurn away all that came near him, although he were young and fat, and wanted neither food nor water; nor did the servants imagine what could possibly ail him. And the only remedy they found was to set him to hard work, after which he would infallibly come to himself. To this I was silent out of partiality to my own kind; yet here I could plainly discover the true seeds of spleen,[8] which only seizeth on the lazy, the luxurious, and the rich; who, if they were forced to undergo the same regimen, I would undertake for the cure.

His Honor had farther observed, that a female Yahoo would often stand behind a bank or a bush, to gaze on the young males passing by, and then appear, and hide, using many antic gestures and grimaces; at which time it was observed, that she had a most offensive smell; and when any of the males advanced, would slowly retire, looking back, and with a counterfeit show of fear, run off into some convenient place where she knew the male would follow her.

At other times, if a female stranger came among them, three or four of her own sex would get about her, and stare and chatter, and grin, and smell her all over; and then turn off with gestures that seemed to express contempt and disdain.

Perhaps my master might refine a little in these speculations, which he had drawn from what he observed himself, or had been told by others; however, I could not reflect without some amazement, and much sorrow, that the rudiments of lewdness, coquetry, censure, and scandal, should have place by instinct in womankind.

I expected every moment that my master would accuse the Yahoos of those unnatural appetites in both sexes, so common among us. But nature it seems hath not been so expert a school-mistress; and these politer pleasures are entirely the productions of art and reason, on our side of the globe.

CHAPTER VIII

The Author relateth several particulars of the Yahoos. The great virtues of the Houyhnhnms. The education and exercises of their youth. Their general assembly.

As I ought to have understood human nature much better than I supposed it possible for my master to do, so it was easy to apply the character he gave of the Yahoos to myself and my countrymen; and I believed I could yet make farther

8. Hypochondria.

discoveries from my own observation. I therefore often begged his honor to let me go among the herds of Yahoos in the neighborhood; to which he always very graciously consented, being perfectly convinced that the hatred I bore those brutes would never suffer me to be corrupted by them; and his honor ordered one of his servants, a strong sorrel nag, very honest and good-natured, to be my guard; without whose protection I durst not undertake such adventures. For I have already told the reader how much I was pestered by those odious animals upon my first arrival. I afterwards failed very narrowly three or four times of falling into their clutches, when I happened to stray at any distance without my hanger. And I have reason to believe, they had some imagination that I was of their own species, which I often assisted myself, by stripping up my sleeves, and shewing my naked arms and breast in their sight, when my protector was with me; at which times they would approach as near as they durst, and imitate my actions after the manner of monkeys, but ever with great signs of hatred; as a tame jackdaw with cap and stockings is always persecuted by the wild ones, when he happens to be got among them.

They are prodigiously nimble from their infancy; however, I once caught a young male of three years old, and endeavored by all marks of tenderness to make it quiet; but the little imp fell a squalling, scratching, and biting with such violence, that I was forced to let it go; and it was high time, for a whole troop of old ones came about us at the noise; but finding the cub was safe (for away it ran) and my sorrel nag being by, they durst not venture near us. I observed the young animal's flesh to smell very rank, and the stink was somewhat between a weasel and a fox, but much more disagreeable. I forgot another circumstance (and perhaps I might have the reader's pardon, if it were wholly omitted) that while I held the odious vermin in my hands, it voided its filthy excrements of a yellow liquid substance, all over my clothes; but by good fortune there was a small brook hard by, where I washed myself as clean as I could; although I durst not come into my master's presence until I were sufficiently aired.

By what I could discover, the Yahoos appear to be the most unteachable of all animals, their capacities never reaching higher than to draw or carry burdens. Yet I am of opinion, this defect ariseth chiefly from a perverse, restive disposition. For they are cunning, malicious, treacherous and revengeful. They are strong and hardy, but of a cowardly spirit, and by consequence insolent, abject, and cruel. It is observed that the red-haired of both sexes are more libidinous and mischievous than the rest, whom yet they much exceed in strength and activity.

The Houyhnhnms keep the Yahoos for present use in huts not far from the house; but the rest are sent abroad to certain fields, where they dig up roots, eat several kinds of herbs, and search about for carrion, or sometimes catch weasels and *luhimuhs* (a sort of wild rat) which they greedily devour. Nature hath taught them to dig deep holes with their nails on the side of a rising ground, wherein they lie by themselves; only the kennels of the females are larger, sufficient to hold two or three cubs.

They swim from their infancy like frogs, and are able to continue long under water, where they often take fish, which the females carry home to their young. And upon this occasion, I hope the reader will pardon my relating an odd adventure.

Being one day abroad with my protector the sorrel nag, and the weather exceeding hot, I entreated him to let me bathe in a river that was near. He consented, and I immediately stripped myself stark naked, and went down softly into the stream. It happened that a young female Yahoo standing behind a bank, saw the whole proceeding; and inflamed by desire, as the nag and I conjectured, came running with all speed, and leaped into the water within five yards of the place where I bathed. I was never in my life so terribly frighted; the nag was grazing at some distance, not suspecting any harm; she embraced me after a most fulsome manner; I roared as loud as I could, and the nag came galloping towards me, whereupon she quitted her grasp, with the utmost reluctancy, and leaped upon the opposite bank, where she stood gazing and howling all the time I was putting on my clothes.

This was matter of diversion to my master and his family, as well as of mortification to myself. For now I could no longer deny that I was a real Yahoo, in every limb and feature, since the females had a natural propensity to me as one of their own species; neither was the hair of this brute of a red color (which might have been some excuse for an appetite a little irregular) but black as a sole, and her countenance did not make an appearance altogether so hideous as the rest of the kind; for I think, she could not be above eleven years old.

Having already lived three years in this country, the reader I suppose will expect that I should, like other travelers, give him some account of the manners and customs of its inhabitants, which it was indeed my principal study to learn.

As these noble Houyhnhnms are endowed by Nature with a general disposition to all virtues, and have no conceptions or ideas of what is evil in a rational creature; so their grand maxim is to cultivate reason, and to be wholly governed by it. Neither is reason among them a point problematical as with us, where men can argue with plausibility on both sides of a question; but strikes you with immediate conviction; as it must needs do where it is not mingled, obscured, or discolored by passion and interest. I remember it was with extreme difficulty that I could bring my master to understand the meaning of the word "opinion," or how a point could be disputable; because reason taught us to affirm or deny only where we are certain; and beyond our knowledge we cannot do either. So that controversies, wranglings, disputes, and positiveness in false or dubious propositions are evils unknown among the Houyhnhnms. In the like manner when I used to explain to him our several systems of natural philosophy, he would laugh that a creature pretending to reason should value itself upon the knowledge of other people's conjectures, and in things, where that knowledge, if it were certain, could be of no use. Wherein he agreed entirely with the sentiments of Socrates, as Plato delivers them, which I mention as the highest honor I can do that prince of philosophers. I have often since reflected what destruction such a doctrine would make in the libraries of Europe; and how many paths to fame would be then shut up in the learned world.

Friendship and benevolence are the two principal virtues among the Houyhnhnms; and these not confined to particular objects, but universal to the whole race. For a stranger from the remotest part is equally treated with the nearest neighbor, and wherever he goes, looks upon himself as at home.

They preserve decency and civility in the highest degrees, but are altogether ignorant of ceremony. They have no fondness for[9] their colts or foals; but the care they take in educating them proceedeth entirely from the dictates of reason. And I observed my master to show the same affection to his neighbor's issue that he had for his own. They will have it that nature teaches them to love the whole species, and it is reason only that maketh a distinction of persons, where there is a superior degree of virtue.

When the matron Houyhnhnms have produced one of each sex, they no longer accompany with their consorts, except they lose one of their issue by some casualty, which very seldom happens; but in such a case they meet again; or when the like accident befalls a person whose wife is past bearing, some other couple bestows on him one of their own colts, and then go together a second time, until the mother be pregnant. This caution is necessary to prevent the country from being overburdened with numbers. But the race of inferior Houyhnhnms bred up to be servants is not so strictly limited upon this article; these are allowed to produce three of each sex, to be domestics in the noble families.

In their marriages they are exactly careful to choose such colors as will not make any disagreeable mixture in the breed. Strength is chiefly valued in the male, and comeliness in the female; not upon the account of love, but to preserve the race from degenerating; for, where a female happens to excel in strength, a consort is chosen with regard to comeliness. Courtship, love, presents, jointures, settlements, have no place in their thoughts, or terms whereby to express them in their language. The young couple meet and are joined, merely because it is the determination of their parents and friends; it is what they see done every day; and they look upon it as one of the necessary actions in a reasonable being. But the violation of marriage, or any other unchastity, was never heard of; and the married pair pass their lives with the same friendship and mutual benevolence that they bear to all others of the same species who come in their way, without jealousy, fondness, quarreling, or discontent.

In educating the youth of both sexes, their method is admirable, and highly deserveth our imitation. These are not suffered to taste a grain of oats, except upon certain days, till eighteen years old; nor milk, but very rarely; and in summer they graze two hours in the morning, and as many in the evening, which their parents likewise observe; but the servants are not allowed above half that time; and a great part of the grass is brought home, which they eat at the most convenient hours, when they can be best spared from work.

Temperance, industry, exercise, and cleanliness are the lessons equally enjoined to the young ones of both sexes; and my master thought it monstrous in us to give the females a different kind of education from the males, except in some articles of domestic management; whereby, as he truly observed, one half of our natives were good for nothing but bringing children into the world; and to trust the care of their children to such useless animals, he said was yet a greater instance of brutality.

But the Houyhnhnms train up their youth to strength, speed, and hardiness, by exercising them in running races up and down steep hills, or over hard stony grounds; and when they are all in a sweat, they are ordered to

9. Attachment to.

leap over head and ears into a pond or a river. Four times a year the youth of certain districts meet to show their proficiency in running, and leaping, and other feats of strength or agility; where the victor is rewarded with a song made in his or her praise. On this festival the servants drive a herd of Yahoos into the field, laden with hay, and oats, and milk for a repast to the Houyhnhnms; after which these brutes are immediately driven back again, for fear of being noisome to the assembly.

Every fourth year, at the vernal equinox, there is a representative council of the whole nation, which meets in a plain about twenty miles from our house, and continueth about five or six days. Here they inquire into the state and condition of the several districts; whether they abound or be deficient in hay or oats, or cows or Yahoos? And wherever there is any want (which is but seldom) it is immediately supplied by unanimous consent and contribution. Here likewise the regulation of children is settled: as for instance, if a Houyhnhnm hath two males, he changeth one of them with another who hath two females, and when a child hath been lost by any casualty, where the mother is past breeding, it is determined what family in the district shall breed another to supply the loss.

CHAPTER IX

A grand debate at the general assembly of the Houyhnhnms, and how it was determined. The learning of the Houyhnhnms. Their buildings. Their manner of burials. The defectiveness of their language.

One of these grand assemblies was held in my time, about three months before my departure, whither my master went as the representative of our district. In this council was resumed their old debate, and indeed, the only debate that ever happened in their country; whereof my master after his return gave me a very particular account.

The question to be debated was whether the Yahoos should be exterminated from the face of the earth. One of the members for the affirmative offered several arguments of great strength and weight, alleging that, as the Yahoos were the most filthy, noisome, and deformed animal which nature ever produced, so they were the most restive and indocile, mischievous, and malicious; they would privately suck the teats of the Houyhnhnms' cows; kill and devour their cats, trample down their oats and grass, if they were not continually watched; and commit a thousand other extravagancies. He took notice of a general tradition, that Yahoos had not been always in their country, but that many ages ago, two of these brutes appeared together upon a mountain; whether produced by the heat of the sun upon corrupted mud and slime, or from the ooze and froth of the sea, was never known. That these Yahoos engendered, and their brood in a short time grew so numerous as to overrun and infest the whole nation. That the Houyhnhnms to get rid of this evil, made a general hunting, and at last enclosed the whole herd; and destroying the older, every Houyhnhnm kept two young ones in a kennel, and brought them to such a degree of tameness as an animal so savage by nature can be capable of acquiring, using them for draft and carriage. That there seemed to be much truth in this tradition, and that those creatures could not be *ylnhniamshy* (or aborigines of the land) because of the violent hatred the Houyhnhnms as well as all other animals bore them; which although their evil disposition sufficiently deserved, could never have arrived at so high a degree, if they had been aborigines, or else they would have long since been rooted out. That the inhabitants taking a fancy to use the service of the Yahoos, had very imprudently neglected to cultivate the breed of asses, which were a comely animal, easily kept, more tame and orderly, without any offensive smell, strong enough for labor, although they yield to the other in agility of body; and if their braying be no agreeable sound, it is far preferable to the horrible howlings of the Yahoos.

Several others declared their sentiments to the same purpose, when my master proposed an expedient to the assembly, whereof he had indeed borrowed the hint from me. He approved of the tradition, mentioned by the honorable member, who spoke before; and affirmed, that the two Yahoos said to be first seen among them, had been driven thither over the sea; that coming to land, and being forsaken by their companions, they retired to the mountains, and degenerating by degrees, became in process of time much more savage than those of their own species in the country from whence these two originals came. The reason of his assertion was that he had now in his possession a certain wonderful Yahoo (meaning myself) which most of them had heard of, and many of them had seen. He then related to them how he first found me; that my body was all covered with an artificial composure of the skins and hairs of other animals; that I spoke in a language of my own, and had thoroughly learned theirs; that I had related to him the accidents which brought me thither; that when he saw me without my covering, I was an exact Yahoo in every part, only of a whiter color, less hairy and with shorter claws. He added how I had endeavored to persuade him that in my own and other countries the Yahoos acted as the governing, rational animal, and held the Houyhnhnms in servitude; that he observed in me all the qualities of a Yahoo, only a little more civilized by some tincture of reason, which however was in a degree as far inferior to the Houyhnhnm race as the Yahoos of their country were to me; that among other things, I mentioned a custom we had of castrating Houyhnhnms when they were young, in order to render them tame; that the operation was easy and safe; that it was no shame to learn wisdom from brutes, as industry is taught by the ant, and building by the swallow (for so I translate the world *lyhannh*, although it be a much larger fowl). That this invention might be practiced upon the younger Yahoos here, which, besides rendering them tractable and fitter for use, would in an age put an end to the whole species without destroying life. That in the meantime the Houyhnhnms should be exhorted to cultivate the breed of asses, which, as they are in all respects more valuable brutes, so they have this advantage, to be fit for service at five years old, which the others are not till twelve.

This was all my master thought fit to tell me at that time, of what passed in the grand council. But he was pleased to conceal one particular, which related personally to myself, whereof I soon felt the unhappy effect, as the reader will know in its proper place, and from whence I date all the succeeding misfortunes of my life.

The Houyhnhnms have no letters, and consequently, their knowledge is all traditional. But there happening few events of any moment among a people so well united, naturally disposed to every virtue, wholly governed by reason, and cut off from all commerce with other nations, the historical part is easily preserved without burdening their memories. I have already observed that they are subject to no diseases, and therefore can have no need of physicians. However, they have excellent medicines composed of herbs, to cure accidental bruises and cuts in the pastern or frog of the foot by sharp stones, as well as other maims and hurts in the several parts of the body.

They calculate the year by the revolution of the sun and the moon, but use no subdivisions into weeks. They are well enough acquainted with the motions of those two luminaries, and understand the nature of eclipses; and this is the utmost progress of their astronomy.

In poetry they must be allowed to excel all other mortals; wherein the justness of their similes, and the minuteness, as well as exactness of their descriptions, are indeed inimitable. Their verses abound very much in both of these, and usually contain either some exalted notions of friendship and benevolence, or the praises of those who were victors in races and other bodily exercises. Their buildings, although very rude and simple, are not inconvenient, but well contrived to defend them from all injuries of cold and heat. They have a kind of tree, which at forty years old loosens in the root, and falls with the first storm; it grows very straight, and being pointed like stakes with a sharp stone (for the Houyhnhnms know not the use of iron), they stick them erect in the ground about ten inches asunder, and then weave in oat straw, or sometimes wattles, betwixt them. The roof is made after the same manner, and so are the doors.

The Houyhnhnms use the hollow part between the pastern and the hoof of their forefeet as we do our hands, and this with greater dexterity than I could at first imagine. I have seen a white mare of our family thread a needle (which I lent her on purpose) with that joint. They milk their cows, reap their oats, and do all the work which requires hands in the same manner. They have a kind of hard flints, which by grinding against other stones they form into instruments that serve instead of wedges, axes, and hammers. With tools made of these flints, they likewise cut their hay, and reap their oats, which there groweth naturally in several fields; the Yahoos draw home the sheaves in carriages, and the servants tread them in certain covered huts, to get out the grain, which is kept in stores. They make a rude kind of earthen and wooden vessels, and bake the former in the sun.

If they can avoid casualties, they die only of old age, and are buried in the obscurest places that can be found, their friends and relations expressing neither joy nor grief at their departure; nor does the dying person discover the least regret that he is leaving the world, any more than if he were upon returning home from a visit to one of his neighbors; I remember my master having once made an appointment with a friend and his family to come to his house upon some affair of importance; on the day fixed, the mistress and her two children came very late; she made two excuses, first for her husband, who, as she said, happened that very morning to *lhnuwnh*. The word is strongly expressive in their language, but not easily rendered into English; it signifies, *to retire to his first Mother*. Her excuse for not coming sooner was that her husband dying late in the morning, she was a good while consulting her servants about a convenient place where his body should be laid; and I observed she behaved herself at our house, as cheerfully as the rest; she died about three months after.

They live generally to seventy or seventy-five years, very seldom to fourscore; some weeks before their death they feel a gradual decay, but without pain. During this time they are much visited by their friends, because they cannot go abroad with their usual ease and satisfaction. However, about ten days before their death, which they seldom fail in computing, they return the visits that have been made by those who are nearest in the neighborhood, being carried in a convenient sledge drawn by Yahoos; which vehicle they use, not only upon this occasion, but when they grow old, upon long journeys, or when they are lamed by any accident. And therefore when the dying Houyhnhnms return those visits, they take a solemn leave of their friends, as if they were going to some remote part of the country, where they designed to pass the rest of their lives.

I know not whether it may be worth observing, that the Houyhnhnms have no word in their language to express anything that is evil, except what they borrow from the deformities or ill qualities of the Yahoos. Thus they denote the folly of a servant, an omission of a child, a stone that cuts their feet, a continuance of foul or unseasonable weather, and the like, by adding to each the epithet of Yahoo. For instance, *hhnm Yahoo, whnaholm Yahoo, ynlhmnd-wihlma Yahoo,* and an ill-contrived house, *ynholmhnmrohlnw Yahoo.*

I could with great pleasure enlarge farther upon the manners and virtues of this excellent people; but intending in a short time to publish a volume by itself expressly upon that subject, I refer the reader thither. And in the meantime, proceed to relate my own sad catastrophe.

CHAPTER X

The Author's economy, and happy life among the Houyhnhnms. His great improvement in virtue, by conversing with them. Their conversations. The Author hath notice given him by his master that he must depart from the country. He falls into a swoon for grief, but submits. He contrives and finishes a canoe, by the help of a fellow servant, and puts to sea at a venture.

I had settled my little economy to my own heart's content. My master had ordered a room to be made for me after their manner, about six yards from the house; the sides and floors of which I plastered with clay, and covered with rush mats of my own contriving; I had beaten hemp, which there grows wild, and made of it a sort of ticking; this I filled with the feathers of several birds I had taken with springes made of Yahoos' hairs, and were excellent food. I had worked two chairs with my knife, the sorrel nag helping me in the grosser and more laborious part. When my clothes were worn to rags, I made myself others with the skins of rabbits, and of a certain beautiful animal about the same size, called *nnuhnoh,* the skin of which is covered with a fine down. Of these I likewise made very tolerable stockings. I soled my shoes with wood which I cut from a tree, and fitted to the upper leather, and when this was worn out, I supplied it with the skins of Yahoos, dried in the sun. I often got honey out of hollow trees, which I mingled with water, or eat it with my bread. No man could more verify the truth of these two maxims, that *Nature is very easily satisfied;* and, that *Necessity is the mother of invention.* I enjoyed perfect health of body, and tranquility of mind; I did not feel the treachery or inconstancy of a friend, nor the inquiries of a secret or open enemy. I had no occasion of bribing, flattering, or pimping to procure the favor of any great man, or of his minion. I wanted no fence against fraud or oppression; here was neither physician to destroy my body, nor lawyer to ruin my fortune; no informer to watch my words and actions, or forge accusations against me for hire; here were no gibers, censurers, backbiters, pickpockets, highwaymen, housebreakers, attorneys, bawds, buffoons, gamesters, politicians, wits, splenetics, tedious talkers, controvertists, ravishers, murderers, robbers, virtuosos; no leaders or followers of party and faction; no encouragers to vice, by seducement or examples; no dungeons, axes, gibbets, whipping posts, or pillories; no cheating shopkeepers or mechanics; no pride, vanity or affectation; no fops, bullies, drunkards, strolling whores, or poxes; no ranting, lewd, expensive wives; no stupid, proud pedants; no importunate, overbearing, quarrelsome, noisy, roaring, empty, conceited, swearing companions; no scoundrels raised from the dust upon the merit of their vices; or nobility thrown into it on account of their virtues; no lords, fiddlers, judges, or dancing masters.

I had the favor of being admitted to several Houyhnhnms, who came to visit or dine with my master; where his honor graciously suffered me to wait in the room, and listen to their discourse. Both he and his company would often descend to ask me questions, and receive my answers. I had also sometimes the honor of attending my master in his visits to others. I never presumed to speak, except in answer to a question; and then I did it with inward regret, because it was a loss of so much time for improving myself; but I was infinitely delighted with the station of an humble auditor in such conversations, where nothing passed but what was useful, expressed in the fewest and most significant words; where (as I have already said) the greatest decency was observed, without the least degree of ceremony; where no person spoke without being pleased himself, and pleasing his companions; where there was no interruption, tediousness, heat, or difference of sentiments. They have a notion, that when people are met together, a short silence doth much improve conversation; this I found to be true; for during those little intermissions of talk, new ideas would arise in their minds, which very much enlivened the discourse. Their subjects are generally on friendship and benevolence; on order and economy; sometimes upon the visible operations of nature, or ancient traditions; upon the bounds and limits of virtue; upon the unerring rules of reason; or upon some determinations, to be taken at the next great assembly; and often upon the various excellencies of poetry. I may add, without vanity, that my presence often gave them sufficient matter for discourse, because it afforded my master an occasion of letting his friends into the history of me and my country, upon which they were all pleased to discant in a manner not very advantageous to human kind; and for that reason I shall not repeat what they said; only I may be allowed to observe that his honor, to my great admiration, appeared to understand the nature of Yahoos much better than myself. He went through all our vices and follies, and discovered many which I had never mentioned to him; by only supposing what qualities a Yahoo of their country, with a small proportion of reason, might be capable of exerting; and concluded, with too much probability, how vile as well as miserable such a creature must be.

I freely confess, that all the little knowledge I have of any value was acquired by the lectures I received from my master, and from hearing the discourses of him and his friends; to which I should be prouder to listen, than to dictate to the greatest and wisest assembly in Europe. I admired the strength, comeliness, and speed of the inhabitants; and such a constellation of virtues in such amiable persons produced in me the highest veneration. At first, indeed, I did not feel that natural awe which the Yahoos and all other animals bear towards them; but it grew upon me by degrees, much sooner than I imagined, and was mingled with a respectful love and gratitude, that they would condescend to distinguish me from the rest of my species.

When I thought of my family, my friends, my countrymen, or human race in general, I considered them as they really were, Yahoos in shape and disposition, perhaps a little more civilized, and qualified with the gift of speech; but making no other use of reason than to improve and mutiply those vices, whereof their brethren in this country had only the share that nature allotted them. When I happened to behold the reflection of my own form in a lake or fountain, I turned away my face in horror and detestation of myself, and could better endure the sight of a common Yahoo than of my own person. By conversing with the Houyhnhnms, and looking upon them with delight, I fell to imitate their gait and gesture, which is now grown into a habit; and my friends often tell me in a blunt way, that I trot like a horse; which, however, I take for a great compliment; neither shall I disown, that in speaking I am apt to fall into the voice and manner of the Houyhnhnms, and hear myself ridiculed on that account without the least mortification.

In the midst of this happiness, when I looked upon myself to be fully settled for life, my master sent for me one morning a little earlier than his usual hour. I observed by his countenance that he was in some perplexity, and at a loss how to begin what he had to speak. After a short silence, he told me, he did not know how I would take what he was going to say; that, in the last general assembly, when the affair of the Yahoos was entered upon, the representatives had taken offense at his keeping a Yahoo (meaning myself) in his family more like a Houyhnhnm than a brute animal. That he was known frequently to converse with me, as if he could receive some advantage of pleasure in my company; that such a practice was not agreeable to reason or nature, or a thing ever heard of before among them. The assembly did therefore exhort him, either to employ me like the rest of my species, or command me to swim back to the place from whence I came. That the first of these expedients was utterly rejected by all the Houyhnhnms who had ever seen me at his house or their own; for, they alleged, that because I had some rudiments of reason, added to the natural pravity of those animals, it was to be feared, I might be able to seduce them into the woody and mountainous parts of the country, and bring them in troops by night to destroy the Houyhnhnms' cattle, as being naturally of the ravenous kind, and averse from labor.

My master added that he was daily pressed by the Houyhnhnms of the neighborhood to have the assembly's exhortation executed, which he could not put off much longer. He doubted[1] it would be impossible for me to swim to another country; and therefore wished I would contrive some sort of vehicle resembling those I had described to him, that might carry me on the sea; in which work I should have the assistance of his

---

1. Suspected.

own servants, as well as those of his neighbors. He concluded that for his own part he could have been content to keep me in his service as long as I lived; because he found I had cured myself of some bad habits and dispositions, by endeavoring, as far as my inferior nature was capable, to imitate the Houyhnhnms.

I should here observe to the reader, that a decree of the general assembly in this country is expressed by the word *hnhloayn*, which signifies an exhortation, as near as I can render it; for they have no conception how a rational creature can be compelled, but only advised, or exhorted; because no person can disobey reason without giving up his claim to be a rational creature.

I was struck with the utmost grief and despair at my master's discourse; and being unable to support the agonies I was under, I fell into a swoon at his feet; when I came to myself, he told me that he concluded I had been dead (for these people are subject to no such imbecilities of nature). I answered, in a faint voice, that death would have been too great an happiness; that although I could not blame the assembly's exhortation, or the urgency of his friends; yet in my weak and corrupt judgment, I thought it might consist with reason to have been less rigorous. That I could not swim a league, and probably the nearest land to theirs might be distant above an hundred; that many materials, necessary for making a small vessel to carry me off, were wholly wanting in this country, which, however, I would attempt in obedience and gratitude to his honor, although I concluded the thing to be impossible, and therefore looked on myself as already devoted[2] to destruction. That the certain prospect of an unnatural death was the least of my evils; for, supposing I should escape with life by some strange adventure, how could I think with temper[3] of passing my days among Yahoos, and relapsing into my old corruptions, for want of examples to lead and keep me within the paths of virtue. That I knew too well upon what solid reasons all the determinations of the wise Houyhnhnms were founded, not to be shaken by arguments of mine, a miserable Yahoo; and therefore after presenting him with my humble thanks for the offer of his servants' assistance in making a vessel, and desiring a reasonable time for so difficult a work, I told him I would endeavor to preserve a wretched being; and, if ever I returned to England, was not without hopes of being useful to my own species by celebrating the praises of the renowned Houyhnhnms, and proposing their virtues to the imitation of mankind.

My master in a few words made me a very gracious reply, allowed me the space of two months to finish my boat, and ordered the sorrel nag, my fellow servant (for so at this distance I may presume to call him), to follow my instructions, because I told my master that his help would be sufficient, and I knew he had a tenderness for me.

In his company my first business was to go to that part of the coast where my rebellious crew had ordered me to be set on shore. I got upon a height, and looking on every side into the sea, fancied I saw a small island towards the northeast; I took out my pocket glass, and could then clearly distinguish it about five leagues off, as I computed; but it appeared to the sorrel nag to be only a blue cloud; for, as he had no conception of any country besides his

2. Doomed.   3. Equanimity.

own, so he could not be as expert in distinguishing remote objects at sea, as we who so much converse in that element.

After I had discovered this island, I considered no farther; but resolved, it should, if possible, be the first place of my banishment, leaving the consequence to fortune.

I returned home, and consulting with the sorrel nag, we went into a copse at some distance, where I with my knife, and he with a sharp flint fastened very artificially,[4] after their manner, to a wooden handle, cut down several oak wattles about the thickness of a walking staff, and some larger pieces. But I shall not trouble the reader with a particular description of my own mechanics; let it suffice to say, that in six weeks time, with the help of the sorrel nag, who performed the parts that required most labor, I finished a sort of Indian canoe; but much larger, covering it with the skins of Yahoos, well stitched together, with hempen threads of my own making. My sail was likewise composed of the skins of the same animal; but I made use of the youngest I could get, the older being too tough and thick; and I likewise provided myself with four paddles. I laid in a stock of boiled flesh, of rabbits and fowls; and took with me two vessels, one filled with milk, and the other with water.

I tried my canoe in a large pond near my master's house, and then corrected in it what was amiss, stopping all the chinks with Yahoo's tallow, till I found it staunch, and able to bear me and my freight. And when it was as complete as I could possibly make it, I had it drawn on a carriage very gently by Yahoos, to the seaside, under the conduct of the sorrel nag and another servant.

When all was ready, and the day came for my departure, I took leave of my master and lady, and the whole family, my eyes flowing with tears and my heart quite sunk with grief. But his honor, out of curiosity, and perhaps (if I may speak it without vanity) partly out of kindness, was determined to see me in my canoe; and got several of his neighboring friends to accompany him. I was forced to wait above an hour for the tide, and then observing the wind very fortunately bearing towards the island to which I intended to steer my course, I took a second leave of my master; but as I was going to prostrate myself to kiss his hoof, he did me the honor to raise it gently to my mouth. I am not ignorant how much I have been censured for mentioning this last particular. Detractors are pleased to think it improbable that so illustrious a person should descend to give so great a mark of distinction to a creature so inferior as I. Neither have I forgot how apt some travelers are to boast of extraordinary favors they have received. But, if these censurers were better acquainted with the noble and courteous disposition of the Houyhnhnms, they would soon change their opinion. I paid my respects to the rest of the Houyhnhnms in his honor's company; then getting into my canoe, I pushed off from shore.

4. Adroitly.

CHAPTER XI

The Author's dangerous voyage. He arrives at New Holland, hoping to settle there. Is wounded with an arrow by one of the natives. Is seized and carried by force into a Portuguese ship. The great civilities of the Captain. The Author arrives at England.

I began this desperate voyage on February 15, 1714/5,[5] at 9 o'clock in the morning. The wind was very favorable; however, I made use at first only of my paddles; but considering I should soon be weary, and that the wind might probably chop about, I ventured to set up my little sail; and thus, with the help of the tide, I went at the rate of a league and a half an hour, as near as I could guess. My master and his friends continued on the shore, till I was almost out of sight; and I often heard the sorrel nag (who always loved me) crying out, *"Hnuy illa nyha maiah Yahoo"* ("Take care of thyself, gentle Yahoo").

My design was, if possible, to discover some small island uninhabited, yet sufficient by my labor to furnish me with necessaries of life, which I would have thought a greater happiness than to be first minister in the politest court of Europe, so horrible was the idea I conceived of returning to live in the society and under the government of Yahoos. For in such a solitude as I desired, I could at least enjoy my own thoughts, and reflect with delight on the virtues of those inimitable Houyhnhnms, without any opportunity of degenerating into the vices and corruptions of my own species.

The reader may remember what I related when my crew conspired against me, and confined me to my cabin, how I continued there several weeks, without knowing what course we took; and when I was put ashore in the longboat, how the sailors told me with oaths, whether true or false, that they knew not in what part of the world we were. However, I did then believe us to be about 10 degrees southward of the Cape of Good Hope, or about 45 degrees southern latitude, as I gathered from some general words I overheard among them, being I supposed to the southeast in their intended voyage to Madagascar. And although this were but little better than conjecture, yet I resolved to steer my course eastward, hoping to reach the southwest coast of New Holland, and perhaps some such island as I desired, lying westward of it. The wind was full west, and by six in the evening I computed I had gone eastward at least eighteen leagues; when I spied a very small island about half a league off, which I soon reached. It was nothing but a rock with one creek,[6] naturally arched by the force of tempests. Here I put in my canoe, and climbing a part of the rock, I could plainly discover land to the east, extending from south to north. I lay all night in my canoe; and repeating my voyage early in the morning, I arrived in seven hours to the southeast point of New Holland.[7] This confirmed me in the opinion I have long entertained, that the maps and charts place this country at least three degrees more to the east than it really is; which thought I communicated many years ago to my worthy friend Mr. Herman Moll,[8] and gave him my reasons for it, although he hath rather chosen to follow other authors.

I saw no inhabitants in the place where I landed; and being unarmed, I

---

5. I.e., 1714. The year began on March 25.   6. A bay.   7. Present-day Republic of South Africa.
8. A famous contemporary mapmaker.

was afraid of venturing far into the country. I found some shellfish on the shore, and eat them raw, not daring to kindle a fire, for fear of being discovered by the natives. I continued three days feeding on oysters and limpets, to save my own provisions; and I fortunately found a brook of excellent water, which gave me great relief.

On the fourth day, venturing out early a little too far, I saw twenty or thirty natives upon a height, not above five hundred yards from me. They were stark naked, men, women, and children round a fire, as I could discover by the smoke. One of them spied me, and gave notice to the rest; five of them advanced towards me, leaving the women and children at the fire. I made what haste I could to the shore, and getting into my canoe, shoved off; the savages observing me retreat, ran after me; and before I could get far enough into the sea, discharged an arrow, which wounded me deeply on the inside of my left knee. (I shall carry the mark to my grave.) I apprehended the arrow might be poisoned; and paddling out of the reach of their darts (being a calm day) I made a shift to suck the wound, and dress it as well as I could.

I was at a loss what to do, for I durst not return to the same landing place, but stood to the north, and was forced to paddle; for the wind, although very gentle, was against me, blowing northwest. As I was looking about for a secure landing place, I saw a sail to the north northeast, which appearing every minute more visible, I was in some doubt whether I should wait for them or no; but at last my detestation of the Yahoo race prevailed; and turning my canoe, I sailed and paddled together to the south, and got into the same creek from whence I set out in the morning, choosing rather to trust myself among these barbarians than live with European Yahoos. I drew up my canoe as close as I could to the shore, and hid myself behind a stone by the little brook, which, as I have already said, was excellent water.

The ship came within half a league of this creek, and sent out her longboat with vessels to take in fresh water (for the place it seems was very well known), but I did not observe it until the boat was almost on shore; and it was too late to seek another hiding place. The seamen at their landing observed my canoe, and rummaging it all over, easily conjectured that the owner could not be far off. Four of them well armed searched every cranny and lurking hole, till at last they found me flat on my face behind the stone. They gazed a while in admiration at my strange uncouth dress; my coat made of skins, my wooden-soled shoes, and my furred stockings; from whence, however, they concluded I was not a native of the place, who all go naked. One of the seamen in Portuguese bid me rise, and asked who I was. I understood that language very well, and getting upon my feet, said I was a poor Yahoo, banished from the Houyhnhnms, and desired they would please to let me depart. They admired to hear me answer them in their own tongue, and saw by my complexion I must be an European; but were at a loss to know what I meant by Yahoos and Houyhnhnms, and at the same time fell a laughing at my strange tone in speaking, which resembled the neighing of a horse. I trembled all the while betwixt fear and hatred; I again desired leave to depart, and was gently moving to my canoe; but they laid hold on me, desiring to know what country I was of? whence I came? with many other questions. I told them I was born in England, from whence I came about five years ago, and then their country and ours was at peace. I therefore hoped they would not treat me as an enemy, since I meant them no harm, but was a poor Yahoo, seeking some desolate place where to pass the remainder of his unfortunate life.

When they began to talk, I thought I never heard or saw any thing so unnatural; for it appeared to me as monstrous as if a dog or a cow should speak in England, or a Yahoo in Houyhnhnmland. The honest Portuguese were equally amazed at my strange dress, and the odd manner of delivering my words, which however they understood very well. They spoke to me with great humanity, and said they were sure their Captain would carry me *gratis* to Lisbon, from whence I might return to my own country; that two of the seamen would go back to the ship, to inform the Captain of what they had seen, and receive his orders; in the meantime, unless I would give my solemn oath not to fly, they would secure me by force. I thought it best to comply with their proposal. They were very curious to know my story, but I gave them very little satisfaction; and they all conjectured, that my misfortunes had impaired my reason. In two hours the boat, which went laden with vessels of water, returned with the Captain's commands to fetch me on board. I fell on my knees to preserve my liberty; but all was in vain, and the men having tied me with cords, heaved me into the boat, from whence I was taken into the ship, and from thence into the Captain's cabin.

His name was Pedro de Mendez; he was a very courteous and generous person; he entreated me to give some account of myself, and desired to know what I would eat or drink; said I should be used as well as himself, and spoke so many obliging things, that I wondered to find such civilities from a Yahoo. However, I remained silent and sullen; I was ready to faint at the very smell of him and his men. At last I desired something to eat out of my own canoe; but he ordered me a chicken and some excellent wine, and then directed that I should be put to bed in a very clean cabin. I would not undress myself, but lay on the bedclothes; and in half an hour stole out, when I thought the crew was at dinner; and getting to the side of the ship, was going to leap into the sea, and swim for my life, rather than continue among Yahoos. But one of the seamen prevented me, and having informed the Captain, I was chained to my cabin.

After dinner Don Pedro came to me, and desired to know my reason for so desperate an attempt; assured me he only meant to do me all the service he was able; and spoke so very movingly, that at last I descended to treat him like an animal which had some little portion of reason. I gave him a very short relation of my voyage; of the conspiracy against me by my own men; of the country where they set me on shore, and of my five years residence there. All which he looked upon as if it were a dream or a vision; whereat I took great offense; for I had quite forgot the faculty of lying, so peculiar to Yahoos in all countries where they preside, and consequently the disposition of suspecting truth in others of their own species. I asked him whether it were the custom of his country to *say the thing that was not?* I assured him I had almost forgot what he meant by falsehood; and if I had lived a thousand years in Houyhnhnmland, I should never have heard a lie from the meanest servant. That I was altogether indifferent whether he believed me or no; but however, in return for his favors, I would give so much allowance to the corruption of his nature, as to answer any objection he would please to make; and he might easily discover the truth.

The Captain, a wise man, after many endeavors to catch me tripping in some part of my story, at last began to have a better opinion of my veracity. But he added that since I professed so inviolable an attachment to truth, I must give him my word of honor to bear him company in this voyage without attempting anything against my life; or else he would continue me a prisoner till we arrived at Lisbon. I gave him the promise he required; but at the same time protested that I would suffer the greatest hardships rather than return to live among Yahoos.

Our voyage passed without any considerable accident. In gratitude to the Captain I sometimes sat with him at his earnest request, and strove to conceal my antipathy against humankind, although it often broke out; which he suffered to pass without observation. But the greatest part of the day, I confined myself to my cabin, to avoid seeing any of the crew. The Captain had often entreated me to strip myself of my savage dress, and offered to lend me the best suit of clothes he had. This I would not be prevailed on to accept, abhorring to cover myself with anything that had been on the back of a Yahoo. I only desired he would lend me two clean shirts, which having been washed since he wore them, I believed would not so much defile me. These I changed every second day, and washed them myself.

We arrived at Lisbon, Nov. 5, 1715. At our landing, the Captain forced me to cover myself with his cloak, to prevent the rabble from crowding about me. I was conveyed to his own house; and at my earnest request, he led me up to the highest room backwards.[9] I conjured him to conceal from all persons what I had told him of the Houyhnhnms; because the least hint of such a story would not only draw numbers of people to see me, but probably put me in danger of being imprisoned, or burned by the Inquisition. The Captain persuaded me to accept a suit of clothes newly made; but I would not suffer the tailor to take my measure; however, Don Pedro being almost of my size, they fitted me well enough. He accoutred me with other necessaries, all new, which I aired for twenty-four hours before I would use them.

The Captain had no wife, nor above three servants, none of which were suffered to attend at meals; and his whole deportment was so obliging, added to very good human understanding, that I really began to tolerate his company. He gained so far upon me, that I ventured to look out of the back window. By degrees I was brought into another room, from whence I peeped into the street, but drew my head back in a fright. In a week's time he seduced me down to the door. I found my terror gradually lessened, but my hatred and contempt seemed to increase. I was at last bold enough to walk the street in his company, but kept my nose well stopped with rue, or sometimes with tobacco.

In ten days, Don Pedro, to whom I had given some account of my domestic affairs, put it upon me as a point of honor and conscience that I ought to return to my native country, and live at home with my wife and children. He told me there was an English ship in the port just ready to sail, and he would furnish me with all things necessary. It would be tedious to repeat his arguments, and my contradictions. He said it was altogether impossible to find such a solitary island as I had desired to live in; but I might command in my own house, and pass my time in a manner as recluse as I pleased.

I complied at last, finding I could not do better. I left Lisbon the 24th day

---

9. At the rear.

of November, in an English merchantman, but who was the Master I never inquired. Don Pedro accompanied me to the ship, and lent me twenty pounds. He took kind leave of me, and embraced me at parting; which I bore as well as I could. During this last voyage I had no commerce with the Master, or any of his men; but pretending I was sick kept close in my cabin. On the fifth of December, 1715, we cast anchor in the Downs about nine in the morning, and at three in the afternoon I got safe to my house at Redriff.

My wife and family received me with great surprise and joy, because they concluded me certainly dead; but I must freely confess, the sight of them filled me only with hatred, disgust, and contempt; and the more, by reflecting on the near alliance I had to them. For, although since my unfortunate exile from the Houyhnhnm country, I had compelled myself to tolerate the sight of Yahoos, and to converse with Don Pedro de Mendez; yet my memory and imaginations were perpetually filled with the virtues and ideas of those exalted Houyhnhnms. And when I began to consider that by copulating with one of the Yahoo species, I had become a parent of more, it struck me with the utmost shame, confusion, and horror.

As soon as I entered the house, my wife took me in her arms, and kissed me; at which, having not been used to the touch of that odious animal for so many years, I fell in a swoon for almost an hour. At the time I am writing, it is five years since my last return to England; during the first year I could not endure my wife or children in my presence, the very smell of them was intolerable; much less could I suffer them to eat in the same room. To this hour they dare not presume to touch my bread, or drink out of the same cup; neither was I ever able to let one of them take me by the hand. The first money I laid out was to buy two young stone-horses,[1] which I keep in a good stable, and next to them the groom is my greatest favorite; for I feel my spirits revived by the smell he contracts in the stable. My horses understand me tolerably well; I converse with them at least four hours every day. They are strangers to bridle or saddle; they live in great amity with me, and friendship to each other.

CHAPTER XII

The Author's veracity. His design in publishing this work. His censure of those travelers who swerve from the truth. The Author clears himself from any sinister ends in writing. An objection answered. The method of planting colonies. His native country commended. The right of the crown to those countries described by the Author is justified. The difficulty of conquering them. The Author takes his last leave of the reader; proposeth his manner of living for the future; gives good advice, and concludeth.

Thus, gentle reader, I have given thee a faithful history of my travels for sixteen years, and above seven months; wherein I have not been so studious of ornament as of truth. I could perhaps like others have astonished thee with strange improbable tales; but I rather chose to relate plain matter of fact in the simplest manner and style; because my principal design was to inform, and not to amuse thee.

---

1. Stallions.

It is easy for us who travel into remote countries, which are seldom visited by Englishmen or other Europeans, to form descriptions of wonderful animals both at sea and land. Whereas a traveler's chief aim should be to make men wiser and better, and to improve their minds by the bad as well as good example of what they deliver concerning foreign places.

I could heartily wish a law were enacted, that every traveler, before he were permitted to publish his voyages, should be obliged to make oath before the Lord High Chancellor that all he intended to print was absolutely true to the best of his knowledge; for then the world would no longer be deceived as it usually is, while some writers, to make their works pass the better upon the public, impose the grossest falsities on the unwary reader. I have perused several books of travels with great delight in my younger days; but, having since gone over most parts of the globe, and been able to contradict many fabulous accounts from my own observation, it hath given me a great disgust against this part of reading, and some indignation to see the credulity of mankind so impudently abused. Therefore, since my acquaintance were pleased to think my poor endeavors might not be unacceptable to my country; I imposed on myself as a maxim, never to be swerved from, that I would *strictly adhere to truth;* neither indeed can I be ever under the least temptation to vary from it, while I retain in my mind the lectures and example of my noble master, and the other illustrious Houyhnhnms, of whom I had so long the honor to be an humble hearer.

> ———*Nec si miserum Fortuna Sinonem*
> *Finxit, vanum etiam, mendacemque improba finget.*[2]

I know very well how little reputation is to be got by writings which require neither genius nor learning, nor indeed any other talent, except a good memory, or an exact *Journal.* I know likewise, that writers of travels, like dictionary-makers, are sunk into oblivion by the weight and bulk of those who come last, and therefore lie uppermost. And it is highly probable that such travelers who shall hereafter visit the countries described in this work of mine, may be detecting my errors (if there be any) and adding many new discoveries of their own, jostle me out of vogue, and stand in my place, making the world forget that ever I was an author. This indeed would be too great a mortification if I wrote for fame; but, as my sole intention was the PUBLIC GOOD, I cannot be altogether disappointed. For, who can read the virtues I have mentioned in the glorious Houyhnhnms, without being ashamed of his own vices, when he considers himself as the reasoning, governing animal of his country? I shall say nothing of those remote nations where Yahoos preside; amongst which the least corrupted are the Brobdingnagians, whose wise maxims in morality and government it would be our happiness to observe. But I forbear descanting further, and rather leave the judicious reader to his own remarks and applications.

I am not a little pleased that this work of mine can possibly meet with no censurers; for what objections can be made against a writer who relates only plain facts that happened in such distant countries, where we have not the

---

2. Fortune has made a derelict of Sinon / but the bitch won't make an empty liar of him, too (Latin; from Virgil's *Aeneid* 2).

least interest with respect either to trade or negotiations? I have carefully avoided every fault with which common writers of travels are often too justly charged. Besides, I meddle not the least with any party, but write without passion, prejudice, or ill-will against any man or number of men whatsoever. I write for the noblest end, to inform and instruct mankind, over whom I may, without breach of modesty, pretend to some superiority, from the advantages I received by conversing so long among the most accomplished Houyhnhnms. I write without any view towards profit or praise. I never suffer a word to pass that may look like reflection, or possibly give the least offense even to those who are most ready to take it. So that, I hope, I may with justice pronounce myself an Author perfectly blameless; against whom the tribes of answerers, considerers, observers, reflectors, detecters, remarkers will never be able to find matter for exercising their talents.

I confess it was whispered to me that I was bound in duty as a subject of England, to have given in a memorial to a secretary of state, at my first coming over; because, whatever lands are discovered by a subject, belong to the Crown. But I doubt whether our conquests in the countries I treat of would be as easy as those of Ferdinando Cortez[3] over the naked Americans. The Lilliputians, I think, are hardly worth the charge of a fleet and army to reduce them; and I question whether it might be prudent or safe to attempt the Brobdingnagians; or, whether an English army would be much at their ease with the Flying Island over their heads. The Houyhnhnms, indeed, appear not to be so well prepared for war, a science to which they are perfect strangers, and especially against missive weapons. However, supposing myself to be a minister of state, I could never give my advice for invading them. Their prudence, unanimity, unacquaintedness with fear, and their love of their country would amply supply all defects in the military art. Imagine twenty thousand of them breaking into the midst of an European army, confounding the ranks, overturning the carriages, battering the warriors' faces into mummy, by terrible yerks[4] from their hinder hoofs: for they would well deserve the character given to Augustus, *Recalcitrat undique tutus*.[5] But instead of proposals for conquering that magnanimous nation, I rather wish they were in a capacity or disposition to send a sufficient number of their inhabitants for civilizing Europe; by teaching us the first principles of Honor, Justice, Truth, Temperance, Public Spirit, Fortitude, Chastity, Friendship, Benevolence, and Fidelity. The names of all which Virtues are still retained among us in most languages, and are to be met with in modern as well as ancient authors, which I am able to assert from my own small reading.

But I had another reason which made me less forward to enlarge his majesty's dominions by my discoveries: to say the truth, I had conceived a few scruples with relation to the distributive justice of princes upon those occasions. For instance, a crew of pirates are driven by a storm they know not whither; at length a boy discovers land from the topmast; they go on shore to rob and plunder; they see an harmless people, are entertained with kindness, they give the country a new name, they take formal possession of it for the king, they set up a rotten plank or a stone for a memorial, they murder two or three dozen of the natives, bring away a couple more by force for a

---

3. Hernando Cortés (1485–1547), who destroyed the Aztec empire.   4. Kicks. *Mummy*: pulp.   5. He kicks backward, at every point on his guard (Latin; Horace's *Satires* 2.20).

sample, return home, and get their pardon. Here commences a new dominion acquired with a title by Divine Right. Ships are sent with the first opportunity; the natives driven out or destroyed, their princes tortured to discover their gold; a free license given to all acts of inhumanity and lust; the earth reeking with the blood of its inhabitants: and this execrable crew of butchers employed in so pious an expedition is a *modern colony* sent to convert and civilize an idolatrous and barbarous people.

But this description, I confess, doth by no means affect the British nation, who may be an example to the whole world for their wisdom, care, and justice in planting colonies; their liberal endowments for the advancement of religion and learning; their choice of devout and able pastors to propagate Christianity; their caution in stocking their provinces with people of sober lives and conversations from this the Mother Kingdom; their strict regard to the distribution of justice, in supplying the civil administration through all their colonies with officers of the greatest abilities, utter strangers to corruption: and to crown all, by sending the most vigilant and virtuous governors, who have no other views than the happiness of the people over whom they preside, and the honor of the king their master.

But, as those countries which I have described do not appear to have any desire of being conquered, and enslaved, murdered, or driven out by colonies, nor abound either in gold, silver, sugar, or tobacco, I did humbly conceive they were by no means proper objects of our zeal, our valor, or our interest. However, if those whom it may concern, think fit to be of another opinion, I am ready to depose, when I shall be lawfully called, that no European did ever visit these countries before me. I mean, if the inhabitants ought to be believed.

But, as to the formality of taking possession in my sovereign's name, it never came once into my thoughts; and if it had, yet as my affairs then stood, I should perhaps in point of prudence and self-preservation have put it off to a better opportunity.

Having thus answered the only objection that can be raised against me as a traveler, I here take a final leave of my courteous readers, and return to enjoy my own speculations in my little garden at Redriff; to apply those excellent lessons of virtue which I learned among the Houyhnhnms; to instruct the Yahoos of my own family as far as I shall find them docible animals; to behold my figure often in a glass, and thus if possible habituate myself by time to tolerate the sight of a human creature; to lament the brutality of Houyhnhnms in my own country, but always treat their persons with respect, for the sake of my noble master, his family, his friends, and the whole Houyhnhnm race, whom these of ours have the honor to resemble in all their lineaments, however their intellectuals came to degenerate.

I began last week to permit my wife to sit at dinner with me, at the farthest end of a long table; and to answer (but with the utmost brevity) the few questions I ask her. Yet the smell of a Yahoo continuing very offensive, I always keep my nose well stopped with rue, lavender, or tobacco leaves. And although it be hard for a man late in life to remove old habits, I am not altogether out of hopes in some time to suffer a neighbor Yahoo in my company, without the apprehensions I am yet under of his teeth or his claws.

My reconcilement to the Yahoo kind in general might not be so difficult, if they would be content with those vices and follies only which nature hath entitled them to. I am not in the least provoked at the sight of a lawyer, a pickpocket, a colonel, a fool, a lord, a gamester, politician, a whoremonger, a physician, an evidence, a suborner, an attorney, a traitor, or the like: this is all according to the due course of things. But when I behold a lump of deformity, and diseases both in body and mind, smitten with pride, it immediately breaks all the measures of my patience; neither shall I be ever able to comprehend how such an animal and such a vice could tally together. The wise and virtuous Houyhnhnms, who abound in all excellencies that can adorn a rational creature, have no name for this vice in their language, which hath no terms to express anything that is evil, except those whereby they describe the detestable qualities of their Yahoos, among which they were not able to distinguish this of pride, for want of thoroughly understanding human nature, as it showeth itself in other countries, where that animal presides. But I, who had more experience, could plainly observe some rudiments of it among the wild Yahoos.

But the Houyhnhnms, who live under the government of reason, are no more proud of the good qualities they possess, than I should be for not wanting a leg or an arm, which no man in his wits would boast of, although he must be miserable without them. I dwell the longer upon this subject from the desire I have to make the society of an English Yahoo by any means not insupportable; and therefore I here entreat those who have any tincture of this absurd vice, that they will not presume to appear in my sight.

A Modest Proposal[1]

for Preventing the Children of poor People in Ireland, *from being a Burden to their Parents or Country; and for making them beneficial to the Publick.*

Written in the year 1729

It is a melancholy object to those who walk through this great town,[2] or travel in the country, when they see the streets, the roads, and cabin-doors crowded with beggars of the female sex, followed by three, four, or six children, all in rags, and importuning every passenger for an alms. These mothers, instead of being able to work for their honest livelihood, are forced to employ all their time in strolling to beg sustenance for their helpless infants: who, as they grow up, either turn thieves for want of work, or leave their dear native country to fight for the Pretender in Spain, or sell themselves to the Barbadoes.[3]

I think it is agreed by all parties, that this prodigious number of children in the arms, or on the backs, or at the heels of their mothers, and frequently of their fathers, is, in the present deplorable state of the kingdom, a very great additional grievance; and, therefore, whoever could find out a fair,

1. The complete text edited by Herbert Davis. 2. Dublin. 3. At this time a British possession, with a prosperous sugar industry. Workers were needed in the sugar plantations. *The Pretender:* James Edward (1688–1766), son of the Catholic king James II of England, called the "Old Pretender" (in distinction to his son Charles, nine years old at the time of this work, called the "Young Pretender"). Many thought him a legitimate claimant to the throne.

cheap, and easy method of making these children sound and useful members of the commonwealth, would deserve so well of the public, as to have his statue set up for a preserver of the nation.

But my intention is very far from being confined to provide only for the children of professed beggars; it is of a much greater extent, and shall take in the whole number of infants at a certain age, who are born of parents in effect as little able to support them as those who demand our charity in the streets.

As to my own part, having turned my thoughts for many years upon this important subject, and maturely weighed the several schemes of other projectors,[4] I have always found them grossly mistaken in their computation. It is true, a child, just dropped from its dam, may be supported by her milk for a solar year with little other nourishment; at most, not above the value of two shillings, which the mother may certainly get, or the value in scraps, by her lawful occupation of begging; and it is exactly at one year old that I propose to provide for them in such a manner, as, instead of being a charge upon their parents or the parish, or wanting food and raiment for the rest of their lives, they shall, on the contrary, contribute to the feeding, and partly to the clothing, of many thousands.

There is likewise another advantage in my scheme, that it will prevent those voluntary abortions, and that horrid practice of women murdering their bastard children, alas, too frequent among us, sacrificing the poor innocent babes, I doubt more to avoid the expense than the shame, which would move tears and pity in the most savage and inhuman breast.

The number of souls in this kingdom being usually reckoned one million and a half, of these I calculate there may be about two hundred thousand couple whose wives are breeders; from which number I subtract thirty thousand couple, who are able to maintain their own children (although I apprehend there cannot be so many, under the present distresses of the kingdom); but this being granted, there will remain an hundred and seventy thousand breeders. I again subtract fifty thousand for those women who miscarry, or whose children die by accident or disease within the year. There only remain a hundred and twenty thousand children of poor parents annually born. The question therefore is how this number shall be reared and provided for? which, as I have already said, under the present situation of affairs, is utterly impossible by all the methods hitherto proposed. For we can neither employ them in handicraft or agriculture; we neither build houses (I mean in the country) nor cultivate land: they can very seldom pick up a livelihood by stealing until they arrive at six years old, except where they are of towardly parts;[5] although I confess they learn the rudiments much earlier; during which time they can, however, be properly looked upon only as probationers; as I have been informed by a principal gentleman in the county of Cavan, who protested to me, that he never knew above one or two instances under the age of six, even in a part of the kingdom so renowned for the quickest proficiency in that art.

I am assured by our merchants that a boy or a girl before twelve years old is no saleable commodity; and even when they come to this age they will not

4. Planners.   5. Particularly talented, unusually gifted.

yield above three pounds or three pounds and half-a-crown at most, on the exchange; which cannot turn to account either to the parents or kingdom, the charge of nutriment and rags having been at least four times that value.

I shall now, therefore, humbly propose my own thoughts, which I hope will not be liable to the least objection.

I have been assured by a very knowing American of my acquaintance in London, that a young healthy child, well nursed, is, at a year old, a most delicious, nourishing, and wholesome food, whether stewed, roasted, baked, or boiled; and I make no doubt that it will equally serve in a fricassee or a ragout.

I do therefore humbly offer it to public consideration, that of the hundred and twenty thousand children already computed, twenty thousand may be reserved for breed, whereof only one-fourth part to be males; which is more than we allow to sheep, black cattle, or swine; and my reason is, that these children are seldom the fruits of marriage, a circumstance not much regarded by our savages, therefore one male will be sufficient to serve four females. That the remaining hundred thousand may, at a year old, be offered in sale to the persons of quality and fortune through the kingdom; always advising the mother to let them suck plentifully in the last month, so as to render them plump and fat for a good table. A child will make two dishes at an entertainment for friends; and when the family dines alone, the fore or hind quarter will make a reasonable dish, and, seasoned with a little pepper or salt, will be very good boiled on the fourth day, especially in winter.

I have reckoned, upon a medium,[6] that a child just born will weigh twelve pounds, and in a solar year, if tolerably nursed, increaseth to twenty-eight pounds.

I grant this food will be somewhat dear,[7] and therefore very proper for landlords, who, as they have already devoured most of the parents, seem to have the best title to the children.

Infants' flesh will be in season throughout the year, but more plentifully in March, and a little before and after: for we are told by a grave author, an eminent French physician,[8] that fish being a prolific diet, there are more children born in Roman Catholic countries about nine months after Lent than at any other season; therefore, reckoning a year after Lent, the markets will be more glutted than usual, because the number of popish infants is at least three to one in this kingdom; and therefore it will have one other collateral advantage, by lessening the number of papists among us.

I have already computed the charge of nursing a beggar's child (in which list I reckon all cottagers, labourers, and four-fifths of the farmers) to be about two shillings per annum,[9] rags included; and I believe no gentleman would repine to give ten shillings for the carcass of a good fat child, which, as I have said, will make four dishes of excellent nutritive meat, when he has only some particular friend, or his own family, to dine with him. Thus the squire will learn to be a good landlord, and grow popular among his tenants; the mother will have eight shillings net profit, and be fit for work till she produces another child.

6. Average.   7. Expensive.   8. François Rabelais (1494?–1553), French satirist and author of *Gargantua and Pantagruel* (1532–52).   9. Per year (Latin).

Those who are more thrifty (as I must confess the times require) may flay the carcass; the skin of which, artificially dressed, will make admirable gloves for ladies, and summer-boots for fine gentlemen.

As to our city of Dublin, shambles[1] may be appointed for this purpose in the most convenient parts of it, and butchers we may be assured will not be wanting; although I rather recommend buying the children alive, and dressing them hot from the knife, as we do roasting pigs.

A very worthy person, a true lover of his country, and whose virtues I highly esteem, was lately pleased, in discoursing on this matter, to offer a refinement upon my scheme. He said, that many gentlemen of this kingdom, having of late destroyed their deer, he conceived that the want of venison might be well supplied by the bodies of young lads and maidens, not exceeding fourteen years of age, nor under twelve; so great a number of both sexes in every country being now ready to starve for want of work and service; and these to be disposed of by their parents, if alive, or otherwise by their nearest relations. But, with due deference to so excellent a friend, and so deserving a patriot, I cannot be altogether in his sentiments; for as to the males, my American acquaintance assured me from frequent experience, that their flesh was generally tough and lean, like that of our schoolboys, by continual exercise, and their taste disagreeable; and to fatten them would not answer the charge. Then as to the females, it would, I think, with humble submission, be a loss to the public, because they soon would become breeders themselves: and besides, it is not improbable that some scrupulous people might be apt to censure such a practice (although indeed very unjustly) as a little bordering upon cruelty; which, I confess hath always been with me the strongest objection against any project, how well soever intended.

But in order to justify my friend, he confessed that this expedient was put into his head by the famous Psalmanazar,[2] a native of the island Formosa, who came from thence to London above twenty years ago; and in conversation told my friend, that in his country, when any young person happened to be put to death, the executioner sold the carcass to persons of quality as a prime dainty; and that in his time the body of a plump girl of fifteen, who was crucified for an attempt to poison the emperor, was sold to his Imperial Majesty's prime minister of state, and other great mandarins of the court, in joints from the gibbet,[3] at four hundred crowns. Neither indeed can I deny, that if the same use were made of several plump young girls in this town, who, without one single groat to their fortunes, cannot stir abroad without a chair,[4] and appear at playhouse and assemblies in foreign fineries which they never will pay for, the kingdom would not be the worse.

Some persons of a desponding spirit are in great concern about the vast number of poor people who are aged, diseased, or maimed; and I have been desired to employ my thoughts what course may be taken to ease the nation of so grievous an encumbrance. But I am not in the least pain upon that matter, because it is very well known, that they are every day dying, and rotting, by cold and famine, and filth and vermin, as fast as can be reasonably

---

1. Slaughterhouses.   2. George Psalmanazar (1679?–1763), a literary impostor born in southern France who claimed to be a native of Formosa and a recent Christian convert. He published a catechism in an invented language that he called Formosan, as well as a description of Formosa with an introductory autobiography.   3. The post from which the bodies of criminals were hung in chains after execution. *Joints:* portions of a carcass carved up by a butcher.   4. I.e., a sedan chair, an enclosed seat carried on poles by men.

expected. And as to the younger labourers, they are now in almost as hopeful a condition: they cannot get work, and consequently pine away for want of nourishment, to a degree, that if at any time they are accidentally hired to common labour, they have not strength to perform it; and thus the country and themselves are happily delivered from the evils to come.

I have too long digressed, and therefore shall return to my subject. I think the advantages by the proposal which I have made are obvious and many, as well as of the highest importance.

For first, as I have already observed, it would greatly lessen the number of papists, with whom we are yearly overrun, being the principal breeders of the nation as well as our most dangerous enemies; and who stay at home on purpose with a design to deliver the kingdom to the Pretender, hoping to take their advantage by the absence of so many good Protestants, who have chosen rather to leave their country than stay at home and pay tithes against their conscience to an idolatrous Episcopal curate.

Secondly, the poorer tenants will have something valuable of their own, which by law may be made liable to distress,[5] and help to pay their landlord's rent; their corn and cattle being already seized, and money a thing unknown.

Thirdly, whereas the maintenance of an hundred thousand children, from two years old and upwards, cannot be computed at less than ten shillings a piece per annum, the nation's stock will be thereby increased fifty thousand pounds per annum; besides the profit of a new dish introduced to the tables of all gentlemen of fortune in the kingdom who have any refinement in taste. And the money will circulate among ourselves, the goods being entirely of our own growth and manufacture.

Fourthly, the constant breeders, besides the gain of eight shillings sterling per annum by the sale of their children, will be rid of the charge of maintaining them after the first year.

Fifthly, this food would likewise bring great custom to taverns; where the vinters will certainly be so prudent as to procure the best receipts[6] for dressing it to perfection, and, consequently, have their houses frequented by all the fine gentlemen, who justly value themselves upon their knowledge in good eating: and a skilful cook, who understands how to oblige his guests, will contrive to make it as expensive as they please.

Sixthly, this would be a great inducement to marriage, which all wise nations have either encouraged by rewards, or enforced by laws and penalties. It would increase the care and tenderness of mothers towards their children, when they were sure of a settlement for life to the poor babes, provided in some sort by the public, to their annual profit instead of expense. We should soon see an honest emulation among the married women, which of them could bring the fattest child to the market. Men would become as fond of their wives during the time of their pregnancy, as they are now of their mares in foal, their cows in calf, or sows when they are ready to farrow; nor offer to beat or kick them (as is too frequent a practice) for fear of a miscarriage.

Many other advantages might be enumerated. For instance, the addition of some thousand carcasses in our exportation of barrelled beef; the propagation of swine's flesh, and improvement in the art of making good bacon,

---

5. The legal seizing of goods to satisfy a debt, particularly for unpaid rent.   6. Recipes.

so much wanted among us by the great destruction of pigs, too frequent at our tables, which are no way comparable in taste or magnificence to a well-grown, fat yearling child, which, roasted whole, will make a considerable figure at a Lord Mayor's feast, or any other public entertainment. But this, and many others, I omit, being studious of brevity.

Supposing that one thousand families in this city would be constant customers for infants' flesh, besides others who might have it at merry meetings, particularly weddings and christenings. I compute that Dublin would take off annually about twenty thousand carcasses; and the rest of the kingdom (where probably they will be sold somewhat cheaper) the remaining eighty thousand.

I can think of no one objection that will possibly be raised against this proposal, unless it should be urged, that the number of people will be thereby much lessened in the kingdom. This I freely own, and it was indeed one principal design in offering it to the world. I desire the reader will observe that I calculate my remedy *for this one individual kingdom of Ireland, and for no other that ever was, is, or I think ever can be, upon earth.* Therefore let no man talk to me of other expedients: *of taxing our absentees at five shillings a pound: of using neither clothes nor household-furniture except what is of our own growth and manufacture: of utterly rejecting the materials and instruments that promote foreign luxury: of curing the expensiveness of pride, vanity, idleness, and gaming in our women; of introducing a vein of parsimony, prudence, and temperance: of learning to love our country, wherein we differ even from Laplanders, and the inhabitants of Topinamboo:*[7] of quitting our animosities and factions, nor act any longer like the Jews,[8] who were murdering one another at the very moment their city was taken: of being a little cautious not to sell our country and consciences for nothing: of teaching landlords to have at least one degree of mercy towards their tenants: lastly, of putting a spirit of honesty, industry, and skill into our shopkeepers; who, if a resolution could now be taken to buy only our native goods, would immediately unite to cheat and exact upon us in the price, the measure, and the goodness, nor could ever yet be brought to make one fair proposal of just dealing, though often and earnestly invited to it.[9]

Therefore I repeat, let no man talk to me of these and the like expedients, till he hath at least some glimpse of hope that there will ever be some hearty and sincere attempts to put them in practice.

But, as to myself, having been wearied out for many years with offering vain, idle, visionary thoughts, and at length utterly despairing of success, I fortunately fell upon this proposal; which, as it is wholly new, so it hath something solid and real, of no expense and little trouble, full in our own power, and whereby we can incur no danger in disobliging England. For this kind of commodity will not bear exportation, the flesh being of too tender a consistence to admit a long continuance in salt, although perhaps I could name a country[1] which would be glad to eat up our whole nation without it.

After all, I am not so violently bent upon my own opinion as to reject any offer proposed by wise men which shall be found equally innocent, cheap,

---

7. In Brazil.   8. Referring to the factionalism under Herod Agrippa II at the time of the destruction of Jerusalem by the Roman emperor Titus.   9. The italicized proposals are Swift's serious suggestions for remedying the situation of Ireland.   1. England.

easy, and effectual. But before something of that kind shall be advanced in contradiction to my scheme, and offering a better, I desire the author, or authors, will be pleased maturely to consider two points. First, as things now stand, how they will be able to find food and raiment for a hundred thousand useless mouths and backs? And, secondly, there being a round million of creatures in human figure throughout this kingdom, whose whole subsistence put into a common stock would leave them in debt two millions of pounds sterling, adding those who are beggars by profession, to the bulk of farmers, cottagers, and labourers, with the wives and children who are beggars in effect; I desire those politicians who dislike my overture, and may perhaps be so bold as to attempt an answer, that they will first ask the parents of these mortals, whether they would not at this day think it a great happiness to have been sold for food at a year old, in the manner I prescribe, and thereby have avoided such a perpetual scene of misfortunes as they have since gone through, by the oppression of landlords, the impossibility of paying rent without money or trade, the want of common sustenance, with neither house nor clothes to cover them from the inclemencies of weather, and the most inevitable prospect of entailing the like, or greater miseries, upon their breed for ever.

I profess, in the sincerity of my heart, that I have not the least personal interest in endeavouring to promote this necessary work, having no other motive than the public good of my country, by advancing our trade, providing for infants, relieving the poor, and giving some pleasure to the rich. I have no children by which I can propose to get a single penny; the youngest being nine years old, and my wife past child-bearing.

ALEXANDER POPE
1688–1744

"If Pope be not a poet, where is poetry to be found?" Samuel Johnson inquired. Transmuting the commonplace, claiming as subject matter everything from the minutiae of social existence to speculation about the nature of universal order, Alexander Pope made unlikely raw material into brilliant poetry.

Born to Roman Catholic parents in the year of the Glorious Revolution that deposed Catholic James II in favor of Protestant William and Mary, Pope lived when repressive legislation against Catholics restricted his financial, educational, professional, and residential possibilities. He could not attend a university or hold public employment; he had to live ten miles outside London. Sickly and undersized (he probably suffered a tubercular infection in infancy), he was educated largely at home. He also educated himself by literary friendships beginning in his youth; throughout his life, he enjoyed close associations with other men and with a few women, in particular his neighbor and intimate friend Martha Blount, to whom he left his estate. Increasingly, he won wealth and reputation by his writing, notably his translations of Homer. Following Candide's course of cultivating his garden, he perfected his grounds and grotto at Twickenham, living in retirement from the city. He died of asthma and edema.

Pope's work ranged through most of the poetic genres of his period. Beginning, as

Virgil had done, with pastorals, he later produced *An Essay on Criticism,* versified advice about proper literary and critical procedure, and went on to publish a great philosophic poem, *An Essay on Man,* and to edit Shakespeare's plays. The bulk of his verse, however, was satiric. In *The Dunciad* (1743), he provided a satiric epic for his age, a history of the progress of dullness.

Writing to a woman friend, Pope described *The Rape of the Lock* (1717) as "at once the most a satire, and the most inoffensive, of anything of mine. . . . 'Tis a sort of writing very like tickling." He thus suggests the tonal complexity of a work that conveys serious social criticism through a fanciful and playful fable narrated in verse of surpassing grace and elegance. The joke of the poem, as well as its serious point, derives from the cataclysmic disturbance a young woman makes over her loss of a lock of hair. Pope adapts epic conventions to his narrative of trivia, including even a supernatural species—the sylphs—parodying the functions of the Greek gods. These reminders of the epic, a genre by definition concerned with important matters, emphasize the poet's consciousness of the relative triviality of eighteenth-century high-society preoccupations. The world Belinda inhabits confuses small things with great; "Puffs, powders, patches, Bibles, billet-doux" occupy her dressing table in indiscriminate assembly. Members of this society take their own pleasure more seriously than anything else: "wretches hang that jurymen may dine." Men and women coexist in fascinated tension, tension that, given even slight provocation, explodes in hostilities. Sexual issues govern the conflict: women guard their "honor," the reputation of chastity, more intently than they preserve their physical purity; men seek to violate both. The ideals of good sense and good humor, expressed in the poem by Clarissa, govern no one in action. Instead, both sexes value beauty (which, as Clarissa points out, fades) and accept it as an excuse for emotional self-indulgence (the theme of Umbriel's excursion to the Cave of Spleen). In its accounts of moral and psychological confusion, of hysterical fits and battles, the poem employs the familiar satiric techniques of exaggeration and distortion intended to reveal the truth and to inspire reform.

But *The Rape of the Lock* celebrates as well as criticizes. The delicacy and grace of the verse, the ethereal beauty of the sylphs, recapitulate Belinda's genuine grace and beauty: "If to her share some female errors fall, / Look on her face, and you'll forget 'em all." Belinda's world operates mainly on the basis of style. In its separation of style from moral substance, the society demands criticism; but the beauty it values—elegant conversation, boat trips on the Thames, magnificent women—like the beauty the poet creates, has meaning in itself. When the disputed lock of hair ascends to the constellations, when the poet calls attention to his own preservation of Belinda's beauty and fame, *The Rape of the Lock* reminds us that praise and blame sometimes appropriately attach to the same objects. Its mixture of playfulness and seriousness, of beauty and harshness, mark the poem's unique achievement.

In *An Essay on Man* (1733–34), a very different work, Pope set out to consider, in successive epistles, humanity in relation to the universe, to itself, to society, and to happiness: an enterprise of ambition almost comparable to Milton's in *Paradise Lost.* Indeed, in the first section of the poem Pope alludes specifically to his predecessor, describing the world as a "Garden, tempting with forbidden fruit" and declaring his own intention to "vindicate [Milton had used *justify*] the ways of God to man." Unlike Milton, Pope pursues this goal not through a dramatic fable but by an extended versified meditation on the philosophic issues involved. That meditation, however, generates its own drama.

Pope draws on a number of intellectual traditions to define the human condition in both cosmic and social terms. The breadth of his reference—to Catholic and Protestant theology, to Platonic and Stoic philosophy, to his period's notions of plenitude and natural order—itself reinforces the underlying assumption of universal, unchanging human nature. The poet evokes a timeless vision of humanity in the universe, poised at the middle of the Great Chain of Being that extends from God to the most minute forms of life, with the fullest possible range of being above and below human-kind. Complaints that the poem's philosophy is shallow ignore the complexity of its synthesis and the seriousness of its ideas. The resounding assertion that concludes the first epistle, for instance ("One truth is clear, WHATEVER IS, IS RIGHT"), implies no unawareness of human misery or evil. Abundant examples of both have been presented in the text. The point is, rather, that the nature of God's plan—by definition not fully comprehensible to human reason—must allow evil for the sake of larger good. And human beings, to possess free will, must have available to them the choice of evil. Such assumptions belong to the intellectual position called "philosophical optimism"—by no means equivalent to what we usually think of as optimism, the faith that everything will turn out well in the long run. The belief expounded in *An Essay on Man,* on the contrary, allows the possibility that matters may turn out badly for individual men and women but assumes that personal misfortune takes its place in a larger, essentially benign, pattern.

The first epistle of the poem, printed here, progresses through ten logically con-nected sections. It begins by insisting on the necessary limitation of human judgment: we see only parts, not the whole. Nonetheless, this fact does not imply the imperfection of humankind; it means, rather, that we are adapted to our position in the general order of things. Our ignorance of future events and our hope for eternal life give us the possibility of happiness. The poem then indicts human beings for pride and impiety (we claim more power of judgment and more knowledge than we can have), for the absurdity of assuming themselves the center of the created universe, and for the unreasonableness of complaints against the providential order (we demand, the poet suggests, both the perfection of angels and the physical sensitivities of animals, although increase in our capacities would bring misery). Turning to the nature of the universal order, the argument insists on the gradations of faculties from the lower animals to humankind, then suggests that this order extends farther than we can know: any interference with it would destroy the whole. Even the speculative possibility of such interference suggests the insanity of human pride. Our only proper course is absolute submission to Providence.

This logical sequence structures the *Essay on Man,* but we should not read the poem only as a versified handbook of eighteenth-century philosophy. Here, as in *The Rape of the Lock,* Pope displays his poetic brilliance, converting philosophic argument into a rich emotional and intellectual texture. He draws us into the poem by address-ing us directly, reminding us of our own tendencies to presumption, our own inevi-table desire to understand the universe as revolving around us. "In Pride, in reas'ning Pride, our error lies": we all share bewilderment at our situation, we all need to interpret it, we all face, every day, our necessary limitations. The poet rapidly shifts tone, sometimes berating his readers, sometimes reminding us (and himself) of his own participation in the universal dilemma, sometimes assuming a godlike perspec-tive and suggesting his superior knowledge. By his changing voice, his changing forms of address, he makes dramatic the futile, yet noble, effort to understand what only the deity can fully comprehend.

At its best, *An Essay on Man* transforms philosophy into emotional experience. It generates drama out of shifting, intersecting perspectives: the lamb licking the hand of its butcher, the Indian looking forward to a heaven his dog will share, the scientist trying to interpret the physical universe. It also makes the abstract vividly specific and concrete, as when reflection on the necessary limitation of human faculties produces the penetrating image of someone dying "of a rose in aromatic pain." Pope's imagi-nation summons up a vast range of concrete reference, and it does not avoid the disturbing: we are invited to think of the human condition in the universe as comparable to that of the ox, which tills the fields, goes to slaughter, or finds itself worshiped as a god, according to accidents of situation. The fly's "microscopic eye" excels our powers; we resemble weeds more than oaks. Yet the poet, ranging from the conversational ease of his opening lines to the ringing certainties of his conclusion, incorporates perceptions of human inadequacy into assertions of a grand scheme, which he makes not only rational but exciting.

Pope has been the subject of a great deal of writing. Biographies include G. Sherburn, *The Early Career of Alexander Pope* (1934), and M. Mack, *Alexander Pope* (1985). A range of responses is represented in M. Mack and J. A. Winn, eds., *Pope: Recent Essays by Several Hands* (1980); H. Bloom, ed., *Alexander Pope* (1985); and W. Jackson and R. P. Yoder, eds., *Critical Essays on Alexander Pope* (1993). Perceptive critical books include R. A. Brower, *Alexander Pope: The Poetry of Allusion* (1959), and T. R. Edwards, *This Dark Estate: A Reading of Pope* (1963). Other useful studies include D. B. Morris, *The Genius of Sense* (1984); L. Damrosch Jr., *The Imaginative World of Alexander Pope* (1987); and Helen Deutsch, *Resemblance and Disgrace: Alexander Pope and the Deformation of Culture* (1996), an investigation that focuses on the importance of Pope's deformed body to his literary effects. An unusually valuable edition of *The Rape of the Lock* has been edited by C. Wall (1998); it includes eighteenth-century material that illuminates Pope's text and places the poem firmly in its cultural context.

PRONOUNCING GLOSSARY

The following list uses common English syllables and stress accents to provide rough equivalents of selected words whose pronunciation may be unfamiliar to the general reader.

Borgia: *bohr'-jah*

Le Comte de Gabalis: *leu kahmt du gah'-bah-lee*

Rosicrucian: *roh-zee-kru'-shan*

Scylla: *sil'-ah*

The Rape of the Lock[1]

An Heroi-Comical Poem

*Nolueram, Belinda, tuos violare capillos;
sed juvat hoc precibus me tribuisse tuis.*[2]
—MARTIAL

TO MRS. ARABELLA FERMOR

MADAM,

It will be in vain to deny that I have some regard for this piece, since I dedicate it to you. Yet you may bear me witness, it was intended only to divert a few young ladies, who have good sense and good humor enough to laugh not only at their sex's little unguarded follies, but at their own. But as it was communicated with the air of a secret, it soon found its way into the world. An imperfect copy having been offered to a bookseller, you had the good nature for my sake to consent to the publication of one more correct; this I was forced to, before I had executed half my design, for the machinery was entirely wanting to complete it.

The machinery, Madam, is a term invented by the critics, to signify that part which the deities, angels, or demons are made to act in a poem; for the

---

1. Text and notes by Samuel Holt Monk.   2. "I was unwilling, Belinda, to ravish your locks; but I rejoice to have conceded this to your prayers" (Martial, *Epigrams* XII. lxxxiv. 1–2). Pope substituted his heroine for Martial's Polytimus. The epigraph is intended to suggest that the poem was published at Miss Fermor's request.

ancient poets are in one respect like many modern ladies: let an action be never so trivial in itself, they always make it appear of the utmost importance. These machines I determined to raise on a very new and odd foundation, the Rosicrucian[3] doctrine of spirits.

I know how disagreeable it is to make use of hard words before a lady; but 'tis so much the concern of a poet to have his works understood, and particularly by your sex, that you must give me leave to explain two or three difficult terms.

The Rosicrucians are a people I must bring you acquainted with. The best account I know of them is in a French book called *Le Comte de Gabalis*,[4] which both in its title and size is so like a novel, that many of the fair sex have read it for one by mistake. According to these gentlemen, the four elements are inhabited by spirits, which they call Sylphs, Gnomes, Nymphs, and Salamanders. The Gnomes or Demons of earth delight in mischief; but the Sylphs, whose habitation is in the air, are the best-conditioned creatures imaginable. For they say, any mortals may enjoy the most intimate familiarities with these gentle spirits, upon a condition very easy to all true adepts, an inviolate preservation of chastity.

As to the following cantos, all the passages of them are as fabulous as the vision at the beginning, or the transformation at the end; (except the loss of your hair, which I always mention with reverence). The human persons are as fictitious as the airy ones; and the character of Belinda, as it is now managed, resembles you in nothing but in beauty.

If this poem had as many graces as there are in your person, or in your mind, yet I could never hope it should pass through the world half so uncensured as you have done. But let its fortune be what it will, mine is happy enough, to have given me this occasion of assuring you that I am, with the truest esteem,

MADAM,
Your most obedient, humble servant,

A. POPE

CANTO I

What dire offense from amorous causes springs,
What mighty contests rise from trivial things,
I sing—This verse to Caryll,[5] Muse! is due:
This, even Belinda may vouchsafe to view:
Slight is the subject, but not so the praise,   5
If she inspire, and he approve my lays.
    Say what strange motive, Goddess! could compel
A well-bred lord t' assault a gentle belle?
Oh, say what stranger cause, yet unexplored,
Could make a gentle belle reject a lord?   10
In tasks so bold can little men engage,
And in soft bosoms dwells such mighty rage?
    Sol through white curtains shot a timorous ray,

---

3. A system of arcane philosophy introduced into England from Germany in the 17th century.   4. By the Abbé de Montfaucon de Villars, published in 1670.   5. John Caryll (1666?–1736), a close friend of Pope's who suggested that he write this poem.

And oped those eyes that must eclipse the day.
Now lapdogs give themselves the rousing shake,   15
And sleepless lovers just at twelve awake:
Thrice rung the bell, the slipper knocked the ground,
And the pressed watch[6] returned a silver sound.
Belinda still her downy pillow pressed,
Her guardian Sylph prolonged the balmy rest: 20
'Twas he had summoned to her silent bed
The morning dream that hovered o'er her head.
A youth more glittering than a birthnight beau[7]
(That even in slumber caused her cheek to glow)
Seemed to her ear his winning lips to lay,   25
And thus in whispers said, or seemed to say:
    "Fairest of mortals, thou distinguished care
Of thousand bright inhabitants of air!
If e'er one vision touched thy infant thought,
Of all the nurse and all the priest have taught,   30
Of airy elves by moonlight shadows seen,
The silver token, and the circled green,[8]
Or virgins visited by angel powers,
With golden crowns and wreaths of heavenly flowers,
Hear and believe! thy own importance know,   35
Nor bound thy narrow views to things below.
Some secret truths, from learned pride concealed,
To maids alone and children are revealed:
What though no credit doubting wits may give?
The fair and innocent shall still believe.   40
Know, then, unnumbered spirits round thee fly,
The light militia of the lower sky:
These, though unseen, are ever on the wing,
Hang o'er the box,[9] and hover round the Ring.
Think what an equipage thou hast in air,   45
And view with scorn two pages and a chair.[1]
As now your own, our beings were of old,
And once enclosed in woman's beauteous mold
Thence, by a soft transition, we repair
From earthly vehicles to these of air.   50
Think not, when woman's transient breath is fled,
That all her vanities at once are dead:
Succeeding vanities she still regards,
And though she plays no more o'erlooks the cards.
Her joy in gilded chariots, when alive,   55
And love of ombre,[2] after death survive.
For when the Fair in all their pride expire,
To their first elements[3] their souls retire:

---

6. A watch that chimes the hour and the quarter hour when the stem is pressed down. *Thrice rung the bell:* Belinda thus summons her maid.   7. Courtiers wore especially fine clothes on the sovereign's birthday.   8. According to popular belief, fairies skim off the cream from jugs of milk left standing overnight and leave a coin in payment. *The circled green:* rings of bright green grass, which are common in England even in winter, were held to be due to the round dances of fairies.   9. *Box* in the theater and the fashionable circular drive (*Ring*) in Hyde Park.   1. Sedan chair.   2. The popular card game. See III.27ff. and note.   3. The four elements out of which all things were believed to have been made were fire, water, earth, and air. One or another of these elements was supposed to be predominant in both the physical and psychological makeup of each human being. In this context they are spoken of as "humors."

The sprites of fiery termagants in flame
Mount up, and take a Salamander's name.[4]   60
Soft yielding minds to water glide away,
And sip, with Nymphs, their elemental tea.[5]
The graver prude sinks downward to a Gnome,
In search of mischief still on earth to roam.
The light coquettes in Sylphs aloft repair,   65
And sport and flutter in the fields of air.
    "Know further yet; whoever fair and chaste
Rejects mankind, is by some Sylph embraced:
For spirits, freed from mortal laws, with ease
Assume what sexes and what shapes they please.   70
What guards the purity of melting maids,
In courtly balls, and midnight masquerades,
Safe from the treacherous friend, the daring spark,
The glance by day, the whisper in the dark,
When kind occasion prompts their warm desires,   75
When music softens, and when dancing fires?
'Tis but their Sylph, the wise Celestials know,
Though Honor is the word with men below.
    "Some nymphs there are, too conscious of their face,
For life predestined to the Gnomes' embrace.   80
These swell their prospects and exalt their pride,
When offers are disdained, and love denied:
Then gay ideas[6] crowd the vacant brain,
While peers, and dukes, and all their sweeping train,
And garters, stars, and coronets appear,   85
And in soft sounds, 'your Grace' salutes their ear.
'Tis these that early taint the female soul,
Instruct the eyes of young coquettes to roll,
Teach infant cheeks a bidden blush to know,
And little hearts to flutter at a beau.   90
    "Oft, when the world imagine women stray,
The Sylphs through mystic mazes guide their way,
Through all the giddy circle they pursue,
And old impertinence expel by new.
What tender maid but must a victim fall   95
To one man's treat, but for another's ball?
When Florio speaks what virgin could withstand,
If gentle Damon did not squeeze her hand?
With varying vanities, from every part,
They shift the moving toyshop[7] of their heart;   100
Where wigs with wigs, with sword-knots sword-knots strive,
Beaux banish beaux, and coaches coaches drive.
This erring mortals levity may call;
Oh, blind to truth! the Sylphs contrive it all.
    "Of these am I, who thy protection claim,   105
A watchful sprite, and Ariel is my name.
Late, as I ranged the crystal wilds of air,

---

4. Pope borrowed his supernatural beings from Rosicrucian mythology. Each element was inhabited by a spirit, as the following lines explain. The salamander is a lizardlike animal, in antiquity believed to live in fire.   5. Pronounced *tay*.   6. Images.   7. A shop stocked with baubles and trifles.

In the clear mirror of thy ruling star
I saw, alas! some dread event impend,
Ere to the main this morning sun descend,   110
But Heaven reveals not what, or how, or where:
Warned by thy Sylph, O pious maid, beware!
This to disclose is all thy guardian can:
Beware of all, but most beware of Man!"
    He said; when Shock,[8] who thought she slept too long,   115
Leaped up, and waked his mistress with his tongue.
'Twas then, Belinda, if report say true,
Thy eyes first opened on a billet-doux;
Wounds, charms, and ardors were no sooner read,
But all the vision vanished from thy head.   120
    And now, unveiled, the toilet stands displayed,
Each silver vase in mystic order laid.
First, robed in white, the nymph intent adores,
With head uncovered, the cosmetic powers.
A heavenly image in the glass appears;   125
To that she bends, to that her eyes she rears.
The inferior priestess, at her altar's side,
Trembling begins the sacred rites of Pride.
Unnumbered treasures ope at once, and here
The various offerings of the world appear;   130
From each she nicely culls with curious toil,
And decks the goddess with the glittering spoil.
This casket India's glowing gems unlocks,
And all Arabia breathes from yonder box.
The tortoise here and elephant unite,   135
Transformed to combs, the speckled and the white.
Here files of pins extend their shining rows,
Puffs, powders, patches, Bibles, billet-doux.
Now awful Beauty puts on all its arms;
The fair each moment rises in her charms,   140
Repairs her smiles, awakens every grace,
And calls forth all the wonders of her face;
Sees by degrees a purer blush arise,
And keener lightnings quicken in her eyes.
The busy Sylphs surround their darling care,   145
These set the head, and those divide the hair,
Some fold the sleeve, whilst others plait the gown;
And Betty's[9] praised for labors not her own.

CANTO II

    Not with more glories, in the ethereal plain,
The sun first rises o'er the purpled main,
Than, issuing forth, the rival of his beams
Launched on the bosom of the silver Thames.
Fair nymphs and well-dressed youths around her shone,   5
But every eye was fixed on her alone.

---

8. Belinda's lapdog.   9. Belinda's maid, the "inferior priestess" mentioned in line 127.

On her white breast a sparkling cross she wore,
Which Jews might kiss, and infidels adore.
Her lively looks a sprightly mind disclose,
Quick as her eyes, and as unfixed as those: 10
Favors to none, to all she smiles extends;
Oft she rejects, but never once offends.
Bright as the sun, her eyes the gazers strike,
And, like the sun, they shine on all alike.
Yet graceful ease, and sweetness void of pride,   15
Might hide her faults, if belles had faults to hide:
If to her share some female errors fall,
Look on her face, and you'll forget 'em all.
    This nymph, to the destruction of mankind,
Nourished two locks which graceful hung behind   20
In equal curls, and well conspired to deck
With shining ringlets the smooth ivory neck.
Love in these labyrinths his slaves detains,
And mighty hearts are held in slender chains.
With hairy springes we the birds betray,   25
Slight lines of hair surprise the finny prey,
Fair tresses man's imperial race ensnare,
And beauty draws us with a single hair.
    The adventurous Baron the bright locks admired,
He saw, he wished, and to the prize aspired.   30
Resolved to win, he meditates the way,
By force to ravish, or by fraud betray;
For when success a lover's toil attends,
Few ask if fraud or force attained his ends.
    For this, ere Phoebus rose, he had implored   35
Propitious Heaven, and every power adored,
But chiefly Love—to Love an altar built,
Of twelve vast French romances, neatly gilt.
There lay three garters, half a pair of gloves,
And all the trophies of his former loves.   40
With tender billet-doux he lights the pyre,
And breathes three amorous sighs to raise the fire.
Then prostrate falls, and begs with ardent eyes
Soon to obtain, and long possess the prize:
The powers gave ear, and granted half his prayer,   45
The rest the winds dispersed in empty air.
    But now secure the painted vessel glides,
The sunbeams trembling on the floating tides,
While melting music steals upon the sky,
And softened sounds along the waters die.   50
Smooth flow the waves, the zephyrs gently play,
Belinda smiled, and all the world was gay.
All but the Sylph—with careful thoughts oppressed,
The impending woe sat heavy on his breast.
He summons straight his denizens of air;   55
The lucid squadrons round the sails repair:
Soft o'er the shrouds aërial whispers breathe
That seemed but zephyrs to the train beneath.

Some to the sun their insect-wings unfold,
Waft on the breeze, or sink in clouds of gold.   60
Transparent forms too fine for mortal sight,
Their fluid bodies half dissolved in light,
Loose to the wind their airy garments flew,
Thin glittering textures of the filmy dew,
Dipped in the richest tincture of the skies,   65
Where light disports in ever-mingling dyes,
While every beam new transient colors flings,
Colors that change whene'er they wave their wings.
Amid the circle, on the gilded mast,
Superior by the head was Ariel placed;   70
His purple[1] pinions opening to the sun,
He raised his azure wand, and thus begun:
    "Ye Sylphs and Sylphids, to your chief give ear!
Fays, Fairies, Genii, Elves, and Daemons, hear!
Ye know the spheres and various tasks assigned   75
By laws eternal to the aërial kind.
Some in the fields of purest ether play,
And bask and whiten in the blaze of day.
Some guide the course of wandering orbs on high,
Or roll the planets through the boundless sky.   80
Some less refined, beneath the moon's pale light
Pursue the stars that shoot athwart the night,
Or suck the mists in grosser air below,
Or dip their pinions in the painted bow,
Or brew fierce tempests on the wintry main,   85
Or o'er the glebe distill the kindly rain.
Others on earth o'er human race preside,
Watch all their ways, and all their actions guide:
Of these the chief the care of nations own,
And guard with arms divine the British Throne.   90
    "Our humbler province is to tend the Fair,
Not a less pleasing, though less glorious care:
To save the powder from too rude a gale,
Nor let the imprisoned essences exhale;
To draw fresh colors from the vernal flowers   95
To steal from rainbows e'er they drop in showers
A brighter wash;[2] to curl their waving hairs,
Assist their blushes, and inspire their airs;
Nay oft, in dreams invention we bestow,
To change a flounce, or add a furbelow.   100
    "This day black omens threat the brightest fair,
That e'er deserved a watchful spirit's care;
Some dire disaster, or by force or slight,
But what, or where, the Fates have wrapped in night:
Whether the nymph shall break Diana's[3] law,   105
Or some frail china jar receive a flaw,
Or stain her honor or her new brocade,

---

1. In 18th-century poetic diction, the word might mean "blood-red," "purple," or simply (as is likely here) "brightly colored." The word derives from Virgil, *Eclogue* IX.40, *pupureus.* 2. Cosmetic lotion. 3. Diana was the goddess of chastity.

Forget her prayers, or miss a masquerade,
Or lose her heart, or necklace, at a ball;
Or whether Heaven has doomed that Shock must fall.   110
Haste, then, ye spirits! to your charge repair:
The fluttering fan be Zephyretta's care;
The drops[4] to thee, Brillante, we consign;
And, Momentilla, let the watch be thine;
Do thou, Crispissa,[5] tend her favorite Lock;   115
Ariel himself shall be the guard of Shock.
    "To fifty chosen Sylphs, of special note,
We trust the important charge, the petticoat;
Oft have we known that sevenfold fence to fail,
Though stiff with hoops, and armed with ribs of whale.   120
Form a strong line about the silver bound,
And guard the wide circumference around.
    "Whatever spirit, careless of his charge,
His post neglects, or leaves the fair at large,
Shall feel sharp vengeance soon o'ertake his sins,   125
Be stopped in vials, or transfixed with pins,
Or plunged in lakes of bitter washes lie,
Or wedged whole ages in a bodkin's eye;[6]
Gums and pomatums shall his flight restrain,
While clogged he beats his silken wings in vain,   130
Or alum styptics with contracting power
Shrink his thin essence like a riveled[7] flower:
Or, as Ixion fixed,[8] the wretch shall feel
The giddy motion of the whirling mill,
In fumes of burning chocolate shall glow,   135
And tremble at the sea that froths below!"
    He spoke; the spirits from the sails descend;
Some, orb in orb, around the nymph extend;
Some thread the mazy ringlets of her hair;
Some hang upon the pendants of her ear: 140
With beating hearts the dire event they wait,
Anxious, and trembling for the birth of Fate.

CANTO III

    Close by those meads, forever crowned with flowers,
Where Thames with pride surveys his rising towers,
There stands a structure of majestic frame,
Which from the neighboring Hampton[9] takes its name.
Here Britain's statesmen oft the fall foredoom   5
Of foreign tyrants and of nymphs at home;
Here thou, great Anna! whom three realms obey,
Dost sometimes counsel take—and sometimes tea.
    Hither the heroes and the nymphs resort,
To taste awhile the pleasures of a court;   10

4. Diamond earrings.   5. From Latin *crispere*, to curl.   6. A blunt needle with a large eye, used for drawing ribbon through eyelets in the edging of women's garments.   7. To "rivel" is to "contract into wrinkles and corrugations" (Johnson's *Dictionary*).   8. In the Greek myth Ixion was punished in the underworld by being bound on an ever-turning wheel.   9. Hampton Court, the royal palace, about fifteen miles up the Thames from London.

In various talk the instructive hours they passed,
Who gave the ball, or paid the visit last;
One speaks the glory of the British Queen,
And one describes a charming Indian screen;
A third interprets motions, looks, and eyes;   15
At every word a reputation dies.
Snuff, or the fan, supply each pause of chat,
With singing, laughing, ogling, and all that.
    Meanwhile, declining from the noon of day,
The sun obliquely shoots his burning ray;   20
The hungry judges soon the sentence sign,
And wretches hang that jurymen may dine;
The merchant from the Exchange returns in peace,
And the long labors of the toilet cease.
Belinda now, whom thirst of fame invites,   25
Burns to encounter two adventurous knights,
At ombre[1] singly to decide their doom
And swells her breast with conquests yet to come.
Straight the three bands prepare in arms to join,
Each band the number of the sacred nine.   30
Soon as she spreads her hand, the aërial guard
Descend, and sit on each important card:
First Ariel perched upon a Matadore,
Then each according to the rank they bore;
For Sylphs, yet mindful of their ancient race,   35
Are, as when women, wondrous fond of place.
    Behold, four Kings in majesty revered,
With hoary whiskers and a forky beard;
And four fair Queens whose hands sustain a flower,
The expressive emblem of their softer power;   40
Four Knaves in garbs succinct,[2] a trusty band,
Caps on their heads, and halberts in their hand;
And parti-colored troops, a shining train,
Draw forth to combat on the velvet plain.
The skillful nymph reviews her force with care;   45
"Let Spades be trumps!' she said, and trumps they were.
    Now move to war her sable Matadores,
In show like leaders of the swarthy Moors.
Spadillio first, unconquerable lord!
Led off two captive trumps, and swept the board.   50
As many more Manillio forced to yield,
And marched a victor from the verdant field.
Him Basto followed, but his fate more hard
Gained but one trump and one plebeian card.
With his broad saber next, a chief in years,   55
The hoary Majesty of Spades appears,

---

1. The game that Belinda plays against the baron and another young man is too complicated for complete
explication here. Pope has carefully arranged the cards so that Belinda wins. The baron's hand is strong
enough to be a threat, but the third player's is of little account. The hand is played exactly according to the
rules of ombre, and Pope's description of the cards is equally accurate. Each player holds nine cards (line
30). The "Matadores" (line 33), when spades are trumps, are "Spadillio" (line 49), the ace of spades;
"Manillio" (line 51), the two of spades; "Basto" (line 53), the ace of clubs; Belinda holds all three of these.
2. Girded up.

Puts forth one manly leg, to sight revealed,
The rest his many-colored robe concealed.
The rebel Knave, who dares his prince engage,
Proves the just victim of his royal rage. 60
Even mighty Pam,[3] that kings and queens o'erthrew
And mowed down armies in the fights of loo,
Sad chance of war! now destitute of aid,
Falls undistinguished by the victor Spade.
 Thus far both armies to Belinda yield; 65
Now to the Baron fate inclines the field.
His warlike amazon her host invades,
The imperial consort of the crown of Spades.
The Club's black tyrant first her victim died,
Spite of his haughty mien and barbarous pride. 70
What boots the regal circle on his head,
His giant limbs, in state unwieldy spread?
That long behind he trails his pompous robe,
And of all monarchs only grasps the globe?
 The Baron now his Diamonds pours apace; 75
The embroidered King who shows but half his face,
And his refulgent Queen, with powers combined
Of broken troops an easy conquest find.
Clubs, Diamonds, Hearts, in wild disorder seen,
With throngs promiscuous strew the level green. 80
Thus when dispersed a routed army runs,
Of Asia's troops, and Afric's sable sons,
With like confusion different nations fly,
Of various habit, and of various dye,
The pierced battalions disunited fall 85
In heaps on heaps; one fate o'erwhelms them all.
 The Knave of Diamonds tries his wily arts,
And wins (oh, shameful chance!) the Queen of Hearts.
At this, the blood the virgin's cheek forsook,
A livid paleness spreads o'er all her look; 90
She sees, and trembles at the approaching ill,
Just in the jaws of ruin, and Codille,[4]
And now (as oft in some distempered state)
On one nice trick depends the general fate.
An Ace of Hearts steps forth: the King unseen 95
Lurked in her hand, and mourned his captive Queen.
He springs to vengeance with an eager pace,
And falls like thunder on the prostrate Ace.
The nymph exulting fills with shouts the sky,
The walls, the woods, and long canals reply. 100
 O thoughtless mortals! ever blind to fate,
Too soon dejected, and too soon elate:
Sudden these honors shall be snatched away,
And cursed forever this victorious day.
 For lo! the board with cups and spoons is crowned, 105

3. The knave of clubs, the highest trump in the game of loo.   4. The term applied to losing a hand at cards.

The berries crackle, and the mill turns round;[5]
On shining altars of Japan[6] they raise
The silver lamp; the fiery spirits blaze:
From silver spouts the grateful liquors glide,
While China's earth receives the smoking tide.   110
At once they gratify their scent and taste,
And frequent cups prolong the rich repast.
Straight hover round the fair her airy band;
Some, as she sipped, the fuming liquor fanned,
Some o'er her lap their careful plumes displayed,   115
Trembling, and conscious of the rich brocade.
Coffee (which makes the politician wise,
And see through all things with his half-shut eyes)
Sent up in vapors to the Baron's brain
New stratagems, the radiant Lock to gain.   120
Ah, cease, rash youth! desist ere 'tis too late,
Fear the just Gods, and think of Scylla's fate![7]
Changed to a bird, and sent to flit in air,
She dearly pays for Nisus' injured hair!
    But when to mischief mortals bend their will,   125
How soon they find fit instruments of ill!
Just then, Clarissa drew with tempting grace
A two-edged weapon from her shining case:
So ladies in romance assist their knight,
Present the spear, and arm him for the fight.   130
He takes the gift with reverence, and extends
The little engine on his fingers' ends;
This just behind Belinda's neck he spread,
As o'er the fragrant steams she bends her head.
Swift to the Lock a thousand sprites repair,   135
A thousand wings, by turns, blow back the hair,
And thrice they twitched the diamond in her ear,
Thrice she looked back, and thrice the foe drew near.
Just in that instant, anxious Ariel sought
The close recesses of the virgin's thought;   140
As on the nosegay in her breast reclined,
He watched the ideas rising in her mind,
Sudden he viewed, in spite of all her art,
An earthly lover lurking at her heart.
Amazed, confused, he found his power expired,   145
Resigned to fate, and with a sigh retired.
    The Peer now spreads the glittering forfex[8] wide,
T' enclose the Lock; now joins it, to divide.
Even then, before the fatal engine closed,
A wretched Sylph too fondly interposed;   150
Fate urged the shears, and cut the Sylph in twain
(But airy substance soon unites again):

---

5. That is, coffee is roasted and ground.   **6.** That is, small, lacquered tables. The word "altars" suggests the ritualistic character of coffee drinking in Belinda's world.   **7.** Scylla, daughter of Nisus, was turned into a sea bird because, for the sake of her love for Minos of Crete, who was besieging her father's city of Megara, she cut from her father's head the purple lock on which his safety depended. She is not the Scylla of the "Scylla and Charybdis" episode in the *Odyssey*.   **8.** Scissors.

The meeting points the sacred hair dissever
From the fair head, forever, and forever!
    Then flashed the living lightning from her eyes,   155
And screams of horror rend the affrighted skies.
Not louder shrieks to pitying heaven are cast,
When husbands, or when lapdogs breathe their last;
Or when rich china vessels fallen from high,
In glittering dust and painted fragments lie!   160
"Let wreaths of triumph now my temples twine,"
The victor cried, "the glorious prize is mine!
While fish in streams, or birds delight in air,
Or in a coach and six the British Fair,
As long as *Atalantis*[9] shall be read,   165
Or the small pillow grace a lady's bed,
While visits shall be paid on solemn days,
When numerous wax-lights in bright order blaze,
While nymphs take treats, or assignations give,
So long my honor, name, and praise shall live!   170
What Time would spare, from Steel receives its date,
And monuments, like men, submit to fate!
Steel could the labor of the Gods destroy,
And strike to dust the imperial towers of Troy;
Steel could the works of mortal pride confound,   175
And hew triumphal arches to the ground.
What wonder then, fair nymph! thy hairs should feel,
The conquering force of unresisted Steel?"

CANTO IV

    But anxious cares the pensive nymph oppressed,
And secret passions labored in her breast.
Not youthful kings in battle seized alive,
Not scornful virgins who their charms survive,
Not ardent lovers robbed of all their bliss,   5
Not ancient ladies when refused a kiss,
Not tyrants fierce that unrepenting die,
Not Cynthia when her manteau's[1] pinned awry,
E'er felt such rage, resentment, and despair,
As thou, sad virgin! for thy ravished hair.   10
    For, that sad moment, when the Sylphs withdrew
And Ariel weeping from Belinda flew,
Umbriel,[2] a dusky, melancholy sprite
As ever sullied the fair face of light,
Down to the central earth, his proper scene,   15
Repaired to search the gloomy Cave of Spleen.[3]
    Swift on his sooty pinions flits the Gnome,
And in a vapor[4] reached the dismal dome.
No cheerful breeze this sullen region knows,

---

9. Mrs. Manley's *New Atalantis* (1709) was notorious for its thinly concealed allusions to contemporary scandals.   1. Negligee, or loose robe.   2. The name suggests shade and darkness.   3. Ill humor. 4. Punning on *vapor* as (1) mist and (2) an excessively emotional (even peevish) state of mind, appropriate to the realm of "spleen."

The dreaded east is all the wind that blows.   20
Here in a grotto, sheltered close from air,
And screened in shades from day's detested glare,
She sighs forever on her pensive bed,
Pain at her side, and Megrim[5] at her head.
    Two handmaids wait the throne: alike in place,   25
But differing far in figure and in face.
Here stood Ill-Nature like an ancient maid,
Her wrinkled form in black and white arrayed;
With store of prayers for mornings, nights, and noons,
Her hand is filled; her bosom with lampoons.   30
    There Affectation, with a sickly mien,
Shows in her cheek the roses of eighteen,
Practiced to lisp, and hang the head aside,
Faints into airs, and languishes with pride,
On the rich quilt sinks with becoming woe,   35
Wrapped in a gown, for sickness and for show.
The fair ones feel such maladies as these,
When each new nightdress gives a new disease.
    A constant vapor[6] o'er the palace flies,
Strange phantoms rising as the mists arise;   40
Dreadful as hermit's dreams in haunted shades,
Or bright as visions of expiring maids.
Now glaring fiends, and snakes on rolling spires,[7]
Pale specters, gaping tombs, and purple fires;
Now lakes of liquid gold, Elysian scenes,   45
And crystal domes, and angels in machines.[8]
    Unnumbered throngs on every side are seen
Of bodies changed to various forms by Spleen.
Here living teapots stand, one arm held out,
One bent; the handle this, and that the spout: 50
A pipkin[9] there, like Homer's tripod, walks;
Here sighs a jar, and there a goose pie talks;
Men prove with child, as powerful fancy works,
And maids, turned bottles, call aloud for corks.
    Safe passed the Gnome through this fantastic band, 55
A branch of healing spleenwort[1] in his hand.
Then thus addressed the Power: "Hail, wayward Queen!
Who rule the sex to fifty from fifteen:
Parent of vapors and of female wit,
Who give the hysteric or poetic fit,   60
On various tempers act by various ways,
Make some take physic, others scribble plays;
Who cause the proud their visits to delay,
And send the godly in a pet to pray.
A nymph there is that all your power disdains,   65

5. Headache.   6. Emblematic of "the vapors"—hypochondria, melancholy, peevishness, often affected by fashionable women.   7. Coils.   8. Mechanical devices used in the theaters for spectacular effects. The fantasies of neurotic women here merge with the sensational stage effects popular with contemporary audiences.   9. An earthen pot. In *Iliad* XVIII.434–40, Vulcan furnishes the gods with self-propelling "tripods" (three-legged stools).   1. An herb, efficacious against the spleen. Pope alludes to the golden bough that Aeneas and the Cumaean sybil carry with them for protection into the underworld in *Aeneid* VI.

And thousands more in equal mirth maintains.
But oh! if e'er thy Gnome could spoil a grace,
Or raise a pimple on a beauteous face,
Like citron-waters[2] matrons' cheeks inflame,
Or change complexions at a losing game;   70
If e'er with airy horns[3] I planted heads,
Or rumpled petticoats, or tumbled beds,
Or caused suspicion when no soul was rude,
Or discomposed the headdress of a prude,
Or e'er to costive lapdog gave disease,   75
Which not the tears of brightest eyes could ease,
Hear me, and touch Belinda with chagrin:[4]
That single act gives half the world the spleen."
   The Goddess with a discontented air
Seems to reject him though she grants his prayer.   80
A wondrous bag with both her hands she binds,
Like that where once Ulysses held the winds;[5]
There she collects the force of female lungs,
Sighs, sobs, and passions, and the war of tongues.
A vial next she fills with fainting fears,   85
Soft sorrows, melting griefs, and flowing tears.
The Gnome rejoicing bears her gifts away,
Spreads his black wings, and slowly mounts to day.
   Sunk in Thalestris'[6] arms the nymph he found,
Her eyes dejected and her hair unbound.   90
Full o'er their heads the swelling bag he rent,
And all the Furies issued at the vent.
Belinda burns with more than mortal ire,
And fierce Thalestris fans the rising fire.
"O wretched maid!" she spread her hands, and cried   95
(While Hampton's echoes, "Wretched maid!" replied),
"Was it for this you took such constant care
The bodkin, comb, and essence to prepare?
For this your locks in paper durance bound,
For this with torturing irons wreathed around?   100
For this with fillets strained your tender head,
And bravely bore the double loads of lead?[7]
Gods! shall the ravisher display your hair,
While the fops envy, and the ladies stare!
Honor forbid! at whose unrivaled shrine   105
Ease, pleasure, virtue, all, our sex resign.
Methinks already I your tears survey,
Already hear the horrid things they say,
Already see you a degraded toast,
And all your honor in a whisper lost!   110

---

2. Brandy flavored with orange or lemon peel.   **3.** The symbol of the cuckold; here "airy," because they exist only in the jealous suspicions of the husband, the victim of the mischievous Umbriel.   **4.** Ill humor. **5.** Aeolus (later conceived of as god of the winds) gave Ulysses a bag containing all the winds adverse to his voyage home. When his ship was in sight of Ithaca, his companions opened the bag and the storms that ensued drove Ulysses far away (*Odyssey* X.19ff.).   **6.** The name is borrowed from a queen of the Amazons, hence a fierce and warlike woman. Thalestris, according to legend, traveled thirty days in order to have a child by Alexander the Great. Plutarch denies the story.   **7.** The frame on which the elaborate coiffures of the day were arranged.

How shall I, then, your helpless fame defend?
'Twill then be infamy to seem your friend!
And shall this prize, the inestimable prize,
Exposed through crystal to the gazing eyes,
And heightened by the diamond's circling rays,   115
On that rapacious hand forever blaze?
Sooner shall grass in Hyde Park Circus grow,
And wits take lodgings in the sound of Bow;[8]
Sooner let earth, air, sea, to chaos fall,
Men, monkeys, lapdogs, parrots, perish all!"   120
     She said; then raging to Sir Plume repairs,
And bids her beau demand the precious hairs
(Sir Plume of amber snuffbox justly vain,
And the nice conduct of a clouded cane).
With earnest eyes, and round unthinking face,   125
He first the snuffbox opened, then the case,
And thus broke out—"My Lord, why, what the devil!
Z—ds! damn the lock! 'fore Gad, you must be civil!
Plague on't! 'tis past a jest—nay prithee, pox!
Give her the hair'—he spoke, and rapped his box.   130
     "It grieves me much," replied the Peer again,
"Who speaks so well should ever speak in vain.
But by this Lock, this sacred Lock I swear
(Which never more shall join its parted hair;
Which never more its honors shall renew,   135
Clipped from the lovely head where late it grew),
That while my nostrils draw the vital air,
This hand, which won it, shall forever wear."
He spoke, and speaking, in proud triumph spread
The long-contended honors[9] of her head.   140
     But Umbriel, hateful Gnome, forbears not so;
He breaks the vial whence the sorrows flow.
Then see! the nymph in beauteous grief appears,
Her eyes half languishing, half drowned in tears;
On her heaved bosom hung her drooping head,   145
Which with a sigh she raised, and thus she said:
     "Forever cursed be this detested day,
Which snatched my best, my favorite curl away!
Happy! ah, ten times happy had I been,
If Hampton Court these eyes had never seen!   150
Yet am not I the first mistaken maid,
By love of courts to numerous ills betrayed.
Oh, had I rather unadmired remained
In some lone isle, or distant northern land;
Where the gilt chariot never marks the way,   155
Where none learn ombre, none e'er taste bohea![1]
There kept my charms concealed from mortal eye,
Like roses that in deserts bloom and die.
What moved my mind with youthful lords to roam?

---

8. A person born within sound of the bells of St. Mary-le-Bow in Cheapside is said to be a cockney. No fashionable wit would have so vulgar an address.   9. Ornaments, hence locks; a Latinism.   1. A costly sort of tea.

Oh, had I stayed, and said my prayers at home! 160
'Twas this the morning omens seemed to tell,
Thrice from my trembling hand the patch box² fell;
The tottering china shook without a wind,
Nay, Poll sat mute, and Shock was most unkind!
A Sylph too warned me of the threats of fate, 165
In mystic visions, now believed too late!
See the poor remnants of these slighted hairs!
My hands shall rend what e'en thy rapine spares.
These in two sable ringlets taught to break,
Once gave new beauties to the snowy neck; 170
The sister lock now sits uncouth, alone,
And in its fellow's fate foresees its own;
Uncurled it hangs, the fatal shears demands,
And tempts once more thy sacrilegious hands.
Oh, hadst thou, cruel! been content to seize 175
Hairs less in sight, or any hairs but these!"

CANTO V

She said: the pitying audience melt in tears.
But Fate and Jove had stopped the Baron's ears.
In vain Thalestris with reproach assails,
For who can move when fair Belinda fails?
Not half so fixed the Trojan³ could remain, 5
While Anna begged and Dido raged in vain.
Then grave Clarissa graceful waved her fan;
Silence ensued, and thus the nymph began:
"Say why are beauties praised and honored most,
The wise man's passion, and the vain man's toast? 10
Why decked with all that land and sea afford,
Why angels called, and angel-like adored?
Why round our coaches crowd the white-gloved beaux,
Why bows the side box from its inmost rows?
How vain are all these glories, all our pains, 15
Unless good sense preserve what beauty gains;
That men may say when we the front box grace,
'Behold the first in virtue as in face!'
Oh! if to dance all night, and dress all day,
Charmed the smallpox, or chased old age away, 20
Who would not scorn what housewife's cares produce,
Or who would learn one earthly thing of use?
To patch, nay ogle, might become a saint,
Nor could it sure be such a sin to paint.
But since, alas! frail beauty must decay, 25
Curled or uncurled, since locks will turn to gray;
Since painted, or not painted, all shall fade,
And she who scorns a man must die a maid;
What then remains but well our power to use,

---

2. A box to hold the ornamental patches of court plaster worn on the face by both sexes. Cf. *Spectator* 81.
3. Aeneas, who forsook Dido at the bidding of the gods, despite her reproaches and the supplications of her sister Anna. Virgil compares him to a steadfast oak that withstands a storm (*Aeneid* IV.437–43).

And keep good humor still whate'er we lose?   30
And trust me, dear, good humor can prevail
When airs, and flights, and screams, and scolding fail.
Beauties in vain their pretty eyes may roll;
Charms strike the sight, but merit wins the soul."[4]
   So spoke the dame, but no applause ensued;   35
Belinda frowned, Thalestris called her prude.
"To arms, to arms!" the fierce virago cries,
And swift as lightning to the combat flies.
All side in parties, and begin the attack;
Fans clap, silks rustle, and tough whalebones crack;   40
Heroes' and heroines' shouts confusedly rise,
And bass and treble voices strike the skies.
No common weapons in their hands are found,
Like Gods they fight, nor dread a mortal wound.
   So when bold Homer makes the Gods engage,   45
And heavenly breasts with human passions rage;
'Gainst Pallas, Mars; Latona, Hermes arms;
And all Olympus rings with loud alarms:
Jove's thunder roars, heaven trembles all around,
Blue Neptune storms, the bellowing deeps resound: 50
Earth shakes her nodding towers, the ground gives way,
And the pale ghosts start at the flash of day!
   Triumphant Umbriel on a sconce's height
Clapped his glad wings, and sat to view the fight:
Propped on their bodkin spears, the sprites survey   55
The growing combat, or assist the fray.
   While through the press enraged Thalestris flies,
And scatters death around from both her eyes,
A beau and witling perished in the throng,
One died in metaphor, and one in song.   60
"O cruel nymph! a living death I bear,"
Cried Dapperwit, and sunk beside his chair.
A mournful glance Sir Fopling upwards cast,
"Those eyes are made so killing"—was his last.
Thus on Maeander's flowery margin lies   65
The expiring swan, and as he sings he dies.
   When bold Sir Plume had drawn Clarissa down,
Chloe stepped in, and killed him with a frown;
She smiled to see the doughty hero slain,
But, at her smile, the beau revived again.   70
Now Jove suspends his golden scales in air,
Weighs the men's wits against the lady's hair;
The doubtful beam long nods from side to side;
At length the wits mount up, the hairs subside.
   See, fierce Belinda on the Baron flies,   75
With more than usual lightning in her eyes;
Nor feared the chief the unequal fight to try,
Who sought no more than on his foe to die.

---

4. The speech is a close parody of Pope's own translation of the speech of Sarpedon to Glaucus, first published in 1709 and slightly revised in his version of the *Iliad* (XII.371–96).

But this bold lord with manly strength endued,
She with one finger and a thumb subdued: 80
Just where the breath of life his nostrils drew,
A charge of snuff the wily virgin threw;
The Gnomes direct, to every atom just,
The pungent grains of titillating dust.
Sudden, with starting tears each eye o'erflows,   85
And the high dome re-echoes to his nose.
    "Now meet thy fate," incensed Belinda cried,
And drew a deadly bodkin⁵ from her side.
(The same, his ancient personage to deck,
Her great-great-grandsire wore about his neck,   90
In three seal rings; which after, melted down,
Formed a vast buckle for his widow's gown:
Her infant grandame's whistle next it grew,
The bells she jingled, and the whistle blew;
Then in a bodkin graced her mother's hairs,   95
Which long she wore, and now Belinda wears.)
    "Boast not my fall," he cried, "insulting foe!
Thou by some other shalt be laid as low.
Nor think to die dejects my lofty mind:
All that I dread is leaving you behind!   100
Rather than so, ah, let me still survive,
And burn in Cupid's flames—but burn alive."
    "Restore the Lock!" she cries; and all around
"Restore the Lock!" the vaulted roofs rebound.
Not fierce Othello in so loud a strain   105
Roared for the handkerchief that caused his pain.⁶
But see how oft ambitious aims are crossed,
And chiefs contend till all the prize is lost!
The lock, obtained with guilt, and kept with pain,
In every place is sought, but sought in vain: 110
With such a prize no mortal must be blessed,
So Heaven decrees! with Heaven who can contest?
    Some thought it mounted to the lunar sphere,
Since all things lost on earth are treasured there.
There heroes' wits are kept in ponderous vases,   115
And beaux' in snuffboxes and tweezer cases.
There broken vows and deathbed alms are found,
And lovers' hearts with ends of riband bound,
The courtier's promises, and sick man's prayers,
The smiles of harlots, and the tears of heirs,   120
Cages for gnats, and chains to yoke a flea,
Dried butterflies, and tomes of casuistry.
    But trust the Muse—she saw it upward rise,
Though marked by none but quick, poetic eyes
(So Rome's great founder⁷ to the heavens withdrew,   125
To Proculus alone confessed in view);

---

5. An ornamental pin shaped like a dagger, to be worn in the hair.   6. *Othello* III.4.   7. Romulus, the "founder" and first king of Rome, was snatched to heaven in a storm cloud while reviewing his army in the Campus Martius (Livy I.16).

A sudden star, it shot through liquid air,
And drew behind a radiant trail of hair.
Not Berenice's[8] locks first rose so bright,
The heavens bespangling with disheveled light.   130
The Sylphs behold it kindling as it flies,
And pleased pursue its progress through the skies.
   This the beau monde shall from the Mall[9] survey,
And hail with music its propitious ray.
This the blest lover shall for Venus take,   135
And send up vows from Rosamonda's Lake.[1]
This Partridge soon shall view in cloudless skies,
When next he looks through Galileo's eyes;[2]
And hence the egregious wizard shall foredoom
The fate of Louis, and the fall of Rome.   140
   Then cease, bright nymph! to mourn thy ravished hair,
Which adds new glory to the shining sphere!
Not all the tresses that fair head can boast,
Shall draw such envy as the Lock you lost.
For, after all the murders of your eye,   145
When, after millions slain, yourself shall die:
When those fair suns shall set, as set they must,
And all those tresses shall be laid in dust,
This Lock the Muse shall consecrate to fame,
And 'midst the stars inscribe Belinda's name.   150

An Essay on Man

To Henry St. John, Lord Bolingbroke

EPISTLE I

ARGUMENT OF THE NATURE AND STATE OF MAN, WITH RESPECT TO THE UNI-
VERSE. Of man in the abstract—I. That we can judge only with regard to our
own system, being ignorant of the relations of systems and things, ver. 17,
&c.—II. That man is not to be deemed imperfect, but a being suited to his
place and rank in the creation, agreeable to the general order of things, and
conformable to ends and relations to him unknown, ver. 35, &c.—III. That
it is partly upon his ignorance of future events, and partly upon the hope of
a future state, that all his happiness in the present depends, ver. 77, &c.—
IV. The pride of aiming at more knowledge, and pretending to more perfection, the cause of man's error and misery. The impiety of putting himself in
the place of God, and judging of the fitness or unfitness, perfection or imperfection, justice or injustice of his dispensations, ver. 113, &c.—V. The
absurdity of conceiting himself the final cause of the creation, or expecting
that perfection in the moral world which is not in the natural, ver. 131, &c.—

---

8. Berenice, the wife of Ptolemy III, dedicated a lock of her hair to the gods to ensure her husband's safe
return from war. It was turned into a constellation.   9. A walk laid out by Charles II in St. James's Park,
a resort for strollers of all sorts.   1. In St. James's Park; associated with unhappy lovers.   2. A tele-
scope. John Partridge was an astrologer whose annually published predictions had been amusingly satirized
by Swift and other wits in 1708.

VI. The unreasonableness of his complaints against Providence, while on the one hand he demands the perfections of the angels, and on the other the bodily qualifications of the brutes; though, to possess any of the sensitive faculties in a higher degree, would render him miserable, ver. 173, &c.—VII. That throughout the whole visible world, an universal order and gradation in the sensual and mental faculties is observed, which causes a subordination of creature to creature, and of all creatures to man. The gradations of sense, instinct, thought, reflection, reason: that reason alone countervails all the other faculties, ver. 207.—VIII. How much further this order and subordination of living creatures may extend, above and below us; were any part of which broken, not that part only, but the whole connected creation must be destroyed, ver. 233—IX. The extravagance, madness, and pride of such a desire, ver. 259.—X. The consequence of all, the absolute submission due to Providence, both as to our present and future state, ver. 281, &c., to the end.

Awake, my St. John![1] leave all meaner things
To low ambition, and the pride of Kings.
Let us (since Life can little more supply
Than just to look about us and to die)
Expatiate free o'er all this scene of Man;   5
A mighty maze! but not without a plan;
A Wild, where weeds and flowers promiscuous shoot;
Or Garden, tempting with forbidden fruit.
Together let us beat this ample field,
Try what the open, what the covert yield;   10
The latent tracts, the giddy heights, explore
Of all who blindly creep, or sightless soar;
Eye Nature's walks, shoot Folly as it flies,
And catch the Manners living as they rise;
Laugh where we must, be candid where we can;   15
But vindicate the ways of God to man.[2]

    I. Say first, of God above, or Man below,
What can we reason, but from what we know?
Of Man, what see we but his station here,
From which to reason, or to which refer?   20
Through worlds unnumbered though the God be known,
'Tis ours to trace him only in our own.
He, who through vast immensity can pierce,
See worlds on worlds compose one universe,
Observe how system into system runs,   25
What other planets circle other suns,
What varied Being peoples every star,
May tell why Heaven has made us as we are.
But of this frame the bearings, and the ties,
The strong connections, nice dependencies,   30
Gradations just, has thy pervading soul

---

1. Pope's friend, who had thus far neglected to keep his part of their friendly bargain: Pope was to write his philosophical speculations in verse; Bolingbroke was to write his in prose.   2. Cf. Milton's *Paradise Lost* I.26. Pope's theme is essentially the same as Milton's, and even the opening image of the garden reminds one of the earlier poet's Paradise.

Looked through? or can a part contain the whole?
  Is the great chain,[3] that draws all to agree,
And drawn supports, upheld by God, or thee?

    II. Presumptuous Man! the reason wouldst thou find,   35
Why formed so weak, so little, and so blind?
First, if thou canst, the harder reason guess,
Why formed no weaker, blinder, and no less?
Ask of thy mother earth, why oaks are made
Taller or stronger than the weeds they shade?   40
Or ask of yonder argent fields above,
Why Jove's satellites[4] are less than JOVE?
    Of Systems possible, if 'tis confest.
That Wisdom infinite must form the best,
Where all must full[5] or not coherent be,   45
And all that rises, rise in due degree;
Then, in the scale of reasoning life,'tis plain,
There must be, somewhere, such a rank as Man:
And all the question (wrangle e'er so long)
Is only this, if God has placed him wrong?   50
    Respecting Man, whatever wrong we call,
May, must be right, as relative to all.
In human works, though laboured on with pain,
A thousand movements scarce one purpose gain;
In God's, one single can its end produce;   55
Yet serves to second too some other use.
So Man, who here seems principal alone,
Perhaps acts second to some sphere unknown,
Touches some wheel, or verges to some goal;
'Tis but a part we see, and not a whole.   60
    When the proud steed shall know why Man restrains
His fiery course, or drives him o'er the plains;
When the dull Ox, why now he breaks the clod,
Is now a victim, and now Egypt's God:
Then shall Man's pride and dullness comprehend   65
His actions', passions', being's use and end;
Why doing, suffering, checked, impelled; and why
This hour a slave, the next a deity.
    Then say not Man's imperfect, Heaven in fault;
Say rather, Man's as perfect as he ought: 70
His knowledge measured to his state and place;
His time a moment, and a point his space.
If to be perfect in a certain sphere,
What matter, soon or late, or here or there?
The blest to-day is as completely so,   75
As who began a thousand years ago.

    III. Heaven from all creatures hides the book of Fate,
  All but the page prescribed, their present state:

---

3. A reference to the popular 18th-century notion of the Great Chain of Being, in which elements of the universe took their places in a hierarchy ranging from the lowest matter to God.   4. Here pronounced *satéllités*.   5. According to the principle of plenitude, there can be no gaps in the Chain.

From brutes what men, from men what spirits know:
Or who could suffer Being here below?   80
The lamb thy riot dooms to bleed to-day,
Had he thy Reason, would he skip and play?
Pleased to the last, he crops the flowery food,
And licks the hand just raised to shed his blood.
Oh blindness to the future! kindly given,   85
That each may fill the circle marked by Heaven:
Who sees with equal eye, as God of all,
A hero perish, or a sparrow fall,
Atoms or systems into ruin hurled,
And now a bubble burst, and now a world.   90
   Hope humbly then; with trembling pinions soar;
Wait the great teacher Death; and God adore.
What future bliss, he gives not thee to know,
But gives that Hope to be thy blessing now.
Hope springs eternal in the human breast: 95
Man never Is, but always To be blest:
The soul, uneasy and confined from home,
Rests and expatiates in a life to come.
   Lo, the poor Indian! whose untutored mind
Sees God in clouds, or hears him in the wind;   100
His soul, proud Science never taught to stray
Far as the solar walk, or milky way;
Yet simple Nature to his hope has given,
Behind the cloud-topt hill, an humbler heaven;
Some safer world in depth of woods embraced,   105
Some happier island in the watery waste,
Where slaves once more their native land behold,
No fiends torment, no Christians thirst for gold.
To Be, contents his natural desire,
He asks no Angel's wing, no Seraph's fire;   110
But thinks, admitted to that equal sky,
His faithful dog shall bear him company.

   IV. Go, wiser thou! and, in thy scale of sense,
Weigh thy Opinion against Providence;
Call imperfection what thou fanciest such,   115
Say, here he gives too little, there too much:
Destroy all Creatures for thy sport or gust,
Yet cry, If Man's unhappy, God's unjust;
If Man alone engross not Heaven's high care,
Alone made perfect here, immortal there: 120
Snatch from his hand the balance and the rod,
Re-judge his justice, be the GOD of GOD.
In Pride, in reasoning Pride, our error lies;
All quit their sphere, and rush into the skies.
Pride still is aiming at the blest abodes,   125
Men would be Angels, Angels would be Gods.
Aspiring to be Gods, if Angels fell,
Aspiring to be Angels, Men rebel:

And who but wishes to invert the laws
Of ORDER, sins against the Eternal Cause. 130

V. Ask for what end the heavenly bodies shine,
Earth for whose use? Pride answers, "'Tis for mine:
For me kind Nature wakes her genial Power,
Suckles each herb, and spreads out ev'ry flower;
Annual for me, the grape, the rose, renew, 135
The juice nectareous, and the balmy dew;
For me, the mine a thousand treasures brings;
For me, health gushes from a thousand springs;
Seas roll to waft me, suns to light me rise;
My footstool earth, my canopy the skies." 140
But errs not Nature from this gracious end,
From burning suns when livid deaths descend,
When earthquakes swallow, or when tempests sweep
Towns to one grave, whole nations to the deep?
"No," 'tis replied, "the first Almighty Cause 145
Acts not by partial, but by general laws;
The exceptions few; some change since all began:
And what created perfect?"—Why then Man?
If the great end be human happiness,
Then Nature deviates; and can man do less? 150
As much that end a constant course requires
Of showers and sunshine, as of man's desires;
As much eternal springs and cloudless skies,
As Men forever temperate, calm, and wise.
If plagues or earthquakes break not Heaven's design, 155
Why then a Borgia, or a Catiline?[6]
Who knows but He whose hand the lightning forms,
Who heaves old Ocean, and who wings the storms;
Pours fierce Ambition in a Caesar's mind,
Or turns young Ammon[7] loose to scourge mankind? 160
From pride, from pride, our very reasoning springs;
Account for moral, as for natural things:
Why charge we Heaven in those, in these acquit?
In both, to reason right is to submit.
Better for Us, perhaps, it might appear, 165
Where there all harmony, all virtue here;
That never air or ocean felt the wind;
That never passion discomposed the mind.
But ALL subsists by elemental strife;
And Passions are the elements of Life. 170
The general ORDER, since the whole began,
Is kept in Nature, and is kept in Man.

VI. What would this Man? Now upward will he soar,
And little less than Angel, would be more;
Now looking downwards, just as grieved appears 175

---

6. Roman who conspired against the state in 63 B.C. Cesare Borgia (1476–1507), an Italian prince notorious for his crimes.   7. Alexander the Great, who when he visited the oracle of Zeus Ammon in Egypt was hailed by the priest there as son of the god.

To want the strength of bulls, the fur of bears.
Made for his use all creatures if he call,
Say what their use, had he the powers of all?
Nature to these, without profusion, kind,
The proper organs, proper powers assigned;   180
Each seeming want compénsated of course,
Here with degrees of swiftness, there of force;
All in exact proportion to the state;
Nothing to add, and nothing to abate.
Each beast, each insect, happy in its own: 185
Is Heaven unkind to Man, and Man alone?
Shall he alone, whom rational we call,
Be pleased with nothing, if not blessed with all?
   The bliss of Man (could Pride that blessing find)
Is not to act or think beyond mankind;   190
No powers of body or of soul to share,
But what his nature and his state can bear.
Why has not Man a microscopic eye?
For this plain reason, Man is not a Fly.
Say what the use, were finer optics[8] given,   195
T' inspect a mite, not comprehend the heaven?
Or touch, if tremblingly alive all o'er,
To smart and agonize at every pore?
Or quick effluvia[9] darting through the brain,
Die of a rose in aromatic pain?   200
If nature thundered in his opening ears,
And stunned him with the music of the spheres,[1]
How would he wish that Heaven had left him still
The whispering Zephyr, and the purling rill?
Who finds not Providence all good and wise,   205
Alike in what it gives, and what denies?

   VII. Far as Creation's ample range extends,
The scale of sensual, mental powers ascends:
Mark how it mounts, to Man's imperial race,
From the green myriads in the peopled grass: 210
What modes of sight betwixt each wide extreme,
The mole's dim curtain, and the lynx's[2] beam:
Of smell, the headlong lioness between,
And hound sagacious[3] on the tainted green:
Of hearing, from the life that fills the Flood,   215
To that which warbles through the vernal wood:
The spider's touch, how exquisítely fine!
Feels at each thread, and lives along the line:
In the nice bee, what sense so subtly true
From poisonous herbs extracts the healing dew?   220
How Instinct varies in the grovelling swine,
Compared, half-reasoning elephant, with thine!
'Twixt that, and Reason, what a nice barriér,

8. Eyes.   9. Stream of minute particles.   1. The old notion that the movement of the planets created a "higher" music.   2. According to legend, one of the keenest sighted animals. *Dim curtain:* the mole's poor vision.   3. Here, exceptionally quick of scent.

For ever separate, yet for ever near!
Remembrance and Reflection how allied;   225
What thin partitions Sense from Thought divide:
And Middle natures,[4] how they long to join,
Yet never pass the insuperable line!
Without this just gradation, could they be
Subjected, these to those, or all to thee?   230
The powers of all subdued by thee alone,
Is not thy Reason all these powers in one?

    VIII. See, through this air, this ocean, and this earth,
All matter quick, and bursting into birth.
Above, how high, progressive life may go!   235
Around, how wide! how deep extend below!
Vast chain of Being! which from God began,
Natures ethereal, human, angel, man,
Beast, bird, fish, insect, what no eye can see,
No glass can reach; from Infinite to thee,   240
From thee to Nothing.—On superior powers
Were we to press, inferior might on ours:
Or in the full creation leave a void,
Where, one step broken, the great scale's destroyed:
From Nature's chain whatever link you strike,   245
Tenth or ten thousandth, breaks the chain alike.
    And, if each system in gradation roll
Alike essential to the amazing Whole,
The least confusion but in one, not all
That system only, but the Whole must fall.   250
Let Earth unbalanced from her orbit fly,
Planets and Suns run lawless through the sky;
Let ruling angels from their spheres be hurled,
Being on Being wrecked, and world on world;
Heaven's whole foundations to their center nod,   255
And Nature tremble to the throne of God.
All this dread ORDER break—for whom? for thee?
Vile worm!—oh Madness! Pride! Impiety!

    IX. What if the foot, ordained the dust to tread,
Or hand, to toil, aspired to be the head?   260
What if the head, the eye, or ear repined
To serve mere engines to the ruling Mind?
Just as absurd for any part to claim
To be another, in this general frame:
Just as absurd, to mourn the tasks or pains,   265
The great directing MIND of ALL ordains.
    All are but parts of one stupendous whole,
Whose body Nature is, and God the soul;
That, changed through all, and yet in all the same;
Great in the earth, as in the ethereal frame;   270
Warms in the sun, refreshes in the breeze,

---

4. Animals that seem to share the characteristics of several different classes, e.g., the duck-billed platypus.

Glows in the stars, and blossoms in the trees,
Lives through all life, extends through all extent,
Spreads undivided, operates unspent;
Breathes in our soul, informs our mortal part,   275
As full, as perfect, in a hair as heart;
As full, as perfect, in vile Man that mourns,
As the rapt Seraph that adores and burns:
To him no high, no low, no great, no small;
He fills, he bounds, connects, and equals all.   280

    X. Cease then, nor ORDER imperfection name:
Our proper bliss depends on what we blame.
Know thy own point: this kind, this due degree
Of blindness, weakness, Heaven bestows on thee.
Submit.—In this, or any other sphere,   285
Secure to be as blest as thou canst bear:
Safe in the hand of one disposing Power,
Or in the natal, or the mortal hour.
All Nature is but Art, unknown to thee;
All Chance, Direction, which thou canst not see;   290
All Discord, Harmony not understood;
All partial Evil, universal Good:
And, spite of Pride, in erring Reason's spite,
One truth is clear, WHATEVER IS, IS RIGHT.[5]

5. Epistle II deals with "the Nature and State of Man with respect to himself, as an Individual"; Epistle III examines "the Nature and State of Man with respect to Society"; and the last epistle concerns "the Nature and State of Man with Respect to Happiness."

FRANÇOIS-MARIE AROUET DE VOLTAIRE
1694–1778

Voltaire's *Candide* (1759) brings to near perfection the art of black comedy. It subjects its characters to an accumulation of horrors so bizarre that they provoke a bewildered response of laughter as self-protection—even while they demand that the reader pay attention to the serious implications of such extravagance.

    Voltaire had prepared himself to write such a work by varied experience—including that of political imprisonment. He was born François-Marie Arouet, son of a minor treasury official in Paris. After attending a Jesuit school, he took up the study of law, which, however, he soon abandoned. In his early twenties (1717–18), he spent eleven months in the Bastille for writing satiric verses about the aristocracy. His incarceration did not dissuade him from a literary career; by 1718 he was using the name Voltaire and beginning to acquire literary and social reputation—as well as some wealth (his speculations in the Compagnie des Indes made him rich by 1726). Money, however, did not protect him from spending more time in the Bastille during that year; after his release, he passed three years in exile, mainly in England. From 1734 to 1749, he studied widely, living with Madame du Châtelet on her estate at Cirey. For the next three years he stayed with Frederick the Great of Prussia at his Potsdam court; after that arrangement collapsed, Voltaire bought property in Switzerland and in adjacent France, settling first at his own château, Les Delices, outside Geneva, and later at nearby Ferney, in France. His international reputation as writer and social critic steadily increased; in the year of his death, he returned triumphantly to Paris.

Like his English contemporary Samuel Johnson, Voltaire wrote in many important genres: tragedy, epic, history, philosophy, fiction. His *Philosophical Dictionary* (1764), with its witty and penetrating definitions, typifies his range and acumen and his participation in his period's effort to take control of experience by intellect. While still a young man, Voltaire wrote a *History of Charles XII* of Sweden, a work unusual for its time in its novelistic technique and its assumption that "history" includes the personal lives of powerful individuals and has nothing to do with divine intervention. Before *Candide* he had published another philosophic tale, *Zadig* (1748), following the pattern of Asian narrative. Like Candide, Zadig goes through an experiential education; it teaches him inconclusive lessons about life's unforeseeable contingencies.

Candide mocks both the artificial order of fiction (through its ludicrously multiplied recognition scenes and its symmetrical division of the protagonist's travels into three equal parts) and what Voltaire suggests is the equally artificial order posited by philosophic optimists. The view of the universe suggested by Pope's *Essay on Man,* for instance, insists on the rationality of a pattern ungraspable by human reason. *Candide* implicitly argues, however, that it does so only by attending to the abstract and undemonstrable and ignoring the omnipresent pain of immediate experience. Gottfried Leibniz, the German philosopher, provides Voltaire's most specific target in *Candide,* with the complexities of his version of optimism reduced for satiric purposes to the facile formula "Everything is for the best in this best of all possible worlds." The formulation is, of course, unfair to Leibniz, whose philosophic optimism, like Pope's, implies belief in an unknowable universal order—roughly equivalent to Christian Providence—but no lack of awareness about the actual misery and depravity human beings experience.

The exuberance and extravagance of Voltaire's imagination force us to laugh at what we may feel embarrassed to laugh at: the plight of the woman whose buttock has been cut off to make rump steak for her hungry companions, the weeping of two girls whose monkey-lovers have been killed, the situation of six exiled, poverty-stricken kings. Like Swift, Voltaire keeps his readers off balance. Raped, cut to pieces, hanged, stabbed in the belly, the central characters of *Candide* keep coming back to life at opportune moments, as though no disaster could have permanent or ultimately destructive effects. Such reassuring fantasy suggests that we don't need to worry, it is all a joke, an outpouring of fertile fancy designed to ridicule an outmoded philosophic system with no particular relevance to us. On the other hand, historical reality keeps intruding. Those six hungry kings are real, actual figures, actually dispossessed. Candide sees Admiral Byng executed: an admiral who really lived and really died by firing squad for not engaging an enemy with sufficient ferocity. The Lisbon earthquake actually occurred; thirty to forty thousand people lost their lives in it. The extravagances of reality equal those of the storyteller; Voltaire demands that the reader imaginatively confront and somehow come to terms with horrors that surround us still.

The real problem, *Candide* suggests, is not natural or human disaster so much as human complacency. When Candide sees Admiral Byng shot, he comments on the injustice of the execution. "That's perfectly true, came the answer; but in this country it is useful from time to time to kill one admiral in order to encourage the others." Early in the nineteenth century, William Wordsworth wrote, "much it grieved my heart to think / What man has made of man." His tone and perspective differ dramatically from Voltaire's, but his point is the same: human beings use their faculties to increase corruption. Failure to take seriously any human death is a form of moral corruption; failure to acknowledge the intolerability of war, in all its concrete detail of rape and butchery, epitomizes such corruption at its worst.

In a late chapter of *Candide,* the central character, less naive than he once was, inquires about whether people have always massacred one another. Have they, he asks, "always been liars, traitors, ingrates, thieves, weaklings, sneaks, cowards, back-biters, gluttons, drunkards, misers, climbers, killers, calumniators, sensualists, fanat-ics, hypocrites, and fools?" His interlocutor, Martin, responds that, just as hawks have always devoured pigeons, human beings have always manifested the same vices. This ironic variation on the period's conviction of the universality and continuity of human nature epitomizes Voltaire's sense of outrage, which in some respects parallels Swift's in the fourth part of *Gulliver's Travels*. Swift demonstrates the implications of "rea-son" considered as an ideal and shows its irrelevance to actual human behavior; Voltaire shows how the claim of a rational universal order avoids the hard problems of living in a world where human beings have become liars, traitors, and so on. His Swiftian catalog of vice and folly expresses the moral insufficiency and perversity of humankind. Martin's cynical assumption that people are naturally corrupt, as hawks naturally eat smaller birds, constitutes another form of avoidance. The assumed inev-itability of vice, like belief that all is for the best, justifies passivity. Nothing *can* be done, nothing *should* be done, or nothing *matters* (the view of Lord Pococurante, another figure Candide encounters). So the characters of this fiction, including Can-dide himself, mainly pursue self-gratification. Even this course they do not follow judiciously: when Candide and Cacambo find themselves in the earthly paradise of Eldorado, "the two happy men resolved to be so no longer," driven by fantasies of improving their condition. Yet, unlike Gulliver, they acquire wisdom at last, learning to withstand "three great evils, boredom, vice, and poverty," by working hard at what comes to hand and avoiding futile theorizing about the nature of the universe.

Although Voltaire's picture of the human condition reveals the same indignation that marks Swift's, he allows at least conditional hope for moderate satisfaction in this life. Candide's beloved Cunégonde loses all her beauty, but she becomes an accomplished pastry cook; Candide possesses a garden he can cultivate. Greed, mal-ice, and lust do not make up the total possibility for humankind. If Voltaire's tone sometimes expresses outrage, at other times it verges on the playful. When, for exam-ple, he mocks the improbabilities of romance by his characters' miraculous resusci-tations or parodies the restrictions of classical form by sending Candide and his friends on an epic journey, one can feel his amused awareness of our human need to make order and our human desire to comfort ourselves by fictions. But as he insists that much of the order we claim to perceive itself comprises a comforting fiction, as he uses satire's fierce energies to challenge our complacencies, he reveals once more the underside of the Enlightenment ideal of reason. That we human beings have reason, Voltaire tells us, is no ground on which to flatter ourselves; rightly used, it exposes our insufficiencies.

Biographies and critical studies of Voltaire include R. Aldington, *Voltaire* (1934); T. Besterman, *Voltaire* (1969); I. O. Wade, *Voltaire and "Candide"* (1959); and M. Hayden, *Voltaire: A Biography* (1981). A good general introduction is P. E. Richter and Ilona Ricardo, *Voltaire* (1980). A work placing Voltaire in a broad context is F. M. Keener, *The Chain of Becoming* (1983), on Voltaire and his English contemporaries. Useful works specifically about *Candide* are William Bottiglia, *Voltaire's Candide: Analysis of a Classic* (1964); Haydn Mason, *Candide: Optimism Demolished* (1992); and D. Williams, *Candide* (1997), a critical guide intended for inexperienced readers. *Candide*, edited by D. Gordon (1999), provides accompanying material that helps establish Voltaire's work in its cultural context.

PRONOUNCING GLOSSARY

The following list uses common English syllables and stress accents to provide rough equiv-alents of selected words whose pronunciation may be unfamiliar to the general reader.

Abare: *a-bahr'*

Cacambo: *ka-kahm'-bo*

Candide: *kahn-deed'*

Cunégonde: *kew-nay-gohnd'*

Giroflée: *zhee-roh-flay'*

Issachar: *ee-sahk-ahr'*

Pangloss: *pan-glaws'*

Paquette: *pah-ket'*

Pococurante: *poh-koh-ku-rahn'-te*

Thunder-Ten-Tronckh: *tun-dayr'—ten—*
trawnk

Candide, or Optimism[1]

translated from the German of Doctor Ralph with the additions which were found in the Doctor's pocket when he died at Minden in the Year of Our Lord 1759

CHAPTER 1

How Candide Was Brought up in a Fine Castle and How He Was Driven Therefrom

There lived in Westphalia,[2] in the castle of the Baron of Thunder-Ten-Tronckh, a young man on whom nature had bestowed the perfection of gentle manners. His features admirably expressed his soul; he combined an honest mind with great simplicity of heart; and I think it was for this reason that they called him Candide. The old servants of the house suspected that he was the son of the Baron's sister by a respectable, honest gentleman of the neighborhood, whom she had refused to marry because he could prove only seventy-one quarterings,[3] the rest of his family tree having been lost in the passage of time.

The Baron was one of the most mighty lords of Westphalia, for his castle had a door and windows. His great hall was even hung with a tapestry. The dogs of his courtyard made up a hunting pack on occasion, with the stable-boys as huntsmen; the village priest was his grand almoner. They all called him "My Lord," and laughed at his stories.

The Baroness, who weighed in the neighborhood of three hundred and fifty pounds, was greatly respected for that reason, and did the honors of the house with a dignity which rendered her even more imposing. Her daughter Cunégonde,[4] aged seventeen, was a ruddy-cheeked girl, fresh, plump, and desirable. The Baron's son seemed in every way worthy of his father. The tutor Pangloss was the oracle of the household, and little Candide listened to his lectures with all the good faith of his age and character.

Pangloss gave instruction in metaphysico-theologico-cosmoloonigology.[5]

---

1. Translated and with notes by Robert M. Adams.   2. A province of western Germany, near Holland and the lower Rhineland. Flat, boggy, and drab, it is noted chiefly for its excellent ham. In a letter to his niece, written during his German expedition of 1750, Voltaire described the "vast, sad, sterile, detestable countryside of Westphalia."   3. Genealogical divisions of one's family-tree. Seventy-one of them is a grotesque number to have, representing something over 2,000 years of uninterrupted nobility.   4. Cunégonde gets her odd name from Kunigunda (wife to Emperor Henry II) who walked barefoot and blindfolded on red-hot irons to prove her chastity; Pangloss gets his name from Greek words meaning all-tongue.   5. The "looney" buried in this burlesque word corresponds to a buried *nigaud*—"booby" in the French. Christian Wolff, disciple of Leibniz, invented and popularized the word "cosmology." The catch phrases in the following sentence, echoed by popularizers of Leibniz, make reference to the determinism of his system, its linking of cause with effect, and its optimism.

He proved admirably that there cannot possibly be an effect without a cause and that in this best of all possible worlds the Baron's castle was the best of all castles and his wife the best of all possible Baronesses.

—It is clear, said he, that things cannot be otherwise than they are, for since everything is made to serve an end, everything necessarily serves the best end. Observe: noses were made to support spectacles, hence we have spectacles. Legs, as anyone can plainly see, were made to be breeched, and so we have breeches. Stones were made to be shaped and to build castles with; thus My Lord has a fine castle, for the greatest Baron in the province should have the finest house; and since pigs were made to be eaten, we eat pork all year round.[6] Consequently, those who say everything is well are uttering mere stupidities; they should say everything is for the best.

Candide listened attentively and believed implicitly; for he found Miss Cunégonde exceedingly pretty, though he never had the courage to tell her so. He decided that after the happiness of being born Baron of Thunder-Ten-Tronckh, the second order of happiness was to be Miss Cunégonde; the third was seeing her every day, and the fourth was listening to Master Pangloss, the greatest philosopher in the province and consequently in the entire world.

One day, while Cunégonde was walking near the castle in the little woods that they called a park, she saw Dr. Pangloss in the underbrush; he was giving a lesson in experimental physics to her mother's maid, a very attractive and obedient brunette. As Miss Cunégonde had a natural bent for the sciences, she watched breathlessly the repeated experiments which were going on; she saw clearly the doctor's sufficient reason, observed both cause and effect, and returned to the house in a distracted and pensive frame of mind, yearning for knowledge and dreaming that she might be the sufficient reason of young Candide—who might also be hers.

As she was returning to the castle, she met Candide, and blushed; Candide blushed too. She greeted him in a faltering tone of voice; and Candide talked to her without knowing what he was saying. Next day, as everyone was rising from the dinner table, Cunégonde and Candide found themselves behind a screen; Cunégonde dropped her handkerchief, Candide picked it up; she held his hand quite innocently, he kissed her hand quite innocently with remarkable vivacity and emotion; their lips met, their eyes lit up, their knees trembled, their hands wandered. The Baron of Thunder-Ten-Tronckh passed by the screen and, taking note of this cause and this effect, drove Candide out of the castle by kicking him vigorously on the backside. Cunégonde fainted; as soon as she recovered, the Baroness slapped her face; and everything was confusion in the most beautiful and agreeable of all possible castles.

---

6. The argument from design supposes that everything in this world exists for a specific reason; Voltaire objects not to the argument as a whole, but to the abuse of it.

CHAPTER 2

What Happened to Candide Among the Bulgars[7]

Candide, ejected from the earthly paradise, wandered for a long time without knowing where he was going, weeping, raising his eyes to heaven, and gazing back frequently on the most beautiful of castles which contained the most beautiful of Baron's daughters. He slept without eating, in a furrow of a plowed field, while the snow drifted over him; next morning, numb with cold, he dragged himself into the neighboring village, which was called Waldberghoff-trarbk-dikdorff; he was penniless, famished, and exhausted. At the door of a tavern he paused forlornly. Two men dressed in blue[8] took note of him:

—Look, chum, said one of them, there's a likely young fellow of just about the right size.

They approached Candide and invited him very politely to dine with them.

—Gentlemen, Candide replied with charming modesty, I'm honored by your invitation, but I really don't have enough money to pay my share.

—My dear sir, said one of the blues, people of your appearance and your merit don't have to pay; aren't you five feet five inches tall?

—Yes, gentlemen, that is indeed my stature, said he, making a bow.

—Then, sir, you must be seated at once; not only will we pay your bill this time, we will never allow a man like you to be short of money; for men were made only to render one another mutual aid.

—You are quite right, said Candide; it is just as Dr. Pangloss always told me, and I see clearly that everything is for the best.

They beg him to accept a couple of crowns, he takes them, and offers an I.O.U.; they won't hear of it, and all sit down at table together.

—Don't you love dearly . . . ?

—I do indeed, says he, I dearly love Miss Cunégonde.

—No, no, says one of the gentlemen, we are asking if you don't love dearly the King of the Bulgars.

—Not in the least, says he, I never laid eyes on him.

—What's that you say? He's the most charming of kings, and we must drink his health.

—Oh, gladly, gentlemen; and he drinks.

—That will do, they tell him; you are now the bulwark, the support, the defender, the hero of the Bulgars; your fortune is made and your future assured.

Promptly they slip irons on his legs and lead him to the regiment. There they cause him to right face, left face, present arms, order arms, aim, fire, doubletime, and they give him thirty strokes of the rod. Next day he does the drill a little less awkwardly and gets only twenty strokes; the third day, they give him only ten, and he is regarded by his comrades as a prodigy.

Candide, quite thunderstruck, did not yet understand very clearly how he was a hero. One fine spring morning he took it into his head to go for a walk,

---

7. Voltaire chose this name to represent the Prussian troops of Frederick the Great because he wanted to make an insinuation of pederasty against both the soldiers and their master. Cf. French *bougre,* English "bugger." 8. The recruiting officers of Frederick the Great, much feared in 18th-century Europe, wore blue uniforms. Frederick had a passion for sorting out his soldiers by size; several of his regiments would accept only six-footers.

stepping straight out as if it were a privilege of the human race, as of animals in general, to use his legs as he chose.[9] He had scarcely covered two leagues when four other heroes, each six feet tall, overtook him, bound him, and threw him into a dungeon. At the court-martial they asked which he preferred, to be flogged thirty-six times by the entire regiment or to receive summarily a dozen bullets in the brain. In vain did he argue that the human will is free and insist that he preferred neither alternative; he had to choose; by virtue of the divine gift called "liberty" he decided to run the gauntlet thirty-six times, and actually endured two floggings. The regiment was composed of two thousand men. That made four thousand strokes, which laid open every muscle and nerve from his nape to his butt. As they were preparing for the third beating, Candide, who could endure no more, begged as a special favor that they would have the goodness to smash his head. His plea was granted; they bandaged his eyes and made him kneel down. The King of the Bulgars, passing by at this moment, was told of the culprit's crime; and as this king had a rare genius, he understood, from everything they told him of Candide, that this was a young metaphysician, extremely ignorant of the ways of the world, so he granted his royal pardon, with a generosity which will be praised in every newspaper in every age. A worthy surgeon cured Candide in three weeks with the ointments described by Dioscorides.[1] He already had a bit of skin back and was able to walk when the King of the Bulgars went to war with the King of the Abares.[2]

CHAPTER 3

How Candide Escaped from the Bulgars, and What Became of Him

Nothing could have been so fine, so brisk, so brilliant, so well-drilled as the two armies. The trumpets, the fifes, the oboes, the drums, and the cannon produced such a harmony as was never heard in hell. First the cannons battered down about six thousand men on each side; then volleys of musket fire removed from the best of worlds about nine or ten thousand rascals who were cluttering up its surface. The bayonet was a sufficient reason for the demise of several thousand others. Total casualties might well amount to thirty thousand men or so. Candide, who was trembling like a philosopher, hid himself as best he could while this heroic butchery was going on.

Finally, while the two kings in their respective camps celebrated the victory by having *Te Deums* sung, Candide undertook to do his reasoning of cause and effect somewhere else. Passing by mounds of the dead and dying, he came to a nearby village which had been burnt to the ground. It was an Abare village, which the Bulgars had burned, in strict accordance with the laws of war. Here old men, stunned from beatings, watched the last agonies of their butchered wives, who still clutched their infants to their bleeding

---

9. This episode was suggested by the experience of a Frenchman named Courtilz, who had deserted from the Prussian army and been bastinadoed for it. Voltaire intervened with Frederick to gain his release. But it also reflects the story that Wolff, Leibniz's disciple, got into trouble with Frederick's father when someone reported that his doctrine denying free will had encouraged several soldiers to desert. "The argument of the grenadier," who was said to have pleaded preestablished harmony to justify his desertion, so infuriated the king that he had Wolff expelled from the country.   1. Dioscorides' treatise on *materia medica,* dating from the 1st century A.D., was not the most up to date.   2. A tribe of semicivilized Scythians, who might be supposed at war with the Bulgars; allegorically, the Abares are the French, who opposed the Prussians in the Seven Years' War (1756–63). According to the title page of 1761, "Doctor Ralph," the dummy author of *Candide,* himself perished at the battle of Minden (Westphalia) in 1759.

breasts; there, disemboweled girls, who had first satisfied the natural needs of various heroes, breathed their last; others, half-scorched in the flames, begged for their death stroke. Scattered brains and severed limbs littered the ground.

Candide fled as fast as he could to another village; this one belonged to the Bulgars, and the heroes of the Abare cause had given it the same treatment. Climbing over ruins and stumbling over corpses, Candide finally made his way out of the war area, carrying a little food in his knapsack and never ceasing to dream of Miss Cunégonde. His supplies gave out when he reached Holland; but having heard that everyone in that country was rich and a Christian, he felt confident of being treated as well as he had been in the castle of the Baron before he was kicked out for the love of Miss Cunégonde.

He asked alms of several grave personages, who all told him that if he continued to beg, he would be shut up in a house of correction and set to hard labor.

Finally he approached a man who had just been talking to a large crowd for an hour on end; the topic was charity. Looking doubtfully at him, the orator demanded:

—What are you doing here? Are you here to serve the good cause?

—There is no effect without a cause, said Candide modestly; all events are linked by the chain of necessity and arranged for the best. I had to be driven away from Miss Cunégonde, I had to run the gauntlet, I have to beg my bread until I can earn it; none of this could have happened otherwise.

—Look here, friend, said the orator, do you think the Pope is Antichrist?[3]

—I haven't considered the matter, said Candide; but whether he is or not, I'm in need of bread.

—You don't deserve any, said the other; away with you, you rascal, you rogue, never come near me as long as you live.

Meanwhile, the orator's wife had put her head out of the window, and, seeing a man who was not sure the Pope was Antichrist, emptied over his head a pot full of———Scandalous! The excesses into which women are led by religious zeal!

A man who had never been baptized, a good Anabaptist[4] named Jacques, saw this cruel and heartless treatment being inflicted on one of his fellow creatures, a featherless biped possessing a soul;[5] he took Candide home with him, washed him off, gave him bread and beer, presented him with two florins, and even undertook to give him a job in his Persian-rug factory—for these items are widely manufactured in Holland. Candide, in an ecstasy of gratitude, cried out:

—Master Pangloss was right indeed when he told me everything is for the best in this world; for I am touched by your kindness far more than by the harshness of that black-coated gentleman and his wife.

Next day, while taking a stroll about town, he met a beggar who was covered with pustules, his eyes were sunken, the end of his nose rotted off, his

---

3. Voltaire is satirizing extreme Protestant sects that have sometimes seemed to make hatred of Rome the sum and substance of their creed.   4. Holland, as the home of religious liberty, had offered asylum to the Anabaptists, whose radical views on property and religious discipline had made them unpopular during the 16th century. Granted tolerance, they settled down into respectable burghers. Since this behavior confirmed some of Voltaire's major theses, he had a high opinion of contemporary Anabaptists.   5. Plato's famous minimal definition of man, which he corrected by the addition of a soul to distinguish man from a plucked chicken.

mouth twisted, his teeth black, he had a croaking voice and a hacking cough, and spat a tooth every time he tried to speak.

CHAPTER 4

How Candide Met His Old Philosophy Tutor, Doctor Pangloss, and What Came of It

Candide, more touched by compassion even than by horror, gave this ghastly beggar the two florins that he himself had received from his honest Anabaptist friend Jacques. The phantom stared at him, burst into tears, and fell on his neck. Candide drew back in terror.

—Alas, said one wretch to the other, don't you recognize your dear Pangloss any more?

—What are you saying? You, my dear master! you, in this horrible condition? What misfortune has befallen you? Why are you no longer in the most beautiful of castles? What has happened to Miss Cunégonde, that pearl among young ladies, that masterpiece of Nature?

—I am perishing, said Pangloss.

Candide promptly led him into the Anabaptist's stable, where he gave him a crust of bread, and when he had recovered:—Well, said he, Cunégonde?

—Dead, said the other.

Candide fainted. His friend brought him around with a bit of sour vinegar which happened to be in the stable. Candide opened his eyes.

—Cunégonde, dead! Ah, best of worlds, what's become of you now? But how did she die? It wasn't of grief at seeing me kicked out of her noble father's elegant castle?

—Not at all, said Pangloss; she was disemboweled by the Bulgar soldiers, after having been raped to the absolute limit of human endurance; they smashed the Baron's head when he tried to defend her, cut the Baroness to bits, and treated my poor pupil exactly like his sister. As for the castle, not one stone was left on another, not a shed, not a sheep, not a duck, not a tree; but we had the satisfaction of revenge, for the Abares did exactly the same thing to a nearby barony belonging to a Bulgar nobleman.

At this tale Candide fainted again; but having returned to his senses and said everything appropriate to the occasion, he asked about the cause and effect, the sufficient reason, which had reduced Pangloss to his present pitiful state.

—Alas, said he, it was love; love, the consolation of the human race, the preservative of the universe, the soul of all sensitive beings, love, gentle love.

—Unhappy man, said Candide, I too have had some experience of this love, the sovereign of hearts, the soul of our souls; and it never got me anything but a single kiss and twenty kicks in the rear. How could this lovely cause produce in you such a disgusting effect?

Pangloss replied as follows:—My dear Candide! you knew Paquette, that pretty maidservant to our august Baroness. In her arms I tasted the delights of paradise, which directly caused these torments of hell, from which I am now suffering. She was infected with the disease, and has perhaps died of it. Paquette received this present from an erudite Franciscan, who took the pains to trace it back to its source; for he had it from an elderly countess, who picked it up from a captain of cavalry, who acquired it from a marquise, who caught it from a page, who had received it from a Jesuit, who during his novitiate got it directly from one of the companions of Christopher Columbus. As for me, I shall not give it to anyone, for I am a dying man.

—Oh, Pangloss, cried Candide, that's a very strange genealogy. Isn't the devil at the root of the whole thing?

—Not at all, replied that great man; it's an indispensable part of the best of worlds, a necessary ingredient; if Columbus had not caught, on an American island, this sickness which attacks the source of generation and sometimes prevents generation entirely—which thus strikes at and defeats the greatest end of Nature herself—we should have neither chocolate nor cochineal. It must also be noted that until the present time this malady, like religious controversy, has been wholly confined to the continent of Europe. Turks, Indians, Persians, Chinese, Siamese, and Japanese know nothing of it as yet; but there is a sufficient reason for which they in turn will make its acquaintance in a couple of centuries. Meanwhile, it has made splendid progress among us, especially among those big armies of honest, well-trained mercenaries who decide the destinies of nations. You can be sure that when thirty thousand men fight a pitched battle against the same number of the enemy, there will be about twenty thousand with the pox on either side.

—Remarkable indeed, said Candide, but we must see about curing you.

—And how can I do that, said Pangloss, seeing I don't have a cent to my name? There's not a doctor in the whole world who will let your blood or give you an enema without demanding a fee. If you can't pay yourself, you must find someone to pay for you.

These last words decided Candide; he hastened to implore the help of his charitable Anabaptist, Jacques, and painted such a moving picture of his friend's wretched state that the good man did not hesitate to take in Pangloss and have him cured at his own expense. In the course of the cure, Pangloss lost only an eye and an ear. Since he wrote a fine hand and knew arithmetic, the Anabaptist made him his bookkeeper. At the end of two months, being obliged to go to Lisbon on business, he took his two philosophers on the boat with him. Pangloss still maintained that everything was for the best, but Jacques didn't agree with him.

—It must be, said he, that men have corrupted Nature, for they are not born wolves, yet that is what they become. God gave them neither twenty-four-pound cannon nor bayonets, yet they have manufactured both in order to destroy themselves. Bankruptcies have the same effect, and so does the justice which seizes the goods of bankrupts in order to prevent the creditors from getting them.[6]

—It was all indispensable, replied the one-eyed doctor, since private misfortunes make for public welfare, and therefore the more private misfortunes there are, the better everything is.

While he was reasoning, the air grew dark, the winds blew from all directions, and the vessel was attacked by a horrible tempest within sight of Lisbon harbor.

---

6. Voltaire had suffered losses from various bankruptcy proceedings.

CHAPTER 5

Tempest, Shipwreck, Earthquake, and What Happened to Doctor Pangloss, Candide, and the Anabaptist, Jacques

Half of the passengers, weakened by the frightful anguish of seasickness and the distress of tossing about on stormy waters, were incapable of noticing their danger. The other half shrieked aloud and fell to their prayers, the sails were ripped to shreds, the masts snapped, the vessel opened at the seams. Everyone worked who could stir, nobody listened for orders or issued them. The Anabaptist was lending a hand in the after part of the ship when a frantic sailor struck him and knocked him to the deck; but just at that moment, the sailor lurched so violently that he fell head first over the side, where he hung, clutching a fragment of the broken mast. The good Jacques ran to his aid, and helped him to climb back on board, but in the process was himself thrown into the sea under the very eyes of the sailor, who allowed him to drown without even glancing at him. Candide rushed to the rail, and saw his benefactor rise for a moment to the surface, then sink forever. He wanted to dive to his rescue; but the philosopher Pangloss prevented him by proving that the bay of Lisbon had been formed expressly for this Anabaptist to drown in. While he was proving the point *a priori,* the vessel opened up and everyone perished except for Pangloss, Candide, and the brutal sailor who had caused the virtuous Anabaptist to drown; this rascal swam easily to shore, while Pangloss and Candide drifted there on a plank.

When they had recovered a bit of energy, they set out for Lisbon; they still had a little money with which they hoped to stave off hunger after escaping the storm.

Scarcely had they set foot in the town, still bewailing the loss of their benefactor, when they felt the earth quake underfoot; the sea was lashed to a froth, burst into the port, and smashed all the vessels lying at anchor there. Whirlwinds of fire and ash swirled through the streets and public squares; houses crumbled, roofs came crashing down on foundations, foundations split; thirty thousand inhabitants of every age and either sex were crushed in the ruins.[7] The sailor whistled through his teeth, and said with an oath:— There'll be something to pick up here.

—What can be the sufficient reason of this phenomenon? asked Pangloss.

—The Last Judgment is here, cried Candide.

But the sailor ran directly into the middle of the ruins, heedless of danger in his eagerness for gain; he found some money, laid violent hands on it, got drunk, and, having slept off his wine, bought the favors of the first streetwalker he could find amid the ruins of smashed houses, amid corpses and suffering victims on every hand. Pangloss however tugged at his sleeve.

—My friend, said he, this is not good form at all; your behavior falls short of that required by the universal reason; it's untimely, to say the least.

—Bloody hell, said the other, I'm a sailor, born in Batavia; I've been four

---

7. The great Lisbon earthquake and fire occurred on November 1, 1755; between thirty and forty thousand deaths resulted.

times to Japan and stamped four times on the crucifix;[8] get out of here with your universal reason.

Some falling stonework had struck Candide; he lay prostrate in the street, covered with rubble, and calling to Pangloss:—For pity's sake bring me a little wine and oil; I'm dying.

—This earthquake is nothing novel, Pangloss replied; the city of Lima, in South America, underwent much the same sort of tremor, last year; same causes, same effects; there is surely a vein of sulphur under the earth's surface reaching from Lima to Lisbon.

—Nothing is more probable, said Candide; but, for God's sake, a little oil and wine.

—What do you mean, probable? replied the philosopher; I regard the case as proved.

Candide fainted and Pangloss brought him some water from a nearby fountain.

Next day, as they wandered amid the ruins, they found a little food which restored some of their strength. Then they fell to work like the others, bringing relief to those of the inhabitants who had escaped death. Some of the citizens whom they rescued gave them a dinner as good as was possible under the circumstances; it is true that the meal was a melancholy one, and the guests watered their bread with tears; but Pangloss consoled them by proving that things could not possibly be otherwise.

—For, said he, all this is for the best, since if there is a volcano at Lisbon, it cannot be somewhere else, since it is unthinkable that things should not be where they are, since everything is well.

A little man in black, an officer of the Inquisition,[9] who was sitting beside him, politely took up the question, and said:—It would seem that the gentleman does not believe in original sin, since if everything is for the best, man has not fallen and is not liable to eternal punishment.

—I most humbly beg pardon of your excellency, Pangloss answered, even more politely, but the fall of man and the curse of original sin entered necessarily into the best of all possible worlds.

—Then you do not believe in free will? said the officer.

—Your excellency must excuse me, said Pangloss; free will agrees very well with absolute necessity, for it was necessary that we should be free, since a will which is determined . . .

Pangloss was in the middle of his sentence, when the officer nodded significantly to the attendant who was pouring him a glass of port, or Oporto, wine.

CHAPTER 6

How They Made a Fine Auto-da-Fé to Prevent Earthquakes, and How Candide Was Whipped

After the earthquake had wiped out three quarters of Lisbon, the learned men of the land could find no more effective way of averting total destruction

---

8. The Japanese, originally receptive to foreign visitors, grew fearful that priests and proselytizers were merely advance agents of empire and expelled both the Portuguese and Spanish early in the 17th century. Only the Dutch were allowed to retain a small foothold, under humiliating conditions, of which the notion of stamping on the crucifix is symbolic. It was never what Voltaire suggests here, an actual requirement for entering the country.   9. Specifically, a *familier* or *poursuivant*, an undercover agent with powers of arrest.

than to give the people a fine auto-da-fé;[1] the University of Coimbra had established that the spectacle of several persons being roasted over a slow fire with full ceremonial rites is an infallible specific against earthquakes.

In consequence, the authorities had rounded up a Biscayan convicted of marrying a woman who had stood godmother to his child, and two Portuguese who while eating a chicken had set aside a bit of bacon used for seasoning.[2] After dinner, men came with ropes to tie up Doctor Pangloss and his disciple Candide, one for talking and the other for listening with an air of approval; both were taken separately to a set of remarkably cool apartments, where the glare of the sun is never bothersome; eight days later they were both dressed in *san-benitos* and crowned with paper mitres;[3] Candide's mitre and *san-benito* were decorated with inverted flames and with devils who had neither tails nor claws; but Pangloss's devils had both tails and claws, and his flames stood upright. Wearing these costumes, they marched in a procession, and listened to a very touching sermon, followed by a beautiful concert of plainsong. Candide was flogged in cadence to the music; the Biscayan and the two men who had avoided bacon were burned, and Pangloss was hanged, though hanging is not customary. On the same day there was another earthquake, causing frightful damage.[4]

Candide, stunned, stupefied, despairing, bleeding, trembling, said to himself:—If this is the best of all possible worlds, what are the others like? The flogging is not so bad, I was flogged by the Bulgars. But oh my dear Pangloss, greatest of philosophers, was it necessary for me to watch you being hanged, for no reason that I can see? Oh my dear Anabaptist, best of men, was it necessary that you should be drowned in the port? Oh Miss Cunégonde, pearl of young ladies, was it necessary that you should have your belly slit open?

He was being led away, barely able to stand, lectured, lashed, absolved, and blessed, when an old woman approached and said,—My son, be of good cheer and follow me.

CHAPTER 7

How an Old Woman Took Care of Candide, and How He Regained What He Loved

Candide was of very bad cheer, but he followed the old woman to a shanty; she gave him a jar of ointment to rub himself, left him food and drink; she showed him a tidy little bed; next to it was a suit of clothing.

—Eat, drink, sleep, she said; and may Our Lady of Atocha, Our Lord St. Anthony of Padua, and Our Lord St. James of Compostela watch over you. I will be back tomorrow.

Candide, still completely astonished by everything he had seen and suffered, and even more by the old woman's kindness, offered to kiss her hand.

—It's not *my* hand you should be kissing, said she. I'll be back tomorrow; rub yourself with the ointment, eat and sleep.

1. Literally, "act of faith," a public ceremony of repentance and humiliation. Such an auto-da-fé was actually held in Lisbon, June 20, 1756.　2. The Biscayan's fault lay in marrying someone within the forbidden bounds of relationship, an act of spiritual incest. The men who declined pork or bacon were understood to be crypto-Jews.　3. The cone-shaped paper cap (intended to resemble a bishop's mitre) and flowing yellow cape were customary garb for those pleading before the Inquisition.　4. In fact, the second quake occurred December 21, 1755.

In spite of his many sufferings, Candide ate and slept. Next day the old woman returned bringing breakfast; she looked at his back and rubbed it herself with another ointment; she came back with lunch; and then she returned in the evening, bringing supper. Next day she repeated the same routine.

—Who are you? Candide asked continually. Who told you to be so kind to me? How can I ever repay you?

The good woman answered not a word; she returned in the evening, and without food.

—Come with me, says she, and don't speak a word.

Taking him by the hand, she walks out into the countryside with him for about a quarter of a mile; they reach an isolated house, quite surrounded by gardens and ditches. The old woman knocks at a little gate, it opens. She takes Candide up a secret stairway to a gilded room furnished with a fine brocaded sofa; there she leaves him, closes the door, disappears. Candide stood as if entranced; his life, which had seemed like a nightmare so far, was now starting to look like a delightful dream.

Soon the old woman returned; on her feeble shoulder leaned a trembling woman, of a splendid figure, glittering in diamonds, and veiled.

—Remove the veil, said the old woman to Candide.

The young man stepped timidly forward, and lifted the veil. What an event! What a surprise! Could it be Miss Cunégonde? Yes, it really was! She herself! His knees give way, speech fails him, he falls at her feet, Cunégonde collapses on the sofa. The old woman plies them with brandy, they return to their senses, they exchange words. At first they could utter only broken phrases, questions and answers at cross purposes, sighs, tears, exclamations. The old woman warned them not to make too much noise, and left them alone.

—Then it's really you, said Candide, you're alive, I've found you again in Portugal. Then you never were raped? You never had your belly ripped open, as the philosopher Pangloss assured me?

—Oh yes, said the lovely Cunégonde, but one doesn't always die of these two accidents.

—But your father and mother were murdered then?

—All too true, said Cunégonde, in tears.

—And your brother?

—Killed too.

—And why are you in Portugal? and how did you know I was here? and by what device did you have me brought to this house?

—I shall tell you everything, the lady replied; but first you must tell me what has happened to you since that first innocent kiss we exchanged and the kicking you got because of it.

Candide obeyed her with profound respect; and though he was overcome, though his voice was weak and hesitant, though he still had twinges of pain from his beating, he described as simply as possible everything that had happened to him since the time of their separation. Cunégonde lifted her eyes to heaven; she wept at the death of the good Anabaptist and at that of Pangloss; after which she told the following story to Candide, who listened to every word while he gazed on her with hungry eyes.

CHAPTER 8

Cunégonde's Story

—I was in my bed and fast asleep when heaven chose to send the Bulgars into our castle of Thunder-Ten-Tronckh. They butchered my father and brother, and hacked my mother to bits. An enormous Bulgar, six feet tall, seeing that I had swooned from horror at the scene, set about raping me; at that I recovered my senses, I screamed and scratched, bit and fought, I tried to tear the eyes out of that big Bulgar—not realizing that everything which had happened in my father's castle was a mere matter of routine. The brute then stabbed me with a knife on my left thigh, where I still bear the scar.

—What a pity! I should very much like to see it, said the simple Candide.

—You shall, said Cunégonde; but shall I go on?

—Please do, said Candide.

So she took up the thread of her tale:—A Bulgar captain appeared, he saw me covered with blood and the soldier too intent to get up. Shocked by the monster's failure to come to attention, the captain killed him on my body. He then had my wound dressed, and took me off to his quarters, as a prisoner of war. I laundered his few shirts and did his cooking; he found me attractive, I confess it, and I won't deny that he was a handsome fellow, with a smooth, white skin; apart from that, however, little wit, little philosophical training; it was evident that he had not been brought up by Doctor Pangloss. After three months, he had lost all his money and grown sick of me; so he sold me to a Jew named Don Issachar, who traded in Holland and Portugal, and who was mad after women. This Jew developed a mighty passion for my person, but he got nowhere with it; I held him off better than I had done with the Bulgar soldier; for though a person of honor may be raped once, her virtue is only strengthened by the experience. In order to keep me hidden, the Jew brought me to his country house, which you see here. Till then I had thought there was nothing on earth so beautiful as the castle of Thunder-Ten-Tronckh; I was now undeceived.

—One day the Grand Inquisitor took notice of me at mass; he ogled me a good deal, and made known that he must talk to me on a matter of secret business. I was taken to his palace; I told him of my rank; he pointed out that it was beneath my dignity to belong to an Israelite. A suggestion was then conveyed to Don Issachar that he should turn me over to My Lord the Inquisitor. Don Issachar, who is court banker and a man of standing, refused out of hand. The inquisitor threatened him with an auto-da-fé. Finally my Jew, fearing for his life, struck a bargain by which the house and I would belong to both of them as joint tenants; the Jew would get Mondays, Wednesdays, and the Sabbath, the inquisitor would get the other days of the week. That has been the arrangement for six months now. There have been quarrels; sometimes it has not been clear whether the night from Saturday to Sunday belonged to the old or the new dispensation. For my part, I have so far been able to hold both of them off; and that, I think, is why they are both still in love with me.

—Finally, in order to avert further divine punishment by earthquake, and to terrify Don Issachar, My Lord the Inquisitor chose to celebrate an auto-da-fé. He did me the honor of inviting me to attend. I had an excellent seat;

the ladies were served with refreshments between the mass and the execution. To tell you the truth, I was horrified to see them burn alive those two Jews and that decent Biscayan who had married his child's godmother; but what was my surprise, my terror, my grief, when I saw, huddled in a *san-benito* and wearing a mitre, someone who looked like Pangloss! I rubbed my eyes, I watched his every move, I saw him hanged; and I fell back in a swoon. Scarcely had I come to my senses again, when I saw you stripped for the lash; that was the peak of my horror, consternation, grief, and despair. I may tell you, by the way, that your skin is even whiter and more delicate than that of my Bulgar captain. Seeing you, then, redoubled the torments which were already overwhelming me. I shrieked aloud, I wanted to call out, 'Let him go, you brutes!' but my voice died within me, and my cries would have been useless. When you had been thoroughly thrashed: 'How can it be,' I asked myself, 'that agreeable Candide and wise Pangloss have come to Lisbon, one to receive a hundred whiplashes, the other to be hanged by order of My Lord the Inquisitor, whose mistress I am? Pangloss must have deceived me cruelly when he told me that all is for the best in this world.'

—Frantic, exhausted, half out of my senses, and ready to die of weakness, I felt as if my mind were choked with the massacre of my father, my mother, my brother, with the arrogance of that ugly Bulgar soldier, with the knife slash he inflicted on me, my slavery, my cookery, my Bulgar captain, my nasty Don Issachar, my abominable inquisitor, with the hanging of Doctor Pangloss, with that great plainsong *miserere* which they sang while they flogged you—and above all, my mind was full of the kiss which I gave you behind the screen, on the day I saw you for the last time. I praised God, who had brought you back to me after so many trials. I asked my old woman to look out for you, and to bring you here as soon as she could. She did just as I asked; I have had the indescribable joy of seeing you again, hearing you and talking with you once more. But you must be frightfully hungry; I am, myself; let us begin with a dinner.

So then and there they sat down to table; and after dinner, they adjourned to that fine brocaded sofa, which has already been mentioned; and there they were when the eminent Don Issachar, one of the masters of the house, appeared. It was the day of the Sabbath; he was arriving to assert his rights and express his tender passion.

CHAPTER 9

What Happened to Cunégonde, Candide, the Grand Inquisitor,
and a Jew

This Issachar was the most choleric Hebrew seen in Israel since the Babylonian captivity.

—What's this, says he, you bitch of a Christian, you're not satisfied with the Grand Inquisitor? Do I have to share you with this rascal, too?

So saying, he drew a long dagger, with which he always went armed, and, supposing his opponent defenceless, flung himself on Candide. But our good Westphalian had received from the old woman, along with his suit of clothes, a fine sword. Out it came, and though his manners were of the gentlest, in short order he laid the Israelite stiff and cold on the floor, at the feet of the lovely Cunégonde.

—Holy Virgin! she cried. What will become of me now? A man killed in my house! If the police find out, we're done for.

—If Pangloss had not been hanged, said Candide, he would give us good advice in this hour of need, for he was a great philosopher. Lacking him, let's ask the old woman.

She was a sensible body, and was just starting to give her opinion of the situation, when another little door opened. It was just one o'clock in the morning, Sunday morning. This day belonged to the inquisitor. In he came, and found the whipped Candide with a sword in his hand, a corpse at his feet, Cunégonde in terror, and an old woman giving them both good advice.

Here now is what passed through Candide's mind in this instant of time; this is how he reasoned:—If this holy man calls for help, he will certainly have me burned, and perhaps Cunégonde as well; he has already had me whipped without mercy; he is my rival; I have already killed once; why hesitate?

It was a quick, clear chain of reasoning; without giving the inquisitor time to recover from his surprise, he ran him through, and laid him beside the Jew.

—Here you've done it again, said Cunégonde; there's no hope for us now. We'll be excommunicated, our last hour has come. How is it that you, who were born so gentle, could kill in two minutes a Jew and a prelate?

—My dear girl, replied Candide, when a man is in love, jealous, and just whipped by the Inquisition, he is no longer himself.

The old woman now spoke up and said:—There are three Andalusian steeds in the stable, with their saddles and bridles; our brave Candide must get them ready: my lady has some gold coin and diamonds; let's take to horse at once, though I can only ride on one buttock; we will go to Cadiz. The weather is as fine as can be, and it is pleasant to travel in the cool of the evening.

Promptly, Candide saddled the three horses. Cunégonde, the old woman, and he covered thirty miles without a stop. While they were fleeing, the Holy Brotherhood[5] came to investigate the house; they buried the inquisitor in a fine church, and threw Issachar on the dunghill.

Candide, Cunégonde, and the old woman were already in the little town of Avacena, in the middle of the Sierra Morena; and there, as they sat in a country inn, they had this conversation.

CHAPTER 10

In Deep Distress, Candide, Cunégonde, and the Old Woman Reach Cadiz; They Put to Sea

—Who then could have robbed me of my gold and diamonds? said Cunégonde, in tears. How shall we live? what shall we do? where shall I find other inquisitors and Jews to give me some more?

—Ah, said the old woman, I strongly suspect that reverend Franciscan friar who shared the inn with us yesterday at Badajoz. God save me from judging him unfairly! But he came into our room twice, and he left long before us.

---

5. A semireligious order with police powers, very active in 18th-century Spain.

—Alas, said Candide, the good Pangloss often proved to me that the fruits of the earth are a common heritage of all, to which each man has equal right. On these principles, the Franciscan should at least have left us enough to finish our journey. You have nothing at all, my dear Cunégonde?

—Not a maravedi, said she.

—What to do? said Candide.

—We'll sell one of the horses, said the old woman; I'll ride on the croup behind my mistress, though only on one buttock, and so we will get to Cadiz.

There was in the same inn a Benedictine prior; he bought the horse cheap. Candide, Cunégonde, and the old woman passed through Lucena, Chillas, and Lebrixa, and finally reached Cadiz. There a fleet was being fitted out and an army assembled, to reason with the Jesuit fathers in Paraguay, who were accused of fomenting among their flock a revolt against the kings of Spain and Portugal near the town of St. Sacrement.[6] Candide, having served in the Bulgar army, performed the Bulgar manual of arms before the general of the little army with such grace, swiftness, dexterity, fire, and agility, that they gave him a company of infantry to command. So here he is, a captain; and off he sails with Miss Cunégonde, the old woman, two valets, and the two Andalusian steeds which had belonged to My Lord the Grand Inquisitor of Portugal.

Throughout the crossing, they spent a great deal of time reasoning about the philosophy of poor Pangloss.

—We are destined, in the end, for another universe, said Candide; no doubt that is the one where everything is well. For in this one, it must be admitted, there is some reason to grieve over our physical and moral state.

—I love you with all my heart, said Cunégonde; but my soul is still harrowed by thoughts of what I have seen and suffered.

—All will be well, replied Candide; the sea of this new world is already better than those of Europe, calmer and with steadier winds. Surely it is the New World which is the best of all possible worlds.

—God grant it, said Cunégonde; but I have been so horribly unhappy in the world so far, that my heart is almost dead to hope.

—You pity yourselves, the old woman told them; but you have had no such misfortunes as mine.

Cunégonde nearly broke out laughing; she found the old woman comic in pretending to be more unhappy than she.

—Ah, you poor old thing, said she, unless you've been raped by two Bulgars, been stabbed twice in the belly, seen two of your castles destroyed, witnessed the murder of two of your mothers and two of your fathers, and watched two of your lovers being whipped in an auto-da-fé, I do not see how you can have had it worse than me. Besides, I was born a baroness, with seventy-two quarterings, and I have worked in a scullery.

—My lady, replied the old woman, you do not know my birth and rank; and if I showed you my rear end, you would not talk as you do, you might even speak with less assurance.

These words inspired great curiosity in Candide and Cunégonde, which the old woman satisfied with this story.

6. Actually, Colonia del Sacramento. Voltaire took great interest in the Jesuit role in Paraguay, which he has much oversimplified and largely misrepresented here in the interests of his satire. In 1750 they did, however, offer armed resistance to an agreement made between Spain and Portugal. They were subdued and expelled in 1769.

CHAPTER 11

The Old Woman's Story

—My eyes were not always bloodshot and red-rimmed, my nose did not always touch my chin, and I was not born a servant. I am in fact the daughter of Pope Urban the Tenth and the Princess of Palestrina.[7] Till the age of fourteen, I lived in a palace so splendid that all the castles of all your German barons would not have served it as a stable; a single one of my dresses was worth more than all the assembled magnificence of Westphalia. I grew in beauty, in charm, in talent, surrounded by pleasures, dignities, and glowing visions of the future. Already I was inspiring the young men to love; my breast was formed—and what a breast! white, firm, with the shape of the Venus de Medici; and what eyes! what lashes, what black brows! What fire flashed from my glances and outshone the glitter of the stars, as the local poets used to tell me! The women who helped me dress and undress fell into ecstasies, whether they looked at me from in front or behind; and all the men wanted to be in their place.

—I was engaged to the ruling prince of Massa-Carrara; and what a prince he was! as handsome as I, softness and charm compounded, brilliantly witty, and madly in love with me. I loved him in return as one loves for the first time, with a devotion approaching idolatry. The wedding preparations had been made, with a splendor and magnificence never heard of before; nothing but celebrations, masks, and comic operas, uninterruptedly; and all Italy composed in my honor sonnets of which not one was even passable. I had almost attained the very peak of bliss, when an old marquise who had been the mistress of my prince invited him to her house for a cup of chocolate. He died in less than two hours, amid horrifying convulsions. But that was only a trifle. My mother, in complete despair (though less afflicted than I), wished to escape for a while the oppressive atmosphere of grief. She owned a handsome property near Gaeta.[8] We embarked on a papal galley gilded like the altar of St. Peter's in Rome. Suddenly a pirate ship from Salé swept down and boarded us. Our soldiers defended themselves as papal troops usually do; falling on their knees and throwing down their arms, they begged of the corsair absolution *in articulo mortis.*[9]

—They were promptly stripped as naked as monkeys, and so was my mother, and so were our maids of honor, and so was I too. It's a very remarkable thing, the energy these gentlemen put into stripping people. But what surprised me even more was that they stuck their fingers in a place where we women usually admit only a syringe. This ceremony seemed a bit odd to me, as foreign usages always do when one hasn't traveled. They only wanted to see if we didn't have some diamonds hidden there; and I soon learned that it's a custom of long standing among the genteel folk who swarm the seas. I learned that my lords the very religious knights of Malta never overlook this ceremony when they capture Turks, whether male or female; it's one of those international laws which have never been questioned.

7. Voltaire left behind a comment on this passage, a note first published in 1829: "Note the extreme discretion of the author; hitherto there has never been a pope named Urban X; he avoided attributing a bastard to a known pope. What circumspection! what an exquisite conscience!"   8. About halfway between Rome and Naples.   9. Literally, when at the point of death. Absolution from a corsair in the act of murdering one is of very dubious validity.

—I won't try to explain how painful it is for a young princess to be carried off into slavery in Morocco with her mother. You can imagine everything we had to suffer on the pirate ship. My mother was still very beautiful; our maids of honor, our mere chambermaids, were more charming than anything one could find in all Africa. As for myself, I was ravishing, I was loveliness and grace supreme, and I was a virgin. I did not remain so for long; the flower which had been kept for the handsome prince of Massa-Carrara was plucked by the corsair captain; he was an abominable negro, who thought he was doing me a great favor. My Lady the Princess of Palestrina and I must have been strong indeed to bear what we did during our journey to Morocco. But on with my story; these are such common matters that they are not worth describing.

—Morocco was knee deep in blood when we arrived. Of the fifty sons of the emperor Muley-Ismael,[1] each had his faction, which produced in effect fifty civil wars, of blacks against blacks, of blacks against browns, halfbreeds against halfbreeds; throughout the length and breadth of the empire, nothing but one continual carnage.

—Scarcely had we stepped ashore, when some negroes of a faction hostile to my captor arrived to take charge of his plunder. After the diamonds and gold, we women were the most prized possessions. I was now witness of a struggle such as you never see in the temperate climate of Europe. Northern people don't have hot blood; they don't feel the absolute fury for women which is common in Africa. Europeans seem to have milk in their veins; it is vitriol or liquid fire which pulses through these people around Mount Atlas. The fight for possession of us raged with the fury of the lions, tigers, and poisonous vipers of that land. A Moor snatched my mother by the right arm, the first mate held her by the left; a Moorish soldier grabbed one leg, one of our pirates the other. In a moment's time almost all our girls were being dragged four different ways. My captain held me behind him while with his scimitar he killed everyone who braved his fury. At last I saw all our Italian women, including my mother, torn to pieces, cut to bits, murdered by the monsters who were fighting over them. My captive companions, their captors, soldiers, sailors, blacks, browns, whites, mulattoes, and at last my captain, all were killed, and I remained half dead on a mountain of corpses. Similar scenes were occurring, as is well known, for more than three hundred leagues around, without anyone skimping on the five prayers a day decreed by Mohammed.

—With great pain, I untangled myself from this vast heap of bleeding bodies, and dragged myself under a great orange tree by a neighboring brook, where I collapsed, from terror, exhaustion, horror, despair, and hunger. Shortly, my weary mind surrendered to a sleep which was more of a swoon than a rest. I was in this state of weakness and languor, between life and death, when I felt myself touched by something which moved over my body. Opening my eyes, I saw a white man, rather attractive, who was groaning and saying under his breath: 'O che sciagura d'essere senza coglioni!'[2]

---

1. Having reigned for more than fifty years, a potent and ruthless sultan of Morocco, he died in 1727 and left his kingdom in much the condition described.　　2. "Oh what a misfortune to have no testicles!"

CHAPTER 12

The Old Woman's Story Continued

—Amazed and delighted to hear my native tongue, and no less surprised by what this man was saying, I told him that there were worse evils than those he was complaining of. In a few words, I described to him the horrors I had undergone, and then fainted again. He carried me to a nearby house, put me to bed, gave me something to eat, served me, flattered me, comforted me, told me he had never seen anyone so lovely, and added that he had never before regretted so much the loss of what nobody could give him back.

'I was born at Naples,' he told me, 'where they caponize two or three thousand children every year; some die of it, others acquire a voice more beautiful than any woman's, still others go on to become governors of kingdoms.[3] The operation was a great success with me, and I became court musician to the Princess of Palestrina . . . '

'Of my mother,' I exclaimed.

'Of your mother,' cried he, bursting into tears; 'then you must be the princess whom I raised till she was six, and who already gave promise of becoming as beautiful as you are now!'

'I am that very princess; my mother lies dead, not a hundred yards from here, buried under a pile of corpses.'

—I told him my adventures, he told me his: that he had been sent by a Christian power to the King of Morocco, to conclude a treaty granting him gunpowder, cannon, and ships with which to liquidate the traders of the other Christian powers.

'My mission is concluded,' said this honest eunuch; 'I shall take ship at Ceuta and bring you back to Italy. *Ma che sciagura d'essere senza coglioni!*'

—I thanked him with tears of gratitude, and instead of returning me to Italy, he took me to Algiers and sold me to the dey of that country. Hardly had the sale taken place, when that plague which has made the rounds of Africa, Asia, and Europe broke out in full fury at Algiers. You have seen earthquakes; but tell me, young lady, have you ever had the plague?

—Never, replied the baroness.

—If you had had it, said the old woman, you would agree that it is far worse than an earthquake. It is very frequent in Africa, and I had it. Imagine, if you will, the situation of a pope's daughter, fifteen years old, who in three months' time had experienced poverty, slavery, had been raped almost every day, had seen her mother quartered, had suffered from famine and war, and who now was dying of pestilence in Algiers. As a matter of fact, I did not die; but the eunuch and the dey and nearly the entire seraglio of Algiers perished.

—When the first horrors of this ghastly plague had passed, the slaves of the dey were sold. A merchant bought me and took me to Tunis; there he sold me to another merchant, who resold me at Tripoli; from Tripoli I was sold to Alexandria, from Alexandria resold to Smyrna, from Smyrna to Con-

---

3. The castrato Farinelli (1705–1782), originally a singer, came to exercise considerable political influence on the kings of Spain, Philip V and Ferdinand VI.

stantinople. I ended by belonging to an aga of janizaries, who was shortly ordered to defend Azov against the besieging Russians.[4]

—The aga, who was a gallant soldier, took his whole seraglio with him, and established us in a little fort amid the Maeotian marshes,[5] guarded by two black eunuchs and twenty soldiers. Our side killed a prodigious number of Russians, but they paid us back nicely. Azov was put to fire and sword without respect for age or sex; only our little fort continued to resist, and the enemy determined to starve us out. The twenty janizaries had sworn never to surrender. Reduced to the last extremities of hunger, they were forced to eat our two eunuchs, lest they violate their oaths. After several more days, they decided to eat the women too.

—We had an imam,[6] very pious and sympathetic, who delivered an excellent sermon, persuading them not to kill us altogether.

'Just cut off a single rumpsteak from each of these ladies,' he said, 'and you'll have a fine meal. Then if you should need another, you can come back in a few days and have as much again; heaven will bless your charitable action, and you will be saved.'

—His eloquence was splendid, and he persuaded them. We underwent this horrible operation. The imam treated us all with the ointment that they use on newly circumcised children. We were at the point of death.

—Scarcely had the janizaries finished the meal for which we furnished the materials, when the Russians appeared in flat-bottomed boats; not a janizary escaped. The Russians paid no attention to the state we were in; but there are French physicians everywhere, and one of them, who knew his trade, took care of us. He cured us, and I shall remember all my life that when my wounds were healed, he made me a proposition. For the rest, he counselled us simply to have patience, assuring us that the same thing had happened in several other sieges, and that it was according to the laws of war.

—As soon as my companions could walk, we were herded off to Moscow. In the division of booty, I fell to a boyar who made me work in his garden, and gave me twenty whiplashes a day; but when he was broken on the wheel after about two years, with thirty other boyars, over some little court intrigue,[7] I seized the occasion; I ran away; I crossed all Russia; I was for a long time a chambermaid in Riga, then at Rostock, Vismara, Leipzig, Cassel, Utrecht, Leyden, The Hague, Rotterdam; I grew old in misery and shame, having only half a backside and remembering always that I was the daughter of a Pope; a hundred times I wanted to kill myself, but always I loved life more. This ridiculous weakness is perhaps one of our worst instincts; is anything more stupid than choosing to carry a burden that really one wants to cast on the ground? to hold existence in horror, and yet to cling to it? to fondle the serpent which devours us till it has eaten out our heart?

—In the countries through which I have been forced to wander, in the taverns where I have had to work, I have seen a vast number of people who hated their existence; but I never saw more than a dozen who deliberately put an

4. Azov, near the mouth of the Don, was besieged by the Russians under Peter the Great in 1695–96. *Janizaries*: an elite corps of the Ottoman armies. 5. The Roman name of the so-called Sea of Azov, a shallow swampy lake near the town. 6. In effect, a chaplain. 7. Voltaire had in mind an ineffectual conspiracy against Peter the Great known as the "revolt of the streltsy" or musketeers, which took place in 1698. Though easily put down, it provoked from the emperor a massive and atrocious program of reprisals.

end to their own misery: three negroes, four Englishmen, four Genevans, and a German professor named Robeck.[8] My last post was as servant to the Jew Don Issachar; he attached me to your service, my lovely one; and I attached myself to your destiny, till I have become more concerned with your fate than with my own. I would not even have mentioned my own misfortunes, if you had not irked me a bit, and if it weren't the custom, on shipboard, to pass the time with stories. In a word, my lady, I have had some experience of the world, I know it; why not try this diversion? Ask every passenger on this ship to tell you his story, and if you find a single one who has not often cursed the day of his birth, who has not often told himself that he is the most miserable of men, then you may throw me overboard head first.

CHAPTER 13

How Candide Was Forced to Leave the Lovely Cunégonde and the Old Woman

Having heard out the old woman's story, the lovely Cunégonde paid her the respects which were appropriate to a person of her rank and merit. She took up the wager as well, and got all the passengers, one after another, to tell her their adventures. She and Candide had to agree that the old woman had been right.

—It's certainly too bad, said Candide, that the wise Pangloss was hanged, contrary to the custom of autos-da-fé; he would have admirable things to say of the physical evil and moral evil which cover land and sea, and I might feel within me the impulse to dare to raise several polite objections.

As the passengers recited their stories, the boat made steady progress, and presently landed at Buenos Aires. Cunégonde, Captain Candide, and the old woman went to call on the governor, Don Fernando d'Ibaraa y Figueroa y Mascarenes y Lampourdos y Souza. This nobleman had the pride appropriate to a man with so many names. He addressed everyone with the most aristocratic disdain, pointing his nose so loftily, raising his voice so mercilessly, lording it so splendidly, and assuming so arrogant a pose, that everyone who met him wanted to kick him. He loved women to the point of fury; and Cunégonde seemed to him the most beautiful creature he had ever seen. The first thing he did was to ask directly if she were the captain's wife. His manner of asking this question disturbed Candide; he did not dare say she was his wife, because in fact she was not; he did not dare say she was his sister, because she wasn't that either; and though this polite lie was once common enough among the ancients,[9] and sometimes serves moderns very well, he was too pure of heart to tell a lie.

—Miss Cunégonde, said he, is betrothed to me, and we humbly beg your excellency to perform the ceremony for us.

Don Fernando d'Ibaraa y Figueroa y Mascarenes y Lampourdos y Souza twirled his moustache, smiled sardonically, and ordered Captain Candide to go drill his company. Candide obeyed. Left alone with My Lady Cunégonde, the governor declared his passion, and protested that he would marry her

---

8. Johann Robeck (1672–1739) published a treatise advocating suicide and showed his conviction by drowning himself at the age of sixty-seven.   9. Voltaire has in mind Abraham's adventures with Sarah (Genesis 12) and Isaac's with Rebecca (Genesis 26).

tomorrow, in church or in any other manner, as it pleased her charming self. Cunégonde asked for a quarter-hour to collect herself, consult the old woman, and make up her mind.

The old woman said to Cunégonde:—My lady, you have seventy-two quarterings and not one penny; if you wish, you may be the wife of the greatest lord in South America, who has a really handsome moustache; are you going to insist on your absolute fidelity? You have already been raped by the Bulgars; a Jew and an inquisitor have enjoyed your favors; miseries entitle one to privileges. I assure you that in your position I would make no scruple of marrying My Lord the Governor, and making the fortune of Captain Candide.

While the old woman was talking with all the prudence of age and experience, there came into the harbor a small ship bearing an alcalde and some alguazils.[1] This is what had happened.

As the old woman had very shrewdly guessed, it was a long-sleeved Franciscan who stole Cunégonde's gold and jewels in the town of Badajoz, when she and Candide were in flight. The monk tried to sell some of the gems to a jeweler, who recognized them as belonging to the Grand Inquisitor. Before he was hanged, the Franciscan confessed that he had stolen them, indicating who his victims were and where they were going. The flight of Cunégonde and Candide was already known. They were traced to Cadiz, and a vessel was hastily dispatched in pursuit of them. This vessel was now in the port of Buenos Aires. The rumor spread that an alcalde was aboard, in pursuit of the murderers of My Lord the Grand Inquisitor. The shrewd old woman saw at once what was to be done.

—You cannot escape, she told Cunégonde, and you have nothing to fear. You are not the one who killed my lord, and, besides, the governor, who is in love with you, won't let you be mistreated. Sit tight.

And then she ran straight to Candide:—Get out of town, she said, or you'll be burned within the hour.

There was not a moment to lose; but how to leave Cunégonde, and where to go?

CHAPTER 14

How Candide and Cacambo Were Received by the Jesuits of Paraguay

Candide had brought from Cadiz a valet of the type one often finds in the provinces of Spain and in the colonies. He was one quarter Spanish, son of a halfbreed in the Tucuman;[2] he had been choirboy, sacristan, sailor, monk, merchant, soldier, and lackey. His name was Cacambo, and he was very fond of his master because his master was a very good man. In hot haste he saddled the two Andalusian steeds.

—Hurry, master, do as the old woman says; let's get going and leave this town without a backward look.

Candide wept:—O my beloved Cunégonde! must I leave you now, just when the governor is about to marry us! Cunégonde, brought from so far, what will ever become of you?

—She'll become what she can, said Cacambo; women can always find something to do with themselves; God sees to it; let's get going.

1. Police officers.   2. A province of Argentina, to the northwest of Buenos Aires.

—Where are you taking me? where are we going? what will we do without Cunégonde? said Candide.

—By Saint James of Compostela, said Cacambo, you were going to make war against the Jesuits, now we'll go make war for them. I know the roads pretty well, I'll bring you to their country, they will be delighted to have a captain who knows the Bulgar drill; you'll make a prodigious fortune. If you don't get your rights in one world, you will find them in another. And isn't it pleasant to see new things and do new things?

—Then you've already been in Paraguay? said Candide.

—Indeed I have, replied Cacambo; I was cook in the College of the Assumption, and I know the government of Los Padres[3] as I know the streets of Cadiz. It's an admirable thing, this government. The kingdom is more than three hundred leagues across; it is divided into thirty provinces. Los Padres own everything in it, and the people nothing; it's a masterpiece of reason and justice. I myself know nothing so wonderful as Los Padres, who in this hemisphere make war on the kings of Spain and Portugal, but in Europe hear their confessions; who kill Spaniards here, and in Madrid send them to heaven; that really tickles me; let's get moving, you're going to be the happiest of men. Won't Los Padres be delighted when they learn they have a captain who knows the Bulgar drill!

As soon as they reached the first barricade, Cacambo told the frontier guard that a captain wished to speak with My Lord the Commander. A Paraguayan officer ran to inform headquarters by laying the news at the feet of the commander. Candide and Cacambo were first disarmed and deprived of their Andalusian horses. They were then placed between two files of soldiers; the commander was at the end, his three-cornered hat on his head, his cassock drawn up, a sword at his side, and a pike in his hand. He nods, and twenty-four soldiers surround the newcomers. A sergeant then informs them that they must wait, that the commander cannot talk to them, since the reverend father provincial has forbidden all Spaniards from speaking, except in his presence, and from remaining more than three hours in the country.

—And where is the reverend father provincial? says Cacambo.

—He is reviewing his troops after having said mass, the sergeant replies, and you'll only be able to kiss his spurs in three hours.

—But, says Cacambo, my master the captain, who, like me, is dying from hunger, is not Spanish at all, he is German; can't we have some breakfast while waiting for his reverence?

The sergeant promptly went off to report this speech to the commander.

—God be praised, said this worthy; since he is German, I can talk to him; bring him into my bower.

Candide was immediately led into a leafy nook surrounded by a handsome colonnade of green and gold marble and trellises amid which sported parrots, birds of paradise,[4] hummingbirds, guinea fowl, and all the rarest species of birds. An excellent breakfast was prepared in golden vessels; and while the Paraguayans ate corn out of wooden bowls in the open fields under the glare of the sun, the reverend father commander entered into his bower.

3. The Jesuit fathers.   4. In this passage and several later ones, Voltaire uses in conjunction two words, both of which mean hummingbird. The French system of classifying hummingbirds, based on the work of the celebrated Buffon, distinguishes *oiseaux-mouches* with straight bills from *colibris* with curved bills. This distinction is wholly fallacious. Hummingbirds have all manner of shaped bills, and the division of species must be made on other grounds entirely. At the expense of ornithological accuracy, I have therefore introduced birds of paradise to get the requisite sense of glitter and sheen.

He was a very handsome young man, with an open face, rather blonde in coloring, with ruddy complexion, arched eyebrows, liquid eyes, pink ears, bright red lips, and an air of pride, but a pride somehow different from that of a Spaniard or a Jesuit. Their confiscated weapons were restored to Candide and Cacambo, as well as their Andalusian horses; Cacambo fed them oats alongside the bower, always keeping an eye on them for fear of an ambush.

First Candide kissed the hem of the commander's cassock, then they sat down at the table.

—So you are German? said the Jesuit, speaking in that language.

—Yes, your reverence, said Candide.

As they spoke these words, both men looked at one another with great surprise, and another emotion which they could not control.

—From what part of Germany do you come? said the Jesuit.

—From the nasty province of Westphalia, said Candide; I was born in the castle of Thunder-Ten-Tronckh.

—Merciful heavens! cries the commander. Is it possible?

—What a miracle! exclaims Candide.

—Can it be you? asks the commander.

—It's impossible, says Candide.

They both fall back in their chairs, they embrace, they shed streams of tears.

—What, can it be you, reverend father! you, the brother of the lovely Cunégonde! you, who were killed by the Bulgars! you, the son of My Lord the Baron! you, a Jesuit in Paraguay! It's a mad world, indeed it is. Oh, Pangloss! Pangloss! how happy you would be, if you hadn't been hanged.

The commander dismissed his negro slaves and the Paraguayans who served his drink in crystal goblets. He thanked God and Saint Ignatius a thousand times, he clasped Candide in his arms, their faces were bathed in tears.

—You would be even more astonished, even more delighted, even more beside yourself, said Candide, if I told you that My Lady Cunégonde, your sister, who you thought was disemboweled, is enjoying good health.

—Where?

—Not far from here, in the house of the governor of Buenos Aires; and to think that I came to make war on you!

Each word they spoke in this long conversation added another miracle. Their souls danced on their tongues, hung eagerly at their ears, glittered in their eyes. As they were Germans, they sat a long time at table, waiting for the reverend father provincial; and the commander spoke in these terms to his dear Candide.

CHAPTER 15

How Candide Killed the Brother of His Dear Cunégonde

—All my life long I shall remember the horrible day when I saw my father and mother murdered and my sister raped. When the Bulgars left, that adorable sister of mine was nowhere to be found; so they loaded a cart with my mother, my father, myself, two serving girls, and three little murdered boys, to carry us all off for burial in a Jesuit chapel some two leagues from our ancestral castle. A Jesuit sprinkled us with holy water; it was horribly salty, and a few drops got into my eyes; the father noticed that my lid made a little tremor; putting his hand on my heart, he felt it beat; I was rescued, and at the end of three weeks was as good as new. You know, my dear Candide, that I was a very pretty boy; I became even more so; the reverend father Croust,[5] superior of the abbey, conceived a most tender friendship for me; he accepted me as a novice, and shortly after, I was sent to Rome. The Father General had need of a resupply of young German Jesuits. The rulers of Paraguay accept as few Spanish Jesuits as they can; they prefer foreigners, whom they think they can control better. I was judged fit, by the Father General, to labor in this vineyard. So we set off, a Pole, a Tyrolean, and myself. Upon our arrival, I was honored with the posts of subdeacon and lieutenant; today I am a colonel and a priest. We are giving a vigorous reception to the King of Spain's men; I assure you they will be excommunicated as well as trounced on the battlefield. Providence has sent you to help us. But is it really true that my dear sister, Cunégonde, is in the neighborhood, with the governor of Buenos Aires?

Candide reassured him with a solemn oath that nothing could be more true. Their tears began to flow again.

The baron could not weary of embracing Candide; he called him his brother, his savior.

—Ah, my dear Candide, said he, maybe together we will be able to enter the town as conquerors, and be united with my sister Cunégonde.

—That is all I desire, said Candide; I was expecting to marry her, and I still hope to.

—You insolent dog, replied the baron, you would have the effrontery to marry my sister, who has seventy-two quarterings! It's a piece of presumption for you even to mention such a crazy project in my presence.

Candide, terrified by this speech, answered:—Most reverend father, all the quarterings in the world don't affect this case; I have rescued your sister out of the arms of a Jew and an inquisitor; she has many obligations to me, she wants to marry me. Master Pangloss always taught me that men are equal; and I shall certainly marry her.

—We'll see about that, you scoundrel, said the Jesuit baron of Thunder-Ten-Tronckh; and so saying, he gave him a blow across the face with the flat of his sword. Candide immediately drew his own sword and thrust it up to the hilt in the baron's belly; but as he drew it forth all dripping, he began to weep.

—Alas, dear God! said he, I have killed my old master, my friend, my brother-in-law; I am the best man in the world, and here are three men I've killed already, and two of the three were priests.

Cacambo, who was standing guard at the entry of the bower, came running.

—We can do nothing but sell our lives dearly, said his master; someone will certainly come; we must die fighting.

Cacambo, who had been in similar scrapes before, did not lose his head; he took the Jesuit's cassock, which the commander had been wearing, and put it on Candide; he stuck the dead man's square hat on Candide's head, and forced him onto horseback. Everything was done in the wink of an eye.

5. A Jesuit rector at Colmar with whom Voltaire had quarreled in 1754.

—Let's ride, master; everyone will take you for a Jesuit on his way to deliver orders; and we will have passed the frontier before anyone can come after us.

Even as he was pronouncing these words, he charged off, crying in Spanish:—Way, make way for the reverend father colonel!

CHAPTER 16

What Happened to the Two Travelers with Two Girls, Two Monkeys, and the Savages Named Biglugs

Candide and his valet were over the frontier before anyone in the camp knew of the death of the German Jesuit. Foresighted Cacambo had taken care to fill his satchel with bread, chocolate, ham, fruit, and several bottles of wine. They pushed their Andalusian horses forward into unknown country, where there were no roads. Finally a broad prairie divided by several streams opened before them. Our two travelers turned their horses loose to graze; Cacambo suggested that they eat too, and promptly set the example. But Candide said:—How can you expect me to eat ham when I have killed the son of My Lord the Baron, and am now condemned never to see the lovely Cunégonde for the rest of my life? Why should I drag out my miserable days, since I must exist far from her in the depths of despair and remorse? And what will the *Journal de Trévoux*[6] say of all this?

Though he talked this way, he did not neglect the food. Night fell. The two wanderers heard a few weak cries which seemed to be voiced by women. They could not tell whether the cries expressed grief or joy; but they leaped at once to their feet, with that uneasy suspicion which one always feels in an unknown country. The outcry arose from two girls, completely naked, who were running swiftly along the edge of the meadow, pursued by two monkeys who snapped at their buttocks. Candide was moved to pity; he had learned marksmanship with the Bulgars, and could have knocked a nut off a bush without touching the leaves. He raised his Spanish rifle, fired twice, and killed the two monkeys.

—God be praised, my dear Cacambo! I've saved these two poor creatures from great danger. Though I committed a sin in killing an inquisitor and a Jesuit, I've redeemed myself by saving the lives of two girls. Perhaps they are two ladies of rank, and this good deed may gain us special advantages in the country.

He had more to say, but his mouth shut suddenly when he saw the girls embracing the monkeys tenderly, weeping over their bodies, and filling the air with lamentations.

—I wasn't looking for quite so much generosity of spirit, said he to Cacambo; the latter replied:—You've really fixed things this time, master; you've killed the two lovers of these young ladies.

—Their lovers! Impossible! You must be joking, Cacambo; how can I believe you?

—My dear master, Cacambo replied, you're always astonished by everything. Why do you think it so strange that in some countries monkeys succeed in obtaining the good graces of women? They are one quarter human, just as I am one quarter Spanish.

6. A newspaper published by the Jesuit order, founded in 1701 and consistently hostile to Voltaire.

—Alas, Candide replied, I do remember now hearing Master Pangloss say that such things used to happen, and that from these mixtures there arose pans, fauns, and satyrs, and that these creatures had appeared to various grand figures of antiquity; but I took all that for fables.

—You should be convinced now, said Cacambo; it's true, and you see how people make mistakes who haven't received a measure of education. But what I fear is that these girls may get us into real trouble.

These sensible reflections led Candide to leave the field and to hide in a wood. There he dined with Cacambo; and there both of them, having duly cursed the inquisitor of Portugal, the governor of Buenos Aires, and the baron, went to sleep on a bed of moss. When they woke up, they found themselves unable to move; the reason was that during the night the Biglugs,[7] natives of the country, to whom the girls had complained of them, had tied them down with cords of bark. They were surrounded by fifty naked Biglugs, armed with arrows, clubs, and stone axes. Some were boiling a caldron of water, others were preparing spits, and all cried out:—It's a Jesuit, a Jesuit! We'll be revenged and have a good meal; let's eat some Jesuit, eat some Jesuit!

—I told you, my dear master, said Cacambo sadly, I said those two girls would play us a dirty trick.

Candide, noting the caldron and spits, cried out:—We are surely going to be roasted or boiled. Ah, what would Master Pangloss say if he could see these men in a state of nature? All is for the best, I agree; but I must say it seems hard to have lost Miss Cunégonde and to be stuck on a spit by the Biglugs.

Cacambo did not lose his head.

—Don't give up hope, said he to the disconsolate Candide; I understand a little of the jargon these people speak, and I'm going to talk to them.

—Don't forget to remind them, said Candide, of the frightful inhumanity of eating their fellow men, and that Christian ethics forbid it.

—Gentlemen, said Cacambo, you have a mind to eat a Jesuit today? An excellent idea; nothing is more proper than to treat one's enemies so. Indeed, the law of nature teaches us to kill our neighbor, and that's how men behave the whole world over. Though we Europeans don't exercise our right to eat our neighbors, the reason is simply that we find it easy to get a good meal elsewhere; but you don't have our resources, and we certainly agree that it's better to eat your enemies than to let the crows and vultures have the fruit of your victory. But, gentlemen, you wouldn't want to eat your friends. You think you will be spitting a Jesuit, and it's your defender, the enemy of your enemies, whom you will be roasting. For my part, I was born in your country; the gentleman whom you see is my master, and far from being a Jesuit, he has just killed a Jesuit, the robe he is wearing was stripped from him; that's why you have taken a dislike to him. To prove that I am telling the truth, take his robe and bring it to the nearest frontier of the kingdom of Los Padres; find out for yourselves if my master didn't kill a Jesuit officer. It won't take long; if you find that I have lied, you can still eat us. But if I've told the truth, you know too well the principles of public justice, customs, and laws, not to spare our lives.

The Biglugs found this discourse perfectly reasonable; they appointed

---

7. Voltaire's name is "Oreillons" from Spanish "Orejones," a name mentioned in Garcilaso de Vega's *Historia General del Perú* (1609), on which Voltaire drew for many of the details in his picture of South America.

chiefs to go posthaste and find out the truth; the two messengers performed their task like men of sense, and quickly returned bringing good news. The Biglugs untied their two prisoners, treated them with great politeness, offered them girls, gave them refreshments, and led them back to the border of their state, crying joyously:—He isn't a Jesuit, he isn't a Jesuit!

Candide could not weary of exclaiming over his preservation.

—What a people! he said. What men! what customs! If I had not had the good luck to run a sword through the body of Miss Cunégonde's brother, I would have been eaten on the spot! But, after all, it seems that uncorrupted nature is good, since these folk, instead of eating me, showed me a thousand kindnesses as soon as they knew I was not a Jesuit.

CHAPTER 17

Arrival of Candide and His Servant at the Country of Eldorado, and That They Saw There

When they were out of the land of the Biglugs, Cacambo said to Candide:
—You see that this hemisphere is no better than the other; take my advice, and let's get back to Europe as soon as possible.

—How to get back, asked Candide, and where to go? If I go to my own land, the Bulgars and Abares are murdering everyone in sight; if I go to Portugal, they'll burn me alive; if we stay here, we risk being skewered any day. But how can I ever leave that part of the world where Miss Cunégonde lives?

—Let's go toward Cayenne, said Cacambo, we shall find some Frenchmen there, for they go all over the world; they can help us; perhaps God will take pity on us.

To get to Cayenne was not easy; they knew more or less which way to go, but mountains, rivers, cliffs, robbers, and savages obstructed the way everywhere. Their horses died of weariness; their food was eaten; they subsisted for one whole month on wild fruits, and at last they found themselves by a little river fringed with coconut trees, which gave them both life and hope.

Cacambo, who was as full of good advice as the old woman, said to Candide:—We can go no further, we've walked ourselves out; I see an abandoned canoe on the bank, let's fill it with coconuts, get into the boat, and float with the current; a river always leads to some inhabited spot or other. If we don't find anything pleasant, at least we may find something new.

—Let's go, said Candide, and let Providence be our guide.

They floated some leagues between banks sometimes flowery, sometimes sandy, now steep, now level. The river widened steadily; finally it disappeared into a chasm of frightful rocks that rose high into the heavens. The two travelers had the audacity to float with the current into this chasm. The river, narrowly confined, drove them onward with horrible speed and a fearful roar. After twenty-four hours, they saw daylight once more; but their canoe was smashed on the snags. They had to drag themselves from rock to rock for an entire league; at last they emerged to an immense horizon, ringed with remote mountains. The countryside was tended for pleasure as well as profit; everywhere the useful was joined to the agreeable. The roads were covered, or rather decorated, with elegantly shaped carriages made of a glittering material, carrying men and women of singular beauty, and drawn by great red sheep which were faster than the finest horses of Andalusia, Tetuan, and Mequinez.

—Here now, said Candide, is a country that's better than Westphalia.

Along with Cacambo, he climbed out of the river at the first village he could see. Some children of the town, dressed in rags of gold brocade, were playing quoits at the village gate; our two men from the other world paused to watch them; their quoits were rather large, yellow, red, and green, and they glittered with a singular luster. On a whim, the travelers picked up several; they were of gold, emeralds, and rubies, and the least of them would have been the greatest ornament of the Great Mogul's throne.

—Surely, said Cacambo, these quoit players are the children of the king of the country.

The village schoolmaster appeared at that moment, to call them back to school.

—And there, said Candide, is the tutor of the royal household.

The little rascals quickly gave up their game, leaving on the ground their quoits and playthings. Candide picked them up, ran to the schoolmaster, and presented them to him humbly, giving him to understand by sign language that their royal highnesses had forgotten their gold and jewels. With a smile, the schoolmaster tossed them to the ground, glanced quickly but with great surprise at Candide's face, and went his way.

The travelers did not fail to pick up the gold, rubies, and emeralds.

—Where in the world are we? cried Candide. The children of this land must be well trained, since they are taught contempt for gold and jewels.

Cacambo was as much surprised as Candide. At last they came to the finest house of the village; it was built like a European palace. A crowd of people surrounded the door, and even more were in the entry; delightful music was heard, and a delicious aroma of cooking filled the air. Cacambo went up to the door, listened, and reported that they were talking Peruvian; that was his native language, for every reader must know that Cacambo was born in Tucuman, in a village where they talk that language exclusively.

—I'll act as interpreter, he told Candide; it's an hotel, let's go in.

Promptly two boys and two girls of the staff, dressed in cloth of gold, and wearing ribbons in their hair, invited them to sit at the host's table. The meal consisted of four soups, each one garnished with a brace of parakeets, a boiled condor which weighed two hundred pounds, two roast monkeys of an excellent flavor, three hundred birds of paradise in one dish and six hundred hummingbirds in another, exquisite stews, delicious pastries, the whole thing served up in plates of what looked like rock crystal. The boys and girls of the staff poured them various beverages made from sugar cane.

The diners were for the most part merchants and travelers, all extremely polite, who questioned Cacambo with the most discreet circumspection, and answered his questions very directly.

When the meal was over, Cacambo as well as Candide supposed he could settle his bill handsomely by tossing onto the table two of those big pieces of gold which they had picked up; but the host and hostess burst out laughing, and for a long time nearly split their sides. Finally they subsided.

—Gentlemen, said the host, we see clearly that you're foreigners; we don't meet many of you here. Please excuse our laughing when you offered us in payment a couple of pebbles from the roadside. No doubt you don't have any of our local currency, but you don't need it to eat here. All the hotels established for the promotion of commerce are maintained by the state. You have had meager entertainment here, for we are only a poor town; but everywhere else you will be given the sort of welcome you deserve.

Cacambo translated for Candide all the host's explanations, and Candide listened to them with the same admiration and astonishment that his friend Cacambo showed in reporting them.

—What is this country, then, said they to one another, unknown to the rest of the world, and where nature itself is so different from our own? This probably is the country where everything is for the best; for it's absolutely necessary that such a country should exist somewhere. And whatever Master Pangloss said of the matter, I have often had occasion to notice that things went badly in Westphalia.

CHAPTER 18

What They Saw in the Land of Eldorado

Cacambo revealed his curiosity to the host, and the host told him:—I am an ignorant man and content to remain so; but we have here an old man, retired from the court, who is the most knowing person in the kingdom, and the most talkative.

Thereupon he brought Cacambo to the old man's house. Candide now played second fiddle, and acted as servant to his own valet. They entered an austere little house, for the door was merely of silver and the paneling of the rooms was only gold, though so tastefully wrought that the finest paneling would not surpass it. If the truth must be told, the lobby was only decorated with rubies and emeralds; but the patterns in which they were arranged atoned for the extreme simplicity.

The old man received the two strangers on a sofa stuffed with bird-of-paradise feathers, and offered them several drinks in diamond carafes; then he satisfied their curiosity in these terms.

—I am a hundred and seventy-two years old, and I heard from my late father, who was liveryman to the king, about the astonishing revolutions in Peru which he had seen. Our land here was formerly part of the kingdom of the Incas, who rashly left it in order to conquer another part of the world, and who were ultimately destroyed by the Spaniards. The wisest princes of their house were those who had never left their native valley; they decreed, with the consent of the nation, that henceforth no inhabitant of our little kingdom should ever leave it; and this rule is what has preserved our innocence and our happiness. The Spaniards heard vague rumors about this land, they called it El Dorado;[8] and an English knight named Raleigh even came somewhere close to it about a hundred years ago; but as we are surrounded by unscalable mountains and precipices, we have managed so far to remain hidden from the rapacity of the European nations, who have an inconceivable rage for the pebbles and mud of our land, and who, in order to get some, would butcher us all to the last man.

---

8. The myth of this land of gold somewhere in Central or South America had been widespread since the 16th century. *The Discovery of Guiana,* published in 1595, described Sir Walter Ralegh's infatuation with the myth of Eldorado and served to spread the story still further.

The conversation was a long one; it turned on the form of the government, the national customs, on women, public shows, the arts. At last Candide, whose taste always ran to metaphysics, told Cacambo to ask if the country had any religion.

The old man grew a bit red.

—How's that? he said. Can you have any doubt of it? Do you suppose we are altogether thankless scoundrels?

Cacambo asked meekly what was the religion of Eldorado. The old man flushed again.

—Can there be two religions? he asked. I suppose our religion is the same as everyone's, we worship God from morning to evening.

—Then you worship a single deity? said Cacambo, who acted throughout as interpreter of the questions of Candide.

—It's obvious, said the old man, that there aren't two or three or four of them. I must say the people of your world ask very remarkable questions.

Candide could not weary of putting questions to this good old man; he wanted to know how the people of Eldorado prayed to God.

—We don't pray to him at all, said the good and respectable sage; we have nothing to ask him for, since everything we need has already been granted; we thank God continually.

Candide was interested in seeing the priests; he had Cacambo ask where they were. The old gentleman smiled.

—My friends, said he, we are all priests; the king and all the heads of household sing formal psalms of thanksgiving every morning, and five or six thousand voices accompany them.

—What! you have no monks to teach, argue, govern, intrigue, and burn at the stake everyone who disagrees with them?

—We should have to be mad, said the old man; here we are all of the same mind, and we don't understand what you're up to with your monks.

Candide was overjoyed at all these speeches, and said to himself:—This is very different from Westphalia and the castle of My Lord the Baron; if our friend Pangloss had seen Eldorado, he wouldn't have called the castle of Thunder-Ten-Tronckh the finest thing on earth; to know the world one must travel.

After this long conversation, the old gentleman ordered a carriage with six sheep made ready, and gave the two travelers twelve of his servants for their journey to the court.

—Excuse me, said he, if old age deprives me of the honor of accompanying you. The king will receive you after a style which will not altogether displease you, and you will doubtless make allowance for the customs of the country if there are any you do not like.

Candide and Cacambo climbed into the coach; the six sheep flew like the wind, and in less than four hours they reached the king's palace at the edge of the capital. The entryway was two hundred and twenty feet high and a hundred wide; it is impossible to describe all the materials of which it was made. But you can imagine how much finer it was than those pebbles and sand which we call gold and jewels.

Twenty beautiful girls of the guard detail welcomed Candide and Cacambo as they stepped from the carriage, took them to the baths, and dressed them in robes woven of hummingbird feathers; then the high officials of the crown, both male and female, led them to the royal chamber between two long lines, each of a thousand musicians, as is customary. As they approached the throne room, Cacambo asked an officer what was the proper method of greeting his majesty: if one fell to one's knees or on one's belly; if one put one's hands on one's head or on one's rear; if one licked up the dust of the earth—in a word, what was the proper form?[9]

—The ceremony, said the officer, is to embrace the king and kiss him on both cheeks.

Candide and Cacambo fell on the neck of his majesty, who received them with all the dignity imaginable, and asked them politely to dine.

In the interim, they were taken about to see the city, the public buildings rising to the clouds, the public markets and arcades, the fountains of pure water and of rose water, those of sugar cane liquors which flowed perpétually in the great plazas paved with a sort of stone which gave off odors of gilly-flower and rose petals. Candide asked to see the supreme court and the hall of parliament; they told him there was no such thing, that lawsuits were unknown. He asked if there were prisons, and was told there were not. What surprised him more, and gave him most pleasure, was the palace of sciences, in which he saw a gallery two thousand paces long, entirely filled with mathematical and physical instruments.

Having passed the whole afternoon seeing only a thousandth part of the city, they returned to the king's palace. Candide sat down to dinner with his majesty, his own valet Cacambo, and several ladies. Never was better food served, and never did a host preside more jovially than his majesty. Cacambo explained the king's witty sayings to Candide, and even when translated they still seemed witty. Of all the things which astonished Candide, this was not, in his eyes, the least astonishing.

They passed a month in this refuge. Candide never tired of saying to Cacambo:—It's true, my friend, I'll say it again, the castle where I was born does not compare with the land where we now are; but Miss Cunégonde is not here, and you doubtless have a mistress somewhere in Europe. If we stay here, we shall be just like everybody else, whereas if we go back to our own world, taking with us just a dozen sheep loaded with Eldorado pebbles, we shall be richer than all the kings put together, we shall have no more inquisitors to fear, and we shall easily be able to retake Miss Cunégonde.

This harangue pleased Cacambo; wandering is such pleasure, it gives a man such prestige at home to be able to talk of what he has seen abroad, that the two happy men resolved to be so no longer, but to take their leave of his majesty.

—You are making a foolish mistake, the king told them; I know very well that my kingdom is nothing much; but when you are pretty comfortable somewhere, you had better stay there. Of course I have no right to keep strangers against their will, that sort of tyranny is not in keeping with our laws or our customs; all men are free; depart when you will, but the way out is very difficult. You cannot possibly go up the river by which you miraculously came; it runs too swiftly through its underground caves. The mountains which surround my land are ten thousand feet high, and steep as walls;

9. Candide's questions are probably derived from those of Gulliver on a similar occasion, in the third part of *Gulliver's Travels*.

each one is more than ten leagues across; the only way down is over precipices. But since you really must go, I shall order my engineers to make a machine which can carry you conveniently. When we take you over the mountains, nobody will be able to go with you, for my subjects have sworn never to leave their refuge, and they are too sensible to break their vows. Other than that, ask of me what you please.

—We only request of your majesty, Cacambo said, a few sheep loaded with provisions, some pebbles, and some of the mud of your country.

The king laughed.

—I simply can't understand, said he, the passion you Europeans have for our yellow mud; but take all you want, and much good may it do you.

He promptly gave orders to his technicians to make a machine for lifting these two extraordinary men out of his kingdom. Three thousand good physicists worked at the problem; the machine was ready in two weeks' time, and cost no more than twenty million pounds sterling, in the money of the country. Cacambo and Candide were placed in the machine; there were two great sheep, saddled and bridled to serve them as steeds when they had cleared the mountains, twenty pack sheep with provisions, thirty which carried presents consisting of the rarities of the country, and fifty loaded with gold, jewels, and diamonds. The king bade tender farewell to the two vagabonds.

It made a fine spectacle, their departure, and the ingenious way in which they were hoisted with their sheep up to the top of the mountains. The technicians bade them good-bye after bringing them to safety, and Candide had now no other desire and no other object than to go and present his sheep to Miss Cunégonde.

—We have, said he, enough to pay off the governor of Buenos Aires—if, indeed, a price can be placed on Miss Cunégonde. Let us go to Cayenne, take ship there, and then see what kingdom we can find to buy up.

CHAPTER 19

What Happened to Them at Surinam, and How Candide Got to Know Martin

The first day was pleasant enough for our travelers. They were encouraged by the idea of possessing more treasures than Asia, Europe, and Africa could bring together. Candide, in transports, carved the name of Cunégonde on the trees. On the second day two of their sheep bogged down in a swamp and were lost with their loads; two other sheep died of fatigue a few days later; seven or eight others starved to death in a desert; still others fell, a little after, from precipices. Finally, after a hundred days' march, they had only two sheep left. Candide told Cacambo:—My friend, you see how the riches of this world are fleeting; the only solid things are virtue and the joy of seeing Miss Cunégonde again.

—I agree, said Cacambo, but we still have two sheep, laden with more treasure than the king of Spain will ever have; and I see in the distance a town which I suspect is Surinam; it belongs to the Dutch. We are at the end of our trials and on the threshold of our happiness.

As they drew near the town, they discovered a negro stretched on the ground with only half his clothes left, that is, a pair of blue drawers; the poor fellow was also missing his left leg and his right hand.

—Good Lord, said Candide in Dutch, what are you doing in that horrible condition, my friend?

—I am waiting for my master, Mr. Vanderdendur,[1] the famous merchant, answered the negro.

—Is Mr. Vanderdendur, Candide asked, the man who treated you this way?

—Yes, sir, said the negro, that's how things are around here. Twice a year we get a pair of linen drawers to wear. If we catch a finger in the sugar mill where we work, they cut off our hand; if we try to run away, they cut off our leg: I have undergone both these experiences. This is the price of the sugar you eat in Europe. And yet, when my mother sold me for ten Patagonian crowns on the coast of Guinea, she said to me: 'My dear child, bless our witch doctors, reverence them always, they will make your life happy; you have the honor of being a slave to our white masters, and in this way you are making the fortune of your father and mother.' Alas! I don't know if I made their fortunes, but they certainly did not make mine. The dogs, monkeys, and parrots are a thousand times less unhappy than we are. The Dutch witch doctors who converted me tell me every Sunday that we are all sons of Adam, black and white alike. I am no genealogist; but if these preachers are right, we must all be remote cousins; and you must admit no one could treat his own flesh and blood in a more horrible fashion.

—Oh Pangloss! cried Candide, you had no notion of these abominations! I'm through, I must give up your optimism after all.

—What's optimism? said Cacambo.

—Alas, said Candide, it is a mania for saying things are well when one is in hell.

And he shed bitter tears as he looked at this negro, and he was still weeping as he entered Surinam.

The first thing they asked was if there was not some vessel in port which could be sent to Buenos Aires. The man they asked was a Spanish merchant who undertook to make an honest bargain with them. They arranged to meet in a café; Candide and the faithful Cacambo, with their two sheep, went there to meet with him.

Candide, who always said exactly what was in his heart, told the Spaniard of his adventures, and confessed that he wanted to recapture Miss Cunégonde.

—I shall take good care *not* to send you to Buenos Aires, said the merchant; I should be hanged, and so would you. The lovely Cunégonde is his lordship's favorite mistress.

This was a thunderstroke for Candide; he wept for a long time; finally he drew Cacambo aside.

—Here, my friend, said he, is what you must do. Each one of us has in his pockets five or six millions' worth of diamonds; you are cleverer than I; go get Miss Cunégonde in Buenos Aires. If the governor makes a fuss, give him a million; if that doesn't convince him, give him two millions; you never killed an inquisitor, nobody will suspect you. I'll fit out another boat and go

---

1. A name perhaps intended to suggest VanDuren, a Dutch bookseller with whom Voltaire had quarreled. In particular, the incident of gradually raising one's price recalls VanDuren, to whom Voltaire had successively offered 1,000, 1,500, 2,000, and 3,000 florins for the return of the manuscript of Frederick the Great's *Anti-Machiavel*.

wait for you in Venice. That is a free country, where one need have no fear either of Bulgars or Abares or Jews or inquisitors.

Cacambo approved of this wise decision. He was in despair at leaving a good master who had become a bosom friend; but the pleasure of serving him overcame the grief of leaving him. They embraced, and shed a few tears; Candide urged him not to forget the good old woman. Cacambo departed that very same day; he was a very good fellow, that Cacambo.

Candide remained for some time in Surinam, waiting for another merchant to take him to Italy, along with the two sheep which were left him. He hired servants and bought everything necessary for the long voyage; finally Mr. Vanderdendur, master of a big ship, came calling.

—How much will you charge, Candide asked this man, to take me to Venice—myself, my servants, my luggage, and those two sheep over there?

The merchant set a price of ten thousand piastres; Candide did not blink an eye.

—Oh, ho, said the prudent Vanderdendur to himself, this stranger pays out ten thousand piastres at once, he must be pretty well fixed.

Then, returning a moment later, he made known that he could not set sail under twenty thousand.

—All right, you shall have them, said Candide.

—Whew, said the merchant softly to himself, this man gives twenty thousand piastres as easily as ten.

He came back again to say he could not go to Venice for less than thirty thousand piastres.

—All right, thirty then, said Candide.

—Ah ha, said the Dutch merchant, again speaking to himself; so thirty thousand piastres mean nothing to this man; no doubt the two sheep are loaded with immense treasures; let's say no more; we'll pick up the thirty thousand piastres first, and then we'll see.

Candide sold two little diamonds, the least of which was worth more than all the money demanded by the merchant. He paid him in advance. The two sheep were taken aboard. Candide followed in a little boat, to board the vessel at its anchorage. The merchant bides his time, sets sail, and makes his escape with a favoring wind. Candide, aghast and stupefied, soon loses him from view.

—Alas, he cries, now there is a trick worthy of the old world!

He returns to shore sunk in misery; for he had lost riches enough to make the fortunes of twenty monarchs.

Now he rushes to the house of the Dutch magistrate, and, being a bit disturbed, he knocks loudly at the door; goes in, tells the story of what happened, and shouts a bit louder than is customary. The judge begins by fining him ten thousand piastres for making such a racket; then he listens patiently to the story, promises to look into the matter as soon as the merchant comes back, and charges another ten thousand piastres as the costs of the hearing.

This legal proceeding completed the despair of Candide. In fact he had experienced miseries a thousand times more painful, but the coldness of the judge, and that of the merchant who had robbed him, roused his bile and plunged him into a black melancholy. The malice of men rose up before his spirit in all its ugliness, and his mind dwelt only on gloomy thoughts. Finally, when a French vessel was ready to leave for Bordeaux, since he had no more diamond-laden sheep to transport, he took a cabin at a fair price, and made it known in the town that he would pay passage and keep, plus two thousand piastres, to any honest man who wanted to make the journey with him, on condition that this man must be the most disgusted with his own condition and the most unhappy man in the province.

This drew such a crowd of applicants as a fleet could not have held. Candide wanted to choose among the leading candidates, so he picked out about twenty who seemed companionable enough, and of whom each pretended to be more miserable than all the others. He brought them together at his inn and gave them a dinner, on condition that each would swear to tell truthfully his entire history. He would select as his companion the most truly miserable and rightly discontented man, and among the others he would distribute various gifts.

The meeting lasted till four in the morning. Candide, as he listened to all the stories, remembered what the old woman had told him on the trip to Buenos Aires, and of the wager she had made, that there was nobody on the boat who had not undergone great misfortunes. At every story that was told him, he thought of Pangloss.

—That Pangloss, he said, would be hard put to prove his system. I wish he was here. Certainly if everything goes well, it is in Eldorado and not in the rest of the world.

At last he decided in favor of a poor scholar who had worked ten years for the booksellers of Amsterdam. He decided that there was no trade in the world with which one should be more disgusted.

This scholar, who was in fact a good man, had been robbed by his wife, beaten by his son, and deserted by his daughter, who had got herself abducted by a Portuguese. He had just been fired from the little job on which he existed; and the preachers of Surinam were persecuting him because they took him for a Socinian.[2] The others, it is true, were at least as unhappy as he, but Candide hoped the scholar would prove more amusing on the voyage. All his rivals declared that Candide was doing them a great injustice, but he pacified them with a hundred piastres apiece.

CHAPTER 20

What Happened to Candide and Martin at Sea

The old scholar, whose name was Martin, now set sail with Candide for Bordeaux. Both men had seen and suffered much; and even if the vessel had been sailing from Surinam to Japan via the Cape of Good Hope, they would have been able to keep themselves amused with instances of moral evil and physical evil during the entire trip.

However, Candide had one great advantage over Martin, that he still hoped to see Miss Cunégonde again, and Martin had nothing to hope for; besides, he had gold and diamonds, and though he had lost a hundred big red sheep loaded with the greatest treasures of the earth, though he had always at his heart a memory of the Dutch merchant's villainy, yet, when he

---

2. A follower of Faustus and Laelius Socinus, 16th-century Polish theologians, who proposed a form of "rational" Christianity which exalted the rational conscience and minimized such mysteries as the trinity. The Socinians, by a special irony, were vigorous optimists.

thought of the wealth that remained in his hands, and when he talked of Cunégonde, especially just after a good dinner, he still inclined to the system of Pangloss.

—But what about you, Monsieur Martin, he asked the scholar, what do you think of all that? What is your idea of moral evil and physical evil?

—Sir, answered Martin, those priests accused me of being a Socinian, but the truth is that I am a Manichee.[3]

—You're joking, said Candide; there aren't any more Manichees in the world.

—There's me, said Martin; I don't know what to do about it, but I can't think otherwise.

—You must be possessed of the devil, said Candide.

—He's mixed up with so many things of this world, said Martin, that he may be in me as well as elsewhere; but I assure you, as I survey this globe, or globule, I think that God has abandoned it to some evil spirit—all of it except Eldorado. I have scarcely seen one town which did not wish to destroy its neighboring town, no family which did not wish to exterminate some other family. Everywhere the weak loathe the powerful, before whom they cringe, and the powerful treat them like brute cattle, to be sold for their meat and fleece. A million regimented assassins roam Europe from one end to the other, plying the trades of murder and robbery in an organized way for a living, because there is no more honest form of work for them; and in the cities which seem to enjoy peace and where the arts are flourishing, men are devoured by more envy, cares, and anxieties than a whole town experiences when it's under siege. Private griefs are worse even than public trials. In a word, I have seen so much and suffered so much, that I am a Manichee.

—Still there is some good, said Candide.

—That may be, said Martin, but I don't know it.

In the middle of this discussion, the rumble of cannon was heard. From minute to minute the noise grew louder. Everyone reached for his spyglass. At a distance of some three miles they saw two vessels fighting; the wind brought both of them so close to the French vessel that they had a pleasantly comfortable seat to watch the fight. Presently one of the vessels caught the other with a broadside so low and so square as to send it to the bottom. Candide and Martin saw clearly a hundred men on the deck of the sinking ship; they all raised their hands to heaven, uttering fearful shrieks; and in a moment everything was swallowed up.

—Well, said Martin, that is how men treat one another.

—It is true, said Candide, there's something devilish in this business.

As they chatted, he noticed something of a striking red color floating near the sunken vessel. They sent out a boat to investigate; it was one of his sheep. Candide was more joyful to recover this one sheep than he had been afflicted to lose a hundred of them, all loaded with big Eldorado diamonds.

The French captain soon learned that the captain of the victorious vessel was Spanish and that of the sunken vessel was a Dutch pirate. It was the same man who had robbed Candide. The enormous riches which this rascal

3. Mani, a Persian sage and philosopher of the 3rd century A.D., taught (probably under the influence of traditions stemming from Zoroaster and the worshipers of the sun god Mithra) that the earth is a field of dispute between two almost equal powers, one of light and one of darkness, both of which must be propitiated.

had stolen were sunk beside him in the sea, and nothing was saved but a single sheep.

—You see, said Candide to Martin, crime is punished sometimes; this scoundrel of a Dutch merchant has met the fate he deserved.

—Yes, said Martin; but did the passengers aboard his ship have to perish too? God punished the scoundrel, and the devil drowned the others.

Meanwhile the French and Spanish vessels continued on their journey, and Candide continued his talks with Martin. They disputed for fifteen days in a row, and at the end of that time were just as much in agreement as at the beginning. But at least they were talking, they exchanged their ideas, they consoled one another. Candide caressed his sheep.

—Since I have found you again, said he, I may well rediscover Miss Cunégonde.

CHAPTER 21

Candide and Martin Approach the Coast of France:
They Reason Together

At last the coast of France came in view.

—Have you ever been in France, Monsieur Martin? asked Candide.

—Yes, said Martin, I have visited several provinces. There are some where half the inhabitants are crazy, others where they are too sly, still others where they are quite gentle and stupid, some where they venture on wit; in all of them the principal occupation is love-making, the second is slander, and the third stupid talk.

—But, Monsieur Martin, were you ever in Paris?

—Yes, I've been in Paris; it contains specimens of all these types; it is a chaos, a mob, in which everyone is seeking pleasure and where hardly anyone finds it, at least from what I have seen. I did not live there for long; as I arrived, I was robbed of everything I possessed by thieves at the fair of St. Germain; I myself was taken for a thief, and spent eight days in jail, after which I took a proofreader's job to earn enough money to return on foot to Holland. I knew the writing gang, the intriguing gang, the gang with fits and convulsions.[4] They say there are some very civilized people in that town; I'd like to think so.

—I myself have no desire to visit France, said Candide; you no doubt realize that when one has spent a month in Eldorado, there is nothing else on earth one wants to see, except Miss Cunégonde. I am going to wait for her at Venice; we will cross France simply to get to Italy; wouldn't you like to come with me?

—Gladly, said Martin; they say Venice is good only for the Venetian nobles, but that on the other hand they treat foreigners very well when they have plenty of money. I don't have any; you do, so I'll follow you anywhere.

—By the way, said Candide, do you believe the earth was originally all ocean, as they assure us in that big book belonging to the ship's captain?[5]

—I don't believe that stuff, said Martin, nor any of the dreams which people have been peddling for some time now.

---

4. The Jansenists, a sect of strict Catholics, became notorious for spiritual ecstasies. Their public displays reached a height during the 1720s, and Voltaire described them in *Le Siècle de Louis XIV* (chap. 37), as well as in the article "Convulsions" in the *Philosophical Dictionary*.   5. The Bible: Genesis 1.

—But why, then, was this world formed at all? asked Candide.

—To drive us mad, answered Martin.

—Aren't you astonished, Candide went on, at the love which those two girls showed for the monkeys in the land of the Biglugs that I told you about?

—Not at all, said Martin, I see nothing strange in these sentiments; I have seen so many extraordinary things that nothing seems extraordinary any more.

—Do you believe, asked Candide, that men have always massacred one another as they do today? That they have always been liars, traitors, ingrates, thieves, weaklings, sneaks, cowards, backbiters, gluttons, drunkards, misers, climbers, killers, calumniators, sensualists, fanatics, hypocrites, and fools?

—Do you believe, said Martin, that hawks have always eaten pigeons when they could get them?

—Of course, said Candide.

—Well, said Martin, if hawks have always had the same character, why do you suppose that men have changed?

—Oh, said Candide, there's a great deal of difference, because freedom of the will . . .

As they were disputing in this manner, they reached Bordeaux.

CHAPTER 22

What Happened in France to Candide and Martin

Candide paused in Bordeaux only long enough to sell a couple of Dorado pebbles and to fit himself out with a fine two-seater carriage, for he could no longer do without his philosopher Martin; only he was very unhappy to part with his sheep, which he left to the academy of science in Bordeaux. They proposed, as the theme of that year's prize contest, the discovery of why the wool of the sheep was red; and the prize was awarded to a northern scholar[6] who demonstrated by A plus B minus C divided by Z that the sheep ought to be red and die of sheep rot.

But all the travelers with whom Candide talked in the roadside inns told him:—We are going to Paris.

This general consensus finally inspired in him too a desire to see the capital; it was not much out of his road to Venice.

He entered through the Faubourg Saint-Marceau,[7] and thought he was in the meanest village of Westphalia.

Scarcely was Candide in his hotel, when he came down with a mild illness caused by exhaustion. As he was wearing an enormous diamond ring, and people had noticed among his luggage a tremendously heavy safe, he soon found at his bedside two doctors whom he had not called, several intimate friends who never left him alone, and two pious ladies who helped to warm his broth. Martin said:—I remember that I too was ill on my first trip to Paris; I was very poor; and as I had neither friends, pious ladies, nor doctors, I got well.

However, as a result of medicines and bleedings, Candide's illness became

---

6. Maupertuis Le Lapon, philosopher and mathematician, whom Voltaire had accused of trying to adduce mathematical proofs of the existence of God.   7. A district on the left bank, notably grubby in the 18th century. "As I entered [Paris] through the Faubourg Saint-Marceau, I saw nothing but dirty stinking little streets, ugly black houses, a general air of squalor and poverty, beggars, carters, menders of clothes, sellers of herb-drinks and old hats." Jean-Jacques Rousseau, *Confessions*, Book IV.

serious. A resident of the neighborhood came to ask him politely to fill out a ticket, to be delivered to the porter of the other world.[8] Candide wanted nothing to do with it. The pious ladies assured him it was a new fashion; Candide replied that he wasn't a man of fashion. Martin wanted to throw the resident out the window. The cleric swore that without the ticket they wouldn't bury Candide. Martin swore that he would bury the cleric if he continued to be a nuisance. The quarrel grew heated; Martin took him by the shoulders and threw him bodily out the door; all of which caused a great scandal, from which developed a legal case.

Candide got better; and during his convalescence he had very good company in to dine. They played cards for money; and Candide was quite surprised that none of the aces were ever dealt to him, and Martin was not surprised at all.

Among those who did the honors of the town for Candide there was a little abbé from Perigord, one of those busy fellows, always bright, always useful, assured, obsequious, and obliging, who waylay passing strangers, tell them the scandal of the town, and offer them pleasures at any price they want to pay. This fellow first took Candide and Martin to the theatre. A new tragedy was being played. Candide found himself seated next to a group of wits. That did not keep him from shedding a few tears in the course of some perfectly played scenes. One of the commentators beside him remarked during the intermission:—You are quite mistaken to weep, this actress is very bad indeed; the actor who plays with her is even worse; and the play is even worse than the actors in it. The author knows not a word of Arabic, though the action takes place in Arabia; and besides, he is a man who doesn't believe in innate ideas. Tomorrow I will show you twenty pamphlets written against him.

—Tell me, sir, said Candide to the abbé, how many plays are there for performance in France?

—Five or six thousand, replied the other.

—That's a lot, said Candide; how many of them are any good?

—Fifteen or sixteen, was the answer.

—That's a lot, said Martin.

Candide was very pleased with an actress who took the part of Queen Elizabeth in a rather dull tragedy[9] that still gets played from time to time.

—I like this actress very much, he said to Martin, she bears a slight resemblance to Miss Cunégonde; I should like to meet her.

The abbé from Perigord offered to introduce him. Candide, raised in Germany, asked what was the protocol, how one behaved in France with queens of England.

—You must distinguish, said the abbé; in the provinces, you take them to an inn; at Paris they are respected while still attractive, and thrown on the dunghill when they are dead.[1]

—Queens on the dunghill! said Candide.

---

8. In the middle of the 18th century, it became customary to require persons who were grievously ill to sign *billets de confession*, without which they could not be given absolution, admitted to the last sacraments, or buried in consecrated ground.   9. *Le Comte d'Essex* by Thomas Corneille.   1. Voltaire engaged in a long and vigorous campaign against the rule that actors and actresses could not be buried in consecrated ground. The superstition probably arose from a feeling that by assuming false identities they drained their own souls.

—Yes indeed, said Martin, the abbé is right; I was in Paris when Miss Monime herself[2] passed, as they say, from this life to the other; she was refused what these folk call 'the honors of burial,' that is, the right to rot with all the beggars of the district in a dirty cemetery; she was buried all alone by her troupe at the corner of the Rue de Bourgogne; this must have been very disagreeable to her, for she had a noble character.

—That was extremely rude, said Candide.

—What do you expect? said Martin; that is how these folk are. Imagine all the contradictions, all the incompatibilities you can, and you will see them in the government, the courts, the churches, and the plays of this crazy nation.

—Is it true that they are always laughing in Paris? asked Candide.

—Yes, said the abbé, but with a kind of rage too; when people complain of things, they do so amid explosions of laughter; they even laugh as they perform the most detestable actions.

—Who was that fat swine, said Candide, who spoke so nastily about the play over which I was weeping, and the actors who gave me so much pleasure?

—He is a living illness, answered the abbé, who makes a business of slandering all the plays and books; he hates the successful ones, as eunuchs hate successful lovers; he's one of those literary snakes who live on filth and venom; he's a folliculator . . .

—What's this word *folliculator?* asked Candide.

—It's a folio filler, said the abbé, a Fréron.[3]

It was after this fashion that Candide, Martin, and the abbé from Perigord chatted on the stairway as they watched the crowd leaving the theatre.

—Although I'm in a great hurry to see Miss Cunégonde again, said Candide, I would very much like to dine with Miss Clairon,[4] for she seemed to me admirable.

The abbé was not the man to approach Miss Clairon, who saw only good company.

—She has an engagement tonight, he said; but I shall have the honor of introducing you to a lady of quality, and there you will get to know Paris as if you had lived here for years.

Candide, who was curious by nature, allowed himself to be brought to the lady's house, in the depths of the Faubourg St.-Honoré; they were playing faro;[5] twelve melancholy punters held in their hands a little sheaf of cards, blank summaries of their bad luck. Silence reigned supreme, the punters were pallid, the banker uneasy; and the lady of the house, seated beside the pitiless banker, watched with the eyes of a lynx for the various illegal redoublings and bets at long odds which the players tried to signal by folding the corners of their cards; she had them unfolded with a determination which was severe but polite, and concealed her anger lest she lose her customers.

---

2. Adrienne Lecouvreur (1690–1730), so called because she made her debut as Monime in Racine's *Mithridate*. Voltaire had assisted at her secret midnight funeral and wrote an indignant poem about it.   3. A successful and popular journalist, who had attacked several of Voltaire's plays, including *Tancrède*.   4. Actually Claire Leris (1723–1803). She had played the lead role in *Tancrède* and was for many years a leading figure on the Paris stage.   5. A game of cards, about which it is necessary to know only that a number of punters play against a banker or dealer. The pack is dealt out two cards at a time, and each player may bet on any card as much as he pleases. The sharp practices of the punters consist essentially of tricks for increasing their winnings without corresponding risks.

The lady caused herself to be known as the Marquise of Parolignac.[6] Her daughter, fifteen years old, sat among the punters and tipped off her mother with a wink to the sharp practices of these unhappy players when they tried to recoup their losses. The abbé from Perigord, Candide, and Martin came in; nobody arose or greeted them or looked at them; all were lost in the study of their cards.

—My Lady the Baroness of Thunder-Ten-Tronckh was more civil, thought Candide.

However, the abbé whispered in the ear of the marquise, who, half rising, honored Candide with a gracious smile and Martin with a truly noble nod; she gave a seat and dealt a hand of cards to Candide, who lost fifty thousand francs in two turns; after which they had a very merry supper. Everyone was amazed that Candide was not upset over his losses; the lackeys, talking together in their usual lackey language, said:—He must be some English milord.

The supper was like most Parisian suppers: first silence, then an indistinguishable rush of words; then jokes, mostly insipid, false news, bad logic, a little politics, a great deal of malice. They even talked of new books.

—Have you seen the new novel by Dr. Gauchat, the theologian?[7] asked the abbé from Perigord.

—Oh yes, answered one of the guests; but I couldn't finish it. We have a horde of impudent scribblers nowadays, but all of them put together don't match the impudence of this Gauchat, this doctor of theology. I have been so struck by the enormous number of detestable books which are swamping us that I have taken up punting at faro.

—And the *Collected Essays* of Archdeacon T———[8] asked the abbé, what do you think of them?

—Ah, said Madame de Parolignac, what a frightful bore he is! He takes such pains to tell you what everyone knows; he discourses so learnedly on matters which aren't worth a casual remark! He plunders, and not even wittily, the wit of other people! He spoils what he plunders, he's disgusting! But he'll never disgust me again; a couple of pages of the archdeacon have been enough for me.

There was at table a man of learning and taste, who supported the marquise on this point. They talked next of tragedies; the lady asked why there were tragedies which played well enough but which were wholly unreadable. The man of taste explained very clearly how a play could have a certain interest and yet little merit otherwise; he showed succinctly that it was not enough to conduct a couple of intrigues, such as one can find in any novel, and which never fail to excite the spectator's interest; but that one must be new without being grotesque, frequently touch the sublime but never depart from the natural; that one must know the human heart and give it words; that one must be a great poet without allowing any character in the play to sound like a poet; and that one must know the language perfectly, speak it purely, and maintain a continual harmony without ever sacrificing sense to mere sound.

---

6. A *paroli* is an illegal redoubling of one's bet; her name therefore implies a title grounded in cardsharping.
7. He had written against Voltaire, and Voltaire suspected him (wrongly) of having written the novel *L'Oracle des nouveaux philosophes.*   8. His name was Trublet, and he had said, among other disagreeable things, that Voltaire's epic poem, the *Henriade,* made him yawn and that Voltaire's genius was "the perfection of mediocrity."

—Whoever, he added, does not observe all these rules may write one or two tragedies which succeed in the theatre, but he will never be ranked among the good writers; there are very few good tragedies; some are idylls in well-written, well-rhymed dialogue, others are political arguments which put the audience to sleep, or revolting pomposities; still others are the fantasies of enthusiasts, barbarous in style, incoherent in logic, full of long speeches to the gods because the author does not know how to address men, full of false maxims and emphatic commonplaces.

Candide listened attentively to this speech and conceived a high opinion of the speaker; and as the marquise had placed him by her side, he turned to ask her who was this man who spoke so well.

—He is a scholar, said the lady, who never plays cards and whom the abbé sometimes brings to my house for supper; he knows all about tragedies and books, and has himself written a tragedy that was hissed from the stage and a book, the only copy of which ever seen outside his publisher's office was dedicated to me.

—What a great man, said Candide, he's Pangloss all over.

Then, turning to him, he said:—Sir, you doubtless think everything is for the best in the physical as well as the moral universe, and that nothing could be otherwise than as it is?

—Not at all, sir, replied the scholar, I believe nothing of the sort. I find that everything goes wrong in our world; that nobody knows his place in society or his duty, what he's doing or what he ought to be doing, and that outside of mealtimes, which are cheerful and congenial enough, all the rest of the day is spent in useless quarrels, as of Jansenists against Molinists,[9] parliament-men against churchmen, literary men against literary men, courtiers against courtiers, financiers against the plebs, wives against husbands, relatives against relatives—it's one unending warfare.

Candide answered:—I have seen worse; but a wise man, who has since had the misfortune to be hanged, taught me that everything was marvelously well arranged. Troubles are just the shadows in a beautiful picture.

—Your hanged philosopher was joking, said Martin; the shadows are horrible ugly blots.

—It is human beings who make the blots, said Candide, and they can't do otherwise.

—Then it isn't their fault, said Martin.

Most of the faro players, who understood this sort of talk not at all, kept on drinking; Martin disputed with the scholar, and Candide told part of his story to the lady of the house.

After supper, the marquise brought Candide into her room and sat him down on a divan.

—Well, she said to him, are you still madly in love with Miss Cunégonde of Thunder-Ten-Tronckh?

—Yes, ma'am, replied Candide. The marquise turned upon him a tender smile.

—You answer like a young man of Westphalia, said she; a Frenchman would have told me: 'It is true that I have been in love with Miss Cunégonde; but since seeing you, madame, I fear that I love her no longer.'

9. The Jansenists (from Corneille Jansen, 1585–1638) were a relatively strict party of religious reform; the Molinists (from Luis Molina) were the party of the Jesuits. Their central issue of controversy was the relative importance of divine grace and human will to the salvation of man.

—Alas, ma'am, said Candide, I will answer any way you want.

—Your passion for her, said the marquise, began when you picked up her handkerchief; I prefer that you should pick up my garter.

—Gladly, said Candide, and picked it up.

—But I also want you to put it back on, said the lady; and Candide put it on again.

—Look you now, said the lady, you are a foreigner; my Paris lovers I sometimes cause to languish for two weeks or so, but to you I surrender the very first night, because we must render the honors of the country to a young man from Westphalia.

The beauty, who had seen two enormous diamonds on the two hands of her young friend, praised them so sincerely that from the fingers of Candide they passed over to the fingers of the marquise.

As he returned home with his Perigord abbé, Candide felt some remorse at having been unfaithful to Miss Cunégonde; the abbé sympathized with his grief; he had only a small share in the fifty thousand francs which Candide lost at cards, and in the proceeds of the two diamonds which had been half-given, half-extorted. His scheme was to profit, as much as he could, from the advantage of knowing Candide. He spoke at length of Cunégonde, and Candide told him that he would beg forgiveness for his beloved for his infidelity when he met her at Venice.

The Perigordian overflowed with politeness and unction, taking a tender interest in everything Candide said, everything he did, and everything he wanted to do.

—Well, sir, said he, so you have an assignation at Venice?

—Yes indeed, sir, I do, said Candide; it is absolutely imperative that I go there to find Miss Cunégonde.

And then, carried away by the pleasure of talking about his love, he recounted, as he often did, a part of his adventures with that illustrious lady of Westphalia.

—I suppose, said the abbé, that Miss Cunégonde has a fine wit and writes charming letters.

—I never received a single letter from her, said Candide; for, as you can imagine, after being driven out of the castle for love of her, I couldn't write; shortly I learned that she was dead; then I rediscovered her; then I lost her again, and I have now sent, to a place more than twenty-five hundred leagues from here, a special agent whose return I am expecting.

The abbé listened carefully, and looked a bit dreamy. He soon took his leave of the two strangers, after embracing them tenderly. Next day Candide, when he woke up, received a letter, to the following effect:

—Dear sir, my very dear lover, I have been lying sick in this town for a week, I have just learned that you are here. I would fly to your arms if I could move. I heard that you had passed through Bordeaux; that was where I left the faithful Cacambo and the old woman, who are soon to follow me here. The governor of Buenos Aires took everything, but left me your heart. Come; your presence will either return me to life or cause me to die of joy.

This charming letter, coming so unexpectedly, filled Candide with inexpressible delight, while the illness of his dear Cunégonde covered him with grief. Torn between these two feelings, he took gold and diamonds, and had himself brought, with Martin, to the hotel where Miss Cunégonde was lodging. Trembling with emotion, he enters the room; his heart thumps, his voice breaks. He tries to open the curtains of the bed, he asks to have some lights.

—Absolutely forbidden, says the serving girl; light will be the death of her. And abruptly she pulls shut the curtain.

—My dear Cunégonde, says Candide in tears, how are you feeling? If you can't see me, won't you at least speak to me?

—She can't talk, says the servant.

But then she draws forth from the bed a plump hand, over which Candide weeps a long time, and which he fills with diamonds, meanwhile leaving a bag of gold on the chair.

Amid his transports, there arrives a bailiff followed by the abbé from Perigord and a strong-arm squad.

—These here are the suspicious foreigners? says the officer; and he has them seized and orders his bullies to drag them off to jail.

—They don't treat visitors like this in Eldorado, says Candide.

—I am more a Manichee than ever, says Martin.

—But, please sir, where are you taking us? says Candide.

—To the lowest hole in the dungeons, says the bailiff.

Martin, having regained his self-possession, decided that the lady who pretended to be Cunégonde was a cheat, the abbé from Perigord was another cheat who had imposed on Candide's innocence, and the bailiff still another cheat, of whom it would be easy to get rid.

Rather than submit to the forms of justice, Candide, enlightened by Martin's advice and eager for his own part to see the real Cunégonde again, offered the bailiff three little diamonds worth about three thousand pistoles apiece.

—Ah, my dear sir! cried the man with the ivory staff, even if you have committed every crime imaginable, you are the most honest man in the world. Three diamonds! each one worth three thousand pistoles! My dear sir! I would gladly die for you, rather than take you to jail. All foreigners get arrested here; but let me manage it; I have a brother at Dieppe in Normandy; I'll take you to him; and if you have a bit of a diamond to give him, he'll take care of you, just like me.

—And why do they arrest all foreigners? asked Candide.

The abbé from Perigord spoke up and said:—It's because a beggar from Atrebatum[1] listened to some stupidities; that made him commit a parricide, not like the one of May, 1610, but like the one of December, 1594, much on the order of several other crimes committed in other years and other months by other beggars who had listened to stupidities.

The bailiff then explained what it was all about.[2]

—Foh! what beasts! cried Candide. What! monstrous behavior of this sort from a people who sing and dance? As soon as I can, let me get out of this country, where the monkeys provoke the tigers. In my own country I've lived

1. The Latin name for the district of Artois, from which came Robert-François Damiens, who tried to stab Louis XV in 1757. The assassination failed, like that of Châtel, who tried to kill Henri IV in 1594, but unlike that of Ravaillac, who succeeded in killing him in 1610.   2. The point, in fact, is not too clear since arresting foreigners is an indirect way at best to guard against homegrown fanatics, and the position of the abbé from Perigord in the whole transaction remains confused. Has he called in the officer just to get rid of Candide? If so, why is he sardonic about the very suspicions he is trying to foster? Candide's reaction is to the notion that Frenchmen should be capable of political assassination at all; it seems excessive.

with bears; only in Eldorado are there proper men. In the name of God, sir bailiff, get me to Venice where I can wait for Miss Cunégonde.

—I can only get you to Lower Normandy, said the guardsman.

He had the irons removed at once, said there had been a mistake, dismissed his gang, and took Candide and Martin to Dieppe, where he left them with his brother. There was a little Dutch ship at anchor. The Norman, changed by three more diamonds into the most helpful of men, put Candide and his people aboard the vessel, which was bound for Portsmouth in England. It wasn't on the way to Venice, but Candide felt like a man just let out of hell; and he hoped to get back on the road to Venice at the first possible occasion.

CHAPTER 23

Candide and Martin Pass the Shores of England; What They See There

—Ah, Pangloss! Pangloss! Ah, Martin! Martin! Ah, my darling Cunégonde! What is this world of ours? sighed Candide on the Dutch vessel.

—Something crazy, something abominable, Martin replied.

—You have been in England; are people as crazy there as in France?

—It's a different sort of crazy, said Martin. You know that these two nations have been at war over a few acres of snow near Canada, and that they are spending on this fine struggle more than Canada itself is worth.[3] As for telling you if there are more people in one country or the other who need a strait jacket, that is a judgment too fine for my understanding; I know only that the people we are going to visit are eaten up with melancholy.

As they chatted thus, the vessel touched at Portsmouth. A multitude of people covered the shore, watching closely a rather bulky man who was kneeling, his eyes blindfolded, on the deck of a man-of-war. Four soldiers, stationed directly in front of this man, fired three bullets apiece into his brain, as peaceably as you would want; and the whole assemblage went home, in great satisfaction.[4]

—What's all this about? asked Candide. What devil is everywhere at work?

He asked who was that big man who had just been killed with so much ceremony.

—It was an admiral, they told him.

—And why kill this admiral?

—The reason, they told him, is that he didn't kill enough people; he gave battle to a French admiral, and it was found that he didn't get close enough to him.

—But, said Candide, the French admiral was just as far from the English admiral as the English admiral was from the French admiral.

—That's perfectly true, came the answer; but in this country it is useful from time to time to kill one admiral in order to encourage the others.

Candide was so stunned and shocked at what he saw and heard, that he would not even set foot ashore; he arranged with the Dutch merchant (with-

---

3. The wars of the French and English over Canada dragged intermittently through the 18th century till the peace of Paris sealed England's conquest (1763). Voltaire thought the French should concentrate on developing Louisiana, where the Jesuit influence was less marked.   4. Candide has witnessed the execution of Admiral John Byng, defeated off Minorca by the French fleet under Galisonnière and executed by firing squad on March 14, 1757. Voltaire had intervened to avert the execution.

out even caring if he was robbed, as at Surinam) to be taken forthwith to Venice.

The merchant was ready in two days; they coasted along France, they passed within sight of Lisbon, and Candide quivered. They entered the straits, crossed the Mediterranean, and finally landed at Venice.

—God be praised, said Candide, embracing Martin; here I shall recover the lovely Cunégonde. I trust Cacambo as I would myself. All is well, all goes well, all goes as well as possible.

CHAPTER 24

About Paquette and Brother Giroflée

As soon as he was in Venice, he had a search made for Cacambo in all the inns, all the cafés, all the stews—and found no trace of him. Every day he sent to investigate the vessels and coastal traders; no news of Cacambo.

—How's this? said he to Martin. I have had time to go from Surinam to Bordeaux, from Bordeaux to Paris, from Paris to Dieppe, from Dieppe to Portsmouth, to skirt Portugal and Spain, cross the Mediterranean, and spend several months at Venice—and the lovely Cunégonde has not come yet! In her place, I have met only that impersonator and that abbé from Perigord. Cunégonde is dead, without a doubt; and nothing remains for me too but death. Oh, it would have been better to stay in the earthly paradise of Eldorado than to return to this accursed Europe. How right you are, my dear Martin; all is but illusion and disaster.

He fell into a black melancholy, and refused to attend the fashionable operas or take part in the other diversions of the carnival season; not a single lady tempted him in the slightest. Martin told him:—You're a real simpleton if you think a half-breed valet with five or six millions in his pockets will go to the end of the world to get your mistress and bring her to Venice for you. If he finds her, he'll take her for himself; if he doesn't, he'll take another. I advise you to forget about your servant Cacambo and your mistress Cunégonde.

Martin was not very comforting. Candide's melancholy increased, and Martin never wearied of showing him that there is little virtue and little happiness on this earth, except perhaps in Eldorado, where nobody can go.

While they were discussing this important matter and still waiting for Cunégonde, Candide noticed in St. Mark's Square a young Theatine[5] monk who had given his arm to a girl. The Theatine seemed fresh, plump, and flourishing; his eyes were bright, his manner cocky, his glance brilliant, his step proud. The girl was very pretty, and singing aloud; she glanced lovingly at her Theatine, and from time to time pinched his plump cheeks.

—At least you must admit, said Candide to Martin, that these people are happy. Until now I have not found in the whole inhabited earth, except Eldorado, anything but miserable people. But this girl and this monk, I'd be willing to bet, are very happy creatures.

—I'll bet they aren't, said Martin.

—We have only to ask them to dinner, said Candide, and we'll find out if I'm wrong.

Promptly he approached them, made his compliments, and invited them

---

5. A Catholic order founded in 1524 by Cardinal Cajetan and G. P. Caraffa, later Pope Paul IV.

to his inn for a meal of macaroni, Lombardy partridges, and caviar, washed down with wine from Montepulciano, Cyprus, and Samos, and some Lacrima Christi. The girl blushed but the Theatine accepted gladly, and the girl followed him, watching Candide with an expression of surprise and confusion, darkened by several tears. Scarcely had she entered the room when she said to Candide:—What, can it be that Master Candide no longer knows Paquette?

At these words Candide, who had not yet looked carefully at her because he was preoccupied with Cunégonde, said to her:—Ah, my poor child! so you are the one who put Doctor Pangloss in the fine fix where I last saw him.

—Alas, sir, I was the one, said Paquette; I see you know all about it. I heard of the horrible misfortunes which befell the whole household of My Lady the Baroness and the lovely Cunégonde. I swear to you that my own fate has been just as unhappy. I was perfectly innocent when you knew me. A Franciscan, who was my confessor, easily seduced me. The consequences were frightful; shortly after My Lord the Baron had driven you out with great kicks on the backside, I too was forced to leave the castle. If a famous doctor had not taken pity on me, I would have died. Out of gratitude, I became for some time the mistress of this doctor. His wife, who was jealous to the point of frenzy, beat me mercilessly every day; she was a gorgon. The doctor was the ugliest of men, and I the most miserable creature on earth, being continually beaten for a man I did not love. You will understand, sir, how dangerous it is for a nagging woman to be married to a doctor. This man, enraged by his wife's ways, one day gave her as a cold cure a medicine so potent that in two hours' time she died amid horrible convulsions. Her relatives brought suit against the bereaved husband; he fled the country, and I was put in prison. My innocence would never have saved me if I had not been rather pretty. The judge set me free on condition that he should become the doctor's successor. I was shortly replaced in this post by another girl, dismissed without any payment, and obliged to continue this abominable trade which you men find so pleasant and which for us is nothing but a bottomless pit of misery. I went to ply the trade in Venice. Ah, my dear sir, if you could imagine what it is like to have to caress indiscriminately an old merchant, a lawyer, a monk, a gondolier, an abbé; to be subjected to every sort of insult and outrage; to be reduced, time and again, to borrowing a skirt in order to go have it lifted by some disgusting man; to be robbed by this fellow of what one has gained from that; to be shaken down by the police, and to have before one only the prospect of a hideous old age, a hospital, and a dunghill, you will conclude that I am one of the most miserable creatures in the world.

Thus Paquette poured forth her heart to the good Candide in a hotel room, while Martin sat listening nearby. At last he said to Candide:—You see, I've already won half my bet.

Brother Giroflée[6] had remained in the dining room, and was having a drink before dinner.

—But how's this? said Candide to Paquette. You looked so happy, so joyous, when I met you; you were singing, you caressed the Theatine with such a natural air of delight; you seemed to me just as happy as you now say you are miserable.

6. His name means "carnation" and Paquette means "daisy."

—Ah, sir, replied Paquette, that's another one of the miseries of this business; yesterday I was robbed and beaten by an officer, and today I have to seem in good humor in order to please a monk.

Candide wanted no more; he conceded that Martin was right. They sat down to table with Paquette and the Theatine; the meal was amusing enough, and when it was over, the company spoke out among themselves with some frankness.

—Father, said Candide to the monk, you seem to me a man whom all the world might envy; the flower of health glows in your cheek, your features radiate pleasure; you have a pretty girl for your diversion, and you seem very happy with your life as a Theatine.

—Upon my word, sir, said Brother Giroflée, I wish that all the Theatines were at the bottom of the sea. A hundred times I have been tempted to set fire to my convent, and go turn Turk. My parents forced me, when I was fifteen years old, to put on this detestable robe, so they could leave more money to a cursed older brother of mine, may God confound him! Jealousy, faction, and fury spring up, by natural law, within the walls of convents. It is true, I have preached a few bad sermons which earned me a little money, half of which the prior stole from me; the remainder serves to keep me in girls. But when I have to go back to the monastery at night, I'm ready to smash my head against the walls of my cell; and all my fellow monks are in the same fix.

Martin turned to Candide and said with his customary coolness:

—Well, haven't I won the whole bet?

Candide gave two thousand piastres to Paquette and a thousand to Brother Giroflée.

—I assure you, said he, that with that they will be happy.

—I don't believe so, said Martin; your piastres may make them even more unhappy than they were before.

—That may be, said Candide; but one thing comforts me, I note that people often turn up whom one never expected to see again; it may well be that, having rediscovered my red sheep and Paquette, I will also rediscover Cunégonde.

—I hope, said Martin, that she will some day make you happy; but I very much doubt it.

—You're a hard man, said Candide.

—I've lived, said Martin.

—But look at these gondoliers, said Candide; aren't they always singing?

—You don't see them at home, said Martin, with their wives and squalling children. The doge has his troubles, the gondoliers theirs. It's true that on the whole one is better off as a gondolier than as a doge; but the difference is so slight, I don't suppose it's worth the trouble of discussing.

—There's a lot of talk here, said Candide, of this Senator Pococurante,[7] who has a fine palace on the Brenta and is hospitable to foreigners. They say he is a man who has never known a moment's grief.

—I'd like to see such a rare specimen, said Martin.

Candide promptly sent to Lord Pococurante, asking permission to call on him tomorrow.

---

7. His name means "small care."

CHAPTER 25

Visit to Lord Pococurante, Venetian Nobleman

Candide and Martin took a gondola on the Brenta, and soon reached the palace of the noble Pococurante. The gardens were large and filled with beautiful marble statues; the palace was handsomely designed. The master of the house, sixty years old and very rich, received his two inquisitive visitors perfectly politely, but with very little warmth; Candide was disconcerted and Martin not at all displeased.

First two pretty and neatly dressed girls served chocolate, which they whipped to a froth. Candide could not forbear praising their beauty, their grace, their skill.

—They are pretty good creatures, said Pococurante; I sometimes have them into my bed, for I'm tired of the ladies of the town, with their stupid tricks, quarrels, jealousies, fits of ill humor and petty pride, and all the sonnets one has to make or order for them; but, after all, these two girls are starting to bore me too.

After lunch, Candide strolled through a long gallery, and was amazed at the beauty of the pictures. He asked who was the painter of the two finest.

—They are by Raphael, said the senator; I bought them for a lot of money, out of vanity, some years ago; people say they're the finest in Italy, but they don't please me at all; the colors have all turned brown, the figures aren't well modeled and don't stand out enough, the draperies bear no resemblance to real cloth. In a word, whatever people may say, I don't find in them a real imitation of nature. I like a picture only when I can see in it a touch of nature itself, and there are none of this sort. I have many paintings, but I no longer look at them.

As they waited for dinner, Pococurante ordered a concerto performed. Candide found the music delightful.

—That noise? said Pococurante. It may amuse you for half an hour, but if it goes on any longer, it tires everybody though no one dares to admit it. Music today is only the art of performing difficult pieces, and what is merely difficult cannot please for long. Perhaps I should prefer the opera, if they had not found ways to make it revolting and monstrous. Anyone who likes bad tragedies set to music is welcome to them; in these performances the scenes serve only to introduce, inappropriately, two or three ridiculous songs designed to show off the actress's sound box. Anyone who wants to, or who can, is welcome to swoon with pleasure at the sight of a castrate wriggling through the role of Caesar or Cato, and strutting awkwardly about the stage. For my part, I have long since given up these paltry trifles which are called the glory of modern Italy, and for which monarchs pay such ruinous prices.

Candide argued a bit, but timidly; Martin was entirely of a mind with the senator.

They sat down to dinner, and after an excellent meal adjourned to the library. Candide, seeing a copy of Homer in a splendid binding, complimented the noble lord on his good taste.

—That is an author, said he, who was the special delight of great Pangloss, the best philosopher in all Germany.

—He's no special delight of mine, said Pococurante coldly. I was once made to believe that I took pleasure in reading him; but that constant recital of fights which are all alike, those gods who are always interfering but never decisively, that Helen who is the cause of the war and then scarcely takes any part in the story, that Troy which is always under siege and never taken—all that bores me to tears. I have sometimes asked scholars if reading it bored them as much as it bores me; everyone who answered frankly told me the book dropped from his hands like lead, but that they had to have it in their libraries as a monument of antiquity, like those old rusty coins which can't be used in real trade.

Your Excellence doesn't hold the same opinion of Virgil? said Candide.

—I concede, said Pococurante, that the second, fourth, and sixth books of his *Aeneid* are fine; but as for his pious Aeneas, and strong Cloanthes, and faithful Achates, and little Ascanius, and that imbecile King Latinus, and middle-class Amata, and insipid Lavinia, I don't suppose there was ever anything so cold and unpleasant. I prefer Tasso and those sleepwalkers' stories of Ariosto.

—Dare I ask, sir, said Candide, if you don't get great enjoyment from reading Horace?

—There are some maxims there, said Pococurante, from which a man of the world can profit, and which, because they are formed into vigorous couplets, are more easily remembered; but I care very little for his trip to Brindisi, his description of a bad dinner, or his account of a quibblers' squabble between some fellow Pupilus, whose words he says *were full of pus,* and another whose words *were full of vinegar.*[8] I feel nothing but extreme disgust at his verses against old women and witches; and I can't see what's so great in his telling his friend Maecenas that if he is raised by him to the ranks of lyric poets, he will strike the stars with his lofty forehead. Fools admire everything in a well-known author. I read only for my own pleasure; I like only what is in my style.

Candide, who had been trained never to judge for himself, was much astonished by what he heard; and Martin found Pococurante's way of thinking quite rational.

—Oh, here is a copy of Cicero, said Candide. Now this great man I suppose you're never tired of reading.

—I never read him at all, replied the Venetian. What do I care whether he pleaded for Rabirius or Cluentius? As a judge, I have my hands full of lawsuits. I might like his philosophical works better, but when I saw that he had doubts about everything, I concluded that I knew as much as he did, and that I needed no help to be ignorant.

—Ah, here are eighty volumes of collected papers from a scientific academy, cried Martin; maybe there is something good in them.

—There would be indeed, said Pococurante, if one of these silly authors had merely discovered a new way of making pins; but in all those volumes there is nothing but empty systems, not a single useful discovery.

—What a lot of stage plays I see over there, said Candide, some in Italian, some in Spanish and French.

—Yes, said the senator, three thousand of them, and not three dozen good

8. *Satires* I.vii; Pococurante, with gentlemanly negligence, has corrupted Rupilius to Pupilus. Horace's poems against witches are *Epodes* V, VIII, XII; the one about striking the stars with his lofty forehead is *Odes* I.i.

ones. As for those collections of sermons, which all together are not worth a page of Seneca, and all these heavy volumes of theology, you may be sure I never open them, nor does anybody else.

Martin noticed some shelves full of English books.

—I suppose, said he, that a republican must delight in most of these books written in the land of liberty.

—Yes, replied Pococurante, it's a fine thing to write as you think; it is mankind's privilege. In all our Italy, people write only what they do not think; men who inhabit the land of the Caesars and Antonines dare not have an idea without the permission of a Dominican. I would rejoice in the freedom that breathes through English genius, if partisan passions did not corrupt all that is good in that precious freedom.

Candide, noting a Milton, asked if he did not consider this author a great man.

—Who? said Pococurante. That barbarian who made a long commentary on the first chapter of Genesis in ten books of crabbed verse?[9] That clumsy imitator of the Greeks, who disfigures creation itself, and while Moses represents the eternal being as creating the world with a word, has the messiah take a big compass out of a heavenly cupboard in order to design his work? You expect me to admire the man who spoiled Tasso's hell and devil? who disguises Lucifer now as a toad, now as a pigmy? who makes him rehash the same arguments a hundred times over? who makes him argue theology? and who, taking seriously Ariosto's comic story of the invention of firearms, has the devils shooting off cannon in heaven? Neither I nor anyone else in Italy has been able to enjoy these gloomy extravagances. The marriage of Sin and Death, and the monster that Sin gives birth to, will nauseate any man whose taste is at all refined; and his long description of a hospital is good only for a gravedigger. This obscure, extravagant, and disgusting poem was despised at its birth; I treat it today as it was treated in its own country by its contemporaries. Anyhow, I say what I think, and care very little whether other people agree with me.

Candide was a little cast down by this speech; he respected Homer, and had a little affection for Milton.

—Alas, he said under his breath to Martin, I'm afraid this man will have a supreme contempt for our German poets.

—No harm in that, said Martin.

—Oh what a superior man, said Candide, still speaking softly, what a great genius this Pococurante must be! Nothing can please him.

Having thus looked over all the books, they went down into the garden. Candide praised its many beauties.

—I know nothing in such bad taste, said the master of the house; we have nothing but trifles here; tomorrow I am going to have one set out on a nobler design.

When the two visitors had taken leave of his excellency:—Well now, said Candide to Martin, you must agree that this was the happiest of all men, for he is superior to everything he possesses.

—Don't you see, said Martin, that he is disgusted with everything he possesses? Plato said, a long time ago, that the best stomachs are not those which refuse all food.

---

9. The first edition of *Paradise Lost* had ten books, which Milton later expanded to twelve.

—But, said Candide, isn't there pleasure in criticizing everything, in seeing faults where other people think they see beauties?

—That is to say, Martin replied, that there's pleasure in having no pleasure?

—Oh well, said Candide, then I am the only happy man . . . or will be, when I see Miss Cunégonde again.

—It's always a good thing to have hope, said Martin.

But the days and the weeks slipped past; Cacambo did not come back, and Candide was so buried in his grief, that he did not even notice that Paquette and Brother Giroflée had neglected to come and thank him.

CHAPTER 26

About a Supper that Candide and Martin Had with Six Strangers, and Who They Were

One evening when Candide, accompanied by Martin, was about to sit down for dinner with the strangers staying in his hotel, a man with a soot-colored face came up behind him, took him by the arm, and said:—Be ready to leave with us, don't miss out.

He turned and saw Cacambo. Only the sight of Cunégonde could have astonished and pleased him more. He nearly went mad with joy. He embraced his dear friend.

—Cunégonde is here, no doubt? Where is she? Bring me to her, let me die of joy in her presence.

—Cunégonde is not here at all, said Cacambo, she is at Constantinople.

—Good Heavens, at Constantinople! but if she were in China, I must fly there, let's go.

—We will leave after supper, said Cacambo; I can tell you no more; I am a slave, my owner is looking for me, I must go wait on him at table; mum's the word; eat your supper and be prepared.

Candide, torn between joy and grief, delighted to have seen his faithful agent again, astonished to find him a slave, full of the idea of recovering his mistress, his heart in a turmoil, his mind in a whirl, sat down to eat with Martin, who was watching all these events coolly, and with six strangers who had come to pass the carnival season at Venice.

Cacambo, who was pouring wine for one of the strangers, leaned respect-fully over his master at the end of the meal, and said to him:—Sire, Your Majesty may leave when he pleases, the vessel is ready.

Having said these words, he exited. The diners looked at one another in silent amazement, when another servant, approaching his master, said to him:—Sire, Your Majesty's litter is at Padua, and the bark awaits you.

The master nodded, and the servant vanished. All the diners looked at one another again, and the general amazement redoubled. A third servant, approaching a third stranger, said to him:—Sire, take my word for it, Your Majesty must stay here no longer; I shall get everything ready.

Then he too disappeared.

Candide and Martin had no doubt, now, that it was a carnival masquerade. A fourth servant spoke to a fourth master:—Your Majesty will leave when he pleases—and went out like the others. A fifth followed suit. But the sixth servant spoke differently to the sixth stranger, who sat next to Candide. He said:—My word, sire, they'll give no more credit to Your Majesty, nor to me either; we could very well spend the night in the lockup, you and I. I've got to look out for myself, so good-bye to you.

When all the servants had left, the six strangers, Candide, and Martin remained under a pall of silence. Finally Candide broke it.

—Gentlemen, said he, here's a funny kind of joke. Why are you all royalty? I assure you that Martin and I aren't.

Cacambo's master spoke up gravely then, and said in Italian:—This is no joke, my name is Achmet the Third.[1] I was grand sultan for several years; then, as I had dethroned my brother, my nephew dethroned me. My viziers had their throats cut; I was allowed to end my days in the old seraglio. My nephew, the Grand Sultan Mahmoud, sometimes lets me travel for my health; and I have come to spend the carnival season at Venice.

A young man who sat next to Achmet spoke after him, and said:—My name is Ivan; I was once emperor of all the Russias.[2] I was dethroned while still in my cradle; my father and mother were locked up, and I was raised in prison; I sometimes have permission to travel, though always under guard, and I have come to spend the carnival season at Venice.

The third said:—I am Charles Edward, king of England;[3] my father yielded me his rights to the kingdom, and I fought to uphold them; but they tore out the hearts of eight hundred of my partisans, and flung them in their faces. I have been in prison; now I am going to Rome, to visit the king, my father, dethroned like me and my grandfather; and I have come to pass the carnival season at Venice.

The fourth king then spoke up, and said:—I am a king of the Poles;[4] the luck of war has deprived me of my hereditary estates; my father suffered the same losses; I submit to Providence like Sultan Achmet, Emperor Ivan, and King Charles Edward, to whom I hope heaven grants long lives; and I have come to pass the carnival season at Venice.

The fifth said:—I too am a king of the Poles;[5] I lost my kingdom twice, but Providence gave me another state, in which I have been able to do more good than all the Sarmatian kings ever managed to do on the banks of the Vistula. I too have submitted to Providence, and I have come to pass the carnival season at Venice.

It remained for the sixth monarch to speak.

—Gentlemen, said he, I am no such great lord as you, but I have in fact been a king like any other. I am Theodore; I was elected king of Corsica.[6] People used to call me *Your Majesty,* and now they barely call me *Sir;* I used to coin currency, and now I don't have a cent; I used to have two secretaries of state, and now I scarcely have a valet; I have sat on a throne, and for a long time in London I was in jail, on the straw; and I may well be treated the same way here, though I have come, like your majesties, to pass the carnival season at Venice.

The five other kings listened to his story with noble compassion. Each

---

1. Ottoman ruler (1673–1736); he was deposed in 1730.   2. Ivan VI reigned from his birth in 1740 until 1756, then was confined in the Schlusselberg, and executed in 1764.   3. This is the Young Pretender (1720–1788), known to his supporters as Bonnie Prince Charlie. The defeat so theatrically described took place at Culloden, April 16, 1746.   4. Augustus III (1696–1763), Elector of Saxony and King of Poland, dethroned by Frederick the Great in 1756.   5. Stanislas Leczinski (1677–1766), father-in-law of Louis XV, who abdicated the throne of Poland in 1736, was made Duke of Lorraine and in that capacity befriended Voltaire.   6. Theodore von Neuhof (1690–1756), an authentic Westphalian, an adventurer and a soldier of fortune, who in 1736 was (for about eight months) the elected king of Corsica. He spent time in an Amsterdam as well as a London debtor's prison.

one of them gave twenty sequins to King Theodore, so that he might buy a suit and some shirts; Candide gave him a diamond worth two thousand sequins.

—Who in the world, said the five kings, is this private citizen who is in a position to give a hundred times as much as any of us, and who actually gives it?[7]

Just as they were rising from dinner, there arrived at the same establishment four most serene highnesses, who had also lost their kingdoms through the luck of war, and who came to spend the rest of the carnival season at Venice. But Candide never bothered even to look at these newcomers because he was only concerned to go find his dear Cunégonde at Constantinople.

CHAPTER 27

Candide's Trip to Constantinople

Faithful Cacambo had already arranged with the Turkish captain who was returning Sultan Achmet to Constantinople to make room for Candide and Martin on board. Both men boarded ship after prostrating themselves before his miserable highness. On the way, Candide said to Martin:—Six dethroned kings that we had dinner with! and yet among those six there was one on whom I had to bestow charity! Perhaps there are other princes even more unfortunate. I myself have only lost a hundred sheep, and now I am flying to the arms of Cunégonde. My dear Martin, once again Pangloss is proved right, all is for the best.

—I hope so, said Martin.

—But, said Candide, that was a most unlikely experience we had at Venice. Nobody ever saw, or heard tell of, six dethroned kings eating together at an inn.

—It is no more extraordinary, said Martin, than most of the things that have happened to us. Kings are frequently dethroned; and as for the honor we had from dining with them, that's a trifle which doesn't deserve our notice.[8]

Scarcely was Candide on board than he fell on the neck of his former servant, his friend Cacambo.

—Well! said he, what is Cunégonde doing? Is she still a marvel of beauty? Does she still love me? How is her health? No doubt you have bought her a palace at Constantinople.

—My dear master, answered Cacambo, Cunégonde is washing dishes on the shores of the Propontis, in the house of a prince who has very few dishes

---

7. A late correction of Voltaire's makes this passage read:

> —Who is this man who is in a position to give a hundred times as much as any of us, and who actually gives it? Are you a king too, sir?
> —No, gentlemen, and I have no desire to be.

But this reading, though Voltaire's on good authority, produces a conflict with Candide's previous remark:—Why are you all royalty? I assure you that Martin and I aren't.
Thus, it has seemed better for literary reasons to follow an earlier reading. Voltaire was very conscious of his situation as a man richer than many princes; in 1758 he had money on loan to no fewer than three highnesses, Charles Eugene, Duke of Wurtemburg; Charles Theodore, Elector Palatine; and the Duke of Saxe-Gotha.   8. Another late change adds the following question:—*What does it matter whom you dine with as long as you fare well at table?* I have omitted it, again on literary grounds.

to wash; she is a slave in the house of a onetime king named Ragotski,[9] to whom the Great Turk allows three crowns a day in his exile; but, what is worse than all this, she has lost all her beauty and become horribly ugly.

—Ah, beautiful or ugly, said Candide, I am an honest man, and my duty is to love her forever. But how can she be reduced to this wretched state with the five or six millions that you had?

—All right, said Cacambo, didn't I have to give two millions to Señor don Fernando d'Ibaraa y Figueroa y Mascarenes y Lampourdos y Souza, governor of Buenos Aires, for his permission to carry off Miss Cunégonde? And didn't a pirate cleverly strip us of the rest? And didn't this pirate carry us off to Cape Matapan, to Melos, Nicaria, Samos, Petra, to the Dardanelles, Marmora, Scutari? Cunégonde and the old woman are working for the prince I told you about, and I am the slave of the dethroned sultan.

—What a lot of fearful calamities linked one to the other, said Candide. But after all, I still have a few diamonds, I shall easily deliver Cunégonde. What a pity that she's become so ugly!

Then, turning toward Martin, he asked:—Who in your opinion is more to be pitied, the Emperor Achmet, the Emperor Ivan, King Charles Edward, or myself?

—I have no idea, said Martin; I would have to enter your hearts in order to tell.

—Ah, said Candide, if Pangloss were here, he would know and he would tell us.

—I can't imagine, said Martin, what scales your Pangloss would use to weigh out the miseries of men and value their griefs. All I will venture is that the earth holds millions of men who deserve our pity a hundred times more than King Charles Edward, Emperor Ivan, or Sultan Achmet.

—You may well be right, said Candide.

In a few days they arrived at the Black Sea canal. Candide began by repurchasing Cacambo at an exorbitant price; then, without losing an instant, he flung himself and his companions into a galley to go search out Cunégonde on the shores of Propontis, however ugly she might be.

There were in the chain gang two convicts who bent clumsily to the oar, and on whose bare shoulders the Levantine[1] captain delivered from time to time a few lashes with a bullwhip. Candide naturally noticed them more than the other galley slaves, and out of pity came closer to them. Certain features of their disfigured faces seemed to him to bear a slight resemblance to Pangloss and to that wretched Jesuit, that baron, that brother of Miss Cunégonde. The notion stirred and saddened him. He looked at them more closely.

—To tell you the truth, he said to Cacambo, if I hadn't seen Master Pangloss hanged, and if I hadn't been so miserable as to murder the baron, I should think they were rowing in this very galley.

At the names of 'baron' and 'Pangloss' the two convicts gave a great cry, sat still on their bench, and dropped their oars. The Levantine captain came running, and the bullwhip lashes redoubled.

—Stop, stop, captain, cried Candide. I'll give you as much money as you want.

9. Francis Leopold Rakoczy (1676–1735), who was briefly king of Transylvania in the early 18th century. After 1720 he was interned in Turkey.   1. From the eastern Mediterranean.

—What, can it be Candide? cried one of the convicts.

—What, can it be Candide? cried the other.

—Is this a dream? said Candide. Am I awake or asleep? Am I in this galley? Is that My Lord the Baron, whom I killed? Is that Master Pangloss, whom I saw hanged?

—It is indeed, they replied.

—What, is that the great philosopher? said Martin.

—Now, sir, Mr. Levantine Captain, said Candide, how much money do you want for the ransom of My Lord Thunder-Ten-Tronckh, one of the first barons of the empire, and Master Pangloss, the deepest metaphysician in all Germany?

—Dog of a Christian, replied the Levantine captain, since these two dogs of Christian convicts are barons and metaphysicians, which is no doubt a great honor in their country, you will give me fifty thousand sequins for them.

—You shall have them, sir, take me back to Constantinople and you shall be paid on the spot. Or no, take me to Miss Cunégonde.

The Levantine captain, at Candide's first word, had turned his bow toward the town, and he had them rowed there as swiftly as a bird cleaves the air.

A hundred times Candide embraced the baron and Pangloss.

—And how does it happen I didn't kill you, my dear baron? and my dear Pangloss, how can you be alive after being hanged? and why are you both rowing in the galleys of Turkey?

—Is it really true that my dear sister is in this country? asked the baron.

—Yes, answered Cacambo.

—And do I really see again my dear Candide? cried Pangloss.

Candide introduced Martin and Cacambo. They all embraced; they all talked at once. The galley flew, already they were back in port. A Jew was called, and Candide sold him for fifty thousand sequins a diamond worth a hundred thousand, while he protested by Abraham that he could not possibly give more for it. Candide immediately ransomed the baron and Pangloss. The latter threw himself at the feet of his liberator, and bathed them with tears; the former thanked him with a nod, and promised to repay this bit of money at the first opportunity.

—But is it really possible that my sister is in Turkey? said he.

—Nothing is more possible, replied Cacambo, since she is a dishwasher in the house of a prince of Transylvania.

At once two more Jews were called; Candide sold some more diamonds; and they all departed in another galley to the rescue of Cunégonde.

CHAPTER 28

What Happened to Candide, Cunégonde, Pangloss, Martin, &c.

—Let me beg your pardon once more, said Candide to the baron, pardon me, reverend father, for having run you through the body with my sword.

—Don't mention it, replied the baron. I was a little too hasty myself, I confess it; but since you want to know the misfortune which brought me to the galleys, I'll tell you. After being cured of my wound by the brother who was apothecary to the college, I was attacked and abducted by a Spanish raiding party; they jailed me in Buenos Aires at the time when my sister had just left. I asked to be sent to Rome, to the father general. Instead, I was named to serve as almoner in Constantinople, under the French ambassador. I had not been a week on this job when I chanced one evening on a very handsome young ichoglan.[2] The evening was hot; the young man wanted to take a swim; I seized the occasion, and went with him. I did not know that it is a capital offense for a Christian to be found naked with a young Moslem. A cadi sentenced me to receive a hundred blows with a cane on the soles of my feet, and then to be sent to the galleys. I don't suppose there was ever such a horrible miscarriage of justice. But I would like to know why my sister is in the kitchen of a Transylvanian king exiled among Turks.

—But how about you, my dear Pangloss, said Candide; how is it possible that we have met again?

—It is true, said Pangloss, that you saw me hanged; in the normal course of things, I should have been burned, but you recall that a cloudburst occurred just as they were about to roast me. So much rain fell that they despaired of lighting the fire; thus I was hanged, for lack of anything better to do with me. A surgeon bought my body, carried me off to his house, and dissected me. First he made a cross-shaped incision in me, from the navel to the clavicle. No one could have been worse hanged than I was. In fact, the executioner of the high ceremonials of the Holy Inquisition, who was a subdeacon, burned people marvelously well, but he was not in the way of hanging them. The rope was wet, and tightened badly; it caught on a knot; in short, I was still breathing. The cross-shaped incision made me scream so loudly that the surgeon fell over backwards; he thought he was dissecting the devil, fled in an agony of fear, and fell downstairs in his flight. His wife ran in, at the noise, from a nearby room; she found me stretched out on the table with my cross-shaped incision, was even more frightened than her husband, fled, and fell over him. When they had recovered a little, I heard her say to him: 'My dear, what were you thinking of, trying to dissect a heretic? Don't you know those people are always possessed of the devil? I'm going to get the priest and have him exorcised.' At these words, I shuddered, and collected my last remaining energies to cry: 'Have mercy on me!' At last the Portuguese barber[3] took courage; he sewed me up again; his wife even nursed me; in two weeks I was up and about. The barber found me a job and made me lackey to a Knight of Malta who was going to Venice; and when this master could no longer pay me, I took service under a Venetian merchant, whom I followed to Constantinople.

—One day it occurred to me to enter a mosque; no one was there but an old imam and a very attractive young worshipper who was saying her prayers. Her bosom was completely bare; and between her two breasts she had a lovely bouquet of tulips, roses, anemones, buttercups, hyacinths, and primroses. She dropped her bouquet, I picked it up, and returned it to her with the most respectful attentions. I was so long getting it back in place that the imam grew angry, and, seeing that I was a Christian, he called the guard. They took me before the cadi, who sentenced me to receive a hundred blows with a cane on the soles of my feet, and then to be sent to the galleys. I was chained to the same galley and precisely the same bench as My Lord the Baron. There were in this galley four young fellows from Marseilles, five

---

2. A page to the sultan.   3. The two callings of barber and surgeon, since they both involved sharp instruments, were interchangeable in the early days of medicine.

Neapolitan priests, and two Corfu monks, who assured us that these things happen every day. My Lord the Baron asserted that he had suffered a greater injustice than I; I, on the other hand, proposed that it was much more permissible to replace a bouquet in a bosom than to be found naked with an ichoglan. We were arguing the point continually, and getting twenty lashes a day with the bullwhip, when the chain of events within this universe brought you to our galley, and you ransomed us.

—Well, my dear Pangloss, Candide said to him, now that you have been hanged, dissected, beaten to a pulp, and sentenced to the galleys, do you still think everything is for the best in this world?

—I am still of my first opinion, replied Pangloss; for after all I am a philosopher, and it would not be right for me to recant since Leibniz could not possibly be wrong, and besides pre-established harmony is the finest notion in the world, like the plenum and subtle matter.[4]

CHAPTER 29

How Candide Found Cunégonde and the Old Woman Again

While Candide, the baron, Pangloss, Martin, and Cacambo were telling one another their stories, while they were disputing over the contingent or non-contingent events of this universe, while they were arguing over effects and causes, over moral evil and physical evil, over liberty and necessity, and over the consolations available to one in a Turkish galley, they arrived at the shores of Propontis and the house of the prince of Transylvania. The first sight to meet their eyes was Cunégonde and the old woman, who were hanging out towels on lines to dry.

The baron paled at what he saw. The tender lover Candide, seeing his lovely Cunégonde with her skin weathered, her eyes bloodshot, her breasts fallen, her cheeks seamed, her arms red and scaly, recoiled three steps in horror, and then advanced only out of politeness. She embraced Candide and her brother; everyone embraced the old woman; Candide ransomed them both.

There was a little farm in the neighborhood; the old woman suggested that Candide occupy it until some better fate should befall the group. Cunégonde did not know she was ugly, no one had told her; she reminded Candide of his promises in so firm a tone that the good Candide did not dare to refuse her. So he went to tell the baron that he was going to marry his sister.

—Never will I endure, said the baron, such baseness on her part, such insolence on yours; this shame at least I will not put up with; why, my sister's children would not be able to enter the Chapters in Germany.[5] No, my sister will never marry anyone but a baron of the empire.

Cunégonde threw herself at his feet, and bathed them with her tears; he was inflexible.

—You absolute idiot, Candide told him, I rescued you from the galleys, I paid your ransom, I paid your sister's; she was washing dishes, she is ugly, I

---

4. Rigorous determinism requires that there be no empty spaces in the universe, so wherever it seems empty, one posits the existence of the "plenum." "Subtle matter" describes the soul, the mind, and all spiritual agencies—which can, therefore, be supposed subject to the influence and control of the great world machine, which is, of course, visibly material. Both are concepts needed to round out the system of optimistic determinism.   **5.** Knightly assemblies.

am good enough to make her my wife, and you still presume to oppose it! If I followed my impulses, I would kill you all over again.

—You may kill me again, said the baron, but you will not marry my sister while I am alive.

CHAPTER 30

Conclusion

At heart, Candide had no real wish to marry Cunégonde; but the baron's extreme impertinence decided him in favor of the marriage, and Cunégonde was so eager for it that he could not back out. He consulted Pangloss, Martin, and the faithful Cacambo. Pangloss drew up a fine treatise, in which he proved that the baron had no right over his sister and that she could, according to all the laws of the empire, marry Candide morganatically.[6] Martin said they should throw the baron into the sea. Cacambo thought they should send him back to the Levantine captain to finish his time in the galleys, and then send him to the father general in Rome by the first vessel. This seemed the best idea; the old woman approved, and nothing was said to his sister; the plan was executed, at modest expense, and they had the double pleasure of snaring a Jesuit and punishing the pride of a German baron.

It is quite natural to suppose that after so many misfortunes, Candide, married to his mistress, and living with the philosopher Pangloss, the philosopher Martin, the prudent Cacambo, and the old woman—having, besides, brought back so many diamonds from the land of the ancient Incas—must have led the most agreeable life in the world. But he was so cheated by the Jews[7] that nothing was left but his little farm; his wife, growing every day more ugly, became sour-tempered and insupportable; the old woman was ailing and even more ill-humored than Cunégonde. Cacambo, who worked in the garden and went into Constantinople to sell vegetables, was worn out with toil, and cursed his fate. Pangloss was in despair at being unable to shine in some German university. As for Martin, he was firmly persuaded that things are just as bad wherever you are; he endured in patience. Candide, Martin, and Pangloss sometimes argued over metaphysics and morals. Before the windows of the farmhouse they often watched the passage of boats bearing effendis, pashas, and cadis into exile on Lemnos, Mytilene, and Erzeroum; they saw other cadis, other pashas, other effendis coming, to take the place of the exiles and to be exiled in their turn. They saw various heads, neatly impaled, to be set up at the Sublime Porte.[8] These sights gave fresh impetus to their discussions; and when they were not arguing, the boredom was so fierce that one day the old woman ventured to say:—

I should like to know which is worse, being raped a hundred times by negro pirates, having a buttock cut off, running the gauntlet in the Bulgar army, being flogged and hanged in an auto-da-fé, being dissected and rowing in the galleys—experiencing, in a word, all the miseries through which we have passed—or else just sitting here and doing nothing?

---

6. A morganatic marriage confers no rights on the partner of lower rank or on the offspring.   7. Voltaire's anti-Semitism, derived from various unhappy experiences with Jewish financiers, is not the most attractive aspect of his personality.   8. The gate of the sultan's palace is often used by extension to describe his government as a whole. But it was in fact a real gate where the heads of traitors and public enemies were gruesomely exposed.

—It's a hard question, said Candide.

These words gave rise to new reflections, and Martin in particular concluded that man was bound to live either in convulsions of misery or in the lethargy of boredom. Candide did not agree, but expressed no positive opinion. Pangloss asserted that he had always suffered horribly; but having once declared that everything was marvelously well, he continued to repeat the opinion and didn't believe a word of it.

One thing served to confirm Martin in his detestable opinions, to make Candide hesitate more than ever, and to embarrass Pangloss. It was the arrival one day at their farm of Paquette and Brother Giroflée, who were in the last stages of misery. They had quickly run through their three thousand piastres, had split up, made up, quarreled, been jailed, escaped, and finally Brother Giroflée had turned Turk. Paquette continued to ply her trade everywhere, and no longer made any money at it.

—I told you, said Martin to Candide, that your gifts would soon be squandered and would only render them more unhappy. You have spent millions of piastres, you and Cacambo, and you are no more happy than Brother Giroflée and Paquette.

—Ah ha, said Pangloss to Paquette, so destiny has brought you back in our midst, my poor girl! Do you realize you cost me the end of my nose, one eye, and an ear? And look at you now! eh! what a world it is, after all!

This new adventure caused them to philosophize more than ever.

There was in the neighborhood a very famous dervish, who was said to be the best philosopher in Turkey; they went to ask his advice. Pangloss was spokesman, and he said:—Master, we have come to ask you to tell us why such a strange animal as man was created.

—What are you getting into? answered the dervish. Is it any of your business?

—But, reverend father, said Candide, there's a horrible lot of evil on the face of the earth.

—What does it matter, said the dervish, whether there's good or evil? When his highness sends a ship to Egypt, does he worry whether the mice on board are comfortable or not?

—What shall we do then? asked Pangloss.

—Hold your tongue, said the dervish.

—I had hoped, said Pangloss, to reason a while with you concerning effects and causes, the best of possible worlds, the origin of evil, the nature of the soul, and pre-established harmony.

At these words, the dervish slammed the door in their faces.

During this interview, word was spreading that at Constantinople they had just strangled two viziers of the divan,[9] as well as the mufti, and impaled several of their friends. This catastrophe made a great and general sensation for several hours. Pangloss, Candide, and Martin, as they returned to their little farm, passed a good old man who was enjoying the cool of the day at his doorstep under a grove of orange trees. Pangloss, who was as inquisitive as he was explanatory, asked the name of the mufti who had been strangled.

—I know nothing of it, said the good man, and I have never cared to know the name of a single mufti or vizier. I am completely ignorant of the episode

---

9. Intimate advisers of the sultan.

you are discussing. I presume that in general those who meddle in public business sometimes perish miserably, and that they deserve their fate; but I never listen to the news from Constantinople; I am satisfied with sending the fruits of my garden to be sold there.

Having spoken these words, he asked the strangers into his house; his two daughters and two sons offered them various sherbets which they had made themselves, Turkish cream flavored with candied citron, orange, lemon, lime, pineapple, pistachio, and mocha coffee uncontaminated by the inferior coffee of Batavia and the East Indies. After which the two daughters of this good Moslem perfumed the beards of Candide, Pangloss, and Martin.

—You must possess, Candide said to the Turk, an enormous and splendid property?

I have only twenty acres, replied the Turk; I cultivate them with my children, and the work keeps us from three great evils, boredom, vice, and poverty.

Candide, as he walked back to his farm, meditated deeply over the words of the Turk. He said to Pangloss and Martin:—This good old man seems to have found himself a fate preferable to that of the six kings with whom we had the honor of dining.

—Great place, said Pangloss, is very perilous in the judgment of all the philosophers; for, after all, Eglon, king of the Moabites, was murdered by Ehud; Absalom was hung up by the hair and pierced with three darts; King Nadab, son of Jeroboam, was killed by Baasha; King Elah by Zimri; Ahaziah by Jehu; Athaliah by Jehoiada; and Kings Jehoiakim, Jeconiah, and Zedekiah were enslaved. You know how death came to Croesus, Astyages, Darius, Dionysius of Syracuse, Pyrrhus, Perseus, Hannibal, Jugurtha, Ariovistus, Caesar, Pompey, Nero, Otho, Vitellius, Domitian, Richard II of England, Edward II, Henry VI, Richard III, Mary Stuart, Charles I, the three Henrys of France, and the Emperor Henry IV? You know . . .

—I know also, said Candide, that we must cultivate our garden.

—You are perfectly right, said Pangloss; for when man was put into the garden of Eden, he was put there *ut operaretur eum*, so that he should work it; this proves that man was not born to take his ease.

—Let's work without speculation, said Martin; it's the only way of rendering life bearable

The whole little group entered into this laudable scheme; each one began to exercise his talents. The little plot yielded fine crops. Cunégonde was, to tell the truth, remarkably ugly; but she became an excellent pastry cook. Paquette took up embroidery; the old woman did the laundry. Everyone, down even to Brother Giroflée, did something useful; he became a very adequate carpenter, and even an honest man; and Pangloss sometimes used to say to Candide:—All events are linked together in the best of possible worlds' for, after all, if you had not been driven from a fine castle by being kicked in the backside for love of Miss Cunégonde, if you hadn't been sent before the Inquisition, if you hadn't traveled across America on foot, if you hadn't given a good sword thrust to the baron, if you hadn't lost all your sheep from the good land of Eldorado, you wouldn't be sitting here eating candied citron and pistachios.

—That is very well put, said Candide, but we must cultivate our garden.

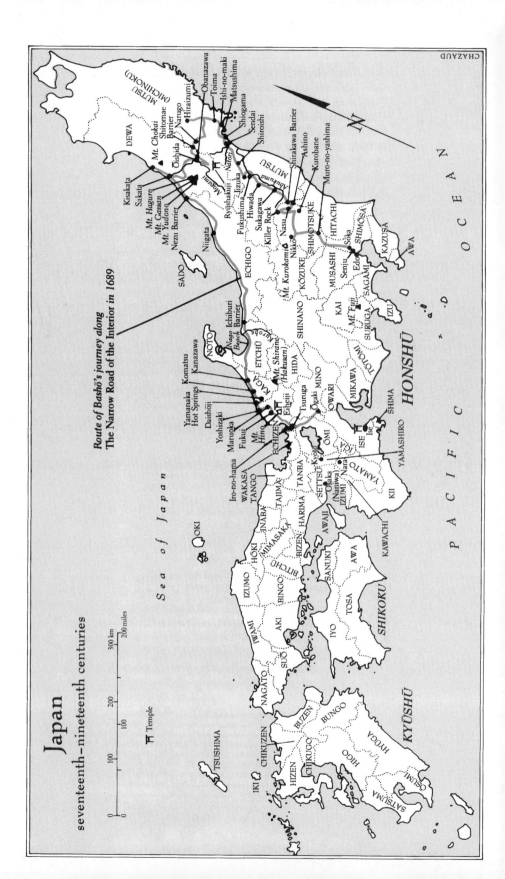

Japan

seventeenth–nineteenth centuries

Route of Bashō's journey along
The Narrow Road of the Interior in 1689

⛩ Temple

0   100   200   300 km
0   100   200 miles

Sea of Japan

PACIFIC OCEAN

HONSHŪ

SHIKOKU

KYŪSHŪ

MUTSU (MICHINOKU)

DEWA

ECHIGO

SADO

OKI

TSUSHIMA

IKI

CHAZAUD

The Rise of Popular Arts
in Premodern Japan

In one of the grand ironies of history, Japan—a country whose prosperity now depends on intense cultivation of foreign markets—began its so-called early modern era as a world recluse. Its leaders chose to seal Japan from foreign influence, fearful that the toehold European traders and Christian missionaries had been gaining in Japan from the mid-sixteenth century through the early seventeenth would end up undermining their political control.

Since the late twelfth century, in the wake of the civil war chronicled in *The Tale of the Heike* (see Volume B), Japan had been governed by a series of military clans who held de facto power as peacekeepers and national administrators on behalf of the emperor, the formal if politically emasculated sovereign. In some periods the reigning military house succeeded as peacekeeper. In others, the country lapsed into disorder as rival clans jousted for supremacy. Gradually, the country splintered until chaos and bloodshed descended on Japan during 150 unruly years lasting from 1467 until the opening of the seventeenth century, when one clan, the Tokugawa, managed to dominate its rivals and thereby reunify the nation under strict but peaceful rule.

The Tokugawa shoguns quickly decided that the foreigners must go. They had seen the Portuguese missionaries play one feudal baron against another and, worse, claim to represent a higher authority to which the converted ranks must ultimately submit. In 1639, therefore, the government of Japan announced a policy of national seclusion. European traders and Christian missionaries were given a choice of expulsion or execution. The building of ocean-going vessels was prohibited, and any Japanese intrepid enough to venture abroad faced certain death if he got homesick. The country closed in on itself for two and a half centuries and, far from withering from a lack of outside stimulation, experienced one of its headiest periods of cultural ferment.

In sum, the shogunal authorities tried to stop time by freezing political, social, and economic conditions in a status quo that favored their predominance. For a remarkably long interval they did succeed in eradicating foreign influence. But they never succeeded in stopping time. When peace and stability returned to Japan, a new class quickly rose in economic and cultural significance. It was a bourgeois, mercantile class, and it came into being as the inevitable consequence of the new political administration. The shogun's vast bureaucracy was staffed by *samurai* retainers. With no more wars to fight, these former soldiers became bureaucrats, and with a government to run they clustered in the cities. Removed from the land and their previous military and agricultural pursuits, the urban *samurai* developed new needs, which were promptly met by enterprising merchants, artisans, and laborers whose numbers swelled in response to economic opportunity. City life and long-distance transport eventually made rice an unwieldy medium of exchange. Coin took its place in business transactions, and the growth of a money economy had a slow but irreversible effect on every aspect of Japanese life. Although the new commercial class was denied access to the political system, as the nation's bankers and suppliers it increasingly held the real power, which was financial.

583

These aggressive, upstart merchants were not hidebound by the traditions of another age, as could be said of both the *samurai* and their political predecessors, the sadly attenuated aristocrats, who barely kept the flame of classical Japanese convention from sputtering and dying out. Now and then the new merchant princes played dress-up with the trappings of high culture, but most of the time they were absorbed in a culture completely of their own making. As a reflection of their world, it was an urban culture. Woodblock prints, short stories, novels, poetry, and plays depicted city life—fast, varied, crowded, and competitive—where people lived by their wits and appreciated wit. Puns and parody took pride of place in the new popular literature, which itself became big business. Publishing proved yet another way of making money in this commercial age, so that for the first time books circulated in printed form rather than in manuscript. Literature came to the masses, or at least the urban masses.

To succeed, it had to meet their tastes. Like metropolitans the world over, Japanese townspeople of the seventeenth and eighteenth centuries moved to a faster beat. They were impatient, and it showed in their fiction. The stately pace of courtly prose yielded to narratives moving at a rapid clip, where action is compressed and any fine-grained analysis of character is likely to be jettisoned as a drag on the reader's fractured attention. The townspeople were also intensely rivalrous. By day they sweat to best the competition; by night they dressed to trump their neighbors in the social contest. Style was an essential component of success, and the new class demanded no less of its writers and artists, who were expected to capture the city scene with acuity and a sense of humor and to execute their work with verbal and visual panache.

Naturally, as tradesmen, the townspeople were nothing if not pragmatic, and naturally too their practical bent affected the literature they supported. The bourgeois audience had little use for tales of noble romance or martial prowess. Like the audience for whom Molière wrote *Tartuffe* (p. 306) and Pope his *Rape of the Lock* (p. 492), the members of this new middle class demanded realism. What was real to them were other people like themselves, the gossip of their own tight world, the perils and the thrills of the marketplace, and the pleasures to be had from prosperity. For the first time, in other words, ordinary people became standard literary characters, and the material and sexual aspects of life were deemed worthy subjects of literature.

Inevitably, at times, there was a certain excess to this exuberant young culture, giddy and energized by the excitement of its own self-creation. It could be, for example, startlingly graphic: every artist of repute enjoyed a lucrative sideline producing erotic woodblock prints. It could also be vulgar, for the nouveaux riches of the merchant class were sometimes prone to a particularly mindless form of conspicuous consumption. A man dallies upstairs at a teahouse with his favorite courtesan. His friend sends over a giant dumpling, so enormous that it cannot be carried up the stairway. Instead of coming down to enjoy the dumpling, he hires six carpenters to widen the stairs. With events like this in the historical record, it is not surprising that caricature and lampoon compose the other side of popular "realism."

For the most part ignored by the *samurai* authorities and removed from foreign influence, the new urban culture developed organically. Actors, courtesans, adventurers, shopkeepers, rice brokers, moneylenders, fashion-plate wives, and precocious sons and daughters created their own cosmopolitan customs. *Kabuki* playwrights, *haiku* poets, woodblock artists, and best-selling novelists all captured in their own genres an intimate glimpse of kinetic bourgeois life—blunt, expansive, iconoclastic, irrepressibly playful. Few here ever heard of the Enlightenment or the scientific revolution. The walled garden of Japan in the seventeenth and eighteenth centuries bloomed nicely without the irrigation of European currents.

A note on the Japanese calendar and time-keeping practices will be helpful in reading the following selections. Until 1873, when Japan adopted the Gregorian calendar of the West, the official calendar was derived from China and was divided into twelve lunations (months) of twenty-nine or thirty days. The resulting lunar year was approximately eleven days shorter than the solar year, which required the insertion of a thirteenth intercalary month every third year or thereabout to align the calendrical year with the solar. In addition, by custom the Japanese year began slightly later than the Western, so that New Year's Day fell anywhere from January 15 to February 15. The beginning of the new year also marked an increase in one's age, in contrast to the Western practice of reckoning age by birthdays. A child born in the twelfth month, for instance, would turn two with the new year.

Years were numbered serially from the year when a reigning emperor ascended the throne. In the modern period (beginning in 1868) the reign of an emperor has one name for its duration. For example, the reign of Emperor Hirohito is called the Shōwa ("enlightened peace") era, which lasted from his ascension in 1926 until his death in 1989. In addition to following the Western practice of numbering years by the Gregorian calendar, the year 1930, say, is reckoned as Shōwa 5. In the premodern period, rather than having one name throughout, an emperor's reign was usually divided into various eras, each with its own name.

Both the months and the hours of the day were designated by the signs of the Chinese zodiac. The day was divided into twelve units, each equivalent to 120 minutes:

Hour		Modern Equivalent
1	Rat	11 P.M.–1 A.M.
2	Ox	1 A.M.–3 A.M.
3	Tiger	3 A.M.–5 A.M.
4	Rabbit	5 A.M.–7 A.M.
5	Dragon	7 A.M.–9 A.M.
6	Snake	9 A.M.–11 A.M.
7	Horse	11 A.M.–1 P.M.
8	Ram	1 P.M.–3 P.M.
9	Monkey	3 P.M.–5 P.M.
10	Rooster	5 P.M.–7 P.M.
11	Dog	7 P.M.–9 P.M.
12	Boar	9 P.M.–11 P.M.

PRONOUNCING GLOSSARY

The following list uses common English syllables to provide rough equivalents of selected words whose pronunciation may be unfamiliar to the general reader.

haiku: *hai-koo*

Heike: *hay-kay*

kabuki: *kah-boo-kee*

nō: *noh*

Tokugawa: *toh-koo-gah-wah*

Zeami: *ze-ah-mee*

TIME LINE

TEXTS	CONTEXTS
	1600–1868 Edo period: Tokugawa family establishes dynasty of shoguns who rule from Edo (present-day Tokyo)
1609 Commercial publishing begins in Japan	
	1616–1660 Imperial family commissions the Katsura Detached Palace (icon of modernism for 20th-century architects)
	1620 The *Mayflower* carries Pilgrims to America
	ca. 1620–1716 Sōtatsu and Kōrin create masterpieces of Japanese screen painting
	1627 Korea becomes a tributary state of China
1639 Aesop's *Fables* translated into Japanese	**1639** Shogun proclaims policy of national isolation, expelling Portuguese and banning Christianity and foreign travel
1682 The *Life of a Sensuous Man* (Ihara Saikaku) launches comic realism and popular fiction	
1686 **The Barrelmaker Brimful of Love** published in Ihara Saikaku's collection *Five Women Who Loved Love*	
1690–1694 **The Narrow Road of the Interior** (Matsuo Bashō), verse inset in a travel memoir written by the foremost *haiku* poet	
1721 The *Love Suicides at Amijima* (Chikamatsu Monzaemon), a masterpiece among tragedies of fatal love written for the puppet theater	
1745 *Haiku* poet Yosa Buson anticipates modern free verse with innovative poems in his *Elegy to Hokuju Rōsen*	

Boldface titles indicate works in the anthology.

TIME LINE

TEXTS	CONTEXTS
1748 *The Treasury of Loyal Retainers* (Takeda Izumo II), a popular play immortalizing the fealty of *samurai* who avenge their master's death	
1758–1801 Studies by Motoori Norinaga revive interest in *The Ten Thousand Leaves,* **The Tale of Genji,** and other Japanese classics	
	1760s Harunobu inaugurates heyday of color woodblock print
	1769–1800 James Watt's refinements of the steam engine fuel Industrial Revolution
1770–1790 Center of literary activity shifts from Kyoto-Osaka area eastward to Edo (present-day Tokyo)	**1770–1790** Glory days of *kabuki* with actor Ichikawa Danjūrō V
ca. 1776 *Tales of Moonlight and Rain* (Ueda Akinari), a collection of supernatural stories, including **Bewitched**	**1776** American colonies adopt the Declaration of Independence
	1790 Utamaro's portraits of women add psychological depth to woodblock print tradition
	1810–1880 Landscapes by Hokusai and Hiroshige take art of woodblock print to its zenith

IHARA SAIKAKU
1642–1693

No writer caught the substance of seventeenth-century Japanese city life as completely as Ihara Saikaku. He knew the foibles of the merchant class inside out,
because he was one of them. Born in Osaka in 1642, when the city was the commercial epicenter of Japan, Saikaku's real name was Hirayama Tōgo. Ihara is thought
to have been his mother's surname, and Saikaku* is the pen name he took when he
became a writer.

It appears that Saikaku's people were tradesmen of substantial means and that at
a young age he inherited the family business, though the nature of that business is
uncertain. Evidence suggests that the family may have been swordsmiths. In any case,
Saikaku had years of economic experience under his belt when, after his young wife
died in 1675, he left the business in the hands of trusted clerks, shaved his head in
the monastic style, and embarked on the life of a retired gentleman, dabbling in
poetry, traveling, and scribbling for his own amusement. Actually, he ended up working as hard as ever, for his talent and drive soon made Saikaku one of Japan's first
professional writers.

By the time of his "retirement," Saikaku was already a well-known amateur poet.
A prime mover in refashioning traditional Japanese verse to the tastes of the new
metropolitan class, he had gained notoriety as a poetic radical. In Saikaku's day a
form of extended, linked verse had all but supplanted the short classical five-line poem
known as the *tanka* (see *The Man'yōshū* and *The Kokinshū,* in Volume B). The new
poetry was usually composed by several people, who took turns penning alternating
units of two and three lines, so that each new link, when yoked to its antecedent,
momentarily completed a verse resembling the traditional five-line poem, before, in
turn, becoming the beginning of another verse, on and on into a sequence that suggested a kind of poetic stream of consciousness. This ingenious form existed well
before Saikaku, but it was in large measure his audacity that brought the genre of
linked poetry completely into the profane world.

Impatient with technical correctness and orthodox poetic conceits, Saikaku turned
"chain poetry" in a new direction. An exhibitionist at heart, he rejected the input of
other poets. His solo sequences gave the illusion of maintaining the linked-verse ideal
of overlapping voices and shifting points of view while concentrating on single-minded
descriptions of the world actually observed. Until now linked poetry had been, essentially, a protracted and often pedantic form of wordplay, but Saikaku used the medium
to fashion a series of fleeting genre scenes of seventeenth-century life. Freewheeling
and down-to-earth, the Saikaku string of slice-of-life vignettes moved with the speed
and vividness of film flying through a projector:

> A thief!
> I thought,
> and feigned sleep.
>
> Between mother and child
> a man crawls in.
>
> His heart aflame,
> he hesitates
> to lift the quilt.

---

*Note that names are given in the Japanese order, with surname first. In the case of writers like Saikaku,
who replace their given names with pen names, Japanese convention designates them by the pen name
rather than the surname—hence Saikaku, not Ihara.

Stage fright:
the first visit to a brothel.

"Hey!
Anything offbeat
for sale?"

"Yesterday again two fools
committed double suicide."*

On a single move
he staked the game†—
and lost.

Already we can see a storyteller in the making, a novelist in search of his medium. Frustrated with the narrative and descriptive limitations of poetry and confident in the colloquial freedom he had carved for himself, Saikaku finally discarded prosodic constraints and tried his hand at fiction. He wrote his first novel in 1682, at the age of forty. *The Life of a Sensuous Man* was a brilliant beginning: a picaresque tale of the amorous exploits of a sexually precocious and ultimately insatiable hero. At seven the young lad falls in love with a maidservant; by nine he is commissioning love letters. A mere youth, he has already found his calling, and by the time the book ends, the sixty-year-old hero has racked up over four thousand conquests.

In his first novel Saikaku managed to preserve both the formal balance and the kaleidoscopic sweep of a linked verse sequence, along with the irreverence that had become his trademark. Structurally, *The Life of a Sensuous Man* is clearly the off-spring of linked poetry. The loosely connected chapters are anecdotal, each intro-duced with a rhetorical flourish in the poetic mode, followed by the "story," a brief episode frequently interrupted when the author pauses to sketch little genre scenes depicting the various mores encountered by the hero as he wends his randy way through life. After a few pages the chapter ends, often abruptly, and the next chap-ter—another link in the narrative chain—takes the hero in a new direction. The novel's structure in fifty-four chapters also parodies *The Tale of Genji* (in Volume B), the classic work of Japanese prose fiction, and the hero's methodic quest for love renders him an updated, if burlesque, version of the romantic noble. It is altogether a more spirited and vulgar world. Merchants replace aristocrats; the customs of the red-light district supersede the rituals of court life. In Saikaku the denizens of this new world had a novelist who spoke their language, and they quickly made the book a best-seller.

Perhaps unintentionally he had launched a new career. In the remaining eleven years of his life Saikaku produced at least twenty-six books (not counting several works considered spurious). He shared with his first hero, the sensuous man, a voracious appetite for life, and in his fiction Saikaku's stamina and curiosity took him every-where: temples, shrines, teahouses, *nō* and *kabuki* theaters, Chinese trading posts, *samurai* barracks, riverboats, pawnshops, law courts, breweries, and brothels. It is hard to imagine a writer more cosmopolitan than Saikaku. The combination of busi-ness experience, ample leisure, and a nose for human mischief made him a shrewd observer of almost every level of Japanese society.

His choice of subject was also wide ranging. He wrote parodies of Confucian ethics, crime stories, lampoons of famous people, and accounts of martial valor. A penchant

---

*Also known as "love suicide." Occasionally, a prostitute and a client would fall in love; the frequent visits could ruin a man financially. The most impassioned lovers escaped their difficulties by committing suicide together. In this verse, the brothel owner mentions the latest case to discourage the young customer from nursing any romantic illusions. †Saikaku switches from the game of love to *go*: like chess, a game of strategy.

for travel led him to publish a collection of regional folktales and the first geographical guide to the whole of Japan. But his richest material by far was the daily life of townspeople. In some works he focused on their love lives, in others on their pocketbooks. Both money and sex were radically new topics for Japanese literature. The subject matter alone would probably have guaranteed Saikaku a certain popularity. What made him an icon was the wit he brought to his material.

Saikaku has been called a realist, but, like Petronius (in Volume A), his art is closer to caricature. The people crowding the pages of his novels and short stories are never fully drawn. Instead, their flaws or idiosyncrasies are exaggerated in a few bold strokes. This representation is realistic not because it paints the whole picture but because the quirks it captures have the immediate ring of truth. No doubt, from the first, readers found Saikaku realistic in comparison with the output of his direct predecessors: fairy tales and sentimental novelettes, juvenile parodies of classical literature, dreary didactic tales, how-to books with a thin veneer of fiction.

As the founder of a new popular "realistic" literature, which cut to the bone of bourgeois experience (more often than not, the funny bone), Saikaku caught both the substance and the spirit of his frenzied age. The immediacy of his subject and his virtuoso style not only won him a full complement of contemporary admirers but a place among the greatest writers of Japan.

The Barrelmaker Brimful of Love is a worthy introduction. The novella is part of a collection of stories, *Five Women Who Loved Love*, written in 1686 when Saikaku had reached his full stride. It should be remembered, though, that this is a writer for whom language is always a bravura performance. Translation, inevitably obscuring linguistic aspects of a text, cannot display the stylist's forte to best advantage. Saikaku's many other strengths, however, do emerge.

For other stories from the same collection, see William Theodore de Bary, *Five Women Who Loved Love* (1956). Numerous translations of Saikaku's fiction are available, of which the following can be recommended: G. W. Sargent, *The Japanese Family Storehouse* (1959); Ivan Morris, *The Life of an Amorous Woman and Other Writings* (1963); Peter Nosco, *Some Final Words of Advice* (1980); Paul Gordon Schalow, *The Great Mirror of Male Love* (1990). For an introduction to Saikaku and his times, see Howard Hibbett, *The Floating World in Japanese Fiction* (1959), and for a history of Japanese literature in the seventeenth and eighteenth centuries see Donald Keene, *World Within Walls* (1976).

PRONOUNCING GLOSSARY

The following list uses common English syllables to provide rough equivalents of selected words whose pronunciation may be unfamiliar to the general reader.

Chozaemon: *choh-zah-e-mohn*

Dotom-bori: *doh-tohm–boh-ree*

Genji: *gen-jee*

Gion-machi: *gee-ohn–mah-chee*

Heike: *hay-kay*

Hirayama Tōgo: *hee-rah-yah-mah toh-goh*

Hokkeji: *hohk-ke-jee*

Ihara Saikaku: *ee-hah-rah sai-kah-koo*

Ise: *ee-say*

Jokyo: *joh-kyoh*

Kawara-machi: *kah-wah-rah–mah-chee*

Kinoe-ne: *kee-noh-e–ne*

Kyushichi: *kyoo-shee-chee*

momme: *mohm-me*

Nabeshima: *nah-be-shee-mah*

Nihei: *nee-hay*

Nokaze: *noh-kah-ze*

Shimmei: *sheem-may*

Shimabara: *shee-mah-bah-rah*

Sumiyoshi: *soo-mee-yoh-shee*

The Barrelmaker Brimful of Love[1]

1

The Cleaning of a Well by a Man Unhappy in Love

Life is short; love is long.

There once was a cooper who, from the coffins he built with his own hands, realized how impermanent the world is. Although he worked his saw and gimlet assiduously for a living, he made very little money and could rent only a thatched hut in Osaka. He lived in a manner befitting the poorer section of Temma.[2]

There was also a girl who surpassed all the others who lived in her remote village. Her complexion was white even to the ears and her feet were not stained by contact with the soil. On New Year's Eve of her thirteenth year her parents were short the sum of silver required as a village tax, which amounted to one-third of their income, and so the girl was sent to serve as a lady's maid in an imposing city-house near Temma.

As time went on her natural disposition and ready wit came to be appreciated. She was solicitous toward the old couple, pleased the lady of the house, and was well thought of by all the others. Later she was allowed free access to the inner storeroom where all the fine things were kept. Everyone thought so highly of her that it was said: "What would happen to this house if Osen were not around?" This was all because of her intelligence.

Osen knew nothing of the ways of love. She had spent all of her nights in a manner which some might think unworthy of her—alone. Once when a light-hearted fellow pulled her dress she responded with a full-throated shriek, leaving the man to bewail this unfortunate turn of events. After that no man would ever speak flirtingly to her. People may criticize Osen for such behavior, but it would probably be a good thing if all men's daughters acted as she did.

Our story begins on the seventh day of autumn, the Tanabata Festival[3] day, when silk clothes—guaranteed never to have been worn before—are piled up seven high, right sleeve over left, to be rented to celebrants. It is amusing to see how the upper-class ladies celebrate by tying familiar poems to juniper twigs while the poor people decorate their houses with gourds and persimmons on the branch.

This particular day was a special occasion for the people of the neighborhood because the common well was being cleaned. The people living in rented houses on the side lanes participated in this cleaning and kept water on the boil for tea to be served to the workmen. After most of the dirty water had been scooped out, the bottom of the well was scraped and up came a variety of things mixed in with pebbles. A kitchen knife, the disappearance of which had puzzled people, came to light, and so did a bunch of seaweed into which a needle had been thrust.[4] I wonder why that was done. Then, on further search, more things came up including some old pony-design

---

1. Translated by and with notes adapted from William Theodore de Bary.   2. A section near the outskirts of Osaka, which was still fairly rustic. A number of coopers, or barrelmakers, located their shops there. 3. Celebrated on the seventh night of the Seventh Month to commemorate the annual meeting of the stars Vega (the weaver maiden) and Altair (the herd boy). According to what was originally Chinese legend, the stars were lovers separated by the Milky Way and could meet only one night a year.   4. To put a curse or cast a spell on someone, an effigy of seaweed with a needle through it was stuck to a tree or cast into a well.

coppers,[5] a naked doll without a face, a one-sided sword-handle peg of crude workmanship, and a patched-over baby's bib. You can never tell just what you will find at the bottom of an uncovered, outside well.

Then, when the well cleaners got down to the barrel planking close to the spring, an old two-headed nail came loose and the planking came apart. They sent for the cooper we have mentioned to make a new hoop for the barrel. When he had succeeded in stopping up the slowly flowing water, the cooper noticed an old woman with a crooked back who was fondling a live lizard.

He asked her what it was, and she answered: "This is a newt which just now was brought up from the well. Don't you recognize one when you see it? If you put this lizard in a bamboo tube and burn it, and then sprinkle its ashes in the hair of the person you love, that person will love you in turn." She spoke with a great deal of conviction.

This woman was formerly an abortionist known as Kosan from Myoto Pond, but when this profession was prohibited she gave up her cruel practice and worked at making noodle-flour with a mortar. Because of the hand-to-mouth nature of such an occupation, she had to work so hard that she did not even hear the temple bell sounding the end of the day. However, as she sank lower and lower in the social scale she learned the lesson of karma[6] and she thought more about the future life.

When she told the cooper about the terrible things that would happen to people who did wrong in this world, he paid no attention to her. Rather, he questioned her the more intently about the efficacy of burning a newt to help in one's love affairs.

Naturally, she became more sympathetic as he talked to her with such earnestness, and she finally asked: "Who is it that you love? I won't tell another soul."

The cooper forgot himself, so much was he thinking of the one he loved, and as he beat on the bottom of the cask he let himself be carried away by his own words, pouring out all of his story to the old woman. "The one I love does not live far away. I love Osen, the maid of the house here. I have sent her a hundred letters without getting a word in reply."

The old woman nodded and said: "You don't need any newts to win her. I can bridge the stream of love for you. I will disperse the clouds and make your love successful in no time at all."

The cooper was surprised to hear her undertake the matter so lightly. "If this will involve a great deal of money, I am afraid I won't be able to supply it, no matter how much I would like to, for this has been a bad season for me. Naturally, if I had the money I wouldn't begrudge it. All I can promise you is a cotton kimono dyed to your liking at New Year's and a set of Nara-hemp[7] clothes of second quality for the mid-summer festival of O-Bon. Is it a bargain?"

"Love that can talk that way must be based on selfishness. I am not looking for that sort of thing at all. You know there is a great art in getting a person to feel love for you. In my lifetime I've helped thousands of people, and

---

5. Coins minted by the private sector, engraved with the image of a pony. They were carried as magic charms to increase one's wealth.   6. The force generated by a person's thoughts, words, and actions believed in Buddhism to determine one's specific destiny in the next existence.   7. Bleached hemp made in Nara (the old capital, south of Kyoto) was used for summer clothing.

always with success. I'll see to it that you meet her before the Chrysanthemum Festival[8] in September."

This set the flames of love burning more fiercely in the cooper's heart and he cried: "My lady, I will supply you with all the firewood you will need to make tea the rest of your life."

In this world no one knows how long a person may live, and it is amusing to think that love should have made him promise so much.

2

After the Dance: A Witch in the Night

There are seven mysterious things in the Temma section of Osaka: the umbrella-shaped flame before the Daikyo Temple; the boy without hands at Shimmei Shrine; the topsy-turvy lady at Sonezaki;[9] the phantom noose of Eleventh Avenue; the crying monk of Kawasaki; the laughing cat of Ikedamachi; and the smouldering Chinese mortar at the Bush-Warbler's Mound.[1] But these are just the magical tricks of old foxes and badgers. Much more to be feared are those demons in human form who play havoc with the lives of ignorant men.

Our souls are dark indeed. And it was so dark the twenty-eighth night of July[2] that hanging lanterns threw no light under the eaves of houseroofs. Street dancers, hoping to sustain their revels till dawn, shouted, "Just one more day to dance till the month is over," but they too reluctantly broke up and returned to their homes. Even the vigilant dog of Four Corners[3] fell fast asleep.

At this late hour old Nanny, the mischievous crone in whom the cooper had put his trust, noticed that the entrance to the great landlord's house was still open. She burst in, slammed the door, and tumbled down onto the kitchen floor, crying: "Oh, oh, it's terrible. Give me a drink of water!"

To those within the house she appeared on the brink of death, but her continued breathing encouraged them to call her back to consciousness, and without more ado she came to life.

"What can you have seen that was so terrifying?" asked the landlord's wife and her aged mother-in-law.

"Well, it's a shameful thing for an old woman to admit, but I went out walking the streets tonight. I went to bed early and couldn't get to sleep, so I decided to go see the dancing. My, it was wonderful! I couldn't get enough of it, especially the Kudoki[4] songs with rhymes made up using *yama* and *matsu*.[5] There was one fellow down in front of the Nabeshima mansion who sang exactly like Nihei, the great Donen[6] singer of Kyoto.

"I pushed my way through a crowd of men and watched the show with my

---

8. Celebrated on the ninth day of the Ninth Month, according to the Chinese calendar. It was one of five major seasonal festivals, as was the Tanabata festival (see n. 3, p. 591).   9. A quarter known for its female prostitutes. *Shimmei Shrine:* a Shinto shrine frequented by homosexual prostitutes.   1. None of these mysteries has been identified.   2. The translation is misleading. In Chapter 1 we are told that it is autumn but here it is July. The lunar calendar followed in Japan at this time was about a month ahead of the Western calendar. Autumn was considered to begin on the seventh day of the Seventh Month, which would normally have corresponded to August in the Western calendar.   3. That is, on the street corner.   4. A long ballad in which one tune was repeated over and over.   5. A word frequently used in poetry for its pun on "pine" and "wait." *Yama:* mountain.   6. *Donen-bushi* was a type of ballad made popular by Donen Ganzaburo of Kyoto around the time this story was written.

fan as an eye-shade so that people couldn't see what an old woman I was. But the men knew what was what, even in the dark. I wiggled my old hips in a most flirtatious way and was really quite sexy in this white gown and black sash. But no one so much as pinched my bottom. 'A woman is a some-time thing.'[7]

"So I started home again, my mind recollecting the old days of my youth, and suddenly near your gate I was hailed by a handsome young fel-low of twenty-four or twenty-five. He was desperately in love, so tortured by his fatal passion that he had only a day or two to live in this Fleeting World.[8] It was the cruel Osen, he said, upon whom his heart had fixed itself so hopelessly.[9] He swore that within a week after his death his ghost would come to kill every member of this household. Oh, he was so fright-some! He had a great nose, his face was flushed with fever, and his eyes gleamed, just as if he were possessed by the *tengu*[1] whose figure is paraded before the Sumiyoshi festival procession. I was so frightened that I had to run in here."

Everyone who had crowded around to hear her story was aghast, and the householder's aged father wept a little.

"To be unhappy in love," he said, "is not unheard of. Osen is old enough to get married now, and we should keep this man in mind if he has a suitable livelihood. Providing he is not a gambler or widow chaser, and is thrifty and frugal, he might make a good choice. Of course, I do not know the man at all, but I can sympathize with him."

By the long silence which followed, it was plain that the others sympa-thized with him too. The shrewd old hen certainly knew her business when it came to promoting a love affair.

It was now past midnight and, after she had been helped to her feet, old Nanny returned to her hovel. While she lay there plotting her next move, dawn broke through the east window. Nearby she could hear the sound of flint on steel, as a neighbor started up his fire. Somewhere an infant began to cry. Sleepily the tenants of that squalid quarter chased out the mosquitoes which had slipped through the breaks in their paper nets and plagued them throughout the night. One minute the women's fingers were pinching at the fleas in their underclothes, the next pinching for some odd coins on the sanctuary shelf[2] with which to buy a few green vegetables. Still, amidst the bitter struggle for existence, pleasure could yet be found by those who, through wedlock, had won partners for their beds. In what delights may they not have indulged, with pillows to the south and mattresses in utter disarray, violating the vigil of Kinoe-ne?[3]

At last the sun rose to shine upon a brisk, breezy autumn day. The old woman tied her head up in a towel and treated herself for a headache, calling upon the services of Dr. Okajima without worrying how the bill would be

---

7. Literal trans.: a woman is something only as long as she is young.   8. Sometimes translated as "Float-ing World," refers to the transitory nature of life in Buddhist teaching and, by extension, to the sensual aspects of human existence.   9. The language used is that associated with a Buddhist belief concerning human passions, according to which obsessions of the soul will, if unsatisfied or unrelieved during a person's lifetime, return after death to wreak vengeance on the object of that passion.   1. A fabulous being with wings and an extremely long nose.   2. A shelf where statues of Buddha were to be kept.   3. On this night a vigil was kept in honor of the god of plenty, and continence was to be observed until midnight. Children conceived at this time were thought to become criminals. *Pillows to the south:* husbands and wives slept with their pillows at the southern end of the bed. Widows and widowers placed their pillows to the north, as a sign of mourning.

paid. She had just served herself some broth of fresh herbs, when Osen came in from the back alley to visit her.

"How are you today?" Osen inquired sweetly, as from her left sleeve she brought forth half a melon pickled in the Nara style and wrapped in a lotus leaf, which she set down on a bundle of firewood. "Perhaps you would like it with some soy sauce," she said modestly and made to go get it without waiting for the other's thanks.

"Wait," the old woman insisted. "It is because of you that I am about to die before my time, and since I have no daughter of my own, you must pray for me when I am gone." Then, reaching into a hemp basket, she brought out a pair of purple socks with red ribbons and a patched-up rosary bag,[4] from which she removed her divorce papers. The socks and bag she gave to Osen, saying they would be keepsakes.

Impressionable, as most women are, Osen believed the story and wept. "If there is truly someone in love with me, why didn't he come for help from a love-wise person like yourself? If I had known his intentions, I should not have spurned him lightly."

Old Nanny saw that this was as good a time as any to come out with the whole story. "There is no reason to hide anything from you now. He did come to me many times, and the deep sincerity of his love for you was more touching and pitiful than I can say. If you should reject him now, my resentment will fall upon no one but you." She spoke with all the cleverness that years of wide experience had given her, and, as was only to have been expected, Osen soon yielded.

"I shall be glad to meet him anytime," she cried, dizzy with emotion.

Thereupon the old crone, delighted to have obtained such a promise, whispered: "It just occurred to me how you might best meet him. On the eleventh day of August you must make a secret pilgrimage to Ise.[5] Traveling alone together, you would become fast friends and could spend your bedtime hours sweetly, heart murmuring to heart of undying love. And you know," she added casually, "he is not at all bad looking."

Without further persuasion and before she had even seen him, Osen was consumed with love for this man. "Can he write letters himself? Does his hair fall long and pretty behind his head? I suppose, since he is a craftsman, his back may be a little stooped. Well, when we set out from here, I should like to stop at noon in Moriguchi or Hirakata, so we can get a room and go to bed early."

She was babbling on like this when the chief maid-servant was heard calling outside: "Miss Osen, you're wanted!"

Osen quickly took her leave: "It's all set for the eleventh then. . . ."

3

As Delicious as the Water of Kyoto:
The Intimacy of Lovers Meeting in Secret

"The morning-glories are in bloom and it would be nice to have a look at them tomorrow early—nice and cool, too," the lady of the house added as

4. To carry beads used for prayer in Buddhism.   5. It was a popular custom to make a pilgrimage to Ise without the knowledge of one's parents or master. When the pilgrim returned, he or she was supposed to be forgiven for absconding.

she began her instructions to the servants that evening. "I want you to arrange some seats out near the back hedge, away from the house. Spread out the flower-mats, put baked rice and toothpicks in the different compartments of the picnic box, and don't forget the tea bottle. I shall take a bath just before six in the morning and then I want my hair done up simply in three plain rolls. As for a gown, let me have the hempen one with open sleeves and a pink lining. I shall wear my gray-satin sash with circle designs on it, the informal, two-piece one dotted with our family crest. I want you to take the utmost care in everything because we may be seen by people in the adjacent streets. So each of you must dress in decent-looking clothes. A litter should be sent at the usual rising time to my sister's house in Tenjinbashi."

She put all the arrangements in the charge of Osen, who attended the lady upon her retirement into an ample mosquito net, at the four corners of which little bells jingled while Osen gently fanned her to sleep. Imagine so much fuss over nothing but some flowers in your back yard!

But perhaps such vanity is not the weakness of women alone. At this time the master of the house was probably wasting himself and his money on Miss Nokaze of Shimabara and Miss Ogino of Shimmachi,[6] buying both of them the same day, one for each end of his carrying-pole.[7] Though he spoke of visiting Tsumura Temple each morning, and carried a shoulder pad[8] for that purpose, it is much more likely that he went straight to the licensed quarter for a morning of sport and pleasure.

Just before dawn on the eleventh of August old Nanny heard a light tapping on the door of her shanty.

"It is Osen," the girl outside whispered as she threw in a bundle which had been hastily wrapped in a large kerchief. Returning immediately to her master's house, Osen did not realize that the old crone would lose no time in searching through the bundle to see what was there: five strings of cash worth about one farthing of silver each, and perhaps eighteen *momme* of pony-engraved silver pieces;[9] nearly a peck of polished rice; a dried bonito;[1] two combs in a charm bag; a one-piece sash of many colors; a silver and brown garment for cooler weather; a lighter gown, well worn, with a fan pattern; cotton socks, the soles of which were unfinished; sandals with loose straps; and a parasol on which Osen had naïvely written her address! The old woman quickly set about erasing the telltale characters in such a way as to leave no unsightly smear upon the parasol. As she did so, someone greeted her from the entranceway.

"Old Nanny, I shall go on ahead now," the cooper called in on his way past.

Later Osen appeared, trembling a little. "Sorry to be late. I was detained at the house."

The old woman then took up the bundle of personal belongings and has-

6. Names of expensive prostitutes in the licensed pleasure quarters of Kyoto and Osaka, respectively. 7. A pole balanced on the shoulders, with items hung at each end for transporting; hence *carrying-pole* is slang for the hiring of two prostitutes at the same time. 8. An item of priestly vestments sometimes worn by lay devotees. 9. Three kinds of currency circulated at the time. In Edo (Tokyo), seat of the shogunal government, gold was the primary currency. In the Kyoto-Osaka region silver prevailed. Copper coins, with a value approximate to pennies, were in use throughout Japan. Gold currency was denominated, but silver had to be measured by weight in *momme*. The silver pieces here are *komagane* ("small silver") coins that weighed one to five *momme* each, the equivalent of several dollars. The homonym *koma* means "pony," thus the translator's *pony-engraved silver pieces*. 1. A favorite fish among townspeople.

tened with Osen down an unfamiliar byway. "It would be a great effort for me, but perhaps for the sake of the pilgrimage I should accompany you to Ise," old Nanny suggested.

Osen was plainly upset. "It's a long trip for an elderly woman and you would find it hard going. Why don't you take the night boat down from Fushimi after you have taken me to meet this man?" she replied tactlessly, for she had now no patience with anything that might upset the headlong progress of her affair.

Just as they were crossing the Capital Bridge, along came Kyushichi, a manservant in the same household as Osen. He had come this way to watch the morning change of guard at Osaka Castle, but, his curiosity aroused when the two women came by, Kyushichi inevitably became a further obstacle in the path of the lovers.

"Why, I have been thinking for some time of making the same pilgrimage and there could be no better companions for the journey than yourselves. Just leave your baggage for me to carry. Fortunately, I have plenty of spending money and can see to it that you suffer no inconvenience on that score." From his excessive politeness one could guess that Kyushichi was inspired by some secret design on Osen, and old Nanny's hostility was immediately aroused.

"A young lady traveling in the company of a man! Now wouldn't that seem most extraordinary to the people who saw us! Besides, the gods of Ise frown on that sort of thing. I have heard and seen enough of people who willfully disgrace themselves before society. Please don't follow us."

"Well, I hardly expected to run into objections of this sort. Believe me, I have no designs on Miss Osen; faith alone moves me to this. In love, the gods will assure my success, without my having to solicit their protection, for my heart is true, true as the road we shall travel together. If the sun and moon favor us and Miss Osen so inclines, we can travel anywhere—to the capital perhaps. This would be just the time to spend four or five days there, seeing the maples of Takao in their bright fall colors and the blooming mushrooms of Saga. The master generally stops at a hotel in Kawara-machi, but I think we would find it awkward there. We could do better," Kyushichi continued as if he would have everything his own way, "by taking some cozy rooms at the western end of Third Avenue. Then the old lady here could visit the Temple of the Original Vow,[2] on Sixth Avenue.

By this time the autumn sun was up over the mountainside, and the travelers were halfway past the pine-shaded banks of the Yodo River when they ran upon a man who looked very conspicuous, seated beneath a cat's-paw willow as if waiting for someone. On closer examination the old crone recognized him as the cooper. From the look in her eyes he could tell that something had gone wrong; it had not worked out as planned after he went on ahead of them.

"You look as if you were going to Ise too," old Nanny addressed him. "But why go alone? You seem to be an agreeable fellow and we'd like to have you spend the night with us somewhere."

The cooper was delighted, of course. "It's so true: 'The kindness of others always brightens a journey.' I am certainly grateful for the invitation."

---

2. Honganji, a Buddhist temple, whose name translates as "Temple of the Original (or True) Vow."

Kyushichi, on the other hand, looked bewildered. "It seems a little odd, especially with this young lady along, to have someone join us when you don't even know where he's going."

"Oh," the old woman replied, "God watches over everything. And with a stout fellow like you along, what can possibly happen?"

Thereafter the four of them slept in the same inn each night. Kyushichi, watching carefully for any opportunity to satisfy his secret desires, removed one of the sliding doors which separated him from the ladies and would peek in at them on his way to the bath. At night, when the four of them slept in a row, he stretched out his hand and tipped up the oil lamp so as to smother the light.

Then, just as it was about to fail, the cooper exclaimed, "It's awfully warm for fall," and opened the window near him so that bright moonlight shone through upon the four sleeping figures.

Again, when Osen made a pretense of snoring and Kyushichi moved his right leg over upon her, he was quickly detected by the cooper, who promptly started up a song about the Soga brothers,[3] "Love plays mischief with all . . ." while beating time with the end of his fan. Osen then abandoned the pretense of sleeping and started to talk with old Nanny.

"There is nothing so calamitous as to bring a girl-child into the world. I have been thinking that it would be a good idea to become a novice at the Fudo Chapel of Kitano[4] next New Year's and eventually become a nun."

"Very good idea," the crone answered sleepily. "Better than to live on in a world full of disappointments."

Thus the two men stood in each other's way the whole night through. The upshot of their bedtime activities was only this: that Kyushichi, who started the evening with his pillow to the west, wriggled around and wound up with his head to the south and his underclothing missing—a shocking piece of carelessness for a pilgrim with money in his waistband; while the cooper slept with a resentful scowl on his face, a wad of tissue paper in his hand, and a clamshell full of clove oil[5] beside him.

The next morning at Mt. Osaka they hired an Otsu man's horse and proceeded on their journey with Osen riding in the middle and the men mounted on either side of her. Funny though an onlooker would have found this arrangement, there was something, whether fatigue or simply pleasure, which made the riders oblivious to their absurdity. On one side Kyushichi fondled Osen's toes; on the other the cooper reached up and put his arm around her waist; and each playfully indulged his secret desires as best he could in a manner that seems somewhat amusing to anyone who knows what each was after.

None of the group had any real interest in the pilgrimage itself. At Ise they failed to visit the Inner Shrine or the sacred beach at which homage is paid to the Sun,[6] stopping only at the Outer Shrine for a few minutes and purchasing as their only souvenirs a purification brooch and some seaweed.

On the way back the two men kept their eyes on each other, so nothing of consequence happened. When they reached the capital, Kyoto, and

---

3. Warriors famous for their daring.　4. A buddhist convent in Osaka. Fudo was a deity who destroys evil.　5. Used as cologne.　6. The sun goddess, mythical ancestor of the imperial family, who is enshrined at Ise.

Kyushichi had guided them to the hotel he knew, the cooper reckoned in his head what he owed Kyushichi for bills the latter had paid, thanked him for his trouble, and took his leave with a bow. Thinking that he would hence-forth have Osen to himself, Kyushichi went out and bought many presents and souvenirs for her. He could hardly wait for night to fall, but decided to while away the time visiting someone he knew in the neighborhood of Karasumaru.

In the meantime old Nanny left the hotel with Osen, ostensibly to visit Kiyomizu Temple. They went directly to Gion-machi, to a little shop which sold box lunches, and there found a card upon which was written "Gimlet and Saw." Recognizing this as the cooper's way of identifying himself, Osen slipped inside almost unnoticeably. Upstairs she found her lover, and together they drank the cup of betrothal,[7] pledging themselves to each other forever.

Thereupon old Nanny retired downstairs. "The water here is simply deli-cious," she exclaimed as she guzzled cups of tea one after another.

Having won from Osen the first installment on their marriage, the cooper left early for Osaka by day boat. Old Nanny and Osen, upon their return to the hotel, gave notice of immediate departure. Kyushichi pleaded with them to stay for a few more days of sight-seeing, but the old woman was determined.

"No, no. What would your mistress say if she thought Osen was chasing around with men?" So off they started.

"I know it's a lot to ask, but this bundle is so heavy. Won't you help us with it, Kyushichi?"

"My back aches. Sorry," he replied.

And when they stopped to rest in a wisteria grove before the Great Buddha of Inari, the women had to pay for their own tea.

4

Shingles Kindle a Fire in the Heart, and so in the Hearth

"If you had told us you wanted to go on a pilgrimage, we would have sent you in a litter or on hired horseback. But to make a secret pilgrimage in the fantastic way you did, and come back with all these presents bought by lord knows whom—why, it's—it's just the sort of thing one never does, not even married couples. And traveling to the capital together, drinking and sleeping together—who would dare go that far?

"Osen is just a woman, and it may be too much to expect that she could resist the urgings of Kyushichi. But Kyushichi, the smart aleck, thinks he must teach the innocent gods what manliness is, and teach this innocent girl . . ."

Their mistress was in a frightful rage. Kyushichi's explanations had no effect on her at all, and the poor, guiltless fellow was finally discharged, without waiting for the regular biannual replacement time of September fifth. Later he worked several terms in a wholesale house called Bizen-ya in Kitano and married a drifter[8] named Longie of Eighthbridge. Now he earns

---

7. Or fidelity.   8. Literal trans.: "lotus-leaf woman"; a prostitute hired by a business to entertain traveling merchants. She floated, like a lotus leaf on the water, from one man to another.

a living as a *sushi*[9] vendor on Willow Lane and has simply forgotten about Osen.

Osen went back to the uneventful routine of household duties, but she was unable to forget her brief romance with the cooper or get him out of her mind. She began to neglect herself, becoming shabby in appearance, careless in conduct, and little by little more gaunt and pale. Finally, losing control of herself, Osen started to wail throughout the night like a sick hen.

About the same time a series of further misfortunes overtook the household. The great cauldron rusted so that its bottom fell out; there was a sudden change between breakfast and supper in the taste of the prepared bean-paste; and lightning struck the roof of the storehouse, setting fire to the shingles. All of these things had a perfectly natural explanation, but people felt that in this case they had some special significance. Someone said: "It is the implacable spirit of the man who is madly in love with Osen—the cooper."

When her master and mistress heard this, they decided to do everything in their power to bring Osen and the cooper together in wedlock. Nanny was called in for a consultation.

"Osen," the old crone said craftily, "has told me several times that she would not have a hand laborer for a husband, and she isn't sure whether or not the cooper will do. But it seems to me that she is being unnecessarily choosy. If, in spite of all, they can just get along in life together, she should be satisfied."

Having heard old Nanny's ideas on the subject, Osen's employers sent for the cooper and concluded a marriage contract with him. Soon afterward, Osen had her sleeves sewn up and her teeth blackened[1] in preparation for the marriage, an auspicious date for which had already been chosen. Her dowry consisted of twenty-three items, including a second-grade chest with a natural finish, a wicker hamper for her trousseau, a folding pasteboard box, two castoff gowns from her mistress, quilted bedclothes, a mosquito net with red lining, and a scarf of classic colors. With all of these, more than a pound of silver was sent to the cooper's house.

The newlyweds proved quite compatible and their luck was good. Honest and industrious, the husband kept his head bent assiduously over the work of his craft, while his good wife took up weaving striped cloth of dark-dyed Fushikane[2] thread. Night and day they worked and never failed to meet their debts on the last day of the year or the day before the Bon Festival.[3] Osen took especially good care of the cooper. In winter, on windy days or when it snowed, she carefully covered his rice to keep it warm when he took it out. In summer she kept a fan close to her pillow to cool him with. When he was out of the house she locked the gate and never looked at another man. If she had occasion to speak of anything, it was always "my husband this, my husband that." Even when, after several years and months, she bore two children, Osen did not forsake her husband for them.

Alas, however, most women are fickle creatures. Captivated by some delicious love story, or deluded by the latest dramatic productions of Dotombori[4] their souls are caught up in giddy corruption. Amidst the falling cherry

9. Small servings of vinegared rice topped, rolled, or mixed with raw seafood, seaweed, or other ingredients.
1. Both are in the adult fashion and are signs that a woman is nubile.   2. A dye process that uses gall (swollen plant tissue caused by an invasion of fungus or other parasites).   3. In honor of the dead; accounts were to be settled the day before.   4. The theater district of Osaka.

blossoms of the Temple of the Heavenly Kings[5] or under a blooming wisteria trellis, they fall head over heels in love with some handsome fellow. And so, upon returning home, they find loathsome the man who has supported them for many long years.

There is no greater folly than this. From the moment of their seduction such women abandon all prudence and frugality, light great fires in their ovens and leave them untended, burn lamps thoughtlessly where no lamp is needed, and while their family fortunes dwindle, wait impatiently for leisure hours to spend away from home. Such marriages are dreadful indeed.

And should their husbands die, in seven days these women are out looking for other husbands. Divorced once, they marry and divorce again, six or seven times. That, unfortunately, is what the morals of the lower classes have sunk to, but this sort of thing, of course, never ever happens among the upper classes. A woman should give herself to only one man during her lifetime. If trouble arises or misfortune strikes, even when she is young, it is quite possible for her to become a nun in the Convent of Kaga or in the Hokkeji Nunnery of the Southern Capital, for this has been done many times before.

There are many others in the Fleeting World[6] who live in sin with secret lovers, but when they are discovered, either their husbands send them home without taking the matter to court, for fear of creating a sensation, or, in the case of husbands greedy for gold, some kind of deal is made and the matter dropped. Thus sinful women are spared through laxity in punishment, and for this reason adultery cannot be stamped out.

But there are gods and there is retribution. Every secret will be made known. How much to be dreaded—this ruinous road!

5

Life Is Shorter Than a Toothpick Made from Woodshavings

This is to announce an informal supper party to be held at my home on the sixteenth next. I should greatly appreciate having the honor of your company. P.S. Guests not listed in order of local prominence.[7]

Chozaemon, the yeast maker, found the years and months passing as if life were only a dream. Already it was fifty years since his father died, and he had reason to congratulate himself on living long enough to celebrate such an anniversary. According to the ancients: "When one goes into mourning on the fiftieth anniversary of his father's death, it is customary to abstain from meat in the morning, but eat fish for supper and drink and sing throughout the evening, having thereafter no further obligations to perform." Since these were to be the last services, Chozaemon did not begrudge a little expense in conducting them properly. The wives of the neighborhood joined in the preparations. They got out the wooden bowls, trays, crockery, and different kinds of wooden plates used only on special occasions, dusted them, and set them on the sideboard.

It happened that the cooper's wife was on friendly terms with these people, so she too dropped in to offer her services. "Isn't there some work to be done in the kitchen?"

---

5. Tenjōji, a Buddhist temple in Osaka known for its cherry trees. 6. See n. 8, p. 594. 7. This is the text of the invitation sent out by Chozaemon.

Osen was known as an intelligent and capable person, and they gave her a delicate job. "There are some sweets in the bedroom. Set them out on the deep trays."

Osen began her job of arranging the imperial persimmons, Chinese walnuts, falling-goose candies, and toothpicks of kaya and cryptomeria wood.[8] When she was almost finished, Master Chozaemon came in to fetch a nest of bowls from the shelf, but in doing so he clumsily dropped one on Osen's head so that her hairdo came apart all at once. He apologized profusely.

"Oh, it didn't hurt at all," Osen assured him as she hastily tied up her hair and went into the kitchen.

When the lady of the house saw her, however, she was immediately aroused. "Until a few minutes ago your hair was done up most beautifully. How could it become disarranged so suddenly?"

Osen, with a clear conscience, replied calmly: "The master was taking some bowls down from the shelf and one fell on me. That's how it happened."

But the lady would not believe her at all. "Indeed! A bowl falling off the shelf in broad daylight! What a playful bowl that must be. If you ask me, somebody fell into bed without going to sleep and her hair came undone. Of all things for an older man to be doing, when he is supposed to be mourning for his father!"

In a violent rage, she picked up some slices of fresh fish, which had been cut and arranged with much care, and began throwing them about the kitchen. No matter what anyone else talked of during the day, vinegar or flour or anything, she would drag in the subject of Osen and not let it drop, to the complete disgust of all who heard about the incident later. Truly it is the greatest of misfortunes for a man to have a wife of such fierce jealousy.

At first Osen put up patiently with the lady's ranting, though she could not help being annoyed by it. Later, the more she thought about it the more bitter and depressed Osen became. "My sleeve is already wet with tears. Having suffered the shame, there is nothing left to lose. I shall make love to Chozaemon and teach that woman a lesson." And, dwelling upon this idea, she aroused in herself a passion for Chozaemon which soon resulted in a secret exchange of promises between the two. They waited only for a suitable occasion to fulfill their desires.

The evening of January twenty-second, in the second year of Jokyo[9] (1685), seemed a propitious one for lovers since the women and children of the neighborhood were amusing themselves at the traditional spring pastime of drawing strings for prizes.[1] On into the night they played, completely absorbed in the game. Some lost and quit, others won and kept on with insatiable enthusiasm. Still others dozed off and started to snore. The cooper turned down his lamp and went to bed early, apparently so tired from the day's toil that he would not have awakened even if someone had pinched his nose.

Chozaemon followed Osen home from the party. "Now is the time to fulfill

8. Japanese cedar. *Falling-goose candies*: confections made from a flour of glutinous rice, barley, chestnuts, or adzuki beans, which are sweetened with sugar, kneaded, shaped in a decorative mold, and toasted. *Kaya*: Japanese nutmeg, or plum yew, an evergreen with edible seeds.   9. The reign name of the current emperor. *January*: better translated as "First Month."   1. A game played during the New Year holidays. Contestants each selected a string, or cord, hoping to draw the one with the winning token attached.

our mutual promise," he urged, and Osen, unable to refuse him, took Chozaemon into her house.

Then began what was to be their first and last attempt at love-making.

No sooner had they removed their underclothes than the cooper awoke. "Hold on! If I catch you, I'll never let you go!" he shouted.

Chozaemon quickly threw off the bedcovers. Naked and terrified, he dashed out and ran a great distance to the house of a close relative, barely escaping with his life.

Osen, realizing that it was a hopeless situation for her, plunged the blade of a carpenter's plane into her heart and died. Her corpse was exposed in the Shame Field[2] with that of the scoundrel Chozaemon when he was at last executed. Their names, known in countless ballads and songs, spread to distant provinces with the warning: This is a stern world and sin never goes unpunished.[3]

2. The execution grounds.   3. Saikaku based this story on an actual event of the year before.

MATSUO BASHŌ
1644–1694

Until the seventeenth century, Japanese literature was privileged property. Court aristocrats and provincial warlords (and the occasional member of the Buddhist clergy) had exclusive access to "books": a narrow supply of manuscript copies. Even when the first printed books began to appear at the beginning of the seventeenth century, they were still luxury items. Connoisseurs underwrote lavishly illustrated printings of the Japanese classics available in limited editions, usually of no more than one hundred copies and intended not for sale but for presentation. Like the manuscripts they replaced, the first printed books were an indulgence. But when printing and publishing became commercial endeavors around the second decade of the new century, books changed from being rare works of art, whose mysteries were known only to the chosen few, into tools and pastimes for the multitude.

The diffusion of literacy, and thus education, was both a cause and an effect of the diffusion of the printed word. Print not only provided new channels of communication, a new medium for artists, and new commercial opportunities, it created for the first time in Japan the conditions necessary for that peculiarly modern phenomenon, celebrity.

The *haiku* poet Matsuo Bashō was an odd candidate for the new renown. Born in 1644 as the second son of a low-ranking provincial *samurai* who cobbled a living by teaching calligraphy, he had little in his background or early years that augured celebrity. Adult life commenced in the most ordinary way, when Bashō entered the service of a cadet branch of the local ruling military house. But he became close to his employer, the young heir, who was a devotee of linked verse, and Bashō too developed a taste for the popular poetry. Together they studied with Kitamura Kigin, one of the leading poets of the day, and they shared the excitement of seeing their compositions—two by Bashō and one by his patron—published in a poetry anthology in 1664. The easygoing days of poetastering and unchallenging service must have been very pleasant for Bashō and must have seemed the shape his days would take for the rest of his life.

But everything changed suddenly with the premature death in 1666 of his master. Bashō lost not only a friend and poetry companion but the protector who would have guaranteed him security and advancement in the ranks of the *samurai*. In 1672 Bashō left for Edo (now Tokyo), the expanding military capital of the shogun's new government, where he decided to make his career as a professional poet. To do so he had to build a following. With some thirty of his verses now in anthologies and his first book recently published, the twenty-eight-year-old Bashō must have conjectured that he had a better chance of establishing himself in a new city, where the competition for income as a teacher and corrector of poetry (an expert paid to correct other people's poetry) would be less intense than in the old capital of Kyoto or the seasoned commercial town of Osaka. This departure for the east was in its own quiet way daring. By leaving his home district and the employ of the local clan, he was forfeiting his status as a *samurai*, a member (however lowly) of the elite ruling class. In relocating to the boomtown of Edo, with a population already over six hundred thousand and growing, Bashō was in fact courting fame.

Not surprisingly, the first years in Edo were not easy. "Sometimes," he would later recall, "I grew weary of poetry and thought I would abandon it. Other times, I vowed to establish my name as the foremost poet. The two alternatives battled within, making me utterly restless." For a while, Bashō was forced to supplement his income with a post in the city's department of waterworks.

But ultimately he succeeded. Linked-verse anthologies sold well in the late seventeenth century, and Bashō's poems appeared in them with increasing frequency. Within eight years he had made a name for himself. He was asked to judge linked-verse competitions, and his published commentaries on these contests found a ready audience. Over time, he had gathered a stable of students large enough by 1680 for him to publish their best poems in an anthology. And Bashō's followers were so devoted that in the same year the more prosperous ones built a cottage for him in a quiet, still rural part of the city.

In front of this cottage, his students planted a banana tree. Its rare flowers were so small as to be unobtrusive, and the large, delicate leaves were easily torn when the wind blew in from the sea. The whole thing looked somehow lonesome. In a climate too cool for it to bear fruit, the tree was deprived of its purpose. Alone inside his hut, Bashō professed an affinity for his banana tree:

> Banana tree in autumn winds:
> a night passed hearing
> raindrops in a basin.

His persona was now complete: the lonely wayfarer who had traveled far from home, the man of simple tastes who had consecrated his life to poetry, the delicate sensibility as fragile as the leaves of a banana tree. It was only fitting that he took the word *banana*—Bashō—for his pen name.

One might well smile at Bashō's canniness. In the choice of his personal metaphor, he managed to join self-image and apparent, actual attributes with a public stance edited seamlessly into his literary product: like an actor so indistinguishable from his interchangeable roles that we think we know the "real" person. Bashō cast himself as a pilgrim, but the purpose of his frequent travels was a poetic devotion to nature— the beauty and truth it alone could reveal—not religious piety. Like a Zen monk, he shaved his head and donned the dark, drab garb of a cleric, setting off, as in *The Narrow Road of the Interior*, on paths by no means always certain, into wilderness not entirely safe. Whether home alone in his rustic cottage or enduring the ardors of the open road, Bashō sought an austere existence, as though he had taken a vow of poverty. *Economy* could have been his watchword.

In person and in art, he was the antithesis of Ihara Saikaku, that prosperous chronicler of rich, material life, and in fact Bashō appears to have disdained Saikaku's prolific literary output. To him, it was vulgar and excessive. (Not surprisingly, Bashō-the-perfectionist's entire oeuvre, about 1,000 *haiku*, is an afternoon's work for Sai-kaku, whose most frenzied single sitting of solo linked-verse composition yielded 23,500 poems in twenty-four hours!) Perhaps Saikaku in turn disdained Bashō's fas-tidiousness, endlessly revising a mere seventeen syllables. In the world of poetry, however, the tortoise won the race. Bashō's lapidary style perfected a kind of epigram that indeed seems to capture the universe in a grain of sand. His sympathy with nature, and particularly with its frailest elements, which speak of the transience and vulnerability of living things, was permanently accepted as the essence of Japanese poetic feeling.

The *haiku* was the perfect form for Bashō's art: a flash of lyric verse as fleeting as the momentary impression it encapsulates—a scene from nature or a natural object that evokes a truth larger than itself—expressed in cryptic, unrhymed lines of five, seven, and five syllables:

> Upon a bare branch
> a crow has descended—
> autumn in evening.

It is a form of poetry that looks effortless. Anyone can string together seventeen syllables and make them sound ponderous or picturesque, which is probably why *haiku* have become so popular (though syntactic differences between Japanese and English can sometimes defeat translation attempts that hold to the exact syllable count). Only a true poet can work within the slender margins of this constricted form and create something beyond aphorism. It was Bashō's gift to fuse the transitory and the eternal, both the moment observed and its greater significance. The crow landing on the branch of a withered tree is the "now" of the poem; time's passing and lone-liness are the universals.

Actually, *haiku* began as part of linked verse, and in this respect too its apparent simplicity is deceptive. In the composition of linked poetry, resulting normally in sequences of thirty-six or one hundred verses (although they could stretch into one thousand verses or more), several poets worked in tandem. They took turns composing alternating links, or verses, in three lines with syllable counts of five, seven, and five (identical in form to *haiku*) and in two lines with syllable counts of seven each. Eventually, anthologies of linked poetry began to appear, excerpting the opening verses from various sequences. Thus these short poems in three lines of seventeen syllables, originally intended as the base to which subsequent lines of verse would be added, came to stand on their own. Poets began to write *haiku* as self-contained lyrics. But however independent they became, for a long time *haiku* retained a vestigial sense that they were somehow part of a larger matrix, or ought to be. This is one reason that poems in *The Narrow Road of the Interior* are embedded in a travel nar-rative, the prose equivalent of a linked sequence. By subtly following some of the structural principles of linked verse, Bashō's narrative achieves a kind of covert unity. And by including an occasional poem by his traveling companion, Sora, it retains something of the feel of linked verse. Once again poets were collaborating.

The Narrow Road of the Interior was written, or begun, in 1689, when Bashō embarked on his most ambitious journey. It would cover fifteen hundred miles of hinterland and take Bashō and Sora to the far corners of northern Japan. Although he is first thought of as a *haiku* poet, many of Bashō's best poems originally appeared in the five travel memoirs that he wrote in the final decade of his life. *The Narrow Road* is the last of these travel diaries, the longest, and the most esteemed. It also represents the climax of a venerable tradition in Japan, where the travel diary as poetic memoir enjoyed a distinguished eight-hundred-year history.

This fact too is an indication that Bashō's poetry involves more than meets the eye. The journey depicted in *The Narrow Road* is another pilgrimage through nature, but it is also a very conscious emulation of the conventions of the past. "Bewitched by the god of restlessness" Bashō describes himself as the trip gets under way. "Seduced by the call of history" would be just as accurate. Bashō, or his literary persona, sets off as the hero on a quest. His goal is to seek inspiration from remote places made famous by literature and history. Reputation, celebrity, tradition intertwine.

In 1943, some 250 years later, a second diary was published. This was Sora's account of their trip together, and it came like a thunderclap. The man who represented himself as a frail pilgrim at the mercy of nature and fate, and who was later deified by the Shinto religion, is described by Sora as a much more practical and wily figure, who altered the facts of his trip, abridged, and deleted to maintain the ascetic tone appropriate for a poetic saint, a man who saw himself as the successor to all poet-travelers of the past and was not about to reveal that among the motives for his trip were cultivating patrons and recruiting new students.

But *The Narrow Road of the Interior* is a literary creation. Its spare, supple prose anchors wise poetic insights. Its *haiku* transcend entertainment. The material has been shaped only by taking great pains, and that is the nature of artistry.

For another, more colloquial rendering of *The Narrow Road of the Interior*, translated by the poet Cid Corman in collaboration with Kamaike Susumu, see *Back Roads to Far Towns* (1986). All five of Bashō's travel journals are found in *The Narrow Road to the Deep North and Other Travel Sketches* (1966), translated by Nobuyuki Yuasa, whose re-creation of *haiku* as four-line poems seems less successful. For examples of Bashō's linked poetry see Earl Miner and Hiroko Odagiri, trans., *The Monkey's Straw Raincoat* (1981). For more poems by Bashō and his followers see Steven D. Carter, *Traditional Japanese Poetry: An Anthology* (1991). Two excellent book-length introductions to Bashō, both by Makoto Ueda, are *Matsuo Bashō* (1982) and *Bashō and His Interpreters* (1991). Shorter introductions are found in two literary histories by Donald Keene: *World Within Walls* (1976) and *Travelers of a Hundred Ages* (1989). For a general study of *haiku* see Kenneth Yasuda, *The Japanese Haiku* (1957); Nippon Gakujutsu Shinkokai, ed., *Haikai and Haiku* (1958), is a basic reference; and for an anthology of *haiku* from Bashō to modern times see Harold G. Henderson, *An Introduction to Haiku* (1958). Haruo Shirane, *Traces of Dreams: Landscape, Cultural Memory, and the Poetry of Bashō* (1998), explores important themes. An interesting comparative study is Earl Miner, *Naming Properties: Nominal References in Travel Writings by Bashō and Sora, Johnson and Boswell* (1996).

PRONOUNCING GLOSSARY

The following list uses common English syllables to provide rough equivalents of selected words whose pronunciation may be unfamiliar to the general reader.

Atsumi: *ah-tsoo-mee*

Benkei: *ben-kay*

Butchō: *boot-choh*

Date: *dah-tay*

Echigo: *e-chee-goh*

Edo: *e-doh*

Fukuura: *foo-koo-oo-rah*

Genji: *gen-jee*

Genroku: *gen-roh-koo*

haikai: *hai-kai*

Heike: *hay-kay*

hototogisu: *hoh-toh-toh-gee-soo*

Ihara Saikaku: *ee-hah-rah sai-kah-koo*

Iizuka: *ee-ee-zoo-kah*

Ji: *jee*

Kanemori: *kah-ne-moh-ree*

Kawai: *kah-wai*

Kisakata: *kee-sah-kah-tah*

Kokinshū: *koh-keen-shoo*

konoshiro: *koh-noh-shee-roh*

koromogae: *koh-roh-moh-gah-e*

Kūkai: *koo-kai*

Kurokamiyama: *koo-roh-kah-mee-yah-mah*

Kyohaku: *kyoh-hah-koo*

Matsuo Bashō: *mah-tsoo-oh bah-shoh*

Minamidani: *mee-nah-mee-dah-nee*

Nikkō: *neek-koh*

Nōin: *noh-een*

Satō Shōji: *sah-toh shoh-jee*

Shinto: *sheen-toh*

Shiogoshi: *shee-oh-goh-shee*

Shirakawa: *shee-rah-kah-wah*

Sōgorō: *soh-goh-roh*

Tsuruga: *tsoo-roo-gah*

Yasuhira: *yah-soo-hee-rah*

Yoichi: *yoh-ee-chee*

Yudono: *yoo-doh-noh*

The Narrow Road of the Interior[1]

The sun and the moon are eternal voyagers; the years that come and go are travelers too. For those whose lives float away on boats, for those who greet old age with hands clasping the lead ropes of horses, travel is life, travel is home. And many are the men of old who have perished as they journeyed.

I myself fell prey to wanderlust some years ago, desiring nothing better than to be a vagrant cloud scudding before the wind. Only last autumn, after having drifted along the seashore for a time, had I swept away the old cobwebs from my dilapidated riverside hermitage. But the year ended before I knew it, and I found myself looking at hazy spring skies and thinking of crossing Shirakawa Barrier.[2] Bewitched by the god of restlessness, I lost my peace of mind; summoned by the spirits of the road, I felt unable to settle down to anything. By the time I had mended my torn trousers, put a new cord on my hat, and cauterized my legs with moxa,[3] I was thinking only of the moon at Matsushima. I turned over my dwelling to others, moved to a house belonging to Sanpū,[4] and affixed the initial page of a linked-verse sequence to one of the pillars at my cottage.

> Even my grass-thatched hut
> will have new occupants now:
> a display of dolls.[5]

It was the Twenty-seventh Day, almost the end of the Third Month. The wan morning moon retained little of its brilliance, but the silhouette of Mount Fuji was dimly visible in the first pale light of dawn. With a twinge of sadness, I wondered when I might see the flowering branches at Ueno and Yanaka again. My intimate friends, who had all assembled the night before, got on the boat to see me off.

We disembarked at Senju.[6] Transitory though I know this world to be, I shed tears when I came to the parting of the ways, overwhelmed by the prospect of the long journey ahead.

1. Translated by Helen Craig McCullough and Steven D. Carter, with notes adapted from McCullough. 2. An old official checkpoint where travelers entered Mutsu Province. 3. A combustible substance used in traditional East Asian medicine. Moxa cones, made from pulverized plant leaves, were burned at specific therapeutic points on the skin, depending on the symptoms. The resulting heat was thought to adjust physical disorders by releasing energy obstructed at a crucial point and returning it to smooth circulation. 4. A disciple and patron. 5. It is the time of the Doll Festival, in the Third Month, when dolls representing the emperor, the empress, and their attendants are displayed in every household. 6. Near Edo (Tokyo). The path of Bashō's journey is traced on the map on p. 582.

> Departing springtime:
> birds lament and fishes too
> have tears in their eyes.

With that as the initial entry in my journal, we started off, hard though it was to stride out in earnest. The others lined up part way along the road, apparently wanting to watch us out of sight.

That year was, I believe, the second of the Genroku[7] era [1689]. I had taken a sudden fancy to make the long pilgrimage on foot to Mutsu and Dewa[8]—to view places I had heard about but never seen, even at the cost of hardships severe enough to "whiten a man's hair under the skies of Wu."[9] The outlook was not reassuring, but I resolved to hope for the best and be content merely to return alive.

We barely managed to reach Sōka Post Station that night. My greatest trial was the pack I bore on my thin, bony shoulders. I had planned to set out with no baggage at all, but had ended by taking along a paper coat for cold nights, a cotton bath garment, rain gear, and ink and brushes, as well as certain farewell presents, impossible to discard, which simply had to be accepted as burdens on the way.

We went to pay our respects at Muro-no-yashima. Sora, my fellow pilgrim, said, "This shrine honors Ko-no-hana-sakuya-hime, the goddess worshipped at Mount Fuji. The name Muro-no-yashima is an allusion to the birth of Hohodemi-no-mikoto inside the sealed chamber the goddess entered and set ablaze in fulfillment of her vow. It is because of that same incident that poems about the shrine usually mention smoke. The passage in the shrine history telling of the prohibition against konoshiro fish[1] is also well known."

On the Thirtieth, we lodged at the foot of the Nikkō Mountains. "I am called Buddha Gozaemon," the master of the house informed us. "People have given me that title because I make it a point to be honest in all my dealings. You may rest here tonight with your minds at ease."

"What kind of Buddha is it who has manifested himself in this impure world to help humble travelers like us—mendicant monks, as it were, on a pious pilgrimage?" I wondered. By paying close attention to his behavior, I satisfied myself that he was indeed a man of stubborn integrity, devoid of shrewdness and calculation. He was one of those, "firm, resolute, simple, and modest, who are near virtue,"[2] and I found his honorable, unassuming nature wholly admirable.

On the First of the Fourth Month, we went to worship at the shrine. In antiquity, the name of that holy mountain was written Nikōsan [Two-Storm Mountain], but the Great Teacher Kūkai changed it to Nikkō [Sunlight] when he founded the temple. It is almost as though the Great Teacher had been able to see 1,000 years into the future, for today the shrine's radiance extends throughout the realm, its beneficence overflows in the eight direc-

---

7. The era name. For information on the Japanese calendar, see the period introduction (pp. 584–85).
8. Two northern provinces.   9. An allusion to a Chinese poem written by someone seeing off a monk on his travels: "Your hat will be heavy with the snows of Wu; / Your boots will be fragrant with the fallen blossoms of Chu." Snow on a traveler's hat was associated with hardships and with whitening hair.
1. Gizzard shad. It was taboo to eat the fish because, when broiled, it gave off a smell like flesh burning.
2. From Confucius's Analects.

tions, and the four classes[3] of people dwell in security and peace. This is an awesome subject of which I shall write no more.

> Ah, awesome sight!
> on summer leaves and spring leaves,
> the radiance of the sun!

Kurokamiyama was veiled in haze, dotted with lingering patches of white snow. Sora composed this poem:

> Black hair shaved off,
> at Kurokamiyama[4]
> I change to new robes.

Sora is of the Kawai family; he was formerly called Sōgorō. He lived in a house adjoining mine, almost under the leaves of the banana plant, and used to help me with the chores of hauling wood and drawing water. Delighted by the thought of seeing Matsushima and Kisakata with me on this trip, and eager also to spare me some of the hardships of the road, he shaved his head at dawn on the day of our departure, put on a monk's black robe, and changed his name to Sōgo. That is why he composed the Kurokamiyama poem. The word koromogae ["I change to new robes"][5] was most effective.

There is a waterfall half a league or so up the mountain. The stream leaps with tremendous force over outthrust rocks at the top and descends 100 feet into a dark green pool strewn with 1,000 rocks. Visitors squeeze into the space between the rocks and the cascade to view it from the rear, which is why it is called Urami-no-take [Rearview Falls].

> In brief seclusion
> at a waterfall—the start
> of a summer retreat.

I knew someone at Kurobane in Nasu, so we decided to head straight across the plain from there. It began to rain as we walked along, taking our bearings on a distant village, and the sun soon sank below the horizon. After borrowing accommodations for the night at a farmhouse, we started out across the plain again in the morning. A horse was grazing nearby. We appealed for help to a man who was cutting grass and found him by no means incapable-of understanding other people's feelings, rustic though he was.

"What's the best thing to do, I wonder?" he said. "I can't leave my work. Still, inexperienced travelers are bound to get lost on this plain, what with all the trails branching off in every direction. Rather than see you go on alone, I'll let you take the horse. Send him back when he won't go any farther." With that, he lent us the animal.

Two small children came running behind the horse. One of them, a little girl, was called Kasane. Sora composed this poem:

---

3. Samurai, farmer, artisan, and merchant. The shrine held the mausoleum of the founder of the Tokugawa shogunate.   4. Or Mount Kurokami, homonymous with "black hair."   5. The first day of the Fourth Month was the date for changing from winter to summer clothing.

> Kasane must be
> a name for a wild pink
> with double petals![6]

Before long, we arrived at a hamlet and turned the horse back with some money tied to the saddle.

We called on Jōbōji, the warden at Kurobane. Surprised and delighted to see us, he kept us in conversation day and night; and his younger brother, Tōsui, came morning and evening. We went with Tōsui to his own house and were also invited to the homes of various other relatives. So the time passed.

One day, we strolled into the outskirts of the town for a brief visit to the site of the old dog shoots, then pressed through the Nasu bamboo fields to Lady Tamamo's tumulus,[7] and went on to pay our respects at Hachiman Shrine. Someone told me that when Yoichi shot down the fan target, it was to this very shrine that he prayed, "and especially Shōhachiman, the tutelary deity of my province."[8] The thought of the divine response evoked deep emotion. We returned to Tōsui's house as darkness fell.

There was a mountain-cult temple, Kōmyōji, in the vicinity. We visited it by invitation and worshipped at the Ascetic's Hall.[9]

> Toward summer mountains
> we set off after prayers
> before the master's clogs.

The site of the Venerable Butchō's[1] hermitage was behind Unganji Temple in that province. Butchō once told me that he had used pine charcoal to inscribe a poem on a rock there:

> Ah, how I detest
> building any shelter at all,
>   even a grass-thatched
> hovel less than five feet square!
> Were it not for the rainstorms . . .

Staff in hand, I prepared to set out for the temple to see what was left of the hermitage. A number of people encouraged one another to accompany me, and I acquired a group of young companions who kept up a lively chatter along the way. We reached the lower limits of the temple grounds in no time. The mountains created an impression of great depth. The valley road stretched far into the distance, pines and cryptomerias rose in dark masses, the moss dripped with moisture, and there was a bite to the air, even though it was the Fourth Month. We viewed all of the Ten Sights[2] and entered the main gate by way of a bridge.

---

6. This poem uses wordplay. The name *Kasane* can mean "double." The word for "wild pink" (a flower) can also mean "beloved child."   7. According to legend, Lady Tamamo was a fox-woman with whom an emperor fell in love. After having been unmasked by a diviner, she fled to Nasu, where local warriors shot her down. Her vindictive spirit survived as Killer Rock, a large boulder that releases poisonous fumes, which Bashō will soon visit on his journey. *Dog shoots:* for a brief time in the 13th century dog shooting had been a sport.   8. Refers to an episode in *The Tale of the Heike* (in Volume B). Yoichi is a minor *samurai* in the service of the Minamoto / Genji. An expert archer, he succeeds in shooting a fan suspended off the prow of an enemy ship, put there to taunt the Genji. Hachiman Shrine was dedicated to the god of war.   9. Dedicated to a miracle-working mountain ascetic of the 8th century, whose enshrined image is believed to have shown a holy man wearing high clogs (referred to in the following poem) and clothes made from leaves, holding a staff, and leaning against a rock.   1. A Zen master with whom Bashō had studied.   2. Various rocks, peaks, buildings, etc., within the temple precincts.

Eager to locate the hermitage, I scrambled up the hill behind the temple to a tiny thatched structure on a rock, a lean-to built against a cave. It was like seeing the holy Yuanmiao's Death Gate or the monk Fayun's[3] rock chamber. I left an impromptu verse on a pillar:

> Even woodpeckers
> seem to spare the hermitage
> in the summer grove.

From Kurobane, I headed toward Killer Rock astride a horse lent us by the warden. When the groom asked if I would write a poem for him, I gave him this, surprised and impressed that he should exhibit such cultivated taste:

> A cuckoo[4] song:
> please make the horse angle off
> across the field.

Killer Rock stands in the shadow of a mountain near a hot spring. It still emits poisonous vapors: dead bees, butterflies, and other insects lie in heaps near it, hiding the color of the sand.

The willow "where fresh spring water flowed"[5] survives on a ridge between two ricefields in Ashino Village. The district officer there, a man called Kohō, had often expressed a desire to show me the tree, and I had wondered each time about its exact location—but on this day I rested in its shade.

> Ah, the willow tree:
> a whole rice paddy planted
> before I set out.

So the days of impatient travel had accumulated, until at last I had reached Shirakawa Barrier. It was there, for the first time, that I felt truly on the way. I could understand why Kanemori had been moved to say, "Would that there were a means somehow to send people word in the capital!"[6]

As one of the Three Barriers, Shirakawa has always attracted the notice of poets and other writers. An autumn wind seemed to sound in my ears, colored leaves seemed to appear before my eyes—but even the leafy summer branches were delightful in their own way. Wild roses bloomed alongside the whiteness of the deutzia, making us feel as though we were crossing snow. I believe one of Kiyosuke's writings preserves a story about a man of the past who straightened his hat and adjusted his dress there.[7] Sora composed this poem:

3. A Chinese priest; he lived in a hut perched atop a high rock. Yuanmiao was a Chinese priest who confined himself for fifteen years to a cave he called Death's Gate.   4. In Japanese *hototogisu*; the name is an onomatopoeia derived from the bird's call: *ho-to-to*. Its song was deemed the quintessence of summer and is so beautiful that Bashō would like his horse to follow after it.   5. Refers to a verse by the famed poet-priest Saigyō (1118–1190): "On the wayside / where a clear spring flowed / in a willow's shade: / 'Just for a moment,' I thought, / but then I lingered there." Saigyō was an inveterate traveler and an important influence on Bashō.   6. Alludes to a poem by Kanemori (d. 990): "Would there were means / To let them know, somehow, / he people of the capital: / 'Today I have crossed / Shirakawa Barrier.'"   7. Fujiwara Kiyosuke (1104–1177) was a court noble and a poet-scholar. The man's actions show respect to Nōin (998–1050?), a monk and early poet-traveler who established Shirakawa Barrier as a place with poetic associations. In earlier times, travelers approaching checkpoints between provinces adjusted their clothes before crossing the barrier.

> With deutzia[8] flowers
> we adorn our hats—formal garb
> for the barrier.

We passed beyond the barrier and crossed the Abukuma River. To the left, the peak of Aizu soared; to the right, the districts of Iwaki, Sōma, and Mihara lay extended; to the rear, mountains formed boundaries with Hitachi and Shimotsuke provinces. We passed Kagenuma Pond, but the sky happened to be overcast that day, so there were no reflections.[9]

At the post town of Sukagawa, we visited a man called Tōkyū, who persuaded us to stay four or five days. His first act was to inquire, "How did you feel when you crossed Shirakawa Barrier?"

"What with the fatigue of the long, hard trip, the distractions of the scenery, and the stress of so many nostalgic associations, I couldn't manage to think of a decent poem," I said. "Still, it seemed a pity to cross with nothing to show for it . . .":

> A start for connoisseurs
> of poetry—rice-planting song
> of Michinoku.

We added a second verse and then a third, and continued until we had completed three sequences.

Under a great chestnut tree in the corner of the town, there lived a hermit monk. It seemed to me that his cottage, with its aura of lonely tranquility, must resemble that other place deep in the mountains where someone had gathered horse chestnuts.[1] I set down a few words:

> To form the character "chestnut," we write "tree of the west."[2] I have heard, I believe, that the bodhisattva Gyōgi perceived an affinity between this tree and the Western Paradise,[3] and that he used its wood for staffs and pillars throughout his life:

> Chestnut at the eaves—
> here are blossoms unremarked
> by ordinary folk.

Asakayama is just beyond Hiwada Post Station, about five leagues from Tōkyū's house. It is close to the road, and there are numerous marshes in the vicinity. It was almost the season for reaping *katsumi*.[4] We kept asking, "Which plant is the flowering *katsumi*?" But nobody knew. We wandered about, scrutinizing marshes, questioning people, and seeking *"katsumi, katsumi"* until the sun sank to the rim of the hills.

---

8. A shrub of the saxifrage family, an ornamental bush with white or pink flowers. It blooms in the Fourth Month.   9. The name of the pond is literally "Shadow Swamp"; with the sun obscured, it does not fulfill its reputation.   1. Refers to Saigyō (see n. 5, p. 611) and one of his poems: "In these remote hills, / I try to trap water / dripping onto the rocks; / I gather horse chestnuts / dropping to the ground."   2. The character for "chestnut" consists of the character for "tree" surmounted by an element resembling the character for "west."   3. One of the various "Buddha worlds" (Buddhist equivalents of Heaven); this one is located in the western sector of the universe and is presided over by Amida, the most popular Buddhist deity of the time. *Bodhisattva*: a person who attains enlightenment but compassionately refrains from entering paradise to save others, a future Buddha. Gyōgi (668–749) was a Buddhist monk known for his asceticism and charisma.   4. Wild rice.

We turned off to the right at Nihonmatsu, took a brief look at Kurozuka Cave,[5] and stopped for the night at Fukushima.

On the following day, we went to Shinobu in search of the Fern-print Rock,[6] which proved to be half buried under the soil of a remote hamlet in the shadow of a mountain. Some village urchins came up and told us, "In the old days, the rock used to be on top of that mountain, but the farmers got upset because the people who passed would destroy the young grain so they could test it. They shoved it off into this valley; that's why it's lying upside down." A likely story, perhaps.

> Hands planting seedlings
> evoke Shinobu patterns
> of the distant past.

We crossed the river at Tsukinowa Ford and emerged at Senoue Post Station. Satō Shōji's[7] old home was about a league and a half away, near the mountains to the left. Told that we would find the site at Sabano in Iizuka Village, we went along, asking directions, until we came upon it at a place called Maruyama. That was where Shōji had had his house. I wept as someone explained that the front gate had been at the foot of the hill. Still standing at an old temple nearby were a number of stone monuments erected in memory of the family. It was especially moving to see the memorials to the two young wives.[8] "Women though they were, all the world knows of their bravery." The thought made me drench my sleeve. The Tablet of Tears[9] was not far to seek!

We entered the temple to ask for tea, and there we saw Yoshitsune's sword and Benkei's pannier,[1] preserved as treasures.

> Paper carp flying!
> Display pannier and sword, too,
> in the Fifth Month.

It was the First Day of the Fifth Month.

We lodged that night at Iizuka, taking advantage of the hot springs in the town to bathe before engaging a room. The hostelry turned out to be a wretched hovel, its straw mats spread over dirt floors. In the absence of a lamp, we prepared our beds and stretched out by the light from a fire-pit. Thunder rumbled during the night, and rain fell in torrents. What with the roof leaking right over my head and the fleas and mosquitoes biting, I got no sleep at all. To make matters worse, my old complaint[2] flared up, causing me such agony that I almost fainted.

At long last, the short night ended and we set out again. Still feeling the effects of the night, I rode a rented horse to Kōri Post Station. It was unsettling to fall prey to an infirmity while so great a distance remained ahead.

---

5. Rich in folklore. A witch was said to be interred beneath Kurozuka, a hillock whose name means "black mound," and the nearby rocky cave was thought a goblins' lair.   6. Said to have been used to imprint cloth with a moss-fern design, a specialty of the area.   7. A brave warrior and supporter of the Genji chieftain Yoshitsune (in *The Tale of the Heike*).   8. Of Satō Shōji's two sons, who died in battle. The young widows were said to have worn their husbands' suits of armor as a way of consoling their grieving mother-in-law, who still hoped to see her sons riding home victorious.   9. A memorial erected in China in honor of a virtuous official. All who saw it were said to weep.   1. A large basket. Yoshitsune is the great hero who leads his clan to victory in the war recounted in *The Tale of the Heike*. Benkei is his faithful lieutenant.   2. Bashō was troubled with stomachaches and hemorrhoids.

But I told myself that I had deliberately planned this long pilgrimage to remote areas, a decision that meant renouncing worldly concerns and facing the fact of life's uncertainty. If I were to die on the road—very well, that would be Heaven's decree. Such reflections helped to restore my spirits a bit, and it was with a jaunty step that I passed through the Great Gate into the Date[3] domain.

We entered Kasajima District by way of Abumizuri and Shiraishi Castle. I asked someone about the Fujiwara Middle Captain Sanekata's[4] grave and was told, "Those two villages far off to the right at the edge of the hills are Minowa and Kasajima. The Road Goddess's shrine and the 'memento miscanthus' are still there."[5] The road was in a dreadful state from the recent early-summer rains, and I was exhausted, so we contented ourselves with looking in that direction as we trudged on. Because the names Minowa and Kasajima suggested the rainy season,[6] I composed this verse.

> Where is Rain Hat Isle?
> Somewhere down the muddy roads
> of the Fifth Month!

We lodged at Iwanuma. It was exciting to see the Takekuma Pine. The trunk forks a bit above the ground, and one knows instantly that this is just how the old tree must have looked. My first thought was of Nōin.[7] Did he compose the poem, "Not a trace this time of the pine" because a certain man, appointed long ago to serve as Governor of Mutsu, had felled the tree to get pilings for a bridge to span the Natori River? Someone told me that generations of people have been alternately cutting down the existing tree and planting a replacement. The present one is a magnificent specimen— quite capable, I should imagine, of living 1,000 years.

Kyohaku[8] had given me a poem as a farewell present:

> Late cherry blossoms:
> please show my friend the pine tree
> at Takekuma.

Thus:

> After three months:
> the twin-trunked pine awaited
> since the cherry trees bloomed.

We crossed the Natori River into Sendai on the day when people thatch their roofs with sweet-flag leaves.[9] We sought out a lodging and stayed four or five days.

I made the acquaintance of a local painter, Kaemon by name, who had been described to me as a man of cultivated taste. He told us he had devoted

3. A clan that included some of the richest and most powerful provincial barons.   4. Fujiwara Sanekata (d. 998) was a court poet whose quarrel with a clansman led to his exile in the northern provinces. 5. Someone had planted a clump of miscanthus, a variety of ornamental grass, at Sanekata's grave in allusion to a memorial poem by Saigyō: "Only his name, / eternally withered, / has escaped decay: / we see, as a memento, / iscanthus on a dry plain."   6. *Mino* can mean "straw raincoat," and *kasa* can mean "rain hat."   7. See n. 7, p. 611.   8. A disciple.   9. On Boys' Day, a holiday on the fifth day of the Fifth Month, it was the custom for families with sons to fly carp streamers, a symbol of vigor and success. On the day before, irises (*sweet-flag*), because they were thought to ward off evil, were hung from the eaves. The holiday was also known as the Iris Festival.

several years to locating famous old places that had become hard to identify, and took us to see some of them one day. The bush clover grew thick at Miyagino; I could imagine the sight in autumn. It was the season when the pieris[1] bloomed at Tamada, Yokono, and Tsutsuji-gaoka. We entered a pine grove where no sunlight penetrated—a place called Konoshita, according to Kaemon—and I thought it must have been the same kind of heavy moisture, dripping from those very trees long ago, that inspired the poem, "Suggest to your lord, attendants, that he wear his hat."[2] We paid our respects at the Yakushidō Hall and at Tenjin Shrine before the day ended.

Kaemon sent us off with a map on which he had drawn famous scenes of Shiogama and Matsushima. He also gave us two pairs of straw sandals, bound with dark blue cords, as a farewell present. The gifts showed him to be quite as cultivated as I had surmised.

> Let us bind sweet-flags
> to our feet, making of them
> cords for straw sandals.

Continuing on our way with the help of the map, we came to the *tofu* [ten-strand] sedge, growing at the base of the mountains where the "narrow road of the interior"[3] runs. I am told that the local people still make ten-strand mats every year for presentation to the provincial Governor.

We saw the Courtyard Monument Stone at Tagajō in Ichikawa Village. It was a little more than six feet tall and perhaps three feet wide. Some characters, faintly visible as depressions in the moss, listed distances to the provincial boundaries in the four directions. There was also an inscription: "This castle was erected in the first year of Jinki [724] by the Inspector-Garrison Commander Ōno no Ason Azumabito. It was rebuilt in the sixth year of Tenpyō Hōji [762] by the Consultant-Garrison Commander Emi no Ason Asakari. First Day, Twelfth Month." That was in the reign of Emperor Shōmu.

Although we hear about many places celebrated in verse since antiquity, most of them have vanished with the passing of time. Mountains have crumbled, rivers have entered unaccustomed channels, roads have followed new routes, stones have been buried and hidden underground, aged trees have given way to saplings. But this monument was a genuine souvenir from 1,000 years ago, and to see it before my eyes was to feel that I could understand the sentiments of the old poets. "This is a traveler's reward," I thought. "This is the joy of having survived into old age." Moved to tears, I forgot the hardships of the road.

From there, we went to see Noda-no-tamagawa and Oki-no-ishi. A temple, Masshōzan, had been built at Sue-no-matsuyama, and there were graves everywhere among the pine trees, saddening reminders that such must be

1. Japanese andromeda (*Pieris japonica*), a broad-leafed evergreen with drooping clusters of white flowers. 2. A poem in the *Kokinshū* (Collection of Ancient and Modern Times; in Volume B), the first of twenty-one imperially commissioned anthologies of classical Japanese poetry; it was completed around 905 and contains 1,111 poems. The poem referred to here is "Suggest to your lord, / attendants, / that he wear his hat, / for beneath the trees of Miyagino / the dew comes down harder than the rain."   3. This road, the source of Bashō's title, extended from what is now northeastern Sendai to Tagajō City (see the map on p. 582).

the end of all vows to "interchange wings and link branches."[4] The evening bell was tolling as we entered Shiogama.

The perpetual overcast of the rainy season had lifted enough to reveal Magaki Island close at hand, faintly illuminated by the evening moon. A line of small fishing boats came rowing in. As I listened to the voices of the men dividing the catch, I felt that I understood the poet who sang, "There is deep pathos in a boat pulled by a rope," and my own emotion deepened.[5] That night, a blind singer recited a Michinoku ballad[6] to the accompaniment of his lute. He performed not far from where I was trying to sleep, and I found his loud, countrified falsetto rather noisy—a chanting style quite different from either *Heike* recitation or the *kōwaka-mai*[7] ballad drama. But then I realized how admirable it was that the fine old customs were still preserved in that distant land.

Early the next day, we visited Shiogama Shrine, which had been restored by the provincial Governor. Its pillars stood firm and majestic, its painted rafters sparkled, its stone steps rose in flight after flight, and its sacred red fences gleamed in the morning sunlight. With profound reverence, I reflected that it is the way of our land for the miraculous powers of the gods to manifest themselves even in such remote, out-of-the-way places as this.

In front of the sanctuary, there was a splendid old lantern with an inscription on its iron door: "Presented as an offering by Izumi no Saburō in the third year of Bunji [1187]." It was rare, indeed, to see before one's eyes an object that had remained unchanged for 500 years. Izumi no Saburō was a brave, honorable, loyal, and filial warrior. His fame endures even today; there is no one who does not admire him. How true it is that men must strive to walk in the Way and uphold the right! "Fame will follow of itself."

Noon was already approaching when we engaged a boat for the crossing to Matsushima, a distance of a little more than two leagues. We landed at Ojima Beach.

Trite though it may seem to say so, Matsushima is the most beautiful spot in Japan, by no means inferior to Dongting Lake or West Lake.[8] The sea enters from the southeast into a bay extending for three leagues, its waters as ample as the flow of the Zhejiang Bore.[9] There are more islands than anyone could count. The tall ones rear up as though straining toward the sky; the flat ones crawl on their bellies over the waves. Some seem made of two layers, others of three folds. To the left, they appear separate; to the right, linked. Here and there, one carries another on its back or cradles it in its arms, as though caring for a beloved child or grandchild. The pines are deep green in color, and their branches, twisted by the salt gales, have assumed natural shapes so dramatic that they seem the work of human hands. The tranquil charm of the scene suggests a beautiful woman who has just completed her toilette. Truly, Matsushima might have been made by Ōyamazumi[1] in the ancient age of the mighty gods! What painter can repro-

---

4. An allusion to the pledge exchanged by the Chinese emperor and his beloved in the *Song of Everlasting Sorrow* by Po Chü-i: "In heaven, may we be birds with shared wings; / On earth, may we be trees with linked branches." The places mentioned here are in the vicinity of Sendai.   5. Reference to a poem in the *Kokinshū*: "However it may be elsewhere / in Michinoku, / there is deep pathos / in a boat pulled by a rope / along Shiogama shore."   6. A local ballad; Bashō is now in the province of Michinoku.   7. Dramatic ballad-dances recounting military episodes from *The Tale of the Heike* (originally performed as an oral narrative) and other warrior stories. *Kōwaka-mai* were one of the precursors of *nō* plays.   8. Chinese sites (which Bashō had never seen) famed for their beauty.   9. In China.   1. A mountain god who was son of the gods who created the Japanese islands.

duce, what author can describe the wonder of the creator's divine handiwork?

Ojima Island projects into the sea just offshore from the mainland. It is the site of the Venerable Ungo's[2] dwelling, and of the rock on which that holy man used to practice meditation. There also seemed to be a few recluses living among the pine trees. Upon seeing smoke rising from a fire of twigs and pine cones at one peaceful thatched hut, we could not help approaching the spot, even though we had no way of knowing what kind of man the occupant might be. Meanwhile, the moon began to shine on the water, transforming the scene from its daytime appearance.

We returned to the Matsushima shore to engage lodgings—a second-story room with a window on the sea. What marvelous exhilaration to spend the night so close to the winds and clouds! Sora recited this:

> Ah, Matsushima!
> Cuckoo, you ought to borrow
> the guise of the crane.[3]

I remained silent, trying without success to compose myself for sleep. At the time of my departure from the old hermitage, Sodō and Hara Anteki[4] had given me poems about Matsushima and Matsu-ga-urashima (the one in Chinese and the other in Japanese), and I got them out of my bag now to serve as companions for the evening. I also had some *hokku,* compositions by Sanpū and Jokushi.[5]

On the Eleventh, we visited Zuiganji.[6] Thirty-two generations ago, Makabe no Heishirō entered holy orders, went to China, and returned to found that temple. Later, through the virtuous influence of the Venerable Ungo, the seven old structures were transformed into a great religious center, a veritable earthly paradise, with dazzling golden walls and resplendent furnishings. I thought with respectful admiration of the holy Kenbutsu[7] and wondered where his place of worship might have been.

On the Twelfth, we left for Hiraizumi, choosing a little-frequented track used by hunters, grass-cutters, and woodchoppers, which was supposed to take us past the Aneha Pine and Odae Bridge. Blundering along, we lost our way and finally emerged at the port town of Ishino-maki. Kinkazan, the mountain of which the poet wrote, "Golden flowers have blossomed," was visible across the water.[8] Hundreds of coastal vessels rode together in the harbor, and smoke ascended everywhere from the cooking fires of houses jostling for space. Astonished to have stumbled on such a place, we looked for lodgings, but nobody seemed to have a room for rent, and we spent the night in a wretched shack.

---

2. A monk who rebuilt a temple at Matsushima. He was the teacher of Butchō, Bashō's Zen master. 3. The gist of the poem is: "Your song is appealing, cuckoo, but the stately white crane is the bird we expect to see at Matsushima [Pine Isles]." Pines and cranes were a conventional pair, both symbols of longevity. Sora's poem alludes to an old poem of uncertain provenance and unstable wording, one version of which reads in part: "[When snow falls] does the plover borrow / The crane's [white] plumage?" 4. Two friends of Bashō, both amateur poets. Hara was also a physician. 5. Bashō's disciples. *Hokku:* the first three lines of a linked-verse sequence, from which *haiku* evolved. 6. The temple restored by Ungo (see n. 2, p. 617). 7. A monk who lived approximately six hundred years earlier and who confined himself to a small temple at Matsushima. 8. Refers to a poem in the *Man'yōshū* (The Collection of Ten Thousand Leaves; in Volume B), which was completed around 759 and is the earliest compilation of Japanese poetry, containing more than forty-five hundred poems. The poem referred to here was written when gold was discovered in the area: "For our sovereign's reign, / an auspicious augury: / among the mountains of Michinoku / in the east, / golden flowers have blossomed."

The next morning, we set out again on an uncertain journey over strange roads, plodding along an interminable dike from which we could see Sode-no-watari, Obuchi-no-maki, and Mano-no-kayahara[9] in the distance. We walked beside a long, dismal marsh to a place called Toima, where we stopped overnight, and finally arrived in Hiraizumi. I think the distance was something over twenty leagues.

The glory of three generations[1] was but a dozing dream. Paddies and wild fields have claimed the land where Hidehira's mansion stood, a league beyond the site of the great gate, and only Mount Kinkeizan looks as it did in the past. My first act was to ascend to Takadachi. From there, I could see both the mighty Kitakami River, which flows down from Nanbu, and the Koromo River, which skirts Izumi Castle and empties into the larger stream below Takadachi. Yasuhira's[2] castle, on the near side of Koromo Barrier, seems to have guarded the Nanbu entrance against barbarian encroachments. There at Takadachi, Yoshitsune[3] shut himself up with a chosen band of loyal men—yet their heroic deeds lasted only a moment, and nothing remains but evanescent clumps of grass.

> The nation is destroyed; the mountains and rivers remain.
> Spring comes to the castle; the grasses are green.[4]

Sitting on my sedge hat with those lines running through my head, I wept for a long time.

> A dream of warriors,
> and after dreaming is done,
> the summer grasses.

> Ah, the white hair:
> vision of Kanefusa[5]
> in deutzia flowers.
> —Sora

The two halls of which we had heard so many impressive tales were open to visitors. The images of the three chieftains are preserved in the Sutra Hall, and in the Golden Hall there are the three coffins and the three sacred images.[6] In the past, the Golden Hall's seven precious substances were scattered and lost; gales ravaged the magnificent jewel-studded doors, and the golden pillars rotted in the frosts and snows. But just as it seemed that the whole building must collapse, leaving nothing but clumps of grass, new walls were put around it, and a roof was erected against the winds and rains. So it survives for a time, a memento of events that took place 1,000 years ago.

> Do the Fifth-Month rains
> stay away when they fall,
> sparing that Hall of Gold?

After journeying on with the Nanbu Road visible in the distance, we spent the night at Iwade-no-sato. From there, we passed Ogurazaki and Mizu-no-

9. All are located between Ishi-no-maki and Toima and had associations with earlier poetry. 1. That is, of the powerful Fujiwara family—Kiyohira, Motohira, and Hidehira—who created the so-called golden age of the north in the 12th century. 2. Son of Fujiwara Hidehira, whose fight with his brother destroyed the clan's prosperity in the region. After killing his brother, Yasuhira was in turn killed by the Minamoto/ Genji chieftain Yoritomo. 3. See n. 1, p. 613. 4. A quote from the Chinese poet Tu Fu, lamenting the devastation caused by a rebellion in 755, from which the T'ang Dynasty never fully recovered. 5. A loyal retainer of Yoshitsune. 6. Of Amida Buddha and his attendants Kannon and Seishi. The coffins contained the mummified remains of Hidehira, his father, and his grandfather.

ojima and arrived at Shitomae Barrier by way of Narugo Hot Springs, intending to cross into Dewa Province. The road was so little frequented by travelers that we excited the guards' suspicions, and we barely managed to get through the checkpoint. The sun had already begun to set as we toiled upward through the mountains, so we asked for shelter when we saw a border guard's house. Then the wind howled and the rain poured for three days, trapping us in those miserable hills.

> The fleas and the lice—
> and next to my pillow,
> a pissing horse.

The master of the house told us that our route into Dewa was an ill-marked trail through high mountains; we would be wise to engage a guide to help us with the crossing. I took his advice and hired a fine, stalwart young fellow, who strode ahead with a short, curved sword tucked into his belt and an oak staff in his hand. As we followed him, I felt an uncomfortable presentiment that this would be the day on which we would come face to face with danger at last. Just as our host had said, the mountains were high and thickly wooded, their silence unbroken even by the chirp of a bird. It was like traveling at night to walk in the dim light under the dense canopy. Feeling as though dust must be blowing down from the edge of the clouds,[7] we pushed through bamboo, forded streams, and stumbled over rocks, all the time in a cold sweat, until we finally emerged at Mogami-no-shō. Our guide took his leave in high spirits, after having informed us that the path we had followed was one on which unpleasant things were always happening, and that it had been a great stroke of luck to bring us through safely. Even though the danger was past, his words made my heart pound.

At Obanazawa, we called on Seifū, a man whose tastes were not vulgar despite his wealth. As a frequent visitor to the capital, he understood what it meant to be a traveler, and he kept us for several days, trying in many kind ways to make us forget the hardships of the long journey.

> I sit at ease,
> taking this coolness
> as my lodging place.

> Come on, show yourself!
> Under the silkworm nursery
> the croak of a toad.

> In my mind's eye,
> a brush for someone's brows:
> the safflower blossom.

> The silkworm nurses—
> figures reminiscent
> of a distant past.[8]
>   —Sora

---

7. To emphasize the murkiness of the atmosphere, Bashō borrows from a poem in which Tu Fu compliments a princess by implying that she lives in the sky: "When I begin to ascend the breezy stone steps, / a dust storm blows down from the edge of the clouds."   8. The silkworm tenders (nurses) dress in an old style. Here, as Bashō does elsewhere, Sora expresses nostalgia for a way of life that had disappeared from the cities to the west.

In the Yamagata domain, there is a mountain temple called Ryū-shakuji, a serene, quiet seat of religion founded by the Great Teacher Jikaku.[9] Urged by others to see it, we retraced our steps some seven leagues from Obanazawa. We arrived before sundown, reserved accommodations in the pilgrims' hostel at the foot of the hill, and climbed to the halls above. The mountain consists of piles of massive rocks. Its pines and other evergreens bear the marks of many long years; its moss lies like velvet on the ancient rocks and soil. Not a sound emanated from the temple buildings at the summit, which all proved to be closed, but we skirted the cliffs and clambered over the rocks to view the halls. The quiet, lonely beauty of the environs purified the heart.

> Ah, tranquility!
> Penetrating the very rock,
> a cicada's voice.

At Ōishida, we awaited fair weather with a view to descending the Mogami River by boat. In that spot where the seeds of the old *haikai*[1] had fallen, some people still cherished the memory of the flowers. With hearts softened by poetry's civilizing touch, those onetime blowers of shrill reed flutes[2] had been groping for the correct way of practicing the art, so they told me, but had found it difficult to choose between the old styles and the new with no one to guide them. I felt myself under an obligation to leave them a sequence. Such was one result of this journey in pursuit of my art.

The Mogami River has its source deep in the northern mountains and its upper reaches in Yamagata. After presenting formidable hazards like Goten and Hayabusa,[3] it skirts Mount Itajiki on the north and finally empties into the sea at Sakata. Our boat descended amid luxuriant foliage, the mountains pressing overhead from the left and the right. It was probably similar craft, loaded with sheaves, that the old song meant when it spoke of rice boats.[4] Travelers can see the cascading waters of Shiraito Falls through gaps in the green leaves. The Sennindō Hall is there too, facing the bank.

The swollen waters made the journey hazardous:

> Bringing together
> the summer rains in swiftness:
> Mogami River!

On the Third of the Sixth Month, we climbed Mount Haguro. We called on Zushi Sakichi[5] and then were received by the Holy Teacher Egaku, the Abbot's deputy, who lodged us at the Minamidani Annex and treated us with great consideration.

On the Fourth, there was a *haikai* gathering at the Abbot's residence:

> Ah, what a delight!
> Cooled as by snow, the south wind
> at Minamidani.

---

9. Better known as Ennin (794–864), a famous priest who helped establish Buddhism in Japan. *Yamagata domain:* from the early 17th century until 1868, Japan was divided into domains, or fiefdoms, held directly by the shogun and his family or by the feudal barons who, to one degree or another, supported him. Yamagata was in the province of Dewa.   1. Nonstandard, or eccentric, linked verse. Masters from two older *haikai* schools had spent time in the area.   2. That is, untutored country people.   3. Two treacherous spots in the river, one with rocks and the other with swift currents.   4. Refers to a folk song whose chief interest lies in its puns on the word *rice*.   5. A dyer by trade and an amateur poet.

On the Fifth, we went to worship at Haguro Shrine. Nobody knows when the founder, the Great Teacher Nōjo, lived. The *Engi Canon*[6] mentions a shrine called "Satoyama in Dewa Province," which leads one to wonder if *sato* might be a copyist's error for *kuro*. Perhaps "Haguroyama" is a contraction of "Dewa no Kuroyama" [Kuroyama in Dewa Province]. I understand that the official gazetteer says Dewa acquired its name because the province used to present birds' feathers to the throne as tribute.[7]

Hagurosan, Gassan, and Yudono are known collectively as the Three Mountains. At Haguro, a subsidiary of Tōeizan Kan'eiji Temple in Edo, the moon of Tendai[8] enlightenment shines bright, and the lamp of the Law of perfect understanding and all-permeating vision burns high. The temple buildings stand roof to roof; the ascetics vie in the practice of rituals. We can but feel awe and trepidation before the miraculous powers of so holy a place, which may with justice be called a magnificent mountain, destined to flourish forever.

On the Eighth, we made the ascent of Gassan. Donning paper garlands, and with our heads wrapped in white turbans, we toiled upward for eight leagues, led by a porter guide through misty mountains with ice and snow underfoot. We could almost have believed ourselves to be entering the cloud barrier beyond which the sun and the moon traverse the heavens. The sun was setting and the moon had risen when we finally reached the summit, gasping for breath and numb with cold. We stretched out on beds of bamboo grass until dawn, and descended toward Yudono after the rising sun had dispersed the clouds.

Near a valley, we saw a swordsmith's cottage. The Dewa smiths, attracted by the miraculous waters, had purified themselves there before forging their famous blades, which they had identified by the carved signature, "Gassan."[9] I was reminded of the weapons tempered at Dragon Spring.[1] It also seemed to me that I could understand the dedication with which those men had striven to master their art, inspired by the ancient example of Gan Jiang and Moye.[2]

While seated on a rock for a brief rest, I noticed some half-opened buds on a cherry tree about three feet high. How admirable that those late blooms had remembered spring, despite the snowdrifts under which they had lain buried! They were like "plum blossoms in summer heat"[3] perfuming the air. The memory of Archbishop Gyōson's touching poem[4] added to the little tree's charm.

It is a rule among ascetics not to give outsiders details about Mount Yudono, so I shall lay aside my brush and write no more.

When we returned to our lodgings, Egaku asked us to inscribe poem cards with verses suggested by our pilgrimage to the Three Mountains:

---

6. An early collection of governmental regulations (compiled 905–927), designed to flesh out the broad administrative structure that was then being adapted from China.   7. The characters representing *sato* and *kuro* are similar in appearance, especially when written in cursive script. The *ha* of "Haguroyama" and the *wa* of "Dewa" can be written with the same phonetic symbol and were once the same sound. The connection between Dewa and birds' feathers is in the orthography: *wa* is written with the character for "feathers."   8. A Buddhist sect.   9. A famous swordsmith in the late 12th century.   1. A spring in China whose waters were used for tempering sword blades.   2. Gan Jiang was a Chinese swordsmith. He and his wife, Moye, forged two famous swords.   3. A Zen metaphor for the rare and unusual and, by extension, for passing beyond this world to enlightenment.   4. A reference to a poem that Gyōson (1055–1135), an ascetic, composed when he discovered cherries blooming out of season: "Let us sympathize / with one another, / cherry tree on the mountain: / were it not for your blossoms, / I would have no friend at all."

Ah, what coolness!
Under a crescent moon,
Mount Haguro glimpsed.

Mountain of the Moon:
after how many cloud peaks
had formed and crumbled?

My sleeve was drenched
at Yudono, the mountain
of which none may speak.

Yudonoyama:
tears fall as I walk the path
where feet tread on coins.[5]

—Sora

After our departure from Haguro, we were invited to the warrior Nagayama Shigeyuki's home, where we composed a sequence. (Sakichi accompanied us that far.) Then we boarded a river boat and traveled downstream to Sakata Harbor. We stayed with a physician, En'an Fugyoku.

Evening cool!
A view from Mount Atsumi
to Fukuura.

Mogami River—
it has plunged the hot sun
into the sea.

I had already enjoyed innumerable splendid views of rivers and mountains, ocean and land; now I set my heart on seeing Kisakata. It was a journey of ten leagues northeast from Sakata, across mountains and along sandy beaches. A wind from the sea stirred the white sand early in the afternoon, and Mount Chōkai disappeared behind misting rain. "Groping in the dark," we found "the view in the rain exceptional too."[6] The surroundings promised to be beautiful once the skies had cleared. We crawled into a fisherman's thatched shanty to await the end of the rain.

The next day was fine, and we launched forth onto the bay in a boat as the bright morning sun rose. First of all, we went to Nōinjima to visit the spot where Saigyō had lived in seclusion for three years. Then we disembarked on the opposite shore and saw a memento of the poet, the old cherry tree that had suggested the verse, "rowing over flowers."[7] Near the water's edge, we noticed a tomb that was said to be the grave of Empress Jingu,[8] together with a temple, Kanmanjuji. I had never heard that the Empress had gone to that place. I wonder how her grave happened to be there.

---

5. The coins have been strewn by pilgrims, but unlike the secular world, no one scrambles to pick them up. Sora sheds tears at this miraculous behavior, which he can only attribute to the power of the gods.
6. Bashō compares Kisakata to the famous West Lake in China, of which Su Tongbo (1037–1101) wrote: "The sparkling, brimming waters are beautiful in sunshine; / The view when a misty rain veils the mountains is exceptional too." *"Groping in the dark"*: probably an allusion to a poem composed at the lake by a visiting Japanese monk, Sakugen (1501–1579): "The sun is setting beyond Yuhangmen; / All sights are indistinct, there is no view. / But I recall the poem, 'Exceptional in rain, beautiful in sunshine'; / Groping in the dark, I feel West Lake's charm."   7. From a poem attributed to Saigyō: "The cherry blossoms / at Kisakata / lie buried under waves: / seafolk in their fishing boat / go rowing over flowers."   8. Legendary empress said to have ruled in the second half of the 4th century.

Seated in the temple's front apartment with the blinds raised, we commanded a panoramic view. To the south, Mount Chōkai propped up the sky, its image reflected in the bay; to the west, Muyamuya Barrier blocked the road; to the east, the Akita Road stretched far into the distance on an embankment; to the north, there loomed the majestic bulk of the sea, its waves entering the bay at a place called Shiogoshi.

The bay measures about a league in length and breadth. It resembles Matsushima in appearance but has a quality of its own: where Matsushima seems to smile, Kisakata droops in dejection. The lonely, melancholy scene suggests a troubled human spirit.

> Xi Shi's[9] drooping eyelids:
> mimosa in falling rain
> at Kisakata.

> At Shiogoshi
> crane legs drenched by high tide—
> and how cool the sea!

A festival:

> A shrine festival:
> what foods do worshippers eat
> at Kisakata?
>   —Sora

> At fishers' houses,
> people lay down rain shutters,
> seeking evening cool.[1]
>   —Teiji, a Mino merchant

Seeing an osprey nest on a rock:

> Might they have vowed,
> "Never shall waves cross here"[2]—
> those nesting ospreys?
>   —Sora

After several days of reluctant farewells to friends in Sakata, we set out under the clouds of the Northern Land Road, quailing before the prospect of the long journey ahead. It was reported to be 130 leagues to the castle town of the Kaga domain. Once past Nezu Barrier, we made our way on foot through Echigo Province to Ichiburi Barrier in Etchū Province, a tiring journey of nine miserably hot, rainy days. I felt too ill to write anything.

> In the Seventh Month,
> even the Sixth Day differs
> from ordinary nights.[3]

9. A Chinese beauty of the 5th century B.C. Originally the consort of the king of Yue, she was later forced to wed his conqueror, the king of Wu.   1. That is, they remove the rain shutters from their houses and put them on the beach, where they sit, enjoying the evening cool.   2. This phrase constitutes a vow of eternal fidelity, derived from a poem in the *Kokinshū*: "Would I be the cast sort / To cast you aside / and turn to someone new? / Sooner would the waves traverse / Sue-no-matsu Mountain."   3. Because people were preparing for the Tanabata Festival, which was held on the seventh day of the Seventh Month in honor of the stars Altair (the herd boy) and Vega (the weaver maiden). Legend held that the two lovers were separated by the Milky Way, except for this one night, when they would meet for their annual rendezvous.

> Tumultuous seas:
> spanning the sky to Sado Isle,
> the Milky Way.

That night I drew up a pillow and lay down to sleep, exhausted after having traversed the most difficult stretches of road in all the north country—places with names like "Children Forget Parents," "Parents Forget Children," "Dogs Go Back," and "Horses Sent Back." The voices of young women drifted in from the adjoining room in front—two of them, it appeared, talking to an elderly man, whose voice was also audible. As I listened, I realized that they were prostitutes from Niigata in Echigo, bound on a pilgrimage to the Grand Shrines of Ise. The old man was to be sent home to Niigata in the morning, after having escorted them as far as this barrier, and they seemed to be writing letters and giving him inconsequential messages to take back. Adrift on "the shore where white breakers roll in," these "fishermen's daughters" had fallen low indeed, exchanging fleeting vows with every passerby.[4] How wretched the karma that had doomed them to such an existence! I fell asleep with their voices in my ears.

The next morning, the same two girls spoke to us as we were about to leave. "We're feeling terribly nervous and discouraged about going off on this hard trip over strange roads. Won't you let us join your party, even if we only stay close enough to catch a glimpse of you now and then? You wear the robes of mercy: please let us share the Buddha's compassion and form a bond with the Way," they said, weeping.

"I sympathize with you, but we'll be making frequent stops. Just follow others going to the same place; I'm sure the gods will see you there safely." We walked off without waiting for an answer, but it was some time before I could stop feeling sorry for them.

> Ladies of pleasure
> sleeping in the same hostel:
> bush clover and moon.[5]

I recited those lines to Sora, who wrote them down.

After crossing the "forty-eight channels" of the Kurobe River and innumerable other streams, we reached the coast at Nago. Even though the season was not spring, it seemed a shame to miss the wisteria at Tako in early autumn. We asked someone how to get there, but the answer frightened us off. "Tako is five leagues along the beach from here, in the hollow of those mountains. The only houses are a few ramshackle thatched huts belonging to fishermen; you probably wouldn't find anyone to put you up for the night." Thus we went on into Kaga Province.

> Scent of ripening ears:[6]
> to the right as I push through,
> surf crashing onto rocks.

---

4. Alludes to a classical poem: "I have no abode, / for I am but the daughter of a fisherman, / spending my life / on the shore / where white waves roll in." Prostitutes went out in small boats to greet in-coming vessels. 5. In this much-discussed poem Bashō is probably not making an invidious comparison between the prostitutes (showy, ephemeral flowers) and himself (the pure remote moon) but simply using aspects of the scene at the inn to comment in amusement on a chance encounter between two very different types of people. It has often been suggested that he may have recorded the meeting at the barrier—or possibly invented it—as a means of including a reference to love, a standard topic in linked verse. 6. That is, of the maturing rice crop.

We arrived at Kanazawa on the Fifteenth of the Seventh Month, after crossing Unohana Mountain and Kurikara Valley. There we met the merchant Kasho,[7] who had come up from Ōsaka, and joined him in his lodgings. A certain Isshō had been living in Kanazawa—a man who had gradually come to be known as a serious student of poetry, and who had gained a reputation among the general public as well. I now learned that he had died last winter, still in the prime of life. At the Buddhist service arranged by his older brother:

> Stir, burial mound!
> The voice I raise in lament
> is the autumn wind.

On being invited to a thatched cottage:

> The cool of autumn:
> let's each of us peel his own
> melons and eggplant.

Composed on the way:

> Despite the red blaze
> of the pitiless sun—
> an autumn breeze.

At Komatsu [Young Pines]:

> An appealing name:
> The wind in Young Pines ruffles
> bush clover and miscanthus.

At Komatsu we visited Tada Shrine, which numbers among its treasures a helmet and a piece of brocade that once belonged to Sanemori.[8] We were told that the helmet was a gift from Lord Yoshitomo[9] in the old days when Sanemori served the Genji—and indeed it was no ordinary warrior's headgear. From visor to earflaps, it was decorated with a gold-filled chrysanthemum arabesque in the Chinese style, and the front was surmounted by a dragon's head and a pair of horns. The shrine history tells in vivid language of how Kiso no Yoshinaka[1] presented a petition there after Sanemori's death in battle, and of how Higuchi no Jirō served as a messenger.

> A heartrending sound!
> Underneath the helmet,
> the cricket.

We could see Shirane's peaks behind us as we trudged toward Yamanaka Hot Springs. The Kannon Hall[2] stood at the base of the mountains to the left. Someone said the hall was founded by Retired Emperor Kazan, who enshrined an image of the bodhisattva there and named the spot Nata after completing a pious round of the Thirty-three Places. (The name Nata was

7. Like others Bashō calls on during his journey, Kasho is an amateur poet.   8. Saitō Sanemori (1111–1183), a *samurai* in the service of the Minamoto / Genji who defects to the Taira / Heike.   9. See n. 1, p. 613.   1. Leader of the northern Genji forces in the war against the Heike.   2. In honor of Kannon, the bodhisattva of compassion and an attendant of the Buddha known as Amida.

explained to us as having been coined from Nachi and Tanigumi.³) It was a beautiful, impressive site, with many unusual rocks, rows of ancient pine trees, and a small thatched chapel, built on a rock against the cliff.

> Even whiter
> than the Ishiyama rocks—
> the wind of autumn.

We bathed in the hot springs, which were said to be second only to Ariake in efficacy.

> At Yamanaka,
> no need to pluck chrysanthemums:⁴
> the scent of the springs.

The master was a youth called Kumenosuke. His father, an amateur of *haikai*, had embarrassed Teishitsu⁵ with his knowledge when the master visited Yamanaka from the capital as a young man. Teishitsu returned to the city, joined Teitoku's⁶ school, and built up a reputation, but it is said that he never accepted money for reviewing the work of anyone from this village after he became famous. The story is an old one now.

Sora was suffering from a stomach complaint. Because he had relatives at Nagashima in Ise Province, he set off ahead of me. He wrote a poem as he was about to leave:

> Journeying onward:
> fall prostrate though I may—
> a bush-clover field!

The sorrow of the one who departed and the unhappiness of the one who remained resembled the feelings of a lapwing wandering lost in the clouds, separated from its friend.

> From this day forward,
> the legend will be erased:
> dewdrops on the hat.⁷

Still in Kaga, I lodged at Zenshōji, a temple outside the castle town of Daishōji. Sora had stayed there the night before and left this poem:

> All through the night,
> listening to the autumn wind—
> the mountain in back.

One night's separation is the same as 1,000 leagues. I too listened to the autumn wind as I lay in the guest dormitory. Toward dawn, I heard clear voices chanting a sutra, and then the sound of a gong beckoned me into the dining hall. I left the hall as quickly as possible, eager to reach Echizen Province that day, but a group of young monks pursued me to the foot of the stairs with paper and inkstone. Observing that some willow leaves had

---

3. Two towns in different provinces; they were the beginning and ending points on an eleven-province tour of thirty-three places sacred to Kannon.   4. These flowers were associated with longevity.   5. An adept of *haikai*.   6. Matsunaga Teitoku (1571–1653), one of the leading practitioners of linked verse.
7. A reference to a common practice when people traveled in pairs. They would write on their hats the phrase "Two persons following the same path."

scattered in the courtyard, I stood there in my sandals and dashed off these lines:

> To sweep your courtyard
> of willow leaves, and then depart:
> that would be my wish!

At the Echizen border, I crossed Lake Yoshizaki by boat for a visit to the Shiogoshi pines.

> Inviting the gale
> to carry the waves ashore
> all through the night,
> they drip moonlight from their boughs—
> the pines of Shiogoshi!
>
> —Saigyō

In that single verse, the poet captures the essence of the scene at Shiozaki. For anyone to say more would be like "sprouting a useless digit."

In Maruoka, I called on the Tenryūji Abbot, an old friend.

A certain Hokushi from Kanazawa had planned to see me off a short distance, but had finally come all the way to Maruoka, reluctant to say good-bye. Always intent on conveying the effect of beautiful scenery in verse, he had produced some excellent poems from time to time. Now that we were parting, I composed this:

> Hard to say good-bye—
> to tear apart the old fan
> covered with scribbles.

I journeyed about a league and a half into the mountains to worship at Eiheiji, Dōgen's[8] temple. I believe I have heard that Dōgen had an admirable reason for avoiding the vicinity of the capital and founding his temple in those remote mountains.

After the evening meal, I set out for Fukui, three leagues away. It was a tedious, uncertain journey in the twilight.

A man named Tōsai had been living in Fukui as a recluse for a long time. He had come to Edo and visited me once—I was not sure just when, but certainly more than ten years earlier. I thought he must be very old and feeble by now, or perhaps even dead, but someone assured me that he was very much alive. Following my informant's directions into a quiet corner of the town, I came upon a poor cottage, its walls covered with moonflower and snake-gourd vines, and its door hidden by cockscomb and goosefoot.[9] That would be it, I thought. A woman of humble appearance emerged when I rapped on the gate.

"Where are you from, Reverend Sir? The master has gone to see someone in the neighborhood. Please look for him there if you have business with him." She was apparently the housewife.

I hurried off to find Tōsai, feeling as though I had strayed into an old romance, and spent two nights at his house. Then I prepared to leave, hopeful of seeing the full moon at Tsuruga Harbor on the Fifteenth of the Eighth

---

8. Founder of one of the main sects of Zen Buddhism.   9. A plant with small greenish blossoms. *Cockscomb*: a plant with fan-shaped clusters of red or yellow blossoms.

Month. Having volunteered to keep me company, Tōsai set out in high spirits as my guide, his skirts tucked jauntily into his sash.

The peaks of Shirane disappeared as Hina-ga-take came into view. We crossed Azamuzu Bridge, saw ears[1] on the reeds at Taema, journeyed beyond Uguisu Barrier and Yunoo Pass, heard the first wild geese of the season at Hiuchi Stronghold and Mount Kaeru, and took lodgings in Tsuruga at dusk on the Fourteenth. The sky was clear, the moon remarkably fine. When I asked if we might hope for the same weather on the following night, the landlord offered us wine, replying, "In the northern provinces, who knows whether the next night will be cloudy or fair?"

That night, I paid a visit to Kehi Shrine, the place where Emperor Chūai[2] is worshipped. An atmosphere of holiness pervaded the surroundings. Moon-light filtered in between the pine trees, and the white sand in front of the sanctuary glittered like frost. "Long ago, in pursuance of a great vow, the Second Pilgrim[3] himself cut grass and carried dirt and rock to fill a marsh that was a trial to worshippers going back and forth. The precedent is still observed; every new Pilgrim takes sand to the area in front of the shrine. The ceremony is called 'the Pilgrim's Carrying of the Sand,' " my landlord said.

> Shining on sand
> transported by pilgrims—
> pure light of the moon.

It rained on the Fifteenth, just as the landlord had warned it might.

> Night of the full moon:
> no predicting the weather
> in the northern lands.

The weather was fine on the Sixteenth, so we went in a boat to Irono-hama Beach to gather red shells. It was seven leagues by sea. A man named Ten'ya provided us with all kinds of refreshments—compartmented lunch boxes, wine flasks, and the like—and also ordered a number of servants to go along in the boat. A fair wind delivered us to our destination in no time. The beach was deserted except for a few fishermen's shacks and a forlorn Nichiren[4] temple. As we drank tea and warmed wine at the temple, I struggled to control feelings evoked by the loneliness of the evening.

> Ah, what loneliness!
> More desolate than Suma,[5]
> this beach in autumn.

> Between wave and wave:
> mixed with small shells, the remains
> of bush-clover bloom.

I persuaded Tōsai to write a description of the day's outing to be left at the temple.

---

1. The spikes on a plant that contain the seeds. 2. According to tradition, the fourteenth emperor, married to Empress Jingū (see n. 8, p. 622). 3. Taa Shōnin (1237–1319). *Pilgrim* was a title given to the patriarch of the Ji sect of Buddhism. 4. Buddhist monk (1222–1282) and founder of a sect that bore his name. 5. A coastal town made famous as the hero's place of exile in *The Tale of Genji* (in Volume B).

Rōtsu came to meet me at Tsuruga and accompanied me to Mino Province. Thus I arrived at Ōgaki, my journey eased by a horse. Sora came from Ise, Etsujin galloped in on horseback, and we all gathered at Jokō's house. Zensenji, Keikō, Keikō's sons, and other close friends called day and night, rejoicing and pampering me as though I had returned from the dead.

Despite my travel fatigue, I set out again by boat on the Sixth of the Ninth Month to witness the relocation of the Ise sanctuaries.[6]

> Off to Futami,
> loath to part as clam from shell
> in waning autumn.

6. The two sanctuaries at the Grand Shrines of Ise, dedicated to the ancestral gods of the imperial family, are rebuilt every twenty years as a kind of repurification.

UEDA AKINARI
1734–1809

In the more than two hundred years since they were first published, the supernatural stories of Ueda Akinari have intrigued generations of Japanese readers. The ghost story has a long history in Japan, but no writer has so successfully insinuated the supernatural into the everyday or better understood the irrational implications of erotic attachment. Akinari's cooly objective mix of realism and the fantastic asserts, long before Freud, that fantasy is part of reality and that our "real" lives embrace much that is "unreal."

Tales of Moonlight and Rain, published in 1776, is a collection of nine short stories that explore the discontinuity between routine life and the abrupt intrusion of the inexplicable. In one story, a money-loving *samurai* receives a visit from the spirit of wealth. In another, a grieving priest, unhinged by the death of his lover, consumes the corpse and thus develops a taste for decomposing flesh. In a work in a very different key, fish depicted by an eccentric artist spring to life, detach themselves from their paintings, and swim to freedom in a lake nearby. Two of the most popular stories recount the misadventures of husbands who abandon their wives. In one, the man finally returns; after a happy reunion he awakens to discover that he has spent the night with the ghost of his dead wife. In the other, the abandoned wife's vengeful spirit haunts her unfaithful husband:

> Taken completely by surprise, he saw that it was the wife he had deserted. She looked pale. Her eyes were dull and ghastly. As she stretched out a bony, emaciated hand and pointed at him, he cried out and fainted in sheer terror. After a while he regained his senses. He opened his eyes and looked around. What had seemed like a house a moment ago was in fact the funeral hut of a graveyard.

The stories range, then, from whimsical to chilling, but each is articulated in a rhythmic poetic prose suffused with eerie beauty and abundant acknowledgment of the authority of Japan's literary past. A product of the merchant milieu, Ueda Akinari was a physician and scholar as well as a writer, and he would probably have been surprised to find that posterity remembers him for his ghost stories rather than his scholarship. His learning, however, permeates this fiction. Its presence is subtle and sometimes veiled in translation, but it is one of the components that raise his supernatural tales above escapist fiction.

As a student of the Japanese classics and the linguistic origins of his native culture, Akinari crafted an agreeable combination of vernacular and literary language. His scholarly command of *The Man'yōshū* (in Volume B), Japan's earliest poetry anthology, inspired both subject and style. The collection served as a sourcebook for stories and geographical settings and also for an archaic diction that seemed, by virtue of its distance, well suited to the spectral. Akinari exploited some of the technical devices of classical poetry and drew on the long-standing Japanese tradition of implanting poetry within a prose context. He was also steeped in *The Tale of the Heike* (in Volume B) and other military chronicles, to which he frequently alludes as part of the realistic fabric he weaves for his tales, made credible in part by recurring references to actual people, places, and events of the historic past. A voracious reader, Akinari appropriated some of his ideas from medieval Japanese folktales (which abound in the sort of miracles that appealed to his imagination) and others from Chinese literature, both classical and current. In fact, Akinari composed his tales during a craze in Japan for Chinese stories of the supernatural, and some of his own stories were elaborate adaptations reworked into the contemporary Japanese idiom.

Of all the various influences he received, however, the legacy of *nō* drama was one of the most important. Like the *nō* playwrights, in some stories Akinari takes a famous poem as the kernel for his narrative. In others he employs a formal device borrowed from the *nō*. Action is set in motion by a journey, and dramatic tension derives from an encounter between the traveler and a ghost. The ghost, of course, as in the *nō*, is the physical manifestation of some gnawing emotion, a restless spirit in the grip of an obsession—hatred, revenge, or jealousy, for example.

In *Bewitched*, Akinari goes further. He incorporates specific myth-making elements from the *nō* play *Dōjōji* (in Volume B). In the play, itself derived from folklore and eleventh-century miracle stories, rejection (or, in the Buddhist scheme of things, passion) transforms a lovesick girl into a serpent. Sexual heat takes a new and deadly form when the venomous snake destroys the man who jilted her: she coils her scaly flesh around his hiding place and roasts him alive. Manago, the heroine of *Bewitched*, is just as lethal. The original title, *A Serpent's Lust*, would have suggested to eighteenth-century readers, if only subliminally, the danger of dragon ladies, a threat already embedded in Japanese literature.

But Akinari reverses the usual narrative. If jealousy can transform a woman into a serpent, he says, then love can turn a serpent into a woman. Drawing on his reading across two cultures and deep into Japan's ancient mythology, he creates one of the great demon-goddesses of Japanese literature. His hypnotic, ethereally beautiful Manago is as weird, mesmerizing, and frightening as the wild serpent-girl in *Dōjōji*. And because *Bewitched* is not a stylized *nō* play but a fairly long short story, Akinari can fashion a vivid image of a woman hell-bent on love, a creature whose passion transcends the ordinary realities of this world.

Like an Alfred Hitchcock of the supernatural, he sets up the story in such a way that the reader has ominous feelings from the very beginning. From the outset we sense that the hero, the handsome, spoiled Toyo-o, a young man with no head for practical matters and no real discipline, is about to get himself caught in something far beyond his ability to control. From the first time he hears Manago's voice, "rich as the sound of rolling jewels," and lays eyes on her "bewitchingly voluptuous" beauty, we know that this is not going to be any ordinary encounter. In due course, both reader and hero discover that Toyo-o is locked in a fatal attraction with a possessive and fiendish apparition.

What is most impressive in *Bewitched* is the way that Akinari controls our descent into the uncanny. Every time Toyo-o's known world is about to rupture, the phantom-woman offers him a plausible excuse for her strange maneuvers, and indeed it is this very plausibility that makes her so frightening. Even after he should know better, Toyo-o hovers on the verge of believing, holding the reader with him. Suspended in uncertainty, we begin to question whether or not the real and the unreal are irreversible opposites, and this is the fantastic's golden opportunity. The tension between logic and fable stretches like a tightrope. As Akinari leads us gingerly across, even modern readers may wonder if rationality's eradication of ghouls and angels is not just another of our own contemporary illusions.

Akinari strives to make the supernatural world credible by finding rational explanations for the fantastic. One could say that in the process *Bewitched* becomes a text that continually denies itself. But one could also say that for Akinari and his readers no denial was necessary. In the spiritual and psychological cosmology of eighteenth-century Japan, the extraordinary was in a certain sense the ordinary. The spirit world had impinged on Japanese life from the country's earliest days, when Shinto, the indigenous religion, taught a kind of nature worship based on the assumption that the boundaries between animate and inanimate, or the living and the dead, are exceedingly permeable. A tree, or river, or mountain, a single rock even, could be the manifestation of a god. The dead could also be gods, and the spirits of ancestors loomed over the living as more than shadowy presences. By the time of *The Tale of Genji* (eleventh century; in Volume B), the supernatural was construed as a normal part of daily life. Directional taboos, for example, often governed one's activities, so that a person could not proceed down a path where diviners sensed a naughty spirit prowling.

Even Buddhism, a much more sophisticated religion than Shinto, helped buttress the Japanese belief in the supernatural. The doctrine of transmigration, for example, taught that the dead are reborn after a brief, uncertain existence in an in-between world. Those who had failed to reconcile their passions could come back to life as ghosts. The most frightening were the "hungry ghosts," whose greed and moral depravity had turned them into the grotesque physical embodiment of their former appetites: skeletal fiends lurking in cesspools, trying futilely to fill their empty though enormous stomachs, bloated not with food but with hunger. When organized religion held that ghosts commingle with human beings, it is not surprising that a whole panoply of spirit-creatures—devils, mountain goblins, magic monkeys, lusty serpents, foxes who transform themselves into temptresses—should be given credence in premodern Japan, or that Akinari, a student of traditional Japanese culture, should take the supernatural for his theme.

One should read a story like *Bewitched* with an understanding that its "unreal" aspects may have seemed a good deal more "real" to its original audience and with an awareness that the presence of ghosts in such fiction is not to be identified with the play of the unconscious. We need to imagine, or reimagine, a mental life that addresses at the conscious level things that we would call the irrational, which modern psychology relegates to the unconscious. Akinari helps us in our reimagining. His ability to paint such a bold picture of desire incarnate and to give his tales the most stunning and delicate atmospherics, thick with fog and mist and midnight apparitions, places him among the forefront of the world's great gothic writers.

For the other stories in Akinari's collection see Kengi Hamada, trans., *Tales of Moonlight and Rain* (1972), and Leon M. Zolbrod, trans., *Ugetsu Monogatari: Tales of Moonlight and Rain* (1974), which contains an extensive introduction. A second collection of Akinari's fiction published posthumously, which contains several more supernatural stories, has been translated by Barry Jackman, *Tales of the Spring Rain* (1975). For biographical and critical studies see Blake Morgan Young, *Ueda Akinari* (1982), and the chapter on Akinari in Donald Keene, *World Within Walls* (1976). An interesting art historical introduction to the supernatural in Japan is found in Stephen Addiss, *Japanese Ghosts and Demons* (1985).

The following list uses common English syllables to provide rough equivalents of selected words whose pronunciation may be unfamiliar to the general reader.

Abe no Yumimaro: *ah-bay noh yoo-mee-mah-roh*

Bunya no Hiroyuki: *boon-yah noh hee-roh-yoo-kee*

Dōjōji: *doh-joh-jee*

Gongen: *gohn-gen*

Hokai Oshō: *hoh-kai oh-shoh*

Kanetada: *kah-ne-tah-dah*

Kii: *kee-ee*

Komatsubara: *koh-mah-tsoo-bah-rah*

Manago: *mah-nah-goh*

Man'yōshū: *mahn-yoh-shoo*

Maroya: *mah-roh-yah*

Miwagasaki: *mee-wah-gah-sah-kee*

Naniwa: *nah-nee-wah*

Suguri: *soo-goo-ree*

Tanabe: *tah-nah-bay*

Toyo-o: *toh-yoh–oh*

Tsubaichi: *tsoo-bah-ee-chee*

Ueda Akinari: *oo-e-dah ah-kee-nah-ree*

Ugetsu: *oo-ge-tsoo*

Yunomine: *yoo-noh-mee-ne*

yū-ō: *yoo–oh*

Bewitched[1]

1

Some time in the remote past, in the coastal village of Miwagasaki, in the province of Kii, there lived a man called Ōya no Takesuke, who was blessed by the sea. He had a good many fishermen working for him, and he caught a great deal of fish every day, both big and small. He was very prosperous indeed.

Ōya no Takesuke had two sons and a daughter. Taro, the elder son, was honest and rugged, devoted to his work, and he carried on the family business. The daughter was married to a man in neighboring Yamato province. Toyo-o, the third child, was a handsome youth with a predilection for learning and cultural pursuits typical of life in Kyoto, the nation's capital. He had no desire or inclination to devote his time and efforts to the family occupation.

Because of this, Toyo-o was something of a problem to his father. Pondering his wayward son's future welfare, Ōya no Takesuke thought of dividing the family wealth and settling upon Toyo-o his portion so that he could live serenely the kind of life that suited him. But then Toyo-o was the sort who, once he came into possession of money, would soon be deceived and robbed of all he owned. If, on the other hand, he were given away for adoption to another family, there might be endless complaints from that family that he was shiftless and irresponsible; that too would be inadvisable.

In the end, Toyo-o's father decided to let him become a scholar or a priest, or whatever his own whims dictated, and thus to allow him to be a burden on his older brother for the rest of his life. Therefore he did not object when Toyo-o went daily to study with his tutor, Abe no Yumimaro, the chief priest of the Kumano Shrine.

1. Translated by Kengi Hamada.

On this particular day, toward the end of September, the sky was clear and the sea calm. Suddenly, clouds began to gather over the sea from the southeast and light rain soon began to fall. Toyo-o borrowed an umbrella from his tutor on his way home. As he reached the spot where he could see the depository of sacred treasures of the Asuka Shrine, the rain became a real downpour. He therefore sought shelter at a nearby fisherman's hut.

An old man emerged to greet him: "Welcome, young master, to this shabby house. Pardon me," he said, dusting off a cushion, "let me offer this for you to sit on."

"Oh, don't bother, please," said Toyo-o. "I just came in from the rain to stay awhile," and he sat down on the raised *tatami*.[2]

At that moment a voice called from outside, rich as the sound of rolling jewels, "May we take shelter in this house for a short while?"

No sooner said than, to Toyo-o's utter amazement, in stepped a beautiful woman less than twenty years of age. Her features, the way she wore her hair, her colorful robe, the perfume she exuded—all this, Toyo-o noted, made her bewitchingly voluptuous. With her was a pretty little maid of fourteen or fifteen carrying a bundle. Both were soaking wet.

2

Toyo-o felt sorry for the woman. And she seemed surprised to see him. Her face lighted up, blushing modestly. There was refinement in her look, and Toyo-o felt instantly attracted to her.

At the same time, it occurred to him that he had never heard of such a beautiful, refined-looking woman living in this neighborhood. She must be a woman from Kyoto, he surmised, who had come on a pilgrimage to the three famous Kumano shrines[3] and had perhaps been strolling on the beach to view the charming scenery when it began to rain. Even so, he felt it was rather unseemly that she was not accompanied by a male escort.

"Come sit here," he invited, making room for her. "The weather will soon clear up, I'm sure."

"Just for a while then, thank you," the woman said.

The house was small and there was barely enough room for her to sit beside him. At such close range, she seemed to Toyo-o more beautiful than ever, almost otherworldly, and his heart leaped with excitement.

"You seem to be a lady of high station in life," he said. "Did you come here on a pilgrimage to the three Kumano shrines? Or to visit the Yunomine Hotspring?[4] But why have you been strolling at such a bare, unattractive beach as this? An ancient poet once commented:

> Oh, how bothersome indeed
> The rain, falling suddenly
> At Sano in Miwagasaki,
> Where there's no shelter for me.

"He probably got caught by just the kind of miserable weather we are having today. This is only a shabby hut, but the owner is a man employed by my father. So please be at ease and rest here. Where, by the way, are you lodging

2. Woven straw mats. These mats are still used in Japan as floor coverings.   3. Among the most popular Shinto shrines, located south of Kyoto and Nara in a mountainous region overlooking the sea. The native deities worshiped there were viewed as manifestations of Buddhist divinities who could prolong life and help the faithful attain rebirth in paradise.   4. Where pilgrims to Kumano often rested.

in the village? I should accompany you there—but perhaps that would be too personal and impolite. Why don't you take this umbrella with you?"

"Thank you for your hospitality," the woman replied. "I shall dry my clothes with the warmth of your kindness and then leave. I am not a visitor from Kyoto. I have lived near this village at Shingū for a long time. Today started out to be a clear day, so I went to offer prayers at the Nachi Shrine. But the downpour forced me to seek shelter here without knowing that you had done the same thing. My lodging is not far from here."

Rising, she continued, "The sky is already clearing, so I shall take my leave while there is still a light rain falling."

Toyo-o delayed her, saying, "The rain has not really stopped yet. Please use this umbrella. You may return it to me whenever it is convenient for you. Better still, where do you live? I can send someone for the umbrella later."

"Ask for Agata no Manago's house in Shingū. It will soon be sundown so I shall have to go now. I will take the umbrella you so graciously offered."

And so Toyo-o saw her off as she spread the umbrella and left, watching until she vanished from his sight. He himself borrowed a straw umbrella from the old man of the hut and went home.

3

That night Toyo-o could not sleep, disturbed by the image of the woman which flittered ceaselessly before his mind's eye. Toward morning, however, fitfully hovering on the edge of sleep, he dreamed that he went calling at Manago's house.

It was a huge structure, as was the front gate. The shutters and the bamboo blinds indicated that Manago lived in elegant style.

Manago herself came to greet him at the door, saying, "I cannot forget your kindness, and I love you. Please come in."

Showing him into an inner chamber, she laid out a feast before him, wine and all kinds of fruit. Made cheerfully drunk by the excesses of her hospitality, he yielded to her caresses and lay down beside her, talking intimately.

Came the dawn, however, and the end of his dream.

Toyo-o thought, if only what had happened were real and not just a dream, how happy he would be! He felt so restless that he even forgot to eat his breakfast, and he literally leaped out of the house, so eager was he to see her. But when he asked around for the house of Agata no Manago, no one seemed to know about it. He kept on searching until late in the afternoon, when he saw Manago's maid coming toward him from the east. Quickly he went to speak to her. "Say," he called, "where is the house of your mistress? I came to get the umbrella."

The maid smiled pleasantly. "I am glad you came. This way, please," and she led the way. Soon she pointed and said, "This is it."

Toyo-o saw that the front gate and the house were huge indeed. The shutters and bamboo blinds were just as impressive as he had imagined in his dream. Strange, he thought, as he walked through the gate. The maid preceded him into the house, announcing, "The man who loaned you the umbrella yesterday was coming this way, so I invited him in."

"Where is he? Bring him here quickly." There was no doubt about it. It was Manago herself who came out to greet Toyo-o.

"I happened to be returning from my studies at the house of my tutor, the Shinto priest Abe no Yumimaro, so I dropped in to get the umbrella. I shall look around your house today and perhaps come again another day."

Manago pressed him to stay. "Maroya," she called to her maid, "don't let Toyo-o leave the house."

Maroya blocked his way. "You forced us to accept your umbrella. It is only right that we force you to stay here now." She pushed him into a room with wooden flooring and a southern exposure, and spread a tatami mat for him to sit on.

It was a splendidly decorated room. The panels on the wall, the shelves, the screens—all seemed to be of valuable classical vintage. This, thought Toyo-o, must be the home, not of an ordinary person, but of someone wealthy and of high station in life.

4

Manago entered. "For certain reasons," she said, "this house no longer has a master. I cannot therefore offer you anything in the way of lavish entertainment. I have brought you some poor wine." So saying, she placed before him a small table and dishes piled high with seafood delicacies, and wine jars. Maroya, the maid, offered to pour the wine.

But Toyo-o was racked with doubts and suspicion. Can I still be dreaming, and will it soon come to an end? All this, however, seemed to be real enough. Still, it was all so mysterious that he could not fathom it.

Guest and hostess drank together immoderately, feeling a pleasant sensation. Manago lifted her wine cup and spoke coquettishly, with an expression reminiscent of a blooming cherry reflected in the water below while a spring zephyr brushed its face. In a bewitching voice like that of a nightingale flitting from branch to branch, she said, "Perhaps I should not tell you this, for it makes me feel ashamed. But if I should die without confessing, people might say something preposterous—that I had been put to death by some angry, vengeful god. So listen to what I have to say without doubting it— trust me that I am not blurting it out on the spur of the moment.

"I was born in Kyoto but my parents died soon afterward and I was brought up by my nurse. Due to family ties, a minor official named Agata in the governor's office of this district brought me here as his wife. My husband died of illness before his term of office expired, and I was left alone and uncared for. My former nurse in Kyoto had meanwhile become a nun and departed on a devotional journey without a fixed destination. And so, Kyoto, my birthplace, has become a strange, distant land to me. I have nowhere else to go.

"Yesterday, while seeking shelter from the rain, I enjoyed the blessings of your hospitality and friendship. I felt certain that you were a sincere man, and that I should devote the rest of my life to you. If you do not dislike me and are willing to accept my love, please drink the wine in this cup to seal our eternal pledge as husband and wife."

Toyo-o hesitated. He himself had felt in his heart the same intention—to marry her, for he was in love with her. And so her proposal caused his heart to leap with joy, like a bird taking flight from its roost. Still, dependent on his father and older brother for his livelihood, he realized he was in no position to make a hasty promise on his own initiative alone—without consulting them and obtaining their consent. Glad though he was, therefore, he told her he could not give her an immediate reply.

Manago, angry and looking miserable, said, "I am afraid I have spoken rather rashly, like a woman crying out from the depths of her heart, and I regret I cannot take back what I said. A woman in my miserable situation should perhaps drown herself in the sea. But if I did, it would weigh heavily on your heart and that, too, would be a serious crime. What I have said is the truth, but please dismiss it as the foolish talk of a drunken woman and forget about it."

Toyo-o relented: "From the beginning I realized you were a cultured woman of Kyoto and I feel now that I have not been mistaken. Brought up as I have been in this rugged region where whales offshore spout seawater, I could not even have dreamed of such a fine proposal, bringing me so much happiness. I cannot, however, accept it immediately because I am still dependent on my parents. I have no property of my own except the hair on my head and the nails on my fingers. I have no power to earn my own living. How could I support you? I feel wretched in my present situation. But, if you are willing to accept these conditions, I shall willingly be of service to you. Confucius said, 'Even a mountain of love crumbles.' And as for myself, how can I help but overlook my obligations of filial piety and sacrifice myself for your sake?"

Manago responded gaily: "Now that you have given me such happy assurances, come and see me from time to time in this poor abode. Here is a sword which was a precious possession of my late husband. Wear it constantly," and she presented it to Toyo-o.

Toyo-o on examining it saw that it was a magnificent long sword with gold and silver trimmings on the scabbard. The blade was a sharp and fearsome thing. He realized it would be inauspicious to reject an engagement gift, so he inserted the sword in his hip sash.

He was repeatedly asked to spend the night there, but he rejected the offer, saying, "I would be chided by my father and older brother if I spent the night here without their permission. I promise you I will invent some kind of excuse to put them at their ease and come tomorrow night."

Thereupon he left without further ado. But at home, the next day dawned before he could sleep soundly.

5

His older brother Taro got up early to supervise the day's work for the fishermen in the family's employ. He peeped into Toyo-o's room through a crack in the door, and in the feeble light of the still-sputtering oil lamp he saw the glittering sword lying beside Toyo-o's pillow.

Strange, Taro thought. Where in the world could he have gotten such a sword?[5] He slid the door open noisily, awakening Toyo-o. Surprised to see Taro in the room, Toyo-o stammered, "Did you call me, Brother?"

"What is that thing glittering beside your pillow?" Taro demanded. "Such a thing is hardly appropriate in a fisherman's house. If Father hears about it, he will surely give you a sound scolding."

---

5. The possession of swords was a privilege of the *samurai* class.

"But I didn't buy it. Someone gave it to me yesterday, so I brought it here."

"There is no one in this village who has such a precious thing to give away. I have always felt it was a waste of money for you to buy books written in Chinese characters,[6] but still I have not interfered because Father has been lenient about it . . ." He added derisively, "Are you going to wear that sword to march and show off in the festival parade here? There is a limit to making a fool of yourself."

Their father heard the loud quarrelsome voice. "What is that good-for-nothing son up to now? Bring him in here."

Taro shouted back, "I don't know where he bought this thing. It is a glittering sword such as a general wears on his hip. To buy such a thing is unseemly, I think. Talk to him about it. I must go now to oversee the fishermen's work; otherwise they would idle their time away."

After Taro left, his mother summoned Toyo-o. "Why have you bought such a thing?" she demanded. "Everything in this house—food, money, goods—belongs to Taro. There is nothing you can claim as your own. We have usually let you do as you pleased. But if you were to incur Taro's displeasure, I am afraid you would have no place in the whole world to go and live. Why can't you, with all your learning, understand this simple truth?"

"I truly did not buy the sword," Toyo-o insisted. "It was given to me for a good reason. Yet Brother has scolded me so roughly just on seeing it."

His father roared, "What have you done to deserve such a precious prize? I cannot imagine! Tell us frankly, without holding back any detail."

"I am ashamed to tell you about it. Let me tell it through another person."

"To whom do you intend to reveal something you are ashamed of telling your own parents or your older brother?"

Taro's wife, who had been listening patiently, could no longer endure the violence of the family quarrel, so she interceded. "Let me hear it from him in his room," she said, pushing Toyo-o there, "though this may be presumptuous on my part."

So Toyo-o told the story to his brother's wife: "Before being found out and scolded by my brother, I had planned to discuss this matter quietly with you. I had not expected things to turn out in this explosive way. The truth is that there is a young widow called Agata no Manago living a lonely life near here, and she asked me to help her, giving me this sword at the same time. As you know, I am inexperienced in the ways of the world and have no means of making an independent living. If, because of this incident, I am driven out of this house, it cannot be helped. I do regret what I have done. But please, Sister, take pity upon me and intercede for me."

His sister-in-law laughed out loud. "I have always felt sorry that a fine young man like you should remain single so long. I think you have done the normal thing. Yes, I will do whatever I can for you."

6

That night she explained the situation to her husband, Taro. "I think it's about time Toyo-o became involved with a woman, don't you? Will you speak to Father about it, so he will approve?"

6. Only the well educated could read Chinese. The brother perhaps makes fun of Toyo-o, because the term *Chinese characters* was also slang for "secret code," suggesting the uselessness of such knowledge.

Taro knit his brows. "This is strange," he said. "I have never heard of a minor official called Agata who served as assistant to the governor of this district. Since our family serves as village headman, we should have been informed if and when any such official died. Anyway, let me see the sword."

When the sword was brought in, Taro examined it thoroughly and seemed to be troubled.

"This is no trifling matter," he said. "Recently ministers of state from the capital arrived at the Kumano Gongen Shrine for special prayers invoking the blessings of the gods and presented numerous precious gifts to the shrine. Then all the valuable gifts were stolen from the shrine depository. The chief priest reported the robbery to the governor's office. And in order to apprehend the robber, the vice governor, Bunya no Hiroyuki, is now conferring with the priest at the priest's house. I have a feeling this sword was not something worn by a minor official here. I shall show it to Father and see what he has to say."

When his father saw the sword and was told about the recent robbery of the precious gifts from the shrine, he turned pale.

"What a terrible thing to happen to us! That good-for-nothing son is the sort who can't even pluck a single hair from another person's head. How such an evil thought as committing this irreverent crime should have entered his head, I cannot understand. If news of this affair leaks out, our family is sure to come to ruin because it is a serious crime, a violation of the code governing shrines. We cannot afford to spare or protect a single member of the family from his misdeed. We must consider our obligations to our ancestors and to our descendants. Tomorrow let us make a clean confession to the authorities."

7

"Yes, indeed," said the surprised chief priest on examining the sword, "this is one of the precious gifts presented to this shrine by the state ministers."

The vice governor, Bunya no Hiroyuki, on receiving the report on the case, said, "Now let us go into the robbery of all the other precious gifts." He gave orders that Toyo-o be arrested immediately for questioning.

A group of some ten samurai, with Taro leading the way, thus went to the Ōya house. Toyo-o, ignorant of what had happened in the meantime, was reading a book in his room. The samurai stamped in unceremoniously, knocked him down, and bound him like a prisoner without even explaining the crime for which he was being arrested. His parents and his brother and his wife wept, saying it was all so sad.

"You have been summoned to the government office," the samurai said. "Now walk quickly."

Bound like a common criminal and surrounded by his captors, Toyo-o was taken to the government office.

Bunya, the vice governor, glared at the prisoner. "You must understand," he roared, "that to steal the offering to the gods of the shrine is a serious, unprecedented crime. Where have you hidden the other precious things you have stolen? Confess the truth without hedging."

At last Toyo-o began to understand that he had been accused of the theft of the sword. With tears flowing, he said, "I swear before the gods that I did not steal anything." He explained how he had been given the sword as a gift by the woman called Manago, who claimed to be the widow of a certain minor official named Agata who had worn the sword while he was still living.

"To prove my innocence," Toyo-o urged, "why don't you arrest that woman at once?"

Bunya, the vice governor, became even more furious. "There has been no one in my employ here by the name of Agata. If you keep on evading the truth, I am warning you that the crime for which you have been arrested will become progressively more serious."

"Why should I keep on lying to you after being arrested for a crime I did not commit?" Toyo-o insisted. "Please, for the sake of the truth, bring the woman here for questioning."

Bunya thereupon said to the samurai, "Where is the house of this Agata no Manago? Go and arrest her."

The samurai, acknowledging the command, pushed Toyo-o ahead of them to lead them to Manago's house.

8

But what had appeared to Toyo-o as imposing pillars on the front gate of Manago's house were sagging with rot; the roof tiles were mostly broken, fallen to the ground. The yard was overgrown with weeds. There were no signs of anyone living in the house. Toyo-o was amazed, to say the least.

The ten samurai searched the neighborhood and rounded up several men, including an aged woodcutter and a rice thrasher. These men squatted in fear before the samurai, one of whom demanded, "Tell me, what manner of people lived here? Is it true that a man called Agata lived in this house?"

An old blacksmith edged forward on his knees and said, "I have not heard of any person by that name. About three years ago a certain man called Suguri lived prosperously in this house. But after his ship loaded with goods bound for Tsukushi was lost at sea, those remaining in the house left for places unknown. It has been unoccupied since then. But I heard from this old dyer that yesterday that young man," he pointed at Toyo-o, "entered the house and left it after a while, which he thought very mysterious indeed."

"Very well," said the samurai. "We shall go into the house and examine it thoroughly to report to the governor." The rest of the samurai, along with Toyo-o, followed the leader through the front gate and into the house itself.

The inside of the building was in a greater state of ruin and desolation than the outside. As they approached the inner courtyard they found what must once have been a lavishly built garden. The pond had dried up, the flowering plants were dead. Wild bushes and weeds flourished everywhere. A lone pine tree, broken by strong winds, looked ghastly.

Opening the latticed door leading to the main hall, they felt a raw-smelling spectral gust of wind and fell back in fearful excitement. Toyo-o, struck with amazement at the change, could not utter a word.

One of the samurai, a big, burly, daring man called Kose no Kumagashi, shouted, "Follow me in!" and stamped his way roughly into the wooden-floored room. A carpet of dust about an inch thick covered the floor, with rat droppings strewn everywhere. And in this filthy room, beside a screen, sat a woman, pretty as a flower.

"In the name of the governor, I arrest you," shouted Kumagashi. "Come with me."

But the woman made no answer. As Kumagashi approached to seize her, there was a sudden clap of thunder, so loud that it seemed as though the earth itself had been split apart. Stunned by the impact, everyone fell to the floor before they could flee the room. When the rumbling ceased they looked around. The woman had disappeared. Nor was there any indication where she might have gone.

But scattered on the floor they saw a great many glittering articles—rolls of imported Korean cotton, Chinese figured silk, colorful linen, *katori*[7] cloth, metal hoes, as well as valuable weapons such as spears, shields, and quivers, the offerings that had been made to the shrine by the ministers of state and were stolen from the shrine depository.

The samurai gathered up the goods and reported back to the vice governor, giving him a detailed description of what had happened at the mysterious, dilapidated house. Both the vice governor and the chief priest of the Kumano Gongen Shrine were convinced that the robbery must have been the work of a spectral monster. The charge against Toyo-o was therefore reduced, but the fact that he had been in possession of the stolen sword could not be officially overlooked. He was thrown into jail and chained to the wall. However, the Ōya family bribed the officials with costly gifts, and Toyo-o was released after serving only a hundred days.

9

But Toyo-o felt that his family could never endure the unpleasant notoriety when his involvement in the affair became the subject of neighborhood gossip. He asked that he be allowed to go to his married sister's house in Nara and live there for a while. The family agreed, fearing that otherwise, after that dreadful experience, he might become seriously ill. And so they sent him off with a traveling companion to look after him.

Toyo-o's sister lived at a place called Tsubaichi in Nara province, married to a merchant called Tanabe no Kanetada. The couple greeted him warmly and, feeling sorry for him after his harrowing experience of the last few months, told him he could stay with them as long as he wanted.

That year passed without further incident. Soon it was February of the following year. The town of Tsubaichi, noted for its many temples and shrines, was near the Hasedera, a temple famous for the blessings of the Goddess of Mercy and known far and wide, even in China. Many were the worshipers from cities and distant villages who went on pilgrimages there each spring. The pilgrims usually lodged at Tsubaichi, and merchants competed for their trade.

Since the Tanabe store dealt in candles, lampwicks, and other lighting goods for religious ceremonies, it enjoyed a lucrative trade. So many customers crowded the shop that movement inside it was almost impossible.

---

7. A thin silk used for summer kimonos.

10

One day in the middle of this prosperous season a woman, seemingly from the city and dazzlingly beautiful, squeezed herself into the Tanabe store, accompanied by a maid, to purchase incense.

The maid, recognizing Toyo-o, shouted, "Here is our master!"

Toyo-o, taken completely by surprise, saw it was Maroya, the maid, and her mistress Manago. "Oh, how dreadful," he cried, and ran into the interior of the shop to hide.

"What is the matter?" asked his sister and her husband, Kanetada.

"That devil has come after me here. Keep away from her!"

The crowd in the shop began screaming: "Where is the devil?"

At this point Manago herself spoke up. "People, you need not fear me. And you, my husband, need not tremble so. I am sorry that I pushed you rashly into committing a crime. I searched for you after that in order to tell you the truth and put you at ease. Fortunately I have found out where you now live.

"I also ask the people of this house to listen carefully to me. If I were really a devil, would I be walking around carelessly in broad daylight, in dense crowds? The garments I am wearing have seams. When I walk against the sun my shadow shows clearly. Consider these things as logical proof and you will be convinced that I am not a devil. So be relieved of your doubts and suspicion."

Toyo-o at last regained his senses, emerged from his hiding place, and said, "I discovered that you are not a human being when I was arrested by the samurai and went back with them to your house. It was in an amazingly wretched state, completely different from the day before. And in that house inhabited only by devils I saw you again, and when the samurai tried to seize you there was a clap of thunder on that sunny day and you disappeared in a flash. I tell you I saw it all with my own eyes. And here you have the effrontery to come chasing after me again. Get out of here, you devil! At once!"

Manago clung to him with tears in her eyes. "I cannot blame you entirely for denouncing me. But please listen to what I have to say. I felt very sorry for you when I heard you were arrested and taken to the government office. So I discussed the matter with an old man in the neighborhood whom I had befriended and had him quickly reduce the house to its hideous state. The thunder that seemed to have rolled when I was about to be seized was a trick played by Maroya. I fled by ship toward Naniwa, but I wanted to find out what had happened to you after that and I prayed to the Goddess of Mercy of the Hasedera.[8] It was revealed to me during my prayer that I should come to the temple here, where the three cryptomeria trees[9] of sacred origin stand. I was thus able to trace you here to Tsubaichi, thanks to the infinite mercy of the goddess Kannon.

"Furthermore, how could a mere woman like me steal and carry away all those precious offerings from the Gongen Shrine depository? The robbery must have been the work of the spirit of my late husband. Please think all this over carefully, trusting the sincerity of my love for you."

8. Famous Buddhist temple south of Nara, established in the 8th century and dedicated to Kannon, goddess of mercy, who was revered for her vow to save all beings.   9. Japanese cedars.

Toyo-o, teetering in an ambivalent state of lingering doubt and pity, could find no words to alienate her further. His sister and her husband, however, were so moved by Manago's seemingly straightforward, singularly feminine pleadings that they had no doubt whatever that she had spoken the truth. And although Toyo-o claimed that Manago was a spectral monster, there could be no such thing in this world, they reasoned. They were impressed by her zeal—and her pitiful state—having come all the way here to search for him. Even though Toyo-o was not convinced, they themselves welcomed her into their household and provided her with a room.

In a day or so Manago, ingratiating herself to her host and hostess, pleaded with them tearfully to win back Toyo-o for her. Completely overcome by her tender pleas, they succeeded in urging Toyo-o to go through with formal wedding rites. Toyo-o, who, in any event, had first been attracted to Manago's physical beauty, daily became less and less intransigent and more attached to her than ever, and finally he pledged eternal love. Now nothing could separate them even for a day, for such was the intensity of their tender love for each other.

11

Then came the month of March, and Kanetada proposed that the whole family go on a picnic to the famed Yoshino.

"This province of Kii," he said, "naturally cannot compare with Kyoto in beauty and elegance, but we have our unrivaled scenic beauties, too. Yoshino[1] is especially beautiful in the spring. You will never tire of seeing Mount Mifune and the Natsumi River, no matter how often you visit there. At this time of year the cherries are in bloom, which makes it all the more beautiful." He urged Toyo-o and Manago, saying "Let us all go on a picnic together."

Manago smiled and said, "There is a saying, Yoshino is a good place which good people look upon as good," quoting the famous verse by Emperor Tenmu which paraphrases the literal implications of the word *yoshi* [good] in Yoshino. "It is the envy of the people of Kyoto, I hear. Yes, it must surely be glorious when the cherries are in bloom. But since childhood I have suffered from a congenital illness which makes me dizzy when I find myself in the midst of a huge throng, or when I have to walk a long distance on the highway. I am sorry to say I cannot accompany you on the picnic. But I shall expect a lot of souvenirs of your trip when you return."

"You need not worry about that," Kanetada replied. "We would never let you walk to the picnic grounds. We do not own a private palanquin[2] but we can always hire one for you. Besides, if you do not come along with us, Toyo-o will be worried and may refuse to go."

Toyo-o added his encouragement: "Since he has made this offer out of kindness, I don't see how we can refuse, even though you might collapse on the wayside."

Thus Manago reluctantly agreed to go along.

---

1. Famous for its cherry blossoms.   2. An enclosed seat, mounted on poles, that was designed to carry a single passenger.

12

Many people along the picnic route were dressed in colorful finery but none could compare with Manago's dazzling beauty.

The family first went calling at a certain temple on Mount Yoshino, where the chief priest was a friend of long standing. In welcoming them the priest said, "You are rather late this spring. The petals of the cherry blossoms are already scattering, and the warbling of the nightingale is waning. But I will escort you to some places where cherry trees are still in bloom."

But first he had a rather tidy supper prepared for them.

At dawn the area was thickly covered with mist. But as the mist cleared they could appreciate the view in all directions, for the temple was situated at a high elevation. Priests' quarters scattered here and there in the lower regions could be seen clearly. The warbling of mountain birds could be heard from hither and yon. Flowers and trees thrived in a riot of colors. The area was so beautiful as to dazzle one's eyes.

For those who were visiting this spot for the first time, the view at a waterfall below was said to be the best, so they were sent in that direction with a guide. As they descended the slope along a circuitous route, they came upon a site where an ancient imperial detached palace was said to have once stood. Nearby was the waterfall. The water below formed a foaming, bubbling whirlpool, in which some small fish were leaping, presenting a pleasing sight.

They sat down to eat their picnic lunch while enjoying the scenery. Presently a man was seen coming from downstream, stepping from boulder to boulder. His hair was as white as newly spun linen. But his legs seemed to be still vigorous with health and vitality. As he approached the waterfall, he stood looking at the picnicking group sitting on the bank. He seemed mystified.

Manago and Maroya deliberately turned their backs on him and pretended not to have seen him standing there. But the old man had already recognized them.

"You devils!" he grumbled. "Again you are bewitching and deceiving human beings. How can you dare assume that shape and form before my very eyes!"

Manago and Maroya stood up in a frenzy of confusion and plunged into the waterfall. The swirling waters suddenly shot up into the air and the two vanished from sight. At the same time a jet black cloud appeared over the spot like a splash of ink, and rain fell in a torrent, rattling noisily like thin bamboo slats.

13

The old man, seeing that the other picnickers in the group had been thrown into excited confusion, calmed them and led them down to a village. "You have been bewitched by that devil who attached itself to you," he told Toyo-o, fixing him with a steady gaze. "If I had not been there to save you, it might have taken your life. Beware of it in the future."

Toyo-o, kneeling on the ground with head bowed in profound thankfulness, revealed to the old man the entire history of his affair with Manago and pleaded earnestly for future protection from the devil.

"I thought so," the old man said. "That devil is really a huge old serpent—a lecherous monster. It mates with a bull and begets a freak calf; it mates with a stallion and begets a freak colt. It has bewitched you because it was fascinated by your good looks. Its evil attachment to its victims is so tenacious that you must be constantly on your guard. Otherwise you will lose your life."

All heard the venerable man with fear in their hearts and prayed to him, saying, "You must be the incarnation of a god."

He laughed. "I am not a god. My name is Tagima no Kibito, and I serve at the Yamato Shrine. I will escort you to your lodging now, so come along." They rose and followed him.

The next day the family returned to Tsubaichi, where the Yamato Shrine was situated. By way of expressing their gratitude to the old man, Tagima no Kibito, they presented him with three rolls of Mino silk and bundles of Tsukushi cotton. They pleaded with him to perform *misogi*[3] rites to ward off future visitations of the devil. He accepted the gifts on behalf of the shrine and distributed them among the priests there, without keeping any for his own use.

"That devil has put you under its spell because you are good looking," he told Toyo-o. "You have been bewitched by the beauty of the temporary abode of that serpent. You must develop a more manly, a more determined spirit, which you now lack, in order to repulse it. By so doing you will not need to rely on my powers to cast off the devil. You must never yield to temptations of passion and lust."

Toyo-o felt as though he had just emerged from a dream, and he thanked the old man profusely for his counsel. To Kanetada, his brother-in-law, he said, "It was due to my wrong thinking that I was subjected to the spell of that serpent for a whole year. I have been remiss in my duties to my parents and my older brother. I can no longer complacently place myself under your roof and favor. I thank you kindly for all you have done for me, and I hope to see you again sometime."

So saying, he left Tsubaichi for his parents' home in Miwagasaki.

14

His parents and his older brother, Taro, on hearing from him about his dreadful experience in Tsubaichi, realized at last that he was in no way to blame for the affair involving Manago and the stolen sword. Pitying him on the one hand, and dreading the evil tenacity of that devil on the other, they decided that they should not let him remain a bachelor any longer and discussed plans to get a wife for him.

At a place called Shiba there lived a petty official named Shōji. Shōji had an only daughter, who was then serving as a lady-in-waiting at the imperial palace in Kyoto. It was said that she would soon be resigning from her work there to return to her father's home in Shiba. Her father thus asked a go-between to call at the Ōya home in Miwagasaki with the proposal that Toyo-o become his son-in-law and live in Shiba. The proposal was immediately accepted as a desirable match.

Tomiko, for such was the girl's name, was sent for. She gladly returned

---

3. Purification.

from Kyoto to become Toyo-o's bride. As she was accustomed to the refined manners of court life, there was a glamorous quality in her appearance and behavior; she looked quite beautiful among provincial girls.

Toyo-o, on taking her as his wife, saw that she had pretty eyes and that she was alert, perspicacious, and assiduous about everything. He recalled how he had been bewitched by Manago and remembered one thing and another about their affair. Teasing Tomiko, he told her, "Since you have been accustomed for years to glamorous court life, surely you must find a provincial like me wanting in many respects. One day a general, the next day a minister of state must have made romantic love to you. I feel envious indeed."

Tomiko looked steadily up at him, saying, "In pampering a woman of no distinction like me and forgetting your own glamorous affair, you force me to be even more envious than you."

Though her appearance was different, her words were spoken precisely as Manago, the devil, would have spoken them. It was her voice!

Toyo-o's hair bristled with terror. He was amazed by the tenacity of that devil.

She laughed. "My dear husband, there is nothing strange about all this. Even if you have forgotten your pledge to me, made across the seas and over the mountains, we meet again because it has been predestined. If you continue to believe in the lies of other people and try to avoid me, vengeance is sure to overtake you. No matter how tall the mountains of Kii may be, it is easy for me to spatter your blood from the highest peak to the valley below. And I warn you, don't ever try to do away with yourself."

Toyo-o, shivering from head to toe, felt as though he were about to die. In fact, he was feeling more dead than alive when someone spoke from behind the screen: "Master, how cross you are tonight on this happy occasion!" It was Maroya, the devil's maid.

Again Toyo-o felt his stomach turn. He closed his eyes and dropped face down on the floor. Manago and her maid tried to mollify and threaten him by turns, but he remained deathlike in this prone position out of sheer terror throughout the night.

15

As the day dawned he leaped out of the bedroom and told his father-in-law about the terrible thing that had happened during the night. "Tell me how I can escape from the wrath of that devil," he said. Even while he spoke, he feared the devil might be listening behind him, so he lowered his voice.

Shōji and his wife turned pale. But Shōji said, "There is a priest here from the Kurama Temple in Kyoto, who comes to perform austerities[4] every year. Since yesterday he has been staying at the temple on the hill across from here. He is particularly effective in invoking divine help against such visitations as the plague, specters, and swarms of crop-destroying locusts. He is held in high esteem by the people of this community. Let us ask him to come and help us."

The priest was sent for in a flurry of excitement, and at length he arrived.

---

4. Renunciations of food and material comforts as forms of self-discipline and religious devotion.

When the frightful circumstances were explained to him, the priest said with a condescending air, "Don't worry. It is easy to catch such a devil." Thus placated, the people felt less uneasy.

He concocted a magic potion consisting of a plant called yū-ō and water, put the mixture in a pot, and proceeded to the bedroom which had now become the devil's den. As the people excitedly sought hiding places, the priest grinned, saying, "Old people and children, you need not hide yourselves out of fear. Stay where you are. I shall seize this serpent and show it to you."

No sooner had he opened the door of the bedroom than the serpent thrust out its head toward the priest. It filled the entire space as the door opened. Glittering whiter than the whitest snowdrift, its eyes like mirrors, its horns like branches of a huge tree, it opened its three-foot-wide mouth, spat out its crimson-colored tongue, and looked as though it would swallow the priest in a mouthful.

"Oh, how terrible!" cried the priest. He dropped the pot of magical potion then and there and fell to the floor. Unable to rise, he barely succeeded in crawling back. "Frightful! Frightful! This is indeed a profound curse of evil gods," he cried. "How can a stupid priest like me destroy the spell with incantations? Without my hands and feet I could never have come back alive." Then he fainted away.

When the people lifted him up, they found his body red, hot, and blackened, as though they were clutching burning wood, perhaps because of the poison spat out by the serpent. His eyes were blinking, as if he wanted to say something, but his voice failed him. The people dashed cold water on his head to revive him, but he finally died. And the people wept over him as though they themselves had been bewitched.

Thereupon Toyo-o seemed to have regained some control of himself. "If the devil is so tenacious as to be impervious to the incantations of such an exalted priest, then it will continue to pursue me as long as I live," he said. "It is not right that so many people should suffer on my account. I will not rely on the help of others any more. I am prepared to die. So please be at ease."

He then walked toward the bedroom. All the members of the household cried, "Are you mad?" and tried to stop him. But he pretended not to have heard them and, walking serenely to the devil's den, opened the door. There was no sign of disturbance. He found Tomiko seated silently opposite Maroya, the devil's maid.

Tomiko asked in the devil's voice, "What manner of grudge are you holding against me, asking others to put me out of the way? If you persist in trying to eliminate me, I shall be forced to be cruel not only to you but also to all the people of this community. Be happy over my undeviating love for you. And never, never transfer your affection to another woman."

She said this last in a coquettish fashion that was intolerable to Toyo-o.

He replied, "There is a saying that human beings have no intention of hurting the tiger. The tiger, on the other hand, is predisposed to hurt human beings. Just so, with an inhuman spirit you have bewitched me cruelly so many times. What is more, over a trifling matter you have threatened me with dire things. There is the worst kind of evil in you. To pursue me out of love may be normally human, but to inflict cruelty on other people in this household is abominable. I beg of you to spare the life of this Tomiko. Then you may take me wherever you wish."

She nodded happily.

16

Toyo-o went out of the bedroom and told Tomiko's father, Shōji, "Since I am being pursued so relentlessly, it is wrong for me to remain in this house and thereby to bring trouble upon others. With your permission, I shall leave forever. That way Tomiko will be free from further molestation."

Shōji would not hear of it. "I have the blood of samurai in my veins," he said. "It would be shameful on my part to submit to such cowardice, and unfair to your family, the Ōyas. Let us plan a better scheme. . . . Oh yes, in Komatsubara, at the Dōjō Temple, there is a priest called Hokai Oshō who is exalted in the performance of incantations. He is an aged person and rarely goes out of his study, but I am sure he will not forsake us in this crisis."

No sooner had he said this than he leaped upon his horse and galloped away. The venerable priest's temple was situated some distance away, so it was late that night when he reached it. Hokai Oshō came out from the back room to greet Shōji. When the priest heard Shōji's story and appeal for help, he said, "It must be a wretched state of affairs indeed. I am an old man now, so I doubt if there would be any effectiveness in my prayers. But I cannot remain idle when your household is faced with such a calamity. Return to your house quickly. I will follow you directly."

He fetched a priest's surplice[5] stained with burned poppy incense and gave it to Shōji, saying, "Try to beguile the monster and coax it into submission, then cover its head with this sacred surplice, pressing down with all your might. If you don't press it hard enough, the monster might escape. Say your prayers as you do it."

Shōji leaped upon his horse again, and galloped homeward with joy in his heart.

He called Toyo-o aside and gave him the surplice, instructing him, as Hokai Oshō had explained, on how to subdue the devil. Toyo-o hid the surplice in the folds of his robe and entered the bedroom. He told the devil, "Shōji has agreed to let me go, so let us depart together."

Tomiko's body responded by rising, very happily, it seemed. Immediately Toyo-o took out the surplice and covered her head with it, pressing it down with all his might, and she fell to the floor.

"Oh, how painful," she cried out, in a muffled voice. "Why are you tormenting me like this? Please quit pressing me here . . . and here." But Toyo-o kept on pressing her down and covering her with all his strength.

Then Hokai Oshō arrived in a palanquin. Escorted into Shōji's house, he kept mumbling an incantation. He went into the bedroom and, shoving Toyo-o aside, lifted the surplice. A serpent lay coiled atop Tomiko's prone, unconscious body. There was no movement. The priest seized the dead snake and put it into an iron pot carried by the acolyte who had accompanied him. He

---

5. A loose outer robe, extending to the knees, worn by priests.

was still mumbling some incantations when another snake, only a foot long, came slithering up from behind the standing screen. This, too, the priest caught and put into the pot, which he covered tightly with the surplice.

And then he got on his palanquin and returned to his temple. He had a grave dug deep in the temple yard and buried the pot, together with its contents. In this way he sealed forever the chances of the serpent reemerging to bedevil and bewitch human beings. Even now, it is said, the serpent's grave mound may be seen in the temple yard.

The people at the Shōji household meanwhile prayerfully shed tears of gratitude. But Tomiko, as a consequence of her horrible experience, became seriously ill and died. Toyo-o, on the other hand, suffered no ill effects but lived a long and healthy life, it is recorded.

A Note on Translation

Reading literature in translation is a pleasure on which it is fruitless to frown. The purist may insist that we ought always read in the original languages, and we know ideally that this is true. But it is a counsel of perfection, quite impractical even for the purist, since no one in a lifetime can master all the languages whose literatures it would be a joy to explore. Master languages as fast as we may, we shall always have to read to some extent in translation, and this means we must be alert to what we are about: if in reading a work of literature in translation we are not reading the "original," what precisely are we reading? This is a question of great complexity, to which justice cannot be done in a brief note, but the following sketch of some of the considerations may be helpful.

One of the memorable scenes of ancient literature is the meeting of Hector and Andromache in Book VI of Homer's *Iliad*. Hector, leader and mainstay of the armies defending Troy, is implored by his wife Andromache to withdraw within the city walls and carry on the defense from there, where his life will not be con stantly at hazard. In Homer's text her opening words to him are these: δαιμόνιε, φθίσει σε τὸ σὸν μένος (daimonie, phthisei se to son menos). How should they be translated into English?

Here is how they have actually been translated into English by capable translators, at various periods, in verse and prose:

1. George Chapman, 1598:

> O noblest in desire,
> Thy mind, inflamed with others' good, will set thy self on fire.

2. John Dryden, 1693:

> Thy dauntless heart (which I foresee too late),
> Too daring man, will urge thee to thy fate.

3. Alexander Pope, 1715:

> Too daring Prince! . . .
> For sure such courage length of life denies,
> And thou must fall, thy virtue's sacrifice.

4. William Cowper, 1791:

> Thy own great courage will cut short thy days,
> My noble Hector. . .

5. Lang, Leaf, and Myers, 1883 (prose):

> Dear my lord, this thy hardihood will undo thee. . . .

6. A. T. Murray, 1924 (prose):

> Ah, my husband, this prowess of thine will be thy doom. . . .

7. E. V. Rieu, 1950 (prose):

"Hector," she said, "you are possessed. This bravery of yours will be your end."

8. I. A. Richards, 1950 (prose):

"Strange man," she said, "your courage will be your destruction."

9. Richmond Lattimore, 1951:

Dearest,
Your own great strength will be your death. . . .

10. Robert Fitzgerald, 1979:

O my wild one, your bravery will be
Your own undoing!

11. Robert Fagles, 1990:

reckless one,
Your own fiery courage will destroy you!

From these strikingly different renderings of the same six words, certain facts about the nature of translation begin to emerge. We notice, for one thing, that Homer's word μένος (menos) is diversified by the translators into "mind," "dauntless heart," "such courage," "great courage," "hardihood," "prowess," "bravery," "courage," "great strength," "bravery," and "fiery courage." The word has in fact all these possibilities. Used of things, it normally means "force"; of animals, "fierceness" or "brute strength" or (in the case of horses) "mettle"; of men and women, "passion" or "spirit" or even "purpose." Homer's application of it in the present case points our attention equally—whatever particular sense we may imagine Andromache to have uppermost—to Hector's force, strength, fierceness in battle, spirited heart and mind. But since English has no matching term of like inclusiveness, the passage as the translators give it to us reflects this lack and we find one attribute singled out to the exclusion of the rest.

Here then is the first and most crucial fact about any work of literature read in translation. It cannot escape the linguistic characteristics of the language into which it is turned: the grammatical, syntactical, lexical, and phonetic boundaries that constitute collectively the individuality or "genius" of that language. A Greek play or a Russian novel in English will be governed first of all by the resources of the English language, resources that are certain to be in every instance very different, as the efforts with μένος show, from those of the original.

Turning from μένος to δαιμόνιε (daimonie) in Homer's clause, we encounter a second crucial fact about translations. Nobody knows exactly what shade of meaning δαιμόνιε had for Homer. In later writers the word normally suggests divinity, something miraculous, wondrous; but in Homer it appears as a vocative of address for both chieftain and commoner, man and wife. The coloring one gives it must therefore be determined either by the way one thinks a Greek wife of Homer's era might actually address her husband (a subject on which we have no information whatever) or in the way one thinks it suitable for a hero's wife to address her husband in an epic poem, that is to say, a highly stylized and formal work. In general, the translators of our century will be seen to have abandoned formality to stress the intimacy; the wifeliness; and, especially in Lattimore's case, a certain chiding tenderness, in Andromache's appeal: (6) "Ah, my husband," (7) "Hector" (with perhaps a hint, in "you are possessed," of the alarmed distaste with which wives have so often viewed their husbands' bellicose moods), (8) "Strange man," (9) "Dearest," (10) "O my wild one" (mixing an almost motherly admiration with reproach and concern), and (11) "reckless one." On the other hand, the older translators have obviously removed Andromache to an epic or heroic distance from her beloved, whence she sees and kindles to his selfless courage, acknowledging, even in the moment of pleading with him to be otherwise, his moral grandeur and the tragic destiny this too certainly implies: (1) "O noblest in desire, . . . inflamed by others' good"; (2) "Thy dauntless heart (which I foresee too late), / Too daring man"; (3) "Too daring Prince! . . . / And thou must fall, thy virtue's sacrifice"; (4) "My noble Hector." Even the less specific "Dear my lord" of Lang, Leaf, and Myers looks in the same direction because of its echo of the speech of countless Shakespearean men and women who have shared this powerful moral sense: "Dear my lord, make me acquainted with your cause of grief"; "Perseverance, dear my lord, keeps honor bright"; etc.

The fact about translation that emerges from all this is that just as the translated work reflects the individuality of the language it is turned into, so it reflects the individuality of the age in which it is made, and the age will permeate it everywhere like yeast in dough. We think of one kind of permeation when we think of the governing verse forms and attitudes toward verse at a given epoch. In Chapman's time, experiments seeking an "heroic" verse form for English were widespread, and accordingly he tries a "fourteener" couplet (two rhymed lines of seven stresses each) in his *Iliad* and a pentameter couplet in his *Odyssey*. When Dryden and Pope wrote, a closed pentameter couplet had become established as the heroic form par excellence. By Cowper's day, thanks largely to the prestige of *Paradise Lost,* the couplet had gone out of fashion for narrative poetry in favor of blank verse. Our age, inclining to prose and in verse to proselike informalities and relaxations, has, predictably, produced half a dozen excellent prose translations of the *Iliad* but only three in verse (by Fagles, Lattimore, and Fitzgerald), all relying on rhythms that are much of the time closer to the verse of William Carlos Williams and some of the prose of novelists like Faulkner than to the swift firm tread of Homer's Greek. For if it is true that what we translate from a given work is what, wearing the spectacles of our time, we see in it, it is also true that we see in it what we have the power to translate.

Of course, there are other effects of the translator's epoch on a translation besides those exercised by contemporary taste in verse and verse forms. Chapman writes in a great age of poetic metaphor and, therefore, almost instinctively translates his understanding of Homer's verb φθίσει (phthisei, "to cause to wane, consume, waste, pine") into metaphorical terms of flame, presenting his Hector to us as a man of burning generosity who will be consumed by his very ardor. This is a conception rooted in large part in the psychology of the Elizabethans, who had the habit of speaking of the soul as "fire," of one of the four temperaments as "fiery," of even the more material bodily processes, like digestion, as if they were carried on by the heat of fire ("concoction," "decoction"). It is rooted too in that characteristic Renaissance élan so unforgettably expressed in characters such as Tamburlaine and Dr. Faustus, the former of whom exclaims to the stars above:

> . . . I, the chiefest lamp of all the earth,
> First rising in the East with mild aspect,
> But fixèd now in the meridian line,
> Will send up fire to your turning spheres,
> And cause the sun to borrow light of you. . . .

Pope and Dryden, by contrast, write to audiences for whom strong metaphor has become suspect. They therefore reject the fire image (which we must recall is not present in the Greek) in favor of a form of speech more congenial to their age, the *sententia* or aphorism, and give it extra vitality by making it the scene of a miniature drama: in Dryden's case, the hero's dauntless heart "urges" him (in the double sense of physical as well as moral pressure) to his fate; in Pope's, the hero's courage, like a judge, "denies" continuance of life, with the consequence that he "falls"—and here Pope's second line suggests analogy to the sacrificial animal—the victim of his own essential nature, of what he is.

To pose even more graphically the pressures that a translator's period brings, consider the following lines from Hector's reply to Andromache's appeal that he withdraw, first in Chapman's Elizabethan version, then in Lattimore's twentieth-century one:

Chapman, 1598:

> The spirit I did first breathe
> Did never teach me that—much less since the contempt of death
> Was settled in me, and my mind knew what a Worthy was,
> Whose office is to lead in fight and give no danger pass
> Without improvement. In this fire must Hector's trial shine.
> Here must his country, father, friends be in him made divine.

Lattimore, 1951:

> and the spirit will not let me, since I have learned to be valiant
> and to fight always among the foremost ranks of the Trojans,
> winning for my own self great glory, and for my father.

If one may exaggerate to make a necessary point, the world of Henry V and Othello suddenly gives way here to our own, a world whose discomfort with any form of heroic self-assertion is remarkably mirrored in the burial of Homer's key terms (*spirit, valiant, fight, foremost, glory*)—five out of twenty-two words in the original, five out of thirty-six in the translation—in a cushioning huddle of harmless sounds.

Besides the two factors so far mentioned (language and period) as affecting the character of a translation, there is inevitably a third—the translator, with a particular degree of talent; a personal way of regarding the work to be translated; a special hierarchy of values, moral, aesthetic, metaphysical (which may or may not be summed up in a "worldview"); and a unique style or lack of it. But this influence all readers are likely to bear in mind, and it needs no laboring here. That, for example, two translators of Hamlet, one a Freudian, the other a Jungian, will produce impressively different translations is obvious from the fact that when Freudian and Jungian argue about the play in English they often seem to have different plays in mind.

We can now return to the question from which we started. After all allowances have been made for language, age, and individual translator, is anything of the original left? What, in short, does the reader of translations read? Let it be said at once that in utility prose—prose whose function is mainly referential—the reader who reads a translation reads everything that matters. "Nicht Rauchen," "Défense de Fumer," and "No Smoking," posted in a railway car, make their point, and the differences between them in sound and form have no significance for us in that context. Since the prose of a treatise and of most fiction is preponderantly referential, we rightly feel, when we have paid close attention to Cervantes or Montaigne or Machiavelli or Tolstoy in a good English translation, that we have had roughly the same experience as a native Spaniard, Frenchman, Italian, or Russian. But *roughly* is the correct word; for good prose points iconically *to* itself as well as referentially beyond itself, and everything that it points to in itself in the original (rhythms, sounds, idioms, wordplay, etc.) must alter radically in being translated. The best analogy is to imagine a Van Gogh painting reproduced in the medium of tempera, etching, or engraving: the "picture" remains, but the intricate interanimation of volumes with colorings with brushstrokes has disappeared.

When we move on to poetry, even in its longer narrative and dramatic forms—plays like Oedipus, poems like the *Iliad* or the *Divine Comedy*—our situation as English readers worsens appreciably, as the many unlike versions of Andromache's appeal to Hector make very clear. But, again, only appreciably. True, this is the point at which the fact that a translation is *always* an interpretation explodes irresistibly on our attention; but if it is the best translation of its time, like John Ciardi's translation of the *Divine Comedy* for our time, the result will be not only a sensitive interpretation but also a work with intrinsic interest in its own right—at very best, a true work of art, a new poem. In these longer works, moreover, even if the translation is uninspired, many distinctive structural features—plot, setting, characters, meetings, partings, confrontations, and specific episodes generally—survive virtually unchanged. Hence even in translation it remains both possible and instructive to compare, say, concepts of the heroic or attitudes toward women or uses of religious ritual among civilizations as various as those reflected in the *Iliad*, the *Mahābhārata*, *Beowulf*, and the epic of *Son-Jara*. It is only when the shorter, primarily lyrical forms of poetry are presented that the reader of translations faces insuperable disadvantage. In these forms, the referential aspect of language has a tendency to disappear into, or, more often, draw its real meaning and accreditation from, the iconic aspect. Let us look for just a moment at a brief poem by Federico García Lorca and its English translation (by Stephen Spender and J. L. Gili):

> ¡Alto pinar!
> Cuatro palomas por el aire van.
>
> Cuatro palomas
> vuelan y tornan.
> Llevan heridas
> sus cuatro sombras.
>
> ¡Bajo pinar!
> Cuatro palomas en la tierra están.

> Above the pine trees:
> Four pigeons go through the air.
>
> Four pigeons
> fly and turn round.
> They carry wounded
> their four shadows.
>
> Below the pine trees:
> Four pigeons lie on the earth.

In this translation the referential sense of the English words follows with remarkable exactness the referential sense of the Spanish words they replace. But the life of Lorca's poem does not lie in that sense. It lies in such matters as the abruptness, like an intake of breath at a sudden revelation, of the two exclamatory lines (1 and 7), which then exhale musically in images of flight and death; or as the echoings of *palomas* in *heridas* and *sombras*, bringing together (as in fact the hunter's gun has done) these unrelated nouns and the unrelated experiences they stand for in a sequence that seems, momentarily, to have all the logic of a tragic action, in which *doves* become *wounds* become *shadows*, or as the external and internal rhyming among the five verbs, as though all motion must (as in fact it must) end with *están*.

Since none of this can be brought over into another tongue (least of all Lorca's rhythms), the translator must decide between leaving a reader to wonder why Lorca is a poet to be bothered about at all and making a new but true poem, whose merit will almost certainly be in inverse ratio to its likeness to the original. Samuel Johnson made such a poem in translating Horace's famous *Diffugere nives*, and so did A. E. Housman. If we juxtapose the last two stanzas of each translation, and the corresponding Latin, we can see at a glance that each has the consistency and inner life of a genuine poem and that neither of them (even if we consider only what is obvious to the eye, the line-lengths) is very close to Horace:

> *Cum semel occideris, et de te splendida Minos*
> *fecerit arbitria,*

> non, Torquate, genus, non te facundia, non te
> restituet pietas.
>
> Infernis neque enim tenebris Diana pudicum
>   liberat Hippolytum
> nec Lethaea valet Theseus abrumpere caro
>   vincula Pirithoo.

Johnson:

> Not you, Torquatus, boast of Rome,
> When Minos once has fixed your doom,
> Or eloquence, or splendid birth,
> Or virtue, shall restore to earth.
> Hippolytus, unjustly slain,
> Diana calls to life in vain;
> Nor can the might of Theseus rend
> The chains of hell that hold his friend.

Housman:

> When thou descendest once the shades among,
>   The stern assize and equal judgment o'er,
> Not thy long lineage nor thy golden tongue,
>   No, nor thy righteousness, shall friend thee more.
>
> Night holds Hippolytus the pure of stain,
>   Diana steads him nothing, he must stay;
> And Theseus leaves Pirithous in the chain
>   The love of comrades cannot take away.

The truth of the matter is that when the translator of short poems chooses to be literal, most or all of the poetry is lost; and when the translator succeeds in forging a new poetry, most or all of the original author is lost. Since there is no way out of this dilemma, we have always been sparing, in this anthology, in our use of short poems in translation.

In this Expanded Edition, we have adjusted our policy to take account of the two great non-Western literatures in which the short lyric or "song" has been the principal and by far most cherished expression of the national genius. During much of its history from earliest times, the Japanese imagination has cheerfully exercised itself, with all the delicacy and grace of an Olympic figure skater, inside a rigorous verse pattern of five lines and thirty-one syllables: the *tanka*. Chinese poetry, while somewhat more liberal to itself in line length, has been equally fertile in the fine art of compression and has only occasionally, even in its earliest, most experimental phase, indulged in verse lines of more than seven characters, often just four, or in poems of more than fifty lines, usually fewer than twenty. What makes the Chinese and Japanese lyric more difficult than most other lyrics to translate satisfactorily into English is that these compressions combine with a flexibility of syntax (Japanese) or a degree of freedom from it (Chinese) not available in our language. They also combine with a poetic sensibility that shrinks from exposition in favor of sequences and juxtapositions of images: images grasped and recorded in, or *as if in,* a moment of pure perception unencumbered by the explanatory linkages, background scenarios, and other forms of contextualization that the Western mind is instinctively driven to establish.

Whole books, almost whole libraries, have been written recently on the contrast of East and West in worldviews and value systems as well as on the need of each for the other if there is ever to be a community of understanding adequate to the realities both face. Put baldly, much too simply, and without the many exceptions and qualifications that rightly spring to mind, it may be said that a central and characteristic Western impulse, from the Greeks on down, has been to see the world around us as something to be *acted on*: weighed, measured, managed, used, even (when economic interests prevail over all others) fouled. Likewise, put oversimply, it may be said that a central and characteristic Eastern counterpart to this over many centuries (witness Taoism, Buddhism, and Hinduism, among others) has been to see that same world as something to be *received*: contemplated, touched, tasted, smelled, heard, and most especially, immersed in until observer and observed are one. To paint a bamboo, a stone, a butterfly, a person—so runs a classical Chinese admonition for painters—you must *become* that bamboo, that stone, that butterfly, that person, then paint from the inside. No one need be ashamed of being poor, says Confucius, putting a similar emphasis on *receiving* experience, "only of not being cultivated in the perception of beauty."

The problem that these differences in linguistic freedom and philosophical outlook pose for the English translator of classical Chinese and Japanese poetry may be glimpsed, even if not fully grasped, by considering for a moment in some detail a typical Japanese *tanka* (*Kokinshu*, 9) and a typical Chinese "song" (*Book of Songs*, 23). In its own language but transliterated in the Latin alphabet of the West, the *tanka* looks like this:

> *kasumi tachi*
> *ko no me mo haru no*
> *yuki fureba*
> *hana naki sato mo*
> *hana zo chirikeru*

In a literal word-by-word translation (so far as this is possible in Japanese, since the language uses many particles without English equivalents and without dictionary meaning in modifying and qualifying functions—for example, *no, mo,* and *no* in line 2), the poem looks like this:

> haze rises
> tree-buds swell
> when snow falls
> village(s) without flower(s)
> flower(s) fall(s)

The three best-known English renderings of this *tanka* look like this:

1. Helen Craig McCullough:

> When snow comes in spring—
> fair season of layered haze
> and burgeoning buds—
> flowers fall in villages
> where flowers have yet to bloom.

2. Laurel Rasplica Rodd and Mary Catherine Henkenius:

> When the warm mists veil
> all the buds swell while yet the
> spring snows drift downward
> even in the hibernal
> village crystal blossoms fall.

3. Robert H. Brower and Earl Miner:

> With the spreading mists
> The tree buds swell in early spring
> And wet snow petals fall—

> So even my flowerless country village
> Already lies beneath its fallen flowers.

The reader will notice at once how much the three translators have felt it desirable or necessary to add, alter, rearrange, and explain. In McCullough's version the time of year is affirmed twice, both as "spring" and as "fair season of . . . haze"; the haze is now "layered"; the five coordinate perceptions of the original (haze, swelling buds, a snowfall, villages without flowers, flowers drifting down) have been structured into a single sentence with one main verb and two subordinate clauses spelling out "when" and "where"; and the original poem's climax, in a scene of drifting petallike snowflakes, has been shifted to a bleak scenery of absence: "flowers have yet to bloom." The final stress, in other words, is not on the fulfilled moment in which snow flowers replace the cherry blossoms, but on the cherry blossoms not yet arrived.

Similar additions and explanations occur in Rodd and Henkenius's version. This time the mist is "warm" and "veil[s] all" to clarify its connection with "buds." Though implicit already in "warm" and "burgeoning," spring is invoked again in "spring snows," and the snows are given confirmation in the following line by the insistently Latinate "hibernal," chosen, we may reasonably guess, along with "veil," "all," "swell," "while," "crystal," and "fall" to replace some of the chiming internal rhyme in the Japanese: ko, no, mo, no, sato, mo, zo. To leave no i undotted, "crystal" is imported to assure us that the falling "blossoms" of line 5 are really snowflakes, and the scene of flowerlessness that in the original (line 4) accounts for a special joy in the "flowering" of the snowflakes (line 5) vanishes without trace.

Brower and Miner's also fills in the causative links between "spreading mists" and swelling buds; makes sure that we do not fail to see the falling snow in flower terms ("wet snow petals"), thus losing, alas, the element of surprise, even magic, in the transformation of snowflakes into flowers that the original poem holds in store in its last two lines; and tells us (somewhat redundantly) that villages are a "country" phenomenon and (somewhat surprisingly) that this one is the speaker's home. In this version, as in the original and Rodd and Henkenius's, the poem closes with the snow scene, but here it is a one-time affair and "already" complete (lines 4 and 5), not a recurrent phenomenon that may appear under certain conditions anywhere at any time.

Some of the differences in these translations arise inevitably from different trade-offs, as in the first version, where the final vision of falling snow blossoms is let go presumably to achieve the lovely lilting echo and rhetorical turn of "flowers fall in villages / where flowers have yet to bloom." Or as in Rodd and Henkenius's version, where preoccupations with internal rhyme have obviously influenced word choices, not always for the better. Or as in all three versions, where different efforts to remind the reader of the wordplay on haru (in the Japanese poem both a noun meaning "spring" and a verb meaning "swell") have had dissimilar but perhaps equally indifferent results. Meantime, the immense force compacted into that small word in the original as both noun and verb, season of springtime and principal of growth, cause and effect (and thus in a sense the whole mighty process of earth's renewal, in which an interruption by snow only foretells a greater loveliness to come) fizzles away unfelt. A few differences do seem to arise from insufficient command of the nerves and sinews of English poetry, but most spring from the staggering difficulties of responding in any uniform way to the minimal clues proffered by the original text. The five perceptions—haze, buds, snowfall, flowerless villages, flowers falling—do not as they stand in the Japanese or any literal translation quite compose for readers accustomed to Western poetic traditions an adequate poetic whole. This is plainly seen in the irresistible urge each of the translators has felt to catch up the individual perceptions, as English tends to require, in a tighter overall grammatical and syntactical structure than the original insists on. In this way they provide a clarifying network of principal and subordinate, time when, place where, and cause why. Yet the inevitable result is a disassembling, a spinning out, spelling out, thinning out of what in the Japanese is an as yet unraveled imagistic excitement, creating (or memorializing) in the poet's mind, and then in the mind of the Japanese readers, the original thrill of consciousness when these images, complete with the magical transformation of snow into the longed-for cherry blossoms, first flashed on the inward eye.

What is comforting for us who must read this and other Japanese poems in translation is that each of the versions given here retains in some form or other all or most of the five images intact. What is less comforting is that the simplicity and suddenness, the explosion in the mind, have been diffused and defused.

When we turn to the Chinese song, we find similarly contesting forces at work. In one respect, the Chinese language comes over into English more readily than Japanese, being like English comparatively uninflected and heavily dependent on word order for its meanings. But in other respects, since Chinese like Japanese lacks distinctions of gender, of singular and plural, of *a* and *the,* and in the classical mode in which the poems in this anthology are composed, also of tenses, the pressure of the English translator to rearrange, straighten out, and fill in to "make sense" for his or her readers remains strong.

Let us examine song no. 23 of the *Shijing.* In its own Chinese characters, it looks like this:

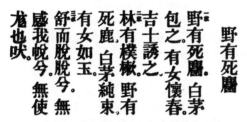

Eleven lines in all, each line having four characters as its norm, the poem seemingly takes shape around an implicit parallel between a doe in the forest, possibly killed by stealth and hidden under long grass or rushes (though on this point as on all others the poem refuses to take us wholly into confidence), and a young girl possibly "ruined" (as she certainly would have been in the post-Confucian society in which the *Shijing* was prized and circulated, though here again the poem keeps its own counsel) by loss of her virginity before marriage.

In its bare bones, with each character given an approximate English equivalent, a translation might look like this:

wild(s)	is	dead	deer	
white	grass(es)	wrap/cover	(it).	
is	girl	feel	spring.	
fine	man	tempt	(her).	
woods	is(are)	bush(es),	underbrush.	5
wild(s)	is	dead	deer.	
white	grass(es)	bind	bundle.	
is	girl	like	jade.	
slow	———	slow	slow.	
not	move	my	sash.	10
not	cause	dog	bark.	

Lines 1 to 4, it seems plain, propose the parallel of slain doe and girl, whatever that parallel may be intended to mean. Lines 5 to 8 restate the parallel, adding that the girl is as beautiful as jade and (apparently) that the doe lies where the "wild" gives way to smaller growth. If we allow ourselves to account for the repetition (here again is a Western mind-set in search of explanatory clues) by supposing that lines 1 to 4 signal at some subliminal level the initiation of the seduction and lines 5 to 8, again subliminally, its progress or possibly its completion, lines 9 to 11 fall easily into place as a miniature drama enacting in direct speech the man's advances and the girl's gradually crumbling resistance. They also imply, it seems, that the seduction takes place not in the forest, as we might have been led to suppose by lines 1 to 8, but in a dwelling with a vigilant guard dog.

Interpreted just far enough to accommodate English syntax, the poem reads as follows:

1. Wai-lim Yip:

> In the wilds, a dead doe.
> White reeds to wrap it.
> A girl, spring-touched.
> A fine man to seduce her.
> In the woods, bushes.   5
> In the wilds, a dead deer.
> White reeds in bundles.
> A girl like jade.
> Slowly. Take it easy.
> Don't feel my sash!   10
> Don't make the dog bark!

Interpreted a stage further in a format some have thought better suited to English poetic traditions, the poem reads:

2. Arthur Waley:

> In the wilds there is a dead doe,
> With white rushes we cover her.
> There was a lady longing for spring,
> A fair knight seduced her.
>
> In the woods there is a clump of oaks,   5
> And in the wilds a dead deer
> With white rushes well bound.
> There was a lady fair as jade.
>
> "Heigh, not so hasty, not so rough.
> "Heigh, do not touch my handkerchief.   10
> "Take care or the dog will bark."

Like the original and the literal translation, this version leaves the relationship between the doe's death and the girl's seduction unspecified and problematic. It holds the doe story in present tenses, assigning the girl story to the past. Still, much has been changed to give the English poem an explanatory scenario. The particular past assigned to the girl story, indeterminate in the Chinese original, is here fixed as the age of knights and ladies; and the seduction itself, which in the Chinese hovers as an eternal possibility within the timeless situation of man and maid ("A fine man *to* seduce her"), is established as completed long ago: "A fair knight seduced her." A teasing oddity in this version is the mysterious "we" who "cover" the slain doe, never to be heard from again.

Take interpretation toward its outer limits and we reach what is perhaps best called a "variation" on this theme:

3. Ezra Pound:

> Lies a dead doe on yonder plain
> whom white grass covers,
> A melancholy maid in spring

                                    is luck
                                    for   5
                                    lovers
                Where the scrub elm skirts the wood
                be it not in white mat bound,
                As a jewel flawless found
                                    dead as a doe is maidenhood.   10
                Hark!
                Unhand my girdle knot.
                                    Stay, stay, stay
                                    or the dog
                                    may   15
                                    bark.

Here too the present is pushed back to a past by the language the translator uses: not a specific past, as with the era of knights and ladies, but any past in which contemporary speech still features such (to us) archaic formalisms as "Unhand" or "Hark," and in which the term "maid" still signifies a virgin and in which virginity is prized to an extent that equates its loss with the doe's loss of life. But these evocations of time past are so effectively countered by the obtrusively present tense throughout (lines 1, 2, 4, 7, 8, 10, 11, 12, 13, and 15) that the freewheeling "variation" remains in this important respect closer to the spirit of the original than Waley's translation. On the other hand, it departs from the original and the two other versions by brushing aside the reticence that they carefully preserve as to the precise implications of the girl-deer parallel, choosing instead to place the seduction in the explanatory framework of the oldest story in the world: the way of a man with a maid in the springtime of life.

   What both these examples make plain is that the Chinese and Japanese lyric, however contrasting in some ways, have in common at their center a complex of highly charged images generating something very like a magnetic field of potential meanings that cannot be got at in English without bleeding away much of the voltage. In view of this, the best practical advice for those of us who must read these marvelous poems in English translations is to focus intently on these images and ask ourselves what there is in them or in their effect on each other that produces the electricity. To that extent, we can compensate for a part of our losses, learn something positive about the immense explosive powers of imagery, and rest easy in the secure knowledge that translation even in the mode of the short poem brings us (despite losses) closer to the work itself than not reading it at all. "To a thousand cavils," said Samuel Johnson, "one answer is sufficient; the purpose of a writer is to be read, and the criticism which would destroy the power of pleasing must be blown aside." Johnson was defending Pope's Homer for those marks of its own time and place that make it the great interpretation it is, but Johnson's exhilarating common sense applies equally to the problem we are considering here. Literature is to be read, and the criticism that would destroy the reader's power to make some form of contact with much of the world's great writing must indeed be blown aside.

                                                            MAYNARD MACK

                              Sources

Brower, Robert H., and Earl Miner. *Japanese Court Poetry*. Stanford: Stanford University Press, 1961.

The Classic Anthology Defined by Confucius. Tr. Ezra Pound. New Directions, 1954.

Kokinshū: A Collection of Poems Ancient and Modern. Tr. Laurel Rasplica Rodd and Mary Catherine Henkenius. Princeton: Princeton University Press, 1984.

Kokin Wakashū: The First Imperial Anthology of Japanese Poetry. Tr. and ed. Helen Craig McCullough. Stanford: Stanford University Press, 1985.

Legge, James. *The Chinese Classics.* Hong Kong: Hong Kong University Press, 1960.

Waley, Arthur. *170 Chinese Poems.* New York, 1919.

PERMISSIONS ACKNOWLEDGMENTS

Cao Xuequin: Excerpts from THE STORY OF THE STONE (DREAM OF THE RED CHAMBER), translated by David Hawkes. Copyright © 1973 by David Hawkes. Reprinted by permission of the translator.

Evliya Çelebi: Excerpts from THE BOOK OF TRAVELS, translated by Pierre McKay. Copyright © 1990 by Pierre McKay from THE BOOK OF TRAVELS. Reprinted by permission of the translator.

Ihara Saikaku: *The Barrelmaker Brimful of Love* from FIVE WOMEN WHO LOVED LOVE by Ihara Saikaku, translated by William Theodore de Bary. Reprinted by permission of Charles E. Tuttle Company, Inc., of Boston, Massachusetts, and Tokyo, Japan.

Sor Juana Inés de la Cruz: *Reply to Sor Filotea de la Cruz* from A WOMAN OF GENIUS, translated by Margaret Sayers Peden. Copyright © 1982 by Lime Rock Press, Inc., Salisbury CT 06086. Reprinted by permission of Lime Rock Press, Inc. No part may be reprinted without express permission of the original publisher.

K'ung Shang-jen: Excerpts from THE PEACH BLOSSOM FAN (T'AO-HUA-SHAN), edited/translated by Chen Shih-hsiang and Harold Acton with the collaboration of Cyril Birch. Copyright © 1976 by The Regents of the University of California. Reprinted by permission of the University of California.

Jean-Baptiste Molière: TARTUFFE, translated by Richard Wilbur. Copyright © 1963 by Richard Wilbur. Copyright renewed © 1991. Reprinted by permission of Harcourt Brace & Company. CAUTION: Professionals and amateurs are hereby warned that this translation, being fully protected under the copyright laws of the United States of America, the British Commonwealth, including Canada, and all other countries are subject to royalty. All rights, including professional, amateur, motion picture, recitation, lecturing, public reading, radio broadcasting, and television, are strictly reserved. Particular emphasis is laid on the question of readings, permission for which must be secured from the author's agent in writing. Inquiries on professional rights (except for amateur rights) should be addressed to Curtis Brown Ltd., 10 Astor Place, New York, NY 10003. The amateur acting rights of *Tartuffe* are controlled exclusively by the Dramatist's Play Service, Inc., 440 Park Ave. South, New York NY 10016. No amateur performance of the play may be given without obtaining in advance the written permission of the Dramatist's Play Service and paying the requisite fee. Inquiries on all other rights should be addressed to Harcourt Brace & Company, Permissions Department, Orlando FL 32887–6777.

Matsuo Bashō: *The Narrow Road of the Interior* from CLASSICAL JAPANESE PROSE: AN ANTHOLOGY, compiled and edited by Helen Craig McCullough, with the permission of the publishers, Stanford University Press. © 1990 by the Board of Trustees of the Leland Stanford Junior University.

Alexander Pope: *The Rape of the Lock* from THE RAPE OF THE LOCK by Alexander Pope, with notes by Samuel Holt Monk. Copyright © 1962, 1968 by W. W. Norton & Company, Inc. Copyright renewed © 1990. Used by permission of W. W. Norton & Company, Inc.

Jean Racine: PHAEDRA, translated by Richard Wilbur. Copyright © 1984, 1986 by Richard P. Wilbur Literary Trust, Trustees C. H. Wilbur, A. L. Schiff, and Multibank National of Western Massachusetts. Reprinted by permission of Harcourt Brace & Company. CAUTION: Professionals and amateurs are hereby warned that this translation, being fully protected under the copyright laws of the United States of America, the British Commonwealth, including Canada, and all other countries which are signatories to the Universal Copyright Convention and the International Copyright Union are subject to royalty. All rights, including professional, amateur, motion picture, recitation, lecturing, public reading, radio broadcasting, and television are strictly reserved. Particular emphasis is laid on the question of readings, permission for which must be secured from the author's agent in writing. Inquiries on professional rights (except for amateur rights) should be addressed to Curtis Brown Ltd., 10 Astor Place, New York NY 10003. Inquiries on translation should be addressed to Harcourt Brace & Company, Permissions Department, Orlando FL 32887–6777.

Jonathan Swift: *A Modest Proposal* from IRISH TRACTS 1727–1733, edited by Herbert Davis. Copyright © 1955. Reprinted by permission of Basil Blackwell.

Ueda Akinari: *Bewitched* from TALES OF MOONLIGHT AND RAIN, translated by Kengi Hamada. Copyright © 1972 by Columbia University Press. Reprinted by permission of Columbia University Press.

François-Marie Arouet de Voltaire: CANDIDE: A NORTON CRITICAL EDITION, second edition by Voltaire, translated by Robert M. Adams. Copyright © 1991, 1966 by W. W. Norton & Company. Used by permission of W. W. Norton & Company, Inc.

Wu Ch'eng-En: Excerpts from MONKEY, translated by Arthur Waley. Copyright © 1943 by the John Day Company. Used by permission of Grove/Atlantic, Inc.

A13

Index

PN 6014 .N66 2001 v.D

The Norton anthology of
 world literature